HISTORY
OF A FREE NATION

HENRY W. BRAGDON

SAMUEL P. MCCUTCHEN

DONALD A. RITCHIE

GLENCOE

Macmillan/McGraw–Hill

New York, New York   Columbus, Ohio   Mission Hills, California   Peoria, Illinois

HISTORY
OF A FREE NATION

Authors

Henry W. Bragdon was for many years a much-admired teacher at the Phillips Exeter Academy in Exeter, New Hampshire, winding up his career there as Cowles Professor in the Humanities Emeritus. In addition to his work on this textbook, he is the author of a biography of President Woodrow Wilson, *Woodrow Wilson: The Academic Years*, which was nominated for a National Book Award. Bragdon also served as president of the New England History Teachers' Association, chief examiner in Social Studies for the College Entrance Examination Board, and lecturer at Harvard College.

Samuel P. McCutchen spent a long career as teacher of high school social studies and as a teacher of social studies teachers. He was professor of education at New York University. On the high school level, he taught at Fayette (Mississippi) High School and was chairman of the social studies department of the John Burroughs School, St. Louis, Missouri. McCutchen also served as president of the National Council for the Social Studies.

Donald A. Ritchie is Associate Historian of the United States Senate Historical Office. Dr. Ritchie received his doctorate in American history from the University of Maryland, after service in the U.S. Marine Corps. He has taught American history at various levels, from high school to the university. He edits the Historical Series of the Senate Foreign Relations Committee and is the author of several books, including *Press Gallery: Congress and the Washington Correspondents,* which received the Organization of American Historians' Richard W. Leopold Prize. Dr. Ritchie has served as president of the Oral History Association and as a council member of the American Historical Association.

Send all inquiries to:
GLENCOE DIVISION
Macmillan/McGraw-Hill
936 Eastwind Drive
Westerville, OH 43081-3374

ISBN 0-02-822753-0   (Student Edition)
ISBN 0-02-822754-9   (Teacher's Wraparound Edition)
Printed in the United States of America.

2 3 4 5 6 7 8 9 10 -RRD-W- 00 99 98 97 96 95 94 93

Consultants

Content Specialists

Colonial and Early National History
Glenda Riley, Ph.D.
Professor of History
University of Northern Iowa
Cedar Falls, Iowa

Antebellum and Civil War History
Delbert A. Jurden, M.A.
Instructor of History
Johnson County Community College
Overland Park, Kansas

Gilded Age and Progressive Era History
Keith Ian Polakoff, Ph.D.
Assistant Vice President and Dean of Graduate Studies
California State University, Long Beach
Long Beach, California

Geography of the United States
Sarah Witham Bednarz, M.A.T.
Lecturer
Department of Geography
Texas A & M University
College Station, Texas

Native American History
Y. Elaine Childers, Ph.D.
Member, Creek Nation
Austin, Texas

John Waukeshon, M.A.
Member, American Indian Resource
and Education Coalition
Austin, Texas

Content Reviewer
Theodore M. Black, Sr.
Chancellor Emeritus
New York State Board of Regents
Port Washington, New York

Twentieth Century History
Stephen E. Ambrose, Ph.D.
Boyd Professor of History and Director of the
  Eisenhower Center
University of New Orleans
New Orleans, Louisiana

K. Austin Kerr, Ph.D.
Professor of History
The Ohio State University
Columbus, Ohio

Conceptual Education
Shirley A. Baugher, Ph.D.
History Teacher
Chicago Public Schools
Chicago, Illinois

Multicultural Education
D. Rosalind Hammond, Ed.D.
Associate Professor of Education
Bowling Green State University
Bowling Green, Ohio

American Religions
Charles R. Kniker, Ed.D.
Professor of Education
Iowa State University
Ames, Iowa

Teacher Reviewers

Glen Blankenship, Ph.D.
Social Studies Coordinator
Gwinnett County Public Schools
Lawrenceville, Georgia

Mary C. Burkett
Social Studies Teacher
Jackson City Schools
Jackson, Mississippi

Lawrence J. Cronin
Chairman, Social Studies
  Department
Greenon High School
Springfield, Ohio

Rose Marie Floyd
Social Studies Teacher
Jefferson Davis High School
Montgomery, Alabama

Jack Gilbert
History Teacher
Carson City High School
Carson City, Nevada

George W. Henry, Jr.
Social Studies Teacher
Highland High School
Salt Lake City, Utah

Marjorie B. Hollowell
Social Studies Teacher
John A. Holmes High School
Edenton, North Carolina

Michael L. Manson, Ed.D.
Social Studies Teacher
Townsend Harris High School
New York City, New York

Simmie G. Plummer
Social Studies Teacher
Valley High School
Albuquerque, New Mexico

Irene Ramnarine
Secondary Social Studies Resource
Teacher
Brevard County School District
Melbourne, Florida

Robert F. Sannicandro
Chairman, Social Studies Department
Marian High School
Framingham, Massachusetts

James M. Wolfe
History Teacher
Suitland University High School
Forestville, Maryland

Loretta Speed
History Teacher
Captain Shreve High School
Shreveport, Louisiana

Richard C. White
Chairman, Social Studies Department
Ames High School
Ames, Iowa

Ernie Woizeschke
Social Studies Department Leader
Coon Rapids Senior High School
Coon Rapids, Minnesota

Contents

★ UNIT 1 ★
A NEW WORLD: PREHISTORY TO 1756

★ UNIT 2 ★
THE STRUGGLE FOR INDEPENDENCE: 1650-1789

JOIN, or DIE.

★ UNIT 3 ★
LAUNCHING THE REPUBLIC: 1789–1824

★ UNIT 4 ★
TOWARD A DEMOCRACY: 1820-1848

★ UNIT 5 ★
DIVISION AND REUNION: 1825-1877

★ UNIT 6 ★
THE EMERGENCE OF MODERN AMERICA: 1860-1900

★ UNIT 7 ★
ENTERING A NEW CENTURY: 1880-1914

★ UNIT 8 ★
CONFLICT, CONFIDENCE, AND COLLAPSE: 1914-1932

★ UNIT 9 ★
TIMES OF CRISIS: 1932-1960

★ UNIT 10 ★
REDEFINING AMERICA'S ROLE: 1954-PRESENT

★ APPENDIX ★

★ FEATURES ★

Connections

Life of the Times

Linking Across Time

American Portraits

Maps

Charts, Graphs, And Tables

The Gifts of History

Dear Student,

Before you start the hundreds of pages that follow—with their thousands of scenes, characters, and ideas—you have every right to ask some questions: So what? What of it? Why should I work hard at teaching myself history?

There are many possible answers. Your teachers will have some; the authors of this book will have some. But think about this: you teach yourself history to give yourself certain gifts that nobody will ever be able to take away from you, no matter how long you live, no matter what happens to you.

What gifts? First, the power of judgment, of good sense about yourself and others, that comes from having many experiences in life and taking time to think about them. Some call it maturity, or growing up. Mainly, of course, we grow up from what happens to us in person—in the family, in school, on the street, at work or play, from our own joy and pain. But there are other human experiences we need to know that we can never have in person. By extending your experience through history, you can at least know something of what it meant to be an explorer, a missionary, a slave, a soldier at Gettysburg, a scared child at Ellis Island, a farm woman in the Depression. Without the power to compare your life with others, you cannot know who you are, how your world got to be the way it is, or what choices you have before you.

The second gift, or power, you gain from studying history is freedom of choice itself. What will you believe? What will you try to do with your life? You can have freedom to choose only by knowing the many ways citizens in the past have thought and acted upon their political, economic, and social problems, and the many private paths they have taken to pursue their own integrity, creativity, and happiness. In sum, teaching yourself history sets you free to question and to judge for yourself everything you hear, see, and read—including, to be sure, everything you read in history books. Not teaching yourself history leaves you as powerless to judge and to choose as if you had lost your own memory.

So think seriously about giving yourself the gifts of history, and read on.

Paul A. Gagnon

—PAUL A. GAGNON
HISTORIAN AND EDUCATOR

Themes

IN AMERICAN HISTORY

*I*magine a United States without computers, telephones, or automobiles, where women and most minorities cannot vote, a place where 8 of 10 people work on farms and higher education is a privilege reserved for the fortunate few.

That we today live in a totally different country—yet one that is indeed still the United States—is no accident. What connects past generations and our own is an unbroken chain of events that shapes our lives. Every event in our personal lives has contributed to who we are today. So too have events throughout our nation's history created the American people of the 1990s. Like individual threads in a cloth, events by themselves may lack substance and seem insignificant. Seen together as part of the whole, however, events gain clarity and form.

To help make sense of countless events in history, historians use themes to organize events into meaningful patterns. Themes are recurrent threads, surfacing within an assortment of events, making up the substance of history's fabric—a rich design emblazoned with brilliant colors on the cloth of time.

American Democracy

Abraham Lincoln perhaps explained the meaning of democracy best when he called it "government of the people, by the people, for the people." Democracy at its best, according to many of our nation's leaders, is "among" the people, as exhibited by this "stump-speaking" politician of the mid-1800s, an era of frontier democracy championed by Andrew Jackson.

Stump Speaking *by George Caleb Bingham, 1853–1854*

Civil Rights and Liberties

The foundation of democracy is the right of every person to take part in government and to voice one's views on issues. Not all people in our nation's past have had this basic right. This lithograph illustrates when all African-American men were granted suffrage in 1870 with the passage of the Fifteenth Amendment. Preservation of such civil rights and liberties for all citizens is how we guarantee that "we the people" control the government.

Missouri's commemoration of the Fifteenth Amendment

Economic Development

Classic Landscape *by Charles Sheeler, 1931*

The Preamble to the Constitution sets out the purposes of American government, one of which is to "promote the general welfare." Framers of the Constitution recognized that one of government's purposes must be to provide a climate in which citizens can better themselves economically. With few government restrictions, the nation's economy was built on the hard work of farmers and agricultural business.

Geography and Environment

Sunset Light, Wind River Range of the Rocky Mountains *by Albert Bierstadt, 1861*

The United States succeeded in part because of its rich natural resources and its vast open spaces. But in most regions of the nation, the natural landscape was transformed to accommodate ambitions that hard work could make dreams come true. The steel plow and the railroad helped Americans settle the West, but the unblemished environment of the native American gave way to the demands of expansion.

Conflict and Cooperation

It has been said that democracy is a poor form of government, but that no better form has been invented. President George Washington established the principle of placing the good of the nation above individual or sectional grievances in 1794, when he led troops against Pennsylvania farmers protesting a tax on whiskey. The conflict over, Washington pardoned the convicted leaders in the spirit of cooperation.

Washington Receiving the Western Army at Fort Cumberland, Maryland *by Frederick Kemmelmeyer, c. 1795*

Influence of Technology

Americans have always been quick to embrace innovations—the country was settled and built by people who gave up old ways and sought new. Americans' lives are profoundly influenced by technology, the use of science and machines. Perhaps no machine has so shaped modern life as the automobile. As the title of this 1920s song shows, the blessings, however, were mixed.

Sheet music cover for a 1920s hit song

The Individual and Family Life

Americans have a strong tradition of individual freedom sheltered by the protective core of the family unit. Families during the 1950s moved to suburban areas outside the central city to provide their families with more living space and protection from the perceived dangers of the city. Our earliest experiences of freedom, which were limited by the rights of other individuals, come from interactions within our homes.

Young suburban family of the 1950s

Humanities and Religion

Some of the earliest European settlers came to America for religious freedom. But a number of these groups turned around and promptly denied others the right to think for themselves and to question the teachings of their ministers. Anne Hutchinson and Roger Williams, among others, believed in their own ability to interpret religious teachings and founded settlements in Rhode Island where genuine religious freedom was practiced.

Anne Hutchinson preaching in her Boston home, from a painting by Howard Pyle

Cultural Diversity

American is not a pure nationality but a peculiar mosaic of ideals and ideas. People from around the world have for generations sung of this "land of the Pilgrims' pride, land where our fathers died" even though their ancestors arrived on these shores long after such events transpired. The public schools were the method by which those seeking a new future were transformed into Americans. These immigrant children in New York in the 1890s pledged allegiance to a flag under which none had been born but which was justly theirs in every way.

Students saluting the flag in New York City's Mott Street Industrial School, *photographed by Jacob Riis, 1889*

U. S. Role in World Affairs

A nation composed of peoples from around the world— buying and selling goods around the world, with economic and military might felt across continents, displaying a form of government emulated in all four corners of the globe— cannot but play a leading role in world affairs. President George Bush carried on a long tradition of American Presidents as champions for democracy when he told the Czechoslovakian people in 1990 that "America will stand with you" during a celebration of that country's 1989 return to democracy.

George Bush meets with the Czechoslovakia Assembly in Prague, 1990

Geography

IN HISTORY

*G*eography—the study of the earth and how people use its resources—is an integral part of the web of history.

Indeed, all history happens somewhere. It is the job of geography to supply answers about where a place is, what it is like, how the people live there, how people from different places interact with one another, and how one place on earth is like others on earth.

The geography of a region not only includes its physical landscape, natural resources, and climate but also the people who have settled there and their distinctive way of life. The history of the American people—the countless events that make up who we are—is notably influenced by the interplay of our nation's geographic features.

Like historians, geographers use themes to help organize their study of geography into purposeful patterns. Organizing information by themes helps make sense of the vast amount of information we have learned about the myriad of distinctive places that make up the United States of America.

Location

A place's position on the earth's surface—its location—constitutes one of the five themes of geography. Location can be either absolute (one particular spot of ground) or relative (position as compared to some other place). *Location* answers the question "Where is that?"

The Southeast, by virtue of its location on the Atlantic Coast, was one of the first parts of North America settled by Europeans. Colonial Williamsburg recreates daily life as it unfolded in the Southeast three centuries ago.

Los Angeles, California, one of the most densely populated urban areas in the United States, is located atop a network of active fault lines. Its Southwest location is a mixed blessing for Los Angeles—the city enjoys a Mediterranean climate, but it lives with the knowledge that earthquakes can strike at any time.

Forty-niners in California hoping to strike it rich knew well the importance of location. "Gold is where you find it," and one miner's claim might yield a bonanza while another only yards away might only produce broken dreams.

GEOGRAPHY IN HISTORY

Place

A place's physical and human characteristics tell what is special about it and what makes it different from all others. Landforms, climate, and culture combine to make up the particular flavor of a particular place. *Place* answers the question "What is that place like?"

Rivers have had a tremendous impact on American history and life. The confluence of the Mississippi (left) and Ohio (right) rivers south of Cairo, Illinois, in the heart of the Midwest imparts a special quality to land that is quite different from that found in the desert Southwest. Water is of paramount importance to both places—in the Midwest for its abundance, in the Southwest for its lack.

The Big Bend area of Texas is quintessential Southwest—vast open spaces hemmed by mountains and blue skies, an arid land where summer rains goad desert plants into a brief frenzy of bloom.

Settlement of the Great Plains coincided with the development of machines for plowing, planting, and harvesting on a grand scale; the combination made the Midwest a supplier of meat and grain to the world.

GEOGRAPHY IN HISTORY

Relationships Within Places

The theme of human-environmental relations describes how people use, affect, and are affected by their surroundings. Through such interaction, people change the environment in which they live. *Relationships within places* answers the question "How do people there live?"

The electrification of the Southeast by the Tennessee Valley Authority brought great changes to human-environmental relations in the region. Once vassals to King Cotton, southeasterners now enjoy a multifaceted economy.

Fishing boats ply the coastal waters of the Northeast in search of such delicacies as lobster. The nutrient-rich waters of the Atlantic drew people to the sea. Yet centuries of fishing have reduced the ocean's bounty.

Warm climate, abundant rainfall, and rich soil combined to make large parts of the Southeast ideally suited for the cultivation of cotton. The use of slave labor for this industry set the stage for a confrontation between North and South that became this nation's bloodiest war.

Movement

People interacting across the globe exemplifies interdependence, the need humans have to utilize skills and resources from around the earth. People travel, communicate, and trade goods, ideas, and information. *Movement* answers the question "How do the people in this place interact with peoples in other places?"

Southwesterners who live along the border between the United States and Mexico can experience dramatic changes in culture and lifestyle by simply walking a few feet from one country to another. The movement of people between countries has political, economic, and social implications. For the United States, a nation of immigrants, these implications are enormous.

New York City in the Northeast has long been the nation's center of international trade, banking, and business. Goods, people, and wealth from around the world ebb and flow in an unceasing tide.

Lewis and Clark, guided by the Shoshone woman Sacajawea, were the vanguard for wave after wave of Americans seeking land and adventure in the West. As the young nation expanded, the definition of the West leaped the Mississippi, spanned the Great Plains, scaled the Rockies, and finally reached the Northwest's Pacific shores.

Regions

Regions is the ultimate theme of geography. Regions—how areas form and change—display unity through their characteristics, some physical, some human. The study of regions allows geographers to answer the question "How is this place like other places on the earth?"

The Pacific Island chain we call Hawaii was built by magma seeping through a "hot spot" on the ocean floor. Kilauea crater adds land area to the United States almost daily with continuous eruptions.

New England is known not only for its brilliant foliage but also for its charming countryside of small villages inhabited by descendants of early settlers whose motto was "Use it up, wear it out, make it do."

The Northeast, like other coastal regions around the world, used its natural advantages to become a center of fishing, shipping, and trade. Yankee clipper ships were the fastest merchant vessels in the world; in 1854 the Flying Cloud set a record of 89 days, 8 hours, between Boston and San Francisco.

UNIT 1

A New World: Prehistory to 1756

...Having landed, they saw trees very green, and much water, and fruits of diverse kinds. The admiral [Columbus] called to the two captains. They said they should bear faithful testimony that he, in the presence of all, had taken possession of the said island for the king and for the queen....

—CHRISTOPHER COLUMBUS
Journal, 1492

SETTING THE SCENE

Time

Prehistory to mid-eighteenth century

Mood

The Americas were first inhabited by peoples who migrated from Asia thousands of years ago. From their descendants evolved a rich variety of cultures. Almost 500 years ago, however, other peoples—Europeans and enslaved Africans—set foot in what to them was a New World. Europeans, filled with dreams of adventure and wealth, explored, conquered, and settled the rich lands of the Western Hemisphere. British North America, in particular, developed and prospered.

Themes

- Geography and the Environment
- The Individual and Family Life
- Humanities and Religion
- Cultural Diversity

Key Events

- First Americans cross the Bering Strait
- Hopewells build mounds in the Ohio River valley
- Height of Mayan culture
- Norse seafarers land at Newfoundland
- Voyages of Columbus
- Spanish conquer Aztec and Incan empires
- Spanish bring enslaved Africans to America
- Founding of New France
- Founding of English colonies

Major Issues

- The environment shapes the development of native American cultures and European colonies in the Americas.
- The search for wealth and a direct route to Asia prompts European exploration and settlement.
- Interaction among native Americans, European colonists, and African Americans leads to the creation of a new American society.

◄ *Water vessel sculpture by Middle Mississippian Indian culture, c. A.D. 1000-1400*

Global Perspectives

Tens of thousands of years ago, people inhabited only some areas of earth. Then, during the last Ice Age—from about 40,000 B.C. to about 10,000 B.C.—a land bridge formed between Asia and North America. For the next several hundred years, bands of people wandered across the bridge and migrated from Asia. They became the first people in the Americas.

Over time, these new Americans evolved, learned skills, and developed tools and weapons. By 7500 B.C., they were farming and living in villages throughout the Western Hemisphere.

In different parts of the globe, great

THE WORLD

	ASIA AND OCEANIA	AFRICA	EUROPE	SOUTH AMERICA	NORTH AND CENTRAL AMERICA	
PREHISTORY		● C. 1,750,000 B.C. *First groups of people appear in Africa*	● 750 B.C. *Greek city-states flourish*		● C. 35,000–20,000 B.C. *First migrants from Asia cross the Bering Strait*	
500 A.D.	● C. 4000 B.C. *Civilizations begin to develop separately in Asia and Africa*		● 509 B.C. *Romans set up a republic*			
1600	● 1368 *Ming Dynasty begins rule of China*		● 1400s *Explorers set out and Age of Discovery begins* ◄	● 1400s *Inca and Aztec empires flourish in Peru and Mexico* ▼	● 1492 *Columbus lands in the Americas* ▲	
1750						

civilizations appeared—in Mesopotamia and Egypt, in the Indus River valley of India and Pakistan, and in the Yellow River valley of China. Influenced by geography and environment, each of these cultures developed distinctive social systems, languages, and religions.

In time, these civilizations began to trade with one another and, in the process, exchanged their beliefs and knowledge. From the Middle East came three major religions of the modern world—Judaism, Christianity, and Islam. From the early Greeks and Romans came philosophies of life and government that became the foundation of modern Western thought.

Throughout the 1500s and 1600s, western Europeans made conquests and founded settlements in the Americas. They were often at odds with native American peoples who struggled to preserve their heritage in the face of a changing world. From this came yet a new culture—an American culture.

THE UNITED STATES

	PACIFIC AND NORTHWEST	SOUTHWEST	MIDWEST	SOUTHEAST	ATLANTIC NORTHEAST
PREHISTORY					
			● 200 B.C.–A.D. 400		
500 A.D.			Hopewell burial-mound culture reaches its zenith		
		● 1050–1200 Great Pueblo period ◄	▲		
1600	● 1578 Sir Francis Drake explores the California coast			● 1607 First permanent English settlement is formed at Jamestown ◄	● 1620 Pilgrims ▲ found Plymouth
1750					● 1735 John Peter Zenger case sets precedent for freedom of the press

AMERICAN LITERARY HERITAGE

from *The Constitution of the Five Nations*

Among the native American groups with the richest oral literary traditions are the Iroquois and Navaho. The Iroquois lived in what is today New York State and were a mighty and warlike people given to infighting. During the 1500s a prophet named Dekanawida (DEK uhn uh WEE duh) appeared among the Iroquois and urged them to lay down their weapons and join hands in the spirit of friendship and peace, which led to the formation of the Iroquois Confederation of the Five Nations.

The Navaho arrived in the Southwest around A.D. 1000. They were an enterprising people who depended on farming and hunting for survival. Like the Iroquois, they expressed themselves in songlike chants and legends that provide a window on their ideals and beliefs.

I am Dekanawida and with the Five Nations confederate lords I plant the Tree of the Great Peace. I name the tree the Tree of the Great Long Leaves. Under the shade of this Tree of the Great Peace we spread the soft white feathery down of the globe thistle as seats for you…and your cousin lords.

We place you upon those seats, spread soft with the feathery down of the globe thistle, there beneath the shade of the spreading branches of the Tree of Peace. There shall you sit and watch the council fire of the confederacy of the Five Nations, and all the affairs of the Five Nations shall be transacted at this place before you.

Roots have spread out from the Tree of the Great Peace, one to the north, one to the east, one to the south and one to the west. The name of these roots is the Great White Roots and their nature is peace and strength.

If any man or any nation outside the Five Nations shall obey the laws of the Great Peace and make known their deposition to the lords of the confederacy, they may trace the roots to the tree and if their minds are clean and they are obedient and promise to obey the wishes of the confederate council, they shall be welcomed to take shelter beneath the Tree of the Long Leaves.

We place at the top of the Tree of the Long Leaves an eagle who is able to see afar. If he sees in the distance any evil approaching or any danger threatening he will at once warn the people of the confederacy….

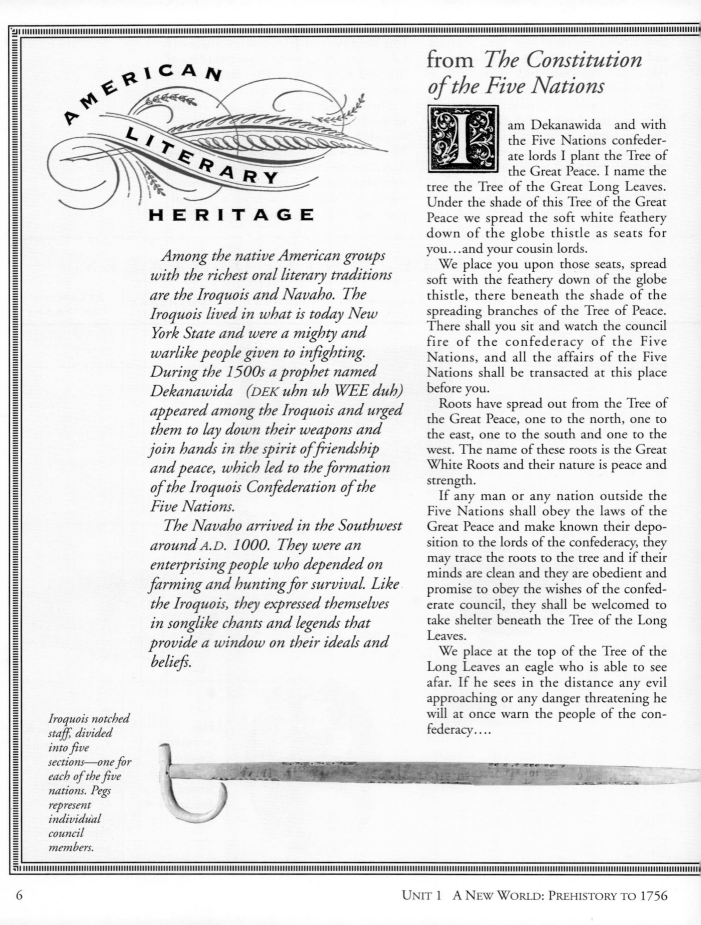

Iroquois notched staff, divided into five sections—one for each of the five nations. Pegs represent individual council members.

All lords of the Five Nations Confederacy must be honest in all things....It shall be a serious wrong for anyone to lead a lord into trivial affairs, for the people must ever hold their lords high in estimation out of respect to their honorable positions.

When a candidate lord is to be installed he shall furnish four strings of shells (or wampum) one span in length bound together at one end. Such will constitute the evidence of his pledge to the confederate lords that he will live according to the constitution of the Great Peace and exercise justice in all affairs.

Navaho blanket

When the pledge is furnished the speaker of the council must hold the shell strings in his hand and address the opposite side of the council fire and he shall commence his address saying: "Now behold him. He has now become a confederate lord. See how splendid he looks." An address may then follow. At the end of it he shall send the bunch of shell strings to the opposite side and they shall be received as evidence of the pledge. Then shall the opposite side say:

"We now do crown you with the sacred emblem of the deer's antlers, the emblem of your lordship. You shall now become a mentor of the people of the Five Nations. The thickness of your skin shall be seven spans—which is to say that you shall be proof against anger, offensive actions and criticism. Your heart shall be filled with peace and good will and your mind filled with a yearning for the welfare of the people of the confederacy. With endless patience you shall carry out your duty and your firmness shall be tempered with tenderness for your people. Neither anger nor fury shall find lodgement in your mind and all your words and actions shall be marked with calm deliberation. In all of your deliberations in the confederate council, in your efforts at law making, in all

your official acts, self-interest shall be cast into oblivion. Cast not over your shoulder behind you the warnings of the nephews and nieces should they chide you for any error or wrong you may do, but return to the way of the Great Law which is just and right. Look and listen for the welfare of the whole people and have always in view not only the present but also the coming generations, even those whose faces are yet beneath the surface of the ground-the unborn of the future nation."

Navaho Song of the Rain Chant

Far as man can see,
Comes the rain,
Comes the rain with me.

From the Rain-Mount,
Rain-Mount far away,
Comes the rain,
Comes the rain with me.

O'er the corn,
O'er the corn, the tall corn,
Comes the rain,
Comes the rain with me.

'Mid the lightnings,
'Mid the lightning zigzag,
'Mid the lightning flashing
Comes the rain,
Comes the rain with me.

'Mid the swallows,
'Mid the swallows blue
Chirping glad together,
Comes the rain,
Comes the rain with me.

Through the pollen,
Through the pollen blest,
All in pollen hidden,
Comes the rain,
Comes the rain with me.

Far as man can see,
Comes the rain,
Comes the rain with me.

INTERPRETING LITERATURE

1. In the Iroquois Constitution, what is the function of the eagle that sits atop the Tree of the Long Leaves?

2. How does the Rain Chant reflect Navaho beliefs about nature?

ANALYZING CULTURE

3. In what ways are the qualities desired for Iroquois leaders similar to or different from those desired for today's leaders in the United States government?

CHAPTER 1
The World in Transition

SETTING THE SCENE

Historical Focus

The first immigrants came to North America long before written history. They arrived by walking across a broad grassy "land bridge" where the Bering Strait now separates Siberia and Alaska. These native Americans developed unique cultures in North and South America. Then a series of events in Europe, Asia, and Africa opened the way to European voyages of discovery and exploration across the Atlantic. From these ventures that began more than 500 years ago, the United States was born.

Concepts to Understand

- Why **diverse cultures** among native Americans came into being.
- How **economic change** developed from trade with East Asia.

People to Know

Dekanawida, Marco Polo, Prince Henry, Vasco de Gama

Places to Locate

Bering Strait, Mesoamerica, Portugal

Terms to Identify

maize, pueblos, manor, serfs, charter, parliament, classical, feudal system, Muslims, samurai, astrolabe

Guided Reading

As you read this chapter, seek answers to the following questions.
1. What were the major native North American groups in 1600?
2. What circumstances in Europe, Asia, and Africa led to voyages of exploration?

SPANNING THE DECADES

POLITICAL	1000 B.C. *Native Americans move onto seacoast of present-day Peru and Ecuador*	A.D. 550 *Collapse of Roman Empire nearly complete*	711 *Moors conquer most of Iberian peninsula*

1000	500 B.C.	A.D. 500

CULTURAL		200 B.C. *Hopewell culture begins to build burial mounds*	900 *Mayan civilization begins to decline*

World map showing Spanish treasure fleet's route from Venice *by Battista Agnese, c.1543–45*

1210
Genghis Khan controls China, central Asia, and the Middle East

1433
Ming rulers in China stop outside trade

1485
Henry Tudor crowned king of England; War of the Roses ends

1000   1500

1085
Anasazi build pueblos, oldest standing buildings in North America

1300
Cahokia is largest North American community

1500
Aztec and Incan empires at their height

…Look at us, hear us…Heart of Heaven, Heart of Earth…May the people have peace, much peace, and may they be happy; and give us good life…grandmother of the sun, grandmother of the light, let there be dawn, and let the light come! …

—MAYAN DAWN PRAYER
Tenth century

9

The First Americans

SETTING THE SCENE

All the people worked the lands of the Inca ruler and of the Sun together, and they went to them with great joy and satisfaction, dressed in the clothes they wore on their grandest festival days...they went through their work with joy and gladness, because it was in the service of the Sun and the Inca ruler.

—GARCILASO DE LA VEGA
Spanish-Inca author, *El Inca*, 1608

Section Focus

The first people to come to the Americas are called native Americans or Indians. After adapting to their new home, they formed many rich and diverse cultures over time. Some of these cultures became elaborate empires, while others remained simple in organization.

Objectives

After studying this section, you should be able to:
- Explain the origins and paths of settlement of the first immigrants to the Americas.
- Compare the Indian cultures in Mexico and South America to those in North America.

Twenty thousand years ago, much of the water in today's oceans was frozen in glaciers. Huge glaciers covered much of what is now Canada and the northern United States. Scientists today believe that people from Asia walked across a "land bridge" that once connected Alaska and Asia.

They did not come all at once or together but in waves often hundreds or thousands of years apart. Most were groups of several families, following great herds of game animals. As these groups reached North America, they moved south along the coasts and mountain valleys. As waves of people continued to come, the people before them moved on to new places and spread out across the land. These waves continued until about 12,000 years ago when rising seawater destroyed the land bridge and separated the continents of Asia and North America.

Not all these people looked alike or were closely related; but short or tall, stocky or thin, they were all Asian and had common characteristics, such as straight black hair and skin ranging from coppery red to yellow-brown.

They gathered wild plants and hunted large animals—horses, mammoths, giant sloths, and beaver. Their spear points have been found with the bones of many animals now extinct in America: mastodons, tapirs, and giant bison. In addition to these and other large animals, the people hunted the smaller deer, antelope, elk, and bison.

Groups of these first Americans moved slowly south until they reached the tip of South America. Over time, these people adapted to their "New World" environment and became the peoples known today as native Americans.

For many thousands of years these people lived in bands of hunter-gatherers, adapting to the land or moving on. Often they became so close to their land that they came to believe that they had always been there. The Lakota Sioux of the Great Plains said:

...Our legends tell us that it was hundreds and perhaps thousands of years ago since the first man sprang from the soil in the midst of the great plains ... so far as we know our people have been born and died on this plain and no people have shared it with us....

Connections

HISTORY AND SCIENCE

PREHISTORY AND ARCHAEOLOGY

Collectors of Indian relics buy and sell arrowheads, spear points, and bits of pottery and jewelry for prices ranging from 50 cents for common arrowheads to hundreds of thousands of dollars for rare ancient specimens. Native Americans and archaeologists object to this practice. They claim that "pothunters" destroy Americans' historic legacy and that an isolated artifact can add little to the understanding of prehistoric cultures.

Although archaeologists "destroy" a site as they excavate, they observe and note details about the placement of each object. Their observations, combined with scientific techniques of dating and classification, can tell much about a particular culture. They can determine how people got their food, whether they built permanent homes, what they used to make tools, and whether they traded with others. Theories can then be developed about a culture's ideas and beliefs. This helps to preserve the prehistoric culture, even though the artifacts have been removed from their original sites.

One pothunter in Kentucky has given up collecting. "This is everybody's history," he says. "It shouldn't be for personal profit. Don't dig," he urges. "You destroy history when you do."

Archaeologist at work

★ ★ ★ ★ ★ ★ ★ ★ ★ ★

MAKING THE SCIENCE CONNECTION

1. What can archaeologists learn about a particular culture from excavating a prehistoric site?

2. Why do archaeologists object to "pothunters"?

LINKING PAST AND PRESENT

3. What are some artifacts of our own culture?

★ ★ ★ ★ ★ ★ ★ ★ ★ ★

Empires in America

Over time some of these hunters took up more sedentary ways of living. In South America groups of these people moved onto the dry seacoast of Peru and Ecuador. By harvesting the rich ocean waters and farming the river valleys, they developed a more complicated culture. By about 1000 B.C., they and the mountain peoples above them began to draw together the abundance of the jungles and sea. From the jungles they got dyes and medicine. These peoples had a gift for farming mountainsides, cultivating potatoes, peanuts, squash, and beans. With their great knowledge of metalwork, they became fine engineers who built great canals and cities. Some of these peoples had cities larger than cities of Europe at the time—with canals, pyramids, temples, markets, even bureaucrats and taxes. Their way of life became more

Examining Fine Art
Many Inca objects, like this intricate sacrificial knife, were made of gold. What other evidence shows that the Inca were highly civilized?

sophisticated and complex with city-states and empires that rose and fell. Because these people had no written language, however, precise knowledge of their history is uncertain.

The last of these great empires in the Andes was the Inca. The Inca were a mountain culture, who, 100 years before Columbus, united South America from its northern coast to the middle of Chile. They had central government, a vast road system, trade networks, irrigation canals, and sets of government storehouses to feed and supply people in case of disasters.

To the north, in the area called Mesoamerica—Central Mexico and Central America— much the same thing was happening. Not too long after the fishing people of Peru began to settle down, the gathering people in the central valley of Mexico cultivated a large-seeded grass. The grass, **maize**, developed over time into corn.

Examining Fine Art *This art shows the legendary origin of Tenochtitlán—an eagle on a cactus became the site of the Aztec capital. What modern city is on this site?*

Along the Gulf of Mexico coast, a group called the Olmecs developed a much more complex society with large villages, temple complexes, and pyramids. The Olmecs were the first Mesoamerican people to handle large masses of stone, sculpting large stone monuments. Their civilization strongly influenced their neighbors.

The Maya farther south were building ever larger pyramids and villages. Their trade networks spread along the coasts. Corn, cocoa, cotton, tomatoes, beans, and squash were traded far distances both north and south. Seeds and cloth of the Maya were traded for the pottery and precious stones of the South Americans. Both peoples became skilled at metalwork and pottery. No doubt ideas also moved back and forth from group to group until, in some cases, origins of ideas and plants are impossible to find.

Again, as people were able to improve their food supply, societies became more and more complex. Small groups grew into city-states and small countries. Market and trade centers sprang up with some groups specializing in products. The Maya developed a vast group of city-states that competed with one another in battle and in building grand public works. Then about A.D. 1000, the Maya changed and scattered over their area. The Maya and their trade routes continued but on a smaller scale. More is known about the Maya because they had a written language with books written on bark paper. Unfortunately, most of these books were lost during the early years of European contact, and it took many years to learn to read them because there were so few samples to study.

The Maya and the people of the Andes had a fascination with mathematics and engineering. The Maya invented the concept of zero. Most of these people had complicated and accurate calendar systems, linked to the study of the stars. Their temple-pyramids show a scientific knowledge of the earth's relation to the sun.

Many other equally advanced groups rose all over Mesoamerica. In the valley of Mexico large groups came and went. Groups from the north would arrive and conquer the people already there, set up a new capital, and fall to a new group of invaders. The last invaders were the Aztec. In about 1325 they settled on some islands in the middle of Lake Texcoco and built their city, Tenochtitlán, the site of modern Mexico City. Tenochtitlán was connected to the mainland by causeways. By the late 1400s, it had gold-adorned temples, floating gardens, and an enormous market. Its population of 100,000 was far larger than any city in Europe at the time.

By this time the Maya trade networks were partially taken over by the Aztec. To the south the Inca had consolidated an empire 3,000 miles long. It had 10,000 miles of roads with woven suspension bridges crossing canyons and rivers. The Inca had terraced hillsides with complicated irrigation systems and were able to feed far more people than lived in their empire. They had systems of moving people wherever they needed them for public works projects. They employed skilled weavers, metalworkers, and builders from other Andean peoples. The Inca had very strict ideas about responsibility of public officials and the duties of people to the state. Much of the system of organization was designed to take care of the people. In 1500, just as the European explorers set sail for the Americas, both the Inca and the peoples of Mexico reached these new heights of power and wealth.

Indian Cultures North of Mexico

The Indians who lived north of Mexico had entered into trade with the natives of Mexico. By 400 B.C., maize had been introduced into what would become the southwestern United States and the fertile Mississippi valley. From these two areas, maize spread throughout North America.

There were not nearly as many people to the north as there were in Mexico and the Inca empire. The Inca ruled perhaps 5 million people, while there were perhaps 4 or 5 million people in Mesoamerica. North of Mexico there were only 1 to 1.5 million people, most of whom lived in small villages and bands with varied cultures and ways of obtaining food. Anthropologists group these people by where they lived and the way they had adapted to the land at the time the Europeans arrived. In North America these groups include: Northwest Coast, California, Southwest, Plains, Southeast, Eastern Woodlands, and Northern Forest, as well as the Inuit (Eskimo and Aleut) in Alaska.

About the time of the fall of the classic Maya and the rise of Mexico Indian cultures, people in what is now the southwestern

HIAWATHA
C. 1570s

The character in the poem *The Song of Hiawatha* is not based on the life of the actual native American leader. The real Hiawatha, a Mohawk, enjoyed a reputation as a magician and a prophet.

Dedicated to ending violence and warfare, Hiawatha devoted his final years to creating a union from among hostile Indian nations. About 1570, he brought together the Mohawk, Onondaga, Oneida, Cayuga, and Seneca into the League of the Five Nations, also known as the Iroquois Confederacy. One remarkable aspect of the league was its ruling council in which each nation had a single vote. This early form of "government based on the consent of the governed" influenced the course of early American democracy. The United States began as a confederacy of states much like the Iroquois Confederacy.

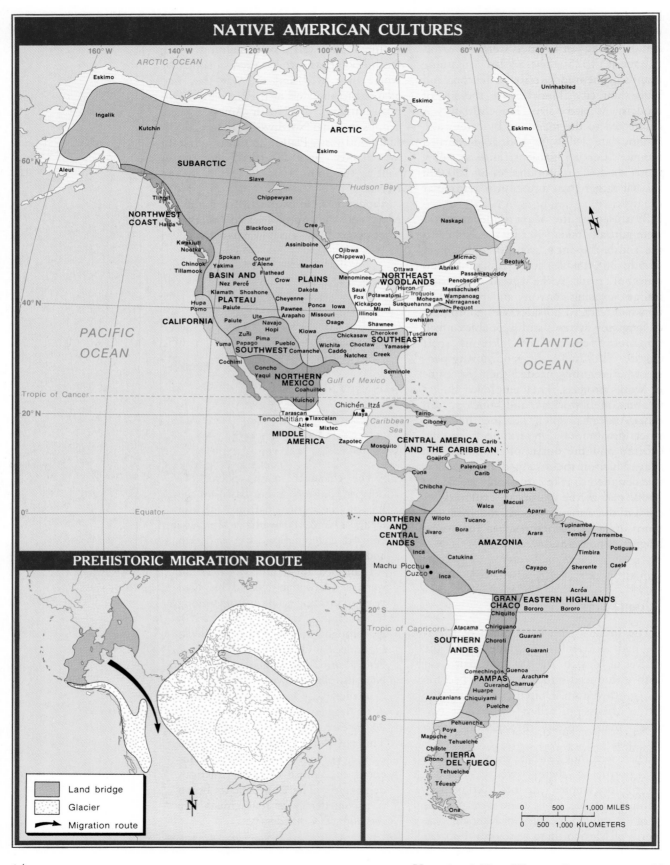

NATIVE AMERICAN CULTURES

ARCTIC OCEAN

Uninhabited

Eskimo

Ingalik

Kutchin

ARCTIC

Eskimo

Aleut

SUBARCTIC

Eskimo

Slave

Hudson Bay

Tlingit

NORTHWEST COAST

Haida

Chippewyan

Cree

Naskapi

Kwakiutl
Nootka

Blackfoot

Micmac

Chinook
Tillamook

Spokan
Yakima

Coeur
d'Alene

Assiniboine

Ojibwa
(Chippewa)

Abnaki

Passamaquoddy

Beotuk

BASIN AND
PLATEAU

Nez Percé

Flathead

Mandan

Menominee

Ottawa
Huron

Penobscot

Klamath

Shoshone

Crow

PLAINS

Iroquois

Massachuset

Hupa
Pomo

Paiute

Cheyenne

Dakota

Sauk
Fox

Potawatomi

Mohegan
Susquehanna

Wampanoag
Narraganset
Pequot

CALIFORNIA

Paiute

Pawnee

Ponca

Iowa

Kickapoo

Miami

Delaware

Ute

Arapaho

Missouri

Illinois

Shawnee

Powhatan

Navajo
Hopi

Kiowa

Osage

Zuñi
Pima

Chickasaw

Cherokee
Tuscarora

Yuma
Papago

Pueblo

Wichita

Choctaw

SOUTHEAST

Yamasee

SOUTHWEST

Comanche

Caddo

Natchez

Creek

Cochimi

Concho
Yaqui

NORTHERN
MEXICO

Seminole

Gulf of Mexico

Coahuiltec

Tropic of Cancer

Huichol

Chichén Itzá

Tarascan

Maya

Taino

Tenochititlán
Aztec

Tlaxcalan

Ciboney

MIDDLE
AMERICA

Mixtec

Caribbean
Sea

Zapotec

Mosquito

CENTRAL AMERICA
AND THE CARIBBEAN

Carib

Goajiro

Cuna

Palenque
Carib

Chibcha

Carib

Arawak

Waica

Macusi

NORTHERN
AND
CENTRAL
ANDES

Witoto

Tucano

Aparai

Jivaro

Bora

Arara

Tupinamba
Tembé

Tremembe

Inca

AMAZONIA

Timbira

Potiguara

Catukina

Ipuriná

Cayapo

Sherente

Caeté

Machu Picchu
Cuzco

Inca

Acróa

GRAN
CHACO

EASTERN HIGHLANDS

Chiquito

Bororo

Bororo

Atacama

Chiriguano

Tropic of Capricorn

SOUTHERN
ANDES

Choroti

Guarani

Guarani

Comechingon

Guenoa

Arachane

Querandi

Araucanians

Huarpe

Chiquiyami

Charrua

PAMPAS

Puelche

Pehuenche

Poya

Mapuche

Tehuelche

Chilote

TIERRA
DEL FUEGO

Chono

Tehuelche

Téuesh

Ona

PACIFIC
OCEAN

ATLANTIC
OCEAN

PREHISTORIC MIGRATION ROUTE

Legend:
- Land bridge
- Glacier
- Migration route

N

---

500   1,000 MILES

0   500   1,000 KILOMETERS

United States began to form larger groups with more complex village structures. Several groups began to build large close-knit villages in the area where Utah, Colorado, Arizona, and New Mexico come together. These people, called Anasazi, built large multi-story apartment-like buildings of adobe and cut stone with connecting causeways and elaborate ceremonial rooms. Early Spanish explorers called these houses **pueblos,** the Spanish word for "villages." The Anasazi pueblos are the oldest standing buildings in North America. Pueblo Bonito, with more than 600 rooms, took about 100 years to build and was finished about A.D. 1130.

To the south in Arizona, the Hohokam were building large villages with elaborate irrigation canals, ball-playing courts, and temple mounds. Their trade goods and decorations show close contact with northern Mexico. Other groups in the area also built large villages and show evidence of extensive trade with the people of Mexico and each other.

Then in about A.D. 1300 all of this changed. Perhaps a severe drought and climate change took place. The Hohokam vanished; other groups scattered and moved closer to established water. The Anasazi moved to the springs on the Hopi Mesas and the Rio Grande. Other groups moved to similar places. Their descendants remain as the Pueblo people of New Mexico and Arizona.

Another area that showed a great growth in population was the Mississippi valley. Around A.D. 900, people along the Mississippi river flourished as farmers and traders. They began to build great temple mounds of earth similar to those in Mexico. Settlements along the river grew into large towns. Cahokia (near present-day St. Louis) had a population of perhaps 10,000 people, with hundreds of temple mounds.

An earlier group of moundbuilders, the Hopewell culture, grew up in the Ohio River valley about 200 B.C. and lasted about 700 years. The Hopewell people farmed their rich land and traded across the Midwest for copper and shells. They built huge mounds of earth as both ceremonial centers and burial sites. Some of the Hopewells' elaborate and enormous mounds—as high as 30 feet—are in the shapes of snakes, turtles, and other animals. Inside the burial mounds, archaeologists have found pearl beads, woven cloth, copper ornaments, and striking objects of stone and mica. Groups such as the Hopewells spread all over the central United States from Wisconsin to the Gulf of Mexico.

On the Great Plains, the last of the hunter-gatherers still hunted the enormous herds of buffalo, which were all that remained of the mighty herds their ancestors followed from Asia. With the arrival of the Spanish and their horses, these people would also undergo a tremendous change. With horses to ride, the buffalo hunters would become a powerful force on the plains.

In other parts of the country, other groups also flourished: the rich fishing cultures of the Pacific Northwest, the seed gatherers of California, the farmers of the Southeast, and the League of the Iroquois in the Northeast.

The Iroquois, an alliance of farming people, dominated their area in the 1500s and 1600s. They were made up of Mohawk, Seneca, Oneida, Onondaga, and Cayuga tribes. Large groups of several families shared a "long house" of poles and bark. A large village might have 50 or more long houses and 300 to 400 people. Their league was a representative **confederation,** or government made up of independent units, probably formed about 1580. It was founded by two of the culture's heroes, Dekanawida and Hiawatha. The women leaders of each clan chose their chief, who would attend league councils. Though the League's Constitution was not written down until 1850, its provisions included:

The object of these laws is to establish peace between the numerous nations of Indians…for the preservation of life, property and liberty…And the number of chiefs in this confederation of the five Indian Nations are fifty….

In the southeastern United States, the Five Civilized Tribes formed another confederation of the Creeks, Cherokee, Choctaw, Seminoles, and Chickasaw. This group later devised a written language and a dictionary. They practiced a loose-knit form of democracy.

Just as the people of Europe and Asia were aware of each other, so widespread groups in the Americas knew about each other and shared similar ideas. For example, despite their diversity, the native American people felt a close relationship with the land and their environment. They felt that all things, themselves included, were all part of one great spirit.

In the 1400s native Americans continued to develop their ways of life isolated from other peoples of the world. The people of other continents were likewise unaware of America. Then a chain of events began to move the peoples of Europe, Asia, and Africa to increased communications and interdependence. The exchange of goods and ideas among civilizations on three continents intensified. By the late 1400s the world stood on the brink of enormous changes. European nations would soon initiate the ventures that led to the colonization of America.

The native American way of life was one that the Europeans who arrived seeking wealth in the new world were not able to appreciate or understand. The Europeans' values, especially their love of gold, seemed strange to the Indians as well. For example, during the conquest of Peru, an Inca citizen asked a European, "What do you do with gold? Do you eat it?" Reportedly, during the conquest of Mexico, Cortés told the ambassador to the Aztec ruler Moctezuma, "We have an illness only gold will cure."

This love of gold was as impossible for the Inca and Aztec to understand as it was impossible for the Europeans to understand human sacrifices. The idea of owning land was as alien to the native people of North America as the idea of not owning land was to the Europeans.

These two different viewpoints and the strong belief on both sides that their point of view was the only correct one would lead to continuing misunderstandings for centuries to come.

★ ★ ★ ★ ★ ★ ★ ★ ★ ★ ★ ★ ★ ★ ★ ★ ★ ★ ★

Section One Review

★ ★ ★ ★ ★ ★ ★ ★ ★ ★ ★ ★ ★ ★ ★ ★ ★ ★ ★

SUMMARY

Twenty thousand years ago, small groups of hunters followed game across a bridge of land that connected Siberia and Alaska. Eventually they spread throughout the Americas. Some remained hunter-gatherers, but others began to farm and raise animals. They built cities and complex cultures. Mesoamerican cultures such as the Inca and Aztec centered around religion with majestic temples and complex rituals. They had written language, numbers, and calendars. Eventually, the Aztec and Inca conquered their neighbors and built empires that included cities, trading centers, and roadways. Meanwhile, many North American peoples also became farmers, and some built villages with complex dwellings.

CHECKING FOR UNDERSTANDING

1. **Identify** Olmecs, Iroquois League, Mesoamerica

2. **Define** pueblos, confederation

3. **Summarize** the process by which the Americas were first settled.

4. **Describe** the characteristics of Mesoamerican culture.

5. **Discuss** three elements of Aztec and Inca cultures.

6. **State** three generalizations about native North American cultures.

THINKING CRITICALLY

7. **Evaluating Causes** Why would towns and complex societies tend to grow up among farmers, rather than among hunter-gatherers?

CONNECTIONS: HISTORY AND GEOGRAPHY

8. **Drawing Conclusions** How did changing physical features of the earth allow settlement of the Americas and then isolate them from the people of other continents for centuries?

★ ★ ★ ★ ★ ★ ★ ★ ★ ★ ★ ★ ★ ★ ★ ★ ★ ★ ★

Study and Writing Skills

Using Literature as a Historical Source

Literature is imaginative or creative writing that can be prose or poetry, fiction or nonfiction. Regardless of its form, literature can transport you across the continent or the ocean, ahead into the future or back in time. The literature of a period provides many insights into history. It helps you to understand the historic setting for events and provides details that make history come alive. For this reason your textbook includes a literature selection at the beginning of every unit.

Explanation

The reading that follows is a Navaho legend of creation. By asking yourself questions when reading the passage, you would receive answers like the ones that appear in italics following the reading.

On the morning of the twelfth day the people washed themselves well. The women dried themselves with yellow cornmeal. Soon after the ablutions were completed, they heard the distant call of the approaching gods. It was shouted, as before, four times—nearer and louder at each repetition—and, after the fourth call, the gods appeared. Blue Body and Black Body each carried two ears of corn, one yellow, one white, each covered at the end completely with grains.

The gods laid one buckskin on the ground with the head to the west; on

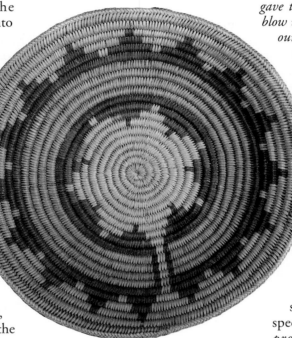

Navaho wedding basket

this they placed the two ears of corn, with their tips to the east, and over the corn they spread the other

buckskin with its head to the east; under the white ear they put the feather of a yellow eagle. Then they told the people to stand at a distance and allow the wind to enter. While the wind was blowing, eight of the Mirage People came and walked around the objects on the ground four times, and as they walked, the eagle feathers, whose tips protruded from between the buckskins, were seen to move. When the Mirage People had finished their walk the upper buckskin was lifted; the ears of corn had disappeared, a man and a

woman lay there in their stead.

The white ear of corn had been changed into a man, the yellow ear into a woman. It was the wind that gave them life....When this ceases to blow we die. In the skin at the tips of our fingers we see the trail of the wind; it shows us where the wind blew when our ancestors were created.

Example

a. What is the theme of the literature selection? *(the creation of people)*

b. Who are the main characters? *(Blue Body, Black Body, and the Mirage People)*

c. Do the events help me understand a historical setting, circumstance, or a specific culture? *(Yes, the legend provides information about Navaho life and values.)*

d. What have I learned from this work about a particular period or culture? *(Religion helped the Navaho to explain the connections between people and the environment. Corn and the wind were the significant natural elements.)*

Practice

For further practice in using literature as an historical source, read American Literary Heritage for Unit One on pages 6 and 7 of this book, and answer the suggested questions for each selection.

The New Europe

I have set you at the center of the world, so that from there you may more easily survey whatever is in the world....You may fashion yourself in whatever form you shall prefer....O highest and marvelous felicity of man! To him it is granted to have whatever he chooses, to be whatever he wills.

—GIOVANNI PICO DELLA
MIRANDOLA
Renaissance philosopher, 1486

Section Focus

During the Middle Ages, the western part of the old Roman Empire recovered from decline and developed a new civilization rooted in Christianity. Powerful monarchs emerged in several countries, and contacts with the Middle East and East Asia stimulated trade, learning, and national rivalries. Western Europe experienced a profound cultural awakening.

Objectives

After studying this section, you should be able to:
- Describe how European society was changed from medieval times.
- Explain the significance of the Renaissance and the Reformation.

The collapse of the Roman Empire was nearly complete by A.D. 550. Small isolated kingdoms replaced the once centralizing influence of Roman rule. When the Roman Empire ended, cities and city life also declined, and travel became dangerous because of the breakdown of law.

The empire's classical civilization nearly disappeared. The Roman Catholic Church remained as the only institution that held together the culture of western Europe.

The Middle Ages

During the Middle Ages,—A.D. 500 to 1500—most of European society was organized by the manorial system. The majority of the people of Europe were peasants who worked on farmlands that belonged to a **manor**, or large estate, held by a noble lord and lady.

Peasants lived in a village on the manor. Most were **serfs**, who were "bound to the soil;" that is, they were considered part of the property. A manor also included woods, common fields and pastures, a church, and shops for weavers, blacksmiths, bakers, and others who made the manor nearly self-sufficient.

In this period, the Church was the center of life in western Europe. Catholic clergy not only performed religious ceremonies but also participated in governing the small feudal manors, and the larger emerging kingdoms.

In 1095 Pope Urban II, head of the Roman Catholic Church, called for a "holy war" against the Seljuk (sehl JOOK) Turks, a Muslim people who held the Christian shrines in Palestine. The Church began a series of holy wars called crusades to recapture the Holy Land, including Jerusalem. The First Crusade was the most successful. Over the next 200 years, other crusaders went to war in the Holy Land. By 1291, however, the Muslims had retaken all the crusaders' kingdoms.

While the crusades were a failure, their effects upon western Europe were enormous. They helped bring western Europe out of isolation into contact with other parts of the world. Trade to satisfy the demand for eastern luxury goods started a series of events that completely changed Europe's economic, political, and social life.

When cities began to revive as centers for trade with the East, new opportunities in the city provided employment for wages. The manorial system began to break down as some serfs demanded higher wages and benefits to stay on the manor. Eventually, many could afford to buy their own land. Others began to pay rent for land with money rather than labor or produce. Farming for profit increased agricultural production, and better conditions caused the population to grow.

Because of their access to trade routes, towns along the Mediterranean Sea—in Italy, southern France, and Spain—grew first. As early as 1200, Venice and Genoa were strong city-states with busy shipyards. By 1423 Tomaso Mocenigo, Doge (mayor) of Venice could report:

…the Florentines send us every year, 16,000 bolts of the finest, fine and medium cloth; we export these to…Syria, Cyprus, Rhodes, Egypt, Romania….And the said Florentines bring in 7000 ducats weekly in all kinds of money, worth a total of 150,000 ducats a year.

Cities in northern Europe also emerged as centers for trade, shipping, and profitable craft industries such as weaving. Those with access to the sea would eventually rival the growth of Italian cities.

The Late Middle Ages

The rise of commerce brought prosperity to much of western and central Europe. The use of money and the need for credit turned some merchants into bankers. They lent money to finance new business ventures and provided credit for shipments of goods. The well-to-do bankers, merchants, and master craftsworkers made up a new town-based middle class that stood between the nobility at the top of the social system and the peasants at the bottom. All through the late Middle Ages, the middle class grew in numbers, importance, and power. It came to include lawyers, doctors, and minor government officials.

The middle class commonly supported the king—who represented stable government—against the feudal nobility— who disrupted trade by conducting local wars. As towns grew in population and wealth, some townspeople were able to buy a **charter** from the local lord and win the right to control their own affairs. In England, townspeople and knights gained a voice in government, sending representatives to meetings of a **parliament,** or assembly.

The power of the towns helped weaken the feudal system and strengthen national governments. Townspeople used their financial power to win rights and favors from an ambitious monarch. In return they supplied funds for ships or soldiers. Some bankers became powerful enough to deal on almost equal terms with European rulers who needed to borrow money. Prosperity, optimism, and an emphasis on human potential set the mood for far-reaching social and cultural changes in the 1400s and 1500s. This period is known as the **Renaissance,** a French word for the "rebirth" of interest in the culture and learning of ancient Greece and Rome. The meaning of the Renaissance, however, went far beyond this definition. Even today, people marvel at the accomplishments of Renaissance artists and scholars.

Examining Illustrations
This scene of peasants farming in front of a castle illustrated a French manuscript in the 1400s. What development weakened the feudal system?

**Examining
Illustrations**
*By the 1400s trade had
created markets in
Europe where Eastern
goods sold for great
profit. How did this
trade bring a Renais-
sance to northern
Italy?*

The Renaissance began about 1350 in the wealthy city-states of northern Italy. Trade with the East enriched merchant and banking families who used their wealth to collect books and paintings, hire architects to design buildings, and support painters and sculptors. Because they saw ruins of Roman monuments and buildings all around them, these wealthy patrons were especially interested in **classical** culture—the arts, literature, and knowledge of ancient Greece and Rome. This interest in the classics came to be called **humanism.**

While the Middle Ages had emphasized the human inner or spiritual nature and the need for self-discipline, the Renaissance awakened human creativity and demanded an outward expression of talent. Renaissance writers, artists, and thinkers admired ancient models, but they were brimming with new and experimental ideas. Writers tried new styles, writing in everyday language instead of scholarly Latin. Painters developed new techniques and tried to portray people realistically. Humanism took on a broader meaning, including an appreciation and concern for all aspects of human life.

The Renaissance in Italy reached its height in the late 1400s. Three of the most famous of the many Italian artists working at that time were Raphael, Michelangelo, and Leonardo da Vinci. Around 1500, Renaissance ideas spread northward into France, the Holy Roman Empire, the Netherlands, and England.

The new craft of printing with movable type, invented about 1440 by a German, Johann Gutenburg, helped spread Renaissance ideas. While only a few handwritten copies of books had been available earlier, by the 1490s there were numerous presses in operation. Because more Europeans could afford books, they were exposed to new ideas.

End of Religious Unity

For most Europeans in the Middle Ages, the Roman Catholic Church was the center of life and the most stable and unifying influence. But by the late 1400s, Europe was in the early stages of an intense religious upheaval.

What would later be known as the Protestant Reformation began simply with demands for reforms in the Roman Catholic Church. Among the leading early reformers were John Wycliffe in England and John Huss in Bohemia, part of the Holy Roman Empire. These early reformers criticized the Church's wealth and the luxurious lifestyles of some of the clergy. They also printed Bibles in the language of the common people rather than the official Latin. The Church feared widespread rebellion against its leadership. Compromises on such serious divisions were often impossible, and fighting broke out between Church supporters and reform groups.

In the early 1500s, Martin Luther, a Catholic and a professor in a German university, challenged several Church practices. Luther believed that salvation was simply by faith, not by good works and acceptance by the Church. In 1521, when he was called before Emperor Charles V to answer charges brought against him by Church authorities, Luther declared:

Unless I be convinced by Scripture and reason, I neither can nor dare retract anything, for my conscience is a captive to God's word, and it is neither safe nor right to go against conscience.

This stand marked the separation of Luther from the Catholic Church. The first Protestant faith, Lutheranism, was born. Soon other Protestant sects developed and became the dominant religions in Scandinavia, parts of modern Germany, the Netherlands, and England. In other parts of Europe, particularly Spain and the Holy Roman Empire, Catholic rulers became the Church's defenders.

The Reformation had far-reaching results. The Catholic Church began its own internal reforms and to counter the spread of Protestantism, encouraged its missionaries to travel and teach in distant parts of the world. Differences in religious beliefs among European monarchs added intensity to national rivalries. The conflict also weakened Church authority, allowing some European rulers to assume more power. Some of the new teachings made people think that it was safe to question other forms of authority.

Emerging Nations

During most of the Middle Ages, Europe was splintered into many small states. Ruled by princes, dukes, barons, and other local lords, these small states were part of a **feudal system.** This system rested on interlocking ties of protection and obligation between landowning nobles and those who lived on their lands.

During the late Middle Ages, strong monarchs and a sense of "nationhood" began to replace feudalism in western Europe. Rulers brought unity to their countries and gained authority over the powerful nobles.

In England it took 30 years of bloody civil war from 1455 to 1485 to unify the kingdom. Hundreds of English nobles, old and young, died in the fighting, destroying some noble families and weakening others. The winning Lancastrian leader, Henry Tudor, came to the throne in 1485 as King Henry VII. He married Elizabeth of York, the daughter of one of his defeated rivals, unifying the kingdom. Henry VII's ruling house, or **dynasty,** produced several outstanding rulers.

The monarchs of France, too, gradually consolidated their power and territory. As the French fought the English in the

Examining Illustrations
Martin Luther's criticisms of Church practices caused a religious revolt. What were two other far-reaching results?

Hundred Years' War from 1337 to 1453, French rulers won the confidence of the entire country. France's victory in the war, aided by the heroism of Joan of Arc, increased the French people's feeling of patriotism and unity.

A different motivation brought political unity to Spain. In about A.D. 711, Muslims, or Moors, from North Africa conquered most of the Iberian peninsula—Spain and Portugal— establishing an advanced culture there. Christian rulers, led by the kingdom of Castile, tried continuously to drive the Moors out of Spain. By the mid-1400s, the Muslims held only the territory around Granada on the southeast coast.

In 1469 Christian unity in Spain was aided by the marriage of the heirs to the largest kingdoms: Isabella of Castile and Leon, and Ferdinand of Aragon. "The Catholic monarchs" believed that Christianity would unify the country. In 1492 they ordered all Jews to leave Spain. In the same year, their armies took Granada from the Moors.

Once part of Spain, Portugal won its independence in the twelfth century. Portugal also defeated the Moors, and by the late 1300s the country was unified under King John I. The Holy Roman Empire, which included the modern nations of Germany, Austria, and parts of Italy, remained the largest European territory. In the late 1400s, however, it faced both internal problems and outside invaders. Poland and Russia would likewise lack the unified direction to participate in exploration and discovery with the western European kingdoms: Spain, Portugal, France, and England. All four had seaports on the Atlantic Ocean—soon to become a great avenue of trade and exploration.

In a few hundred years, Europeans, once isolated from the rest of the world and bound by a rigid feudal system, developed a widespread spirit of curiosity and adventure. Unified monarchies and national rivalry led to competition for trade with Asia. The search for an all-water route to East Asia encouraged western European explorers to cross unknown oceans and seek new lands.

★ ★ ★ ★ ★ ★ ★ ★ ★ ★ ★ ★ ★ ★ ★ ★ ★ ★ ★

Section Two Review

★ ★ ★ ★ ★ ★ ★ ★ ★ ★ ★ ★ ★ ★ ★ ★ ★ ★ ★

SUMMARY

During the 1300s and 1400s, Europe shifted from feudalism to nationalism. As towns and trade developed, a growing middle class of merchants and bankers accumulated wealth and power. They used this power to finance the activities of powerful monarchs, gaining political influence in the process. They financed some of the world's finest art and architecture during the Renaissance, a rebirth of interest in classical culture and the pursuit of knowledge. As nations unified, the unity of the Roman Catholic Church began to break down as reformers questioned Church teaching and policy.

CHECKING FOR UNDERSTANDING

1. **Identify** Martin Luther, Henry Tudor, Moors, Isabella of Castile and Leon, Ferdinand of Aragon

2. **Define** manor, serfs, charter, parliament, Renaissance, classical, humanism, feudal system, dynasty

3. **Discuss** the political changes in Europe in the late 1400s.

4. **Describe** the changes in the European social structure after the close of the Middle Ages.

5. **Explain** the broad meaning of the term *Renaissance* as it applies to art, science, and culture.

6. **Summarize** the development and results of the Reformation.

THINKING CRITICALLY

7. **Analyzing Cause and Effect** Why did the growth of towns and a middle class of bankers and merchants lessen the influence of feudal lords?

CONNECTIONS: HISTORY AND RELIGION

8. **Evaluating Results** What role did religion play in the growth of European culture?

★ ★ ★ ★ ★ ★ ★ ★ ★ ★ ★ ★ ★ ★ ★ ★ ★ ★ ★

Medieval Asia and Africa

In this book it is our design to treat all of the great and admirable achievements of the …Kublai Khan;…in our language Lord of Lords, and of a surety he hath good right to such a title, for in respect to number of subjects, extent of territory, and amount of revenue, he surpasses every sovereign….

—MARCO POLO
Venetian traveler to China, 1298

Section Focus

Europeans' desire for trade had provided a compelling reason for contact with the East. Trade between Asia and Africa, however, had transpired for centuries. The rise of Islam was a major influence on contacts between Europe, Asia, and Africa.

Objectives

After studying this section, you should be able to:
• Explain the impact of Islam.
• Describe the extent and importance of the Mongol Empire.
• Identify some of the trading kingdoms of Africa.

Since ancient times, trade had linked the different peoples and cultures of the "Old World"—Europe, Asia, and Africa. Both the Greeks and Romans had established profitable routes of trade with Asia and Africa. Seeking slaves and luxuries such as silks, spices, and precious stones, traders also carried ideas and information over great distances.

With the fall of the Roman Empire, Europe's participation in foreign trade had declined. Roads and bridges fell into disrepair and robbers preyed on travelers because there was no government to keep order. While most people in Europe lived in the country, isolated into small villages, trade between Asia and Africa continued.

Spread of the Muslim World

The most important influence in medieval Asia and Africa—with consequences for Europe as well—was the rise of the religion of Islam. Founded by the prophet Mohammed in the 600s, Islam spread quickly from the Arabian peninsula by conquest through the Middle East to Asia and North Africa, into Spain and the Mediterranean region. About 682 an Arab general, Achbar Ben Nafi Al-Fahri, and his warriors had reached the Atlantic in North Africa. Achbar expressed his zeal for Islam:

Did not these waters present an insuperable barrier, I would carry the faith and the law of the faithful to countries reaching from the rising of the sun to the setting thereof!

The original Islamic empire led by Arabs was soon divided. Rival groups of Muslims—the name for followers of Islam—organized and took control over different areas in Asia, Africa, and parts of Europe. In some places—for example, Spain—they met fierce resistance and eventually lost power.

By the late 1400s, the rapidly growing empire of the Ottoman Turks was the leading Muslim power. From their base in Asia Minor—modern Turkey—the Ottomans had taken over Greece and much of the Balkan peninsula.

As Islam spread, Muslims and Christians came into direct conflict. Knights from Christian Europe fought to recapture lands that the Muslims occupied in Spain and Sicily. In 1095, at the urging of the Pope, the knights' main goal became control of Palestine and its Christian shrines.

Examining Illustrations *Islamic doctors' discoveries helped develop European medicine in the 1100s. Where did Arabic numerals originate?*

In the long run, these Crusades into the Holy Land, which was sacred to both Christians and Muslims, had a great influence on trade and learning. From Middle Eastern and Islamic cultures, the returning knights and soldiers learned about new foods and products—spices, sugar, silk, cotton, dyes, perfumes, tapestries, and fruits such as peaches and melons. Wealthy Europeans could afford to buy these luxuries from the East. Increased trade enriched the Italian city-states.

Contact with the Muslim world also brought new ideas. Arab scholars had made important advances in medicine, astronomy, mathematics, and other sciences. While learning had declined in medieval Europe, the Arabs had preserved much of Greek and Roman science and philosophy. From the Arabs, Europeans learned algebra and the system of Arabic numerals, which the Arabs had learned in India. In Spain the Muslims introduced the Arabian horse as well as oranges and lemons.

One of the early targets of Muslim expansion was the huge subcontinent of India. Beginning in A.D. 712, groups of Muslim invaders from Persia (Iran) and Afghanistan occupied parts of northern India. The beliefs of the Muslim conquerors clashed with the ancient Hindu traditions of India. While some Indians converted to Islam, religious conflict led to deep divisions within the country.

In the late fifteenth century, a weak Muslim kingdom known as the Delhi sultanate was in power in northern India. The rest of the country was divided among many small states and kingdoms controlled by princes and rajas, most of whom were Hindu. Early in the 1500s, another group of Muslims established the powerful Mogul Empire, which would unite and rule India for several hundred years.

Empires of the East

In the early 1200s the ancient empire of China was conquered by the invading "Golden Horde" of Mongols from central Asia. Genghis Khan and his army of fierce, swift riders also swept westward across central Asia, through Russia, terrorizing the Slavic people in Poland, Hungary, and Austria. For nearly 200 years, the Mongols ruled one of the largest empires in history, including China, central Asia, Russia, and the Middle East.

Although the Chinese considered the Mongols "foreign barbarians," China prospered under their rule. Overland travel between Europe and China was safe while the Mongols controlled the huge central Eurasian plain. East-west trade was revived, along with cultural exchanges among China, Europe, and Muslim Asia. European traders, travelers, and missionaries went to China. They returned not only with silks and spices but also with important inventions like the compass, printing, and gunpowder.

European traders also brought back knowledge and exciting descriptions of the wonders they had seen in Asia. The most famous was a young merchant from Venice, Marco Polo, who traveled to the court of Kublai Khan in 1275 and stayed

Examining Illustrations *Marco Polo arrives at the court of Kublai Khan in this illustration from a thirteenth-century manuscript. Polo stayed in China as an aide to the Khan. Upon returning to Europe he wrote the popular* Descriptions of the World. *Europeans were impressed by Chinese civilization. What luxuries were in the Khan's palace?*

on till the 1290s. Marco Polo's description of the luxury of the "Great Khan's" court stirred the imaginations of his readers in medieval Europe:

———— ◦◦◦ ————

The palace is completely surrounded by a square wall, each side being a mile in length. . . Inside, the walls and halls and chambers are all covered with gold and silver and decorated with pictures of dragons and birds and horsemen and various breeds of beasts and scenes of battle. The ceiling is similarly adorned so that there is nothing to be seen anywhere but gold and pictures. The hall is so vast that a meal might be served there for more than 6,000 men.

———— ◦◦◦ ————

By the late 1400s, when the inquiring spirit of the Renaissance was changing Europe, the mood in China was to preserve tradition. Following the death of the Great Khan in 1294, the Chinese overthrew their Mongol rulers. The conservative rulers of the new Ming Dynasty wanted to restore the old, purely Chinese heritage. New ideas were discouraged, and students studied only the ancient classic books. At first the Ming rulers did encourage trade. In the early 1400s their admiral Zheng He [CHENG HOH] led expeditions around the Indian Ocean and to the coast of east Africa. Then in 1433—perhaps to avoid foreign influences—the Ming rulers halted trade and cut China's contacts with the outside world. China would remain relatively isolated for centuries.

Like medieval Europe, Japan had a feudal society, based on the bonds between landowning nobles and the knights who served them. **Samurai,** the warriors of feudal Japan, lived by a strict code of honor. Since the 1100s, the country had been led by **shoguns,** military dictators who had far more power than the emperor.

Japan's island location had helped protect it from conquest during Mongol rule in China. When Kublai Khan's navy tried to invade Japan in 1281, a typhoon destroyed the fleet. Fighting off the Mongols, however, weakened the shoguns' government. In the late 1400s, local lords, backed by their private armies of samurai, were almost constant-

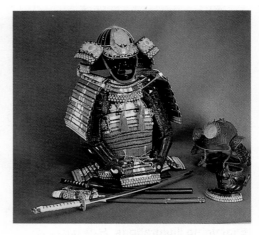

Examining Illustrations *The samurai wore loose-fitting armor and fought with curved steel swords. How was Japanese society in 1100 like European society?*

ly at war. Nonetheless, towns and trade were prospering in medieval Japan. Japan, China, Korea, and Southeast Asia had long been exchanging both goods and ideas.

African Trading Kingdoms

From ancient times, trade linked different areas of the continent of Africa with other cultures and peoples. While Egypt and other parts of North Africa were part of the Mediterranean world, North African merchants also followed caravan trails south across the Sahara to exchange precious salt for gold and slaves.

The earliest African civilizations developed east of the Sahara. Egypt dominated the region for more than 2,000 years. Kushites from the southern Nile then became an independent kingdom. During the time of the Roman Empire, another powerful state, Axum, expanded to challenge the Kushite rule. Axum, strongly influenced by the early Christian church, made Christianity the official religion of the kingdom in A.D. 330. When Islam spread across northern Africa in the A.D. 600s, Axum lost much of its coastal territory. Its rulers set up the Christian kingdom of Ethiopia. While Ethiopian rulers attempted to spread

Life of the Times

GOLDEN AGE OF MALI

The harmony that characterized everyday life during the golden age of Mali contradicts the myth of African "barbarity" that Europeans perpetuated after the slave trade had begun. A firsthand account of life in Mali was given by the Arab geographer ibn-Battutu. Traveling through Mali in the fourteenth century, he marveled at the law, order, and racial tolerance of the African kingdom.

"The Negroes possess some admirable qualities. They are seldom unjust and have a greater abhorrence of injustice than any other people. Their Sultan shows no mercy to any one guilty of the least act of it. There is complete security in their country. Neither traveler nor inhabitant in it has anything to fear from robbers or men of violence. They do not confiscate the property of any white man who dies in their country, even if it be uncounted wealth. On the contrary, they give it into the charge of some trust-worthy person among the whites, until the rightful heir takes possession of it."

Many African nations in the late 1400s were as advanced as Mali. Slave traders, however, ignored the cultural values of these societies and only saw the people as a means to quick profit.

Examining Illustrations *Hide hats with gold trim were worn by the Ashanti clan of West Africa. What city was the center of trade in West Africa in the 1300s?*

Christianity throughout Africa, civil war and Muslim expansion weakened and isolated their nation

Between A.D. 500 and 1500, three wealthy trading kingdoms—Ghana, Mali, and Songhai—developed one after the other in the western Sudan, the grasslands south of the Sahara. The Muslim conquest of North Africa greatly increased trade, and Muslim culture spread to the area.

In the 1300s the trading city of Timbuktu in Mali became a leading center of Islamic culture, with a university and a great mosque. In 1468—the time of the Wars of the Roses in England—the Songhai people rebelled and captured Timbuktu. Askia Mohammed, a strong general and devout Muslim, ruled Songhai between 1493 and 1528.

East Africa, on the other hand, looked eastward, trading with Arabia, Persia, India, and even China. Wealthy city-states such as Kilwa were trading centers for African gold, ivory, cinnamon, palm oil, and slaves. The city-states had white stone houses and mosques. Swahili, an African-based language mixed with Arabic words, was widely used in trade.

Civil wars brought internal disorder to Bantu nations in Central and South Africa. The resulting loss of power left little defense against Europeans who arrived in the 1500s.

★ ★ ★ ★ ★ ★ ★ ★ ★ ★ ★ ★ ★ ★ ★ ★ ★ ★ ★

Section Three Review

★ ★ ★ ★ ★ ★ ★ ★ ★ ★ ★ ★ ★ ★ ★ ★ ★ ★ ★

SUMMARY

Muslims and Christians came into conflict. Two hundred years of Crusades failed to force the Muslims out of Palestine—the Holy Land. But the crusaders stimulated trade, science, and scholarship by bringing back to Europe the goods, inventions, and ideas they acquired in the East. Muslim conquerors developed powerful trading empires and added elements of their own culture to the highly developed cultures they found in India and Africa. The Mongols conquered highly developed civilizations in China, central Asia, Russia, and the Middle East. Marco Polo's accounts of his observations in Asia fueled interest in routes to the Far East.

CHECKING FOR UNDERSTANDING

1. **Identify** Muslims, Ottomans, Crusades, Marco Polo, Axum, Swahili

2. **Define** samurai, shoguns

3. **Analyze** the way in which the spread of Islam affected Europe, Asia, and Africa.

4. **Discuss** the extent and importance of the Mongol Empire.

5. **List** some of the trading kingdoms of western and eastern Africa.

THINKING CRITICALLY

6. **Predicting Outcomes** How might interest in exploration have increased as a result of the Crusades?

LINKING PAST AND PRESENT

7. **Comparing Actions** In the 1970s and 1980s, Islamic nations came into frequent conflict with their Jewish and Christian neighbors. Saudi Arabia, for example, restricted visitors to prevent foreign influences from changing the Islamic way of life. How are these events similar to those described in this section?

★ ★ ★ ★ ★ ★ ★ ★ ★ ★ ★ ★ ★ ★ ★ ★ ★ ★ ★

Europeans Seek the East

On Friday, the 18th of May…we sighted lofty mountains.…They asked what he [the captain-major] sought so far away from home, and he told them that we came in search of Christians and of spices.

—VASCO DA GAMA
Portuguese explorer, from his logbook, 1498

Section Focus

By the last decades of the fifteenth century, technological and economic changes in Europe made long sea voyages possible. The prime goal of these ventures was a sea route from Europe to Asia, in search of spices and luxury goods. Encouraged by their rulers, Portuguese sea captains were the first to find this route.

Objectives

After studying this section, you should be able to:
- Explain the changes in commerce and in technology that enabled Europeans to sponsor long ocean voyages.
- State the importance of the Portuguese discovery of a sea route to Asia.

The new spirit of curiosity and adventure that swept over Europe with the Renaissance helped launch the bold voyages of the Age of Exploration. Many other motivations sent these sailors across unknown oceans: Europeans wanted luxury goods from Asia, as well as the spices—pepper, nutmeg, cinnamon, cloves—that preserved foods and made them taste better. European merchants hoped to break the monopoly that Arab traders and Venetian merchants had on the overland routes to Asia. European monarchs hoped to enrich and strengthen their countries—and themselves. When new lands were discovered, the Roman Catholic Church sent missionaries to bring Christianity to millions of new souls.

While six countries on the Atlantic coast—Portugal, Spain, France, the Netherlands, Sweden, and England—would eventually undertake voyages of discovery, the pioneer in these ventures was Portugal.

A Revolution in Commerce

Italian city-states had proven that great profit awaited those willing to take risks to trade with the distant East. They had a monoply on trade through the Mediterranean, but northern European merchants and bankers would soon use their accumulated wealth to sponsor voyages. They would lend money to outfit ships and pay the captains and crew, and they would insure ships.

The great expense of ocean voyages made new ways of raising finances necessary. In England, France, and the Netherlands, the **joint-stock company** became a useful form for raising money. The company would sell shares, called **stock**, to a number of investors, thus providing money or **capital**, for its venture. Each shareowner then received a portion of the venture's profits—or losses.

The joint-stock company let small investors, who could not afford to outfit an entire ship, take part in overseas commercial ventures by buying one or more shares of stock. It also enabled wealthy people to spread their risks by investing in several joint-stock companies at the same time. A joint-stock company might have hundreds of shareholders, thus creating strong organizations rich enough to support long expeditions or found colonies.

No matter how strongly motivated or well financed, long voyages of discovery could not have succeeded without improvements in technology: new ship designs and better navigational instruments.

In the Mediterranean, for thousands of years, ship captains had tried to sail within sight of land, guided mainly by written descriptions of coasts and harbors, such as:

The landmark for Barcelona is a high, abrupt, and isolated mountain called Monserrate. When you are northeast of it, you will see a low mountain with a tower on it.

By the fifteenth century, captains also had precise maps for both the Mediterranean and the Atlantic coasts of Europe and North Africa. In addition, they had learned from Arab sailors how to use several improved navigational instruments. The **compass,** which was invented in China, reliably showed the direction of magnetic north—even at night or in cloudy weather. The **astrolabe** and the **quadrant** measured the positions of the sun and stars, allowing the navigator to determine distance north and south from a given point.

Ships built to new designs were faster and more seaworthy. The **carrack,** for example, had several masts and a rudder. Smaller but easier to handle was the Portuguese **caravel,** a double-rigged ship with both square and triangular sails. On Columbus's first voyage, the flagship *Santa María* was a carrack of about 1 hundred tons; the *Niña* and the *Pinta* were caravels.

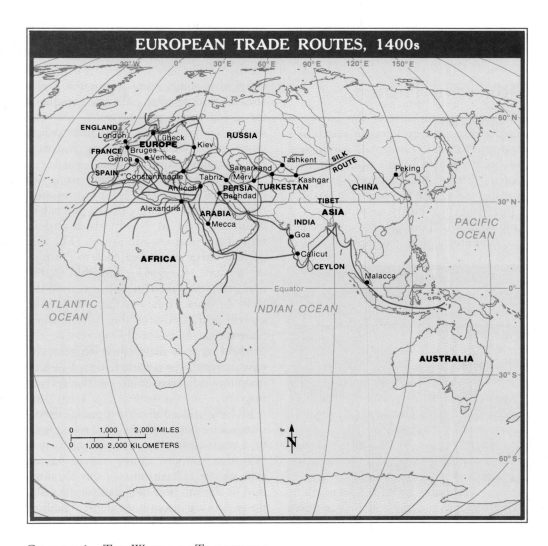

Examining Maps
Italian cities controlled trade through the Mediterranean, forcing northern Europe to take more difficult land routes. What changed this by 1500?

Examining Fine Art *Henry the Navigator is shown in this detail of the painting,* Panel of the Infanta. *What studies did he support beginning in 1419?*

Pioneering Portuguese

Portugal was the first of the European kingdoms to send explorers in search of a sea route to Asia. This small nation had not been troubled by the wars that were ravaging France and England nor by the ongoing war against the Moors in Spain.

In 1419 Prince Henry, a younger son of King John I of Portugal, set up a center for astronomical and geographical studies at Sagres, on the southwestern tip of Portugal. There he invited mapmakers, astronomers, and shipbuilders from throughout the Mediterranean world to study and plan voyages of exploration.

With this collected knowledge, Prince Henry sent expeditions beyond the safety of the Mediterranean. Portuguese ships began to travel southward along the African coast. As expeditions returned, Henry's mapmakers corrected and improved their sailing charts, which the Portuguese kept secret.

For people at that time, these were fearsome voyages. Europeans were convinced that great dangers awaited in the open ocean: a Sea of Darkness, sea monsters, oceans that boiled at the equator. There were, in fact, some dangerous currents and treacherously shallow waters along the African coast. By the time Prince Henry—known as "the Navigator"—died in 1460, his ships had reached only Cape Verde, the westernmost tip of Africa.

By this time, the Portuguese were already trading with African merchants for gold, ivory, pepper, palm oil, and slaves. Soon they had profitable trading posts on the West African coast and were establishing sugar plantations.

Slavery and the slave trade were not new in the region. Using war captives and others as slaves had long been a practice in Muslim society in North Africa and in other parts of the world as well. The first African slaves were taken back to Portugal as servants in 1441. Probably 1,000 Africans were taken to Portugal over the next 5 years. But by the 1490s, the growth and profits of the African sugar plantations had greatly increased the demand for local slave labor. To meet the new demand, slave traders turned to kidnapping and "slave raids" in the African interior.

In 1487 and 1488 a Portuguese expedition led by Bartholomeu Dias was caught in a storm that blew the ships off course near the southern tip of Africa. As the skies cleared, Dias realized from the position of the sun that they had rounded the tip of Africa without knowing it. The Portuguese ruler, King John II, hopefully

Examining Fine Art
The Slave Deck, *painted by Meynell from his memories of the voyage on the* Albanoz, *shows African slaves in cramped quarters. When did European slave trade begin?*

named the area the "Cape of Good Hope" because it seemed to promise the existence of a new sea route to India.

Ten years later another Portuguese expedition set sail, headed by Vasco da Gama. After almost a year's travel, they rounded the Cape of Good Hope and sailed up the eastern coast of Africa past the rich Muslim city-states of Kilwa and Malindi. With an Arab pilot, the expedition crossed the Indian Ocean to Calicut on the coast of India.

The voyage home took another year and was much more difficult. So many sailors died of **scurvy**, a sickness caused by a lack of fresh fruits and vegetables, that there were only enough left to sail two ships. Da Gama finally returned home to Portugal in September 1499. It is said that the profits on his cargo of cinnamon, cloves, nutmeg, ginger, and pepper covered the cost of his expedition 60 times over.

The trade rivalry among Italian city-states had been intense. Now Portugal's successful sea venture would cost the Italian cities their monopoly on trade. When news of da Gama's voyage reached Venice, the effect was dramatic. A Venetian writer reported:

———◆◆◆———

...if this voyage should continue,
the King of Portugal could call himself
the King of Money, because
all would convene to that country to obtain
spices, and the money
would accumulate greatly in Portugal....
this news was held by the learned to
be the worst news which the Venetian
Republic could have had....

———◆◆◆———

Da Gama's ships had traveled 24,000 miles. The sea route that he opened brought Portugal wealth and challenged the other European nations to make their own explorations. In the following four centuries, western Europe's quest for empire across the oceans would affect the lives of people on every continent.

Section Four Review

SUMMARY

The joint-stock company made voyages of exploration easier to finance. Improvements in navigation and sailing technology, new maps, and knowledge from the East made navigation safer. New designs made ships faster and more seaworthy. These developments were furthered under the sponsorship of Prince Henry of Portugal, who gathered experts to plan voyages of exploration. Following each voyage, mapmakers revised their sailing charts to reflect knowledge gained on these expeditions. Finally, Bartholomeu Dias discovered the route around Africa when a storm blew him off course, and 10 years later, Vasco da Gama used this route to sail from Portugal to India.

CHECKING FOR UNDERSTANDING

1. **Identify** Prince Henry "the Navigator," Bartholomeu Dias, Vasco da Gama

2. **Define** joint-stock company, stock, capital, compass, astrolabe, quadrant, carrack, caravel, scurvy

3. **Enumerate** the reasons the Europeans undertook voyages of discovery.

4. **List** new inventions, and explain their importance to exploration.

5. **Describe** the effects of the Portuguese discovery of a sea route around Africa to Asia.

THINKING CRITICALLY

6. **Making Deductions** Why would wealthy investors want to buy a small share in several overseas voyages rather than a large share in one?

CONNECTIONS: HISTORY AND ECONOMICS

7. **Evaluating Results** How did the introduction of the joint-stock company result in more voyages of exploration?

★ Chapter 1 Review ★

★ Summary

After traveling across a land bridge from Asia between 20,000 and 12,000 years ago, native Americans built cities and complex cultures—especially Mesoamerican nations such as the Inca and Aztec. Islamic empires grew to include Palestine—the Christian Holy Land—and 200 years of Crusades resulted. The crusaders brought back to Europe the goods, inventions, and ideas they acquired from highly developed Eastern cultures. Marco Polo's accounts of his observations in China fueled interest in routes to East Asia. A renewed interest in classical learning, called the Renaissance, brought new knowledge and a curiosity about the world. Meanwhile, during the 1300s and 1400s, most of Europe shifted from feudalism to nationalism. Church unity, however, broke down as reformers questioned Church teaching and policy. The joint-stock company made voyages of exploration easier to finance, and improvements in navigation and sailing technology made them more effective. Under the direction of Prince Henry of Portugal, navigators gained knowledge used to improve ocean voyages. Finally, Bartholomeu Dias discovered the route around Africa, and 10 years later, Vasco da Gama used this route to sail from Portugal to India, opening an ocean route to the East.

★ Using Vocabulary

Classify each of the terms listed below into one of the following categories:

Political Structures and Systems

Economic Activity and Systems

Inventions and Technology

Religion and Culture

astrolabe	compass	pueblos
capital	feudal system	quadrant
caravel	humanism	Renaissance
carrack	joint-stock company	samurai
charter	manor	serfs
classical	Parliament	shoguns

★ Reviewing Facts

1. **Discuss** the major changes in the political and social structure of Europe in the late 1400s.
2. **Describe** the characteristics of the Renaissance.
3. **Identify** advanced cultures of Africa and Asia and the importance of their trade with Europe.
4. **Report** on the effects of religious conflicts during this time period.
5. **Compare** the cultures of Mesoamerican and North American native peoples.
6. **List** the motives of the nations interested in voyages of discovery.
7. **Summarize** the development of the middle class and its role in the voyages of exploration.
8. **Enumerate** the achievements of the Portuguese voyages of discovery.

★ Understanding Concepts

DIVERSE CULTURES

1. Compare the differences and similarities between each of the following sets of cultures: medieval Europeans and medieval Japanese; West African trading kingdoms and Aztecs.
2. Both European Renaissance scholars and Ming Dynasty rulers restored interest in ancient classic works of their cultures. How did their motives differ?

ECONOMIC CHANGE

3. How did the middle class gain economic power comparable to that of feudal landowners?
4. What new form of investment made more voyages of exploration possible? How did it affect economic opportunity in general?

★ Thinking Critically

1. **Classifying Causes** What factors facilitated the change from feudalism to nationalism? Label each cause political, economic, or religious.
2. **Analyzing Motivation** What forces and events motivated voyages of exploration?
3. **Understanding Global Events** How did the spread of Islam contribute to the growth of nationalism? the Renaissance? the interest in exploration?

4. Recognizing Motives Had Europeans known that native American cultures existed, which would they have wanted to visit? Why?

5. Relating Past and Present Today investors watch the rise and fall of stock market prices, regarding them as a measure of economic strength. What new form of investment described in this chapter eventually led to the development of the stock market? How does the stock market differ today from this earlier form of investment?

★ Writing About History

NARRATION

Refer to the description of how to write a narrative essay in the History Writer's Handbook in the Appendix of this book. Your teacher will give you more specific instructions on the essay's length and the assignment's due date.

Imagine you are captain of one of Vasco da Gama's ships. Write a few days' entries in the ship's log book, relating the day's events and challenges and detailing the crew's reactions. You may need to conduct research for authentic details, but imaginary details are also acceptable.

★ Learning Cooperatively

Working in a group of four, make a set of four parallel time lines covering the years 600 to 1500. Indicate major events and developments in China, among the Indians in what is now Mexico, among the Europeans in what is now Italy, and among major Arab Muslim groups. Each member should research the history of one culture and show the major events on that culture's time line.

★ Mastering Skills

READING A CHAPTER

Every book you read is organized in a certain way. This book is organized to present certain factual material in a way that is interesting, informative, and not too difficult to understand. To accomplish this, it is divided into units and chapters, each of which focuses on specific themes of American history. Each chapter is divided into sections that focus on topics and concepts within these themes.

Knowing how to read a chapter systematically will make it easier for you to learn the material and will save you time in studying. One way to do this is to follow these steps:

a. Review the unit-opening organizer, "Setting the Scene," to understand how this chapter relates to the others in this unit.

b. Read the chapter organizer to learn the specific historical focus and important concepts in the chapter.

c. Review the features, look at the illustrations, and skim through the review material at the end of the chapter.

d. Survey the chapter by reading the section and subsection headings and each section focus in the section organizers. As you do this, write the chapter title on a sheet of paper. Under the title make a list of the headings and subheadings that will serve later as an outline of topics.

e. Now you are ready to begin reading the chapter. As you read, make a question from each section heading and write it on your paper. Read to discover the answer to your question, and recite this answer to yourself when you finish reading the section. Repeat this step for each section of the chapter. When you have completed all of the sections, compare your notes to the summaries in the section review that are located at the end of each section. This will help you learn to identify the main ideas in each section.

Example Following the guidelines outlined above, you would learn this material in systematically reading this chapter:

Chapter One surveys thousands of years of history. It begins the study of United States history by relating developments in America from the time of the arrival of native Americans. The concepts are diverse cultures and economic change. Illustrations include native American art and artifacts, and art from Europe, Asia, and Africa. Features are about native Americans and ancient cultures. The title of the chapter is The World in Transition. *The section heading is* The First Americans; *the subheadings are* Empires in America *and* Indian Cultures North of Mexico. *Prereading section question:* "Who were the first Americans, and how did they live?"

Practice Add section headings and subheadings to make a complete outline for Chapter 1. Follow these steps as you study each chapter in the text.

CHAPTER 2
Discovery and Exploration

SETTING THE SCENE

Historical Focus

The first Europeans to visit North America were Norse seafarers who reached Newfoundland about 1000. Interest in exploration and settlement of the Americas, however, did not truly begin until the first voyage of Christopher Columbus in 1492. Thereafter, until the early 1600s, various nations—Spain, Portugal, France, England, and the Netherlands sent explorers to the New World. These adventurers were looking for gold and silver as well as a shortcut through the Americas to the riches of the East.

Concepts to Understand

- How European nations sought wealth through voyages of **discovery and exploration** to the New World.
- How European **values and beliefs** differed from those of the native American population.

People to Know

Christopher Columbus, Ferdinand Magellan, Hernan Cortés, Moctezuma, Junípero Serra, Samuel de Champlain

Places to Locate

Newfoundland, Hispañiola, Tenochtitlán, Mississippi River, New Amsterdam

Terms to Identify

sagas, *Santa María, conquistadores, mestizos,* viceroys, northwest passage, Spanish Armada

Guided Reading

As you read this chapter, seek answers to the following questions.

1. Why did European nations want to explore the New World?
2. How did the Spanish and French treat native Americans?

SPANNING THE DECADES

POLITICAL	1000 *Norse seafarers establish settlements in Iceland, Greenland, and Newfoundland*		1492 *First voyage of Christopher Columbus to the New World*	1519 *Magellan begins voyage around the world*
	1000	1450	1500	
CULTURAL	1050 *European traders bring home astrolabes from East Asia*		1518 *Spanish bring African slaves to the New World*	1534 *The Church of England separates from the Roman Catholic Church*

Landing of Leif Eriksson, *by Edward Moran, 1898*

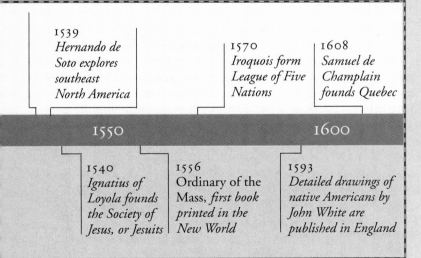

1539
Hernando de Soto explores southeast North America

1570
Iroquois form League of Five Nations

1608
Samuel de Champlain founds Quebec

1550

1600

1540
Ignatius of Loyola founds the Society of Jesus, or Jesuits

1556
Ordinary of the Mass, *first book printed in the New World*

1593
Detailed drawings of native Americans by John White are published in England

...the Indians were totally deprived of their freedom and were put in the harshest, fiercest, most horrible servitude and captivity, which cannot be understood by someone who has not seen it. Even beasts enjoy more freedom when they are allowed to graze in the fields....

—BARTOLOMÉ DE LAS CASAS
History of the Indies, 1562

Voyages of Columbus

It was this year of 1492 that your Highnesses...decided to send me, Christopher Columbus, to the regions of India...to see peoples...and to learn of...the measures which could be taken for their conversion to our Holy Faith.

—CHRISTOPHER COLUMBUS
In the *Santa Maria's* log, August 1492

Section Focus

In their eagerness to find easier routes for trade in Asia, some Europeans had a new idea: instead of sailing south and east around Africa, they could sail west. The idea led to discoveries that altered life in Europe and brought drastic change to those who lived on the continents that lay between Europe and Asia.

Objectives

After studying this section, you should be able to:
- Compare the purposes and results of the four voyages of Columbus.
- Discuss the purpose and results of Magellan's expedition.

The first Europeans to arrive in the Americas were Norse seafarers from Scandinavia. Between A.D. 800 and 1100 the Norse established settlements in Iceland, Greenland, and present-day Newfoundland, which they called Vinland. The Norse settlements in Vinland were unsuccessful because of conflicts with Indians and lack of support from home. The Vinland settlements soon disappeared—forgotten except in Norse **sagas,** or long heroic stories.

It was not until the voyage of Christopher Columbus in 1492 that the age of European discovery and exploration of the Americas began in earnest. After Europeans learned that Columbus had discovered continents not yet known to them, Spain, Portugal, France, the Netherlands, and England sent expeditions to the New World. They pursued a passage to Asia through or around the Americas in search of precious metals. In time these nations all established colonies in the Americas.

Columbus's First Venture

Christopher Columbus was born in Genoa, Italy, in 1451. His early interest in navigation led him to Lisbon, Portugal, in 1477. There, Portuguese explorations of the African-Atlantic coast brought him new knowledge of geography and cartography.

Columbus had studied the atlas of the ancient Greek geographer, Ptolemy, who believed the earth was a sphere. But Ptolemy underestimated its size. In 1477, Columbus was one of the first to read the newly printed "Travels" of Marco Polo. On the basis of this information Columbus shrank Ptolemy's calculations. He figured the distance between Japan and the Canary Islands, off the northeastern coast of Africa, at only 2,400 miles. His calculations resulted in an obsession to undertake a voyage to Asia by sailing west.

For years Columbus sought in vain for financial backing. Portuguese explorations had proven Ptolemy wrong on so many points that Columbus was promptly rejected in Portugal. Having no success with the kings of France or England, he spent six years trying to persuade Ferdinand and Isabella of Spain, that his scheme would bring them wealth, empire, and converts to Catholicism. Finally, Isabella and Ferdinand provided Columbus with three ships, the *Niña,* the *Pinta,* and the *Santa Maria.*

Columbus left Spain in August 1492 with about 90 sailors. He sailed south to the Canary Islands where he repaired his ships and took on fresh supplies. Columbus then charted his course westward,

Connections

HISTORY AND GEOGRAPHY

"TWAS A SMALL WORLD," COLUMBUS THOUGHT

Around the sixth century B.C. Greek philosopher Thales proposed the idea that the earth was a disc floating in water. Shortly after, Pythagoras advanced the idea that the earth was a sphere. Several centuries later Aristotle tested this idea by observing the circular shadow of the earth on the moon during eclipses.

The size of the earth was more difficult to determine than its shape. Greek geographer Erastosthenes, however, almost correctly calculated the circumference of the earth at about 25,000 miles by measuring the angles of the sun's rays at separated points. This figure was known by Columbus, but he chose to use the calculations made by a number of later scholars who underestimated the size of the earth by nearly one-half. Mapmakers compounded the errors by showing Europe, Asia, and Africa much larger than they actually are and by showing the Atlantic Ocean as a narrow gulf.

Columbus died believing he had reached Asia. After all, he had found it just where he had calculated it should be.

★ ★ ★ ★ ★ ★ ★ ★ ★

MAKING THE GEOGRAPHY CONNECTION

1. What contributions did early Greeks make to geography?

2. Why did Columbus think he had reached Asia?

LINKING PAST AND PRESENT

3. What distance can scientists determine today?

★ ★ ★ ★ ★ ★ ★ ★ ★

---

noting "…nothing to the north, nothing to the south."

By early October the fleet had already gone farther than Columbus thought would be necessary to reach Japan. The sailors were frightened and wanted to turn back. On October 9 the crew "heard birds passing all night long" and believed they were close to land. On October 11 Columbus wrote in his log:

The crew of the Pinta spotted some…reeds and some other plants; they also saw what looked like a small board or plank. A stick was recovered that looks man-made, perhaps carved with an iron tool…. but even these few [things] made the crew breath easier; in fact the men have even become cheerful.

In the early morning of October 12, 1492, the lookout aboard the *Pinta* saw white cliffs glistening in the moonlight. At dawn, Columbus went ashore onto a small island in the Bahamas (San Salvador) and claimed it for Spain. Believing he had reached the East Indies off the coast of Asia, he called the native people Indians. On the nearby coasts of Cuba and Hispañiola [HIS puhn YOH luh]—present-day Haiti and the Dominican Republic—Columbus found enough gold to raise his hopes for wealth and glory.

In April 1493, Columbus returned triumphantly to the Spanish court. The king and queen gave him the titles "Admiral of the Ocean Sea" and "Viceroy and Governor of the Indies." All were fascinated by both the copper-skinned people Columbus brought back and his reports of lands where every bird, tree, and flower were new to Europeans. Isabella and Ferdinand were most enthusiastic about the gold.

**Examining
Illustrations**
*This idyllic painting
depicts native Ameri-
cans welcoming
Columbus and his
ships (in the back-
ground). Columbus
made four voyages to
the Americas between
1492 and 1504. Why
do you think he failed
to realize that he had
reached a new world
and not the East?*

Columbus made three more voyages across the Atlantic, exploring many Caribbean islands and the east coast of Central America. Despite his achievements, he never found the wealth desired by Spain. Columbus died in 1506 a broken, frustrated dreamer, unaware that he had reached new continents in the Western Hemisphere.

Spain and Portugal Divide the World

Accounts of Columbus's discoveries soon set off a flurry of exploration particularly by Spain and Portugal. When seafaring explorers realized that the lands reached by Columbus formed a barrier between Europe and Asia, they sought to find a way around them. They also wanted to claim and conquer this New World.

Columbus's 1492 discovery put Spain and Portugal in direct competition for trade and empire-building. In 1493, because of potential conflict, Pope Alexander VI convinced the two Catholic nations to divide the new overseas territories between them. A **line of demarcation,** a north-south line drawn on a map through the Atlantic Ocean by the pope, gave Spain all the non-Christian lands to the west of the line and Portugal all those

to the east. The Portuguese, objecting that the line favored Spain, threatened war. In 1494 Spain and Portugal resolved their differences "for the sake of peace and concord" in the Treaty of Tordesillas (TAWRD uh SEE uhs). The treaty moved the demarcation line nearly 1,000 miles further westward—about 48° west longitude—and extended it around the earth to secure Portuguese claims in Asia.

In 1500 a fleet of Portuguese ships under the command of Pedro Álvares Cabral (PAY throo AHL vuh reesh kuh BRAHL) set out for India by going east around the coast of Africa. Swinging west to get favorable winds, Cabral's expedition was blown off course and unintentionally reached present-day Brazil. Because Brazil's eastern bulge lay to the east of the line set by the treaty, Portugal claimed it.

In 1499 on another Portuguese expedition, with an Italian-born navigator and merchant, Amerigo Vespucci (vay SPOO chee), sailed along the coast of South America. In a long letter Vespucci wrote about his voyage, he concluded that the land he had explored was a vast new continent—a New World. In 1504 Vespucci's sensational account, which he purposely redated 1497, was published, and he erroneously received credit for reaching the mainland of the New World before Columbus. German mapmakers named the New World "America," and the name stuck.

In 1511 Vasco Núñez de Balboa (VAHS koh NOO nyayth day bal BOH uh) was the acting governor of a Spanish-built town on the northern coast of South America called Darien. On expeditions into what is now Panama, Balboa learned from the native people of "great waters" to be found on the west side of this narrow strip of land. Balboa led an expedition to find this body of water, guided by the Indians who knew trails through the difficult countryside. They did indeed reach a huge body of water, which Balboa claimed for Spain. Having climbed a peak alone to see the water first, Balboa indeed became the first European to see the eastern coast of the Pacific Ocean. It was now certain that the lands Columbus had reached were not part of Asia. They were separated from Asia by this seemingly endless ocean.

VOYAGES OF EXPLORATION

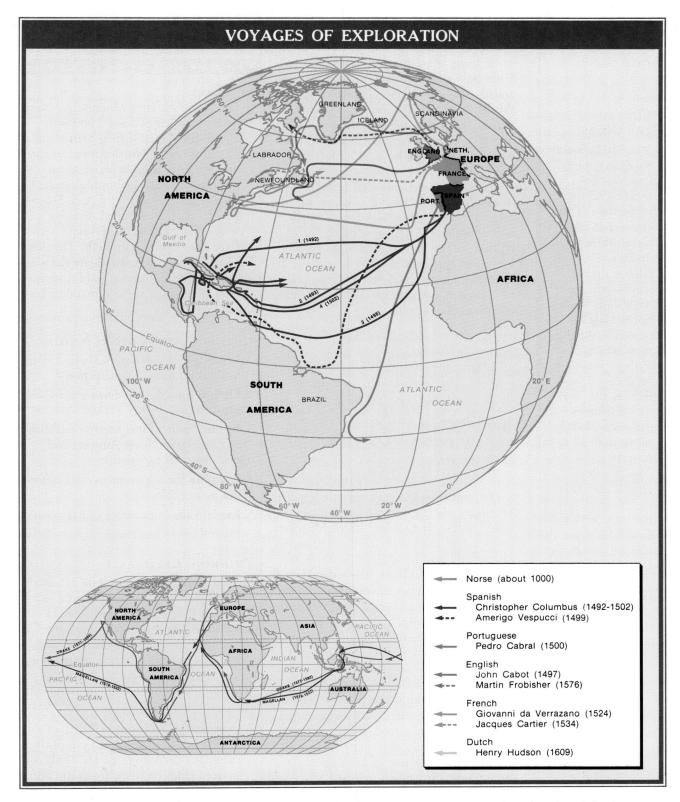

Legend:

Norse (about 1000)

Spanish
Christopher Columbus (1492-1502)
Amerigo Vespucci (1499)

Portuguese
Pedro Cabral (1500)

English
John Cabot (1497)
Martin Frobisher (1576)

French
Giovanni da Verrazano (1524)
Jacques Cartier (1534)

Dutch
Henry Hudson (1609)

Examining Maps *Several European explorers visited the Caribbean area and the coast of the Americas following Columbus's voyages of discovery. These explorers were in the service of different countries. Who claimed for the Portuguese the land that is now Brazil?*

Magellan's Voyage

Balboa's expedition did, however, revive some hope of sailing west to reach Asia. Since only a strip of land, or **isthmus**, separated the oceans in Panama, it was thought that perhaps there was a **strait,** or narrow waterway, between the two bodies of water. Portuguese navigator Ferdinand Magellan believed he could find such a passage.

Magellan hoped to sail around the world to the Spice Islands, a center for the valuable spice trade located in what is now Indonesia. After the king of Portugal refused to give him financial backing, Magellan approached King Charles I of Spain with his plan. A Spanish missionary to America, Bartolemé de Las Casas, described this meeting:

———◦◦◦———

Magellan brought with him a well-painted globe, and thereon traced the course he proposed to take…he intended to follow the coast up [south] until he found the strait [passage to the other ocean.]

———◦◦◦———

The Spanish king agreed to finance Magellan, and in 1519 Magellan set sail with 5 ships. By October 1520, Magellan had reached the strait that now bears his name at the southern tip of South America. The strait, with its fierce winds and strong tides, was so difficult to navigate that it took over a month for the expedition to finally enter the waters south of the isthmus. Because the ocean seemed so calm, Magellan called it the Pacific, meaning "peaceful." During the voyage across the Pacific that followed, the sailors suffered extreme hardships from a lack of fresh food and water, and many died. Magellan met his own death in April 1521 as the result of a local war in the Philippines. Only one of his ships, carrying 18 survivors, finally reached Spain in 1522. These survivors and their ship were the first to circumnavigate the world. Magellan's expedition succeeded in revealing the true size of the earth.

Linking Across Time

THE DISCOVERERS

The first native Americans Christopher Columbus met hid in fright of these strangely clothed men brought by a type of sailing craft they had never seen. Four and a half centuries later, the first human to travel in space landed in a Russian field populated by a cow and two women. "Have you come from outer space?" the frightened women wanted to know. Yuri Gagaran assured them that he was a Soviet citizen, not a creature from another world.

Early and modern explorers share more common experiences than one might expect. The level of technology has greatly changed during the course of history, but human nature has not. The basic theme of exploration is that it takes people into unknown realms. Test pilots have a phrase for it: *pushing the envelope.* Sailors of Columbus's time might have called it tempting fate.

Columbus used only a compass and his knowledge of the seas to set a course. Aboard the *Santa María* was the most advanced navigational aid of the day, the astrolabe, but Columbus did not know how to use it. He calculated the ship's speed by timing how fast bubbles or objects on the ocean's surface passed astern. Lookouts at the top of the ship's mast—the fifteenth-century version of radar—kept a sharp eye for signs of land. When Columbus landed at San Salvador, he thought he had found the East Indies. In 1969 Neil Armstrong and Buzz Aldrin had landing radar, computers, and an autopilot to guide their descent to the moon's surface. Yet despite

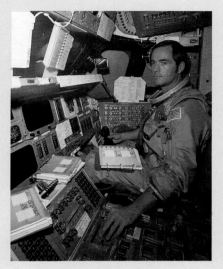

Astronaut Robert Crippen in the cabin of Columbia

their sophisticated gadgetry, they too did not know their precise location. Because they were headed for a crater, Armstrong manually piloted the *Eagle* to a smoother landing site. It took hours to pinpoint their exact location using another ancient navigation aid, the sextant.

Voyages of discovery throughout the ages have owed much to writers who fired the imagination and inspired exploration. The findings of Greek geographer Ptolemy contributed to Columbus's inspiration through his calculating the circumference of the globe at 18,000 miles, making the distance between western Europe and eastern Asia sound relatively short— and actually very much in error. By the time Columbus reached North America, he thought he had traveled far enough to be in India. Modern generations of explorers have been inspired and challenged

by science fiction accounts of space travel.

Fear of the unknown is another link between early and modern explorers. While well-read people of Columbus's day knew the world was round, there were nevertheless many unknown dangers awaiting them in vast uncharted areas beyond the primitive maps. So fearful were the sailors Columbus commanded that he kept two accounts of how far he estimated they had traveled. In a secret journal he recorded how far he really thought the ship traveled each day. In the ship's log available to the crew, he put down a considerably lesser distance.

Space travelers had worries like weightlessness and exposure to radiation in outer space. No one knew how the human body would react to floating for days where there was no up or down. Would the astronauts be able to swallow food? Would their hearts become weak from having to do less work? The problems facing early and modern explorers were different, but they all sprang from the same source—pushing the envelope.

★ ★ ★ ★ ★ ★ ★ ★ ★ ★

MAKING CONNECTIONS

1. Compare the level of technology available to Columbus with that used by modern astronauts.

2. How were problems faced by early and modern explorers different?

★ ★ ★ ★ ★ ★ ★ ★ ★ ★

Spain in America

When they were given these presents, the Spaniards burst into smiles; their eyes shone with pleasure.... They picked up the gold and fingered it like monkeys; they seemed to be transported by joy, as if their hearts were illumined and made new....

—AZTEC ENVOY, 1519

Section Focus

Europeans had not found a new trade route to Asia, but they soon began to look upon the Americas as a source of wealth. Explorers heard stories of fabulously rich cities in the interior. Among the most vigorous in searching for treasure in the Americas were Spanish explorers. Their activities, along with those of the Christian missionaries who often accompanied them, would permanently change the world of the native peoples of the Americas.

Objectives

After studying this section, you should be able to:
- Describe the Spanish exploration and conquest of the South and Central American mainlands.
- Discuss life in the Spanish colonies.

I n the 25 years after Columbus's first voyage, Spaniards carved out small outposts through the West Indies—on Cuba, Jamaica, Puerto Rico, and Hispaniola. Generally they were not interested in creating permanent settlements in the Americas. Instead, they flocked to the islands in search of precious metals. The native Indians of these islands suffered greatly, however, because of Spanish ambition.

The Conquistadores

The many **conquistadores** (kohn KEES tuh DOHR ays)—Spanish conquerors who made their way to the Caribbean islands in the late 1400s and early 1500s—were eager to find great wealth, especially gold and silver. They did not hesitate to use harsh means to obtain these precious metals. The natives of the Caribbean, many of whom were enslaved and put to work washing for gold or raising crops, were virtually exterminated in less than 20 years. Many died of overwork. Most, however, succumbed to such European diseases as smallpox and measles, from which they had no immunity. By 1520 the Spanish were importing Africans as slaves to replace the Indian populations.

The Spaniards did not confine themselves to the Caribbean islands for very long. Stories of fantastic riches on the mainland soon sent bold Spanish adventurers into the interior of Mexico, Central America, and South America.

Among the most successful of these *conquistadores* was Hernán Cortés (kawr TEHZ). In 1519 Cortés led an expedition from Cuba to the eastern shore of Mexico.

Although Cortés's army numbered only 600, the Spaniards had luck—and sophisticated weapons—on their side. The Spanish also had horses, which the Indians had never seen, that they used in cavalry charges.

Cortés gained invaluable help from Doña Marina, an enslaved native the Aztec had given to him. She may have told Cortés of Quetzalcoatl (keht SAHL KWAHT uhl), the legendary god who had promised to return as a fair-skinned man.

When Cortés landed on the Mexican coast, reports of "floating mountains bearing fair-skinned gods" were sent to Moctezuma, the Aztec emperor. Moctezuma believed that Cortés may indeed have been Quetzalcoatl, and he sent the Spaniards dazzling gifts. Seeing this wealth, the Spaniards were determined to obtain more of it.

As Cortés marched inland toward the Aztec capital of Tenochtitlán (tay NOHK tee LAHN), subjects of the Aztec allied with him, hoping to free themselves from Aztec rule. At first Moctezuma reluctantly welcomed the Spaniards and lodged them in Tenochtitlán. Cortés wrote:

The city itself is as big as Seville or Cordoba ....[it] has many squares where...markets are held continuously.... There are...many temples.... Amongst these temples there is one...whose great size and magnificence no human tongue could describe.

The Spaniards soon feared that the Aztec would realize they were not gods. Therefore, to insure their safety, they took Moctezuma captive. They also looted the city of gold and silver. Eight months later, when Moctezuma was killed by a stone thrown by one of his subjects, the Aztec rose up against the Spanish. Many Spaniards were killed during a retreat.

In 1521 Cortés returned to the Aztec capital, having amassed huge numbers of Indian allies who wanted freedom from Aztec rule. He cut off supplies to Tenochtitlán and, after a long siege, destroyed this city whose magnificence had so impressed him. Mexico City was built on its ruins, and the area's rich silver mines soon produced vast wealth.

The conquest of Mexico encouraged other *conquistadores* to seek vast riches in the Americas. One such *conquistador* was Francisco Pizarro, an illiterate soldier who had been stirred by rumors of fabulously rich cities on the Pacific coast of South America.

In 1531 Pizarro set sail from Panama with an army of only 180 soldiers. His destination was the Inca empire in what is now Peru. After an exhausting journey, the Spaniards reached the city of Cajamarca (kah huh MAHR kuh). The Inca empire had been badly weakened by a civil war from which the new emperor Atahualpa (ah tah WAHL pah) had emerged victorious. The Spaniards greeted him with swords and guns, taking him captive. In

Examining Illustrations

Cortés, with only a small army and Indian allies, marched on the Aztec capital of Tenochtitlán in 1519 and eventually destroyed this magnificent city. What new city was built on its site?

an effort to save his life, Atahualpa gave the Spaniards a room filled with gold objects and other treasures. Despite the ransom, the Spanish later executed Atahualpa. Within a short time, many Spanish settlers immigrated to Peru, where they mined silver and gold.

As Cortés and Pizarro conquered the native civilizations in Mexico and Peru, other Spanish *conquistadores* explored areas to the north. Juan Ponce de León, the governor of Puerto Rico, was one of the first Spaniards to head to northern lands. He had sailed on Columbus's second voyage to America in 1493 and settled in the Caribbean. De León had heard native tales of a wondrous fountain whose water would restore youth. In 1513 he set sail northward in search of this magical fountain. When the Spaniards reached land near what is now the city of St. Augustine, they named the area Florida for the blooming wild flowers and fragrant plants. De León never found the mythical "Fountain of Youth," but he claimed the land for Spain.

After 1542 the Spanish worked to consolidate their empire in South America, Central America, Mexico, and the Caribbean. Because the northern lands did not provide the riches the Spanish had found in the south, the northern borderlands were considered unsuitable for colonization.

AMERICAN PORTRAITS

JUNÍPERO SERRA
1713-1784

Most Spanish conquests in the New World were marked by a terrible slaughter of the local people. In contrast, a gentle priest established Spanish control in California by setting up a string of missions to care for and convert the American Indians.

Born on an island off the Spanish coast, Junípero Serra became a Franciscan priest and professor of philosophy. But he wanted to work as a missionary among American Indians, and in 1749 he left Spain for Mexico. At the age of 55, he was sent to take control of Upper California. He established a mission at San Diego, and later founded several missions stretching up the California coast to San Francisco. Taking as his motto "Always go forward and never turn back," Junípero Serra traveled by foot from mission to mission, making sure that Indians were not abused.

Colonial Life

The people of Spain's American colonies formed a structured society, where position was determined by birth, income, and education. At the top were *peninsulares*—high government and church officials who had been born in Spain. Below the peninsulares were *creoles*—those born in the Spanish colonies of Spanish parents. Many creoles were wealthy, but the high colonial positions were reserved only for *peninsulares*. *Mestizos* (meh STEE zohs), those born of Indian and Spanish parents, made up the next level of colonial society. At the lowest levels of society were Indians, African slaves, and *mulattoes*—people of Spanish and African or Indian and African ancestry.

Many people in the Spanish colonies lived under the *encomienda* system. Through this system the Spanish monarch rewarded *conquistadores* and others with vast tracts of land and the right to demand both taxes and labor from the Indians who lived on the land. The *encomenderos* were supposed to protect the Indians, teach them Catholicism, and pay them for their labor. In reality, the Spanish colonists often treated the natives cruelly, overworking them, and using their forced labor to gain vast personal wealth.

The mingling of Spanish and Indian cultures produced a new kind of society in the Spanish colonies. Spanish became the language of the colonies though many Indians continued to speak their original languages. The Spanish introduced European crops, such as wheat, alfalfa, oranges, and figs. Their livestock—horses, cattle, and chickens—were also introduced as well as iron products, wheeled carts, and firearms.

Likewise, products from the Americas made significant changes in Europe when the Spaniards returned with plants they had first sighted among native cultures. For example, the American Indian potato radically decreased Europeans' reliance on flour—to the extent that towns whose economies centered around mills declined.

Spain's system for governing its huge colonial empire included the appointment of **viceroys**—Spanish nobles appointed by the monarch to look after the interests of the crown. The Spanish monarch also set up a special court in Mexico City known as the *audiencia*. The purpose of this court was to oversee the viceroys and control the behavior of the *conquistadores*. It also was supposed to provide a forum for justice to the native peoples.

The Spaniards established missions in their colonies, from which clergy could convince Indians to become loyal Spanish subjects and Catholics. Some priests sought to protect the natives from the *conquistadores*. Father Bartolomé de Las Casas insisted that, like all humans, Indians were children of God and therefore should be protected by the Church and the king.

Spanish priests also founded missions in the northern part of Spain's empire. Beginning in 1769 Father Junípero Serra began a chain of missions in California. A road linking these missions was called The Royal Highway, or *El Camino Real* (EHL kah MEE noh ray AHL). **Presidios**, or forts, were generally built nearby to protect the missions. Native peoples were taken from their own settlements and brought to the missions to be fed, clothed, and taught European methods of agriculture and handicrafts. They were usually required to stay at the missions, attend religious instruction and services, and labor for the priests.

★★★★★★★★★★★★★★★★★★

Section Two Review

★★★★★★★★★★★★★★★★★★

SUMMARY

Following voyages of exploration, Spaniards set out to exploit America for its wealth. *Conquistadores* such as Cortés in Mexico and Pizarro in Peru extended the Spanish empire by conquering and looting the Indian nations. The Spanish then mined vast amounts of gold and silver, using native peoples and later Africans as slave labor. In the North American borderlands, Spanish explorers found little wealth, so colonization was very slow. However, Junípero Serra, in an effort to extend Christianity, founded a chain of missions in California.

CHECKING FOR UNDERSTANDING

1. **Identify** Hernán Cortés, Francisco Pizarro, Junípero Serra, *El Camino Real*

2. **Define** conquistadores, peninsulares, creoles, mestizos, mulattoes, encomienda

3. **Discuss** the effects of Spanish colonization on the native Americans who inhabited the West Indies.

4. **Summarize** the Spanish exploration and conquest of the American mainland.

5. **Describe** life in the colonies established in America by Spain.

THINKING CRITICALLY

6. **Verifying Predictions** Spanish explorers introduced horses to native Americans. Predict how the lives of the Plains Indians in North America might be significantly altered by having horses. Consult Chapter 17, Section One, to verify your predictions.

CONNECTIONS: HISTORY AND RELIGION

7. **Analyzing Relationships** How did the religious beliefs of the Aztec work to the advantage of Cortés?

★★★★★★★★★★★★★★★★★★

Study and Writing Skills

Asking Effective Questions

Imagine that your teacher asks you and three of your friends in class to do a group report on the Spanish *conquistadores* in America. After you tell the teacher that you are not sure how to begin, she suggests that you start by asking effective questions.

Explanation

Effective questions are questions that serve a specific purpose and provide desired information. Asking effective questions involves a three-step process. If you ask questions without having a carefully planned strategy for doing so, much time can be wasted and confusion may result. Effective questions help you "get to the point" and allow you to better understand any given topic.

The three steps involved in developing effective questions are:

a. Determine what information you need to know.

b. Decide what materials or people you should consult.

c. Consider what questions you should ask.

By following these guidelines, the questions you ask will be effective ones.

Example

Note how the above steps have been applied to asking effective questions about the Spanish *conquistadores:*

a. What is it you need to know?

1534 book illustration of conquistadores *in America*

• the historical role and significance of the Spanish *conquistadores*
• the nature of the *conquistadores'* activities in America

b. Who or what should you consult for information?
• your textbook
• encyclopedias and other reference books
• a person who is familiar with Spanish history, or perhaps someone who was born or has lived in Spain or Latin America

• magazines such as *National Geographic, American Heritage,* or *American History Illustrated.*

c. What questions should you ask?
• Who were the *conquistadores?*
• What were they doing in Spain before they came to America?
  • How were they funded?
  • What were their reasons for coming to America?
  • What were their specific goals?
  • Where were their areas of activity in America?
  • What problems and challenges did they encounter?
  • What was their success in reaching their goals?
  • Where were their areas of permanent settlement (if any)?
  • What effect did their activities have on the people they encountered?

Having determined what it is you need to understand, the sources of information, and the topics that could be covered, you are prepared to ask effective questions as you read and absorb materials during your study of American history.

Practice

For further practice in asking effective questions, apply the above steps to preparing a research report on the explorations of Amerigo Vespucci.

English, French, and Dutch Ventures

These white men must have fallen from the clouds. How else could they have reached us through the woods and rapids, which even we find hard to pass? The French chief [Champlain] can do anything. All that we have heard of him must be true.

—NIBACHIS
Algonquian chief, 1613

Section Focus

Like the Spanish, the English, French, and Dutch sought a water route through the New World. In this search they explored the northern regions of the continent. Unlike the Spanish, though, they did not quickly establish colonies. For the first century or so, these nations' activities in the New World were neither as far-reaching nor as forceful as those of Spain.

Objectives

After studying this section, you should be able to:
• Describe early English exploration of North America.
• Discuss French and Dutch colonization in North America.

Although the English participated in early voyages of exploration, they failed to establish permanent colonies in America until the early 1600s. Poor finances, religious conflict at home, preoccupation with colonizing Ireland, and the threat of war with Spain overshadowed English interest in the New World. Yet it was these early explorations by the English that gave them claim to land for later colonization in North America.

In 1497 King Henry VII of England authorized John Cabot "to sayle to all partes, countreys, and seas, of the East, of the West, and of the North" and to discover new lands unknown to Christians. English merchants hoped that Cabot would discover a route to Asia. Cabot explored the shores of present-day Nova Scotia, Newfoundland, and Labrador. Like Columbus, Cabot believed he had found Asia. But when a second expedition found only the barren coasts of Labrador and Greenland, English interest in westward exploration and settlement waned.

Rivalry Between England and Spain

By the 1570s, however, Queen Elizabeth I became increasingly anxious about Spain's growing global power. Wishing to challenge Spain's influence in the New World—but fearing to do so openly—she secretly financed voyages by Martin Frobisher, whose purpose was to search for a **northwest passage** through North America to Asia. Frobisher explored the Atlantic coast of what is now Canada, but he too failed to find a route to the East.

Elizabeth also gave her unofficial approval to piracy against Spanish ships and settlements. Daring English sea captains, such as Francis Drake, cruised the shores of Spanish America, capturing treasure ships and looting towns. These English "sea dogs" inflicted heavy damage to the Spanish. Because Spain was still the strongest power in Europe, however, the English did not attempt colonization in America or take any open action against the Spanish.

The eventual challenge to open conflict came from Spain rather than England. In 1588, seeking revenge for English attacks on Spanish ships and colonies, King Phillip II of Spain dispatched a huge fleet of ships, known as the **Spanish Armada,** to sail against the English fleet. The "invincible armada" included 130 ships, and 27,000 troops.

Although the English fleet was greatly outnumbered, their ships were faster and far easier to handle than the slow, heavy Spanish galleons. The English ships attacked the Spanish vessels one by one. Before a Spanish galleon could get close enough for its soldiers to board an English warship, it was pounded by artillery. The result was devastating to the Spanish fleet.

The badly damaged armada was forced up the English Channel and into the North Sea. A fierce storm off the coast of Scotland further crippled the Spanish fleet. Only 60 to 70 ships returned to Spain. In a single battle, Spain had lost most of its naval forces; they could no longer be considered the dominant power on the sea. The way was now cleared for English colonization in the Americas.

French Presence in America

French colonization in North America began relatively late. In 1524 the French king, Francis I, had sent Italian sea captain

Examining Illustrations *This early map of New France shows Jacques Cartier meeting with Indians and scenes of Indian life. What river valley did Cartier explore and claim for France?*

Giovanni da Verrazano to search for a northwest passage. Verrazano sailed the Atlantic coast from Newfoundland south to North Carolina. In 1534 Jacques Cartier made the first of three voyages to northern North America, searching for the elusive passage. Although he explored the St. Lawrence River as far as what is now Montreal, he also failed to find the passage. While French fishers sometimes visited North American waters, it was not until the early 1600s that the French made a serious attempt to establish a colony. In 1608 Samuel de Champlain founded Quebec on the banks of the St. Lawrence River. Few French settlers, however, were attracted to this northern outpost. In 1609 Champlain joined the Algonquian and Huron peoples in a raid against the Iroquois confederacy. Champlain described the hostilities:

When I saw them getting ready to shoot their arrows at us, I leveled my arquebuse [gun]…and aimed straight at one of the three chiefs. The shot brought down two and wounded another…. The Iroquois were greatly astonished and frightened to see two of their men killed so quickly…they abandoned the field and fled into the depth of the forest.

As a result of this battle, the Iroquois, the most formidable warriors in eastern North America, became sworn enemies of the French. This enmity was to have far-reaching effects on American history.

The French were generally confined to the northern part of North America until the late 1600s. In 1673 Louis Joliet, an American-born fur trader, and the Jesuit priest Jacques Marquette embarked on a search for a river known to native Americans as the "big river"—the Mississippi. They canoed from St. Ignace on the northern tip of Lake Michigan to the Mississippi along inland waterways and followed it as far as the Arkansas River. In

1682 Robert de La Salle followed the Mississippi to its delta and claimed the vast lands drained by it for France. He named the region Louisiana after the French king, Louis XIV.

The colonies established by France in North America formed a long string of outposts, extending from the Gulf of Mexico to Canada. Although French explorers were disappointed when they did not find gold and silver in North America, they soon found another kind of wealth—fur. Beaver skins sent to France and made into hats were a particularly profitable item in the fur trade.

Except with the Iroquois, the French generally had better relations with native Americans than did the Spanish. French

Life of the Times

FRENCH FUR TRADERS

In the early 1700s, the most stylish Europeans wore hats and other garments fashioned from felt cloth. Beaver furs from North America produced the highest quality and most durable felt. Pelts supplied by French fur traders were therefore highly prized. To keep the supply of furs constant, French traders maintained a close relationship with native Americans who trapped the beaver.

The French government, hoping to keep the lucrative fur trade from the English, encouraged their traders and settlers to live with the Algonquian Indians. Many traders and missionaries moved into Indian villages.

As a result, the Algonquian changed the French colonists in America. Frenchmen married Indian women and raised their children as Indians. Other French settlers adopted Algonquian ways. In 1749 a Swedish traveler observed:

"The French in Canada in many respects follow the customs of the Indians, with whom they have constant relations. They use the tobacco pipes, shoes, gaiters [leg coverings], and girdles [loincloths] of the Indians. They follow the Indian way of waging war exactly and have adopted many other Indian fashions."

trappers and traders known as *coureurs de bois*—"runners of the woods"—did not threaten to take over Indian lands. They lived among the Indians, learned their ways, spoke their languages, and often married among them.

French missionaries, known to the Indians as "black robes," journeyed into the North American wilderness to convert native Americans to Catholicism. Not accompanied by armies as Spanish missionaries were, the French Jesuits often suffered torture and death. In spite of their travails, most of them did not despair. One French priest wrote in the mid-1600s:

Do not imagine that the…loss of many Christians can bring to nought the mystery of the cross of Jesus Christ…. We shall die; we shall be captured, burned, butchered: be it so. Those who die in their beds do not always die the best death.

The French government had difficulty recruiting colonists for its North American settlements for several reasons. First of all, these colonies were not as valuable as

Examining Maps
European explorers searched endlessly for riches in the Americas. Francisco Vásquez de Coronado, who visited the American Southwest, found no gold, but he introduced native Americans to horses. How far north did his expedition explore?

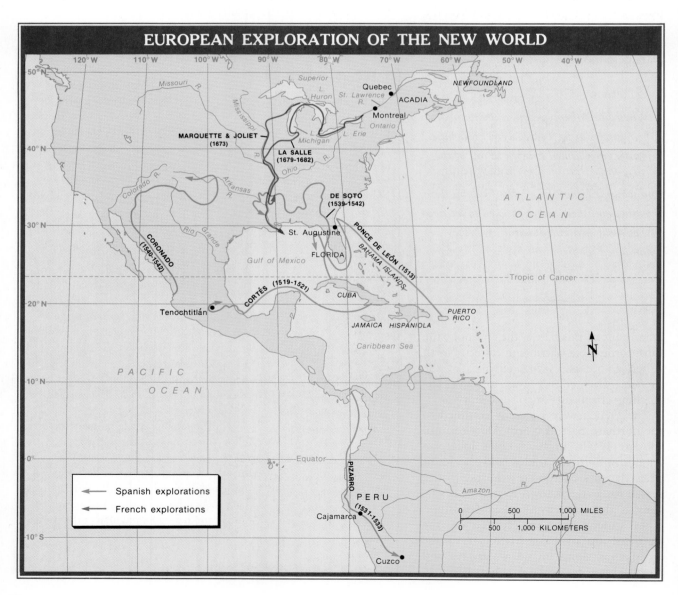

EUROPEAN EXPLORATION OF THE NEW WORLD

the French possessions in the West Indies—the islands of Guadaloupe, Martinique, and Saint Domingue, which all produced rich sugar crops. Secondly, most French rulers were more interested in extending their rule over European territory than in settling North America. In addition, the French missed an opportunity to gain an energetic group of settlers when they forbade French Protestants, known as Huguenots, to settle in America. Persecuted in France, many Huguenots would have gladly emigrated to America.

The Dutch in America

Like the French, the Dutch were late in setting up colonies in North America. By the 1600s the Dutch had ousted the Portuguese from the spice trade. They controlled the East Indies, set up the only trading post in Japan, maintained many West African slave ports, established a colony in Cape Town, South Africa, and had holdings in the Caribbean islands.

Dutch ventures on the North American continent were not nearly so impressive. In 1609 the Dutch East India Company funded an expedition by an English navigator, Henry Hudson. He reached New York Harbor and sailed up the river, which today bears his name, as far as present-day Albany, New York. The Dutch soon set up trading posts on Manhattan Island, which they named New Amsterdam, and along the Hudson River. A profitable fur trade was established with the Indians.

To attract settlers to New Netherland, the Dutch West Indies Company promised to give huge tracts of land along the Hudson and Delaware rivers to proprietors if at least 50 people could be hired and kept on the land. Few settlers, however, were interested. Although the Dutch colony was small, it contained a remarkable ethnic mix. One visitor reported that he had heard "eighteen different languages" being spoken in New Amsterdam in the mid-1600s. Because of poor leadership and weak government, though, New Netherland easily fell to the growing colonial influence of England in 1664.

SUMMARY

In search of new lands and a northwest passage, John Cabot, Martin Frobisher, and Jacques Cartier explored parts of North America. Francis Drake, an English "sea dog," explored the Pacific Coast, looting Spanish ships and towns along the way. But only after the defeat of the Spanish Armada in 1588 was the way opened for English and French colonization in North America. The French founded Quebec and established the fur trade as well as a string of outposts along the St. Lawrence River. The French also enjoyed good relations with the Indians, except for the Iroquois. The Dutch established a small colony along the Hudson River.

CHECKING FOR UNDERSTANDING

1. **Identify** John Cabot, Jacques Cartier, Samuel de Champlain, Robert de La Salle, Henry Hudson

2. **Define** Spanish Armada

3. **Summarize** English voyages of exploration in North America.

4. **Contrast** patterns of French settlement with colonization patterns of other European nations.

5. **Explain** factors that limited the success of early Dutch colonies in North America.

THINKING CRITICALLY

6. **Citing Evidence** What evidence can you find of the importance of the Catholic faith to the French?

CONNECTIONS: HISTORY AND GEOGRAPHY

7. **Understanding Geography** Refer to the world map in the Appendix. How does the location of England and France explain their desire for a northwest passage as an alternative to the route around Cape Horn?

★ ★ ★ ★ ★ ★ ★ ★ ★ ★ ★ ★ ★ ★ ★ ★ ★ ★ ★

★ Chapter 2 Review ★

★ Summary

Even though the first Europeans to set foot on the North American continent were the Scandinavian Norse, their settlements were not lasting. Several centuries later—in search of an ocean route to Asia—Columbus discovered the Americas, and Amerigo Vespucci recognized South America as a new continent. An expedition led by Ferdinand Magellan finally circumnavigated the world and opened a water route around South America to Asia.

Following their exploration, Spaniards exploited America for its gold and silver, conquering native Americans in Mexico and Peru. They used Indians and imported Africans as slave labor and relegated them to the bottom of the colonial class system. Although the Spanish borderlands of North America were not quickly settled, Spanish culture has influenced the language, religion, art and architecture of the American Southwest.

In search of new lands and a northwest passage, English and French adventurers explored parts of North America. The defeat of the Spanish Armada in 1588 opened the way for English and French colonization. The French established the fur trade and a string of outposts, including Quebec. French explorers also claimed for France all the territory drained by the Mississippi River. The Dutch established a small colony along the Hudson River.

★ Using Vocabulary

Match each word or phrase with the correct definition below.

a. sagas   e. strait
b. *creoles*   f. *peninsulares*
c. *encomienda*   g. *mestizos*
d. armada   h. northwest passage

1. people born in the Spanish colonies of Spanish parents
2. people with Indian and Spanish parents
3. a fleet of ships
4. system of awarding *conquistadores* land and the right to collect taxes and labor from Indians
5. fabled water route through North America to the Pacific

6. long narratives
7. in the Spanish colonies, high officials born in Spain
8. a narrow body of water between two landmasses

★ Reviewing Facts

1. **Identify** the first Europeans to attempt to settle North America.
2. **Compare** the significant achievements of Columbus with those of Amerigo Vespucci and his captain.
3. **Report** on the accomplishments of Magellan's crew and their importance.
4. **Summarize** Spanish land exploration, exploitation, and colonization in America.
5. **Describe** life and the class system in the Spanish colonies.
6. **Discuss** French exploration and settlement patterns in North America.
7. **Explain** the failure of Dutch colonies in North America to grow and prosper.

★ Understanding Concepts

DISCOVERY AND EXPLORATION

1. What explorations were undertaken in search of something that was never found?
2. What discoveries were made when searching for something else?

VALUES AND BELIEFS

3. What role did religion play in the colonization of the Americas?
4. How did the religious values of the French rulers interfere with their efforts to attract French colonists to North America?

★ Thinking Critically

1. **Analyzing Motivation** Compare the motives of the early European explorers with those who explore areas such as outer space and the ocean floor today. How are the goals of each group similar? How are they different?

2. Comparing Effects Compare the effects of French and Spanish settlers on native Americans. How did the settlement patterns and economic pursuits of each account for the difference?

3. Determining Cause and Effect Why do you suppose Spanish exploration in the Caribbean, Central America, and South America resulted in more settlements than did the Spanish, French, and Dutch explorations to the north?

★ Writing About History

ARGUMENTATION

Refer to the description of how to write a argumentative essay in the History Writer's Handbook in the Appendix of this book. Your teacher will give you more specific instructions on the essay's length and the assignment's due date.

Imagine you are a friend of Columbus. He is frustrated by his failure to persuade the monarchs of Europe to fund a voyage to find a water route around the world to Asia, and has asked you to "ghost-write" a persuasive letter to King Ferdinand and Queen Isabella of Spain. Begin by describing the hardships of the land route to Asia, then present your solution using the format described in your handbook.

★ Learning Cooperatively

Work in a group of five to map the routes of Columbus, Magellan, Cabral, Cabot, and La Salle. Each member should research one explorer, then trace the route of that explorer on a single map large enough to display in the classroom or elsewhere in the school. Each member of the group should write a short paragraph on the explorer, describing his background, motivations, exploits, and significance. Each paragraph should be attached to the map as informative captions.

★ Mastering Skills

USING A GAZETTEER

What if you wanted to find *Cuba* on a map, but you had no idea where it was located? To find out, you could look up *Cuba* in a gazetteer, a dictionary of

geographical names.

A gazetteer lists geographical place-names in alphabetical order. Gazetteers differ somewhat, but most entries include a description, relative location, and exact location with map coordinates—latitude and longitude. The coordinates for *Cuba* are 22°N/79°W. To find this exact location on a map, simply find the correct latitudinal and longitudinal lines and follow them until they intersect.

A gazetteer entry may also include other data such as historical information, population, altitude, and a map reference page. The gazetteer in the Appendix of this book, for example, includes a reference to pages or maps where additional information may be found.

Columbia River river flowing through southwest Canada and northwestern United States into the Pacific Ocean (46°15′N/124°W) *264*, 403

Concord village northeast of Boston, Massachusetts; site of first battle of the American Revolution in 1775. (42°N/71°W) 111, *115*

Connecticut state in the northeastern United States (41°45′N/73°15′W) *57*, 66

Cuba country in the West Indies, North America (22°N/79°W) 37, *647*

Czechoslovakia country in eastern Europe (49°30′N/16°E) 567, *1094*

Example Study the gazetteer entries on this page, then answer the questions that follow:

1. Which of the locations are found in the United States? Which are outside the United States? *(Concord, Columbia River, and Connecticut are inside the U.S.; Cuba and Czechoslovakia are outside the U.S.)*

2. What is the exact location of the Columbia River? *(46°15′N/124°W)*

3. If *Cuzco,* the Incan capital in Peru, had been listed above, between what two entries would it have been found? *(Cuba and Czechoslovakia)*

Practice Choose four geographic locations from the maps on pages 39 and 50, and write gazetteer entries for each of them, including latitude and longitude coordinates, where possible.

CHAPTER 3
Colonial America

SETTING THE SCENE

Historical Focus

The British entered the race for colonial empire in the New World in the early 1600s. Although their early efforts were not as dramatic as those of the Spanish, the British colonies became the most populous American settlements within a century of colonization. The British used their colonies as a source of raw materials and a market for manufactured goods. In time, a distinctly new American society emerged. This in turn led to tensions and strained relations between the colonies and Great Britain.

Concepts to Understand

- How **migration** from Europe shaped the character of colonial society.
- What political, social, and religious **values and beliefs** the colonists brought to America.

People to Know

James I, John Smith, Squanto, John Winthrop, Anne Hutchinson, William Penn

Places to Locate

Virginia, Massachusetts, New York

Terms to Identify

indentured servant, proprietor, Puritan, Separatist, Quakers, commonwealth, constitution

Guided Reading

As you read this chapter, seek answers to the following questions.

1. What contributed to the growth and success of the Middle Colonies? New England? The Southern Colonies?
2. In what ways did Americans differ from the British by 1750?

SPANNING THE DECADES

POLITICAL	1607 *Founding of Jamestown, first permanent English colony*	1630 *Massachusetts Bay becomes a haven for Puritan dissenters*	1660 *Parliament passes Navigation Acts*	1676 *Bacon's Rebellion in Virginia*
	1600	1640		1680
CULTURAL	1636 *Harvard, first college in British colonies, founded at Cambridge, Mass.*	1647 *Massachusetts establishes elementary schools*	1649 *Maryland passes religious Toleration Act*	1654 *First Jewish colonists arrive in New Amsterdam from Brazil*

Hooker and Company Journeying through the Wilderness from
Plymouth to Hartford in 1636 *by Fredric E. Church, 1846*

1701
*Ft. Detroit
established by French*

1733
*Georgia, last
British colony in
North America,
founded*

1720   **1760**

1690
New England
Primer *first
elementary textbook,
published*

1741
*Height of "Great
Awakening"
religious revival*

*The country itself in its soil, air, water,
season, and produce, both natural and
artificial, is not to be despised. The land
containeth divers sorts of earth…God in His
wisdom having ordered it so, that the
advantages of the country [abound].*

– WILLIAM PENN
Letter to Free Society of Traders, 1683

Jamestown and the Southern Colonies

SETTING THE SCENE

You are to take into yor consideracôn how our severall Plantacôns [Plantations] may be best supplied with servants....that vagrantes and others who remaine here noxious [harmful] and unprofitable, may be soe transplanted to....our Forraine [foreign] Plantacôns.

—CHARLES II
King of England, Instructions for the Councill Appointed for Forraigne [Foreign] Plantacôns [Plantations], 1660

Section Focus

In the century following Columbus's discovery, England's response to Spanish enterprise in America was nothing more creative than piracy of Spanish commerce on the seas. By 1600, however, England had a naval power in the Atlantic, adequate finances for colonization, and a surplus population willing to risk its life for religious, political, or economic reasons.

Objectives

After studying this section, you should be able to:
- Explain the effect of the environment on Virginia's settlement and lifestyle.
- Describe the economic conditions that influenced the development of the Southern Colonies.

As early as 1578, Sir Humphrey Gilbert and his half-brother Sir Walter Raleigh tried to plant a permanent English colony in North America. But on Gilbert's voyage back to England, his ships were lost at sea.

In 1587 Raleigh sent 91 men, 17 women, and 9 children to settle on Roanoke Island near the coast of what is now North Carolina. He named the land "Virginia," in honor of the "Virgin Queen," Elizabeth I. The effort failed because Spanish control of the Atlantic delayed Raleigh's efforts to resupply the colony until after England defeated the Spanish Armada in 1588. When English ships finally returned to Roanoke, they found none of the settlers. The only clue left behind was a word carved on a tree—*CROATOAN*, the name of nearby Indians and of a nearby island. The fate of the "Lost Colony" remains a mystery.

Jamestown, 1607

In 1606 King James I created the Virginia Company from two separate groups of merchants who had petitioned for permission to found colonies. Two divisions, the Virginia Company of London and the Virginia Company of Plymouth, were granted exclusive settlement rights in North America. The London group's charter permitted the planting of a colony in Virginia, where, it was believed, precious metals abounded.

In 1607 the London Company sent out 3 ships carrying 144 settlers. After being driven back by Indians on the first attempted landing in Virginia, they sought a more secure place for a settlement on a peninsula 60 miles up the James River. There they founded Jamestown, naming both the river and the town for their king.

The long ocean voyage, an outbreak of disease in the swampy and unhealthy settlement site, Indian attacks, and starvation worked against the Jamestown colonists. Captain John Smith led the colony through some of its most trying times. Mixing friendship, force, bluff, and bargaining, he saved the starving colony by trading beads, knives, pots, and fish hooks for corn, vegetables, turkeys, and venison from the Indians. Yet the arrival of supply ships early the next year found only 38 colonists still alive.

Some of Jamestown's difficulties resulted from the London Company's poor management. Houses and buildings were the immediate need for the colonists, but the company had sent only four carpenters. Jamestown was a business venture for the London Company, expected to make a profit for its shareholders. For this reason the company supplied jewelers and goldsmiths and "gentlemen" who wanted to look for gold—not carpenters to build houses or farmers to raise crops for survival. The tragic result was that most of the 500 colonists who came in the first few years died. Only 60 survived the "starving time," the winter of 1609 to 1610. George Percy, one of the survivors of the first settlement, wrote of the sufferings at Jamestown:

Our men were destroyed with cruell diseases as Swellings, Flixes, Burning Fevers, and by warres, and some departed suddenly, but for the most part they died of mere famine.

There were never Englishmen left in a forreigne Countrey in such miserie....our food was but a small Can of Barlie sod in water....our drinke cold water taken out of the River, which was at a floud verie salt, at a low tide full of slime and filth, which was the destruction of many of our men....

Examining Maps *England's American colonies were founded along the Atlantic coast from what is now Maine to Georgia. Settlement usually was along rivers and natural harbors. Why was travel between the colonies usually via the Atlantic rather than overland?*

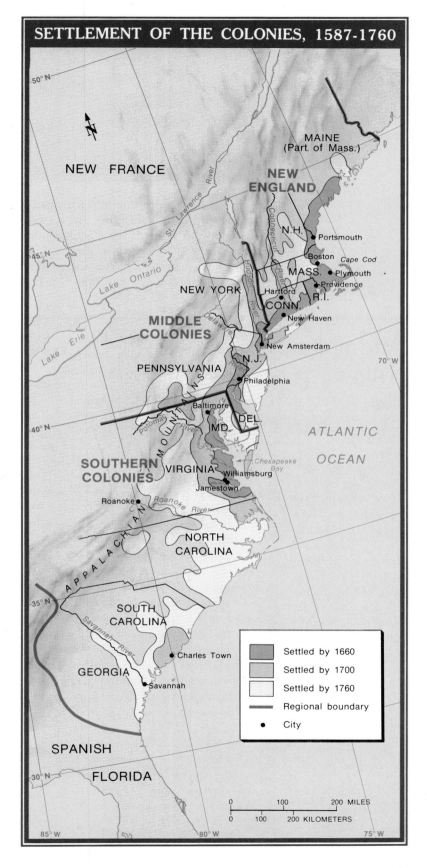

SETTLEMENT OF THE COLONIES, 1587-1760

	Settled by 1660
	Settled by 1700
	Settled by 1760
	Regional boundary
•	City

Examining Illustrations

Tobacco manufacturing, shown in this 1750 engraving, required a large labor force. To meet this need planters often bought and sold slaves. How did Virginia law make slavery a permanent condition?

Effective leadership might have spared Jamestown these hardships. As it was, John Smith, injured in a gunpowder explosion, had returned to England in 1609 and not until 1611 was the company able to supply a new governor.

Mismanagement eventually cost the London Company its charter. By 1616 the investment made by company shareholders had brought no real profits. The company's reform program of 1618 expanded land sales, extended English law and rights to colonists, and allowed settlers to elect a representative assembly. Soon after, new recruits, including various craftspeople, arrived in Virginia. But even an additional 4,000 settlers did not end Virginia's troubles. Poor treatment of nearby Indians resulted in an attack that cost 350 lives. A royal investigation found that the badly governed settlers were dying faster than they could be replaced. King James I dissolved the company and took control of the colony in 1624.

Growth of Virginia

The difference in climate between England and Virginia meant that the settlers would learn to raise new crops. From the native peoples they learned to grow corn, beans, and squash, but these did not make money for the London Company shareholders. After the company lost its charter, Virginia found a profitable cash crop—tobacco. Introduced by the Indians, the use of tobacco soon became popular in England despite the fact that King James I wrote a book in which he called it "a custom Loathsome to the eye, hateful to the Nose, harmfulle to the Braine, daungerous to the Lungs." The native Virginia tobacco was of poor quality compared with that from the Spanish Caribbean islands, but in 1612 John Rolfe secured and planted some West Indies tobacco seeds. After this, Virginia's tobacco exports grew rapidly. In 1640 almost 1.5 million pounds of tobacco entered the port of London.

Tobacco, a labor-intensive crop, produced a great demand for colonists. Thousands of settlers came to Virginia, lured by the promise of free farmland. But this source of labor was not enough. Homeless children from the streets of London were sent to serve as apprentices to trades people in the colony. Convicts, farmers who had lost their lands, and the poor also came. Those who could not pay their own

---

Life of the Times

BRIDE SHIPS

The first colonists sent by the London Company in 1607 to Jamestown were men. Women did not arrive in the colony until several years later. The population remained heavily male for nearly two decades. A ratio of 15 men to 1 woman was the norm. Indeed, the lack of females hindered the London Company's plan for the colony's growth and economic success.

Although the cultivation of tobacco assured the stability of the Virginia colony, the London Company decided that "The Plantacion can never flourish till families be planted and the respect of wives and Children fix the people on the Soyle." In 1619 the members of the first legislative assembly agreed: "In a newe plantation it is not knowen whether man or women be more necessary." To solve the problem of the shortage of women, the London Company sent the first "bride ship" to America. Its passengers included nearly 100 "young, handsome, and honestly educated maids" suitable for marriage.

Cost of transport for these maidens was paid by the London Company. The average payment for a bride by a Virginia colonist was 120 pounds of tobacco, or about $20.00.

After a few instances in which a woman became engaged to two men at the same time, the London Company stopped sending bride ships. Instead, a type of travel brochure was written boasting of the advantages of living in the New World.

way became **indentured servants,** working from four to seven years to pay off their passage across the Atlantic.

Land was a source of wealth and social status in England. Consequently, the London Company's directors offered 50 acres to settlers who paid their own fare to Virginia or sent someone else. Wealthy settlers who acquired plantations used indentured servants as laborers. After the period of indenture, they were free to start their own farms.

In 1619 a Dutch warship brought 20 enslaved Africans to Jamestown. Virginians, desiring an additional source of labor for their tobacco fields, purchased the slaves. At first Africans were treated somewhat like indentured servants, many earning their freedom by several years of work. Slavery was first recognized in Virginia law in 1661. The following year, Virginia law declared that the status of a newborn child depended on the status of the mother. Slavery became a permanent, inherited condition.

From 1600 to 1850 Europeans brought 15 million enslaved West Africans to the Americas. Before 1600 Africans had used prisoners of war and criminals as slaves. Europeans, however, sold enslaved people for profit. Most enslaved Africans were taken to the plantations of the West Indies. Virginians continued to use indentured servants as the primary labor supply until 1670. Then changing economic conditions in Virginia made African slaves more desirable than indentures.

Governing Virginia

In the 1660s an oversupply of tobacco pushed down its price. Only the very largest plantations were able to remain profitable.

Examining Maps *The American colonies carried on trade among themselves and with distant ports across the Atlantic. Make a list of the items that the colonies imported and those they exported.*

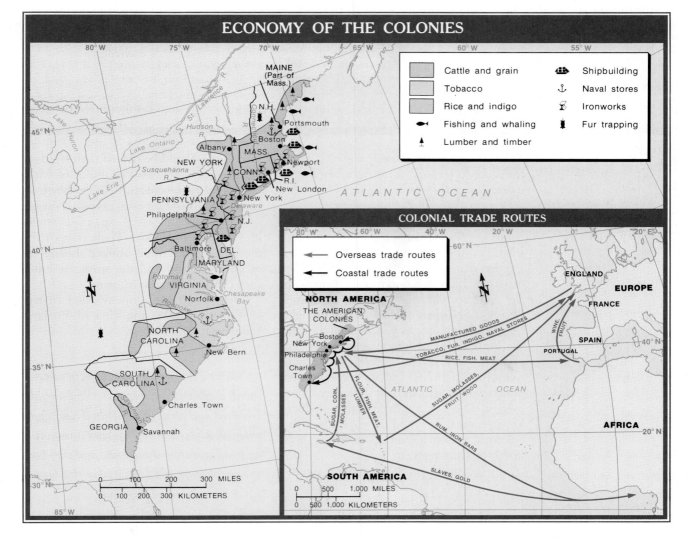

Connections

H I S T O R Y   A N D   E C O N O M I C S

STOCK EXCHANGES

Merchants in the sixteenth century reduced the risk of ocean trade by forming trading companies. Governments of western European states controlled the trade of their merchants and provided company charters that included the rights of stock ownership.

The early trading companies eventually led to the formation of joint-stock compa-

A merchant's counting house

nies such as the Dutch United East India Company formed in the early 1600s. In order to sell large blocks of shares to investors, this company created a stock exchange in Amsterdam. The money raised became a permanent fund from which the company could initiate trading ventures.

In 1650 the English adopted the Dutch method of creating a permanent fund for trading enterprises. Before 1773, however, English investors who wanted to buy or sell shares of stock had to locate a broker to transact their business. Then the London brokers founded the first English stock exchange.

Not all the trading companies made money. England's Virginia Company was a costly failure, as were other European companies. By 1700, however, joint-stock companies had proven that free enterprise could raise the capital necessary for costly ventures, regardless of the risk.

MAKING THE ECONOMICS CONNECTION

1. Why did merchants form joint-stock companies?

2. What advantage did the Dutch United East India Company have over English companies in 1590?

LINKING PAST AND PRESENT

3. What is a stock exchange?

Many former indentured servants, now free, had to rent farmland from plantation owners or move west to the interior, where they were exposed to Indian attack. These depressed economic conditions produced bands of homeless people who roved through the colony. Frontier settlers charged that the government, controlled by eastern planters, failed to protect them from the Indians. In June 1676, Nathaniel Bacon, a freedman of the frontier, brought together many people who were angry with the government of Virginia in the largest popular revolt before the American Revolution. In September Bacon's force burned Jamestown; Bacon died of dysentery, however, in October. Leaderless, the rebellion lost its momentum, and the governor of the colony took revenge on 23 of Bacon's followers by hanging them.

The potential menace of these unemployed people caused wealthy planters to rely less upon indentured servants and more upon enslaved people. Unlike inden-

tures, slaves could be denied their freedom permanently and could be punished without appeal to the courts. Because they were black, identification was easy and escape difficult. African slavery expanded rapidly in Virginia after 1670. Planters with the most land and slaves soon held the highest social status and had the strongest influence in Virginia's government.

In the London Company's first charter of Virginia (1606) the king of England had agreed that:

…all and every of….Our subjects, which shall dwell and inhabit …the said several colonies and plantations,…shall have and enjoy all liberties, franchises and immunities …to all intents and purposes, as if they had been abiding and born within this Our Realm of England….

While colonial charters extended the rights of the English people to the colonists, the government in England exercised only loose control over its American colonies. Eventually the colonists enjoyed more self-government than the English at home.

In the beginning Virginia had been strictly ruled by a council and an appointed governor with almost absolute power. In 1619, however, the London Company gave the settlers a voice in the government by permitting the first representative assembly in America, the House of Burgesses. These burgesses and a council appointed by the governor together had power to make laws. When King James I took control from the London Company, making Virginia a royal colony, he appointed the governor but allowed the House of Burgesses to continue. Over the years the House of Burgesses gained more power. Eventually it assumed control over taxes that paid the governor's and other officials' salaries—the "power of the purse."

Other Southern Colonies

In 1632 King Charles I gave his friend George Calvert, Lord Baltimore, a grant of 10 million acres north of Virginia. Calvert became **proprietor** of the colony, meaning that he had authority over its government. By 1634 his son, Cecil Calvert, sent the first 200 settlers to Maryland, named at Charles I's suggestion after his Catholic queen, Henrietta Maria. From the beginning the Calverts intended Maryland to be a refuge for Catholics. Soon, however, more Protestants than Catholics were arriving. To protect Catholics from persecution, Cecil, the second Lord Baltimore, offered religious freedom to all Christian settlers. Later the legislative assembly of Maryland affirmed this freedom by the Religious Toleration Act of 1649, the first of its kind in America.

Necessity prompted religious toleration in Maryland, but nothing advanced women's rights. Margaret Brent was an able administrator of the Calvert estates, whose judgment had helped prevent an

armed revolt. The assembly, however, denied her request for the right to vote.

Like Virginia, Maryland grew tobacco. Because of extensive farming, its towns were few and small. Baltimore, the chief city, had only 7,000 inhabitants by 1765.

Profits from tobacco in Virginia and Maryland enticed other English nobles to become proprietors of colonies farther south along the Atlantic coast. In 1663 eight nobles received from Charles II a grant to settle Carolina. Land in northern Carolina attracted pioneer farmers from Virginia. From the start, this was an area of **subsistence farming** where farmers grew only enough to live on and sometimes a

AMERICAN PORTRAITS

MARGARET BRENT
1601(?)-1671(?)

Born a Roman Catholic at a time when England was denying Catholics many civil rights, Margaret Brent moved to Maryland in 1638. She quickly became one of the largest landowners, and, according to colonial records, was the first woman to own land in her own name.

Brave and forceful, Brent helped put down a rebellion from neighboring Virginia, and she took charge of paying Maryland's troops. Refusing to be confined to the restricted life of most colonial women, she later served as attorney for Lord Baltimore, Maryland's proprietor. She came into conflict with the colonial government when she appeared before the assembly and demanded the right to vote. After the governor denied her claim, she moved to a large plantation in Virginia. There "America's first feminist" lived the rest of her life.

little tobacco for sale as a cash crop. As northern Carolina grew, its principal exports became **naval stores**—tar, pitch, and turpentine—products of its pine forests that are used in ship-building.

Southern Carolina offered a better harbor than in the north and attracted more settlers. The first English colonists came from the West Indies island of Barbados to found the only major city in the South, Charles Town—present-day Charleston—in 1669. Some of these settlers had used slave labor on their sugar plantations in the Caribbean. With the knowledge of rice-growing that enslaved Africans brought from their homelands, these settlers built great plantations, importing many more slaves to work the malaria-ridden fields. Eliza Lucas, a settler from the West Indies, introduced the growing of indigo, a plant that produced a blue dye. By 1746 indigo had also become an important cash crop grown for export.

Sir Anthony Ashley Cooper, one of the proprietors, persuaded John Locke, an English political philosopher, to write a framework of government for South Carolina. The result was The Fundamental Constitutions of Carolina, providing for a legislature of weathly nobles chosen by landholders. The proprietors surrendered control in 1729, and the king made both Carolinas royal colonies.

Georgia, named after King George II, was the last of the 13 English colonies. Its proprietor, James Oglethorpe (OH guhl THAWRP), a wealthy philanthropist and soldier, wanted Georgia to be both a refuge for poor English debtors and a military outpost against the Spaniards in Florida. The first settlement, founded in 1733, was Savannah.

At first, Oglethorpe governed with strict controls, forbidding slavery and rum and controlling land sales. These restrictions limited Georgia's growth, causing some unhappy settlers to move across the border to South Carolina. In the 1740s the trustees who controlled Georgia lifted the restrictions against slavery and rum. They also gave the colonists an elected assembly, but Georgia failed to prosper until after control was returned to the king in 1752.

★★★★★★★★★★★★★★★★★★★
Section One Review
★★★★★★★★★★★★★★★★★★★

SUMMARY

The London Company settled Virginia. Proprietors colonized Maryland, Georgia, and the Carolinas. These colonies built their economies on crops suited to the land and climate. At first most of the labor was supplied by indentured servants—soon replaced by enslaved Africans. The governors allowed government by elected representatives. Eventually the King assumed control.

CHECKING FOR UNDERSTANDING

1. **Define** indentured servants, plantations, proprietors, subsistence farming, naval stores

2. **Compare** the organizations that established and governed the Southern Colonies with those that governed European nations.

3. **Explain** the factors that created hardships and initially limited the success of the Virginia colonies.

4. **Relate** the economic activity and conditions that prevailed in early Virginia to the development of the class system and slavery.

THINKING CRITICALLY

5. **Evaluating Social Changes** Southern planters prospered by introducing and spreading the use of tobacco. Today we know tobacco is an unhealthy substance. If tobacco were discovered today, do you think our government would permit its production and sale? Explain.

CONNECTIONS:
HISTORY AND ECONOMICS

6. **Recognizing Cause and Effect** How did the location and physical characteristics of Virginia force settlers into a different economic activity from what they had planned? How did this economic activity affect the development of social life in Virginia?

★★★★★★★★★★★★★★★★★★★

New England

Every man,…free or not free, shall have libertie to come to any publique Court, Councell, or Towne meeting, and either by speech or writing to move any lawfull, seasonable, and materiall question or to present any necessary motion, complaint, petition, Bill, or affirmation.

—MASSACHUSETTS BODY OF LIBERTIES, 1641

Section Focus

While the Virginia Company of London struggled to plant a colony at Jamestown, the Virginia Company of Plymouth hesitated to make such an investment. Its only accomplishment was sending Captain John Smith to explore the region north of Virginia, which he named "New England." When New England was settled, it was by accident rather than design, by people seeking a religious haven, not investors seeking a fortune.

Objectives

After studying this section, you should be able to:
• Explain the relationship of church and state in the New England colonies.
• List three reasons why self government developed in the New England colonies.

The Church of England—the Anglican Church—broke away from the Catholic Church in 1534. Some Anglicans, called Puritans, believed that the Church of England had not done enough "to purify" itself of all symbols of Catholic worship. Most Puritans wanted to reform the Church of England. One group, called Separatists, believed that it was better to separate themselves entirely and to form their own church. Because the Anglican Church was the official state church, Separatists, like all other religious **dissenters**, or protesters, faced persecution, jail, and even death.

Separatists Move to Plymouth

In 1607 a group of Separatists, soon to be known as Pilgrims, left England to escape persecution. They settled in Holland, (known today as The Netherlands) where, despite the freedom to worship as they pleased, they were dissatisfied. Their children grew up speaking a different language and learning new customs. Where might they maintain their language, customs, and form of worship? America beckoned.

In 1619 the Pilgrims secured a grant of land in Virginia from the London Company. After much preparation, in September 1620, 73 men and boys and 29 women and girls set sail on the *Mayflower* from Plymouth, England. In November the ship landed far to the north of Virginia at Cape Cod on the Massachusetts coast. Because they had no charter for an area outside the control of the London Company, the Pilgrims drew up and signed the Mayflower Compact, an agreement to live under the laws of the community.

The Pilgrims searched for nearly a month before they found Plymouth harbor. On December 25, they began to build the first large house for common use. In the bleak, cold, snowy New England winter, the Pilgrims, like the Virginia colonists, had their "starving time." By spring almost half of them had died. Even the few survivors might have starved if it had not been for Squanto, an Indian who taught them about their new environment. William Bradford, one of the colonists, wrote that Squanto "directed them how to set their corn, where to take fish, and to procure other commodities" and that he was also their pilot "to bring them to unknown places for their profit, and never left them until he died."

The Pilgrims' deep sense of religious purpose and determination to endure hardships sustained the colony. In 1621 the survivors elected Bradford governor, a post that he would hold for more than 30 years. In the spring they planted crops. A good harvest in the autumn and the arrival of more provisions on the ship *Fortune* inspired a day of thanksgiving to God.

Additional settlers from England built a cluster of small villages near Plymouth, but the colony never became very large. It elected its own officials and ran its own affairs until 1691, when it became part of the larger Massachusetts Bay Colony.

Puritan Massachusetts

In 1625 when Charles I became king of England, he decided to rule without Parliament and to suppress Puritanism. When friends of the king within the Church of England deprived Puritan ministers of their pulpits, the dissenters turned their thoughts to America. Several prominent Puritans bought a trading company, changed its name to the Massachusetts Bay Company, and secured a charter directly from the king. Twelve members signed an agreement at Cambridge in 1629:

...[I]t is fully and faithfully agreed amongst us,...that we will so really endeavour the execution of this worke, as by God's assistance we will be ready in our persons, and with such...familyes as are to go with us,...to embark for the said plantation by the first of March next....

This marked the beginning of the great Puritan migrations to New England to build a Christian society they believed would be a lighthouse for all the world.

The first governor of Massachusetts, John Winthrop, called the colony "a city upon a hill."

In 1630, 17 ships with about 1,000 Puritan settlers sailed for Massachusetts. During the next 10 years, 20,000 settlers followed. Boston, the leading town, and surrounding settlements such as Dorchester, Roxbury, Watertown, and Charlestown, flourished.

When they left England, the Puritans thought of themselves as members of the Anglican Church. As they settled Massachusetts, they organized their churches under ministers elected by each **congregation,** or a body of church members. The ministers set about reforming religious ceremonies, while the congregation became the final authority on church decisions. Compared to the Anglican clergy, the New England minister had limited authority. He was to teach, preach, pray, and administer; but the congregation held power over membership and church discipline. In the American colonies, the Puritans became known as Congregationalists.

The Massachusetts Bay charter, unlike those of other colonies, did not specify the location of the company's headquarters or where its shareholders' meetings would be held. Taking advantage of this loophole, the shareholders voted to move the company from England to Massachusetts. Winthrop carried the charter across the Atlantic Ocean, where shareholders would have more freedom from the king's control. Upon arriving in America, Winthrop transformed The Massachusetts Bay Company from a trading company into a **commonwealth**, a self-governing political unit, the first of its kind in America.

At first, the few shareholders of the Massachusetts Bay Company, called "freemen," held all the power in the colony. Under Winthrop, they made up the General Court, or the lawmaking body. Soon, however, over 100 colonists demanded to be admitted to the company as freemen. Under pressure, Winthrop consented. A law passed in 1631 gave all Puritan men who were church members admission to the

General Court as freemen. When the population grew too large to operate the government in this way, the Massachusetts Bay Company allowed the free men in each town to elect two representatives to the General Court. What began as a directors' meeting of a trading company ended up as a colonial legislature with power to make law.

Dissent and Division

The Puritans who came to Massachusetts to worship as they pleased had no intention of granting this freedom to others. They drove out Baptists, Quakers, and others who disagreed with them on religious issues. Others simply left to find more fertile farmland. Those who left

Massachusetts founded other colonies in New England.

Roger Williams arrived in the Massachusetts Bay Colony in 1631. According to William Bradford, Williams was "a man godly and zealous but very unsettled in judgment." When Williams became pastor of a church in Salem, he began to raise embarrassing issues. He preached that the church and the government should be separate because concern with political affairs would corrupt the church, and he asserted that the colonists had no right to settle on the land unless they bought it from the Indians. Finally, he challenged the right of Puritan rulers to compel people to engage in religious services. Because Williams's views threatened basic Puritan ideas, Winthrop and the

Examining Fine Art *Several Indians are present in this painting of the first Thanksgiving in the Plymouth colony. Perhaps they include Squanto and Samoset, who offered advice on planting and fishing, which helped the Pilgrims survive. After the first harvest, Governor Bradford called for a three-day feast. The celebration became a tradition in America, and in 1942 Congress made Thanksgiving a national holiday. What happened to the Plymouth Colony in 1691?*

THE AMERICAN COLONIES, 1607–1776

Colony and date of settlement	Founders	Reasons for founding	Type of government	Major occupations or Major items of trade
NEW ENGLAND COLONIES				
Plymouth Colony 1620	Pilgrims	Religious freedom	Charter, 1620–1686 Part of Massachusetts, 1691–1776	Farming
New Hampshire 1623	Puritans, Proprietors	Land grant, opposition to Massachusetts	Proprietary, 1629–1679 Royal, 1679–1776	Ship timber, rum
Massachusetts Bay Colony 1630	Puritans	To set up a Puritan society	Charter, 1629–1686 Royal, 1691–1776	Shipping, shipbuilding, fishing, forest products, rum, household manufactures
Rhode Island 1636	Roger Williams	Religious freedom	Charter, 1644–1776	Shipbuilding, diversified manufactures, rum
Connecticut 1636	Thomas Hooker	Land, trade with Indians	Charter, 1662–1776	Shipbuilding, furs, wheat
MIDDLE COLONIES				
New York (New Netherland) 1626	Dutch West India Company	Land, trade with Indians	Dutch charter, 1626–1664 Proprietary, 1664–1685 Royal, 1685-1776	Furs, forest products, grain, livestock, shipping
New Jersey (as part of New Netherland) 1626	Dutch West India Company	Land, trade with Indians	Dutch charter, 1626–1664 Proprietary, 1664–1702 Royal, 1702-1776	Iron, leather goods, diversified farming
Delaware (New Sweden) 1638	Swedish West India Company	Land, trade with Indians	Swedish charter, 1638–1655 Dutch charter, 1655–1664 Proprietary, 1664–1776	Diversified farming
Pennsylvania 1682	William Penn	Religious freedom for Quakers	Proprietary, 1681–1776	Household manufactures, iron, wheat, flax, flour, beef, livestock, forest products, glass, shipping
SOUTHERN COLONIES				
Virginia 1607	London Company	To find gold, land	Charter, 1606–1624 Royal, 1624–1776	Tobacco, cattle, iron, grain, furs
Maryland 1634	George Calvert (Lord Baltimore)	Religious freedom for Catholics	Proprietary, 1632–1691 Royal, 1691–1715 Proprietary, 1715–1776	Tobacco, iron
North Carolina 1650	Proprietors	Land, trade with Indians	Proprietary, 1663–1729 Royal, 1729–1776	Food products, furs, household manufactures, tobacco, naval stores
South Carolina 1670	Proprietors	Land, trade with Indians	Proprietary, 1663–1729 Royal, 1729–1776	Rice, indigo, cattle, furs
Georgia 1733	James Oglethorpe	Fresh start for debtors, a buffer against Spanish Florida	Proprietary, 1732–1752 Royal, 1752–1776	Rice, indigo, hides

Examining Charts *Most of the 13 colonies (Plymouth became part of Massachusetts) were founded under charters issued to investing companies. By 1752, however, 8 colonies had come under the direct control of the monarch. How many colonies that were once controlled by proprietors became royal colonies?*

General Court banished him from the colony.

Facing deportation to England, Williams fled south and spent the winter with friendly Indians. In 1636, with several followers from Massachusetts Bay, he started the colony of Rhode Island on land purchased from the native Americans. The new colony, chartered in 1644, welcomed Jews as well as all Christians, and guaranteed their religious freedom. In Rhode Island church and state were completely separate, a principle that was to become an important part of America's political heritage.

Not long after Williams departed, Massachusetts faced a similar challenge. Anne Hutchinson began to openly challenge Puritan ministers and their interpretations of the Bible. When her teachings attracted a growing band of disciples and threatened the serenity of Boston, authorities brought her to trial. Ordered to leave the colony, she went to Rhode Island to begin a new settlement later called Portsmouth.

In 1637 the Reverend John Wheelwright, one of the few ministers Anne Hutchinson admired, was also expelled from Massachusetts for criticizing Puritan teaching. He and his followers settled in New Hampshire. Following the example of the Mayflower Compact, they created and signed the Exeter Compact and set up a civil government. In 1679 New Hampshire obtained a charter from King Charles II. Other pioneer settlers pushed farther north into Maine, which remained part of Massachusetts until 1820.

In 1636 settlers who wanted richer farmland and more freedom followed Thomas Hooker, a Puritan minister, to the fertile valley of the Connecticut River. Hartford and a series of other "river towns" sprang up along the river from Saybrook to Springfield. In 1662 these communities annexed New Haven and other towns to form the colony of Connecticut. In 1639 the colony adopted the Fundamental Orders of Connecticut, the first written **constitution,** or plan of government in America.

Section Two Review

SUMMARY

To escape persecution by the Anglican Church, the Puritans and Pilgrims settled Massachusetts. The Massachusetts Bay Company became the first commonwealth, and extended the vote to all Puritan men. Colonists escaping persecution from the Pilgrims and Puritans or simply desiring richer farmland settled Rhode Island, New Hampshire, and Connecticut, where they established civil governments with religious freedom. Connecticut adopted the first written constitution.

CHECKING FOR UNDERSTANDING

1. **Identify** Massachusetts Bay Company, Mayflower Compact, Roger Williams, John Wheelwright, Exeter Compact

2. **Define** dissenters, congregation, commonwealth, constitution

3. **Explain** the objectives of the Puritans and Pilgrims in settling the Massachusetts Bay Colony.

4. **Discuss** the relationship of church and state in New England.

5. **Summarize** what led to self-government in New England.

6. **Detail** the causes of the creation of Rhode Island, New Hampshire and Connecticut.

THINKING CRITICALLY

7. **Analyzing Motives** Most New England colonies were settled by people escaping religious persecution. Which of these groups sought true religious freedom? How did they differ from the others?

CONNECTIONS:
HISTORY AND GEOGRAPHY

8. **Understanding Motives** Compare the motives of the colonists who immigrated to New England with those of the colonists who settled Virginia.

Interpreting Primary Sources

Puritans subjecting wrongdoers to public ridicule

Women in the Colonies

Women were not as inactive in public life as colonial law suggests. Historians have used documents, such as the following from the records of the Suffolk County Court in Massachusetts, to uncover information about colonial women. Note some symbols from Elizabethian English are used; for example, ye stands for the word "the", y^t means "that," and "bene" stands for "been."

Order abt Hitt (8 July, 1674)

Jn Answer to the request of Anne Hitt widdow... that Shee might haue Liberty to dispose of & put to Sale some part of [her husband's] Estate for the paiment of debts & Legacies & maintenance of herselfe & Children: The Court Orders & Empowres the saide Anne Hitt (with the consent & advice) of those that are Sureties for her true Administracion upon the saide Estate) to dispose of & put to Sale the house & ground at Charlestown valued in the Jnventory at £:170. Shee rendring an Account of s^d Sale unto the Court of this County.

Walsebee's discharge (28 April, 1674)

The wife of David Walsebee of Brantery being presented for her Idleness and sottish carriage. upon hearing of the case The Court judge there is noe ground for the presentment & soe discharge her.

Licenses (28 April, 1674)

Anne Puglice upon certificate from the Selectmen of Boston had her Licence renewed to distill & retail strong waters by small quantities for ye yeare ensuing; provided shee did not sell to any of the inhabitants of the Town to drincke it in her house and George Puglice her husband as principall in ten pounds & Richard Collicot & William Bartholmew as Sureties in five pounds apiece acknowledged themselves respectiuely bound to the Treasuror of the County of Suffolke on condicion that Anne Puglice should observe all the Laws concerning distilling and retailing of strong waters & that shee should not sell any to the inhabitants of the Town to bee dranck in her house.

EXAMINING THE PRIMARY SOURCE

1. List examples in the colonial documents of alphabetical, spelling, and capitalization changes that have appeared in the English language since these documents were written in the seventeenth century.

2. What freedom was originally denied Anne Hitt that resulted in the court order?

THINKING CRITICALLY

3. What does the charge against the wife of David Walsebee indicate about the manners expected of women in colonial America?

4. Some historians have pointed out that women's actual status in colonial America was higher than their legal status. Do the documents support or contradict that observation? Explain your answer.

The Middle Colonies

In my newly laid out Germantown there are already sixty-four families in a very prosperous condition. Such persons, therefore, and all those who still arrive, have to fall to work and swing the axe most vigorously....to throw down these gigantic oak and other forest trees,...

—FRANCIS D. PASTORIUS
German Settler in Pennsylvania, 1700

Section Focus

From 1640 to 1660 a bitter struggle for power between the king and Parliament postponed further colonization in America. Parliament overthrew King Charles I in 1649 and established a commonwealth under Puritan Oliver Cromwell. When the monarchy was restored in 1660, the new king, Charles II, revived English interest in starting new colonies. He rewarded some of his supporters by granting them proprietorships. These became the Middle Colonies.

Objectives

After studying this section, you should be able to:
• Describe the role of proprietors in the development of the Middle Colonies.
• Give reasons for Pennsylvania's rapid growth.

England's neglect of the American colonies between 1640 and 1660 enabled traditions of self-government to firmly develop in America. Colonial legislatures in New England and the South made their own laws, and local courts enforced them. Colonists frequently defied or ignored orders from England and even from their own colonial governors. The Middle Colonies also developed a degree of independence from England, primarily because of the authority the king gave his proprietors. These proprietors permitted their colonists to elect representative assemblies, not because they wanted to surrender power, but because they found it a good way to attract and keep settlers. Proprietors had learned that more settlers meant greater profits.

New Netherland Becomes New York

In 1664 King Charles II granted his brother James, the Duke of York, the land west and south of New England, from the Connecticut River to the Delaware River. He did this even though the territory had already been settled by the Dutch. For years the English had viewed the Dutch colony as a threat because of its trade, its expanding settlements, and its location as a wedge between New England to the north and Virginia to the south. Consequently, in 1664 the Duke of York sent a fleet of four English warships to capture the settlement of New Amsterdam. Peter Stuyvesant (STY vuh sant), the Dutch governor of New Netherland, tried to defend the colony. But he lacked the support of his own colonists and was forced to surrender New Netherland without a struggle. The Duke of York did not hesitate to change the colony's name to New York.

A series of governors appointed by the Duke of York ruled New York until 1683 when the Duke agreed to the colonists' demands for an elected representative assembly. Two years later, however, the Duke of York became King James II, making New York a royal colony. He proceeded to dissolve the assembly and to return full power to the governor. When the English overthrew James II in the Glorious Revolution of 1688, Jacob Leisler, a German trader, led a rebellion in New York. He established a government

Linking Across Time

BROADWAY

Today's Broadway, New York City's most famous street, bears no resemblance to the Broadway of 1679. Instead of ending in Brooklyn it runs 17 miles from the tip of Manhattan Island to a point four miles past the borough known as The Bronx. Among the sites found along its route are Wall Street, Times Square, and Spanish Harlem.

Examining Fine Art
This view of Bethlehem, Pennsylvania, was painted about 1757. Settled by German-speaking Moravians, Bethlehem had natural beauty, but life required hard work. What was the first major task in a new settlement?

with an elected assembly that lasted until 1690, when a new British royal governor arrived in the colony. The new governor captured Leisler, tried him, and had him hanged. The governor, however, permitted the colony to continue to elect an assembly.

New York's varied population included Dutch, Swedes, native Americans, Africans, Jews, some English and French settlers, and people of many other nationalities. But Dutch customs remained strong, and the Dutch Calvinist churches endured. The city, as it appeared in 1679, was described by a Dutch traveler, Jasper Dankers:

[The fort] has only one gate, and that is on the land side, opening upon a broad plain or street, called the Broadway or Beaverway. Over this gate are the arms of the Duke of York....We went on up the hill, along open roads and a little woods, through the first village, called Breukelen [Brooklyn], which has a small and ugly little church standing in the middle of the road.

Several factors delayed New York's rapid growth. Immigration was discouraged because large landowners called **patroons** still held much of the land along the Hudson River. The French in Canada prevented expansion to the north, and the powerful Iroquois Confederacy blocked expansion westward. New York City's magnificent harbor made it a natural trade center, but for many years the small population of the colony did not supply enough goods for export.

New Jersey

Shortly after the Duke of York received his enormous grant of land in 1664, he started giving out parts of it to his friends. He gave New Jersey to John Lord Berkeley and Sir George Carteret. Finding it sparsely inhabited, these proprietors offered religious freedom, large land grants, and the right for landowners to elect a legislative assembly.

In 1674 Berkeley sold his proprietary rights in western New Jersey to a few members of a religious group called the Society of Friends, or Quakers, who were seeking refuge from persecution. In 1682 the heirs of Carteret sold eastern New Jersey to another group of Quakers. The English government created the royal colony of New Jersey by combining the two parts, placing it under the authority of the governor of New York in 1702. Not until 1738 was New Jersey given its own governor.

Pennsylvania and Delaware

William Penn started the most successful colony in America. The son of a British admiral, Penn won the favor of both King Charles II and King James II. But, to his father's dismay, Penn had joined the Quakers when he was a student at Oxford. Quakers were considered religious radicals in England because they believed that paid clergy were unnecessary and that every person could know God's will through his or her own "inner light." They also refused to perform military service, or to swear oaths. They were detested in England and persecuted as anarchists in America.

Neither his father's anger nor jail could make Penn give up his religious views, and King Charles II remained his friend.

Penn wanted to start a colony in America that would serve as a refuge for persecuted Quakers. After his father's death, Penn took advantage of a debt that Charles II owed Admiral Penn, asking the king for a grant of land in America. In 1681 Charles II made Penn the proprietor of a vast area west of the Delaware named "Penn's Woods," or Pennsylvania.

Arriving in Pennsylvania in 1682, Penn worked out a plan for a "city of brotherly love," Philadelphia. His agents advertised for settlers in England, France, the Netherlands, and Germany. Their promises of religious freedom attracted many besides the Quakers, especially Germans.

Because Penn believed in equality, he drew up a "Frame of Government" that provided for an elected council and an assembly. Pennsylvania gave the right to vote to a large number of colonists. Penn also insisted that the Indians be paid for their land and be treated fairly.

These measures meant rapid growth for the colony. By the time Penn left for England in 1684, there were 7,000 colonists. When he returned in 1699, Philadelphia rivaled Boston and New York City as both a commercial and cultural center. Thousands of prosperous farms dotted the countryside. A boundary dispute with Maryland to the south led to the hiring of two surveyors, Mason and Dixon, to draw borders between the two colonies. This border, known as the Mason and Dixon line, later would become famous as the dividing line between slave states and nonslave states.

In 1682 William Penn bought the three counties south of Pennsylvania along the Atlantic Coast from the Duke of York. These "lower counties," known as Delaware, had first been settled by the Dutch, then the Swedes, before the English captured them in 1664. Although Delaware was not part of Penn's grant from the king, he drew up a Charter of Privileges, permitting the lower counties to elect their own assembly. Until the American Revolution, the governor of Pennsylvania also served as the governor of Delaware.

Section Three Review

SUMMARY

King Charles II granted the Duke of York a territory previously settled by the Dutch. The Duke attacked and captured the colony, renaming it New York. He gave two friends two grants of land that later became New Jersey. In order to provide a home for persecuted Quakers, William Penn obtained a grant of land and founded Pennsylvania, where he established an elective government with freedom for all religions. He attracted colonists with advertisements and promises of rights and freedoms. Native Americans were paid for their land. Penn then purchased the land that later became Delaware.

CHECKING FOR UNDERSTANDING

1. **Identify** Duke of York, William Penn, Mason and Dixon

2. **Define** patroons, Quakers

3. **Discuss** the role of proprietors in the political and economic development of the Middle Colonies.

4. **Explain** the conditions, in England and in the Middle Colonies, that supported the development of self-government in the Middle Colonies.

5. **Compare** the early immigrant populations of New York, New Jersey, Pennsylvania and Delaware.

THINKING CRITICALLY

6. **Supporting an Opinion** Argue for or against this statement: in the Middle Colonies, democracy developed more because of its economic advantages than because of ideology.

CONNECTIONS: HISTORY AND RELIGION

7. **Recognizing Values** Which religious beliefs of the Quakers might account for Pennsylvania's advanced democracy, including fairness to native Americans?

People of the Colonies

The day is short, the work great, the workman lazy, the wages high, the master urgeth. Up then, and be doing.

—POOR RICHARD'S ALMANAC, 1775

Section Focus

Colonial society differed in many ways from English society. A new environment, a diversity of peoples, and new economic opportunities helped to produce a society uniquely American. The history of social development in colonial America is a story of progress for many, but it is blemished by the enslavement of Africans and the eviction of native Americans from their lands. It is not a simple tale—for social, political, economic, and religious motivations all interacted to weave the fabric of colonial society.

Objectives

After studying this section, you should be able to:
- Describe social class and the role of women in the colonies.
- Identify the roles of indentured servants and African Americans in the colonies.
- Discuss the relationship between English colonists and native Americans.

By European standards the society of Elizabethan England was remarkably mobile. An apprentice might become rich and marry his daughter to a noble. In turn, a noble's younger son, who inherited no property, might become an apprentice or hire himself out as a soldier. English women were less restrained socially than the women on the Continent. Like England, the colonies' social structure had many classes, but from the start it was more democratic. English society was aristocratic, dominated by great lords and ladies. Immigrants to America were mostly common people, although social class in the colonies remained important.

Colonial Social Classes

In each of the 13 colonies there was an upper class, socially superior by law or custom. In New England, merchants, shipowners, and the clergy composed this class. In the South and along the Hudson River in New York, great landowners imitated the country gentry, or upper class, of England. Early colonial laws permitted only upper-class men to wear silver buttons and upper-class women and girls to wear silk dresses. Social rank was indicated on marriage certificates and even on tombstones.

Near the bottom of society were indentured servants, bound by contract to work in the colonies in return for their passage to America. When the contract expired, the servant was free to work for wages. Because labor was scarce, wages in the colonies were 2 or 3 times those in England. In some colonies after the term of indenture, the law gave each person as much as 50 acres of land. Indentured servants could move up in society. For example, in the 1660s 13 of 28 members of the Virginia House of Burgesses had come to the colony as indentured servants.

For most people, life in colonial America was better than it had been in Europe. Still, many died within the first year because of hardships encountered during the ocean voyage. Frontier settlements faced conflict with Indians, starvation due to crop failures, disastrous fires, and epidemics of smallpox, dysentery, malaria, diphtheria, and yellow fever.

By the 1700s conditions had improved, although epidemics continued to make life uncertain. There was widespread prosperity—a product of cheap land, a ready market for colonial exports, and hard work. Idleness was generally regarded as a sin like drunkenness or gluttony. There were few beggars and paupers. Organized crime was almost unknown, except for occasional piracy on the high seas and banditry on the frontier. Just as there were few beggars at the bottom, there were few idle rich at the top. Many of the wealthiest people, whether New England merchants, Hudson Valley patroons, or Virginia plantation owners, habitually rose at dawn and worked until dark.

The population of the American colonies was diverse. By 1775 people of English origin accounted for just under half the population. The high birth rate— an average of seven births per woman in New England—and the long period of colonial history—1607 to 1776—meant that most of these were born in the colonies. From about the time of the founding of Pennsylvania in 1681, people of different European nationalities and religions—Scots, Irish Catholics, French Huguenots, Spanish Jews, and German Protestants—arrived in increasing numbers. Together with the Dutch in New York, these accounted for nearly one-third of the colonists.

Beginning in Virginia in 1619, the first African slaves were brought by the Dutch from the West Indies. Africans, both slave and free, made up about 20 percent of the total population. Like the English, by 1775 most of these had been born in America. The proportion of African Americans was highest in the Southern Colonies because slave labor proved profitable on rice and tobacco plantations. In South Carolina three out of four people were African slaves.

Women in the Colonies

English colonial population grew rapidly because proportionately there were more women than in the Spanish and French colonies. Colonial women were considered fortunate because they easily found husbands. The only respectable career for women at that time was thought to be marriage. As in all European societies of the time, women were denied higher education. Women generally married in their early twenties and had five or six children. Their principal task was rearing children, although most women died during the child-bearing years.

The second occupation for most women was farming. A farm could not carry on without the skills of women in making cloth, garments, candles, soap, and breadstuffs. Life on the frontier made women more self-reliant. A visitor to the North Carolina-Virginia backcountry in 1710 gave this description of a frontierswoman:

…[S]he is a very civil woman and shows nothing of ruggedness or Immodesty in her carriage, yett she will carry a gunn in the woods and kill deer, turkeys, etc., shoot down wild cattle, catch and tye hoggs, knock down beeves with an axe and perform the most manful exercises.

Examining Maps *The American colonies belonged to England, but immigrants represented a variety of ethnic and racial backgrounds. What immigrant group was predominant along the Atlantic coast?*

NATIONAL ORIGINS OF THE AMERICAN COLONISTS, 1760

Legend:
- English
- German
- Scotch-Irish
- Africans
- Dutch
- Scottish

In the South plantation wives helped in directing the work force. When seafaring New England husbands left their wives, sometimes for years at a time, women were successful as merchants or storekeepers. Widespread home manufacturing allowed wives to learn trades. Some women were printers, newspaper publishers, druggists, and doctors.

Colonial laws gave women more protection than English laws. In England, for example, the common law allowed a husband to beat his wife but only with a "reasonable instrument"; according to Massachusetts law, he could beat her only in self-defense.

Slavery in the Colonies

At first it was not clear that enslaved Africans were to be treated differently from white indentured servants. Gradually legal distinctions were adopted. Indentured servants retained the rights of English people and the protection of the law. Africans were protected by no law or tradition. While the Catholic Church in the Spanish colonies offered some protection to enslaved people, no similar institution protected them in the English colonies. The South gave slave marriages no legality and children could be sold away from their mothers. Slaves could own no property and had little legal protection against irresponsible or cruel owners. Practically, their protection was only their value to the owner who provided food, clothing, and shelter to keep them reasonably healthy.

Slave labor was well adapted to the southern plantation system, where the work was done in fields and easily overseen. The profits of large plantations made slavery seem necessary to the South's prosperity. Southern colonial laws declared blacks to be enslaved for life, and their children after them. It was illegal to teach Africans to read for fear that learning would spoil them for physical labor. There were, in the South, owners who disapproved of slavery but hesitated to free their slaves because free blacks faced serious discrimination. In addition, whites feared them as possible leaders of slave insurrections. So most southern colonies passed laws that made it difficult or impossible to give enslaved people their freedom.

In the North, slavery was less profitable and enslaved people less numerous. New England, not only allowed, but required people who were enslaved to marry; they could acquire property and testify in court. An owner might punish a slave, but an owner who killed a slave could be charged with murder. A growing number of people argued that slavery was a moral wrong.

In 1700 Samuel Sewall, a Massachusetts judge, published *The Selling of Joseph,* a pamphlet that maintained that slavery was contrary to the Bible. In Pennsylvania, Quakers and Mennonites, a German religious sect, denounced slavery. The number of free blacks increased, and a few even became prosperous. In Jaffrey, New Hampshire, Amos Fortune bought other blacks out of slavery and left money for the town school. But the northern colonies did not permit equality to free blacks. Custom usually kept them in menial positions, and the laws denied them the right to vote or hold office.

Native Americans and Colonists

The first meetings between English settlers and Indians gave little evidence to the eventual destruction of the native Americans' ways of life. A few colonial leaders, notably Roger Williams and William Penn, tried to treat them fairly, and some Protestant ministers regarded the Indians principally as souls to be brought to knowledge of Christ.

The expansion of colonial farms into Indian lands became the principal cause of numerous conflicts. The colonists reasoned that since the Indians did not have settled dwellings, but were on the move like "the foxes and wild beasts...so it is lawful now to take a land which none useth; and make use of it." The historian James Truslow Adams wrote:

*When a French trader or trapper
plunged into the forest, and the green leaves
closed behind him, it was to mingle
with the life of the natives, which,
in its main aspects, flowed on
uninterrupted by his presence. When,
on the other hand...the English frontier
crept ever farther and farther inland, and
town succeeded town, it was as if, adding
stone to stone, great dikes were being built,
which more and more dammed up
the waters of native life.*

Some of the conflicts resulted from great misunderstandings each culture had of the other's values. Europeans viewed land ownership as essential to an individual's progress. Individual Indians did not own land, but jointly shared territory with all the members of the group. Native Americans who sold or by treaty gave up lands, did so without any authority, since no chief could dispose of land.

Colonists justified wars against native Americans in many ways. Some Puritan ministers even claimed that Indians were children of the devil, so they could be killed in good conscience.

Individually, a colonist may not have been a match for the Indian brave who had learned the art of war in struggles over territory with other Indians, but because of sheer numbers and weapons the whites were destined to win. They also had grim allies in diseases such as smallpox. European diseases sometimes wiped out whole Indian communities because the native Americans had not developed immunities. Of the estimated 120,000 native Americans who had lived in the area occupied by the 13 colonies, perhaps only 20,000 survived. Most Indian nations, too small to resist, simply disappeared as social units. The Iroquois Confederacy was the only group that had the ability to protect its members from destruction.

SUMMARY

The American colonies were prosperous, with an upper class that included merchants, ship owners, the clergy, and large landowners. The indentured servants could improve their standing once free. Women could not vote, but they were full partners in running farms and sometimes businesses. Enslaved Africans became property, with no legal protection in the South. In the North, opposition to slavery began to grow. Thousands of native Americans perished in battles with colonists and in epidemics.

CHECKING FOR UNDERSTANDING

1. **Identify** Iroquois Confederacy
2. **Discuss** the social class system in the colonies.
3. **Describe** the position of indentured servants, women, and African Americans in the colonies.
4. **Explain** how conflicts developed between English colonists and native Americans.

THINKING CRITICALLY

5. **Evaluating Causes** Most colonists were common people, rather than titled aristocracy. What became the new basis for class structure and how did it lead to class mobility?

GLOBAL PERSPECTIVES

6. **Applying Principles** In 1755, Jean-Jacques Rousseau, a French philosopher, blamed European society's evils on "The first man who, having enclosed a piece of ground, bethought himself of saying 'This is mine'...." To this he added, "...you are undone if you once forget that the fruits of the earth belong to us all, and the earth itself to nobody." How might Rousseau have helped the colonists understand native Americans?

★ ★ ★ ★ ★ ★ ★ ★ ★ ★ ★ ★ ★ ★ ★ ★ ★ ★ ★ ★

The Colonies Become America

Be a master of your trade; count it a disgrace to be no workman....Why do you find so many occupations mentioned in the Scriptures? 'Tis partly that so you may think on the Scriptures in the midst of your occupations.

—COTTON MATHER
Puritan minister, in a sermon, 1701

Section Focus

Colonial society developed from British foundations. By the mid-1700s, however, colonial society differed from Britain in many ways. This was partly because the colonies were a haven for a variety of religious beliefs. Religious toleration became necessary in colonies where no one church dominated. In many areas the church was at the center of community life and the clergy, in many cases, swayed political decisions.

Objectives

After studying this section, you should be able to:
• Explain why religious toleration and freedom developed during the colonial period.
• Identify three sources of democratic government and individual rights in the colonies.

I n the South the planter aristocracy usually belonged to the Anglican Church, while the middle and poorer classes included Roman Catholics, Methodists, Baptists, and Presbyterians. In New England the great majority of the people were Puritan Congregationalists, but there were small groups of other Protestant sects. The Middle Colonies had the greatest variety—Dutch Calvinists, German Lutherans, Scot Presbyterians, Mennonites, Jews, Quakers, and Presbyterians. In New England and the Southern Colonies, a single official church was "established"—that is, supported by taxes.

The Colonial Mind

Although many people came to America to worship as they pleased, this did not mean that they were ready to grant others the same privilege. Massachusetts Puritans believed that religious toleration was a weakness inspired by the devil. Anyone who advocated it must be "either an atheist or a heretic or a hypocrite or at best a captive of some lust." While they expelled many like Roger Williams, they hanged Quakers on Boston Common. Virginia, on the other hand, expelled ministers who came from Massachusetts.

Some who were persecuted learned the value of religious toleration. In Rhode Island Roger Williams claimed that it was:

...the will and command of God...that a permission of the most Paganish, Jewish, Turkish, or Antichristian consciences and worships be granted to all men.

In the seventeenth century no other colony went that far, but, as we have seen, Maryland granted liberty of worship to Christians, and later Pennsylvania welcomed anyone who worshiped God.

In the 1740s the colonies experienced a religious revival called the Great Awakening. Some Puritan ministers in Massachusetts, concerned over declining religious fervor in their communities, began to preach sermons that warned of the impending dangers of hell. They were influenced by Jonathan Edwards of Northampton, who was one of America's greatest colonial Christian theologians. Within a few years, George Whitefield, an English evangelist and follower of John Wesley's revivals in Britain, came to America. In 7 trips from Britain, he preached from one end of the colonies to the other, sometimes to outdoor crowds of 20,000.

As ministers took sides favoring or opposing the revivalists, new churches sprang up. By the 1770s, people felt free to shop around for a preacher and a religion that suited them. The diversity of churches helped to make religious toleration even more essential. Other products of the revival were new colleges such as Princeton, Brown, Rutgers, and Dartmouth.

By the late 1700s, open religious persecution in the colonies was largely a thing of the past, although all religious groups were not equal before the law. Visitors from other countries were especially struck by the freedom granted Jews, who still suffered severe persecution in most European countries. A foreign traveler to New York in about 1750 was astonished to find that Jews owned prosperous shops, farms, and trading vessels.

The Puritans believed that citizens should learn enough English to read the Bible and understand the laws. The Massachusetts General School Act of 1647 stated two principles of education that remain today: local communities have a duty to set up schools, and this duty is enforced by law.

In the Middle Colonies, schooling was not as universal as in New England, but it was widespread. In the Southern Colonies, formal education was generally limited to children of large landowners and professionals. Governor William Berkeley of Virginia supported this belief in a letter to England:

...there are no free schools, or printing, and I hope we shall not have them these hundred years, for learning has brought disobedience and heresy and sects into the world ...God keep us from both!

Examining Fine Art
A Quaker Meeting *gave each person the chance to speak. The Quakers' democratic and peace-loving ways brought persecution by less tolerant groups. What two factors helped to bring about religious toleration?*

Even where schools were desired, the widely separated plantations and farms of the South made them impractical.

By modern standards colonial schools were primitive. One New England teacher wrote of his schoolhouse, "one might as well nigh as good keep school in a hog stie." There were few books, and instruction was given only two or three months a year. Most girls received little formal education. Two-thirds of the women whose names appear on Massachusetts legal documents in the early 1700s could not write their signatures. Despite the shortcomings of colonial education, no other region of equal size in the world had such a high proportion of the population that could read and write.

Religion was the principal force behind most institutions of higher learning in the colonies. The earliest colleges Harvard, William and Mary, and Yale were founded to train young men for the ministry. Colleges were also attended by sons of wealthy families and by ambitious poorer boys anxious to improve their situations in life.

By the middle of the eighteenth century, the college curriculum began to change, as an interest in science and a demand for practical subjects increased or grew. Thus when King's College—later

Examining Illustrations *This engraving is of Jonathan Edwards, a Puritan theologian and minister in Northampton, Massachusetts. His preaching helped start the Great Awakening. What colleges were products of this religious movement?*

Columbia—was opened in New York City in 1754, it announced that the comprehensive scheme of studies would include not only the traditional Latin, Greek, and Hebrew, but also:

Surveying and Navigation, Geography, History, Husbandry, Commerce, Government, the Knowledge of All Nature in the Heavens above us and in the Air, Water, and Earth Around us, Meteors, Stones, Mines and Minerals, Plants and Animals, and of everything useful for the Comfort, Convenience and Elegance of Life.

This interest in science, which produced a new confidence in human reason, originated in Europe, where it was known as the Enlightenment. The English philosopher John Locke produced works that were widely read in America. In *An Essay Concerning Human Understanding*, Locke maintained that people could best gain knowledge of the universe by observing and by experimenting. This knowledge would guide them in developing a reasonable society. In the second of two *Treatises on Government,* Locke taught that people were born with certain natural rights to life, liberty, and property; that people formed governments to protect these rights; and that a government interfering with these might rightfully be overthrown. Practical Americans readily accepted the

Linking Across Time

FREEDOM OF THE PRESS

In 1735 John Peter Zenger faced charges of libel for printing a critical report about the royal governor of New York. Andrew Hamilton defended Zenger in court by asking the jury to base its decision on whether the charges were true, not whether they were offensive. The jury found Zenger not guilty. When the nation became independent, freedom of the press was included in the Bill of Rights. In 1931 the Supreme Court expanded this right by declaring "prior restraint" laws against malicious or slanderous articles unconstitutional.

idea that government was the agent of the people, not their ruler.

The Press in America

In addition to schools and colleges, newspapers, almanacs, books, and circulating libraries all helped to raise the level of public information. Because paper and type were expensive and the reading public in America small, most books came from Britain. But by 1750 there were 25 or 30 American newspapers, mostly 4 pages long, printed weekly. The subscription lists contained only a few thousand names, but readers were more numerous. Printed on tough rag paper, these newspapers were passed from hand to hand at the local inn until half the men in a village often read a single copy. European travelers in the colonies were amazed to find that political discussions in public inns were joined intelligently by everybody from the college-educated to stable help.

Colonial editors occasionally criticized British laws or officials. In 1735 Peter Zenger of the *New York Weekly Journal* accused the royal governor of corruption. As a result, copies of the paper were publicly burned by the sheriff, and Zenger was brought to trial on a charge of libel. His lawyer, Andrew Hamilton, argued that the editor was not guilty, since the charges were true, and since free speech was a basic right of English people. Zenger was acquitted. At the time the case attracted little attention, but today it is regarded as a landmark in the development of free press in America.

Economy and Government

By 1776, the close of the colonial period, 30 percent of the ships in the British merchant marine were American, and most of these sailed from New England ports. New Englanders carried on a share of the African slave trade. They were the first to hunt whales in the Antarctic; in 1774, 360 whaling ships sailed from the island of Nantucket alone. While New England was a formidable competitor in trade, no colony offered much competition to the British in manufacturing. Colonists usually obtained manufactured goods from Britain .

To pay for fine European goods like clothing, books, wine, and cutlery the colonies had to trade staples that Europeans needed or to pay in gold or silver. Trade with the West Indies netted Spanish dollars, the common colonial currency. Later the new nation, the United States, would adopt the dollar instead of the British pound as its monetary unit. Gradually the colonies developed a culture distinctly different from Europe.

The degree of power exercised by British officials varied from colony to colony, but it was limited everywhere. In all colonies the voters elected their own legislature, and in charter colonies their governor as well. In proprietary colonies the governor was appointed by the proprietor or by his heirs; in royal or crown colonies the governor was chosen by the king. The governor of a proprietary or crown colony had wide powers, such as a veto over the legislature and control of land grants. Yet he was often at the mercy of the legislature, which might refuse to vote him his salary.

Government at the town and county levels was run entirely by the colonists themselves. In New England, the important local unit was the township. Decisions were made at the town meeting, which most heads of families had a right to attend. The town meeting was the most direct form of democracy in the colonies. In the Southern and Middle colonies, local government was usually less democratic but, nevertheless, entirely independent of British control.

None of the colonies was so democratic as to allow full political rights to all men or to *any* women. Active citizenship and the right to vote and hold office were limited to adult white males owning property, who usually had to be members of the established church. In spite of these limitations, a higher proportion of people was involved in government in the British colonies than anywhere in the European world. This wide participation gave Americans training that was valuable when the colonies later became independent.

SUMMARY

Religious groups played important roles in shaping colonial values, institutions, and society. Established churches were tax-supported, and usually only male members of established churches could vote or hold office. Churches established most schools and colleges. Eventually, religious diversity made religious toleration necessary. The influence of the Enlightenment and its philosophers combined with an active press to create a climate favorable to democratic traditions—already established in local government and the elected legislatures.

CHECKING FOR UNDERSTANDING

1. **Identify** the Great Awakening, the comprehensive scheme of studies, John Locke

2. **Give Reasons** for the development of religious freedom and toleration in the British colonies.

3. **Compare** the importance and availability of education in the three geographic regions of the colonies. What accounts for the difference?

4. **List** factors contributing to the growth of democracy and rights in the American colonies.

THINKING CRITICALLY

5. **Recognizing Relationships** What evidence do you find in this chapter that church and state were not separate in most of the American colonies? In what ways did religious groups exert their influence?

CONNECTIONS:
HISTORY AND PHILOSOPHY

6. **Applying Ideas** Ancient philosophers who believed monarchs ruled by divine right encouraged support for monarchies. How did John Locke's ideas make a similar contribution to belief in democracy?

★ ★ ★ ★ ★ ★ ★ ★ ★ ★ ★ ★ ★ ★ ★ ★ ★ ★

★ Chapter 3 Review ★

★ Summary

In the 1600s and early 1700s, thirteen English colonies were established—some for profit by proprietors and private trading companies, and others by religious groups seeking freedom.

New England, Middle, and Southern colonies developed differently. Diverse economies were built on crops or enterprises suited to regional climates. England largely left the colonies to govern themselves. Religious diversity eventually made religious toleration necessary. With a thriving export and trade economy, many people moved between the classes. Women could not vote, but they were full partners in running farms and sometimes businesses. Slaves became property, with no legal protection in the South. Native Americans suffered from battles with colonists over land and epidemics of European diseases. At first, churches provided most schools and colleges, but public education began to emerge, especially in New England.

★ Using Vocabulary

Use all the terms below in one of four sentences or paragraphs, each about one of the following: the class hierarchy in the colonies, the religious groups who colonized New England, government in the colonies, major exports.

indentured servants	plantations
proprietors	subsistence farming
naval stores	dissenters
congregation	commonwealth
constitution	patroons

★ Reviewing Facts

1. **Describe** the role of religion in settling the American colonies.
2. **Summarize** the growth of self-government in the colonies.
3. **Explain** the role economics played in the settlement of the colonies.
4. **Detail** the government in three types of colonies.
5. **Analyze** why slavery became more prevalent in the South than in New England.

6. **Compare** the class system in the Southern colonies with that in New England.
7. **Discuss** how democratic ideas gradually became an important part of colonial thought.

★ Understanding Concepts

MIGRATION

1. The colonists who left England to settle in America endured formidable hardships. List three reasons why different groups of colonists migrated to America in the face of these risks and hardships. How do their motives compare to the reasons people migrate today?
2. Compare the motives of the Pilgrims and Puritans who migrated to Massachusetts with those of Williams, Penn, and Wheelwright.

VALUES AND BELIEFS

3. What values and beliefs were instrumental in establishing democratic institutions in the American colonies?
4. Explain why Puritans, who left England to escape religious persecution, denied religious freedom to other groups. In what societies today is religious freedom denied?

★ Thinking Critically

1. **Proposing Solutions** Imagine you are appointed to resolve disputes between native Americans and colonists wanting farmland. Propose a fair plan for expansion. Remember that native Americans did not own land.
2. **Analyzing Trends** Women's rights movements in the United States have generally sought the vote, full citizenship, property rights, equal pay and economic opportunity, equality in marriage, and the right to work in traditionally male occupations. Which of these did women have to some extent during the colonial period? Why?
3. **Linking Past and Present** Some southern slaveholders feared to free their slaves because of the discrimination the former slaves might face. Consider what you know of the experiences of African Americans. What evidence can you find to suggest that their fears were not justified?

4. Recognizing Bias The colonial class system allowed great mobility, yet for generations the descendants of the first families to settle New England enjoyed more prestige than other citizens. What does this form of stature have in common with the class structure in England?

★ Writing About History

DESCRIPTION

Refer to the instructions of how to write a description in the History Writer's Handbook in the Appendix of this book. Your teacher will give you more specific instructions on the description's length and the assignment's due date.

Imagine you are an author who traveled in the first supply ship to reach Jamestown the year after it was settled. Write a description, to be published in Britain, of the condition of the colony when you arrived.

★ Learning Cooperatively

Working in a group with four members, study slavery around the world and throughout history. Assign each member one or more cultures or geographic areas to study. For example, one member might study slavery in ancient Europe, another in Africa, and so on. Report your findings and conduct a discussion comparing and contrasting slavery in other cultures with slavery of African Americans in the colonies. Select a recorder to take notes, and a spokesperson to share your comparison with the rest of the class.

★ Mastering Skills

READING A THEMATIC MAP

No doubt you have seen and studied maps in textbooks, magazines, atlases, even on television weather or news reports. Although there is almost no limit to the kinds of information that maps can show, most maps, depending on the type of information they present, fit into one of two broad categories. Maps that show general information such as countries, cities, rivers, and other features are called *general reference maps*. A second category of maps is *thematic maps*. These maps depict or emphasize more specific information than general reference maps. Often the

information is on a single topic. The map below is a thematic map because it depicts information about a particular topic—land holdings in New England during the 1600s and early 1700s.

Example To read this or any other thematic map, follow the guidelines below:

- Read the title to determine the topic of the map.
- Locate the map legend, or key, if one is given. Often the legend uses symbols and colors to represent the categories of information that can be found in the map.
- Now look at the map itself. Locate and study the symbols and colors on the map. From this information, you can hypothesize or make generalizations about the map's theme.

Practice Use the map and what you have read in the chapter to answer the following questions.

1. Based on the title, what can you learn from the map?

2. In what year was the Rhode Island Grant bestowed?

3. What grants of land were made in 1629?

4. **Drawing Conclusions** The map shows that there were many grants of land made during the 1600s and early 1700s. What do you think the British Crown was trying to accomplish by making these land grants?

★ ★ ★ Unit 1 Digest ★ ★ ★

For thousands of years, cultures around the world developed in relative isolation. Then Europe entered an age of discovery and exploration during the 1400s and 1500s. Western Europeans crossed the Atlantic Ocean to find the Americas, vast continents rich in precious metals and other natural resources. They then proceeded to explore and conquer lands that they previously had not known existed. In this "New World" the blending of diverse cultures gave birth to a unique American civilization.

Chapter 1
The World in Transition

The first Americans were immigrants who traveled across a land bridge that once connected Siberia and Alaska. Eventually these people spread throughout North and South America. Although some remained hunter-gatherers, others learned agriculture and raised animals. In Central America the Olmec, Maya, and Aztec civilizations, and the Inca of South America, developed highly organized and sophisticated societies. In North America the Anasazi developed pueblos and the Hopewell constructed huge burial mounds. Elsewhere, the Iroquois language groups formed a strong, lasting political confederation.

Meanwhile, in western Europe, a new Europe was emerging as Christianity unified the people and strong monarchs unified their territories. A wealthy middle class developed from the increase in commerce and growth of cities. Peace, prosperity, and optimism helped to set in motion a far-reaching rebirth of interest in the classical heritage of Greece and Rome called the Renaissance. The Renaissance brought a profound cultural awakening in Italian, French, English, and German lands.

Religious leaders like John Wycliffe, John Huss, Martin Luther, and John Calvin called for the reform of the Roman Catholic Church. During the Reformation, some groups broke entirely with the Church and founded Protestant churches.

In Asia and Africa, Muslim leaders established empires and expanded their territories. The trade that had flourished on these continents since ancient times continued to grow. Traders carried ideas as well as goods between the East and the West, usually along overland routes or a combination of overland and water routes. China, however, turned inward, halting trade to free its people from outside influences.

The development of nation-states, the Renaissance, the Reformation, and the growth of trade caused many Europeans to turn outward. Improved technology gave navigators the compass, the astrolabe, the quadrant, and faster, more seaworthy ships. Bankers, merchants, and joint-stock companies provided the money to finance expeditions. In search of spices and luxury goods, explorers braved the uncharted seas to find an all-water route from Europe to Asia. Portuguese sailors rounded the tip of Africa and charted an eastern waterway to India.

Chapter 2
European Discovery and Exploration

Soon European nations other than Portugal were looking to establish direct trading links with the East. Not until the voyages of Christopher Columbus in the late 1490s, however, were Europeans aware that North America and South America existed. Yet by 1500, Spain and Portugal were competing for territory in the Americas. The pope drew a line of demarcation between Portuguese and Spanish lands in South America. Soon this line was shifted and extended around the earth. Meanwhile, Portugal grew rich because it controlled the eastern route to the Indies. In 1519 Spain made its bid for wealth from Asia by sending Ferdinand Magellan to find a westerly route. His expedition was the first to circumnavigate the world.

Commerce led to empire building. The Spaniards wanted wealth from the New World, but also glory and an opportunity to spread Christianity. In 1519 Hernán Cortés began his conquest of the Aztecs. He defeated their emperor Moctezuma and shipped huge amounts of Aztec gold to Spain. His success encouraged other *conquistadores,* such as Francisco Pizarro who conquered the Incan empire, to seek their fortunes in the Americas. In the process, the Spaniards claimed vast territories that eventually formed a great colonial empire. The people of Spain's colonies formed a structured society, with government officials at the top and native Americans and African slaves at the bottom.

Other countries envied the riches that Spain's conquests in Central and South America brought. As a result France, England, and the Netherlands searched for a northwest passage to the East and made claims in the New World during the 1500s and the 1600s. The French established a permanent colony at Quebec in 1608 along the St. Lawrence River and developed a lucrative trade in beaver furs. By 1682 French explorers had claimed the Mississippi River basin. The Dutch settled in the rich Hudson River valley.

Chapter 3
Colonial America

After the English destroyed the Spanish invasion fleet, the Armada, in 1588, their interest in the Americas deepened. The first English colony on Roanoke Island failed in 1578. But in 1607 the English founded Jamestown in Virginia—their first permanent settlement in the New World. Despite many hardships, the Jamestown colonists survived. Profits from the tobacco they grew lured new settlers to Virginia. In time, the colonists there formed the first representative government body in North America, the House of Burgesses. The first Africans were brought to Jamestown in 1619.

The Jamestown settlers came to America looking for wealth. Others, like the Pilgrim and Puritan settlers in New England, wanted freedom from religious persecution. Upon arrival in North America in 1620, the Pilgrims signed the Mayflower Compact and established the Plymouth colony in what is now Massachusetts. With the help of the American Indian Squanto, they adapted to their environment. By 1629 thousands of Puritans, hoping to build a model Christian society, had migrated to Massachusetts. However, religious differences soon forced some of them to move on and found settlements in Rhode Island and Connecticut.

Other colonies were created when the king granted huge tracts of land to proprietors. These proprietorships included the southern colonies of Maryland, the Carolinas, and Georgia, and the middle colonies of New York, New Jersey, Pennsylvania, and Delaware.

Although many diverse groups of people populated the colonies, their values and beliefs, government, and educational institutions grew out of English traditions. By the mid-1700s, these aspects of colonial society had a unique, and many times religious, character. Over time, the social and political structure of the colonies became more democratic than in England. For example, the House of Burgesses, not the English Parliament, controlled the taxes that paid the governor's salary, and the Act of Toleration in Maryland protected the religious freedom of all Christian settlers there. In short, the colonies offered a better life to most of the people who settled there.

However, many women, Africans, and native Americans did not share in this better life. Women were given little formal education and were banned from participation in government. Most Africans in the colonies were slaves. And native Americans fought constantly with the colonists over territory. Although few colonists were as skilled as Indian warriors at fighting, the colonists' numbers and superior weapons gave them an advantage. European diseases wiped out whole native American communities because they had not developed immunities.

SYNTHESIZING UNIT THEMES

RELATING IDEAS

1. How did religion help shape events between the 1400s and the 1700s?

IDENTIFYING TRENDS

2. How did technology influence the exploration and the settlement of the New World?

MAKING COMPARISONS

3. Compare the culture in England with the culture that American colonists developed.

★ Unit 1 Review ★

★ Analyzing Unit Themes

GEOGRAPHY AND THE ENVIRONMENT

1. How did the location of Asian centers of trade relative to Europe lead to colonies in the Americas?

THE INDIVIDUAL AND FAMILY LIFE

2. Compare the lives and obligations of medieval serfs and colonial indentured servants.

HUMANITIES AND RELIGION

3. What roles did religion play in motivating voyages of exploration and in colonizing America?

4. What major developments in the arts were taking place in Europe during the age of exploration and colonization?

CULTURAL DIVERSITY

5. What role did cultural diversity play in the colonization of North and South America?

★ Reviewing Chronology

Study the unit time line on pages 4 and 5, then answer the questions that follow.

1. How much time elapsed between Columbus's arrival in the Americas and the first permanent English settlement?

2. As the Hopewell culture declined in North America, what dynasty came to power in China?

★ Linking Past and Present

- 1990 Iraq attacked and occupied Kuwait. The United Nations threatened and then used military force against Iraq.

- 1990 Conflict between Muslims and Hindus in India erupted in bloody riots over a Muslim mosque built by the first Mogul emperor in 1528 on the site where Hindus believe Ram, a Hindu god, was born.

Study the information above, then answer the questions that follow.

1. **Predicting Outcomes** Had the United Nations been founded as early as 1200, could it have prevented the Spanish, Mongols, and Ottomans from conquering so many of the world's peoples? Explain your answer.

2. **Proposing Alternatives** How could the Mogul emperor have shown respect for the beliefs of the Hindus and avoided bloody conflict more than four centuries later?

★ Demonstrating Citizenship

Acquiring and Using Information Consult an almanac or other reference book to identify the official language of each nation in Central and South America. Based on this information, what second language might an English-speaking citizen of the Americas wish to study?

★ Interpreting Illustrations

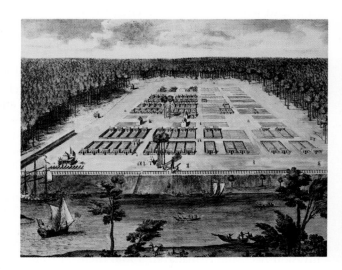

Examine closely the engraving above of Savannah, the first settlement in the Georgia colony, as it looked in 1734. Then answer the questions that follow.

1. Why do you think this particular site was selected by the settlers for a colony?

2. What evidence is there that Savannah was one of the first planned cities in America?

3. As the first capital of the Georgia colony, what advantages might Savannah have had over settlements that came later?

★ Unit 1 Review ★

★ Thinking Globally

1. Comparing Attitudes The Magna Carta in 1215 compelled England's monarchs to govern according to law. In 1295 a representative government body, Parliament, further limited the monarch's power. Therefore, during the 1500s and 1600s, English monarchs were bound by laws passed by a representative legislative body. By contrast, Spanish monarchs of the 1500s held absolute power. Believing they ruled by divine right, Spanish monarchs concentrated power in their own hands. What attitudes toward authority might you expect in each country?

2. Tracing Origins What relationship would you expect to see between views of government in the colonies and those of the founding country in the Spanish and British empires?

★ Relating Geography and History

LOCATION: RELATIVE LOCATION

In the 1300s and 1400s, most goods from Asia were delivered by Arab merchants to Mediterranean ports. Italian states such as Genoa and Venice dominated most of the Mediterranean trade. By contrast, Portugal sought an ocean route to Asia.

Study the map on page 29, then answer the questions that follow.

1. How might the locations of Italian states account for their domination of Mediterranean trade?

2. How might the location of Portugal account for its initiative in seeking an ocean route to Asia?

★ Practicing Skills

USING LITERATURE AS A HISTORICAL SOURCE

Refer to the skills lesson on Using Literature as a Historical Source on page 17 to help you practice this study and writing skill.

The following reading is taken from William Bradford's *Of Plymouth Plantation*. Written between 1630 and 1647, this work is a nonfiction description of the Separatists from their origins in England through their settlement and growth in Massachusetts. Bradford was

elected the colony's governor 30 times between 1621 and 1656.

Read the excerpt, then answer the questions that follow.

All this while the Indians came skulking about them [Pilgrims], and would sometimes show themselves aloof off, but when any approached near them, they would run away; and once they stole away their tools where they had been at work and were gone to dinner. But about the 16th of March, a certain Indian came boldly amongst them and spoke to them in broken English, which they could well understand but marveled at it. At length they understood by discourse with him that he was not off these parts, but belonged to the eastern parts where some English ships came to fish, with whom he was acquainted and could name sundry of them by their names, amongst whom he had got his language. He became profitable to them in acquainting them with many things concerning the state of the country in the east parts where he lived, which was afterwards profitable unto them; also of the people here, of their names, number and strength, of their situation and distance from this place, and who was chief amongst them. His name was Samoset. He told them also of another Indian whose name was Squanto, a native of this place, who had been in England and could speak better English than himself.

1. What is the theme of this literature selection?

2. Who is the main character?

3. Do the events help you understand a historical setting, circumstance, or a specific culture?

4. What have you learned from this excerpt about a particular period or culture?

ASKING EFFECTIVE QUESTIONS

Refer to the skill lesson on Asking Effective Questions on page 46 to help you practice this study and writing skill.

You are asked to write a research report about the German immigrants who settled in colonial Pennsylvania. You have determined that you need to know reasons why these immigrants would want to leave their homeland for an uncertain future in an English colony. As you consult textbooks, encyclopedias, and history magazines, what questions should you ask to understand why Germans came to America?

Write a list of 5 to 10 effective questions on this topic.

UNIT 2
The Struggle for Independence: 1650-1789

By the rude bridge that arched the flood,
Their flag to April's breeze unfurled,
Here once the embattled farmers stood
And fired the shot heard round the world.

—RALPH WALDO EMERSON
Concord Hymn, 1867

SETTING THE SCENE

Time

Late seventeenth century to late eighteenth century

Mood

For the 13 English colonies, the years following the crushing defeat of the French in North America were filled with resentment, anger, an emerging patriotism, and hope. Harsh measures passed by Parliament in an effort to control the colonies were met with outrage and hostile countermeasures. Gradually united, the colonists joined together and rebelled against their parent country. Their independence thus secured, Americans created for themselves a remarkable new form of democratic government.

Themes

- American Democracy
- Civil Rights and Liberties
- Economic Development
- Conflict and Cooperation

Key Events

- French and Indian War
- Fall of Quebec
- Treaty of Paris, 1763
- Stamp Act
- Boston Tea Party
- Battles of Lexington and Concord
- Declaration of Independence
- Battle of Saratoga
- British defeat at Yorktown
- Treaty of Paris, 1783
- Ratification of the Constitution

Major Issues

- British defeat of the French in North America prompts Parliament to attempt tightening commercial and political control of the 13 English colonies.
- Patriot determinism, military skill, and French aid enable the colonies to win independence from Britain.
- Key compromises lead to the formation of a strong and democratic central government.

George Washington Before the Battle of Trenton *by John Trumbull, 1792*

Global Perspectives

The United States was not the only country that engaged in a bloody revolution. France, too, saw an uprising that was to change the shape of its history. In 1789 French artisans and shopkeepers stormed and captured the hated prison-fortress, the Bastille, and sparked numerous other outbreaks throughout the country. The ultimate result was a new government that instituted democracy and abolished France's monarchy.

Great Britain had earlier limited the power of its monarchy. By this period Britain was in the midst of a different sort of revolution—the Industrial Revolution.

THE WORLD

	ASIA AND OCEANIA	AFRICA	EUROPE	SOUTH AMERICA	NORTH AND CENTRAL AMERICA
1650		● 1652 *Capetown is founded at Cape of Good Hope* ● 1660 *Several small kingdoms are established on the upper Niger* ➤			● 1650 *Spanish introduction of horses to the Plains alters native Americans' lives*
1700				● 1693 *Gold rush begins in Brazil*	
1750			● 1727 *Robert Walpole becomes Britain's first prime minister* ● 1769 *James Watt perfects the steam engine* ➤		
1800	● 1770 *Captain James Cook discovers Australia* ▲		● 1789 *Revolution breaks out in France*		● 1789 *Alexander Mackenzie reaches Arctic Ocean*

This transformation, which changed Britain from a rural, agricultural society to an urban, industrial one, was marked by many inventions and developments. In 1769, for example, James Watt, a Scots mathematician and instrument maker, perfected the steam engine, giving industrialists the option to locate their factories away from rivers.

Britain continued to expand its influence overseas. In 1770 Captain James Cook claimed Australia for Britain. A few years earlier, the British East India Company had gained great influence in India's affairs. And in 1789 Alexander Mackenzie, a Scots explorer, reached the Arctic Ocean after a journey of 2,990 miles in 120 days.

The Industrial Revolution, combined with increasing knowledge of the world, laid the groundwork for changes that would occur in the newly independent 13 American colonies. The young United States would soon be swept up in these events.

	PACIFIC AND NORTHWEST	SOUTHWEST	MIDWEST	SOUTHEAST	ATLANTIC NORTHEAST
1650					
			1673 Jacques Marquette and Louis Joliet explore the		
1700	1697 Jesuit missionaries enter California	1689 Spaniards establish missions in Texas ▼	Upper Mississippi River for France ▲	1718 French found city of New Orleans	
1750					1754 ▲ French and Indian War begins
	1778 James Cook discovers Hawaiian Islands		1787 Northwest Ordinance provides a plan for governing the Northwest Territory		1776 ▼ Declaration of Independence signed
1800					

AMERICAN LITERARY HERITAGE

The call to arms during the Revolution was heard not only on fields of battle but off, echoed by the leading writers of the day. Some of the most inspiring words that rang out against British tyranny were those of Thomas Paine, a sometime teacher, sailor, and grocer, who turned journalist in his late thirties. A chance meeting with Benjamin Franklin in London provided Paine the motivation he needed to immigrate to the colonies.

The first essay from his collection, The American Crisis, *issued in December 1776, was read by Washington at Valley Forge to buoy the spirits of his beleaguered troops. As you read this passage, notice the language Paine uses to rally support for the American cause.*

Thomas Paine

from *The American Crisis, Number 1*

These are the times that try men's souls. The summer soldier and the sunshine patriot will in this crisis, shrink from the service of his country; but he that stands it NOW deserves the love and thanks of man and woman. Tyranny, like hell, is not easily conquered; yet we have this consolation with us, that the harder the conflict, the more glorious the triumph. What we obtain too cheap, we esteem too lightly; 'tis dearness only that gives everything its value. Heaven knows how to put a proper price upon its goods; and it would be strange indeed, if so celestial an article as FREEDOM should not be highly rated. Britain, with an army to enforce her tyranny, has declared that she has a right (*not only to* TAX) but "to BIND *us in* ALL CASES WHATSOEVER," and if being *bound in that manner,* is not slavery, then is there not such a thing as slavery upon earth. Even the expression is impious, for so unlimited a power can belong only to God....

I have as little superstition in me as any man living, but my secret opinion has ever been, and still is, that God Almighty will not give up a people to military destruction, or leave them unsupportedly to perish, who have so earnestly and so repeatedly sought to avoid the calamities of war, by every decent method which wisdom could invent. Neither have I so much of the infidel in me, as to suppose that he has relinquished the government of the world, and given us up to the care of devils; and as I do not, I cannot see on what grounds the king of Britain can look up to heaven for help against us: a common murderer, a highwayman, or a housebreaker, has as good a pretense as he....

I once felt all that kind of anger which a man ought to feel against the mean [small-minded] principles that are held by the Tories. A noted one, who kept a tavern at Amboy, was standing at his door, with as pretty a child in his hand, about eight or nine years old, as I ever saw, and after speaking his mind as freely as he thought was prudent, finished with this unfatherly expression, "Well, give me peace in my day." Not a man lives on the continent but fully believes that a separation must some time or other finally take place; and a generous parent should have said, "If there must be

sometimes cease to shine, the coal can never expire....

...Let it be told to the future world that in the depth of winter, when nothing but hope and virtue could survive, that the city and the country, alarmed at one common danger, came forth to meet and to repulse it. Say not that thousands are gone, turn out your tens of thousands; throw not the burden of the day upon Providence, but *"show your faith by*

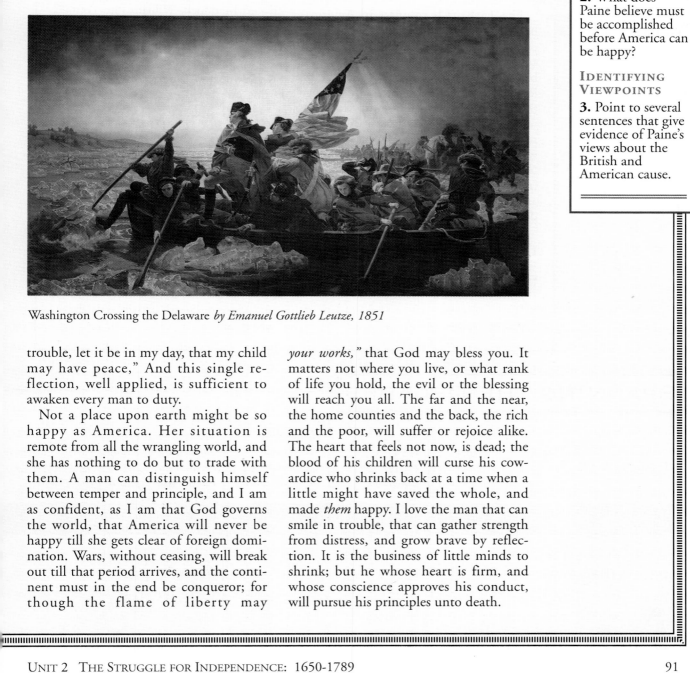

Washington Crossing the Delaware *by Emanuel Gottlieb Leutze, 1851*

INTERPRETING LITERATURE

1. What does Paine mean by the phrase "the summer soldier and the sunshine patriot"?

2. What does Paine believe must be accomplished before America can be happy?

IDENTIFYING VIEWPOINTS

3. Point to several sentences that give evidence of Paine's views about the British and American cause.

trouble, let it be in my day, that my child may have peace," And this single reflection, well applied, is sufficient to awaken every man to duty.

Not a place upon earth might be so happy as America. Her situation is remote from all the wrangling world, and she has nothing to do but to trade with them. A man can distinguish himself between temper and principle, and I am as confident, as I am that God governs the world, that America will never be happy till she gets clear of foreign domination. Wars, without ceasing, will break out till that period arrives, and the continent must in the end be conqueror; for though the flame of liberty may

your works," that God may bless you. It matters not where you live, or what rank of life you hold, the evil or the blessing will reach you all. The far and the near, the home counties and the back, the rich and the poor, will suffer or rejoice alike. The heart that feels not now, is dead; the blood of his children will curse his cowardice who shrinks back at a time when a little might have saved the whole, and made *them* happy. I love the man that can smile in trouble, that can gather strength from distress, and grow brave by reflection. It is the business of little minds to shrink; but he whose heart is firm, and whose conscience approves his conduct, will pursue his principles unto death.

CHAPTER 4
The Road to Revolution

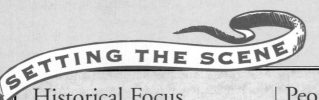

SETTING THE SCENE

Historical Focus

The 13 British colonies in America began with very little help from the parent country. Through hard work, the colonists created a prosperous economy based on agriculture and trade, and they learned to govern themselves. In settling this new land, colonists also developed a sense that they were part of the birth of a new society, different from Europe, where men and women were able to better themselves. Once their need for British protection ended with the French and Indian War, the road to independence was not far behind.

Concepts to Understand

- How Parliament sought to tighten **political control** over the colonies.
- Why colonists resorted to **political protest** against British policies.

People to Know

Edward Braddock, William Pitt, Pontiac, George Grenville, Patrick Henry, George III

Places to Locate

Ft. Duquesne, Quebec, Ohio Valley, Lexington

Terms to Identify

duty, salutary neglect, militia, land speculators, writs of assistance, direct tax, boycott, monopoly

Guided Reading

As you read this chapter, seek the answers to the following questions.
1. What were the causes and results of the French and Indian War?
2. What events led the colonists to armed resistance of British control over the colonies?

SPANNING THE DECADES

POLITICAL						
	1752 *Georgia becomes a royal colony*	**1754** *Albany Congress*	**1759** *British force French and Canadians to surrender Quebec*	**1763** *Treaty of Paris ends French and Indian War*	**1765** *Stamp Act passed*	**1767** *Townshend Acts passed*

1750   **1760**

CULTURAL				
	1750 *More than 25 weekly newspapers published among the colonies*	**1754** *Columbia University founded in New York City*	**1763** *Benjamin Franklin perfects the harmonica*	**1767** Letters from a Farmer in Pennsylvania *published by John Dickinson*

Patrick Henry Before the Virginia House of Burgesses,
Peter F. Rothermel, 1851

1773
*Boston
Tea
Party*

1770
*Boston
Massacre*

1775
*Revolutionary
War began*

1770

1780

1769
*Students at Harvard
and Yale are listed
alphabetically, not by
social position as before*

1772
*Charles Wilson
Peale completed
painting of George
Washington*

1775
*Quakers established
first antislavery
society in the
United States*

*...The Revolution was effected before the
war commenced. It was in the hearts and
minds of the people....This radical change
in the principles, opinion, sentiments and
affections of the people, was the real
American Revolution....*

—JOHN ADAMS
Letter to Hezekiah Niles, 1818

English Colonial Policy

Great Britain has confined all our trade to herself....We are obliged to take from Great Britain commodities that we could purchase cheaper elsewhere.

—JOHN ADAMS
Delegate to the First Continental Congress, 1774

Section Focus

Although the American colonies were prosperous and produced most of the food and goods they needed to survive, they were by no means self-sufficient. The colonies needed the benefit of trade with one another as well as with other countries. When Parliament passed a series of laws restricting their right to trade freely, the colonists found ways to evade the restrictions.

Objectives

After studying this section, you should be able to:
- Explain the economic motives that shaped British colonial policy.
- Discuss the development of an American character and way of life during the colonial period.

While allowing the colonies to run local affairs with little interference, Great Britain attempted to control their foreign trade. From the British point of view, the colonies existed to supply raw materials and to provide markets for British goods. Guided by these ideas, Britain tried to tighten its control over the colonial economy.

The Acts of Trade and Navigation

Beginning in 1651, Parliament passed a series of laws known as Trade and Navigation Acts. The Navigation Act of 1651 stated that all goods shipped between England and the colonies had to be carried in ships built either in England or in the colonies. Then in 1660 Parliament listed, or enumerated, specific colonial products that could be shipped only to Britain. These **enumerated commodities** included tobacco, cotton, indigo, and sugar. This was a profitable arrangement for British merchants, who could resell the goods not used in England to other countries. Another measure required American ships returning from Europe to make a "broken voyage," stopping at an English port on the way home to pay a **duty,** or tax, on the goods they had purchased on the European continent. As a result, the colonies received less for some of their exports and paid more for some of their imports than if they had been permitted to trade freely.

A number of other laws were designed to help special groups at the expense of the 13 colonies. For example, the Molasses Act of 1733 helped the owners of sugar plantations in the British West Indies by putting a heavy tax on the importation of sugar and molasses from any other place. Development of colonial industry was slowed by the Woolen Act of 1699, which forbade the colonies to export woolen goods; the Hat Act of 1732, which made it illegal for hatmakers in the colonies to sell their goods outside the colonies; and the Iron Act of 1750, which restricted the manufacture of iron goods in the colonies.

More often than not, these restrictions were the result of pressure on Parliament by British manufacturers who wanted to kill colonial competition. Benjamin Franklin's reaction was typical of the views of American manufacturers:

A colonist cannot make a button, a horse shoe, nor a hobnail but some sooty ironmonger or respectable buttonmaker of Britain shall bawl and squall that his honor's worship is ...maltreated, injured, cheated and robbed by the rascally Americans.

Enforcing the Laws

Despite these laws Britain regulated colonial trade less strictly than did other European nations. Colonists could ship fish, lumber, and grain—products for which Britain had no need—wherever they could find a market. A few navigation laws actually helped the colonists. One law required British merchants to buy tobacco only from the colonies. Another prohibited tobacco-raising in Britain itself.

Most of the navigation laws, however, restricted colonial trade. Had Britain exercised a policy of strict enforcement from the beginning, events might have turned out differently. During the early colonial years, Parliament opted for a policy of **salutary neglect,** or non-interference, which allowed the colonists to do what they wished. One reason for the policy was distance—it was simply too difficult to control a situation 3,000 miles away. Another reason was that few revenue officers bothered to go to America; instead they appointed deputies who were often lax in their duties. Soon colonists got into the easy habit of evading British laws, and smuggling became an accepted practice. Even when smugglers were brought to trial, sympathetic colonial juries seldom found them guilty.

Although British trade regulations were designed to place restrictions on the colonies, in practice they may have helped as much as they hindered. The colonists took advantage of those regulations that favored them and ignored those that hurt them. After a time it became clear that stricter enforcement of the laws by Parliament would have serious repercussions in the colonies.

The Making of Americans

The colonies had been founded with little help from the British government and had developed their prosperous agriculture and extensive trade on their own. In a fertile area many times larger than England, they were doubling their population every 25 or 30 years. They had learned to govern themselves, but above all, they had developed an American character different from that of the Europeans.

Linking Across Time

FREE TRADE

American's desire for free unlimited trade with other countries sparked revolution. This desire did not end when America separated from Great Britain. From the Confederation period to today, people have disagreed over how much protection from foreign competition American industry needs. Today taxing foreign automakers to protect the American automobile industry is an issue that Congress and the President frequently debate.

Examining Fine Art
Benjamin Franklin journeyed to London to present the colonists' views on taxation to the Lords of the Privy Council. Why was it difficult for the British government to enforce laws strictly in the colonies?

The American character became based on success through individual effort—the work ethic. In 1766 John Adams wrote:

I always consider the settlement of America as the opening of a grand scheme and design in Providence for the illumination of the ignorant and the emancipation of the slavish part of mankind all over the earth.

Still, the colonists needed British protection. Without it colonists could not defend themselves from the French in Canada. Not until France was expelled from North America did the 13 colonies start on the road to revolution.

Life of the Times

COLONIAL DANCE

Even though the colonists gradually moved toward conflict with Britain, there was still time for recreation. The long work week of most colonists was filled with physically draining labor. The few moments spent on leisure activities generally centered around quiet activities such as reading or card games. Spectator sports for men—horse racing and turkey shoots—were also popular. The major exception to sedentary pastimes for men and women was dancing.

From rural farms to urban mansions, dance in colonial America was one of the most common forms of recreation. While some clergy condemned dancing as evil, others recommended it as healthy exercise. "Dancing masters"—teachers—opened schools in communities throughout the colonies and were employed by wealthy families to demonstrate the latest steps.

Taverns were often the site of impromptu dances. Couples performed line dances such as the reel to the accompaniment of a fiddler. The reel soon gave way to a more daring dance called the cotillion, a dance imported from the courts of France. In this forerunner of modern square dancing, four couples—who under these circumstances were permitted to enjoy publicly some physical contact—formed a group and moved to the directions of a "caller."

SUMMARY

Between 1650 and 1750, Parliament passed laws regulating colonial trade. By doing so, it hoped to establish a system that served the best interest of the British Empire. The colonists were less interested in British interests than in their own economic development. For a time, the colonies and Britain were able to pursue their separate interests without serious problems. Sooner or later, those interests would have to clash.

CHECKING FOR UNDERSTANDING

1. **Identify** Trade and Navigation Acts, British West Indies, broken voyage, American character

2. **Define** enumerated commodities, duty, salutary neglect

3. **List** three ways in which British trade laws limited the colonists' freedom of action.

4. **Explain** why the colonists did not revolt right away when Parliament passed navigation laws.

5. **State** two ways in which the interests of the British and the colonists were different during this period.

THINKING CRITICALLY

6. **Making Judgments** Imagine that you operate an American rum distillery in 1733. The British have passed the Molasses Act placing a duty on foreign molasses, which you have been purchasing from the French West Indies. List three reasons why you will ignore the Act, and justify your disobedience.

CONNECTIONS: HISTORY AND GEOGRAPHY

7. **Drawing Conclusions** Weather and climate conditions affect the kinds of crops that can be grown in different areas. Why did Parliament enumerate certain colonial products to be shipped only to Britain?

Struggle for Empire

SETTING THE SCENE

The parts of North America which may be claimed by Great Britain or France are of as much worth as either kingdom. That fertile country to the west of the Appalachian Mountains.... "Garden of the World!"

—NATHANIEL AMES
Astronomical Diary and Almanack, 1758

Section Focus

In 1689 England and France began a contest for empire that went on for generations with only short intervals of peace. War was on a world-wide scale with active military operations in Europe and the Mediterranean, in the East Indies and India, in the Caribbean, and in North America. The long rivalry for the control of North America was a drama played against the backdrop of a vast wilderness. This conflict had a direct impact on the future of the 13 colonies. The outcome would determine whether the British or French would control the western territories.

Objectives

After studying this section, you should be able to:
• Explain the causes and describe the stages of the French and Indian War.
• Summarize the results of the war.

The Anglo-French contest for North America had two phases. The wars fought between 1689 and 1713 were known in the 13 colonies as King William's War (1689-1697) and Queen Anne's War (1702-1713). In Europe they were called the War of the League of Augsburg and the War of the Spanish Succession. At the close of this first phase, Great Britain gained Nova Scotia, Newfoundland, and Hudson's Bay Territory. The second phase, from 1742 to 1763, included the wars known in the colonies as King George's War (1742–1748) and the French and Indian War (1754–1763); in Europe they were called the War of the Austrian Succession and the Seven Years' War. This struggle ended in victory for Great Britain—with the French losing all their holdings on the North American mainland.

Strengths of Britain and France

It is not as difficult to see why Great Britain won the war in America as it is to understand why France was able to hold out for so long. The French were outnumbered by British colonists by at least 20 to 1, and the British navy generally had control of the sea. Still, the question of how much assistance the 13 colonies would contribute to the British war effort remained. Distrusting the motives of one another, the colonies had argued bitterly over boundary claims and rarely aided one another in Indian wars. Could they now set aside their differences?

The Albany Plan

In 1754 on the eve of the Seven Years' War, delegates from seven northern colonies met with representatives of the Iroquois nations in Albany, New York. The stated purpose of the meeting was to persuade the powerful Iroquois to ally with the British against the French. But many delegates harbored another purpose—to create a union of the colonies. Benjamin Franklin presented to the conference the Albany Plan of Union, in which he proposed that the colonies form a Grand Council with the power to levy taxes, raise troops, and regulate trade with the Indians. The actions of this Grand Council would be subject to veto by the British crown.

JOIN, or DIE.

Although Franklin's plan was adopted by the delegates, it was rejected by both the colonial and British governments who feared loss of power. The lack of cooperation seriously handicapped the war effort. Americans seldom consented to fight outside their own colonies and colonies ignored taxes imposed by Britain for their own defense. Nor would they tax themselves.

The French and Indian War

The final round of the struggle between England and France for control of North America began in the Ohio Valley. Determined to possess this rich area, the French drove out English fur traders, and in 1754 built Fort Duquesne (doo KAYN) at the point where the Monongahela (muh NAHN guh HEE luh) and Allegheny rivers meet to form the Ohio River. The fort, located in territory claimed by both Virginia and Pennsylvania, was a threat to the safety of these colonies and a barrier to expansion.

Facing this threat the colonists sent a force of Virginia **militia**—a group of civilians trained as soldiers to fight in emergencies—to attack the fort. Under the command of an inexperienced 22-year-old major from Virginia named George Washington, the militia advanced on the fort, and in 1754 ambushed a French scouting party. The French retaliated by capturing Washington's entire force at Fort Necessity, but later released them. War had begun even though there had been no formal declaration.

In the summer of 1755, British General Edward Braddock led 1,450 British and colonial soldiers, including Washington and Daniel Boone, in another attack on

Fort Duquesne. Once more, the British forces were driven back. More than 900 of Braddock's soldiers were killed or wounded, and Braddock himself was killed.

Braddock's defeat caused many native Americans to switch their support from the British to the French. The French were winning the war, and French fur traders, who mixed peacefully with the native Americans, seemed less a threat to their way of life than did the land-hungry English settlers. Along the Ohio Valley, native American allies of the French attacked outlying settlements.

Disasters continued after Great Britain and France formally declared war in 1756. French Canada had a brilliant military commander to lead their campaigns; British generals were no match for Louis Montcalm. British expeditions that tried to control the St. Lawrence River by

Examining Maps *In 1754 Great Britain, France, Spain, and Russia all claimed land in North America. Which two countries controlled the most land on the continent?*

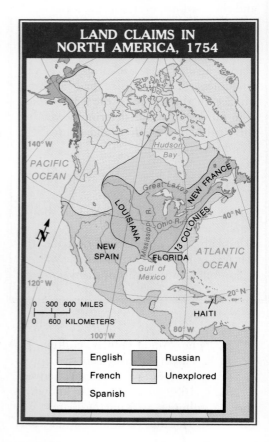

LAND CLAIMS IN NORTH AMERICA, 1754

English
French
Spanish
Russian
Unexplored

taking Montreal and the French fort of Louisburg met with utter failure.

The complexion of the war changed, however, when William Pitt became Britain's minister of war in 1758. Supremely self-confident, Pitt declared, "I know that I can save this country and that no one else can." By giving aid to France's enemies in Europe, Pitt forced France to split its forces. Pitt also sent talented, young officers to lead the campaigns in North America. Through his maneuvers Pitt quickly reversed the course of events. By the end of 1758, Louisburg and Fort Duquesne were in British hands; and in June 1759, a British army of 9,000 was encamped on the St. Lawrence River a few miles below the great French fortress of Quebec.

For more than two months, British commander James Wolfe had tried in vain to find a weak spot in the French defenses at Quebec. Time was running short, for the winter would soon set in. Finally, Wolfe outlined a daring plan to his skeptical staff. He proposed to have his troops land at night and scale a wooded cliff located under the guns of the fortress. Wolfe had hit upon the idea when he observed Canadian women washing clothes in the river and hanging them to dry on the cliffs above. He realized that there had to be a pathway up the sheer cliffs to the fortress! Gambling on the element of surprise, Wolfe suspected that the French would not have a strong guard at a point considered safe from attack.

Led by Scottish Highlanders, Wolfe's soldiers climbed the cliffs and overpowered the few guards. Before daybreak 4,500 soldiers were drawn up for battle on the open fields at the top of the cliffs known as the Plains of Abraham. Commander Montcalm quickly gathered his forces to meet them. In the battle that followed, the volleys of British infantry mowed down the

Examining Illustrations
General James Wolfe led British forces in a daring attack on Quebec. What was the significance of the fall of Quebec?

Examining Maps *The French and Indian War lasted nine years and was fought over a vast area. What route did British General Wolfe take to reach Quebec?*

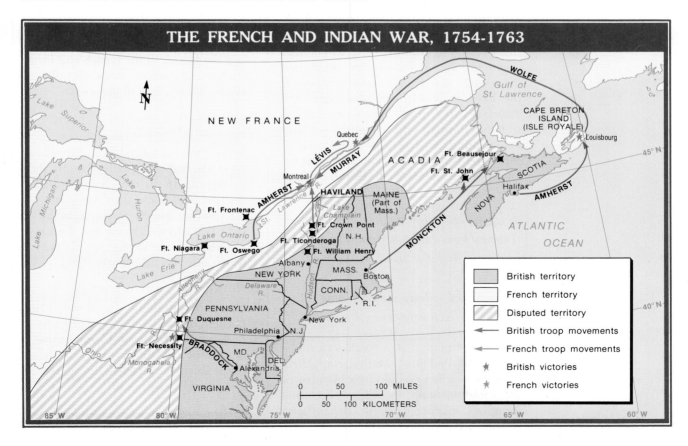

French and Canadians, who were driven back into town and forced to surrender. The fall of Quebec meant the end of the French Empire in North America.

Treaty of Paris, 1763

Great Britain won its war with France—in America, Europe, and Asia. Under the terms of the Treaty of Paris of 1763, Britain secured control of the largest amount of territory ever gained by one nation in a single treaty. From France, Great Britain obtained all of Canada they did not already control and all the land east of the Mississippi River. From Spain, France's ally, Great Britain gained Florida. To repay Spain for its losses and to protect France from losing it to Great Britain, France transferred the Louisiana Territory to Spain. North America was now divided between Great Britain and Spain with the Mississippi River forming the boundary.

For the French, defeat was bitter. France was left with no land on the continent of North America. After 150 years of colonization, the enterprise and heroism of French pioneers, missionaries, and soldiers were halted. There was only one small crumb of comfort—the 13 colonies might revolt. A French leader likened them to a "ripe fruit," ready to drop off the branch. Within two years after the Treaty of Paris, French agents would travel secretly through the English colonies investigating the chances of a revolution.

In 1763 Benjamin Franklin celebrated the loyalty of the colonies to the British crown:

Know ye, bad neighbors, who aim to divide
The sons from the mother, that she's still our
pride, And if ye attack her, we're all
on her side,
Which nobody can deny, deny,
Which nobody can deny.

By 1776 Franklin would completely reverse himself; he would be a member of the Continental Congress declaring America's independence of Britain and fighting a war to make it good.

SUMMARY

From 1689 to 1763, France and Britain fought a series of wars in Europe and other parts of the world. In 1763 focus shifted to the colonies with the outbreak of the French and Indian War. Victory on the Plains of Abraham gave Great Britain control of Canada and all of North America east of the Mississippi River.

CHECKING FOR UNDERSTANDING

1. **Identify** Albany Plan of Union, George Washington, Benjamin Franklin, William Pitt, James Wolfe, Treaty of Paris

2. **Define** militia

3. **Describe** the role played by the native Americans in the French and Indian War and why they preferred French to English settlers.

4. **Explain** why the French, the British, the native Americans, and the colonists all wanted to control the Ohio Valley.

5. **List** important officers for the French and the British in the French and Indian War and describe how each influenced the outcome of the war.

THINKING CRITICALLY

6. **Recognizing Stereotypes** In a war, the two sides are usually categorized as good and bad or the right side and the wrong side. In the French and Indian war, the British and their American colonists are usually portrayed as the right side and the French and the native Americans as the wrong side. Discuss which side you believe was right.

LINKING PAST AND PRESENT

7. **Comparing Actions** In 1990 Saddam Hussein of Iraq annexed the oil-rich Arab nation of Kuwait. Compare the motives of Saddam Hussein with those of the British and French during the French and Indian War.

★★★★★★★★★★★★★★★★★★★

Control and Protest

SETTING THE SCENE

I rejoice that America has resisted ...the gentleman asks, when were the colonies emancipated? But I desire to know, when were they made slaves?...I beg leave to tell the House what is really my opinion. It is, that the Stamp Act be repealed absolutely, totally, and immediately.

—WILLIAM PITT
In an address to Parliament, 1766

Section Focus

Although the colonists failed to realize it at the time, the French and Indian War changed their relationship with Britain forever. Freed from the danger of French attack, the Americans no longer needed British regiments and warships. The British Parliament, on the other hand, was convinced that it had to exercise stricter control over the colonies. With the passage of each new law, the colonists became more outraged and resentful.

Objectives

After studying this section, you should be able to:
• List and explain British attempts to tighten control over the colonies after the French and Indian War.
• Identify the ways in which the colonies resisted British control.

With the end of the French and Indian War, Britain turned its attention to America. Victory had brought Britain vast new territories—and a host of new problems. The British government first had to cope with the huge debt left by the war. Then it needed to decide what to do with the recently acquired western territory beyond the Appalachian and Allegheny mountains.

The Proclamation of 1763

In 1763 Pontiac's Rebellion broke out in the West. Pontiac, chief of the Ottawas, had foreseen that Britain's defeat of France meant a hard fate for his people. The French had traded with the native Americans, protected them, and intermarried with them. By contrast, the ever-advancing settlers of the British colonies threatened to wipe them out. Pontiac welded several native American peoples into a fighting force and formed a confederacy of native Americans in the Ohio Valley. Pontiac's forces captured a chain of British forts northwest of the Ohio River, but failed to drive the settlers back across the Appalachian Mountains.

During Pontiac's Rebellion, the British government issued the Proclamation of 1763, which ended all settlement west of a line running along the crest of the Appalachian Mountains. The government also maintained thousands of troops along the frontier—as much to protect the Indians from the settlers as the settlers from the Indians.

Although Americans at first accepted the Proclamation of 1763, they soon resented it. Colonists protested that the Proclamation deprived them of land they had a right to settle and interfered with charter rights of colonies whose grants extended "from sea to sea." Perhaps the biggest outcry came from **land speculators**—people who purchased land to resell it for profit. They claimed American interests were being sacrificed to fill the pockets of British fur traders who wished to leave the native Americans undisturbed.

Stricter Enforcement

The selection of George Grenville as Britain's minister of finance in 1763 signaled a change in policy. Grenville was an

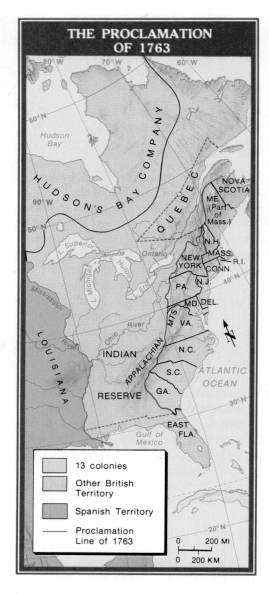

THE PROCLAMATION OF 1763

13 colonies

Other British Territory

Spanish Territory

Proclamation Line of 1763

0   200 MI

0   200 KM

swearing out a particular warrant for every building they entered. Grenville also mandated that colonists accused of smuggling be tried in admiralty courts, where the accused was denied the right of trial by jury and the judges pocketed a percentage of the fines they imposed.

New Taxes

Between 1764 and 1767, Parliament levied new taxes that shifted part of the burden of the war debt to the colonies. With the acquisition of Canada and other territories after the war, the size of the British Empire had more than doubled, and the problems of governing it grew more complicated and expensive. The war left the British government with a national debt more than twice what it was in 1754, and the people of Britain objected strongly to paying any more in taxes. They felt it was only fair that the colonists pay a part of the cost of defending and administering the empire. Grenville also persuaded Parliament to levy new duties on colonial imports, the most important of these being the Sugar Act of 1764. Although this law cut in half the rates of the Molasses Act of 1733, the British government had always winked at evasions of the Molasses Act. The troubling thing about the Sugar Act was that the British intended to enforce it. Colonial merchants realized that strict enforcement would wipe out the profits of the trade with the Spanish and French West Indies that brought much-needed **specie**—gold and silver coins—into the colonies. In that same year, Parliament forbade colonial governments to issue paper money. Caught in a two-way squeeze of lower profits and scarcity of hard currency, many merchants faced bankruptcy.

The Stamp Act

In 1765 Parliament, on Grenville's advice, passed another revenue law called the Stamp Act. This law differed from previous tax measures because it was a **direct tax**—a tax paid directly to the government rather than being included in the

energetic administrator who believed that laws should be strictly enforced. He was said to be the first minister in a generation who read dispatches from American revenue collectors and was aware of the extent of smuggling in the colonies. In addition, Grenville noted that the revenue service in the 13 colonies was costing the British government 4 times as much as it collected.

Grenville required customs officers to go to their posts in America rather than stay in England and hire deputies as before. These officers were armed with **writs of assistance**—general search warrants allowing them to seek smuggled goods without

Connections

HISTORY AND GEOGRAPHY

NATIVE AMERICAN AND EUROPEAN LAND VALUES

Native Americans were quick to understand European desire for their own territory, but colonists seemed unable—or unwilling—to understand how deeply the

Native American village

Indians valued the land. Ottawa chief Pontiac, speaking to Englishman Alexander Henry, explained: "These lakes, these woods, and mountains were left us by our ancestors. They are our inheritances, and we will part with them to no one....you ought to know that He, the Great Spirit and Master of Life, has provided food for us in these spacious lakes and on the woody mountains...."

Englishman George Thomas, when negotiating the price paid to the Iroquois for lands in New York, stated a very different view: "It is very true, that the lands are of later become more valuable, but what raises their value? Is it not entirely owing to the industry and labor used by the white people, in their cultivation and improvement? Had not they come amongst you, these lands would have been of no use to you...and the value of land is no more than it is worth in money."

★ ★ ★ ★ ★ ★ ★ ★ ★ ★

MAKING THE GEOGRAPHY CONNECTION

1. What was the value of the land to the Indians?

2. How did the colonists' idea of land value differ from the Indians' view?

LINKING PAST AND PRESENT

3. How does Thomas's view compare with the current practice of valuing land?

★ ★ ★ ★ ★ ★ ★ ★ ★ ★

price of goods. It required that stamps be placed on many kinds of articles and documents, including wills, playing cards, newspapers, dice, almanacs, and licenses. Duties ranged from 1 cent on newspapers to $10 for college diplomas, and payment had to be made in specie.

While Grenville's previous tax laws had affected those engaged in foreign trade, namely New England merchants and shippers, the Stamp Act affected colonists everywhere. It especially offended the most powerful and articulate groups in the colonies: lawyers, newspaper editors, and ministers. Because of the Stamp Act, colonists were drawn to the realization that their interests were not necessarily the same as British interests. On the day the Stamp Act was to go into effect, men and women wore mourning clothes and church bells tolled all the way from Portsmouth, New Hampshire, to Savannah, Georgia.

Colonists backed their protests with a **boycott**—a refusal to buy British goods. Men and women made solemn promises to wear homespun clothing instead of British woolens. Colonial merchants signed **nonimportation agreements**, promising not to buy British goods until Parliament repealed the unpopular law. Soon imports from Britain dropped, and British merchants, saying that they were faced with "utter ruin," besieged Parliament with petitions against the Stamp Act. Under such pressure, Parliament backed down and repealed the law in 1766.

The next year Parliament tried to raise revenue through the Townshend Acts, which placed import duties on tea, paper, glass, and paint. The British could not effectively collect these taxes either, and all the Townshend duties were repealed in 1770, except the tax on tea, which was retained to assert the principle of Parliament's authority.

Threats to Colonial Self-Government

Grenville's new customs collectors and admiralty judges were followed by 10,000 British soldiers. These troops were sent, it was said, to protect the Americans. But to protect them from whom? The French had been defeated, and the native Americans were at peace. Colonists noted that the British soldiers, called **redcoats** because of the color of their uniforms, were not stationed in frontier posts, but in towns such as Boston and New York where there was no more danger from native Americans than in London. But the presence of the redcoats served other purposes—to strengthen the hand of colonial governors and to frighten colonial legislatures into line.

It was also clear that the British wanted to free royal officials from colonial control. For this reason, the British government shifted customs cases to the admiralty courts and ruled that royal judges and governors were to be paid out of customs revenues that British revenue officers collected. Now colonial legislatures could no longer check the power of royal governors by holding up their salaries.

Disobedience of British Laws

The efforts of the British government to tighten control met such determined resistance that it surprised even the Americans themselves. The resistance took a variety of forms, including disobedience of British laws, protests, increased cooperation among the 13 colonies, boycotts, and violence.

The Americans, long accustomed to evading British revenue laws, did not hesitate to disobey new ones. In spite of a stronger British customs service, smuggling went on much as usual. The long coast of America prevented revenue officers from inspecting all incoming ships, especially when the local inhabitants were constantly trying to thwart them.

In 1765 Parliament passed the Quartering Act directing the colonies to provide barracks and supplies for the British troops ordered to America. The New York and Massachusetts legislatures regarded the act as concealed taxation and flatly refused to provide funds. Most of the other colonies found other ways to disobey the law.

After 1765 many colonists crossed the Appalachian Mountains and began to establish settlements in the western lands. Led by Daniel Boone and others, settlers spilled into western New York, Kentucky, and Tennessee, staking their land claims on native American land. Although this westward movement met the colonists' need for expansion, it violated the Proclamation Act of 1763. Governor Dunmore of Virginia advised Parliament that it was very nearly impossible to control the settlers' movement:

I have learnt from experience that the established authority of any government in America, and the policy of government at home, are both insufficient to restrain the Americans....they do not conceive that Government has any right to forbid their taking possession of a Vast Tract of Country, either uninhabited, or which serves as a shelter to a few scattered tribes of Indians.

The Question of Representation

One of the first public colonial protests took place in Virginia in May 1765 when the House of Burgesses met to consider the Stamp Act. Patrick Henry introduced the Virginia Resolutions protesting Parliament's action. Henry claimed that, since Americans elected no members to the British Parliament, they could not be taxed by that body. The House of Burgesses had "the only exclusive right and power to lay taxes" upon Virginians. This bold stand by the largest of the colonies encouraged the other colonies to follow suit, and the principle of "no taxation without representation" was accepted as a basic right.

To most people in Britain the argument against "taxation without representation" was faulty. The colonies were represented under the principle of "virtual" representation. It did not matter that Americans did not elect members to the House of Commons, the only branch of the government that could tax. Many other citizens were not directly represented either. It did not matter where these citizens lived or even if they had the right to vote because the House of Commons was pledged to represent every person in Britain and the empire. Americans had little regard for the idea of virtual representation, largely because, since the time of the earliest settlements, the people had always had direct representation—electing colonial assembly members to represent their interests.

Resistance to the Stamp Act brought about the first real cooperation among the 13 colonies. A committee of the Massachusetts legislature sent letters to leaders of the other colonial legislatures urging them to send delegates to a convention to decide on a common policy toward the British government. As a result, the Stamp Act Congress met in New York in October 1765. Nine colonial legislatures were represented, and the colonies that did not participate sent messages of support.

The delegates drew up resolutions and organized a boycott of British-made goods. In 1768 the Massachusetts legislature issued a Circular Letter calling on all the other colonial legislatures to join in protest against the measure.

John Dickinson helped promote colonial unity in his *Letters from a Farmer in Pennsylvania,* published in the *Pennsylvania Gazette* in 1767 and 1768. Dickinson argued that the people of the 13 colonies, "separated from the rest of the world, and firmly bound together by the same rights, interests, and dangers," formed "one political body of which each colony is a member."

Along with this new spirit of cooperation came a rising spirit of patriotism. In a speech to the Stamp Act Congress, Christopher Gadsden of South Carolina declared, "There ought to be no New England Man, no New Yorker, known on the continent, but all of us Americans."

Section Three Review

SUMMARY

After 1763 Parliament passed a series of revenue acts to strengthen control over the colonies and make the colonists assume part of the debt incurred by long years of war. Accustomed to levying their own taxes, colonists refused to obey the laws. Great Britain had failed to recognize that their colonies had grown apart. Americans were no longer members of the English family, but a new people with a separate destiny.

CHECKING FOR UNDERSTANDING

1. **Identify** Pontiac, Proclamation of 1763, Stamp Act, Townshend Acts, Stamp Act Congress

2. **Define** land speculators, writs of assistance, specie, direct tax, boycott, redcoats

3. **Explain** why Great Britain ended salutary neglect of the colonies after 1763.

4. **Compare** British reasons for issuing the Proclamation of 1763 with colonists' interpretations of the action.

5. **State** why colonists opposed direct taxes.

THINKING CRITICALLY

6. **Understanding Cause and Effect** Compose a series of American newspaper headlines that describe British actions (causes) and American reactions (effects) between 1763 and 1770.

LINKING PAST AND PRESENT

7. **Making Comparisons** In 1989 Chinese students in Beijing staged a huge peaceful demonstration to gain greater freedom of thought and action. The government ordered the students to return to their homes. When they refused, government troops fired on them. Compare the actions of American colonists against Britain in 1763 with those of the Chinese students against their government in 1989.

Interpreting Primary Sources

The Stamp Act Crisis

An Effigy of a New Hampshire Stamp Master

During the decade between the passage of the Stamp Act in 1765 and the outbreak of the Revolution, colonial resistance to Parliament took several forms. Colonial legislatures sent numerous resolutions and petitions to the Crown criticizing their perceived loss of rights and "taxation without representation." But early colonial successes—notably the repeal of the Stamp Act—came from boycotting English goods and other acts of defiance by ordinary citizens.

Open protest by commoners against unjust rulers and laws had long been an accepted part of English political life. In the colonies, efforts to bring about political change through protest was significantly aided by weak British control. Although colonial officials had the authority to suppress "disturbances of the peace," they frequently did not have the means to do so. In rural areas, police power consisted only of a county sheriff and, sometimes, a deputy. In towns, the sheriff might have had a night watch, but this was seldom effective. In New York, for example, the night watch was described as a "parcel of idle, drinking vigilant snorers, who never quelled any nocturnal tumult in their lives."

The hated Stamp Act placed a tax on every type of legal document, newspapers, almanacs—even playing cards and dice. Colonists, taking advantage of a weak law enforcement system, reacted swiftly. The 1829 woodcut engraving shown above depicts the unrest that convinced stamp agents throughout the colonies to resign their posts. Images such as this, a type of early political cartoon, also served to justify the violent action that was sometimes taken. At the center, the crowd is stoning an effigy, or likeness, of the New Hampshire stamp agent. On the left, leading the crowd through the streets of Portsmouth, New Hampshire, protesters are carrying a coffin.

EXAMINING THE PRIMARY SOURCE

1. Describe the mood of the crowd. What details in the picture help you determine this?

2. What time of day is depicted in the engraving? How can you tell?

3. Identify two types of buildings shown in the engraving.

4. What do you think the coffin symbolizes?

THINKING CRITICALLY

5. What circumstances today, if any, might justify using fear and intimidation tactics to protest unjust laws? Explain your answer.

6. Under what circumstances in recent times have you seen political effigies?

The Breach Widens

SETTING THE SCENE

In our own native land, in defense of the freedom that is our birthright....for the protection of our property...we have taken up arms.

—DECLARATION OF THE CAUSES AND NECESSITY OF TAKING UP ARMS, 1775

Section Focus

The period between 1770 and 1773 marked a slowdown in the struggle between the colonies and Great Britain. This respite ended when Parliament granted a monopoly on the sale of tea in the colonies to the East India Company. After that every British action triggered an American response—the Boston Tea Party, the Intolerable Acts, and the First Continental Congress. Even as late as the winter of 1775, colonists hoped for a reconciliation with Britain but events were leading to separation.

Objectives

After studying this section, you should be able to:
- List the Intolerable Acts, and describe how the colonists responded to them.
- Describe the events that led to war between Great Britain and the American colonies.

Although most colonial leaders who opposed efforts of the British Parliament to tax Americans were from the wealthy planter and merchant classes, they were supported by shopkeepers, clerks, and laborers. These colonists were the driving force behind two vital resistance groups—the Sons and Daughters of Liberty.

Boycotts and Violence

The Sons of Liberty carried out organized resistance by keeping watch on shopkeepers suspected of selling British goods. They publicly denounced or threatened those they caught. When the Sons of Liberty learned that Andrew Oliver was going to be appointed Distributor of Stamps for Boston, they hung his **effigy,** or likeness, on the Liberty Tree and stoned it. Then they looted his house and coerced him to refuse the job. When Massachusetts Lieutenant-Governor Thomas Hutchinson defended Oliver, a mob attacked Hutchinson's home and destroyed the finest collection of books and documents in the colonies. Although such actions forced British sympathizers into silence, they also frightened many supporters of the American cause. Some colonial leaders attempted to prevent the use of violence; still the colonies took no action against the Sons of Liberty.

American and British opposition to the Stamp Act forced Parliament to repeal it. In an effort to save face, Parliament passed the Declaratory Act, which affirmed its right as the supreme legislator of the British empire "to bind the colonies in all cases whatsoever."

Parliament was following the principle of this law when it passed the Townshend (TOWN zehnd) Acts in 1767, but the colonists argued that any law designed to raise revenue from them without their consent was a violation of their liberties. Again they drew up nonimportation agreements. Again the Sons of Liberty patrolled docks where English goods might be landed and shops where they might be sold.

Colonial women organized the Daughters of Liberty to boycott British goods. The Daughters of Liberty gave up imported clothes, made tea out of local herbs, and produced homespun cloth. New England ministers organized the women of their congregations in great spinning contests. On one occasion, over 100

Linking Across Time

SONS AND DAUGHTERS OF LIBERTY

Private citizens defending or opposing a cause has been a recurring feature throughout United States history. Americans, often impatient with their political leadership, have organized groups to protest or support such issues as abolition, women's suffrage, child labor, and abortion. With the exception of the Second World War, groups have opposed every war the United States has fought. However, this right to voice grievance is so basic to America it is enshrined in the Bill of Rights.

Examining Fine Art *Mercy Otis Warren of the Daughters of Liberty was a witty and skillful propagandist. In what other way did the Daughters help the resistance?*

Daughters of Liberty ran spinning wheels all day, while hundreds of spectators cheered them on. One of the most influential of the Daughters was Mercy Otis Warren who published political pamphlets supporting the resistance—although she had to use a man's name to be published.

The Boston Massacre

In the same year that Parliament repealed the Townshend duties, the first clash between Americans and British troops took place. Two regiments of redcoats had been sent to Boston to support the governor and to intimidate the Sons and Daughters of Liberty who were making Massachusetts a center of opposition to Britain. On the night of March 5, 1770, a crowd of 50 or 60 men and boys gathered to taunt British soldiers outside the Boston Customs House. When the crowd threw sticks and snowballs at the redcoats, the soldiers panicked and opened fire, killing five men. News of the event, which became known as the "Boston Massacre," spread throughout the colonies. It soon became a symbol of British force and tyranny.

An Uneasy Calm

From 1770 to 1773 a lull quieted the controversy between Great Britain and the 13 colonies. Part of this was because of prosperous times, largely a result of increasing demand for American farm products. Having won relief from some taxes, the Americans allowed the British to collect others. Imports of British goods rose—from $8 million in 1768 to $21 million in 1771.

Despite the calmer relations, basic issues had not been settled. Parliament still maintained its right to legislate for the colonies "in all cases whatsoever." The Americans, on the other hand, insisted that they were no more obliged to pay taxes levied by Parliament than the British had to pay taxes levied by the Virginia House of Burgesses.

The calm was interrupted periodically by acts of violence. In 1771 a British customs schooner that had taken a smugglers' ship into custody was attacked at night. The captive ship was released, the customs officials locked into the hold, and their schooner badly damaged. When another British revenue boat, the *Gaspée,* ran aground off Rhode Island, "persons unknown" attacked and burned it.

Meanwhile, leaders of the American resistance were busy forming a variety of organizations to translate popular discontent into action. The most effective of these were the committees of correspondence. Under such able leaders as Patrick Henry and Samuel Adams, the committees sought to inform colonists of events throughout the colonies. They were greatly assisted by the efficient postal service that Benjamin Franklin had organized. Keeping in contact with each other, these committees helped keep the resistance movement going.

The Boston Tea Party

The period of calm between the colonies and Britain came to an end with the Boston Tea Party. This dramatic event started a chain reaction that led to war and broke the ties between Great Britain and the colonies.

By 1773 the British East India Company was experiencing severe financial problems because of famine in the Indian province of Bengal, the shrinking of the American tea market, and mismanagement. Facing bankruptcy, the company appealed to Parliament for assistance. Parliament quickly voted to relieve it of most of its import and export duties to grant it a **monopoly**, or sole control of the trade, for tea in the American market. Despite the 3-cents-per-pound Townshend duty the East India Company had to pay, the company would still be able to sell its tea at a lower price in the colonies than tea brought in from France and Holland, the colonies' main sources of tea.

Announcement of the plan produced an outcry in America. Colonists argued that if Parliament could give the East India Company a monopoly of trade in tea, it could arrange monopolies for other products as well. Above all, colonists objected to the tea monopoly because they suspected its real purpose was to bribe them into acknowledging Parliament's right to tax the colonies. "The baneful [harmful] chests [of tea] contain a slow poison," wrote Benjamin Rush of Philadelphia, "something worse than death—the seeds of SLAVERY."

Opposition groups mobilized to prevent the sale of the East India tea. Ships arriving in the Atlantic ports were unable to sell a pound of tea. At Charleston the tea was kept in a warehouse until after the Revolutionary War broke out. At New York and Philadelphia the tea ships were forced to turn back. In Boston, however, Governor Hutchinson ordered that no ship could leave the harbor without unloading its tea. Colonists led by Sam Adams were just as determined that no tea would come ashore. For days crowds milled in the street and attended rallies where the sole topic of conversation was what action to take. Then on December 16, about 8,000 people attended a public meeting in and near the Old South Church. There the colonists learned that Hutchinson had no intention of backing down. On a signal from Sam Adams, a group of colonists, disguised as Mohawks, rushed to the wharf. In full sight of a cheering crowd, they boarded the tea ships and heaved 342 chests of tea valued at $75,000 into the harbor.

The Intolerable Acts

Benjamin Franklin called the Boston Tea Party "an act of violent injustice," and some Boston merchants were willing to start a collection to pay for the damage. To the British government, however, it was an act of lawlessness that deserved swift and severe punishment. In March 1774, Parliament passed a series of laws known as the Coercive Acts. One of the acts closed the port of Boston until

AMERICAN PORTRAITS

CRISPUS ATTUCKS
1723(?)-1770

Little is known about the life of Crispus Attucks before the evening of March 5, 1770. Attucks may well have been a runaway slave in Boston, where he probably worked on the docks. But for one brief moment that night, Attucks stood at the forefront of American resistance to British rule.

After Attucks finished his dinner in an inn, he joined a nearby crowd that had formed on King Street. Young boys were taunting British soldiers, hurling snowballs and sticks. Tensions grew between the soldiers and the unruly mob. A soldier's musket suddenly fired, and Attucks fell to the ground and died instantly. Four others were also killed, and several were wounded in what has become known as the Boston Massacre. Attucks became a martyr to the patriot cause—a black man who gave his life in the name of liberty.

Examining Fine Art

The unwillingness of George III to compromise made it increasingly difficult to solve the growing problems between the colonists and Great Britain. What was the purpose of the declaration the First Continental Congress sent to George III?

payment was made for the tea. Another act stipulated that British officials accused of a crime were to be tried in English rather than American courts. Still another provided that British troops could be quartered in any town in Massachusetts—even in private homes. Finally, the Massachusetts charter was amended to greatly reduce the colony's right of self-government. The end result was that Boston and the colony of Massachusetts were to suffer for the actions of the handful of unknown persons who had staged the protest. Colonists considered the provisions of the Coercive Acts so harsh that they were called the "Intolerable Acts" throughout the colonies.

Passed at the same time, and considered by the colonists as one of the Intolerable Acts, was the Quebec Act, which extended the Canadian province of Quebec south to the Ohio River. It also allowed French Canadians use of their own legal system, which did not provide for trial by jury, and which recognized the legality of the Roman Catholic Church within the enlarged province. In their excited state, Americans saw the Quebec Act as the first step toward doing away with jury trials and Protestantism in the 13 colonies. They also believed the boundary changes were made to keep American settlers out of western lands forever.

The Intolerable Acts revealed that the British government now intended once and for all to show the colonists who had authority. This was partly because of the attitude of King George III. During the reigns of George III's predecessors, the leaders of Parliament had taken over direction of British affairs. When George III was a little boy, his mother had urged him to "be a king!" and he was determined to follow that advice. George III did not begin the quarrel between the British government and the colonies, but he made it worse because he believed that he had to rule the colonies with a strong hand. After the Boston Tea Party, George III refused compromise. "The colonies," he said, "must submit or triumph."

The First Continental Congress

When Parliament passed the Coercive Acts, British leaders expected that the other colonies would agree that Massachusetts deserved punishment. William Pitt had warned, however, that the acts would give the colonies a new reason to unite.

Pitt proved to be right. The acts convinced many Americans that the leaders of Britain were conspiring to take away their liberties. What happened to Massachusetts could happen to other colonies. The Virginia House of Burgesses passed a resolution, which was widely circulated by committees of correspondence, calling for a congress, and every colony, except Georgia, chose delegates.

Numbering 56 in all, the delegates to the First Continental Congress met in Philadelphia in September 1774. The Congress petitioned the king for relief from the Intolerable Acts and vowed to stop trade with Britain until the acts were repealed. A Declaration of Rights and Grievances was designed to appeal to moderate people—its tone was conciliatory and it expressed devotion to George III. But it denounced every revenue-raising or power-limiting step taken by Britain since 1763 as a violation of colonial charters and the rights of colonists as British citizens.

"The Association"

The intent of the boycott proposed by the First Continental Congress was to cut off all trade with Britain. To endure such a self-inflicted blow to their economy, the

Congress urged Americans to engage in local manufactures. Appealing to the spirit of self-sacrifice, the Congress also resolved to:

...discourage every species of extravagance and dissipation, especially all horse-racing, and all kinds of gambling, cockfighting, exhibitions of shows, plays and other extensive diversions and entertainments.

Congress tried to enforce its boycott by setting up "in every county, city, and town," an organization known as "the Association." The Association exerted a surprising degree of control over Americans, telling them what they should eat, drink, and wear, as well as how they should behave in public. The Association did its work effectively; imports of British goods into New York, for example, dropped from more than $2 million in 1774 to $6,000 in 1775.

Lexington and Concord

Meanwhile, in every colony a volunteer army was organizing, and military supplies were being collected. In New England, minutemen assembled to drill on village greens, while town officials collected ammunition, uniforms, and food. In the Southern Colonies, planters undertook to recruit and equip companies of soldiers at their own expense. It appeared that the dispute between Great Britain and the colonies would be settled only by force.

Fighting between the Americans and the British broke out near Boston, which had been occupied in 1774 by a British army under General Thomas Gage. Early on April 19, 1775, a detachment of 700 British soldiers was secretly sent to destroy the military supplies colonists had collected at Concord, 21 miles from Boston. Learning of the soldiers' destination, the Boston Sons of Liberty sent Paul Revere and William Dawes to alert the minutemen in the towns and villages along the way. When the British reached the town of Lexington,

about 70 armed minutemen awaited them. The colonists were ordered to drop their weapons and disperse. Then someone fired a shot. A spontaneous skirmish ensued, and the colonists fled. Eight colonists were killed, and ten were wounded; only one British soldier was wounded. The British pushed on to Concord and burned what little gunpowder the colonists had not used for themselves.

By the time the British began their march toward Boston, the countryside was swarming with minutemen, who fired at the redcoats from behind trees, buildings, and stone walls. Only a brigade sent out from Boston saved the British from annihilation. About 250 British and 100 Americans were killed or wounded at Concord.

The Colonists Mobilize

News of Lexington and Concord, carried by riders on horseback, electrified the colonies. The Massachusetts Committee of Public Safety, which directed the resistance organizations in the colony, called for an army of 30,000 men "to defend our wives and children from the butchering hands of an inhuman soldiery." Groups of militia from all over New England marched toward Boston, one New Hampshire company covering 54 miles in 18 hours. General Gage found himself besieged.

Examining Fine Art
John Trumbull painted the Battle of Bunker Hill, which actually took place on Breed's Hill, 11 years after the battle was fought. Why was the battle significant for the colonists?

On June 17, 1775, the British discovered that Americans occupied Breed's Hill, a peninsula overlooking Boston from the north. The American army could easily have been trapped from behind, but the British commander decided to make a frontal attack uphill. The redcoats advanced in close order, each carrying a heavy pack in addition to a 15-pound musket. Because the range of a musket was scarcely more than 50 yards, the Americans were ordered to hold their fire until they could see the "whites of their enemies' eyes."

The Americans turned back two attacks, inflicting heavy losses, but were finally driven back when they ran out of ammunition. The Battle of Bunker Hill, as it came to be called, was a moral victory for the Americans because their untrained militia had stood up to professional troops. The British, whose casualties in the battle were more than 40 percent, made no further attempt to attack.

Meanwhile, in May 1775, a handful of volunteers from Vermont known as the Green Mountain Boys captured the small garrisons guarding the fortresses of Crown Point and Ticonderoga on the vital Lake George-Lake Champlain route. The forts were not only strategically placed but rich in military supplies.

On May 10, 1775, the day that Fort Ticonderoga fell, a Second Continental Congress met in Philadelphia. Originally called to plan further protests against British actions, the Congress assumed the powers of a central government and took steps to conduct the war that had, in fact, begun at Lexington. The Congress voted to ask the colonies for supplies and troops, to send agents to France to obtain financial assistance, and to encourage rebellion among French Canadians. It also voted to dignify the motley group of volunteers besieging Boston with the name "Continental Army." For commander in chief, Congress chose George Washington. It valued his experience and ability, but the fact that he was a Virginian was also important because it would keep the Southern and Middle colonies from thinking of the conflict as New England's war. Although it would be more than a year until independence was declared, the American Revolution had begun.

Section Four Review

SUMMARY

Before 1773 British actions and American reactions took a predictable course. Parliament passed acts taxing the colonies; the colonists protested, refused to obey the laws, and boycotted British goods. Goaded to a showdown on the issue of power, George III declared that the "colonists would have to submit or triumph." The stage was set for revolution.

CHECKING FOR UNDERSTANDING

1. **Identify** Declaratory Act, Boston Massacre, Boston Tea Party, Intolerable (Coercive) Acts, Lexington and Concord, Breed's Hill, Second Continental Congress

2. **Define** monopoly

3. **Describe** three violent encounters between the colonists and redcoats between 1770 and 1776.

4. **Compare** the British reason for giving the East India Company a monopoly on tea with the colonists' reasons for opposing it.

5. **Explain** the purpose and significance of the two Continental Congresses.

THINKING CRITICALLY

6. **Supporting an Opinion**   Some historians place the cause of the Revolution on the series of tax laws passed after 1763. Others believe that the underlying cause for separation was not taxation but a growing national consciousness of Americans. Point out the strengths of each theory.

CONNECTIONS:
HISTORY AND MUSIC

7. **Interpreting Songs**   Obtain the lyrics to *The Liberty Song,* the official song of the Sons of Liberty. Examine the words and explain how this song expresses the feelings of Americans about the right of Parliament to tax the colonies.

Critical Thinking Skills

Identifying Cause and Effect

It is 6:00 A.M. on Monday, when you turn on your radio and hear that schools have been closed because of a heavy snowfall. You may not realize it, but you have just heard about a cause-and-effect relationship. The snow caused the school closing—the snow is the cause; the school closing is the effect.

Explanation

Everything that happens does so because something makes it happen. What happens is called the *effect*. The person, condition, or event that makes the thing happen is called the *cause*. The connection between what happens and what makes it happen is known as a cause-and-effect relationship.

The following guidelines will aid you in identifying cases of cause-and-effect relationships in written material:

a. Often statements contain "clue words" that alert you to cause and effect. Be aware of and look for words or phrases such as *because, led to, brought about, produced, as a result of, so that, thus, since, outcome, as a consequence, resulted in, gave rise to, and therefore.*

b. At times there are no "clue words." In their place, however, may be the word *and* or a comma.

c. Cause and effect is usually expressed in more than one sentence or paragraph. In a cause-and-effect description, ask yourself if economics, religion, geography, or technology is involved in the event or condition being studied. These are major forces in history that make things happen.

CONFLICT IN BOSTON, 1773

CAUSES

- Britain granted East India Company a monopoly on tea sales in America.
- Colonists boycotted tea.
- Tea ships not allowed to unload in colonial harbors.

↓

EVENT

- Boston Tea Party

↓

EFFECTS

- Colonists threw $75,000 of tea into Boston Harbor.
- Boston merchants offer to pay for tea.
- British Parliament passes Coercive Acts.

Example

Read the following examples, and note how the guidelines have been applied to the following statements about the 1750s and 1760s:

a. As a result of the Boston Tea Party, the British Parliament passed a series of Coercive Acts.

(The "clue" is "as a result of." The cause was the Boston Tea Party. The effect was the passing of the Coercive Acts by the British Parliament.)

b. The Virginia House of Burgesses was convinced that the Coercive Acts would take away American liberties, and so it decided to form a Continental Congress.

(The "clue word" is and. *If you are not sure if a cause-and-effect relationship is indicated by the word* and, *reword the sentence using the word* because: Because the Virginia House of Burgesses was convinced that the Coercive Acts would take away American liberties, they decided to form a Continental Congress. It is now clear that the cause was the conviction in the House of Burgesses that American liberties would be taken away, and the effect was the formation of the Continental Congress.)*

c. The First Continental Congress proposed a boycott on all trade with Great Britain. "The Association" was formed to enforce this boycott throughout the colonies.

(A cause-and-effect relationship is expressed using more than one sentence. In this case, the effect—the formation of "The Association" to enforce the boycott—appears in the second sentence. The cause—the proposed boycott of all trade with Great Britain—appears in the first sentence. Note that economics was involved.)

Practice

For further practice with this skill, write out three examples of cause and effect from this chapter. Underline the part of the sentence or paragraph that states the *cause.* Underline twice the part that represents the *effect.* Circle any "clue words" that point out these relationships.

★ Chapter 4 Review ★

★ Summary

Actions of the colonists from 1770 on show that, after a long period of salutary neglect, Americans did not want Great Britain to be directly involved in colonial affairs. When Parliament passed a series of laws restricting American freedom of action, the colonists reacted, often violently, to prevent change in their accepted way of governing. The demands made on Britain by colonial legislatures and by the Continental Congress were actually pleas to return to the old relationship: repeal the Stamp Act, repeal the Townshend Acts, repeal the Intolerable Acts, restore trial by jury, remove restrictions placed on western migration. Both sides realized, however, that this was not possible. After Lexington, Americans accepted the inevitability of separation.

★ Using Vocabulary

Using the words below, write an editorial for the *Boston Gazette* that might have appeared the day after the battle at Lexington.

salutary neglect	**direct tax**
customs duties	**boycott**
writs of assistance	**redcoats**

★ Reviewing Facts

1. **Describe** the British strategy and execution of the battle fought against the French on the Plains of Abraham.
2. **State** how the series of laws passed by Parliament after 1763 differed from those passed before 1763.
3. **Explain** how the Proclamation of 1763 affected the colonists and tell why they were angry over it.
4. **Identify** the incidents that became turning points in the relationship between the colonies and Britain.
5. **List** the acts of Parliament between 1763 and 1774 that colonists considered direct taxes.
6. **List** the organizations that came into being in the colonies to protest British tax laws and describe the ways in which they defied those laws.
7. **Define** the purpose of the Coercive (Intolerable) Acts and show how they backfired in terms of expected colonial responses.

★ Understanding Concepts

POLITICAL CONTROL

1. After 1763, the British had the problem of governing and defending the new territories gained in the French and Indian War. Parliament passed laws to obtain revenue from the colonists. Make a chart showing the names of these acts and how they would raise money for Britain.
2. When the colonists refused to pay the taxes imposed by Parliament, the crown took measures to force obedience. List these measures and tell what effect they had on British-American relations.

POLITICAL PROTEST

3. Describe three forms of political protest used by the colonists.
4. Protest documents helped unite Americans against the British crown. Cite two of these documents, along with the names of their authors and a summary of their contents.

★ Thinking Critically

1. **Linking Past and Present**   British manufacturers were protected by Parliament's regulations limiting American manufacturing. What advantages are there when competition exists among businesses?
2. **Determining Motives**   The Albany Plan of Union was an early forerunner of the later Stamp Act Congress and the First and Second Continental congresses. Why were colonial governments so reluctant to form a union of colonies as envisioned by the Albany Plan?
3. **Expressing Point of View**   Imagine that you are a citizen living in Great Britain after 1763. You read in the newspaper that American colonists are disturbed by your government's actions in enforcing the collection of revenues. Write a letter to the editor, expressing your reactions.
4. **Identifying Alternatives**   Historians argue whether any war is inevitable. How could war between Britain and the American colonies have been avoided?

★ Writing About History

DEFINITION

Refer to the description of how to write a definition in

the History Writer's Handbook in the Appendix of this book. Your teacher will give you more specific instructions on the length and the assignment's due date.

Write a letter from Benjamin Franklin to Parliament following passage of the Coercive Acts. In the letter, attempt to explain the reasons for the Boston Tea Party, the colonial position on taxation, and recommendations for policy changes that would make the colonists consider remaining part of the British Empire.

★ Learning Cooperatively

Your group will write a play in three acts about the incidents leading to the American Revolution. Your play should have British and American characters. Each act should have one scene that takes place in Britain and one that follows it in America. Use these time periods in writing the acts: Act I, 1763-1767; Act II, 1767-1773; Act III, 1773-1776.

★ Mastering Skills

READING MILITARY MAPS

As you read about the battles of Lexington and Concord, you might find it confusing to keep track of where the British soldiers and American minutemen were, which direction they were marching, and how many miles they were covering.

A map can give you a visual representation that helps you "see" what you are reading. The map that follows shows the battles of Lexington and Concord. By studying it, you might be able to picture Paul Revere racing down the road on his famous midnight ride. You might also see the minutemen who lived in the countryside, getting ready to meet the British at Lexington.

Military maps, besides giving you a visual representation of an event, can provide helpful information that sometimes the text does not include. For example, a map might show what kind of terrain is involved. You could tell if the soldiers had to march over hills or through rivers. A military map could also show which ports had to be protected, how much area the soldiers covered, and what their advances and retreats were.

Military maps usually use symbols to show battle sites. From this, you might be able to determine how one event might have led to another. Color is also important on military maps. On the following map,

red shows the British troops' routes and black and blue shows the Americans' routes.

To help you read military maps, follow the guidelines explained below.

- Look at the title to determine the subject.
- Find the legend. It will include symbols to help you find routes and battle sites.
- Study the mileage chart to get an idea of how much land they covered. For example, in this map, you can see that it is about 21 miles from Boston to Concord. Remember that Paul Revere and the other riders were covering this on horseback.
- If the map is *topographical,* or shows land features, consider what the soldiers had to deal with in marching and fighting battles.

Practice   Study the map below and then answer the questions that follow.

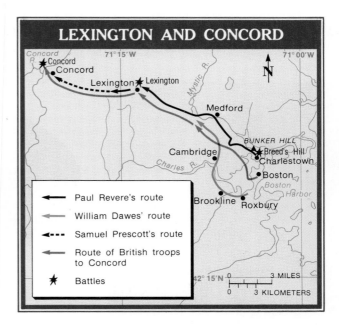

1. Who took over for Paul Revere when he was captured?
2. Why did Paul Revere and William Dawes take different routes?
3. **Drawing Inferences** Considering what you've read about trade between England and the colonies, why would it be important for the colonists to control Boston and its harbor?

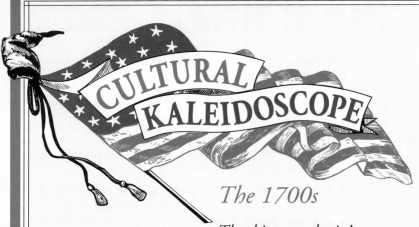

CULTURAL KALEIDOSCOPE

The 1700s

The thirteen colonies' quest for independence in the eighteenth century was apparent not only on the battlefields at Saratoga and Yorktown, but also in the gradual emergence of a uniquely American cultural identity. Frontier struggles, patriotism, and the Revolutionary War were currents running through expressions of this budding culture.

Technology

INVENTIONS

A leading politician of the age, Benjamin Franklin, was also an important inventor. One of Franklin's most lasting inspirations—the bifocal lens—proved necessity *is* the mother of invention: the "good doctor" was himself near-sighted. Franklin also devised the first lightning rod and an improved iron stove that spread heat more evenly. His famous but extremely dangerous key-and-kite experiment connected lightning and electricity.

Another inventor of note was David Bushnell, a student at Yale. His *Turtle*, a one-person, hand-powered torpedo-firing submarine, might have aided the Revolutionary war effort had its bite been as terrible as its bark. The sub's first and only mission, an assault on the British warship *Eagle* in 1776, left the crew and vessel intact but shaken. Even so, the *Turtle's* mission was the first use of submarine warfare.

◄ *Painting from the side of a fire engine of the Franklin Volunteer Company of Philadelphia, c.1835*

◄ *Chandler Wedding Tapestry, 1756*

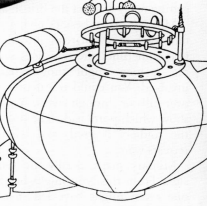

► *Sketch of Bushnell's* Turtle

Entertainment and Recreation

THEATRE

In the realm of entertainment, the eighteenth century was an era of "firsts." The year 1716 marked the opening at Williamsburg, Virginia, of the first theater in the colonies. The physical structure itself was a converted barn. Later in the century, the first American play—Thomas Godfrey's *The Prince of Parthia, a tragedy in five acts*—was produced in Williamsburg.

NEWSPAPERS

In 1704 the earliest colonial newspaper, *The Boston News-Letter,* issued its first edition. Close on its heels came the Philadelphia-based *Pennsylvania Gazette,* whose owner sold the paper within a year of its start-up. The new owner? Ben Franklin.

The first strides toward standardizing English spelling came with Noah Webster's "Blue-backed Speller," published in 1783.

FOOD

It was cold, it was creamy, and it was featured in 1744 on the menu of a dinner hosted by Maryland governor Thomas Bladen. This frozen confection—which we know today as *ice cream*—became so popular in the colonies that in 1784 George Washington himself bought "a cream machine for Ice." Vanilla only.

▲ *Title page of Webster's spelling book, 1789*

▼ *America's first newspaper, 1704*

▼ *Hornbook for learning the alphabet*

▲ *Benjamin Franklin's printing press*

Literature

MAJOR POETS

Celestial choir! enthron'd in realms of light,

Columbia's scenes of glorious toils I write.

These heroic words, addressed to "His Excellency, General Washington" were penned by a slave who also happened to be a gifted poet. Her name was Phillis Wheatley, and in 1770, at age 20, she became the first published female black author.

Philip Freneau, another outstanding poet of the age, is today regarded as America's earliest important producer of lyric, or richly musical, verse.

BROADSIDE BALLADS

The Patriots' cause during the Revolution was defended not only in deed but in word. Broadside ballads—emotionally charged story poems printed on a single sheet of paper—helped fuel colonists' passion for freedom.

FICTION

The literature of Colonial America was filled with action and controversy, primarily appearing in newspapers, pamphlets, and magazines, only infrequently in books. But booksellers in 1789 were given a new item to peddle. It was *The Power of Sympathy*, the first American novel to appear in print. Dedicated to the "young ladies of America," the story depicted the sad fate of a young woman who had been corrupted. William Hill Brown, the book's author, for obvious reasons chose to keep his identity secret. The novel, however, was a best-seller.

◀ *Portrait of Phillis Wheatley, 1773*

▼ *Title page from* The Power of Sympathy, *1789*

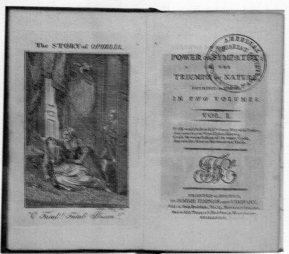

▲ The Yankees Return from Camp, *a 1765 broadside ballad*

The Arts

PAINTING

Through the mid-eighteenth century, art in America was dominated by *limners*. These were artists who painted portraits without faces, then sought out patrons whose gold would inspire them to "fill in the blanks."

Later in the century, three highly talented artists— John Singleton Copley, Benjamin West, and Gilbert Stuart—emerged on the scene as forerunners of a style of painting that was unmistakably American. Stuart, perhaps the best known of the three, is remembered for his enduring portrait of the nation's first President.

MUSIC

The appearance in 1770 of William Billings's book of hymns, *The New England Psalm-Singer,* launched his career as America's first professional composer. Another of his tunes, "Chester," became a favorite chant among Patriot foot soldiers during the Revolution.

ARCHITECTURE

The first colonial buildings were primarily functional. In time, builders began to use more refined structures that they borrowed from public buildings in Europe. The Georgian style (named after King George I) was adapted from the classical architecture of ancient Greece and Rome. It flourished in America from the 1730s until well after the Revolution.

ANALYZING CULTURE

1. In what ways might patriotism be considered as the guiding force behind much of American eighteenth-century culture?

2. Pick three milestones of early American culture. Explain how the initial achievements connected with them have changed.

◄ *Engraving by Paul Revere in frontispiece of* The New England Psalm-Singer, *1770*

▲ *Georgian-style architecture, Derby House in Salem, Massachusetts*

◄ Paul Revere *by John Singleton Copley, 1768-70*

CHAPTER 5
War for Independence

SETTING THE SCENE

Historical Focus

Even after the first skirmishes, the colonists still hoped to reconcile with the British crown. Events during the winter of 1775-1776, however, propelled them toward separation. The writings of Thomas Paine, the king's inflexible attitude, and his use of German mercenaries—all led the Second Continental Congress to issue a Declaration of Independence on July 4, 1776. Under Washington's leadership, the new United States fought its momentous war for independence over six long years.

Concepts to Understand

- Why **revolution** against Great Britain seemed the only option left for the colonies.
- How colonists believed their **civil rights and liberties** could be secured and protected.

People to Know

Thomas Jefferson, Charles Cornwallis, Marquis de Lafayette, Abigail Adams, Benedict Arnold

Places to Locate

Trenton, Saratoga, Valley Forge, Yorktown

Terms to Identify

treason, mercenaries, Patriots, Loyalists, Declaration of Independence, Treaty of Paris

Guided Reading

As you read this chapter, seek the answers to the following questions.
1. What factors caused the American Revolution?
2. Why were the Americans able to win the war?

SPANNING THE DECADES

POLITICAL	1775 *Second Continental Congress meets*	1776 *Declaration of Independence*	1777 *Battle of Saratoga*	1778 *George Rogers Clark's forces capture Kaskaskia*	1781 *Cornwallis surrenders at Yorktown*

1775   **1780**

CULTURAL	1775 *Daniel Boone and 30 men clear Kentucky's Wilderness Road*	1776 *Common Sense by Thomas Paine*	1777 *Gilbert Stuart studies painting and assists Benjamin West in London*		1781 *Franciscan Fathers found Los Angeles in California*

Molly Pitcher at the Battle of Monmouth
by Dennis Malone Carter, 1854

1782
Great Britain and United States sign provisional treaty of peace in Paris

1783
Treaty of Paris signed

1785

1783
Noah Webster publishes first spelling book

1784
American Methodist Church formed in Baltimore, Maryland

...The blood of the slain, the weeping voice of nature cries, Tis time to part. *Even the distance at which the Almighty has placed England and America is a strong and natural proof that the authority of the one over the other was never the design of heaven...*

—THOMAS PAINE
Common Sense, 1776

SECTION ONE

Foundations of Freedom

I am well aware of the toil, and blood, and treasure, that it will cost to maintain this declaration, and support and defend these States. Yet, through all the gloom, I can see the rays of ravishing light and glory. I can see that the end is more than worth all the means, and that posterity will triumph in that day's transaction....

—JOHN ADAMS
Massachusetts delegate to the Second Continental Congress in a letter to his wife, Abigail, July 3, 1776

Section Focus

Delegates to the Second Continental Congress faced a difficult decision—whether to separate from or to seek reconciliation with Great Britain. Congress would weigh carefully any official action announcing independence, since the leaders would be committing treason against the British crown.

Objectives

After studying this section, you should be able to:
• List the arguments for American independence.
• Explain the purposes and principles of the Declaration of Independence.

After the bloodshed in Massachusetts, people like Patrick Henry of Virginia appealed for separation from Great Britain. But most colonists were not ready for independence and neither was the Second Continental Congress that convened in Philadelphia in May 1775. Instead, most of the members wanted the colonies to remain part of the British empire and at the same time rule themselves through their own legislatures. Even after selecting George Washington of Virginia as the commander in chief of the new Continental Army, the Congress declared, "We have not raised armies with ambitious designs of separating from Great Britain, and establishing independent states." In a petition that tried to appease the king, the delegates blamed all their troubles on his ministers, "those artful and cruel enemies who abuse your royal confidence and authority for the purpose of effecting our destruction."

But the British government adopted an inflexible attitude. King George III refused to read the conciliatory petition from the Continental Congress and denounced the "diverse wicked and desperate persons" leading the rebels. He called on loyal subjects to charge the American leaders with **treason**, or attempting to overthrow the government, and to punish them according to British law:

...that the offender be drawn on a hurdle to the place of execution, that there he be hanged by the neck but not till he be dead, that while yet alive he be disembowelled and that then his body be divided into four quarters, the head and each quarter to be at the disposal of the crown.

The king then took direct action. In October 1775, a British naval force burned to the ground the defenseless port of Falmouth, Maine. Finally in December, George III declared the American colonies entirely outside his protection and placed all their ports under blockade by the British fleet. Unable to raise sufficient troops in Great Britain because the war was unpopular, the king hired **mercenaries,** or paid soldiers, from the rulers of small German states. They were generally

Connections

H I S T O R Y   A N D   R E L I G I O N

THE REVOLUTIONARY PULPIT

"If the Americans shall be taught to believe Resistance to be lawful...it will not be long before...[they] publicly appear in Arms," remarked an English citizen in 1774. His fears were well-founded. The Revolutionary War effort

George Whitefield preaching

drew powerful support from Congregational, Presbyterian, and other Christian churches, whose clergy had no official ties with England. Boston minister Samuel West interpreted the New Testament discussion on submitting to civil authority as applying only to those leaders who "punish the wicked and encourage the good." Those who do not, he continued, "forfeit their authority to govern the people."

In contrast, the Episcopal church in America had strong ties with the Church of England. Episcopal clergy, who were ordained in England, saw opposition to British rule as a danger to all authority. Their support of the Crown found receptive ears among the colonial aristocracy, particularly in the Southern Colonies.

MAKING THE RELIGION CONNECTION

1. How did the strength of their ties with England affect the support or opposition of American clergy to the Revolution?

LINKING PAST AND PRESENT

2. Describe a current political issue on which American clergy are divided.

---

known as "Hessians," because a large number were supplied by the Prince of Hesse. By 1776 it was becoming obvious that compromise between the colonies and Britain was impossible. Yet the American Congress held back, unwilling to declare the final separation.

Moving Toward Independence

At this critical moment, a most persuasive and widely read pamphlet was published. Entitled *Common Sense,* it was written in January 1776 by Thomas Paine, an English radical who had recently arrived in America. Paine attacked the strongest bond still keeping America tied to Britain—loyalty to the king. He assaulted monarchy in general and George III in particular, discrediting hereditary kingship as a superstition that had been

sold to the ignorant by means of lies and fables. In *Common Sense* Paine stated that a king was usually "the principal ruffian of some ruthless gang," and George III, "the royal brute of Great Britain," was typical of his breed. Paine pointed to the advantages Americans might gain if they were free of British commercial restrictions and of Britain's quarrels with its European neighbors. He appealed to the Americans' belief that they were a chosen people, pioneers of liberty:

Freedom hath been haunted around the globe, Asia and Africa have long expelled her. Europe regards her like a stranger, and England hath given her warning to depart. O receive the fugitive, and prepare in time an asylum for mankind!

Examining Illustrations *In an engraving by Francois Xavier Habermann colonists pull down the statue of King George III. On what grounds could the colonists argue that English subjects had the right to overthrow a king?*

Common Sense had a large circulation and served to divide Americans into either **Patriots,** who favored separation, or **Loyalists,** who supported the British government. The early successes of American Patriots supported Paine's arguments. In Virginia they expelled the royal governor and the soldiers defending him; in North Carolina the militia, the colony's emergency forces, repulsed an attempted landing of redcoats; in South Carolina a full-scale British attack on Charleston was brilliantly driven back.

The greatest American success occurred in New England. When Washington arrived to take charge of the Continental Army near Boston, he had almost no **artillery,** or large guns, but during the winter the rebels seized over 50 cannons from Fort Ticonderoga. Weighing two to six tons apiece, they were lashed to sledges and dragged by oxen 200 miles over snowy trails and frozen rivers to Dorchester Heights overlooking Boston. During the night of March 4, 1776, about 2,000 militiamen positioned groups of these cannons. In the morning this threat greeted General William Howe, who had replaced General Thomas Gage as commander of the British force, leaving him no choice but to abandon the city. On March 17 he sailed north for Halifax, Nova Scotia, carrying with him 1,000 Loyalists who preferred exile to rebellion.

Colonists made strong arguments for independence from their need for military supplies and for reopening foreign trade. The Americans lacked guns, gunpowder, ammunition, uniforms, tents, and medical supplies as well as the facilities to produce them in quantity. The cutoff of trade with the British Empire caused acute distress among American shippers and merchants who had to scramble to find new markets. Commercial treaties with other nations had to be arranged and such treaties could only be written by an independent nation—not by rebellious colonies.

Furthermore, the members of the Continental Congress hoped for aid from France. Since 1763 the French had desired revenge on Great Britain for the terrible defeat they suffered in the Seven Years' War. As early as November 1775, a French agent secretly conferred with members of the Congress. Within a few months the French government started to smuggle arms to the Americans. Nevertheless, France refused to enter into a formal alliance or sign a commercial treaty until the Americans declared themselves an independent nation.

Beginning with North Carolina in April 1776, the colonies advised their delegates in Congress to vote for independence. On June 7, Richard Henry Lee of Virginia introduced a brief "Resolution of Independence." The delegates debated for nearly a month while the moderates in Congress made a last stand for reconciliation. On July 2, 1776, the Continental Congress adopted Lee's resolution "that these united colonies are, and of right ought to be free and independent states." The official Declaration of Independence had been in preparation for almost a month before it was agreed upon by Congress on July 4. Its purpose was to justify the revolution, to notify the world and Great Britain that the colonies were independent, and to state the principles upon which the new nation was founded.

The Declaration of Independence

The Declaration of Independence is principally the work of Thomas Jefferson, a young Virginian who had been an inconspicuous member of Congress. A poor public speaker and shy by nature,

Jefferson was known as an able writer. When Congress appointed a committee to draw up a public statement justifying independence, he was naturally included. Two prominent and busier members of the committee, Benjamin Franklin and John Adams, asked Jefferson to write the first draft of the declaration.

Since time was so limited, Jefferson did not write an entirely original document. He drew upon several sources—a declaration of **grievances,** or complaints, he had written earlier, the new Virginia Bill of Rights, Lee's resolution, and writings of European political philosophers. Beginning in the 1600s scientists such as Isaac Newton had promoted a belief in an orderly universe governed by scientific principles. This thinking became the foundation of "Enlightenment" philosophy that spread from Europe to America. Jefferson was one of many Americans who accepted and built upon principles derived from these thinkers. In particular, he was influenced by the ideas of "natural rights" and government by social contract written by the English philosopher, John Locke. Jefferson gave the idea of natural rights its most eloquent expression in the Declaration of Independence.

When Jefferson submitted his draft to Franklin, the old scholar made a few changes before the committee finally sent the document to Congress. There, additional changes were made before its final acceptance.

The Declaration has four main parts: the **preamble,** or introduction, which states why the Continental Congress chose to explain their separation from Britain formally and publicly; a declaration of rights which describes the general theories of government upon which the American Revolution was founded; a long list of grievances against George III; and finally, the formal resolution of independence. The declaration of rights sets forth a philosophy of human rights that has influenced generations of people around the world. Much was derived from John Locke's *Second Treatise on Government* that was originally intended to justify the right of the English to overthrow King James II in the "Glorious Revolution" of 1688.

After a statement in the preamble that the Americans were publishing the Declaration out of "a decent respect to the opinions of mankind," Jefferson wrote the famous sentence, the basis for all that follows:

We hold these truths to be self-evident, that all men are created equal, that they are endowed by their Creator with certain unalienable Rights, that among these are Life, Liberty, and the pursuit of Happiness.

Examining Illustrations
"Raising the Liberty Pole" reveals the change to colonial dispositions the idea of freedom brought. On what European philosophy were the ideas expressed in the Declaration based?

Jefferson did not mean that everyone has the same abilities nor the same circumstances. True equality of condition for men and women was not a subject for consideration by even the most enlightened leaders of the eighteenth century. Many delegates to Congress, including Jefferson himself, owned slaves. Equal rights and equality before the law were distant dreams that would unfold over the next two centuries in America. The self-evident truths to which Jefferson referred were that rights are God-given or "natural," not subject to the whim of a monarch or even an elected government.

The next lines of the Declaration set forth the idea of government by social contract:

That to secure these rights, Governments are instituted among Men, deriving their just powers from the consent of the governed, That whenever any Form of Government becomes destructive of these ends, it is the Right of the People to alter or to abolish it, and to institute new Government, laying its foundation on such principles and organizing its powers in such form, as to them shall seem most likely to effect their Safety and Happiness.

Like Locke, Jefferson suggested that the purpose of government is to secure natural rights. Locke had argued that in a "state of nature" people were all free, equal, and independent. They gave up their complete freedom in order to join a community for their own safety and comfort. Jefferson agreed that the origin of government was a **social contract** in which people granted power to the rulers in exchange for protection of their rights. In truth, most eighteenth-century governments had their origin in conquest or seizure of power in the distant past, not in any agreement by the people to protect their rights. This passage, however, notably insisted that the only *rightful* aim of government is to protect the individual, and that government is the agent of the people.

If a just government rests on popular consent, the document continues, the people may refuse their consent to an unjust government, may "alter or abolish it," and may set up another government. This passage, then, justified revolution. In the twentieth century it has sometimes been called the **right of self-determination**, meaning the right of people to be free from foreign rule. Having its foundation in such a principle, the United States has been challenged throughout its history about conducting its foreign relations accordingly. Whether it has done so has often caused heated debates about American foreign policy.

Next the Declaration charges that the British government had attempted to put Americans under the king's power. An early version of the document blamed British misdeeds on Parliament, but this was altered to read "the present King of Great Britain." This change increased the effectiveness of the Declaration because revolt against a tyrannical monarch was politically more acceptable than revolt against representatives in Parliament.

The largest section of the Declaration is a list of grievances against this "present King of Great Britain." Relentlessly, Jefferson heaped wrong upon wrong. Note his use of monotonous repetition: "He has refused.... He has forbidden.... He has utterly neglected.... He has obstructed.... He has plundered.... He has.... He has.... He has...." These charges were not entirely fair. George III did not begin the quarrel with the colonies nor did he play an important role in shaping policy toward America until 1774. From that point on, however, the king resisted conciliation.

The Declaration of Independence closes by maintaining that the Americans did everything possible to preserve peace with "our British brethren" and were spurned. There was nothing left for them but to declare that "these United Colonies are, and of right ought to be,

Free and Independent States." To defend this action, the Americans pledged their lives, their fortunes, and their sacred honor.

Influence of the Declaration

Even though it contained few original ideas, the Declaration of Independence became one of the world's most important political documents. In it Americans made a commitment, as Lincoln later stated in the Gettysburg Address, "to the proposition that all men are created equal." As a result, the Declaration has been a continual lever for change in American society—toward equal rights, equal opportunities, and equal voice in government. At different times in our history, it has operated toward ending slavery, giving women the right to vote, enlarging job opportunities, and extending opportunities for education. With a genius for simple and eloquent prose, Jefferson managed to plant the ideals of equality and self-government in the American tradition.

Up to 1776 colonists based their claims to self-government within the British Empire on colonial charters and on the traditional "rights of Englishmen." The Declaration demanded independence from Britain on the basis of the natural, inborn rights of all persons. Thus, the Declaration of Independence acquired worldwide significance. When the Marquis de Lafayette returned to France after fighting for the American cause in the Revolutionary War, he hung a copy of the Declaration in a niche in his dining room; another empty niche beside it awaited a similar French declaration of human rights. When the Spanish-American colonies revolted in the early nineteenth century, several drew up declarations based on the United States' model. In the twentieth century, Jawaharlal Nehru (juh WAH huhr LAHL NAY roo), the first prime minister of India, called the Declaration of Independence a "landmark in human freedom."

SUMMARY

Despite the efforts of moderates in the colonies and in Parliament, a war no one really wanted was declared in 1776. Americans used theories of natural rights and contract government to declare their independence from the British empire. After compiling a long list of grievances against a tyrannical George III, they concluded that separation was their only possible course of action. The United States of America came into being.

CHECKING FOR UNDERSTANDING

1. **Identify** Hessians, Thomas Paine, General William Howe, Richard Henry Lee, Thomas Jefferson, John Locke

2. **Define** mercenaries, Patriots, Loyalists, grievances, preamble, natural rights, social contract, right of self-determination

3. **Name** three important reasons for separating from Great Britain as described in *Common Sense*.

4. **Cite** the four main sections of the Declaration of Independence and tell what each contains.

THINKING CRITICALLY

5. **Making Value Judgments** Explain why unalienable rights were so important that the colonists would fight a war to preserve them.

LINKING PAST AND PRESENT

6. **Making Comparisons** In the winter of 1989, a civil war broke out in Romania between communists and revolutionaries. Rebel soldiers captured and executed the president and his wife and declared Romania a free and independent state. A few months later, democratic elections were held and communists were thrown out of office. Compare this revolution with the American Revolution.

★ ★ ★ ★ ★ ★ ★ ★ ★ ★ ★ ★ ★ ★ ★ ★ ★ ★ ★

The Declaration of Independence

*D*elegates at the Second Continental Congress faced an enormous task. The war against Great Britain had begun but to many colonists the purpose for fighting was unclear. As sentiment increased for a complete break with Britain, Congress decided to act. A committee was appointed to prepare a document that declared the 13 colonies free and independent from Britain. More important, the committee needed to explain why separation was the only fitting solution to long standing disputes with Parliament and the British Crown. Thomas Jefferson was assigned to prepare a working draft of this document, which was then revised. It was officially adopted, July 4, 1776. More than any other action of the Congress, the Declaration of Independence served to make the American people one people.

The printed text of the document shows the spelling and punctuation of the parchment original. To aid in comprehension, selected words and their definitions appear in the side margin along with other explanatory notes.

impel *force*

endowed *provided*

People create governments to insure that their natural rights are protected.

If a government does not serve its purpose, the people have a right to abolish it. Then the people have the right and duty to create a new government that will safeguard their security.

In Congress, July 4, 1776. The unanimous Declaration of the thirteen united States of America,

PREAMBLE

When in the Course of human events, it becomes necessary for one people to dissolve the political bands which have connected them with another, and to assume among the powers of the earth, the separate and equal station to which the Laws of Nature and Nature's God entitle them, a decent respect to the opinions of mankind requires that they should declare the causes which impel them to the separation.—

DECLARATION OF NATURAL RIGHTS

We hold these truths to be self-evident, that all men are created equal, that they are endowed by their Creator with certain unalienable Rights, that among these are Life, Liberty, and the pursuit of Happiness.—

That to secure these rights, Governments are instituted among Men, deriving their just powers from the consent of the governed,—

That whenever any Form of Government becomes destructive of these ends, it is the Right of the People to alter or to abolish it, and to institute new Government, laying its foundation on such principles and organizing its powers in such form, as to them shall seem most likely to effect their Safety and Happiness. Prudence, indeed, will dictate that Governments long established should not be changed for light and transient causes; and accordingly all experience hath shewn, that mankind are more disposed to suffer, while evils are sufferable, than to right themselves by abolishing the forms to which they are accustomed. But when a long train of abuses and usurpations, pursuing invariably the same

Declaration of Independence in Congress, John Trumbull

Object evinces a design to reduce them under absolute Despotism, it is their right, it is their duty, to throw off such Government, and to provide new Guards for their future security.—

LIST OF GRIEVANCES

Such has been the patient sufferance of these Colonies; and such is now the necessity which constrains them to alter their former Systems of Government. The history of the present King of Great Britain is a history of repeated injuries and usurpations, all having in direct object the establishment of an absolute Tyranny over these States. To prove this, let Facts be submitted to a candid world.—

He has refused his Assent to Laws, the most wholesome and necessary for the public good.—

He has forbidden his Governors to pass Laws of immediate and pressing importance, unless suspended in their operation till his Assent should be obtained; and when so suspended, he has utterly neglected to attend to them.—

He has refused to pass other Laws for the accommodation of large districts of people, unless those people would relinquish the right of Representation in the Legislature, a right inestimable to them and formidable to tyrants only.—

He has called together legislative bodies at places unusual, uncomfortable, and distant from the depository of their public Records, for the sole purpose of fatiguing them into compliance with his measures.—

He has dissolved Representative Houses repeatedly, for opposing with manly firmness his invasions on the rights of the people.—

Despotism
unlimited power

usurpations
unjust uses of power
Each paragraph lists reported crimes of George III.

relinquish *give up*
inestimable *priceless*

He has refused for a long time, after such dissolutions, to cause others to be elected; whereby the Legislative powers, incapable of Annihilation, have returned to the People at large for their exercise; the State remaining in the meantime exposed to all the dangers of invasion from without, and convulsions within.—

He has endeavoured to prevent the population of these States; for that purpose obstructing the Laws for Naturalization of Foreigners; refusing to pass others to encourage their migrations hither, and raising the conditions of new Appropriations of Lands.—

He has obstructed the Administration of Justice, by refusing his Assent to Laws for establishing Judiciary powers.—

He has made Judges dependent on his Will alone, for the tenure of their offices, and the amount and payment of their salaries.—

He has erected a multitude of New Offices, and sent hither swarms of Officers to harass our people, and eat out their substance.—

He has kept among us, in times of peace, Standing Armies without the Consent of our legislatures.—

He has affected to render the Military independent of and superior to the Civil power.—

He has combined with others to subject us to a jurisdiction foreign to our constitution, and unacknowledged by our laws; giving his Assent to their Acts of pretended Legislation:—

For quartering large bodies of troops among us:—

For protecting them, by a mock Trial, from punishment for any Murders which they should commit on the Inhabitants of these States:—

For cutting off our Trade with all parts of the world:—

For imposing Taxes on us without our Consent:—

For depriving us in many cases, of the benefits of Trial by Jury:—

For transporting us beyond Seas to be tried for pretended offences:—

For abolishing the free System of English Laws in a neighbouring Province, establishing therein an Arbitrary government, and enlarging its Boundaries so as to render it at once an example and fit instrument for introducing the same absolute rule into these Colonies:—

For taking away our Charters, abolishing our most valuable Laws, and altering fundamentally the Forms of our Governments:—

For suspending our own Legislatures, and declaring themselves invested with power to legislate for us in all cases whatsoever.—

He has abdicated Government here, by declaring us out of his Protection and waging War against us.—

He has plundered our seas, ravaged our Coasts, burnt our towns, and destroyed the Lives of our people.—

He is at this time transporting large Armies of foreign Mercenaries to compleat the works of death, desolation and tyranny, already begun with circumstances of Cruelty & perfidy scarcely paralleled in the most barbarous ages, and totally unworthy the Head of a civilized nation.—

He has constrained our fellow Citizens taken Captive on the high Seas to bear Arms against their Country, to become the executioners of their friends and Brethren, or to fall themselves by their Hands.—

He has excited domestic insurrections amongst us, and has endeavoured to bring on the inhabitants of our frontiers, the merciless Indian Savages, whose known rule of warfare, is an undistinguished destruction of all ages, sexes and conditions.

In every stage of these Oppressions We have Petitioned for Redress in the most humble terms: Our repeated Petitions have been answered only by repeated injury. A Prince, whose character is thus marked by every act which may define a Tyrant, is unfit to be the ruler of a free people.

Nor have We been wanting in attentions to our British brethren. We have warned them from time to time of attempts by their legislature to extend an unwarrantable jurisdiction over us. We have reminded them of the circumstances of our emigration and settlement here. We have appealed to their native justice and magnanimity, and we have conjured them by the ties of our common kindred to disavow these usurpations, which would inevitably interrupt our connections and correspondence. They too have been deaf to the voice of justice and of consanguinity. We must, therefore, acquiesce in the necessity, which denounces our Separation, and hold them, as we hold the rest of mankind, Enemies in War, in Peace Friends.—

RESOLUTION OF INDEPENDENCE BY THE UNITED STATES

We, therefore, the Representatives of the united States of America, in General Congress, Assembled, appealing to the Supreme Judge of the world for the rectitude of our intentions, do, in the Name, and by Authority of the good People of these Colonies, solemnly publish and declare, That these United Colonies are, and of Right ought to be Free and Independent States; that they are Absolved from all Allegiance to the British Crown, and that all political connection between them and the State of Great Britain, is and ought to be totally dissolved; and that as Free and Independent States, they have full Power to levy War, conclude Peace, contract Alliances, establish Commerce, and to do all other Acts and Things which Independent States may of right do.—

And for the support of this Declaration, with a firm reliance on the protection of divine Providence, we mutually pledge to each other our Lives, our Fortunes and our sacred Honour.

unwarrantable jurisdiction *unjustified authority*

consanguinity *originating from the same ancestor*

rectitude *rightness*

The signers, as representatives of the American people, declared the colonies independent from Great Britain. Most members signed the document on August 2, 1776.

John Hancock
President
from Massachusetts

Georgia
Button Gwinnett
Lyman Hall
George Walton

North Carolina
William Hooper
Joseph Hewes
John Penn

South Carolina
Edward Rutledge
Thomas Heyward, Jr.
Thomas Lynch, Jr.
Arthur Middleton

Maryland
Samuel Chase
William Paca
Thomas Stone
Charles Carroll
of Carrollton

Virginia
George Wythe
Richard Henry Lee
Thomas Jefferson
Benjamin Harrison
Thomas Nelson Jr.
Francis Lightfoot Lee
Carter Braxton

Pennsylvania
Robert Morris
Benjamin Rush
Benjamin Franklin
John Morton
George Clymer
James Smith
George Taylor
James Wilson
George Ross

Delaware
Caesar Rodney
George Read
Thomas McKean

New York
William Floyd
Philip Livingston
Francis Lewis
Lewis Morris

New Jersey
Richard Stockton
John Witherspoon
Francis Hopkinson
John Hart
Abraham Clark

New Hampshire
Josiah Bartlett
William Whipple
Matthew Thornton

Massachusetts
Samuel Adams
John Adams
Robert Treat Paine
Elbridge Gerry

Rhode Island
Stephen Hopkins
William Ellery

Connecticut
Samuel Huntington
William Williams
Oliver Wolcott
Roger Sherman

Linking Across Time

THE SHOT HEARD ROUND THE WORLD

Of the Battle of Lexington, American author Ralph Waldo Emerson later wrote in his "Concord Hymn:"

By the rude bridge that arched the flood,
Their flag to April's breeze unfurled,
Here once the embattled farmers stood,
And fired the shot heard round the world.

Echoes of the American Revolution still reverberate. The American colonists' struggle for life, liberty, and the pursuit of happiness two centuries ago continues to inspire people around the world. Writing about the wave of political and social changes sweeping the Communist world at the end of the 1980s, George F. Will observed that:

"...the American Revolution unleashed the most potent force surging through the last two centuries. The force is the passion for freedom grounded in respect for right....The philosophic core of the American Revolution...made America, as Lincoln said, a nation dedicated to a 'proposition.' It is that all persons are created equal in their right to freedom....Lincoln's political vocabulary...expresses the aspirations that are growing like grass in the slowly widening fissures in the foundations of oppressive states."

First to catch the flame of freedom from the new United States was France. Leading political thinkers in the two countries shared ideas about the basic rights of humankind. The Marquis de Lafayette, a French nobleman who fought for the American cause, returned to his native land and

Storming the Bastille, July 14, 1789

championed freedom. At his suggestion French revolutionaries in 1789 adopted a Declaration of the Rights of Man and Citizen. This document proclaimed ideas that were at the foundation of the American Revolution, namely, that laws are an expression of the general will. All persons born equal in the eyes of the law and in opportunity, have rights to liberty, property, security, and to resist oppression; and they have freedom of opinion, religion, speech, and writing. When French insurgents wrenched open the doors of the Bastille prison in 1789 and freed its prisoners, Lafayette symbolically acknowledged French debt to the American Revolution by sending President Washington the key to the prison.

Soon a wave of revolution swept through Spain's colonies in Latin America. South American revolutionaries drew inspiration from both the American and French examples. Antonio Nariño, a hero of Colombian independence, was exiled for translating and publishing a copy of the French Declaration.

Simón Bolívar, the great South American liberator, echoed revolutionary French and American ideals when he said in 1815 that *"South Americans have made efforts to obtain...civil societies founded on the principles of justice, liberty and equality."* In so doing, Bolívar restated once again the dream made reality by volley fire from New England Patriot farmers in April 1775.

★ ★ ★ ★ ★ ★ ★ ★ ★ ★ ★

MAKING CONNECTIONS

1. What is the 'proposition' to which Lincoln believed the nation was dedicated?

2. How does the French Declaration of the Rights of Man and Citizen echo and go beyond the Declaration of Independence?

ANALYZING IDEAS

3. What recent events in world affairs show that the struggle begun by the American Revolution continues?

★ ★ ★ ★ ★ ★ ★ ★ ★ ★ ★

Fighting For Independence

These are the times that try men's souls. The summer soldier and the sunshine patriot will, in this crisis, shrink from the service of his country; but he that stands it now deserves the love and thanks of man and woman.

—THOMAS PAINE
The Crisis, December 19, 1776

Section Focus

Having announced their separation from Britain, the Americans faced a draining military struggle to maintain independence. The British would not willingly surrender so large a part of their colonial empire to a band of rebels. During the early stages of the war, it was all Washington could do to prevent the capture of his entire army.

Objectives

After studying this section, you should be able to:

- List two reasons why the American victories at Trenton and Princeton were important.
- Compare the difficulties faced by the Americans and the British in the Revolutionary War.

Early in 1776 Parliament authorized an army of 55,000, including 30,000 German mercenaries. In August 1776, perhaps the largest single military force ever sent from Europe to America appeared off the coast of New York City—more than 400 transports bearing 32,000 troops, guarded by 30 warships, under the command of Sir William Howe. With his brother, Admiral Richard Howe, he addressed a conciliatory letter to "George Washington, Esq.," offering to pardon the rebels if they laid down their arms, restored the local governments that existed before 1775, and accepted royal governors and councils. When Washington refused to consider proposals that offered nothing but pardons, the British war machine moved into action. Easily defeating an ill-trained militia of 20,000 under Washington's command, the British took New York City and held it until the war ended seven years later. They followed Washington's army up the Hudson River and, when he crossed to New Jersey, pursued him southward to the Delaware River. Through desertions, deaths, and captures, the American army was now reduced to 5,000, and the Continental Congress was forced to flee from Philadelphia to Baltimore.

Trenton and Princeton

When all seemed lost, Washington planned a bold move. On the evening of December 25, the first issue of *The Crisis* by Thomas Paine was read to the troops. "These are the times that try men's souls…." Hoping to win at least one battle before his troops' terms were up, Washington ferried his soldiers back across the Delaware River in a freezing winter wind. Nine miles away lay Trenton, held by 1,300 Hessians under the command of Colonel Johann Gottlieb Rall, who regarded the Americans as "country clowns." Rall had taken few precautions against attack. Washington guessed correctly that these German troops would celebrate Christmas by getting thoroughly drunk and took a chance on surprising them the morning after. He attacked at dawn on December 26, killing or capturing more than 1,000 Hessians in only three-quarters of an hour. Rall, gravely wounded, was carried back to his headquarters. As doctors cut away his clothes to treat his wounds, they found an unopened note from a Loyalist who had tried to warn him the night before that Washington was coming. Had the colonel read this note, he might have ambushed Washington and changed the course of history.

When General Howe heard of the defeat at Trenton, he sent General Charles Cornwallis from New York with 8,000 soldiers to capture Washington's force. Washington, whose troops now numbered only 1,500, pretended to be trapped, then slipped away and surprised a British force at Princeton on January 3, 1777. He then moved his army into the highlands of New Jersey out of Cornwallis's reach.

These victories saved the American cause. Philadelphia celebrated when the captured Hessians were paraded through the streets. Because of his earlier failures, Washington had been in danger of being removed from command. Now Congress gave him more power, and new enlistments joined his army as it moved to winter quarters at Morristown, New Jersey.

Financial Problems

Victory was sweet, but harder tests of Patriot endurance lay ahead. Raising a volunteer army for short-term duty was difficult enough; keeping troops in service was nearly impossible. Although some 300,000 persons eventually took up arms as Patriots, Washington could never count on more than 20,000 under his command at any point. Most soldiers served during the winter months, then returned home for the spring planting, and many refused to fight outside their own home areas. Throughout the war Washington begged for more troops, but Congress was powerless to do anything more than pass these requests along to the states.

Paying for the war was equally difficult. Lacking the power to tax, Congress issued paper money. These "Continentals," which had nothing to support their value, soon became nearly worthless. Fortunately Robert Morris, a Pennsylvania merchant and banker, personally pledged large amounts of money for the war effort. A member of the Continental Congress, Morris was elected superintendent of finance in 1781, a position that earned him the title "financier of the American Revolution." Largely through his efforts, sufficient funds were raised to move Washington's army from New York to the final campaign at Yorktown.

American Advantages

Washington's leadership was undoubtedly America's greatest asset, even though he lost more battles than he won. He may have been mistaken in training his army on strictly European lines. He sometimes annoyed his troops by his stiff manner and a tendency to talk as though all were lost. But no one did more to win the war. While British commanders often returned to England for the winter, Washington remained at his post. He saw his home at Mount Vernon only once during the war, and then only for a few hours. He alone

AMERICAN PORTRAITS

HAYM SALOMON
1740(?)-1785

Forced to flee from his native Poland after championing the cause of Polish freedom, Haym Salomon went first to England and then to America. Arriving in New York in 1772, he soon joined the Patriot struggle.

A Jewish businessman of remarkable ability, Salomon acquired wealth, all of which he risked during the American Revolution. Twice arrested as a spy, he was condemned to death for plotting to burn British ships at anchor outside New York City. He escaped by bribing his jailer and fled to Philadelphia. There he opened a prosperous private banking business and donated thousands of dollars for military supplies and government salaries. He also worked with Robert Morris to secure loans for the war effort. As a result of his devotion to America—and business problems after the war—Salomon died penniless.

commanded sufficient respect to keep the frail Continental Army from dissolving. As one former soldier later told his grandchildren, "He was a fine man, General Washington—he was everything a man should be."

Great Britain's military strength should have been sufficient to defeat the rebels. The British government had hard cash to pay its troops and to buy food from Loyalist farmers. The disciplined army, well-trained officers, and a strong navy kept supplies flowing. But the British faced several major hurdles. First, the war was unpopular in Britain. General Gage, who was relieved of his command in 1775, observed:

They [colonists] give out that they expect peace on their own terms through the inability of Britain to contend with them; and it is no wonder that such reports gain credit with the people, when letters from England and English newspapers give so much encouragement to rebellion.

In addition, Britain's sprawling colonial empire, threatened by other European powers, demanded that troops stretch around the globe. While American soldiers defended their homes, the British, thousands of miles from home, fought for a cause that many did not understand or even support. Finally, in order to win, the British had to gain control of a vast American territory. This task was especially difficult because the American's hit-and-run tactics frustrated British generals, and Washington established an effective spy system that brought information from behind British lines at critical times.

Despite these problems, British generals believed that they could defeat the poorly equipped Americans. Lieutenant General John Burgoyne devised a plan that would divide and conquer the rebels. Neither he nor the Americans could foresee that this effort would backfire, resulting in America obtaining the key ingredient for its success—French aid.

Section Two Review

SUMMARY

At the outset, the United States had serious problems carrying out a revolution they were ill-prepared to execute. George Washington had to raise, train, and equip a colonial army to face the most powerful military establishment in the world. With no power to tax or draft professional soldiers, Congress could only ask states for help, which they generally refused. Despite early losses, Washington's victories in 1777 boosted morale and offered Americans hope.

CHECKING FOR UNDERSTANDING

1. **Identify** Trenton and Princeton, General Cornwallis, Robert Morris, General Thomas Gage

2. **List** the American and British advantages at the beginning of the war. Considering the advantages held by both sides, which side do you think had the better chance of winning?

3. **Describe** the strategy used by George Washington to capture the Hessians at Trenton.

THINKING CRITICALLY

4. **Analyzing Ideas**   It has been said that George Washington was America's greatest asset in winning the Revolution. Analyze this thesis using the battles at Trenton and Princeton, the winter at Valley Forge, and Washington's personal commitment to duty to support your argument.

CONNECTIONS:
HISTORY AND POLITICAL SCIENCE

5. **Synthesizing Information**   Between 1773 and 1804, all the northern states moved to abolish slavery. The Continental Congress also prohibited the importation of enslaved people. Show how these acts followed the principles stated in the Declaration of Independence.

SECTION THREE

The War Deepens

Being on the left of the road as we marched along, I discovered lying upon the ground something with appearance of a man. Upon approaching him, he proved to be a youth about sixteen who, having come out to view the British through curiosity, for fear he might give information to our troops, they had run him through with a bayonet and left him for dead....

–MOSES HALL
North Carolina soldier, 1780

Section Focus

The American Revolution aroused strong emotions and divided opinions both in America and in Europe. While European rulers hoped that Britain would be humbled and the balance of power restored, they were concerned that their open support for a revolution might arouse rebellion in their own colonies or even at home.

Objectives

After studying this section, you should be able to:
- List two reasons why France supported the American Revolution.
- Describe the roles of women, African Americans, and Native Americans in the war.

The first efforts to secure French assistance came as early as 1776 when Silas Deane was sent to Paris. Deane was successful in securing secret aid, but after the Declaration of Independence, the United States desired open support. Benjamin Franklin became the principal American **envoy** [OHN voy], or delegated representative, to France. Perhaps no foreign diplomat in history was as popular as Franklin in Paris. His face appeared everywhere, in books and pamphlets, on rings, watches, brooches, and snuffboxes. Women even did their hair in a style *"á la Franklin,"* designed to imitate his beaver hat. The middle class admired him because of his successful publishing career and the sayings of *Poor Richard's Almanac.* Intellectuals admired him as a scientist. To liberals, he represented the way a free society allowed people to rise by their own talents. The French officials, whom he pressed for more troops, money, and supplies, were won over by his ability, courage, cheerfulness, and tact. But Franklin's charms may have been wasted had not the Americans proved that they could win a crucial battle. France, its treasury already strained, would not provide funds for the American struggle unless there was some hope of success. News of the British defeat at Saratoga settled the issue.

British Attack from Canada

Although an American attempt to conquer Canada in 1776 had failed, it forced the British to divert to Canada troops that might have been better used in New York and New Jersey. In 1777 General John Burgoyne planned a great three-pronged attack that would divide the colonies along the line of Lake Champlain and the Hudson Valley. According to the plan, while General Howe moved up the Hudson River from New York City, Burgoyne's army would move south from Montreal. A lesser force under British officer Barry St. Leger would invade by way of Lake Ontario and the Mohawk River. The three armies would meet near Albany.

Because the British war office failed to keep in touch with him, Howe's army never participated in the plan. Hoping to catch Washington, Howe led an expedition from New York to Philadelphia, the capital. He captured Philadelphia in September, overcoming Washington at the Battle of Brandywine and inflicting a further defeat on the Americans at Germantown, Pennsylvania, in October. This time Congress fled to York, Pennsylvania.

Meanwhile, Burgoyne's force of 8,000 troops, unaware that Howe's army would not meet them—started south toward Albany. They easily recaptured Fort Ticonderoga in midsummer. Their comfortable success was primarily because American soldiers opposing Burgoyne were poorly trained and badly equipped. Their officers employed so much energy quarreling among themselves they could scarcely direct the troops.

After such an effortless victory, however, Burgoyne faced one obstacle after another. A force of 1,000 Americans felled trees across the only road to Albany, so that Burgoyne's army could move no more than 1 mile a day. A British force sent toward Bennington, Vermont, for rations was surrounded by volunteers under General John Stark who inspired his troops with:

My men, yonder are the Hessians. They were bought for seven pounds and ten pence a man. Are you worth more? Prove it. Tonight, the American flag floats from yonder hill or Molly Stark sleeps a widow!

To further delay Burgoyne's master plan, St. Leger's advance from Lake Ontario was slowed by his own troops' bloody ambush of Americans at Oriskany, New York. The stage was set for a dramatic American victory.

Saratoga, The Turning Point

In spite of his difficulties near Philadelphia, Washington sent some of his best troops to General Horatio Gates, commanding officer for the northern campaigns. Meanwhile, with their homes threatened by the British advance and Burgoyne's Indian allies, New York and New England militia began to gather at Bemis Heights. Eventually, Burgoyne was surrounded by a force nearly twice as large as his own. He was unable to get food, to retreat to Ticonderoga, or to advance on Albany. After making one unsuccessful attempt to cut through the American lines, his force surrendered at Saratoga in October 1777.

The victory at Saratoga proved crucial. British ministers offered to grant the Americans generous rights of self-government within the British Empire. Fearing that the offer might be accepted, France signed two treaties with the Continental Congress—the first recognized American independence and granted commercial

Examining Maps
Between August and October 1777, the fortunes of the war changed. A British plan to divide the colonies failed. Describe the battles at Bennington, Oriskany, and Saratoga.

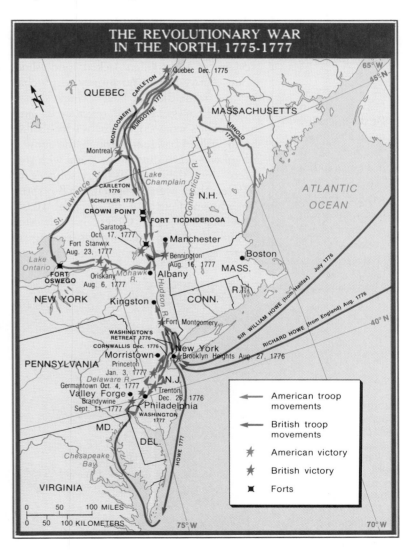

The American Revolution forged a bond between the United States and France that has sometimes been strained but never broken. In 1876, the centennial of the American Revolution, France gave the United States a monument to freedom, the Statue of Liberty. One of General John J. Pershing's aides, upon landing with American troops in France during World War I, recalled French aid in the American Revolution by declaring, "Lafayette, we are here."

privileges; the second offered an alliance on favorable terms.

From 1778 on, the Continental Army was partly supplied and paid with French gifts and loans and reinforced by disciplined French regiments. The French navy prevented the British from moving troops as they pleased up and down the Atlantic Coast. Following the lead of France, Spain and the Netherlands entered the war against England, while Russia, Prussia, Denmark, Sweden, and Portugal formed a League of Armed Neutrality to resist British sea power.

The Winter at Valley Forge

Before French aid reached America, Washington's army had to endure the unusually harsh winter of 1777 and 1778 encamped at Valley Forge, Pennsylvania. Many of the soldiers lacked food, shoes, and coats and had no money to purchase them. Some did not have a single shirt or pair of pants. Huddled together in small huts, they wrapped themselves in blankets and walked barefoot through the snow to haul water. On duty, some stood with their feet inside their hats. When a soldier's feet froze, they were amputated. By spring nearly one-fourth of the original 10,000 soldiers had died. Others had deserted. While the American army was freezing and starving, farmers around Valley Forge sold

their meat and grain to British troops in Philadelphia who paid not in "Continentals" but in silver coin.

The Prussian Baron Friedrich W.A. von Steuben and the French Marquis de Lafayette joined Washington at Valley Forge, bringing discipline and encouragement. By spring, the tattered army began to regain morale as new provisions arrived from France. Several European nations joined with France to lend financial and military support. Individual volunteers such as Count Casimir Pulaski of Poland, von Steuben, and Lafayette were evidence of the widespread sympathy generated by the Revolution.

Difficult Choices

When the Declaration of Independence called the United States "one people," it expressed a hope rather than a fact. Only about one-third of the American people actively supported the war. Another third were indifferent to the Patriot cause, except when fighting reached their doorsteps. The rest supported the British.

The American Revolution was a civil war as well as a war against Great Britain. In every one of the 13 colonies, Loyalists, sometimes called Tories by the Patriots, refused to abandon allegiance to George III. In some areas Loyalists remained in control, and thousands joined the British army. The struggle between the Patriots and the Loyalists was as bitter as the

Examining Fine Art
Washington and his tired band of soldiers march into Valley Forge for the winter encampment. The army included many teenagers. Why might the winter of 1777 and 1778 be called the low point for American morale?

struggle between the rebels and the British. Patriots thought of the Loyalists as traitors to the American cause. Loyalists thought of Patriots as traitors to Britain.

Many Loyalists were wealthy; some were royal officials, military officers, Anglican ministers, college presidents, large landowners, doctors, lawyers, and merchants. They found rebels like the Sons of Liberty threatening. Said one Loyalist: "If I must be devoured, let me be devoured by the jaws of a lion [Britain], and not gnawed to death by rats." But not all the Loyalists were wealthy. In upstate New York, poor tenant farmers joined the Loyalists because the landowners supported the Revolution. In some southern states, backcountry farmers became Loyalists because they disliked the Patriot merchants and planters of the coastal areas.

It is not surprising that Loyalists were most numerous in British-occupied cities such as New York, Philadelphia, Charleston, and Savannah. To prove their loyalty to the crown, they sometimes spied and informed on the rebels. Later, when the British army withdrew from these areas, the Loyalists feared for their lives. Over 400 Loyalist families fled from Savannah to Jamaica, taking with them more than 5,000 slaves. From all the colonies, perhaps 100,000 Loyalists packed their belongings, sold whatever they could, and left hurriedly for Canada, Bermuda, and Great Britain. Those who remained behind were often persecuted by their neighbors. Many lost their property; others were imprisoned or tarred and feathered. A few were executed.

Many women actively served the American cause. As secret agents they supplied Washington and other generals with information about British positions and plans. They raised money to equip troops. They ran farms and businesses while their husbands were away at war. John Adams's family would have gone bankrupt had not Abigail Adams capably managed their family farm in Braintree, Massachusetts.

During the war it was common for women to accompany the troops—both American and British—serving as cooks, medics, laundresses, and guides. Sarah Osburn went with her husband's regiment from West Point to Yorktown, washing, mending, and cooking for the soldiers. Once, while carrying food supplies, she met General Washington, who asked her if she was "not afraid of the cannonballs." "No," she replied, "it would not do for the men to fight and starve too."

A few women fought in the ranks, the most famous being Mary Ludwig Hays, better known as Molly Pitcher. Carrying water to the gunners during the battle of Monmouth, New Jersey, in 1778, she saw her husband fall and took his place at the cannon. For her services she later received a pension of $50 a year. Deborah Sampson disguised herself as a man and enlisted in a Massachusetts regiment. She fought in many battles and was seriously

Life of the Times

YANKEE PEDDLER

Farm families during the Revolution had difficulty producing all the materials required for food, shelter, and clothing. Money was scarce. Barter, or trading one item for another, increased in popularity. Peddlers—traveling hawkers of dry goods— canvased the countryside with pack horses and wagons laden with merchandise. Such Yankee vendors dated from early colonial times and were a prominent fixture in rural America for generations.

Wherever crowds assembled—at political events, religious gatherings, or other meetings—a peddler selling wares was also likely to be present. In between times the peddler traveled house to house and was a welcome visitor. His sundry inventory varied, of course, but goods ranged from such notions as pins, combs, buttons, and ribbon to necessities such as clocks, tinware, drugs, shoes, spices, cloth, even books. The peddler, who was a careful observer of human nature as well as a shrewd trader, brought news and gossip, gave advice, and sometimes even treated the sick. Due to customary shortages of currency and coin, barter for goods was the usual practice. Some successful peddlers eventually established themselves with a general store. For others the appeal of the road was simply too great to resist.

**Examining
Illustrations**
*Deborah Sampson
served in the army
under the name of
Robert Shurtleff. What
did she do after the
war?*

all people equal, they reserved full privileges of citizenship for white males.

When the colonies rebelled against Great Britain, African Americans and native Americans were faced with difficult choices. Each side in the conflict wanted their support, but which side should they join? Would the British or the Americans give African Americans their freedom? Which side would protect the territorial rights of native Americans?

From the beginning of the war, at Lexington, Concord, and Bunker Hill, black soldiers fought for the American cause. But slave owners were afraid to give guns to black people, whether slave or free. In November 1775, orders went out to discharge all African American soldiers in the Continental Army and not to permit others to enlist. Soon after, the royal governor of Virginia promised to free any slave or indentured servant who joined the British army. Many slaves were reportedly crossing into the British lines. As a result, the Continental Congress reversed its policy and allowed free blacks to reenlist and to be recruited into the army and navy. Most African American soldiers served in integrated regiments, although some states organized all-black companies.

Jehu Grant, a slave in Rhode Island, joined the American army fearing that his

wounded. Sampson was honorably discharged from the army and returned home to marry and raise a family. She expressed her regret, however, in having to give up her uniform, which had allowed her to travel about "safe from insult and annoyance."

Women who supported the Revolution expected to gain from its ideals of democracy and equality. When John Adams was serving in the Continental Congress, his wife Abigail sent him this message:

By the way, in the new Code of Laws which I suppose it will be necessary for you to make, I desire you would remember the Ladies and be more generous and favourable to them than your ancestors! Do not put unlimited power in the hands of husbands. Remember all Men would be tyrants if they could. If particular care and attention is not paid to the Ladies, we are determined to foment a rebellion, and will not hold ourselves bound by any Laws in which we have no voice or Representation.

Abigail Adams's words went unheeded. The American Revolution did very little to change the political rights of women. Although new state bills of rights declared

Examining Fine Art *Abigail Adams was an early crusader for women's rights. Her letters demonstrate the careful thought of educated women of the colonial period. To what group did the new state bills of rights reserve the full privileges of citizenship?*

Loyalist master planned to send him to work on a British ship. He later recalled:

But when I saw the liberty poles and the people all engaged for the support of freedom, I could not but like and be pleased with such thing (God forgive me if I have sinned in so feeling). And living on the borders of Rhode Island, where whole companies of colored people enlisted, it added to my fears and dread of being sold to the British. These considerations induced me to enlist into the American army, where I served for about ten months, when my master found me and took me home.

Jehu Grant later achieved freedom. Other slaves who were recruited into the army either won freedom from the start or at the end of their military service.

In 1775 the Continental Congress sent a message to the Iroquois Nation. "This is a family quarrel between us and old England." It asked the native Americans "to remain at home, and not join on either side...." Some groups of native Americans remained neutral, but many joined the British. They knew the Americans opposed the British Proclamation of 1763, which reserved the land west of the Appalachian Mountains for the native Americans.

British agents encouraged the native Americans to attack frontier settlements. They provided weapons and ammunition to Cherokees to raid the Virginia, Georgia, and Carolina frontiers. These actions diverted many state militia from fighting against British troops. The British stirred up similar trouble in Ohio and throughout the Northwest and enlisted native Americans into the British army.

In New York four nations of the Iroquois Confederation supported the British. Washington sent troops against the Iroquois and broke their confederation. Many Indians—including most of the Mohawks —moved permanently to Canada.

SUMMARY

With superior land and naval forces, adequate financing, and experienced military leadership, the British were assuming a victory. Using guerrilla tactics, Americans surprised the English by winning a stunning victory at Saratoga. This victory foretold that the United States might have a chance and brought about an American-French alliance that turned the course of the war. The period from 1777 to 1780 was also marked by significant contributions of women and black soldiers to the war effort.

CHECKING FOR UNDERSTANDING

1. **Identify** Silas Deane, *Poor Richard's Almanac*, John Burgoyne, Saratoga, Horatio Gates, Baron Friedrich W.A. von Steuben, Count Casimir Pulaski, Marquis de Lafayette, Tories, Molly Pitcher, Abigail Adams

2. **Cite** both military and diplomatic reasons why the victory at Saratoga was crucial to the American cause.

3. **Describe** the ways in which France and other foreign nations assisted the American people during the Revolution.

4. **Explain** the decisions facing African Americans and native Americans during the Revolutionary War.

THINKING CRITICALLY

5. **Analyzing Beliefs** The Revolution has been described as a civil war as well as a rebellion against Great Britain. Analyze this theory based on the conflict between Loyalists and Patriots. Consider each group's political beliefs.

CONNECTIONS: HISTORY AND ENVIRONMENT

6. **Describing Cause and Effect** Describe the devastating effects of the winter weather conditions at Valley Forge in 1777-1778 on Washington's army.

★ ★ ★ ★ ★ ★ ★ ★ ★ ★ ★ ★ ★ ★ ★ ★ ★ ★

The War Ends

Howe and Burgoyne and Clinton too,
With Prescott and Cornwallis joined,
Together plot our overthrow
In one infernal league combined.
The foe comes on with haughty stride,
Our troops advance with martial noise,
Their veterans flee before our youth.
And generals yield to beardless boys.

—WILLIAM BILLINGS
"Let Tyrants Shake" from *The Singing Master's Assistant*, 1778

Section Focus

Throughout the war Britain hoped to prevent the rebels from securing arms from France and other nations. Yet the rebels held on, continuing to frustrate redcoat generals by avoiding direct confrontation and capture. The rebellion had broken out in the north, but the conclusion would be played out in the south in dramatic fashion at Yorktown, Virginia.

Objectives

After studying this section, you should be able to:
- Identify the problems that the British and Americans faced in continuing the war effort.
- Explain the military strategy that defeated Lord Cornwallis.

In 1778 the British evacuated Philadelphia and marched across New Jersey toward New York. On their way, Washington attacked General Henry Clinton's 12-mile baggage train at Monmouth. A mistaken order and perhaps treachery prevented an American victory, but Clinton was not able to take advantage of American blunders. He escaped to Manhattan where he would remain until the end of the war. While New York City remained in British hands, Washington kept an eye on the enemy from his camp in nearby White Plains, New York.

British Focus on the South

Unable to capture Washington's army or to put down the rebellion in the north, the British turned their main military efforts to the south. For three years, beginning in 1778, the redcoats marched through Georgia, the Carolinas, and Virginia, their main forces never suffering defeat.

The British were not as successful in the southwest. General Bernardo de Galvez, the governor of Spanish Louisiana, gave secret assistance to the Americans, allowing them to ship arms, ammunition, and supplies up the Mississippi River. When Spain officially entered the war in 1779, Galvez's troops defeated the British at Baton Rouge, Natchez, and Pensacola. These battles were important because they forced the British to divert troops away from their campaigns along the Atlantic coast.

The American cause suffered a year of gloom in 1780. When 6,000 French troops landed at Newport, Rhode Island, a British fleet promptly blockaded them. The Continental Army had not been paid for a month and was on the verge of mutiny. Civilians suffered from high prices as a result of the flood of paper money that had been printed by states and the Continental Congress. American morale received its most severe blow when a major general turned traitor.

Benedict Arnold, a brilliant military leader, had won several battles for the American cause. After Arnold was wounded at Saratoga, Washington assigned him the post of military governor of Philadelphia. In February 1779, the Council of Pennsylvania brought charges against Arnold for abuse of power and self-serving business dealings. Washington issued a mild rebuke but continued to include Arnold in plans for the coming campaign. Arnold, however, had already decided to join the British Army. In 1780 he attempted to turn over to the British the American fort on the Hudson River at West Point. Arnold tried to deliver a secret message to Major John André, head of British secret service, but three American militiamen intercepted his notes. Washington was given the evidence in Arnold's own writing. "Arnold has betrayed me," he said, "Whom can we trust now?"

The British were having their troubles, too. Ireland had rebelled, and pro-American riots erupted in London. The British armies could not keep their conquests in the south because they could not win the loyalty of the inhabitants. A British officer compared his company to a ship at sea: it moved in any direction it wished but left no trace behind. The British were also harassed by guerrilla fighters under the leadership of Francis Marion, "the Swamp Fox." Sometimes commanding as few as 30 men, sometimes as many as 900, Marion repeatedly surprised and defeated small British forces.

Beginning of the End

Believing that Georgia and South Carolina were secure, Lord Cornwallis, the British commander of forces in the south, moved into North Carolina. At King's Mountain, on October 7, 1780, back-country rebels ambushed an army of 1,100 Loyalists. After this victory Daniel Morgan and General Nathaniel Greene defeated part of a British force under Cornwallis at Cowpens in January, but were forced to retreat at Guilford Courthouse in March 1781.

The most serious setbacks for the British in 1780 and 1781 were naval defeats at the hands of the French, causing them to lose command of the Atlantic. This made possible the capture of the principal British force in the south under Lord Cornwallis, who had moved out of North Carolina to what he believed to be the safety of Yorktown, Virginia.

General Washington, outside New York with the main body of the Continental Army, learned that a French fleet under Admiral de Grasse was heading for the Chesapeake Bay. At the urging of General Jean Baptiste Rochambeau (ROH SHAHM BOH), commander of the French troops in America, Washington agreed to a remarkable combined operation against the British. Leaving a few troops behind to fool Clinton, Washington sped south with a large force. The French fleet blocked the entrance to Chesapeake Bay, beating back a British fleet sent to relieve Cornwallis. Meanwhile, a French army sailed from Rhode Island to Virginia. Additional forces under Anthony Wayne and Lafayette converged on Yorktown. Besieged on land and hemmed in by sea, Cornwallis was forced to surrender on October 19, 1781. Upon learning the news, Lord North, the British Prime Minister, cried out repeatedly, "Oh God! it is all over."

Examining Maps *After Cornwallis moved his troops to Yorktown, Virginia, he was trapped by the French and Americans. Trace and describe the routes taken by the colonial forces of Washington and de Grasse and the British troops of Cornwallis.*

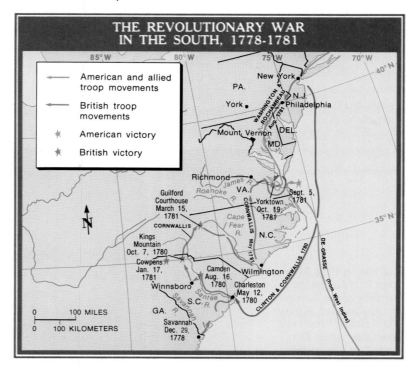

Although the objectives were not the same, America's military experience in Vietnam in the 1960s and 1970s proved to be bitterly similar to Britain's experience in the American Revolution. Years of bombing and fighting against the Vietcong did not weaken the enemy's will to fight. Just as many British protested against their government over the Revolutionary War, as Americans protested against the war in Vietnam. American leaders, convinced that a military victory was too costly, followed the same course the British adopted in 1783, a negotiated peace.

It was not quite over. Because the war included French and Spanish alliances, the fighting in Europe dragged on for two more years. But there were no significant battles in America after Yorktown.

The Treaty of Paris, 1783

A combination of events, positions, and interests enabled the United States to achieve a favorable peace settlement. The British knew that Spain was not eager to see the United States extend its boundaries beyond the Appalachians and threaten Spanish control of Louisiana and Florida. Great Britain hoped to drive a wedge between the United States and its allies by offering generous peace terms. Originally Congress instructed the American commissioners to conclude no settlement unless the French agreed. However, when it was discovered that the French might secretly encourage the British to offer the Americans a boundary well east of the Mississippi, the commissioners violated their instructions. They negotiated directly with the British representatives, played on British desires to destroy the American-French alliance, and were able to secure valuable western territories.

A brilliant war-time expedition of 180 Virginia soldiers under George Rogers Clark in 1778 had helped to establish the American position. Clark's capture of the British posts of Kaskaskia (kas KAS kee uh) and Vincennes (vihn SEHNZ), located in present day Illinois and Indiana, established the United States' claim to the trans-Appalachian West.

The Treaty of Paris in 1783 acknowledged American independence and granted the new nation land from the Atlantic Ocean to the Mississippi River. Although several provisions of the treaty led to later disputes, it was a great diplomatic victory. The United States gained an area four times the size of France and nearly ten times that of the British Isles.

Influence of the American Revolution

When British troops marched out of Yorktown to lay down their arms, American bands played a march called "The World Turn'd Upside Down." Perhaps it had. The American victory gave new hope to the oppressed in Europe and endangered the old system of monarchy and aristocracy.

The American Revolution was one of the causes of the French Revolution. The large sums of money France poured into the American Revolution brought its government to the verge of bankruptcy. When the king's ministers proposed new loans or taxes to balance the budget in 1778, French people raised the familiar cry of "no taxation without representation" and forced King Louis XVI to call representatives of the people together in a body known as the Estates-General. The American example of rebellion against a tyrant inspired French revolutionaries.

The British defeat in the Revolutionary War discredited George III and put an end to his attempt to "be a king" by buying

Examining Fine Art
John Trumbull painted this view of the surrender at Yorktown. Nearly 8,000 British troops laid down their arms. Why did Britain offer generous peace terms?

AMERICAN CASUALTIES IN THE REVOLUTION

	Militia	Naval	Total
Killed in action	5,992	832	6,824
Died as prisoners	—	—	8,500
Total American deaths in service 15,324			
Wounded	7,988	457	8,445
Captured	15,427	2,725	18,152
Missing	1,426	—	1,426
Deserted	99	1	100

Howard H. Peckham. *The Toll of Independence.* Chicago: University of Chicago Press, 1974.

Examining Tables *The American Revolution was costly in terms of lives lost. The casualty rate discouraged General Washington. How does the total number of deaths in service compare with the number wounded? What might account for the high death rate?*

control of Parliament. However, in a letter the king wrote in 1782, he refused any blame for the loss of the colonies:

I cannot conclude without mentioning how sensibly I feel the dismemberment of America from this empire, and that I should be miserable indeed if I did not feel that no blame on that account can be laid at my door....

After the defeat at Yorktown, Parliament voted Lord North, George III's prime minister, out of office and took steps to assure that no king could ever again corrupt and control its members as George III had done. Thus, the American Revolution helped to make the British monarch a figurehead. It also persuaded the British to allow their remaining colonies more self-government. Ralph Waldo Emerson did not exaggerate when he wrote in the "Concord Hymn" that the shot fired by the minutemen on April 19, 1775, was "heard round the world."

SUMMARY

The American cause suffered setbacks early in 1780, including military defeats, treason, lack of money, and inflation. The fortunes of war changed, primarily because of guerrilla tactics that resulted in victories for the Continental army. By 1781 the advantage was completely with the Americans. A joint campaign with the French ended in victory at Yorktown, the last important battle of the war. The Treaty of Paris gave the United States independence and territory from the Atlantic Ocean to the Mississippi River.

CHECKING FOR UNDERSTANDING

1. **Identify** Benedict Arnold, Francis Marion, Yorktown, General Clinton, Lord Cornwallis, Treaty of Paris

2. **List** three problems that the Americans and the British each faced toward the end of the war.

3. **Detail** the French-American operation that brought about the end of the war.

4. **Cite** the terms of the Treaty of Paris.

5. **Describe** how the American Revolution caused the French Revolution.

THINKING CRITICALLY

6. **Analyzing Results** A military band played "The World Turn'd Upside Down" when British troops marched out of Yorktown to surrender. Analyze and explain how the world had been turned upside down by the United States' victory in the Revolution and how the course of British and American history was changed.

LINKING PAST AND PRESENT

7. **Making Comparisons** In 1990 United States military forces were sent overseas to Saudi Arabia. In 1776 British military forces were sent overseas to America. Explain how the situation faced by American soldiers in Saudi Arabia and by British soldiers in America compare.

★ ★ ★ ★ ★ ★ ★ ★ ★ ★ ★ ★ ★ ★ ★ ★ ★

★ Chapter 5 Review ★

★ Summary

The United States entered the Revolutionary War in 1776 with a determination to maintain self-government without British interference. They were conservative revolutionaries in that they were not seeking drastic social, political, or economic changes. They fought to maintain an American way of life based on human inalienable rights: life, liberty, and equality before the law.

Americans won the war, despite tremendous odds. They gained independent status among nations, and they extended their continental frontiers to the Mississippi, beginning the march toward their manifest destiny—from sea to shining sea.

★ Using Vocabulary

Each of the following terms pertains to the Declaration of Independence. Use these terms to explain the four parts of the Declaration.

grievances	**preamble**
social contract	**natural rights**
resolution	

★ Reviewing Facts

1. **Compare** the plan the British devised to win the war in 1777 with that of the Americans and French in 1780, noting similarities and differences in the two plans.
2. **Describe** the guerrilla tactics used by General Francis Marion and the effect of these methods on the British army.
3. **List** three important military leaders on both sides of the conflict, and tell how each influenced the war's outcome.
4. **Explain** the significant contributions and achievements made by women to the war effort.
5. **Tell** how the participation of black soldiers in the war enhanced the American cause.
6. **Name** three contributions of the French that helped turn the tide of war for the Americans.
7. **Define** the terms of the Treaty of Paris, and explain how they achieved the goals for which Americans fought.

★ Understanding Concepts

REVOLUTION

1. It has been said that the American Revolution was something new under the sun. This was the first time colonials successfully rebelled against the parent country. Analyze the effect this would have on the colonial empires of France, Spain, and Portugal.
2. *The American Revolution has been described as the most conservative revolution in history.* After looking up the definition of *conservative,* prove or refute the above statement based on what Americans wanted to "conserve," as stated in the Declaration of Independence, and how successful they were in their endeavor.

CIVIL RIGHTS AND LIBERTIES

3. American revolutionaries said many times that they were fighting to preserve the basic English rights they had always enjoyed. Describe these rights using the Magna Carta, English Bill of Rights, Mayflower Compact, and Declaration of Independence as references to support your answer.
4. Jefferson turned to natural rights and the contract theory of government when he was writing the Declaration of Independence. Explain why he used these particular concepts.

★ Thinking Critically

1. **Linking Past and Present** Detail the relationship you see between the theory of government as outlined in the Declaration of Independence and political changes that have occurred in Eastern Europe in recent years.
2. **Understanding Cause and Effect** Analyze the effects of a long and indecisive war on citizen morale and war support. Describe the factors that produce positive effects and negative effects.

★ Writing About History

NARRATION

Refer to the description of how to write a narrative essay in the History Writer's Handbook in the Appendix of this book. Your teacher will give you more specific instructions on the essay's length and the assignment's due date.

Imagine that you are George Washington, Commander-in-Chief of the Continental Army. Keep a diary of your thoughts, and experiences during the awful winter at Valley Forge, 1777-1778. Include items from your expense ledger, and accounts of how the men reacted to the cold, the lack of food and clothing, no pay, and the failure of Congress to provide even basic necessities for fighting the war. Tell how you managed to hold everything together until help came from the French in the spring. Base the details in this diary upon some facts about Valley Forge you have located through research.

★ Learning Cooperatively

You and a partner will take sides in the Revolutionary cause. Decide which one will assume the Loyalist position and the Patriot position. Adopt an appropriate name for the characters you portray and choose a role that includes personal information such as your occupation, your family, and your community. Write a series of letters to your partner in which you convey your feelings before, during, and after the war. Include your reactions to such events as the Stamp Act, the Boston Massacre, the Boston Tea Party, the Declaration of Independence, the various campaigns and battles of the war, and the Treaty of Paris. Date your letters so that they follow each event that you include. Remember that your personal circumstances and your age will change over the course of the 20 years in which these events took place. In reacting to the events, explain how each relates to the position you took as a Patriot or a Loyalist. Write a final letter that concludes by telling what happened to you and your family at the end of the war. When you finish present several letters to the class as if it were a script of a play.

★ Mastering Skills

IDENTIFYING THE MAIN IDEA

Written material generally is divided into paragraphs, each of which contains at least one sentence that presents the *main idea,* or principal focus, or that paragraph. The other sentences explain or give detail about the main idea.

When the main idea is expressed in the first sentence, it is known as the *topic sentence.* If the main idea is expressed in the last sentence, it is known as a *summary sentence.* At times, however, the main idea is stated in a sentence in the middle of the paragraph or is not stated directly at all.

The following steps will help you identify the main idea of a paragraph:

- Read the paragraph carefully, and determine the general focus or subject.
- Read the paragraph again, sentence by sentence. For each, ask yourself what would happen if that sentence were not in the paragraph. Would the rest of the sentences tie together and make sense? If the answer to the question is no, you probably have found the sentence that contains the main idea. In that case, identify the idea.
- Check the remaining sentences to determine if they support the idea put forth in the sentence you have just chosen. Do they describe, explain, or give details about what you have identified as the main idea?

Example Read the following statement by Jehu Grant, a slave who joined the American army during the Revolutionary War:

But when I saw the liberty poles and the people all engaged for the support of freedom, I could not but like and be pleased with such thing (God forgive me if I have sinned in so feeling). And living on the borders of Rhode Island, where whole companies of colored people enlisted, it added to my fears and dread of being sold to the British. These considerations induced me to enlist into the American army, where I served for about ten months, when my master found me and took me home.

In this example, the first sentence tells why Jehu liked the idea of joining the American army. The second sentence gives another reason why he wished to enlist and why it was possible for him to enlist. But it isn't until the last sentence that the reader is told that Jehu enlisted and served in the American army. The last sentence sums up what the paragraph is about, while the first two sentences support the idea put forth in the last sentence. Thus, the last sentence expresses the main idea and is the summary sentence for the paragraph.

Practice Apply the three steps to the message that Abigail sent to her husband, John Adams, on page 140 of your textbook.

CHAPTER 6
A More Perfect Union

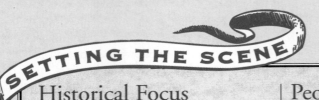

SETTING THE SCENE

Historical Focus

Although victorious on the battlefield, Americans faced serious problems as they launched their new nation. They successfully met the challenge of establishing state governments and a national government under the Articles of Confederation. It soon became apparent, however, that weaknesses of this new national government might break it apart. During this period of experiment and uncertainty, farsighted American political leaders laid the foundations of a free and democratic government embodied in a new constitution.

Concepts to Understand

- How **political control** was allocated within the government under the Articles of Confederation.
- Why a strong central **authority** was needed to keep the republic intact.

People to Know

John Jay, Daniel Shays, James Madison, William Paterson

Places to Locate

New Orleans, Barbary coast, Tennessee, Northwest Territory, Philadelphia

Terms to Identify

bicameral, franchise, emancipation, ratify, public land, right of deposit

Guided Reading

As you read this chapter, seek the answers to the following questions.

1. Why did people consider the government under the Articles of Confederation weak?
2. What important compromises made the Constitution possible?

SPANNING THE DECADES

POLITICAL					
	1776 *New Hampshire adopts the first written state constitution*	**1777** *The Articles of Confederation completed*	**1779** Bonhomme Richard *wins battle against* Serapis	**1781** *Articles of Confederation ratified*	**1783** *British evacuate New York City*

1775   **1780**

CULTURAL				
	1775 *Smallpox epidemic throughout colonies*		**1780** *The first Universalist Church in the nation built in Gloucester, Mass.*	**1780** *American Academy of Arts and Sciences founded in Boston*

The Signing of the Constitution *by Howard Chandler Christy, 1940*

1785
Land
Ordinance
passed

1787
Constitutional
Convention
meets in
Philadelphia

1788
Constitution
is ratified

1785   1790

1784
Empress of
China *sails from*
New York to
Canton, China

1786
Va. law
provides for
separation
of church
and state

1787
The Contrast
—first successful
stage comedy in
New York

1789
*University
of North
Carolina
founded*

*...Sir, I agree to this Constitution
with all its faults...because I think a general
government necessary for us....I doubt too
whether any other Convention we can
obtain may be able to make a better
Constitution....*

—BENJAMIN FRANKLIN,
Constitutional Convention, 1787

Government in Transition

SETTING THE SCENE

The Americans will have no Center of Union among them, and no Common Interest to pursue, when the Power and Government of England are finally removed....the Americans never can be united....Their fate seems to be—A DISUNITED PEOPLE, till the End of Time.

—JOSIAH TUCKER
English clergyman, 1781

Section Focus

As the Revolution progressed, some Americans recognized the need for unity in fighting the British, as well as the need to maintain rule of law. While soldiers on the battlefield fought for freedom, their leaders struggled to create a government to replace British authority. The result was a unique blend of British political heritage and the American experience.

Objectives

After studying this section, you should be able to:
- Describe the governments that resulted from state constitutions.
- List the strengths and weaknesses of the Articles of Confederation.

As the fighting spread from Massachusetts in 1775, royal governors throughout the colonies watched their authority collapse. Although at first a few tried to organize Loyalist resistance, eventually all royal governors abandoned their offices and fled. In May 1776, Congress urged the colonies to "adopt such government as shall best conduce to the happiness and safety of their constituents." For most colonies that meant replacing their colonial charters with new constitutions.

New State Governments

Most state constitutions established state governments similar to the colonial governments they replaced. All states except Pennsylvania and Georgia created **bicameral,** or two-house, legislatures. Members of each house represented geographic districts and, in nearly all the states, were directly elected by the voters.

Major changes were made in the executive branch, however. Many Americans had come to distrust strong executive power, the result of their unhappy experience with royal governors and George III. So most state governors were elected to one-year terms by their legislatures and had no power to **veto,** or reject, bills passed by the legislature.

For the most part, citizenship was restricted to white male property-owners. Neither women nor blacks could vote in most states, and all states established strict property requirements for officeholders. Some Americans, especially in the North, compared their state constitutions to the promise of equality expressed in the Declaration of Independence and questioned whether the **franchise,** or right to vote, should be so limited.

Although the Revolution did not win for all Americans the full equality and democracy promised in the Declaration of Independence, it did move American society in that direction. Because it was difficult to claim that "all men are created equal" in a society where some people were owned by others, many Americans began to question the institution of slavery. Some states passed laws to prohibit the importation of more slaves, and by 1804 every state north of Maryland had provided for the **emancipation,** or freeing, of black slaves. The states accomplished this in different ways. New York simply declared that children of enslaved parents were free at birth. Pennsylvania required that all slaves born after 1780 be freed at age 28. Some merely paid slaveholders to free their slaves. An enslaved person in Massachusetts sued for his freedom because the state constitution declared "all men are born free and equal." The state court agreed and declared slavery unconstitutional in Massachusetts in 1783.

In the South there also were those who felt slavery was wrong. In 1782, when Virginia passed a law allowing emancipation of slaves, 10,000 were freed within 8 years. Despite personal feelings, however, little was done elsewhere. In the North the economy did not rely on slavery. In the South, however, enslaved people were a large proportion of the wealth, and the plantation system depended on their labor. Even Thomas Jefferson, who hated slavery, did not free his slaves until his death. Like others, Jefferson could see no practical way to end slavery in the South.

Another significant victory of the Revolution was an increase in religious freedom. As the Southern colonies gained independence, the Church of England was **disestablished**—that is, no longer supported by taxation. In Virginia a bill for religious freedom written by Jefferson proclaimed that:

…[N]o man shall be compelled to frequent or support any religious worship, place or ministry…nor shall otherwise suffer on account of his religious opinions or belief, but that all men shall be free to profess, and by argument to maintain, their opinion in matters of religion.

In New England, however, the descendants of the Puritans continued tax support of the Congregational Church and allowed only Protestants to vote. In addition, Roman Catholics could not hold office in five states, and Jews were barred from office in nine.

Although states discriminated against their residents on the basis of race, sex, religion, and economic standing, most state constitutions included bills of rights spelling out the "unalienable rights" that government must recognize and protect. State bills of rights guaranteed trial by jury, freedom of the press, and other rights to be protected against tyranny.

The Articles of Confederation

When the Revolution began, the Second Continental Congress simply assumed most functions of a central government, such as appointing army officers and conducting diplomacy, even though it had no legal basis to exercise such powers. While the individual states were drafting their constitutions, Congress developed a plan to unite the states and establish its own legal authority. In 1777 Congress completed the document, called the Articles of Confederation, and proposed that it go into effect only after every state had approved it.

Not until 1781, however, did all the states **ratify**, or agree to, the Articles of Confederation. The main reason for delay was that several states claimed large tracts of western land. Based mainly on colonial charters that had granted land "from sea to sea," these claims often overlapped, causing confusion and conflict. In addition, the six states without western land claims, led by Maryland, argued that the West should become **public land**, or land belonging to the national government. Maryland refused to ratify the Articles

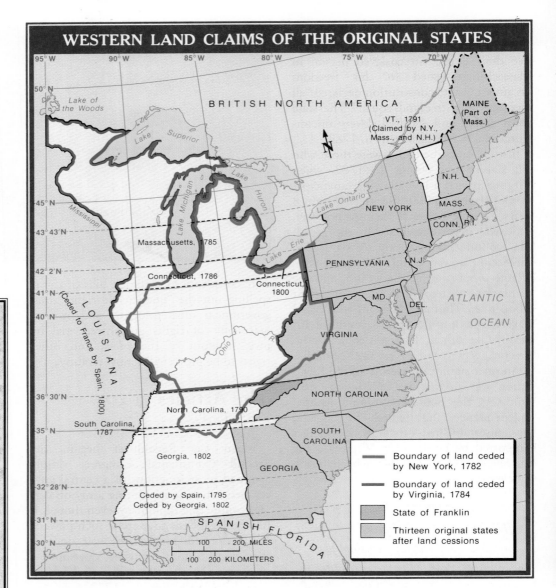

WESTERN LAND CLAIMS OF THE ORIGINAL STATES

Legend:
- Boundary of land ceded by New York, 1782
- Boundary of land ceded by Virginia, 1784
- State of Franklin
- Thirteen original states after land cessions

Examining Maps *States without western land claims feared that states with western lands would expand to become so rich and powerful that they would dominate any central government. Therefore, states without western lands refused to agree to a central government until the other states surrendered their land claims. Which state had the largest land claims in the West?*

Linking Across Time

THE EXECUTIVE BRANCH

American distrust of executive power exists even to this day.

Until the middle of the twentieth century, most state constitutions limited governors' terms to two years. Many states now allow four-year terms but limit the number of terms a governor may serve.

Until Franklin Roosevelt was elected to four terms as President, custom had restricted Presidents to two terms.

In 1951 the Constitution was amended to limit Presidents to two terms in office.

until this demand was met. But Virginia, which had huge claims—what is now Kentucky, West Virginia, Ohio, Indiana, Illinois, Michigan, and Wisconsin—refused to cooperate. Finally, in 1781, with Lord Cornwallis and the British army moving toward Virginia, the state agreed to give up its land claims. Maryland ratified the Articles, and at last the rebelling states were united.

Most members of the Continental Congress were quite wary of a strong central government. They took Benjamin Franklin's Albany Plan of Union as their guide and created what John Dickinson, the main author of the Articles, called a "firm league of friendship" among the states. Governing authority was placed in a **unicameral,** or one-house, Congress in which each state had one vote. Congress could wage war and make treaties—powers that were denied to the states. It could raise an army and navy, borrow money, establish a postal system, and manage native American affairs.

The states agreed to "give full faith and credit to the public acts of other states," such as wills and legal decisions, so that citizens of one state could do business in another. Each state also agreed to return escaped criminals and runaway slaves. There was freedom of movement across state lines. No passports were required for travelers from one state to another, and there were no barriers to immigration. Finally, the states agreed to settle their disputes by arbitration rather than by war.

Despite these features, the national government under the Articles proved too weak to operate effectively. There was no executive branch to carry out laws, and no federal courts existed to interpret them. Executive power was divided among several congressional committees. Two important functions, both related to the dispute with Great Britain, were denied to Congress—the power to tax and the power to regulate commerce. Having thrown off their British masters, the states did not intend to put themselves under another.

Unable to collect taxes, Congress had to depend on the generosity of the states for its income—"government by supplication," or begging, as one frustrated member observed. Between 1781 and 1789, however, the states gave Congress only about one-sixth of the funds it requested. Without money or real power over the states, the Confederation Congress commanded so little respect that its members often did not bother to attend sessions. In 1783 it was difficult even to convene enough members to ratify the treaty ending the Revolutionary War. That same year, the threats of a few hundred unpaid soldiers drove Congress out of Philadelphia. For a time it moved from city to city, like a company of actors, finally settling in New York. Washington called Congress "a shadow without substance." He told John Jay, the Confederation's chief diplomat, that he feared for the future of the nation.

Section One Review

SUMMARY

After the Revolution, the now independent states established new governments. Bills of rights in each state guaranteed trial by jury, religious freedom, and freedom of the press. Universal liberty was not granted since many new governments did not abolish slavery. Although the Articles of Confederation created a central government to deal with national and international matters, real power rested with the states that maintained authority to tax, regulate interstate commerce, and coin money. The inability of the Confederation government to provide strong leadership emphasized its weakness both at home and abroad.

CHECKING FOR UNDERSTANDING

1. **Identify** Articles of Confederation, Confederation Congress

2. **Define** bicameral, veto, franchise, emancipation, disestablished, ratify, public land, unicameral

3. **Explain** why the newly formed states made major changes in their executive branches.

4. **Describe** the positive and negative features of the Articles of Confederation.

THINKING CRITICALLY

5. **Expressing Viewpoints** Imagine that you live in the new United States after the Revolution. Based on your own sex, race, and religion, tell to what extent the Revolution has brought about equality for you.

CONNECTIONS: HISTORY AND RELIGION

6. **Determining Consequences** Churches are supported by donations from their members. What difference did it make that the Church of England was supported by taxes paid by all?

The Confederation Government

They [the difficulties of the United States] exhibit a melancholy proof of what our transatlantic foe has predicted; and of another thing, perhaps, which is still more to be regretted, . . . that mankind, when left to themselves, are unfit for their own government. I am mortified beyond expression when I view the clouds that have spread over the brightest morn that ever dawned on any country.

—GEORGE WASHINGTON
Letter to Henry Lee, 1786

Section Focus

The United States under the Articles of Confederation was an unstable nation. America expanded westward, but it continued to have problems with other nations. There was constant bickering among the states and many groups in society were discontented.

Objectives

After studying this section, you should be able to:
- Discuss the problems between the United States and other nations.
- Explain the process of settling the West.
- Identify the domestic problems of the new nation.

One of the blessings of independence predicted by Thomas Paine in *Common Sense* was that America would at last be free of European rivalries that had dragged the colonies into war. Even before the Treaty of Paris was ratified, the Confederation Congress resolved that "the true interest of these states requires that they should be as little as possible entangled in the politics and controversies of European nations." Yet total isolation from Europe was impossible. The prosperity of the United States depended, as before the Revolution, on trade with European nations and their colonies. Satisfactory trading arrangements required that the United States make commercial treaties with those nations. There also were problems with the Spanish in Florida and New Orleans to the south, and with the British in the north. These, too, could be settled only by diplomacy.

Foreign Relations

Predictably, the United States did not enjoy good relations with its recent foe, Great Britain. The British agreed to receive John Adams as minister from the United States, even though he had been a prominent rebel during the war. They refused, however, to send a minister to the United States, explaining that they did not know whether to send 1 or 13.

Neither country carried out the terms of the Treaty of Paris. The United States had agreed that British creditors could recover prewar debts by suing in American courts, and that Congress would ask the states to cease persecution of Loyalists. But when British merchants sued in state courts, unfriendly judges and juries usually sided with American debtors. The states also ignored Congress and continued to treat Loyalists harshly, subjecting them to confiscation of property, exile, and even lynching. The British government used these treaty violations as an excuse to remain in northern forts they had agreed to abandon. These posts were the centers

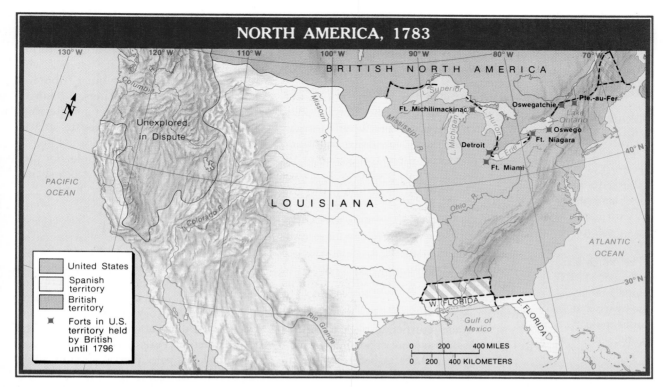

NORTH AMERICA, 1783

BRITISH NORTH AMERICA

Unexplored, in Dispute

PACIFIC OCEAN

LOUISIANA

ATLANTIC OCEAN

Ft. Michilimackinac
Oswegatchie
Pte.-au-Fer
Detroit
Oswego
Ft. Niagara
Ft. Miami

W. FLORIDA
E. FLORIDA
Gulf of Mexico

United States
Spanish territory
British territory
Forts in U.S. territory held by British until 1796

0   200   400 MILES
0   200   400 KILOMETERS

Examining Maps *The Treaty of Paris in 1783 established the boundaries of the new United States. The newly independent nation shared the North American continent with British territory to the north and Spanish territory to the west and south. What boundary dispute did the United States have with Spain after the Treaty of Paris?*

of a million-dollar annual fur trade with the Indians that Great Britain was determined to keep.

American trade suffered because the former colonies now lay outside the British Empire. American tobacco and naval stores no longer enjoyed a preferred position in British markets. American ships were banned from the British West Indies, and they were allowed to enter English ports only with the products of their home states—a ship from Massachusetts could not carry New York furs or North Carolina turpentine to London. When the United States tried to negotiate a trade treaty, Great Britain showed little desire to grant economic privileges to its former colonies.

Difficulties with Spain during the Confederation period were as serious as those with Great Britain. The Spanish were unhappy about the vast western lands the United States acquired in the Treaty of Paris, fearing that the future expansion of

the United States would threaten the Spanish empire in America. Spain insisted that the southern boundary of the United States was not the border described in the Treaty of Paris, but a line nearly 100 miles to the north. To protect its claims, Spain formed alliances with the Cherokee, Creek, and Chickasaw Indians and incited them against American settlers in the disputed territory. They also found American citizens who were willing, for a price, to act as Spanish secret agents.

By controlling the mouth of the Mississippi River, Spain also was able to threaten western trade. Bulky goods from the West—lumber, grain, and deerskins—could not be easily carried over the mountains to the east coast, but had to float down the Ohio and Mississippi rivers on rafts and flatboats. Westerners wanted the **right of deposit** at New Orleans—that is, permission to put goods ashore for transfer to ocean-going ships without paying duties. When Spain refused, westerners

The Land Ordinance of 1785 established a system of land survey and settlement that we still use today.

The Northwest Ordinance of 1787 created a procedure by which territories could become self-governing and achieve equal status with the founding states. Thirty-seven states have entered the Union through this procedure, each of them the equal of the thirteen original states.

If the British Parliament had adopted this system before 1776, history might have been different.

asked Congress for a treaty with Spain that would grant free navigation of the Mississippi River. Although a treaty was proposed, it paid no attention to western interests.

Relations with France were not entirely happy either. During the Revolutionary War, French loans helped keep American armies in the field. Now rising debt interest on loans and the extravagance of the court created serious problems in France. Hoping to stave off bankruptcy, the government introduced reforms and universal land taxes. The French were also disappointed that few commercial opportunities resulted from American independence. Benjamin Franklin had predicted that with the end of British trade regulations, American commerce would be largely transferred to France. But, in general, postwar trade returned to old patterns. By 1789 the British were exporting as much to the United States as before, while the French share of the American market increased only slightly.

The most humiliating foreign relations problem for the nation was its treatment by the Barbary Pirates. Four North African states—Morocco, Tunis, Tripoli, and Algiers—made a practice of capturing the ships and crews of nations who refused to pay them an annual **tribute**, a payment to sail in their waters. No longer protected by the British fleet and treasury, American ships were subject to attack. Having neither funds for tribute nor a fleet for defense, Congress could not prevent American commerce from being driven out of the Mediterranean Sea.

Settling the West

Until the end of the 1800s, "the West" was not a specific geographic region of the United States. Instead, it was a term for the next area of settlement, as pioneers invaded the territory of native Americans and moved them off the land. During the Confederation period, the West lay just beyond the Appalachian Mountains. Only three roads connected this region with the east coast. Yet so many settlers crossed the mountains between 1780 and 1790 that the population grew from 2,000 to

Examining Fine Art *In this painting by George Caleb Bingham, Daniel Boone leads pioneers west into Kentucky. Who was living on the land settled by these pioneers?*

100,000. Congress was powerless to meet these westerners' needs. It could not dislodge the British from their forts in the north or persuade Spain to grant the right of deposit in the south. It could prevent neither the Spanish nor the British from arming the Indians against western pioneers. Without money, Congress could neither purchase Indian land nor provide troops to protect settlers.

Westerners had other grievances with the national government as well. Many resented that eastern speculators held large tracts of western land. In 1785 a convention of Kentucky settlers declared:

…To grant any Person a larger quantity of land than he designs…to seat himself or his Family on, is a greevance, Because it is subversive of the fundamental Principles of a free republican Government to allow any individual or Company or Body of Men to possess such large tracts of Country in their own right as may at a future Day give them undue influence.

In 1784, after making a journey to the West, George Washington reported that the region was hanging to the Confederation by a thread. In what is now Tennessee, settlers created a government called the State of Franklin, paying their governor in whiskey and deerskins. Unable to obtain statehood from Congress, some Tennessee leaders considered **seceding**, or withdrawing, from the Union. Settlers in the Kentucky territory also talked of secession.

The Confederation Congress was alarmed about the problems some westerners were causing in its territories. To protect against "uninformed, and perhaps licentious people, as the greater part of those who go there are," its president urged "that a strong toned government exist" in the West. Congress responded with two laws that established a precedent for the future growth of the nation.

Life of the Times

HOME REMEDIES

There were few medical doctors in the thinly settled West. Even if medical help had been available, recovery from sickness and disease in the early nineteenth century was often more a matter of chance than scientific treatment. In an age before germs and proper sanitation were understood, home remedies for illness became an everyday, and perhaps necessary, part of pioneer life. While some folk remedies, such as herbal teas, might have had positive effects, others cures could make the patient worse. Consider these examples.

For venomous snakebite, a part of the reptile that inflicted the wound was placed on top of the incision. This, it was thought, would draw out the poison.

Mumps were treated by rubbing the afflicted person's spine with garlic.

One cure for measles was to make a warm broth of water and sheep dung. The patient sipped the broth until recovery.

Indigestion was a common problem. A mixture of Cayenne pepper and alcohol applied to the stomach supposedly spelled relief.

Worms in children could be treated by boiling sage in milk, turning it to whey with vinegar or alum, then having the child drink it. If the worms did not harden in the stomach, the child would live.

Some of the best cures were learned from the native Americans, who used native plants in pastes and teas.

Determined not to repeat the problems in Kentucky and Tennessee—and also to raise money—Congress passed the Land Ordinance of 1785. This law provided a more orderly method for settling public land north of the Ohio River. The land would be surveyed and divided into townships six miles square. Every township was to contain 36 sections of one square mile, 640 acres, each. The land would sell for $1 per acre. To attract land speculators, the law required that buyers take at least one whole section. Speculators could divide their sections into smaller rectangular tracts and sell them to settlers at a profit. The ordinance also provided the first federal subsidy to education. Proceeds from the sale of Section 16 in each township had to be used to establish public schools.

To provide for "strong toned government," Congress passed the Northwest Ordinance of 1787. The region bounded by the Ohio River, the Great Lakes, and the Mississippi River was to be divided into not fewer than three territories nor more than five. Whenever 5,000 adult male citizens settled in a territory, they could set up a territorial government modeled on a British royal colony. The settlers would elect a territorial legislature. The national government appointed and paid judges and a territorial governor so that the territorial legislature could not control them.

Although Congress was trying to govern its western territories as tightly as Great Britain had tried to control the colonies, the Northwest Ordinance provided a democratic model for national expansion that has been followed ever since. When the population of a territory reached 60,000, its people could organize a new state and apply for admission to the Union as the equal of the other states. Never before had a nation promised political equality to its colonies or set up a procedure to carry out such a promise.

The Northwest Ordinance also extended into the territories personal rights guaranteed in the constitutions of the original 13 states, such as freedom of religion, speech, and assembly. Perhaps more importantly, it prohibited slavery north of the Ohio River, an act that had a lasting

Examining Maps *In the Southern colonies, persons granted land went out to select the best land they could find, resulting in scattered settlement and conflicting claims. So for the northwest, Congress patterned the Land Ordinance of 1785 after New England's practice of granting land only after it had been surveyed, a system that resulted in more orderly development. What states came out of the Northwest Territory?*

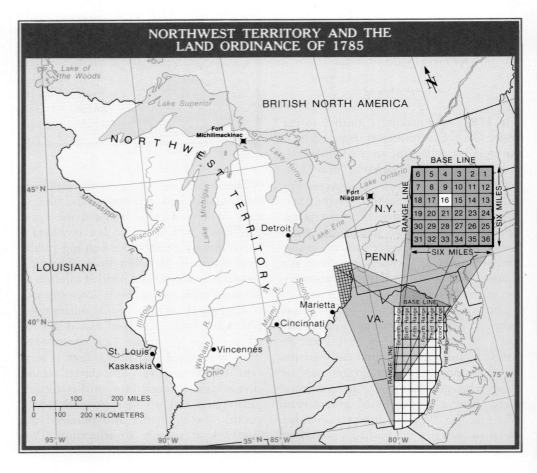

Examining Illustrations *Jacobb Shattucks and Daniel Shays led the farmers' rebellion in western Massachusetts. What grievances did these rebelling farmers have?*

effect on the political geography and history of the United States.

Disputes Among the States

While the Confederation Congress was providing for stability in the West, the eastern part of the nation was moving closer to crisis as the states engaged in disputes with one another. There were even struggles between groups within some states. These difficulties resulted from suspicion and rivalry, from the postwar **depression**—or economic slowdown—, and from the weak central government.

Serious conflicts erupted over territory as states engaged in boundary disputes. For example, parts of present-day Vermont were claimed by New York, New Hampshire, and Massachusetts. A conflict between Connecticut and Pennsylvania almost resulted in war. In the spring of 1784, Connecticut settlers living in the disputed territory were attacked and driven out by the Pennsylvania militia.

Because Congress was powerless to regulate commerce, each state passed laws taxing goods from its neighbors. New York taxed firewood from Connecticut and cabbage from New Jersey. New Jersey retaliated by charging New York for a harbor lighthouse on the New Jersey side of the Hudson River. Virginia taxed Pennsylvania farmers who shipped wheat through the state to North Carolinian customers.

When the Continentals issued during the Revolution lost their value, there was no national **currency,** or paper money. Since there was not much specie in the country

Examining Artifacts
Some states printed so much paper money that it became virtually worthless. Rhode Island, whose currency is shown here, was so notorious for this practice that it was nicknamed "Rogues Island." Why did states print paper money?

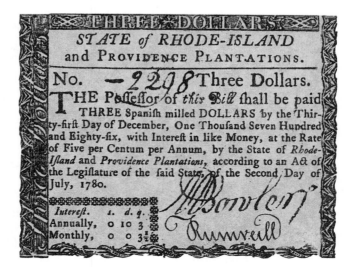

either, each state decided to print its own paper money. Because the value of these paper notes differed from state to state, they often were not accepted as payment outside the states issuing them. This situation presented yet another obstacle to trade.

In Massachusetts the economic situation became explosive. Unable to pay their debts, farmers in western Massachusetts were jailed or had their property seized by the courts. Having recently fought the British, these farmers felt the new government was just another variety of tyranny. In September 1786, led by former Continental Army captain Daniel Shays, they closed the courts in 2 Massachusetts counties and stopped land confiscations. In early 1787, wearing his faded blue Continental Army uniform, Shays led 1,000 men against the Springfield arsenal to get more guns. Only through donations from wealthy merchants was the state able to raise a militia force strong enough to meet Shays at Springfield.

Although his rag-tag band was easily defeated by the militia, Shays's Rebellion caused great alarm throughout the United States, and people who believed in orderly government were fearful. Most of the nation's leaders shared the horror of George Washington, who shared his concern in a letter to his friend Henry Lee:

———— ·◦◦◦· ————

Let us have a government by which our lives, liberties, and properties will be secured, or let us know the worst at once.... To be more exposed in the eyes of the world, and more contemptible than we already are, is hardly possible.... Let the reins of government then be braced and held with a steady hand....

———— ·◦◦◦· ————

In 1787, as the young nation began its sixth year under the Articles of Confederation, it seemed that the prophecies of those who said the United States could not form an effective system of government were coming true.

Section Two Review

SUMMARY

The United States suffered a number of humiliating experiences under the Articles of Confederation that pointed to the need for a stronger central government. Britain refused to give up northern trading posts and would not negotiate a commercial treaty with its former colonies. Spain formed alliances with the Indians and refused to allow right of deposit at New Orleans. States quarreled with each other over commerce and boundaries. A change was needed if the nation was to survive.

CHECKING FOR UNDERSTANDING

1. **Identify** John Adams, Cherokee, New Orleans, Barbary Pirates

2. **Define** right of deposit, tribute, secede, depression, currency

3. **Account for** the decrease in American trade with Great Britain after 1783.

4. **Describe** the difficulty between the United States and Spain over right of deposit at New Orleans.

5. **Explain** the problems that arose among the states during the Confederation period.

6. **Cite** the main provisions of the Land Ordinance of 1785 and the Northwest Ordinance of 1787.

7. **Specify** the reasons for Shays's Rebellion and show how it led to the Constitutional Convention.

THINKING CRITICALLY

8. **Contrasting Ideas** This period saw the beginnings of a "sectional" awareness within the new United States. Contrast the economic interests in various areas of the country at this time.

LINKING PAST AND PRESENT

9. **Recognizing Similarities** What problems does the federal government face today that are similar to those the Confederation government faced?

Toward a New Constitution

SETTING THE SCENE

We, the People of the United States, in Order to form a more perfect Union, establish Justice, insure domestic Tranquility, provide for the common defence, promote the general Welfare, and secure the Blessings of Liberty to ourselves and our Posterity, do ordain and establish this Constitution for the United States of America.

—PREAMBLE
Constitution of the United States, 1787

Section Focus

As the nation struggled, some Americans became convinced that the Articles of Confederation were an inadequate framework for government. One proposed solution was to strengthen them, and a meeting was called for that purpose. Out of that meeting came a new constitution.

Objectives

After studying this section, you should be able to:

• Explain how each of the conflicts at the Philadelphia Convention was resolved.
• Explain how the Constitution corrected the weaknesses of the Confederation government.

After the war, George Washington had retired to Mount Vernon, his Virginia estate on the Potomac River. But concern about the nation's problems moved him to action once again. In 1785 he invited representatives of Virginia and Maryland to Mount Vernon to discuss their differences.

At this meeting the two groups agreed on joint control of currencies, import duties, and navigation on the Potomac River and Chesapeake Bay. This success inspired Maryland and Virginia to invite all states to meet at Annapolis, Maryland, to discuss common problems.

When the Annapolis Convention met in September 1786, delegates from only five states were present, so they could do little. Included in this group, however, was Alexander Hamilton of New York, an outspoken supporter of a strong national government. With Shays and his followers threatening the government of Massachusetts, Hamilton persuaded the delegates to propose another convention. Its purpose would be to regulate commerce and to propose measures making the national government more effective. Congress responded by calling a meeting of the states in Philadelphia, "for the sole and express purpose of revising the Articles of Confederation."

The Philadelphia Convention

The date set for the Philadelphia Convention was May 14, 1787, but it was May 24 before enough delegates arrived to do business. Eventually 12 of the 13 states were represented, although some delegates did not arrive until midsummer.

The 55 delegates included many of the most able political leaders in the United States. Most were lawyers or judges; 21 had college degrees, a high number in a time when few people had any formal education. Nearly all the delegates had practical experience in government. Most had helped write their state constitutions. More than half had sat in the Continental Congress or the Confederation Congress and so had seen the consequences of a weak central government.

Several important leaders of the Revolution were missing. Thomas Jefferson, John Adams, and Thomas Paine were in Europe. Massachusetts did not send Samuel Adams or John Hancock. Patrick Henry of Virginia, who opposed a strong national government, was selected but refused to attend because he "smelled a rat." Despite the absence of such notables, the gathering at Philadelphia brought together one of the greatest combinations of intelligence, knowledge, and ability in American history. "An assembly of demigods," Jefferson called them.

Franklin, the oldest delegate at 81, was in poor health and did not attend regularly. Washington was elected to preside over the proceedings, so, like Franklin, his participation in the discussions was limited. But they were the best-known Americans of their time and their presence gave the convention great prestige. The house guest of a Pennsylvania delegate, Washington walked every day to the

AMERICAN PORTRAITS

THOMAS JEFFERSON
1743-1826

The young Virginia lawyer first came to public attention in 1774 as a political thinker and writer when he penned a pamphlet in defense of colonial rights. Jefferson acquired his lifelong love of books on science, philosophy, and literature from his childhood teachers, and as a student at William and Mary College.

Jefferson's effectiveness as a writer went way beyond his literary style. His writings reflected careful reading and study. Jefferson loved ideas—as well as book collecting. His enormous library later became the basis of the Library of Congress. As minister to France from 1785 to 1789, he shipped nearly 200 volumes to his good friend James Madison. These books—mostly works on political theory—had a profound impact on Madison's thinking about a new government for the United States.

convention sessions. Most others were less conscientious. Rarely were more than 30 in attendance at any one time.

Despite a late start and poor attendance, the delegates worked hard. They were in session almost every day for sixteen weeks, usually both morning and afternoon. It was agreed that the meetings would be private, and members were forbidden to let the public know the content of the debates. Although this secrecy aroused public suspicion, it made compromise easier by shielding the delegates from outside political pressures.

James Madison, a 36-year-old Virginian, was the first delegate to arrive at the convention, and he was the most prepared. He came to Philadelphia with a draft of a completely new framework of government. As soon as the convention was ready for business, Virginia governor Edmund Randolph immediately rose and presented Madison's proposal, known as the Virginia Plan. This document became the basis for discussion in the convention; it is the foundation for the Constitution of the United States.

Conflicts and Compromises

Although almost all delegates at the convention agreed that the Articles were hopelessly weak, there were two serious conflicts that proved difficult to resolve. Differences developed between large states and small states over representation in Congress, and between northern and southern states over economic issues and the institution of slavery.

The dispute between large and small states nearly broke up the convention. The large states demanded that each state be represented by population in the bicameral Congress Madison had proposed. By what possible right, they asked, should Delaware's 59,000 inhabitants have equality with Virginia's 692,000? The small states insisted that they would never give up the equal power they enjoyed under the Articles of Confederation to be swallowed up by the large states. William Paterson of New Jersey said his state would "rather submit to a monarch, to a despot, than to

Examining Fine Art *This portrait of James Madison was painted about the time of the Philadelphia Convention. What contribution did Madison make to the Constitution?*

representation in the lower house of Congress would be based on population; in the upper house each state would have an equal vote. The delegates' ability to resolve this dispute increased their confidence in compromise as the key to a successful convention. For this reason, the Constitution that emerged from Philadelphia has been called a "bundle of compromises." Compromise can be found in nearly every section of the document.

A dispute arose between the commercial interests of the North and the plantation interests of the South. Southerners wanted to count slaves to determine representation to Congress but not for direct taxation. The North wanted to count slaves for taxation but not for representation. A "three-fifths compromise" established that five slaves would be equal to three free persons for both representation and taxation.

South Carolina and Georgia, afraid that a strong national government might act against slavery, insisted that the Constitution forbid interference with the slave trade. The delegates agreed that for 20 years the national government would not prevent the importation of slaves nor charge an import duty of more than ten dollars a head.

Another dispute between North and South concerned commerce. Northern merchants and shippers wanted a government with power to protect shipping from foreign competition. Southern planters, fearing that this would increase the cost of

such a fate." He presented an alternative proposal, known as the New Jersey Plan, which would have merely strengthened the Articles of Confederation.

Disagreement also arose over the structure of the new government. Large-state delegates generally favored Madison's plan for a national government with separate executive, legislative, and judicial branches and with the states subordinate to the national government. Most small-state delegates supported the New Jersey Plan, which continued the Confederation and left the states supreme.

For two weeks, bitter debate raged over these differences. There seemed no middle ground between the large and the small states. Washington wrote a friend that he had lost all hope for the convention and regretted having anything to do with it. Franklin proposed that each session be opened with prayer, to ask divine guidance in finding an acceptable compromise.

The deadlock was broken when the delegates took a day off to celebrate the Fourth of July. During the recess, a committee worked out what became known as the "Great Compromise." According to this agreement, state

Examining Photographs
George Washington sat at this platform desk (center) in Philadelphia's Independence Hall to preside over the Constitutional Convention. Why was his presence so important?

Connections

H I S T O R Y   A N D   S C I E N C E

ASTRONOMY AND THE CONSTITUTION

Like most delegates to the Constitutional Convention, James Madison was greatly influenced by the ideas of the European Enlightenment. Consequently, he believed that there were "natural laws" that governed human behavior, much like the laws that governed the physical universe.

Madison was much impressed by an intricate working model of the solar system, an orrery (AWR uh ree), built in 1767 by Philadelphia astronomer David Rittenhouse. Rittenhouse used this ingenious device to illustrate the theories of Isaac Newton. Newton believed that the solar system was held in place by a balance between centrifugal force and the power of gravity.

Just as the solar system was stabilized by equal but opposing forces, Madison reasoned, so might a stable government result from a balance of political powers. Thus Madison found in the theories of Isaac Newton support for federalism—a strong national government balanced by the power of the states.

Rittenhouse's Orrery

★ ★ ★ ★ ★ ★ ★ ★ ★ ★

MAKING THE SCIENCE CONNECTION

1. What was Rittenhouse's orrery supposed to demonstrate?

2. How did Newtonian theory influence Madison?

LINKING PAST AND PRESENT

3. What other examples of balances in power are there in national government today?

★ ★ ★ ★ ★ ★ ★ ★ ★ ★

shipping their products abroad, insisted that a two-thirds vote in both houses of Congress be required to pass such laws, a provision that would have given the South veto power over such legislation. Southerners also feared that the new government would raise money by placing duties on exports such as tobacco, creating an unfair tax burden on their section. Here too, a compromise was arranged. Trade laws might be passed by a simple majority in Congress, but the national government was forbidden to tax exports.

These compromises allowed the delegates to complete their two essential tasks: to give the national government more power and to provide a framework for a workable government. The delegates granted to the central government the powers it had needed most under the Articles of Confederation. The new government could levy and collect taxes, provided such taxes were "uniform throughout the United States." Thus it would be able to pay its own way rather than begging from the states. It could regulate commerce with foreign nations and between the states. Thus it could write and enforce commercial treaties that would increase foreign trade, and it could keep trade among the states free of barriers. It could coin money and regulate its value, so there could be a national standard of money instead of state currencies with differing values.

Many of the other powers granted the central government were not new but were simply carried over from the Articles of Confederation. For example, the Articles had granted power to Congress to raise armies and navies and borrow money. But because the Confederation Congress could not raise money by taxation, such powers existed only on paper. The new national government could carry out all the powers given to it.

Although the greatest disputes at the convention were over the structure and powers of the legislative branch, the delegates also disagreed about the executive branch. Everyone at the convention agreed on the need for an executive branch to operate the government, but some delegates favored a group executive, so that no one individual could become too powerful. However, the executive committees of the Confederation Congress had not worked out well, and Hamilton's proposal for a single executive chosen by Congress for life was not acceptable either. It smacked too much of monarchy. In the final weeks of the convention two more compromises were achieved. A single executive would serve a four-year term. This person would not be chosen directly by the people, but by special electors named by the legislature of each state.

As the long hot summer drew to a close, the exhausted delegates merely roughed out the framework of the judicial branch. In so doing, they created only a Supreme Court and empowered the new government to create "such inferior Courts as the Congress may from time to time ordain and establish."

Their work concluded, the delegates reviewed their efforts. No one was completely happy with the final plan, but most agreed it was a vast improvement on the Articles they hoped it would replace. Madison recorded the reaction of the United States' most eminent citizen, Benjamin Franklin:

Doctor Franklin, looking toward the President's chair, at the back of which a rising sun happened to be painted... "I have," said he, "often and often in the course of the Session...looked at that [sun] behind the President without being able to tell whether it was rising or setting; but now, at length I have the happiness to know it is a rising and not a setting Sun.

SUMMARY

Once the delegates convened in Philadelphia in 1787, they recognized that they could not create an effective government merely by revising the Articles of Confederation. If the nation were to continue, a union would have to be forged based on shared powers between the states and the central government. Although there was disagreement over representation in Congress, how slaves were to be counted, methods of taxation, and the nature of the chief executive, the Framers overcame their differences and worked out compromises that resulted in the Constitution.

CHECKING FOR UNDERSTANDING

1. **Identify** Annapolis Convention, Alexander Hamilton, Philadelphia Convention, James Madison, Virginia Plan, New Jersey Plan

2. **Cite** the reasons for and results of the Annapolis Convention.

3. **Detail** the key features of the Virginia and New Jersey Plans.

4. **Describe** the key compromises that were made concerning representation, slavery, and the executive branch.

5. **Outline** the powers granted to the central government under the Constitution that it did not have under the Articles of Confederation.

THINKING CRITICALLY

6. **Inferring Causes** Why did the delegates at the Philadelphia Convention think it best to keep their meetings secret?

LINKING PAST AND PRESENT

7. **Recognizing Parallels** Delegates at the Constitutional Convention compromised on several issues. Why does compromise continue to be important today in government?

★ ★ ★ ★ ★ ★ ★ ★ ★ ★ ★ ★ ★ ★ ★ ★ ★ ★ ★

The Ratification Struggle

SETTING THE SCENE

It seems to have been reserved to the people of this country, by their conduct and example, to decide the important question, whether societies of men are really capable or not of establishing good government from reflection and choice, or whether they are forever destined to depend for their political constitutions on accident and force.

—ALEXANDER HAMILTON
The Federalist, No.1, 1787

Section Focus

Although the Constitution was complete, the delegates' work was not. They now faced another challenging task—convincing the American people to accept the new government. As details of the Constitution became public, they aroused great controversy throughout the nation. Approval was by no means assured.

Objectives

After studying this section, you should be able to:
• Explain the arguments for and against the new Constitution.
• List the advantages of the Federalists in the campaign for ratification.

O n September 17, 1787, after four months of exhausting effort, the delegates to the Constitutional Convention gathered one last time to sign their work. Of the 55 who had come to Philadelphia that spring, 42 were still on hand, and all but three agreed to sign the document. Then the delegates adjourned to a nearby tavern for a farewell dinner before beginning their journeys home to campaign for ratification.

The Constitution Opposed

The Framers of the Constitution anticipated that ratification would be difficult. Rhode Island, which had boycotted the convention, certainly would not approve. So it seemed foolish to insist on the unanimous approval required to amend the Articles. Instead, the Constitution provided that "the ratification of nine States shall be sufficient for the establishment of this Constitution."

To get even nine states to ratify the Constitution was no small task. Some states objected to surrendering their power and independence to the national government. Mercy Otis Warren, an influential political writer, observed:

Not one legislature in the United States had any idea when they sent delegates to the convention at Philadelphia that it would destroy their state governments and offer them a consolidated system instead.

Nor were supporters of states' rights pleased that the new Constitution bypassed state governments in the ratification process. Ratification was to be decided by special conventions to be called in each state, a process implementing the idea expressed in the Declaration of Independence that governments "derive their just powers from the consent of the governed."

Even among the "governed," however, opposition was strong. Debtors and paper-money advocates were opposed to any plan forcing full payment of debts and restoring sound currency. There was certainly suspicion of a powerful central government. Why revolt from Great Britain, people asked, simply to fall under a new kind of tyranny? Popular leaders, such as John Hancock and Samuel Adams in Massachusetts, opposed it. In Virginia, Patrick Henry warned:

This proposal of altering our federal government is of a most alarming nature....you ought to be extremely cautious, watchful, jealous of your liberty; for instead of securing your rights, you may lose them forever... a wrong step made now will plunge us into misery, and our republic will be lost.

Those who favored the new plan of government called themselves "Federalists." They took this name to emphasize that the Constitution was based on the principle of **federalism**, a system in which power is divided between a central government and regional governments, and to remind Americans that the states would retain many of their powers. Of course, those who opposed the Constitution were "federalists" too, because the league of states created by the Articles also was based on federalism. The real issue was whether the national government or the state governments would be supreme. By taking the name "Federalists," however, the supporters of the Constitution caused their opponents to be tagged with the negative-sounding label "Anti-Federalists."

The Ratification Campaign

Although the two sides were almost equally divided, several factors worked against the Anti-Federalists. Their campaign was a negative one. They attacked almost everything about the Constitution, complaining that the central government had too much power, that there was no mention of God in the document, and that it failed to protect basic liberties such as freedom of speech and religion. But the Anti-Federalists had nothing to offer other than to continue with the hapless Articles of Confederation or to call a new constitutional convention.

The Federalists, on the other hand, presented a definite program to meet the difficulties facing the nation. They promised that if the Constitution were ratified, **amendments,** or additions and changes, would be made to provide a Bill of Rights to protect the people.

The Federalists also made better use of communications. They were supported by most of the nation's newspapers. They presented their case more convincingly in sermons, pamphlets, and debates in state conventions.

The Federalists' campaign for ratification produced one of the finest pieces of political writing in the history of the world, *The Federalist*—a collection of 85 essays written by Hamilton, Madison, and John Jay. Originally published as newspaper articles in the *New York Journal*, the essays explained in detail the importance of the Constitution to the success of the nation.

The Federalists succeeded in getting the Constitution ratified not merely because they were good writers and speakers, but also because the were politically shrewd. In states where strong opposition existed, they were able to outmaneuver their

Examining Political Cartoons *This 1788 cartoon celebrates Virginia and New York becoming the tenth and eleventh states to ratify the Constitution. When approval of only nine states was needed, why was the approval of Virginia and New York so important?*

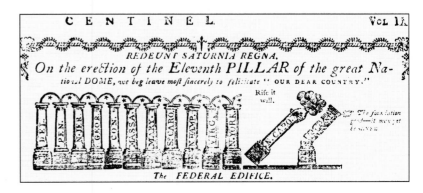

RATIFICATION OF THE CONSTITUTION		
State	**Date**	**Vote**
Delaware	Dec. 7, 1787	30–0
Pennsylvania	Dec. 12, 1787	46–23
New Jersey	Dec. 18, 1787	38–0
Georgia	Jan. 2, 1788	26–0
Connecticut	Jan. 9, 1788	128–40
Massachusetts	Feb. 6, 1788	187–168
Maryland	Apr. 28, 1788	63–11
South Carolina	May 23, 1788	149–73
New Hampshire	June 21, 1788	57–47
Virginia	June 25, 1788	89–79
New York	July 26, 1788	30–27
North Carolina	Nov. 21, 1789	194–77
Rhode Island	May 29, 1790	34–32

Examining Tables *The entire ratification process took more than two years, beginning with Delaware's approval and concluding with Rhode Island's. Why is it not surprising that Rhode Island was last to ratify?*

opponents. In Pennsylvania, the Federalists called the election to the state's ratifying convention before the Anti-Federalists had a chance to organize. In the Massachusetts ratifying convention, the Federalists used influential Anti-Federalist leader John Hancock to gain support for the Constitution. They suggested to Hancock that if the Constitution were ratified, he could be the first President of the United States. In New York, two-thirds of the State Convention were Anti-Federalists. But the persuasiveness of John Jay and the news that ten states had already ratified convinced enough Anti-Federalists to change sides so that New York became the "eleventh pillar" of the new federal roof.

The vote in several key states was extremely close: in the Massachusetts ratifying convention 187 voted in favor of the Constitution, 168 opposed; in Virginia the vote was 89 to 79; and in New York 30 to 27. By July 1788, however, all the states except Rhode Island and North Carolina had ratified, and preparations were made to launch the new government without them.

Section Four Review

SUMMARY

Once the Framers of the Constitution had finished their work, the document had to be ratified by nine states to go into effect. Ratification was not assured. The Framers knew that state governments would not give up their powers willingly and designated that special conventions should carry out ratification. The population divided into Federalists, who supported a federal union with powers shared by states and the central government, and Anti-Federalists, who feared strong central government and believed essential powers should remain with the states. In the end, strong leadership and organization gave the advantage to the Federalists.

CHECKING FOR UNDERSTANDING

1. **Identify** Federalists, Anti-Federalists

2. **Define** federalism, amendments

3. **State** three reasons why some thought it would be difficult to ratify the Constitution.

4. **Distinguish** between the positions of the Federalists and the Anti-Federalists.

5. **Indicate** the advantages of the Federalists in the struggle for ratification.

THINKING CRITICALLY

6. **Making Inferences** Why would it have been considered significant when people such as John Hancock, Samuel Adams, and Patrick Henry opposed the new Constitution?

LINKING PAST AND PRESENT

7. **Recognizing Parallels** George Washington, Ben Franklin, and John Adams came out in favor of the Constitution and helped win popular support for its ratification. Today many causes are endorsed by famous people. Give some examples.

Study and Writing Skills

Taking Notes

A committee of delegates to the Second Continental Congress designed the Articles of Confederation. The committee members had heard Richard Henry Lee's original proposal of a confederation. No doubt, while they were listening to Lee, delegates dashed down notes about the plan and their opinions about it.

Explanation

Experts agree that one of the best ways to remember something is to write it down. *Taking notes*—writing down information in an orderly and brief form—not only helps you remember but it also makes your studying easier.

There are several styles of notetaking, but all clarify and put information in a logical order. When taking notes in class or as you are reading your text, it will help to keep in mind these guidelines:

- Identify the subject, and write it at the top of the page. In your text, for example, look for chapter or section headings.

- Be selective in what information you include in your notes. For example, anything your teacher writes on the chalkboard or shows you from a transparency should be included. If your teacher emphasizes a point or spends a considerable amount of time on a given topic, this is also a clue to its importance. Similarly, if your

textbook covers a single topic over several pages, take notes by seeking the topic sentences of paragraphs on the topic. Be certain to write down all words in bold type in your text.

Your major goal is to listen or read carefully, paying attention to the main ideas or key points. That way you won't be furiously writing down every word your

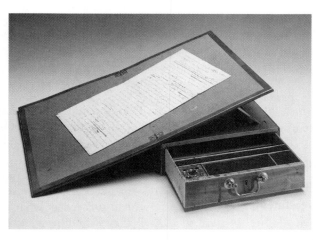

Lap desk invented by Thomas Jefferson

teacher says, including some trivial points, while you pass over the main theme. Your notes should consist of the main ideas and supporting details on the subject.

- Paraphrase the information. That is, put the information in your own words rather than trying to take it down word for word. That will make you think about what the author or speaker meant.

In order to save time, you might want to develop a personal "shorthand." For example, eliminate vowels from words: "develop"

becomes "dvlp". Use symbols, arrows, or rough drawings: "+" for "and." Practice your shorthand in all of your classes.

- Make sure your notes are legible and neat so that you will be able to understand them when you read them again.

Example

If you were taking study notes following the guidelines above while reading the subsection, "Foreign Relations," beginning on page 154, your notes may resemble the following:

Foreign Relations (undr Confed.)

G.B.—nt gd rel. w/U.S.; yes 2 J Adams as U.S. mnstr; no 2 G.B. mnstr 2 U.S.

U.S. + G.B. nt fllw Trty/Paris:

—U.S. judges pro Am dbtrs when G.B. crdtrs sued in ct.

—sts. treat Loy. badly

—G.B. stayed in frts N bec. U.S. nt fllw Trty (fur trade-$)

Am trde suffr:

1. no pref. pos. in G.B. mkt

2. Am shps ban'd fr. Br. W. Ind.

3. G.B.—no 2 trde trty

Practice

After you have carefully read Section 4, follow the general guidelines to note-taking and create shorthand notes for the subsection "The Ratification Campaign."

★ Chapter 6 Review ★

★ Summary

After the Revolution, the thirteen colonies became free and independent states, each with its own sovereignty, constitution, and elected officials. A weak central government was created with no executive, taxing power, or control over interstate commerce.

Postwar problems and bickering among the states emphasized the inadequacy of this arrangement. Before political anarchy and financial irresponsibility destroyed the ideals for which Americans had fought, a bold group of leaders met and drafted a new plan of government. States put aside jealousies and compromised on the crucial issues of representation and slavery. They added new executive and judicial branches of government. Nine states ratified the Constitution by July 1788. A new age had begun.

★ Using Vocabulary

Each of the following terms has a meaning that relates to government. Find the definition of each word and then write a sentence in which you give an example of its meaning.

bicameral	**franchise**
federalism	**veto**
ratify	**amendments**

★ Reviewing Facts

1. **Describe** the problems faced by the United States under the Articles of Confederation.
2. **List** reasons why England and Spain refused to negotiate trade treaties with the United States after the Revolution.
3. **Explain** why right of deposit at New Orleans was essential to western farmers.
4. **State** the main purposes for passage of the Land Ordinance of 1785 and the Northwest Ordinance of 1787.
5. **Explain** why the delegates' backgrounds at the Constitutional Convention were helpful.
6. **Identify** the disagreements that divided the delegates to the Constitutional Convention.
7. **Detail** why *The Federalist* helped win public support for the new Constitution.

★ Understanding Concepts

POLITICAL CONTROL

1. How were the political values of the newly independent states reflected in the form of government created in the Articles of Confederation?
2. Show how the changes made by the Framers of the Constitution preserved those same political values.

AUTHORITY

3. The states gave their legislatures a great deal of power after the war. Explain the view of authority that prompted them to do so.
4. Propose possible reasons why a distrust of strong central authority after the Revolutionary War gradually gave way to its acceptance at the Constitutional Convention.

★ Thinking Critically

1. **Analyzing Ideas** Explain why phrases such as "government by supplication" and "a shadow without substance" so well described the Confederation government.
2. **Formulating Alternatives** If Tennessee settlers had seceded from the Union and Shays's Rebellion had succeeded, what immediate effects do you think they would have had on Americans?
3. **Applying Concepts** Define the term *compromise* in your own words, and show how it can solve a problem between opposing points of view.
4. **Supporting an Argument** You are a Federalist trying to convince an audience to accept the new Constitution. Outline your speech, detailing the arguments you would use.

★ Writing About History

CAUSE AND EFFECT

Refer to the description of how to write a cause-and-effect essay in the History Writer's Handbook in the Appendix of this book. Your teacher will give you more specific instructions on the essay's length and the assignment's due date.

Imagine that you are an observer at the Constitutional Convention, listening to the delegates argue about how to set up a legislative branch. Record their various proposals and what effect each proposal would have.

★ Learning Cooperatively

In order for people to operate effectively in a free society, individuals must give up some personal freedoms and agree to live by rules that operate in the best interests of all citizens. Imagine that you are part of a group that is being sent to the moon in order to establish a colony there. Together, write a constitution by which you agree to be governed while you are living on the moon. Decide which portions of the United States Constitution will work for your new situation and what changes will need to be made to serve the best interests of your group.

★ Mastering Skills

ANALYZING PRIMARY AND SECONDARY SOURCES

Suppose your drivers' education teacher told you that it is acceptable to cross a double line. But later, as you study the driving laws in your state, you read that driving across double lines is a traffic violation. Which source should you believe—your drivers' education teacher or the book of traffic laws?

The laws themselves are a primary source. Your teacher, who must read the laws and then interprets them to the class, is a secondary source. Usually, a primary source is more reliable than a secondary source but not always. In this case, however, you should believe the book of traffic laws and not your teacher.

In written material a *primary source* is the original source of information, usually an original document or first-person account. Laws, contracts, diaries, autobiographies, and scripts are examples of primary sources. A *secondary source* is a secondhand account by someone who is retelling, interpreting, or summarizing the information provided in the primary source. Textbooks, brochures, lectures, nonfiction by historians, or any accounts that give information that was originally from another source are secondary sources.

Based on the definitions given above, you can determine whether any source of information that you consult is a primary source or a secondary source. The following tests will help you analyze either a primary source or a secondary source in order to determine its dependability, and to assess the accuracy of the information that it provides.

- If the material comes from a secondary source, determine if the author is qualified to interpret the primary source from which original information is drawn.

- For either a primary source or a secondary source, decide if the account has been influenced by emotion, opinion, exaggeration, or for some special purpose. Even authors of original sources can have reasons to distort the truth to suit their personal purposes.

- Look for good *documentation* of the primary or secondary source, that is, evidence or other information that supports the account given.

- Try to consult more than one primary or secondary source. If they agree, the account is more likely to be accurate.

- If possible, compare the information in a secondary source to the primary source on which the account is based.

Example The following examples demonstrate how these tests can be applied to analyzing primary and secondary sources:

1. You watch a TV documentary movie about Admiral Robert E. Peary's expedition to the North Pole. Later you read excerpts from his diary that seem to disagree with the information provided by the movie. *(The diary, a primary source, usually would be the more reliable source.)*

2. Your uncle insists that the limit on walleyes is seven in your state, but a game warden who spoke to your class, and a brochure the warden handed out, say the limit is six fish. *(Although all sources are secondary, the warden and the brochure are more reliable sources. Also two accounts say the limit is six fish, while only one source says the limit is seven fish.)*

Practice Review *The Constitution of the United States,* a primary source, and the information about the Constitution, a secondary source, in the Constitutional Handbook that follows. Determine if the primary source (Constitution) indicates that the secondary source (textbook) is accurate.

★ ★ ★ Unit 2 Digest ★ ★ ★

In a few short years, the United States went from 13 colonies to an independent nation. The path was marked by a revolution in which the colonists demonstrated to the world their belief in independence, individual rights, and democracy. These cherished values formed the basis for their Constitution, which would serve as the law of the land.

Chapter 4
The Road to Revolution

The road from colonies to nation was a gradual one that began with Parliament's attempt to control the colonies' foreign trade. The first efforts toward this goal were a series of laws, beginning in 1651, known as Trade and Navigation Acts. This legislation was intended to ultimately kill colonial competition. Most of these laws, however, were not enforced—in part because of the distance that separated Britain from the colonies and in part because the appointed revenue officers were lax in their duties.

Parliament's concern about colonial trade was part of a larger issue, the struggle between Britain and France over control of North America. In the final round, the French and Indian War, Britain emerged victorious after William Pitt became minister of war in 1758. With the Treaty of Paris in 1763, France was eliminated as a contender for power in North America.

Britain's victory brought it a host of new problems, among them a huge war debt and a question of how to administer their newly acquired territory. To solve the former problem, Parliament levied new taxes that shifted part of the financial burden onto the colonies. To solve the latter problem, Parliament passed the Proclamation of 1763, which forbid all settlement west of the Appalachians. The colonist's protested through petitions and representatives in London. They felt their rights as subjects of the Crown had been violated. As tensions grew, so did the means of protest. After the 1765 Stamp Act, the colonists staged boycotts, and sometimes became violent. In their challenge to British authority, the colonies discovered a sense of unity and patriotism and began to act together.

As time progressed the breach between Britain and the colonies gradually widened. Then, in 1773, colonists reacted to a monopoly granted to the British East India Tea company by throwing thousands of pounds of tea into the Boston Harbor. Parliament responded with the Coercive Acts, which the colonists dubbed the "Intolerable Acts."

King George III refused to compromise, arguing that the colonies must "submit or triumph." The colonists responded by calling the First Continental Congress and organizing volunteer armies. Soon fighting broke out between Massachusetts "minutemen" and British troops near Boston at Concord. News of the battle spread quickly and electrified the colonies. Although it would be another year before the colonies formally declared their independence, the American Revolution had begun.

Chapter 5
War for Independence

Most colonists were not ready for independence. They wanted to remain part of the British empire as long as they could govern themselves through their own legislatures. The British government, though, was inflexible and wanted to punish the rebels.

The move toward independence got a boost from Thomas Paine, a political philosopher who in January 1776 published the persuasive and widely read pamphlet, *Common Sense*. In it, Paine argued against monarchy in general, for separation from Britain, and appealed to the American belief that they were a select people.

The Patriots, supporters of separation, began to prevail. Beginning with delegates from North Carolina in April 1776, the colonies advised their delegates in Congress to vote for independence. The Declaration of Independence, drafted by Thomas Jefferson, formally notified the world on July 4 that the colonies were indeed independent.

Announcing their independence was not as challenging as maintaining it. Britain, unwilling to surrender its large territory in North America, dispatched perhaps the largest single military force ever sent from Europe to America. The success of these troops and short-term enlistments reduced George Washington's ill-prepared forces. Two early victories at Trenton and Princeton helped save the American cause.

The Americans faced a long struggle with a volunteer army and insufficient funds to pay for the war. The struggle was eased when France allied itself with the American cause following a major victory over British forces at Saratoga. Soon Spain and the Netherlands also entered the war against Britain.

Women courageously served the American war effort, acting as secret agents, raising money, and running farms and businesses while their husbands were away. A few women even fought in the ranks. African Americans and native Americans also served in the Revolutionary War; the former were more likely to support the Patriot army, and the latter, the British.

The fighting gradually moved from north to south. For three years, beginning in 1778, the main British forces did not suffer a defeat in the South. Then in 1780, British General Cornwallis surrendered at Yorktown, Virginia, marking the last significant battle of the war. The colonies were, at last, independent.

Chapter 6
A More Perfect Union

With independence, the colonies needed new constitutions to replace colonial charters. Most adopted a bicameral legislature and restricted the executive branch.

The right to vote, however, was restricted to white males who owned property. Some of the new states also began to question the institution of slavery. Other changes included an increase in religious freedom.

While the states were writing new constitutions, Congress developed a plan to unite them. Known as the Articles of Confederation, this document placed governing authority in Congress in which each state had one vote. It also curtailed the executive branch, which was a committee of delegates.

Under the Articles, the national government was weak. Domestically, the government was unable to collect taxes, enforce the laws, or interpret them. It also faced difficulties dealing with settling the West, although the Congress passed two important documents—the Land Ordinance of 1785 and the Northwest Ordinance of 1787. In addition, there were disputes between the states over boundaries, commerce, and currency, all of which the Congress was powerless to solve. Internationally, the new nation experienced difficulties with Britain, Spain, France, and Barbary States. As a result, trade declined.

Because of these problems, it became apparent that the Articles were inadequate and that a new framework for government was needed. A convention was called, which met in Philadelphia over the summer of 1787, to resolve these problems. For a time differences between large states and small states over representation in Congress, and between northern and southern states over economic issues, including slavery, threatened to break up the deliberations. Ultimately, a series of compromises was reached that created a powerful two-house Congress, a strong chief executive, and a national judiciary. Most delegates believed that the new plan—the Constitution—was a vast improvement over the Articles.

Ratification of the Constitution was difficult, however, primarily because some states were cautious about surrendering their power. Finally, though, supporters of the Constitution, the Federalists, emerged victorious. The new government was set to be launched in 1789.

SYNTHESIZING UNIT THEMES

RELATING IDEAS

1. How did the new state constitutions strive for democratic ideals?

IDENTIFYING TRENDS

2. What events led the colonies to declare their independence?

MAKING COMPARISONS

3. Compare life for the colonists under British rule with life under the Articles of Confederation.

★ Unit 2 Review ★

★ Analyzing Unit Themes

AMERICAN DEMOCRACY

1. What democratic principles did Americans include in their constitution that were not a part of their English heritage?

CIVIL RIGHTS AND LIBERTIES

2. What civil rights were denied colonists by British laws and actions before the Revolutionary War?

ECONOMIC DEVELOPMENT

3. How did Great Britain's view of the American colonies before the Revolution and its view of the new United States after the war affect trade relations between the the two nations?

CONFLICT AND COOPERATION

4. How did the conflicting interests of the British and Americans lead to the Revolutionary War?

5. Describe colonial attempts at cooperation before the Revolution. How did the war bring about the first successful colonial confederation?

★ Reviewing Chronology

1. Cite British legislative actions during the 1760s and 1770s that led to the separation of the colonies from Britain.

2. Divide the period 1650-1789 into at least five time periods. Indicate your reasons for each of the segments.

★ Linking Past and Present

- 1960   First massive antiapartheid demonstrations occur in black township of Sharpeville, South Africa.

- 1984   Tensions between ruling white minority and nonwhite majority push South Africa toward civil war.

- 1989   President Frederick W. de Klerk frees black nationalist leader Nelson Mandela.

- 1990   South African public beaches and hospitals are desegregated; racial violence against blacks and whites continues.

Study the information above, then answer the questions that follow.

1. **Making Comparisons**   In what way does the struggle for freedom of blacks in South Africa today resemble the struggle of the colonists in 1776?

2. **Making Judgments**   Nelson Mandela believes that, in time, violence will end and blacks will gain equality. Given events in South Africa and the example of the American Revolution, do you agree? Give reasons why or why not.

★ Demonstrating Citizenship

Cooperating   The success of the Revolution depended on commitment to freedom and the protection of basic rights. Colonists cooperated to keep these rights, risking their lives and their country's future. State three areas in which American citizens cooperate today to preserve basic rights and freedoms. What forms can these cooperative efforts take?

★ Interpreting Illustrations

Examine closely the painting above, *A View of the Town of Concord, 1775*, attributed to Ralph Earl. Then answer the questions that follow.

1. While British troops march through the town of Concord, where was the Patriot militia?

2. In the background, the British are destroying barrels of gunpowder and throwing them into the river. What was the objective of the British march on Concord, and did it meet its objective?

3. What was the significance of the British march on

Lexington and Concord and the fighting that took place for the British occupation of Boston and the Patriot cause?

★ Thinking Globally

1. **Analyzing Motives** In 1778 the British Parliament entertained a motion to abolish the slave trade. In 1788 the U.S. Constitution was ratified with a compromise agreement not to interfere with the slave trade for 20 years. How do you account for the differences in legislative actions of the two countries regarding slavery?

2. **Making Comparisons** In 1789 the National Constitutional Assembly in France issued the Declaration of the Rights of Man which proclaimed all men were "born and remain free and equal in rights." It assured liberty, property, and security and said that government existed to protect citizens' rights. This document was modeled after the Virginia Declaration of Rights adopted in 1776. Compare the motives behind the creation of both documents.

★ Relating Geography and History

PLACE: PHYSICAL CHARACTERISTICS

Two views of American society developed in the late eighteenth century. Alexander Hamilton predicted that the population of the United States would be focused in cities; that the country's economy would be based on manufacturing; and that government would rest in the hands of a business elite. Thomas Jefferson said the nation would have an agrarian society; that people would live on small farms and in villages; that they would be essentially self-sufficient; and that they would be governed by an elite group of planters.

Given the physical characteristics and population characteristics of the time, which view seemed likely to prevail? Explain the reasons for your answer.

★ Practicing Skills

IDENTIFYING CAUSE AND EFFECT

Refer to the skills lesson on Identifying Cause and Effect on page 113 to help you practice this critical thinking skill. Underline the cause and underline twice the effect. Circle any "clue words."

1. A force of 1,000 Americans felled trees across the only road to Albany, so that Burgoyne's army could move no more than one mile a day.

2. Many slaves were reportedly crossing into the British lines. As a result, the Continental Congress reversed its policy and allowed free blacks, but not slaves, to reenlist and to be recruited into the army and navy.

3. The British armies could not keep their conquests in the South because they could not win the loyalty of the inhabitants.

4. Many Americans had come to distrust strong executive power, the results of their unhappy experience with royal governors and George III.

5. The national government under the Articles proved too weak to operate effectively. There was no executive branch to carry out laws, no federal courts existed to interpret them, and Congress had no power to collect taxes.

6. Since it was difficult to claim that "all men are created equal" in a society where some people were owned by others, many Americans began to question the institution of slavery.

TAKING NOTES

Refer to the skills lesson on Taking Notes on page 169 to help you practice this study and writing skill. Study the following notes. Then write out the notes in longhand.

Stamp Act 65
–drect tx
–pd 2 gov't
–txd 54 things
–1¢ 2 $10
–dcmnets, wills, crds, nwspaprs, etc.
Rstance 2 Stmp Act made colns coop
–Stmp Act Cong.
–in NY Oct 65
–9 colns rep'd
–rsolvd 2 bycott Br. gds
–Mass. Circ Ltr 68
–calld on othr colns 2 prtst
Stmp agnts rsign
Parl rpeal March 66

Launching a New Government

I

Launching a New Government

2

The Constitution of the United States with Annotations

SETTING THE SCENE

Thirteen newly elected representatives and 8 senators arrived in New York City on March 3, 1789. They would be part of the new Congress that was forming just six months after the state of New York had become the eleventh to ratify the Constitution. In the city they found lodging in private homes and boarding houses to await the arrival of a quorum to do business. The representatives waited a full month before the House, with 30 members, was ready to convene; the Senate did not have a sufficient number to begin until April 6.

Some members of Congress worried that the new government would lose credibility, or at least respect, if they did not organize soon. On April 1 the House of Representatives opened its first session at New York's old City Hall in lower Manhattan, remodeled and renamed Federal Hall. It met downstairs and was open to the public. The Senate convened April 6, on the second floor where noisy spectators would not disturb deliberations.

The House elected its first speaker, Frederick Muhlenberg of Pennsylvania, and began to establish rules and procedures. The Senate chose a temporary president until the electoral vote count for President and Vice President could be counted, because the Constitution named the Vice President as permanent president of that body.

When the Senate announced that it was ready, House members climbed the stairs for the first Joint Session of Congress. The first task was counting the Electoral College votes and declaring George Washington President.

CONSTITUTIONAL TIMELINE

LANDMARK SUPREME COURT DECISIONS

- 1803 Marbury v. Madison *establishes judicial review*
- 1861 Exparte Merryman *—challenge to writ of* habeas corpus
- 1877 Munn v. Illinois—*first "Granger Case"*

1790 — 1860

SELECTED AMENDMENTS

- 1791 *The Bill of Rights is ratified*
- 1804 *Twelfth Amendment divides election of President and Vice President*
- 1868 *Fourteenth Amendment defines and protects "citizens"*

U.S. Capitol and the reflecting pool at night, Washington, D.C.

1896
Plessy v.
Ferguson
*"separate but
equal" doctrine*

1919
Schenck v. United
States—*first "clear and
present danger" test*

1954
Brown v. Bd. of
Education of Topeka
*overturns "separate
but equal"*

1966
Miranda v.
Arizona—*suspects
must be informed
of their rights*

1930

2000

1913
*Sixteenth
Amendment provides
Congress with power
to levy income tax*

1920
*Nineteenth
Amendment gives
women the right
to vote*

1992
*Twenty-seventh
Amendment controls
timing of congressional
salary increases*

Federal Government

The entire system of federal government in the United States rests on a single document: the Constitution. It has served as the "supreme law of the land" for more than 200 years, making it the oldest written constitution in the world. Institutions that we take for granted—the Congress, the President, the Supreme Court—were created by the Constitution. Major governmental decisions that are made every day depend upon constitutional authority. Yet, many Americans, whose rights are protected by the Constitution, know little of its structure or development.

Examining Photographs *Tourists gather in the rotunda of the Capitol to view art depicting the history of the United States. How has United States history been affected by the Constitution?*

National Powers

Before 1789 some compared America to a barrel without a hoop—in desperate need of something to hold it together. Sharing this sentiment, the authors of the Constitution created a strong central government. Article I, Section 8, which has been called the "heart of the Constitution," gave the new Congress various powers not possessed by the Confederation Congress, including the critical ones of levying taxes and regulating interstate commerce.

The power to levy taxes enabled Congress to finance the federal government. It was briefly challenged by a rebellion in western Pennsylvania against a tax on whiskey, but Washington used the army to enforce the law. When the Congress decided to levy an income tax, objections that it was unconstitutional led to the Sixteenth Amendment in 1913.

The power that the Constitution gave Congress over interstate commerce and the "elastic clause" both strengthened the national government at the expense of state power. The interstate commerce power grew alongside the development of a national economy beginning in the 1800s. Through its authority over interstate commerce, Congress has been able to enact laws ranging from prohibitions against racial discrimination to regulations on consumer credit transactions.

The "elastic clause" that appears in Article I, Section 8, says that Congress shall make all laws "necessary and proper" for putting into effect its enumerated powers. Determining what laws are necessary and proper has provided an arena for ongoing debate over the years, beginning with the debate over the National Bank in 1790. Those who wish to restrain the power of the central government emphasize the word "necessary." These **strict constructionists** interpret the Constitution as narrowly as possible. Those **loose constructionists** who wish to expand the central government emphasize the word "proper." They interpret the Constitution more broadly, to allow the government to exercise both the powers explicitly listed in Article I, Section 8, and the "implied" powers of that provision.

DIVISION OF POWERS

EXCLUSIVE POWERS GRANTED TO THE FEDERAL GOVERNMENT	CONCURRENT POWERS SHARED BY THE FEDERAL AND STATE GOVERNMENTS	RESERVED POWERS SET ASIDE FOR THE STATES
• Regulate interstate and foreign commerce • Establish an army and navy • Declare war • Coin money • Establish postal system • Establish federal courts • Set standards for weights and measures • Regulate patents and copyrights • Admit new states • Establish laws of citizenship • Pass laws needed to carry out its powers	• Enforce the laws • Borrow money • Lay and collect taxes • Establish courts • Charter banks • Provide for the general welfare	• Regulate intrastate commerce • Conduct elections • Determine voting requirements • Establish local governments • Provide for public safety • Tenth Amendment reserves to the state governments all powers not granted to the federal government or prohibited by the Constitution

Examining Charts *When the Constitution was written, the states, being older than the federal government, reserved certain powers to themselves. The Constitution gave certain powers and rights to the national government. Who retained all other rights?*

State Powers

While the central government was strengthened by the Constitution, the document itself reinforced the idea that the states were to remain sovereign in some matters. Through their authority in common law and criminal law, the state governments were left in control of local affairs. Their separate identities were retained and protected, and their authority in matters not specifically given to the national government was limited only by the rights of the people within each state. The Tenth Amendment assured this basic protection of the people's and each state's sovereignty.

A final assurance of state and popular sovereignty is provided by the amending process. Because the Constitution and the states both derive their authority from the people, provisions for changing the Constitution depend upon the representatives in Congress and the will of the people. This careful arrangement has resulted in only 27 amendments. The first 10 were added almost immediately—in 1791—as a Bill of Rights to protect against national government encroachments on individual freedom.

Since the earliest years of constitutional government, the popular belief has been that federal and state governments operate in two separate spheres. In reality, the national government and the states have cooperated on joint projects since the 1800s. The first cooperative ventures were in the areas of banking and railroad- and canal-building. Today federal and state powers continue to overlap. In such fields as education, welfare, commerce, and law enforcement, it is sometimes difficult to tell where one level of power begins and the other ends.

There has also been a general belief that the federal government has a tendency to infringe on state powers. In 1952 Dwight Eisenhower emphasized this concern by running for President on a platform that promised to protect "states rights." More recently, Ronald Reagan used the term New Federalism to express his concern that the federal government had encroached on state powers. New Federalism generally meant state control of federal-grant moneys.

House and Senate

The first senators and representatives to Congress were educated and politically experienced. Of the original 88 members of Congress, 54 had already served the national government; 20 had helped write the Constitution in Philadelphia. Although Article I imposes some requirements for election to Congress, such as a minimum age of 25 for the House, most members of Congress have historically been over 40 years of age and have been above average in wealth and education.

The Senate was originally intended to resemble the British House of Lords in its separation from popular control. Its members were given a longer term of office, and it was looked upon as the quieter, more deliberate chamber. Originally, Senators were chosen by state legislatures, but the Seventeenth Amendment, adopted in 1913, opened their election to popular vote.

Originally each state determined how it would elect its House members. But in 1842 Congress passed a law requiring each state to divide into districts for the purposes of House elections. The districts, having nearly equal populations, would assure that people were equally represented.

Many states ignored this rule, however, as political parties sought advantages for their own candidates. District boundaries were drawn in such a way as to assure the election of the controlling party's candidates. In *Wesberry v. Sanders* in 1964, the Supreme Court ruled that large differences in population among Georgia's districts failed to meet constitutional guidelines for fair representation. Since 1970 new districts formed in every state are of nearly equal population.

Legislative Powers

The Constitution not only established different qualifications and terms for the Senate and House, it provided different legislative powers for each chamber. The Senate approves treaties and presidential appointments and tries all **impeachments,** or cases in which a government official has been formally accused of wrongdoing in office; the House originates all revenue bills, and has the power to impeach members of the executive and judicial branches. Legislation must pass both Houses before it can be sent to the President to be signed into law.

Many of the enumerated powers that the Constitution gives Congress leave little room for interpretation. When the Constitution says that Congress has authority to provide punishment for counterfeiting, it is quite clear. There have been, however, lengthy national debates over other powers. Congress may authorize the sale of savings bonds as a means of borrowing money, but in the 1980s, when the nation's debt from borrowing seemed out of control, some government leaders sought a remedy in a constitutional amendment. Such an amendment is unlikely, as members of Congress are not inclined to vote for an amendment that would, in effect, restrict their control of the national budget.

Examining Photographs *The idea of representative democracy works well when the legislature is responsive to the will of the people. Congressman John Conyers listens to the opinions of some of his Michigan constituents in his Washington office. Which chamber was not originally elected by the people?*

Another area where the division between the powers of Congress and the President is unclear is in control of the military. The Constitution gives Congress power to declare war and to raise and support armies. It makes the President, however, Commander in Chief of these forces. How far can the President go in using the army without an official declaration of war? The War Powers Act of 1973 attempted to clarify this issue, but the question arose again in 1990 when President Bush sent American troops to Saudi Arabia in response to Iraq's invasion of nearby Kuwait.

Separation of Powers

When the constitutional authority of Congress seems to conflict with the authority of the President, it is often because of a deliberate effort by the Constitutional Convention to limit the power of government. The Framers of the Constitution, fearing unrestricted power in the hands of government, chose to divide government powers among three separate branches. This **separation of powers** is one of the most distinctive features of the Constitution.

The federal government is separated into legislative, executive, and judicial branches. These branches, described in the first three articles of the Constitution, are each given separate authority. Article I ensures this separation by providing that no member of Congress may serve simultaneously in the executive or judicial branch.

Under this separation of powers, each branch exercises a check on the powers of the other two because each branch's powers counterbalance the others. Consider the power to enact legislation. The lawmaking authority of Congress is checked by the President's power to veto laws that

Examining Charts *The balance of powers and the system of checks and balances are fundamental principles found throughout the Constitution. What phrase describes the division into executive, legislative, and judicial branches?*

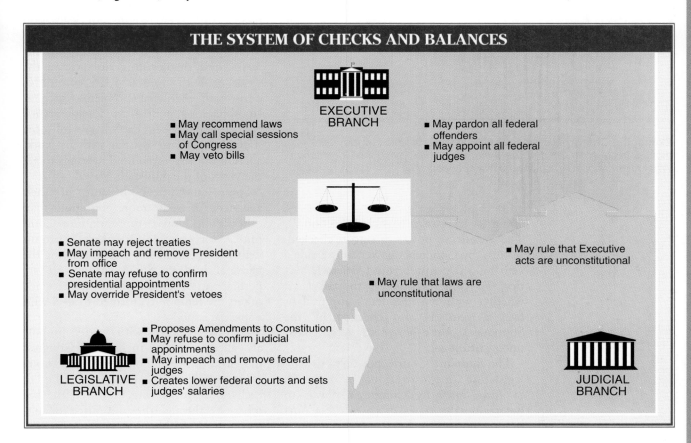

THE SYSTEM OF CHECKS AND BALANCES

EXECUTIVE BRANCH

- May recommend laws
- May call special sessions of Congress
- May veto bills

- May pardon all federal offenders
- May appoint all federal judges

- Senate may reject treaties
- May impeach and remove President from office
- Senate may refuse to confirm presidential appointments
- May override President's vetoes

- May rule that Executive acts are unconstitutional

- May rule that laws are unconstitutional

- Proposes Amendments to Constitution
- May refuse to confirm judicial appointments
- May impeach and remove federal judges
- Creates lower federal courts and sets judges' salaries

LEGISLATIVE BRANCH

JUDICIAL BRANCH

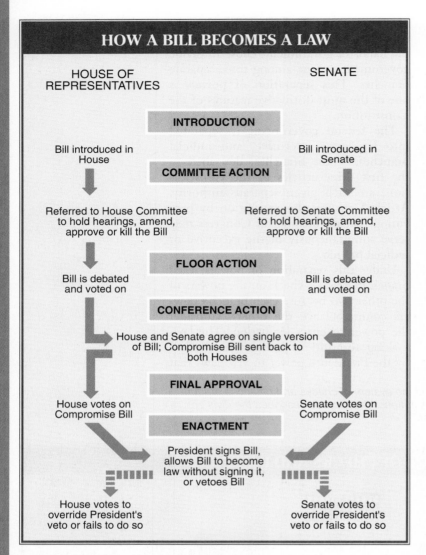

HOW A BILL BECOMES A LAW

HOUSE OF REPRESENTATIVES   SENATE

INTRODUCTION

Bill introduced in House   Bill introduced in Senate

COMMITTEE ACTION

Referred to House Committee to hold hearings, amend, approve or kill the Bill   Referred to Senate Committee to hold hearings, amend, approve or kill the Bill

FLOOR ACTION

Bill is debated and voted on   Bill is debated and voted on

CONFERENCE ACTION

House and Senate agree on single version of Bill; Compromise Bill sent back to both Houses

FINAL APPROVAL

House votes on Compromise Bill   Senate votes on Compromise Bill

ENACTMENT

President signs Bill, allows Bill to become law without signing it, or vetoes Bill

House votes to override President's veto or fails to do so   Senate votes to override President's veto or fails to do so

Examining Charts *The process of enacting a bill into law may take months because of the deliberate method spelled out in the Constitution. What might happen if a budget bill is not passed?*

jurisdiction, (Article III, Section 2), and by the President's power to appoint justices, or members, of the high court (Article II, Section 2).

Finally, the President's power to appoint Supreme Court justices is checked by the requirement that all appointments have the consent of the majority of the Senate (Article II, Section 2).

These and many other checks and balances in the Constitution maintain a careful balance among the three branches.

This protection, however, has a price. If two branches of government disagree, decisive action may be difficult, even impossible. Thus, if the President and Congress cannot agree on a federal budget, the entire federal government may be forced to shut down—as almost happened as recently as 1990.

Process of Lawmaking

The Constitution describes the duties of the three branches, but it does not detail how those duties are to be carried out. To handle the heavy volume of legislation efficiently, both houses of Congress from the very beginning divided into committees. These smaller units do most of the work of both houses. Each committee deals with particular problems, such as labor, banking, agriculture, foreign affairs, and armed services. Each has a full-time staff of experts to assist it with its work, and committees often hold hearings to get the views of the public.

Some committees, because of their assigned duties, are more prestigious than others. The House Appropriations Committee, for example, is especially prominent because of its key role in shaping the national budget. Some committees are permanent, or standing committees, while others are temporary, formed to deal with a specific issue.

Legislation begins with written proposals called bills. Any member of Congress may introduce a bill on any subject. Long before going to the full membership of each house for a vote, however, the bill must pass through the committee (or subcommittee) with responsibility for the

Congress has passed (Article I, Section 7). The President's power to veto is checked, in turn, by Congress's power to override a veto by a two-thirds vote (Article I, Section 7). Congress's power to pass laws, whether with the President's approval or over a veto, is also checked by the Supreme Court's power to declare laws unconstitutional.

The Supreme Court's power to declare legislation unconstitutional is checked, in turn, both by Congress's power to determine the types of cases the Court has authority to hear, or the Court's

Examining Photographs *Although some of the work of the legislature is done on the floor of Congress, most of it is done outside the chambers by committees. Each member of Congress has a staff of legislative assistants and other aides who research issues, draft bills, and organize the member's office. Why does Congress need elaborate administrative support and rules?*

Linking Across Time

THE WAR POWER

The issue of whether the President can legally send troops into combat without a declaration of war by Congress is still unsettled. When President Bush sent American troops to Saudi Arabia in 1990, his defense secretary told the Senate Armed Services Committee that the President, as Commander in Chief, has that authority. The House Democratic Caucus, however, said no. In a non-binding resolution, they said the President must have congressional approval for offensive action in the Persian Gulf. The legal dilemma was sidestepped when Congress approved action against Iraq early in 1991.

subject in question. The two main political parties in the United States are both represented on virtually all congressional committees but one party—and this could be one party in the Senate and a different one in the House—will always have a majority, and hence voting control, on each committee.

Because all bills must pass through a committee, the committee's chair who has substantial control over the committee's daily schedule, has immense power to expedite or prevent passage of a given bill. The chair is usually the member of the majority party with the most seniority, that is, the one who has served on the committee for the longest time.

The Constitution provided for a deliberate and sometimes slow method of passing legislation by establishing two legislative houses. One factor that may slow down passage of a bill is the requirement that the legislation passed by both houses be exactly the same. At times a bill passed by one house is altered slightly by the other. In these instances Congress may turn to a conference committee. This committee composed of members of both houses, usually drafts a compromise proposal that the House and Senate can vote for or against. In a recent term, over 11,000 separate bills were presented to Congress. While only 534 of these were passed into law, it is easy to see why Congress has needed an elaborate set of administrative rules to handle its workload. Fortunately, the Framers, who could not foresee the increasing workload of Congress, allowed the Congress to develop its own rules for procedure.

The Presidency

The presidency may seem common-place today, but the Framers of the Constitution engaged in lengthy debates over almost every aspect of the office. The method of election, the length of a presidential term, and the powers of the office caused such controversy that the convention finally turned to a committee consisting of one delegate from each state to prepare a final proposal. Most of this committee's proposals were written into the Constitution.

Executive Powers

The Constitution gives the President extensive powers. Four of the most important are: the command of the country's military forces, the power to conduct foreign affairs, the power to appoint the cabinet and other executive officers, as well as all federal judges, and the legislative veto power.

Examining Photographs *Presidents use the annual State of the Union Address to outline yearly goals. How many such addresses may a President give?*

There are, however, checks and balances on the President's power. Article I, Section 8, gives Congress the power "To make rules for the government and regulation of the land and naval forces." As mentioned earlier, Congress alone has the power to declare war. The President's power to conduct foreign affairs is limited by the requirement that all treaties have the approval of two-thirds of the Senate, and the power to appoint executive officers and judges is subject to the approval of the majority of the Senate.

Originally the Constitution allowed the President a term of four years without limiting the number of consecutive elections—a generous provision since many state governors in the 1780s could hold office for only one year and were not allowed to run for reelection. In addition, many governors had no veto power. Little wonder the Anti-Federalists made the presidency a principal point of attack during the battle over ratification.

The presumption that George Washington would be the first President served to calm many fears about the potential power of the office. Washington, as President, exercised caution in nearly every decision that he made because, as he said, "As the first of everything, in our situation, will serve to establish a Precedent, it is devoutly wished on my part, that these precedents may be fixed on true principles." As a result, the presidency from the beginning was a respected institution. Washington's refusal to serve more than two terms in office established a precedent that was not broken until Franklin Roosevelt won four elections beginning in 1932. In 1951 the Twenty-second Amendment officially limited Presidents to two terms.

Expansion of Presidential Powers

Virtually all the President's stated powers have expanded since the Constitution first took effect. For example, the first 6 Presidents exercised the veto power only 10 times. But Andrew Jackson vetoed 12 bills, prompting critics to dub him "King

Connections

RANKING THE PRESIDENTS

Americans expect greatness from every person they choose as President. History reveals, however, that not all Presidents are esteemed as equal.

In 1948 historian Arthur M. Schlesinger asked 55 historians to rank the past Presidents by rating them as great, near great, average, below average, or failures. They rated Lincoln, Washington, F. D. Roosevelt, Wilson, and Jefferson as great. As near great were T. Roosevelt, Cleveland, J. Adams, and Polk. Grant and Harding were rated failures.

Presidential seal

Schlesinger's 1962 poll added two new Presidents—Truman as near great and Eisenhower as average. The other results were much the same as the first poll. In 1981 Eisenhower moved from average to near great, an indication that historians' views of a President may change over time.

Critics of presidential ratings point out that Presidents rated as great or near great have served at times of national crisis. When average citizens rate the Presidents, however, the results are different. A recent Harris Poll ranked Kennedy first, followed by F. D. Roosevelt, and Reagan.

★ ★ ★ ★ ★ ★ ★ ★ ★ ★

MAKING THE GOVERNMENT CONNECTION

1. How did historians' views of Eisenhower change?

2. Who are historians most likely to keep at the top of their ratings list?

LINKING PAST AND PRESENT

3. What Presidents do your parents rate as great?

4. How would you rate the last four Presidents?

★ ★ ★ ★ ★ ★ ★ ★ ★ ★

Andrew the First." His successors have used the veto power even more frequently.

Other presidential powers have also been magnified. Abraham Lincoln used his authority as commander-in-chief of the military to take the extraordinary step of issuing the Emancipation Proclamation, which freed the slaves in the states that rebelled against the Union. This kind of decision normally falls within the responsibilities of Congress.

During the wars in Korea and Vietnam, Presidents stretched the commander-in-chief's power to even greater lengths by engaging American soldiers in combat without a declaration of war by Congress. A similar constitutional challenge was mounted against George Bush's transfer of troops to Saudi Arabia following Iraq's invasion of Kuwait in 1990. So far the Supreme Court has declined to rule on such challenges, citing its policy of not getting involved in political disputes, only legal ones.

The Constitution did not foresee the development of political parties, one source of additional presidential power. As head of one of the two major political parties, the President can exert pressure for legislation and can give or withhold support for a senator's or representative's reelection.

In addition, as Grover Cleveland put it, "The presidency is the people's office." That is, while members of Congress represent particular states or districts within states, the President represents the whole country. Every presidential action attracts nationwide attention by the press and electronic media.

The personality and goals of those who hold the office affect the extent of its power. Andrew Jackson, Theodore Roosevelt, and Franklin D. Roosevelt used the force of personality to enhance their power. In contrast, because of his less assertive personality, President Calvin Coolidge wielded less influence.

CLASSIFIED INFORMATION

When United States forces began air strikes against Iraq in January 1991, news coverage was more intense than at any other time in the history of war. Within the first few days, however, news reporters began to complain of the military's censorship of information. They were reminded of an earlier time of censorship during the war in Vietnam, when even Congress was unaware of certain vital information. The issue of the people's or their representatives' rights to information conflicts with the administration's need to keep its war strategy secret.

Examining Photographs *Presidents sometimes visit troops who are engaged in war in order to lend encouragement. Most Presidents, however, leave war strategy to the military. Why is the President usually better informed about wars than Congress is?*

Times of crisis often present opportunities for enhancement of presidential power. Abraham Lincoln took great liberties with the Constitution during the Civil War. On his own authority he increased the size of the federal army—something Congress alone is permitted to do (Article I, Section 8, paragraph 12). He ordered payment of federal funds to private citizens for military purposes—which the Constitution authorizes only Congress to do (Article I, Section 9, paragraph 6). He even suspended the writ of *habeas corpus,* which protects against wrongful imprisonment, despite a Supreme Court ruling that Congress alone could take such action (Article I, Section 9, paragraph 2). Congress eventually took action to bring the President's powers back in line with peacetime norms.

Presidential power increases during crises involving actual or perceived danger from abroad. It is affected by the tendency of Congress to yield much of its power to the President for the duration of the crisis. For several decades beginning in 1941, American Presidents governed a country at war: first the struggle against Germany and Japan, then the Cold War against the Soviet Union, then two "police actions" in Korea and Vietnam.

The President, who has access to a vast military and foreign service network, can control information that Congress receives. This factor has contributed to the increase in presidential power over foreign affairs, especially in the twentieth century. In addition, Congress, working as a whole or through committees, is inherently less capable of exercising decisive action quickly.

In domestic policy the Constitution clearly gives "the power of the purse" to Congress. Over time, the President has come to dominate many processes of raising and spending the government's money. The creation of the Bureau of the Budget in 1921 (now called the Office of Management and Budget), whose director was appointed by the President, heralded the transfer of major budgetary power out of the hands of Congress.

Since its creation by the Constitution, the office of the presidency has grown greatly. Its expanded power and its role, however, continue to be limited by constitutional checks and balances.

The Courts

The judiciary is only briefly described in the Constitution. Article III provides that there shall be "one Supreme Court" and such lower courts as Congress may establish. The Framers left the details to be worked out later.

The first Congress passed the Judiciary Act of 1789. This law set up the federal court system, the basics of which are still in place today. The federal judiciary may be envisioned as a three-tiered pyramid, with many district courts at the bottom, a smaller number of circuit courts in the middle, and one Supreme Court at the top.

The comparatively numerous district courts are spread around the country. Cases from a district court may be appealed, or taken for review (where one side believes the district judge has made an error) to the circuit court for the area in which the district court is located. There are 12 circuit courts around the country.

The Supreme Court

Cases may be appealed from the circuit courts to the Supreme Court, which currently consists of nine members: eight associate justices and one Chief Justice. Because the cases that reach them are so complex and time-consuming, the justices must decline to rule upon all but a small fraction of the cases they are asked to hear. Thus, although someone who believes he or she has been wronged may vow to take the case "all the way to the Supreme

Examining Photographs *In the front row, left to right, are Associate Justices John Paul Stevens and Byron White, Chief Justice William Rehnquist, and Associate Justices Harry Blackmun and Sandra Day O'Connor. In the second row are Justices David Souter, Antonin Scalia, Anthony Kennedy, and Clarence Thomas. Which article of the Constitution provides this court?*

Court," the case is likely to get no higher than one of the circuit courts.

The principal purpose of the federal judiciary is to provide a forum for disputes involving federal laws. The Framers did not want the federal government to rely on state courts to enforce its laws.

The most important power of the federal courts, that of **judicial review,** is not stated in the Constitution. This is the power of the Court to decide whether a given law, federal or state, conflicts with the Constitution. If the Court decides that it does, the law is declared unconstitutional, or invalid, and ceases to have effect. This amounts to a form of veto power over all laws.

Judicial review has been a fundamental part of our government since 1803, when it was first announced by Chief Justice John Marshall in the famous case of *Marbury v. Madison.* Marshall, who presided over the Supreme Court for 34 years, ruled in this case that part of the Judiciary Act of 1789 conflicted with the Constitution and was therefore invalid. This was bold indeed, in a young nation where no one had ever nullified an act of Congress. The Constitution is a law, Marshall courageously declared, and it is the job of the courts "to say what the law is." This assumed power of the Court remains unchallenged.

The power of judicial review does not necessarily mean the Supreme Court always has the last say. If the Supreme Court rules a law unconstitutional, the Congress or the states may initiate an amendment to the Constitution. This, in fact, happened when the Sixteenth Amendment provided for an income tax.

There are additional limits on the Supreme Court's power. First, the Court cannot rule on just any law, but only on those that come before it. In this sense its role is passive; it cannot take the initiative to correct problems that the justices see or hear about, but must wait for others to file lawsuits charging that an injustice has been done. Second, lacking any army or police force, the Court must rely on the President to enforce its rulings.

During Andrew Jackson's administration, a dispute arose over Georgia's attempt to evict the Cherokees from its borders. When the Supreme Court, under Chief Justice John Marshall, voted to uphold the rights of the Cherokees, Jackson, a veteran Indian fighter, reportedly declared, "John Marshall has made his decision. Now let him enforce it." Such a refusal, or threatened refusal, by a President to enforce a court decision has been used sparingly because of its obvious disregard for the constitutional powers of the federal courts.

Another way to override a Supreme Court ruling is to limit federal courts' jurisdiction. The Constitution gave Congress control over jurisdiction—another aspect of the system of checks and balances.

AMERICAN PORTRAITS

JOHN MARSHALL
1755-1835

The Supreme Court's rapid rise to equality with Congress and the presidency is due mainly to the influence of one man, John Marshall.

The first born of 14 brothers and sisters, Marshall was raised on a family farm in Virginia. In the Revolutionary War, he spent the difficult winter at Valley Forge with George Washington.

After a brief study of law, Marshall was admitted to the Virginia bar in 1780. He then served in the Virginia legislature until he was called by President John Adams to join a mission to France. Marshall returned as one of the heroes of the XYZ Affair. Elected to the House of Representatives, he quickly became the leader of the moderate Federalists. In 1801, Adams appointed Marshall Chief Justice of the Supreme Court. For the next 34 years Marshall led the Court in landmark decisions.

In 1868 Congress used this power to limit the Supreme Court's authority. William McCardle, an antiblack publisher in Vicksburg, Tennessee, advocated violent opposition to Congress's Reconstruction laws. When the army arrested him, McCardle's lawyers sought his release on a writ of *habeas corpus.* Congress, fearing that the Supreme Court would side with McCardle and thus damage its reconstruction efforts, passed a law withdrawing jurisdiction from the Supreme Court in all habeas corpus cases. Having no authority to rule, the Court dismissed McCardle's appeal.

More recently, congressional opponents of the Supreme Court have proposed several bills that would withdraw the Court's jurisdiction over such cases as those involving school prayer, busing, abortion, and gender discrimination. If, however, Congress could remove jurisdiction in any or all cases that it chose, it could effectively block any provision of the Constitution from being enforced. Such action is not likely because it would disregard the separation of powers, a basic principle of the United States constitutional government.

Federal Judiciary

Unlike Congress and the President, federal judges do not have to face the people at election time. The Constitution provides that they shall hold office "during good behavior"—which generally means for life or until they choose to resign—and that their salaries may not be reduced. The Framers wanted to insulate federal judges from political pressures so they could rule fairly and wisely, without fear that popular hostility could cost them their jobs or salaries. Indeed, one of the main functions of any court is to stand *against* the popular tide, such as by protecting unpopular individuals against "the tyranny of the majority."

A federal judge can be removed through the difficult process of impeachment by Congress (the same process as that required to remove a President). This is another aspect of the system of checks and balances. The fact that very few federal judges have faced impeachment is evidence of the care taken in selecting them.

The Constitution Today

When the Constitution reached its bicentennial year in 1989, it inspired a fresh interest in the meaning and significance of the document. Two broadly different views emerged. Some people saw the limitations and problems that the federal government faced and suggested a new constitutional convention to restructure the government to meet today's difficult challenges. Others emphasized the remarkable enduring quality of the Constitution and its basic principles that remain important today.

It is likely that if changes are to be made in basic principles of government, they will come by amendment or interpretation. Amendment, however, has historically been approached with caution. The Founders wanted the Constitution to be safe from the unruly passions of the public and schemes of the politicians. When the Supreme Court ruled that the burning of the United States flag was a form of free expression protected by the First Amendment, President George Bush sought an amendment outlawing the desecration of the flag. Many viewed this idea as the kind of manipulation that the Framers wanted to prevent when they provided for the amending process.

One amendment, the Fourteenth, has provided a broad basis for interpretation by the courts. Originally written to make former slaves citizens, the amendment set forth the "equal protection" and "due process" clauses. It is striking that two short rules—that everyone shall receive the equal protection of the laws, and that no one may be deprived of life, liberty, or property without due process of law—could accomplish so much, as well as generate so much controversy.

The original intent of the Fourteenth Amendment was obstructed for many years. In 1883 the Supreme Court in the

decisions regarding racial discrimination and many personal freedoms.

Court decisions constantly define constitutional amendments. In 1966, in *Miranda v. Arizona*, the Supreme Court set strict guidelines for police questioning—a decision that further defined the Fifth Amendment protection against self-incrimination.

Court interpretations limit the need for continual constitutional amendment. The last change in the Constitution was adopted in 1992—the Twenty-seventh Amendment, concerning congressional pay raises.

The Constitution's adaptability to new circumstances has made it a lasting framework of government. It has permitted, perhaps even encouraged, debate over the proper role of each branch of government, or of government itself. Through the first two centuries of federal government, the Constitution has served to moderate change in government. It has also ably guarded those freedoms that we the people have entrusted it to preserve.

Examining Photographs *When a suspect is arrested, police read a list of rights to the accused. What court case set these guidelines?*

Civil Rights Cases rejected the Fourteenth Amendment as a basis for protecting individual rights, ruling that the equal protection clause applies only to the states, not to "private action." In 1896 the Court decided in *Plessy v. Ferguson* that "separate but equal" public facilities for blacks and whites were constitutional, denying the protection of the Fourteenth Amendment.

Finally, in 1954 the Court ruled in *Brown v. Board of Education of Topeka* that separate educational facilities were not equal. Since then the Supreme Court has often used the due process and equal protection clauses in decisions to support basic individual rights.

In a landmark ruling in 1965, the Supreme Court held that "due process," in conjunction with the personal protections of the Bill of Rights, implies a right of privacy. Then, in *Roe v. Wade* (1973), the Court ruled that the right of privacy includes abortion within limits. Since the 1960s the Court has incorporated most of the Bill of Rights into the Fourteenth Amendment. The due process and equal protection clauses have been the basis of

Examining Photographs *President Richard Nixon signs into law the Twenty-sixth Amendment to the Constitution. When was it adopted?*

The Constitution of the United States

*The Constitution of the United States
is truly a remarkable document. It was one of the
first written constitutions in modern history. The Framers
wanted to devise a plan for a strong central government that would
unify the country, as well as preserve the ideals of the Declaration of
Independence. The document they wrote created a representative
legislature, the office of president, a system of courts, and a process for
adding amendments. For over 200 years the flexibility and strength of
the Constitution has guided the nation's political leaders. The
document has become a symbol of pride and a force for national unity.
In studying the Constitution, those passages that have been set aside or
changed by the adoption of amendments have been crossed out. Also
included are explanatory notes that will help clarify
the meaning of each article and section.*

The Preamble introduces the Constitution and sets forth the general purposes for which the government was established. The preamble also declares that the power of the government comes from the people.

The printed text of the document shows the spelling and punctuation of the parchment original.

Article I. The Legislative Branch

Section 1. Congress
The power to make laws is given to a Congress made up of two chambers to represent different interests: the Senate to represent the states; the House to be more responsive to the people's will.

Section 2. House of Representatives
1. Election and Term of Office
"Electors" means voters. Every two years the voters choose new Congress members to serve in the House of Representatives. The Constitution states that each state may specify who can vote. But the 15th, 19th, 24th, and 26th Amendments have established guidelines that all states must follow regarding the right to vote.

2. Qualifications
Representatives must be twenty-five years old, citizens of the United States for seven years, and residents of the state they represent.

3. Division of Representatives among the States
The number of representatives from each state is based on the size of the state's population. Each state is divided into congressional districts, with each district required to be equal in population. Each state is entitled to at least one representative. The number of representatives in the House was set at 435 in 1929. Since then, there has been a reapportionment of seats based on population shifts rather than on addition of seats.

Only three-fifths of a state's slave population was to be counted in determining the number of representatives elected by the state. Native Americans were not counted at all.

The "enumeration" referred to is the census, the population count taken every ten years since 1790.

4. Vacancies
Vacancies in the House are filled through special elections called by the state's governor.

5. Officers
The Speaker is the leader of the majority party in the House and is responsible for choosing the heads of various House committees. "Impeachment" means indictment, or bringing charges against an official.

Preamble

We, the people of the United States, in Order to form a more perfect Union, establish Justice, insure domestic Tranquility, provide for the common defence, promote the general Welfare, and secure the Blessings of Liberty to ourselves and our Posterity, do ordain and establish this Constitution for the United States of America.

Article I

Section 1
All legislative Powers herein granted shall be vested in a Congress of the United States, which shall consist of a Senate and House of Representatives.

Section 2
1.   The House of Representatives shall be composed of Members chosen every second Year by the People of the several States, and the Electors in each State shall have the Qualifications requisite for Electors of the most numerous Branch of the State Legislature.

2.   No Person shall be a Representative who shall not have attained to the Age of twenty-five Years, and been seven Years a Citizen of the United States, and who shall not, when elected, be an Inhabitant of that State in which he shall be chosen.

3.   Representatives and direct Taxes shall be apportioned among the several states which may be included within this Union, according to their respective Numbers, ~~which shall be determined by adding to the whole Number of free Persons, including those bound to Service for a Term of Years, and excluding Indians not taxed, three fifths of all other Persons.~~ The actual Enumeration shall be made within three Years after the first Meeting of the Congress of the United States, and within every subsequent Term of ten Years, in such Manner as they shall by Law direct. The Number of Representatives shall not exceed one for every thirty Thousand, but each state shall have at Least one Representative; ~~and until such enumeration shall be made, the State of New Hampshire shall be entitled to chuse three; Massachusetts eight, Rhode Island and Providence Planatations one, Connecticut five, New York six, New Jersey four, Pennsylvania eight, Delaware one, Maryland six, Virginia ten, North Carolina five, South Carolina five, and Georgia three.~~

4.   When vacancies happen in the Representation from any State, the Executive Authority thereof shall issue Writs of Election to fill such Vacancies.

5.   The House of Representatives shall chuse their Speaker and other Officers; and shall have the sole Power of Impeachment.

Section 3

1.   The Senate of the United States shall be composed of two Senators from each State, chosen ~~by the Legislature thereof~~; for six Years; and each Senator shall have one Vote.

2.   Immediately after they shall be assembled in Consequence of the first Election, they shall be divided as equally as may be into three Classes. The Seats of the Senators of the first Class shall be vacated at the Expiration of the second Year, of the second Class at the Expiration of the fourth Year, and of the third Class at the Expiration of the sixth Year, so that one-third may be chosen every second Year; and if Vacancies happen by Resignations, or otherwise, ~~during the Recess of the Legislature of any State, the Executive thereof may make temporary Appointments until the next Meeting of the Legislature, which shall then fill such Vacancies.~~

3.   No person shall be a Senator who shall not have attained to the Age of thirty Years, and been nine Years a Citizen of the United States, and who shall not, when elected, be an Inhabitant of that State in which he shall be chosen.

4.   The Vice President of the United States shall be President of the Senate, but shall have no vote, unless they be equally divided.

5.   The Senate shall chuse their Officers, and also a President pro tempore, in the absence of the Vice-President, or when he shall exercise the Office of the President of the United States.

6.   The Senate shall have the sole Power to try all empeachments. When sitting for that purpose, they shall be on Oath or Affirmation. When the President of the United States is tried, the Chief Justice shall preside: And no person shall be convicted without the Concurrence of two-thirds of the Members present.

7.   Judgment in Cases of Impeachment shall not extend further than to removal from Office, and disqualification to hold and enjoy any Office of Honor, Trust or Profit under the United States: but the Party convicted shall nevertheless be liable and subject to Indictment, Trial, Judgment and Punishment, according to Law.

Section 4

1.   The Times, Places, and Manner of holding Elections for Senators and Representatives, shall be prescribed in each state by the Legislature thereof; but the Congress may at any time by Law make or alter such Regulations, except as to the Places of Chusing Senators.

2.   The Congress shall assemble at least once in every Year, ~~and such Meeting shall be on the first Monday in December, unless they shall by Law appoint a different Day.~~

Section 3. The Senate
1. Number of Members, Terms of Office, and Voting Procedure

Originally, senators were chosen by the state legislators of their own states. The 17th Amendment changed this, so that senators are now elected directly by the people. There are 100 senators, two from each state.

2. Staggered Elections; Vacancies

One third of the Senate is elected every two years. The terms of the first Senate's membership was staggered: one group served two years, one four, and one six. All senators now serve a six-year term.

The 17th Amendment changed the method of filling vacancies in the Senate.

3. Qualifications

Qualifications for the Senate are more restrictive than those for the House. Senators must be at least 30 years old and they must have been citizens of the United States for at least nine years. The Framers of the Constitution made the Senate a more elite body in order to produce a further check on the powers of the House of Representatives.

4. President of the Senate

The Vice President's only duty listed in the Constitution is to preside over the Senate. The only real power the Vice President has is to cast the deciding vote when there is a tie. However, modern Presidents have given their Vice Presidents new responsibilities.

5. Other Officers

The Senate selects its other officers, including a presiding officer (president pro tempore) who serves when the Vice President is absent or has become President of the United States.

6. Trial of Impeachments

When trying a case of impeachment brought by the House, the Senate convenes as a court. The Chief Justice of the Supreme Court acts as the presiding judge, and the Senate acts as the jury. A two-thirds vote of the members present is necessary to convict officials under impeachment charges.

7. Penalty for Conviction

If the Senate convicts an official, it may only remove the official from office and prevent that person from holding another federal position. However, the convicted official may still be tried for the same offense in a regular court of law.

Section 4. Elections and Meetings
1. Holding Elections

In 1842 Congress required members of the House to be elected from districts in states having more than one Representative rather than at large. In 1845 it set the first Tuesday after the first Monday in November as the day for selecting presidential electors.

2. Meetings

The 20th Amendment, ratified in 1933, has changed the date of the opening of the regular session of Congress to January 3.

Section 5. Organization and Rules of Procedure

1. Organization

Until 1969 Congress acted as the sole judge of qualifications of its own members. In that year, the Supreme Court ruled that Congress could not legally exclude victorious candidates who met all the requirements listed in Article I, Section 2.

A "quorum" is the minimum number of members that must be present for the House or Senate to conduct sessions. For a regular House session, a quorum consists of the majority of the House, or 218 of the 437 members.

2. Rules

Each house sets its own rules, can punish its members for disorderly behavior, and can expel a member by a two-thirds vote.

3. Journals

In addition to the journals, a complete official record of everything said on the floor, as well as the roll call votes on all bills or issues, is available in the *Congressional Record,* published daily by the Government Printing Office.

4. Adjournment

Neither house may adjourn for more than three days or move to another location without the approval of the other house.

Section 6. Privileges and Restrictions

1. Pay and Privileges

To strengthen the federal government, the Founders set congressional salaries to be paid by the United States Treasury rather than by members' respective states. Originally, members were paid $6 per day. Salaries for Senators and Representatives are $129,500.

The "immunity" privilege means members cannot be sued or be prosecuted for anything they say in Congress. They cannot be arrested while Congress is in session, except for treason, major crimes, or breaking the peace.

2. Restrictions

"Emoluments" means salaries. The purposes of this clause is to prevent members of Congress from passing laws that would benefit them personally. It also prevents the President from promising them jobs in other branches of the federal government.

Section 7. Passing Laws

1. Revenue Bills

"Revenue" is income raised by the government. The chief source of government revenue is taxes. All tax laws must originate in the House of Representatives. This insures that the branch of Congress which is elected by the people every two years has the major role in determining taxes. This clause does not prevent the Senate from amending tax bills.

Section 5

1. Each House shall be the Judge of the Elections, Returns and Qualifications of its own Members, and a Majority of each shall constitute a Quorum to do Business; but a smaller Number may adjourn from day to day, and may be authorized to compel the Attendance of absent Members, in such Manner, and under such Penalties as each House may provide.

2. Each House may determine the Rules of its Proceedings, punish its Members for disorderly Behaviour, and, with the Concurrence of two-thirds, expel a Member.

3. Each House shall keep a Journal of its Proceedings, and from time to time publish the same, excepting such Parts as may in their Judgment require Secrecy; and the Yeas and Nays of the Members of either House on any question shall, at the desire of one-fifth of those Present, be entered on the Journal.

4. Neither House, during the Session of Congress, shall, without the Consent of the other, adjourn for more than three days, nor to any other Place than that in which the two Houses shall be sitting.

Section 6

1. The Senators and Representatives shall receive a Compensation for their Services, to be ascertained by Law, and paid out of the Treasury of the United States. They shall in all Cases, except Treason, Felony and Breach of the Peace, be privileged from Arrest during their attendance at the Session of their respective Houses, and in going to and returning from the same; and for any Speech or Debate in either House, they shall not be questioned in any other place.

2. No Senator or Representative shall, during the Time for which he was elected, be appointed to any civil Office under the Authority of the United States, which shall have been created, or the Emoluments whereof shall have been encreased, during such time; and no Person holding any Office under the United States, shall be a Member of either House during his continuance in Office.

Section 7

1. All Bills for raising Revenue shall originate in the House of Representatives; but the Senate may propose or concur with Amendments as on other bills.

2. Every Bill which shall have passed the House of Representatives and the Senate, shall, before it become a Law, be presented to the President of the United States; If he approve he shall sign it, but if not he shall return it, with his Objections, to that House in which it shall have originated, who shall enter the Objections at large on their Journal, and proceed to reconsider it. If after such Reconsideration two-thirds of that House shall agree to pass the bill, it shall be sent, together with the objections, to the other House, by which it shall likewise be reconsidered, and if approved by two-thirds of that House, it shall become a Law. But in all such Cases the Votes of both Houses shall be determined by Yeas and Nays, and the Names of the Persons voting for and against the Bill shall be enterd on the Journal of each House respectively. If any Bill shall not be returned by the President within ten Days (Sundays excepted) after it shall have been presented to him, the Same shall be a Law, in like Manner as if he had signed it, unless the Congress by their Adjournment prevent its Return, in which Case it shall not be a Law.

3. Every Order, Resolution, or Vote to which the Concurrence of the Senate and House of Representatives may be necessary (except on a question of Adjournment) shall be presented to the President of the United States; and before the Same shall take Effect, shall be approved by him, or, being disapproved by him, shall be repassed by two-thirds of the Senate and House of Representatives, according to the Rules and Limitations prescribed in the case of a Bill.

2. How Bills Become Laws

A bill may become a law only by passing both houses of Congress and by being signed by the President. If the President disapproves, or vetoes, the bill, it is returned to the house where it originated, along with a written statement of the President's objections. If two-thirds of each house approves the bill after the President has vetoed it, it becomes law. In voting to override a President's veto, the votes of all members of Congress must be recorded in the journals or official records. If the President does not sign or veto a bill within ten days (excluding Sundays), it becomes law. However, if Congress has adjourned during this ten-day period, the bill does not become law. This is known as a "pocket veto."

3. Presidential Approval or Veto

The Framers included this paragraph to prevent Congress from passing joint resolutions instead of bills to avoid the possibility of a presidential veto. A bill is a draft of a proposed law, whereas a resolution is the legislature's formal expression of opinion or intent on a matter.

The Capitol in Washington, D. C., houses the seat of the nation's government. Congressional lawmakers meet in the Capitol to hear arguments and vote on bills put before them that eventually become part of the nation's law.

Section 8. Powers Granted to Congress

1. Revenue
This clause gives Congress the power to raise and spend revenue. Taxes must be levied at the same rate throughout the nation.

2. Borrowing
The federal government borrows money by issuing bonds.

3. Commerce
The exact meaning of "commerce" has caused controversy. The trend has been to expand its meaning and, consequently, the extent of Congress's powers.

4. Naturalization and Bankruptcy
"Naturalization" refers to the procedure by which a citizen of a foreign nation becomes a citizen of the United States.

5. Currency
Control over money is an exclusive federal power; the states are forbidden to issue currency.

6. Counterfeiting
"Counterfeiting" means illegally imitating or forging.

7. Post Office
In 1970 the United States Postal Service replaced the Post Office Department.

8. Copyrights and Patents
Under this provision, Congress has passed copyright and patent laws.

9. Courts
This provision allows Congress to establish a federal court system.

10. Piracy
Congress has the power to protect American ships on the high seas.

11. Declare War
While the Constitution gives Congress the right to declare war, the United States sent troops into combat without a congressional declaration.

12. Army
This provision reveals the Framers' fears of a standing army.

13. Navy
This clause allows Congress to establish a navy.

14. Rules for Armed Forces
Congress may pass regulations that deal with military discipline.

15. Militia
The "militia" is now called the National Guard. It is organized by the states.

16. National Guard
Even though the National Guard is organized by the states, Congress has the authority to pass rules for governing its behavior.

17. Nation's Capital
This clause grants Congress the right to make laws for Washington, D.C.

Section 8

The Congress shall have the Power

1. To lay and collect Taxes, Duties, Imposts and Excises, to pay the Debts and provide for the common Defence and general Welfare of the United States; but all Duties, Imposts and Excises shall be uniform throughout the United States;

2. To borrow money on the credit of the United States;

3. To regulate Commerce with foreign Nations, and among the several States, and with the Indian Tribes;

4. To establish an uniform Rule of Naturalization, and uniform Laws on the subject of Bankruptcies throughout the United States;

5. To coin Money, regulate the Value thereof, and of foreign Coin, and fix the Standard of Weights and Measures;

6. To provide for the Punishment of counterfeiting the Securities and current Coin of the United States;

7. To establish Post Offices and post Roads;

8. To promote the Progress of Science and useful Arts, by securing for limited Times to Authors and Inventors the exclusive Right to their respective Writings and Discoveries;

9. To constitute Tribunals inferior to the Supreme Court;

10. To define and punish Piracies and Felonies committed on the high Seas, and Offenses against the Law of Nations;

11. To declare War, grant Letters of Marque and Reprisal, and make Rules concerning Captures on Land and Water;

12. To raise and support Armies, but not Appropriation of Money to that Use shall be for a longer Term than two Years;

13. To provide and maintain a Navy;

14. To make Rules for the Government and Regulation of the land and naval forces;

15. To provide for calling forth the Militia to execute the Laws of the Union, suppress Insurrections, and repel Invasions;

16. To provide for organizing, arming, and disciplining, the Militia, and for governing such Part of them as may be employed in the Service of the United States, reserving to the States respectively, the Appointment of the Officers, and the Authority of training the Militia according to the discipline prescribed by Congress;

17. To exercise exclusive Legislation in all Cases whatsoever, over such District (not exceeding ten Miles square) as may, by Cession of particular States, and the acceptance of Congress, become the Seat of Government of the United States, and to exercise like Authority over all Places purchased by the Consent of the Legislature of the State in which the Same shall be, for the Erection of Forts, Magazines, Arsenals, dock-Yards, and other needful Buildings;—And

18. To make all Laws which shall be necessary and proper for carrying into Execution the foregoing Powers, and all other Powers vested by this Constitution in the Government of the United States, or in any Department or Officer thereof.

Section 9

1. ~~The Migration or Importation of such Persons as any of the States now existing shall think proper to admit, shall not be prohibited by the Congress prior to the Year one thousand eight hundred and eight, but a tax or duty may be imposed on such importation, not exceeding ten dollars for each Person.~~

2. The privilege of the Writ of Habeas Corpus shall not be suspended, unless when in Cases of Rebellion or Invasion the public Safety may require it.

3. No Bill of Attainder or ex post facto Law shall be passed.

4. No capitation, or other direct, Tax shall be laid unless in Proportion to the Census or Enumeration herein before directed to be taken.

5. No Tax or Duty shall be laid on Articles exported from any State.

6. No Preference shall be given by any Regulation of Commerce or Revenue to the Ports of one State over those of another: nor shall Vessels bound to, or from, one State, be obliged to enter, clear, or pay Duties in another.

7. No Money shall be drawn from the Treasury, but in Consequence of Appropriations made by Law; and a regular Statement and Account of the Receipts and Expenditures of all public Money shall be published from time to time.

8. No Title of Nobility shall be granted by the United States: —And no Person holding any Office of Profit or Trust under them, shall, without the Consent of the Congress, accept of any present, Emolument, Office, or Title, of any kind whatever, from any King, Prince, or foreign State.

Section 10

1. No State shall enter into any Treaty, Alliance, or Confederation; grant Letters of Marque and Reprisal; coin Money; emit Bills of Credit; make any Thing but gold and silver Coin a Tender in Payment of Debts; pass any Bill of Attainder; ex post facto Law, or Law impairing the Obligation of Contracts, or grant any Title of Nobility.

2. No State shall, without the Consent of the Congress, lay any Imposts or Duties on Imports or Exports, except what may be absolutely necessary for executing its inspection Laws: and the net Produce of all Duties and

18. Elastic Clause

This is the so-called "elastic clause" of the Constitution and one of its most important provisions. The "necessary and proper" laws must be related to one of the 17 enumerated powers.

Section 9. Powers Denied to the Federal Government.

1. Slave Trade

This paragraph contains the compromise the Framers reached regarding regulation of the slave trade in exchange for Congress's exclusive control over interstate commerce.

2. Habeas Corpus

"Habeas corpus" is a Latin term meaning "you may have the body." A writ of habeas corpus issued by a judge requires a law official to bring a prisoner to court and show cause for holding the prisoner. The writ may be suspended only during wartime.

3. Bills of Attainder

A "bill of attainder" is a bill that punishes a person without a jury trial. An "ex post facto" law is one that makes an act a crime after the act has been committed.

4. Direct Taxes

The 16th Amendment allowed Congress to pass an income tax.

5. Tax on Exports

Congress may not tax goods that move from one state to another.

6. Uniformity of Treatment

This prohibition prevents Congress from favoring one state or region over another in the regulation of trade.

7. Appropriation Law

This clause protects against the misuse of funds. All of the President's expenditures must be made with the permission of Congress.

8. Titles of Nobility

This clause prevents the development of a nobility in the United States.

Section 10. Powers Denied to the States

1. Limitations on Power

The states are prohibited from conducting foreign affairs, carrying on a war, or controlling interstate and foreign commerce. States are also not allowed to pass laws that the federal government is prohibited from passing, such as enacting ex post facto laws or bills of attainder. These restrictions on the states were designed, in part, to prevent an overlapping in functions and authority with the federal government that could create conflict and chaos.

The inauguration is held on January 20 following a presidential election. Generally held on the steps of the Capitol, the ceremony centers on swearing into office the new President.

2. Export and Import Taxes

This clause prevents states from levying duties on exports and imports. If states were permitted to tax imports and exports they could use their taxing power in a way that weakens or destroys Congress's power to control interstate and foreign commerce.

3. Duties, Armed Forces, War

This clause prohibits states from maintaining an army or navy and from going to war, except in cases where a state is directly attacked. It also forbids states from collecting fees from foreign vessels or from making treaties with other nations. All of these powers are reserved for the federal government.

Article II. The Executive Branch
Section 1. President and Vice President

1. Term of Office

The President is given power to enforce the laws passed by Congress. Both the President and the Vice President serve four-year terms. The 22nd Amendment limits the number of terms the President may serve to two.

Imposts, laid by any State on Imports and Exports, shall be for the Use of the Treasury of the United States; and all such Laws shall be subject to the Revision and Controul of the Congress.

3. No State shall, without the Consent of Congress, lay any duty of Tonnage, keep Troops, or Ships of War in time of Peace, enter into any Agreement or Compact with another State, or with a foreign Power, or engage in War, unless actually invaded, or in such imminent Danger as will not admit of delay.

Article II
Section 1

1. The executive Power shall be vested in a President of the United States of America. He shall hold his Office during the Term of four years, and, together with the Vice-President chosen for the same Term, be elected, as follows:

2. Each State shall appoint, in such Manner as the Legislature thereof may direct, a Number of Electors, equal to the whole Number of Senators and Representatives to which the State may be entitled in the Congress: but no Senator or Representative, or Person holding an Office of Trust or Profit under the United States, shall be appointed an Elector.

3. ~~The Electors shall meet in their respective States, and vote by Ballot for two Persons, of whom one at least shall not be an Inhabitant of the same State with themselves. And they shall make a List of all the Persons voted for, and of the Number of Votes for each; which List they shall sign and certify, and transmit sealed to the Seat of the Government of the United States, directed to the President of the Senate. The President of the Senate shall, in the Presence of the Senate and House of Representatives, open all the Certificates, and the Votes shall then be counted. The Person having the greatest Number of Votes shall be the President, if such Number be a Majority of the whole Number of Electors appointed; and if there be more than one who have such Majority, and have an equal Number of Votes, then the House of Representatives shall immediately chuse by Ballot one of them for President; and if no Person have a Majority, then from the five highest on the List the said House shall in like Manner chuse the President. But in chusing the President, the Votes shall be taken by States, the Representation from each State having one Vote; a quorum for this Purpose shall consist of a Member of Members from two-thirds of the States, and a Majority of all the States shall be necessary to a Choice. In every Case, after the Choice of the President, the Person having the greatest Number of Votes of the Electors shall be the Vice-President. But if there should remain two or more who have equal votes, the Senate shall chuse from them by Ballot the Vice President.~~

4. The Congress may determine the Time of chusing the Electors, and the Day on which they shall give their Votes; which Day shall be the same throughout the United States.

5. No person except a natural born Citizen, or a Citizen of the United States, at the time of the Adoption of this Constitution, shall be eligible to the Office of President; neither shall any Person be eligible to that Office who shall not have attained to the Age of thirty-five years, and been fourteen Years a Resident within the United States.

6. In Case of the Removal of the President from Office, or of his Death, Resignation, or Inability to discharge the Powers and Duties of the said Office, the same shall devolve on the Vice-President, and the Congress may by Law provide for the Case of Removal, Death, Resignation or Inability, both of the President and Vice-President, declaring what Officer shall then act as President, and such Officer shall act accordingly, until the disability be removed, or a President shall be elected.

2. Election

The Philadelphia Convention had trouble deciding how the President was to be chosen. The system finally agreed upon was indirect election by "electors" chosen for that purpose. The President and Vice President are not directly elected. Instead, the President and Vice President are elected by presidential electors from each state who form the electoral college. Each state has the number of presidential electors equal to the total number of its senators and representatives. State legislatures determine how the electors are chosen. Originally, the state legislatures chose the electors, but today they are nominated by political parties and elected by the voters. No senator, representative, or any other federal officeholder can serve as an elector.

3. Former Method of Election

This clause describes the original method of electing the President and Vice President. According to this method, each elector voted for two candidates. The candidate with the most votes (as long as it was a majority) became President. The candidate with the second highest number of votes became Vice President. In the election of 1800, the two top candidates received the same number of votes, making it necessary for the House of Representatives to decide the election. To prevent such a situation from recurring, the 12th Amendment was added in 1804.

4. Date of Elections

Congress selects the date when the presidential electors are chosen and when they vote for President and Vice President. All electors must vote on the same day. The first Tuesday after the first Monday in November has been set as the date for presidential elections. Electors cast their votes on the Monday after the second Wednesday in December.

5. Qualifications

The President must be a citizen of the United States by birth, at least thirty-five years old, and a resident of the United States for fourteen years. See Amendment 22.

6. Vacancies

If the President dies, resigns, is removed from office by impeachment, or is unable to carry out the duties of the office, the Vice President becomes President. (Amendment 25 deals with presidential disability.) If both the President and Vice President are unable to serve, Congress has the power to declare by law who acts as President. Congress set the line of succession in the Presidential Succession Act of 1947.

7. Salary

Originally, the President's salary was $25,000 per year. The President's current salary of $200,000 plus a $50,000 taxable expense account per year was enacted in 1969. The President also receives numerous fringe benefits including a $120,000 nontaxable allowance for travel and entertainment, and living accommodations in two residences, the White House and Camp David. However, the President cannot receive any other income from the United States Government or state governments while in office.

8. Oath of Office

The oath of office is generally administered by the chief justice, but can be administered by any official authorized to administer oaths. All Presidents-elect except Washington have been sworn into office by the chief justice. Only Vice Presidents John Tyler, Calvin Coolidge, and Lyndon Johnson in succeeding to the office have been sworn in by someone else.

Section 2. Powers of the President
1. Military, Cabinet, Pardons

Mention of "the principal officer in each of the executive departments" is the only suggestion of the President's Cabinet to be found in the Constitution. The Cabinet is a purely advisory body, and its power depends on the President. Each Cabinet member is appointed by the President and must be confirmed by the Senate. This clause also makes the President, a civilian, the head of the armed services. This established the principle of civilian control of the military.

2. Treaties and Appointments

The President is the chief architect of American foreign policy. He or she is responsible for the conduct of foreign relations, or dealings with other countries. All treaties, however, require approval of two-thirds of the senators present. Most federal positions today are filled under the rules and regulations of the civil service system. Most presidential appointees serve at the pleasure of the President. Removal of an official by the President is not subject to congressional approval. But the power can be restricted by conditions set in creating the office.

3. Vacancies in Offices

The President can temporarily appoint officials to fill vacancies when the Senate is not in session.

Section 3. Duties of the President

Under this provision the President delivers annual State-of-the-Union messages. On occasion, Presidents have called Congress into special session to consider particular problems.

7. The President shall, at stated Times, receive for his Services, a Compensation, which shall neither be encreased nor diminished during the Period for which he shall have been elected, and he shall not receive within that Period any other Emolument from the United States, or any of them.

8. Before he enter on the execution of his Office, he shall take the following Oath or Affirmation: "I do solemnly swear (or affirm) that I will faithfully execute the Office of President of the United States, and will to the best of my Ability, preserve, protect and defend the Constitution of the United States."

Section 2

1. The President shall be Commander in Chief of the Army and Navy of the United States, and of the Militia of the several States, when called into the actual Service of the United States; he may require the Opinion, in writing, of the principal Officer in each of the executive Departments, upon any subject relating to the Duties of their respective Offices, and he shall have Power to Grant Reprieves and Pardons for Offences against the United States, except in Cases of Impeachment.

2. He shall have Power, by and with the Advice and Consent of the Senate, to make Treaties, provided two-thirds of the Senators present concur; and he shall nominate, and by and with the Advice and Consent of the Senate, shall appoint Ambassadors, other public Ministers and Consuls, Judges of the supreme Court, and all other Officers of the United States, whose Appointments are not herein otherwise provided for, and which shall be established by Law. But the Congress may by Law vest the Appointment of such inferior Officers, as they think proper, in the President alone, in the Courts of Law, or in the Heads of Departments.

3. The President shall have Power to fill up all Vacancies that may happen during the Recess of the Senate, by granting Commissions which shall expire at the End of their next Session

Section 3

He shall from time to time give to Congress Information of the State of the Union, and recommend to their Consideration such Measures as he shall judge necessary and expedient; he may, on extraordinary occasions, convene both Houses, or either of them, and in Case of

As commander in chief of the United States armed forces, the President is the people's check on the power of the military. Throughout history, Presidents have used this power to call upon the military to defend the nation.

Disagreement between them, with respect to the Time of Adjournment, he may adjourn them to such Time as he shall think proper; he shall receive Ambassadors and other public Ministers; he shall take Care that the Laws be faithfully executed, and shall Commission all the Officers of the United States.

Section 4

The President, Vice-President and all civil Officers of the United States, shall be removed from Office on Impeachment for, and Conviction of, Treason, Bribery, or other high Crimes and Misdemeanors.

Article III

Section 1

The Judicial Power of the United States, shall be vested in one supreme Court, and in such inferior Courts as the Congress may from time to time ordain and establish. The judges, both of the supreme and inferior Courts, shall

The President's duty to receive foreign diplomats also includes the power to ask a foreign country to withdraw its diplomatic officials from this country. This is called "breaking diplomatic relations" and often carries with it the implied threat of more drastic action, even war. The President likewise has the power of deciding whether or not to recognize foreign governments.

Section 4. Impeachment

This section states the reasons for which the President and Vice President may be impeached and removed from office. (See annotations of Article I, Section 2, Clauses 6 and 7.)

Article III. The Judicial Branch
Section 1. Federal Courts

The term "judicial" refers to courts. The Constitution set up only the Supreme Court but provided for the establishment of other federal courts. There are presently nine justices on the Supreme Court.

Congress has created a system of federal district courts and courts of appeals, which review certain district court cases. Judges of these courts serve during "good behavior," which means that they usually serve for life or until they choose to retire.

Section 2. Jurisdiction

1. General Jurisdiction

Use of the words "in law and equity" reflects the fact that American courts took over two kinds of traditional law from Great Britain. The basic law was the "common law," which was based on over five centuries of judicial decisions. "Equity" was a special branch of British law developed to handle cases where common law did not apply.

Federal courts deal mostly with "statute law," or laws passed by Congress, treaties, and cases involving the Constitution itself. "Admiralty and maritime jurisdiction" covers all sorts of cases involving ships and shipping on the high seas and on rivers, canals, and lakes.

2. The Supreme Court

When a court has "original jurisdiction" over certain kinds of cases, it means that the court has the authority to be the first court to hear a case. A court with "appellate jurisdiction" hears cases that have been appealed from lower courts. Most Supreme Court cases are heard on appeal from lower courts.

3. Jury Trials

Except in cases of impeachment, anyone accused of a crime has the right to a trial by jury. The trial must be held in the state where the crime was committed. Jury trial guarantees were strengthened in the 6th, 7th, 8th, and 9th Amendments.

hold their Offices during good Behaviour, and shall, at stated Times, receive for their Services, a Compensation, which shall not be diminished during their Continuance in Office.

Section 2

1. The judicial Power shall extend to all Cases, in Law and Equity, arising under this Constitution, the Laws of the United States, and treaties made, or which shall be made, under their Authority; to all Cases affecting ambassadors, other public ministers and consuls; to all cases of admiralty and maritime Jurisdiction; to Controversies to which the United States shall be a party; to Controversies between two or more states; ~~between a State and Citizens of another State; between Citizens of different States~~; between Citizens of the same State claiming Lands under Grants of different States, and between a State, or the Citizens thereof, and foreign States, Citizens or Subjects.

2. In all Cases affecting Ambassadors, other public Ministers and Consuls, and those in which a State shall be Party, the supreme Court shall have original Jurisdiction. In all the other Cases before mentioned, the supreme Court shall have appellate Jurisdiction, both as to Law and Fact, with such Exceptions, and under such Regulations as the Congress shall make.

3. The trial of all Crimes, except in Cases of Impeachment, shall be by Jury; and such Trial shall be held in the State where the said Crimes shall have been committed; but when not committed within any State, the Trial shall be at such Place or Places as the Congress may by Law have directed.

In this room Supreme Court proceedings are held. The Constitution established the jurisdiction of the federal courts by defining the kinds of cases these courts may hear.

Section 3

1. Treason against the United States, shall consist only in levying War against them, or in adhering to their Enemies, giving them Aid and Comfort. No Person shall be convicted of Treason unless on the Testimony of two Witnesses to the same overt Act, or on Confession in open Court.

2. The Congress shall have power to declare the Punishment of Treason, but no Attainder of Treason shall work Corruption of Blood, or Forfeiture except during the Life of the Person attainted.

Article IV

Section 1

Full Faith and Credit shall be given in each State to the public Acts, Records, and judicial Proceedings of every other State. And the Congress may by general Laws prescribe the Manner in which such Acts, Records, and Proceedings shall be proved, and the Effect thereof.

Section 2

1. The Citizens of each State shall be entitled to all Privileges and Immunities of Citizens in the several States.

2. A Person charged in any State with Treason, Felony, or other Crime, who shall flee from Justice, and be found in another State, shall on demand of the executive Authority of the State from which he fled, be delivered up, to be removed to the State having Jurisdiction of the crime.

3. ~~No Person held to Service or Labour in one State, under the Laws thereof, escaping into another, shall, in Consequence of any Law or Regulation therein, be discharged from such Service or Labour, but shall be delivered up on Claim of the Party to whom such Service or Labour may be due.~~

Section 3

1. New States may be admitted by the Congress into this Union; but no new State shall be formed or erected within the Jurisdiction of any other State; nor any State be formed by the Junction of two or more States, or parts of States, without the Consent of the Legislatures of the States concerned as well as of the Congress.

2. The Congress shall have Power to dispose of and make all needful Rules and Regulations respecting the Territory or other Property belonging to the United States; and nothing in this Constitution shall be so construed as to Prejudice any Claims of the United States, or of any particular State.

Section 3. Treason
1. Definition

Knowing that the charge of treason often had been used by monarchs to get rid of people who opposed them, the Framers of the Constitution defined treason carefully, requiring that at least two witnesses be present to testify in court that a treasonable act was committed.

2. Punishment

Congress is given the power to determine the punishment for treason. The children of a person convicted of treason may not be punished nor may the convicted person's property be taken away from the children. Convictions for treason have been relatively rare in the nation's history.

Article IV. Relations Among the States
Section 1. Official Acts

This provision insures that each state recognize the laws, court decisions, and records of all other states. For example, a marriage license or corporation charter issued by one state must be accepted in other states.

Section 2. Mutual Duties of States
1. Privileges

The "privileges and immunities," or rights of citizens, guarantee each state's citizens equal treatment in all states.

2. Extradition

"Extradition" means that a person convicted of a crime or a person accused of a crime must be returned to the state where the crime was committed. Thus, a person cannot flee to another state hoping to escape the law.

3. Fugitive-Slave Clause

Formerly this clause meant that slaves could not become free persons by escaping to free states.

Section 3. New States and Territories
1. New States

Congress has the power to admit new states. It also determines the basic guidelines for applying for statehood. One state, Maine, was created within the original boundaries of another state (Massachusetts) with the consent of Congress and the state.

2. Territories

Congress has power over federal land. But neither in this clause nor anywhere else in the Constitution is the federal government explicitly empowered to acquire new territory.

Section 4. Federal Protection for States

This section allows the federal government to send troops into a state to guarantee law and order. The President may send in troops even without the consent of the state government involved.

Article V. The Amending Process

There are now 26 Amendments to the Constitution. The Framers of the Constitution deliberately made it difficult to amend or change the Constitution. Two methods of proposing and ratifying amendments are provided for. A two-thirds majority is needed in Congress to propose an amendment, and at least three-fourths of the states (38 states) must accept the amendment before it can become law. No amendment has yet been proposed by a national convention called by the states, though in the 1980s a convention to propose an amendment requiring a balanced budget had been approved by 32 states.

Article VI. National Supremacy
1. Public Debts and Treaties

This section promised that all debts the colonies had incurred during the Revolution and under the Articles of Confederation would be honored by the new United States government.

2. The Supreme Law

The "supremacy clause" recognized the Constitution and federal laws as supreme when in conflict with those of the states. It was largely based on this clause that Chief Justice John Marshall wrote his historic decision in *McCulloch v. Maryland*. The 14th Amendment reinforced the supremacy of federal law over state laws.

3. Oaths of Office

This clause also declares that no religious test shall be required as a qualification for holding public office. This principle is also asserted in the First Amendment, which forbids Congress to set up an established church or to interfere with the religious freedom of Americans.

Section 4

The United States shall guarantee to every State in this Union a Republican Form of Government, and shall protect each of them against Invasion; and on Application of the Legislature, or of the Executive (when the Legislature cannot be convened) against domestic Violence.

Article V

The Congress, whenever two-thirds of both Houses shall deem it necessary, shall propose Amendments to this Constitution, or, on the Application of the Legislatures of two-thirds of the several States, shall call a Convention for proposing Amendments, which, in either Case, shall be valid to all Intents and Purposes, as part of this Constitution, when ratified by the Legislatures of three-fourths of the several States, or by Conventions in three-fourths thereof, as the one or the other Mode of Ratification may be proposed by the Congress; Provided that no Amendment which may be made prior to the Year One thousand eight hundred and eight shall in any Manner affect the first and fourth clauses in the Ninth Section of the first Article; and that no State, without its Consent, shall be deprived of its equal Suffrage in the Senate.

Article VI

1. All Debts contracted and Engagements entered into, before the Adoption of this Constitution, shall be as valid against the United States under this Constitution as under the Confederation.

2. This Constitution, and the Laws of the United States which shall be made in Pursuance thereof; and all Treaties made, or which shall be made, under the Authority of the United States, shall be the supreme Law of the Land; and the Judges in every State shall be bound thereby, any Thing in the Constitution or Laws of any State to the Contrary notwithstanding.

3. The Senators and Representatives before mentioned, and the Members of the several State Legislatures, and all executive and judicial Officers, both of the United States and of the several States, shall be bound by Oath or Affirmation, to support this Constitution; but no religious Test shall ever be required as a Qualification to any Office or public Trust under the United States.

Article VII

The Ratification of the Conventions of nine States shall be sufficient for the Establishment of this Constitution between the States so ratifying the same.

Done in Convention, by the Unanimous Consent of the States present, the Seventeenth Day of September, in the Year of our Lord one thousand seven hundred and Eighty-seven, and of the Independence of the United States of America the Twelfth. In Witness whereof We have hereunto subscribed our Names.

Article VII. Ratification of the Constitution

Unlike the Articles of Confederation, which required approval of all thirteen states for adoption, the Constitution required approval of only nine of thirteen states. Thirty-nine of the 55 delegates at the Constitutional Convention signed the Constitution. The Constitution went into effect in June 1788.

Signers

George Washington, President and Deputy from Virginia

New Hampshire
John Langdon
Nicholas Gilman

Massachusetts
Nathaniel Gorham
Rufus King

Connecticut
William Samuel Johnson
Roger Sherman

New York
Alexander Hamilton

New Jersey
William Livingston
David Brearley
William Paterson
Jonathan Dayton

Pennsylvania
Benjamin Franklin
Thomas Mifflin
Robert Morris
George Clymer
Thomas FitzSimons
Jared Ingersoll
James Wilson
Gouverneur Morris

Delaware
George Read
Gunning Bedford, Jr.
John Dickinson
Richard Bassett
Jacob Broom

Maryland
James McHenry
Daniel of St. Thomas Jenifer
Daniel Carroll

Virginia
John Blair
James Madison, Jr.

North Carolina
William Blount
Richard Dobbs Spaight
Hugh Williamson

South Carolina
John Rutledge
Charles Cotesworth Pinckney
Charles Pinckney
Pierce Butler

Georgia
William Few
Abraham Baldwin

Attest: William Jackson, Secretary

Amendment I

Congress shall make no law respecting an establishment of religion, or prohibiting the free exercise thereof; or abridging the freedom of speech, or of the press; or the right of the people peaceably to assemble, and to petition the Government for a redress of grievances.

Amendment II

A well-regulated Militia, being necessary to the security of a free State, the right of the people to keep and bear Arms, shall not be infringed.

Amendment 1.

Freedom of Religion, Speech, Press, and Assembly (1791)

The 1st Amendment protects the civil liberties of individuals in the United States. The 1st Amendment freedoms are not absolute, however. They are limited by the rights of other individuals.

Amendment 2.

Right to Bear Arms (1791)

The purpose of this amendment is to guarantee states the right to keep a militia.

Several amendments protect the rights of the accused. While awaiting trial, a defendant may be released by posting bail, a procedure regulated by the Eighth Amendment.

POST BAIL
BOND HERE

Amendment 3.
Quartering Troops (1791)

This amendment is based on the principle that people have a right to privacy in their own homes. It also reflects the colonists' grievances against the British government before the Revolution. Britain had angered Americans by quartering (housing) troops in private homes.

Amendment 4.
Searches and Seizures (1791)

Like the 3rd Amendment, the 4th Amendment reflects the colonists' desire to protect their privacy. Britain had used writs of assistance (general search warrants) to seek out smuggled goods. Americans wanted to make sure that such searches and seizures would be conducted only when a judge felt that there was "reasonable cause" to conduct them. The Supreme Court has ruled that evidence seized illegally without a search warrant may not be used in court.

Amendment 5.
Rights of Accused Persons (1791)

To bring a "presentment" or "indictment" means to formally charge a person with committing a crime. It is the function of a grand jury to see whether there is enough evidence to bring the accused person to trial. A person may not be tried more than once for the same crime (double jeopardy).

Amendment III

No soldier shall, in time of peace be quartered in any house, without the consent of the Owner, nor in time of war, but in a manner to be prescribed by law.

Amendment IV

The right of the people to be secure in their persons, houses, papers, and effects, against unreasonable searches and seizures, shall not be violated, and no Warrants shall issue, but upon probable cause, supported by Oath or affirmation, and particularly describing the place to be searched, and the persons or things to be seized.

Amendment V

No person shall be held to answer for a capital, or otherwise infamous crime, unless on a presentment or indictment of a Grand Jury, except in cases arising in the land or naval forces, or in the Militia, when in actual service in time of War or public danger; nor shall any person be subject for the same offence to be twice put in jeopardy of life or limb; nor shall be compelled in any criminal case to be a witness against himself, nor be deprived of life, liberty, or property, without due process of law; nor shall private property be taken for public use, without just compensation.

Members of the armed services are subject to military law. They may be tried in a court martial. In times of war or a natural disaster, civilians may also be put under martial law.

The 5th Amendment also guarantees that persons may not be forced in any criminal case to be a witness against themselves. That is, accused persons may refuse to answer questions on the ground that the answers might tend to incriminate them.

Amendment VI

In all criminal prosecutions, the accused shall enjoy the right to a speedy and public trail, by an impartial jury of the State and district wherein the crime shall have been committed, which district shall have been previously ascertained by law, and to be informed of the nature and cause of the accusation; to be confronted with the witnesses against him; to have compulsory process for obtaining witnesses in his favor, and to have the Assistance of Counsel for his defence.

Amendment 6.
Right to Speedy, Fair Trial (1791)
The requirement of a "speedy" trial insures that an accused person will not be held in jail for a lengthy period as a means of punishing the accused without a trial. A "fair" trial means that the trial must be open to the public and that a jury must hear witnesses and evidence on both sides before deciding the guilt or innocence of a person charged with a crime. This amendment also provides that legal counsel must be provided to a defendant. In 1963, the Supreme Court ruled, in *Gideon v. Wainwright,* that if a defendant cannot afford a lawyer, the government must provide one to defend the accused person.

Amendment VII

In suits at common law, where the value in controversy shall exceed twenty dollars, the right of trial by jury shall be preserved, and no fact tried by a jury, shall be otherwise reexamined in any Courts of the United States, than according to the rules of common law.

Amendment 7.
Civil Suits (1791)
"Common law" means the law established by previous court decisions. In civil cases where one person sues another for more than $20, a jury trial is provided for. But customarily, federal courts do not hear civil cases unless they involve a good deal more money.

Amendment VIII

Excessive bail shall not be required, nor excessive fines imposed, nor cruel and unusual punishments inflicted.

Amendment 8.
Bail and Punishment (1791)
"Bail" is money that an accused person provides to the court as a guarantee that he or she will be present for a trial. This amendment insures that neither bail nor punishment for a crime shall be unreasonably severe.

Amendment IX

The enumeration in the Constitution, of certain rights, shall not be construed to deny or disparage others retained by the people.

Amendment 9.
Powers Reserved to the People (1791)
This amendment provides that the people's rights are not limited to those mentioned in the Constitution.

Amendment 10.
Powers Reserved to the States (1791)

This amendment protects the states and the people from an all-powerful federal government. It provides that the states or the people retain all powers except those denied them or those specifically granted to the federal government. This "reserved powers" provision is a check on the "necessary and proper" power of the federal government provided in the "elastic clause" in Article I, Section 8, Clause 18.

Amendment 11.
Suits against States (1795)

This amendment provides that a lawsuit brought by a citizen of the United States or a foreign nation against a state must be tried in a state court, not in a federal court. This amendment was passed after the Supreme Court ruled that a federal court could try a lawsuit brought by citizens of South Carolina against a citizen of Georgia. This case, *Chisholm v. Georgia,* decided in 1793, was protested by many Americans, who insisted states would lose authority if they could be sued in federal courts.

Amendment 12.
Election of President and Vice President (1804)

This amendment changes the procedure for electing the President and Vice President as outlined in Article II, Section 1, Paragraph 3.

To prevent the recurrence of the election of 1800 whereby a candidate running for Vice President (Aaron Burr) could tie a candidate running for President (Thomas Jefferson) and thus force the election into the House of Representatives, the Twelfth Amendment specifies that the electors are to cast

The Constitution did not provide for the existence of political parties, which today play a major role in the election of the President and Vice President.

Amendment X

The powers not delegated to the United States by the Constitution, nor prohibited by it to the States, are reserved to the States respectively, or to the people.

Amendment XI

The Judicial power of the United States shall not be construed to extend to any suit in law or equity, commenced or prosecuted against one of the United States by Citizens of another State, or by Citizens or Subjects of any Foreign State.

Amendment XII

The Electors shall meet in their respective States and vote by ballot for President and Vice-President, one of whom, at least, shall not be an inhabitant of the same State with themselves; they shall name in their ballots the person voted for as President, and in distinct ballots the person voted for as Vice-President, and they shall make distinct lists of all persons voted for as President, and of all persons voted for as Vice-President, and of the number of votes for each, which lists they shall sign and certify, and transmit sealed to the seat of the government of the United States, directed to the President of the Senate;—The President of the Senate shall, in the presence of the Senate and House of Representatives, open all the certificates and the votes shall then be counted;—The person having the greatest number of votes for President, shall be the President, if such number be a majority of the whole number of Electors appointed; and if no person have such majority, then from the persons having the highest numbers not exceeding three on the list of those voted for as President, the House of Representatives shall choose immediately, by ballot, the President. But in choosing the President, the votes shall be taken by states, the representation from each state having one vote; a quorum for this purpose shall consist of a member or members from two-thirds of the states, and a majority of all the states shall be necessary to a choice. And if the House of Representatives shall not choose a President whenever the right of choice shall devolve upon them, ~~before the fourth day of March next following,~~ then the Vice-President shall act as President, as in the case of the death or other constitutional disability of the President.—The person having the greatest number of votes as Vice-President, shall be the Vice-President, if such number be a majority of the whole number of Electors appointed, and if no person have a majority, then from the two highest numbers on the list, the Senate shall choose the Vice-President; a quorum for the purpose shall consist of two-thirds of the whole number of Senators, and a majority of the whole number shall be necessary to a choice. But no person constitutionally ineligible to the office of President shall be eligible to that of Vice-President of the United States.

Amendment XIII

Section 1
Neither slavery nor involuntary servitude, except as a punishment for crime whereof the party shall have been duly convicted, shall exist within the United States, or any place subject to their jurisdiction.

Section 2
Congress shall have power to enforce this article by appropriate legislation.

separate ballots for each office. The votes for each office are counted and listed separately. The results are signed, sealed, and sent to the president of the senate. At a joint session of Congress, the votes are counted. The candidate who receives the most votes, providing it is a majority, is elected President. Other changes include: (1) a reduction from five to the three highest candidates receiving votes among whom the House is to choose if no candidate receives a majority of the electoral votes, and (2) provision for the Senate to choose the Vice President from the two highest candidates if neither has received a majority of the electoral votes.

The Twelfth Amendment does place one restriction on electors. It prohibits electors from voting for two candidates (President and Vice President) from their home state.

Amendment 13.
Abolition of Slavery (1865)
This amendment was the final act in ending slavery in the United States. It also prohibits the binding of a person to perform a personal service due to debt. In addition to imprisonment for crime, the Supreme Court has held that the draft is not a violation of the amendment.

This amendment is the first adopted to be divided into sections. It is also the first to contain specifically a provision granting Congress power to enforce it by appropriate legislation.

The cannon on the battlefield at Gettysburg stands as a reminder of the nation's struggle over slavery, abolished by the Thirteenth Amendment.

Amendment 14.
Rights of Citizens (1868)

The clauses of this amendment were intended 1) to penalize southern states that refused to grant African Americans the vote, 2) to keep former Confederate leaders from serving in government, 3) to forbid payment of the Confederacy's debt by the federal government, and 4) to insure payment of the war debts owed the federal government.

Section 1. Citizenship Defined By granting citizenship to all persons born in the United States, this amendment granted citizenship to former slaves. The amendment also guaranteed "due process of law." By the 1950s, Supreme Court rulings used the due process clause to protect civil liberties. The last part of Section 1 establishes the doctrine that all citizens are entitled to equal protection of the laws. In 1954 the Supreme Court ruled, in *Brown v. Board of Education* of Topeka, that segregation in public schools was unconstitutional because it denied equal protection.

Section 2. Representation in Congress This section reduced the number of members a state had in the House of Representatives if it denied its citizens the right to vote. This section was not implemented, however. Later civil rights laws and the 24th Amendment guaranteed the vote to African Americans.

Section 3. Penalty for Engaging in Insurrection The leaders of the Confederacy were barred from state or federal offices unless Congress agreed to revoke this ban. By the end of Reconstruction all but a few Confederate leaders were allowed to return to public life.

Section 4. Public Debt The public debt incurred by the federal government during the Civil War was valid and could not be questioned by the South. However, the debts of the Confederacy

According to the Supreme Court, equality of education is guaranteed by the Fourteenth Amendment, which was ratified in 1868.

Amendment XIV

Section 1

All persons born or naturalized in the United States, and subject to the jurisdiction thereof, are citizens of the United States and of the State wherein they reside. No State shall make or enforce any law which shall abridge the privileges or immunities of citizens of the United States; nor shall any State deprive any person of life, liberty, or property, without due process of law, nor deny to any person within its jurisdiction the equal protection of the laws.

Section 2

Representatives shall be apportioned among the several States according to their respective numbers, counting the whole number of persons in each State, excluding Indians not taxed. But when the right to vote at any election for the choice of electors for President and Vice-President of the United States, Representatives in Congress, the Executive and Judicial officers of a State, or the members of the Legislature thereof, is denied to any of the male inhabitants of such State, being twenty-one years of age, and citizens of the United States, or in any way abridged, except for participation in rebellion, or other crime, the basis of representation therein shall be reduced in the proportion which the number of such male citizens shall bear to the whole number of male citizens twenty-one years of age in such State.

Section 3

No person shall be a Senator or Representative in Congress, or elector of President and Vice-President, or hold any office, civil or military, under the United States, or under any State, who, having previously taken an oath, as a member of Congress, or as an officer of the United States, or as a member of any State legislature, or as an executive or judicial officer of any State, to support the Constitution of the United States, shall have engaged in insurrection or rebellion against the same, or given aid or comfort to the enemies thereof. But Congress may by a vote of two-thirds of each House, remove such disability.

Section 4

The validity of the public debt of the United States incurred for payment of pensions and bounties for service, authorized by law, including debts in suppressing insurrections or rebellion, shall not be questioned. But neither the United States nor any State shall assume or pay any debt or obligation incurred in aid of resurrection or rebellion against the

United States, or any claim for the loss or emancipation of any slave; but all such debts, obligations and claims shall be held illegal and void.

Section 5

The Congress shall have power to enforce, by appropriate legislation, the provisions of this article.

Amendment XV

Section 1

The right of citizens of the United States to vote shall not be denied or abridged by the United States or by any State on account of race, color, or previous condition of servitude.

Section 2

The Congress shall have power to enforce this article by appropriate legislation.

Amendment XVI

The Congress shall have power to lay and collect taxes on incomes, from whatever source derived, without apportionment among several States, and without regard to any census or enumeration.

Amendment XVII

Section 1

The Senate of the United States shall be composed of two Senators from each State, elected by the people thereof, for six years; and each Senator shall have one vote. The electors in each state shall have the qualifications requisite for electors of the most numerous branch of the state legislatures.

Section 2

When vacancies happen in the representation of any State in the Senate, the executive authority of such State shall issue writs of election to fill such vacancies: *Provided,* that the legislature of any State may empower the executive thereof to make temporary appointments until the people fill the vacancies by election as the legislature may direct.

Section 3

This amendment shall not be so construed as to affect the election or term of any Senator chosen before it becomes valid as part of the Constitution.

were declared to be illegal. And former slave owners could not collect compensation for the loss of their slaves.

Section 5. Enforcement Congress was empowered to pass civil rights bills to guarantee the provisions of the amendment.

Amendment 15.
The Right to Vote (1870)
Section 1. Suffrage for African Americans

The 15th Amendment replaced Section 2 of the 14th Amendment in guaranteeing blacks the right to vote, that is, the right of blacks to vote was not to be left to the states. Yet, despite this prohibition, African Americans were denied the right to vote by many states by such means as poll taxes, literacy tests, and white primaries.

Section 2. Enforcement Congress was given the power to enforce this amendment. During the 1950s and 1960s, it passed successively stronger laws to end racial discrimination in voting rights.

Amendment 16.
Income Tax (1913)

The origins of this amendment went back to 1895, when the Supreme Court declared that a federal income tax unconstitutional. To overcome this Supreme Court decision, this amendment authorized an income tax that was levied on a direct basis.

Amendment 17.
Direct Election of Senators (1913)
Section 1. Method of Election The right to elect senators was given directly to the people of each state. It replaced Article I, Section 2, Clause 1, which empowered state legislatures to elect senators. This amendment was designed not only to make the choice of senators more democratic but also to cut down on corruption and to improve state government.

Section 2. Vacancies A state must order an election to fill a senate vacancy. A state may empower its governor to appoint a person to fill a Senate seat if a vacancy occurs until an election can be held.

Section 3. Time in Effect This amendment was not to affect any senate election or temporary appointment until it was in effect.

Amendment 18.
Prohibition of Alcoholic Beverages (1919)

This amendment prohibited the production, sale, or transportation of alcoholic beverages in the United States. Prohibition proved to be difficult to enforce, especially in states with large urban populations. This amendment was later repealed by the 21st Amendment.

Amendment 19.
Women's Suffrage (1920)

This amendment, extending the vote to all qualified women in federal and state elections, was a landmark victory for the women's suffrage movement, which had worked to achieve this goal for many years. The women's movement had earlier gained full voting rights for women in four western states in the late nineteenth century.

Amendment 20.
"Lame-Duck" Amendment (1933)
Section 1. New Dates of Terms This amendment had two major purposes: 1) to shorten the time between the President's and Vice President's election and inauguration, and 2) to end "lame-duck" sessions of Congress.

When the Constitution first went into effect, transportation and communication were slow and uncertain. It often took many months after the election in November for the President and Vice President to travel to Washington, D.C., and prepare for their inauguration on March 4. This amendment ended this long wait for a new administration by fixing January 20 as inauguration day.

Section 2. Meeting Time of Congress "Lame-duck" sessions occurred every two years, after the November congressional election. That is, the Congress that held its session in December of an election year was not the newly elected Congress

Amendment XVIII

Section 1
After one year from ratification of this article the manufacture, sale, or transportation of intoxicating liquors within, the importation thereof into, or the exportation thereof from the United States and all territory subject to the jurisdiction thereof for beverage purposes is hereby prohibited.

Section 2
The Congress and the several states shall have concurrent power to enforce this article by appropriate legislation.

Section 3
This article shall be inoperative unless it shall have been ratified as an amendment to the Constitution by the legislatures of the several States, as provided in the Constitution, within seven years from the date of the submission hereof to the states of the Congress.

Amendment XIX

Section 1
The right of citizens of the United States to vote shall not be denied or abridged by the United States or by any state on account of sex.

Section 2
Congress shall have power to enforce this article by appropriate legislation.

Amendment XX

Section 1
The terms of the President and Vice president shall end at noon on the 20th day of January, and the terms of the Senators and Representatives at noon on the 3rd day of January, of the years in which such terms would have ended if this article had not been ratified; and the terms of their successors shall then begin.

Section 2
The Congress shall assemble at least once in every year, and such meeting shall begin at noon on the 3rd day of January, unless they shall by law appoint a different day.

Section 3
If, at the time fixed for the beginning of the term of the President, the President elect shall have died, the Vice President elect shall become President. If a President shall not have been chosen before the time fixed for the

beginning of his term, or if the President elect shall have failed to qualify, then the Vice President elect shall act as President until a President shall have qualified; and the Congress may by law provide for the case wherein neither a President elect nor a Vice President elect shall have qualified, declaring who shall then act as President, or the manner in which one who is to act shall be selected, and such person shall act accordingly until a President or Vice President shall have qualified.

Section 4

The Congress may by law provide for the case of the death of any of the persons from whom the House of Representatives may choose a President whenever the right of choice shall have devolved upon them, and for the case of the death of any of the persons from whom the Senate may choose a Vice President whenever the right of choice shall have devolved upon them.

Section 5

Sections 1 and 2 shall take effect on the 15th day of October following the ratification of this article.

Section 6

This article shall be inoperative unless it shall have been ratified as an amendment to the Constitution by the legislatures of three-fourths of the several States within seven years from the date of its submission.

but the old Congress that had been elected two years earlier. This Congress continued to serve for several more months, usually until March of the next year. Often many of its members had failed to be re-elected and were called "lame-ducks." The 20th Amendment abolished this lame-duck session, and provided that the new Congress hold its first session soon after the November election, on January 3.

Section 3. Succession of President and Vice President This amendment provides that if the President-elect dies before taking office, the Vice President-elect becomes President. In the cases described, Congress will decide on a temporary President.

Section 4. Filling Presidential Vacancy If a presidential candidate dies while an election is being decided in the House, Congress may pass legislation to deal with the situation. Congress has similar power if this occurs when the Senate is deciding a vice-presidential election.

Section 5. Beginning the New Dates Sections 1 and 2 affected the Congress elected in 1934 and President Roosevelt, elected in 1936.

Section 6. Time Limit on Ratification The period for ratification by the states was limited to seven years.

Amendment XXI

Section 1

The eighteenth article of amendment to the Constitution of the United States is hereby repealed.

Section 2

The transportation or importation into any State, Territory, or possession of the United States for delivery or use therein of intoxicating liquors, in violation of the laws thereof, is hereby prohibited.

Section 3

This article shall be inoperative unless it shall have been ratified as an amendment to the Constitution by conventions in the several States, as provided in the Constitution, within seven years from the date of the submission hereof to the States by the Congress.

Amendment 21. Repeal of Prohibition Amendment (1933)

This amendment nullified the 18th Amendment. It is the only amendment ever passed to overturn an earlier amendment. It remained unlawful to transport alcoholic beverages into states that forbade their use. It is the only amendment ratified by special state conventions instead of state legislatures.

Amendment 22.
Limit on Presidential Terms (1951)

This amendment wrote into the Constitution a custom started by Washington, Jefferson, and Madison, whereby Presidents limited themselves to two terms in office. Although both Ulysses S. Grant and Theodore Roosevelt sought third terms, the two-term precedent was not broken until Franklin D. Roosevelt was elected to a third term in 1940 and then a fourth term in 1944. The passage of the 22nd amendment insures that no President is to be considered indispensable. It also provides that anyone who succeeds to the presidency and serves for more than two years of the term may not be elected more than one more time.

Amendment 23.
Presidential Electors for the District of Columbia (1961)

This amendment granted people living in the District of Columbia the right to vote in presidential elections. The District casts three electoral votes. The people of Washington, D.C., still are without representation in Congress.

Amendment XXII

Section 1

No person shall be elected to the office of the President more than twice, and no person who had held the office of President, or acted as President, for more than two years of a term to which some other person was elected President shall be elected to the office of the President more than once.

But this Article shall not apply to any person holding the office of President when this Article was proposed by the Congress, and shall not prevent any person who may be holding the office of President, or acting as President, during the term within which this Article becomes operative from holding the office of President or acting as President during the remainder of such term.

Section 2

This article shall be inoperative unless it shall have been ratified as an amendment to the Constitution by the legislatures of three-fourths of the several States within seven years from the date of its submission to the States by the Congress.

Amendment XXIII

Section 1

The District constituting the seat of Government of the United States shall appoint in such manner as the Congress may direct:

A number of electors of President and Vice President equal to the whole number of Senators and Representatives in Congress to which the District would be entitled if it were a State, but in no event more than the least populous State; they shall be in addition to those appointed by the States, but they shall be considered, for the purposes of the election of President and Vice President, to be electors appointed by a State; and they shall meet in the District and perform such duties as provided by the twelfth article of amendment.

Section 2

The Congress shall have power to enforce this article by appropriate legislation.

Amendment XXIV

Section 1
The right of citizens of the United States to vote in any primary or other election for President or Vice President, for electors for President or Vice President, or for Senator or Representative in Congress, shall not be denied or abridged by the United States or any State by reason of failure to pay any poll tax or other tax.

Section 2
The Congress shall have power to enforce this article by appropriate legislation.

Amendment XXV

Section 1
In case of the removal of the President from office or his death or resignation, the Vice President shall become President.

Section 2
Whenever there is a vacancy in the office of the Vice President, the President shall nominate a Vice President who shall take the office upon confirmation by a majority vote of both houses of Congress.

Section 3
Whenever the President transmits to the President pro tempore of the Senate and the Speaker of the House or of Representatives his written declaration that he is unable to discharge the powers and duties of his office, and until he transmits to them a written declaration to the contrary, such powers and duties shall be discharged by the Vice President as Acting President.

Section 4
Whenever the Vice President and a majority of either the principal officers of the executive departments or of such other body as Congress may by law provide, transmit to the President pro tempore of the Senate and the Speaker of the House of Representatives their written declaration that the President is unable to discharge the powers and duties of his office, the Vice President shall immediately assume the power and duties of the office of Acting President.

Thereafter, when the President transmits to the President pro tempore of the Senate and the Speaker of the House of Representatives his written declaration that no inability exists, he shall resume the powers and duties of his office unless the Vice President and a majority of either the

---

Amendment 24.
Abolition of the Poll Tax (1964)
A "poll tax" was a fee that persons were required to pay in order to vote in a number of Southern states. This amendment ended poll taxes as a requirement to vote in any presidential or congressional election. In 1966 the Supreme Court voided poll taxes in state elections as well.

Amendment 25.
Presidential Disability and Succession (1967)
Section 1. Replacing the President The Vice President becomes President if the President dies, resigns, or is removed from office.

Section 2. Replacing the Vice President The President is to appoint a new Vice President in case of a vacancy in that office, with the approval of the Congress.

The 25th Amendment is unusually precise and explicit because it was intended to solve a serious constitutional problem. Sixteen times in American history, before passage of this amendment, the office of Vice President was vacant, but fortunately in none of these cases did the President die or resign.

This amendment was used in 1973, when Vice President Spiro Agnew resigned from office after being charged with accepting bribes. President Nixon then appointed Gerald R. Ford as Vice President in accordance with the provisions of the 25th Amendment. A year later, President Richard Nixon resigned during the Watergate scandal, and Ford became President. President Ford then had to fill the Vice Presidency, which he had left vacant upon assuming the Presidency. He named Nelson A. Rockefeller as Vice President. Thus both the presidency and vice-presidency were held by men who had not been elected to their offices.

Section 3 Replacing the President With Consent If the President informs Congress, in writing, that he or she cannot carry out the duties of the office of President, the Vice President becomes Acting President.

Section 4 Replacing the President Without Consent If the President is unable to carry out the duties of the office but is unable or unwilling to so notify Congress, the Cabinet and the Vice

President are to inform Congress of this fact. The Vice President then becomes Acting President. The procedure by which the President may regain the office if he or she recovers is also spelled out in this amendment.

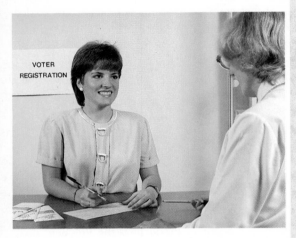

The Twenty-sixth Amendment, ratified in 1971, extended the right and the responsibility of voting to those who were 18 years of age or older.

Amendment 26.
Eighteen-Year-Old Vote (1971)
This amendment made 18-year-olds eligible to vote in all federal, state, and local elections. Until then, the minimum age had been 21 in most states.

Amendment 27.
Restraint on Congressional Salaries (1992)
Any increase in the salaries of members of Congress will take effect in the subsequent session of Congress.

principal officers of the executive departments or of such other body as Congress may by law provide, transmit within four days to the President pro tempore of the Senate and the Speaker of the House of Representatives their written declaration that the President is unable to discharge the powers and duties of his office. Thereupon Congress shall decide the issue, assembling within forty-eight hours for that purpose if not in session. If the Congress within twenty-one days after receipt of the latter written declaration, or, if Congress is not in session, within twenty-one days after Congress is required to assemble, determines by two-thirds vote of both houses that the President is unable to discharge the powers and duties of his office, the Vice President shall continue to discharge the same as Acting President; otherwise, the President shall resume to the power and duties of his office.

Amendment XXVI

Section 1
The right of citizens of the United States, who are eighteen years of age or older, to vote shall not be denied or abridged by the United States or by any State on account of age.

Section 2
The Congress shall have power to enforce this article by appropriate legislation.

Amendment XXVII
No law, varying the compensation for the services of Senators and Representatives, shall take effect, until an election of Representatives shall have intervened.

★ Summary

The Constitution is the foundation of the government of the United States. Because it is flexible, it has been able to endure for more than 200 years. The Constitution establishes a federal system, with a strong central government and separate state governments. State and popular sovereignty are retained by the Tenth Amendment and by the amending process itself. The three branches of the national government balance power between the legislature, the executive, and the judiciary. Occasionally the powers of one branch comes into conflict with the others. The power of the President grows in times of crisis, but over the years power tends to return to balance. Changes that have been made in the Constitution sometimes come by amendment, but more often they are the result of Court decisions or the flexibility of the Constitution itself. The Supreme Court constantly reinterprets the Constitution as it decides cases. Many of these cases apply guarantees of the Fourteenth Amendment to provisions in the Bill of Rights. The Constitution has served to moderate change in the United States for more than 200 years.

★ Using Vocabulary

Use each of the following terms in sentences that relate to the Constitution:

strict construction   **loose construction**

judicial review   **quorum**

★ Reviewing Facts

1. **Discuss** the development of the method of selecting members of the House of Representatives from 1842 to 1979.
2. **Describe** the idea of "separation of powers."
3. **Summarize** the work of committees in the House and Senate.
4. **Compare** the Supreme Court decision in *Plessy v. Ferguson* to its decision in *Brown v. Board of Education of Topeka.*
5. **List** three ways in which the power of the federal government has been expanded.
6. **Report** three examples of the expansion of presidential powers in time of crisis.

★ Thinking Critically

1. **Recognizing Effects** Describe three historic developments in which the power of Congress over interstate commerce and the "elastic clause" have expanded the authority of the federal government.
2. **Analyzing Ideas** The Preamble to the Constitution begins with "We the People." How does the Constitution assure that the people have sovereignty over the government?
3. **Determining Motivations** The delegates to the Constitutional Convention intended that the Senate be a more dignified body than the House. Why did the delegates believe this was important? What provisions in the Constitution give the Senate higher status than the House?
4. **Supporting an Argument** Some people believe that the separation of powers into three branches has led to a slow and often ineffective government, as each branch contends for dominance. Others believe that this separation is essential to protect the people from tyrannical government. Choose one of these opinions and support it with evidence from history.
5. **Applying Concepts** Judicial review has played an important role in shaping the laws under which we live. As a matter of course, the Supreme Court interprets the law, determining whether it is constitutional. This great power of the Court has been challenged, sometimes by individuals or groups, sometimes by one of the other branches of government. Trace the application of judicial review to the Fourteenth Amendment during the period from the Civil War to the present.

★ Linking Past and Present

The rights of citizens have developed gradually since the Constitution went into effect in 1789. Amendments to the Constitution, laws, court decisions, and presidential actions have served to clarify, define, or even limit rights. Choose one of the following rights and trace its historical development in the United States from the time the Constitution was ratified to the present:

suffrage   freedom of religion

freedom of speech   freedom of the press

due process of law   equal protection of law

UNIT 3

Launching the Republic: 1789-1824

The great bond of union to every people is its government.
This destroyed or distrusted, there is no center left of
intelligence, counsel, or action; no system of purposes or measures;
no point of rallying or confidence.

—REVEREND TIMOTHY DWIGHT
Fourth of July sermon, 1798

SETTING THE SCENE

Time

Late eighteenth century to early nineteenth century

Mood

The American people faced with confidence an uncertain future under the Constitution. Within the span of three decades, the new government—under capable leadership—had put finances in order, witnessed the birth of political parties, improved its transportation system, and more than doubled its territory. Victory in a second war with England led to a strong spirit of unity and nationalism. By 1824 the United States had been transformed into a strong, independent nation.

Themes

- American Democracy
- Geography and Environment
- Conflict and Cooperation
- U.S. Role in World Affairs

Key Events

- Washington's Inauguration
- Bill of Rights ratified
- Whiskey Rebellion
- Treaty of Greenville
- "Revolution of 1800"
- *Marbury v. Madison*
- Louisiana Purchase
- Lewis and Clark Expedition
- War of 1812
- Battle of New Orleans
- Acquisition of Florida
- The Monroe Doctrine

Major Issues

- The plan for a strong central government, as set forth in the Constitution, becomes a working reality.
- Disagreements within Congress and Washington's cabinet result in the formation of political parties.
- Backed by the Supreme Court, the power and authority of the national government grows at the expense of the states.

CHAPTERS

7

The Federalist Era

8

Jefferson and the Republicans

9

Nationalism and Change

◄ Liberty in the Form of the Goddess of Youth, *based on an engraving by Edward Savage, 1796*

Global Perspectives

I n the 1780s the United States was but a fledgling among the nations of the world. Older, more established nations were busy building empires at the same time. While France, under Napoleon Bonaparte, was amassing an empire that included much of Europe, Britain's vast empire was reaching deep into southern Asia. In 1819 Britain turned Singapore into one of its leading seaports. Britain also tightened its control over India.

Unrest was brewing closer to home. In 1791 a former slave, Toussaint L'Ouverture, led a revolt that led to Haiti's independence in 1804. In Spanish

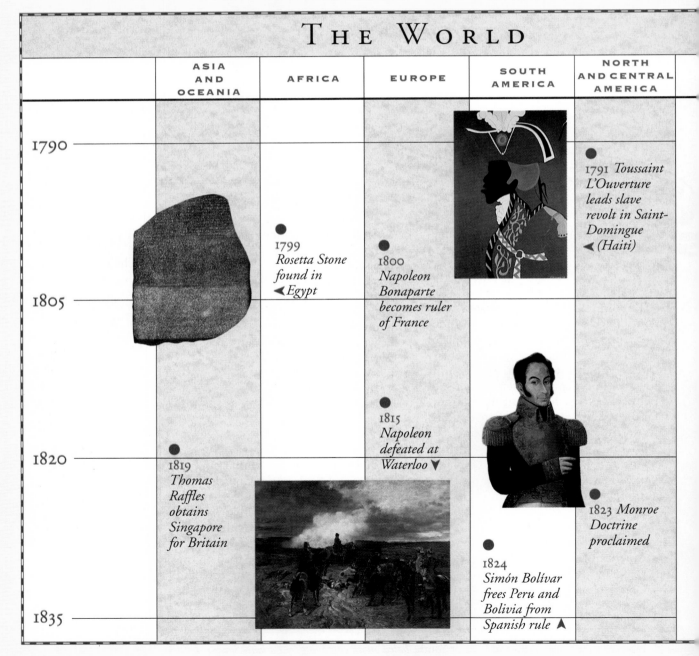

THE WORLD

	ASIA AND OCEANIA	AFRICA	EUROPE	SOUTH AMERICA	NORTH AND CENTRAL AMERICA
1790					**1791** *Toussaint L'Ouverture leads slave revolt in Saint-Domingue ◄ (Haiti)*
		1799 *Rosetta Stone found in ◄ Egypt*	**1800** *Napoleon Bonaparte becomes ruler of France*		
1805					
			1815 *Napoleon defeated at Waterloo ▼*		
1820	**1819** *Thomas Raffles obtains Singapore for Britain*				**1823** *Monroe Doctrine proclaimed*
				1824 *Simón Bolívar frees Peru and Bolivia from Spanish rule ▲*	
1835					

America, independence movements were also fermenting. One of the earliest occurred in Mexico where a priest, Miguel Hidalgo, began a revolt that laid the groundwork for Mexico's independence in 1824. In 1819 Simón Bolívar secured independence for the new nation of Gran Colombia, which included the present-day countries of Colombia, Venezuela, Panama, and Ecuador. Bolívar also led bloody independence movements in Peru and Bolivia, securing Peru's independence in 1824 and Bolivia's the following year.

The United States applauded the independence of its neighbors and strongly opposed Spain's plan to regain its colonies. To solidify this position, in 1823, President James Monroe issued a warning that came to be known as the Monroe Doctrine. This doctrine became the foundation of American foreign policy for many years and was expanded upon by later United States Presidents.

THE UNITED STATES

	PACIFIC AND NORTHWEST	SOUTHWEST	MIDWEST	SOUTHEAST	ATLANTIC NORTHEAST
1790					1790 First copyright law passes
				1793 Eli Whitney with backing of Catherine Greene invents the cotton gin	
1805			1804 Lewis and Clark explore the Louisiana Territory ▲		1807 Robert Fulton's steamboat, The Clermont, speeds river travel
			1813 Commodore Oliver H. Perry defeats the British in Battle of Lake Erie in War of 1812		
1820	1820 First missionaries reach Hawaii	1821 Stephen Austin settles Americans in Texas ▲		1819 Florida is purchased from Spain	1821 Public schools open in Massachusetts
1835					

AMERICAN LITERARY HERITAGE

from *The Prairie*

In light of the nation's westward expansion and its promise of prosperity, American writers abandoned the political soapbox and turned to cultivating an American literary style. Romanticism, a movement that emphasized imagination and inner feelings, won adherents among many writers of the era.

One of the most celebrated was James Fenimore Cooper. Largely regarded in his own day as a producer of "pop" fiction, Cooper left a legacy of five novels whose central character, Natty Bumppo, is a trapper forced increasingly westward by the encroachment of civilization on his beloved frontier. In the following excerpt, Natty Bumppo, surrounded by the Pawnees who have become his family, is near death.

James Fenimore Cooper

hen he had placed his guests in front of the dying man, Hard-Heart…[a young Pawnee chief and Natty Bumppo's adopted son] leaned a little forward and demanded: "Does my father hear the words of his son?"

"Speak," returned the trapper, in tones that issued from his chest, but which were rendered awfully distinct by the stillness that reigned in the place. "I am about to depart from the village of the…[Pawnees] and shortly shall be beyond the reach of your voice."

"Let the wise chief have no cares for his journey," continued Hard-Heart with an earnest solicitude that led him to forget, for the moment, that others were waiting to address his adopted parent; "a hundred …[Pawnees] shall clear his path from briars."

"Pawnee, I die as I have lived, a Christian man," resumed the trapper with a force of voice that had the same startling effect upon his hearers as is produced by the trumpet when its blast rises suddenly and freely on the air after its obstructed sounds have been heard struggling in the distance: "as I came into life so will I leave it. Horses and arms are not needed to stand in the presence of the Great Spirit of my people. He knows my color, and according to my gifts will he judge my deeds…."

A little disappointed, the young partisan stepped modestly back, making way for the recent comers to approach. Middleton [an army officer whose life Natty Bumppo has saved] took one of the meager hands of the trapper, and, struggling to command his voice, he succeeded in announcing his presence. The old man listened like one whose thoughts were dwelling on a very different subject; but when the other had succeeded in making him understand that he was present, an expression of joyful recognition passed over his faded features.

"I hope you have not so soon forgotten those whom you so materially served!" Middleton concluded. "It would pain me to think my hold on your memory was so light."

"Little that I have ever seen is forgotten," returned the trapper; "I am at the close of many weary days, but there is not one among them all that I could wish to overlook. I remember you with the whole of your company; aye, and your gran'ther that went before you. I am glad that you have come back upon these plains, for I had need of one who speaks the English, since little faith can be put in the traders of these regions. Will you do a favor to an old and dying man?"

"Name it," said Middleton; "it shall be done."

"It is a far journey to send such trifles," resumed the old man, who spoke at short intervals, as strength and breath permitted; "a far and weary journey is the same; but kindnesses and friendships are things not to be forgotten. There is a settlement among the Otsego hills—"

"I know the place," interrupted Middleton, observing that he spoke with increasing difficulty; "proceed to tell me what you would have done."

"Take this rifle and pouch and horn, and send them to the person whose name is graven on the plates of the stock—a trader cut the letters with his knife—for it is long that I have intended to send him such a token of my love."

"It shall be so. Is there more that you could wish?"

"Little else have I to bestow. My traps I give to my Indian son; for honestly and kindly has he kept his faith. Let him stand before me."

Middleton explained to the chief what the trapper had said, and relinquished his own place to the other.

"Pawnee," continued the old man, always changing his language to suit the person he addressed, and not infrequently according to the ideas he expressed, "it is a custom of my people for the father to leave his blessing with the son before he shuts his eyes forever. This blessing I give to you; take it, for the prayers of a Christian man will never make the path of a just warrior to the blessed prairies either longer or more tangled. May the God of a white man look on your deeds with friendly eyes, and may you never commit an act that shall cause him to darken his face. I know not whether we shall ever meet again. There are many traditions concerning the place of Good Spirits. It is not for one like me, old and experienced though I am, to set up my opinions against a nation's. You believe in the blessed prairies, and I have faith in the sayings of my fathers. If both are true, our parting will be final; but if it should prove that the same meaning is hid under different words, we shall yet stand together, Pawnee, before the face of your Wahcondah, who will then be no other than my God. There is much to be said in favor of both religions, for each seems suited to its own people, and no doubt it was so intended. I fear I have not altogether followed the gifts of my color, inasmuch

An illustration on a 1777 map of Canada, showing fur trade between the French and native Americans

as I find it a little painful to give up forever the use of the rifle and the comforts of the chase. But then the fault has been my own, seeing that it could not have been His...."

The old man made a long and apparently a musing pause. At times he raised his eyes wistfully, as if he would again address Middleton, but some innate feeling appeared always to suppress his words. The other, who observed his hesitation, enquired in a way most likely to encourage him to proceed whether there was aught else that he could wish to have done.

Last of the Mohicans *by Thomas Cole, 1827*

"Not so, not so, Captain. Let me sleep, where I have lived, beyond the din of the settlements! Still I see no need why the grave of an honest man should be hid, like a redskin in his ambushment. I paid a man in the settlements to make and put a graven stone at the head of my father's resting place. It was of the value of twelve beaver skins, and cunningly and curiously was it carved! Then it told to all comers that the body of such a Christian lay beneath; and it spoke of his manner of life, of his years, and of his honesty...."

"I am without kith or kin in the wide world!" the trapper answered; "when I am gone, there will be an end of my race. We have never been chiefs; but honest, and useful in our way. I hope it cannot be denied, we have always proved ourselves. My father lies buried near the sea, and the bones of his son will whiten on the prairies—"

"Name the spot, and your remains shall be placed by the side of your father," interrupted Middleton.

"And such a stone you would have at your grave?"

"I! no, no, I have no son, but Hard-Heart, and it is little that an Indian knows of white fashions and usages. Besides I am his debtor, already, seeing it is so little I have done since I have lived in his tribe. The rifle might bring the value of such a thing—but then I know it will give the boy pleasure to hang the piece in his hall, for many is the deer and the bird that he has seen it destroy. No, no, the gun must be sent to him whose name is graven on the lock!"

"But there is one who would gladly prove his affection in the way you wish: he who owes you not only his own deliverance from so many dangers, but who inherits a heavy debt of gratitude from his ancestors. The stone shall be put at the head of your grave."

The old man extended his emaciated hand, and gave the other a squeeze of thanks....

Middleton and Hard-Heart placed themselves on the opposite sides of his seat, and watched with melancholy solicitude the variations of his countenance. For two hours there was no very sensible alteration. The expression of his faded and timeworn features was that of a calm and dignified repose. From time to time he spoke, uttering some brief sentence in the way of advice, or asking some simple questions concerning those in whose fortunes he still took a friendly interest. During the whole of that solemn and anxious period each individual of the tribe kept his place, in the most self-restrained patience. When the old man spoke, all bent their heads to listen; and when his words were uttered, they seemed to ponder on their wisdom and usefulness.

As the flame drew nigher to the socket, his voice was hushed, and there were moments when his attendants doubted whether he still belonged to the living. Middleton, who watched each wavering expression of his weather-beaten visage with the interest of a keen observer of human nature, softened by the tenderness of personal regard, fancied he could read the workings of the old man's soul in the strong lineaments of his countenance. Perhaps what the enlightened soldier took for the delusion of mistaken opinion did actually occur—for who has returned from that unknown world to explain by what forms, and in what manner, he was introduced into its awful precincts?...

...Suddenly, Middleton felt the hand which he held, grasp his own with incredible power, and the old man, supported on either side by his friends, rose upright to his feet. For a moment he looked about him, as if to invite all in presence to listen (the lingering remnant of human frailty), and then, with a fine military elevation of the head, and with a voice that might be heard in every part of that numerous assembly, he pronounced the word:

"Here!"

A movement so entirely unexpected, and the air of grandeur and humility which was so remarkably united in the mien of the trapper, together with the clear and uncommon force of his utterance, produced a short period of confusion in the faculties of all present. When Middleton and Hard-Heart, each of whom had involuntarily extended a hand to support the form of the old man, turned to him again, they found that the subject of their interest was removed forever beyond the necessity of their care. They mournfully placed the body in its seat, and Le Balafré [an aging Pawnee chief] arose to announce the termination of the scene to the tribe. The voice of the old Indian seemed a sort of echo from that invisible world to which the meek spirit of the trapper had just departed.

"A valiant, a just, and a wise warrior has gone on the path which will lead him to the blessed grounds of his people!" he said. "When the voice of the Wahcondah called him, he was ready to answer. Go, my children; remember the just chief of the palefaces, and clear your own tracks from briars!"

The grave was made beneath the shade of some noble oaks. It had been carefully watched to the present hour by the Pawnees of the Loup, and is often shown to the traveler and the trader as a spot where a just white man sleeps. In due time the stone was placed at its head, with the simple inscription, which the trapper had himself requested. The only liberty, taken by Middleton, was to add, *"May no wanton hand ever disturb his remains!"*

INTERPRETING LITERATURE

1. What two requests does Natty Bumppo make of Middleton?

2. Describe the trapper's feelings about Pawnee customs.

3. What support can you find for the view that Natty Bumppo is a product of the prairie?

Determining Relevance

4. What symbolism can be witnessed in Natty Bumppo's death?

CHAPTER 7
The Federalist Era

SETTING THE SCENE

Historical Focus

With the ratification of the Constitution and national elections, a new government was in place by the spring of 1789. However, many problems faced President Washington and Congress. One of the most urgent was the poor financial condition of the country. Largely through the efforts of Alexander Hamilton and Federalist leaders, broad and sound policies were implemented. Controversy developed over Hamilton's program, however, resulting in the formation of political parties.

Concepts to Understand

- How George Washington's strong **leadership** brought stability to the new government.
- How **political values** shaped the formation of political parties.

People to Know

Alexander Hamilton, Anthony Wayne, Blue Jacket, Edmond Genêt, Thomas Pinckney, John Adams

Places to Locate

Kentucky, Cincinnati

Terms to Identify

cabinet, quorum, protective tariff, bonds, excise tax, implied powers, nonpartisan, nullification, Federalists, Republicans

Guided Reading

As you read this chapter, seek the answers to the following questions.

1. What were some of the major issues that Washington faced as President?
2. How did foreign affairs contribute to the growth of American political parties?

SPANNING THE DECADES

POLITICAL	1787 *Northwest Ordinance passed*	1789 *George Washington inaugurated*	1790 *Alexander Hamilton proposed funding and assumption*	1791 *Bank of the United States is chartered*

1785   **1790**

CULTURAL	1786 Pittsburgh Gazette *became first newspaper west of the Appalachians*	1789 *Church of England became the Protestant Episcopal Church*	1790 *Samuel Slater built first cotton mill*	1791 *Washington, D.C., is surveyed*

The Inspection of the First U.S. Coins *by John W. Dunsmore, 1914*

1794	1795			
Whiskey Rebellion in western Pennsylvania	*Treaty of Greenville opened Northwest Territory for settlement*	1797 *John Adams inaugurated*	1798 *Undeclared naval war with France*	

1795   **1800**

1794	1796	1799
Eli Whitney patented cotton gin	*Boston African Society founded as benevolent group for blacks*	*American Review and Literary Journal published; first quarterly literary review*

…From the situation where I now am, I see a scene of ambition beyond all my former suspicions or imaginations…which will turn our government topsy-turvey. Jealousies and rivalries have…never stared me in the face in such horrid forms as at present….

—JOHN ADAMS
Letter to Abigail Adams, 1797

Organizing the Government

The preservation of the sacred fire of liberty and the destiny of the republican model of government are justly considered, perhaps, as deeply, as finally, staked on the experiment entrusted to the hands of the American people.

—GEORGE WASHINGTON
First Inaugural Address, 1789

Section Focus

With the ratification of the Constitution in 1788, a new framework of government was in place. The obvious choice as leader of the new government was the hero of the Revolution, George Washington. Although he was reluctant to take the job, his reputation and stature were critical to the nation's success.

Objectives

After studying this section, you should be able to:
• List the precedents set by Washington as first President.
• Describe the first Congress under the Constitution.

George Washington accepted the presidency reluctantly. On the day he left for his inauguration, he confided in his diary:

About ten o'clock I bade adieu to Mt. Vernon, to private life, and to domestic felicity, and with a mind oppressed with more anxious and painful sensations than I care to express, set out for New York.

At almost every town and village on the way from Virginia to the nation's temporary capital, Washington was met by welcoming speeches, cheering crowds, and troops of cavalry. When he reached New York on April 23, 1789, he was rowed across the Hudson River on a barge built especially for the occasion and staffed with 13 harbor pilots in white uniforms. Most of New York's 33,000 residents lined the wharves and cheered as the barge neared shore. Seven days later, Washington took the oath of office and gave the first inaugural address. In reporting the event, a correspondent for the *Federal Gazette* of Philadelphia wrote:

…[T]he concourse of spectators, the devout fervency with which he repeated the oath, and the reverential manner in which he bowed down and kissed the sacred volume—all these conspired to render it one of the most august and interesting spectacles ever exhibited on this globe. It seemed, from the number of witnesses, to be a solemn appeal to Heaven and earth at once.

After the inauguration ceremony concluded, the festivities began with the ringing of church bells and the firing of cannons. Throughout the land there was public rejoicing for the man many believed to be the United States' greatest national asset.

Washington as President

Washington's background was as plantation manager and soldier. Because he lacked experience in government and had only limited knowledge of political theory and history, he felt he was unprepared to be the chief executive. Although Washington doubted his own qualifications, many Americans regarded him with admiration bordering on awe. As early in his career as his first military victories at Trenton and Princeton, a Philadelphia newspaper wrote of Washington: "If there are any spots in his character they are like the spots on the sun, only discernible through a telescope." Such hero worship had its value to the new government. As a visible symbol of unity and power, Washington provided a focus for loyalty to the nation.

Yet Washington was far more than a national symbol or figurehead. He knew the United States as well as any person alive, having traveled in every state except Georgia and having met or exchanged letters with most of the nation's prominent

Examining Illustrations *Washington's first cabinet included, (left to right) Henry Knox, Thomas Jefferson, Edmund Randolph, and Alexander Hamilton. Washington (far right) held no regular meetings with these officers, but did rely on their expert opinions. Hamilton became the most influential because the Treasury post gave him a strong position in proposing legislation. Washington claimed to have no particular political expertise. What other qualifications did he bring to the presidency?*

leaders. From the time he took charge of the Continental army in 1775, he worked, as he said, to "discourage all local attachments" and to substitute "the greater name of American."

Even with Washington in office and Congress in session, the Constitution was still little more than a paper plan. It would be months before the government could be functioning effectively. Laws had to be passed to establish executive departments such as the Treasury and the Post Office. A federal court system was needed to fill the gap left by the Framers of the Constitution.

Once federal offices were established, hundreds of people had to be found who were willing to give up their current jobs to serve as judges, tax collectors, and postmasters. Here, Washington's wide range of acquaintances and his reputation were invaluable in helping him find competent government officials.

Washington himself proved to be a first-rate administrator. On important matters, he sought the advice of his department heads, establishing what became known as the **cabinet,** a group of advisers to the President that continues to serve the same function today.

Creating a cabinet was only one of several precedents set by Washington in areas where the Constitution was silent or unclear. He determined that the Senate's approval power over presidential appointments did not extend to their removal from office. He took control of foreign affairs, limiting the Senate's role of advice and consent to ratifying or rejecting treaties only after they were made.

Although he headed the executive branch, Washington assumed leadership in legislative affairs as well. In written messages to Congress, and indirectly through reports prepared by his secretary of the treasury, Alexander Hamilton, Washington urged passage of laws he believed were in the public interest. With such encouragement Congress almost invariably followed his lead. Later Presidents would follow suit and become what some have called "chief legislator."

The First Congress

When the Confederation came to an end in 1788, it left behind 70 unpaid clerks, a military of 672 soldiers, and millions of dollars in debts. Before it disbanded, the Confederation Congress had arranged for the new government to be elected in November 1788, and start work on March 4, 1789. When March arrived, however, less than one-third of the senators and one-quarter of the representatives had reached New York. "The people will forget the new government before it is born," lamented a senator from Massachusetts. Not until April did each house of Congress have a **quorum,** or a majority of its members present in order to conduct business.

The Senate was a small body consisting of two members from each state elected by their state legislature. The Framers of the Constitution had expected the Senate to serve as an advisory body to the President. With this in mind, Washington came to the Senate in August 1789 with an Indian treaty and asked for the senators' advice as well as their consent to the treaty. Because some senators felt uncomfortable discussing the treaty in the presence of the President, they instead referred it to a committee for study. Senator William Maclay described Washington's reaction in his personal journal:

I rose and supported the mode
of doing business by committees;...
As I sat down,
the President of the United States
started up in a violent fret.
"This defeats every purpose
of my coming here,"
were the first words that he said....
He cooled, however, by degrees.

Washington then left the Senate, departing, wrote Maclay, "with a discontented air." Although he returned later to watch the Senate debate, amend, and ratify the treaty, it was the last time that any President formally sought the advice of the Senate.

The Senate was a quiet and formal body. Its members dressed in powdered wigs, lace, and velvet. For its first five years, the Senate conducted its business in private. Not until 1794 was a gallery built for the public and the press. By contrast, the House of Representatives was more informal. Elected by the people, the House welcomed the public and the press from the beginning. Debate was loud, and members often wore their hats inside the chamber. The House took the lead in legislative matters, especially in dealing with the nation's troubled finances and in providing a Bill of Rights.

After debates that lasted through the summer of 1789, Congress established three executive departments: a Department of State to take charge of foreign affairs, a Department of the Treasury to handle the nation's finances, and a Department of War to manage the military. Congress also created the position of Attorney General to handle the government's legal matters. None of these offices were specifically called for in the Constitution.

Congress then turned its attention to the judicial branch and passed the Judiciary Act of 1789, setting up the Supreme Court and lower federal courts as called for by the Constitution. President Washington quickly named the first Supreme Court Justices, deliberately choosing three from northern and three from southern states.

Although a majority in both the Senate and the House had supported ratification of the Constitution, the Anti-Federalist minority insisted that Congress quickly provide the Bill of Rights promised during the ratification campaign. In his inaugural address, Washington also urged that careful attention be given to such demands. Finally in September 1789, after much debate, Congress proposed 12 amendments. Of these, 10 were ratified by the states and added to the Constitution in 1791.

Section One Review

SUMMARY

The period from 1788 to 1796 was characterized by the precedent-setting leadership of George Washington and by the establishment of a new government. Washington took control of both foreign and domestic affairs. To assist him he set up a cabinet and made key appointments. He acted with wisdom and authority to assure the success of the Constitution.

CHECKING FOR UNDERSTANDING

1. **Identify** Judiciary Act of 1789

2. **Define** cabinet, quorum

3. **List** the characteristics that made George Washington the ideal choice to become the first President of the United States.

4. **Describe** the precedents set by Washington that are still practiced by Presidents in our own time.

5. **Outline** the executive departments that were created, describe the responsibility each had, and name the heads of each of the original departments.

6. **Characterize** the two houses of the first Congress.

THINKING CRITICALLY

7. **Evaluating Performance** Given his lack of experience in government and politics, explain why Washington was able to head a new framework of government.

CONNECTIONS: HISTORY AND GEOGRAPHY

8. **Using a Reference Source** George Washington was the first President from the state of Virginia. Find the four states which lead as birthplaces of future Presidents. In what regions of the country are they? Hypothesize on why more Presidents came from these regions than from others.

Linking Across Time

PRESIDENTS AND PRECEDENTS

Washington's presidency, simply by virtue of being the first, established precedents that still guide the conduct of Presidents. Washington was acutely aware that his every act would be scrutinized. "Few...can realize the difficult and delicate part which a man in my situation has to act....I walk on untrodden ground. There is hardly any part of my conduct which may not hereafter be drawn into precedent."

As soon as Washington was elected, he was beset with requests for jobs. His refusal to hire friends and relatives established the idea that the office is public, not private. Washington's use of the cabinet as a source of advice set a precedent that continues today. So too did his appearance in person before Congress to deliver his State of the Union addresses, although this method was abandoned by Thomas Jefferson and not renewed until Woodrow Wilson. Future Presidents took another cue from Washington's periodic tours of the country, although today such tours often assume political overtones, as when the President campaigns for fellow party members. Later Presidents also modified the precedent by taking frequent vacation trips, a practice for which they have sometimes been criticized. In 1990 George Bush, for example, was flayed by critics for taking a scheduled month-long vacation at the same time he was sending American troops to Saudi Arabia.

The thorny problem of whether to recognize new governments, especially ones that overthrew regimes with which the United States had diplomatic ties, also presented itself to Washington. He argued that "we surely cannot deny to any nation the right whereon our own government is founded, that

Washington's Inaugural

every nation may govern itself according to whatever form it pleases." This precedent has been modified as well. Presidents still exercise the power to grant recognition, but by implication they also have the power to withhold it. The denial of diplomatic recognition was made a powerful tool of international diplomacy by later Presidents.

In 1794 the Whiskey Rebellion presented Washington with one of his strongest challenges—and yet another precedent was set. His use of federal troops to enforce the law fell within his right as commander in chief of the armed forces. Washington chose to lead the expedition personally. While President Eisenhower did not personally lead the force in 1957, he did send troops to Little Rock, Arkansas, to enforce school integration.

Washington's first administration began with a mere skeleton crew of clerks. In appointing workers to carry out the functions of the executive office, Washington indirectly assumed the role of party leader, appointing only those he perceived to be sympathetic with his political views. Future Presidents took increasingly active roles in the leadership of political parties.

Perhaps Washington's strongest legacy was the idea that a President should serve no more than two terms in office. It was not broken until World War II, when Franklin D. Roosevelt persuaded American voters to elect him President four times. So strong was Washington's precedent that it was made part of the basic law of the land by the Twenty-second Amendment to the Constitution.

★ ★ ★ ★ ★ ★ ★ ★ ★ ★ ★

MAKING CONNECTIONS

1. What were three important precedents that Washington established?

2. Why do you think some precedents have been modified while others have not?

ANALYZING IDEAS
3. What considerations do you think future Presidents would face when deciding whether to break a precedent established by President Washington?

★ ★ ★ ★ ★ ★ ★ ★ ★ ★ ★

Solving National Problems

The support of government—the support of troops for the common defense—the payment of the public debt, are the true final causes for raising money.

—ALEXANDER HAMILTON
Secretary of the Treasury, 1791

Section Focus

The United States needed money to pay its war debts and to finance national growth. Raising these funds was the huge but vital task of the secretary of the treasury, Alexander Hamilton. His plans would bring financial stability to the new government. The plans, however, also would rekindle debate over the amount of power exercised by the national government.

Objectives

After studying this section, you should be able to:

• Discuss Hamilton's financial program for the United States and the opposition to it.
• Describe the problems settlers faced during western expansion.

If the United States were to survive, the new government had to be able to pay its way. All members in both houses of Congress agreed that as soon as possible the federal government should begin to collect **tariffs,** or taxes on imports.

But a tariff law was not passed until July 1789 because some sections of the nation wanted a **protective tariff**—a high tax on imports to protect their products from foreign competition—while they opposed protection for goods produced in other sections. For example, the South wanted a high tariff on imported hemp, which was used in making rope, to protect its own hemp crop. But New England opposed this because it would cost more to rig ships. New England, in turn, wanted a high tariff to protect its rum distilleries, while the South preferred to import rum directly from Jamaica.

The tariff of 1789 represented a compromise between the South and New England. Representatives to Congress from both sections of the country dropped their demands for protection and agreed to a **revenue tariff,** a low tax on imports designed to provide income for the government rather than protection for private business. Although there were a few exceptions, tariffs on imports averaged between 5 percent and 8 percent.

Hamilton's Program

Most of the money raised by the tariff was needed to pay off the United States' $54 million national debt. The nation owed $12 million to France and the Netherlands for loans made during and after the Revolutionary War. The Continental Congress also had borrowed more than $40 million from individual Americans by selling them **bonds,** or certificates that promised repayment with interest. In addition, the government felt responsible for paying soldiers and army suppliers as the Continental Congress had promised. Finally, the individual states owed money totaling $25 million.

In the debate over federal finances, the dominant figure was 33-year-old Alexander Hamilton. An aide to General Washington during the Revolution, Hamilton had now been chosen by Washington to be secretary of the treasury. A poor man who married into a wealthy family, Hamilton believed in a strong government that favored prosperous merchants and large

Linking Across Time

THE FEDERAL RESERVE SYSTEM

Today the Federal Reserve System, consisting of twelve District Reserve Banks, a Board of Governors, and several advisory councils, serves as the central bank for the United States.

In addition to regulating currency and supervising banking, the "Fed" is charged with maintaining a stable economy, a high level of employment, and a favorable balance of trade with other nations.

landowners. He distrusted small farmers and laborers and expressed this view by writing:

All communities divide themselves into the few and the many. The first are the rich and well-born, the other the mass of the people....The people are turbulent and changing; they seldom judge or determine right. Give therefore to the first class a distinct permanent share of the government.

When Congress asked Hamilton to prepare a financial plan, his proposals reflected his attitudes about wealth, power, and government. In a two-part *Report on the Public Credit* and a *Report on Manufactures,* he convinced Congress to pass a series of laws in 1790 and 1791. His recommendations, however, produced conflict and controversy.

Hamilton believed it was vital to the nation that the government have enough income to operate, pay the interest on the national debt, and gradually reduce the debt itself. So, in addition to the tariff, Hamilton proposed an **excise tax** on American whiskey. An excise tax is a tax paid by the manufacturer of a product and passed on to those who buy the product. In 1791 Congress approved Hamilton's proposal by enacting an excise tax on whiskey.

In dealing with the national debt, Hamilton proposed that foreign creditors be paid at once. As long as the United States owed money to other nations, he argued, it could not be truly independent. Congress responded by repaying France and the Netherlands in full by 1796.

Hamilton believed that the domestic debt also should be paid in full, even though the value of the bonds issued by the Continental Congress had fallen in value to as little as 20 cents on the dollar. Hamilton argued that in paying these bonds in full, the United States would tell its citizens and the world that its promises were good. After much debate, Congress passed the Funding Bill in 1790.

Hamilton proposed that the federal government also pay the states' debts. The

Examining Illustrations   *The United States mint began operations under the Coinage Act of 1792 and minted the $10 gold piece, called an eagle, beginning in 1795. Because of a shortage of United States coins, America continued to use foreign coins until 1857, when Congress removed all foreign coins from circulation. What did Hamilton believe would establish confidence in Bank of the United States notes?*

states had fought for the entire nation, he argued, so the cost of their help during the Revolution should be assumed by the national government. Hamilton also believed that federal payment of state debts would give the states a strong and selfish interest in the success of the central government. Congress agreed and in 1790 passed the Assumption Act.

A key element of Hamilton's financial proposals was that the federal government establish a national bank modeled on the Bank of England. The bank would be a place for the federal government to deposit its tax receipts, as well as a place where tax revenues and private deposits could be used for large loans to government and to businesses.

Most importantly, the proposed bank would issue paper money backed by gold and silver in the bank's vaults. The public could have confidence in this currency because it could be exchanged for coins on demand. The notes of a Bank of the United States, circulating throughout the country, would provide a national currency that would stimulate commerce and promote business growth.

Hamilton believed that the federal government should encourage development of American industries. In his *Report on Manufactures* he argued that industrial growth would make the country wealthier, because investing in manufacturing often yielded higher profits than did agriculture. Industrial growth would also encourage the immigration of skilled laborers to the nation. He proposed protective tariffs and government aid to new or expanding businesses. Although Congress did not act on this part of Hamilton's program, later events would prove that his vision was a clear one.

On the whole, Hamilton's program had immediate success in restoring the credit of the United States. By 1792, for example, bonds that had sold at a discount just four years earlier, were selling for 120 percent to 125 percent of face value.

There was another, more personal motive behind Hamilton's proposals. Because he believed in government by the wealthy and distrusted common people, his plans were intended to enlist the "rich

and well-born" to support the federal government. He hoped to make such people selfishly interested in its survival. Although most of his proposals were enacted by Congress, the debate over many of them became bitter and divisive.

Opposition to Hamilton

Despite its merits, Hamilton's program encountered great opposition, much of it led by Thomas Jefferson, Washington's secretary of state. Although tensions between Hamilton and Jefferson involved a personal struggle for power in Washington's cabinet, they also reflected larger differences in the vision each man had of the nation.

The self-made Hamilton called democracy "poison" and characterized the general public as selfish, unreasonable, and violent. He believed that a powerful central government was needed to keep order, and he wanted to reduce the power of the states.

Jefferson, born to wealth and social position, believed that if people were

Examining Illustrations
The Bank of the United States was built on Third Street in Philadelphia. On what grounds did Madison oppose the Bank?

Examining Maps
General Anthony Wayne, with a strong force, marched north from Fort Washington to fight Blue Jacket in 1794. Where was the battle of Fallen Timbers fought?

one anti-Hamilton newspaper called them. As time had passed, the original holders of these bonds, facing hard times and fearing that they would never be paid, sold their bonds to speculators at a discount. Madison was outraged that New England merchants who had paid as little as $10 for a $100 bond now would receive full value while the Patriot who bought the bond during the Revolution got nothing. In addition, because federal funds would pay these speculators, tax money from the South would end up in New England pockets.

Madison's objection to the Assumption Bill was based on similar sectional concerns. Most of the southern states had already paid their debts and did not want their taxes to pay the debts of the northern states. This dispute was settled when Hamilton, Madison, and Jefferson struck a deal. Southerners in Congress would vote for Hamilton's debt assumption plan. In return, the nation's capital would move from New York to Philadelphia for 10 years, and then to a new federal city on the Potomac River between Maryland and Virginia.

When Congress debated the bill to establish a national bank, Madison attacked it on constitutional grounds. Congress had no power to establish a bank, he argued, because it was not among the **enumerated powers,** or powers mentioned specifically, in the Constitution. Nor was it an **implied power,** a power that, while not directly stated in the Constitution, is suggested and does allow Congress to exercise its stated powers. If the federal government were allowed to establish a national bank, he feared there would be no limits to federal power.

Despite Madison's arguments, Congress passed the Bank bill by an almost two-to-one majority. But Washington hesitated to act, realizing that whether he signed this controversial bill or vetoed it, he would be setting an important precedent. Instead, he asked Attorney General Edmund Randolph and Secretary of State Jefferson, both fellow Virginians, for written opinions on the constitutionality of a national bank. Each

given the opportunity, they would be decent and reasonable. A defender of human liberty, Jefferson believed in a minimum of government and favored power at the local level. Because Jefferson could not block Hamilton in the executive branch, the conflict was played out in Congress, where Jefferson's political ally, James Madison, represented Virginia.

Led by Madison, Hamilton's critics attacked the Funding Bill as unfair to the original purchasers of the bonds issued by the Continental Congress—"the warworn soldiers" and their "widows and orphans,"

INDIAN CAMPAIGNS IN OHIO

Battle of Fallen Timbers, 1794 — Fort Miami

St. Clair's defeat, 1791 — Fort Randolph

PA.

Fort Recovery

40° N

NORTHWEST TERRITORY

0   100 MI
0   100 KM

Cincinnati

KENTUCKY   85° W   VIRGINIA   80° W

Land ceded by Indians in Treaty of Greenville, 1795

→ Route of General Arthur St. Clair

→ Route of General Anthony Wayne

★ Battle

opposed it using the same argument as Madison—that it was an over-extension of federal power. Washington passed Jefferson's and Randolph's opinions on to Hamilton. Working day and night, Hamilton composed a reply that convinced President Washington he should sign the Bank bill. In a classic statement of implied powers, Hamilton argued that because the Bank's functions were among the powers given Congress, the Constitution gave Congress the right to choose any legal means to carry out those functions. In 1791 the Bank of the United States was established for a 20-year period with a capital investment of $10 million. Within two hours after shares in the Bank went on sale, wealthy investors had purchased $8 million worth of its stock.

Problems in the West

In addition to the financial problems left by the Confederation Congress, the new government faced continuing concerns about the western territories. The most immediate cause for alarm was relations with Indian nations, to which President Washington devoted most of his annual message to Congress in 1791. Armed to defend their lands, encouraged by the British and Spanish, and unimpressed by the Confederation government, the Indians battled settlers over frontier land. Thousands of people were killed in almost constant conflict. Washington hoped to improve relations, but the bloodshed had to stop.

South of the Ohio River, treaties were signed with the Cherokees in 1791 and the Chickamaugas in 1794—and the Creeks asked the federal government for protection from the settlers. Once these Indians in southern regions had been approached, the bluegrass meadows of Kentucky and the rich bottom lands along the rivers of Tennessee drew more than 300,000 settlers between 1790 and 1800. With such great population increases, Kentucky gained admission to the Union in 1792 and Tennessee in 1796.

Relations in parts north of the Ohio River were not as conciliatory. In 1791,

after a military expedition into the Northwest Territory was badly beaten by the Miami chief Little Turtle, Washington ordered the governor of the territory, General Arthur St. Clair, to the area with the largest force the West had ever seen— 2,300 regular troops plus several companies of militia. As St. Clair moved north from Cincinnati, desertion and disease reduced his army to 1,400. But lacking respect for his enemy and rejecting the pleas of his weakened troops, St. Clair continued into Indian territory. In November 1791, near what is now the Ohio-Indiana border, he was attacked. Only 500 of his command survived one of the worst defeats in American military history.

Life of the Times

FRONTIER WEDDINGS

Weddings were major social events on the frontier. Unlike marriage celebrations in more settled areas and in the East, western settings frequently lacked a religious service. Traveling clergy were scarce, and a resident minister even more uncommon. Instead, a justice of the peace would hear the couple's vows. This union was followed with festivities orchestrated by neighbors and friends that lasted for days.

The party typically began at the bride's home when her father placed a jug of whiskey on his doorstep. Male guests positioned one mile from the house, then raced to seize the jug. The winner carried the jug to the groom who took the first drink. Next, the groom and his party traveled to the bride's home for a daylong party. Around 9 o'clock in the evening, the female guests carried the bride to a bed in her parent's cabin. Later the male guests brought the groom to the bed. Guests would continue their party outside the cabin, often looking in on the newlyweds. The next morning the couple led a procession of guests to the groom's parents' cabin. Another daylong party or "infare," followed. On the third day the new couple moved into their own cabin. In the evening a "shivaree," or housewarming, took place. Guests surrounded the cabin armed with noisemaking devices. On a designated signal, the woods erupted in a din of noise. The newlyweds opened their home for yet another party that generally ended at dawn, finally marking the end of the wedding celebration.

The President then tried negotiation. The Indians' victory made them unwilling to compromise, however, and they demanded that all settlers north of the Ohio River leave the territory. Washington turned to General Anthony Wayne, who had distinguished himself in the Revolutionary War. In August 1794, his force defeated 800 Indians under the Shawnee chief Blue Jacket at the battle of Fallen Timbers. Wayne pursued his foes all the way to Fort Miami, near present-day Toledo, Ohio, a British fur post that had been

supplying weapons to the Indians. In 1795 the Indians agreed to surrender most of the present state of Ohio. As a result, settlers flocked to the new land, and in 1803 Ohio was admitted to the Union.

While Wayne was chasing Indians, another uprising was occurring in the West. In the days before canals and railroads, Westerners could not sell their grain east of the Appalachian Mountains because the cost of wagon transportation was prohibitive. Because a wagonload of whiskey was worth much more than a wagonload of grain,

Examining Maps *Westward settlement was rapid in the years between 1790 and 1820. Within eight years of the Treaty of Greenville that opened the territory to settlement, Ohio was admitted to the Union. What river was the avenue to the West?*

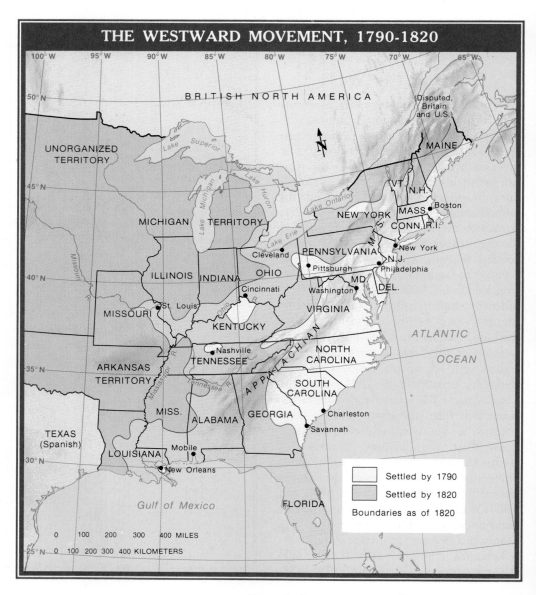

Western farmers distilled their grain into whiskey so they could transport it to market and make a profit. Whiskey was also used as currency in the West, where gold and silver coins or bank notes were scarce.

Westerners believed that Hamilton's excise tax on whiskey, first levied in 1791, was aimed directly at them. There may have been some truth to this claim. Hamilton viewed the excise tax not only as a source of revenue for the national government but also as a way to get the West to recognize federal authority.

Anti-tax sentiment was especially strong in western Pennsylvania, where citizens refused to pay the tax, attacked revenue officers, and burned the barns of neighbors who told authorities where stills were located. Known as the Whiskey Rebellion, this revolt was as much a challenge to law and order as Shays's Rebellion had been eight years before. The outcome under the new government, however, was very different. The Massachusetts militia had suppressed Shays without help from the nearly bankrupt Confederation government. When the governor of Pennsylvania hesitated to take action against the Whiskey Rebellion, the federal government stepped in and crushed it. President Washington, with Hamilton at his side, personally led 12,000 militia into western Pennsylvania, a force so overwhelming that when it approached, resistance to the whiskey tax melted. Some rebellion leaders were seized and taken to Philadelphia for trial. Two were found guilty of treason, but Washington pardoned both of them. The new government had shown its strength, he felt. Now it could afford to be merciful.

The rapid settlement of the West had a profound effect on politics. Reflecting the spirit of the frontier, the new western states extended **suffrage,** or voting rights. Because land was so plentiful in the West, the constitutions of Kentucky and Tennessee required no property qualifications for voting. All white males over 21 years of age had the franchise. The argument for extending suffrage was that any man who helped clear the land and fight Indians had a right to a say in the government. Like Jefferson, westerners tended to believe in common people.

★★★★★★★★★★★★★★★★★★

Section Two Review

★★★★★★★★★★★★★★★★★★

SUMMARY

The Washington administration had to deal with serious problems: revenues, the national debt, and westward expansion. Congress passed a revenue tariff on imported items. Alexander Hamilton established a program for paying the nation's debts and for creating a banking system to handle financial affairs. Washington himself attempted to make the West safer for settlement by sending federal troops to put down Indian attacks and to end a farmers' rebellion against a federal excise tax on whiskey.

CHECKING FOR UNDERSTANDING

1. **Identify** *Report on Manufactures,* Fallen Timbers, Whiskey Rebellion

2. **Define** tariffs, protective tariff, revenue tariff, bonds, excise tax, enumerated powers, implied power, suffrage

3. **Describe** why protective tariffs created sectional disagreements.

4. **Explain** the purpose and function of the national bank.

5. **Name** two problems in the West, and tell how Washington handled them.

THINKING CRITICALLY

6. **Predicting Outcomes** Predict why Hamilton's and Jefferson's differing views might eventually lead to the formation of political parties.

CONNECTIONS:
HISTORY AND MATHEMATICS

7. **Interpreting Statistics** The national debt in 1790 was $54 million, and the population was estimated at 4 million. The national debt in 1990 was about $3 trillion, and the population was estimated at about 250 million. Use these figures to estimate how much of the national debt was owed by each person in 1790 and in 1990. How many times greater had the debt grown over these 200 years?

★★★★★★★★★★★★★★★★★★

Critical Thinking Skills

Distinguishing Between Fact and Value Judgment

Suppose that you are starting a part-time job after school. There are things you want to buy, but you also have to budget your money. You tell a friend that you make $350 per month. He tells you that you should put most of it in a savings account. You stated a fact. He stated a value judgment.

Explanation

A fact is a statement that can be proved by evidence. This evidence can be empirical (something you can actually see or feel), or a reliable written account such as in a book or document. In contrast, a value judgment is a statement that includes a person's opinions based on one's values or feelings.

At one time or another, everyone is faced with the need to make a decision based on facts and value judgments. The following guidelines will help you in distinguishing between these two kinds of statements:

a. When reading or listening to any statement, keep in mind the definitions of fact and value judgment. Could the statement be supported with evidence?

b. Which statements are you being asked to accept as fact?

Example

Read the following statements and note how the guidelines have

been applied:

Hamilton said in 1790 that a central Bank of the United States would be "an institution of primary importance to the prosperous administration of the finances." (Could this statement have been supported with evidence? *No. This is a value judgment. The statement*

Congress Hall, center, site of the debate over a national bank in 1790

was Hamilton's belief that a central bank would be of primary importance, yet there was no evidence or proof to support it.)

Hamilton stated that the bank and its branches would provide places where the government could deposit money obtained through taxes. (*This is a fact—if created, the bank would provide such places.*)

Madison, however, argued that the federal government had no right to establish a central bank

because it was not among the enumerated powers of Congress found in the Constitution. (*This is a fact. Such authority was not among the powers of Congress. Evidence therefore supported it.*)

Madison also stated that establishing a central bank was not "necessary." He was referring to the "elastic clause" of Article 1, Section 8. (Could this have been supported with evidence? *No. This statement was not a fact, but Madison's opinion, a value judgment. He was also asking Congress to accept this statement as fact because he said it "is not" necessary. He did not say it "would not" be necessary.*)

Madison stated that if the federal government were allowed to set up a central bank, there would be no limits to the power of the federal government. (What evidence did Madison have to support this statement? *None. He was personally against too much governmental control over the states, and was therefore suspicious of federal power. This was a value judgment, or personal belief.*)

Practice

For further practice in this skill, find two examples of both factual statements and value judgments or opinions of the authors in Section One of this chapter.

Foreign Affairs Under Washington

The English know very well that the Americans would give their lives in defense of their national soil....Some day, perhaps, they will be the avengers of the seas, but that day is still far off. The Americans will become great slowly, or not at all.

—NAPOLEON BONAPARTE
French military leader, 1769-1821

Section Focus

Although an ocean away from Europe, the United States could not hope to exist in isolation. Along with new domestic policies, the nation had to forge a response to overseas pressures as well. Treaties brought improved relations for a time. But the end of Washington's presidency found the United States facing renewed problems with other nations.

Objectives

After studying this section, you should be able to:
- Describe the effects of the French Revolution on the United States.
- Explain the importance of the Jay and Pinckney treaties.

Shortly after Washington was inaugurated in 1789, the French Revolution began. At first, Americans sympathized with the revolutionaries because they were demanding the same rights that Americans had won a few years earlier. The French "Declaration of the Rights of Man and the Citizen" proclaimed that all "men are born and remain free and equal in rights," and declared the rights of "liberty, property, security and resistance to oppression." The French revolutionaries readily acknowledged their debt to the United States in the expression and defense of these rights.

In this country, popular enthusiasm for France became for a time almost a madness. Americans sang French revolutionary songs such as the "Marseillaise," erected "liberty poles" and wore "liberty caps," and even took to calling each other Citizen and Citizeness instead of Mr. and Mrs. In New York, King Street was renamed Liberty Street, and in Boston, Royal Exchange Alley became Equality Lane.

Cheers for France were often joined with damnation of Britain. Not only was the memory of the American Revolution still strong, but there was resentment because of the British refusal to give up the fur posts and to stop arming the Indians of the Northwest.

America's European Problems

When war broke out between France and Great Britain in 1793, the French expected American aid. According to treaties signed in 1778 between France and the American revolutionaries, France would have been justified in asking for American military assistance against Great Britain. They did not go that far, but they hoped to recruit American volunteers for the French army and navy and to use American ports as bases to attack British merchant ships.

France's expectations placed the United States in a difficult position. To be dragged into hostilities with Great Britain, whatever American sentiment for France,

Connections

HISTORY AND MATHEMATICS

PLANNING WASHINGTON, D.C.

By using inspiration, imagination, and his skill in geometry, engineer Pierre Charles L'Enfant created the design for a national capital unlike any other. When L'Enfant, who fought in the Revolution, heard that Congress was planning a new national capital, he quickly offered his services.

Souvenir handkerchief of the capital

Although L'Enfant's design was soon modified, his basic plan allowed a spacious modern city to develop. He envisioned a rationally laid-out metropolis that would embody the new nation's republican ideals, with wide boulevards connecting the branches of government, national monuments, parks, and entry gates.

L'Enfant began by choosing the spots for the Capitol and President's house. The Congress building became the central point in a square grid of streets occupying the terrain between the Potomac and Anacostia rivers. The grid was slashed by avenues that radiated from the capitol hill like spokes on a wheel. These avenues provided a direct route to different parts of the city. At strategic spots, L'Enfant's unique blend of topography and geometric symmetry called for circular intersections to join three or more avenues.

MAKING THE MATHEMATICS CONNECTION

1. What geometric forms did L'Enfant use in planning Washington, D.C.?

2. What are the advantages of locating a capitol in a planned city?

LINKING PAST AND PRESENT

3. What kinds of geometric shapes are found in modern government buildings?

---

would have been a disaster. Three-fourths of America's trade was with Britain, and tariff duties on British products provided the bulk of federal revenues. Because the British fleet controlled the seas, war would have ended foreign trade and meant bankruptcy for the new government.

Upon hearing of the outbreak of war in Europe, Washington called a cabinet meeting to discuss whether he should issue a declaration of neutrality. All cabinet members supported neutrality, even though Jefferson did so reluctantly. Jefferson, who had served as American minister to France and greatly respected the French people, believed that a formal declaration of neutrality would help Britain, and so he cautioned Washington against it. Hamilton, who despised the democracy of the French Revolution, argued that Britain was more to be feared than France, and he urged Washington to

announce America's neutrality. Again, Hamilton's arguments prevailed, and in April 1793, Washington issued a Proclamation of Neutrality. The President declared that the conduct of the United States toward the warring powers was to be "friendly and impartial." He warned that Americans who helped either side would be denied the protection of the government and would be subject to punishment.

The arrival of a new French minister, Citizen Edmond Genêt (zhuh NAY), put Washington's neutrality proclamation to the test. Arriving in South Carolina, Genêt traveled overland to the capital at Philadelphia. Along the way he was invited to so many dinners and pro-French celebrations that his journey became a triumphant procession. He arranged to place American crews on French **privateers,** or armed private ships, and offered George Rogers Clark a commission in the French army.

Arriving confidently in Philadelphia, Genêt demanded that the United States advance him money to pay his new recruits.

The French minister's efforts to involve the United States in war were soon thwarted. Washington received him with icy politeness. Hamilton used all his influence against Genêt. Even Jefferson flatly refused Genêt's demands and came to dislike him intensely. Finally, an outraged Washington demanded that he be recalled to France. Genêt, however, begged to remain in the United States, because changes in France's revolutionary government caused him to fear for his life. Washington granted his request, and he spent the rest of his life in obscurity.

Great Britain also tested American foreign policy. When the British realized that the new federal government was more powerful than its predecessor, they at last consented to send a minister to the United States. But once war began in Europe, they issued a series of orders forbidding neutral ships to trade with the French West Indies, to carry French West Indian produce, or to carry any weapons or food to France. These restrictions fell most heavily on the United States, which had the largest neutral merchant marine. British warships seized hundreds of American vessels and confiscated their cargoes, a clear violation of the rights of a neutral nation under international law.

In the spring of 1794, these provocations, coupled with news of British involvement with the Indians in the Northwest Territory, pushed Congress to the brink of war. Hamilton urged Washington to make one last effort to come to a peaceful solution to the outstanding United States-Britain disputes by sending John Jay, Chief Justice of the Supreme Court, as a special envoy to Great Britain.

The British were willing to sign a treaty. A war with the United States would only make it harder to carry on the war with France. And the United States was Britain's best market. Jay got rather poor treaty terms, however, partly because Alexander Hamilton committed a serious mistake; he let the British know Jay's instructions.

Treaties with Britain and Spain

The Jay Treaty was completed late in 1794 and was presented by Washington to the Senate the next year. The British promised once again to evacuate their forts in American territory if the United States let them keep the fur trade with the Indians. American ships were allowed into ports in the British Isles on the same terms as British ships in American ports. The treaty permitted the United States a very limited trade with the British West Indies, but none with Canadian ports. On the whole, it seemed that the British gave fewer concessions than they received. There was no promise that the violation of American neutral rights at sea would cease. Nor was there any assurance that British agents would stop giving weapons to American Indians. When the news of the Jay Treaty became known, there was a tremendous public outcry against it. Jay's effigy was hanged, burned, and guillotined in city squares throughout the nation. Hamilton, speaking in support of the treaty in New York City,

Examining Illustrations
The Arch Street Ferry *engraving by William Birch shows a busy trade center in Philadelphia. How did Britain threaten American trade?*

was stoned by a mob. Despite the public's outrage, the Senate narrowly ratified the treaty by a two-thirds vote, 20 to 10. Dissatisfied with the treaty and dismayed by public reaction, Washington hesitated but finally signed it. Resistance continued in the House, where opponents of the treaty, led by Madison, refused to vote funds necessary to put it into effect. But a growing fear that the alternative to an unsatisfactory treaty was war with Britain resulted in a 50 to 49 vote to release the funds.

Ironically, Jay's treaty helped the United States win concessions from Spain. When the treaty's pro-British terms became public, Spain's government suspected that a secret agreement had been made providing British support for an American attack on Spanish New Orleans and Florida. Thomas Pinckney was sent to Spain to try once again to settle longstanding differences between the two nations. In 1795 the Pinckney Treaty granted the United States all the concessions it had been seeking

since the end of the Revolutionary War—free navigation of the Mississippi River, the right of deposit at New Orleans, acknowledgement of the United States' southern boundary at the 31st parallel and western boundary at the Mississippi.

Washington Steps Down

Washington had wanted to retire after his first term as President, saying he would rather dig ditches than continue. He agreed to serve a second term only after prominent leaders, including both Jefferson and Hamilton, urged him to do so, saying it was his patriotic duty. In 1792, as in 1789, he received no opposition in the electoral college. But Washington enjoyed his second term even less than his first. Forced to choose in the bitter conflict between Jefferson and Hamilton, he continued to favor Hamilton. When Jefferson

Examining Cartoons *Federalists depicted Jefferson in this cartoon trying to hinder Washington's progress by hanging onto the carriage wheel. What major step did Jefferson take in 1793?*

resigned from the cabinet in 1793, Washington came under increasingly harsh attacks from Jefferson's supporters who accused the President of selling out to Great Britain. When he left office, the *Philadelphia Aurora*, a leading anti-administration newspaper, proclaimed:

If ever there was a period for rejoicing this is the moment. Every heart in unison with the freedom and happiness of the people ought to beat high with exultation that the name of Washington from this day ceases to give a currency to political iniquity and legalized corruption.

By the end of his second term, Washington had become sensitive to such criticism. He confessed that he wished to escape these attacks made "in such exaggerated and indecent terms as could scarce be applied to a Nero, a notorious defaulter, or even a common pickpocket."

The last major act of Washington's presidency was his Farewell Address, which was published in the *American Daily Advertiser* on September 17, 1796. This address was Washington's explanation for not seeking a third term as President. But more importantly, in this famous document, he gave the young republic his best advice on the conduct of politics and foreign affairs.

Upon returning to his beloved Mount Vernon, Washington had every reason to feel proud of his achievements during eight years as President. Most of the major difficulties of the Confederation had been overcome. As a result of Hamilton's financial program, America's credit was as good as any nation in Europe. The suppression of the Whiskey Rebellion had demonstrated the power of the new government. The major demands of the West had been fulfilled. In the difficult situation presented by war between France and Britain, Washington had steered a course that kept the United States prosperous and at peace.

Section Three Review

SUMMARY

The United States proclaimed neutrality in the war between France and Britain in 1793. Britain tried to block American trade with France, and preyed upon American ships. While many in Congress clamored for war, Washington relied on diplomacy to ease tensions. The Jay and Pinckney treaties improved trade relations and enhanced America's public image abroad.

CHECKING FOR UNDERSTANDING

1. **Identify** Declaration of the Rights of Man, Proclamation of Neutrality, Citizen Edmond Genêt, Jay Treaty, Pinckney Treaty, Farewell Address

2. **Describe** the activities of Citizen Genêt that caused President Washington to demand his recall.

3. **Show** how Great Britain's actions against the United States nearly resulted in war.

4. **Specify** which terms of the Jay Treaty created American opposition to it.

5. **State** which sectional area of the United States most benefited by the Pinckney Treaty and why.

THINKING CRITICALLY

6. **Supporting Positions** In his Farewell Address Washington warned against political divisions at home and foreign entanglements abroad. Cite three events in American history after 1796 that prove Washington's warnings were not taken seriously.

LINKING PAST AND PRESENT

7. **Comparing Actions** Britain's embargo of trade against France when war broke out in the 1790s was aimed at defeating France. The United Nations' trade sanctions against Iraq when it seized Kuwait in 1990 was aimed at avoiding a war. Compare how both actions are alike and different.

SECTION FOUR

President John Adams

SETTING THE SCENE

Let fame to the world sound America's voice;

No intrigue can her sons from their government sever;

Her pride is her Adams— his laws are her choice,

And shall flourish, till liberty slumber forever!

—ROBERT TREAT PAINE
Adams and Liberty, 1794-1796

Section Focus

It was inevitable that a nation of people holding different political philosophies and ideologies would sooner or later establish political parties. Foreign affairs provided further reasons for partisan politics. Led by a new President, the government would soon have to deal with problems on foreign soil as well as suspected treason at home.

Objectives

After studying this section, you should be able to:
- Explain why political parties arose.
- Describe the problems John Adams encountered as President.

The origins of America's two-party political system are found in the conflicts within Washington's cabinet and in Congressional debates over Hamilton's financial program. Shortly after Washington took office, it became clear that Hamilton had the President's ear on almost every government matter. To counter Hamilton's strong influence, Madison and Jefferson began to gather support for their views both inside the government and out. From their effort emerged America's first political party.

The Formation of Parties

Washington's first administration was **nonpartisan**—that is, there were no permanent divisions based on politics or causes. Differences arose over specific issues, which were hotly debated. But harmony returned after a cause triumphed or lost. Jefferson's resignation from Washington's cabinet, however, signaled a formal split in the ranks of the nation's political leadership.

After resigning, Jefferson openly allied with Madison, who was already opposing the Washington administration in Congress, to form what they called the "Republican" interest. They chose this name to suggest that they were defending freedom and self-government from the anti-democratic influence of Hamilton.

Hamilton's supporters retaliated by taking the name "Federalists," the label previously used by supporters of the Constitution during the ratification campaign. This clever maneuver was intended to imply that the Republicans were the Anti-Federalists and that they did not support the Constitution.

The Federalists included people who stood to profit from Hamilton's financial program—creditors, merchants, and bondholders. Federalists gained mass support from wage earners in the shipping industry and from residents of states that benefited when the federal government assumed state debts. Reflecting Hamilton's distrust of the people, the Federalists hoped to put the direction of government into the hands of the "rich, well-born, and able." The Republicans' strength was among southern planters, subsistence farmers of the backcountry, and "mechanics" such as carpenters, shoemakers, and masons. The Republicans advocated limiting the power of the central government.

As the presidential election of 1796 drew near, both sides increasingly acted like traditional political parties. Under Madison's leadership, the Republicans tried to gain public support by opposing the unpopular Jay Treaty. Washington gave the Federalists an election advantage by delaying his retirement announcement. The Republicans were unwilling to offer any candidate to oppose a national hero.

When Washington withdrew two months before the election, the Federalists selected Vice President John Adams, who was highly respected in the country at large and had solid support from his native New England. The Republicans countered with a candidate of equal national reputation and sectional strength—Thomas Jefferson. In selecting its candidate for Vice President, each party tried to achieve geographic balance between its candidates. The Federalists chose Thomas Pinckney of South Carolina, who was currently popular because of his successful treaty negotiations with Spain. The Republicans balanced Jefferson, the Virginian, with Aaron Burr of New York.

Because the Framers of the Constitution had not anticipated political parties, the nation's first partisan presidential election was a confusing contest. The Constitution provided that the candidate with the highest number of votes in the electoral college would become President, and the runner-up, Vice President. Therefore, some New England Federalist electors left Pinckney off their ballots in order to make sure that Adams would get the highest vote. The result was that Adams, a Federalist, was elected President with 71 electoral votes, while Jefferson, a Republican, became Vice President with 68.

Adams as President

John Adams had spent most of his life in public service. An early leader of the revolutionary movement in Massachusetts, he was a prominent member of the First and Second Continental Congresses. During the war, he served as envoy to France and Holland. He was one of the American representatives at the Treaty of Paris ending the Revolutionary War, and later became the nation's first minister to Great Britain. Under Washington, he served two terms as Vice President. In each office, he served with distinction.

Despite his many administrative talents, Adams was not a successful President. For one thing, he was too aware of his own virtues. During the Revolution he had written of himself: "At such times as this there are many dangerous things to be done which nobody else will do, and therefore I cannot help attempting them." Enemies satirized both his love of ceremony and his roly-poly figure by nicknaming him "His Rotundity." He was difficult to deal with because he was reluctant to compromise, often being as suspicious of others' motives as he was sure of his own.

Adams inherited the dispute with France. French disappointment over Washington's Neutrality Proclamation turned to hostility after the Jay Treaty. During the election of 1796, the French minister to the United States actively campaigned against Adams. When Charles C. Pinckney was sent as minister to France in 1796, he was ordered out of the country. Meanwhile, the French navy started to prey on American shipping.

Adams was anxious to make peace. Immediately after taking office, he sent envoys to Paris to negotiate a treaty. When the Americans arrived, they were approached by representatives of Charles Maurice de Talleyrand, the French minister of foreign affairs, who refused to meet with

Linking Across Time

NATURALIZATION

Persons who wish to become naturalized citizens today must maintain legal residency in the United States for five years before making application. Foreign spouses of U.S. citizens can apply after three years. Applicants must be at least 18 years old, be able to speak, read, and write English; be of good moral character; and demonstrate a knowledge of U.S. history. They also must pay a $50 fee and take an oath of allegiance to the United States.

them. In a letter to the secretary of state, the American envoys reported that the French government was:

...exceedingly irritated at some passages of the President's speech, and desired that they should be softened; and that this step would be necessary previous to our reception. That, besides this, a sum of money was required for the pocket of the [government leaders], which would be at the disposal of M. Talleyrand.

AMERICAN PORTRAITS

BENJAMIN BANNEKER
1731-1806

Born into a free black family in Maryland, Benjamin Banneker attended a private school, but he was largely self-educated. When his father died, Banneker sold the family farm and devoted the rest of his life to mathematics and natural science.

Banneker's skill in mathematics prompted Thomas Jefferson to secure him a job surveying the land for the new national capital at Washington, D.C. When the French architect—Pierre L'Enfant—was removed from the project, he took his detailed maps with him. Banneker amazed everyone by redrawing the missing maps from memory! From 1791 to 1796 he made astronomical and tide calculations for a yearly almanac. Known as "the sable genius," Banneker became a symbol for racial justice in a land not yet ready to grant him rights of citizenship.

Unwilling to pay this bribe, the Americans broke off negotiations. Because their reports labeled Talleyrand's agents as X, Y, and Z, this situation came to be known as the XYZ Affair, and it produced an outburst of popular anger against France. Adams was cheered in Congress when he declared that he would never send another minister without France assuring its respect to "the representative of a great, free, powerful, and independent nation." The slogan of the day became: "Millions for defense, but not one cent for tribute." Congress created a Department of the Navy in May 1798, and soon warships and privateers were waging an undeclared naval war with France.

War fever suited Federalist party leaders. The national emergency strengthened the federal government, made the Federalists popular, and discredited the pro-French Republicans. If war continued, Federalists expected to win reelection in 1800. But President Adams refused to let election politicking dominate American foreign policy. When Talleyrand changed his mind and was willing to receive American diplomats, Adams sent to the Senate a nomination for an American minister to France. Federalist senators were furious, but they could not long oppose an effort to make peace. By the end of Adams's presidency, peace with France had been restored.

Adams's action in making peace against the wishes of most of his party was an extremely courageous act. Proud of his nonpartisan accomplishment, Adams later wrote that he wished his gravestone to be inscribed, "Here lies John Adams who took upon himself the responsibility of the peace with France in the year 1800."

Partisan Legislation

Many Federalists were convinced that prominent Republicans were actively in league with France "to burn all our cities and cut the throats of all our inhabitants," as one Federalist newspaper reported it. So in 1798, in the midst of war fever, the Federalist majority in Congress pushed through three laws designed to hurt the Republican party—a Naturalization Act, an Alien Act, and a Sedition Act.

Many French and Irish refugees had recently come to America. Because they were anti-British, most supported the Republican party. The Naturalization Act tried to weaken this Republican strength by extending the residency requirement for citizenship from 5 to 14 years. The Alien Act reflected an almost hysterical fear that French agents were using Republicans as dupes. It required all immigrants to register with the federal government and allowed the President to deport without trial any alien whom he considered "dangerous to the peace and safety of the United States." The Sedition Act attempted to muzzle the Republican press by making it a crime to speak or publish anything false or malicious against the federal government or any of its officers.

Both Adams and Hamilton had warned fellow Federalists against abusing their power. Instead of weakening the Republican party, Federalists—through these laws—gave Republicans the issues that broadened their public support. Republicans were horrified by the Federalist attack on the Bill of Rights, which guaranteed freedom of speech and press. In 1798 and 1799, the Republican legislatures of Kentucky and Virginia passed resolutions, secretly written by Jefferson and Madison, denouncing the Sedition Act as unconstitutional. The Kentucky Resolutions are especially important because they first presented the theory of **nullification**. According to this theory, the Constitution was an agreement among the states to establish a central government. If an act of this government exceeded the powers given it in the Constitution, a state had the right to refuse to obey.

The nullification theory was denounced by other state legislatures as threatening to the Union. If any state could nullify any federal law it considered unconstitutional, the power of the federal government would cease. The Kentucky and Virginia resolutions were intended as campaign material for the presidential election of 1800 and were not followed by action that undermined federal authority. Once raised, however, the issue would return to haunt a later generation and confirm the worst fears of the Federalists.

Section Four Review

SUMMARY

The presidency of John Adams was marked by controversy and divisiveness. Federalists and Republicans clashed over federal power, the nature of society, and foreign policy. Incensed over the XYZ Affair and French interference with American shipping, Federalists wanted to declare war on France. Adams' willingness to send another diplomatic mission to France restored peace. Republicans countered the controversial Alien and Sedition Acts with the Kentucky and Virginia Resolutions, introducing the nullification theory and reinforcing their commitment to states' rights.

CHECKING FOR UNDERSTANDING

1. **Identify** XYZ Affair, Naturalization Act, Alien and Sedition Act, Kentucky and Virginia Resolutions

2. **Define** nonpartisan, nullification

3. **List** the main differences between the Republicans and the Federalists.

4. **Point out** John Adams's public service background prior to his becoming President.

5. **Describe** the XYZ Affair and its effect on American events.

THINKING CRITICALLY

6. **Evaluating Ideas**   List what you consider to be the strengths and weaknesses of having political parties. Use your list to write an opinion statement of 3-4 sentences explaining why you favor or oppose having political parties.

LINKING PAST AND PRESENT

7. **Using Resources**   Like John Adams, George Bush had wide experience in government service before he became President. Look in current reference books to find the various government positions that President Bush previously held.

★ Chapter 7 Review ★

★ Summary

Between 1789 and 1800, the Federalists probably accomplished more than any other party in our nation's history. They transformed a Constitution on parchment into a workable instrument of government. They opened the West for settlement and made it possible for western farmers to get their produce safely to market. They established the reputation and power of the United States among other nations of the world. They created a sound economic and financial system. Much of their success was due to the character of George Washington, the genius of Alexander Hamilton, and the integrity of John Adams. As one historian said, they "found America disunited, poor, insolvent, weak, discontented, and wretched. It hath left her united, wealthy, respectable, strong, happy, and prosperous." But by 1800 their usefulness was over. The youth, vigor, and optimism of the country were drawn to the party of more democratic principles—to the Republicans and Thomas Jefferson.

★ Understanding Vocabulary

For each term below, write a sentence explaining why it had either a unifying effect or a divisive effect on the new government.

cabinet	enumerated powers
protective tariff	implied power
revenue tariff	nonpartisan
excise tax	nullification

★ Reviewing Facts

1. **List** the actions taken during Washington's presidency that reflected the Federalist principle of strong central government authority.
2. **Outline** the causes that gradually led to the development of political parties.
3. **Identify** the economic problems facing the nation in 1789 and how Hamilton's financial program addressed those problems.
4. **State** the causes, their effects, and the final outcomes of the problems that the United States faced with France and Britain between 1789 and 1800.
5. **Show** how the actions of George Washington and improved foreign relations opened up the West for settlement.

★ Understanding Concepts

LEADERSHIP

1. Characterize the leadership style that George Washington exercised as President.
2. Describe the kind of leadership the Federalists provided in relation to the kind provided in the Confederation government.

POLITICAL VALUES

3. Describe the political values that motivated President Washington.
4. Explain the ideals of the Republicans under Thomas Jefferson, and compare them with Federalist principles.

★ Thinking Critically

1. **Drawing Conclusions** Washington was the first of several generals who later became President. Why do people think that a good general will make a good President?
2. **Making Hypotheses** Suggest reasons why Thomas Jefferson, Franklin D. Roosevelt, and John F. Kennedy, who all came from wealthy family backgrounds, devoted their public lives to a concern for the common people.
3. **Formulating Causes** Explain why events in Europe have so often had an effect in the United States.
4. **Linking Past and Present** Some people feel that there is very little difference between the Republican party and Democratic party today. Do you agree or disagree with this statement? Explain why you feel the way you do.

★ Writing About History

CLASSIFICATION AND DIVISION

Refer to the description of how to write a classification and division essay in the History Writer's Handbook in the Appendix of this book. Your teacher will give you more specific instructions on the essay's length and the assignment's due date.

Read an encyclopedia article about the life of George Washington. Then divide the many facts about Washington's life into several different periods

★ Chapter 7 Review ★

or categories. Write a report on George Washington's life and be prepared to explain why you have classified Washington's life into the categories you have chosen.

★ Learning Cooperatively

You and four class members will portray a banker and the following persons asking for a loan: 1) a New England manufacturer wanting to build a furniture factory, 2) a western farmer wanting to buy 100 acres of land, 3) a southern plantation owner wanting to buy more land and slaves, 4) a land speculator wanting to buy a million acres of land in the West. Each team member should portray a different person. After interviews are finished, decide together whether and why each of the loans should be granted or denied.

★ Mastering Skills

RECOGNIZING HISTORICAL REASONING

Just as you sometimes have different opinions from your friends, people in the past had differing opinions as well. Some differences, such as Hamilton's and Jefferson's, are now quite famous. In order to present a clear view of what actually happened hundreds of years ago, historians use *historical reasoning* to write their opinions and to support the stories they tell. *Reasoning* is the process by which one judgment is deduced from others that are given. This means that to support an argument (or in this case, to tell a story from history), certain techniques can be used to prove a point.

When historians write about history, they often use certain words to connect the facts to other words that help the reader understand their meaning. These clue words point out the deductions they have made.

The chart that follows lists four kinds of historical reasoning. By learning to recognize these four methods, you can better determine for yourself whether or not an historian has supported his or her argument adequately. Four kinds of historical reasoning are:

- *Cause-and-effect reasoning* explains why things might have happened.
- *Analogies,* or comparisons, show how two things are alike or different.
- *Generalizations* point out how one aspect of the story relates to the whole picture.
- *Proof* uses specific facts or details.

KINDS OF HISTORICAL REASONING

KIND	CLUE WORDS
Cause and Effect	led to, brought on, resulted in
Example: *The ratification of the Constitution in 1788 resulted in a new framework for government.*	
Analogies	like, as, similar to, different from
Example: *Westerners tended, like Jefferson, to believe in common people.*	
Generalizations	some, most, all, few
Example: *Most people were opposed to the Jay Treaty.*	
Proof	for example, this statement shows
Example: *Washington made it clear that he wanted to retire after his first term. For example, he pointed out that he would rather dig ditches than continue.*	

Example After studying the chapter and the kinds of historical reasoning shown in the chart, the following questions concerning the story told about the Federalist Era by this text's authors can be answered.

1. What statements in Section 1 give *proof* to Washington's leadership skills? *(Military victories, character, knew the country)*

2. How is *cause and effect* used in Section 2 to explain how settlement north of the Ohio River caused conflict with the Indians? *(Indians battled settlers, Washington sent in troops)*

Practice Read the following statement Thomas Jefferson made in regards to his differences with Hamilton. *"Every difference of opinion is not a difference in principle. We have called by different names brethren of the same principle. We are all Republicans, we are all Federalists."* What kind of reasoning do you think Jefferson was using to make his point? Explain.

CHAPTER 8

Jefferson and the Republicans

SETTING THE SCENE

Historical Focus

Between 1800 and 1815 the United States experienced rapid expansion as well as the challenge of war. The Louisiana Territory doubled the size of the nation, creating remarkable new opportunities, and Americans looked to the future confidently. However, when war between France and Great Britain was renewed, the United States found its peace and neutrality threatened. By 1812 the United States and Great Britain had once more plunged into war.

Concepts to Understand

- How **geographic expansion** changed the social and economic character of the United States.
- How expansion, economic change, and conflict unified Americans and helped them form a **national identity**.

People to Know

Aaron Burr, John Marshall, Meriwether Lewis, Sacajawea, Tecumseh

Places to Locate

Missouri River, Rocky Mountains, Lake Erie, Baltimore, Washington, D.C.

Terms to Identify

laissez-faire, judicial review, writ of mandamus, Louisiana Purchase, impressment, "War Hawks," War of 1812

Guided Reading

As you read this chapter, seek the answers to the following questions.

1. What opportunities resulted from the Louisiana Purchase?
2. What factors caused the War of 1812?

SPANNING THE DECADES

POLITICAL	1801 *Jefferson is elected President*	1803 *Louisiana Purchase*		1807 *Chesapeake is attacked*
	1800		**1805**	
CULTURAL	1801 *"Second Great Awakening" religious revival in the West began*		1805 *Mercy Otis Warren published* History of the...American Revolution	1807 *Inventor Robert Fulton perfects the steamboat* Clermont

A View of New Orleans *by John L. Boqueta de Woiseri, 1803*

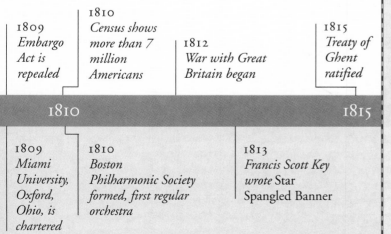

...Each generation is as independent of the one preceding as that was of all which had gone before. It has then, like them, a right to choose for itself the form of government it believes most promotive of its own happiness....

—THOMAS JEFFERSON
Letter to Samuel Kercheval, 1816

The Changing Political Scene

A just and solid republican government maintained here will be a standing monument and example for the aim and imitation of the people of other countries.

—THOMAS JEFFERSON
President of the United States, 1801

Section Focus

The election of 1800 marked a turning point for the United States. For the first time, the Federalist party was not in power. Its political philosophy of rule by "the good, the wise, and the rich" was considered outdated. The growing democratic spirit of the nation found its expression in the Republican party.

Objectives

After studying this section, you should be able to:
- Compare the views of the Federalist and Republican parties on economy, democracy, and the role of government.
- Explain Thomas Jefferson's views on government.

During his vice-presidency under John Adams, Thomas Jefferson became the active leader of the Republican party. He was in an ideal situation for the task—at the center of the government, and yet his job as Vice President carried with it very few official duties. Through personal contact with members of Congress and through thousands of letters, he kept in touch with Republicans all over the country.

Above all, however, Jefferson spread his views and ideas through newspapers. He once said that if he had to choose between government without newspapers or newspapers without a government, he would choose the latter. Jefferson raised money to start dozens of Republican newspapers, and these newspapers were a tremendous force in turning public opinion toward the Republican viewpoint.

The Election of 1800

As the presidential election of 1800 approached, the Federalists selected John Adams and Charles Pinckney as their candidates; the Republicans, Jefferson and Aaron Burr. During the campaign, Jefferson suggested that his followers concentrate their fire on the Sedition Act and heavier taxes brought on by the undeclared war with France. The Federalists countered by predicting that Jefferson would cancel the public debt and abolish the navy. Speakers for both parties made deceitful charges. Republicans pictured Adams as a tyrant who wanted to be king. Federalists, on the other hand, portrayed Jefferson as a drunkard, an atheist, and a French agent. One of the leading Federalist newspapers, *The Hartford Courant*, voiced the opinion that:

Mr. Jefferson has long felt a spirit of deadly hostility against the Federal Constitution…. If he should be elected President, the Constitution will inevitably fall…. The result will be dreadful to the people of the United States.

Realizing that lack of support in all the states north of Pennsylvania had cost them the election in 1796, the Republicans worked hard in 1800 to gain the backing of laborers and recent immigrants in northeastern cities. The contest was close; so close that the voters in the state of New York would ultimately determine which party would win the election. Here the

Republicans had a stroke of good fortune. Aaron Burr's organization was so effective in getting out the vote in New York City that the Republicans carried every district in the city. That victory gave them the state and, with it, the national election.

The election results posed a new question: the Republicans had won but *which* Republican candidate became President? There was no doubt that the party had intended Jefferson as President and Burr Vice President. But unlike today's election practices, candidates in 1800 were not designated as the candidate for President or the candidate for Vice President. Because every Republican elector had two votes and voted separately for both Jefferson and Burr, each candidate received 73 electoral votes. In such a situation where there was no majority, the Constitution stipulates that the House of Representatives selects the President. A group of die-hard Federalists schemed to deny Jefferson the presidency and elect Burr—and came close to doing just that. The House was so evenly divided that it took 6 days and 36 ballots to reach a decision. The deadlock was broken only after a group of Federalists led by Hamilton threw their support to Jefferson because they considered him better suited for the job and abler than Burr.

Although the Federalists were unhappy at losing the presidency, they accepted it and surrendered control of the federal government. This marked the first time in modern history that the political control of a country had been transferred through a democratic election. Despite animosity between Federalists and Republicans, the party system was beginning to work for the nation. The political parties that Washington had feared and warned against had developed national organizations that selected competent candidates for public office, maintained communications between federal officials and their constituents, and dealt effectively with factional and sectional differences.

Although the election of 1800 marked the end of the Federalist party as a viable political force, the party had made some lasting and important contributions. The Constitution was working and the problems of the Confederation period had been

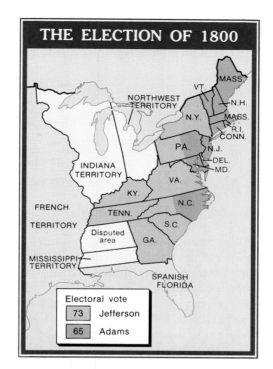

Examining Maps *The election of 1800 pitted Republican Thomas Jefferson against Federalist John Adams. Which states split their electoral votes between the two candidates?*

solved, at least for a time. Given these accomplishments it seems surprising that the Federalists went into such a drastic decline. An important reason for this is that its members had little trust in the people. While Jefferson and the Republicans often praised the wisdom of the common people, many Federalists were apt to think of them, in the words of one Federalist newspaper, as "the stupid populace, too abject in ignorance to think rightly, and too depraved to draw honest deductions."

Jefferson the Individual

If the Washington, D.C., of 1801— with its muddy streets and half-finished buildings—was an odd sort of national capital, the first President inaugurated there was in many ways an odd sort of man to be the founder of a political party and head of state. Thomas Jefferson hated crowds, avoided making speeches, and was too thin-skinned to enjoy rough-and-tumble politics. The Marquis de Chastellux, who met Jefferson near the end of the Revolutionary War, was amazed at finding in backcountry Virginia:

…an American, who without ever having quitted [left] his own country, is at once a musician, skilled in drawing, a geometrician, an astronomer, a natural philosopher, legislator, and statesman.

This description only begins to list Jefferson's skills and accomplishments. Jefferson's interest in agriculture led him to import hundreds of foreign plants into this country and to send hundreds of American plants abroad. One of the finest architects of his day, Jefferson designed his own home, Monticello, and was the chief architect of the Virginia Capitol and a complex of buildings for the University of Virginia. His many inventions included an improved plow, a swivel chair, and a folding carriage top. A lover of English, French, and classical literature, he collected a library that eventually became the nucleus of the Library of Congress.

In appearance and manner, Jefferson had little of Washington's dignity. He deliberately tried to reduce the ceremony surrounding the office of President because he felt both Washington and Adams had acted too much like British royalty. For example, instead of riding in a coach, Jefferson chose to walk the 200 yards from the boarding house to his inauguration. He also sent written messages to Congress instead of appearing in person, beginning a custom that lasted more than a century. Visitors from other countries were amazed to see him riding through the dusty streets of Washington on horseback, dressed in faded corduroy overalls, with a bag of clover seed in front of the saddle. A British diplomat described Jefferson as having the appearance of a "tall, large-boned farmer."

Jefferson and Government

Jefferson brought both a political and a philosophical change to the presidency. He believed the people were the source of a government's power, an idea he expressed in his Inaugural Address. In relatively few words, Jefferson explained his theory of government. Pleading for national harmony after the bitter election, Jefferson said:

Let us restore to social intercourse that harmony and affection without which liberty and even life itself are but dreary things.… We are all Republicans, we are all Federalists.

By this he meant that despite their distrust of democracy, Federalists recognized the principle that problems are finally settled by the will of the people, and that despite their distrust of centralized power, the Republicans did not propose to destroy the federal government.

Jefferson addressed three issues in his address that he considered to be of great importance. First, there was the question of what to do with persons who wished to dissolve the Union or change its republican form. Should these persons be jailed or exiled? Or should they be forced to register with the police as the Alien and Sedition Acts had required? There was genuine and widespread fear of disloyalty

Examining Fine Art
In addition to being an inventor and a scientist, Thomas Jefferson helped design the University of Virginia. Jefferson brought a new outlook to the presidency as well. Why did Jefferson focus on the theme of unity in his Inaugural Address?

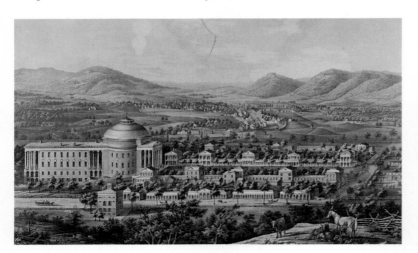

UNIT 3 LAUNCHING THE REPUBLIC: 1789-1824

and foreign influence, but Jefferson had such a strong belief in human freedom and such faith in human reason that he refused to be alarmed. He recommended letting those who wish to alter or destroy the Union "stand undisturbed as monuments of the safety with which error of opinion may be tolerated."

Jefferson also addressed whether or not a government by the people would be strong enough to meet crises. The federal government lacked a strong police system and a large standing army, and many Americans feared the government was too weak to last. Jefferson said that he thought it was, on the contrary, the strongest in the world because each citizen had a personal interest in fighting to keep it free.

Finally, Jefferson addressed the question of the ability of human beings to govern themselves. Jefferson turned the question around by asking who was good enough to govern someone else. He asked if people "had found angels in the form of kings to govern?" *King* in Jefferson's time meant dictator.

Jefferson described what he thought were the principles of "wise and frugal government." In contrast to Hamilton's idea that the federal government should actively promote banking, commerce, and industry, Jefferson advocated his belief in a "hands-off" policy called **laissez-faire**, meaning literally, "let people do as they choose." Governments adhering to *laissez-faire* should not control the way people do business or farm but should keep its role to restraining people from injuring each other and allowing them to be "free to regulate their own pursuits."

Jefferson's views on democracy and individual freedom quieted the fears of the Federalists. He called for "the preservation of the General Government in its whole constitutional vigor," which surely did not suggest his earlier theory of nullification presented in the Kentucky and Virginia resolutions of 1798 and 1799. He also spoke of "the honest payment of our debts." This came as a great relief to owners of federal bonds who feared that, as an opponent of Hamilton's financial policies, Jefferson would prevent repayment to the bondholders.

SUMMARY

The election of 1800 officially marked the end of the Federalists in power. Jefferson brought to the presidency a different set of political values. His interests in agriculture, architecture, inventions, and literature contributed further to changing values in government. In his address to the nation, Jefferson described his views on the principles of government, democracy, and individual freedom. Jefferson regarded the election of 1800 as a "revolution," in the sense that, with the defeat of the Federalists, people who did not trust democracy were replaced by those who believed strongly in democracy.

CHECKING FOR UNDERSTANDING

1. **Identify** Charles Pinckney, Aaron Burr, Monticello

2. **Define** *laissez-faire*

3. **Explain** how Alexander Hamilton brought about the election of Thomas Jefferson even though they were political enemies.

4. **State** the main points of Jefferson's political philosophy.

5. **List** the main points made by Jefferson in his Inaugural Address.

THINKING CRITICALLY

6. **Comparing Actions** Compare Jefferson's and Washington's administrations based on appearance and manner.

CONNECTIONS: HISTORY AND PHILOSOPHY

7. **Recognizing Similarities** In 1806 Asher Benjamin published *American Builders' Companion*. These "how-to" books contained the same principles found in elaborate professional books, but in a condensed, practical form, aimed for village carpenters and amateur architects. Show how Benjamin's manuals are related to Jefferson's philosophical and political views.

Interpreting Primary Sources

Female Equality

In the early 1800s, some American women began to challenge the accepted notion of female inferiority to men. They began to demand a greater role in public life and seek more education for themselves. An organized movement for women's rights, with a substantial number of supporters however, did not begin until the Seneca Falls Convention in 1848.

Prior to this a few public leaders attempted to both satisfy these women and to contain them at the same time. For example, Massachusetts minister Thomas Bernard urged women to stay in their "sphere," where, as mothers, they wielded "extensive power over the fortunes of man in every generation."

The following letter shows a young woman trying to make sense of the contradictory doctrines of female subordination and sexual equality.

From Eliza Southgate's letter to a male cousin, 1801—

But every human being who has contemplated human nature on a large scale will certainly justify me when I declare that the inequality of privilege between the sexes is very sensibly felt by us females, and in no instance is it greater than in the liberty of choosing a partner in marriage; true, we have the liberty of refusing those we don't like, but not of selecting those we do. This is undoubtedly as it should be....

Educated woman of the period

I never was of opinion that the pursuits of the sexes ought to be the same; on the contrary, I believe it would be destructive to happiness, there would a degree of rivalry exist each should have a separate sphere of action—in such a case there could be no clashing unless one or the other should leap their respective bounds. Yet to cultivate the qualities with which we are endowed can never be called infringing the prerogatives of man....

The cultivation of the power we possess, I have ever thought a privilege (or I may say duty) that belonged to the human species, and not man's exclusive prerogative. Far from destroying the harmony that ought to subsist, it would fix it on a foundation that would not totter at every jar. Women would be under

the same degree of subordination that they now are; enlighten and expand their minds, and they would perceive the necessity of such a regulation to preserve the order and happiness of society....

EXAMINING THE PRIMARY SOURCE

1. What does Southgate suggest is a prime example of the inequality of privilege between the sexes?

2. What disadvantage does Southgate see to men and women following the same pursuits?

3. What advantage to men does Southgate see in women's developing their minds to the highest possible degree?

THINKING CRITICALLY

4. Identify parts of the letter that reveal Southgate's ambivalence about female subordination.

5. Do you agree or disagree with Southgate's assertion that competition between men and women creates unhappiness in male-female relationships? Explain your answer.

LINKING PAST AND PRESENT

6. To what extent do men and women today function in separate spheres? Give examples to support your answer.

Jefferson in Office

SETTING THE SCENE

[The election of 1800] is as real a revolution in the principles of government as that of 1776 was in its form.

—THOMAS JEFFERSON
President of the United States, 1801

Section Focus

The partisan bitterness of the campaign still lingered when Jefferson and the Republicans took office. Jefferson realized that his primary task was to unite the nation and prove that he would represent not only the members of his party but all Americans. Partly for this reason, Jefferson left intact many Federalist programs.

Objectives

After studying this section, you should be able to:
• Compare similarities and differences between Jefferson's administration and those of Washington and Adams.
• Discuss the significance of judicial review.

J efferson liked to speak of his election in 1800 as a "revolution." Perhaps it was a revolution in the sense that leaders who distrusted democracy were replaced by those who believed in it; but it was surely one of the mildest revolutions ever. Not only was there no violence, but surprisingly few laws passed by the Federalists were repealed. The Alien and Sedition Acts had expired and were not renewed; the waiting period necessary for immigrants to become American citizens was reduced

from 14 years to 5; and the excise tax on whiskey was abolished. The major features of Hamilton's financial program—the Bank of the United States, the Funding Act, and the assumption of state debts—remained untouched.

Jefferson the Leader

Once in office, President Jefferson and the other Republican leaders found they had to modify their views on governing. Before he became President, Jefferson argued that the executive branch held too much power. In his Inaugural Address, he hinted that he would allow Congress to guide policy. As President, Jefferson reduced the outward signs of his authority and made gestures toward giving Congress more control over day-to-day affairs of government. He soon found, however, that he had to provide strong leadership or watch his party divide into factions.

For this reason Jefferson used his position as party leader to influence legislation. By working with Republican leaders in Congress and by giving his supporters key positions, Jefferson became just as much chief legislator as Washington had been.

The congressional elections of 1800 gave the Republicans solid majorities in both the House and Senate, putting them in the position to repeal any Federalist legislation they disliked. The only change

Examining Illustrations
Some Federalists feared that the Jefferson administration would reverse every Federalist policy and possibly destroy the young government. What actions did Jefferson take regarding Hamilton's financial program?

they attempted to make, however, was to cut back the power of the federal judiciary and remove some federal judges from office.

Republicans feared the judiciary for three reasons. One was that federal judges, holding their positions "during good behavior," or life, were beyond the control of the people. Another was that federal courts had declared several state laws unconstitutional, thereby strengthening the power of the federal government while reducing that of the states. Finally, Federalists had "packed" the judiciary during their last month in office. The number of federal judges was increased by the Judiciary Act of 1801, and Adams promptly filled several positions with members of his party. These new judges were known as "midnight judges" because Adams supposedly signed appointments until midnight of his last day in office.

One of the first acts of Congress after Jefferson took office was to repeal the Judiciary Act of 1801. After doing away with the "midnight judges" by abolishing their offices, the Republicans tried to remove other Federalists from the judiciary by impeachment. In 1804 a Federalist district judge named John Pickering was impeached by the House and convicted by the Senate for actions that indicated he was mentally unstable. The House then impeached Supreme Court Justice Samuel Chase, who had attacked democracy in general and Jefferson in particular while addressing a Baltimore jury. The Senate, however, refused to convict Chase because it was not convinced that he had been proven guilty of "treason, bribery, or other high crimes and misdemeanors."

Judicial Review

In 1801, shortly before leaving office, President Adams appointed John Marshall Chief Justice of the United States. Marshall was an ardent Federalist and detested his cousin and fellow Virginian, Thomas Jefferson. In *Marbury v. Madison* (1803), one of the first cases to come before him, Marshall greatly strengthened the power of the federal judiciary. In his decision he claimed that the federal courts had the power of **judicial review** over acts of Congress—that is, the power to decide whether or not laws passed by Congress were constitutional.

When James Madison took over as secretary of state in the Jefferson administration, he found on his desk the commissions of a number of justices of the peace for the new District of Columbia. President Adams had signed the commissions, but they had not been delivered, and Jefferson instructed Madison to withhold the commissions. One of the appointees, William Marbury, petitioned the Supreme Court for a **writ of mandamus**—a court order requiring specific action—instructing Madison to give him his commission.

Life of the Times

TELLING TIME

An unscheduled pace characterized both the lives of the small farmers whom Jefferson saw as the nation's future, and those of the propertied elite whose interests Hamilton espoused. Whether rich or poor, urban or rural, Americans measured their activity primarily in days, months, and seasons—not in hours or minutes.

Most families in the early 1800s could afford neither clocks nor watches. Although accurate clocks existed, the few timepieces within a community often told different times. People used the position of the sun during the various seasons to estimate time during the day and to determine when they slept and rose from bed. Church bells tolled to announce worship services and town meetings, not the hour of the day.

The routine of daily life moved at a different pace without standardized time.

Nature, for example, arranged the farmer's schedule. Farm families planted, cultivated, and harvested their crops according to the cycle of the seasons. Weather patterns influenced when families could set out for town or market—by wagon, over dirt roads—or when visitors were likely to arrive. A storm could easily upset plans by turning the roads to mud.

The Supreme Court was faced with a difficult decision. If it ruled that Marbury was entitled to be a judge and issued a writ, Jefferson and Madison could simply ignore it, diminishing the power and prestige of the Court. If the Court did not issue a writ, the Republicans would win by default. Marshall came up with a brilliant solution. Acknowledging that Marbury had a legal right to his commission, Marshall argued that the Supreme Court could not issue the writ because the Constitution specifically listed the cases in which the Court had *original* jurisdiction. The writ of mandamus was not among them. In attempting to extend the Court's original jurisdiction to issue writs, the Judiciary Act of 1789 was in direct conflict with the Constitution, so the law was void.

Marshall went on to say that the Constitution was the supreme law of the land. It could not be changed at the whim of the legislative branch. By this decision Marshall had neatly sidestepped his political dilemma. He gave the Republicans the final result they sought by not issuing the writ. He even limited the original jurisdiction of the Court. Far more importantly, however, he managed to lay down the very cornerstone of the Supreme Court's power, judicial review, the authority to interpret the Constitution, which gives the judicial branch a "check of the legislative branch" in the system of checks and balances.

Aside from this setback, Jefferson viewed his first term as tranquil and a success. War had broken out in Europe, but its first effect in the United States was to increase foreign trade. Taxes had been reduced, and the income of the federal government from tariffs was sufficient to pay everyday expenses and reduce the national debt. Nearly everything that had happened during President Jefferson's first term added to the popularity of the Republican party, and Jefferson's reelection was a foregone conclusion. Running against Charles Pinckney of South Carolina, Jefferson received 162 of 176 electoral votes. The prospects for continuing what he had started looked good, but Jefferson's second term was to be far less successful than his first.

★ ★ ★ ★ ★ ★ ★ ★ ★ ★ ★ ★ ★ ★ ★ ★ ★

Section Two Review

★ ★ ★ ★ ★ ★ ★ ★ ★ ★ ★ ★ ★ ★ ★ ★ ★

SUMMARY

Jefferson viewed his first term as tranquil and successful. Like Washington, he became a chief legislator, but his attempt to limit the judiciary failed. Not only did Chief Justice John Marshall establish the principle of judicial review in *Marbury v. Madison*, but he also confirmed the judiciary as the third great branch of government and gave the judiciary a check in the system of checks and balances. From that point on, the judicial branch, with the power and authority to interpret the Constitution, was provided with a veto over federal laws.

CHECKING FOR UNDERSTANDING

1. **Identify** John Marshall, *Marbury v. Madison*

2. **Define** writ of mandamus, judicial review

3. **Name** three important accomplishments of Jefferson during his first term in office.

4. **List** three reasons why Republicans feared the judiciary.

5. **Describe** how President Jefferson attempted to curb the power of the judicial branch.

THINKING CRITICALLY

6. **Analyzing Issues** In *Marbury v. Madison*, Marshall strengthened the power of the federal judiciary. How did Marshall go beyond the issues of the case to establish the power of the Court for all time?

CONNECTIONS: HISTORY AND ECONOMICS

7. **Analyzing Differences** In 1990 Congress passed a bill to reduce the budget deficit by increasing taxes, raising revenues, and decreasing government spending. Describe the difference between Jackson's first term and the bill of 1990.

★ ★ ★ ★ ★ ★ ★ ★ ★ ★ ★ ★ ★ ★ ★ ★ ★

Looking Westward

SETTING THE SCENE

These lands are ours. No one has a right to remove us, because we were the first owners. The Great Spirit above has appointed this place for us, on which to light our fires, and here we will remain....

—TECUMSEH
Chief of the Shawnee nation, to the messenger of President Madison, 1810

Section Focus

The purchase of the Louisiana Territory from France was a notable achievement of the Jefferson administration. Yet the decision to make the purchase was not an easy one. Committed to interpreting the Constitution in its strictest sense, Jefferson doubted that he possessed the power to make the purchase. On the other hand, the opportunity to gain the land west of the Mississippi River might never come again.

Objectives

After studying this section, you should be able to:
* Explain the significance of the Louisiana Purchase.
* Identify the reasons why unrest between native Americans and the American government was increasing.

The news that Spain had ceded Louisiana, including New Orleans, to France in 1800 was of great concern to the United States. The French were now ruled by Napoleon Bonaparte, whose conquests kept Europe in turmoil for many years.

Napoleon increased France's power in Europe and planned to create a new French empire in North America.

Jefferson was alarmed at the prospect of New Orleans being in French hands. The city was a major trade center for the United States, especially as a market for western goods. Jefferson feared that the French might close New Orleans to American trade, thus blocking the development of the American West. He wrote Robert Livingston, United States minister stationed in Paris, that:

...there is on the globe one single spot, the possessor of which is our national and habitual enemy. It is New Orleans, through which the produce of three-eighths of our territory must pass to market.

Jefferson feared that French control of New Orleans meant that the United States would have to "marry" itself to the British navy for protection. Before allying with Britain, however, Jefferson authorized Livingston to offer France $10 million for New Orleans and West Florida and sent James Monroe as a special envoy to Paris to negotiate the purchase.

The Louisiana Purchase

It is unlikely that American arguments, threats, or dollars would have moved Napoleon if his plans for a French empire had not suffered a great defeat in the most valuable of France's American colonies, Sainte Domingue (Haiti). During the 1700s, its exports of sugar, indigo, coffee, and cotton were almost equal in value to the combined exports of the 13 colonies. In 1791 its enslaved blacks rebelled. Under the leadership of a remarkable general, Pierre Toussaint L'Ouverture, (TOO sahn LOO vehr tyoor) "the black Napoleon," Haitian blacks attempted to make their island an independent state.

In 1801 Napoleon sent soldiers to put down the Haitian revolt. Toussaint

L'Ouverture organized such effective resistance that the French expedition failed, although he himself was captured. The disaster was so complete—the French lost almost all their troops to battle and yellow fever—that Napoleon was forced to abandon his American ambitions.

Meanwhile, Livingston had been urging the French to sell New Orleans. In April 1803, Talleyrand, the French foreign minister, asked Livingston how much the United States would give for the entire Louisiana Territory. Livingston, who had been joined by James Monroe, took only a few days to reach an agreement by which the United States was to pay about $15 million for the territory—about 4 cents an acre.

When news of the French offer reached the United States, Jefferson was torn between a desire to extend the boundaries of the United States west of the Mississippi River and concern over whether the federal government had the legal power to acquire foreign territory. Since the Constitution does not specifically grant this power, he wanted a constitutional amendment to assure that the sale was legal. Livingston warned the President and the Senate, which must approve all treaties, that Napoleon might change his mind. Jefferson asked the Senate to ratify the treaty and the Senate gave its consent, despite opposition from New England Federalists. Although this action did not follow Jefferson's belief in strict construction of the Constitution, he justified the acquisition on the grounds that it was part of the President's implied powers to protect the nation. The Louisiana Purchase doubled the size of the United States and opened the way for westward expansion by removing the threat of French interference.

Lewis and Clark

Very little was known about the area west of the Mississippi, and it excited Jefferson's curiosity. He sent an expedition led by two officers in the U.S. Army, Meriwether Lewis and William Clark, up the Missouri River to explore the new territory. The expedition was the first scientific project to receive federal funds, and Jefferson himself drew up their instructions. He told Lewis and Clark to find the sources of the Missouri River, to try to find a usable route across the Rocky Mountains to the Pacific Ocean, and to observe the customs of the Indians they met. They were also instructed to carefully note features of the land, the weather, and the plants and animals they saw.

The expedition left St. Louis in May 1804. It returned over two years later with its mission accomplished, having surmounted hardships ranging from "ticks and musquiters" to near-starvation and floods.

Among the members of the expedition was York, a black slave. York's skills in hunting and fishing made him a valuable member of the expedition. He was particularly successful in making friends with the Indians they met along the way. Sacajawea (sak uh juh WAY uh), a Shoshone woman, and her French-Canadian husband later joined the party as interpreters and guides. Her role was important because Lewis and Clark wanted to build peaceful relations with the Indian peoples living in the newly acquired territory.

The Lewis and Clark expedition added immensely to the knowledge of the huge area that had been purchased. It also helped the United States lay claim to the northern region between the Rocky Mountains and the Pacific Ocean known as Oregon. Within a few years, fur traders based in St. Louis were traveling to the Rockies, and by 1812 there were about 70,000 people living in the southern section of the Louisiana Territory.

Burr's Conspiracies

The Louisiana Purchase troubled diehard Federalists in the Northeast. They feared that westward expansion would weaken New England's power in national affairs and would subordinate its commercial interests to the agricultural interests of the South and West. A group of Federalists drafted a plan to take New England out of the Union and form a northern confederacy. The plotters realized that, if the confederacy were to last, it had to

Linking Across Time

THE FRENCH IN NORTH AMERICA

Rivalry between Britain and France for domination of North America and Europe helped the young United States. France, following the loss of its North American empire in the French and Indian War, was anxious to aid the 13 colonies in their struggle against Britain. Later, after France took Louisiana from Spain, the young United States acquired this vast inland domain. In 1803, following the defeat of French troops in Haiti, Napoleon sold Louisiana, partially to prevent the British from seizing it.

include New York as well as New England. They found an ally in Aaron Burr, who was willing to desert the Republican party and run for governor of New York on the Federalist ticket in 1804.

The plan went awry, however, when Burr was soundly defeated, in large part, because Alexander Hamilton, who had worked to prevent Burr's election to the presidency in 1800, campaigned against him. When Hamilton continued after the election to criticize his integrity, Burr challenged Hamilton to a duel.

Even though Hamilton had a wife and young children, was burdened with debts, and his eldest son had recently been killed in a duel, he accepted the challenge. On a July morning in 1804, Hamilton, Burr, their assistants, and a physician rowed across the Hudson River to a rock shelf at the foot of the Palisades. At the signal Burr, an excellent shot, fired a bullet into Hamilton's body. Hamilton died the next day. When a New York coroner's jury indicted Burr for murder, he escaped from New York but not from his troubles.

He headed west and took part in arranging a conspiracy. Sometimes Burr talked of secession of the western territories, sometimes of the conquest of Mexico—with himself as emperor. Whatever Burr's final goal, he collected arms, bought flatboats on the Ohio River, and floated down toward New Orleans with between 80 and 100 followers. His movements became so widely known, however, that the federal government had time to prepare for anything he might do. When President Jefferson ordered his arrest, Burr fled to Spanish Florida, only to be

Examining Maps *The Louisiana Purchase doubled the size of the United States and prepared the way for the growth of the United States as a great continental power. The geography of the far-flung territory was revealed through a series of explorations that began soon after the territory was purchased. What was the farthest western point that the Lewis and Clark expedition reached?*

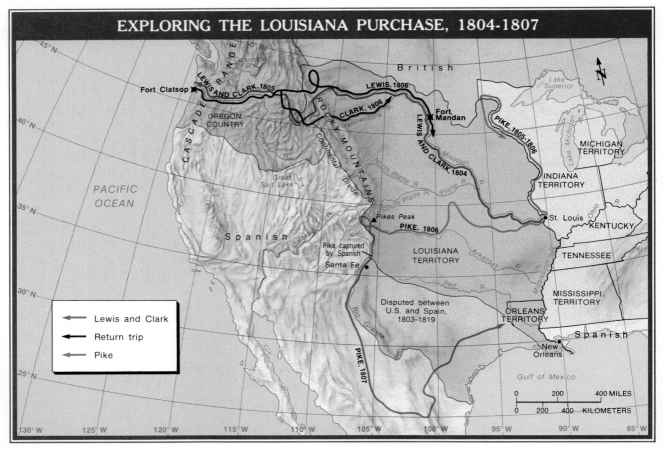

EXPLORING THE LOUISIANA PURCHASE, 1804-1807

Connections

EXPLORING THE LOUISIANA PURCHASE

What lay in the vast Louisiana Territory? How far was it to the Pacific Ocean? Certainly, the members of the Lewis and Clark expedition had little idea what distances and difficulties they would face on their trek. Starting from St. Louis, the expedition traveled northward up the Missouri River into what is now North

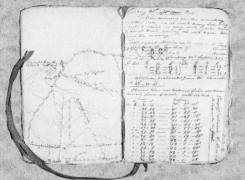

William Clark's Journal, September 30, 1805

Dakota. Eventually, it crossed the Rocky Mountains and sailed on the Columbia River to the Pacific Ocean. The members had traveled more than 7,600 miles to the Pacific. They returned with maps and information that helped make possible the great western migration during the mid-1800s.

William Clark constructed 60 maps—some eight feet in length—depicting the expedition's route. Although the expedition carried various surveying and measuring instruments, Clark seems to have relied primarily on the compass and his own estimates of distances in making his maps. It is likely that Clark took a series of back sightings to render his maps. For example, after reaching an easily identifiable landmark such as a bend in a stream, Clark would turn and take a compass reading back to his previous point of sighting. Clark could then plot each shift in the route on the map.

MAKING THE GEOGRAPHY CONNECTION

1. What do you think was the major obstacle facing Lewis and Clark?

2. Would you classify Clark's method of mapmaking scientific? Explain.

LINKING PAST AND PRESENT

3. How might an unknown region of the earth be mapped today?

---

captured in 1807 and taken to Richmond, Virginia, to stand trial for treason. At the trial, Chief Justice Marshall, following the Constitution's provisions regarding the rights of a person accused of treason, insisted that the prosecution produce two witnesses to an "overt act" on Burr's part. Because there were no trustworthy witnesses against him, Burr was acquitted and went into exile.

Conflict with the Indians

During both Jefferson's administration and James Madison's that followed, settlers, hunters, and land speculators pressured hard on the Indians. Jefferson, himself, favored moving the Indians who lived east of the Mississippi River to unoccupied lands in the Louisiana Territory. He insisted that the Chickasaw and Cherokee nations give up their lands in Alabama and Georgia and move to what is now Arkansas.

North of the Ohio River, the Treaty of Greenville had not satisfied the pioneers' desire for land. By persuasion, force, and fraud, native Americans were forced to give up more and more land. In spite of treaty promises that were to last "as long as the sun shall climb the heavens or the waters shall run in the streams," white settlers persisted in moving into Indian land. William Henry Harrison, governor of the Indiana Territory, has been described as "the most talented American at depriving the native Americans from their ancestral lands." In the 15 treaties he negotiated, Indians gave up nearly all of present-day Indiana and Illinois.

During these difficult times, a remarkable leader named Tecumseh (Tuh KUM suh) became chief of the Shawnees. He wanted to unite all the tribes of the Mississippi Valley into a great federation to protect themselves against the white intruders. Tecumseh went to Harrison and urged that the United States give up

The Shawnee leader Tecumseh was a bold and imaginative leader who hoped to unite many native American peoples into a confederation. Tecumseh's death destroyed any chance of such a union. What did Tecumseh hope to achieve by establishing the confederation?

some recently "purchased" territory on the ground that the chiefs who signed the treaty had no authority to do so. Harrison replied that only the President of the United States could answer such a request. Tecumseh answered:

*Well, as the great chief is to decide
the matter, I hope the Great Spirit will put
sense enough into his head to induce
him to give up this land. It is true, he is so
far off he will not be injured by
the war; he may sit still in his town
and drink his wine, while you and I will
have to fight it out.*

The prediction came true. In 1811 Harrison launched a war against Tecumseh's followers, knowing that the great Indian leader had journeyed south to persuade Indian communities to join the confederation. Harrison became a national hero after leading American troops in battle at Tippecanoe near what is today West Lafayette, Indiana. Tecumseh's death in 1813 destroyed the dream of a native American confederation. Afterwards, several native American nations made peace with Harrison.

Section Three Review

SUMMARY

Jefferson went against his own political philosophy of strict construction of the Constitution and limited executive power when he approved the Louisiana Purchase—the greatest achievement of his presidency. This acquisition, along with vast amounts of territory in the South and Midwest ceded by the Indians, paved the way for extensive frontier expansion, while the expedition of Lewis and Clark added to the nation's knowledge of the North American continent. However, the purchase was not popular with some northeastern Federalists, who toyed with ideas of secession to maintain their political power.

CHECKING FOR UNDERSTANDING

1. **Identify** Louisiana Purchase, Lewis and Clark, York, Sacajawea, Tecumseh
2. **State** why New Orleans was a city important to the nation.
3. **Specify** Jefferson's reasons for making the Louisiana Purchase.
4. **Describe** the purpose and outcome of the Lewis and Clark expedition into the Louisiana Territory.
5. **Explain** the importance of the battle of Tippecanoe.

THINKING CRITICALLY

6. **Predicting Outcomes** Aaron Burr was tried for treason but was acquitted. How did his acquittal affect future treason charges?

CONNECTIONS: HISTORY AND SCIENCE

7. **Comparing Actions** Neil Armstrong and Edwin Aldrin lived up to President Kennedy's promise of putting a man on the moon before 1970. In 1969 they landed the *Eagle* on the moon. How did the expeditions of Lewis and Clark and Armstrong and Aldrin affect the nation's frontier?

Foreign Affairs

We have seen...nations with which we have the most friendly and useful relations, engaged in mutual destruction. While we regret the miseries...let us bow with gratitude to that kind providence which guarded us.

—THOMAS JEFFERSON
Address to Congress, October 17, 1803

Section Focus

Thomas Jefferson had entered the presidency committed to Washington's policy of neutrality. Yet the United States and Europe had grown economically dependent upon each other. When Britain and France tried to manipulate trade with the United States as a weapon against the other, the United States sought ways to fight back.

Objectives

After studying this section, you should be able to:
- Identify the problems that the United States faced in its attempt to remain neutral in the conflict between Great Britain and France.
- Identify three ways in which the United States tried to maintain its freedom of the seas.
- Explain the reasons for the increasing demand for war.

Jefferson hoped that "nature and a wide ocean" would keep the United States entirely isolated from European rivalries. "Peace," he wrote to an English friend, "is our passion." As his Federalist opponents had forecasted years before, Jefferson proposed to do away with the navy and entrust the defense of the United States to militia instead of a standing army. For the United States to remain unarmed, however, proved impossible.

The first threat to peace came not from one of the great powers of Europe, but from Tripoli (part of present-day Libya), a small country on the north coast of Africa. **Piracy**, or preying on ships at sea, was a principal business of Tripoli and the other Barbary Coast states of Morocco, Algiers, and Tunis. The ships of countries that did not pay tribute to the Barbary states were likely to be captured and their sailors enslaved. Between 1789 and 1801, the United States paid over $2 million in tribute. At the time of the XYZ Affair, when Americans were chanting "Millions for defense, but not one cent for tribute," a United States warship was on its way to Algiers carrying 26 barrels of silver dollars to pay the pirates for "protection."

Despite his desire for peace, Jefferson was determined that the United States would not be robbed by the Barbary pirates. Consequently, he carried on a four-year war with Tripoli. The American navy eventually had 14 ships stationed in the Mediterranean Sea.

In 1805 the American counsel in Egypt, William Eaton, put together a small force of American, Greek, and Arab mercenaries. Crossing 500 miles of the desolate Sahara, they invaded and captured a small fort in Tripoli. The ruler of Tripoli made peace after receiving a ransom of $60,000 for captured American sailors. For a time, this discouraged the other Barbary Coast states from asking for additional tribute. But in 1807, after President Jefferson withdrew the American navy, attacks on American ships started again. The piracy of the Barbary states did not end until 1815, when an American fleet of ships under Stephen Decatur, joined by warships of European nations, once and for all, put an end to the practice.

Britain and France

Most of Jefferson's second term, coinciding with war in Europe, was spent trying to maintain American neutrality. In

1803 Great Britain and France had once again gone to war. The United States was an important source of supply to both sides. Each side took measures to limit what it saw as aid to the enemy and, in doing so, violated American freedom of the seas. Napoleon issued the Berlin and Milan decrees, which forbade any country under French control to import British goods or to allow British ships to enter its harbors. Neutral ships bringing British goods, stopping at British ports, or even submitting to search by British naval vessels, were to be seized.

Great Britain answered the Napoleonic decrees with the Orders in Council, which were directed mainly at the United States. British traders were already alarmed at the increase in the United States' merchant marine. If American ships now took over the trade with Europe forbidden to the British by Napoleon, the United States might replace Britain as the greatest trading nation in the world. Therefore, the Orders in Council of 1807 forbade neutral ships to trade with Europe unless they stopped in Britain first.

If enforced, the Napoleonic decrees and the Orders in Council might have ended American trade with Europe. An American ship that entered a British harbor was likely to be seized by the French afterward; if it sailed directly to Europe, it was likely to be seized by the British on its way home. British warships cruised outside American harbors to search ships and learn their destinations. French officials confiscated hundreds of United States' ships in European ports. Neither blockade was complete, and the profits made from successful evasion were so great that the merchant marine prospered.

Even more distressing than the attempt to cut off the United States' trade was the British practice of taking sailors from American ships. Discipline in the British navy was so strict and the pay so low that it was impossible to get enough volunteers. For centuries Britain had secured sailors by a legalized form of kidnapping known as **impressment**. Sailors were impressed in port and taken off merchant ships at sea. British sailors frequently deserted and signed on American vessels, where the conditions and pay were better. Sometimes a British warship calling in an American port found it difficult to sail away because so many of the crew deserted. To combat this problem, Britain

THE IMPRESSMENT OF AN
American Sailor Boy,

THE youthful sailor mounts the bark,
  And bids each weeping friend adieu :
Fair blows the gale, the canvass swells :
  Slow sinks the uplands from his view.

Three mornings, from his ocean bed,
  Resplendent beams the God of day :
The fourth, high looming in the mist,
  A war-ship's floating banners play.

Her yawl is launch'd ; light o'er the deep,
  Too kind, she wafts a ruffian band :
Her blue track lengthens to the bark,
  And soon on deck the miscreants stand.

Around they throw the baleful glance—
  Suspense holds mute the anxious crew—
Who is their prey ? poor sailor boy !
  The baleful glance is fix'd on you.

Nay, why that useless scrip unfold ?
  They damn'd the "lying yankee scrawl,"
Torn from thine hand, it strews the wave—
  They force thee trembling to the yawl.

Sick was thine heart as from the deck,
  The hand of friendship wav'd farewell ;
Mad was thy brain, as far behind,
  In the grey mist thy vessel fell.

One hope, yet, to thy bosom clung,
  The captain mercy might impart ;

Vain was that hope, which bade thee look,
  For mercy in a Pirate's heart.

What woes can man on man inflict,
  When malice joins with uncheck'd power ;
Such woes, unpitied and unknown,
  For many a month the sailor bore !

Oft gem'd his eye the bursting tear,
  As mem'ry linger'd on past joy ;
As oft they flung the cruel jeer,
  And damn'd the "chicken liver'd boy."

When sick at heart, with "hope defer'd,"
  Kind sleep his wasting form embrac'd,
Some ready minion ply'd the lash,
  And the lov'd dream of freedom chas'd.

Fast to an end his miseries drew :
  The deadly hectic flush'd his cheek :
On his pale brow the cold dew hung,
  He sigh'd, and sunk upon the deck !

The sailor's woes drew forth no sigh ;
  No hand would close the sailor's eye :
Remorseless, his pale corse they gave,
  Unshrouded to the friendly wave.

And as he sunk beneath the tide,
  A hellish shout arose ;
Exultingly the demons cried,
  "So fare all Albion's Rebel Foes !"

claimed the right to stop American ships, search for former British subjects, and force them back into service.

In June 1807, a United States' warship, the *Chesapeake,* was leaving the United States for the Mediterranean Sea when it was stopped by a British naval vessel, the *Leopard.* The commander of the *Leopard* demanded that he be allowed to search the *Chesapeake* for British deserters. When he was refused, the British ship fired three broadsides at the *Chesapeake,* killing 3 and wounding 18. After the *Chesapeake* surrendered, the British boarded the ship and carried off 4 sailors.

The attack on the *Chesapeake* aroused great anger, and American newspapers clamored for war. Jefferson, however, delayed calling Congress into session until tempers had time to cool. Although the President did not intend to let these actions by the British go unanswered, he sought a course of action other than war.

Jefferson thought he had found a substitute for war in the use of an economic boycott. Jefferson reasoned that both Britain and France were so dependent upon American goods that if the United States cut off trade with them, they would stop violating the nation's neutral rights. With the President's urging, Congress passed the Embargo Act in December 1807, forbidding United States' ships to sail for foreign ports anywhere in the world.

The Embargo Act caused some suffering in Britain, hurt France very little, but was nothing short of disastrous for the United States. Stores of wheat, cotton, and tobacco piled up on wharves. Thousands of sailors were put out of work. Ships rotted at the docks. Exports fell from $198 million in 1807 to $22 million in 1808. Imports fell from $138 million to $55 million.

Seldom has a law been so bitterly resisted. Merchant ships made secret runs to European ports. Smuggling between the northeastern states and Canada grew by leaps and bounds. To stop violations of the embargo, Jefferson stationed militia along the Canadian border and permitted officials to search for smuggled goods without proper warrants. Ironically,

President Jefferson was accused of using his great power at the expense of the Bill of Rights, which he himself had championed years before as a check against tyranny.

Drifting Into War

After two terms, Jefferson was glad to retire to Monticello. During his tenure he had often been compelled to violate principles he held dear, such as individual freedom and limited federal power, for the good of the country as a whole. In the epitaph he wrote for himself, Jefferson asked to be remembered only as the author of the Declaration of Independence and the Virginia Bill for Religious Freedom and founder of the University of Virginia.

Jefferson used his influence to secure the nomination of his close friend and secretary of state, James Madison. In the

election of 1808, Madison easily defeated the Federalist candidate, Charles Pinckney. This was in spite of the fact that, because of opposition to the Embargo Act, all of New England except Vermont went Federalist.

Even before Jefferson left office in March 1809, Congress had repealed the unpopular Embargo Act. This measure was replaced by another, the Non-Intercourse Act, which banned trade with ports under British or French control but allowed trade with the rest of the world. Although less harmful to American trade than the Embargo Act, the Non-Intercourse Act was no more successful in forcing France and Britain to respect the rights of the United States.

In May 1810, Congress tried another tactic and passed Macon's Bill No. 2, which stated that, if either France or Britain agreed to respect neutral rights, the United States would cut off trade with the other nation. In August Napoleon responded with offers to remove his decrees. Not even waiting for the actual repeal of the French decrees, Madison cut off trade with Great Britain, effective March 2, 1811. Napoleon revealed how insincere his offer was when the French navy continued to seize American ships.

Although neither Britain nor the United States really wanted war, their actions steered them in that direction. In May 1811, an American ship attacked a British warship. Americans saw it as revenge for the British attack on the *Chesapeake*.

Some young members of Congress, most of them Republicans from the West and the South, called for an all-out confrontation. Hunger for land heightened this war fever. The Westerners were eager to take Canada while the Southerners wanted Spanish Florida.

Alone, the War Hawks did not have enough votes in Congress to pass a declaration of war. But as more Americans became angry over British seizure of American sailors and ships, pressure to fight increased. Finally, the Republican majority in Congress decided that the United States must accept the risks of war rather than allow itself to be pushed around.

War of 1812

This morning on awakening we were greeted with the sad news, that our city was taken, the bridges and public buildings burnt, our troops flying in every direction.... I do not suppose Government will ever return to Washington. All those whose property was invested in this place, will be reduced to poverty.

—MARGARET SMITH
Washington, D.C., resident, 1814

Section Focus

President Madison listed a number of grievances against Great Britain in his war message, including impressment, blockades, inciting Indian uprisings, and rejecting diplomatic efforts. Yet the war that some hailed as the "Second War for American Independence" was not a popular one, especially in New England. The fighting ended in 1814 with the Treaty of Ghent, but the agreement did nothing to settle the issues that had caused the war.

Objectives

After studying this section, you should be able to:

• Describe the major campaigns of the War of 1812.
• Summarize the results of the War of 1812 and the Treaty of Ghent.

The British government repealed the Orders in Council on June 23, 1812. British harvests had been poor, and the British desperately needed grain from the United States. British manufacturers had bombarded Parliament with pleas that they faced utter ruin unless trade with the United States was reestablished. The repeal came too late, however. The United States had declared war 4 days earlier. Declaring war against Great Britain did not suggest an alliance with France. A proposal to also include France in the declaration was defeated in the Senate by a vote of 18 to 14.

The War in Canada

General Andrew Jackson expressed a popular opinion when he predicted that the conquest of Canada by the United States would be a "mere military promenade." There were indeed a number of reasons why an attack northward was feasible. Canada was sparsely populated, and the French Canadians were lukewarm toward their British rulers. The narrow strip of settlement running up the St. Lawrence River and north of Lake Ontario was so close to the United States that it was open to attack at all points. Montreal, the strategic center of Canada, was only 30 miles from New York State.

Yet the conquest of Canada proved to be an exercise in frustration, mainly because the military forces of the United States were almost totally unprepared. The regular army, numbering about 6,000 soldiers, was scattered throughout the frontier posts. The top commanders, veterans of the Revolution, were too old for warfare. There was no single commanding general and no overall plan of how the war should be fought.

To compensate for the small size of the army, Madison called on the states to furnish militia. Some New England governors refused to supply any troops at all because they were opposed to "Mr. Madison's War." Members of New York's militia refused to cross the Niagara River into Canada, maintaining that they had enlisted only to defend their state from invasion.

The United States' lack of preparation was immediately evident. Small but ably led Canadian forces took Detroit and two forts on Lake Michigan. On the other hand, an American attack across the Niagara River was turned back. No serious attempt was made to take Montreal.

In 1813 matters improved at the western end of the war zone. Commodore Oliver Hazard Perry, having constructed a small fleet, won a brilliant victory over a British squadron and established American control of Lake Erie. Perry's victory made possible an invasion of Canada by way of Detroit. A group of Kentucky volunteers under William Henry Harrison advanced into Canada and defeated a British army at the battle of the Thames, about 60 miles northeast of Detroit. In the East, however, incompetent commanders failed dismally in attempted invasions of Canada from Sackett Harbor and Lake Champlain.

AMERICAN PORTRAITS

DOLLEY MADISON
1768-1849

Born in North Carolina, Dolley Payne grew up in Virginia until, at age 15, she moved with her parents to Philadelphia. There she married John Todd, Jr. Dolley Todd gave birth to two children, but in the yellow-fever epidemic in 1793, she lost one of her children and her husband.

The following year Dolley Todd married James Madison. When James became secretary of state, Dolley served as unofficial first lady, entertaining White House guests of widower Thomas Jefferson. As official first lady from 1809 to 1817, Dolley was known for her elaborate parties—including the first inaugural ball. She also displayed remarkable bravery during the War of 1812. Packing up Gilbert Stuart's famous painting of George Washington and White House belongings, she conveyed them safely out of town before the British burned the White House in 1814.

During 1812 and 1813, the British, preoccupied with the war against France, had put little effort into the war against the United States. But when Napoleon was defeated and forced into exile in 1814, the British were free to strike hard at the United States. In late summer an army of more than 14,000 British veterans advanced southward from Montreal to invade New York. Blocking its way was an American army stationed at Plattsburg on Lake Champlain. Although outnumbered nearly 3 to 1, American forces drove back the attacks, and the British retreated to Montreal. The northern border of the United States was safe.

The British Offensive

In 1814 the British sent two other expeditions into the United States—one to attack Washington and Baltimore; the other to take New Orleans. In August British transports landed an army of about 4,000 soldiers at Chesapeake Bay. It marched into the capital and very nearly captured Madison. To retaliate against the burning of public buildings in York (now Toronto) in 1813, the British burned the public buildings of Washington, destroying the Capitol and the White House. From there the British proceeded to Baltimore but were turned back by the forces guarding the city. It was during the bombardment of Fort McHenry in Baltimore harbor that Francis Scott Key wrote what became the national anthem, the "Star-Spangled Banner."

Unable to crack the defenses at Baltimore, the British army joined forces with the expedition attempting to capture New Orleans. The British, now almost 10,000 strong, reached the mouth of the Mississippi River in December 1814. Awaiting them were 4,500 Americans under the command of Andrew Jackson. His army consisted of regular soldiers and militia, with a few pirates recruited for their ability to handle artillery. Jackson also called upon the free blacks of New Orleans to volunteer for service, promising them the same wages as the white soldiers. Two all-black battalions contributed to the American victory at New Orleans.

When the final British attack came on January 8, 1815, American forces were sheltered behind a barricade of cotton bales. The British, advancing in the open, were no match for Jackson's well-protected soldiers. More than 2,000 soldiers were killed or wounded before the British surrendered. However, the battle of New Orleans, the greatest American victory of the war, was a useless slaughter. News traveled slowly in those days and it was learned only after the battle that a peace treaty had been signed in Europe two weeks earlier.

The War at Sea

At the beginning of the war, the pitifully small navy of the United States appeared to be no match for the British fleet. Only four small ships plus a few small gunboats for coastal defense were built during the administrations of Jefferson and Madison. During John Adams's administration, however, half a dozen excellent **frigates**—medium-sized warships—had been built. These frigates had more firepower than any European ships of the same size and were speedy enough to escape from larger warships.

When war broke out, the frigates put to sea and within a few months had won a series of victories in battles with British vessels. The victories had little effect on Britain, however, since its navy outnumbered that of the United States at least 20 to 1. Still, Britain had ruled the sea so long that even a few defeats to the United States came as a shock to British leaders.

Examining Illustrations *On August 19, 1812, the U.S. frigate* Constitution *decisively defeated the British warship* Guerriere. *Why was it surprising that American ships were victorious in many early battles?*

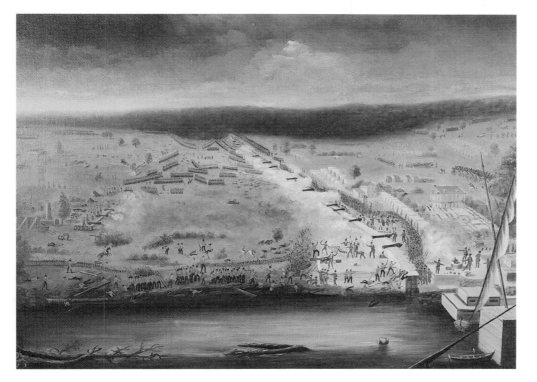

Examining Illustrations *In the Battle of New Orleans, fought on January 8, 1815, the outnumbered American troops resoundingly defeated the British forces. What effect did the battle have on the treaty that ended the war?*

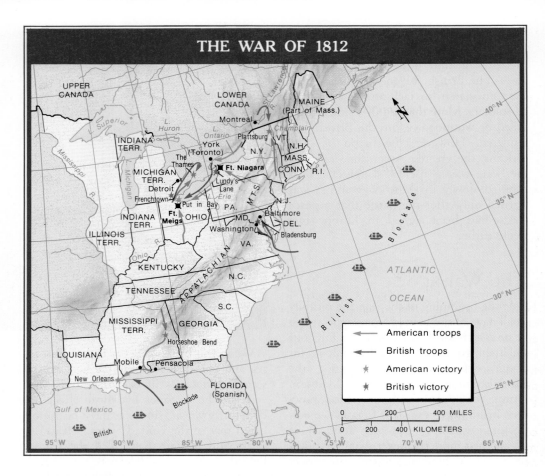

THE WAR OF 1812

Examining Maps *Until 1814, the British had been waging a defensive war. After Napoleon was defeated, the British were free to concentrate their forces against the United States. The British planned a multi-pronged attack. One army from Canada would move south into the United States. A second army would attack Washington, D.C., and a third army would land at New Orleans. What were the major American victories in the south?*

After yet another loss, a British newspaper lamented:

Can this be true? Will the English people read this unmoved? Any man who foretold such disasters this day last year would have been treated as a madman or a traitor….[U.S. frigates] leave their ports when they choose and return when it suits their convenience.

In addition to the frigates, the United States sent more than 500 privateers to sea. They captured more than 1,300 British vessels, some within sight of Britain.

As the war went on, however, American victories at sea grew fewer and fewer.

With overwhelmingly superior numbers, the British fleet was able to blockade the entire Atlantic coast from Boston to Savannah. United States trade with other countries virtually ceased, and the United States' navy, bottled up in port, never again enjoyed its early successes.

The War's End

As the war dragged on, opposition grew. Nowhere was opposition stronger than in New England where people balked at buying United States bonds issued to cover the cost of the war and held public meetings to protest the conflict. New Englanders believed that no navy was strong enough to protect them and disliked fighting on the same side as "the monster" Napoleon.

Above all, they foresaw that the war would be damaging, even ruinous to their economies:

About three fourths of our townsmen depend on the sea for the means of subsistence for themselves and their families. By the recent declaration of war more than one half of that proportion is liable to fall into the hands of the enemy.... We feel it therefore most strongly incumbent...to seek a speedy termination of the present war.

In December 1814, delegates from the New England states met in secret sessions at Hartford, Connecticut, to recommend action. The Hartford Convention did not insist that New England leave the Union, but it did demand seven constitutional amendments to increase the region's political power. The Convention insisted that southern states no longer be allowed to count three-fifths of their slaves in determining representation in Congress. Moreover, it urged a two-thirds vote of Congress for admitting new states and for declaring war.

The Hartford Convention sent commissioners to present its demands to President Madison and Congress. Their arrival in the capital coincided with the news of the victory at New Orleans and the signing of the treaty ending the war. Amidst the great celebrations, the commissioners had no choice but to return to their homes.

Almost from the moment the War of 1812 began, both sides tried to end it. Great Britain had no wish to be diverted from fighting Napoleon. The United States would have stopped fighting at once if Great Britain had agreed to stop impressment. The Treaty of Ghent did not contain a word about neutral rights or impressment. Not a square mile of territory changed hands. The warring nations simply agreed to stop fighting, to restore the old boundaries, and to put other problems off for future settlement. Signed on Christmas Eve, 1814, the treaty was unanimously ratified by the Senate in February 1815.

Section Five Review

SUMMARY

The United States declared war against England in 1812 as a matter of national honor. Despite a number of humiliating defeats, Americans performed well at sea and received a great psychological boost from Jackson's victory at New Orleans. The performance of the United States military forced Britain to admit that the new nation was working and that it could conduct itself effectively in a war. Although the war had been extremely unpopular in certain regions of the country and the Treaty of Ghent failed to resolve the problems that caused the war, the conflict gave Americans the recognition abroad that they had sought since the American Revolution.

CHECKING FOR UNDERSTANDING

1. **Identify** Andrew Jackson, Mr. Madison's War, Oliver Perry, Francis Scott Key, Battle of New Orleans, Hartford Convention, Treaty of Ghent

2. **Define** frigates

3. **Explain** why American troops failed to capture Canada.

4. **State** why the battle of New Orleans was a useless slaughter.

5. **Explain** the Hartford Convention's purpose and outcome.

THINKING CRITICALLY

6. **Comparing Actions** The United States entered the war in Vietnam in 1965 and left it in 1973 without winning or losing. Compare the goals and outcomes of the War of 1812 and the Vietnam War.

CONNECTIONS: HISTORY AND MUSIC

7. **Assessing Motivations** A great many of the songs of the 1970s were about the Vietnam War. Did the songwriters of the 1970s have the same motive as Francis Scott Key? Why?

★ Chapter 8 Review ★

★ Summary

The Republican victory in 1800 resulted in the first peaceful political transition in history. Although they professed to be champions of the common man, the administrations of Jefferson and Madison were not so different from those of their predecessors. Jefferson appointed an agrarian elite to serve the nation and stretched the elastic clause of the Constitution to its limits through the Louisiana Purchase. The expedition of Lewis and Clark added immeasurably to knowledge of the nation's geography and paved the way for frontier expansion. What might have been a disastrous war with Great Britain only enhanced the country's prestige by proving, once again, that the American military could hold its own against the most powerful nation on earth.

★ Using Vocabulary

Use the vocabulary words to create a newspaper article on the main events of the War of 1812.

laissez-faire	**writ of mandamus**
judicial review	**piracy**
impressment	**frigates**

★ Reviewing Facts

1. **Compare** the views of Thomas Jefferson and Alexander Hamilton on the role of government and society.
2. **Explain** why *Marbury v. Madison* was a great victory for Federalists and the judiciary.
3. **Indicate** how Jefferson planned to use some of the territory gained within the Louisiana Purchase to relocate the Indians.
4. **Explain** how the Louisiana Purchase caused the champions of implied powers to become strict constructionists.
5. **Describe** the military accomplishments of Andrew Jackson between 1813 and 1815.
6. **State** where the Republicans wanted Native Americans to move and the measures Jefferson and Madison took to force that move.

★ Understanding Concepts

NATIONAL IDENTITY

1. In his inaugural address, Jefferson reminded Americans, "We are all Republicans, we are all Federalists." Explain how that statement was meant to create a national identity.
2. Show how the Treaty of Ghent enhanced the nation's identity even though the United States gained none of its goals in fighting the war.

GEOGRAPHIC EXPANSION

3. When Jefferson doubled the size of the United States through the Louisiana Purchase, many people believed it was God's will that the United States should extend from sea to sea. Explain why Americans held this belief.
4. American expansion also occurred through the cession of Indian lands. How did William Henry Harrison handle the conflict with the Indians?

★ Thinking Critically

1. **Making Judgments**   Imagine that you are walking along a Washington street and see President Jefferson dressed in faded corduroy overalls. How would you feel about Jefferson running the country? On what criteria have you based your judgment?
2. **Comparing Policy**   Describe ways Jefferson was like Washington.
3. **Cause and Effect**   What effects did the Louisiana Purchase have on the United States politically and economically?
4. **Linking Past and Present**   Describe any similarities or differences you see between the impressment of American sailors in the 1800s and the Iraqi guests (hostages) of 1990.
5. **Analyzing Results**   Explain why neither side won or lost under the terms of the Treaty of Ghent.

★ Writing About History

NARRATION

Refer to the description of how to write a narrative essay in the History Writer's Handbook in the

★ Chapter 8 Review ★

Appendix of this book. Your teacher will give you more specific instruction on the essay's length and the assignment's due date.

Although they were political enemies in office, Thomas Jefferson, a Republican, and John Adams, a Federalist, later became friends. They kept up a correspondence until they died. Select a partner and write a series of letters that Adams and Jefferson might have written to each other on the state of the nation after 1808—the War of 1812, the Indians affairs, and the settlement of the West.

★ Learning Cooperatively

Organize a group within your classroom to simulate a discussion among George Bush, John Adams and Thomas Jefferson. Possible discussion topics might include the budget deficit, the situation in the Middle East, civil rights, and any other foreign or domestic issues you think relevant. Present the group discussion to your class.

★ Mastering Skills

DESCRIBING EXACT AND RELATIVE LOCATION

Any point on Earth can be determined by finding the *latitude* and *longitude* lines that run through it. Together, the lines form a sort of imaginary grid on the earth. Latitude lines, also called *parallels*, run east and west on the grid. The equator is at 0° latitude and is at the midpoint between the North and South poles. Latitude lines are measured in degrees north and south of the equator. Places north of the equator, from 0° to 90°N, are said to be located in the northern latitudes, and places south of the equator, from 0° to 90°S, in the southern latitudes.

Longitude lines, also called *meridians,* are the lines of the global grid that run north and south. They are numbered based on how far east or west they are of the prime, or first, meridian that runs through Greenwich, England. Meridians are numbered from 0° at the Prime Meridian to 180°E and 180°W. Areas of the globe east of the Prime Meridian are east longitude. Areas west of the Prime Meridian are west longitude. The meridians meet at the International Date Line in the Pacific Ocean.

Example Geographers use lines of latitude and longitude to locate places on Earth's surface. The degrees at which the latitude and longitude lines meet is the *exact location* of that place. For example, to describe the exact location of a city, geographers would first find on the map the line of latitude nearest to the city. Then they would follow this line until it intersects the nearest line of longitude. The latitude and longitude coordinates together provide the city's exact location. On the map of the Barbary States, the exact location of Tripoli is 32°N and 13°E.

Besides exact location, places also have *relative location.* Relative location is indicated by using the cardinal directions—north, south, east, and west—as well as the intermediate directions—northeast, southeast, northwest, and southwest—to describe the location of one place in relation to another. For example, Tripoli is located west of the city of Derna and southeast of Algiers. The use of latitude and longitude can also be helpful in determining the relative location of one place to another.

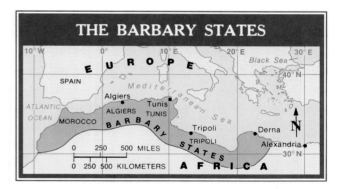

Practice Study the map and then answer the questions that follow.

1. What body of water borders the Barbary States to the north?

2. What is the exact location of Tunis?

3. In which direction would a traveler go from Tunis to reach Tripoli?

4. In between approximately which lines of longitude do the Barbary States fall?

5. Describe the relative location of the Barbary States in relation to Spain. Then, use a map of the world to describe the relative location of Tripoli to the places that follow: Moscow; Johannesburg, South Africa; Bombay, India; and the Suez Canal.

CULTURAL KALEIDOSCOPE

Circa 1800

The Louisiana Purchase and victory in the War of 1812 sent a clear message to the world: the United States was here to stay. An ever-growing sense of national pride and a spirit of romance and adventure infused the culture of the period from 1789 to 1824.

Literature

ROMANTIC WRITERS

Romanticism, a European literary movement, took a distinctively American turn when it crossed the Atlantic. Readers loved the frontier adventures told by James Fenimore Cooper in his *Leatherstocking Tales.*

The sentimental story of *Charlotte Temple, A Tale of Truth,* by Susanna Rowson, became America's first bestseller. And Washington Irving's humorous *A History of New York* entertained an especially large audience.

▲ *Diedrich Knickerbocker from Irving's* A History of New York

◄ Kindred Spirits *by Asher B. Durand, 1849*

The Arts

POETS

By 1811 17-year-old William Cullen Bryant had completed a first draft of the poem "Thanatopsis." The work, his best-known, earned Bryant worldwide recognition. A year later, Francis Scott Key witnessed the British shelling of Ft. McHenry and hastily scribbled a stirring tribute to America's navy. His poem, "The Star Spangled Banner," became the lyrics of the country's national anthem. The tune, however, is English.

ARCHITECTURE

Some have called him the architect of American independence. But Thomas Jefferson was also one of the leading American architects of his time. An admirer of the Roman republic, he borrowed features from Roman-inspired English buildings for his home, Monticello. Its distinctive portico, or porch, and white columns and trim were hallmarks of a popular style of architecture called Georgian— named, ironically, for English kings.

▼ *Monticello at Charlottesville, Virginia*

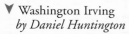
▼ Washington Irving
by Daniel Huntington

➤ View of the Bombardment of Fort McHenry by British Fleet, 1814
by John Bower

Entertainment and Recreation

FASHION

Americans came into their own around 1800 as creatures of style. In 1794 the century-old fashion of powdering men's hair passed out of vogue, although men wore a short ponytail tied with a black ribbon until about 1800. At the same time, a sandal of sorts decorated with bows and ribbons became all the rage among women. High heels, which had once been high fashion, were now flat out.

PASTIMES

Americans of leisure devoted themselves to 2 pastimes: billiards and horse racing. In 1796 Francis Baily, an English traveler in America, noted that Norfolk, Virginia, alone boasted 12 billiard tables. The next year the

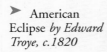

➤ American Eclipse *by Edward Troye, c.1820*

Williams Race Track was erected near Lexington, Kentucky. Soon after, several winners of the English Derby were brought over for breeding. The price per horse: about $250.

GATHERING PLACES

The opening in New Orleans of the Théâtre de St. Pierre in 1791 established the Crescent City as a center for opera—a distinction it would hold until the Civil War.

The opening of the American Museum in New York City reflected popular interest in science and art. However, the museum was sold lock, stock, and barrel to circus promoter P.T. Barnum in 1841.

▲ *Portraits of Col. and Mrs. Thomas Pinckney by E.G. Malbone, 1777-1807*

➤ Liberty and Washington, *anonymous*

Technology

FOOD

That Americans of means ate well in 1800 is evident from a Christmas dinner menu at Mount Vernon during the Washington administration. The feast, which opened with onion soup, included 34 different dishes, 5 of them meat.

FARMING

In 1797 an inventor named Newbold revolutionized agriculture with the cast-iron plow. John Taylor and Edmund Ruffin carried out a number of vital experiments on soil with the help of a fellow Virginian, the many-talented and ever-inquiring Thomas Jefferson.

TRANSPORTATION

In 1785 John Stevens of Hoboken, New Jersey and Marc Brunel, a Frenchman, co-piloted a crude propeller-driven steamboat up the Passaic River. The 16-bladed propeller that the two men used in their trial run had been patented by an English inventor, Joseph Bramah, who is best remembered for another of his inventions: the flush toilet.

ANALYZING CULTURE

1. Name cultural developments driven by national pride and by a spirit of romance or adventure.

2. Trace the evolution to the present of two aspects of culture you read about.

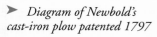

➤ *Diagram of Newbold's cast-iron plow patented 1797*

▼ *The* Archimedes *of 1838, one of the first successful commercial propeller-driven steamships*

◄ *American Museum, New York, (on left)*

CHAPTER 9
Nationalism and Change

SETTING THE SCENE

Historical Focus

During the peacetime that followed the War of 1812, a powerful spirit of nationalism swept through American life. A diverse movement, nationalism was reflected in many ways. It included the push for internal improvements, better economic ties among sections of the country, the death of the Federalist Party, and a strengthening of the central government. This new sense of American pride also resulted in a more forceful foreign policy.

Concepts to Understand

- How a feeling of **national community** emerged during the presidency of James Monroe.
- How foreign policy helped shape the United States as an emerging **world power.**

People to Know

James Monroe, John Quincy Adams, Robert Fulton, Simón Bolívar

Places to Locate

National Road, Erie Canal, Florida

Terms to Identify

nationalism, internal improvements, turnpikes, locks, Adams-Onís Treaty, Monroe Doctrine

Guided Reading

As you read this chapter, seek the answers to the following questions.
1. What forces helped unite the United States after the War of 1812?
2. What international circumstances prompted President Monroe to proclaim the Monroe Doctrine?

SPANNING THE DECADES

POLITICAL

1816	1817	1818	1819
Second Bank of the United States chartered	*Construction of Erie Canal begins*	*National Road reaches Wheeling, Virginia*	McCulloch v. Maryland

1815   1820

CULTURAL

1816	1817	1819	1820
African Methodist Episcopal Church organized	*Steamboat service available on Mississippi River*	*University of Virginia founded*	*First U.S. missionaries travel to Hawaii*

Fourth of July Celebration in Center Square, Philadelphia *by John Lewis Krimmel, 1819*

1821
Moses Austin receives Spanish grant in Texas

1823
Monroe Doctrine proclaimed

1824
Gibbons v. Ogden

1825
Erie Canal opens

1825

1821
First Roman Catholic cathedral dedicated in Baltimore

1823
"A Visit from St. Nicholas," better known as "Twas the Night Before Christmas," published anonymously

1824
Robert Owen founded New Harmony, Indiana

…The existing state of things as well as the "prospect before us," is most happy for the American people. The republic, reposing on the laurels of a glorious war, gathers the rich harvest of an honorable peace.…

—HEZEKIAH NILES
Niles' Weekly Register, Baltimore, Maryland, September 2, 1815

The Era of Good Feelings

SETTING THE SCENE

In war we are one people. In making peace we are one people. In all commercial relations we are one and the same people. In many other respects the American people are one.

—JOHN MARSHALL
Chief Justice of the U.S. Supreme Court in *Cohens v. Virginia*, 1821

Section Focus

After the War of 1812, United States economic growth continued to be limited by geography. Because long-range commercial activity was difficult, most Americans traded close to home. As industry grew in northern cities, manufacturers wanted to expand their markets, receive protection from overseas competition, and enjoy conditions at home that encouraged growth. Rural Americans also desired prosperity. After the war people cooperated to develop a more unified nation.

Objectives

After studying this section you should be able to:
• Identify events after the War of 1812 that showed a spirit of nationalism.
• Explain how the Supreme Court increased the national government's power.

Nationalism is a feeling of intense loyalty and devotion to one's country. It is a spirit that unifies diverse groups who share a geographic area into one nation. Nationalism can be demonstrated by people's actions, illustrated by such symbols as a flag and expressed in a nation's art, literature, and music.

Nationalism has been one of the most powerful forces in the history of the modern world. In the nineteenth century, nationalism was the glue that cemented numerous small states into the nations of Germany and Italy. In the twentieth century, nationalism inspired colonies in Africa and Asia to break away from their European rulers and declare independence. Eastern Europe's rejection of Soviet control and the recent reunification of Germany demonstrate the continuing power of nationalism.

Nationalistic Legislation

In the United States, the spirit of nationalism has not always been evident. It declined after the Revolution but was revived by the War of 1812. The conduct of the war revealed the dangers of disunion, and the war's outcome increased national pride and self-confidence. Albert Gallatin, one of the United States commissioners at the peace conference in Ghent, recognized the revival of nationalism in a letter written shortly after the war's end:

The war had renewed & reinstated the National feelings & character, which the Revolution had given, & which were daily lessened. The people...are more American: they feel & act more as a Nation, and I hope that the permanency of the Union is thereby better secured.

In 1816 James Monroe, a Virginia Republican, was elected President over New York Federalist Rufus King. On a national goodwill tour the new President promoted a spirit of unity everywhere he went. His warm reception by cheering crowds in Boston caused a local Federalist newspaper to proclaim that an "Era of Good Feelings" had begun. By 1820 the Federalists, discredited by their anti-war position during the war of 1812, had vanished from national politics, and President Monroe was reelected without opposition.

Postwar nationalism was revealed in legislation as well as in politics. The War of 1812 had clearly demonstrated that Jefferson's ideal of a central government with strictly limited functions could not meet the needs of a nation in crisis. After the war, a Republican Congress passed a series of laws that sounded as though they had been written by Federalists.

Henry Clay of Kentucky and John C. Calhoun of South Carolina, nationalist leaders in Congress, proposed an ambitious program that Clay called the "American System," based on protection and **internal improvements**—roads, canals, and other transportation needs. They advocated a protective tariff for manufacturers, an improved market for farmers, and better transportation for agricultural and industrial goods. Transportation improvements would be financed with money raised by the tariff. Both leaders wanted to reinstate the national bank to create a national currency and encourage economic growth. They hoped that this nationalistic program would bring prosperity to all sections of the country and, to the nation, economic independence from the rest of the world.

Republicans traditionally had opposed the idea of a national bank. They blocked the recharter of the first bank of the United States in 1811 and substituted nothing in its place. The results were disastrous because the notes of the Bank of the United States had become the national currency. Without a currency and lacking sufficient gold and silver for coins, the country had only the notes of state-chartered banks. These notes were backed by inadequate resources, which gave them little or no value. They generally were accepted only in the localities where they were issued. Without a national bank, the federal government also had a difficult time borrowing money during the War of 1812 .

Because of the nation's financial problems, the Republicans changed their minds after the war and supported creation of a new national bank. In 1816 Congress passed a bill to establish a second Bank of the United States. Like its predecessor, the second Bank of the United States could issue notes to be used as national currency and act in a number of ways to control state banks. President Madison, who in 1791 had opposed the first national bank as unconstitutional, signed the legislation.

Protection for manufacturers was another example of postwar nationalism. During the War of 1812 Americans had difficulty obtaining British products, thus encouraging the growth of American industry. But once the war was over, Britain dumped goods in the United States at such low prices they threatened to put American companies out of business. Protecting

AMERICAN PORTRAITS

HENRY CLAY
1777-1852

Virginia-born and raised, Henry Clay moved to Kentucky, a state that kept him in Congress—and in the forefront of national politics—for nearly 50 years.

A fierce political rivalry soon developed between Clay and another westerner, Andrew Jackson of Tennessee. The two first clashed in 1819 when Clay blasted Jackson's Florida invasion. The election of 1824 made them bitter enemies. Ignoring instructions from Kentucky to back Jackson for President, Clay supported John Quincy Adams, who appointed Clay secretary of state. Jackson's revenge came when he defeated Clay in the presidential election of 1832. Clay sought the presidency three more times before retiring. In 1849, however, he returned to Congress and put together a compromise between North and South that helped delay the Civil War.

Examining Political Cartoons *Representatives of the nation's regions compete in a card game—each card symbolizing a political issue. Henry Clay (left) plays cards for "U. S. Bank" and "Tariff." What role did these issues have in his plan for national growth?*

American industry meant that consumers would pay more for imported products, but to business leaders and nationalists alike, this price seemed a fair exchange for economic independence.

Congress responded with the Tariff of 1816. Unlike earlier revenue tariffs, which provided income for the federal government, this tariff was designed to protect American manufacturers by placing high taxes on imports.

To opponents of a protective tariff, the nationalists explained that by discouraging the sale of imported goods they were helping the entire nation become more prosperous and self-sufficient. Manufacturers would buy raw materials from American sources and in turn sell their products within the country.

Even as the Federalist party faded away, Republicans were carrying out their old opponents' plans for a strong national government encouraging and protecting private business. Indeed, Federalist ideals would outlast both the Era of Good Feelings and Jefferson's Republican party. Long after Federalists disappeared from Congress, their influence continued to be felt.

Supreme Court Nationalism

Nationalism in the years after the War of 1812 also was demonstrated in a series of Supreme Court decisions by Chief Justice

John Marshall. Marshall was appointed in 1801 as one of the last acts of President John Adams, a Federalist. By 1815 the majority of the justices had been appointed by Republican Presidents, but Marshall still dominated the Court. He was a brilliant debater and possessed such strong convictions, friendliness, and persuasiveness that, according to one historian, he "molded his fellow judges like putty." During his 34 years as Chief Justice, Marshall was in the minority on only one case dealing with a constitutional issue. Between 1819 and 1824, Marshall ruled in three important court cases that established the dominance of the nation over the states and that shaped the future of American government.

McCulloch v. Maryland (1819) involved an attempt by Maryland to tax the Baltimore branch of the newly created second Bank of the United States. The case answered basic questions about the federal government's power and its relationship with the states.

The national bank was constitutional, Marshall said, even though the Constitution did not specifically give Congress the power to create one. He repeated Alexander Hamilton's 25-year-old argument that the federal government was not limited to the powers listed in the Constitution:

Let the end be legitimate, let it be within the scope of the constitution, and all means which are appropriate…which are not prohibited, but consist with the letter and spirit of the constitution, are constitutional.…

Marshall observed that the Constitution specifically permitted Congress to issue money, borrow money, and collect taxes. He noted that the national bank would assist in exercising these enumerated powers. Therefore, he concluded, the federal government could choose any method that was "necessary and proper" to exercise the powers the Constitution had given it.

Marshall noted that the people, acting collectively, had created the federal government. Thus it was a truly "national" government, not created by the states or subordinate to them. Therefore, he reasoned, no state had the power to tax the national bank, a legal creation of the federal government. A heavy tax would make it difficult or impossible for the Bank to operate in that state because, he noted, "The power to tax involves the power to destroy." Thus Marshall established that a state could not interfere with any federal agency within its borders.

The second important decision of the Marshall court during this period was *Dartmouth College v. Woodward* (1819). This case was one of several in which the Supreme Court handed down decisions protecting contracts and property rights from state power. Dartmouth College was a private school chartered in 1769 by King George III. In 1815 the New Hampshire state legislature passed a law to change the charter, allowing Dartmouth to become a state college. But Dartmouth officials did not want to give up their private school, and they refused

Examining Tables   *Long after the Federalist party ceased to exist, the Supreme Court continued to express the party's ideals. Chief Justice John Marshall, a Federalist, dominated the Court until his death in 1835, spanning the administrations of five Republican and Democratic Presidents. The Marshall Court handed down a series of decisions, shown below, that increased federal power over state governments. How has* Gibbons v. Ogden *affected daily life today?*

THE MARSHALL COURT AND THE NATIONAL INTEREST	
Case and Year	**Issue and Decision**
Marbury v. *Madison* (1803)	Declared an act of Congress unconstitutional. Court given power of judicial review and power to declare congressional and state legislation unconstitutional.
Fletcher v. *Peck* (Yazoo land fraud case, 1810)	Declared sanctity of contracts. Gave Supreme Court right to overturn state laws that ran counter to specific provisions of Constitution.
Martin v. *Hunter's Lessee* (1816)	Gave Supreme Court right to reverse decisions of state courts.
Trustees of Dartmouth College v. *Woodward* (1819)	Reaffirmed sanctity of contracts. Protected banks and corporations with state charters from meddling by state legislators.
Sturges v. *Crowninshield* (1819)	Tested constitutionality of state bankruptcy laws. Court determined that in absence of federal regulation, states were free to legislate.
McCulloch v. *Maryland* (1819)	Challenged constitutionality of Bank of the United States. Court said "implied powers" enabled Congress to enact any legislation within letter and spirit of Constitution.
Cohens v. *Virginia* (1821)	Tested constitutionality of Judiciary Act of 1789. Court said states gave up some sovereignty in ratifying Constitution so state courts must accept federal jurisdiction.
Gibbons v. *Ogden* (1824)	Invalidated a state monopoly. Court gave Congress right to regulate interstate commerce, a decision of great importance for national development.

The Guide to American Law, vol. 7 (1984)

Linking Across Time

POLITICAL PARTIES

Only one Federalist President was ever elected, and the party had disappeared by 1820. However, Federalist ideals—chief among them a strong central government—are alive and well today in the foundation of the Democratic party. The oldest American political party, the Democrats are direct descendants of the very same Republicans who took over Federalist concepts. The Republicans became Democrat-Republicans for several years, then dropped "Republican," becoming Democrats with Andrew Jackson's election.

to turn over college records and funds to the state. When New Hampshire courts upheld the legislature, Dartmouth appealed to the Supreme Court. In writing the Court's decision, Marshall noted that in the Constitution "the state legislatures were forbidden 'to pass any law impairing the obligation of contracts,' that is, of contracts respecting property." A college charter is a contract, he said, and a state has no right to interfere with it. Thus, the state's attempt to seize this private college was unconstitutional.

The *Gibbons v. Ogden* (1824) case became known as a landmark decision on interstate commerce. The case involved a company that operated steamboats in New York. The company had been given a monopoly over steamboat traffic in New York waters. The company took it upon itself to extend its monopoly to include traffic across the Hudson River between New York and New Jersey. Marshall declared this monopoly unconstitutional. The decision stated that in allowing the extension, the state legislature overstepped its power according to the Constitution, which gave the federal government control over interstate commerce.

In writing the Court's decision, Marshall defined interstate commerce in a way that went far beyond the mere exchange of trade goods between states. By ruling, in effect, that anything crossing state boundaries comes under federal control, Marshall provided the federal government with the constitutional basis for many of the broad and sweeping powers it exercises today. In this 1824 Supreme Court decision may be found the constitutional authority for such diverse federal activities as licensing radio and TV stations, setting standards for clean air and water, pursuing criminals who flee across state lines to avoid prosecution, inspecting and grading of meat, and protecting migratory birds.

In these cases and others, Marshall's nationalism strengthened the power of the federal government at the expense of the states. Although he was bitterly attacked for his decisions by defenders of states' rights, Marshall's views made the Constitution flexible enough to meet the changing needs of a growing country.

Section One Review

SUMMARY

Monroe's presidency was marked by a revival of nationalism. Laws passed by Congress were aimed at national rather than local concerns. Thus, the American System advocated building better transportation links between the country's different sections, imposing protective tariffs to promote American manufacturing, and chartering a new national bank. Supreme Court decisions upheld the authority of the federal government, the sanctity of contracts against state interference, and federal jurisdiction over interstate commerce.

CHECKING FOR UNDERSTANDING

1. **Identify** Era of Good Feelings, American System, Tariff of 1816, John Marshall, *McCulloch v. Maryland, Gibbons v. Ogden*

2. **Define** nationalism, internal improvements

3. **Compare** the powers of the Second Bank of the United States with the powers of the First Bank.

4. **List** two ways in which the Republicans adopted a Federalist point of view of government after 1812.

5. **Explain** the difference between a protective tariff and a revenue tariff.

THINKING CRITICALLY

6. **Determining Relevance** Explain how John Marshall's ruling in *McCulloch v. Maryland* was an example of "the end justifies the means."

CONNECTIONS: HISTORY AND GOVERNMENT

7. **Drawing Conclusions** The Supreme Court on occasion overturns decisions made by state supreme courts. What does such action say about the power of the Supreme Court?

Tying the Nation Together

Let it not be forgotten, let it be forever kept in mind, that the extent of our republic exposes us to the greatest of all calamities, next to the loss of liberty...disunion.... Let us, then, bind the republic together with a perfect system of roads and canals.

—JOHN C. CALHOUN
Representative, in a speech to Congress, 1817

Section Focus

The United States had a need for better transportation. The number of states nearly doubled by 1820, and 9 of the 11 new states were west of the Appalachians. Yet there was no easy way to move industrial and farm products long distances. As a transportation network began to crisscross the country, it stimulated movement of people and products and helped build a stronger nation.

Objectives

After studying this section, you should be able to:

- Explain the advantages and disadvantages of each type of transportation improvement.
- Discuss the ways that internal improvements changed the nation.

The War of 1812 made the need for a better transportation system clear. It had been extremely difficult to move armies, cannon, and supplies from one place to another. Indeed, American plans to invade and annex Canada during the war had failed, in part because America lacked good roads. Now, in peacetime, the only way to move products long distances overland was in wagons on roads that weather made impassable much of the year. With the steamboat in its infancy, travel on the Mississippi River was still one-way. Goods could be floated downriver on flatboats or keelboats, but very little could be powered upstream. Some Americans, especially in the West, felt it was the federal government's responsibility to improve transportation. One such westerner was Henry Clay.

Although a protective tariff and national bank were acceptable to Clay's fellow Republicans, not all were ready to support federal financing of internal improvements. In 1816 Representative John C. Calhoun of South Carolina proposed a "Bonus Bill" to build roads and canals with the $1.5 million fee paid by the Bank of the United States for its charter. The bill passed but President Madison vetoed it, arguing that to spend money improving transportation was an unconstitutional extension of federal power.

Transportation by Road

An east-west national road, already underway when Madison vetoed the Bonus Bill, was the first major step in the creation of a national transportation system. In 1806 Congress funded the National Road from the sale of western lands, and construction started from the Potomac River at Cumberland, Maryland, in 1811. By 1818 the road reached Wheeling, Virginia, spanning the Ohio River on the longest suspension bridge in the world—an engineering marvel. The bridge was 1,010 feet long and hung from towers rising 153 feet above the river.

The National Road went west to Vandalia, Illinois, cutting a path 80 feet wide through the wilderness. The center 30 feet were "paved" with crushed stone, and the road crossed streams and rivers on stone

Examining Fine Art *A Conestoga wagon travels the National Road in this 1814 painting by American landscape artist Thomas Birch. What problems did travel by road present in early America?*

bridges. Great Conestoga wagons drawn by oxen or teams of four, six, or eight horses moved westward along this route.

The National Road turned out to be the only great federal transportation project. In general, states or private businesses undertook such improvements in transportation. State-chartered private companies constructed hundreds of miles of **turnpikes,** roads that were barricaded at intervals by poles that stopped travelers until they paid a **toll,** or fee. However, turnpikes were profitable only on main routes, such as between Albany and Lake Erie, or in populated areas where traffic was heavy. In the West, highways usually were constructed by the states themselves, at times with the aid of federal funds.

Although by 1840 the country was crisscrossed with roads, they did not provide satisfactory transportation. Except in the East few were surfaced or spanned by adequate bridges. When the routes passed through woods, foot-high stumps remained in the road bed. Spring rains turned roads to mud and mired wagons up to their axles. In swampy places, "corduroy"—logs laid sideways across the road bed—hurt horses' legs and jolted wagons to pieces. David

Stevenson described a journey by stagecoach along a typical route of the time in his book *Sketch of the Civil Engineering of North America* published in 1838:

Sometimes our way lay for miles through extensive marshes, which we crossed by corduroy-roads....At others the coach stuck fast in mud, from which it could be extricated only by the combined efforts of the coachman and passengers; and at one place we traveled...through a forest flooded with water, which stood to a height of several feet....The distance of the route from Pittsburg to Erie is 128 miles, which was accomplished in forty-six hours...although the conveyance by which I travelled carried the mail, and stopped only for breakfast, dinner and tea, but there was considerable delay by the coach being once upset and several times "mired."

Such difficult travel was necessary for families moving west with their belongings and for farmers herding cattle and hogs to market. But bulky goods, such as farm crops or manufactured products, could not be quickly or profitably moved long distances by land. The price of products was out of reach for many people, because merchants passed shipping costs on to consumers. Far more important to commerce, therefore, were America's inland waterways.

Transportation by Water

Rivers had long been the primary means of moving commercial goods. But travel was one-way—flatboats and rafts floating downstream. Trips against the current were slow and difficult. When steamboats became commonplace the country's rivers were transformed into highways. Although steamboats were built before 1800, they initially did not attract much attention. In 1807, however, Robert Fulton's steamboat, the *Clermont*,

Examining Maps In the early nineteenth century, inland travel in America was generally limited to navigable rivers. But by 1840 the United States east of the Mississippi River was crisscrossed by a network of roads and canals, making the movement of people and commerce easier and less expensive. By what route could farm goods from Lexington, Kentucky, reach New York City?

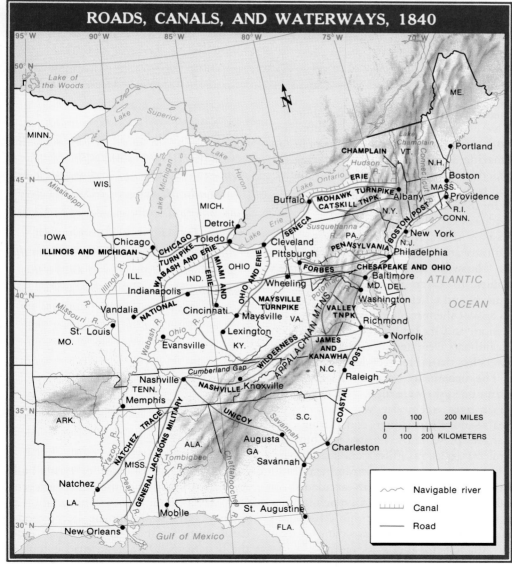

made its first voyages on the Hudson River, chugging the 150 miles from New York City to upstream Albany in an amazing 32 hours. By demonstrating the practicality of two-way river travel, Fulton launched the steamboat era.

In 1811 the first steamboat in Western waters steamed down the Ohio and Mississippi rivers from Pittsburgh to New Orleans and then returned upriver as far as Louisville. Steamboats proved their ability to carry passengers and goods quickly and efficiently, and by 1850 nearly 800 of them regularly traveled the Mississippi and its tributaries. Flat-bottomed steamboats were developed to navigate on rivers less than three feet deep.

The benefits of steamboat travel were great, but risks were high. The average life of a river steamboat was three to six years—not surprising considering the dangers presented by snags, ice, bursting boilers, collisions, fires, and sand bars. About one-third of the steamboats built before 1850 were lost in accidents. In 1839 Michael Chevalier, a French traveler in America, noted that his Mississippi steamboat trip posed more dangers than his Atlantic crossing:

There have been many accidents by fire in the steamers, and many persons have perished in this way.... The Brandywine was burnt near Memphis, in 1832, and every soul on board, to the number of 110, was lost. The Americans show a singular indifference in regard to fire, not only in the steamboats, but also in their houses; they smoke without the least concern in the midst of half open cotton-bales, with which a boat is loaded; they ship gunpowder with no more precaution than if it were so much maize or salt pork....it matters little, if they move at a rapid rate, and are navigated at little expense.

The thousands of miles of canals built during the first part of the nineteenth century were as important to transportation as the river systems. For moving heavy goods, canals were far more efficient than even the best roads. On a good road it took 4 horses to haul a 1.5 ton load; 2 horses or mules could pull a canal boat with a load of 50 tons. Before 1815 a number of short canals had been built, most of them around rapids and falls in rivers. A few canals connected nearby natural waterways. The canal-building craze did not really begin, however, until completion of the Erie Canal in 1825.

Begun by New York state in 1817, the Erie Canal was 40 feet wide, 4 feet deep and 363 miles long—running from Albany on the Hudson River to Buffalo on Lake Erie. The canal lowered the cost of moving a ton of goods from almost 20 cents per mile to less than 2 cents and reduced travel time from 20 days to 6. It quickly made New York City the greatest port in America and brought instant prosperity to rural areas upstate.

The success of the Erie Canal encouraged other states to invest in canals. Pennsylvania built a canal system across the Appalachian mountains, linking Pittsburgh with the east and allowing Philadelphia to challenge New York as the nation's major port. Ohio went deeply into debt to build 500 miles of canals connecting the Ohio River and Lake Erie. Indiana's canal-building program nearly bankrupted the state.

In an era before dynamite, concrete, and steel, building canals took astonishing physical effort by countless workers. By 1840 more than 3,000 miles of canals were dug by workers using shovels and scoops pulled by horses and oxen. **Locks**—enclosures with gates at each end to raise or lower the water level—were constructed as canals crossed hills and valleys. The stone for these locks had to be cut and set completely by hand.

Construction workers labored on the canals from dawn to dusk for wages that averaged less than $1 a day. Many farmers earned extra income by working on nearby canal projects. But farmers were not available during the growing season, and in areas other than cities, the population was too small to supply enough workers. So construction depended on thousands of Irish immigrants who moved from project to project as canal-building spread. Canals also created opportunities for new businesses to supply food, shelter, and other necessities to workers—and later to travelers on the canals. In rural areas, towns sprang up along canals, especially at locks, which were typical stopping points for boats. Soon, however, an even quicker means of transportation was developing.

Examining Illustrations   *Canals speeded the movement of goods and people, but their usefulness was limited. They froze in winter, dried up in summer, and flooded with spring rains—collapsing their banks and requiring expensive repairs. Why did New York City benefit from the Erie Canal?*

Connections

HISTORY AND TECHNOLOGY

CANAL LOCKS

Get up there mule, here comes a lock
We'll make Rome 'fore 6 o'clock
And back we'll go to our home dock
Right back home to Buffalo.

The "lock" in the verse of this popular early nineteenth-century song was one of 83 along the Erie Canal. Locks are

Lockport, Erie Canal

chambers, with gates at each end, that raise and lower ships to compensate for elevation changes along a waterway.

A ship traveling downstream enters a lock and remains there while a gate is closed behind it, creating a watertight chamber. Water is slowly released through the downstream gate to lower the water level in the lock. The downstream gate is then opened, and the ship continues on its way at a lower elevation. To raise a ship, water is added to the lock through the upstream gate.

In places where elevation changes are great, such as at a waterfall, locks are combined in a sort of water staircase. Ships pass from one lock to another, each lock like a step on the staircase.

Locks remain important even today on the Ohio and Mississippi rivers. Many locks from times past can be found still standing in towns, forests, and fields—remnants of the nineteenth century.

★ ★ ★ ★ ★ ★ ★ ★ ★ ★

MAKING THE TECHNOLOGY CONNECTION

1. What do canal locks do?

2. What materials and technologies common today were not available for building or operating nineteenth-century locks?

LINKING PAST AND PRESENT

3. What canals are important in world commerce today?

★ ★ ★ ★ ★ ★ ★ ★ ★ ★

Transportation by Rail

Railroads proved the most practical of all internal improvements. They were faster than roads and were passable in almost all weather. They did not freeze in winter or dry up in summer like canals and rivers; nor were they limited by topography.

Early trains were nearly as unsafe as steamboats. Engineers operated locomotives at top speed down hills and around curves, giving passengers the nineteenth-century equivalent of a roller-coaster ride. Sparks from belching smokestacks ignited wooden railroad cars, haystacks, and buildings along the track. To save money,

Examining Illustrations *A train wins a race with a horse-drawn coach in the 1830s. Sparks and soot from smokestacks often ruined the clothes of passengers riding in open cars. What advantages did railroads have over roads and canals?*

only a single set of tracks was laid to carry trains in both directions, so collisions were frequent. Experienced travelers rode in the middle cars.

Despite their dangers, railroads excited Americans. In his book *Walden*, Henry David Thoreau captured this spirit:

When I hear the iron horse make the hills echo with his snort like thunder, shaking the earth with his feet and breathing fire and smoke from his nostrils...it seems as if the earth had got a race now worthy to inhabit it.

Yet despite such enthusiasm, railroads were slow to take hold, mainly because of opposition from state governments, which had heavy investments in roads and canals. New York, for example, attempted to protect the Erie Canal by prohibiting trains from carrying freight. By 1840 the number of miles of track laid equaled the number of miles of canals that had been dug. But not until the second half of the century would railroads dominate the nation's transportation system.

Transportation and Daily Life

Roads, canals, steamboats, and railroads created a truly national economy in the United States by the mid-1800s, and they contributed to the establishment of a national identity. People could now buy goods produced in distant places. Rural Americans could have glass in the windows of their homes and hang curtains sewn from cloth manufactured in the

Examining Illustrations   *In the era before electric lights or kerosene lanterns, most rural homes were lit by candlelight. Candle-making was a major household chore until roads and canals made manufactured candles available in rural areas. How did internal improvements change American life?*

mills of New England. Citizens of Illinois could enjoy the same foods, fashions, and household furnishings as residents of Vermont. Food prices fell in the Northeast, while farm production more than doubled. By 1840 more western farm products were being shipped on the Erie Canal than down the Mississippi River to New Orleans.

Transportation changed America in other ways as well. Information joined the flow of products as mail became deliverable throughout the nation. In 1825 Congress established home delivery of letters, and in 1847 created the first national postage stamps. With the mail came newspapers, which brought national issues to the attention of the most remote rural communities and helped integrate them into national life and politics. Improved transportation also brought circuit-riding preachers more frequently. No longer did Americans in isolated areas wait months for formal religious services, marriage ceremonies, or baptism of their children.

For women, the effects of the transportation revolution were mixed. The constant need to make such household necessities as candles, soap, and cloth once required the help of the whole family. But the availability of manufactured goods nation-wide changed the division of labor and status of women. Household work required less time and became the sole responsibility of women. It also became less valued than labor that produced income for the family, and many women moved into paid employment outside the home.

Another important result of the transportation system was that it connected the Northeast with the old Northwest Territory. The natural geographic connection of the West was with the South, by way of the Mississippi River. But the best market for western farm products was the populous industrial Northeast. Opening up that market created a strong economic tie between the West and the Northeast—a tie that later would have important political consequences for the nation.

Section Two Review

SUMMARY

In the early 1800s roads and canals were built to unite the different sections of the country. When Madison's veto of the Bonus Bill reduced federal financing for internal improvements, private companies and state governments stepped in to fill the gap. Steamboats, roads, and canals improved transportation, joined the West with the South and East, carried raw materials and manufactured goods, and hastened migration of settlers into western territories. They also encouraged an information revolution by making postal service and newspapers available to citizens along the frontier.

CHECKING FOR UNDERSTANDING

1. **Identify** Bonus Bill, National Road, Robert Fulton, Erie Canal

2. **Define** turnpike, toll, locks

3. **Describe** the environmental problems that were involved in building early roads and canals.

4. **Identify** three kinds of transportation improvements and an example of places that each linked together.

5. **Explain** the effect the transportation revolution had on women.

THINKING CRITICALLY

6. **Linking Past and Present** Roads, canals, steamboats, and railroads were early transportation links between East and West. What are examples of other major links that tie different sections of the country together today?

CONNECTIONS: HISTORY AND GEOGRAPHY

7. **Using a Road Map** In the 1950s the federal and state governments began construction of a federal interstate highway system. Identify some of the major interstate roads and the areas that they join.

Monroe and Foreign Affairs

SETTING THE SCENE

Great Britain … is the nation which can do us the most harm of any one, or on all earth; and with her on our side we need not fear the whole world.

—THOMAS JEFFERSON
Letter to President James Monroe, 1823

Section Focus

The nationalism that inspired developments at home also affected the young nation's foreign affairs. Americans approved from afar as Spain's colonies in Latin America gained independence. At the same time, the United States worked to establish peace along its borders and to expand them where possible. Out of these events came a policy that for the next 150 years guided America's attitude toward European involvement in the affairs of the Western Hemisphere.

Objectives

After studying this section, you should be able to:
- Describe America's problems with Britain and Spain and how they were settled.
- Explain the foreign policy principles established by the Monroe Doctrine.

United States foreign affairs after the War of 1812 were dominated by John Quincy Adams, Monroe's secretary of state until becoming President himself in 1825. Few Americans could match his qualifications. He had spent 18 years abroad in diplomatic service, as the United States minister to the Netherlands, Portugal, Russia, and Great Britain. Furthermore, as the son of a former Federalist President and a native New Englander, his appointment to the cabinet was in the spirit of national unity sought by President Monroe.

Disputes and Diplomacy

Although peace with Great Britain had been achieved in 1815, bitter feelings remained. The Treaty of Ghent was widely regarded as a mere truce because it had not resolved the differences between the two nations. "That man must be blind to the indications of the future," declared Henry Clay in 1816, "who cannot see that we are destined to have war after war with Great Britain." Disputes over fishing rights at the mouth of the St. Lawrence River led to violence between Canadians and New Englanders. Britain and the United States competed for naval supremacy on the Great Lakes. From Maine to Oregon the boundary between the United States and Canada was unsettled, and in several places it was disputed.

There were strong reasons for improving relations with Great Britain. Chief among these was trade. Britain remained a buyer of American raw materials and America a market for British manufactured goods. Realizing that neither country had anything to gain by continued hostilities, Britain made attempts to smooth out relations. For example, it ended assistance to native Americans in United States territory south of the Great Lakes. Between 1815 and 1817, Great Britain and the United States were able to work out several of their disputes peacefully.

As minister to England, John Quincy Adams used Great Britain's desire for better relations with the United States to negotiate the famous Rush-Bagot Agreement of 1817, the first mutual naval disarmament in history. The United States and Britain agreed to remove all warships from the Great Lakes, except for a few small vessels to control smuggling. This precedent later encouraged the United States and Canada to demilitarize their entire 3,000-mile border, creating what continues to be the longest unfortified international boundary in the world.

The Rush-Bagot Agreement also set the stage for the Convention of 1818, which specified where American ships could fish in Canadian waters and set the northern boundary of the Louisiana Purchase by running the forty-ninth parallel from the Lake of the Woods in Minnesota to the Rocky Mountains. Beyond the Rockies, the treaty provided "joint occupation" of the disputed Oregon territory for ten years. Each country would be free to carry on fur trade and settle the region without interference from the other. The dispute over ownership of Oregon was thereby suspended.

Spanish Florida remained a source of friction, however, as it had been since the Louisiana Purchase. Spain insisted that Florida's western boundary was the Missis-sippi River, while the United States claimed that it was the Perdido River, 200 miles farther east. During the War of 1812 the United States resolved the controversy by simply seizing the disputed territory.

Because Spain was an ally of Great Britain in the War of 1812, Florida became a base of British and Indian operations against the United States. After the war, it remained a refuge for Seminole and Creek Indians, who continued to battle the Georgia settlers who had taken their land. In 1818 Andrew Jackson, commanding the Tennessee militia, ignored the international boundary and pursued a Seminole force into Florida, where he seized Spanish settlements at Pensacola and St. Marks.

The Spanish government demanded that the United States pay for the "outrage" and punish Jackson. But Adams defended Jackson and argued that true blame lay in Spain's failure to keep order in Florida. He convinced Monroe to issue Spain an ultimatum—either govern Florida effectively or surrender it to the United States.

Occupied with problems throughout its Latin American empire, Spain gave in and ceded Florida to the United States in the Adams-Onís Treaty of 1819. In return the United States agreed to pay $5 million to American citizens who had claims against Spain. The treaty also set the western boundary of the Louisiana Purchase from the Gulf of Mexico northwest to the Oregon Territory and west to the Pacific. In addition, the United States gave up a weak claim to Texas as part of the Louisiana Territory, while Spain gave up a much stronger claim to Oregon. Secretary of State Adams had used Spain's world problems to negotiate a treaty extremely favorable to his own nation.

The Monroe Doctrine

The most significant accomplishment of Secretary of State Adams was the Monroe Doctrine of 1823. This famous statement of foreign policy had a complex background that involved events in Latin America, in Europe, and on the Pacific coast of North America.

Between 1814 and 1824, Spain's Latin American colonies declared independence.

Examining Illustrations
President Monroe consulted his cabinet before issuing the Monroe Doctrine. What warning did the Monroe Doctrine contain?

Armies led by Simón Bolívar (See MOHN Buh LEE vahr) and José San Martín (Hoh SAY SAHN MAHR TEEN) exceeded even the Patriots' heroics in the American Revolution. Bolívar's advance to Peru through more than 2,000 miles of mountains and San Martín's expedition from Argentina, as he led 5,000 troops through mountain passes over 12,000 feet high, captured the attention of the American people.

Sympathy for the Latin Americans was increased by events in Europe. After defeating Napoleon in 1815, the victorious European monarchies formed the Quadruple Alliance to suppress the democratic ideas of the French Revolution. Klemens von Metternich (MEHT uhr NIHK), prime minister of Austria, branded democracy "the disease which must be cured, the volcano which must be extinguished, the gangrene which must be burned out with the hot iron." The Quadruple Alliance helped defeat revolutions in Italy and Spain.

The success of the Quadruple Alliance caused some European leaders to talk of taking similar action in the Americas. Although there was little chance that they could carry out such action, rumors of it caused concern in the United States and Great Britain. Both the British and the Americans were enjoying a profitable trade with Latin American nations. If the Quadruple Alliance returned the region to Spain, restrictions would reappear and this trade would be lost. The British government looked for a way to discourage moves to restore Spanish rule in Latin America.

In August 1823, the British foreign minister suggested to the U.S. minister in London that the two nations issue a joint statement about the independence of Latin America. The statement would say that the United States and Britain opposed intervention in Latin America by any power, and that neither nation would acquire any part of Latin America for itself—a surprising proposal from an old enemy. The American minister informed President Monroe.

Examining Maps
The American Revolution of 1776 and the French Revolution of 1789 inspired Spain's Latin American colonies to seek independence. What European nations had colonies in South America after 1825?

LATIN AMERICA, 1825

Date is date of independence

The British proposal was an attractive and timely one. The Monroe administration was wrestling with a number of foreign policy concerns. Russia already claimed Alaska and was making aggressive moves on the Pacific coast. For years Russian settlers had been operating an iron foundry north of San Francisco. In 1821 the Russian tsar announced that his empire extended south into Oregon, which conflicted with American and British claims there.

Should the United States allow Russia to expand its holdings in the Western Hemisphere? How should the United States meet the threat of intervention in Latin America—accept the British offer of cooperation or act alone? President Monroe discussed these questions with his cabinet and consulted his fellow Virginians, Jefferson and Madison. The two former Presidents favored a joint statement with Great Britain. But Secretary of State Adams argued that it would look as though the United States was following "in the wake of the British man-of-war." He urged that the United States act alone. The nationalism of John Quincy Adams prevailed.

For what would become a landmark of American foreign policy, the Monroe Doctrine was presented in an undramatic way. It appeared in two widely separated passages in President Monroe's annual message to Congress on December 2, 1823. It provided both a warning and a reassurance to Europe (see Appendix).

Despite its lasting importance, the Monroe Doctrine had no great significance at the time it was issued. If the nations of the Quadruple Alliance ever seriously contemplated intervention in the Americas, it was the British navy, not Monroe's warning, that made them back down. In 1824 the Russians, already in possession of more land than they could effectively govern, agreed to withdraw from Oregon.

The significance of the Monroe Doctrine is in later events. Its bold warnings gained meaning only when the United States was able to back them up without relying on British sea power—a development that took nearly a century. Nor did the Monroe Doctrine protect Latin America from the nationalism, expansion, and intervention of the United States itself over the next 150 years.

★ ★ ★ ★ ★ ★ ★ ★ ★ ★ ★ ★ ★ ★ ★ ★ ★ ★

Section Three Review

★ ★ ★ ★ ★ ★ ★ ★ ★ ★ ★ ★ ★ ★ ★ ★ ★

SUMMARY

After the War of 1812, bitter relations between the United States and Britain improved, beginning with the Rush-Bagot Agreement, which removed each other's warships from the Great Lakes. Later treaties negotiated fishing rights and settled territorial issues. Spain agreed to sell Florida and recognized the boundary of the Louisiana Purchase in the Adams-Onís treaty. The United States was sympathetic when Spain's colonies in Latin America fought for and gained independence. The government subsequently issued the Monroe Doctrine that would define future American foreign policy. It closed the Western Hemisphere to additional European colonization.

CHECKING FOR UNDERSTANDING

1. **Identify** John Quincy Adams, Rush-Bagot Agreement, Adams-Onís Treaty, Simón Bolívar, José San Martín, Quadruple Alliance, Monroe Doctrine

2. **List** the disputes that the United States had with Britain and Spain.

3. **Explain** why diplomacy won out over war in solving the United States' problems with Britain and Spain.

4. **Describe** the chain of events in Latin America and Europe that formed the background to the Monroe Doctrine.

THINKING CRITICALLY

5. **Applying Principles**   Argue how U.S. government involvement in Central American affairs could be interpreted as violating the principles of the Monroe Doctrine.

GLOBAL PERSPECTIVES

6. **Synthesizing Ideas**   The American Revolution, the French Revolution, and revolutions in Latin America all occurred within a span of 50 years. What political ideas were prevalent at the time to cause these revolutions?

★ ★ ★ ★ ★ ★ ★ ★ ★ ★ ★ ★ ★ ★ ★ ★ ★

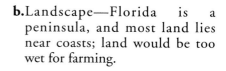

Map and Graph Skills

Drawing Conclusions from Maps

Your best friend comes back from a backpacking trip through Colorado. Pulling out a map, he describes a dangerous situation he survived near the top of Pikes Peak. After talking about all the factors that could have created the situation, and looking closely at the map, you decide that he must have lost the trail at about 10,000 feet. You *drew a conclusion.*

Drawing conclusions is a process of making decisions or judgments through careful analysis of available information. In order to draw your conclusion, you knew about Pikes Peak and how to read a hiking map. A conclusion is reached after you have made a series of *inferences,* or deductions based on such facts or circumstances. These inferences act as clues that help you make the decision or judgment.

The following guidelines will help you draw conclusions from these maps:

a. Study the map for bodies of water. How might they be used in the future? Are they strategic for trade or defense?

b. Study the landscape. Is the terrain mountainous or flat?

Does the land have agricultural potential?

c. Study the boundaries. Do physical boundaries match natural boundaries? Are there any border disputes?

d. Study other map data. Examine routes, resources, labels, etc.

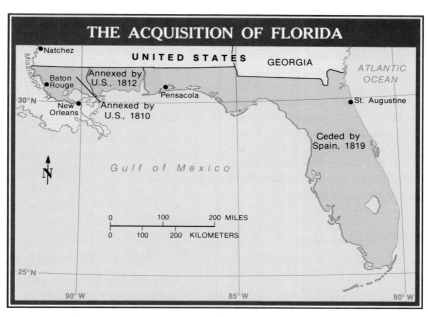

Example

Examine the historical map of Florida on this page. Following the guidelines, you can draw a conclusion as to why Florida was acquired by the United States in 1819:

a. Bodies of water—Gulf of Mexico, Atlantic Ocean, Mississippi River. All locations along these waterways would provide ports for trade and strategic locations for defense.

b. Landscape—Florida is a peninsula, and most land lies near coasts; land would be too wet for farming.

c. The borders are clearly defined, except for the New Orleans area. Spain, England, France, and the United States all had interests in this area. Florida is clearly part of the same landmass as the United States.

d. Data primarily deals with border disputes—land in 3 different areas between the Mississippi River and the eastern coast of Florida was annexed or ceded between 1810 and 1819.

You conclude that the need to expand to its natural borders, obtain good ports, and a strategic position for defense made the acquisition of Florida appealing for the United States.

Practice

Apply these same guidelines to the map of roads, canals, and rivers in 1840 in this chapter, and draw conclusions as to why the states of New York, Ohio, and Indiana had the most mileage of canals.

★ Chapter 9 Review ★

★ Summary

After the War of 1812, America experienced a period of intense nationalism characterized by attempts to achieve a national economic, geographic, and political community. State and federal legislation promoted internal improvements to join the sections of the nation, while Supreme Court decisions strengthened the authority of the national government.

As the sections were physically joined by a network of roads and canals, settlers streamed westward and cities sprang up in the wilderness. Raw materials and manufactured goods went back and forth, and trading between the sections expanded. An information network eliminated the local character of communications and brought news of national and international affairs over new American highways and byways.

American pride was evidenced in the conduct of foreign affairs. While the United States acquired territory from Spain, Americans voiced their support for Spain's Latin American colonies struggling for the independence the United States had so recently won. The Monroe Doctrine closed the Western Hemisphere to further foreign colonization and announced the United States' intention to stay out of Europe's affairs.

★ Using Vocabulary

Write a paragraph describing the awakening of American nationalism from 1812 to 1823 using the following terms:

internal improvements	**Era of Good Feelings**
protective tariffs	**American System**
turnpikes	**Monroe Doctrine**

★ Reviewing Facts

1. **Describe** how establishing the Second Bank of the United States contributed to nationalism.
2. **Compare** Republicans' attitudes on internal improvements, banking, and federal power with their previous positions on these issues.
3. **Explain** how the federal judiciary strengthened nationalism in key decisions from 1819 to 1824.
4. **Cite** Madison's reason for vetoing the Bonus Bill.
5. **Summarize** the changes that resulted from internal improvements in transportation.

6. **List** transportation improvements of the era and the advantages and disadvantages of each.
7. **Describe** the diplomatic agreements with Great Britain and Spain that had a bearing on United States territory.

★ Understanding Concepts

NATIONAL COMMUNITY

1. How did the United States change from local communities to a more national community in the Era of Good Feelings?
2. Latin Americans created a community of states in 1823 that they called the Confederation of the United Provinces of Central America. What events in the United States might have influenced this development?

WORLD POWER

3. How was Europe's shift in attitude toward the United States as a growing power seen in the Rush-Bagot Agreement and Adams-Onís Treaty?
4. What was the perception of U.S. power resulting from the Monroe Doctrine?

★ Thinking Critically

1. **Recognizing Stereotypes** Early nineteenth-century backwoods and frontier settlers were generally regarded as crude country bumpkins in coonskin caps with no education or interest in world affairs. Describe how a lack of internal improvements could have spawned such a view.
2. **Understanding Cause and Effect** How did the transportation revolution bring about a communications revolution in the West?
3. **Making Judgments** Give President Monroe's reasons for issuing the Monroe Doctrine independently of Great Britain, and show how he could not possibly have enforced this policy.
4. **Linking Past and Present** When Iraq marched into Kuwait in 1990, the United States sent troops to Saudi Arabia and declared that the Persian Gulf states were closed to further territorial aggression. Compare this action with the provisions stated in the Monroe Doctrine.

★ Writing About History

COMPARISON

Refer to the description of how to write a comparison essay in the History Writer's Handbook in the Appendix of this book. Your teacher will give you more specific instructions on the essay's length and the assignment's due date.

Compare the advantages of each of the following means of transportation during the early 1800s: roads, rivers, canals, railroads.

★ Learning Cooperatively

Imagine that you work for a local newspaper in Cincinnati, Ohio, in 1823. Like most newspapers even today, your news staff holds daily meetings to discuss which news items to print in the upcoming edition. Discuss with other members of your staff what international, national, and local topics should be included in tomorrow's newspaper. Also determine on what you will base your decision to include certain articles.

★ Mastering Skills

EXPRESSING A VIEWPOINT

You may find yourself at times holding a viewpoint different from others. You can best express your viewpoint on any topic if you present it clearly and give evidence that supports your viewpoint persuasively. The following guidelines will help you do this:

• Before stating your viewpoint on a topic, research the subject thoroughly. Find out what viewpoints others hold on the same topic.

• Decide what your position is and list as many statements to support it as you cam. Study the list to make certain that all supporting statements relate directly to the topic, to one another, and to the point of view you have chosen. Check to make sure they are in a logical, easy-to-follow order and that they support your point of view in a clear enough manner for others to understand. Each statement should define, clarify, explain, give a reason for, or state the consequence(s) of holding your point of view.

• State your position. Then, present your supporting statements. Leave for last the supporting statement that is most impressive and will have the most impact. Your concluding statement should also restate your viewpoint, but in different words than your opening statement.

Example The statement below expresses a viewpoint about Americans after the War of 1812. Read the viewpoint, its supporting statements, and the restatement of the viewpoint. Note how they all follow the guidelines for expressing a viewpoint.

Opening statement of viewpoint:

1. The American people felt like one nation.

Supporting statements:

2. Tariffs on international goods protected internal trade.

3. A national banking system was created.

4. The dominance of the nation over the states was established, as the power of the federal government increased while states' rights decreased.

5. Improved transportation made trade between the states easier.

6. Improved communication such as a federal postal system and newspapers carrying national news made easier the exchange of information from state to state.

Concluding restatement of viewpoint:

7. The War of 1812 renewed the national feelings that the Revolution had given, and subsequent internal improvements lead the people now to feel more American, more like a nation.

Practice Use the guidelines, and write a paragraph that expresses your viewpoint on the principles set forth in the following passage from the Monroe Doctrine.

[T]he American continents, by the free and independent condition which they have assumed and maintain, are henceforth not to be considered as subjects for future colonization by any European powers....In the wars of the European powers in matters relating to themselves we have never taken any part, nor does it comport with our policy so to do. It is only when our rights are invaded or seriously menaced that we resent injuries or make preparation for our defense....We owe it, therefore, to candor and to the amicable relations existing between the United States and those powers to declare that we should consider any attempt on their part to extend their system to any portion of this hemisphere as dangerous to our peace and safety.

★ ★ ★ Unit 3 Digest ★ ★ ★

After the ratification of the Constitution, the young United States chose a leader and established domestic policies. It was also thrust into foreign affairs. Many wondered whether the nation would survive these pressures. In the end not only did it survive but it emerged as a world leader.

Chapter 7
The Federalist Era

To lead the new nation, the people elected the hero of the Revolution, George Washington, who inspired confidence and loyalty to the nation. As the first President, Washington set several precedents, such as creating a cabinet, directing foreign affairs, and serving as "chief legislator."

Washington also tackled the nation's war debts. He delegated much of the nation's financial policy to Alexander Hamilton, his secretary of the treasury. Hamilton recommended an excise tax on whiskey to provide revenue for the government, payment of foreign and domestic debts, assistance with state debts, the establishment of a central bank, and the development of home industries. On the whole, Hamilton's program restored the credit of the United States, although it met with bitter opposition, particularly from Thomas Jefferson, who believed the federal government should not wield such power.

To deal with the Indians who were resisting settlers entering the western territories, Washington called on General Anthony Wayne to drive the native Americans out of Ohio. The defeat of the Miami Confederation and the Treaty of Greenville opened the way for settlement in the Northwest. Washington also snuffed out the Whiskey Rebellion staged by western farmers to protest the excise tax on whiskey.

Another of Washington's tasks was to establish a foreign policy. At the outbreak of the Anglo-French War, he issued the Proclamation of Neutrality, which stated that the nation would be "friendly and impartial" toward both warring parties. This proclamation withstood the efforts of French minister Edmund Genêt to gain American support for his nation's cause.

Washington faced difficulties with England, which interfered with American trade. In an effort to stave off war, Washington's chief justice John Jay negotiated what became known as the Jay Treaty. Following this treaty, the United States signed the Pinckney Treaty with Spain, giving the United States the right to deposit goods at the mouth of the Mississippi River and established a southern boundary for the United States.

John Adams succeeded Washington as the nation's leader. Resistant to the skill of compromise, he faced a difficult term in office. Adams's tenure was marked by the XYZ affair, in which the French attempted to bribe American envoys; an undeclared war with France; anti-Republican legislation that ultimately hurt Adams's Federalist party; and the first appearance of the theory of nullification in the Virginia and Kentucky Resolutions.

Chapter 8
Jefferson and the Republicans

Adams sought reelection in 1800 but was defeated by Republican Thomas Jefferson in a close contest. Jefferson brought a political and philosophical change to the presidency. The thrust of his beliefs were the people were the source of a government's power. He also believed that people who thought that the Union should be dissolved should not be punished; that the United States government was the strongest in the world; and that people were able to govern themselves. Once in office, however, Jefferson found that he had to provide strong leadership to prevent his party from dividing into factions.

During Jefferson's first term, for the most part, foreign and domestic affairs remained tranquil, with much of the earlier Federalist legislation remaining in effect. An exception was the power of the federal judiciary, which the Republicans cut back. In addition, foreign trade was increased; taxes and the national debt were reduced; and the principle of judicial review, in which the Supreme Court ruled on the constitutionality of laws, was established. Jefferson's accomplishments led to an easy victory for a second term.

A major event during Jefferson's presidency was the Louisiana Purchase, which doubled the size of the United States. Despite doubts over whether the federal government had the legal power to acquire foreign territory, Jefferson agreed to the purchase because it extended the boundaries of the United States west of the Mississippi. Not all people supported the purchase, however. In particular, die-hard Federalists in the Northeast feared that it would ultimately weaken New England's power in national affairs.

During Jefferson's presidency, he tried to remain neutral in foreign affairs despite such threats as attacks on ships by the Barbary pirates, the French Napoleonic decrees, the British Orders in Council, and the British policy of searching American ships for former British subjects. In response to the latter, Congress passed the Embargo Act, which sanctioned an economic boycott. Because American trade suffered severely as a consequence, the act was repealed.

Under James Madison, Jefferson's successor, the United States became embroiled in an unpopular war with Britain. The war of 1812 dragged on three years, with fighting taking place in Canada, in the United States, and at sea. The war finally ended in 1814 with the Treaty of Ghent.

Chapter 9
Nationalism and Change

The period following the War of 1812 was marked by the spirit of nationalism, in which Americans cooperated to develop a stronger, more unified nation. Internal improvements were encouraged, and a new national bank stimulated the economy and encouraged economic growth. In addition, protective tariffs were instituted to protect American manufacturers from goods manufactured abroad.

Nationalism was also demonstrated in a series of Supreme Court decisions by Chief Justice John Marshall, which strengthened the power of the federal government at the expense of the states. These included *McCulloch v. Maryland*, *Dartmouth College v. Woodward*, and *Gibbons v. Ogden*.

The early 1800s were also marked by a transportation revolution, taking place on America's inland waterways at a time when highway and turnpike development in its infancy. Railroads were also slow to take hold. One development was Fulton's steamboat, which turned rivers into two-way navigation paths. Another was the building of thousands of miles of canals during this period. Both developments dramatically lowered the time and cost of shipping goods from place to place.

Transportation improvements helped unite Americans, who could now buy goods produced in distant places and improve their lifestyles. Other important consequences of transportation improvements were the increase in the spread of information and the changes to the geographic landscape of the country.

While the United States was making internal improvements, it was also looking after its foreign affairs. Relations between the United States and Britain improved with the Rush-Bagot Agreement, which was the first example of mutual naval disarmament in history. Differences between Spain and the United States were settled by the Adams-Onís Treaty, which gave Florida to the United States. One of the greatest foreign policy accomplishments, however, was the Monroe Doctrine, which proclaimed that the western hemisphere was closed to further European colonization. Although insignificant when it was issued, it has had lasting importance in American foreign policy and has helped keep the nation out of European affairs.

★ Unit 3 Review ★

★ Analyzing Unit Themes

AMERICAN DEMOCRACY

1. How did Chief Justice John Marshall reinforce the principles of American government established by the Constitution?

GEOGRAPHY AND ENVIRONMENT

2. As settlers poured into the country's expanded western lands, what effects did they have on the American environment?

3. How did the environment of the United States influence the development of a uniquely American character?

CONFLICT AND COOPERATION

4. Why did some issues threaten to disrupt the spirit of American nationalism and unity?

U.S. ROLE IN WORLD AFFAIRS

5. Explain Washington's rationale for recommending a policy of noninvolvement in European affairs.

6. Explain how the Monroe Doctrine was an affirmation or a denial of United States isolationism.

★ Reviewing Chronology

For each of the following events in Europe, indicate what event it caused in the United States and when it occurred.

1. 1793 War between Britain and France
2. 1797 XYZ Affair
3. 1803 France sells Louisiana
4. 1815 Quadruple Alliance

★ Linking Past and Present

- 1969 Thousands demonstrate against the Vietnam War.
- 1970 National Guard kills four student demonstrators at Kent State University in Ohio.
- 1973 United States signs cease-fire agreement with North Vietnam and South Vietnam.

Study the information above, then answer the questions that follow.

1. **Making Comparisons** How did popular support for the Vietnam War compare with popular support

for the War of 1812?

2. **Making Judgments** What was different about the aftermath of the two wars?

★ Demonstrating Citizenship

Communicating Cooperation and communication among Washington, Hamilton, Adams, and their colleagues helped successfully launch the new government. In what ways can you communicate with the government to improve conditions in your community and nation?

★ Interpreting Illustrations

Study the political cartoon shown above, then answer the questions that follow.

1. Who do the various figures in the cartoon represent?

2. What is going on in this cartoon?

3. **Recognizing Satire** Explain the words "O grab me."

★ Thinking Globally

1. **Analyzing Motives** In 1802 Napoleon was forced to send troops to Sainte Domingue (Haiti) to put down the rebellion led by L'Ouverture. In 1803 Britain and France went to war. How did these two events affect Napoleon's decision to sell Louisiana?

2. Drawing Conclusions In 1821 population figures were revealed for major European countries and for the United States. The figures represent millions.

France	30.4
German Confederation	26.0
Great Britain	20.8
Italian States	18.0
Austria	12.0
United States	9.6

What significance can you draw from these figures?

★ Relating Geography and History

PLACE: RELATIONSHIPS WITHIN PLACES

Very early in its history, the South developed an agrarian economy that focused on one or two cash crops and used slave labor. As the nation expanded, the South insisted on trying to extend its economic philosophy into other geographic regions.

Answer the questions that follow.

1. What features of the environment led southerners to grow cash crops?

2. What one feature of the environment did southerners feel was conducive to slave labor? Why?

3. For the South's economy to expand, what geographic regions appeared suitable?

★ Practicing Skills

DISTINGUISHING BETWEEN FACTS AND VALUE JUDGMENTS

Refer to the skills lesson on Distinguishing Between Fact and Value Judgment on page 240 to help you practice this critical thinking skill.

Distinguish whether each of the following quotes is a factual statement or a value judgment.

1. "A just and solid republican government maintained here will be a standing monument and example for the aim and imitation of the people of other countries."

2. "Mr. Jefferson has long felt a spirit of deadly hostility against the Federal Constitution."

3. "Jefferson is at once a musician, skilled in drawing, a geometrician, an astronomer, a natural philosopher, legislator, and statesman."

4. "We are all Republicans, we are all Federalists."

5. It is New Orleans, through which the produce of three-eighths of our territory must pass to market."

6. "We have seen nations with which we have the most friendly and useful relations, engaged in mutual destruction."

7. "This morning on awakening we were greeted with the sad news, that our city was taken, the bridges and public buildings burnt, our troops flying in every direction."

8. "I do not suppose Government will ever return to Washington. All those whose property was invested in this place, will be reduced to poverty."

9. "Any man who foretold such disasters this day last year would have been treated as a madman or a traitor."

10. "About three-fourths of our townsmen depend on the sea for the means of subsistence for themselves and their families."

11. "We feel it therefore most strongly incumbent to seek a speedy termination of the present war."

DRAWING CONCLUSIONS FROM MAPS

Refer to the skills lesson on Drawing Conclusions from Maps on page 301 to help you practice this map and graph skill. Study the map of the Louisiana Purchase on page 264. Then determine whether or not each of the following conclusions can be drawn from the map.

1. Most of the Louisiana Territory consisted of dry desert land.

2. The Louisiana Territory now gave the United States a buffer between itself and areas controlled by Europe.

3. The Louisiana Territory provided very few means of access for traveling through its area.

4. Acquiring the Louisiana Territory was natural to some Americans because then the United States could expand all the way to the Pacific Coast.

5. Access to Pacific Ocean trade through the river system running through the Louisiana Territory and the Oregon Country severely weakened the importance of the Mississippi River as a trade link.

UNIT 4

Toward A Democracy: 1820-1848

...Of all the countries in the world, America is that in which the spread of ideas and of human industry is most continual and most rapid....

—ALEXIS DE TOCQUEVILLE
American Notes, 1831

SETTING THE SCENE

Time

Early nineteenth century

Mood

The years between 1820 and 1848 were a time of national optimism and growth. Andrew Jackson helped shape the character of the age by supporting the growth of democracy. At the same time, the nation's economy grew with the development of the factory system in the Northeast, settlement of the Northwest, and the expansion of slavery in the South. Confident of their future, Americans also experimented with social reform movements aimed at bettering society.

Themes

- American Democracy
- Economic Development
- Humanities and Religion
- Conflict and Cooperation

Key Events

- Missouri Compromise
- Founding of New Harmony
- Tariff of Abominations
- Maysville Road veto
- The Liberator published
- Indian Removal
- Nullification Crisis
- Bank Recharter Bill veto
- American Anti-Slavery Society
- Panic of 1837
- Seneca Falls Convention

Major Issues

- Distinct sections—North, South, and West—cooperate and compete for economic development.
- Jacksonian democracy results in increased power of the President and popular participation in political life.
- Religious motivation and democratic ideals spark the Abolitionist movement and other efforts form social reform.

◄ The County Election *by George Caleb Bingham, 1852*

Global Perspectives

The years between 1820 and 1848 were ones of change, conflict, and cooperation all over the world. In South America, Venezuela and Ecuador became separate nations. At the same time, some Latin American leaders sought more cooperation through Pan-Americanism. In Europe France rebelliously ousted an unpopular king, and Great Britain celebrated the crowning of their new young queen, Victoria.

In western nations the Industrial Revolution was at work. It had begun in Britain but soon spread to the rest of Europe and to the United States. With

THE WORLD

	ASIA AND OCEANIA	AFRICA	EUROPE	SOUTH AMERICA	NORTH AND CENTRAL AMERICA
1820				**1821** *Peru becomes independent of Spain*	
					1826 *Pan-Americanism gets underway at Panama Congress*
1830			**1830** *July Revolution in France* ▲	**1830** *Venezuela and Ecuador become nations*	
		1835 *Boer farmers start the "Great Trek"*	**1837** *Victoria becomes Queen of Great Britain* ▼		
1840	**1839** *Britain and China battle in First Opium War* ▲				**1840** *Act of Union unites Upper and Lower Canada*
1850					

the revolution's diffusion, it dramatically altered the industrial, political, and social life of the entire western world.

In the United States new industrial ideas fostered the growth of manufacturing and changed the lives of industrial workers. As in Europe, it aided the growth of transportation, which in turn led to the rise of cities. It also helped bring more people to the United States in search of jobs.

During this time, political life in the United States changed as well. With the election of Andrew Jackson as President in 1828, more people began to take part in political affairs. Many of Jackson's supporters believed strongly in democracy and such social reforms as women's rights and improvements in education. The most controversial issue, however, was the abolition of slavery. Great Britain outlawed slavery in 1833, but in the United States slavery became entrenched in the southern economy. Slavery ultimately threatened the unity of the nation.

THE UNITED STATES

	PACIFIC AND NORTHWEST	SOUTHWEST	MIDWEST	SOUTHEAST	ATLANTIC NORTHEAST

1820

● 1820 *Missouri Compromise creates a balance between slave and free states* ▼

● 1821 *California becomes a Mexican province*

● 1827 *Mission era ends with expulsion of all Franciscans from New Mexico and Arizona* ▲

● 1826 *Educational lyceum movement begins in Mass.*

1830

● 1830 *Joseph Smith founds Church of Latter-Day Saints*

● 1838 *Cherokee Indians endure the "Trail of Tears"* ◄

● 1839 *Charles Goodyear makes first vulcanized rubber*

1840

1850

The country's rapid physical and technological growth during the early 1800s caused Americans to look to the future with unbridled optimism.

Many Transcendental works of poetry and prose were penned during the period, but none more fully embodies Transcendental ideals than Henry David Thoreau's Walden. *Part journal, part social commentary, and part sermon, the work summarizes and enlarges upon Thoreau's experiences at Walden Pond, near Concord, Massachusetts, where he built a cabin and lived in solitude for two years.*

As you read this passage, look for Thoreau's criticisms of American society, his call for personal freedom, and what he says we must do to live in society.

Henry David Thoreau

from Walden

When first I took up my abode in the woods, that is, began to spend my nights as well as days there, which, by accident, was on Independence Day, or the Fourth of July, 1845, my house was not finished for winter, but was merely a defense against the rain, without plastering or chimney, the walls being of rough, weather-stained boards, with wide chinks, which made it cool at night. The upright white hewn studs and freshly planed door and window casings gave it a clean and airy look, especially in the morning, when its timbers were saturated with dew, so that I fancied that by noon some sweet gum would exude from them. To my imagination it retained throughout the day more or less of this auroral character, reminding me of a certain house on a mountain which I had visited a year before. This was an airy and unplastered cabin, fit to entertain a travelling god, and where a goddess might trail her garments. The winds which passed over my dwelling were such as sweep over the ridges of mountains, bearing the broken strains, or celestial parts only, of terrestrial music. The morning wind forever blows, the poem of creation is uninterrupted; but few are the ears that hear it....

I went to the woods because I wished to live deliberately, to front only the essential facts of life, and see if I could not learn what it had to teach, and not, when I came to die, discover that I had not lived. I did not wish to live what was not life, living is so dear; nor did I wish to practice resignation, unless it was quite necessary. I wanted to live deep and suck out all the marrow of life, to live so sturdily and Spartan-like as to put to rout all that was not life, to cut a broad swath and shave close, to drive life into a corner, and reduce it to its lowest terms, and, if it proved to be mean, why then to get the whole and genuine meanness of it, and publish its meanness to the world; or if it were sublime, to know it by experience, and be able to give a true account of it in my next excursion. For most men, it appears to me, are in a strange uncertainty about it, whether it is of the devil or of God, and have *somewhat hastily* concluded that it is the chief end of man here to "glorify God and enjoy him forever."

Still we live meanly, like ants….Our life is frittered away by detail. An honest man has hardly need to count more than his ten fingers, or in extreme cases he may add his ten toes, and lump the rest. Simplicity, simplicity, simplicity! I say, let your affairs be as two or three, and not a hundred or a thousand; instead of a million count half a dozen, and keep your accounts on your thumb-nail. In the midst of this chopping sea of civilized life, such are the clouds and storms and quicksands and thousand-and-one items to be allowed for, that a man has to live, if he would not founder and go to the bottom and not make his port at all, by dead reckoning, and he must be a great calculator indeed who succeeds. Simplify, simplify. Instead of three meals a day, if it be necessary eat but one; instead of a hundred dishes, five; and reduce other things in proportion. Our life is like a German Confederacy, made up of petty states, with its boundary forever fluctuating, so that even a German cannot tell you how it is bounded at any moment. The nation itself, with all its so-called internal improvements, which, by the way, are all grown establishment, cluttered with furniture and tripped up by its own traps, ruined by luxury and heedless expense, by want of calculation and a worthy aim, as the million house-holds in the land; and the only cure for it, as for them, is in a rigid economy, a stern and more than Spartan simplicity of life and elevation of purpose. It lives too fast. Men think that it is essential that the *Nation* have commerce, and export ice, and talk through a telegraph, and ride thirty miles an hour, without a doubt, whether *they* do or not; but whether we should live like baboons or like men, is a little uncertain….

Let us spend one day as deliberately as Nature, and not be thrown off the track by every nutshell and mosquito's wing that falls on the rails. Let us rise early and fast, or break fast, gently and without perturbation; let company come and let company go, let the bells ring and the children cry,—determined to make a day of it. Why should we knock under and go with the stream?…

Time is but the stream I go a-fishing in. I drink at it; but while I drink I see the sandy bottom and detect how shallow it is. Its thin current slides away, but eternity remains. I would drink deeper; fish in the sky, whose bottom is pebbly with stars. I cannot count one. I know not the first letter of the alphabet. I have always been regretting that I was not as wise as the day I was born. The intellect is a cleaver; it discerns and rifts its way into the secret of things. I do not wish to be any more busy with my hands than is necessary. My head is hands and feet. I feel all my best faculties concentrated in it. My instinct tells me that my head is an organ for burrowing, as some creatures use their snout and fore paws, and with it I would mine and burrow my way through these hills. I think that the richest vein is somewhere hereabouts; so by the divining-rod and thin rising vapors I judge; and here I will begin to mine.

Walden Pond

INTERPRETING LITERATURE

1. What motivated Thoreau to go and live alone in the wilderness?

2. What is Thoreau's assessment of life at mid-century? To what does he compare life?

3. What do you think the phrase "every nutshell and mosquito's wing" means?

SEEING RELATIONSHIPS

4. What trends and tendencies of the period go hand in hand with the ideals Thoreau expresses?

CHAPTER 10
Sectionalism and Growth

Historical Focus

At the same time that national spirit and pride were evident throughout the country, a strong sectional rivalry was also developing. Each region—the North, South, and West—wanted to further its own economic and political interests. Issues such as land policy, the tariff, and internal improvements were favored or opposed by different sections. The question of extending slavery, however, became the issue that proved the most difficult to resolve.

Concepts to Understand

- Why early labor movements challenged the **free enterprise** system.
- How **economic and cultural change** brought about by the Industrial Revolution led to the creation of the factory system.

People to Know

Samuel Slater, Eli Whitney, James Tallmadge, Andrew Jackson, Henry Clay

Places to Locate

Liberia, Pittsburgh, Missouri

Terms to Identify

textile, emigration, closed shop, "squatters' rights," Tallmadge Amendment, favorite sons, "corrupt bargain"

Guided Reading

As you read this chapter, seek the answers to the following questions.

1. How did the Industrial Revolution affect the textile industry?

2. How did each section view the major issues faced by the nation?

SPANNING THE DECADES

POLITICAL	1791 *Bill of Rights ratified*	1800 *Nation's capital moved from Philadelphia to Washington, D.C.*	1803 Marbury v. Madison
	1790	**1800**	**1810**
CULTURAL	1790 *Samuel Slater builds first cotton mill, at Pawtucket, Rhode Island*	1793 *Eli Whitney receives patent for the cotton gin*	1800 *Library of Congress founded*

Where Cotton Is King *by Konstantin Rodko*

1819
*Tallmadge
Amendment
prohibits slavery
in Missouri*

1820
*Missouri
Compromise*

1824
*House
decides
Presidential
election*

1820

1816
*African
Colonization
Society formed*

1818
*Illinois is
admitted to
the Union*

1825
*Erie
Canal
completed*

*...It is among the very evils of slavery that it
taints the very sources of moral
principle...for what can be more false and
heartless than this doctrine which make the
first and holiest rights of humanity to
depend upon the color of the skin...*

—JOHN QUINCY ADAMS
From his diary, March 3, 1820

Growth in the North

How many men at this hour are living in a state of bondage to the machines? How many spend their whole lives, from the cradle to the grave in tending them by night and day?

—SAMUEL BUTLER
English novelist, 1872

Section Focus

The late eighteenth and early nineteenth centuries brought developments that would forever change life in all regions of the United States. With newly developed machines, goods could be produced more quickly and efficiently than ever before. But with the growth of industry came new problems for American workers.

Objectives

After studying this section, you should be able to:
- Discuss the impact of the Industrial Revolution on the American way of life.
- Examine the conditions that prompted the formation of trade societies in the United States.
- Explain why early attempts at unionization in the United States failed.

In the thousands of years between the building of the first pyramids in 2650 B.C. and the construction of log cabins in the eighteenth century, there was not much change with regard to building tools or sources of power. Hand implements and beasts of burden remained as important to the colonist as to the ancient Egyptian. Then came the Industrial Revolution—a revolution that would change ways of life more in the next 200 years than they had changed in the previous 4,500.

The Industrial Revolution

The Industrial Revolution consisted of several basic developments: in industry there were shifts from simple tools to complex machines; from natural sources of power, such as draft animals and falling water, to artificial sources, such as the steam engine and the electric motor; from regional to nationwide distribution of products. Jobs became more specialized, so that many workers concentrated on particular, narrow tasks rather than on creating an entire product. In addition, new inventions made transportation and communication faster and more efficient.

The Industrial Revolution began in Great Britain. Between 1730 and 1800, new mechanical methods of spinning and weaving cotton cloth transformed Britain's clothing industry. These machines operated so efficiently that cotton cloth, formerly a luxury, became the cheapest **textile,** or woven fabric, in the world.

Initially, manufacturing was a British monopoly; many of the machines that characterized the Industrial Revolution were developed by British inventors. Furthermore, British laws forbade the export of this machinery, as well as the **emigration**—the leaving of one's country permanently for another country—of skilled workers. Many Americans believed it was time to start producing their own goods. As Thomas Jefferson wrote in 1816:

...to be independent for the comforts of life we must fabricate them ourselves.... [S]hall we make our own comforts or go without them at the will of a foreign nation?

The new technology finally reached America in 1789 with the arrival of Samuel Slater. While a young man in Britain, Slater apprenticed in a textile factory, where he memorized every detail of the finest textile machinery. Soon after arriving on American soil, he formed a partnership with two other men in Providence, Rhode Island, and began to duplicate British textile machinery from memory. In 1790 America's first textile mill, built on the banks of the Seekonk River, opened its doors for business under the name of Almy, Brown, and Slater. The Industrial Revolution had come to America.

The embargo against England in 1812 had given the cotton-textile industry a chance to develop in the United States. This industry, which soon became more prosperous than the North's lucrative trade, was centered in New England for a number of reasons. The region boasted many swift-flowing streams, an abundant source of water power. New England's shippers were seeking additional enterprises in which to invest their profits. And, after the 1820s, European immigration to the region provided a large labor force. By 1840, 800 cotton mills and 500 woolen mills in New England employed nearly 50,000 workers. In addition, shipping continued to thrive in the region, and there also were many small factories turning out such products as shoes, clocks, carriages, and paper.

Manufacturing also took hold in the Middle Atlantic states—Pennsylvania, New Jersey, and New York. Although there were textile mills in this region, too, the area was better known for its coal and iron ore resources. Improved roads and expansion of the nation's railway systems opened western markets, and increased the demand for machinery. It was discovered that coal could be used in the manufacture of iron, which was used to make machines. The coal fields of Pennsylvania quickly turned the area into a great center for the iron industry and for the manufacture of machinery. Pittsburgh, located near plentiful deposits of coal and iron ore, became a great center of these industries.

Early Effects

The Industrial Revolution transformed the Northeast from a region where families lived and worked together at farming, crafts, and home-based businesses to one in which people lived mostly in cities and earned their livings by working for others in industry. Factories that required a large

Linking Across Time

THE TEXTILE INDUSTRY

As was the case in the 1810s and 1820s, the United States continues to import more textiles than it manufactures. Great Britain, however, has been replaced as the major supplier. Imported textiles today come primarily from the Pacific Rim countries, which include Singapore, Malaysia, the Philippines, Indonesia, Taiwan, and South Korea. This region, like New England in the early decades of the nineteenth century, has an abundance of cheap labor.

Examining Illustrations
Technology from the Industrial Revolution was used by Samuel Slater in a mill he built at Pawtucket, Rhode Island, in 1790. How was this textile mill powered?

**Examining
Illustrations**
*As the Industrial Revo-
lution spread, factories
sprang up in many New
England towns. What
types of products did
these factories pro-
duce?*

**Examining
Fine Art**
*The serenity of rural
farming life made a
striking contrast with
the hustle of the
expanding factory sys-
tem in New England
and the Northeast. Why
did young people leave
the farm?*

labor force and nearby sources of power sprang up in existing cities, such as New York and Philadelphia. Such new cities as Lowell and Lawrence in Massachusetts were built along the falls and rapids of New England's rivers. As the cities grew, so did the demand for better transportation to carry raw materials to the factories and finished products to markets. Improved transportation brought food into the cities to feed the thousands of factory workers.

Industrialization created two new classes of people—the industrial capitalists who built and owned the factories, and the industrial laborers who worked in them. These new owners and workers performed distinctly different functions. The differences even extended to their dress, and these differences became symbols that are still understood today: in political cartoons, a top hat and frock coat designate a capitalist; a cap and overalls, a factory worker.

Much of the profit from the Northeast's manufacturing and shipping went back into business, but a great deal of money was also invested all over the country. Banks loaned money to speculators in the West, to companies building Mississippi River steamboats, and to Alabama cotton producers. Thus, even though the regions of the nation developed in different ways, the whole country began to be tied together by a web of credit.

The Labor Movement

Although industrialization eventually raised the standard of living of many people by creating cheaper and more abundant goods, its immediate result was to create several new difficulties for workers.

As machines replaced hand tools, jobs for skilled craftsworkers became scarcer, and many such workers were reduced to performing unskilled labor. Before industrialization, there had been enjoyment in skilled work and pride in good handicraft. But tending machines proved monotonous, and workers could take little pride in the completed product. Moreover, though craftspeople worked long hours, they could begin and end the day at the times they themselves chose. If they wanted to take a day off to go fishing or to sleep, the decision was theirs. Factory workers, by contrast, kept hours that were fixed by the employer.

Dramatic social changes occurred as a result of such industrialization. In the small-community society before the Industrial Revolution, laborers often owned their own cottages, with gardens to help supplement their earnings and help feed their families during periods of unemployment. Now big-city workers were crowded into dingy rented apartments and could not produce any of their own food. In addition, before the age of industry, owner and employee knew each other and might even have married into each other's families. After industrialization, however, owners and workers lived in different sections of town and moved in different social circles.

In an effort to improve working conditions, workers organized into labor unions. In the United States, the first labor unions were formed by skilled craftspeople, such as carpenters, shoemakers, and printers. By 1830 most of the major crafts had "trade societies" in all the major northeastern cities. The trade societies worked to improve the lives of their members by demanding higher wages, shorter hours, and the **closed shop**, a place of employment open only to union members.

In some cities, different crafts joined together to form citywide federations. In 1835 the Philadelphia trade societies called a citywide strike to force the employers to grant members a 10-hour day. In addition, city trade societies from several cities formed a National Trades Union, which claimed 300,000 members.

Unskilled factory workers were less successful in forming unions. Strikes could be easily broken by employers who simply hired recent immigrants to fill vacant factory positions. Incentive to organize was low, too, among textile workers, many of whom were young women from poor farms. To these hardworking young women, $3 a week was good pay and a 12- or 13-hour workday not unusual. Some factory owners even provided these women with educational opportunities, comfortable quarters, and chaperones.

As competition for jobs in the textile mills increased, however, conditions worsened, and some of the female workers decided to organize. This led to the first women's strike, which occurred in 1824 among the weavers of Pawtucket, Rhode Island. In 1833 a union for women factory workers appeared in Lynn, Massachusetts, followed shortly by a "Factory Girls' Association," designed to include all female workers.

Examining Fine Art *Winslow Homer's painting* Morning Bell *depicts young women, carrying their lunches, going off to work in a New England textile mill. About how many hours per day did laborers such as these young women work?*

Often these early labor unions were ineffective. As Harriet Hanson Robinson wrote of an 1836 textile strike in Lowell, where she had worked as a child:

It is hardly necessary to say that so far as results were concerned this strike did no good....[T]hough the authorities did not accede to their demands, the majority returned to their work, and the corporation went on cutting down the wages.

ELIZABETH ANN SETON
1774-1821

Elizabeth Ann Seton was 31 years old when she converted from the Episcopal Church to Roman Catholicism. Newly widowed with five young children, she drew strength from her new faith and determined that her children would receive a Catholic education.

Elizabeth Ann opened a free Catholic elementary school—the first in the nation—in Baltimore, Maryland, in 1809. Not only did she provide the children of newly arrived immigrants with schooling but she also fed them lunch! She later founded the American Sisters of Charity, guided the Sisters into aiding the sick, founding orphanages, and bringing new converts to the Roman Catholic faith. In 1975, "Mother Seton" became the first native-born American to be declared a Roman Catholic saint.

Nonetheless, such unions represented the first attempts at large-scale organizations of women workers in the United States.

Demands of Labor

The unions stood behind many of the demands for reform that characterized this period. No groups were more interested in the founding of public schools than the trade societies, whose members wanted to eliminate competition from children in the labor market. Unions also led the movement to abolish imprisonment for being unable to pay one's debts. In the 1830s, this was a critical issue. An estimated 75,000 people were thrown into jail for unpaid debts each year, often for trifling amounts. Another labor demand was for **mechanics' lien** (leen) laws, which would require that the wages owed to workers be the first payments a bankrupt employer would have to make.

In order to obtain their goals, laborers began to enter politics. In 1829 the Workingmen's party put up candidates for local offices in New York City and won a surprising 6,000 out of 20,000 votes. This party and others like it did not last long, for they were torn apart by infighting between radicals and moderates and between representatives of different unions. Professional politicians lured many workers into the major parties by including some of labor's demands in their platforms. The Democrats were especially successful in encouraging workers to support Andrew Jackson. In 1840 Martin van Buren revealed his debt to the labor vote by establishing a 10-hour day for federal government workers.

The early trade societies faced severe legal difficulties. In 1806 a Pennsylvania court ruled against a strike by Philadelphia's shoemakers' union—the Federal Society of Journeymen Cordwainers— stating that workers organizing to force employers to raise wages constituted criminal conspiracy and was punishable by fines or imprisonment. This ruling became a precedent followed in other states. In 1835 employers successfully prosecuted another group of shoemakers, this time in Geneva, New York. In finding the workers guilty of conspiracy because their trade society demanded that they be paid at least $1 to make a pair of shoes, the court said:

Competition is the life of trade.
If the defendants cannot make coarse boots
for less than one dollar per pair,
let them refuse to do so:
but let them not directly or indirectly
undertake to say that others
shall not do the same work
for less price.

The legal right of trade societies to carry on collective action against employers was finally recognized in 1842 in the case of *Commonwealth v. Hunt*. The Massachusetts Supreme Court held that an attempt by a trade society to improve the lot of its members through organized pressure, such as a strike or a boycott, might be legal if the methods employed were peaceful. This rather cautious tolerance of trade societies had force only in Massachusetts, however, and employers were still able to use the courts to break many strikes.

In any event, the decision came too late to help most of the early unions. The Panic of 1837 had already caused their collapse. Unemployment was so widespread that in order to avoid starvation, workers accepted whatever wages were offered. It would be nearly a generation before labor again tried to organize on a large scale.

The labor movement of the Jacksonian period did secure some permanent gains, however. Labor influence was a major force in promoting public schools and in making it easier for settlers to acquire public lands. Several states passed laws limiting the workday to 10 hours. Many states passed mechanics' lien laws, and imprisonment for debt was almost universally abandoned.

★ ★ ★ ★ ★ ★ ★ ★ ★ ★ ★ ★ ★ ★ ★ ★ ★ ★

Section One Review

★ ★ ★ ★ ★ ★ ★ ★ ★ ★ ★ ★ ★ ★ ★ ★ ★ ★

SUMMARY

The Industrial Revolution began in America as new technology replaced craftspeople. With its many rivers and power mills, New England became the leader of the textile industry. Because of its coal resources, the Middle Atlantic states became a center for the iron industry. Improved transportation systems moved necessities and manufactured goods. Industrialization led to workers experiencing long hours and low wages. In response, workers began to form trade unions, but their efforts were only modestly successful.

CHECKING FOR UNDERSTANDING

1. **Identify** Samuel Slater, National Trades Union, Factory Girls' Association, *Commonwealth v. Hunt*

2. **Define** emigration, closed shop, mechanics' lien laws

3. **Describe** the effects of the Industrial Revolution on the economy and lifestyles of the Northeast.

4. **Explain** the conditions that led workers to form trade societies.

5. **List** two or more factors that limited the success of worker organizations during this period.

THINKING CRITICALLY

6. **Analyzing Viewpoints** United States law prohibits "industrial espionage," or theft of technology between firms, and the export of certain technologies to foreign countries. Give your opinion of such laws and of Samuel Slater's conduct.

CONNECTIONS:
HISTORY AND GEOGRAPHY

7. **Recognizing Relationships** What geographic features favored industrial growth in the Northeast over the other regions?

★ ★ ★ ★ ★ ★ ★ ★ ★ ★ ★ ★ ★ ★ ★ ★ ★ ★

Changes in the South and West

SETTING THE SCENE

First settlers [in the West]—a mixed set of hunters and farmers. They possess more property and comforts than the [hunters]; yet they are a half barbarous race. They follow open land, selling out when the Country begins to be well settled....

—ELIAS P. FORDHAM
British traveler in his journal, 1818

Section Focus

During this time of industry, ingenuity, and migration, the people of the nation quickly adapted to the changing times. They altered production methods to take advantage of new technology. They also redefined the westward-moving frontier. In doing so these people influenced the shape of American life and society for years to come.

Objectives

After studying this section, you should be able to:
- Explain how industrialization contributed to wider acceptance of slavery in southern states.
- Describe the importance of cotton to the South.
- Identify reasons for the rapid growth experienced by the Northwest.

The effects of the Industrial Revolution were felt in the South even earlier than they were felt in the Northeast. As British cotton mills produced cheaper goods for a worldwide market, they demanded more and more raw cotton. Much of this cotton came from the southern states. To produce more cotton, southern planters needed a technological advancement.

Plantation Slavery

Before the Industrial Revolution, some southern planters profited greatly from their use of enslaved people—especially owners of large rice fields and tobacco plantations. Most other planters, however, made little profit from slave labor. Keeping slaves fed and clothed was costly. To prevent slaves from attempting to run away from the cruel and harsh working conditions, slaveowners had to supervise their work force continually.

With Eli Whitney's cotton gin in 1793, however, slave labor was made profitable throughout the South. Because of the cotton gin, it was now possible to process cotton quickly, cheaply, and efficiently, thus significantly increasing production. Cotton fibers, which had to be painstakingly removed by hand from the seeds after it was picked, could be cleaned by Whitney's machine instead. Now, rather than cleaning 1 pound of cotton per day, a slave could clean 50. If the cotton gin was operated with water power, this total was increased to 1,000 pounds a day.

British demand for cotton, as well as the increased production made possible by the cotton gin, changed southern attitudes toward slavery. Cotton production proved to be ideally suited to the use of slave labor. The planting, hoeing, picking, and ginning all required manual labor, and slaves provided a fairly cheap source. Furthermore, most of the field work was done in groups and could thus be easily supervised. Because the growing and harvesting of cotton continued throughout much of the year in the deep South,

Examining Illustrations *The invention of the cotton gin made cotton the most important southern agricultural product. Bountiful cotton harvests, particularly in the newer growing regions of Alabama and Mississippi, were the basis of the South's increasing prosperity. The cultivation of cotton, however, required intensive hand labor. What tasks in cotton production did slaves perform?*

enslaved people did not have to be supported through long periods of idleness. Thus, slave labor suddenly became profitable for cotton growers.

More and more southerners began to think of slavery as a "positive good." Biblical arguments were used to suggest that slavery was a natural institution, ordained by God. Criticism of this "peculiar institution" virtually died out in slave states. Between the invention of the cotton gin and the beginning of the Civil War, the number of enslaved persons in the United States more than quintupled, even though slaves could not be legally imported after 1808, when the slave trade was ended.

Cotton Is King

Cotton first became a major crop in South Carolina and Georgia, but its production quickly spread throughout the South. Cotton, however, was not the only important southern crop. The climate of the upper South was unsuited to cotton-growing. In Virginia, Kentucky, and North Carolina, tobacco was a more

successful crop, and Louisiana produced sugar. And throughout the South, farmers raised corn, wheat, hogs, and cattle.

Still "Cotton is king" was a common southern phrase that accurately reflected the importance of cotton to the South's economy. Because the South had few factories, cotton continued to be sent out of the region for manufacture. Cotton was the greatest export, not only of the South but of the nation.

Examining Engravings
Eli Whitney's 1793 cotton gin was a remarkably simple machine. A revolving cylinder studded with wire hooks tore the cotton lint from the seed. How did this machine improve cotton production?

Connections

HISTORY AND MUSIC

SONGS OF SLAVERY

Slaves used music to help endure long hours of forced labor and to relax when they were released from chores. Although masters forbade slaves to play horns or drums, for fear that they could be used to send messages about planned rebellions, they were permitted to sing.

Slaves resting after the long day's work

The repertoire of slave songs was much more extensive than the slaveowners knew. It was not uncommon for slaves to sneak out of their quarters at night for secret meetings. In these secret gatherings, slaves poked fun at their masters by telling folk tales and with songs such as "… They Give Us The Husk."

THEY GIVE US THE HUSK

We raise the wheat,
They give us the corn;
We bake the bread,
They give us the crust;
We sift the meal,
They give us the husk;
We peel the meat,
They give us the skin;
And that's the way,
They take us in.

The profound influence of cotton on the South was reflected in the class structure of southern society. The institution of slavery, which had been abolished in the North, led to the formation of a rigid system of social classes in the South. At the top were a few wealthy planters, who enslaved 50 to 200 or more people and cultivated the best land. Below these rich owners was a larger class of less wealthy planters who owned medium-sized farms and usually had fewer than 20 slaves. Then there were the owners of small farms, who made up a large majority of southern farmers and owned either a few slaves or none at all. They raised crops and meat for their own needs and some cash crops, such as cotton or sugar.

Near the bottom of the social scale was a class of impoverished white people, about 1 percent of the white population. They were usually illiterate and did not have regular employment, obtaining food by hunting, raising a few hogs or cows, and farming the exhausted soils for which cotton growers had no use. Seen as lowest on this cotton-created scale were the blacks. All but a few were enslaved, and nearly all performed heavy labor or menial tasks.

To keep up with the demand for raw cotton, cotton plantations sprang up to the west, in the fertile "black belt" (so-called for its rich, black soil) of Mississippi and Alabama, and in the rich bottom lands along the Mississippi River and its tributaries. This westward movement of the cotton crop contributed to the population growth that led to statehood for Mississippi in 1817, for Alabama in 1819, and for Arkansas in 1836.

The rapid movement of cotton production was not merely the result of the increased demands of British mills, however. It also came from the movement of plantation owners, who depleted the soil by planting one cotton crop after another in the same location. When the fertility of the soil was exhausted, they had to move on. It was cheaper to migrate than to restore fertility to the earth.

Many southerners, including Thomas Jefferson, George Washington, and Patrick Henry, publicly condemned slavery. In 1787 many southerners even supported passage of the Northwest Ordinance, which prohibited slavery north of the Ohio River. This same group advocated the abolition of the slave trade at the earliest date allowed by the Constitution.

Few southern planters were as enthusiastic about freeing their slaves. Many southerners feared that if too many blacks were freed in the South, it would create new social and cultural problems for southern society. And the majority, as well, did not believe that freed blacks should have equality with whites. In response to these concerns, in 1817 slaveowners in Virginia, Maryland, and Kentucky formed the American Colonization Society, whose purpose was to plant colonies of freed slaves back in Africa, the home of the slaves' ancestors.

Members of the society encouraged blacks already living as free men and women to emigrate. In 1819 Congress appropriated $100,000 to support the project, and in 1822 the society founded the republic of Liberia—"land of freedom"—on the west coast of Africa as a haven for American ex-slaves. But the society lacked funds to relocate more than a few thousand people. More important, most blacks felt that America, not Africa, was their home. One group wrote:

This is our home, and this is our country.
Beneath its sod lies the bones of our fathers:
for it, some of them fought,
bled, and died.
Here we were born,
and here we will die.

By 1860 the group had relocated about 12,000 African Americans to Africa.

Examining Illustrations
The journey across the mountains into the Ohio Valley on roads such as the Wilderness Trail was difficult and often took several weeks. What draft animals were used to pull carts and wagons?

Settlement of the Northwest

Like the expanding South, the Northwest Territory also experienced tremendous growth as pioneers poured over the Appalachian Mountains into the region, clearing and settling the land, readying it for a future as part of the United States. "All America is moving westward," wrote a British traveler who passed through Pittsburgh in 1816. The census of 1820 revealed that one-fourth of the population of the United States lived west of the Appalachians.

Examining Illustrations *Northwest cities such as Detroit, Chicago, and Milwaukee (shown below) began as forts or trading posts. Why did these outposts develop into major cities?*

Life of the Times

MOVING WEST

Rich, virgin soil and cheap land drew American farmers to the Northwest like a magnet. Between 1800 and 1840, thousands upon thousands of settlers poured into the region. They came from all sections of the United States—cotton planters from the upland South, cattle and sheep farmers from New England, grain farmers from Virginia. All were looking for new economic opportunities.

Conestoga wagons, developed by Pennsylvania's German Americans during the colonial era, typically carried all the family's possessions on their journey west. These sturdy wagons, pulled by yoked oxen, had canvas tops.

Once the pioneers had arrived at their destinations, their survival depended upon becoming proficient with the long-handled axe and rifle. With the axe the farmer not only cleared trees from the land, but fashioned the wood from those trees into cabins and crude furniture.

A good rifle was essential equipment for people moving West. It was used for defense from enemies—human and otherwise—and for providing game for food. Until the 1840s, the weapon most settlers chose was the "Kentucky Rifle." With its long barrel, small bore, and accurate sights, a skilled pioneer could split a sapling at over 200 yards.

Because of the hostilities between settlers and Indians, settlement of the Northwest had been tentative until the end of the War of 1812. But that war resulted in the breakup of Tecumseh's Indian league and put an end to British support of the northern nations. After the defeat of the Sauk (sawk) chief Black Hawk in 1832, the Indians were driven west of the Mississippi.

Perhaps the greatest lure of the Northwest was vast, rich, unsettled land. According to the English economist and novelist Harriet Martineau, who made an extended tour of the United States from 1834 to 1836:

The possession of land is the aim of all actions, generally speaking, and a cure for all social evils, among men in the United States. If a man is disappointed in politics or love, he goes and buys land....If a citizen's neighbours rise above him in the towns, he betakes himself where he can be a monarch of all he surveys.

Available land was cheap. Many settlers "squatted" on whatever unoccupied acres they could find.

Examining Photographs *Cincinnati, the "Queen City of the West," had become a major transportation and manufacturing center by the 1840s. In this early photograph, what type of riverboats are at the docks?*

Settlers poured into the Northwest. From the South came independent farmers and impoverished whites anxious to get away from slavery and the plantation system. From the Northeast came farmers lured by tales of the almost unbelievable fertility of western lands. Eventually, Europe supplied a third stream of immigrants, often arriving in New York or Philadelphia and traveling west by the Erie Canal or the Ohio River to the nation's frontier.

Growth of Towns

Farmers alone did not develop the West. They needed sawmills for lumber and flour mills for grain; barges and wagons to carry produce to market; merchants to buy it; and storekeepers to provide the goods they could not make themselves. These suppliers gathered in towns where cargo was transferred, such as Cincinnati (where three tributaries flow into the Ohio River), Louisville (at the falls of the Ohio River), and Nashville (at the head of steamship navigation on the Cumberland River).

Thus, manufacturing began to develop in these cities. The largest manufacturing center in the West, however, was Pittsburgh. Located at the site where the Allegheny and Monongahela rivers flow into the Ohio River, Pittsburgh had access to the area's mineral resources. Here were glass factories, which in 1815 produced glassware worth $235,000. The whole region benefited from Pittsburgh's iron works.

In western towns, people could often make more money in manufacturing than they could on the farms. Such skilled workers as masons and wheelwrights were so scarce that they demanded and received high wages. Manufacturers could charge high prices because of the increasing demand for their articles and because of the cost of transporting products across or around the Appalachians. Western towns offered such prospects of wealth that selling lots in future cities of the West became a standard way for speculators to take money from investors.

Section Two Review

SUMMARY

Slavery became profitable after the Industrial Revolution increased demand for cotton and the cotton gin made large-scale production of cotton possible. As cotton became the South's greatest export, it led to a class system of large, slaveholding planters, small farmers, poor whites, and African Americans. Meanwhile, settlers were attracted to the Northwest: farmers by abundant fertile land, businesses and workers by demand for goods and services, and manufacturers by high prices. Midwest cities and towns became centers where cargo was transferred before moving to the Northwest.

CHECKING FOR UNDERSTANDING

1. **Identify** Eli Whitney, Northwest Ordinance, American Colonization Society, Liberia

2. **Analyze** the effects of the Industrial Revolution on attitudes toward slavery in the South.

3. **Explain** the importance of cotton to the South and its effect on the region's way of life.

4. **Summarize** the reasons for the rapid growth of the Northwest and western cities.

THINKING CRITICALLY

5. **Examining Causes**   In what way did the Industrial Revolution and the growth of the plantation system encourage southerners to move to and settle in the Northwest?

CONNECTIONS:
HISTORY AND TECHNOLOGY

6. **Predicting Effects**   Based on the information in this section, do you believe that slavery in the South would have died out on its own without the inventions of the Industrial Revolution? Why or why not?

Linking Across Time

SLAVERY IN WORLD HISTORY

Evidence of slavery is found in the Hebrew scriptures and in ancient Greek and Roman writings. Only in the last two hundred years has humanity shown a fundamental revulsion toward the practice. Systems of forced labor may be practiced secretly in a few areas.

Historically, slavery has taken two principal forms. Ownership of one person by another as personal property is known as chattel slavery. In another form, serfdom, people are tied to the land. Although not owned by others, serfs have no legal right to change occupations, their places of residence, or employers.

Slaves or serfs could be of the same race as their masters or of a different race. Greeks, Romans, and medieval lords principally practiced the enslavement of people of their own race. Later, the ownership of people of another race—mainly blacks—became the rule in the Americas, where slavery was practiced to an extent undreamed of in the ancient world.

Many slave practices in the ancient world resulted from constant warfare. Captives taken in battle were put to work building cities, tilling fields, and erecting monuments to conquerors. Babylonians and Hittites had well-established laws dealing with slavery as early as 1750 B.C. One of the best-known stories of slavery and eventual freedom in the Mid-dle East concerns the ancient Israelites, who were held as captives in Egypt.

Iron casting from Benin showing slaves in western clothes

Greece's golden age was underpinned by slave labor. Captives were plentiful due to constant wars; Athens at its height was said to have more than 55,000 slaves and 155,000 citizens. Philosophers such as Socrates, Plato, and Aristotle could devote themselves to the pursuit of knowledge because the work of ordinary living was done by slaves. Roman civilization was also built on slavery. About one-third the population of the early Roman Empire consisted of slaves, but in Rome the practice took on a cruel twist. Gladiators were enslaved warriors who were forced to butcher one another for the amusement of the public.

The modern English word *slave* comes from medieval European slave practices. So many Slavic peoples were forced into servitude by Germans that the word "slav" came to stand for a person in bondage. Serfdom developed in western and eastern Europe in order to allow free men to fight in battle. Small landowners who could not afford the equipment required for war sought the protection of stronger neighbors and eventually became their servants.

Following the voyages of Columbus to the Americas, Spanish adventurers enslaved native Americans. By the 1520s European traders had brought thousands of slaves from western Africa to the Caribbean. Soon black slaves were supplying the labor force needed to develop lands in all the Americas. Not until the United States Civil War was the evil practice outlawed in this country.

★ ★ ★ ★ ★ ★ ★ ★ ★ ★ ★

MAKING CONNECTIONS

1. How is serfdom different from chattel slavery?

2. Why do you think Europeans enslaved people of other races?

ANALYZING IDEAS

3. How might American society be different if Europeans rather than blacks had been enslaved in the United States?

★ ★ ★ ★ ★ ★ ★ ★ ★ ★ ★

Sectional Rivalry and Compromise

ETTING THE SCENE

This momentous question [Missouri's joining the Union as a slave state], like a fireball in the night, awakened and filled me with terror. I consider it at once as the knell of the Union.

—THOMAS JEFFERSON
Letter to John Holmes, April 27, 1820

Section Focus

The issue of the expansion of slavery, which caused Thomas Jefferson such grave concern, was only one issue that threatened the nation's unity. Despite these issues, leaders of the United States struggled to cooperate, and the term "compromise" became part of the national vocabulary.

Objectives

After studying this section, you should be able to:
• Identify four areas of sectional conflict.
• Explain how the Missouri Compromise temporarily maintained a balance between slave states and free states.
• Explain how John Quincy Adams won the 1824 presidential election.

Given the physical differences between the regions of the United States—the harsh and unforgiving land of the Northeast, the warm, fertile southern region, and the forests and mountains of the West—it is not surprising that Americans in these regions had different concerns and reacted differently to important issues. How to apportion public lands, how to protect American products, how to improve life in the United States, and what to do about slavery were questions whose resolutions would affect each region differently. Solutions to these problems would have to be reached by compromise.

Points of Conflict

Politicians were those who assumed the task of finding compromises to smooth over the sectional differences that threatened the Union. One of the issues they tackled was public land policy. Should land be offered to settlers at a low price or a high one? Should land be opened for settlement rapidly or slowly? Should squatters, who occupied lands before they were opened for sale, have any rights to the lands they farmed?

Each region of the nation had different answers to these questions. Western frontier farmers naturally favored cheap land, rapid settlement, and "squatters' rights." Eastern manufacturers were opposed to such policies for fear the West would draw off their labor supply. Eastern farmers were convinced that cheap western lands would result in unfair competition. Southerners were divided on this issue. Plantation owners wanted lands opened for sale but were opposed to "squatters' rights," because the squatters might claim the best lands first.

Another caustic issue was a protective tariff. Should there be high tariffs to protect United States industries? Or should tariffs be kept low, to allow foreign goods to come into the country cheaply? Northeastern manufacturers and laborers naturally favored protective tariffs to ensure that American factories could compete successfully with foreign manufacturers. As southerners came to realize that their region would not become a manufacturing center, they became more and more opposed to the system of protection. High tariffs caused them to pay more for manufactured goods.

Surprisingly, the Northwest, a farming region, was the section most completely in favor of protection. This was because they thought that the growth of industrial cities would increase the market for farm products. In addition, westerners believed that protection might encourage manufacturing west of the Appalachians; revenue from the tariffs could then be used for building much-needed roads and canals.

Money was at the core of arguments over internal improvements. Should the federal government spend money to build roads and canals, or at least help states and private companies to build them? The West was overwhelmingly in favor of using federal money for such purposes because it needed roads and canals to get its goods to market. The South, with a fine river system for transportation, was opposed. The Northeast generally favored internal improvements at federal expense, partly because tariffs would be required to pay for them.

Among all the issues, the extension of slavery into territories seemed to raise the most feverish emotion. Should the territories be closed to slavery, following the precedent set in the Northwest Ordinance? Because cotton production demanded the movement of plantations onto new lands and the plantation system depended on slave labor, southerners insisted that they be allowed to take their slaves with them anywhere but into the free states. In the northern and western states, which were not economically dependent on the slave system, there was an increasing conviction that slavery was a moral wrong. While conceding that southern states had a right to maintain slavery where it already existed, northerners protested it should not be allowed to be extended to the territories. To southerners, this meant that no new slave states

could be formed, and the political power of the South would decrease.

These conflicting sectional interests loomed as major problems the national government had yet to address.

The Missouri Compromise

The question of the expansion of slavery became politically controversial in 1819 when Missouri applied for admission to the Union as a slave state. As soon as the bill reached the floor of Congress, Representative James Tallmadge of New York proposed an amendment that would gradually abolish slavery in Missouri and forbid future importation of slaves into the state. His amendment stated, in part:

...That the further introduction of slavery or involuntary servitude be prohibited...and that all children of slaves, born within the said state... shall be free....

The impact of the Tallmadge Amendment, if passed, was immediately apparent. Slavery would gradually be ended in an area where it already existed. The amendment, which passed the House on a strictly sectional vote, caused a violent outcry from southerners. The amendment, and with it the question of Missouri's admission to the Union, was held up for more than a year, while debates in Congress grew increasingly bitter.

A new twist to the debate was introduced when Maine petitioned to be separated from Massachusetts and admitted to the Union as a free state. At this time there were 11 free and 11 slave states. Thus, slave and nonslave states were evenly represented in the Senate, although the North's population gave it a majority in the House of Representatives. If Missouri alone were admitted, the slave states would enjoy an important advantage in the Senate. However, if Maine were admitted as a free state at the same time, the balance in the Senate would continue unchanged.

Finally a compromise was reached. Missouri and Maine were admitted to the Union together. In the still unsettled portions of the Louisiana Purchase, slavery would be forbidden north of the parallel 36° 30′, a line running west from the southern boundary of Missouri.

This solution gave southerners their immediate goal—the admission of Missouri as a slave state. But the area closed to the future expansion of slavery was far greater than the area potentially open to slaveowners. The South allowed the North this advantage partly because of a widely held belief that the prairie region west of the Mississippi River was unfit for human settlement. Misinformation fueled this myth. Explorer Zebulon Pike described the area as an arid desert. Army officer Stephen H. Long considered the area between the Missouri River and

THE MISSOURI COMPROMISE, 1820

Legend:
- Free states
- Free territories
- Slave states
- Slave territories
- Non-United States territory

Examing Photographs *Early in his political career John C. Calhoun of South Carolina was a nationalist. As sectional tensions grew he increasingly spoke for the South. What was his role in the election of 1824?*

the Rocky Mountains as unsuitable for farming and uninhabitable. When southerners realized that this region was not "a great American desert," they began to demand changes in the provisions of the Missouri Compromise.

The Election of 1824

In 1824 there was only one national political party, the Jeffersonian Republicans. Yet the lack of opposing parties did not mean that the nation was politically unified. The struggle for the presidency took place not between parties but between sectional interests and personalities. As a result, the Republican party broke apart.

The four candidates who ran for president in 1824 were **favorite sons,** that is, candidates supported by the political leaders from their own state and region. Two of the candidates, Henry Clay of Kentucky and Andrew Jackson of Tennessee, were from the West. John Quincy Adams of Massachusetts received his strongest support from New England, while

Examining Maps *The Missouri Compromise was an attempt to resolve the question of slavery in the western territories. What boundary did the 36° 30′ parallel line form and how far westward did this line extend?*

William Crawford of Georgia represented the South. John C. Calhoun of South Carolina withdrew from the race early and ran for the vice-presidency, which he easily won.

Political infighting among the supporters of each candidate was fierce, although the public seemed to take little interest. Only one-fourth of the electorate bothered to vote. When the results were tallied, Jackson received a plurality of the popular vote but he did not have a majority in the electoral college. Here he led with 99 votes, followed by Adams with 84. Crawford and Clay were far in the rear with 41 and 37 respectively.

In such situations, the Twelfth Amendment to the Constitution provides that the President is to be chosen by the House of Representatives, each state having one vote. The state delegations are to select the President from the three candidates who received the highest number of electoral votes.

Clay was eliminated because he had placed fourth. Crawford was President Monroe's choice, the official candidate of the Republican caucus, and he was popular with many congressional leaders. A severe illness following the general election, however, took him out of the running. The choice was between Jackson and Adams. As Speaker of the House, Clay was in a position to swing the election either way, and he had his own political future to consider. Not wanting to aid the fortunes of a rival westerner, he threw his support to Adams. Adams easily won on the first ballot, which was taken February 9, 1825. Clay was even able to convince his own Kentucky delegation—under clear instructions from the state legislature to support Jackson—to switch their vote. The tally was 13 states for Adams, against only 7 for Jackson and 4 for Crawford.

Controversy surrounding the election, however, did not end with Adams's victory. The new President named Clay his secretary of state, a position then considered to be an important stepping stone to the presidency. Jackson and his supporters were furious and thought they smelled a deal. An anonymous letter to the newspapers

Examining Political Cartoons *As this cartoon showing Adams's ship and Jackson's ship illustrates, the presidential election of 1824 was fought more over sectional interests and personalities than national issues. What sections did the major candidates represent?*

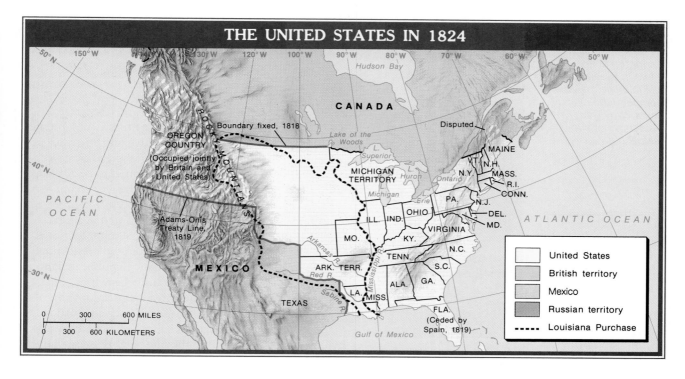

THE UNITED STATES IN 1824

	United States
	British territory
	Mexico
	Russian territory
- - - -	Louisiana Purchase

Examining Maps *The United States in 1824 was a young and vigorous country with distinct sections—the North, South, and West. Politically, the nation consisted of 24 states, the territories of Florida, Michigan, and Arkansas, and the vast unorganized northern region of the Louisiana Purchase. What international boundary was in dispute in 1824?*

charged that Clay was given the job as the result of a "corrupt bargain." The story claimed that Adams had promised to make Clay secretary of state in return for his leverage over key votes in the House of Representatives. Adams, a devoutly religious man, protested his innocence, as did Clay. But their denials failed to remove suspicion. For the next three years, critics of the Adams administration repeated the cry of "bargain and corruption" that betrayed the will of the people. Denouncing Clay as "the Judas of the West," Jackson resigned his seat in the Senate and returned home. The Tennessee legislature nominated him again for President and the election campaign of 1828 was underway.

Adams's Presidency

Perhaps no United States President has been more able than John Quincy Adams, and no American official has served the country with more dedication than he.

Yet his one failure in a long, distinguished career in public life was as President of the United States.

Jackson supporters were determined that Adams's presidency should not succeed, and throughout his administration the differences among Jeffersonian Republicans deepened. Those who supported Adams and Clay became known as National Republicans. They generally favored a strong role for federal government in funding internal improvements and other national projects. They were vigorously opposed by the Jacksonians, soon to call themselves Democrats, who favored a less powerful federal government.

In his first message to Congress, Adams set forth a program of nationalist legislation. He urged the use of federal funds not merely for roads and canals but also for a national university, exploration, and scientific research. Suggesting the building of astronomical observatories, Adams pointed out that:

Examining Photographs

This image, the first photograph of an American President while in office, reveals a somber John Quincy Adams. Why was his presidency not successful?

Linking Across Time

THE SMITHSONIAN INSTITUTION

John Quincy Adams was a lifelong supporter of the arts and education. Largely through his efforts after his presidency, Congress was persuaded to accept the bequest of James Smithson, an English scientist. Smithson left £100,000 to establish in Washington, D.C., an institution "for the increase and diffusion of knowledge."

Today the Smithsonian Institution serves the public through a zoological park, a performing arts center, several renowned museums, art galleries, and research institutes.

...scarcely a year passes over our heads without bringing some new astronomical discovery to light, which we fain receive at second hand from Europe....

But Adams's eloquence was to no avail. His opponents ridiculed his proposals. How extravagant, they said, to spend the taxpayers' money on such frills. And later, when Adams and Clay proposed to send delegates to a Pan-American Congress called by Latin American liberator Simón Bolívar, Congress delayed action until it was too late for the United States to be represented.

Adams's problems did not end when Jackson left the Senate in 1825. Although he could have strengthened his following by discharging Jackson supporters from federal jobs and filling those vacancies with people faithful to him, he refused to play politics on his own behalf. Adams's strict code of propriety also prevented him from answering opponents publicly. Thus his ambitious federal programs received little support, and his power as President was neutralized by opponents in the House. The stage was set for Adams's defeat in the presidential election of 1828.

Section Three Review

SUMMARY

Differing economic interests created sectional conflicts over four issues: public land policy, a protective tariff, internal improvements, and the spread of slavery. When Missouri petitioned to be admitted to the Union as a slave state, a major political crisis developed. In a compromise, Missouri was admitted as a slave state and Maine as a free state. Sectional interests also dominated the presidential election of 1824. Four Republican candidates, Jackson, Adams, Crawford, and Clay, split the vote along sectional lines. Because no candidate received a majority in the electoral college, the contest was thrown into the House of Representatives where Adams, with Clay's backing, was declared the winner.

CHECKING FOR UNDERSTANDING

1. **Identify** Tallmadge Amendment, Missouri Compromise, Henry Clay
2. **Define** favorite sons
3. **Describe** the sectional conflict the Missouri Compromise attempted to resolve.
4. **Explain** why Adams was accused of a "corrupt bargain" with Henry Clay.
5. **List** two reasons for Adams's failure as President to implement his ideas and policies.

THINKING CRITICALLY

6. **Predicting Outcomes** Do you think Adams would have become President had sectional conflicts not divided the country? Explain.

LINKING PAST AND PRESENT

7. **Comparing Policies** Controversy still exists over tariffs and other legislation to protect American industry from foreign competition. How do such measures affect American consumers and workers?

Study and Writing Skills

Using Reference Works in Research

A term paper has been assigned and you decide to research the presidency of John Quincy Adams. The first step is to go to the library to use reference works.

Explanation

Standard reference works are general encyclopedias, biographical dictionaries, periodical guides, books of quotations, atlases, and almanacs. These are found in the Reference section of the library. Each type of reference work provides specific kinds of information.

General encyclopedias are sets of books that contain relatively short articles on many subjects. Because encyclopedia reading levels and the amount of detail in content coverage vary, check several to see which is the most appropriate for you.

Biographical dictionaries offer condensed biographies of famous individuals. They are useful when you need more information than an encyclopedia provides, but less than a full biography or auto-biography.

Periodical guides help you find articles in magazines and newspapers. Articles are indexed by subject or by the author's last name. Under a subject heading the entry will contain the title of the article;

author name(s); and the title of the publication, date, and page number(s). Periodicals that you should become familiar with as a history student are *American History Illustrated, American Heritage,* and *Smithsonian.* Periodical guides are especially helpful when you need to have current information.

Books of quotations contain statements by individuals. Quotations may be arranged by the author's last name or by subject. Make it a habit to use quotations to support your main ideas and "add color" to your writing.

Atlases contain maps and charts, and *almanacs* contain statistics. Each also includes additional data that may give supporting evidence for your report. If the report is to contain illustrations, atlases and almanacs may provide ideas or suggestions.

Example

For your report on Adams, follow these steps:

- Check several encyclopedias to see which one has the appropriate reading level and best coverage of Adams.

- Locate and read about Adams in a biographical dictionary. Does the material add to what was in the encyclopedia?

  • Look up "Adams, John Q." in a periodical guide under "Subjects." With the assistance of a librarian, obtain the periodicals listed.

  • Locate books of quotations, and scan the index for quotes by Adams. Read them and decide if any could be used in your report.

- Check atlases and almanacs on United States history or United States Presidents for illustrations or maps pertaining to Adams's administration.

Practice

For further practice make a list of the titles of all the reference works in your school library that you could use to complete a report on Samuel Slater and the early American textile industry.

★ Chapter 10 Review ★

★ Summary

The Industrial Revolution drastically changed how Americans lived and worked. In the Northeast, independent skilled workers became industrial wage earners, living in cities. In the South, the cotton gin made slavery profitable. Farmers and merchants developed the area north and west of the Ohio River.

Sectional conflicts arose over land policy, tariffs, transportation improvements, and the extension of slavery. The Missouri Compromise temporarily kept the balance between free and slave states. In the election of 1824, however, sectional conflict split the vote. This resulted in the election of John Quincy Adams by the House of Representatives.

★ Using Vocabulary

Use each vocabulary word in a sentence about the Industrial Revolution or its effect on sectional conflict.

emigration	**closed shop**
mechanics' lien laws	**favorite sons**

★ Reviewing Facts

1. **Compare** the effects of the Industrial Revolution on different sections.
2. **Describe** the conditions that organized workers tried to change and what limited their success.
3. **List** four issues on which the sections had major differences.
4. **Identify** factors that led to the rapid development of the Northwest.
5. **Explain** why "Cotton was King" in the South.
6. **Name** the plan that temporarily resolved sectional conflict over slavery.
7. **State** why the Tallmadge Amendment angered southerners.
8. **Summarize** the events that brought Adams to the presidency.

★ Understanding Concepts

FREE ENTERPRISE

1. What were some of the abuses of the free enterprise system that factory workers experienced, and how were these abuses addressed?
2. Describe how trade unions in the 1820s and 1830s might have changed the free enterprise system.

ECONOMIC AND CULTURAL CHANGE

3. What factors caused a shift from small-scale production by independent workers to large scale production in factories owned by a few capitalists?
4. How might the shift from home-based industry to the industrial factory system eventually contribute to congested roadways, air pollution, and a shortage of energy?

★ Thinking Critically

1. **Making Comparisons** Compare the capitalist factory system and the plantation system with the class structures they created, and related human rights issues.
2. **Evaluating Choices** Imagine you are a slave and the American Colonization Society wants to buy you and send you to Liberia. List reasons for accepting or refusing their offer.
3. **Analyzing Problems** What problems would immediate freedom for slaves have presented for freed slaves and for white southerners? Propose a plan to address these problems.
4. **Linking Past and Present** What similarities do you see in the practice of clearing rain forests worldwide in the 1980s and cotton farmers who wore out the soil and then moved West?

★ Writing About History

DESCRIPTION

Refer to the description of how to write a descriptive essay in the History Writer's Handbook in the Appendix of this book. Your teacher will give you more specific instructions on the essay's length and the assignment's due date.

Imagine it is 1800. You have moved to the city to work in a factory or textile mill. Write a letter to your family on the farm, describing something they have not seen, such as a spinning frame, a factory, a tenement, or the city. For details, refer to the information and illustrations in this text, an encyclopedia, refer-

★ Chapter 10 Review ★

ence and other books on the Industrial Revolution.

★ Learning Cooperatively

Working in a group of three, research the current status of tariffs and protection of American industry from foreign competition. Have one member research the existing systems of protection, another member examine the arguments that favor or oppose tariffs, and the third member research the foreign countries that protect their industry from American competition. Agree upon a fair policy regarding tariffs. Choose a spokesperson to share your policy with other groups.

★ Mastering Skills

ANALYZING TABULAR DATA

The skill of analysis helps to answer the "hows" and "whys" of history. Analyzing involves breaking information into smaller pieces so that it can be examined more easily. Tabular data can often help you analyze information because tables summarize a large amount of information in a small space. Tabular data is presented in rows and columns that make it easy to read.

Suppose you were answering a review question that asked you to explain how or why about a topic in the chapter. If some of the information needed to answer this question is available in a table, the guidelines below should be followed:

a. Read carefully the how or why question. Assess what information you need to know.

b. Determine what kind of information is given in the table. Look first at the table's title, then read the table's headings.

c. Review the chapter content, then scan the data by row and column. Compare the data and apply what you have learned to answer the question.

Example You are asked to explain why the growth rate for industrial workers grew more rapidly than slave labor between 1800 and 1830. Note how the above guidelines have been followed.

a. Information needed for question—*(growth rates for industrial labor and slave labor between 1800 and 1830)*

b. Information in table—*(labor force growth between 1800 and 1830)*

c. Analysis required—determine the increase in slave

GROWTH OF THE LABOR FORCE (IN THOUSANDS)

Year	Free	Slave	Farm	Industrial
1800	1,370	530	1,400	1
1810	1,590	740	1,950	15
1820	2,185	950	2,470	17
1830	3,020	1,180	2,965	75

and industrial laborers from 1800 through 1830; calculate the percentage of growth for each. Compare the two growth rates and what you have learned about the development of industry and slavery during this period. Explain why the industrial labor force grew more rapidly than slave labor. *(Industrial labor grew by 750 percent; slave labor by 223 percent. Industry had natural resources, capital, and a labor supply that grew through immigration. The increase in slaves came from large cotton plantations that were expanding west. The number of slaves was limited to natural increase since importing slaves after 1808 was illegal.)*

Practice Use the following table and your understanding of Chapter 10 content to answer the two analyzing questions that follow.

ELECTION OF 1824

Candidate	Electoral Vote	Popular Vote	House Vote
Jackson	99	153,544	7
Adams	84	108,740	13
Crawford	41	46,618	4
Clay	37	47,136	—

1. How did Adams succeed in winning the presidency in 1824?
2. How could Clay receive more popular votes but fewer electoral votes than Crawford?

CHAPTER 11
Age of Jackson

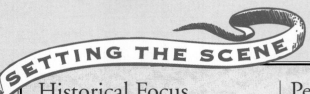

SETTING THE SCENE

Historical Focus

Andrew Jackson's victory in the election of 1828 marked the beginning of a new era. His election symbolized the growth of popular democracy, and Jackson himself became a symbol for the age. Although a westerner, he fought sectionalism by insisting upon the supremacy of federal laws over the states. He also fought economic injustice and social inequality. Jackson's political movement resulted in the formation of the Democratic party, and also an opposition party, the Whigs.

Concepts to Understand

- How **political change** in state voting laws advanced Jacksonian democracy.
- How **economic policy** shaped controversies over the tariff and national banking system.

People to Know

Daniel Webster, John C. Calhoun, Martin Van Buren, John Tyler

Places to Locate

Illinois, Oklahoma

Terms to Identify

spoils system, Trail of Tears, pocket veto, nullification, "pet banks," Specie Circular, platform

Guided Reading

As you read this chapter, seek the answers to the following questions.

1. In what ways was Andrew Jackson a symbol of his times?
2. Explain how Jackson's nationalism was shown during the nullification crisis and his war on the national bank.

SPANNING THE DECADES

POLITICAL	1825 *New parties Democratic Republicans and National Republicans emerge*	1828 *Andrew Jackson elected President*	1830 *Webster-Hayne debate in the Senate*	1832 *Nullification crisis in South Carolina*

1825   1830

CULTURAL	1827 *John Audubon begins publishing his* Birds of America *series*	1828 Cherokee Phoenix *published; first newspaper in an Indian language*	1830 *Church of Jesus Christ of Latter-day Saints (Mormons) organized in New York*	1833 New York Sun *begins publication; first popular "penny" newspaper*

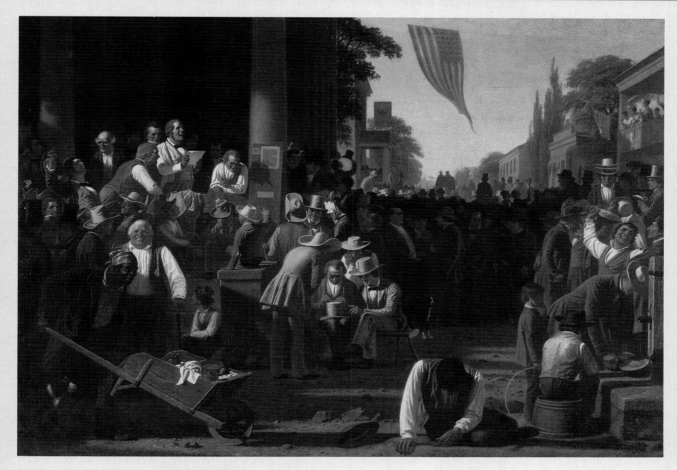

Verdict of the People by George Caleb Bingham, 1854-1855

… [E]very man is equally entitled to protection by law; but when the laws undertake to add to these natural and just advantages artificial distinctions…the humble members of society…have a right to complain of the injustice of their Government.

—ANDREW JACKSON
Veto of the Bank Recharter Bill, 1832

Growth of Democracy

SETTING THE SCENE

When a nation begins to modify the elective qualifications, it may easily be foreseen that, sooner or later, that qualification will be entirely abolished.

—ALEXIS DE TOCQUEVILLE
Democracy in America, 1835

Section Focus

Although sectional rivalries overshadowed the national spirit and proved divisive during John Quincy Adams's presidency, a powerful force was rising that would influence American politics more than sectionalism or nationalism. The spirit of democracy soon would provide a standard to assess candidates, affect the rules for elections, and significantly influence government decisions. The presidency of Andrew Jackson would give this spirit momentum and would itself be carried along by democracy's swelling tide.

Objectives

After studying this section, you should be able to:
- Describe campaign methods used by both political parties in the election of 1828.
- Summarize the life and political career of Andrew Jackson.

W ell before the presidential election of 1828, it was clear that President John Quincy Adams and challenger Andrew Jackson would be the only candidates. Without much help from the President, Adams's supporters had built a loosely organized following, primarily in the Northeast. They tended to represent established property interests and favored nationalist legislation. Jackson's supporters, on the other hand, included farmers of the South and West, skilled workers, and owners of small businesses. Like the Republican party of Jefferson's time, Jacksonians favored limiting federal power. The Adams supporters called themselves National Republicans, and the Jackson followers took the name Democratic Republicans, or simply Democrats.

The Election of 1828

The United States in the 1820s was undergoing rapid change. Conflicting sectional interests and a shifting population made political forecasts difficult. In this environment both political parties decided not to risk the presidential election of 1828 by taking a strong position on any issue. Instead, they focused on comparisons of the candidates' personal traits. The electioneering soon turned to mudslinging.

The National Republicans portrayed Jackson as a barbarian who "misspelled every fourth word," a Julius Caesar who would destroy American liberties, and a "butcher" who had murdered a score of men. The Democrats revived the "bargain and corruption" smear from the 1824 election. They went on to charge that Adams had allowed the federal civil service to become scandalously dishonest and had wasted the people's money on "gaming tables"—actually a billiard table and a chess set bought with Adams's own money for the White House. Adams's backers went so far as to accuse Jackson of adultery based on a technicality concerning his wife's divorce from a former husband years earlier. Rachel Jackson suffered terribly from this attack and died shortly after the election—a tragedy for which Andrew never forgave the slanderers.

While both parties were equally adept at misrepresentation, the Democrats found an advantage in their candidate's humble beginnings. Democratic newspapers called Andrew Jackson "the candidate of the people."

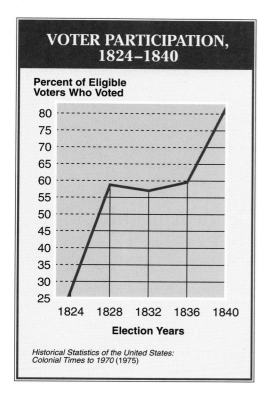

VOTER PARTICIPATION, 1824–1840

Percent of Eligible Voters Who Voted

	1824	1828	1832	1836	1840

(Election Years)

Historical Statistics of the United States: Colonial Times to 1970 (1975)

Examining Graphs *A significant rise in the number of eligible voters who actually voted in a presidential election occurred in 1828. How much did the percent increase and what accounted for it?*

The election of 1828 was a decisive victory for Jackson—178 electoral votes to 83. Adams was strong only in New England. Jackson swept nearly every southern and western state and carried Pennsylvania and New York.

Although the campaign was a national disgrace, the election was one of the most significant in American history. For the first time a candidate from the region west of the Appalachians was elected President. The rapid growth of the western states was swinging the political center of gravity away from the eastern seaboard. The results also showed the developing political split between the nation's sections.

Three times as many people voted for President in 1828 than had in 1824. This was partly because many states had lowered or eliminated property ownership as a voting qualification, and also because twice as many eligible voters participated. Many reasons have been given for the

elimination of property ownership as a qualification for voting in the early 1800s, including the ideals of the Declaration of Independence and the social equality of frontier life. In addition, as cities and towns grew, the percentage of working people who did not own property increased. These people paid taxes and had an interest in the political affairs of their communities. By the 1820s Pennsylvania, Massachusetts, and New York recognized this interest and substituted the payment of taxes for property ownership as a basis for voting rights. By 1852 the last state, Virginia, had given the franchise to all adult white males.

Andrew Jackson's victory in 1828 was partly the result of his party's appeal to the

Life of the Times

GETTING OUT THE VOTE

The election of Andrew Jackson in 1828 signaled a new era in American political life. Property-holding qualifications for voting had been gradually and quietly abolished by the states, which extended the franchise to most adult white males. With this dramatic increase in the number of voters, political party organizations and candidates soon learned to make appeals tailored for mass audiences.

Voter support hinged on candidates or party officials making contact with the electorate. In most areas of the country this meant that candidates and political parties participated in every kind of community gathering. Political rallies featuring parades, flags, speeches, and free-flowing liquor became hallmarks of electioneering.

The potential for vote fraud was everywhere. The polls might be open for several days, which made it easier for enterprising voters to cast more than one ballot. None of the states used a secret ballot. Rather, parties printed their own ballots, or "tickets" with the names of candidates. Voters going to the polls might be harassed by high-pressured ballot hawkers from rival parties into accepting their ticket.

State nominating conventions also encouraged participation in elections. Convention proceedings were reported in the local press, which aroused citizens to work for their party's choices.

Linking Across Time

"Mudslinging" Tactics

A political consultant of today has compared modern campaign ads to "mud wrestling in a pig sty." Much like the mudslinging campaign tactics of Jackson's time, in the Bush-Dukakis 1988 presidential race, a television ad paired photographs of Governor Dukakis and a convicted killer who had attacked a couple while on furlough from a Massachusetts prison. In chilling tones, the narrator blamed Dukakis because he supported his state's prison-furlough program. That and similar ads are said to have cost Dukakis the 1988 election.

new voters. Jackson's supporters believed that he represented the "common man." All former Presidents had enjoyed the advantages of inherited wealth or education or both. Jackson, orphaned at 14, had made his way entirely on his own. He became the symbol of the growing power of democracy.

Andrew Jackson was such a controversial figure that it is difficult to find the truth between the slander of his enemies and the praise of his admirers. According to James Parton, his first important biographer, the evidence could be interpreted to show Jackson as either a patriot or a traitor:

He was one of the greatest of generals and wholly ignorant of the art of war. A writer, brilliant, elegant, eloquent, without being able to compose a correct sentence or spell words of four syllables.... A democratic autocrat. An urbane savage. An atrocious saint.

Gentleman and Soldier

Born in a log cabin on the North Carolina frontier, Jackson rose to the highest

Examining Fine Art *Andrew Jackson was a courageous Indian fighter and successful general. Why would military heroism help a candidate capture the presidency?*

office—a visible evidence of the American success story. In his time Jackson became almost a mythical figure. George Bancroft, a New Englander and an ardent Democrat, wrote:

Behold, then, the unlettered man of the West, the nursling of the wilds, the farmer of the Hermitage, little versed in books, unconnected by science with the tradition of the past, raised by the will of the people to the highest pinnacle of honor, to the central post of republican freedom, to the station where all the nations of the earth would watch his actions—where his words would vibrate through the civilized world, and his spirit be the moving-star to guide the nations.

Jackson was elected Tennessee's first representative to Congress before the age of 30. In the War of 1812, he had been one of the few generals who could get ill-trained militia to stand up to the British redcoats. His most obvious trait was his force of will, a characteristic that became evident when someone tried to defy him.

Jackson's early life was notable for violent personal quarrels. He took part in five duels, once killing a man. From that encounter, a bullet lodged next to his heart remained with him for the rest of his life, surgeons believing it too dangerous to operate. As Jackson grew older, his temper and actions became milder; by the time he reached the White House, he had become a person of dignity and courtesy. A visiting English woman at his inauguration said he looked like "a gentleman and a soldier."

Entering office at age 62, Jackson was tortured by several physical agonies: headaches, digestive disorders, coughing spells, and old wounds. His wife Rachel's death before the inauguration in 1829 added bereavement and loneliness. Still, his inner toughness enabled him to perform the duties of the office with a firm and steady hand.

★ Section One Review ★

SUMMARY

The supporters of President John Quincy Adams and challenger Andrew Jackson conducted a mudslinging campaign in 1828. Jackson's victory reflected significant changes in the political landscape of America. The fact that the new President was from the West, and of frontier origins, indicated the growing political power of that section and the emerging influence of the "common man" in national politics. A newly enfranchised group of landless voters, including laborers and small business owners, contributed to Jackson's victory. Jackson's rise from humble beginnings gave hope to many Americans in similar circumstances. For the first time able to vote, they supported "the candidate of the people" on election day. The President they helped elect was decisive and combative. His strong will was his great asset and also a source of great controversy.

CHECKING FOR UNDERSTANDING

1. **Identify** National Republicans, Democratic Republicans

2. **Describe** the focus of the 1828 election.

3. **Explain** why the campaigning parties chose not to take positions on the issues.

4. **Contrast** the opinion Jackson's attackers held of him with his image in the eyes of his admirers.

THINKING CRITICALLY

5. **Analyzing Results** How might changes during the Industrial Revolution have become factors in the extension of voting privileges?

LINKING PAST AND PRESENT

6. **Comparing Campaigns** Research the campaign between George Bush and Michael Dukakis in 1988. How are the campaigns of 1828 and 1988 similar?

Interpreting Primary Sources

The Light

A self-taught artist, George Catlin (1796-1872) devoted his life to documenting the history and culture of native Americans through the art of painting. Catlin moved westward from Pennsylvania in 1830 and became the first painter to shape the national image of the proud Plains Indians. During the mid 1830s, Catlin spent several summers among various native American peoples. He saw and recorded with his brush the earthlodge villages of the Pawnees, the scalp dance of the Sioux, and the practices of Blackfoot medicine men. He was so accurate and detailed in his paintings that descendants of those he immortalized easily recognized their ancestors.

By 1840 Catlin had made almost 500 portraits and sketches. He established Catlin's Indian Gallery, a traveling exhibition of painting, costumes, and artifacts that toured major cities in Great Britain and France as well as the United States. During the 1850s Catlin traveled to South America and to the Pacific coast of North America and recorded the appearances, surroundings, and ways of life of the native Americans of these regions. Many of the thousands of paintings Catlin produced can be viewed in the Smithsonian Institution in Washington, D.C., and in the American Museum of

The Light

Natural History in New York.

Through his work, Catlin came to realize that traditional tribal life was doomed to destruction from whiskey, disease, and forcible removal from ancestral lands. His paintings record a way of life obliterated by the constant march of white expansion during the nineteenth century. They are a highly valuable primary source of information for more than 40 Indian nations.

The two-pose painting shown here is of Wi-jun-jon, or Pigeon's Egg Head—also known as The Light—the son of an Assiniboin chief that Catlin painted in 1832. The Assiniboin lived on the northern Plains and were distant relatives of the Dakota Sioux. Wi-jun-jon was part of a delegation of Plains Indians who, in 1831, traveled to Washington, D.C., where they met with President Jackson.

Catlin shows Wi-jun-jon resplendent in native American dress upon his arrival in Washington and ridiculous in a colonel's uniform (a gift from the President) on his way back to his people. The Assiniboin barely recognized Wi-jun-jon when he arrived and dismissed his stories of the life he had seen in Washington as preposterous lies. Once respected by his people, the Light lost his credibility while in the white man's land.

EXAMINING THE PRIMARY SOURCE

1. Compare the clothing, accessories, and posture of The Light in each pose.

2. Identify and explain the significance of the scenery that The Light faces in each pose.

THINKING CRITICALLY

3. What point does the artist make by showing The Light back-to-back with himself?

4. Catlin uses dress to symbolize two different ways of life. What are the potential advantages and disadvantages of The Light's adopting the clothing white Americans wear?

Jacksonian Democracy

...[T]he best government rests on the people and not on the few, on persons and not on property, on the free development of public opinion and not on authority....the people collectively are wiser than the most gifted individual....

—GEORGE BANCROFT
Nineteenth-century historian in a speech at Williamtown College, 1835

Section Focus

While Jackson's name is used to describe this period of American history, the spirit and direction of American democracy in these years had much broader sources than the character of the President. Jacksonian democracy is also defined by the political optimism of his time. It was a period of celebration for the rights of the "common man."

Objectives

After studying this section, you should be able to:
• List three important democratic changes that developed during this period.
• Describe attitudes toward native Americans and African Americans during this period.

As the time for Jackson's inauguration approached, thousands of his admirers poured into Washington. They slept five or six to a bed; when no more beds were to be had, they spent the night on sofas, billiard tables, and floors. Seized with fear, dignified Washingtonians thought of Rome, overrun by hordes of barbarians. Outgoing President John Quincy Adams left the capital rather than attend the ceremony that, in his opinion, might mean the end of the republic.

The People's Government

Some Americans thought Jackson would turn the inauguration into a grand military pageant. Instead he followed Jefferson's precedent and walked to the inaugural ceremony. His hands shook as he quietly read a cautious and colorless address. What happened later, however, seemed to justify those who had gloomily predicted that Jackson's election meant the reign of "King Mob." Following the address at the Capitol, Jackson rode on horseback to the White House, surrounded by a cheering crowd. There a reception had been prepared for invited guests and important officials only. The crowd, however, began to push inward. Chairs and china were broken. Admirers pressed around Jackson so heavily that he had to be helped to escape through a back window. Some of the crowd was influenced to leave the presidential mansion when buckets of punch were placed on the White House lawn.

During the Jackson era the American definition of democracy and popular expectations of the political system changed greatly. Americans had always believed it possible for common people to climb up the social ranks through hard work and thrift. One of their rewards might be a voice in political affairs. Now, however, politicians sought the support of ordinary voters.

Before Jackson's time, voters expected public officials to use their own best judgment. Now they came to believe that officials should act according to the demands of the people. To make government respond more directly to popular will, state and local governments began to fill some positions such as judges, constables, and public surveyors by election rather than appointment. The terms of office were also shortened so that popular opinion had a more direct effect on the actions of elected officials.

As new voters made demands on government, they learned the power of political organization. National issues became as much topics of conversation as local issues had always been. As national parties built stronger state and local ties, they began to rely upon a growing number of professional or career politicians. These changes helped to initiate the **spoils system,** the practice of appointing people to government positions on the basis of party loyalty and party service. This was not an entirely new development; George Washington had often used the support of Federalist principles as a test for appointment. But Jackson was the first to oust large numbers of government employees in order to appoint his followers to office. He based his action on the principle that there should be rotation in office—a point he emphasized in his first state of the union message:

The duties of all public officers are...so plain and simple that men of intelligence may readily qualify themselves for their performance; and I cannot but believe that more is lost by the long continuance of men in office than is generally to be gained by their experience.

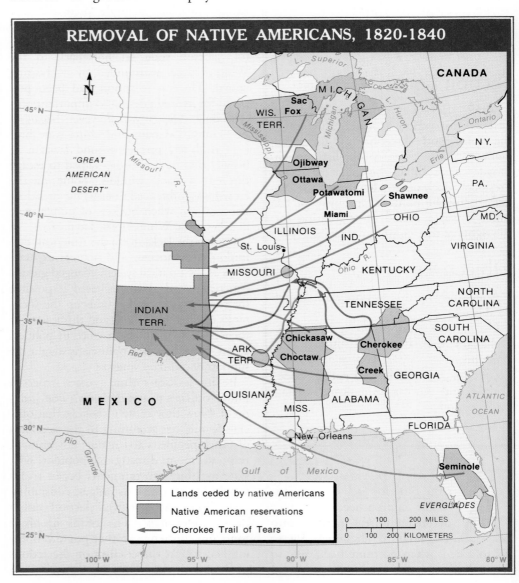

REMOVAL OF NATIVE AMERICANS, 1820-1840

Lands ceded by native Americans

Native American reservations

Cherokee Trail of Tears

Examining Maps *The federal government relocated Indian tribes living in the United States to reservations in Indian Territory. Identify the Indian tribes that were removed and compare the environments of the Indian homelands to their new homes on the Western reservations.*

Some believed that the spoils system set a poor precedent. A contemporary observer not unfriendly to Jackson noted that "office-seeking and office-getting was becoming a regular business, where impudence [boldness] triumphed over worth."

Jackson amplified presidential power by using the veto more than all previous Presidents. He was also one of the first Presidents to use the **pocket veto,** killing a bill by taking no action on it and waiting for Congress to adjourn.

Jacksonian democracy did not offer women suffrage, but women did make some gains in rights and liberties. Emma Willard, Catharine Beecher, and Mary Lyon established female academies, promoting education among women. By 1850 most white women were literate, a major change from the eighteenth century. And in the 1830s some states passed the first women's property acts, guaranteeing women the right to control property.

Native Americans and African Americans

Jacksonian democracy had nothing to offer two oppressed minorities—native Americans and African Americans. The administrations under Jackson and his successor, Martin Van Buren, pursued an Indian policy begun by Jefferson—removing these peoples to territory west of the Mississippi River. In an annual message to Congress in 1835, Jackson explained:

All preceding experiments for the improvement of the Indians have failed. It seems now to be an established fact that they cannot live in contact with a civilized community and prosper.... A country West of Missouri and Arkansas has been assigned to them, into which the white settlements are not to be pushed.

Because mapmakers had labeled the area between the Missouri River and the Rocky Mountains "The Great American Desert," most Americans believed that this land

AMERICAN PORTRAITS

SEQUOYA
1760(?)-1843

Although the son of a white trader, Sequoya was raised among his mother's Cherokee people. He never learned English, but he was fascinated by the "talking leaves" of books. He was convinced that reading and writing gave whites power. After being disabled by an accident, he dedicated himself to creating written symbols for the Cherokee language.

At first, Sequoya tried to create simple pictures to represent Cherokee words, but later he developed 86 symbols to represent all syllables in Cherokee speech. He then had his six-year-old daughter demonstrate his system of reading and writing to Cherokee leaders. Following their approval of his system, thousands of Cherokees learned how to read and write. Sequoya even published a Cherokee newspaper and translated parts of the Bible into Cherokee.

would provide a permanent Indian reservation. Jackson, and later President Van Buren, spoke of protecting the Indians from fraud and of how humane and just the government's removal policy was, but the policy as carried out was cruel.

In Georgia the Cherokee had developed a comfortable lifestyle that included schools, mills, and turnpikes. In the 1820s, under pressure from the state of Georgia to give up their lands, they wrote a constitution, hired lawyers, and sued in the Supreme Court. Chief Justice John Marshall upheld the rights of the Cherokee against the state of Georgia. However, Jackson refused to carry out the decision ordering Georgia to return Cherokee lands. "Marshall has made his opinion," he reportedly said, "now let him enforce it." When the Cherokee resisted the government's "generous" offer of lands farther west, Jackson sent in the army. Forced to move from their homes to what is now Arkansas and Oklahoma, an estimated 4,000 died of starvation, disease, or exposure on the march that the Cherokee called the "Trail of Tears."

Another tragedy took place in Illinois. The Sac and Fox people were forced to move to Iowa where the Sioux and the settlers both harassed them. In 1832 Black Hawk, the Sac and Fox leader, moved them back into Illinois to recover their old lands. When farmers in Illinois panicked, the state militia trapped and massacred Black Hawk's entire group.

By 1840 the government had moved the few native Americans still living east of the Mississippi to reservations, except for the Seminole of Florida. After years of fighting, Osceola, their chief, was captured and later died in prison. Some Seminole settled deep in the Everglades, where they remain today.

Although most citizens supported Jackson's Indian removals, a few National Republicans, like Henry Clay, said that Jackson's attitude stained the nation's honor. Missionary-minded religious denominations, especially Methodists and Quakers, denounced the harsh treatment of native Americans, but these voices were a small minority.

In the South, the cotton culture had firmly established the institution of slavery in the 1830s, and criticism of the system became increasingly unwise. Those who spoke out against slavery were highly unpopular and risked physical harm. In the North, blacks were free, but were generally second-class citizens.

The debates of the 1820s leading to the Missouri Compromise had shown the slavery issue to be so explosive that a policy called "the great silence" began, and discussion of slavery as a national issue faded. Anti-slavery literature was often barred from the mails. From 1836 to 1844 anti-slavery petitions to Congress were automatically "laid on the table"—that is, ignored. Jackson did not oppose these policies, even though he himself was a slaveowner.

SUMMARY

In several ways, Jackson's election represented a kind of revolution in American politics. Jackson did not create Jacksonian democracy, but in his time the voting rights were extended to ordinary people, and he drew his political strength from this trend. In addition, Jackson extended the power of the presidency with his "spoils system" and his use of the veto. As common people exercised increasing political power, they came to expect their officials to implement the voters' wishes, and more offices became elective. Despite the growth of democracy, women, African Americans, and native Americans did not benefit from it. The fortunes of these three groups in society remained for the most part largely in the hands of the white male majority.

CHECKING FOR UNDERSTANDING

1. **Identify** John Marshall, Black Hawk, Osceola

2. **Define** spoils system, pocket veto

3. **Summarize** the political changes that took place in the Jacksonian period.

4. **Compare** the fates of African Americans and native Americans during this era.

5. **List** the gains made by women in the Jacksonian period.

THINKING CRITICALLY

6. **Evaluating Leadership**   In what way did the Jackson administration violate the constitutional system of checks and balances?

GLOBAL PERSPECTIVES

7. **Recognizing Differences**   In the last 20 years, the Supreme Court has returned land and money to native Americans. How did the Cherokee experience of the 1820s differ from more modern trends?

★ ★ ★ ★ ★ ★ ★ ★ ★ ★ ★ ★ ★ ★ ★ ★ ★ ★

Political Controversies

I have not accustomed myself to hang over the precipice of disunion, to see whether, with my short sight, I can fathom the depth of the abyss below....

—DANIEL WEBSTER
Speech in Congress, January 27, 1830

Section Focus

Although Andrew Jackson was the people's President, the people in 1828 had diverse interests. Westerners believed that Jackson would favor internal improvements and curb the power of the Bank of the United States while inflating the currency. Southern Democrats began to oppose high tariffs and national spending on internal improvements. The northeastern wing of the party was split on the tariff issue, but strongly opposed inflationary money policies. It was a setting ripe for conflict. Debates on these issues would test Jackson's leadership even as they strained the federal system of government.

Objectives

After studying this section, you should be able to:
• Identify the various sectional interests of the nation in this period.
• Explain how the tariff and nullification issue developed into a crisis.

Both supporters and opponents were interested in President Jackson's position on such matters as internal improvements, tariffs, and banking. In his first term of office, Jackson made bold decisions on these issues—sometimes delighting, sometimes dismaying, fellow Democrats.

Jackson surprised the West with his answer to the issue of federally financed roads. Congress had passed a bill promising to pay for half the cost of extending the Cumberland Road inside the state of Kentucky. This legislation, known as the Maysville Road bill, was vetoed by Jackson. He said that the Constitution did not grant the federal government power to spend money on local transportation—the road was to be entirely inside one state. In his veto message he explained that grants of federal money:

....[H]ave always been professedly under the control of the general principle that the works which might be thus aided should be "of a general, not local, national, not state," character. A disregard of that distinction would of necessity lead to the subversion of the federal system.

The fact that the proposed extension was to be inside the home state of Henry Clay, Jackson's chief political adversary, probably influenced his strict interpretation of the Constitution.

Sectional Issues

The Northeast and the West were divided over federal land policy. Senator Samuel A. Foot of Connecticut represented eastern manufacturers who were worried about losing their labor supply. In 1830 he proposed a limit on western land sales, to discourage people from moving west. Senator Thomas Hart Benton of Missouri angrily attacked Foot for promoting the interests of the Northeast at the expense of the West. Senator Robert Y. Hayne of South Carolina supported Benton. In several days of debate, senators from both the South and the Northeast attempted to win the support of western politicians. With Vice President Calhoun of South Carolina presiding, Hayne and Daniel Webster of Massachusetts eventually engaged in a full-scale discussion of

Examining Illustrations *During the Webster-Hayne debate in the Senate, Daniel Webster argued that the Union was a national government of all people in all states, and if it passed laws that infringed on the rights of the states, the Supreme Court would declare the laws unconstitutional. What was Robert Hayne's major argument?*

Linking Across Time

TARIFFS TODAY

Like manufacturers in the early 1800s, American business firms continue to demand protective tariffs on cheaper foreign imports that hurt profits. In 1987, however, Harley-Davidson, the only motorcycle maker in the United States, requested that a 1983 tariff against Japanese motorcycles be lifted early. The tariff, which they originally requested, had so improved business, that protection was no longer needed. Frequently, however, Congress extends such tariffs for several years beyond the initial time limit.

many of the issues. When the debate turned to the question of the tariff, the resulting crisis threatened the federal Union. It also affected Calhoun's political career because many of the ideas expressed by Hayne were originally written in an essay published anonymously by the Vice President.

Webster's political career followed a course exactly opposite Calhoun's. Calhoun had been a War Hawk during the War of 1812. Webster opposed the war, even to the extent of considering **nullification,** or making null and void federal laws calling for raising troops. When Calhoun supported nationalist legislation after the war, Webster supported the Northeast. By 1830, however, the two reversed positions. To preserve his political future in South Carolina, Calhoun changed his views. South Carolina was suffering from low cotton prices and a depressed economy. Calhoun could no longer support high tariffs because the people of his home state believed that high tariffs were a cause of their local economic problems. Opposing the tariff, Calhoun became a states' rights advocate, while Webster's support for a protective tariff made him favor a strong federal government.

A man of imposing appearance—it was said no man could be as great as Webster looked—the senator from Massachusetts was also the greatest orator of his day. In a "Second Reply to Hayne," he pointed out that nullification could only mean the end of the Union. Webster said the Union was not a creature of the states: it was the people's government, forged for their own welfare and meant to endure. Thousands of copies of the speech were published. School children memorized the closing paragraph with the famous final words: "Liberty and Union, now and forever, one and inseparable!"

The antitariff forces rallied around Calhoun's ideas published anonymously in a work called *The South Carolina Exposition.* Calhoun denounced the tariff of 1828, claiming that it made the South a servant of northern industrialists. In brief, Calhoun's argument was that the federal government was created by a **compact,** or contract among the states. Each state gave up only such powers as were expressly granted in the Constitution. If the federal government passed laws that infringed on the remaining state powers, each individual state, not the Supreme Court, had the right to decide whether or not that federal law was constitutional. A state could declare the law null and void within its own borders. Behind this doctrine of nullification lurked the threat to secede from the Union.

The nullification issue moved the debate to the broad and potentially dangerous issue of the nature of the federal Union. The Tariff of 1832 would threaten the Union by pushing South Carolina to the brink of secession.

The protective tariff of 1816 was not costly enough to satisfy American manufacturers. In response to their demands, duties on imported manufactures and on some raw materials were raised twice more—in 1824 and 1828. These laws aroused increasing resentment in the South, especially in South Carolina where the cotton economy was depressed. Increased cotton production on rich lands farther west had reduced cotton prices. Instead of blaming local causes,

South Carolinians attributed their ills to the tariff. When the news of the Tariff of 1828, called by its enemies the "Tariff of Abominations," reached Charleston, people were indignant. Flags were hung at half-mast; college students threatened to buy no northern goods; and there was talk of leaving the Union. But South Carolina held back from formal action against the Tariff of 1828 because John C. Calhoun, the state's leading politician, was Andrew Jackson's running mate for Vice President. Calhoun's influence in a new administration might bring about tariff reduction.

The Nullification Crisis

Which side would Jackson take in the argument over nullification? Southerners hoped that the President, a slaveholder and planter himself, would support their interests. Jackson's first annual message to Congress in December 1829 had raised the hopes of the states' rights defenders.

The President warned Congress against "all encroachments upon the legitimate sphere of state sovereignty," a position that also signaled his veto of the Maysville Road bill in 1830.

The nullifiers tried to get Jackson to show his hand at a dinner celebrating Jefferson's birthday on April 13, 1830. Controlling the committee in charge of the banquet, they had antitariff and nullification toasts printed on the menu. It was hoped that the President would fall into the mood of the occasion. But Jackson chose the national interest over the states. When his turn came, the old warrior asked everyone to rise, looked straight at Calhoun, and proposed a toast that echoed Webster: "Our Federal Union: it must be preserved." Calhoun, pale and trembling, responded, "Our Union, next to our liberty, the most dear."

The break between Jackson and Calhoun over nullification was personal as well as political. Major John Eaton, Jackson's

Examining Political Cartoons *Published during the nullification controversy, this cartoon shows the manufacturing North getting fat at the expense of the South. Why did Southerners have this point of view?*

secretary of war, had married a young woman who was not socially approved by Mrs. Calhoun and the other cabinet members' wives. Of the cabinet members, only Martin Van Buren, a widower, could afford to be pleasant to Peggy Eaton. Jackson, remembering his own wife's suffering from social slander, stopped meeting with most of his cabinet advisers. Jackson's final break with Calhoun came when he discovered that, years earlier, Calhoun had wanted to have "Old Hickory" censured for mistreatment of the Indians in Florida. From this point on, Van Buren became Jackson's choice to succeed him in office.

In 1832 Congress passed a new tariff law. The rates, while lower than those of 1828, were still high. South Carolina immediately called a special convention that passed an Ordinance of Nullification declaring that the tariff was "null, void, and no law, nor binding upon this state, its officers, or its citizens." The ordinance threatened secession, and the state began to arm and drill a volunteer military force.

In response, Jackson issued a "Proclamation to the People of South Carolina," pointing out that nullification meant disunion and disunion meant treason. Privately, he warned Senator Hayne that if there was bloodshed he would hang the first nullificationist he could get his hands on from the first tree he could find. Hayne resigned from the Senate to become governor of South Carolina and Calhoun resigned the vice-presidency to lead the fight in the Senate.

Compromise settled the nullification crisis. Jackson asked Congress to pass a Force Bill to give him the powers necessary to suppress disunion in South Carolina. While Congress debated the measure, Henry Clay introduced a compromise tariff bill. It provided for gradual scaling down of duties to the 1816 level. The Tariff of 1833, supported by both Webster and Calhoun, and the Force Bill were passed the same day. Thus Congress removed South Carolina's grievance about the tariff and at the same time denied its right to nullify a law. South Carolina withdrew its Ordinance of Nullification, claiming it had won its major purpose—lowering the tariff.

★ ★

Section Three Review

★ ★

SUMMARY

Opposing sectional interests continued to divide the country over tariffs, internal improvements and money policies. States' rights versus national power became a major controversy, especially after a series of tariffs led to the Ordinance of Nullification in South Carolina. John C. Calhoun, a South Carolina states' rights advocate who opposed Jackson's nationalist policies, resigned as Vice President after Jackson threatened to respond to nullification with force. Only when Henry Clay introduced a compromise tariff was the crisis resolved.

CHECKING FOR UNDERSTANDING

1. **Identify** Daniel Webster, John C. Calhoun, Ordinance of Nullification

2. **Define** nullification, compact

3. **Describe** the differing interests of the sections of the United States during Jackson's presidency.

4. **Summarize** the crisis over the tariff and nullification and its resolution.

5. **List** characteristics of Jackson's presidential leadership.

6. **Explain** the reasons for the hostilities between Calhoun and Jackson.

THINKING CRITICALLY

7. **Inferring Values** At a celebration, Jackson and Calhoun exchanged toasts to the Union. Although they used similar words, they planted themselves firmly on opposing sides of a sensitive issue. In your own words restate the implied messages they were giving to each other.

CONNECTIONS: HISTORY AND ECONOMICS

8. **Recognizing Motives** Calhoun began his political career with a nationalist philosophy. What economic and political factors forced him to abandon that philosophy?

★ ★

Jackson's War on the Bank

ETTING THE SCENE

> *...Matters worse and worse in Wall Street as far as I can learn; everyone discouraged; prospect of universal ruin and general insolvency of the banks, which will be terrible indeed if it takes place. Workingmen thrown out of employ by the hundreds daily.*
>
> —GEORGE TEMPLETON STRONG
> Student at Columbia University, from his diary, 1837

Section Focus

The national debates over internal improvements and tariffs divided the country along sectional and economic lines. Although the threats of nullification and secession were real, leaders in Congress managed to compromise on these issues. The fight over the Second Bank of the United States, however, divided business interests from labor, creditors from debtors, and commercial interests from agriculture. Instead of compromise, this issue caused panic and depression.

Objectives

After studying this section, you should be able to:
• List the main arguments regarding the Second Bank of the United States.
• Explain the role of the Bank in the election of 1832.

At the time the question of nullification was dividing the nation, Jackson was also engaged in a dramatic struggle with the Bank of the United States. Chartered in 1816, the "B.U.S.," as it was nicknamed, was a useful institution. Like the original Bank of the United States, it performed much of the financial business of the country and controlled the supply of currency.

Popular Distrust of Banks

Despite its importance, the Bank had many enemies who called it such names as "Monster," "Octopus," and "Mammoth of the East." Opposition came from smaller banks chartered by state legislatures, because the B.U.S. was a powerful competitor, and because it prevented state banks from lending too freely. Another group, mostly farmers, were against all banks. They believed the only honest currency was "hard money"—silver and gold. Farmers respected real wealth—corn, hogs, grain, cotton, tobacco—and resented paying tribute to those who controlled paper wealth, such as mortgages and bank notes.

The Bank also suffered because of a rising feeling against monopolies. Although 80 percent of the Bank of the United States was owned by private individuals, it enjoyed a monopoly of all government business. State legislatures granted somewhat similar privileges to state banks and also made monopoly grants to companies running toll bridges, steamship lines, and turnpikes. Feeling against this sort of privilege was strong in the Northeast among small businesses and workers who believed that monopolistic charters created an unfair advantage. They made certain people wealthy and kept others from acquiring property. Thomas Sedgwick, a writer and typical Jacksonian, argued that the right to incorporate and to issue paper money should belong to everyone, not just banking monopolies:

> *Will it be said that money would not have been loaned if the legislature had not granted any exclusive privilege of doing it to a certain number of individuals? No! As compared with what would have been effected under a free trade system, the banks have been a clog upon the industry of this country....*

Jackson versus the Bank

The Bank of the United States had not been especially successful in its first few years. A new president, Nicholas Biddle of Philadelphia, beginning in 1819 made improvements that helped to enhance the Bank's reputation. Sound investments, high dividend rates for its stockholders, and a sense of responsibility to serve the government had made the Bank a respected institution among business and commercial interests.

Poorer people, especially in the South and West did not share this opinion, however. Farmers, wishing easy credit, were unhappy with the Bank's strict lending policies. Laborers in the East disliked the paper currency issued by the Bank because it caused higher prices.

Jackson, like most westerners, was a hard-money man who distrusted all banks and all paper money. While the President believed that high finance was dangerous, he also remembered that the Bank had opposed his candidacy in 1828 and had refused jobs and loans to his supporters.

For the first three years of his presidency, however, Jackson took no action against the Bank except to express the opinion that it had too much power. The President's inaction may have encouraged Nicholas Biddle's supporters to use the difference of opinion on the Bank issue to challenge Jackson in the election of 1832.

The National Republicans fired the first shots in the bank war when they decided to make the Bank the main issue of the 1832 election. In the summer of 1832, Henry Clay, the likely presidential challenger, introduced a bill to give the Bank a new charter, even though the old one did not run out until 1836. Clay hoped to embarrass Jackson by forcing him either to sign a bill he disliked or to veto it. He did not believe Jackson could defend a veto in the presidential campaign. When Congress passed the Recharter Bill, Jackson remarked, "The Bank, Mr. Van Buren, is trying to kill me; *but I will kill it.*" His veto message to Congress showed little knowledge of banking but great understanding of why many people disliked the B.U.S. Jackson wrote that the

Bank favored the few against the many; it made "the rich richer and the potent more powerful." He called it un-American because more than a quarter of its valuable stock had been purchased by foreigners. Finally, he said it was an overextension of federal power because the Constitution nowhere explicitly granted the federal government the right to establish a central bank.

Jackson's veto was so sharp that Nicholas Biddle described it as having "all the fury of a chained panther biting the bars of his cage." Bank forces campaigned hard for Henry Clay, hiring speakers, subsidizing newspapers, printing handbills that included Jackson's veto, and spending a lot of money. Clay and Daniel Webster campaigned hard across the country countering the speeches of Jackson supporters.

Election of 1832

The Bank issue did determine the presidential election, but not in the way Henry Clay anticipated. The National Republicans accused Jackson of "appealing to the worst passions of the uninformed part of the people and endeavoring to stir up the poor against the rich." They produced arguments to show the value of the Bank to the nation's finances. But the bank issue backfired. Jackson's veto message appealed to a majority of the people. When the returns were counted, they showed that Jackson had won an overwhelming victory. He received 687,000 popular votes to Clay's 530,000 and carried the electoral college by 219 to 49.

The election of 1832 introduced a new method of nominating candidates. A new minor party called the Anti-Masons ran a slate of candidates that it had selected at a national nominating convention. Previously, nominations had been made either by state legislatures or by a caucus of party members in Congress. The Anti-Masons' procedure, giving more people a role in presidential nominations, was soon adopted by the major parties and has been followed ever since.

Connections

HISTORY AND ECONOMICS

BANKS AND THE MONEY SUPPLY

In the 1800s a bank served three functions in the community: it provided a secure place to deposit gold and silver coins; it loaned its deposits to individuals and local businesses; and it issued paper notes to borrowers—the value on each bank note representing a like amount of coins in its vault. These notes then circulated in the economy as money.

In theory, a bank's loans could not exceed its deposits. But the interest on loans was profit, and by issuing more notes, banks could loan many times the specie in their vaults. If enough people who held a bank's notes wanted hard cash, however, all its assets would be paid out and its depositors' funds would be lost.

The Second Bank of the United States sought to regulate the nation's economy by controlling bank notes. By purchasing huge amounts of notes and redeeming them at the issuing banks, the B.U.S. could exhaust the assets of unsound banks and force them to close. But even this crude central banking system ended when the B.U.S. lost its charter. Not until the Federal Reserve System was created in 1913 was banking brought under effective control.

An early bank note issued by the Bank of the United States.

★ ★ ★ ★ ★ ★ ★ ★ ★ ★

MAKING THE ECONOMICS CONNECTION

1. How did banks get the paper money they printed into the nation's money supply?

LINKING PAST AND PRESENT

2. What clues on modern paper money show that the government is involved in banking today?

★ ★ ★ ★ ★ ★ ★ ★ ★ ★

Jackson Destroys the Bank

Jackson took his reelection as a directive from the people to destroy the power of the Bank at once, even though its charter did not run out until 1836. Although the law required funds of the federal government to be deposited in the Bank, Jackson resolved to remove them. This required an order from the secretary of the treasury. Two secretaries resigned rather than sign the order. Finally, a third secretary agreed, and the government began to gradually withdraw deposits from the vaults of the B.U.S. New funds from taxation and land sales were placed in strong state banks that National Republicans scornfully called "pet banks."

The removal of the deposits caused a great outcry among Jackson's opponents, who branded the action unconstitutional.

Nicholas Biddle, president of the Bank, claimed that removal of the deposits forced him to call in its loans and stop lending. Biddle's policy created such a scarcity of credit that hundreds of business people were driven into bankruptcy and scores of banks failed. Factories closed down and workers were laid off. Since Jackson had vetoed the Bank bill, business people sent petitions urging him to save the country from depression. The President replied, "Go to Nicholas Biddle!" Eventually, Democrats shifted the blame to Biddle, arguing that if one man at the head of a private institution could drive the country into depression, then Jackson was right in saying the Bank had too much power. Finally Biddle gave in. The B.U.S. reversed its policies and began to extend easy credit to state banks. With money once again plentiful, the administration threw millions of acres of public land on the market. The resulting land boom sparked a time of reckless investment. Congress stimulated the boom by issuing $30 million in surplus funds to the states, triggering a host of internal improvement schemes in turnpikes, canals, and railroads.

The Panic of 1837

The free spending, speculation, and resulting inflation worried Jackson's hard-money supporters. Jackson decided to halt the trend by issuing the Specie Circular, ordering that all payments for public lands be in silver or gold. This drastic reversal of policy virtually stopped land sales, eliminated easy credit, and helped bring on a severe panic and depression in 1837.

Jackson's victory over the Bank had appeared to be a victory for free enterprise. It encouraged a movement toward "free banking" laws that permitted any individual or group to establish a state-chartered bank as long as certain regulations designed to protect the depositors and the public were observed. Comparable to free bank legislation were the general incorporation laws, which were designed to allow all businesspeople to form corporations on the same terms. Jacksonians wanted to free business from government controls and to allow business concerns to succeed on the basis of efficiency rather than on special favors.

While Jackson increased the power of the presidency, he believed his mission was to reduce the sphere of the central government, reflecting the *laissez-faire* philosophy that the Jacksonians inherited from Thomas Jefferson. But the war against the Bank of the United States reduced confidence in the banking system and removed government controls over speculation, inflation, and rapid expansion. The administration's erratic policies proved that leaders had much to learn about government's role in a free economy. Soon Democrats would learn that in times of depression, the party in power loses the presidential election.

SUMMARY

The Bank of the United States stabilized the nation's economy by controlling the supply of currency and by preventing smaller banks from lending too freely. It drew opposition from other banks, borrowers, and even hard-money advocates. Having vetoed a bill to extend the Bank's charter, Jackson won re-election in 1832. He then withdrew government funds from the Bank, which tightened credit, causing widespread business failures and unemployment. The return to easy credit made possible by Jackson's final destruction of the Bank led to overspeculation and inflation. Jackson responded by issuing the Specie Circular, ordering that payment for public land be in gold or silver. This policy reversal dried up credit again and set the stage for the Panic of 1837.

CHECKING FOR UNDERSTANDING

1. **Identify** Anti-Masons, Specie Circular

2. **State** the functions and advantages of the Bank of the United States.

3. **List** the objections to the Bank of the United States.

4. **Describe** the role the Bank of the United States played in the election of 1832.

5. **Explain** how Jackson destroyed the Bank of the United States.

THINKING CRITICALLY

6. **Analyzing Causes**   Explain how public fear of an economic crisis can bring on a depression or worsen it.

GLOBAL PERSPECTIVES

7. **Recognizing Similarities**   Some nations respond to economic hard times with easy credit and liberal monetary policies, resulting in runaway inflation. What similarities do you see between such developments and events in the United States in the 1830s?

Rise of the Whig Party

The sum of the whole is that there is but one power, one control, one will in the state. All is concentrated in the President.... The source of the legislative power is no longer to be found in the Capitol but in the palace of the President.

—HENRY CLAY
Campaign speech in support of William Henry Harrison, June 27, 1840

Section Focus

Opposition to Jackson resulted in the formation of a new party called the Whigs. Taking their name from the British party that in the eighteenth century had resisted the power of the Crown, they fought the growth of presidential power under "King Andrew I." Their principal leaders were Clay and Webster. The Whig party succeeded in electing two presidents, but both died in office and the party itself split over slavery in the 1850s.

Objectives

After studying this section, you should be able to:
• List three causes of the panic and depression of 1837.
• Explain why the government became ineffective under President Tyler.

As the election of 1836 approached, Jackson used his control of the Democratic party to pick his successor. His choice was Martin Van Buren, the Vice President, a New York politician whose reputation for craftiness earned him the nickname "the Fox of Kinderhook."

The Whigs were so divided they could not agree on one candidate. Instead, they nominated three favorite sons, or leading politicians from different states, hoping to divide the electoral college vote. If they could prevent Van Buren from getting a majority, the election would be thrown into the House of Representatives, controlled by the Whigs. Jackson's continuing popularity and the nation's perceived prosperity were enough to give the Democrats the election. Van Buren won 170 electoral votes against a combined total of 124 votes for all his opponents, although his edge in the popular vote was small.

Panic and Depression

Van Buren had hardly taken office when the country was hit by the panic of 1837 and one of the most severe depressions in American history. Jackson's Specie Circular had sent the economy into a tailspin, but like most depressions, that of 1837 had several causes. One factor was a withdrawal of British investments. British gold and silver deposits in American banks had supported American economic growth in the 1830s. In 1837 Great Britain suffered from hard times, and British investors became more cautious.

As British and American investors in state banks withdrew deposits, banks failed. There was no Bank of the United States to restore confidence in the banking system. People hoarded their gold and silver, merchandise went unsold, crops found no markets, and businesses closed. Thousands of farmers lost their farms through mortgage foreclosures. Unemployment soared among eastern factory workers, and work on canals and railroads nearly ceased. As the depression deepened, workers fought over the meager relief that city governments provided.

Today, faced with such a crisis, the people would demand action by the federal government, and the federal government would respond with legislation. In the 1830s, however, a depression was regarded as an act of nature like a drought or a hurricane. Instead of recognizing that both state and federal

governments had helped to cause the depression, *laissez-faire* philosophers said it was not the function of the government to do much about the problem. Van Buren emphasized this in his inaugural address when he said that "all communities are apt to look to government for too much." His one great legislative effort was to try to get the federal government entirely out of banking. He shared Jackson's disapproval of a great central bank like the B.U.S., but recognized that depositing federal funds in pet banks had also failed.

Van Buren proposed an Independent Treasury System, under which the federal government would collect its taxes in specie to be stored in vaults throughout the country. Federal expenditures would be paid in specie, making federal credit literally as good as gold. This would discourage inflated bank notes because state banks would have to keep a sufficient reserve to allow their depositors and those holding their notes to do business with the government. The Independent Treasury Act successfully passed in 1840.

"Log Cabin" Campaign of 1840

The Whigs eagerly looked forward to the election of 1840, even though they were so divided on major issues that they did not even try to write a **platform**, or statement

of beliefs. Their campaign plan was simple: nominate a military hero and attack Van Buren. For their presidential candidate they passed over known leaders of the party and chose General William Henry Harrison, whose principal attraction was that he had fought Indians at the battle of Tippecanoe in 1811. Nicholas Biddle warned that Harrison should not make speeches:

Let him say not one single word about his principles, or his creed—let him say nothing—promise nothing. Let no committee, no convention, no town meeting ever extract from him a single word about what he thinks nor what he will do hereafter. Let the use of pen and ink be wholly forbidden.

Democrats jeered that all Harrison was fit for was to sit in front of a log cabin, drink hard cider, and draw a pension. The Whigs adopted the very methods the Jacksonians had used against Adams in 1828. Harrison—born to wealth and social position—was pictured as a simple frontiersman, while Van Buren—born in humble circumstances—was portrayed as a champagne-drinking aristocrat with cologne-scented whiskers. John Tyler, a former Democrat who had left the party in protest over Jackson's nullification policy, was selected as Harrison's running mate. The Whigs' campaign slogan became "Tippecanoe and Tyler too." Blaming the Democrats for the depression, the Whigs boasted that Van Buren's policy was "fifty cents a day and French soup; our policy—two dollars a day and roast beef." The result of this rollicking campaign was a decisive victory for Harrison—234 electoral votes to 60—although the popular vote was quite close.

The election of 1840 was the first to illustrate a recurring principle of American politics: during a depression, the party in power is likely to be punished at the polls. Twelve years before, when Jackson defeated Adams, a little more than 50 percent of the eligible voters went to the polls. In 1840 nearly 80 percent of those eligible voted—in some states almost 90 percent. The high turnout revealed that the party organizations had penetrated every county, village, and city precinct. Parties had set up machinery for informing the electorate and had assured that voters came to the polling places.

Tyler and the Whigs Split

While the Whigs gained office by ignoring differences and discrediting Van Buren, once in power they had to address the diverse needs of the nation. Henry Clay, now in the Senate, had worked out a legislative program designed to appeal to as many different interests as possible. The elderly Harrison was expected to be a figurehead, while Clay and Webster ran the party. But just a month after his inauguration, President Harrison died of pneumonia.

John Tyler of Virginia became the first Vice President to become President by the death of the incumbent. Placed on the Whig ticket simply to attract southern support, Tyler was opposed to most of the Clay and Webster programs. They were nationalists; the new President was a believer in states' rights. Nevertheless, he did sign the first of several bills in Clay's program. The Tariff of 1842 pleased eastern manufacturers by raising the rates to about what they had been ten years earlier. The Pre-emption Act of 1841 satisfied the western demand that "squatters" on public lands have first right to buy the lands they had settled. Tyler, however, vetoed a bill establishing another national bank and vetoed a second bill that was drawn up to meet his objections. In disgust at the President's actions, all the Whigs except Daniel Webster resigned from the cabinet, and Clay resigned from the Senate. Divided, without a program or leadership, the Whigs lost heavily in the congressional elections of 1842, and John Tyler became a President without a party. Yet, while Jacksonian democracy finally had proven powerless to solve the nation's growing sectional stalemate, the democratic spirit continued to show great promise in addressing the nation's social needs.

★★★★★★★★★★★★★★★★★★★

Section Five Review

★★★★★★★★★★★★★★★★★★★

SUMMARY

The panic of 1837 caused banks to fail and British investors to withdraw their deposits. Public panic led to hoarding of cash and discouraged buying, which led to business failures and unemployment. Lacking a national bank to restore stability, Van Buren created an Independent Treasury System, while political opponents organized the Whig party. Divided on major issues, the Whigs did not develop a platform in the presidential election of 1840, but focused on personalities. William Henry Harrison, their candidate, won but died in office. John Tyler, his successor, clashed with the nationalist program of the Whigs.

CHECKING FOR UNDERSTANDING

1. **Identify** Whigs, Martin Van Buren, John Tyler

2. **Define** platform

3. **List** factors that led to the panic and depression of 1837.

4. **Explain** why the Whigs had no platform and how they conducted their campaign in 1840

5. **Specify** the circumstances that distinguished the election of 1840.

6. **State** the reasons government became ineffective under Tyler.

THINKING CRITICALLY

7. **Evaluating Political Systems**   Six Vice Presidents have, like Tyler, become President. So, in effect, they have been chosen by the presidential candidate, not by the voters. Suggest another method by which the Vice President might be chosen.

CONNECTIONS: HISTORY AND POLITICS

8. **Analyzing Voter Behavior**   Why does the party in power usually lose elections held during a depression?

★★★★★★★★★★★★★★★★★★★

★ Chapter 11 Review ★

★ Summary

Andrew Jackson's victory in the presidential election of 1828 indicated a westward shift of the political center and the emerging influence of the "common man." After voting rights were extended, politicians began to seek the support of ordinary people. More offices became elective. Jacksonian democracy, however, did not extend to native Americans, African Americans, or women.

Despite his belief in limited federal powers, Jackson extended presidential power through the spoils system and frequent use of the veto. When states rights versus national power became an issue, Jackson supported the national government and responded forcefully when South Carolina tried to nullify the federal tariff law.

Jackson also asserted presidential authority in his struggle with the Second Bank of the United States. His destruction of the Bank's power eventually led to panic and depression in 1837, causing widespread business failure and unemployment. But these were the problems of the new President, Martin Van Buren, who attempted to restore economic stability. The Whig party was organized in these troubled times and elected William Henry Harrison President in 1840. After Harrison's death on April 4, 1841, John Tyler, his successor, clashed with the Whigs' nationalist program.

★ Using Vocabulary

Use the following terms in writing a short essay about presidential leadership style.

platform   **pocket veto**   **spoils system**

★ Reviewing Facts

1. **Compare** the campaigns of 1828 and 1840.
2. **Identify** the important democratic changes that developed during the Jackson era.
3. **Identify** the groups that did not benefit from democracy under Jackson and explain why.
4. **List** examples of Jackson's authoritative style and extension of presidential power.
5. **State** the reasons Jackson and others objected to the Second Bank of the United States.
6. **Describe** the panic of 1837 and its causes.
7. **Summarize** the rise of the Whigs and the reasons for their failure.

★ Understanding Concepts

POLITICAL CHANGE

1. What political and democratic changes aided Jackson's election victory in 1828?
2. How was the election of 1840 significant?

ECONOMIC POLICY

3. How did the tariff and nullification issue develop into a crisis?
4. What changes, in the United States and abroad, contributed to the panic of 1837?

★ Thinking Critically

1. **Linking Past and Present**   Political parties often choose vice-presidential candidates for the reasons the Whigs selected Tyler: to attract voters with views different from those of the presidential candidate. Review news accounts of the 1988 presidential election. Do you think the Democrats should have chosen Jesse Jackson as Michael Dukakis's running mate instead of Lloyd Bentsen? Explain your answer.

2. **Analyzing Executive Performance**   Did Andrew Jackson's conduct as President reflect the growing spirit of democracy? Use examples to support your opinion.

3. **Evaluating Policy**   Argue for or against the spoils system.

4. **Comparing Institutions**   Compare the Bank of the United States with the Independent Treasury System created to replace it. What were the advantages of each?

5. **Recognizing Causes**   In the early 1800s, democracy expanded. Yet slavery became more entrenched and native Americans were further deprived of rights. How might the Industrial Revolution and westward expansion account for these apparently contradictory developments?

★ Chapter 11 Review ★

★ Writing About History

CAUSE AND EFFECT

Refer to the description of how to write a cause-and-effect essay in the History Writer's Handbook in the Appendix of this book. Your teacher will give you more specific instructions on the essay's length and due date.

Imagine you are a financial reporter in 1838. Write a newspaper article explaining to your readers the chain of causes and effects that led to the panic of 1837. Prepare before you begin writing by organizing your ideas as shown graphically on page 113.

★ Learning Cooperatively

Working in pairs, research the history of the governments' and settlers' dealings with Black Hawk's nation. Divide the research assignments, assigning separate responsibilities to each partner. Imagine it is 1832 and Black Hawk has returned with his followers to reclaim Iowa lands that farmers now own and work. You and your partner have been appointed by Jackson to recommend a solution. Agree on a fair plan and present it to your class.

★ Mastering Skills

DISTINGUISHING RELEVANT FROM IRRELEVANT INFORMATION

Suppose a friend promises to pick you up at 7 o'clock. When he isn't there by 8, you begin to wonder why: Is he lost? Was he in an accident? When your friend finally arrives, you express your concern about his lateness. But instead of offering an explanation he responds, "How do you like my car? We're going to make a really great impression tonight." You reply, "That's irrelevant."

An important part of critical thinking is being able to distinguish relevant from irrelevant information. *Relevant information* is information that deals with the main topic or idea. *Irrelevant information* is information that does not deal with the main idea. In the above case, the car's appearance is irrelevant because the topic of discussion was that your friend was late and not the car. The impression that the car will make has nothing to do with your friend's lateness.

The following guidelines will help you to distinguish between relevant and irrelevant information in written material:

- Read the material, and determine the main idea, or topic of discussion.
- For each statement, determine if it relates directly to the topic by asking yourself if the statement defines, explains, illustrates, serves as an example, or describes a cause or consequence of the topic.
- Any statement that does not do one of the things named in the second guideline is information that is irrelevant.

Example   These guidelines are used to tell the difference between relevant and irrelevant information in the following paragraph. The first sentence states the main idea, that Andrew Jackson had a negative attitude toward native Americans.

Andrew Jackson was no friend of America's Indians. (*topic*) Since colonial days, settlers had been pushing native Americans off their lands. (*irrelevant*) The general's reputation in the West was largely built as an Indian fighter. (*illustrates*) After the War of 1812, he led the Tennessee militia against the Creeks and the Cherokees. (*example*) The Cherokee nation was trying to live in peace with their white neighbors. (*irrelevant*) Like other westerners, Jackson believed that Indians blocked western expansion. (*cause*) As President, he moved the Cherokees from their Georgia home to new territory in Oklahoma. (*illustrates*)

Practice   Use the above guidelines to decide which of the following sentences are relevant or irrelevant to the topic "The Cherokee's experience in Georgia." Give reasons for your decisions.

(1) The Cherokees established schools for their children and even wrote a constitution.   (2) They did these things to better fit in with the settlers that surrounded their territory.   (3) The Cherokees hoped that if they lived like their neighbors, that the state would accept their presence and not take their land. (4) The Creeks and Seminoles, however, were more hostile to the demands of Georgia settlers for Indian land.   (5) When cooperation did not help the Cherokees, they sued Georgia to force the state to return their land.   (6) Although the Cherokees won their case, President Jackson refused to enforce the Supreme Court's decision. (7) The Cherokees call their removal from Georgia to Oklahoma the "Trail of Tears."

CHAPTER 12
The Spirit of Reform

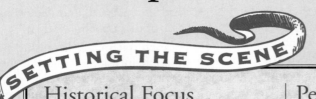

SETTING THE SCENE

Historical Focus

American reformers during the first half of the nineteenth century worked selflessly to create a more perfect society. Some even sought to create a "heaven on earth." Many reformers, particularly those who sought to end slavery, were religiously motivated. Others traced their reform spirit to ideas in the Declaration of Independence. In either case, the noble goal of achieving a truly benevolent and just American society would serve as model for the rest of the world.

Concepts to Understand

- Why social **reform** movements were so widespread during this period.
- How new **values and beliefs** influenced educators, reformers, artists, and writers.

People to Know

Horace Mann, Dorthea Dix, Frederick Douglass, Herman Melville

Places to Locate

Oberlin, Seneca Falls

Terms to Identify

lyceum, abolitionists, Underground Railroad, Hudson River School

Guided Reading

As you read this chapter, seek the answers to the following questions.

1. What factors motivated the wide variety of reform movements in the first half of the nineteenth century?
2. How did the spirit of reform affect the status of prisoners, women, and African Americans?

SPANNING THE DECADES

	POLITICAL		
	1825 *John Quincy Adams inaugurated as sixth U.S. President*	1830 *Maysville Road Bill is vetoed*	1832 *Black Hawk War*

1825   **1830**

	CULTURAL			
	1825 *Robert Owen organizes utopian community at New Harmony, Indiana*	1829 *First school for the blind, New England Asylum, opened in Boston*	1831 *The Liberator, abolitionist newspaper published*	1833 *National temperance movement founded*

The Pic-Nic *by Thomas Cole, 1846*

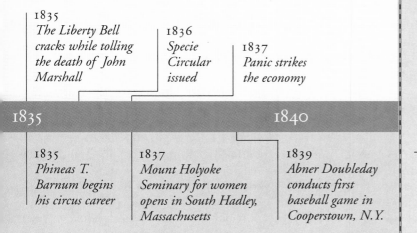

1835
The Liberty Bell cracks while tolling the death of John Marshall

1836
Specie Circular issued

1837
Panic strikes the economy

1835   1840

1835
Phineas T. Barnum begins his circus career

1837
Mount Holyoke Seminary for women opens in South Hadley, Massachusetts

1839
Abner Doubleday conducts first baseball game in Cooperstown, N.Y.

...Let us then, be up and doing
With a heart for any fate;
Still achieving, still pursuing,
Learn to labor, and to wait.

—WILLIAM WADSWORTH LONGELLOW
The Psalm of Life, 1838

Advances in Education

What a fertility of projects for the salvation of the world! One apostle taught that use of money was the cardinal evil; another that the mischief was in our diet....With this din of opinion and debate there was a keener scrutiny of institutions and of domestic life than any we have known....

—RALPH WALDO EMERSON
American poet and essayist, 1803-1882

Section Focus

The "keener scrutiny of institutions" to which Emerson referred meant that Americans were examining their society on the basis of ideas in the Declaration of Independence. During the early 1800s, many Americans in search of a better, more democratic world formed organizations to persuade others to their way of thinking. Perhaps never before or since the Jacksonian period have Americans shown such optimistic faith in improving the quality of life.

Objectives

After studying this section, you should be able to:
- Identify improvements in education made in the 1800s.
- Discuss the obstacles to establishing public schools.

Although the idea of universal education had a long history, dating back as far as the Massachusetts General School Act of 1647, public school systems had not developed adequately. As late as 1834, 250,000 of the 400,000 children in Pennsylvania did not attend school. In the 1830s and 1840s, however, there was a tremendous increase in the number of tax-supported schools.

Public Education

The drive for public education was rooted in the vision of the United States as a land of equal opportunity. To deny a child education was to close the door to it.

As more people gained the right to vote, the need for education grew. Nonwhites, women, and white men without property had all been denied the vote in the early days of the Republic. In the 1820s and 1830s, however, most states amended their laws, extending the vote to white men who did not own land. In addition, it became necessary to educate the increasing number of immigrants who came to the United States in the mid-1800s. Thus, the increase in the number of eligible voters became a compelling reason for free public education. Democracy demanded an informed, educated electorate, a goal not easy to achieve.

One legislator who tackled this goal was Horace Mann. As president of the Massachusetts Senate, he pressed for public education and signed a bill in 1837 creating a state board of education in Massachusetts. He then stepped down from his post to serve as secretary of the state board of education. During his 12 years in that position, he doubled teachers' salaries, opened 50 new high schools, grouped students by grades, and established schools for teacher training called "normal schools." Massachusetts quickly became the model for all other northern states.

The establishment of public schools was not achieved without a fight. Communities that declared themselves in favor of public schools were often unwilling to tax their citizens to raise the necessary money. Lutherans, Roman Catholics, and other religious groups ran private schools of their own. Many of these people wondered why they should pay taxes to support public schools. Many people without children were also opposed. "Why should

I be taxed," they protested, "to educate other people's children?"

In answer, Thaddeus Stevens, a rising young politician from Pennsylvania, said:

The industrious, thrifty, rich farmer pays a heavy county tax…which is necessary to support and punish convicts, but loudly complains of that which goes to prevent his fellow being from becoming a criminal.…

Educating blacks presented even more difficult problems. It was flatly illegal in the South, and in the northern states people wavered on the need to provide education for blacks—whether with whites, separately, or at all. Although there were 15,000 blacks in New York City in 1828, there were only 2 schools for them; in Philadelphia, only 3 schools for 20,000 blacks.

Efforts to educate blacks were sometimes met with violence even in the more liberal North. Prudence Crandall's white students withdrew when she admitted one black girl to her Connecticut school in 1831. When her school filled with black girls from all over the Northeast, the school was vandalized. Food had to be secretly brought in to the students. Connecticut then made it illegal to educate "a person of color" from out of state, which led to Crandall's arrest and conviction. The verdict, however, was reversed. When Crandall reopened the school, it was again attacked, and she was forced to give up her efforts there.

Others, especially in the West, saw no reason why children should learn more than the "three Rs." As an Indiana newspaper put it:

…Give them a little spelling, a little ciphering, and a little handwriting, with a liberal sprinkling of the rod, and they'll have more than their fathers had before them. Did Tippecanoe Harrison graduate from a seminary? Did Old Hickory Jackson know any Latin or Greek?…

Examining Illustrations
Horace Mann said "Be ashamed to die until you have won some victory for humanity." Why did some groups resist Mann's ideas about public education?

Even less public support could be mustered for education for children with special needs. Reformers who worked for this cause went to great lengths to give these children an equal opportunity for a better life. Reverend Thomas Gallaudet traveled to Europe to learn how to help people with impaired hearing. He became adept at hand signals, or signs, for communicating with hearing-impaired persons that he learned about in France. When he returned in 1817, he opened a school in Hartford, Connecticut, that became a model in education for the hearing impaired.

Samuel Gridley Howe, head of the New England Asylum for the Blind, taught the unsighted to read by pasting string on cards to make raised letters. His prize student was Laura Bridgman, a girl who entered the school at age eight and learned to read, write, and sew. She became the first sight- and hearing-impaired person to be successfully educated.

Often teachers were untrained and undedicated young men or women. As

Examining Tables
The number of students enrolled in school more than doubled between 1840 and 1860. In which 10-year period covered by the table did enrollments increase the most?

U.S. STUDENT ENROLLMENT, 1840–1860

	1840	1850	1860
Total population (in millions)	17.1	23.2	31.4
Total students: primary, secondary and higher education (in millions)	2.0	3.6	5.5
Students as percent of total population	11.7	15.5	17.5
Total white population, age 5–19 (in millions)	5.3	7.2	9.5
Students as percent of total white population, age 5–19	37.7	50.0	57.8

Lawrence A. Cremin, *American Education: The National Experience, 1783–1876* (1980)

teachers were paid salaries of only $155 a year for men and as little as one-third of that for women, schools could not attract skilled professionals to teach. Because teacher training was not yet widely available, classroom instruction was characterized by memorization and harsh discipline.

Fortunately, the spirit of reform was strong enough to influence lawmakers. By 1850 most of the free states provided tuition-free elementary education. In the South, which was dominated by plantation owners, public schools were far less common. But in the North, free high schools had replaced many private academies. Most boys and girls, however, did not take advantage of the high schools. Many lacked interest in "book learning," or believed that the quality of education was poor, or that free schools were charity. The new laws supporting free public education were, however, an important step in the development of the United States educational system.

An American Language

Despite a popular mistrust of "book learning," Noah Webster's *American Spelling Book* became a bestseller after it was first published in 1783. By 1837 sales had reached 15 million copies. In 1880 it was still going strong. The publishers reported:

It has the largest sale of any book in the world except the Bible. We sell a million copies a year, and we have been selling it at that rate for forty years.... They are bought by all the large dry goods and supply houses, and furnished by them to every crossroads store.

A young schoolteacher when he wrote the speller, Webster was dedicated to "a uniformity and purity of language." He was eager not simply to preserve the language for its own sake; but he saw it as a way to promote national spirit. "A national language," he wrote, "is a band of national union." His spelling book contained a preface encouraging Americans to respect their own literature. Webster also wrote the famous dictionaries that bore his name.

William McGuffey, a cleric and college president, had similar ideas. In 1836 he introduced the first of six McGuffey's Readers. Filled with moral instructions and patriotic sayings, these literature anthologies influenced schoolchildren for generations. Between 1836 and 1920, 122 million McGuffey's Readers were published. They were eventually adopted as textbooks in 37 states.

The influence of McGuffey's reader and Webster's spelling book and dictionary was great indeed. These texts helped promote uniformity of language and provided children with a shared cultural background.

Higher Education

New approaches to education were adopted at the college and university levels as well. North Carolina opened a state university in 1795. Jefferson helped to establish the University of Virginia, which opened its doors in 1825. The university was an exception in that its students were offered a broad spectrum of subjects and were free to take any course.

Although many state universities were established after 1820, most colleges and universities were private, church-related schools that offered professional training to aspiring ministers. As the practice of apprenticeship was still common in many professions, formal education for those students seeking careers in law, medicine, or engineering was slow to develop.

In the face of limited offerings and inadequate facilities in United States universities, many students sought higher education in the more progressive schools of Europe, especially in Germany. American students returned to the United States enthusiastic and full of new ideas for changing higher education.

Interest in training teachers helped the cause of higher education for women. One argument for training women as teachers was that it was more economical because women teachers could be paid less than men. Although many men feared that higher education for women would disrupt home life, feminist leaders such as Emma Willard, Catharine Beecher, and Mary Lyon argued that chemistry could be used in cooking and math in household finance. Their schools, founded in the 1820s and 1830s, were front-runners in higher education for women. Mount Holyoke College, founded in Massachusetts by Lyon in 1836, is still a women's college.

Oberlin College in Ohio, the first coeducational school, saw its first female student graduate in 1841. Oberlin—and Bowdoin College in Maine—were the first institutions to admit black students. These achievements were rarities, however. Because black men and women were generally barred from educational opportunities, there were fewer than 15 black college students in the United States before 1840. Aside from one black college, Lincoln University, which opened in Pennsylvania in 1854, there was little progress in education for blacks until after the Civil War.

While opportunities for formal higher education were limited for most people, there was a move toward adult education for the common person. Libraries, once accessible only by subscription, began to take hold as free public institutions. The first was established in Peterboro, New Hampshire, in 1833.

Even more popular was the **lyceum** (ly SEE uhm) movement, begun in 1826 in Millbury, Massachusetts, by Josiah Holbrook. A lyceum was a voluntary organization designed to promote "the improvement of its members in useful knowledge." Supporting their organization with small membership fees, the group might purchase books, scientific equipment, and specimens for study. Most popular were the traveling lecturers sponsored by the lyceums. Through the work of lyceums, many people were exposed to the great ideas of the times.

★ ★ ★ ★ ★ ★ ★ ★ ★ ★ ★ ★ ★ ★ ★ ★ ★ ★

Section One Review

★ ★ ★ ★ ★ ★ ★ ★ ★ ★ ★ ★ ★ ★ ★ ★ ★ ★

SUMMARY

In the early 1800s, few public schools existed. As more people gained the right to vote, the number of tax-supported schools increased substantially. Many citizens and groups opposed taxes for public schools. Public schools operated with meager facilities and young, poorly-trained, and underpaid teachers. Educating blacks and children with special needs brought less public support. The spirit of reform led to the establishment of free high schools, colleges, and universities. Webster's *American Spelling Book,* and *McGuffey's Readers* enjoyed wide circulation.

CHECKING FOR UNDERSTANDING

1. **Identify** Noah Webster, William McGuffey, Horace Mann
2. **Define** lyceum
3. **Summarize** the progress in public education during the 1800s, including the problems of those who wanted to educate black children.
4. **List** the groups that objected to public education and the reasons for their objections.
5. **Discuss** the qualifications of teachers in the 1800s.

THINKING CRITICALLY

6. **Analyzing Causes**   In what ways did the *McGuffey's Readers* and Webster's dictionaries and spelling book play a part in keeping American English uniform?

LINKING PAST AND PRESENT

7. **Recognizing Recurring Issues**   In the 1980s some groups asked for a tax credit for parents paying tuition to send their children to private schools. What similarities do you see in the opposition to tax-supported schools in the 1800s and the 1980s?

★ ★ ★ ★ ★ ★ ★ ★ ★ ★ ★ ★ ★ ★ ★ ★ ★ ★

Critical Thinking Skills

Making Comparisons

Imagine that your younger brother cannot decide between joining the debate team or playing intramural baseball. He has limited free time, so he asks you to help him compare the two. You tell him that you cannot because that is "like comparing apples and oranges." Your friend hears the conversation and comes in to tell you that you indeed can compare the debate team to baseball.

Explanation

To compare means to examine in order to identify similarities and differences. You can compare any two things. To be an accurate comparison, however, you must note at least one similarity and one difference.

Making comparisons does not involve analysis or evaluation. There are no judgments being made, and no conclusions being drawn.

In the above example, there are obvious differences between debating and baseball, yet there are at least two similarities. Both are group activities, and both are competitive in the nature in which points are scored. This means that a comparison is possible.

No matter what you are comparing, there are questions that can be asked that help in making effective comparisons. They are:

1. What is it that I want to compare?

2. What do they have in common that I can compare?

3. On which common area do I want to concentrate?

Daguerreotype of the Emerson School

4. What similarities are there in this common area? What differences are there in this common area?

Example

Note how the above questions are applied in making a comparison between public and private schools in the 1800s:

1. What is being compared? *(Public and private schools in the 1800s.)*

2. What did they have in common? *(A belief in education for the young; a concern for values; the need for acquiring money with which to operate their schools.)*

3. On which common area should there be concentration? *(The need for acquiring money can be chosen, although you could have chosen any area.)*

4. What similarities are there in this common area? *(Both had to pay teachers; pay for books; pay for heating fuel and building expenses.)*

What differences are there in this common area? *(Public schools acquired money through community taxation. Private schools generally acquired money through churches or other sponsoring groups and through fees or donations only from those parents whose children actually went to those schools.)*

This completes a comparison between public and private schools in the 1800s. This method can be applied to other movements or institutions in your study of history.

Practice

For further practice in making comparisons, read Section 2 and apply the above questions in making a comparison between the women's rights movement and the antislavery movement.

Struggle for Rights

What is man born for but to be a Reformer, a Re-maker of what man has made, a renouncer....

—RALPH WALDO EMERSON
Lecture to the Mechanics' Apprentices' Library Association, 1841

Section Focus

Numerous reforms were advocated during the Jacksonian period. There were organizations to do away with flogging in the navy, drinking alcohol, and eating meat. There was even a society that encouraged reformers called The Friends of Universal Reform.

The great reform movements of the 1830s and 1840s could boast of solid achievement, especially in state legislation dealing with such problems as prisons, the mentally ill, child labor, liquor, and public schools.

Objectives

After studying this section, you should be able to:
- List reform movements of the 1800s and discuss their achievements.
- Explain the ways in which women were treated as second-class citizens.
- Discuss the efforts made to end slavery.

Calling for action on such issues as care for the mentally ill, women's rights, and abolition of slavery, reformers appealed to their state legislatures and the federal government with little success. The persistent message of the reformers eventually awakened the United States to many of the needs of more than one-half of the population.

Prison Reform

As Emerson had suggested, there was a wealth of opportunity for reform; one had only to turn a critical eye to the world and make a choice.

Prisons, too, began to experiment with ways to reform criminals. Unfortunately, the results were more severe punishments. For example, in Pennsylvania criminals were put in solitary confinement day and night to allow convicts to meditate on their crimes and, thus, reform. At Auburn, New York, treatment was less severe. There group labor in absolute silence was allowed. Instead of public hangings—commonplace before the 1830s—reformers sought the more humane change to private executions.

Obviously, much reform remained to be done. When Dorothea Dix began visiting prisons in 1841, she found that mentally ill persons were still treated as criminals. In her report to the Massachusetts legislature, she wrote:

I proceed, gentlemen, briefly to call your attention to the present state of insane persons confined within this commonwealth, in cages, closets, cellars, stalls, pens! Chained, naked, beaten with rods, and lashed into obedience....

Miss Dix's findings were so shocking and so accurate that Massachusetts passed a law establishing asylums where mental illness could be treated as a disease rather than as a crime. Miss Dix traveled throughout the United States visiting more than 800 jails and almshouses, or homes for the poor. Largely as a result of her influence, 20 more states founded insane asylums. Later she traveled overseas, helping to promote better treatment of the mentally ill in every major

European country. Through her friendship with a Japanese diplomat, the first insane asylums in Japan were built.

Women's Rights Movement

Even though the Declaration of Independence promised equality for all, the promise for women rang hollow. Women had actually lost ground in their political equality since colonial times. While certain women had suffrage under colonial charters, that privilege was revoked after the colonies declared their independence from Great Britain. Despite the fact that by 1850 nearly all white males could vote, women were still denied an active part in politics.

Examining Illustrations *Dorothea Dix's careful documentation of the treatment of mental illness led to state-operated asylums. Why was this a remarkable achievement for a woman in the 1840s?*

Women were perceived as "second-class citizens" in other ways, too. According to English common law that formed the basis of American law, "husband and wife are one and that one is the husband." Even before a woman married, however, she lost the right to manage her own personal matters. According to one law book, it was unfair to her betrothed to allow a woman to control her own finances because he might be disappointed if she did not bring all of her anticipated wealth into the marriage. Similarly, a woman had no legal right to manage the affairs of her own children, and only in the state of Ohio could a woman make a will.

As factories opened in the Northeast, many new jobs for women were created. As in teaching, women received considerably less pay than men did, and when they took it home, the money became their husbands'. Women also felt social pressures directed against those who took these jobs.

In spite of little formal education, women learned by reading. One important influence was the women's magazine *Godey's Lady's Book,* which published such important authors as Emerson, Longfellow, Poe, and Hawthorne and had a circulation of 150,000.

Still, almost all institutions of higher education and most professional careers were closed to women. It took Elizabeth Blackwell years to be allowed to take medical courses. When she finally completed her training to become the country's first woman physician, sexist prejudice nearly kept her from practicing.

Even in the reform movements themselves, women were often forced to defer to men. It was considered improper, for example, for a woman to address a mixed audience. When nine women went as United States delegates to the World Antislavery Convention, they were greeted with cries of "Turn out the women!" from American clerics. The women, Lucretia Mott and Elizabeth Cady Stanton among them, refused to leave and, as a compromise, were seated behind a curtain and allowed only to listen.

Frustrated by the limits on their actions, women reformers began a campaign for their own rights. In 1848 Mott and Stanton organized the Seneca Falls Convention. This gathering of women reformers drew up a "Declaration of Sentiments and Resolutions" that echoed the words of the Declaration of Independence:

We hold these truths to be self-evident: that all men and women are created equal; that they are endowed by their Creator with certain inalienable rights; that among these are life, liberty, and the pursuit of happiness....

Stanton shocked many of the women present when she proposed a resolution that they devote themselves to gaining the right to vote. Frederick Douglass, a black antislavery reformer, stepped into the shocked silence to second the resolution, giving a speech in support. The resolution passed, but narrowly.

Most politicians were either indifferent or hostile to the issue of women's rights. During this time women gained neither the right to vote nor admission to professions; most colleges continued to exclude them. They did, however, gain relief from some of their worst legal handicaps. For example, many states passed laws permitting women to retain and manage their own property. Above all, women drew attention to their cause and to the seriousness of their purpose.

Antislavery Crusade

The most glaring violation of democratic principles in the United States was black slavery. How could the nation claim to be "the land of the free" when human beings were bought and sold like chattel

AMERICAN PORTRAITS

AMELIA BLOOMER
1818-1894

One episode in Amelia Bloomer's life so catapulted her to fame that today few remember she was a leading reformer. Publisher of the *Lily,* her own newspaper, Bloomer called for just marriage laws, temperance, and women's suffrage.

It was, however, the clothing she first wore in 1851 that made Amelia Bloomer a household name. Seeking a more practical style than the hoopskirt, she donned a short skirt over loose pants gathered at the ankles. She did not invent the fashion, but her insistence on wearing it—despite ridicule— led to calling the outfit "bloomers." Large crowds came to hear her lecture. The novelty of seeing a woman wearing pants accounted for much of her popularity. She finally concluded, that her bloomers distracted attention away from her reform efforts, and she returned to more traditional garb.

Examining Illustrations   *Harriet Tubman (far left) risked 19 trips into the South to liberate slaves. Sojourner Truth (second to right) traveled throughout the North as a lecturer promoting abolition and women's rights. Her strong arguments convinced many to work for abolition. At first abolition had supporters in the South, but after 1831 Southerners who opposed slavery kept silent or moved to the North. What may have caused this change?*

or common property? The question became increasingly acute by 1840. By that time most Latin American countries had abolished slavery, and Great Britain had banned the practice. It is not surprising then that the upsurge of democratic feeling in the Jacksonian period made antislavery the dominant reform effort.

The organized movement to abolish slavery began among religious groups. As early as 1776, the Quakers—in the South as well as in the North—had agreed not to hold slaves. In Virginia in 1789 the Baptists recommended "every legal measure to extirpate this horrid evil from the land." The abolition movement at first made many converts in the South. Benjamin Lundy, a native of New Jersey, spent most of his active career organizing antislavery societies in southern communities. James G. Birney, an Alabama lawyer and cotton planter, freed his own slaves and attempted to get other owners to do the same.

The voices of **abolitionists**, or those persons in favor of doing away with slavery, grew stronger. On January 1, 1831, the first edition of *The Liberator*, a Boston antislavery newspaper, was published.

Editor William Lloyd Garrison wrote in a strong, unrelenting tone:

I will be as harsh as truth, and as uncompromising as justice. On this subject, I do not wish to think, or speak, or write, with moderation.... I am in earnest. I will not equivocate. I will not excuse. I will not retreat a single inch. AND I WILL BE HEARD.

Garrison denounced both Northerners who refused to be shocked by slavery and Southerners who held slaves. He demanded immediate freedom for enslaved blacks without compensation for the owners, whom he regarded as "not...within the pale of Christianity, of Republicanism, of humanity." He denounced the Constitution as being in "a league with death and a covenant with Hell" because it protected slavery. Garrison and his followers made no attempt to win their way by political action. They were willing to divide the

Union to rid the free states of the shame of being tied to the slave states.

Garrison had a talent for antagonizing even his own supporters. Many abolitionists refused to follow him. A group who proposed to abolish slavery by the use of the ballot box founded the Liberty party. It nominated James G. Birney for the presidency in 1840 and 1844, but Birney received only a few thousand votes.

Another leader who favored political action was Frederick Douglass, a self-educated former slave, who edited an abolitionist newspaper, *The North Star.* The title was meant to remind people of the Underground Railroad. This secret abolitionist organization, which had hiding places, or stations, throughout the northern states and even into Canada, brought slaves out of the South and set them free. Moving at night, the agents of the Underground Railroad had only Polaris, the fixed star in the northern skies, to guide them. They not only took care of slaves after they had come North, but they

risked their lives to go into the slave states and lead blacks to freedom. One of the most successful of these agents was Harriet Tubman, the "Black Moses," who had herself been born into slavery. After making her own escape, she returned to the South again and again, liberating more than 300 slaves. Tubman always avoided arrest, even though a reward of $40,000 was promised for her capture.

It had been no mere coincidence that the first publication of *The Liberator* coincided with a slave insurrection in Virginia in 1831. That revolt was led by Nat Turner, a black preacher and slave who believed himself divinely inspired to lead his people from bondage. Turner's rebellion was quelled, but only after about 60 whites had been killed. The revolt spread panic throughout the South. The belief that Turner had been inspired by abolitionist propaganda effectively ended the antislavery movement in the South. From that time on, Southerners who favored abolition of slavery usually remained silent or moved north.

Examining Fine Art *Before the Civil War, thousands of slaves fled hundreds of miles and endangered their lives to reach the first station on the Underground Railroad. The refugees in this painting are arriving at Levi Coffin's Indiana Farm. Coffin, a Quaker abolitionist, was one of 3,000 active sympathizers who provided shelter to runaways. What service did Polaris provide?*

Among Southern abolitionists who fled to the North were sisters Sarah and Angelina Grimké (GRIHM kee). As daughters of a slaveowner in South Carolina, they had learned through firsthand experience to abhor slavery. They moved to Philadelphia, became Quakers, and were among the first women to speak out for both abolition and women's rights. Angelina explained the connection between the two movements:

Women ought to feel a peculiar sympathy in the colored man's wrong for, like him, she has been accused of mental inferiority and denied the privilege of a liberal education.

One of the few Southerners who did not leave was Cassius Marcellus Clay, a distant relative of Henry Clay, who edited abolitionist newspapers in Kentucky. As a Southerner who held unpopular beliefs, Clay habitually went about armed with two pistols and a bowie knife. He even fortified his office with two cannons and a keg of gunpowder set to go off. When he was absent one day, however, a mob seized his presses and sent them across the Ohio River to Cincinnati.

Southern hostility to abolition grew stronger. The South demanded the suppression of abolitionist material as a condition for remaining in the Union. Southern postal workers refused to deliver abolitionist newspapers. In 1835 a bill to bar abolitionist literature from the mails passed the Senate, although it eventually was abandoned. In 1836, under Southern pressure, the House of Representatives passed a "gag rule" providing that all abolitionist petitions should be shelved without debate.

Despite the excitement it aroused, the antislavery movement affected politics very little at first. The Missouri Compromise had supposedly averted civil war by fixing the boundary between slave and free territory. No prominent politician, however, proposed endangering the Union by attacking slavery where it was already protected by law.

Section Two Review

SUMMARY

The reform movements of the 1830s and 1840s led to improved conditions for prisoners and the mentally ill. Women were not allowed to vote nor be admitted to professions. They could, in some states, retain and manage their own property. Slavery, in spite of democratic changes, persisted. The abolitionist movement began among religious groups. It established newspapers and the Underground Railroad. Despite its growing hostility to slavery, the antislavery movement had little effect on politics.

CHECKING FOR UNDERSTANDING

1. **Identify** Dorothea Dix, Seneca Falls Declaration, Frederick Douglass, William Lloyd Garrison, Harriet Tubman

2. **Define** abolitionists, Underground Railroad

3. **Discuss** the reform movements of the 1800s and their achievements.

4. **Explain** discrimination against women in the 1800s and the methods women used to address this issue.

5. **Describe** the contributions of three key individuals to the antislavery movement.

THINKING CRITICALLY

6. **Making Decisions** Imagine that you are a northern male teacher who has strong feelings against slavery. Would you join the abolitionists? Why or why not?

CONNECTIONS: HISTORY AND MATHEMATICS

7. **Comparing Purchasing Power** At the time of Tubman's reward, about $25 would buy goods that cost $400 in 1990. What is the approximate value of the $40,000 reward in 1990 dollars?

SECTION THREE

Social and Cultural Change

SETTING THE SCENE

If a man does not keep pace with his companions, perhaps it is because he hears a different drummer. Let him step to the music which he hears, however measured or far away.

—HENRY DAVID THOREAU
American philosopher and writer,
Walden, 1854

Section Focus

The Pilgrims had come to the New World with a vision of a different life. The years that followed were filled with the work of carving out an existence in a new land. Americans wanted to prove that their country was truly independent of Europe. They wanted to create a distinct civilization, rivaling that of the Old World. They were concerned not only with rights but with the quality and flavor of life in the United States.

Objectives

After studying this section, you should be able to:
- Identify the prominent artists, writers, and scientists of the 1800s.
- Explain the goals of nineteenth-century religious movements.
- Discuss the temperance movement.

(1820), in England and tried to attract readers by promoting the rumor that he was "a prominent Englishman." In 1820 the Reverend Sydney Smith, writing in a British magazine, sneered at the low cultural level of Americans and the lack of artistic and scientific achievement in the United States:

The Americans are a brave, industrious, and acute people; but they have hitherto given no indication of genius.... In the four quarters of the globe, who reads an American book? Or goes to an American play? Or looks at an American picture or statue? What does the world yet owe to American physicians and surgeons? What new substances have their chemists yet discovered? What old ones have they analyzed?

Almost as if in answer to Sydney Smith's taunt, the second quarter of the nineteenth century saw many advances by American scientists and an outpouring of books by American writers that are still read on both sides of the Atlantic.

Writers and the American Scene

Editors such as Garrison, Clay, and Douglass had been using their talents to directly influence social reform. American writers had somewhat different motivations—to reform America's attitude toward itself.

Washington Irving invented a literary past out of the history of the Hudson River valley, once an area of Dutch settlement. With this material he created

Americans themselves had a sense of inferiority. People could not write poetry without "a legendary past nor a poetic present," remarked one young scholar. "Large mountains, extensive prairies, tall cataracts, long rivers [and] millions of dirty acres" did not seem suitable subjects for literature. James Fenimore Cooper set the scene of his first novel, *Precaution*

Connections

HISTORY AND SCIENCE

THE SCIENTISTS OF NEW HARMONY

The short-lived economic community that Robert Owen founded at New Harmony, Indiana, was an exciting place. Although isolated, it boasted an excellent

New Harmony

library, school, musical societies, art collections, even a public lecture series. This environment attracted some of the finest scientific minds of the day. Primarily naturalists, these scientists collected and classified specimens, and wrote on biological and geological subjects.

A key supporter of Owen's community was geologist William Maclure. In 1817 Maclure had produced a detailed U.S. geological map, the first of its scope. A member of New Harmony until its failure in 1827, he had hoped to put into practice new European teaching methods. Another New Harmony geologist, Gerard Troost, a native of Holland, acquired an impressive mineral collection.

Entomologist Thomas Say settled at New Harmony permanently and published a descriptive work on insects, the third volume of *American Entomology*. Say later edited books on shells and birds.

★ ★ ★ ★ ★ ★ ★ ★ ★ ★

MAKING THE SCIENCE CONNECTION

1. Why were scientists like Maclure, Troost, and Say attracted to life at New Harmony?

2. What scientific interests did the New Harmony naturalists pursue?

LINKING PAST AND PRESENT

3. What is the interest of naturalists today?

★ ★ ★ ★ ★ ★ ★ ★ ★ ★

---

characters like Rip Van Winkle. As a result of reading James Fenimore Cooper's novels, generations of children—not only here but in France and Great Britain—gloried in the drama of native Americans and pioneers on the New York frontier. In his novels and short stories, Nathaniel Hawthorne mined the Puritan history of his native New England. In *Moby Dick,* Herman Melville used his experience as a sailor to write a fascinating account of whaling that was also an allegorical drama of the human struggle itself.

American poets, too, began to use American subjects. Henry Wadsworth Longfellow immortalized the native American hero Hiawatha. John Greenleaf Whittier in "Snow-Bound" described winter on a New England farm. William Cullen Bryant in "To a Waterfowl," drew a haunting picture of sunset over a lonely marsh. Edgar Allan Poe wrote of the terrors that lurk in the world of imagination and dream.

Many American writers took an active part in reform movements. Whittier and Longfellow joined the crusade against slavery, as did poet James Russell Lowell and poet and novelist Lydia Maria Child. Henry David Thoreau himself spent a night in jail rather than pay taxes to support the Mexican War.

Scientific Advances

Men and women in the United States also won fame in the field of science. As a child in Nantucket, Massachusetts, Maria Mitchell taught herself astronomy while checking navigational instruments for whaling captains. She discovered a new comet, several groups of distant stars, and wrote important studies of Jupiter and Saturn. Mitchell was the first woman elected to several learned societies. Joseph Henry, the inventor of the electromagnetic motor, headed the Smithsonian Institution, established in 1846. Research there laid the basis for the accurate prediction of weather.

Matthew Maury, an officer of the United States Navy, developed tables predicting winds and ocean tides at different seasons and gave directions for the shortest travel time. These tables helped reduce the average sailing time from New York to San Francisco by 47 days. His findings aided worldwide navigation so greatly that 13 foreign nations honored him. Known as the founder of the science of oceanography, Maury also made a systematic study of the ocean bottom and selected the route for the first transatlantic cable.

One of the most important advances in the history of medicine is credited to two physicians from the United States. Working independently, Dr. Crawford W. Long of Georgia in 1842 and Dr. W. T. G. Morton of Boston in 1846 were the first physicians to use ether as an anesthetic during surgery.

The Arts

Painters and sculptors were eager to produce works as great as those of Europe. Samuel F. B. Morse, the inventor of the telegraph, began his career as a painter who wanted to "rival the genius of a Raphael, a Michelangelo, a Titian," in order to refute the charge that the United States "has produced no men of genius." American art, however, did not develop quickly. American artists had little opportunity for the skilled training

Examining Fine Art   *Thomas Cole's* River in the Catskills *is a beautiful example of Hudson River School art that flourished in the mid-1800s. The landscapes painted by Cole, Thomas Doughty, Asher B. Durand, and others reflect both Americans' pride in their country's natural beauty and their love of nature. Theirs was a distinct departure from European styles of painting. Why did painters, including Samuel F.B. Morse, seek to excel in their art?*

available abroad, and European styles were still the standard by which art was judged.

American artists did best, when, like the writers, they turned their attention to the American scene. Such an artist was George Caleb Bingham, who painted the life he had seen on the Missouri frontier as a boy. Of importance also was a group of landscape painters in the East known as the Hudson River School. Their romantic paintings of the Catskill Mountains and Hudson River are highly prized.

Early nineteenth-century American architects continued to use classical models developed in the Renaissance. In New England, Charles Bulfinch, influenced by English models, developed a distinctive "Federal" style of architecture that can be seen in the Massachusetts State House, the largest building in America at the time it was designed. Bulfinch later worked for 14 years in Washington D.C., and helped to complete the design of the Capitol. His influence can be seen especially in architecture in the Northeast. The type of architecture that most appealed to the American taste, however, was the style known as "Greek Revival." Based on classical Greek and Roman forms, it was used both in domestic architecture and in public and private buildings, the most famous of which is Virginia's State Capitol. "A Greek Revival town," remarked a historian of American architecture, "is a fine and handsome assembly of stately colonnades and well-turned building masses."

By the middle of the nineteenth century, American architects had abandoned the simplicity and clean lines of the Federal and Greek Revival styles and begun to imitate the Gothic style of the Middle Ages. Characterized by elaborate detail, pointed windows, and colored glass, this style was originally developed for churches and stone construction. When adapted to other purposes and to wooden buildings, however, it often seemed inappropriate. Among the few signs of real originality in American architecture were the "octagon houses," designed to give maximum light and space with a minimum of wall space and supporting rafters.

International Peace

While American artists were creating an American culture, a small group of social reformers turned their attention to a problem affecting all human-kind—abolition of war. Since the formation of this nation had apparently solved the problem of bringing together independent states and because the United States seemed in no danger from its neighbors, it was natural for Americans to think that universal peace was attainable. In 1828 the American Peace Society was formed to promote international understanding. Its principal founder was William Ladd, who abandoned successful careers, first as ship captain and then as farmer, to devote his entire energy to the cause of peace. Ladd agitated for a Congress of Nations with courts of international justice to settle all disputes.

Social Experiments

From Europe at this period came a new idea—**socialism.** Socialists believed that the means of production should be owned by society, not by private individuals. They believed that business competition and individual ownership of property caused poverty and inequality. Socialists proposed to substitute cooperation for competition and common ownership for individual ownership. The early followers of the idea proposed to start small, voluntary communities where their ideas could be put into practice. Most of these experiments took place in the United States because land was so easy to acquire. A famous English socialist, Robert Owen, started a cooperative venture at New Harmony, Indiana. Even more influential than he were the disciples of the Frenchman, Charles Fourier, who proposed to organize society into "phalanxes" of just 1,620 people, living in villages called "phalansteries." His converts included Horace Greeley, editor of the New York *Tribune,* the most widely read newspaper in the United States.

The goal of the founders of the Brook Farm community in Massachusetts was to free its members for intellectual activity by running a self-sufficient farm. Members became disillusioned, however, because of the time, energy, and hard work required by farm labor. The New England writer Nathaniel Hawthorne was persuaded to live at Brook Farm for a time. He, too, found it difficult to write—his primary aim—because of the hard work required on the farm. He wrote to his fiancée:

It is my opinion…that a man's soul may be buried under a dungheap, or in a furrow of the field, just as well as under a pile of money….

The community ultimately collapsed after a large fire left the group greatly in debt.

Religious Movements

Religious groups, having an additional basis for unity, were more successful in community living. One rapidly growing religious body was The Church of Jesus Christ of Latter-Day Saints, more commonly known as the Mormon Church. This church was founded in 1830 by a New Englander, Joseph Smith, who claimed to have been called to restore the Christian church to its original form. Smith wrote the *Book of Mormon* from golden plates that he said an angel had led him to discover. Mormonism enjoyed a rapid growth and established a distinctive pattern of communal living at Kirtland, Ohio. Persecution finally drove the Mormons west to Utah.

Another religious group, the Shakers, was founded by Mother Ann Lee in 1772, as an offshoot of the Quakers. Supporting themselves by small industry in orderly communities that were isolated from the rest of the world, the Shakers reached their peak in the mid-1800s with some 6,000 members. They did not marry or have children; the society survived by making converts. Few Shakers are left, but their handiwork—especially Shaker furniture, with its clean lines—is highly valued by collectors today.

Examining Fine Art The Methodist Camp Meeting *of the early 1800s emphasized religious experiences. Other religious movements sprang from new revealed truth. Name three religious groups that practiced communal living.*

Linking Across Time

TEMPERANCE

The temperance movement continued under the leadership of the National Women's Christian Temperance Union (WCTU), formed in 1874. In 1920 the Eighteenth Amendment banned the manufacture and sale of liquor, but it was repealed by the Twenty-first Amendment. The WCTU has helped enact state laws requiring public schools to teach about the harmful effects of alcohol and drugs. Another organization, Mothers Against Drunk Driving (MADD), promotes legislation to stop drunk driving.

Examining Illustrations *Ralph Waldo Emerson, a Transcendentalist thinker, expressed optimism about the self-reliant individual in his writing and lectures. Why were Unitarians attracted to Transcendentalism?*

The Oneida Community in central New York state was another group that aspired to found a successful utopian society. Practicing a form of Christian socialism, members supported themselves by manufacturing steel game traps and silver plate. The group prospered for some 30 years but then broke up.

Religious communities were just one aspect of the great ferment in religious thought in the first half of the nineteenth century. During this period a number of other new religious denominations arose. The creed for the Unitarian Church was formulated in New England in 1819 by Reverend William Ellery Channing. Breaking away from the Congregational Church, Unitarians rejected the doctrine of the Trinity, preferring the concept of the oneness of Deity. The Unitarians also believed that human beings were by nature good, not evil.

Unitarians were attracted to the philosophy of Transcendentalism. A distinctly American movement, it emphasized the relationship between human beings and nature as well as the importance of the individual conscience. Writers such as Margaret Fuller, Ralph Waldo Emerson, and Henry David Thoreau were among the leading Transcendentalist thinkers of the time. Through her life and writings, Fuller advocated rights for women. In his poems and essays, Emerson urged people to trust themselves, to listen to the inner voice of conscience, and to break the bonds of custom and prejudice. In *Walden* (1854) Thoreau extolled a life of thoughtful solitude.

Alexis de Tocqueville (TAWK veel), a French political scientist who studied American institutions during the Jacksonian period, observed that American ministers of all faiths did not "attempt to draw or fix all the thoughts of man upon the life to come." Life on earth was no longer a mere preparation for the hereafter; instead, people had the capacity and the duty to improve the environment in which they found themselves. Such religious zeal was often intimately tied to the spirit of reform.

Protestantism experienced a renewal, a "Second Great Awakening." Throughout the country, beginning in New England and spreading westward, the immense growth of Protestant denominations was marked by great revival meetings, the building of thousands of new churches, and the founding of scores of colleges and universities. In cities a similar stirring of religious activity arose in the Catholic churches. In Boston and New York, for example, the Roman Catholic Church provided not only places of worship for Catholic European immigrants, but also schools, orphanages, and charitable organizations.

The Temperance Movement

While some religious groups attempted to revise their philosophies or create alternative societies, others put their energies into changing what they felt undermined the quality of life. This was how many groups, especially Baptists and Methodists, viewed liquor. The temperance movement, which began in the United States and spread to England, attempted to ban the use of alcohol.

Most of the movement's leaders were clergy interested in doing away with social evils, poverty, and crime, often brought on by heavy drinking. Like many other reform groups, temperance groups formed a national organization, the United States Temperance Union, founded in 1833. Heavy drinkers were persuaded to "take the pledge" to give up alcohol. Temperance propaganda even included a "Cold Water Army" of children with uniforms and marching songs. The revivalist spirit of the temperance movement is revealed by a stanza from one of its songs, entitled "One More Drink":

Stay, mortal stay! nor heedless thus
Thy sure destruction seal;
Within that cup there lurks a curse
Which all who drink shall feel.
Disease and death forever nigh,
Stand ready at the door,
And eager wait to hear the cry
"O give me one glass more!"

In addition to trying to persuade people not to drink, temperance societies demanded laws to put an end to the sale of liquor. They were able to convince many politicians of the justice of their cause. Abraham Lincoln, for example, favored prohibition by state action, arguing that just as the American Revolution freed people from the tyranny of Britain, so would prohibition free people from the tyranny of alcohol. In 1851 Maine passed the first state prohibition law, an example followed by about a dozen states. Other states passed "local option" laws, which allowed towns and villages to prohibit the sale of liquor within their boundaries.

Many aspects of the reform movement may seem odd today. The achievements of the 1830s and 1840s, however, often had beneficial and long-lasting results. The years of reform helped establish the spirit of free thinking in the American character.

Section Three Review

SUMMARY

American artists and writers came into their own in the 1800s as they began to feature American subject matter and evolve American styles. American scientists made outstanding contributions in astronomy, meteorology, oceanography, and medicine. Social and religious groups began experiments in communal living. Protestants split into diverse sects, and new religious philosophies developed. Owing partly to increasing religious attention to life on earth, religious groups became leaders in reform movements such as abolition and the emerging temperance movement.

CHECKING FOR UNDERSTANDING

1. **Identify** Hudson River School, Maria Mitchell, Charles Bulfinch, William Ladd, Greek Revival, Brook Farm community, Transcendentalism, Second Great Awakening

2. **Define** socialism

3. **List** the prominent American artists and writers of the 1800s.

4. **Explain** the goals of the major religious movements.

5. **Describe** the temperance movement in the 1800s.

THINKING CRITICALLY

6. **Analyzing Reform** The reform movements of the 1800s were initiated to extend rights and freedom of choice. What movement was an exception? What laws that have similar goals exist today?

CONNECTIONS: HISTORY AND SCIENCE

7. **Evaluating Technological Impact** Matthew Maury improved transportation and communication. How have his contributions helped our modern world?

★ Chapter 12 Review ★

★ Summary

In the 1800s the spirit of reform was evident in America's advances in education, the struggle for rights, and social and cultural changes. As more people gained the right to vote, the need for education grew. The number of tax-supported schools increased, and a number of free high schools, colleges, and universities opened.

Women gained the right to own and manage property, but not the right to vote nor enter most professions. Other reform movements included education for the deaf and blind and improved conditions for prisoners and the mentally ill.

New religious sects emerged, and an increasing focus on the need to improve life on earth led many groups to embrace the spirit of reform. Religious groups lead such movements as temperance and abolition. Slavery persisted, but abolitionists did establish newspapers and an Underground Railroad.

Culturally, the United States came into its own, producing some outstanding artists and writers. In addition, Americans made valuable contributions in science.

★ Using Vocabulary

Context clues help a reader determine the meaning of an unfamiliar word. A clue might take the form of a definition, an explanation, a synonym or antonym, or further details that make the meaning clear. Write a sentence using each of the pairs of related words below. Include context clues so that the meaning of both words would be clear to a reader unfamiliar with them.

lyceum	socialism
abolitionists	Underground Railroad

★ Reviewing Facts

1. **Summarize** advances in American education in the early 1800s.
2. **Describe** how Garrison, Douglass, and Clay influenced the abolitionist movement.
3. **Specify** the goals and achievements of the women's rights movement during this period.
4. **List** other reform movements of the period and their accomplishments.
5. **Identify** the major religious groups and movements that emerged during the 1800s.

★ Understanding Concepts

REFORM

1. Which of the nineteenth-century reform movements was hampered by opposition from groups concerned about their own economic interests? Explain.
2. What factors might account for the prevalence of reform movements during and after the Jacksonian period?

VALUES AND BELIEFS

3. What reasons can you give for why both the abolitionist and temperance movements began among religious groups?
4. The Underground Railroad was run by decent people who broke the law. Under the law these people were technically stealing property. What values did they consider to be above the law? Do you think breaking the law is ever justified under certain circumstances? Explain.

★ Thinking Critically

1. **Recognizing Causes**   In what way did sexist discrimination actually help open doors to higher education for women?
2. **Making Global Comparisons**   Slavery was abolished in Great Britain, France, and Latin America before it was abolished in the United States. What economic and political differences probably account for this?
3. **Citing Evidence**   What evidence can you find that at the beginning of the 1800s, European art and literature were superior to that of the United States?
4. **Linking Past and Present**   Today the law requires all students to attend school until a certain age. During the 1800s, high school attendance was voluntary. Why might a democratic society prefer compulsory education to voluntary attendance?

★ Writing About History

EXAMPLES

Refer to the description of how to use examples in writing essays in the History Writer's Handbook in the Appendix of this book. Your teacher will give you more specific instructions on the essay's length and the assignment's due date.

Imagine you are the editor of a prominent newspaper in 1830. Write an editorial pointing out injustices that exist even as democratic changes are sweeping the country. Give examples of failure to provide freedom and equal opportunity for all people in the United States.

★ Learning Cooperatively

Working in pairs, research the life of one American writer or poet of the 1800s, and review one of the writer's works. Have one partner write a biography and a description of the writer's contribution to American culture. Have the other partner write a review of the writer's work. Bind them into one booklet with the writer's name as a title. Display the booklets for other students to read.

★ Mastering Skills

IDENTIFYING EVIDENCE

You probably understand the dictionary's definition of *evidence*—"the data on which a judgment or conclusion may be based, or by which proof or probability may be established." You might not be able to identify what is legal evidence, however.

There are two kinds of evidence—that which is *admissible* (allowable or acceptable) in court and that which is not. For example, a statement made about an event by someone who was not present at that event is not admissible evidence. Only four kinds of evidence are admissible:

• eyewitness accounts—statements by people who saw an event take place

• written documents—diaries, letters, memos

• visual evidence, such as photographs

• physical objects, such as weapons or clothing

These definitions of evidence can help you identify evidence to support your studies. You can imagine that when Dorothea Dix spoke out against the treatment of the mentally ill, she had to gather evidence to support her claims.

Example Consider this claim: *Insane people are treated like criminals and are forced to live like animals in cages.* Read the information about Dorothea Dix in the chapter on pages 369-370. Then read the answers to the following questions. They will help you to understand how to identify evidence to support claims.

1. Are there statements by eyewitnesses? *(Yes, Dix herself visited the prisons; some prison or court officials might report what they had observed.)*

2. Are there written documents? *(Yes, the court and prison records of the treatment of insane people.)*

3. Is there visual evidence? *(Some photographs might have existed or sketches might be drawn by an eyewitness.)*

4. Are there physical objects? *(Yes, the chains, rods, stalls, etc.)*

Practice Suppose that you read a claim that African Americans actually lost some of their earlier rights in northern states beginning in the 1820s. Researching this claim you find a document entitled *Appeal of Forty Thousand Citizens, Threatened with Disfranchisement to the People of Pennsylvania, 1838.* Read the following excerpt from the document and identify evidence that supports the claim.

We appeal to you from the decision of the "Reform Convention," which has stripped us of a right peaceably enjoyed during forty-seven years under the constitution of this commonwealth.... It may be objected to us, that in point of fact we have lost by the recent decision of the [Pennsylvania] Supreme Court, in the case of Fogg v. Hobbs, *whatever claim to the right of suffrage we may have had under the constitution of 1790.... Not so. We hold our rights under the present constitution none the cheaper for that decision.... The blessings of the broad and impartial charter of Pennsylvania rights can no more be wrested from us by legal subtlety than the beams of our common sun or the breathing of our common air.... Our fathers fought by the side of yours in the struggle which made us an independent republic.... All we ask is, that no man shall be excluded on account of his* color; *that the same rule be applied to all.*

★ ★ ★ Unit 4 Digest ★ ★ ★

With the 1820s came the Industrial Revolution, which brought industrialization, growth, conflict, migration, and compromise—social, economic, and political—to the United States. At the same time, the decade began an age of democracy and social reform. Americans improved their lives and learned the advantages and disadvantages of freedom and unity.

Chapter 10
Sectionalism and Growth

The Industrial Revolution brought changes to all sections of the United States. In the Northeast, New England's textile industry expanded rapidly due to the abundance of water power and workers. Other manufacturing and shipping industries also grew in importance. As a result, goods became cheaper and more widely available. Meanwhile, craft workers who once worked in shops and owned their own tools found their lives more difficult and restricted in factories—their sense of security was gone. The plight of unskilled factory workers was even worse. To improve their lives, craft workers organized trade societies, and unskilled workers formed labor unions. When strikes failed to achieve the workers' goals, their organizations formed political parties. Even though political action brought about some reforms, the workers' parties were short lived, and the societies and unions soon collapsed.

In the South the cotton gin and Britain's increased demand for cotton boosted the economy beyond southerners' wildest dreams. Cotton became the major export not only of the South but of the nation. Plantations grew in size and number. As a result, many southerners' disapproval of slavery faded away because owning slaves was now profitable and more popular than ever.

In the Northwest, food, land, and other resources abounded. Pioneers streamed over the Appalachian Mountains to settle the region. Storekeepers and millers followed to supply the pioneers' needs. Soon towns became cities like Cincinnati, Louisville, and Chicago, and in these cities, manufacturing sprang up. By 1820 more than one-fourth of the people in the United States lived west of the Appalachian Plateau.

Each section of the country had its own wants and needs. The Northeast favored a protective tariff to stimulate the sale of its manufactured goods. The South insisted on the expansion of slavery to maintain its cotton economy. The Northwest demanded internal improvements like roads to get its goods to markets. Often people in different sections quarreled over whether the national government should support a particular issue. These quarrels threatened American unity.

To save the Union, politicians sought compromises like Henry Clay's "American System," designed to benefit the economies of all sections. But the compromises brought unity for only a while. In the presidential election of 1824, sectionalism resurfaced. Four National Republicans, representing different sections, sought the office. Since no candidate won a majority in the electoral college, the election was thrown into the House of Representatives. With Clay's help, John Quincy Adams emerged victorious, much to the disgust of Andrew Jackson, who had received the most popular votes. Jackson then resigned his seat in the Senate to begin campaigning for the 1828 election.

Chapter 11
The Age of Jackson

By the election of 1828, sectional interests had strengthened, and the population was shifting from the Northeast to the South and the Northwest. As a result, the political parties avoided discussing the issues and indulged in mudslinging.

Andrew Jackson became the new

President. Jackson was a man of the people and his supporters became known as Democrats. During Jackson's administration, the power of the presidency increased, the American definition of democracy broadened, and the people began to expect more from their political system. Politicians now recognized the importance of the individual voter, and the American government became more of a government by the people.

However, the new democracy did not extend to native Americans and African Americans. The government forced American Indians to move from their lands. Thousands of Indians died during the removal process, African Americans did not fare much better. In the South most remained slaves. In the North free blacks were second-class citizens.

Meanwhile, tariffs, banking, and internal improvements were still controversial and triggered sectional disputes. When Senator Hayne from the South and Senator Webster from the Northeast debated the issues of nullification and high tariffs, many feared that the southern states might secede.

The banking issue divided the nation still further. Andrew Jackson's stand against the Second Bank of the United States helped him win the 1832 election but, in the end, led to the panic and depression of 1837.

In the election of 1840, the Whig party captured the presidency for its candidate, William Henry Harrison, by avoiding dangerous issues and trying to overcome sectionalism. Once in power, the Whigs realized that they had to meet the diverse needs of the nation. However, Harrison died after only a month in office, and Vice President John Tyler became President. Unfortunately for the Whigs, Tyler, a southerner, disagreed with them on many issues, especially states' rights.

Chapter 12
The Spirit of Reform

Between 1820 and 1850, many Americans focused on social needs rather than political issues. Reformers wanted to better their world, and through organizations and reform movements, they accomplished enduring changes.

Thanks in part to Horace Mann and his example as public school board secretary for Massachusetts, many states provided free elementary education by 1850. In addition, Noah Webster's *American Spelling Book* and William McGuffey's *McGuffey's Reader* were helping establish a uniform language throughout the United States. State universities began to spring up, and Emma Willard and Catharine Beecher founded some of the first schools for the academic education of women. Programs for adult education and free public libraries became widespread.

Other reformers championed the causes of prisoners and the disabled. Blind children were taught to read with their fingers, and the deaf were taught to speak with signs. Due to the persistence of Dorothea Dix, many states opened insane asylums to care for the mentally ill who formerly lived in jails.

Also in the 1840s, women began to organize for their rights. They failed to gain universal suffrage or general acceptance into professions, but for the first time in many states women were allowed to retain and to manage their property. The first womens' rights convention was held in Seneca Falls, New York, in 1848.

The dominant reform effort of the time was the abolitionist movement. Some abolitionist leaders, such as Frederick Douglass, worked to abolish slavery through political means. Meanwhile, the Underground Railroad quietly smuggled slaves out of the South, and the black preacher Nat Turner led an unsuccessful slave rebellion that panicked southerners into restricting black privileges more than ever.

American culture reflected the social changes going on. Poets, artists, and novelists described the American scene. Part of the scene was a religious renewal, a "Second Great Awakening," during which existing religions were strengthened and new religious groups formed. Among the new religious organizations were several utopian communities, such as the Shakers.

SYNTHESIZING UNIT THEMES

RELATING IDEAS

1. How did economic growth deepen sectional conflicts?

IDENTIFYING TRENDS

2. What changes did reformers effect between 1820 and 1850?

MAKING COMPARISONS

3. Compare the political issues and strategies of the 1828 presidential election with those of the 1840 election.

★ Analyzing Unit Themes

AMERICAN DEMOCRACY

1. What important democratic changes developed during the Industrial Revolution?
2. What groups did not benefit from American democracy? Why?

ECONOMIC DEVELOPMENT

3. How did the Industrial Revolution lead to changes in the American economy, its lifestyle, and its values?
4. In what ways did the Industrial Revolution divide the country?

HUMANITIES AND RELIGION

5. How did changes in religious philosophy relate to the growing leadership of religious groups in social reform?

CONFLICT AND COOPERATION

6. How did sectional interests over economic issues develop into conflicts within the Union?

★ Reviewing Chronology

List the following events in chronological order.
- Henry David Thoreau's *Walden* is published.
- The United States Temperance Union is founded.
- John Quincy Adams becomes President.
- Black Hawk and the Sauk are driven west of the Mississippi River.
- Andrew Jackson issues the Specie Circular.

★ Linking Past and Present

- In 1990, 50 women from prominent Saudi-Arabian families drove automobiles through a city to protest their ineligibility to obtain driver's licenses. Some lost their government jobs. Others lost their university teaching jobs.
- Saudi-Arabian women do not have the right to vote, cannot eat out in public, cannot come in contact with men in public, and cannot drive cars. Many, however, do not seek the equality enjoyed by women in western nations.

Study the information above, then answer the questions that follow.

1. **Relating Issues** How does the Saudi protest relate to American women being treated as second-class citizens during the Jacksonian period?
2. **Comparing Values and Attitudes** Compare the Saudi protest and outcome with the Seneca Falls Declaration and outcome.

★ Demonstrating Citizenship

Making Decisions American poets and writers of the 1830s and 1840s wanted to reform America's attitude toward itself. As a writer or poet, explain how you would present this attitude to the public.

★ Interpreting Illustrations

The Rats leaving a Falling House.

Study the political cartoon above depicting Andrew Jackson and his cabinet members. Then answer the questions that follow.

1. To what incident does this cartoon refer? What happened?

2. What do the title and the items in the background suggest about the cartoonist's assessment of Jackson's administration?

★ Thinking Globally

1. **Comparing Reform Strategies** Following the Industrial Revolution, an exiled German named Karl Marx deplored the abuses of capitalism. The capitalist system, he charged, concentrated wealth in the hands of a few capitalists, widened the gulf between the rich and the poor, denied workers a fair share of their labor, and led to abominable working conditions and other abuse of the worker. In 1848, he and Frederick Engels, in the *Communist Manifesto,* proposed public ownership of land and all means of production. How did American reformers differ in their approach to correcting the abuses of capitalism?

2. **Testing Hypotheses** The Soviet Union, the first country to install a political and economic system based on Marx's theories, began to reintroduce limited private enterprise in the 1980s and 1990s. Review news reports from this period to explain what might have prompted this decision.

★ Relating Geography and History

RELATIONSHIPS WITHIN PLACES: HUMAN-ENVIRONMENT INTERACTIONS

The Industrial Revolution affected each area of the country differently due to its physical characteristics. The North was rocky and mountainous with a short growing season, abundant moving water and coal deposits. The South was lush and fertile with warm temperatures and a long growing season. The West had abundant fertile land but was distant from markets, goods and services and separated from the rest of the country by rugged terrain.

Answer the questions that follow.

1. How did the physical characteristics explain the economies that developed in each section?

2. How did workers and settlers adapt to their environment?

★ Practicing Skills

USING REFERENCE WORKS IN RESEARCH

Refer to the skills lesson on Using Reference Works in Research on page 335 to help you practice this study and writing skill.

a) **encyclopedia**   b) **biographical dictionary**
c) **periodical guide**   d) **book of quotations**
e) **atlas**   f) **almanac**

Indicate which of the above reference works would be most suitable to research the following kinds of information.

1. a detailed description of the 1828 election campaign

2. a definition and example of a pocket veto

3. a brief description of Rachel Jackson

4. an 1828 election map

5. more detailed information about Andrew Jackson's early years

6. Andrew Jackson's personal views on democracy

7. popular and electoral vote counts of the 1840 presidential election

8. a study of the impact of Jacksonian democracy on the United States

9. Jackson's treatment of native Americans

10. route of the "Trail of Tears"

11. statistics on Cherokee and Seminole populations today

12. examples of Daniel Webster's oratory

13. a list of Presidents and the years of their terms of office

MAKING COMPARISONS

Refer to the skills lesson on Making Comparisons on page 368 to help you practice this critical thinking skill.

Use information from Section Two of chapter 11 on pages 345-348 to compare Jeffersonian and Jacksonian democracy in the following areas.

1. election wins in 1800 and 1828

2. the people

3. public officials

4. federal authority

5. voting rights

UNIT 5

Division and Reunion
1825-1877

We are not enemies, but friends...Though passion may have strained, it must not break our bonds of affection. The mystic chords of memory, stretching from every battle-field and patriot grave to every living heart and hearthstone all over this broad land, will yet swell the chorus of the Union ....

—ABRAHAM LINCOLN
First Inaugural Address, March 4, 1861

SETTING THE SCENE

Time

Early to late nineteenth century

Mood

The slavery issue dominated American life during the first half of the nineteenth century. Compromise had worked in the past but a growing antislavery movement would not let the moral shame of slavery die. Convinced that they were at the mercy of a national government dominated by Northern interests, 11 slave states seceded from the Union, resulting in a bloody and bitter Civil War. Union victory, followed by a period of Reconstruction, meant the end of slavery but not racial inequality.

Themes

• Civil Rights and Liberties
• Conflict and Cooperation
• Cultural Diversity
• U. S. Role in World Affairs

Key Events

• Monroe Doctrine
• Treaty of Guadalupe Hidalgo
• Compromise of 1850
• Confederate States formed
• Battles of Gettysburg and Vicksburg
• Surrender of General Lee
• Assassination of Lincoln
• Radical Reconstruction
• Compromise of 1877

Major Issues

• A belief in manifest destiny results in war with Mexico.
• The breakdown of the political party system with the death of the Whigs produces an inability to compromise over slavery.
• During the Civil War, the nation's welfare over individual rights leads to a suspension of civil liberties.
• Although harsh, Reconstruction of the Southern states gradually leads to a renewed Union.

◄ Return of the Colors,1865 *by Edward Simmons, 1902*

Global Perspectives

Beginning in 1803 with the Louisiana Purchase, the United States began a move westward— its "manifest destiny." The question of slavery in these western territories was a major cause of the Civil War, a bloody conflict that divided the young nation.

Conflict racked other parts of the world as well. In 1848 nationalist revolutions, in which citizens sought to end political absolutism, shocked many European nations. After these uprisings had been put down, the use of force often kept citizens from rising up against their rulers.

THE WORLD

	ASIA AND OCEANIA	AFRICA	EUROPE	SOUTH AMERICA	NORTH AND CENTRAL AMERICA
1825					
1845					
	1853 Commodore Matthew Perry arrives in Japan ▲		1848 Nationalist revolutions throughout Europe ▲	1850 Slave trade, but not slavery, ends in Brazil	1861 Benito Juârez becomes President of Mexico ▲
1865			1854 Crimean War begins		
		1869 Suez Canal opens ◄			1867 Dominion of Canada is formed ◄
1885					

Other parts of the world also felt the effects of change. In 1854 Great Britain and France declared war on Russia. This conflict, known as the Crimean War, curbed Russia's influence over the weakening Ottoman Empire. In India in 1857 sepoys—Indian soldiers who served in the British army—rebelled against mistreatment and religious discrimination. Nonetheless, the British strengthened their empire in India, totally subjecting the vast subcontinent.

The United States, meanwhile, turned its attention toward Japan. In 1853 Commodore Matthew Perry sailed into Japan's Edo Bay, demanding that Japan grant trading privileges to the United States. Japan, awed by the power of the United States navy, bowed to American demands. After the Civil War, the United States increased its influence in Latin America. Its involvement there would culminate in an expansionist war before the century was over.

THE UNITED STATES

	PACIFIC AND NORTHWEST	SOUTHWEST	MIDWEST	SOUTHEAST	ATLANTIC NORTHEAST

1825

1830
Fur traders open the Oregon Trail

1836
Texas Revolution, Battle of the Alamo ▲

1831
Cyrus McCormick invents the reaper ▼

1825
Erie Canal completed ▼

1845

1848
Gold discovered in California ▲

1848
Mexican Cession

1852
Uncle Tom's Cabin *published*

1865

1861
Civil War begins ➤

1867
Alaska purchased from Russia

1872
Yellowstone National Park created

1885

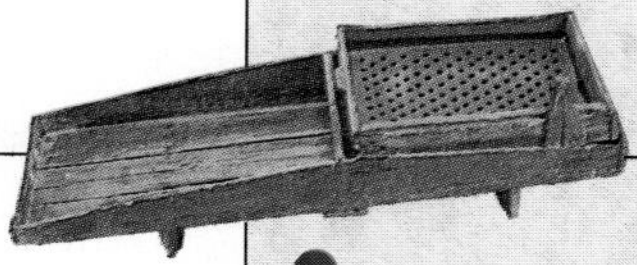

AMERICAN LITERARY HERITAGE

The struggles that tore the nation apart at midcentury were reflected in much of the period's writing. Spirituals—songs of salvation— provided the enslaved African Americans who wrote and chanted them not only with a measure of solace in bleak times but with a means for communicating secretly among themselves under their masters' watchful eye. On the other side of the fence were the writings of Confederate sympathizers, one of whom was Mary Chesnut, wife of a wealthy South Carolina lawyer and senator. Her recently published diary offers a vivid firsthand account of the war and its senseless waste.

As you read, be alert to the authors' attitudes toward their own predicaments.

Mary Chesnut

Follow the Drinking Gourd

hen the sun comes back and the first quail calls,
  Follow the drinking gourd,
  For the old man is a-waiting
for to carry you to freedom
  If you follow the drinking gourd.

Follow the drinking gourd,
  Follow the drinking gourd,
For the old man is a-waiting for to carry you to freedom
  If you follow the drinking gourd.

The river bank will make a very good road,
  The dead trees show you the way,
Left foot, peg foot traveling on
  Follow the drinking gourd,

The river ends between two hills
  Follow the drinking gourd,
There's another river on the other side,
  Follow the drinking gourd,

Where the little river meets the great big river,
  Follow the drinking gourd,
For the old man is a-waiting for to carry you to freedom
  If you follow the drinking gourd.

Go Down, Moses

hen Israel was in Egypt land,
  Let my people go!
  Oppressed so hard they
  could not stand,
  Let my people go!

CHORUS

Go down, Moses,
  Way down in Egypt land
Tell ole Pharoah,
  Let my people go!

Thus say the Lord, bold Moses said,
  Let my people go!
If not I'll smite your first-born dead,
  Let my people go!

No more shall they in bondage toil,
  Let my people go!
Let them come out with Egypt's spoil,
  Let my people go!

Swing Low, Sweet Chariot

Swing low, sweet chariot,
  Coming for to carry me
home,
  Swing low, sweet chariot,
Coming to carry me home.

I looked over Jordan and what did I see
Coming for to carry me home,
A band of angels coming after me.
Coming to carry me home.

If you get there before I do,
Coming for to carry me home,
Tell all my friends I'm coming too,
Coming to carry me home.

Swing low, sweet chariot,
Coming for to carry me home,
Swing low, sweet chariot,
Coming to carry me home.

from Mary Chesnut's Civil War

April 7, 1861....Things are
happening so fast....
    My husband has been
made an aide-de-camp of
[Confederate] General Beauregard....

....he tells me the attack on Fort
Sumter [in Charleston Harbor] may begin
tonight. Depends on [Major] Anderson
[commander of the Union forces occupying the fort] and the troops outside....

The Banjo Lesson
*by Henry Tanner,
1893*

Today at dinner there was no allusion to
things as they stand in Charleston
Harbor. There was an undercurrent of
intense excitement. There could not have
been a more brilliant circle. In addition to
our usual quartet (Judge Withers,
Langdon Cheves, and Trescot), our two
governors dined with us. Means and
Manning.

These men all talked so delightfully. For
once in my life I listened.

That over, business began. In earnest,
Governor Means rummaged a sword and
red sash from somewhere and brought it
for Colonel Chesnut, who had gone to
demand the surrender of Fort Sumter.

And now, patience—we must wait....

Why did that green goose Anderson go into Fort Sumter? Then everything began to go wrong.

Now they have intercepted a letter from him, urging them to let him surrender. He paints the horrors likely to ensue if they will not.

He ought to have thought of all that before he put his head in the hole.

April 12, 1861....Yesterday was the merriest, maddest dinner we have had yet. Men were more audaciously wise and

Colonel Anderson had been deeply interesting—but was not inclined to be communicative, wanted his dinner. Felt for Anderson. Had telegraphed to President [of the Confederacy,] Davis for instructions.

What answer to give Anderson, etc., etc. He has gone back to Fort Sumter with additional instructions....

I do not pretend to go to sleep. How can I? If Anderson does not accept terms—at four—the orders are—he shall be fired upon.

Bombardment of Fort Sumter, Charleston Harbor *by Currier and Ives, 1861*

witty. We had an unspoken foreboding it was to be our last pleasant meeting. Mr. Miles dined with us today. Mrs. Henry King rushed in: "The news, I come for the latest news—all of the men of the King family are on...[Morris] island [a strategic point near Fort Sumter]"—of which fact she seemed proud.

While she was here, our peace negotiator—or envoy—came in. That is, Mr. Chesnut returned—his interview with

I count four—St. Michael chimes. I begin to hope. At half-past four, the heavy booming of a cannon.

I sprang out of bed. And on my knees —prostrate—I prayed as I never prayed before.

There was a sound of stir all over the house—pattering of feet in the corridor— all seemed hurrying one way. I put on my double gown and a shawl and went, too. It was to the housetop.

The shells were bursting. In the dark I heard a man say "waste of ammunition."

I knew my husband was rowing about in a boat somewhere in that dark bay. And that the shells were roofing it over—bursting toward the fort. If Anderson was obstinate—he was to order the forts on our side to open fire. Certainly he had begun. The regular roar of the cannon—there it was. And who could tell what each volley accomplished of death and destruction.

The women were wild, there on the rooftop. Prayers from the women and imprecations from the men, and then a shell would light up the scene. Tonight, they say, the forces are to attempt to land....

We watched up there—everybody wondered. Fort Sumter did not fire a shot.

Today Miles and Manning, colonels now—aides to Beauregard—dined with us. The latter hoped I would keep the peace. I give him only good words, for he was to be under fire all day and night, in the bay carrying orders, etc.

Last night—or this morning truly—up on the housetop I was so weak and weary I sat down on something that looked like a black stool.

"Get up, you foolish woman—your dress is on fire," cried a man. And he put me out. It was a chimney, and the sparks caught my clothes. Susan Preston and Mr. Venable then came up. But my fire had been extinguished before it broke out into a regular blaze.

Do you know, after all that noise and our tears and prayers, nobody has been hurt. Sound and fury, signifying nothing. A delusion and a snare....

Somebody came in just now and reported Colonel Chesnut asleep on the sofa in General Beauregard's room. After two such nights he must be so tired as to be able to sleep anywhere....

April 13, 1861. Nobody hurt, after all. How gay we were last night.

Reaction after the dread of all the slaughter we thought those dreadful cannon were making such a noise in doing.

Not even a battery the worse for wear.

Fort Sumter has been on fire. He has not yet silenced any of our guns. So the aides—still with swords and red sashes by way of uniform—tell us.

But the sound of those guns make regular meals impossible. None of us go to table. But tea trays pervade the corridors, going everywhere.

Some of the anxious hearts lie on their beds and moan in solitary misery. Mrs. Wigfall and I solace ourselves with tea in my room.

These women have all a satisfying faith.

April 15, 1861. I did not know that one could live such days of excitement.

They called, "Come out—there is a crowd coming."

A mob indeed, but it was headed by Colonels Chesnut and Manning.

The crowd was shouting and showing these two as messengers of good news. They were escorted to Beauregard's headquarters. Fort Sumter had surrendered.

Those up on the housetop shouted to us, "The fort is on fire." That had been the story once or twice before.

When we had calmed down, Colonel Chesnut, who had taken it all quietly enough—if anything, more unruffled than usual in his serenity—told us how the surrender came about.

Wigfall was with them on Morris Island when he saw the fire in the fort, jumped in a little boat and, with his handkerchief as a white flag, rowed over to Fort Sumter. Wigfall went in through a porthole.

When Colonel Chesnut arrived shortly after and was received by the regular entrance, Colonel Anderson told him he had need to pick his way warily, for it was all mined.

As far as I can make out, the fort surrendered to Wigfall.

But it is all confusion. Our flag is flying there. Fire engines have been sent to put out the fire.

Everybody tells you half of something and then rushes off to tell something else or to hear the last news....

INTERPRETING LITERATURE

1. What is the message from slave to slave in "Follow the Drinking Gourd"?

2. Which spiritual equates the plight of the slaves with that of another group? Which group?

3. Describe the mood of the spirituals.

4. What is Mary Chesnut's view of events at Fort Sumter? Explain.

EVALUATING REACTIONS

5. Compare the themes of the spirituals with Mary Chesnut's comments on events of the day.

CHAPTER 13
Manifest Destiny

SETTING THE SCENE

Historical Focus

The drive to expand the boundaries of the United States across North America became a single-minded goal for many Americans in the 1830s and 1840s. Through war with Mexico and diplomatic negotiations with Great Britain, the United States acquired Texas, Oregon, California, Utah, and the remainder of the Southwest. By 1850 thousands and thousands of settlers had crossed the Great Plains for new homes. They carried with them a fervent belief in democratic institutions.

Concepts to Understand

- Why geographic **expansion** to the Pacific became a national mission.
- How westward **migration** shaped the political development of Oregon and California.

People to Know

Joseph Smith, Brigham Young, Stephen Austin, Antonio Santa Anna, James K. Polk, Zachary Taylor, Matthew Perry

Places to Locate

Oregon Trail, Rio Grande

Terms to Identify

Webster-Ashburton treaty, mountain men, dark horse, consul, Ostend Manifesto

Guided Reading

As you read this chapter, seek the answers to the following questions.

1. What made Americans so determined to expand the size of the country?
2. What were the causes and results of the Mexican War?

SPANNING THE DECADES

POLITICAL	1836 *Battle of the Alamo* *Texas wins independence*		1842 *Webster-Ashburton Treaty ratified*	

1835   1840

CULTURAL	1838 *First trans-Atlantic steamship voyage*	1839 *Charles Goodyear develops vulcanized rubber*	1841 *Ralph Waldo Emerson publishes* Self Reliance *and* Essays	1844 *First telegraph message sent*

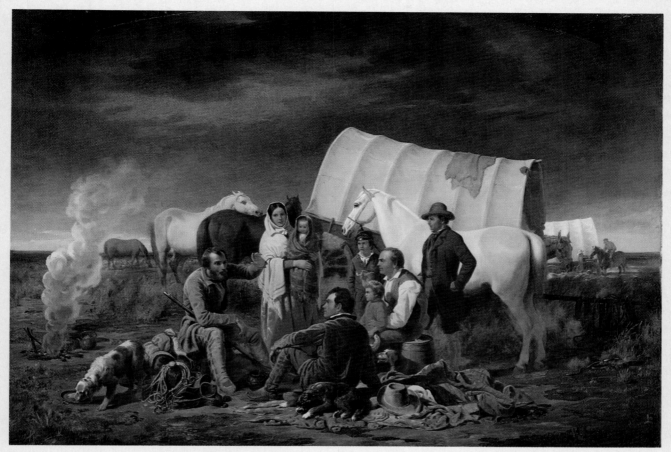

Advice on the Prairie *by William Ranney, 1853*

…[O]ur people, increasing to many millions, have filled the eastern valley of the Mississippi, adventurously ascended the Missouri to its headsprings, and are already engaged in establishing the blessing of self government in valleys of which the rivers flow to the Pacific….

—JAMES K. POLK
Inaugural Address, March 4, 1845

SECTION ONE

The Thirst for New Lands

Sir, our natural boundary is the Pacific Ocean. The swelling tide of our population must and will roll on until that mighty ocean interposes its waters, and limits our territorial empire.

—FRANCIS BAYLIES
Congressman from Massachusetts, 1821

Section Focus

The idea that the United States was bound to extend its borders from the Atlantic to the Pacific oceans became known as "manifest destiny." It found its greatest expression in the decade of the 1840s, when the United States acquired territories even more vast than the Louisiana Purchase of 1803.

Objectives

After studying this section, you should be able to:
• Give reasons Americans wanted to expand their territory to the Pacific.
• Describe negotiations with Britain over disputed lands.

S everal factors combined to produce the expansionist movement known as manifest destiny. Chief among these was the seemingly habitual ambition, nurtured by the restlessness of the American pioneer spirit, to move on to new land. Fulfilling the nation's manifest destiny, settlers pushed westward all the way to the Pacific coast—one of the great migrations of history. Yet, why would Americans move beyond the existing boundaries of the United States when most of the land within those boundaries was still sparsely settled, and most of the area between the Mississippi River and the Rocky Mountains was still not tilled?

Westward to the Pacific

The push to the Pacific Ocean resulted in part from the assumption that the tree-less plains between the 98th meridian and the Rockies were unsuited to farming and should therefore be left to the Indians and the buffalo. The federal government set apart portions of this "Great American Desert" for Indian nations expelled from their homes in the East. In 1825 the government declared that there was to be no further white settlement beyond a line drawn along the western boundaries of existing states and territories. Reinforcing this policy, Congress in 1834 not only forbade settlement in Indian territories but required a special license to trade with Indians. Thus, if newcomers wanted available land, especially the forested and well-watered land they were used to, they had to cross the Rockies.

Land-hungry settlers proved willing to risk their lives in crossing the wide grass-lands and steep mountains to reach the Pacific Coast. The spirit of manifest destiny was flavored with the boastfulness of the frontiersman who said that he could:

...wade the brown Mississippi, jump the Ohio, step across the Nolachucky, ride a streak of lightning, slip without a scratch down a honey locust tree, whip my weight in wildcats, and strike a blow like a falling tree.

Commercial interests as well as the desire for land promoted manifest destiny. Excited by the recent opening of China, eastern traders and shipowners saw the harbors of San Diego and San Francisco as necessary way-stations on the route to Asia. Fearing that the British were also interested in acquiring good harbors and would seize California before the United States, eastern mercantile interests pushed hard for expansion. They also wanted the question of who controlled the Oregon territory to be settled in such a way that the United States would acquire the excellent harbor at Puget Sound.

Perhaps the strongest aspect of the patriotic impulse toward expansion was pride in American institutions and a desire to spread them. Andrew Jackson expressed this idea clearly when he argued that the United States had a mission to "extend the area of freedom." It was political idealism that motivated a New York editor, John L. O'Sullivan, who gave a name to the expansionist movement when he wrote:

Away, away with all those cobweb issues of rights of discovery, exploration, settlement, continuity, etc. Our claims are based on the right of our manifest destiny to overspread and to possess the whole continent which Providence has given us for the development of the great experiment in liberty and federative self-government entrusted to us.

Rivals for the Land

Expanding the United States to the Pacific involved risks, for it meant taking land claimed or settled by other peoples. The United States, with limited military power, had to carefully weigh the possibility of hostilities with Indians on the Plains, with Mexico in Texas, and with Britain on the Pacific Coast.

Fortunately for the United States, the vast region of southwestern plains and plateaus was a "power vacuum." Mexico claimed the land but had almost no presence there. The Indians who lived there were at a technological disadvantage in defending themselves against whites. The Arapaho and Comanche Indians of the Plains and the Apaches of the Southwest were divided into small bands and fought each other as readily as they did whites. In the 1840s, they did not realize that their entire way of life was in danger.

Mexico lacked not only settlements in the region but political stability at the center of its government. With a revolution occurring about once every three years, Mexico was unable to carry on a war with another nation effectively. It could not prevent the advance of the United States to the Rio Grande or to California.

Manifest destiny also propelled the United States toward confrontation with the British on the Pacific Coast. Although Great Britain's superior naval power would probably have been able to keep Oregon and take California, British political leaders had little desire to add to an empire that they thought to be already overextended.

Great Britain, however, was quite capable of defending land that served its vital interests. For this reason the first area where the advance of American settlement caused serious friction with Britain was not in the West, but in the extreme Northeast. Because of confusing language in the Treaty of Paris after the Revolution, the northern and eastern boundaries of Maine had been uncertain. As long as the region was unoccupied, this was not a serious matter. In 1838, however, the British decided to construct an overland road to connect St. John on the Bay of Fundy with Montreal and Quebec. The road was just one part of an overall plan to suppress a Canadian independence movement by giving British troops ease of travel. In February 1839, settlers from Maine, pushing into the fertile Aroostook (uh ROOS tuhk) Valley, met and clashed with British workers who were felling trees for the road project. The struggle, fought mostly with fists, is known as the Aroostook War. It nearly led to something more serious when Maine and New Brunswick called out their militias, and Congress authorized President Van Buren to call for 50,000 soldiers in case a war with Great Britain should develop.

A general atmosphere of ill will made it seem likely that sooner or later some petty dispute would plunge the United States and Great Britain into war. American orators and school textbooks kept alive bitter memories of the Revolution and the War of 1812. Beginning in 1838 along the border between the United States and Canada, Americans formed secret "Hunters' Lodges" whose avowed purpose was to help the Canadians throw off British rule.

On the other side of the Atlantic, Britons harbored their own resentments against Americans. British authors wrote books that jeered at every unpleasant feature of American life from tobacco-chewing to slavery. Many British investors were angry over losses from land swindles or debts that some states had refused to honor after the Panic of 1837.

The Webster-Ashburton Treaty

In spite of friction and ill feeling, there were practical reasons for pursuing peace. The most important reason was that the United States and Great Britain each profited from the other's trade. Great Britain was the largest foreign buyer of American wheat, tobacco, and cotton, and the United States was Britain's biggest market for manufactured goods. Fortunately, both the British and American governments were aware of the advantages of peace.

In 1842 Lord Aberdeen, the British foreign secretary, and Daniel Webster, the American secretary of state, arranged a meeting to attempt to settle outstanding disputes. Showing his goodwill, Aberdeen sent Lord Ashburton, the husband of an American heiress, to Washington, D.C.

Eager to reach an agreement, the men decided that it was impossible to fix the correct boundary of Maine. Instead, they divided the disputed territory as fairly as they could. Great Britain got what it wanted most—enough of the northern section to make possible a direct land route from the St. Lawrence River to New Brunswick. The United States received what it wanted—the Aroostook Valley—along with other concessions on the northern boundaries of New Hampshire, Vermont, and New York.

Webster and Ashburton failed to reach agreement on several other disputes involving such matters as American ships illegally carrying slaves from Africa, the debts owed British investors, and the ownership of the Oregon territory. While the Webster-Ashburton Treaty did not remove all points of Anglo-American friction, it did clear the air and put an end to the threat of war.

SUMMARY

In the 1840s the quest for land and commercial interests pushed American pioneers westward to the Pacific Ocean. Americans considered the Great Plains unproductive, but California and Oregon were attractive to settlers and to eastern merchants, eager to claim coastal harbors for their trade with China. Patriotism fueled Americans' wish to spread their democratic beliefs across the continent and nearly brought war with Great Britain over territorial disputes in Maine. The need for good economic and trade relations with Great Britain led to the Webster-Ashburton Treaty.

CHECKING FOR UNDERSTANDING

1 **Identify** manifest destiny, Aroostook War, Webster-Ashburton Treaty

2. **Explain** how mistaken beliefs about the land between the 98th meridian and the Rockies fueled westward migration.

3. **List** the three rivals to American settlers for western lands.

4. **Name** three factors that led to the manifest destiny movement.

5. **Cite** two factors that prevented native Americans from stopping westward migration.

THINKING CRITICALLY

6. **Identifying Assumptions** Do you believe Americans had the right to settle western lands? What assumptions did the idea of manifest destiny make about the rights of Indians and others to this land?

CONNECTIONS: HISTORY AND GEOGRAPHY

7. **Analyzing Motives** What are the characteristics of a good harbor? Why were harbors important in the 1840s? Explain how the quest for good harbors affected western migration.

★ ★ ★ ★ ★ ★ ★ ★ ★ ★ ★ ★ ★ ★ ★ ★ ★ ★

Oregon and Texas

SETTING THE SCENE

There are at the present time two great nations in the world....I allude to the Russians and the Americans....All other nations seem to have nearly reached their natural limits, and they have only to maintain their power; these alone are proceeding...along a path to which no limit can be perceived.

—ALEXIS DE TOCQUEVILLE
French writer, *Democracy in America,* 1835

Section Focus

Americans had begun moving to Texas in the 1820s. By the 1830s and 1840s, they were making their way to Oregon, California, and Utah. What began as a trickle of immigrants swelled to a flood; these American settlements, in turn, gave weight to arguments in favor of expansion and annexation.

Objectives

After studying this section, you should be able to:
- Describe the overland migrations to Oregon and Utah.
- Explain why Texas wanted independence from Mexico and how it became part of the United States.

The Oregon Territory extended from the Pacific Ocean to the Rocky Mountains, bordering Russian Alaska to the north and California to the south. Until the early 1800s, Spain, France, Russia, Great Britain, and the United States held claims to Oregon. The United States acquired the French claim by the Louisiana Purchase in 1803 and the Spanish claim by the Florida-purchase treaty of 1819. Russia fixed the southern boundary of Alaska in 1824, giving up its claims to the area. In 1818 Great Britain and the United States agreed to a curious arrangement known as "joint occupation" of the Oregon Territory, leaving the question of ownership unsettled. While Webster and Ashburton were determining the Maine boundary, the rivalry between Great Britain and the United States in the Oregon territory intensified.

The Opening of Oregon

The interest of the United States in Oregon began in 1787 when a Boston ship, the *Columbia,* made a very profitable pioneer trading voyage. The ship left port with a supply of ginseng, the root of a common New England weed highly prized by the Chinese as a medicine. Rounding Cape Horn, South America, the *Columbia* sailed to the coast of Oregon to take on other cargo in demand in China—sea-otter furs. After a voyage across the Pacific, the ginseng and furs were exchanged for Chinese tea and silk. These in turn were sold to Americans at high prices when the vessel returned to the United States after a trip around the world in 1790.

The *Columbia* inaugurated a regular trade route, with profits that were sometimes enormous. In exchange for trinkets valued at less than $2, one trader got from the Indians sea-otter pelts that brought $22,000 in China. Small wonder that in 1800, 5 years before the arrival of Lewis and Clark, no fewer than 15 New England ships cruised the coast of Oregon to gather furs for the China trade.

The beavers found in inland waterways drew even more people to Oregon than the sea otters of the coast. Beaver pelts had been the chief export of French Canada before 1763 and of the British fur traders after that. By 1800, the eastern supply had been reduced so much that the discovery of beavers in the streams draining from the Rockies was like a gold strike. Fierce competition developed between three great fur companies: the British Hudson's Bay Company, the

Examining Fine Art
Frederic Remington vividly depicts the fur trade. Where were these furs marketed for huge profits?

Examining Illustrations *In the late 1830s, "Oregon fever" began to entice Americans to a 2000-mile moving adventure. Who sent back the first reports of rich Oregon soil?*

Woodcraft, forest craft, and river craft were his skill. To read the weather, the streams, the woods; to know the ways of animals and birds; to find food and shelter; to find the Indians when they were his customers or to battle them from stump to stump when they were on the warpath and to know which caprice was on them; to take comfort in flood or blizzard; to move safely through the wilderness, to make the wilderness his bed, his table and his tool—this was his vocation.

American Fur Company headed by John Jacob Astor of New York, and the Missouri Company of St. Louis. The bitter struggle among the fur companies verged on actual warfare. The three companies played politics in rivalries among the Indian nations, bribed away each other's agents, and sometimes stole each other's furs. As accessible regions were trapped out, the rugged individuals who carried on the dangerous business of trapping and trading in Indian country penetrated farther and farther into the Rocky Mountain wilderness searching for new sources of furs.

In *The Year of Decision, 1846,* Bernard DeVoto wrote of the bravery, skill, and self-reliance of these trappers, who became known as "mountain men":

While their heyday lasted only about 10 years and they never numbered more than a few hundred at any one time, the mountain men played an important part in opening overland routes to Oregon and California. They discovered the best passes through the mountains and places where rivers could be crossed. They also served as guides to parties of settlers crossing the mountains by wagon train. The pursuits of the mountain men, however, were devastating to the native Americans. They introduced whiskey and new diseases, which corrupted and weakened these Americans.

Settlers Move West

Until shortly before 1840 the joint occupation of Oregon was almost entirely a British affair, with the Hudson's Bay Company acting as the government of the region. In the mid-1830s, however, American churches sent missionaries to Christianize the Indians. When the missionaries began to farm, they sent back glowing reports of the fertility of the soil.

Missionaries Marcus and Narcissa Whitman, together with Eliza and Henry Spalding, joined a band of mountain men on their journey to Oregon in 1836. Narcissa Whitman and Eliza Spalding were the first white women known to cross the continent. Reading the Whitmans' letters, people in the East were convinced that the Oregon country could be settled. In 1838

a party of American pioneers arrived by ship in the valley of the Willamette River; most newcomers, however, came by covered wagon over the Oregon Trail. By 1842 there were perhaps 500 Americans in Oregon, and in the next year a single party of immigrants numbered 900.

The long, slow journey from Missouri to Oregon demanded courage and endurance. Heavy Conestoga wagons carried a family's belongings in a space only about 10 feet long, 4 feet wide, and 2 feet deep. Teams of 6 or 8 oxen pulled the wagons; when the going was good, they covered about 2 miles in an hour. The trip usually took from May to November, when there was grass along the trail for the cattle to graze. Crossing rivers involved the risk of tipping the wagons or drowning the oxen. Through much of the journey there was an ever-present danger from Indians. To meet such difficulties, parties of immigrants had to be thoroughly organized. The members of a wagon train often chose officers by election. One person would have responsibility for the cattle, another for posting sentries, and another for leading the advance party, which chose the route. The group as a whole voted on major decisions.

By 1843 so many Americans had arrived in Oregon that they set up a government of their own. Like the Pilgrims and the Mayflower Compact, they drew up their own constitution. Its preamble, similar to the U.S. Constitution Preamble, read:

We the people of Oregon territory,
for the purpose of mutual protection
and to secure peace and prosperity among
ourselves, agree to adopt the following
laws and regulations until such time
as the United States of America
extend their jurisdiction over us.

The last phrase shows that the settlers were determined that the United States and not Britain should rule Oregon. By 1845, 5,000 Americans were living south of the Columbia River and demanding that their government take possession of the Oregon Territory.

Another group of settlers moved west, not to expand United States territory but to escape from it. The Mormon Church and its founder Joseph Smith were forced to move several times to escape persecution. Many people resented the new religion because of its communal organization and Smith's teachings that a man could have more than one wife. The Mormons moved first to Ohio, then to Missouri, and then to Illinois. At Nauvoo, Illinois, they built a thriving community of 20,000 people. But in 1844 Joseph Smith was jailed for ordering the destruction of a printing press that belonged to people who

Life of the Times

MOUNTAIN MEN

In the early nineteenth century, fashionable Europeans wore felt hats made of beaver fur. Milliners used the short-haired fur from a beaver's belly to produce the soft nap needed for felt. These hats came in all shapes—top hats, felt bonnets, and tricorns—the three-cornered hats associated with the American Revolution. At one time milliners obtained their furs from Russia, but hunters exhausted the supply of beaver there. The next source was the woodlands of eastern North America until the beaver was hunted out there too. Then beaver were discovered in the Rocky Mountains.

Fur companies hired free-lance trappers who over time became known as mountain men. Few rules, except the law of survival, governed their behavior. While only some mountain men could read, almost all were good horsemen and marksmen. As year-round wilderness residents, they learned to live independently. They also knew everything about capturing beavers.

A mountain man called the bait he used to lure the beaver "medicine." Actually it was a musky liquid that came from the glands of other beavers. The mountain man spread the liquid on a branch suspended above the trap.

Since beavers are water animals, a mountain man set his trap under water to mask his smell. An animal caught in the underwater trap drowned quickly, and so the trapper did not have to worry about struggling with his catch and possibly getting hurt or damaging the pelt of the animal.

Examining Fine Art *Some poorer Mormons traveled to Utah in handcarts. What nation owned Utah in 1847?*

The move took place in 1847. The Mormons soon established several flourishing settlements near the Great Salt Lake in Utah. They developed an advanced system for controlling the water supply in the semiarid regions of the Far West. Around Salt Lake City, irrigation transformed the desert into a garden spot. In 1848 the Mormons learned that the Mexican territory to which they had fled had become a part of the United States as the result of a war with Mexico over the southern border of Texas.

Texas Independence

Texas—a vast, ill-defined area extending southwest from Louisiana to the Rio Grande and west to the foothills of the Rocky Mountains—belonged to Mexico. The original Spanish settlements in Texas were limited to a few hundred people and a dozen Indian missions.

When Mexico broke away from Spain in 1821, its government sought settlers to develop Texas. In 1822 Stephen Austin,

Examining Maps
Many people died on these trails. What were the geographic hazards on the trail from Independence to Los Angeles?

disagreed with him. An angry mob then killed Smith and his brother. Brigham Young, the new leader, believing that no safe refuge could be found in the United States, sought an isolated haven in territory that belonged to Mexico.

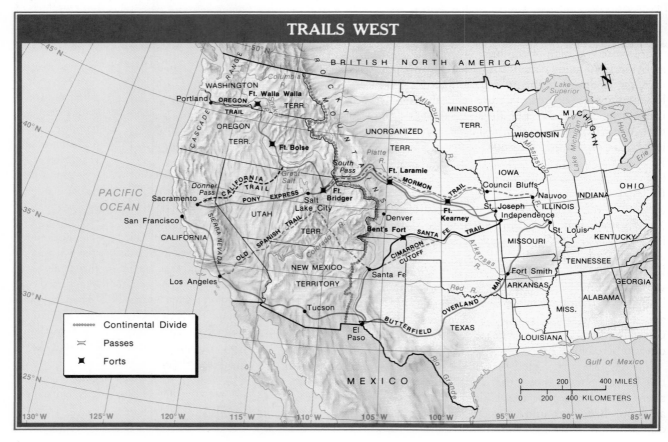

Connections

HISTORY AND RELIGION

AMERICAN MISSIONARIES

Lyman Beecher, Congregationalist pastor and seminary president, in his *Plea for the West* (1832), argued that the future of the nation depended on Christianizing the West. Protestant and Catholic missionaries heeded Beecher's call. Organizations were founded to send missionaries and Bibles to remote western settlements.

Father Pierre DeSmet among the Indians

Along with the strong challenge to repent and accept Christian beliefs, missionaries taught people to read and write.

A few Protestant missionaries also began to work among native Americans in the West—a calling that Franciscans and Jesuits had felt since the early days of exploration. A pioneer Methodist missionary effort began in the Oregon Territory when Marcus and Narcissa Whitman helped establish a string of mission stations along the Columbia River in the 1830s.

Missionaries often tried to secure special protection for Indians but they found it difficult to serve both the needs of the Indians and advancing white settlers. Missionaries also imposed their own values and traditions, which often led to few converts and deep resentment among native Americans.

★ ★ ★ ★ ★ ★ ★ ★ ★ ★

MAKING THE RELIGION CONNECTION

1. Why did Lyman Beecher call for missionary work in the West?

2. Why might missionaries have found it difficult to serve the needs of Indians and white settlers?

LINKING PAST AND PRESENT

3. How does missionary activity today differ from the 1800s?

★ ★ ★ ★ ★ ★ ★ ★ ★ ★

an American, took over a grant of land that the Spanish government had given his father, Moses Austin, before Mexico's independence. Mexican officials agreed that Austin could bring American settlers into Texas, provided that they became Roman Catholics and obeyed Mexican law. Austin's settlement proved so successful that by 1830 Texas had attracted almost 30,000 Americans. In that year Mexico passed a law restricting further immigration because it was concerned about developments in Texas. Americans, knowing that Mexico's law against slavery was not strictly enforced in Texas, had brought thousands of enslaved people. In addition, they had failed to become Catholics, and the flood of settlers now outnumbered local Mexicans 10 to 1.

In 1833 Mexico elected General Antonio Santa Anna as president. When the new president assumed dictatorial powers and abolished local rights, rebellion broke out in Texas. Late in 1835 Santa Anna marched his army north to subdue the rebels. In February 1836, with more than 2,000 troops, Santa Anna besieged 188 Texans in the Alamo, a mission station in San Antonio. After 2 weeks of resistance, the defenders of the Alamo were defeated, but the victory cost Santa Anna over 1,500 soldiers.

The Mexican army pursued Sam Houston, the leader of the Texans, and a band of rebel troops toward the United States border. But at San Jacinto (SAN huh SEENT uh) Creek, Houston's forces turned and attacked. Crying "Remember the Alamo!" they surprised and defeated the Mexican troops and captured Santa Anna. Under pressure, Santa Anna signed a treaty accepting the independence of Texas. As soon as he was free, however, Santa Anna refused to be bound by terms dictated at the point of a sword. The Mexican Congress considered Texas a rebellious province, but could not subdue it.

Texas declared itself the Lone Star Republic in 1836 and immediately voted to seek admission to the United States. Although there was strong southern support to extend the area of cotton-growing by annexing Texas, northern abolitionists charged that the whole history of Texas was a slaveholders' plot to enlarge their power. President Jackson, choosing not to impair the chances of Vice President Martin Van Buren's winning the next presidential election, delayed recognition of the new republic until after the election of 1836. President Van Buren refused to recommend annexation, leaving the question for the next administration.

The issue arose again in 1843. President John Tyler feared that the Republic of Texas would ally itself too closely with Great Britain. The British were also interested in Texas as a new source of cotton—and as a market for their manufactured goods. Moreover, British antislavery societies hoped that the new country might be persuaded to free its slaves. The threat of Texas as a competing source of cotton and a possible haven for runaway slaves greatly alarmed southerners, among them John C. Calhoun, who became secretary of state in 1844. He presented an annexation treaty to the Senate, but the 35-16 vote there did not meet the two-thirds majority needed for ratification. The rejection of annexation sprang from northern opposition to adding more slave territory to the Union and from fears that admission of Texas would bring on a war with Mexico.

Examining Maps
Santa Anna won a costly victory, losing 1,500 soldiers at the Alamo. In what battle did Houston's forces win Texas's independence?

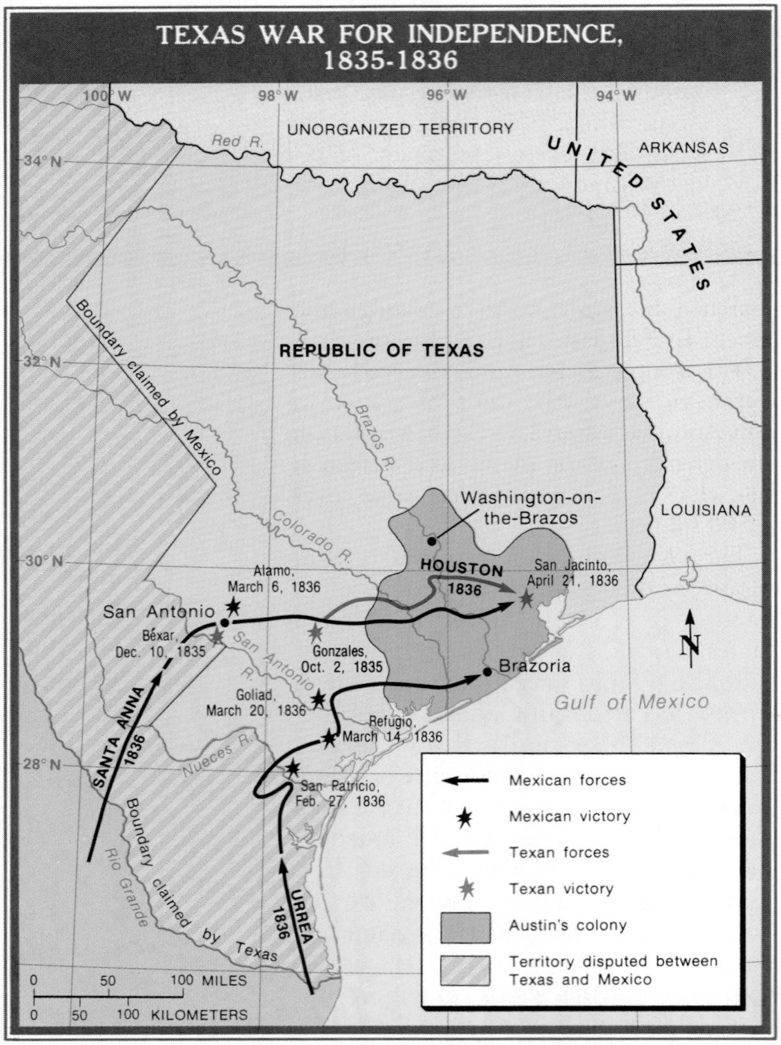

TEXAS WAR FOR INDEPENDENCE, 1835-1836
100° W
98° W
96° W
94° W
34° N
32° N
30° N
28° N
UNORGANIZED TERRITORY
Red R.
UNITED STATES
ARKANSAS
REPUBLIC OF TEXAS
Boundary claimed by Mexico
Brazos R.
Colorado R.
Washington-on-the-Brazos
LOUISIANA
HOUSTON 1836
San Jacinto, April 21, 1836
Alamo, March 6, 1836
San Antonio
Béxar, Dec. 10, 1835
Gonzales, Oct. 2, 1835
San Antonio R.
Brazoria
Goliad, March 20, 1836
Gulf of Mexico
Refugio, March 14, 1836
SANTA ANNA 1836
Nueces R.
San Patricio, Feb. 27, 1836
Rio Grande
Boundary claimed by Texas
URREA 1836
N
Mexican forces
Mexican victory
Texan forces
Texan victory
Austin's colony
Territory disputed between Texas and Mexico
0 50 100 MILES
0 50 100 KILOMETERS

Election of 1844

As the presidential election of 1844 approached, the issue of territorial expansion took center stage. Ex-President Van Buren, a Democrat, and Henry Clay, a Whig, were expected to be the rival candidates. Texas's annexation, with its threat of disunion over slavery, alarmed both men so much that they opposed it in letters to the press published on the same day. Then the unexpected happened. Van Buren failed to receive the Democratic nomination. A coalition of westerners who wanted Oregon and southerners who wanted Texas nominated the first **dark horse,** or unexpected candidate, in the history of the presidency, James K. Polk of Tennessee.

The Democrats dodged the slavery issue by linking the demands for Texas and Oregon. They placed their main emphasis on taking all of Oregon, where slavery would certainly never be established. This was dramatized by the campaign slogan, "Fifty-four forty or fight!" (The parallel 54°40' was the southern boundary of Alaska.) Manifest destiny became the principal issue of the campaign.

To counter this unexpected challenge, the Whigs had only Henry Clay's great personal popularity and the slogan, "Who is James K. Polk?" which called attention to the obscurity of Clay's opponent. Clay backed down from his earlier opposition to admitting Texas by issuing a cautious statement that he would be glad to see the region annexed, if the American people so desired and if war with Mexico could be avoided. Clay's hedging did not quite work, and Polk won the election by a slim margin.

Even though the election had been close, President Tyler, still in office, asserted that Polk's victory was a mandate for the admission of Texas to the Union. He asked Congress to accomplish the admission by a joint resolution that would require only a simple majority, instead of a treaty that required a vote of two-thirds of the Senate. In February 1845, on Tyler's initiative, both houses of Congress, by very narrow majorities, passed the joint resolution offering to annex Texas. In December 1845, the Lone Star Republic became the twenty-eighth state. The Mexico-Texas boundary remained undetermined, and the Mexican government threatened war.

Division of Oregon, 1846

The risk of war with Mexico put pressure on the United States to settle the Oregon question. It was one thing to shout, "Fifty-four forty or fight!" in an election campaign, and another to take on Great Britain, the greatest sea power in the world, and prepare to fight Mexico.

Great Britain also had reasons to settle the Oregon question peacefully. By 1846 the number of American settlers in Oregon had risen to 10,000 and United States expansionists were calling for "thirty thousand rifles" in Oregon to protect American interests. Rather than losing all of the territory, the British government was willing to relinquish the southern half. The Hudson's Bay Company had trapped out the beavers from the region there and had moved its principal base from the Columbia River to Vancouver Island. In 1846 Polk submitted to the Senate a British proposal to divide Oregon along the 49th parallel. In spite of the objections of westerners, who accused the President of backing down on his demand for all of Oregon, the Senate approved the treaty and it was signed on June 15, 1846.

Section Two Review

SUMMARY

Until 1840 the British held the primary interest in Oregon. American interest in and migration to Oregon increased after America joined the fur trade. Missionaries to Oregon fueled a major migration with reports of fertile farmland. Americans also poured into Texas, forcing the Mexican government to ban further immigration. When Texans revolted against the Mexican government, Santa Anna led an army into Texas. Led by Sam Houston, the Texans eventually won a shaky independence. After the United States annexed Texas in 1845, the possibility of war with Mexico unfolded and forced the United States to settle the conflict over the Oregon border with Britain.

CHECKING FOR UNDERSTANDING

1. **Identify** *Columbia,* Mormons, Brigham Young, Santa Anna, Sam Houston

2. **Define** dark horse

3. **Explain** how the fur trade initiated interest in Oregon.

4. **Cite** two reasons why James K. Polk won the 1844 election.

THINKING CRITICALLY

5. **Recognizing Cultural Diffusion** The mountain men who hunted in Oregon had an adverse effect on the Indians who lived there by introducing disease and alcohol. List some possible consequences of this cultural interaction.

GLOBAL PERSPECTIVES

6. **Recognizing Relationships** Animal pelts from Oregon were used by clothiers in Paris and London to line coats. The skins were also made into felt that was used worldwide. Describe the relationship that can be seen between a worldwide clothing industry and the migration of American people westward.

War With Mexico

Now, after reiterated menaces, Mexico has passed the boundary of the United States, has invaded our territory and shed American blood upon the American soil. She has proclaimed that hostilities have commenced, and that the two nations are now at war.

—JAMES K. POLK
Message to Congress, May 11, 1846

Section Focus

James K. Polk had been chosen as a presidential candidate because of his clear commitment to territorial expansion. He was determined to fulfill the pledges he made to his party during the campaign. In undertaking a war with Mexico, however, he would face stiff resistance from northerners and Whigs in Congress.

Objectives

After studying this section, you should be able to:
- Contrast the United States' short-term and long-range goals in the war with Mexico.
- List the terms of the treaty of Guadalupe Hidalgo.

James K. Polk was a man who knew what he wanted. On his first day in office, he told a member of his cabinet that he had four great purposes: to settle the Oregon question, to lower the tariff, to reestablish the independent treasury system abolished by the Whigs in 1842, and to annex California. By his third year in office, Polk's strong will and hard work had accomplished his first three goals. Annexing California would prove much more difficult.

New Englanders had traded with California for cattle hides and tallow for 50 years and had described the region as "the richest, most beautiful, the healthiest country in the world." In the 1840s, it seemed that control of the region might soon change hands. The native population had staged 4 rebellions against the Mexican government, which was too distant and too disorganized to govern the region effectively. American officials feared that Great Britain, or even France, might annex California to acquire the great harbor of San Francisco, large enough to accommodate all the navies of the world.

In his annual message to Congress in December 1845, Polk cautioned Great Britain and France by repeating the "no colonization" principle of the Monroe Doctrine. He also urged the United States **consul,** or official representative, in Monterey, California, to "arouse in the bosoms of the Californians that love of liberty so natural to the American continent"—in other words, to stir up a revolution. Late in 1845 he sent John Slidell as envoy to Mexico to discuss the Texas question and to offer up to $25 million for California. Slidell's mission was completely fruitless. So great was Mexican anger at the loss of Texas that any Mexican official who dared to talk with the American diplomat could have lost his position and possibly his life. Slidell's visit, however, inspired a successful revolt against the Mexican government by those who opposed any negotiations with the United States. The new leaders were determined to go to war to win back Texas, and President Mariano Paredes refused to see Slidell. Because he could not present his case, Slidell returned to Washington, D.C. The Mexican government broke off diplomatic relations when the United States annexed Texas, making further negotiations impossible.

The failure of Slidell's mission did not end attempts by the United States to annex California. Mexico's leaders, already angry with the United States, might easily be provoked into war.

Examining Illustrations
President Polk, an expansionist, spoke of "the right of the United States" to territories beyond the Rocky Mountains. Which territory did he want to annex?

Outbreak of War

The spark that ignited the war between Mexico and the United States resulted from a dispute over the southern boundary of Texas. Mexico claimed it was the Nueces (noo AY suhs) River, while the United States said it was the Rio Grande 130 miles to the south. Both sides prepared troops, but for a time they did not clash. On hearing of the failure of Slidell's mission to Mexico City, Polk immediately ordered General Zachary Taylor to move his troops south to the Rio Grande. Taylor's troops were, in effect, sent looking for trouble, waiting for an incident justifying retaliation.

Late in April 1846, Mexican soldiers crossed the Rio Grande and attacked a small detachment of United States cavalry, which were in Mexican territory according to the Mexican point of view. When news of this attack on Taylor's force reached Washington, D.C., the President hastily revised a war message that he had been preparing in response to Slidell's rejection in Mexico City. Pointing out that his effort to negotiate peaceably with Mexico had failed, Polk argued that war had been begun "by the act of Mexico herself." On May 13, 1846, Congress declared war by overwhelming majorities in both houses.

In spite of the vote in Congress, many Americans refused to support a war of aggression against a weaker neighbor. It was, wrote the New England author James

Linking Across Time

DECLARING WAR

It is doubtful that an American President today would declare war as preemptively as Polk did in 1846. In 1990, although Americans deplored Iraq's invasion of Kuwait and praised President Bush's deployment of United States' troops to the Middle East to protect Saudi Arabia from invasion, many Americans supported force only after the nation joined with the world community in exhausting all other peaceful options.

Examining Illustrations *After six months of difficult fighting, General Winfield Scott forced his way into Mexico City. Scott's 10,000 American troops included young military officers Ulysses S. Grant and Robert E. Lee. Why did some of the troops oppose the war?*

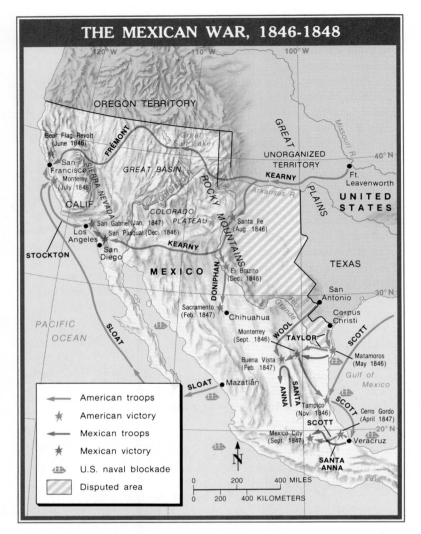

THE MEXICAN WAR, 1846-1848

I have said from the first that the United States are the aggressors.... We have not one particle of right to be here.... It looks as if the government sent a small force on purpose to bring on a war, so as to have a pretext for taking California and as much of this country as it chooses, for, whatever becomes of this army, there is no doubt of a war between the United States and Mexico.... My heart is not in this business...but, as a military man, I am bound to execute orders.

Although attacking Polk for starting the war, the Whigs in Congress supported it by voting for supplies and troops. This action was not as illogical as it may seem, because it is not certain that war could have been prevented. Several months before Polk's message to Congress, the Mexican government had declared itself in favor of "a necessary and glorious war." Aware of the dismal failure of American efforts to invade Canada in the War of 1812, the Mexicans expected victory.

The President himself planned the military campaigns of the Mexican War as a three-part strategy. First, General Taylor and his troops invaded northern Mexico. In May they pushed the Mexican army back across the Rio Grande and by September had taken the city of Monterrey. Taylor and his men then penetrated nearly 300 miles into Mexico and against strong resistance, won the battle of Buena Vista in February 1847.

As the second part of the war strategy, General Stephen Kearny left Missouri with a small force of young recruits in July 1846 and headed west. In August they took Santa Fe, the principal city of New Mexico, with hardly a shot fired in its defense. Kearny and his troops marched on to California, where they helped the Pacific Squadron defeat the Mexicans in Los Angeles in January 1847. A local revolt in northern California, with the assistance of a handful of American

Examining Maps *The Mexican War was spread out over a vast territory. Unable to defend distant California, Mexico concentrated its efforts in the region south of Texas. How many months elapsed between Zachary Taylor's initial invasion and Winfield Scott's victory and occupation of Mexico City?*

Russell Lowell, simply a southern scheme to steal "bigger pens to cram in slaves." Whig members of Congress, including Abraham Lincoln, then a representative from Illinois, challenged Polk's statement that he had tried to avoid war. Lincoln invited Polk to point out the spot where American blood had been spilled on American soil.

Even American soldiers had their doubts about the legitimacy of the war. In 1846 Colonel Ethan Allen Hitchcock wrote:

troops and a small fleet, had already shaken off Mexican authority. Thus California came under United States control, and fighting in the west ended.

When Mexico still refused to make peace, Polk launched the third part of his war strategy, sending General Winfield Scott to conquer Mexico City. With a force of 10,000, Scott sailed south and landed at Veracruz. In September 1847, after six months of difficult fighting, he occupied the capital.

Working to the Americans' advantage was the disorganization of the Mexican government. One group after another seized power in Mexico, so that sometimes it was difficult to know who headed the government; once three different men claimed to be president. Alfonso Toro, a Mexican historian, wrote of his country's hapless condition:

Although Mexico had an enormous war budget, she really lacked an army; for hardly worthy of the name was the assemblage of drafted men, badly armed, and …without confidence in their leaders. The soldiers, who were almost never paid but were maltreated and exploited by their chiefs, deserted whenever they could and even rebelled with arms in their hands when they were ordered to march….

Examining Maps By 1853 manifest destiny was a reality. Some expansionists still talked of the acquisition of Canada and Mexico, but most Americans were satisfied with the vast expanse of unsettled lands now available. What state is the geographic center of the 48 contiguous states?

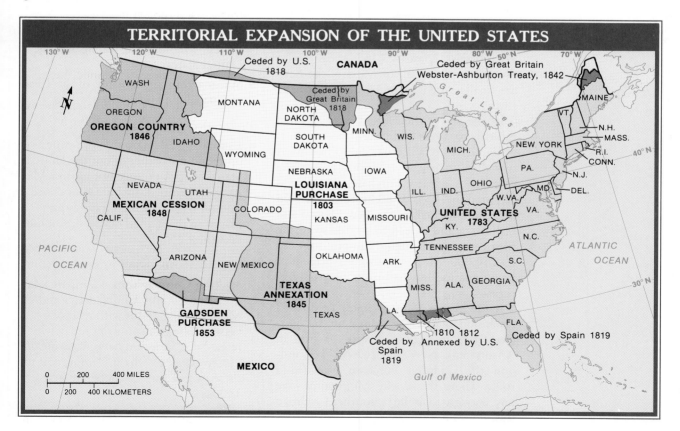

TERRITORIAL EXPANSION OF THE UNITED STATES

Treaty of Guadalupe Hidalgo

After the capture of Mexico City, it was some months before a Mexican government could be organized to sign the peace treaty. Meanwhile, ardent advocates of manifest destiny, including two members of Polk's Cabinet, urged that the United States annex all of Mexico.

President Polk, anticipating Scott's victory in Mexico City, had sent Nicholas P. Trist, a clerk in the state department, to Mexico with instructions to offer the same terms that Slidell had offered earlier. After a long delay, Polk's patience with Trist gave out, and the President ordered him back to Washington. Trist, knowing that he was on the verge of a successful treaty, ignored the orders and stayed on to complete the negotiations.

In February 1848, before the total-annexation movement had proceeded very far, a peace treaty was signed at Guadalupe Hidalgo, outside Mexico City.

While President Polk denounced the "exceptional conduct" of Nicholas Trist, he saw no alternative to submitting this treaty to the Senate. After a round of expansionist oratory by those who favored annexing all of Mexico, the Senate finally voted 38 to 14 in favor of the treaty.

In the treaty the United States gained full title to Texas (with the Rio Grande as a boundary), California, and all of what was then called New Mexico except the so-called Gadsden Purchase, which was acquired in 1853. The United States paid $15 million outright for New Mexico and California and agreed to pay debts of the Mexican government amounting to $3,250,000. Mexico lost only 1 percent of its population but half of its national territory.

In 1853 the United States completed expansion across the continent by purchasing from Mexico a strip of land in Arizona and New Mexico. For $10 million the Gadsden Purchase provided a route where the Rocky Mountains were low enough to build a southern railroad to California.

SUMMARY

President James K. Polk was determined to annex California. Mexico, still angry over Texas, was unwilling to negotiate. War broke out when Polk sent forces into disputed territory. The United States launched a three-pronged attack that ended with American occupation of Mexico City. Though some Americans advocated annexing all of Mexico, a compromise was reached in the Treaty of Guadalupe Hidalgo. California and New Mexico became American territory, and the southern border of Texas was established at the Rio Grande.

CHECKING FOR UNDERSTANDING

1. **Identify** John Slidell, Zachary Taylor, Winfield Scott, Treaty of Guadalupe Hidalgo
2. **Define** consul
3. **List** two reasons for the war between Mexico and the United States.
4. **Cite** the reasons why Mexico had difficulty fighting the war against the United States.
5. **Summarize** the provisions of the Treaty of Guadalupe Hidalgo.

THINKING CRITICALLY

6. **Evaluating an Action** Write your opinion on whether or not the United States' actions to wage war against Mexico were justified. Include your conclusion on what part manifest destiny played in the United States' decision to take these actions.

LINKING PAST AND PRESENT

7. **Making Comparisons** Compare relations between the United States and Mexico in the 1840s with relations between the two countries today by researching in recent newsmagazines. List two reasons why it is important for these two nations to cooperate in the 1990s.

Interpreting Primary Sources

Migration

Shortly after California became United States territory, the gold rush began. Among the thousands of people who made the long and dangerous trek west was Alvin Coffey, a slave. His master took away all the money that Coffey made in the mines but later sold him to a new owner. Coffey eventually earned freedom for himself and his family. His account of the trip to California suggests some of the dangers and hardships faced by many of the forty-niners.

A miner with a pack mule

from *Reminiscences* by Alvin Coffey:

I started from St. Louis, Missouri, on the 2nd of April in 1849. There was quite a crowd of neighbors who drove through the mud and rain to St. Joe to see us off. About the first of May we organized the train. There were twenty wagons in number and from three to five men to each wagon.

We crossed the Missouri River at Savanna Landing. . . . At six in the morning, there were three more went to relieve those on guard. One of the three that came in had cholera so bad that he was in lots of misery. Dr. Bassett, the captain of the train, did all he could for him, but he died at 10 o'clock and we buried him. We got ready and started at 11 the same day and the moon was new just then.

We got news every day that people were dying by the hundreds in St. Joe and St. Louis. It was alarming. When we hitched up and got ready to move, [the] Dr. said, "Boys, we will have to drive day and night.". . . We drove night and day and got out of reach of the cholera. . . .

We got across the plains to Fort Lar[a]mie, the 16th of June and the ignorant driver broke down a good many oxen on the trains. There were a good many ahead of us, who had doubled up their trains and left tons upon tons of bacon and other provisions. . . .

Starting to cross the desert to Black Rock at 4 o'clock in the evening, we traveled all night. The next day it was hot and sandy. . . .

A great number of cattle perished before we got to Black Rock. . . . I drove our oxen all the time and I knew about how much an ox could stand. Between nine and ten o'clock a breeze came up and the oxen threw up their heads and seemed to have new life. At noon, we drove into Black Rock. . . .

We crossed the South Pass on the Fourth of July. The ice next morning was as thick as a dinner-plate.

The wagon train went through Honey Lake to Deer Creek in Sacramento Valley and then to Redding Springs on October 13, 1849.

On the morning of the 15th, we went to dry-digging mining. We dug and dug to the first of November, at night it commenced raining, and rained and snowed pretty much all the winter. We had a tent but it barely kept us all dry. There were from eight to twelve in one camp. We cut down pine trees for stakes to make a cabin. It was a whole week before we had a cabin to keep us dry.

EXAMINING THE PRIMARY SOURCE

1. Why did those who wanted to travel west first stop at St. Joseph, Missouri?

2. What danger did travelers face in St. Louis and St. Joseph?

3. How did Coffey notice that some drivers had little knowledge of oxen?

4. What does the description of ice on the Fourth of July reveal about South Pass?

THINKING CRITICALLY

5. What evidence in Coffey's account indicates that people met unexpected problems on this trip?

6. Do you think that people in 1850 were more willing to take risks than they are today? Give evidence to support your answer.

SECTION FOUR

Global Interests

SETTING THE SCENE

As the United States and Japan are becoming every day nearer and nearer to each other, the President desires to live in peace and friendship with the emperor; but ...no friendship can long exist between them unless Japan should...cease to act toward the people of this country as if they were...enemies....

—C.M. CONRAD
Acting Secretary of State,
November 5, 1852

Section Focus

Victory in the Mexican War and the acquisition of Oregon gave the United States vast new territories but also raised new issues. How would the United States connect its Pacific settlements with the East? Would expansion continue southward? Would manifest destiny continue to move American interests beyond North America to other parts of the globe?

Objectives

After studying this section, you should be able to:
• Explain the events that brought about the Clayton-Bulwer Treaty.
• Compare the motivations for American interest in Cuba, Central America, China, and Japan in the mid-1800s.

The acquisition of territory from Mexico and the division of Oregon completed United States expansion across the continent. The spirit of manifest destiny subsided in the North but not in the South. Whether dictated by law or by geography, the portion of the United States open to slavery was far smaller than the area closed to slavery. Many southerners thought the only way to maintain the sectional balance was to expand southward. In 1848 *De Bow's Review,* a New Orleans financial journal, declared, "We have New Mexico and California. We *will* have old Mexico and Cuba!"

The Caribbean and Central America

Lying so close to Florida, Cuba offered tempting benefits—rich sugar plantations worked by thousands of enslaved people and a strategic location at the mouth of the Caribbean. So strong was the desire for Cuba among southerners and some northern investors that in 1848 the United States offered to buy Cuba from Spain for $100 million. The Spanish foreign minister turned down the bid, saying that he would rather see the island sink into the sea than sell it.

When negotiations failed, determined expansionists lent their support to armed adventurers called "filibusterers," who set off to gain territory that might later be annexed to the United States. One of the best known filibusterers was Narcisco López. With the aid of prominent Southerners, López attempted three armed landings in Cuba with small bands of Americans. His goal was to foment a revolt against Spanish rule, but on his third try he was captured and swiftly executed in 1851.

Interest in expansion to the south did not die with López, however. Prominent northern Democrats who sought southern expansion were called "dough faces." Among these was President Franklin Pierce from New Hampshire. He raised America's offering price for Cuba to $130 million. When Spain still refused, secretary of state William Marcy instructed United States ministers to Spain, Britain, and France to meet and decide how to obtain Cuba. The 3 United States diplomats drew up a statement known as the Ostend Manifesto, which declared that if Spain would not sell the island, the United States should take it by force. In part it said:

After we shall have offered Spain a price for Cuba far beyond its present value, and this shall have been refused, it will then be time to consider the question, does Cuba, in the possession of Spain, seriously endanger our internal peace and existence of our cherished Union? Should this question be answered in the affirmative, then, by every law, human and divine, we shall be justified in wresting it from Spain....

Published in 1854, this infamous document caused such protest that the secretary of state repudiated it, and the effort to buy Cuba was abandoned. Future attempts to expand slave territory were doomed because of northern opposition.

American ambitions turned from expansion to development of the newly acquired territories. Hundreds made the long journey overland across the plains and the Rocky Mountains, but the longest route around Cape Horn, South America, was the safest. In January 1848, gold was discovered in California at Sutter's mill near Sacramento. Stories of instant riches led to a gold rush from the eastern United States and Europe. Many fortune seekers who took the ocean route saved time by crossing the narrow isthmus at Panama to board one of the few ships that would carry them to California. The gold rush aroused new interest in a project that had been discussed since the establishment of the Spanish colonies in the sixteenth century: the construction of a canal across Central America to connect the Atlantic and Pacific oceans. In 1846 the United States signed a treaty with New Granada (later Colombia) by which it gained the right to preserve "free transit" across the Isthmus of Panama.

The British were also interested in controlling canal routes and in extending their influence along the entire Atlantic coast of Central America. Rival ambitions caused such tension that in 1850 Great Britain sent a special agent, Sir Henry Bulwer, to Washington, D.C., to confer with Secretary of State John M. Clayton. In the resulting Clayton-Bulwer Treaty, the United States and Britain agreed to jointly support the building of a canal either through Nicaragua or Panama. The cost and risks of such a venture delayed action by either country until after 1900. Then American interest was reawakened by the commercial and military advantages of a canal to support United States expansion in the Pacific.

AMERICAN PORTRAITS

NARCISCO LÓPEZ
1798?-1851

Narcisco López, a Venezuelan, fought for Spain against Simón Bolívar's South American independence forces, rising to the rank of general in the Spanish Army. Later he took up residence in Cuba, married, and became devoted to the interests of the Cuban people. In 1848 he planned a revolt against Spanish rule, hoping for help from American supporters and for annexation of the island to the United States. When the revolt failed, he fled to America.

López visited New Orleans where, in 1850, he asked for volunteers to join an expedition to win the island from Spain. His force of 600 landed in Cuba but found few Cubans willing to risk revolution. On a later expedition López was captured by the Spanish and executed.

In 1902 an independent Cuba raised its flag—one originally designed by López in red, white, and blue.

The Opening of China and Japan

The acquisition of California gave the United States valuable ports from which to launch its Pacific trade. For centuries the prospect of trade with China had stirred people's imaginations because China produced valuable commodities and its potential 300 million customers were the largest untapped market in the world. United States trade with China had grown since the late eighteenth century, but until the 1840s, this trade was limited to the port of Canton. As the oldest civilization in the world, the Chinese did not think they had much to gain from the outside world.

But a weakened Chinese government could not long resist foreign trade. From 1839 to 1842, the British fought the First Opium War with China. When Great Britain won, it acquired the port of Hong Kong and various privileges for its merchants and missionaries. Among these was the right of **extraterritoriality,** or the right of a foreigner accused of a crime to be tried under his or her own law rather than under Chinese law by Chinese courts. Later the British, aided by other European

Examining Illustrations *Commodore Perry accompanied by his color-bearer delivered gifts to the emperor of Japan. What favor did he seek?*

nations, forced China to grant special privileges to Christian missionaries, to set aside 16 "treaty ports" run by westerners, and to allow European gunboats to patrol Chinese rivers.

The United States also secured privileges in China. In 1844 President Tyler sent Caleb Cushing, an able diplomat, to China with four warships. Cushing persuaded the Chinese to grant generous trade arrangements. Because the United States was not interested, as were some

Examining Illustrations *This Chinese fan commemorates the opening of trade between China and the United States. Captain John Greene's ship* The Empress of China *sailed from New York to Canton in 1784. For many years American trade of furs and sea-otter skins for silks and tea was limited to this one port. How was this arrangement changed?*

nations, in annexing parts of China, the Chinese were friendlier to Americans than to others. By 1850 American clipper ships carried most of the Chinese tea exported to Europe. American missionaries followed the traders; 88 of the 150 Protestant missionaries in China in 1851 were American.

American ships sailing to China needed ports to take on fuel and supplies. Japan's location made it ideal for such ports of call. Japan, however, had shut itself off from contact with most of the outside world for hundreds of years; only the Dutch were allowed trading privileges and only at the port of Nagasaki. The Japanese distrusted foreigners so intensely that sailors from shipwrecked whaling vessels had no guarantee of protection if they washed up on Japanese shores.

In 1853 a small United States fleet under Commodore Matthew C. Perry sailed into Tokyo harbor. Perry stayed only 10 days but left a message for the Mikado, or emperor, of Japan from President Millard Fillmore, who wrote:

These are the only objects for which I have sent Commodore Perry, with a powerful squadron, to pay a visit to your imperial majesty's renowned city of Yedo: Friendship, commerce, a supply of coal and provisions, and protection for our shipwrecked people....

Perry returned the next year with more warships, all guns prepared for action. Perry also brought elaborate presents for the ruler of Japan, including a miniature telegraph and steam railroad. By this mixture of courtesy and threat, the Japanese were persuaded to open relations with the rest of the world. Soon, Japanese leaders were convinced that they should adopt the industrial technology of western nations, and Japan moved quickly to catch up with the West. Within one century Japanese influence rivaled American influence in the Pacific.

Section Four Review

SUMMARY

After the war with Mexico, the United States turned to more global interests. Southern slaveowners and northern merchants wanted to acquire Cuba from Spain, but Spain refused to negotiate for the island. Attempts to annex Cuba by force backfired when shocked Americans became aware of the Ostend Manifesto. Competing American and British plans to build a canal through Central America led to the Clayton-Bulwer Treaty. China was forced to open up its markets to western nations. Japan, intimidated into cooperating with western traders, would soon begin to develop its own industrialized economy.

CHECKING FOR UNDERSTANDING

1. **Identify** Narciso López, Franklin Pierce, Ostend Manifesto, Clayton-Bulwer Treaty, Matthew Perry

2. **Define** extraterritoriality

3. **Explain** how the Ostend Manifesto backfired.

4. **Cite** why so many people went to California after 1848.

5. **Name** two provisions of the Clayton-Bulwer Treaty.

6. **List** two reasons the United States government expressed an interest in China and Japan in the mid-1800s.

THINKING CRITICALLY

7. **Evaluating Foreign Policy** Evaluate Commodore Perry's strategy in Japan. What was the underlying message of Perry's visit?

GLOBAL PERSPECTIVES

8. **Making Predictions** Japan, long isolated from other countries, was impressed by Perry's steam-powered ships with their big guns. How did this contact with western technology change Japanese life?

★ Chapter 13 Review ★

★ Summary

Manifest destiny, the belief that America would extend its boundaries and its political ideology to the Pacific Ocean, motivated foreign policy in the 1840s. Underlying the push to the Pacific was the desire to secure West Coast harbors and the rich resources of Oregon. Expansion had its price, however. Mexicans, native Americans, and the British were also rivals for this land. Ironically, tensions between the United States and Britain erupted over a territorial dispute in the Northeast. Conflict was avoided by the Webster-Ashburton Treaty.

Meanwhile, Oregon attracted increasing numbers of American settlers, and others staked claims in Texas. When Mexico tried to cut off immigration, Texans already had independence on their minds. Texans won their independence and soon asked to be admitted to the United States. President Polk, unable to purchase California from Mexico, sent troops to southern Texas, provoking war. After Mexico's defeat, the Treaty of Guadalupe Hidalgo extended the United States to the Pacific Ocean and set the Texas border at the Rio Grande.

Americans soon turned their sights toward other global interests. Only public outrage prevented the United States from seizing Cuba from Spain. To expand global trade, the United States negotiated with Britain a peaceful solution to controlling canal routes in Central America, took advantage of trading privileges won by European nations in China, and used warships to back up its request that Japan open its ports to American merchants.

★ Using Vocabulary

Imagine yourself an American diplomat in the 1840s assigned to negotiate trade agreements in China and Japan. Explain the challenges and duties of your job with sentences that use each of the terms below.

consul   **extraterritoriality**

★ Reviewing Facts

1. **Specify** both agrarian and commercial reasons that promoted manifest destiny.
2. **List** two resources that made Oregon a valuable territory.

3. **Explain** the reasons for the war between the United States and Mexico.
4. **Name** two important events in the Texas independence movement.
5. **Explain** why some Americans were hesitant to make Texas a state.
6. **Summarize** why the United States was not able to acquire Cuba.
7. **Cite** two reasons why China and Japan were forced to initiate trade with the West.

★ Understanding Concepts

EXPANSION

1. Explain the connection between patriotism and manifest destiny. How did feelings of patriotism help Americans justify expansion?
2. Geography often plays a role in defining the borders of a nation. Explain the role of geography in supporting the belief that it was "natural" for the United States to expand to the Pacific ocean.

MIGRATION

3. The westward migration of pioneers in Conestoga wagons is a cherished part of American folklore. What factors made this migration such an adventure? Why do you think Americans continue to be fascinated by stories about these travels?
4. Explain how the migration of American immigrants into Texas made it difficult for Mexico to control this part of its empire.

★ Thinking Critically

1. **Determining Motivations**   What economic advantages did Americans hope to reap from expansion to the Pacific? Looking back, how would you evaluate the economic impact of manifest destiny?
2. **Distinguishing False from Accurate Images** Many legends have grown up about mountain men. What was it about their way of life that led to the creation of these stories? Why might their accomplishments have been exaggerated?
3. **Assessing Causes**   Was war with Mexico inevitable? Explain the causes that made negotiations between the United States and Mexico nearly impossible, including the Mexican viewpoint.

4. Analyzing Policies Explain how the implied threat of force was used by the United States to open relations with China and Japan.

★ Writing About History

DEFINITION

Refer to the description of how to write a definition in the History Writer's Handbook in the Appendix of this book. Your teacher will give you more specific instructions on the essay's length and the assignment's due date.

Words can have different meanings to different people. Manifest destiny changed the lives of many people in the 1840s, including the lives of people living in other countries. Write four separate definitions of the concept of manifest destiny as each of these four people might have defined it: James K. Polk, Santa Anna, a Plains Indian, and a mountain man.

★ Learning Cooperatively

Was President Polk a shrewd and visionary leader who expanded the power and borders of the United States, or was he a bully who took what he wanted without regard for other people's rights? You and a partner will evaluate Polk's presidency to answer these concerns. One of you will be a Polk supporter and the other an opponent. First, work together to compile a list of Polk's achievements. Then work separately and write an evaluation of each action according to your role as supporter or opponent. When you have finished writing, exchange and discuss each other's evaluations. Then present your findings to the class.

★ Mastering Skills

PREPARING NOTECARDS FOR A RESEARCH REPORT

By now you have had practice selecting a research paper topic, finding resources at the library, and deciding on the main ideas you will cover. The next step to writing a research paper is preparing notecards from your research before writing your first draft.

The following guidelines will help you prepare notecards with the critical information you will need to write your report well. Included as an example is what might appear on your notecard if your topic is "Pioneer Life."

Example

- On the first card, write the name of the author of the resource, the title, location, publisher, copyright date, and page number, according to the bibliographic style approved by your teacher. Later, you will use this same card when preparing your final bibliography.

> Weaver, Robert B. "Pioneer Life." *World Book Encyclopedia*. Vol. 14. Chicago: Field Enterprises, 1991, pages 428-442.

- Start the next card with the author's last name and first name, if more than one author has the same last name. Include the title, too, if you are using more than one resource from this author. Also include the page number.
- Underneath the author's name and page number, take notes on one main idea only. Start by writing a sentence that summarizes the main idea—a generalization. Then list supporting statements.

> Weaver, page 439
>
> Main Idea: The pioneers could not buy soap, so they had to make their own.
>
> Supporting Statements:
>
> 1. The pioneers saved wood ashes in a barrel and fats and grease from cooking and butchering.
> 2. In the spring the pioneers poured water over the ashes in the barrel and allowed it to trickle out through a hole near the bottom.
> 3. This brown liquid called lye was collected and boiled in a kettle with fats and grease until it thickened to form a soft, jellylike, yellow soap.

- After you have taken notes from all your resources using a separate card for each main idea, sort through your cards, placing them in the order you will address the main ideas as you write. Now you are ready to draft a rough draft of your report.

Practice Research and prepare notecards for a report on the history of one of the western states.

CHAPTER 14
Compromise and Conflict

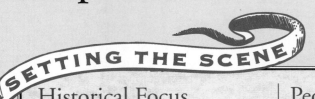

SETTING THE SCENE

Historical Focus

Even though the nation as a whole was prosperous, deep political and social divisions could no longer be ignored. By the late 1840s, southerners were defending slavery as a "positive good," while antislavery feelings in the North and West intensified. Political compromise worked in 1850, but by 1860 compromise was no longer possible. For southerners, the election of Lincoln convinced them that slavery would not be protected within the Union. Secession, they felt, was the only option left.

Concepts to Understand

- How **economic diversity** led to differing views on slavery.
- How **political conflict** over slavery and the nature of the Union led to secession.

People to Know

Stephen A. Douglas, John Deere, Harriet Beecher Stowe, Dred Scott, Abraham Lincoln, John Brown

Places to Locate

California, Freeport, Harpers Ferry

Terms to Identify

popular sovereignty, Know Nothings, Republican party, secession

Guided Reading

As you read this chapter, seek the answers to the following questions.
1. What were the major differences between the North and the South?
2. What events led seven southern states to secede from the Union?

SPANNING THE DECADES

POLITICAL

1848
First presidential election to be held on the same day in all states

1850
Compromise of 1850

1854
Kansas-Nebraska Act is passed

1845

1850

CULTURAL

1846
Elias Howe patents sewing machine

1848
Washington Monument cornerstone set in Washington, D.C.

1849
Longest suspension bridge in the world opens over the Ohio River

1851
Herman Melville publishes Moby Dick

View of Harpers Ferry *by Ferdinand Richardt, 1858*

1857
Supreme Court in Scott v. Sanford *rules the Missouri Compromise unconstitutional*

1858
Lincoln-Douglas debates in Illinois

1860
South Carolina secedes from the Union

1855   **1860**

1856
Gail Borden received a patent for condensed milk

1857
National Teacher's Association organized in Philadelphia

…I will say here…that I have no purpose, directly or indirectly to interfere with the institution of slavery in the states where it exists. I believe I have no lawful right to do so and have no inclination to do so….

—ABRAHAM LINCOLN
Reply to Douglas, August 21, 1858

A Union in Danger

The issue now presented is not whether slavery shall exist unmolested where it now is, but whether it shall be carried to new and distant regions, now free, where the footprint of a slave cannot be found.

—DAVID WILMOT
Speech in the House of Representatives, 1846

Section Focus

The Mexican War and the Treaty of Guadalupe Hidalgo brought into the open the slavery issue that politicians had been trying to avoid ever since the bitter debates over the admission of Missouri to the Union. With the acquisition of New Mexico and California, it became clear that some decision had to be made regarding the legality of slavery in these new areas.

Objectives

After studying this section, you should be able to:
* Evaluate the impact of the issue of slavery on the 1848 presidential election.
* Explain why California's application for admission to the Union incited heated debates on the question of slavery.
* Describe how the Compromise of 1850 temporarily reunited the nation.

E ven before the war with Mexico had ended, growing antislavery sentiment in the North led the House of Representatives, with its northern majority, to pass the Wilmot Proviso. This bill provided that all territory acquired from Mexico should be closed to slavery. Although the Wilmot Proviso was defeated in the Senate, where North and South were equally represented, many southern senators argued that Congress had no constitutional power to forbid slavery in the territories; to do so would be to deny slaveowners their rights as citizens.

There seemed to be no way of reconciling these opposing views on the issue of slavery in the new territories. When the Polk administration ended in 1849, no steps had been taken to provide for civil government in New Mexico and California.

The Election of 1848

In the presidential election of 1848, both northerners and southerners took elaborate precautions to play down discussion of slavery. The Democrats, although controlled by their southern wing, nominated a northern senator, Lewis Cass of Michigan. Cass supported a compromise solution known as **popular sovereignty**, whereby voters within the territories would decide whether slavery would be permitted inside their borders. The statement of policies, or platform, of the Democrats reinforced this idea by stating that Congress had no authority over the question of slavery.

The Whigs, whose principal stronghold was in the North, nominated Zachary Taylor from Louisiana, a slaveowner himself. The Whig platform avoided the issue of slavery altogether by focusing on Taylor's military accomplishments in the Mexican War.

Efforts to keep slavery out of the campaign failed, however. A third party emerged when a group of antislavery northern Democrats and "conscience Whigs" united with the former Liberty party to form the Free Soil party. This party, whose motto was "Free soil, free speech, free labor, and free men," nominated former President Martin Van Buren. Although the Free Soilers gained no electoral votes, they received more popular votes than the Democrats had in New York, Vermont, and Massachusetts. In New York the Free Soilers received enough

Examining Illustrations
The intense debate in the Senate sparked by the California question led to yet another important political compromise. Who arranged this last great intersectional agreement?

Democratic votes to deprive Cass of that state's 36 electoral votes, which gave the election to Taylor with 163 electoral votes—exactly 36 more than Cass had.

The California Question

The issue of slavery in the new territories intensified after gold was discovered in California in 1848. By the end of 1849, an estimated 95,000 "Forty-niners" from all over the world had settled in northern California. Ray Allen Billington, a historian, described the gold-seekers:

In those ramshackle mining camps...where rooms rented for $1,000 a month and eggs cost $10 a dozen, were assembled the most colorful desperadoes ever gathered in one spot. Mingling together were Missouri farmers, Yankee sailors, Georgia crackers, English shopkeepers, French peasants, Australian sheepherders, Mexican peons,... and a liberal sprinkling of "assassins manufactured in Hell."

With this tremendous growth in population came an urgent need for government. Crime and violence had become common in mining camps and towns, and military authorities could not control it. At the suggestion of President Taylor, a convention met in Monterey, California,

in the fall of 1849, and adopted a constitution that, in part, provided a structure for the new government and outlined state boundaries. It also prohibited slavery. The

Life of the Times

FORTY-NINERS

President Polk referred to the rich gold discovery in California in his annual message to Congress in December 1848. The secret was out. Within a year the gold fever attracted some 95,000 people to California. The three principal routes were across the Isthmus of Panama, around Cape Horn, or overland. Half of the '49ers crossed the plains and mountains. Along the California Trail inexperienced travelers died by the hundreds.

Skeletons of horses and oxen marked the toll of death from exhaustion or starvation. The hardships, according to John Lloyd Stephens who described his own struggle, "... are beyond conception. Care and suspense, pained anxiety, fear of losing animals and leaving one to foot it and pack his 'duds' on his back, begging provisions, fear of being left in the mountains to starve and freeze to death... are things of which I may write and you may read, but they are nothing to the reality."

Those who survived the trail found life in California nearly as demanding. One fortune-seeker wrote, "I start at 4 o'clock in the morning and keep on till 12 noon.... I rest for three or four hours ... and then I work again till 8 o'clock in the evening. The nights are extremely cold. . . ."

newly created government immediately applied for admission to the Union as a free state in which slavery was forbidden. California's application for statehood touched off one of the longest, most bitter debates in the history of Congress. Violent threats aimed at senators were common. Admission of California would tip the balance of power in the Senate in favor of the free states, already in the majority in the House. If California were admitted as a free state, southern leaders warned, their states would leave the Union.

To deal with this alarming situation, Henry Clay, who had been in retirement since his defeat in the presidential election of 1844, successfully ran for reelection as senator. The Whig senator from Kentucky, a master of negotiation, proceeded to arrange his last great intersectional compromise. Clay's compromise was a series of measures intended to satisfy northern and southern demands. The principal provisions favoring the North were that California be admitted as a free state and that the slave trade—but not slavery—be forbidden in the District of Columbia. The South, in turn, would gain a stronger Fugitive Slave Law, designed to suppress the Underground Railroad. In addition, the Mexico Cession, gained at the end of the Mexican War, would be divided into two territories, Utah and New Mexico, with the question of slavery to be decided by popular sovereignty when the territories were organized with territorial legislatures. This was, interestingly enough, the same formula as had been proposed by Cass in the 1848 campaign.

At first, Clay's proposals failed to receive sufficient support to pass. President Taylor opposed Clay and offered proposals of his own. However, Taylor died suddenly in the summer of 1850. His successor, Vice President Millard Fillmore, favored the compromise. The young Illinois senator Stephen A. Douglas skillfully put through the compromise as five separate bills, which Fillmore duly signed. The Compromise of 1850 averted immediate disaster, but, unhappily, turned out to be a temporary truce rather than a permanent peace.

★ ★ ★ ★ ★ ★ ★ ★ ★ ★ ★ ★ ★ ★ ★ ★ ★

Section One Review ·

★ ★ ★ ★ ★ ★ ★ ★ ★ ★ ★ ★ ★ ★ ★ ★ ★

SUMMARY

By 1848 the nation had become divided over the issue of slavery. Efforts to downplay the controversy during the presidential election were dashed when a group of northern Democrats, who advocated freedom for the slaves, formed the Free Soil party. The conflict over slavery became centered on the admission of new states, especially California. The Compromise of 1850 temporarily calmed tempers on both sides. Provisions of the Compromise included the admission of California as a free state and a stronger Fugitive Slave Law.

CHECKING FOR UNDERSTANDING

1. **Identify** Wilmot Proviso, Lewis Cass, Zachary Taylor, Free Soil party, Stephen A. Douglas, Compromise of 1850

2. **Define** popular sovereignty

3. **Explain** why the issue of extending of slavery into the territories came to a head over California's application for statehood

4. **Describe** what the emergence of the Free Soil party accomplished to help win the 1848 presidential election for Zachary Taylor.

5. **List** four provisions of the Compromise of 1850.

THINKING CRITICALLY

6. **Evaluating Policies** Explain why acceptance of the idea of popular sovereignty would have been unacceptable to abolitionists.

CONNECTIONS: HISTORY AND ECONOMICS

7. **Analyzing Point of View** Supporters of the Free Soil party were mostly small, independent, family farmers who lived in the Midwest. Explain why Free Soil farmers believed that slaveowners had an unfair competitive edge against them.

★ ★ ★ ★ ★ ★ ★ ★ ★ ★ ★ ★ ★ ★ ★ ★ ★

Map and Graph Skills

Classifying Information

One day you take hundreds of old stamps to a stamp collector and ask how much they are worth. The stamp collector tells you that before the stamps can be appraised, you will first have to classify them.

Explanation

Classifying is a process of separating and arranging information into related groups. The stamp collector wants you to separate the stamps into categories such as United States stamps and stamps of foreign nations or regular-issue stamps and commemorative stamps. This kind of classification will make it easier for you and the collector to see what stamps you have and to evaluate them.

In order to group the stamps into these various categories, you must examine each stamp and compare it to the others. Based on your understanding of the criteria—for example, the differences between a regular-issue stamp and a commemorative stamp—you can then classify each stamp accordingly.

The same process can be done with historical information. Instead of trying to understand all the information about a broad subject, you can break it down into parts and organize it. Taking notes on the subject is one way of organizing the information. Another would be making a chart, which is a graphic view of the information set up in columns and rows. Organizing the information makes it easier to

evaluate, and from studying the information, one can draw conclusions or make generalizations.

Example

One of the many sources of information about history is illustrations. This map of the Compromise of 1850, for example, will be helpful in understanding

COMPROMISE OF 1850

WISCONSIN 1848
MICHIGAN 1837
OREGON TERRITORY
UNORGANIZED TERRITORY
MINN. TERR.
IOWA 1846
UTAH TERRITORY
CALIF. 1850
NEW MEXICO TERRITORY
MEXICO
TEXAS 1845

Free states
Slave states
Territory closed to slavery
Territory open to slavery
Indian territory

what were the results of the compromise. After examining the data on the map, follow the guidelines below to help classify its information.

- Determine what information you need to classify.
  (results of the Compromise of 1850)

- Decide on the major categories by looking closely at how the information can be broken down into parts.
  (The legend of this map shows

categories: *free states, free territories, slave states, territories open to slavery.*)

- Write down the data that fits in each category or, if you are making a chart, place the appropriate information in columns under each category.
  (*free states:* Calif., Conn., Del., Ill., Ind., Iowa, Maine, Mass., Mich., N.H., N.J., N.Y., Ohio, Pa., R.I., Vt., Wisc.; *free territories:* Minn., Oreg., Unorganized Territory; *slave states:* Ala., Ark., Fla., Ga., Ky., La., Md., Miss., Mo., N.C., S.C., Tenn., Tex., Va.; *territories open to slavery:* N.M., Utah)

- After studying the information in each category and combining it with your prior knowledge of the subject you are studying, what conclusions can you make?
  (Possible answers might be: *Free states and territories were in the northern half of the country; In 1850 there was not much territory left that would be open to slavery; More of the nation was free in 1850 than was slave.*)

Practice

For further practice in classifying information, follow these guidelines in taking notes or creating a chart on the Kansas-Nebraska Act map on page 434. Write at least two conclusions about the results of the Kansas-Nebraska Act.

Economic Differences in the North and South

SETTING THE SCENE

I can now sleep of nights. We have gone through the most important crisis that has occurred since the founding of the government, and whatever party may prevail, hereafter the Union stands firm.

—DANIEL WEBSTER
Speech in the United States Senate, 1850

Section Focus

The Compromise of 1850's apparent resolution of the slavery issue took place during a period of remarkable national prosperity. Every major economic interest—cotton planting, wheat farming, manufacturing, and transportation—was booming. The huge gold strike in California paid for imports; the flood of gold expanded United States currency. Also, during these years, increasing numbers of immigrants began arriving in the country.

Objectives

After studying this section, you should be able to:
• Describe the inventions that changed both the northern and southern economies.
• Explain the great impact of increased immigration on the economic growth of the United States.

During the 20 years from 1840 to 1860, rapid and apparently self-sustaining growth became the dominant characteristic of the nation's economy. Among the reasons for this growth were new inventions, sufficient capital with which to build new factories, a class of businesspeople willing to start new enterprises, an increase in agricultural productivity, a growing labor supply, and a transportation system that connected farms to factories.

Inventions and Industry

In 1850 two-thirds of the nation's people were engaged in agriculture. But industry was growing, partly because of a flood of new inventions. By 1861 the telegraph had made possible rapid communication throughout the continent and across the Atlantic. The rotary press allowed newspapers to publish far larger editions than ever before. Some inventions, however, had their greatest impact on Northern industries. For example, the sewing machine, invented by Elias Howe in 1846, revolutionized shirt-making by reducing the time it took to make one shirt from more than 14 hours to little more than an hour; when the technique was adapted for shoemaking, it made possible the mass production of shoes. Charles Goodyear's invention of vulcanized rubber in 1839 was widely used in industry and in the manufacture of waterproof garments.

Textile factories, powered by more efficient steam engines, increased in size as several operations were combined under a single roof. The techniques invented by Eli Whitney and Simeon North for making interchangeable parts and breaking down manufacturing into simple operations now found applications in the mass production of clocks, watches, farm machinery, and sewing machines.

For the first time, goods manufactured in the United States were featured in world markets. At the Crystal Palace Exhibition in London in 1851, American

Connections

H I S T O R Y   A N D   T E C H N O L O G Y

INDUSTRIAL INNOVATION

What is the North, asked a southerner in the 1850s, "but a conglomeration of greasy mechanics, filthy operatives,

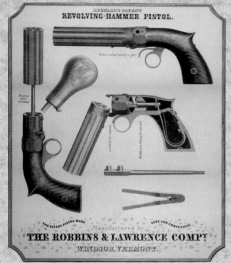

Revolving Hammer Pistol

small-fisted farmers, and moon-struck theorists?" Southerners may have looked scornfully at manufacturing in the North, but Europeans were fascinated by "Yankee Notions" like machine-made clocks and buckets, canned food, and handguns with revolving chambers. These products were the result of Yankee ingenuity and the machine-tool industry, which mass-produced interchangeable parts.

The British called this industry "the American system of manufacturing," but "the Northeastern American system" would have been more accurate. More than half of America's 140,000 factories were concentrated between New York and Massachusetts, and they were the country's largest and most productive. The South had 20,000 factories, but they were small and concentrated on processing local products like cotton or tobacco rather than manufacturing.

MAKING THE TECHNOLOGY CONNECTION

1. How might the level of industrialization affect the ability of the North and the South to wage war?

LINKING PAST AND PRESENT

2. Hypothesize why the South in the 1990s is not among the top few manufacturing centers.

innovations such as mechanical churns, revolvers, and alarm clocks fascinated the crowds. All this activity served to benefit the industrialized North far more than it did the South, whose economy was largely based on agriculture.

Developments in Agriculture

Inventions and innovations allowed agricultural productivity to keep pace with the nation's fast-growing industries. The Middle West, with its fertile plains, attracted farmers from the rocky and hilly lands of the Northeast as well as immigrants from Europe. Public lands could be purchased for as little as 25 cents an acre, and the Pre-emption Act of 1841 allowed squatters the opportunity to buy their land before someone else did.

The first great need was for plows that could cut through tree roots in recently

cleared forest land and turn the tough sod of the prairies. In 1825 Jethro Wood began the manufacture of an iron plow with replaceable parts. John Deere of Moline, Illinois, soon developed a much-improved version made of steel instead of iron; by 1850 the Deere factories were turning out as many as 10,000 plows per year. The new plows enabled farmers to plant more land than they could harvest. To solve this problem, Cyrus McCormick, a Virginia blacksmith, took out a patent in 1834 on a mechanical "reaper," or grain harvester. By 1860 more than 100,000 of McCormick's reapers were in use. These inventions were accompanied by still others: a mechanical drill to plant grain, the threshing machine, and the horse-drawn hay rake.

Although the West benefited more from these inventions than did the South, which still depended on slave labor, Southern economy also improved. Increased demand for raw cotton by an efficient

The hundreds of thousands of immigrants who arrived in the United States before 1860 mainly came from western and northern Europe, particularly Germany and Ireland. By the turn of the century, however, most of the millions of "new" immigrants were from eastern and southern Europe, notably Russia and Italy. But regardless of the country of origin, reasons for coming to America remained much the same, freedom from political unrest and economic opportunity.

British textile industry brought prosperity to the deep South. In the 1850s, cotton production broke all previous records. By 1860 seven-eighths of the world's supply of cotton came from the United States, and raw cotton comprised three-fifths of the nation's exports.

The 1850s also witnessed a revival of tobacco farming. A discovery by Stephen, a black overseer in North Carolina, led to a new method of "curing," or preparing, tobacco, which greatly increased the yield and quality of tobacco crops. Yet despite these advances, the South did not experience the industrial expansion enjoyed by the North. Eventually the West would follow the North and surpass the South in its move toward greater industrialization.

Increased Immigration Fuels Factories

One of the necessities for sustained industrial growth is a sizable labor supply. Until about 1800, immigrants came to the United States at a rate of about 8,000 per year. During the second quarter of the nineteenth century, however, a great migration from Europe to America began. Between 1840 and 1860, an average of more than 200,000 immigrants reached American shores every year. The reasons for this were both political and economic. Thousands of immigrants made the perilous voyage to escape poverty. Many English crafts workers, made jobless by the Industrial Revolution, sailed to America. The Scandinavians and the Dutch, whose native soil could not support rapidly growing populations, also came. So did the Irish, after a failure of their potato crop resulted in economic hardship and the starvation of thousands. Others, like the Germans, came to avoid political persecution. By 1860 one out of every eight Americans was foreign-born.

European agents of railroad companies and steamship lines described America as a land where riches could be had almost for the asking. Several states established immigration agencies to attract northern Europeans; inducements were offered, such as giving the right to vote to newcomers even before they became naturalized citizens.

Perhaps the most persuasive inducements were the "America letters" written by recent immigrants to their families and friends in Europe. One person wrote:

The poorest families adorn the tables three times a day like a wedding dinner—tea, coffee, beef, fowls, pies, eggs, pickles, good bread....Say, is it so in England?

The move to America was difficult and dangerous. Immigrants were packed into overcrowded ships where terrible conditions resulted in death from malnutrition and disease in an estimated 10 percent of the passengers. Unfortunately, the problems of the immigrants continued even after they had found jobs and places to live—immigrants were forced to confront the bigotry of some established Americans who resented their different languages, religions, and customs.

Such resentment, along with the fear that immigrants would bring new and possibly radical political ideas into the United States, led to the formation of secret societies. One of these was a nationwide secret political society called The Order of the Star-Spangled Banner, founded in 1849. Nicknamed "Know Nothings" because members replied "I know nothing" when asked about their organization, they tried to keep recent immigrants from political office. They also demanded that immigration be restricted and that the naturalization period be extended to 21 years.

In spite of such hardships and prejudice, immigrants continued to flock to the United States. Although some went West to its rich farmlands, many remained in the North, often in such port cities as New York and Boston, where their ships had docked. One reason for this was that they had little money to continue their journeys. Also the South already had a source of cheap labor—the black slave. The result was that immigrants supplied the North's growing industries with a steady stream of low-paid workers.

Transportation Ties North and West

With rapidly expanding domestic and foreign markets came great advances in transportation. In the 1850s the United States built the largest merchant marine fleet in the world, inland navigation reached its peak, and on the railroads—the newest form of transportation—track mileage was increased threefold.

In 1849 Great Britain repealed the Navigation Laws that had given special protection to British ships trading within its empire. The United States, however, continued to allow only its own ships to carry cargo between American ports. Competing on even terms with British ships in British ports while enjoying an advantage in their own, United States ships increased in total tonnage from 943,000 tons in 1846 to 2,226,000 tons in 1857.

The greatest triumph at sea for the United States was the clipper ship, which enjoyed its brief heyday between 1845 and 1860. Characterized by very sharp bows, an immense spread of sail, and masts 200 feet high, clippers soon became the fastest ocean-going sailing vessels ever built. The clipper *Lightning* once logged over 500 miles in a 24-hour period.

Alarmed by the superiority of United States sailing ships, the British concentrated on the development of steamships. Between 1850 and 1860, the amount of ocean freight carried in steam vessels rose from 14 to 28 percent, and most of this increase could be attributed to British shipping. By 1860 United States shipyards, which could produce only sailing ships, were closing down.

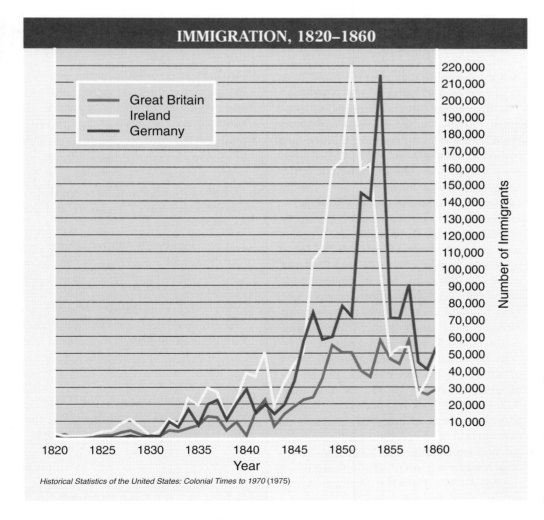

IMMIGRATION, 1820–1860

Historical Statistics of the United States: Colonial Times to 1970 (1975)

Examining Graphs
Immigration into the United States from Great Britain, Ireland, and Germany increased dramatically between 1820 and 1860. In what two years was immigration the greatest?

During this decade inland navigation also reached its peak. The Erie Canal carried so much traffic that it had to be widened and deepened. The Great Lakes gained such importance as a water route that 6,000 ships sailed from Chicago in a single year. This was also the great period of steamboats on the Mississippi River. Mark Twain's *Life on the Mississippi* and *Huckleberry Finn* bear witness to the importance of the great river as a trade route.

But the days of great river traffic were numbered. As inventor Oliver Evans predicted in 1813:

The time will come when people will travel in stages moved by steam engines, from one city to another, almost as fast as birds fly, fifteen or twenty miles an hour.

Railroads were able to reach places that riverboats could not. By 1860 railroads tied the agricultural areas of the Northwest to the cities and ports of the Northeast. The first successful use of the steam locomotive in the United States occurred on the Charleston and Hamburg railroad line in South Carolina in 1831. Other lines began operation almost simultaneously. Early railroads, however, were handicapped by numerous practical problems. Furthermore, railroads were extremely expensive to build and maintain. Whereas state governments had funded the building of canals, private enterprise provided the money for the railroads. The new railroads cost what were then colossal sums. The Erie Railroad cost about $23 million to build, half as much as the United States paid for New Mexico and California.

By 1850 many of the technical problems of railroading had been solved, and an era of great expansion began. By this time 9,000 miles of track had been laid; 10 years later the number of miles had increased to over 30,000, and railroads connecting the Atlantic seaboard to the Mississippi River crisscrossed the East. What continued to set the South apart from the North, however, was its "peculiar institution," black slavery.

Section Two Review

SUMMARY

In the mid-nineteenth century, the United States economy grew at a fantastic rate. Inventions such as the telegraph, sewing machine, and vulcanized rubber created new industries and enlarged established ones. Manufacturing processes were improved and goods transported from American factories by new railroads and ships stormed world markets. In agriculture, an improved steel plow and a mechanical reaper opened up farmland in the Midwest. To accommodate the labor needs of the new industries, immigrants swarmed to cities in the northeastern United States.

CHECKING FOR UNDERSTANDING

1. **Identify** Elias Howe, John Deere, Cyrus McCormick, "Know Nothings," clipper ship

2. **Distinguish** between inventions that helped manufacturing expand and those that helped the growth of agriculture.

3. **Explain** why the expanding economy of the North attracted foreign immigrants.

4. **Identify** two differences between the economic systems of the North and the South.

5. **List** two significant innovations in transportation.

THINKING CRITICALLY

6. **Analyzing Relationships** Explain why transportation is important to economic progress.

CONNECTIONS: LINKING PAST TO PRESENT

7. **Comparing Motives** Compare reasons why immigrants came to the United States in the mid-1800s with the reasons immigrants continue to come to the United States today.

Dispute Over Slavery

Where slavery is, there liberty cannot be; and where liberty is, there slavery cannot be.

—CHARLES SUMNER
U.S. senator, in a speech
at the Cooper Institute, 1864

Section Focus

The 1850s found the South feeling increasingly isolated—isolated from the industrial boom of the North and from the new technologies that were redefining agriculture in the West, isolated by its support of the slave system. Was the Union doomed to be torn apart by the vast political and economic differences that separated North and South?

Objectives

After studying this section, you should be able to:
* Discuss how the majority of southerners viewed and defended the institution of slavery.
* Explain the significance of the Kansas-Nebraska Act.
* Examine the reactions of both the North and the South to the Supreme Court's *Dred Scott* decision.

Southern legislatures made it increasingly difficult for owners to emancipate their slaves. Some states decreed that free blacks must either go somewhere else or be sold back into slavery. All blacks, slave or free, had to carry identification passes when away from their homes. At night, patrols equipped with dogs and guns watched for runaways.

The "Peculiar Institution"

The bondage of blacks assumed many forms. Between house servants and their masters and mistresses, there was often a sense of trust and affection. Some enslaved people, especially in the cities, were hired out to other employees and thus were afforded some freedom of movement. The entire working force of the highly successful Tredegar Iron Works in Richmond, Virginia, was black. Most blacks, however, worked on plantations and lived lives marked by hard labor, cruel discipline, and isolation. Slave marriages were not legally recognized. Families could be broken up by sale. And it was against the law to teach slaves to read, although some white Southerners broke that law.

The few people who enslaved many people made some money out of the slave system. The rise in the price of "prime field hands," from $300 in 1790 to $1,800 in 1860, proved that slaves were a valuable commodity. In general, however, the system proved costly for the South as well as inefficient, mainly because it kept the South from mechanizing its industry. In addition, slavery as an institution lowered the dignity of both the workers and the work.

To support the system, many southerners developed an elaborate defense of slavery. Southerners argued that slavery was necessary to provide an adequate labor supply. Moreover, they said, slavery was "a positive good" because all the enslaved person's material needs were provided. One southerner spoke for many when he said, "The slaves are all well fed, well clad, have plenty of fuel, and are happy. They have no dread of the future—no fear of want." Such apologists also suggested that slavery was better than the unemployment, poverty, and crime that existed in industrial cities of the Northeast and in Great Britain. Finally, defenders of slavery tried to use arguments from science and the Bible to show that slavery was acceptable.

The defenders of slavery were careful to target their appeal to the three-fourths of southern whites who owned no black slaves. The "peculiar institution" gave every southern white person—rich or poor—a feeling of superiority over every

HARRIET TUBMAN
1820-1913

Born to enslaved parents in Maryland, Harriet Tubman worked as a plantation field hand until she was nearly 30 years old. Then she made her break for freedom, escaping to the North with the help of the Underground Railroad.

Knowing full well the risks of being captured, Tubman nonetheless made 19 trips back into the South during the 1850s to help other slaves escape. Altogether she assisted more than 300 blacks—including her aged parents—to escape bondage. While not the founder of the Underground Railroad, she certainly became its most famous and successful conductor. Known as the "Moses" of her people, Tubman maintained iron discipline among the escapees, and—despite huge rewards offered in the South for her capture and arrest—she always managed to elude her enemies.

Abolitionist mobs freed runaway slaves from jail. Under this law, the word of an owner of a runaway slave or even one who claimed to be the owner, was taken as conclusive proof of identity. A suspected runaway (who might in fact be a free person) had no right to testify on his or her own behalf. Any citizen might be required to join in pursuit of a runaway slave.

To counter this injustice, most free state legislatures passed personal liberty laws that nullified the Fugitive Slave Law by forbidding state officials to assist in the capture of runaways. Antislavery feeling in the North was also stimulated by the publication in 1852 of Harriet Beecher

---

black person, whether free or enslaved. In the South, according to Calhoun:

…the two great divisions of society are not the rich and poor, but white and black; and all the former, the poor as well as the rich, belong to the upper classes, and are respected and treated as such.

Opposition to Slavery

For a few years it looked as though the Compromise of 1850 might provide a permanent solution to the slavery controversy. In the presidential election of 1852, both major parties stood by its provisions. Leading business people, plantation owners, and members of Congress joined in condemning any attempt at serious discussion of the issue of slavery.

In the North, however, opposition to the stringent Fugitive Slave Law included in the Compromise of 1850 increased.

Stowe's *Uncle Tom's Cabin,* a novel portraying slavery at its worst. The book sold 10,000 copies in a week and 300,000 copies in its first year of publication.

Bloodshed on Free Soil

In 1854 the political truce over slavery ended with the passage of the Kansas-Nebraska Act. This legislation originated with Senator Stephen A. Douglas of Illinois, the skilled legislator of Compromise of 1850 fame. Douglas did not intend to

reopen intersectional controversy. Rather, he hoped to encourage the rapid settlement of the trans-Missouri region and build a transcontinental railroad with terminals at St. Louis and Chicago. The act provided that the region be divided into two new territories, Nebraska and Kansas. The question of whether or not slavery would exist in the new territories was to be decided by popular sovereignty. This part of the act negated the Missouri Compromise, because the new teritories of Kansas and Nebraska both lay above

Examining Maps *The tough fugitive slave law passed as part of the Compromise of 1850 intensified the efforts of the Underground Railroad. This informal organization secretly assisted runaway slaves in their journey north. Where did the routes of the Underground Railroad take fugitive slaves?*

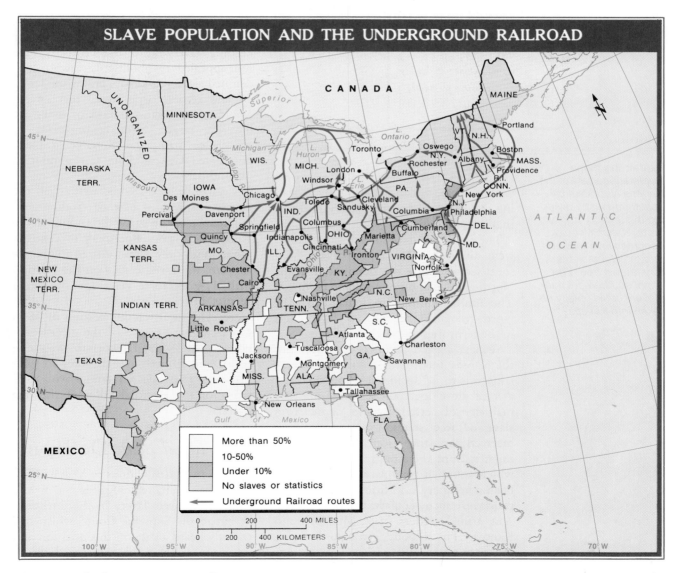

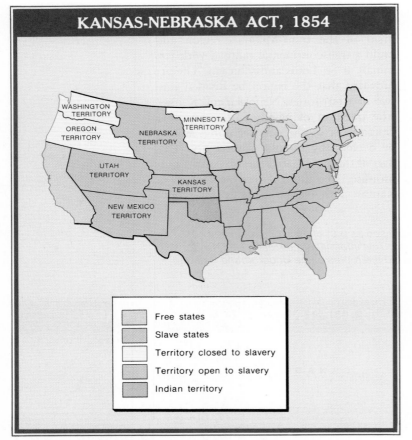

KANSAS-NEBRASKA ACT, 1854

Free states
Slave states
Territory closed to slavery
Territory open to slavery
Indian territory

Examining Maps
Some supporters of the Kansas-Nebraska bill assumed that by dividing the territory into two parts, Kansas would become slave territory and the Nebraska territory remain free. Why might southerners think slavery could easily be taken into Kansas?

latitude 36° 30′. In order to overcome this problem, a clause specifically repealing the Missouri ban on slavery north of that line was added.

The results of the Kansas-Nebraska Act were disastrous. The repeal of the Missouri Compromise was denounced in the North as a violation of a solemn compact. The South continued to demand that the North recognize the rights of slaveholders in the territories of the United States.

Settlers started at once to move into the Kansas Territory. Because the slavery issue was to be decided by popular vote, a race developed to see whether the majority of settlers would come from slave or free states. Northern settlers received assistance from an abolitionist organization, the Emigrant Aid Society, which supplied wagons, tools, livestock, farm machinery, and rifles. Meanwhile, a proslavery secret society, the Blue Lodge, sent armed settlers from Missouri into Kansas. The bloody struggle between the proslavery and antislavery factions

began to assume the proportions of a civil war.

The violence in "bleeding Kansas" reached its peak on the eve of the presidential election of 1856. In the two years since the passage of the Kansas-Nebraska Act, the Whig party had broken up because of friction between the proslavery "Cotton" Whigs of the South and the antislavery "Conscience" Whigs of the North. To fill the void, two new parties—the Americans and the Republicans—appeared. The American party, composed of Know Nothings and some ex-Whigs, tried to divert people's minds from the slavery issue by whipping up feeling against immigrants. Its candidate in 1856 was former President Fillmore. The basic principle of the Republicans (who took their name from the party of Thomas Jefferson) based its platform on "free soil," or keeping slavery out of the territories. Free soil appealed to abolitionists, who condemned slavery, and to many white farmers and laborers who feared that slavery would lower their standard of living by lowering wages. Strongly organized in every free state, the Republican party nominated General John C. Frémont as its candidate.

Meanwhile, the Democrats dodged the slavery issue. To balance Southerners' dominance of the party, they nominated a Northerner, James Buchanan of Pennsylvania. With only a minority of the popular vote, the Democrats won the election with 174 electoral votes for Buchanan against 114 for Frémont and 8 for Fillmore. The result of the election of 1856 was ominous because of the clearly sectional voting—the Democrats swept the South and gained enough votes to win, while the Republican Frémont won two-thirds of the electoral votes of the free states.

The *Dred Scott* Decision

In his inaugural address in March 1857, President Buchanan suggested that the controversy over slavery in the territories be left to the Supreme Court, which had recently heard a case on this question and was soon expected to render a decision.

Dred Scott was a slave taken by a former master from the state of Missouri into territory closed to slavery by the Missouri Compromise and then brought back to Missouri again. For more than 10 years, Scott, with the financial support of abolitionists, had sued for freedom on the grounds that residence in a free territory released him from slavery.

On March 6, 1857, Chief Justice Roger Taney (TAW nee) delivered the majority opinion in *Scott v. Sanford.* Nine separate opinions were written. The seven majority views were from Democrats who upheld completely the southern point of view that Scott had no right to sue in a federal court. Taney ruled against Scott because, he claimed, the founders of the United States did not intend for blacks to be citizens. In addition, when ruling on the constitutionality of the Missouri Compromise ban on slavery north of the 36° 30′ line, the Court said:

…it is the opinion of the court that the Act of Congress which prohibited a citizen from holding and owning property of this kind [slaves] in the territory of the United States north of the line therein mentioned, is not warranted by the Constitution and is therefore void….

Instead of settling the slavery dispute, the *Dred Scott* decision made it more bitter. If the decision stood, the Republican party might as well go out of existence, because its basic principle—free soil—had been declared unconstitutional. Republicans therefore claimed that the decision was not binding, but was an **obiter dictum,** an incidental opinion not called for by the circumstances of the case. Taney's decision, said a Republican newspaper, carried no more weight than "the judgment of the majority of those congregated in any Washington bar-room." Southerners, on the other hand, called on the North to obey the decision as the price of the South's remaining in the Union.

SUMMARY

By the 1850s, slavery was firmly entrenched in the South. To defend the slave system, southerners fostered the belief that slavery was a positive good and that blacks were racially inferior. Antislavery feelings in the North were fueled by hatred of the Fugitive Slave Law and the novel *Uncle Tom's Cabin.* Many northerners were upset by the Kansas-Nebraska Act with its provision for popular sovereignty. The *Dred Scott* decision, which stated that slaves were property and could be taken into the territories, intensified the conflict between proslavery and antislavery factions.

CHECKING FOR UNDERSTANDING

1. **Identify** Harriet Beecher Stowe, James Buchanan, Dred Scott, *Uncle Tom's Cabin*, Republican party

2. **State** three reasons southerners used to defend slavery.

3. **Distinguish** northern and southern reactions to the passage of the Kansas-Nebraska Act.

4. **Summarize** reactions to the *Dred Scott* decision.

THINKING CRITICALLY

5. **Analyzing a Ruling** Chief Justice Roger Taney ruled that Dred Scott could not sue for his freedom because he was not a citizen. Do you think Taney correctly interpreted the Constitution? Write two sentences to support your opinion.

CONNECTIONS: HISTORY AND GEOGRAPHY

6. **Comparing Cultures** One defense of slavery claimed that slaves were well cared for compared with northern industrial workers who suffered from poverty and hunger. Write a short rebuttal to this defense of slavery.

Drifting Toward War

SETTING THE SCENE

...the election of Lincoln, with all of its surroundings, is sufficient [for secession]. What is the significance of his election? It is the endorsement... of all those acts of aggression upon our rights by all these states, legislatures, governors, judges, and people. He is elected by the perpetrators of these wrongs....

—ROBERT TOOMBS
U.S. senator, in a speech to the
Georgia Legislature, 1861

Section Focus

Toombs voiced the fears of many southerners. Both the North and the South watched with dread as events surrounding the election of 1860 led toward the dissolution of the Union. For southerners, Lincoln's election signaled that slavery could not be extended.

Objectives

After studying this section, you should be able to:

• Evaluate the importance of the Lincoln-Douglas debates.
• Identify the purpose of John Brown's raid at Harper's Ferry and reactions to it.
• List the political events that led to the secession of seven Southern states.

The question of slavery in the territories left the nation in a state of almost hopeless confusion. The *Dred Scott* decision, supported in the South, was flatly opposed by the Republicans, dominant in the North. But what about the principle of popular sovereignty? Did the *Dred Scott* decision forbid the people of a territory to decide whether or not they wanted slavery? This became the most important question in the Lincoln-Douglas debates of 1858.

Lincoln-Douglas Debates

Stephen A. Douglas and Abraham Lincoln were rival candidates in the election for senator from Illinois. Douglas—a short, thickset man nicknamed "Little Giant," both for his size and his political influence—had served in the Senate for 12 years and had gained a national reputation for his commitment to the principle of popular sovereignty. The most prominent Democrat in Congress, he hoped to be elected President in 1860.

His challenger was Abraham Lincoln—a man whose tall, angular frame inspired ridicule and who often hid valuable papers in his stovepipe hat. Lincoln had served only a single undistinguished term in the House of Representatives. He defended the Compromise of 1850—even to the point of enforcing the Fugitive Slave Law. But although Lincoln was not an abolitionist, he did believe that if slavery were confined to its existing area, Southerners themselves might eventually abolish it. As a former Whig who had only recently joined the Republican party, Lincoln enjoyed a local reputation as a clever lawyer and keen debater.

During the campaign Lincoln and Douglas traveled to seven Illinois towns to debate the critical issues of the day. Douglas attempted to show that Republicans in general—and Lincoln in particular—were abolitionists in disguise, bent on destroying the Union. During their debate at Freeport, Illinois, Lincoln put Douglas in a difficult position by asking the question, "Can the people of a territory in any lawful way...exclude slavery from their limits prior to the formation of a State Constitution?" Douglas was trapped. If he answered "Yes," he would appear to support popular sovereignty, thereby opposing the *Dred Scott* decision. A "yes" answer would improve his chances for reelection as senator, but at the expense of Southern support

Examining Photographs *John Brown failed in his attempt to start a slave uprising in Virginia. How did he explain his actions?*

continue his work. On October 16, 1859, with only 21 followers, he seized the federal arsenal at Harpers Ferry, Virginia, intending to free and arm the slaves of the surrounding countryside. The siege ended with the capture of Brown by Colonel Robert E. Lee and the death of 10 of his men. At his Virginia trial for treason and murder, Brown expressed no remorse. In his last address to the court, Brown said:

I believe that to have interfered as I have done—as I have always freely admitted I have done—in behalf of [God's] despised poor, was not wrong but right. Now if it is deemed necessary that I should forfeit my life for the furtherance of the ends of justice and mingle my blood...with the blood of millions in this slave country whose rights are disregarded by wicked, cruel, and unjust enactments—I submit; so let it be done!

Found guilty, John Brown was hanged on December 2. Many Northerners regarded Brown as a martyr to the cause of freedom.

for the 1860 presidency. A "no" answer, on the other hand, would make it seem as if he had abandoned the notion of popular sovereignty—the principle on which he had based his political career. This answer would be welcomed by the South but could cost him the senatorial election.

To solve this dilemma, Douglas formulated the so-called Freeport Doctrine. According to this formula, Douglas said he accepted the *Dred Scott* decision that forbade Congress to bar slavery from the territories. However, he pointed out, a territorial legislature might effectively discourage slavery if it failed to pass laws to keep slaves under control. Said Douglas, "Slavery cannot exist a day, or an hour, anywhere, unless it is supported by local police regulations." By admitting that a territorial legislature could practically nullify the *Dred Scott* decision, Douglas won a narrow victory in Illinois' senatorial election—at the price of losing Southern support for the presidency in 1860. Lincoln lost the election but gained a national reputation.

John Brown's Raid

John Brown, a fiery abolitionist, regarded himself as a heaven-sent agent whose mission was to liberate slaves and punish slaveholders. Brown had previously participated in the armed struggle against proslavery forces in Kansas, later traveling East to

Examining Maps
The result of the critical presidential election of 1860 split along sectional lines. Lincoln did not win in any states south of Pennsylvania and the Ohio River. How many states did Douglas carry?

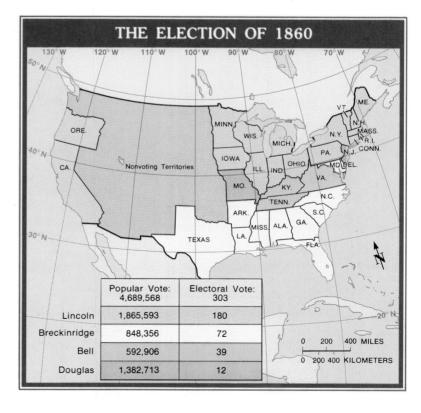

THE ELECTION OF 1860

	Popular Vote: 4,689,568	Electoral Vote: 303
Lincoln	1,865,593	180
Breckinridge	848,356	72
Bell	592,906	39
Douglas	1,382,713	12

The New England poet Ralph Waldo Emerson said that Brown had "made the gallows glorious like the cross." Southerners regarded Brown's punishment as just. They feared nothing so much as a slave revolt.

Even before Brown's raid at Harpers Ferry, Southern fears had already reached crisis proportions with the 1857 publication of *The Impending Crisis of the South,* by Hinton R. Helper, himself a Southerner. Helper attacked slavery because it enriched a few "slaveocrats" at the price of dooming non-slaveholding whites to "galling poverty and ignorance." Many Southern states banned the book from the mails. The Republican party was stirred to distribute 100,000 copies as a campaign document.

The Election of 1860

As the election of 1860 approached, Democrats split over the issue of slavery in the territories. A northern wing of the party nominated Douglas for the presidency and backed popular sovereignty; a southern wing nominated John C. Breckinridge of Kentucky and supported the *Dred Scott* decision. The Constitutional

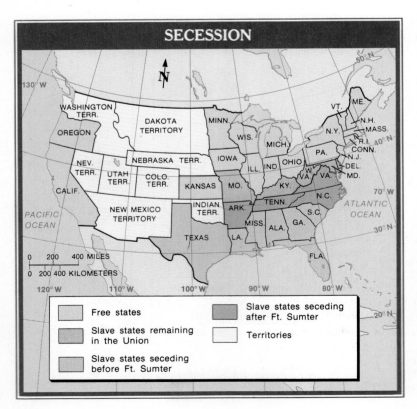

SECESSION

Free states

Slave states remaining in the Union

Slave states seceding before Ft. Sumter

Slave states seceding after Ft. Sumter

Territories

Union party, a third group composed mostly of former southern Whigs, nominated John Bell of Tennessee and attempted to avoid the slavery issue during the campaign.

With such division among their opponents, the door to the presidency stood open for the Republicans. Their platform, designed to attract votes from many quarters, was that slavery should be left undisturbed where it existed, but that it should be excluded from the territories. They denounced John Brown's raid as "among the gravest of crimes." They also called for a protective tariff, free homesteads for settlers, and federal funds for internal improvements, including a railroad to the Pacific. In an attempt to attract recent immigrants, they were harshly critical of Know-Nothing attempts to make naturalization more difficult.

The Republicans nominated Abraham Lincoln as their candidate. Lincoln, the only one of the candidates to make no speeches, stayed quietly at his home in Springfield, Illinois.

The election was a clear victory for the Republicans. Lincoln gained a majority in the electoral college, winning more votes than all three of his opponents combined. Not even listed on the ballot in some southern states, he carried every free state except New Jersey, where the vote was split between Lincoln and Douglas. Breckinridge carried the deep South, and Bell and Douglas divided the border states.

The South Secedes

Southerners viewed Lincoln as a "daring and reckless leader of the abolitionists." In their view, his election meant abolition and slave insurrections. During the four-month interval between Lincoln's election in November 1860 and his inauguration in March 1861, the seven states of the deep South (South Carolina, Mississippi, Florida, Alabama, Georgia, Louisiana, and Texas) voted for **secession**—withdrawal from the Union.

These states based their right to secede on the theory of states' rights: the Constitution, they argued, was a contract among sovereign states. The free states had broken

that contract by refusing to enforce the
Fugitive Slave Law and by denying the
southern states or southerners their equal
_____ territories; therefore, the
_____ were justified in resuming
_____ and equal place among
_____ the seven states drafted
_____ their new alliance—the
_____ es of America—and called
_____ states to join them.
_____ overnment leaders made
_____ npts at compromise. The
_____ was a proposal by Senator
_____ en of Kentucky. The key-
_____ tenden Compromise was
_____ ent of the 36° 30′ line,
_____ tories into slave and non-
_____ coln, however, refused to
_____ osal.
_____ reached Washington,
_____ bruary 1861, only eight
_____ emained in the Union.
_____ s feared for his life.
_____ th generally agreed with
_____ that states did not have
_____ e the Union, no one
_____ to force them back in.
_____ Scott expressed wide-
_____ ntiment when he said,
_____ depart in peace."
_____ ed. In his first inaugural
_____ that "no state upon its
_____ n can lawfully get out of
_____ argued that secession was
_____ asic democratic principle
_____ e majority should prevail.
_____ an before him, Lincoln
_____ ive measures to force the
_____ es back into the Union.
_____ ly to hold military posts
_____ by the Confederates, to
_____ aws where federal agents
_____ ious" to the local popula-
_____ eliver the mail "unless
_____ gh Lincoln still refused to
_____ ssion regarding slavery in
_____ s address did not explicit-
_____ onstitutional amendment
_____ l interference with slavery
_____ states. Finally, he pleaded
_____ South be "not enemies,
_____ said that "there need be
_____ r violence." Sadly, these
_____ dashed.

SUMMARY

Although the Lincoln-Douglas debates sharpened the issue of slavery in the territories, resolution of the issue was not in sight. John Brown, a fervent abolitionist, hoped to start a slave uprising. His failed attempt, however, only fueled southern fears of violence. In the election of 1860, Democrats split over slavery, thus opening the way for a Republican victory. Lincoln had pledged not to interfere with slavery in the South, but even before he took the oath of office, seven southern states seceded from the Union.

CHECKING FOR UNDERSTANDING

1. **Identify** Abraham Lincoln, John Brown, Hinton Helper, Crittenden Compromise, Confederate States of America

2. **Define** secession

3. **Identify** the opposing viewpoints demonstrated during the Lincoln-Douglas debates.

4. **Explain** why John Brown's raid at Harpers Ferry led to further isolation of the South.

5. **List** three issues the Republicans used to their advantage in the election of 1860.

THINKING CRITICALLY

6. **Analyzing Choices** Compile a list of events, other than the election of Lincoln, that might have led the seven southern states to secede from the United States.

LINKING PAST AND PRESENT

7. **Comparing Actions** In the 1990s, the Baltic republics of Estonia, Latvia, and Lithuania struggled to secede from the Soviet Union. Compare this present-day secession movement to the secession by southern states in the 1860s.

★ ★ ★ ★ ★ ★ ★ ★ ★ ★ ★ ★ ★ ★ ★ ★ ★ ★ ★ ★

★ Chapter 14 Review ★

★ Summary

The controversy over slavery boiled during the 1840s and 1850s. The Compromise of 1850 created a temporary lull in the conflict between proslavery and antislavery forces. California entered the union as a free state, and southerners got a tough, new fugitive slave law. Meanwhile, new territories were organized with no restriction on slavery.

A remarkable period of economic growth fueled by new inventions and technological innovations spurred on both the industrial North and the agricultural South. Large numbers of immigrants flooded into the United States to meet the labor needs of the booming industrial economy.

The slavery issue, however, would not go away. The Supreme Court, in the *Dred Scott* decision, ruled that slaves could be taken into the territories and that the Missouri Compromise was unconstitutional. When the Kansas-Nebraska Act was passed, opening this area to slavery, near civil war ensued as slavery and antislavery groups fought for control of the Kansas territorial government. When abolitionist John Brown attacked the arsenal at Harpers Ferry as the first step in a slave revolt, southerners were convinced that compromise with abolitionists was not possible.

Increasingly, the South found itself isolated politically from the rest of the nation. The election of Abraham Lincoln in 1860, perceived as an abolitionist victory by southerners, triggered the secession of seven southern states.

★ Using Vocabulary

Each of the following terms can be considered a "cause" and an "effect." Define the terms below by writing two sentences for each. Write one sentence that explains the term as a cause and another sentence using the term as an effect. Here is an example: "*Secession* by southern states was one cause of the Civil War." "One effect of the election of Abraham Lincoln was the southern states' *secession.*"

popular sovereignty   **platform**

★ Reviewing Facts

1. **Explain** how the slavery issue affected the presidential election of 1848.

2. **Classify** the provisions of the Compromise of 1850 into those that appealed to southern states and those that appealed to northern states.

3. **List** five inventions that hastened economic development between 1830 and 1860.

4. **State** three reasons why large numbers of immigrants came to the United States between 1830 and 1860.

5. **Explain** why the Kansas-Nebraska Act resulted in renewed fighting between slavery and antislavery forces.

6. **Summarize** the *Dred Scott v. Sanford* decision.

7. **Relate** the issue of popular sovereignty to the Lincoln-Douglas debates.

8. **Correlate** Brown's raid at Harpers Ferry to southern attitudes about the North.

★ Understanding Concepts

ECONOMIC DIVERSITY

1. Explain how economic diversity might have affected northern and southern views on slavery. Include in your answer differences between the northern and southern economies.

2. What role did improved transportation play in the expanding United States economy?

POLITICAL CONFLICT

3. How did the southern states explain their right to secede from the Union?

4. Evaluate the impact of John Brown's attack at Harpers Ferry on southern attitudes toward compromise with abolitionists.

★ Thinking Critically

1. **Linking Past and Present** The issues of slavery and popular sovereignty divided Americans in the 1850s. What are some issues today that divide Americans? What distinguishes a divisive issue from one that can be resolved through compromise?

2. **Evaluating Means of Transportation** New railroads cost large sums of money to build. Weigh the initial costs of building a railroad against the potential for earning profits.

3. **Recognizing Bias** Southerners developed an

elaborate defense of slavery. Analyze their defense of slavery and explain why their ideas were based on racial prejudice.

4. **Predicting Outcomes** How likely is it that the slavery issue could have been settled peacefully without states leaving the Union? Explain why a political solution issue was doubtful.

★ Writing About History

CLASSIFICATION

Refer to the description of how to write a classification essay in the History Writer's Handbook in the Appendix of this book. Your teacher will give you more specific instruction on the essay's length and the assignment's due date.

Before writing your essay, compile a list of changes that took place in the years between 1840 and 1860. Divide these changes into three categories: political, technological, and social. Next, create a subcategory that enumerates all the items that created conflict and tension between the North and South. Use these classifications to write an essay entitled, "Factors that Divided the North and South."

★ Learning Cooperatively

You will work with two others in a group to conduct a mock trial to determine whether or not John Brown should be executed. Each member in your group will assume one of the following roles: defending attorney, prosecuting attorney, and judge. The defense and prosecution attorneys must prepare their cases to present before the judge. The judge must prepare at least two questions to ask each attorney. Present your trial to the class and poll them to determine John Brown's innocence or guilt.

★ Mastering Skills

MAKING INFERENCES

Each day you give and receive information both verbally and in writing. Sometimes this information is stated directly, but at other times it is hinted at, or implied. When this happens, a person has to make an *inference,* or a deduction based on facts or circumstances. Inferences are made by "reading between the lines." You make an inference when you use facts to draw a conclusion that is not stated directly. Good inferences are based on sound reasoning and careful analysis of information. Making inferences helps you understand something more completely.

Example The following steps will help you make inferences on information presented below on southern slaveholders.

- Read or listen carefully. Be sure you understand all the facts presented:

    Slaveholders, called planters, were actually a very small percentage of the southern population. To be considered a planter, a person had to hold at least 20 slaves. Only about 4 percent of slaveholders had this many slaves. An extremely small percentage of slaveholders had more than 100 slaves. Jefferson Davis, who became the future president of the Confederacy, held as many as 3,000 slaves. The majority of slaveholders, however, were farmers who kept about 5 slaves.

    About three-fourths of the southerners had no slaves at all. These southerners owned small farms on which they grew their own food and perhaps a cash crop such as tobacco or cotton. About 10 percent of this non-slaveholding southern population were poor whites. They supported themselves by hunting and fishing.

- Summarize the information:

    The majority of the people in the South did not own slaves. Those who did had very few. Only a few planters had large numbers of slaves.

- Decide what inferences or conclusions can be made based on what was read or heard but was not stated directly. Read the following inference based on the above summary.

    The economic benefits of slavery directly affected only a few southerners.

Practice Use the three steps outlined above and what you have learned in this chapter to determine which of the following three inferences seems reasonable.

1. Before the Civil War, the prosperity of the South depended on slave labor.

2. The absence of slavery in the North meant that northerners were not prejudiced against African Americans.

3. The southern economy grew because of advances in farming equipment such as Deere's steel plow and McCormick's grain harvester.

CULTURAL KALEIDOSCOPE

America's Centennial

The decades preceding the nation's hundredth birthday were times of unparalleled growth. They were also times of unparalleled conflict over westward expansion, slavery, and equality for women—issues mirrored in the culture of the years 1825 to 1877.

Literature

PHILOSOPHICAL WRITERS

Quite suddenly in the mid-1800s, America found itself in a literary and intellectual renaissance. It sprang from philosopher Ralph Waldo Emerson's Transcendentalism, a movement which held that all beings are connected through a common universal soul. Among the writers who rose to prominence during this period were Henry David Thoreau, Nathaniel Hawthorne, and Herman Melville.

REGIONAL POETS

New England, the center of the Transcendental movement, was also home to a crop of poets who achieved international acclaim during the 1840s and 1850s. Styled the "Fireside Poets," the group included such luminaries as Henry Wadsworth Longfellow, Oliver Wendell Holmes, James Russell Lowell, John Greenleaf Whittier, and Emily Dickinson. They concentrated on themes of nature and love.

▼ *Woodcut from an abolitionist's letter to Stephen Foster, 1846*

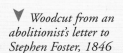

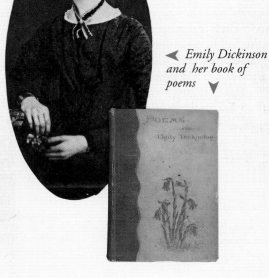

◄ *Emily Dickinson and her book of poems* ▼

▲ Nathaniel Hawthorne *painted by Charles Osgood, 1840*

Technology

CHRONICLERS OF AN ERA

In contrast to the Fireside Poets, other writers dealt with the hardships of slavery and civil war. *Uncle Tom's Cabin,* a novel by Harriet Beecher Stowe, and *My Bondage and My Freedom,* the autobiography of ex-slave Frederick Douglass, detailed the plight of the slave.

Even Walt Whitman, whose philosophic poems in his famed 1855 collection *Leaves of Grass* extol his idealized love of America, responded to the horrors of the Civil War with such poems as "Drum Taps" and "Beat! Beat! Drums!"

LONG-DISTANCE COMMUNICATION

Sending messages from state to state would never again be a struggle. Samuel Morse's telegraph and special code—a system of dots and dashes to represent the alphabet—advanced communication through the sending of electrical impulses along wires strung from one city to another. The first test line between Baltimore and Washington, D.C., with the message "What hath God wrought," was successfully sent in 1844.

MEDICINE

In 1846 anesthesia was first used to control pain during surgery. Not long after, the bearded faces of Pough-keepsie, New York, restaurateurs William and Andrew Smith (also known as the Smith Brothers) began to grace the packages of their wild-cherry-flavored cough remedy.

▼ *Smith Brothers cough drops*

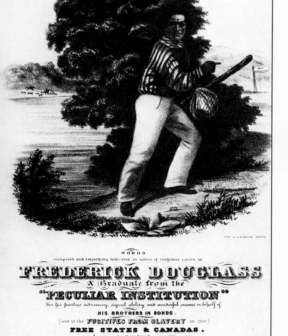

▶ *Dr. John Collins explains the effects of ether to eradicate pain during surgery, 1846*

◀ *Cover of sheet music written for Douglass, 1845*

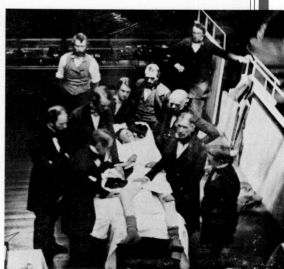

The Arts

MUSIC OF THE CIVIL WAR

Like most wars, the Civil War spawned its share of patriotic tunes. Most frequently sung in support of the Union cause was Julia Ward Howe's "Battle Hymn of the Republic."

Heading the confederate Top 40 were "The Yellow Rose of Texas" and "Dixie." Arguably the most stirring tune composed during the war was a four-note bugle call first sounded in 1862—the year of Shiloh and Antietam. Its name was "Taps."

PAINTING

The call "Westward Ho!" lured many artists of this era to the frontier. One of the most celebrated was George Caleb Bingham, who carefully recorded the sights of river life in Missouri. Bingham also skillfully captured the details of daily life in his scenes of elections in frontier towns.

PHOTOGRAPHY

An entirely different view of western expansion came from the new art of photography. Invented by a French chemist and perfected by French physicist Louis Daguerre, the daguerrotype created a fever in the United States when Samuel F. B. Morse ordered the first camera from Paris in 1839.

Photography made it possible for Americans of the 1860s to glimpse the Civil War "up close and personal." The frank and chilling visual accounts of life—and death—at the front lines by photojournalists Matthew Brady and Alexander Gardner remain unsurpassed to this day.

► Cover of Howe's sheet music

▼ Fur Traders Descending the Missouri
by George Caleb Bingham, c.1845

◄ Dead Boy in the Road at Fredericksburg
by Mathew B. Brady, 1863

Entertainment and Recreation

THE EXPOSITION

For six months Philadelphia was hopping with nearly 10 million visitors paying $3.8 million in admissions to celebrate the nation's first 100 years and to see the new inventions of the time—such as the telephone, the typewriter, and the 2500-horsepower Corliss engine.

VACATION SPOT

Hotel-building reached new heights toward the middle of the 1800s with the completion of Boston's four-story Tremont House. The structure, which boasted 170 rooms, was one of the grandest hotels on any continent. Among the notable figures to sign its guest register was Charles Dickens.

FOOD

Efforts to please a fussy customer one night in 1853 led George Crum, a Saratoga Springs, New York, chef to create one of the most popular snack foods of all time. Crum's name for his paper-thin wafers of potato, Saratoga chips, never took. The custom of munching "potato chips" did.

▲ Program for the hundredth anniversary of the nation

▲ Home of the potato chip

▶ Tremont House

Historical Focus

The Civil War was a major turning point for the American people. It was the "last of the old wars and the first of the new." Still prominent were muzzle-loading rifles, horse cavalry, and chivalrous respect for the enemy. New were the use of railroads, the telegraph, ironclad ships, observation balloons, conscription, and the concept of "total war." When the fighting ended, 600,000 Americans had lost their lives, slavery had been abolished, and much of the South lay in ruins.

Concepts to Understand

- Why it became necessary to curtail civil **rights and freedoms** during the Civil War.
- How military **conflict** led to total war between the North and South.

People to Know

Robert E. Lee, Ulysses S. Grant, William T. Sherman, Clara Barton

Places to Locate

Ft. Sumter, Antietam, Gettysburg, Vicksburg, Appomattox Court House

Terms to Identify

martial law, habeas corpus, conscription, bounty, greenbacks

Guided Reading

As you read this chapter, seek the answers to the following questions.

1. What were the advantages of the Union and Confederacy in the war?
2. How did Lincoln's choice of Grant as commander of the Union armies help the Union war effort?

SPANNING THE DECADES

POLITICAL	1860 *Buchanan sends relief supplies to Ft. Sumter*	1861 *Eleven states secede and form the Confederate States of America*	1862 *Emancipation Proclamation issued*	1863 *Union victories at Gettysburg and Vicksburg*

1860   1862

CULTURAL	1860 *The Pony Express links Missouri with California*	1861 *First transcontinental telegraph message is sent*	1862 *Julia Ward Howe's* Battle Hymn of the Republic *is published*	1863 *First national currency goes into circulation*

Militia Drill Scene, Civil War *by James Walker, 1861*

1864
Lincoln reelected

1865
Lee surrenders to Grant at Appomattox Court House, Virginia

Lincoln assassinated; Andrew Johnson becomes President

1864

1866

1864
Quakers found Swarthmore College in Pennsylvania

1865
Mark Twain publishes The Celebrated Jumping Frog of Calaveras County

…This is essentially a people's contest…it is a struggle for maintaining in the world that form…of government whose leading object is to elevate the condition of [all] to clear the paths of laudable pursuit for all…

—ABRAHAM LINCOLN
War Message to Congress, 1861

SECTION ONE

The Outbreak of War

SETTING THE SCENE

The time to compromise has passed and those who oppose us shall smell powder and feel Southern steel.... No compromise, no reconstruction, no reconciliation can now be entertained.

—JEFFERSON DAVIS
President of the Confederacy, 1861

Section Focus

The new President of the United States and his counterpart in the Confederacy each faced a formidable task. With the attack on Fort Sumter, war became the solution to the long-standing differences between North and South. Each leader was determined to do what was necessary to win a quick victory. Neither could predict the terrible cost of the long war that was to come.

Objectives

After studying this section, you should be able to:
• Compare the strengths and weaknesses of the North and South.
• Explain the strategies of the North and South.
• Discuss the role of wartime diplomacy.

As the Southern states seceded, they seized United States arsenals, mints, fortresses, and other public property within their borders. Fort Sumter, on a rocky island in the harbor of Charleston, South Carolina, was one of only two Southern forts still under federal control. By April 1861, the fort was running short of provisions because a supply ship sent by President Buchanan in January had been turned back by artillery fire from shore. Lincoln decided to resupply Fort Sumter, and he told South Carolina authorities of his decision.

Lincoln's decision placed Jefferson Davis, president of the Confederacy, in a difficult position. How long could the Confederates tolerate the fort of a "foreign" nation in the harbor of their major Atlantic port? If Davis allowed the fort to be resupplied, he would appear to be giving in to Lincoln. If he ordered that Fort Sumter or the relief ships be fired on, he risked war. Davis chose to take the fort before the ships arrived. On April 12, 1861, shore batteries of the South Carolina militia opened fire on Fort Sumter. From inside the fort, Captain Abner Doubleday described the attack:

Showers of balls...and shells...poured into the fort in one incessant stream, causing great flakes of masonry to fall in all directions. When the immense mortar shells, after sailing high in the air, came down in a vertical direction, and buried themselves in the parade ground, their explosion shook the fort like an earthquake.

After 34 hours of bombardment, but no loss of life, Fort Sumter surrendered.

Preparing to Fight

News of the attack on Fort Sumter stirred nationalism in the North. When Lincoln requested 75,000 volunteers for 90 days to suppress the rebellion, more responded than could be equipped or trained. "I never knew what popular excitement could be," wrote a Bostonian to a friend in England. "The whole population, men, women, and children, seem to be in the streets with Union flags.... Nobody holds back." A similar wave of nationalism swept the South, as Jefferson Davis called for 100,000 volunteers. A visitor to the South found "revolutionary fervor in full sway....Young men are dying to fight."

Lincoln knew that conflicting forces existed in the eight slaveholding states that had not yet seceded. Nationalism worked for the Union, while the strongest argument for secession was slavery. He considered Delaware to be safe for the Union. But to remind the others that the war was to preserve the nation, and not to end slavery, the President declared:

The central idea pervading this struggle is the necessity of proving that popular government is not an absurdity. We must settle this question now, whether, in a free government, the minority have the right to break up the government whenever they choose.

Faced with the prospect of fighting their neighbors, however, four more states—Virginia, Arkansas, North Carolina, Tennessee—abandoned the Union. Virginia's secession put Washington, D.C., in danger.

To its west was Virginia. To the east was Maryland, where many people owned slaves and supported the Confederacy. If Maryland seceded, the Union capital would be in enemy territory. Lincoln determined to hold Maryland at all costs.

Only a week after Fort Sumter, as Union troops passed through Baltimore on their way to Washington, D.C., they were attacked by a mob aroused by pro-Confederate newspapers. The President responded by placing Baltimore under **martial law,** a form of military rule that includes suspending Bill of Rights guarantees. Persons who advocated secession or otherwise openly supported the Confederacy were arrested and held without trials. Although tensions in Maryland remained high throughout the war, Lincoln's action kept this strategically important state in the Union.

"I hope to have God on my side," Lincoln said, "but I must have Kentucky." The President's native state and Missouri were important because they controlled the Mississippi and Ohio rivers. Although Kentucky had a pro-Union government, Lincoln eventually put the state under martial law to stabilize it. In Missouri, where slaveholders controlled the state, he supported rebellion against the pro-Confederate elected state government.

Examining Illustrations
Lincoln's strong personality dominated his cabinet. "The President is the best of us," wrote one member, "there is only one vote in the Cabinet and it belongs to him." With what problems did Lincoln and his cabinet have to deal?

Strategies and Advantages

The Civil War was fought across the continent from southern Pennsylvania in the Northeast to New Mexico in the Southwest. Nearly three million soldiers wore the uniforms of the Union or the Confederacy. Countless other men and women supported these troops—on the farm, in the factory, on the battlefield, and behind the lines.

The South had the better army, especially during the early years of the war. Because of a strong military tradition in the South, many Confederate officers had attended the United States Military Academy at West Point in New York. Most of the top officers in the United States Army resigned their commissions to fight for the Confederacy, among them Robert E. Lee. After his native Virginia seceded, Lee decided that he could not "raise my hand against my relatives, my children, my home." He rejected Lincoln's offer to lead the Union armies and took command of Confederate forces in Virginia.

The Union's military strategy was simple: blockade Confederate ports and ruin the South's economy; invade the South and split it into thirds at the Mississippi River and through Tennessee and Georgia; and capture the Confederate capital at Richmond, Virginia. Southern strategy was even simpler. Southerners would be fighting for their independence on familiar terrain. To win, the South did not have to do anything except hold out against enemy attacks.

The South, formerly a region within a nation, was now itself a nation to fight and die for. Southerners felt they were fighting to preserve the cotton economy and the plantation culture. Because Europe was the major market for their cotton, they counted on European nations to provide war materials and other supplies.

The South would need Europe's help because the North was superior in nearly every type of resource. The Union had more than 80 percent of the manufacturing plants and most of America's merchant ships, railroad track, banks, minerals, grain

Examining Graphs *The economic differences between North and South had been developing for decades. What advantages did these differences offer the North?*

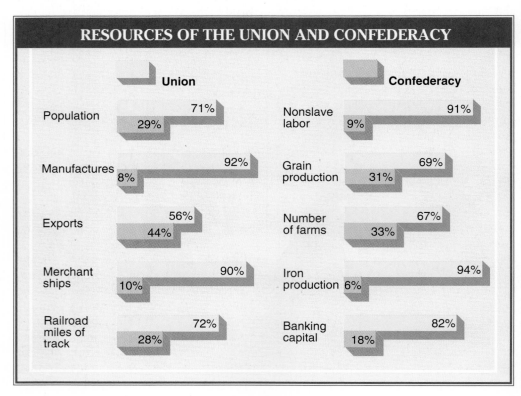

RESOURCES OF THE UNION AND CONFEDERACY

	Union		Confederacy
Population	71% / 29%	Nonslave labor	91% / 9%
Manufactures	92% / 8%	Grain production	69% / 31%
Exports	56% / 44%	Number of farms	67% / 33%
Merchant ships	90% / 10%	Iron production	94% / 6%
Railroad miles of track	72% / 28%	Banking capital	82% / 18%

Examining Illustrations *In the first battle of ironclad ships, the Union's* Monitor *(left) defeated the South's* Merrimac *off Virginia in March 1862. The Union's blockade was saved but the era of wooden warships was over. Why was the blockade important?*

crops, and meat. The Confederacy had less than one-half as many people as the North and more than one-third of these were slaves. The Confederacy was open to attack all along its border with the Union and along its extensive coastline. In short, the South was ill-equipped to wage war, even in its own defense.

The Confederacy also suffered from the very political theories that had created it. The Confederate constitution limited the authority of the central government and emphasized states' rights, a framework of government that was contrary to what was needed in wartime. As the war progressed, some state governments resisted the Confederacy's efforts to raise troops. Not until 1863 was the central government able to levy taxes to finance the war. It was forced to borrow and to issue worthless paper money to pay its bills. State governments also printed paper money and added to the economic chaos, which encouraged hoarding and damaged morale.

Wartime Diplomacy

The principal task of Union diplomacy during the Civil War was to prevent European nations from supporting the Confederacy. Europe's ruling classes continued to be concerned about maintaining their power and status at home, and they were not upset by the disintegration of the world's largest democracy. The British and French governments, in particular, were openly sympathetic to the Confederacy.

The South expected Britain's aid because British textile mills used Southern cotton. In Britain, manufacturers believed that an independent South would be a better market for their products. Lacking industry, the Confederacy would be unlikely to impose protective tariffs. Lincoln reminded the British that they needed Union wheat as much as Confederate cotton. But to prevent Great Britain and the South from developing closer commercial ties, the President also struck his first blow against the South.

Six days after Fort Sumter fell, Lincoln announced a blockade of Southern ports. At the time the action seemed foolish and impossible to enforce. To patrol a Confederate coastline 3,500 miles long, the United States Navy had just 42 wooden ships and fewer than 9,000 sailors, so at first the blockade was selective. But as the Union navy grew to 626 ships and about 59,000 sailors, the blockade reduced Confederate imports and exports to what could be carried in "blockade runners"—small, fast vessels designed to sneak through openings in the sandbars that lined much of the Southern coast. Blockade runners could not begin to replace regular commerce, however, and Southern trade eventually shrank to a fraction of what it had been before the war, depriving Confederate armies of vital supplies.

Unable to break the blockade militarily, Southern leaders hoped to accomplish it diplomatically. If Britain recognized Confederate independence, its powerful navy could keep Southern cotton flowing to British textile mills. In May 1861, Britain declared that a state of war existed between the North and South and announced its neutrality in that war. Because the British stopped short of recognizing Southern independence, Confederate leaders continued to pursue that goal.

In November 1861, Confederate diplomacy brought the North to the brink of war with Great Britain. A United States warship stopped the British steamer *Trent* in the Caribbean and removed two Confederates bound for negotiations in Britain and France. When Britain angrily demanded the release of the two diplomats and an apology for violating its neutrality, some Americans called for war. The British responded by sending 8,000 troops to Canada. Forced to choose between international humiliation if he gave in, or war with England if he refused, Lincoln released the diplomats. "One war at a time," he told his critics.

British relations with the Confederacy remained close after the *Trent* affair, and tensions with the Union high. Southern diplomats arranged for British shipyards to build and outfit Confederate warships to prey on Northern shipping. But these vessels could not break the Union blockade, nor could Britain's need for cotton. Increased cotton production by Britain's colonies in Egypt and India replaced the loss of Southern cotton and eliminated the Confederacy's best hope for European intervention in the Civil War.

★ ★ ★ ★ ★ ★ ★ ★ ★ ★ ★ ★ ★ ★ ★ ★ ★ ★

Section One Review

★ ★ ★ ★ ★ ★ ★ ★ ★ ★ ★ ★ ★ ★ ★ ★ ★ ★

SUMMARY

Besides rallying the North and South to war, the attack on Fort Sumter also persuaded four more Southern states to join the Confederacy. Northern war strategy hinged on the blockade of Southern ports, the invasion and division of the South, and the capture of Richmond. The South planned to fight a defensive war, supplied and financed by trade with Europe. While the North enjoyed many material advantages, the South possessed superior military leadership and a unifying cause. For both sides, diplomacy played a major role, as the Confederacy attempted to obtain Europe's assistance and the North tried to prevent it.

CHECKING FOR UNDERSTANDING

1. **Identify** Confederacy, Fort Sumter, Jefferson Davis, Robert E. Lee, Richmond, *Trent* Affair

2. **Define** martial law

3. **List** three consequences of the attack on Fort Sumter.

4. **Summarize** the advantages of the North and South.

5. **Describe** the effects of the Union blockade and Southern response to it.

THINKING CRITICALLY

6. **Analyzing Causes** The attack on Fort Sumter aroused intense patriotic feelings in the North. Comment on two aspects of this attack that you think contributed to Northerners' outburst of patriotism.

CONNECTIONS: HISTORY AND ECONOMICS

7. **Synthesizing Ideas** Tariffs were of two kinds: protective and revenue. Explain why British manufacturers believed that an independent South would not impose protective tariffs on British industrial products.

★ ★ ★ ★ ★ ★ ★ ★ ★ ★ ★ ★ ★ ★ ★ ★ ★ ★

The War on the Battlefield

It is well that war is so terrible, or we should get too fond of it.

—ROBERT E. LEE
Battle of Fredericksburg, 1862

Section Focus

The fighting began with two armies of immigrants, farm boys, schoolteachers, and store clerks. At first there was a curious, almost eager anticipation of battle. But as blood began to spill and young men on both sides fell wounded and dying, both North and South began to confront the grim reality of a long and bitter war.

Objectives

After studying this section, you should be able to:

• Identify the major battles of the war.
• Explain the significance of the battles of Antietam, Gettysburg, and Vicksburg.

There were two major areas of land warfare. The eastern theater, east of the Appalachians, centered on the region surrounding the two capitals, Washington, D.C., and Richmond, Virginia. Because the two cities were less than 100 miles apart, many battles occurred in this area.

The western theater centered around the Mississippi River and its tributaries. In many ways, the West was critical to victory. If Union armies gained control of the Mississippi River, the Confederacy would lose its western food supplies.

The War in Virginia

On July 21, 1861, with Lincoln's 90-day volunteers nearing the end of their enlistments, the Union army invaded Virginia to capture Richmond. About 30 miles from Washington, D.C., 30,000 Northern troops met a smaller Confederate force near a stream called Bull Run. Expecting victory and a quick end to the war, members of Congress and Washington civilians came along to picnic and watch the battle. What they saw was a confusing clash of two untrained armies. Union troops fought well at first, but the Confederates proved better organized. Using the railroad and telegraph, Confederate officers were able to quickly supply reinforcements. The Union army's retreat was reported for the *London Times* by a correspondent on the scene:

I perceived several wagons coming from the direction of the battlefield;…a thick cloud of dust rose behind them, and running by the side of the wagons were a number of men in uniform…. every moment the crowd increased, drivers and men cried out with the most vehement gestures, "Turn back! Turn back! We are whipped!"

Together, panic-stricken soldiers and civilians fled back to Washington.

Indeed, Yankee predictions of a quick war could have come true. "Give me 10,000 fresh troops, and I will be in Washington tomorrow," Confederate general Thomas "Stonewall" Jackson said after Bull Run. But Jefferson Davis insisted on a defensive war, and the Union was saved.

After the disaster at Bull Run, Lincoln replaced General Irvin McDowell with General George McClellan who trained and reorganized the Union army. But in 1862 the Confederates turned back McClellan at the Seven Days' Battle, General John Pope at the Second Battle of Bull Run, and General Ambrose Burnside at Fredericksburg. In May 1863, at Chancellorsville, Virginia, Lee smashed General Joe Hooker, who lost 17,000 men to an army half his size. "My God, my God," Lincoln cried when he learned of Hooker's terrible defeat, "What will the country say!"

Antietam and Gettysburg

Confederate military success in the eastern theater did not extend onto Northern soil. Lee's victory over bungling Union generals at the Second Battle of Bull Run in August 1862, encouraged him to invade the Union. His plan was to surprise Washington, D.C., from the north and destroy Northern morale. In September 1862, his 45,000 troops slipped into Maryland and disappeared into the mountains, where he split his army and sent "Stonewall" Jackson to seize the federal arsenal at Harpers Ferry. McClellan, who was to protect Washington by keeping between Lee and the capital, frantically chased after his enemy.

At this point, incredible good luck befell McClellan. On a Maryland road a Union patrol found three cigars wrapped in a copy of Lee's plans. McClellan realized that the Confederate forces were divided and that he could destroy Lee's army. On September 17, 1862, McClellan attacked Lee at Antietam (An TEE tuhm) Creek near Sharpsburg, Maryland. In the bloodiest single day of the war, McClellan forced Lee to retreat back into Virginia. The Confederates suffered more than 11,000 casualties. But McClellan lost even more, and his army was too damaged to pursue Lee and finish him.

When news of Antietam was telegraphed to Lincoln, he called his cabinet together and told them:

Examining Illustrations   *While Lincoln searched desperately for a general who could win in the east, the Confederates remained under the able command of General Robert E. Lee (on the white horse). But Lee's brilliant strategist, General Thomas "Stonewall" Jackson, was mortally wounded at Chancellorsville, and Lee mourned the loss of "my right arm." Which Union generals did Lee defeat in Virginia?*

The order was an Emancipation Proclamation, which he issued on September 22, 1862, to free the slaves of the Confederacy (see Appendix). Lincoln's order, which made this conflict a war against slavery, had its greatest impact, however, in the North and in Europe. It had little effect in the South, which first had to be defeated.

Encouraged by nearly destroying Hooker's army of 130,000 at Chancellorsville, Lee crossed the Potomac again in June 1863, and moved into southern Pennsylvania. He was shadowed, however, by a Union army under General George G. Meade. An accidental clash between small units at Gettysburg developed into a bloody battle that marked the turning point of the war.

As both armies gathered to do battle, Union troops took up positions on the crest of a low ridge. It became the Confederates' task to dislodge them from this high ground. Desperate Confederate attacks—concluding on July 3 in a gallant but suicidal charge across an open field by General George Pickett's 15,000 troops—were all repulsed. After 3 days of fighting, Union casualties were more than 23,000. More than 28,000 Confederates were killed or wounded, about 7,000 of them in Pickett's Charge. "Do not let the enemy escape," Lincoln wired the victorious Meade.

On July 4, Lee retreated into Virginia. Once again, the Union army failed to pursue him. "Our army held the war in the hollow of its hand," cried a frustrated Lincoln. "We had only to stretch forth our hands and they were ours. And nothing I could say or do could make the Army move."

Although both sides suffered heavy casualties at Gettysburg, it was a devastating

THE WAR IN THE EAST, 1861-1863

Union forces
Confederate forces
Battle

loss of life from which the sparsely populated South could not recover. On November 19, 1863, President Lincoln visited Gettysburg to dedicate the battlefield cemetery and to honor the soldiers buried there. In this Gettysburg address, the President promised that "these dead shall not have died in vain" (see Appendix).

War in the West

In 1861 the war in the west was a struggle for control of the border states. In Missouri the pro-Union state government that Lincoln supported waged its own civil war against Confederate sympathizers. Thousands were killed in fighting in Missouri before the first shots were fired at Bull Run in the east.

The western counties of Virginia, where pro-Union sentiment ran strong, were detached from the state after it seceded, and in 1863 they were admitted to the Union as the new state of West Virginia. Despite Kentucky's strong pro-Confederate leanings, the Union army held the state throughout the war. Thus Union strategy in the border states deprived the South of a strong line of defense along the Ohio River.

Examining Maps
The Union's military strategy in the eastern theater of the war is shown in this map. What was the Union's war goal in the east?

In the following year the Confederacy was squeezed from both north and south, as opposing forces battled for control of the Mississippi River. The Union advance began when General Ulysses S. Grant attacked two Confederate forts on the Kentucky-Tennessee border. First taking Fort Henry, on the Tennessee River, Grant surrounded Fort Donelson, on the Cumberland River, in February 1862. When the Confederate commander at Fort Donelson tried to negotiate, Grant's reply created his reputation as a tough, no-nonsense soldier: "No terms except unconditional and immediate surrender can be accepted."

The fall of Fort Donelson, with about 13,000 Confederate prisoners, opened the way for a Union advance south toward a railroad center at Corinth, Mississippi. From there Grant planned to move west along the railroad to capture Memphis, Tennessee, on the Mississippi River.

The Union advance was slowed in April 1862 by the bloody, two-day battle of Shiloh on the Tennessee-Mississippi border. Grant's army was surprised near Corinth by the Confederates under General Albert Sidney Johnston. Union forces

Examining Photographs *Before the war, Ulysses S. Grant failed at farming and as a merchant. Although he did not distinguish himself in his class at West Point, Lincoln said of him, "He fights." Why was Grant's victory at Fort Donelson important?*

Examining Maps
As in the east, most fighting in the western theater of the war occurred on Confederate soil. What was the Union's military strategy in the west?

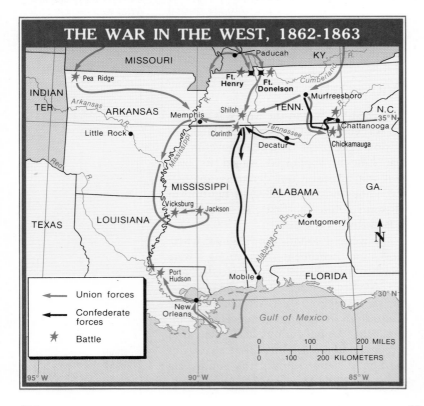

THE WAR IN THE WEST, 1862-1863

Legend:
→ Union forces
→ Confederate forces
★ Battle

escaped disaster when reinforcements arrived and Johnston was killed. But Grant lost 13,000 of his 63,000 troops, and Confederate casualties numbered 11,000 of 40,000. Impressed by the determination of his enemy, Grant later wrote that after Shiloh, "I gave up all idea of saving the Union except by complete conquest."

Meanwhile, Flag Officer David Farragut was ordered to capture New Orleans. To reach the city, his warships had to move upriver from the Gulf of Mexico past two Confederate forts. After failing to destroy the forts, Farragut decided to pass under cover of darkness. As the maneuver began, the moon rose and the forts opened fire, hitting the first ship 42 times. After a 90-minute battle, 20 of 24 ships made it past, and New Orleans surrendered without firing a shot.

By the end of 1862, Union armies occupied all of western Tennessee and were probing south into Mississippi. Other armies were advancing north from New Orleans. Only Vicksburg, Mississippi, blocked Union control of the river and success of the Union's western strategy.

Connections

THE BATTLE OF VICKSBURG

Control of the Mississippi River was crucial to success for both the Union and Confederacy. As long as the South held Vicksburg, it controlled the 150 miles of river between that city and Baton Rouge. Vital supplies from western states flowed into the Confederacy across this stretch. But before Grant could seize Vicksburg,

Union fleet reaches Vicksburg in 1863

he had to deal with a greater enemy—the wicked geography of the delta. Heavily fortified, Vicksburg was perched on a high bluff on the east side of a sharp bend in the Mississippi. North of Vicksburg lay the Yazoo Delta, a vast area of flat, swampy land half under water. Grant descended the river from Memphis where he vainly sought to approach the city through the delta. Grant then boldly crossed the Mississippi to the west bank, slipped south, and recrossed below Vicksburg. Contrary to established military strategy, and against the unanimous advice of his staff, he cut his supply lines, allowing his troops only what food they could carry or get along the way. Unable to track Grant's army, Vicksburg's defenders were taken by surprise when he attacked from the south and east. Pinned against the river and swamp, the Confederates surrendered after a six-week siege.

★ ★ ★ ★ ★ ★ ★ ★ ★ ★

MAKING THE GEOGRAPHY CONNECTION

1. What hazards might Grant have encountered through the delta?
2. Why was control of the Mississippi River important for the Union?

LINKING PAST AND PRESENT

3. What places do you know of today where geography would pose problems for American troops?

★ ★ ★ ★ ★ ★ ★ ★ ★ ★

Vicksburg and Chattanooga

As 1863 began, Union victory on the Mississippi River depended on taking the city of Vicksburg, and in late 1862 and early 1863, Grant made five attempts to capture the city. Finally, in May 1863, he began one of his most daring campaigns. After marching his army down the west bank of the Mississippi, below Vicksburg, he started inland. The Confederate commander at Vicksburg, thinking Grant was trying to trick him into the field, stayed behind his fortifications.

Moving quickly, Union forces reached Jackson, the capital of Mississippi, almost without opposition. Then Grant turned and fought his way back west to the outskirts of Vicksburg. In 17 days his troops marched 180 miles and won 5 battles against larger forces. Then he laid siege to Vicksburg. It was a terrifying time for the

population. Starving residents ate horses, mules, and dogs. As Union artillery bombarded the city, a woman wrote in her diary:

We are utterly cut off from the world, surrounded by a circle of fire.... The fiery shower of shells goes on day and night.... People do nothing but eat what they can get, sleep when they can, and dodge the shells.... We were all in the cellar when a shell came tearing through the roof, burst upstairs, tore up that room;...the pieces coming through both floors down into the cellar....

On July 4, 1863, the same day that Lee began his retreat from Gettysburg, the starving city of Vicksburg surrendered. Five days later Port Hudson, the last Confederate port on the Mississippi River, also fell. Texas and Arkansas, the South's leading food producers were now cut off from the rest of the Confederacy.

Union forces now attempted to cut the Confederacy again—through eastern Tennessee and Georgia. The key was Chattanooga, a rail center on the Tennessee-Georgia border. In September 1863, a Union army under General William Rosecrans was badly defeated by Confederate general Braxton Bragg at the Battle of Chickamauga, in northwest Georgia. A Union officer described his army's retreat:

The march was a melancholy one. All along the road for miles, wounded men were lying. They had crawled or hobbled slowly away from the fury of the battle, become exhausted, and lain down by the roadside to die. Some were calling the names and numbers of their regiments, but many had become too weak to do this.... the army is simply a mob. There appears to be neither organization nor discipline. Were a division of the enemy to pounce down upon us ... I fear the Army of the Cumberland would be blotted out.

Rosecrans retreated to Chattanooga, where the Confederates laid siege to his army and cut off its supplies. He was saved when Grant arrived in October and drove Confederate forces from the heights around the city, opening the way for a Union advance into Georgia.

By the end of 1863, only four states—Georgia, South Carolina, North Carolina, and Virginia—remained to be subdued. In early 1864, Lincoln gave General William T. Sherman command in the west and summoned Grant to accomplish what none of his other generals could do—to crush Robert E. Lee.

★ ★ ★ ★ ★ ★ ★ ★ ★ ★ ★ ★ ★ ★ ★ ★ ★

Section Two Review

★ ★ ★ ★ ★ ★ ★ ★ ★ ★ ★ ★ ★ ★ ★ ★ ★

SUMMARY

The first major battle of the war at Bull Run—a Union disaster—sent a message that this would not be a short or bloodless conflict. In the east, early Confederate victories gave way to Union victories at Antietam and Gettysburg. In the west, the Union's strategy was to gain control of the Mississippi River. Grant's capture of Fort Henry and Fort Donelson began the Union advance, which concluded with Grant's daring victory at Vicksburg. The fall of Vicksburg established Union control of the Mississippi and cut the South in half.

CHECKING FOR UNDERSTANDING

1. **Identify** Bull Run, George McClellan, Antietam, Emancipation Proclamation, Gettysburg, Ulysses Grant, Vicksburg

2. **List** early Confederate victories and when they occurred.

3. **Explain** Lincoln's timing in issuing the Emancipation Proclamation.

4. **State** why the Battle of Gettysburg was so significant.

5. **Describe** Grant's strategy at Vicksburg.

THINKING CRITICALLY

6. **Making Inferences** Bull Run changed people's perception of the war. From this reaction, what can you infer about the way people on both sides viewed the war before Bull Run?

GLOBAL PERSPECTIVES

7. **Analyzing Geography in History** Vicksburg was a key transportation point along the Mississippi River. Strategic points such as this exist in the world today. Compare the tactical location of Vicksburg then to the present-day importance of the Strait of Hormuz and the Panama Canal.

★ ★ ★ ★ ★ ★ ★ ★ ★ ★ ★ ★ ★ ★ ★ ★ ★

Linking Across Time

THE CHANGING NATURE OF WARFARE

Between the time Americans battled the British in the Revolution and each other in the Civil War, a dramatic change in warfare took place. This was due to the invention of a device about the size of the tip of an index finger: the conoidal, or cone-like, bullet for rifled muskets. It is likely that no other technological advance in weaponry has had such an important, or immediate, effect on the battlefield.

The flintlock muskets commonly used by armies before the 1850s were notoriously inaccurate. Smoothbored muzzleloaders, they allowed part of the force of the blast to escape around the round bullet, and it waffled through the air like a knuckleball. Attackers were relatively safe from enemy fire until within about 100 yards. Defenders would hold their fire until they could "see the whites of their eyes," that is, about 50 yards distance. Since it took 12 motions and at least 15 seconds to reload, the soldier often relied on the bayonet once the initial volley was fired.

The conoidal bullet tremendously increased the accuracy and range of rifles, becoming deadly at up to 300 yards. In the Civil War, the common soldier's rifled musket inflicted 85 to 90 percent of casualties.

Battle became increasingly impersonal as men killed and were killed by unseen opponents. The power, accuracy, and rate of rifle fire increased by the time of World War I, but a new invention of the 1880s—the field telephone—brought artillery back to the fore of battle. It helped forward observers direct the fire of artillery positioned thousands of yards behind the front lines, far out of sight of the men they were killing.

World War I also saw the evolution of the airplane from an observation vehicle to an instrument of death from above. Although the first bombs were dropped by hand by pilots in open cockpits, bombing quickly became more sophisticated. By World War II, bombing raids over Great Britain and Germany took place day and night from planes miles high that dropped hundreds of bombs in a single mission.

Modern-day air warfare has become even more impersonal. Ballistic missiles launched from another continent and carrying nuclear warheads, can devastate hundreds of square miles. Similar destruction can come from a ship at sea—or under it.

Warplanes now engage in aerial "dogfights" not with machine gun fire, but with computer-controlled weapons systems. Pilots use radar to fire heat-seeking missiles at an enemy who is still miles away, out of sight far over the horizon.

MAJOR ADVANCES IN WEAPONRY

prehistory	sword, bow	1837	telegraph
c. A.D. 600	stirrup	c. 1838	breech-loading rifle
c. A.D. 1150	English longbow	c. 1850	rifle with conoidal bullet
c. A.D. 1200	gunpowder	c. 1880	field telephone
c. 1364	cannon	1884	maxim machine gun
c. 1425	pistol	1886	high explosive shell
1503	naval mine	1896	wireless radio
c. 1550	musket	1915	poison gas, combat aircraft, aerial bomb
1620	submarine	1916	tank
c. 1690	flintlock musket and bayonet	1918	aircraft carrier
c. 1700	rifle	1938	radar
c. 1783	observation balloon	c. 1940	computer
1790	shrapnel	1945	atomic bomb
1803	steamship	1954	nuclear power
1825	railroad	1960	laser beam

MAKING CONNECTIONS

1. How did technological advances affect battlefield tactics?

LINKING PAST AND PRESENT

2. How does today's radio and television influence the perception of war on the home front?

Behind the Lines

SETTING THE SCENE

I have seen Him in the watch-fires of a hundred circling camps;
*   They have builded Him an altar in the evening dews and damps;*
*   I can read His righteous sentence by the dim and flaring lamps;*
*   His day is marching on.*

—JULIA WARD HOWE
The Battle Hymn of the Republic, 1862

Section Focus

Financial, agricultural, and industrial resources played a major role in determining which side would win the war. But people were the most important resource. The war provided opportunities for blacks and women to make additional contributions to their nation's vital interests.

Objectives

After studying this section, you should be able to:

• Discuss behind-the-lines activity in the North and South.
• Explain the wartime roles played by women, blacks, and native Americans.

The Civil War was the largest war ever fought on the North American continent. Of the 1.5 million Southern white males of fighting age, about 900,000 served in the Confederate armies. Of 4 million such males in the North, about half fought in the war. In addition, more than 200,000 blacks fought and served in the Union military, and thousands of slaves performed manual labor for Confederate armies.

More Americans were killed in this war than in any other conflict in the history of the United States. Even in the early battles the losses were shockingly high. As the war dragged on, the Union suffered terrible casualties but grew stronger. Confederate losses, however, gradually weakened the South's will to fight.

Wartime Government Power

Opposition to the war existed from the very beginning in both North and South. To carry on the war, President Lincoln and President Davis each exerted so much power that both were accused of acting like dictators. The Confederate government seized mules, wagons, food, and slaves for its armies. The Union government took over and operated private telegraph lines and railroads near war zones. Both Presidents suppressed opposition to the war by abusing the civil rights of citizens. Davis declared martial law in parts of the Confederacy, and he suspended the right of **habeas corpus**, which requires that persons who are arrested be brought to court to show why they should be held.

The North was a hotbed of discontent about the war. Abolitionists were irate over Lincoln's accommodating attitude toward slavery and about his refusal to make the end of slavery a goal of the war. They were joined by members of Lincoln's own party in Congress, a faction called the Radical Republicans, who opposed Lincoln's view that the war was only to preserve the Union.

At the other extreme were the "Copperheads," mainly Democrats, who called for ending the war at any price, even if that meant welcoming the South and slavery back into the Union, or letting the slave states leave in peace. Some Copperheads encouraged Northerners to resist the war and others openly supported the South.

Many of the measures Lincoln used to quiet opposition to the war violated constitutional guarantees of free speech, press, and assembly. He prevented a state legislature from meeting. He denied some opposition newspapers use of the mails and used the army to shut others down.

And he ordered hundreds of suspected Confederate sympathizers jailed without the right of habeas corpus.

President Lincoln agonized over his decisions to deny American citizens their civil rights. But he also believed that the survival of the nation during an emergency overrode the Constitution. Near the end of the war, he wrote to a friend that:

I felt that measures, otherwise unconstitutional, might become lawful by becoming indispensable to the preservation of the Constitution through the preservation of the nation.

In May 1863, Clement Vallandigham, a former Ohio congressman, made a speech in which he blamed the President for prolonging the war. He was arrested and sentenced to prison for the remainder of the war by a military court in Cincinnati. Vallandigham appealed to the Supreme Court for his release. But in 1864, in *Ex parte Vallandigham,* the Court refused to challenge the President and ruled that its authority did not extend to military courts.

Not until the war was over and Lincoln dead, did the Supreme Court confront the civil rights violations that had occurred. In 1866, in *Ex parte Milligan,* the Court overturned the conviction of a Copperhead tried for treason by a military court in Indiana. The Court noted that Milligan had been living in a peaceful area where the civil courts were operating, and it rejected the argument that war justified the denial of rights guaranteed by the Constitution:

…it is the birthright of every American citizen when charged with crime, to be tried and punished according to law…. By the protection of law human rights are secured; withdraw that protection, and they are at the mercy of wicked rulers, or the clamor of an excited people.

Although Milligan's alleged crime had been much more serious than Vallandigham's, the Court ordered Milligan released.

The Emancipation Proclamation

When the Civil War began there was not universal support in the North for a war to free the slaves. In many areas of the North there was open hostility to black Americans, and laws that limited their rights. Slavery still existed in Washington, D.C., and in five states that remained in the Union.

Lincoln, himself, was not an abolitionist. He regarded slavery as a moral wrong and a disaster for both blacks and whites, but he recognized the constitutional guarantees for slavery. He assured the South that he had "no purpose, directly or indirectly, to interfere with the institution of slavery where it now exists" but that he only opposed its extension into the territories. Again and again Lincoln declared that his goal was "to save the Union…not either to save or destroy slavery." If he acted any other way, he feared that the border states might join the Confederacy.

As time passed, however, Lincoln came under increasing pressure to turn the war into a crusade against slavery. The abolitionists and the Radical Republicans demanded that Southern slaveholders be punished for the war by loss of their property. As the number of battlefield casualties grew, Northerners increasingly began to feel that such bloodshed was justified only if it destroyed an institution that violated human principles of freedom and dignity. In addition, Great Britain talked of mediating a settlement of the war on behalf of the South. Lincoln realized that public opinion in Europe—and in Britain especially—was strongly opposed to slavery, and that no European government would defend the South in a war to abolish slavery.

After Lee's defeat at Antietam in 1862, Lincoln announced that he would free the slaves in the Confederate states on January 1, 1863. But the Emancipation

Proclamation did not immediately free any slaves, because it applied only to the areas held by the enemy. The Proclamation, however, turned the war into a moral crusade and aroused a renewed spirit in the North. The number of black volunteers for the army increased dramatically. As news of the Proclamation spread through the Confederacy, whenever Northern armies occupied Southern territory, thousands of runaway slaves poured into Union lines. The Emancipation Proclamation is "the greatest event of our nation's history, if not the greatest event of the century," said black abolitionist editor Frederick Douglass.

Slavery in areas where the Emancipation Proclamation did not apply remained a problem, however. There were 800,000 slaves in the border states and many more in areas of the South that the Union armies already had conquered. For these areas Lincoln recommended a policy of compensated emancipation—setting the slaves free, but paying their owners for them. Congress, however, adopted this idea only for the District of Columbia, where there were just 3,000 slaves. Elsewhere, slavery was abolished by the Thirteenth Amendment to the Constitution, ratified in 1865.

Raising the Armies

At first, both North and South relied on volunteers to fill the ranks of their armies, and Lincoln's original 90-day volunteers were replaced by 3-year enlistments. But lengthening lists of casualties, published in newspapers, reduced enthusiasm for the war in both North and South, and enlistments decreased.

As the South's economy collapsed, and the scarcity of clothing and medicine was matched by shortages of food and shelter, Confederate desertions increased. "I am so tired for I never get any rest night or day, and I don't think I will last much longer," wrote a Georgia woman in despair. When Confederate soldiers received such letters, many saw no disgrace in going home to aid their suffering families. In all, 100,000 Confederate soldiers deserted, while Union desertions were 3 times that number.

Both North and South were forced to resort to **conscription,** or the drafting of men for military service. The South, with less than one-half the population of the North, began drafting men aged 18 to 35 in April 1862. Later, as the need to maintain its armies increased, the Confederate congress raised the upper age limit to 50. In March 1863, the United States Congress created a military draft in the North.

The draft laws were incomplete and discriminatory. In both North and South a draftee could avoid military service by hiring a substitute, and a Union draftee could buy his way out by paying the government $300. Such provisions aroused

---

Life of the Times

MESS CALL

One of the more unpleasant features of life in Civil War armies was the food. Neither the Confederacy nor the Union enlisted men as cooks, and no training was available to those who received this assignment. In the Union army recruits could supplement their rations with supplies from a merchant who was licensed to accompany the army—if they had money. Prices, however, were generally high and the quality of items such as pies and canned meat was questionable.

When in quarters, a company would receive a government issue of flour, pork, beans, potatoes, coffee and the like. Initially, six or eight recruits would form a mess team and take turns cooking. If any of them actually knew something about preparing meals, the group was fortunate. Later, the commanding officer assigned men to the cook tent, as often as not to get them out of the ranks.

On the march, rations typically consisted of dried salt pork, hardtack (a saltless hard biscuit made from flour), and coffee. Southern soldiers usually went without coffee, and cornmeal was substituted for hardtack. Veteran soldiers found fresh hardtack palatable enough. With age, however, it might become infested with weevils. Some thought it better to eat it in the dark. Soldiers of both armies frequently supplemented meager rations by stealing crops and livestock from nearby farms.

Examining Photographs *"Company E, 4th U.S. Colored Infantry" mustered for this photograph. More than half the blacks who enlisted in the Union army were from Confederate states. The casualty rate among black troops was higher than for white soldiers. Why did the South not enlist blacks in the Confederate army?*

public criticism everywhere that it was "a rich man's war and a poor man's fight."

In the South, some state governors helped their citizens evade the draft. In the North, opposition to conscription caused terrible draft riots in New York City in July 1863. A local resident reported that for four days:

...there were dreadful scenes enacted in the city. The police were successfully opposed; many were killed, many houses were gutted and burned: the...asylum was burned and all the furniture was carried off by women....

To those who enlisted, the North paid a **bounty,** or lump sum of money, of as much as $1,500 for a single three-year enlistment. This led to the practice of "bounty jumping," whereby a man would enlist, collect his bounty and then desert, only to reenlist somewhere else.

President Lincoln at first resisted appeals to enlist blacks in the Union armies because he feared that such a policy would be resented in the border states. But after the Emancipation Proclamation the policy was changed. Nearly 200,000 free blacks and fugitive slaves enlisted for military service and an additional 150,000 served in the quartermaster and engineering corps. Black soldiers were commanded by white officers, were paid less, and were segregated from white troops, who often resented them. Many black regiments distinguished themselves in combat, however, and 23 black soldiers won the Congressional Medal of Honor during the war.

Until the very end of the war, the South refused to accept blacks for military

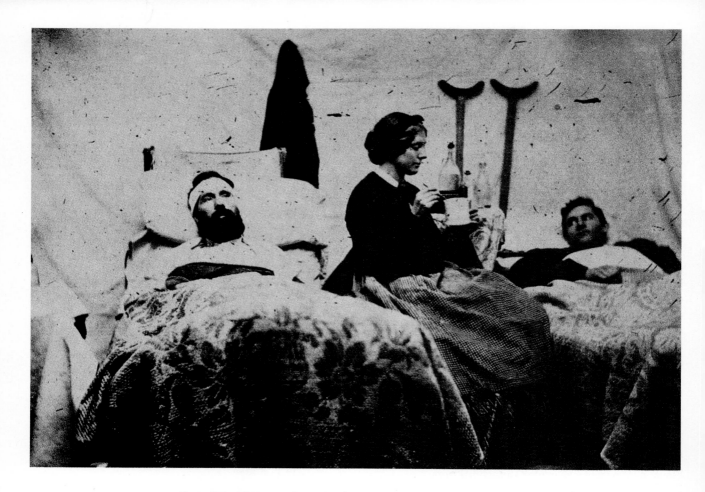

Examining Photographs *Although it was considered unladylike by Southerners, women on both sides became nurses. The Union army required its nurses to be plain: "Their dresses must be brown or black, with no bows, no jewelry, and no hoop skirts." Although they were harassed by their male colleagues, female nurses improved the standard of care. In what other ways did women aid the war effort?*

service, despite its desperate need for soldiers. Confederate armies often used slaves to dig fortifications, cook, drive wagons, and perform other labor, but there was widespread opposition to arming slaves for combat. Not until March 1865, on the advice of General Lee, did the Confederate congress agree to black soldiers. But by then the war was in its final days, and the new troops could not affect its outcome.

The Civil War also dramatically affected the lives of native Americans. The South acted quickly to win the Indians to their side, sending commissioners to the Indian Territory to sign peace treaties with the Indian nations. The Cherokees even fought on the Confederate side.

In 1864 the Union sent troops to restore its authority over the Indians. Federal victories over Confederate and Indian forces in Arkansas and in the Indian Territory showed the Indians the weakness of their Confederate allies. The North then renegotiated treaties with the Indian nations and took land away from those who had fought for the Confederacy.

Women Behind the Lines

The demands the war placed on civilian populations created new roles for women in both the North and South. Southern women were required to run plantations after planters and overseers were called for military service. On smaller farms, women plowed the fields and handled other chores. Southern households became miniature factories, with spinning wheels and looms turning out clothing for the Confederacy. The war forced many Southerners to abandon their romantic view of women as "belles" to be protected from rough work. Many women were needed to replace men as government clerks and factory workers—including dangerous work in munitions factories, making weapons and ammunition for the troops. Some women accompanied the armies in the field, cooking, sewing, and washing. A few went into combat disguised as men, and some acted as spies behind Union lines. Although shortages of food and other necessities made life very difficult in the Confederacy, Southern women managed to keep the home front going under the most desperate conditions during the war.

Although most Northern women did not suffer from invading armies and destruction of their homes and property, they also were deeply affected by the war. In the North, the mechanical reaper and the sulky plow—where the operator rode on top of the plow itself rather than pushed it from behind—allowed women to take the place of husbands and sons who were in the army. Industry's need for labor opened other opportunities for women in Northern factories. Many women whose fathers and husbands had been drafted needed such work to support their families.

On both sides, women took over much of the nursing, a task formerly reserved for men. As nurses, women were exposed to the worst horrors of the war. Dorothea Dix became superintendent of female nurses in the Union army and in this position fought corruption and prejudice against her sex. Even more effective in widening the role of women in hospitals was Clara Barton, who later became the first president of the American Red Cross.

Women also played a large part in America's first great private relief organization—the United States Sanitary Commission. This organization collected millions of dollars for projects to improve the living conditions of Union soldiers. It

is little wonder that after the Civil War there was a renewed demand that women receive the right to vote.

Supplying the Armies

In a long war fought on a vast scale, victors are decided as much behind the lines as on the battlefield. The Confederacy was defeated largely because of its inability to produce industrial goods. Through war contracts, the Confederate government helped to stimulate industry in the South. It encouraged the establishment of clothing and shoe factories to provide uniforms, and munitions factories to supply

AMERICAN PORTRAITS

CLARA BARTON
1821-1912

Clara Barton grew up loving sports and intended to make teaching her career. After 18 years in education, however, she went to work for the U.S. Patent Office. She was in the nation's capital when the guns of the Civil War started blazing.

Though lacking medical training, Clara Barton left her desk job to care for sick and wounded Union soldiers. Traveling to the sites of some of the worst carnage of the war, she even ventured deep into the Confederacy to assist Federal forces laying seige to Charleston. She regularly risked her life by passing through the front lines to deliver supplies and nurse the wounded. After the war—before she founded the American Red Cross in 1881—Clara Barton worked to identify thousands of soldiers who had perished at the Andersonville prison camp in Georgia.

its troops with arms and ammunition. But it lacked the industrial capacity to provide other necessities.

The efforts of the Union government to supply its armies were hindered by overcharging and corruption. Army contractors sometimes supplied shoddy clothing, rotten meat, and defective shoes. But the productivity of Northern factories was so great that, in spite of the graft, Union armies were generally much better equipped than their enemy.

The Confederacy also was less able to finance the war than was the North. The South had intended to obtain money by selling cotton in Europe, but the Union blockade prevented this. To raise money, the Confederacy enacted a graduated income tax and demanded 10 percent of all crops produced. But the most important way that the Confederacy, and its state governments, raised money was simply by printing more of it. The Confederate government was able to operate only by forcing its citizens to accept its worthless currency in exchange for supplies.

The North was far more successful in financing the war. About one-fourth of the $4 billion needed came from taxation, and the rest from borrowing and issuing paper money. For the first time, Congress levied an income tax of 5 percent on incomes from $600 to $5,000, and 10 percent on incomes above that. Excise taxes were placed on food, tobacco, clothing, alcoholic beverages, railroad tickets, and many other items. High wartime tariffs, passed with little opposition because no Southerners remained in Congress, also brought in revenue. Their purpose, however, also was to encourage American manufacturers to increase production, so that the army would not be dependent on imported goods.

During the war the federal government issued more than $2.5 billion worth of bonds. Like the Confederacy, the Union government also inflated its currency, but not to the point where it became worthless. The federal government issued $400 million worth of **greenbacks**, paper money that was not backed by gold or silver, but whose value rose and fell with the success of Union armies in the field.

SUMMARY

During the war both Union and Confederate governments extended their powers. Lincoln's decision to issue the Emancipation Proclamation changed the war into a conflict over human rights. As the war dragged on, both North and South began to draft men to fill the ranks of their armies. Opposition to the draft caused riots, the most violent in New York City. Union armies opened their ranks to blacks, and both the North and South negotiated with Indian nations. Women worked behind the lines—running farms, in factories, and nursing the sick and wounded.

CHECKING FOR UNDERSTANDING

1. **Identify** *Ex parte Milligan,* Clara Barton, Radical Republicans, Copperheads, *Ex parte Vallandigham*

2. **Define** habeas corpus, conscription, bounty, greenbacks

3. **State** what factors caused Lincoln to change his war goals to include freeing the slaves.

4. **List** the contributions made by blacks to the war effort on both sides.

5. **Explain** how women supported the war effort behind the lines.

THINKING CRITICALLY

6. **Assessing Cause and Effect**   The war provided women opportunities that were not open to them before. What effect do you think this had on their views about their status in society?

CONNECTIONS:
HISTORY AND ECONOMICS

7. **Analyzing Policies**   Both North and South printed paper money not redeemable in gold or silver, whose value fluctuated wildly. Explain why a system that uses paper currency must have the support and faith of the general citizenry.

★ ★ ★ ★ ★ ★ ★ ★ ★ ★ ★ ★ ★ ★ ★ ★ ★ ★

Ending the War

> *It is only those who have neither fired a shot nor heard the shrieks and groans of the wounded who cry aloud for blood, more vengeance, more desolation. War is Hell.*

—WILLIAM TECUMSEH SHERMAN
Commencement address at Michigan Military Academy, 1879

Section Focus

In March 1864, it became Ulysses S. Grant's turn to face the brilliant Confederate general, Robert E. Lee. Lincoln brought Grant east and gave him command of all Union forces. At last the President found a commander who could win the war. The President, however, would not live to see the war's end.

Objectives

After studying this section, you should be able to:
- Explain the changes in Union military strategy after Grant took command.
- Discuss the issues in the election of 1864.

General Grant determined that to win the war he would utilize the Union's biggest advantages over the South—its overwhelming superiority in population and in production capacity. To end the South's *ability* to fight, he would not only defeat Confederate armies, but would destroy them. To end the South's *will* to fight, he would engage in "total war"—war against civilians and resources as well as against armies.

Grant in the East

Moving south into Virginia, in May and June 1864, Grant's force of 120,000 engaged the Confederate army of 60,000 almost continuously. At the Battle of the Wilderness, Lee stopped Grant in a forest where the fighting was so heavy that the woods caught fire, trapping the wounded in the flames and burning them to death. But instead of retreating after a defeat, like previous Union commanders had done, Grant kept advancing. He attacked Lee at Spotsylvania in a bloody battle that one soldier called "the most terrible twenty-four hours of our service in the war." In early June, Grant attacked Lee again, at Cold Harbor, where he ordered suicidal charges against fortified Confederate positions.

In less than a month, Union forces had suffered casualties greater in number than Lee's entire army. A Union officer protested that "our men have, in many instances, been foolishly and wantonly sacrificed." But Grant knew that he could replace his losses while his enemy could not, and he promised "to fight it out along this line if it takes all summer."

In mid-June Lee retreated to Petersburg, south of Richmond, where Grant surrounded the Confederates and their capital and laid siege to the city. In July, Lee attempted to break the siege by instructing General Jubal Early to move through Virginia's Shenandoah River valley to threaten Washington, D.C. Grant dispatched the Union cavalry under General Philip Sheridan to drive the Confederates from the area and told him "nothing should be left to invite the enemy to return." He ordered Sheridan to make the valley "a barren waste." By March 1865, Sheridan had carried out his orders so well, he reported to Grant, that a crow flying across the valley would have to carry its food. Meanwhile, Grant continued his siege of Richmond.

Sherman's March

In May 1864, as Grant invaded Virginia, he ordered General William T. Sherman and his 100,000 troops posted

Linking Across Time

HISTORIC RICHMOND

The City of Richmond is actively dedicated to preserving its rich history. Civil War monuments may be seen in many areas, such as the Richmond National Battlefield Park, which contains sites of seven sieges against the Confederate capital. Meadow Farm, an 1850s living history museum, presents authentic reenactments of major Civil War battles. The Museum of the Confederacy boasts the world's largest collection of Civil War artifacts.

in Chattanooga, Tennessee, to engage and destroy the Confederate army in the west. The Confederates were forced to retreat toward Atlanta, Georgia, which Sherman captured in September and occupied until November, when he ordered the city evacuated and destroyed. City officials begged that Atlanta be spared, but Sherman replied:

You might as well appeal against the thunderstorm as against these terrible hardships of war. They are inevitable, and the only way the people of Atlanta can hope once more to live in peace and quiet at home, is to stop the war....

As the Northern army abandoned the city, a Union officer described its destruction:

The heaven is one expanse of lurid fire; the air is filled with flying, burning cinders; buildings covering two hundred acres are in ruins or in flames; every instant there is the sharp detonation or the smothered booming sound of exploding shells and powder....

To segment the South a second time, Sherman adopted Grant's tactics before Vicksburg—strike into enemy territory and live off the land. His army marched

Examining Photographs *Unlike Atlanta, which was occupied and then burned by Union troops, Richmond, shown here in April 1865, was destroyed by Union artillery during Grant's siege of the city. Why did Sherman burn Atlanta?*

Examining Photographs *Union general William T. Sherman brought the horror of war to the civilian population of Georgia and the Carolinas. How did Sherman affect the outcome of the election of 1864?*

southeast and for a month carved a path of destruction 60 miles wide through one of the richest agricultural regions of the South. Sherman reached the Atlantic coast at Savannah, Georgia, and reported to Grant that he had destroyed $100 million of property in Georgia—$20 million in military damage and "the remainder is simply waste and destruction."

As he entered Savannah on December 20, 1864, Sherman learned that five days before, outside Nashville, Tennessee, General George Thomas had destroyed the Confederates' western army. The war in the west was over.

In February 1865, Sherman left Savannah and marched north through the Carolinas, destroying everything in his path and planning to link up with Grant at Richmond.

The Election of 1864

Throughout the war, federal, state, and city elections continued to be held in the North, but the war divided both major parties into War Democrats and Peace Democrats, Radical Republicans and Conservative Republicans. In the presidential election of

Examining Photographs *A Southern family loads what possessions they can before fleeing their home. How did the nature of the war change in Georgia?*

1864, the Republican party temporarily changed its name to the Union party to attract Democrats who supported the war.

The Unionists renominated Lincoln for President and chose a War Democrat for Vice President, Andrew Johnson, military governor of Tennessee. The Democrats nominated George McClellan, the popular general who Lincoln had twice removed from command. But the Democrats drew up a peace platform that branded the war a failure and called for the immediate restoration of the Union.

Lincoln's chances for victory largely depended on the fortunes of the Union armies in the field. In mid-1864 the war was going badly, and Lincoln was certain that he would be defeated. But Sherman's capture of Atlanta in September, coupled with McClellan's refusal to support his party's platform, gave Lincoln the victory. The voters had decided that "it was not best to swap horses while crossing the river," Lincoln said.

In his second inaugural address in March 1865, Lincoln reviewed the causes of the war and hoped for a peace without bitterness. Both sides "read the same Bible and pray to the same God," he noted, so "let us judge not that we be not judged." It may be, Lincoln said, that the war was divine vengeance on both North and South for two centuries of wrong to black people.

Lincoln concluded his short address by extending charity to the defeated South. He directed his generals to offer the Confederate armies the most liberal terms of surrender, and asked Northerners:

With malice toward none, with charity for all ... let us strive on to finish the work we are in, to bind up the nation's wounds,...to do all which may achieve and cherish a just and lasting peace among ourselves and with all nations.

Examining Fine Art

Lee (right) surrenders to Grant at Appomattox Court House. Grant ordered Union troops not to celebrate. "The war is over," he said, "the rebels are our countrymen again." How did Grant's surrender terms compare with Lincoln's attitude toward the South?

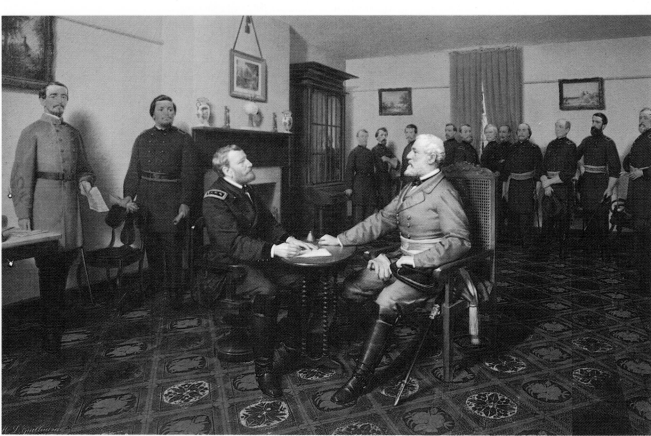

UNIT 5 DIVISION AND REUNION: 1825-1877

The Final Days

While Lincoln was delivering his second inaugural address in March 1865, Grant was pressing in on Richmond and Sherman was marching through the Carolinas. Aware that the situation was hopeless, General Lee advised President Davis that he could no longer defend Richmond. The Confederate government fled south, and Lee's army finally evacuated the city. By April 4, 1865, President Lincoln was able to walk through the streets of the former Confederate capital.

Just days later, Grant's forces cut off Lee's troops as they attempted to unite with other Confederate armies. Grant urged Lee to surrender in order to prevent "further effusion of blood." On April 9, 1865, the two men met at Appomattox Court House in central Virginia. Grant offered Lee generous terms: Southern soldiers could go home if they pledged not to fight again. The officers would keep their pistols and the men their horses.

When Lee's army came to lay down their arms, Union troops saluted each division as it appeared. As the Confederate forces marched before them, the Union troops watched silently, with "not a cheer, nor a word, nor whisper of vainglory," one Union officer described it, "but an awed stillness rather, a breath-holding, as if it were the passing of the dead."

Defying orders from President Davis, by June, all other Confederate generals also surrendered. The long, bitter struggle that split the nation finally came to an end.

President Lincoln did not live to see the end of the war, however. On April 14, 1865, just five days after Lee's surrender, Lincoln was assassinated by John Wilkes Booth, a fanatical Confederate sympathizer. Booth's deed was a tragedy for both North and South, for it removed the one person best equipped to "bind up the nation's wounds." A Richmond newspaper called Lincoln's death "the heaviest blow which has ever fallen upon the people of the South." A young Southern woman confided to her diary, "The most terrible part of the war is now to come."

★ Section Four Review ★

SUMMARY

In 1864 Grant began a steady, deadly advance toward Richmond. At the same time, Sherman began a long, destructive campaign through Georgia. Lincoln just narrowly won reelection in 1864. On April 9, 1865, Lee, facing overwhelming Union forces, surrendered on Grant's generous terms. The nation would no longer benefit from Lincoln's calm leadership, however, as he was assassinated five days later.

CHECKING FOR UNDERSTANDING

1. **Identify** William T. Sherman, Union Party, Andrew Johnson, Appomattox, John Wilkes Booth

2. **List** three major battles which Grant fought against Lee.

3. **Explain** the strategy that Grant adopted to defeat the Confederacy.

4. **Examine** how Sheridan's and Sherman's tactics broadened the war's scope beyond purely military engagements.

5. **Describe** the manner in which Grant conducted the Confederate surrender.

THINKING CRITICALLY

6. **Analyzing a Quotation** To explain his reelection, Lincoln stated, "it was not best to swap horses while crossing the river." Explain the meaning of Lincoln's quotation and how it applied to him.

CONNECTIONS: HISTORY AND MUSIC

7. **Evaluating Sources** *When this Cruel War is Over, Bear this Gently to My Mother,* and *Tell Me, Is My Father Coming Back?*, were titles of popular songs during the Civil War. As the titles indicate, the songs were sad and full of melancholy. Do you think popular songs are a good measure of how the general public feels? Explain your answer.

★ Chapter 15 Review ★

★ Summary

The fall of Fort Sumter kindled patriotism in both North and South and started their preparation for war. As the North drew upon advantages in manufacturing, population, transportation, and wealth, the South relied on superior military leaders.

At first, Southern armies outmaneuvered Union forces in the east, awakening the nation to the reality that it would be a long and costly war. Southern invasions of the North were unsuccessful, however. In the western theater, Union armies gained control of border states. Grant's victory at Vicksburg segmented the South, while Sherman's march from Atlanta to Savannah divided it again.

As the war dragged on, both sides were forced to conscript solders. Lincoln reversed an earlier decision and allowed blacks to enlist in the Union army. The character of the war also changed when Lincoln issued the Emancipation Proclamation, thereby making the end to slavery a reason for the conflict. Shortly after Lincoln was reelected, Lee surrendered. But chances for a peaceful reconciliation were dampened by Lincoln's assassination just five days later.

★ Using Vocabulary

For the first time, photography was used extensively to record history during the American Civil War. Regard each of the terms below as captions for a pictorial history of the Civil War. After each term, describe a photograph that would explain the concept or identify the term.

martial law	**conscription**
greenbacks	**habeas corpus**
bounty	

★ Reviewing Facts

1. **List** two Southern military advantages and two Northern military advantages.
2. **State** the Union army's three principal goals.
3. **Explain** how technology played a role in determining the victor at Bull Run.
4. **Describe** the results of Antietam and Gettysburg for the Southern army.
5. **Summarize** the effects the Emancipation Proclamation had on the war.

6. **State** two methods the North used to raise troops.
7. **State** two reasons why Lincoln was reelected.

★ Understanding Concepts

RIGHTS AND FREEDOM

1. How did Lincoln violate constitutional rights during the war and for what reasons?
2. Why would blacks be anxious to fight for the Union army? Why was Lincoln initially reluctant to use black soldiers?

CONFLICT

3. Why did Union victory come only after its generals decided to fight a ruthless war?
4. How did attitudes about the kind and extent of the war change after Bull Run?

★ Thinking Critically

1. **Evaluating Causes** List five factors that affected the military ability of both the Northern and Southern armies. Rank the items according to their importance in determining the outcome of the Civil War.
2. **Evaluating an Action** Grant's campaign against Vicksburg was a calculated risk. List the pros and cons of Grant's strategy. If he had failed, what likely consequences would he have faced?
3. **Assessing Motivation** Was Lincoln justified in denying citizens their constitutional rights during the Civil War? Suppose a President today took actions similar to Lincoln's—describe how you think Americans would react.
4. **Analyzing a Speech** What can you infer from Lincoln's Gettysburg address (see Appendix) about how he would have treated the South after the war?

★ Writing About History

ARGUMENTATION

Refer to the description of how to write an argumentation essay in the History Writer's Handbook in the Appendix of this book. Your teacher will give you more specific instruction on the essay's length and the assignment's due date.

The Civil War resulted in enormous loss of life. Do you believe this loss was justified? Write an essay on whether or not you believe the war was worth the cost. Write your argument from the perspective of a disabled Union or Confederate soldier or of a Union or Confederate wife whose husband died fighting in the war.

★ Learning Cooperatively

Each member in your group takes one of these roles: Union soldier, Confederate soldier, and British journalist. The journalist would like to get both viewpoints on the war. Each group member must prepare one question to be asked by the journalist. If you are the Union soldier, write a question for the journalist to ask the Confederate soldier and vice versa. If you are the journalist, write one question that you will ask each soldier. Conduct the interview in front of your classmates.

★ Mastering Skills

DRAWING CONCLUSIONS

Put yourself in the place of a Confederate soldier who is in Richmond in March 1865. Union forces led by Grant are about to take the city. Meanwhile, Sherman is marching north. You know that Union troops outnumber Confederate troops by more than two-to-one. There are rumors that General Lee has advised President Davis to leave Richmond because the city can no longer be defended. Based on this information, what conclusions could you draw about the future of the war and the Confederacy?

In this case, of course, you know the outcome—Lee surrendered to Grant on April 9, 1865, and the Confederacy was soon disbanded. But you can look at other aspects of the story to help you draw additional conclusions. *Drawing conclusions*—that is, making judgments or decisions after deliberation—can help you in your studies. After reviewing what you know, ask yourself such questions as:

- Do I have all the information I need to make a valid conclusion?
- Have I weighed all the information fairly?

- How and why might new information cause me to change or modify my conclusion?

Example   The map below shows the final campaigns of the Civil War. Like the early battles, the final struggles between the Union and the Confederacy took place in the eastern theater. From this information you could *conclude* that it might have been unwise for the Confederacy to move their capital to Richmond, which appears to be a poor strategic location.

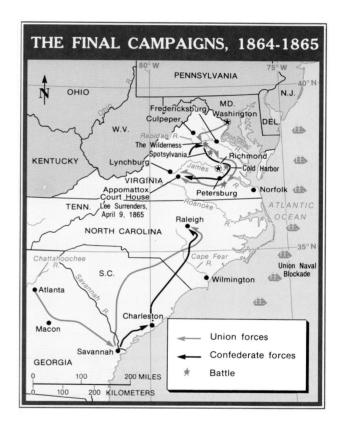

THE FINAL CAMPAIGNS, 1864-1865

Practice   Study the map, and then draw further conclusions by answering the questions that follow.

1. What conclusions can you make about what life must have been like for people living in Virginia during the final months of the war?

2. What conclusions can you make about whether or not the Confederates were fighting offensive or defensive battles?

3. **Analyzing Choices**   What conclusions do you think led General Lee to finally surrender?

CHAPTER 16
Reconstruction

SETTING THE SCENE

Historical Focus

Confederate war veterans who returned home after the war found their land devastated. Black Americans quickly discovered that freedom did not mean equality. The first order of business for the federal government, however, was to readmit the southern states to the Union. This proved difficult because white Southerners were bitter and Radical Republicans in Congress worked to keep their party in power.

Concepts to Understand

- Why **adaptation** to new social conditions was necessary for newly freed slaves and white planters.
- How Radical Republicans sought to exercise **power and authority** over the Reconstruction process.

People to Know

O. O. Howard, Andrew Johnson, Thaddeus Stevens, Rutherford B. Hayes

Places to Locate

Sea Islands, Georgia, Arkansas

Terms to Identify

tenant farmers, sharecroppers, amnesty, "black codes," mandate, disenfranchised, impeach, segregation

Guided Reading

As you read this chapter, seek the answers to the following questions.

1. How did Lincoln, Johnson, and the Radical Republicans differ over Reconstruction?
2. What was the Compromise of 1877?

SPANNING THE DECADES

POLITICAL	1865 *Freedmen's Bureau is established*	1868 *President Johnson impeached by the House of Representatives; Senate fails to convict him*	1873 *New York Stock Exchange closes for 10 days after economic panic begins*

1865   1870

CULTURAL	1866 *Fisk School, later Fisk University, founded in Nashville, Tennessee*	1866 *Ku Klux Klan formally organized in Pulaski, Tennessee*	1871 *P. T. Barnum opens circus in Brooklyn, New York*

A Visit from the Old Mistress *by Winslow Homer, 1876*

1877
Compromise of 1877 gives presidential election to Rutherford B. Hayes

1875

1880

1876
Alexander Graham Bell transmits message on his telephone

1879
The Church of Christ, Scientist, chartered

1881
Kansas passes a prohibition law

...The evidence of an intense hostility to the federal Union, and equally intense love of the late Confederacy, nurtured by the war is decisive. While it appears that nearly all [Southerners] are willing to submit, at least for the time being, to federal authority, it is equally clear that the ruling motive is...representation in Congress....

—REPORT OF THE JOINT COMMITTEE on Reconstruction, June 20, 1866

After Slavery

SETTING THE SCENE

During the war blacks, of course, sided with the North. They believed that if the North should be successful they would be freed....But I hesitate to apply the name of loyalty to their feelings. They have never had a country.

—JOHN RICHARD DENNETT
The Nation, April 11, 1866

Section Focus

The Civil War saved the Union but shook the nation to its roots. The fall of the Confederacy toppled the planter aristocracy that had ruled the South since before the American Revolution. Also gone was slavery, the labor system that was the basis of Southern society. But the end of slavery did not solve the problems that the 3.5 million newly freed blacks were to face.

Objectives

After studying this section, you should be able to:
- Explain the changes in Southern society that occurred after the Civil War.
- Discuss the changes that freedom brought to black families.

When Confederate veterans—tired, ragged, and hungry—went home at the end of the Civil War, they returned to a ravaged land. Large areas of land had been systematically laid waste by the armies of Sherman and Sheridan. The wreckage stretched from South Carolina's Atlantic coast in the east to Tennessee in the west and from Virginia's Shenandoah Valley in the north through Georgia in the south. One Mississippi woman remembered her father's homecoming after the war:

He had come home to a house stripped of every article of furniture. The plantation was stripped of the means of cultivating any but a small portion of it. A few mules and one cow made up the stock.... He owned nothing that could be turned into money without great sacrifice but five bales of cotton.

But it was not only the land that was in ruin. Economically, politically, and socially, the South was in total disarray. Confederate money was worthless, and Southern banks were ruined. Government at every level had all but disappeared. There were no courts, no judges, no sheriffs, and no police—no law or authority except when groups of people took matters into their own hands. The war left the South's transportation systems in complete disorder. Roads were impassable, bridges had been destroyed or washed away, and railroad track rendered unusable. For planters, the greatest economic blow was the loss of their slaves, an investment worth more than $2 billion. When the slaves were freed, the plantation system collapsed.

New Ways of Life

The devastation of war affected all levels of Southern society. After his regiment surrendered at Appomattox, the planter Harry Hammond said he had "a pipe, some tobacco, and literally nothing else." Although Hammond owned a large plantation, he could find no one who could afford to buy his land when he put it up for sale. Hammond was saved from total ruin when most of the 300 blacks on the plantation agreed to stay and work the land. In return for their labor, Hammond provided his former slaves with housing, firewood, weekly food allotments, every other Saturday off, and $15 a year in cash after the crops were harvested. Hammond also agreed to provide the loan of a mule

Examining Photographs *Devastation in the South was widespread after the Civil War. Columbia, South Carolina; Atlanta, Georgia; and Charleston, South Carolina, shown above, were the cities suffering the greatest destruction. In what ways were the communications systems of the South in disarray?*

and a plow so that the workers could grow their own crops.

Not every planter was so fortunate. Southerners who had invested heavily in Confederate currency and bonds were wiped out financially when they became worthless after the war. Many lost their land because of taxes or other debts they could not pay. Some sold their acres to anyone who could pay the outrageously low prices for which Southern farms and plantations were advertised in Northern newspapers. On other plantations and on small farms throughout the South, war widows struggled to hold onto their property and keep it producing.

Poor blacks and whites realized that social and economic status in the South was tied to the land, but few had money to buy land, even at such low prices. So some became **tenant farmers,** that is, they farmed land that they rented. But even this was beyond the means of many poor Southerners and, more often, they became **sharecroppers,** persons who worked the owner's land—sometimes using the

owner's tools, animals, and seed—and received a share of the crops in return.

Although these arrangements seemed a solution that would provide a living for both workers and landowners, the system contained serious defects. For example, debt-ridden landowners wanted to get the highest possible return, so they pressured tenants to grow only cotton or tobacco, cash crops that paid the best. To prevent depletion of the soil, however, tenants could have planted a variety of crops, including food crops.

Tenants, black and white alike, usually had to buy seed, fertilizer, work animals, and food on credit, at interest rates as high as 40 percent. So, no matter how hard they worked, many tenants fell deeply into debt and remained trapped on the land until they paid those debts—no freer to leave than the slaves had been. As late as 1907, a federal investigator estimated that one-third of the farms in the Cotton Belt depended on the labor of tenants tied to the land by their debts. Years later a former slave recalled the frustration that black Southerners felt about this system:

Lincoln got praise for freeing us, but did he do it? He gave us freedom without giving us any chance to live to ourselves and we still had to depend on the southern white man for work, food, clothing, and he held us through our necessity and want in a state of servitude but little better than slavery.

AMERICAN PORTRAITS

FREDERICK DOUGLASS
1817-1895

Born into slavery, Frederick Douglass escaped (after one failed attempt) in 1838 and quickly emerged as a leading abolitionist. During the Civil War, he prodded President Lincoln to free the slaves, and he helped organize black troops to fight for freedom.

After Lincoln was assassinated, Douglass opposed the Reconstruction program of President Johnson. Instead he backed the Radical Republican plan. He used his oratorical ability to insist on full equality for blacks in all parts of the nation, and he was a vigorous backer of the Fourteenth Amendment. But he was particularly outspoken in support of the Fifteenth Amendment, guaranteeing black men the right to vote. To Douglass, being able to vote meant that blacks would not only be full citizens but would also have a weapon to protect their rights.

Even before the end of the war, some slaveholders noticed a change in the attitude of their slaves as they sensed freedom close at hand. Other planters were stunned, however, when slaves they thought happy and content left without a word to try to reach the Union lines.

Freedom strengthened black family ties. Families that had been separated during slavery were now reunited. Newspapers carried advertisements from blacks seeking information about missing relatives:

$200 reward. During the year 1849, Thomas Sample carried away from this city, as his slaves, our daughter Polly, and son, Geo. Washington, to the State of Mississippi, and subsequently to Texas....We will give $100 each for them, to any person who assist them, or either of them, to get to Nashville, or get word to us of their whereabouts, if they are alive.

Freed slaves, many of whom had only first names, now went about choosing family names. Some chose the name of an ancestor or the name of a hero, like Lincoln. Some adopted their former slaveholder's family name, but many blacks rejected such an idea. "That's my old rebel master's title," said one young man, "and I don't see any use in being called for him."

Former slaves who remained on the plantations as paid laborers usually refused to live in the old slave quarters. They objected to the common areas for cooking and washing and sought the privacy of separate cabins. For others, freedom meant leaving the plantation and their former owners and starting a new life. Some settled on the Great Plains and farmed land of their own. Others headed for large cities and jobs they hoped to find there.

The Freedmen's Bureau

At the close of the war, Congress had created within the War Department, a Bureau of Refugees, Freedmen, and

Examining Photographs *Thousands of Southerners after the Civil War faced the problem of finding enough food to stay alive. Many black families farmed land that was owned by others. Sharecropping worked for landowners who could keep their holdings intact. But for blacks, the system simply shackled them to their tiny plots. What options remained for families that did not want to be tied to the sharecropping system?*

Abandoned Lands, which became popularly known as the Freedmen's Bureau. Led by General O.O. Howard, the Bureau at first gave food and clothing to both black and white families in the war-ravaged South. Its primary mission, however, was to help blacks adjust to their new freedom. In addition, the Bureau provided medical help and founded 45 hospitals in 14 states.

Sponsored by the Freedmen's Bureau and the American Missionary Association, hundreds of Northern school teachers went south after the war. Many were young women who had been active in the antislavery and women's rights movements, who now dedicated themselves to educating the freed slaves. The teachers frequently found their students just as dedicated to getting an education. One black teacher from Philadelphia who taught school in Georgia, noted that many of her students worked in the fields in the morning and came to class "after their hard toil in the hot sun, as bright and as anxious to learn as ever." At the end of the day, these same classrooms were filled with adults, equally hungry for the education deprived to them while they were slaves. The Freedmen's Bureau also worked to establish colleges to train black teachers, contributing to the founding of Howard University, the Hampton Institute, Fisk University, and other historically black colleges.

Examining Illustrations *The Freedmen's Bureau set up hundreds of schools in the South for the newly freed slaves. Many adults as well as children attended. In what other ways did the Freedmen's Bureau try to help blacks adjust to a new life?*

In addition, the Freedmen's Bureau tried to find jobs for former slaves. It encouraged them to sign labor contracts with planters to provide work in return for wages or a share of the crops. Because most former slaves could neither read nor write, Bureau agents tried to prevent them from being cheated in these contracts, but the Bureau never had enough agents to do this job fully.

The dream of most freed slaves was to own their land. During the war Union troops had seized large amounts of land from Southern planters, and Congress decided to distribute some of this land to former slaves. On the Sea Islands of South Carolina, the Freedmen's Bureau was permitted to sell or lease confiscated land in parcels of up to 40 acres. Many newly freed black families hoped that 40 acres and a mule would help them start their lives anew. However, when President Andrew Johnson decided to pardon Confederates, he restored their property rights. If their land had been distributed to blacks, it was returned to its former owners. General Howard went to the Sea Islands to tell black farmers that their land was being returned to pardoned Confederates. He urged them to sign labor contracts to work on the land they briefly had owned. Most of the farmers refused to sign contracts, and a large number refused to give up their land. They were evicted against their will—some at bayonet point—by Union troops.

Section One Review

SUMMARY

After the Civil War, the South had to rebuild not only its farms and roads, but its social and political structures as well. A new system of farming soon developed to accommodate the lack of money. Tenant farmers and sharecroppers worked the owners' land in exchange for rent or a share of the crops. Freedom for African Americans meant renewed family ties and a new sense of identity. The Freedmen's Bureau provided services in education and employment for newly freed slaves. In addition, many blacks moved to other regions of the country to find work and start a new life. Yet equality for blacks was still elusive and few were able to realize the dream of owning their own land. Although they were no longer slaves, many African Americans found few opportunities open to them.

CHECKING FOR UNDERSTANDING

1. **Identify** Freedmen's Bureau
2. **Define** tenant farming, sharecroppers
3. **List** three drawbacks to tenant farming.
4. **Describe** three changes in family life for blacks after the war.

THINKING CRITICALLY

5. **Assessing Outcomes** Imagine that you are a newly freed slave living in the South. Write a short account of how freedom affects your life. Include ideas about the Freedmen's Bureau, segregation, former slave owners, and your chances to own land.

LINKING PAST AND PRESENT

6. **Making Comparisons** Some people believe that blacks have not achieved equality with whites. Despite great strides, blacks are still underrepresented in government and in the higher-paying professions. Compare present-day factors that inhibit racial equality with those of the Reconstruction era.

SECTION TWO

Reconstructing the South

...[R]econstruction...is fraught with great difficulty. Unlike a case of war between independent nations,...no one man has authority to give up the rebellion for any other man. We simply must begin with and mold from disorganized and discordant elements.

—ABRAHAM LINCOLN
Speech of April 11, 1865

Section Focus

Northern leaders varied in their opinion over the best way to deal with the defeated South. President Lincoln contended that the task was to restore the nation quickly and without bitterness. Others, however, felt that the South should be punished, and they sought to shape Reconstruction accordingly.

Objectives

After studying this section, you should be able to:
- Compare the Lincoln-Johnson plans for Reconstruction with the plans of the Radical Republicans.
- Explain how the black codes and the return of former Confederates to power affected Reconstruction.

"Reconstruction" involved much more than merely rebuilding and repairing the war damage inflicted on the South. It also meant restructuring Southern society by granting rights to former slaves, and restoring the nation by readmitting Southern states to the Union. Between 1865 and 1877, Congress and the President struggled with, and frequently clashed over, Reconstruction policies and programs.

Presidential Reconstruction

Before the war ended Lincoln began to plan for the peace that would follow the war. Because his primary goal was to restore the Union as quickly as possible, the President favored a generous policy. He offered **amnesty,** or pardon, to all Southerners, except for a few high-ranking Confederate officials, who pledged an oath of loyalty to the United States. Lincoln proposed that when 10 percent of a state's voters in the 1860 presidential election had taken this oath, Congress would readmit the state to the Union.

Lincoln's plan did not address the plight of freed slaves. Although Lincoln strongly supported the Thirteenth Amendment to free the slaves, for a long time he personally had favored colonization of free blacks in Africa and the Caribbean. But he was willing to let the South handle the matter. The President urged, however, that blacks who could read and write, and those who had served in the Union army, be allowed to vote.

Resistance to Lincoln's plan surfaced at once from his Radical Republican opponents in Congress. The Radicals did not share the President's belief that the Southern states could immediately be trusted with determining the status of free blacks, or that loyal state governments could result from his readmission plan. In addition, they maintained that Congress, rather than the President, should determine Reconstruction policies.

The Radicals' alternative to Lincoln's plan came in the Wade-Davis Bill of 1864. This legislation proposed putting the South under military rule and required a majority of a state's electorate to take the loyalty oath as a condition for the state's readmission. When Lincoln killed this bill with a **pocket veto**—that is, he let the session of Congress expire without signing the legislation—Senator Benjamin Wade of Ohio and

Representative Henry Davis of Maryland challenged him in a widely published attack that warned:

The President must understand that the authority of Congress...must be respected...and if he wishes our support he must confine himself to his executive duties—to obey and execute, not make the laws—and leave political reorganization to Congress.

When Arkansas, Tennessee, and Louisiana met the conditions of Lincoln's plan, Congress refused to readmit them to the Union. The President then realized that he would not have a peace based on "malice toward none" and "charity for all," and he began to negotiate with Radical congressional leaders. At this critical point, Lincoln was assassinated.

Andrew Johnson, who succeeded to the presidency, attempted to carry out Lincoln's Reconstruction policies. But he was hampered in this effort because, as an unelected President, he had little popular following. In addition, as a former Democrat, he could not command the support of the Republican majority in Congress and as a Tennessean and former slaveholder, he offended the Radicals. If these handicaps were not enough, he was self-righteous, hot-tempered, stubborn, and crude.

In the summer of 1865, with Congress in recess, Johnson began to implement his Reconstruction program. His conditions for readmission were that each Southern state abolish slavery, repeal its ordinance of secession, and repudiate its war debts. When Congress returned in December, every state except Texas had followed Johnson's formula and asked to return to the Union. The Radicals, however, were alarmed because the leniency of Johnson's plan allowed the return of traditional leadership in each of these states, and Southern voters elected former Confederate officials to power. The new governor

Examining Photographs *President Andrew Johnson soon found himself at odds with the Radical Republicans who wanted a stricter Reconstruction policy. Why did Johnson take no action regarding the status of blacks?*

of South Carolina was a former Confederate senator, for example, and Alexander Stephens, former Vice President of the Confederacy, was elected to the United States Senate. When Congress reconvened, it refused to seat members from the Southern states.

The Radicals were also concerned about the status of blacks in the South. Like Lincoln, President Johnson believed that this was a state matter and that federal jurisdiction stopped with the abolition of slavery. Consequently, the new Southern state governments endorsed the principle stated by the governor of Mississippi, "Ours is and ever shall be a government of white men."

The new Southern state legislatures passed a series of laws known as "black codes" that severely limited the rights of blacks and made it plain that blacks were still to have a subordinate status in the South. State governments made few provisions for black schools. In no Southern state were blacks permitted to vote, testify against whites, handle weapons, or serve on juries. In some states, all blacks were required by law to have steady work. Those who did not were arrested as vagrants, and their labor sold to the highest bidder. Some states permitted blacks to work only as farmers and servants and denied them many of the rights enjoyed by whites.

Northerners were outraged by the black codes, and even Johnson's supporters were alarmed by the actions of the Southern states. Secretary of the Navy Gideon Welles warned that:

The entire South seem to be stupid and vindictive, know not their friends, and are pursuing just the course which their opponents, the Radicals, desire. I fear a terrible ordeal awaits them in the future.

These fears proved well-founded. Events in the South increasingly led moderate Northerners to support the Radicals in Congress against the President.

In 1865, House and Senate leaders created a Joint Committee on Reconstruction to set congressional policy for restoring the Union. Over the next few months, the Joint Committee proposed bills providing economic aid for blacks and protection of their civil rights. Congress passed these bills, but President Johnson vetoed each one. Finally, in April 1866, Congress passed the Civil Rights Bill, which granted citizenship to blacks and gave federal government the power to intervene to protect the rights of freed slaves. When Johnson also vetoed this bill, Congress overrode his veto.

Fearing that the Civil Rights Act might be overturned in court, however, Congress passed the Fourteenth Amendment to the Constitution in June 1866. The amendment defined citizenship to include blacks and required that no state deny any person "the equal protection of the laws." In addition, the amendment barred many Confederate political leaders from holding public office and prohibited any state from paying Confederate war debts.

President Johnson attacked the Fourteenth Amendment and campaigned against its ratification. As the 1866 congressional elections neared, it was clear that they would reveal whether the President or Congress would control the direction of Reconstruction.

In a speaking tour to muster support, Johnson made so many bitter and intemperate remarks that he alienated more voters than he gained. He called powerful Radical Republican leaders traitors who were "opposed to the restoration of the Union of these States." His opponents

Life Of The Times

REBEL PRIDE

Soon after General Lee's surrender, the occupying Union army issued certain ordinances that were aimed at erasing all loyalty to the Confederacy. Many of these laws added insult to the injury of the defeated South. Ingenious Southerners, however, often found ways to circumvent these rules and keep their Rebel pride intact.

A "Button Order," for example, prohibited the wearing of Confederate military buttons. Since buttons of any type were scarce, Southerners resorted to using thorns from thornbushes as fastenings. Realizing that replacement buttons would be difficult to find, a clause permitted the "covering of formerly used buttons with cloth." Ingenious women draped Confederate buttons with black cloth. Thus, in obeying the Button Order, Southerners found a way that they could publicly display mourning for the Confederacy.

Another ordinance stated that the courts of Virginia could not issue any marriage license unless both parties took the oath of allegiance to the United States. More than one former Confederate prospective groom bristled at such an idea. Under much pressure from alarmed prospective brides, the Union General who issued the ordinance delayed its effective date for three days. During this interval, a multitude of hastily planned weddings took place.

Examining Photographs *Thaddeus Stevens of Pennsylvania led Radical Republicans in the bitter fight against President Johnson's Reconstruction program. What were the goals of the Radical Republicans?*

attacked the loyalties of Democrats, even former Democrats like the President:

Every deserter, every sneak who ran away from the draft calls himself a Democrat....Every wolf in sheep's clothing who pretends to preach the gospel but proclaims the righteousness of man-selling and slavery...calls himself a Democrat.

The November election provided an overwhelming victory for the Radicals, who gained control of both House and Senate. They now had the strength to override any presidential veto and could claim that they had a **mandate,** or command, from the public to enact their own Reconstruction program.

Radical Reconstruction

Republican leader Thaddeus Stevens summarized the Radicals' approach to Reconstruction in an 1866 speech in the House of Representatives:

Strip a proud nobility of their bloated estates, reduce them to a level with plain republicans; send them forth to labor, and teach their children to enter the workshops or handle the plow, and you will thus humble proud traitors.

Now firmly in control, the Radical Republicans began implementing their policies for Reconstruction. One goal was to sweep away the new state governments in the South and to replace them with military rule. Other goals were to ensure that former Confederate leaders would have no role in governing the South, and that the freed slaves' right to vote was protected.

Radical plans were inspired by self-interest as well as by concern for the freed slave and a desire to punish the South. The Radicals expected that blacks would express their gratitude for freedom by voting Republican. If the Southern states were readmitted to the Union without providing the franchise to blacks, the Democrats might regain power. Radical plans also were supported by Northern business leaders, who feared that a Congress controlled by Democrats might lower the tariff or destroy the national banking system established during the Civil War.

Many Radicals genuinely cared about the plight of the freed slaves, of course. They had been abolitionists before the Civil War and had pushed Lincoln into making emancipation a goal of the war. They believed in a right to equality and that government must rest on the consent of the governed. Senator Henry Wilson of Massachusetts summarized their position by saying:

> *[Congress] must see to it that the man made free by the Constitution is a freeman indeed; that he can go where he pleases, work when and for whom he pleases…go into the schools and educate himself and his children; that the rights and guarantees of the common law are his, and that he walks the earth proud and erect in the conscious dignity of a free man.*

In March 1867, Congress passed a Reconstruction Act that abolished the South's new state governments and put them under military rule. Except for Tennessee, the former Confederacy was divided into five military districts, each under command of a Union general. To be restored to the Union, each of the states was required to hold a constitutional convention, with delegates elected by all adult males, and to frame a state constitution that gave blacks the right to vote. If the voters ratified the constitution, a state government could be elected. Finally, if Congress approved the constitution, if the state legislature ratified the Fourteenth Amendment, and if the amendment became a part of the Constitution, then the state would be readmitted to the Union. By 1868, six states—Alabama, Arkansas, Florida, Louisiana, North Carolina, and South Carolina—had satisfied these requirements and were restored to the United States.

In 1869 Congress further protected black suffrage by passing the Fifteenth Amendment to the Constitution, providing that the right to vote "shall not be denied…on account of race, color, or previous condition of servitude." Congress required that states not yet complying with the Reconstruction Act—Virginia, Georgia, Mississippi, and Texas—had to ratify the Fifteenth Amendment as a further condition for readmission to the Union.

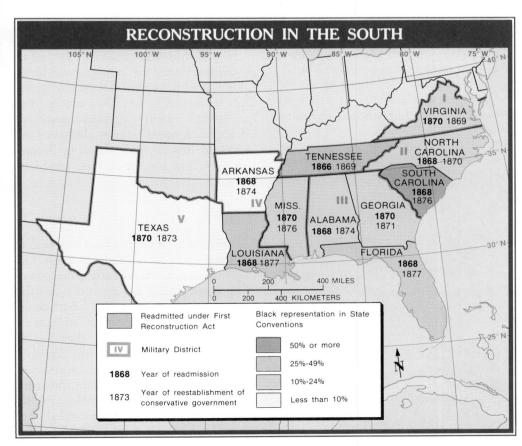

RECONSTRUCTION IN THE SOUTH

Legend:
- Readmitted under First Reconstruction Act
- IV Military District
- **1868** Year of readmission
- 1873 Year of reestablishment of conservative government

Black representation in State Conventions
- 50% or more
- 25%-49%
- 10%-24%
- Less than 10%

VIRGINIA **1870** 1869
NORTH CAROLINA **1868** 1870
TENNESSEE **1866** 1869
ARKANSAS **1868** 1874
SOUTH CAROLINA **1868** 1876
MISS. **1870** 1876
ALABAMA **1868** 1874
GEORGIA **1870** 1871
TEXAS **1870** 1873
LOUISIANA **1868** 1877
FLORIDA **1868** 1877

Examining Maps
Reconstruction in the South began with the readmission of the 11 former Confederate states. How is the end of Reconstruction in each of the former Confederate states shown on the map?

Carpetbag Government

By 1870, each of the 10 states under military rule had been readmitted to the Union. But Radical Reconstruction had **disenfranchised**—or took the right to vote from—many former Confederates, and many other Southern whites boycotted elections. As a result, government in the South was left to a small group of white Southern Union sympathizers called "scalawags" and Northerners who came South—called "carpetbaggers" because they arrived with all their belongings in cheap suitcases made of carpet fabric.

Some carpetbaggers were respectable, honest, and sincerely devoted to the public interest, but enough were self-seeking to give the "carpetbag governments" a reputation for graft, fraud, and waste. Votes in Southern state legislatures were openly bought and sold. One carpetbag governor admitted accepting more than $40,000 in bribes. Railroad franchises, public lands, and government contracts went to white Northerners and Northern businesses. As a result, Southern state debts rose sharply.

Carpetbag rule was not without achievement, however. Most public funds were spent honestly to encourage rebuilding and industrial development in the war-torn states. Carpetbag governments also established public schools, including schools for black children, that had not existed in the South before the Civil War.

Many Southern whites despised carpetbag governments that increased debt and taxes and that educated, protected, and shared power with blacks. A Charleston, South Carolina, newspaper reflected such feelings when it commented on a recently adjourned session of the state legislature:

In life it has been unlovely, and in death it has not belied its record. As it lived, it has died—an uncouth, malformed and abortive monstrosity, its birth a blunder, its life a crime, and its death a blessing.

Black voters, however, saw the carpetbag governments as their best hope and they overwhelmingly voted for Republican candidates. At the height of Radical Reconstruction, 700,000 blacks could vote in the South, compared to 625,000 whites.

Although black voters held the majority at the polls in several states, the carpetbag governments were not run by or for black people. No blacks were elected governors. Only in South Carolina did a state legislature have a majority of black members. Fifteen black members were elected to the House of Representatives during Reconstruction, and two black men served as United States senators.

The Radicals in Power

To ensure their control over the Reconstruction program, the Radicals in Congress attempted to reduce the power of both the judicial and executive branches. Fearing that the Supreme Court could apply its decision in *ex parte Milligan* to the military districts of the South, Congress forbade appeals to the Supreme Court arising under the Reconstruction Act. To prevent President Johnson from appointing justices to vacancies on the Supreme Court, Congress provided that when justices died or resigned, they were not to be replaced.

Examining Illustrations
The first black members of Congress are shown in this Currier and Ives print. The first black Senator, Hiram R. Revels, is at the far left. What were the major achievements of Southern governments during this period?

The Radicals also were determined to reduce the presidential power that Lincoln had assumed during the Civil War and to remove Johnson as an obstacle to their plans. Here, too, the conflict focused on the military districts of the South. In March 1867, Congress passed the Army Appropriation Act, which severely limited the President's power as commander-in-chief. Accompanying this legislation was the Tenure of Office Act, which required Senate approval for the President to remove any government official whose appointment had required its consent.

The Radicals knew that President Johnson wanted to remove Edwin Stanton, Lincoln's secretary of war, who remained in Johnson's cabinet but who openly sided with the Radicals. Characteristically, Johnson ignored these warnings and continued trying to block Radical Reconstruction. He removed commanders in the Southern military districts who supported the Radicals and, while Congress was in recess, he fired Stanton.

To replace Stanton, Johnson appointed General Grant, but when the Senate reconvened, it rejected Grant's nomination, and Grant resigned in favor of Stanton. Outraged, Johnson fired Stanton again—on February 21, 1868—this time replacing him with General Lorenzo Thomas, but Stanton barricaded himself inside his office and refused to leave. The Radicals then came to Stanton's support. Three days later, the House of Representatives voted to **impeach,** or charge, Johnson with "high crimes and misdemeanors" in office. As provided in the Constitution, the President was tried by the Senate, a two-thirds majority being needed for a conviction.

For more than two months, amid intense public excitement, the Senate debated the President's fate. Radical members of the House, led by Thaddeus Stevens, presented the case against Johnson, denouncing him for blocking Reconstruction and even suggesting that Johnson might have been involved in the plot to assassinate Lincoln. Johnson's lawyers argued that Lincoln, not Johnson, had appointed Stanton to the Cabinet and, therefore, that the Tenure of Office Act did not apply. Although Johnson

never attended the trial, his lawyers were successful in arguing his case and winning public sympathy for his position.

On May 16, 1868, the Senate voted 35 to 19 that Johnson was guilty of "high crimes and misdemeanors"—just one vote short of what was needed for conviction. Seven Republican senators were not able to find honest evidence that Johnson was guilty. Under tremendous political pressure, they refused to put partisan politics above the independence of the executive branch. One of them, Senator Lyman Trumbull, explained the reason for his vote:

It is not a party question I am to decide. I must be governed by what my reason and judgment tell me is the truth and the justice and the law of this case....Once set, the example of impeaching a President for what, when the excitement of the hour shall have subsided, will be regarded as insufficient causes, and no future President will be safe who happens to differ with a majority of the House and two thirds of the Senate...what then becomes of the checks and balances of the Constitution so carefully devised and so vital to its perpetuity? They are all gone.

Although Johnson remained in office for the last few months of his term, he was powerless to challenge the Radicals'

Examining Illustrations
In 1868, the House adopted 11 articles of impeachment against President Johnson. Tickets of admission to the trial were sold. What were the results of the trial?

Examining Political Cartoons *Despite having little political experience, Ulysses S. Grant's military achievements and unassuming manners helped him gain the Republican nomination for President in 1868. What factors helped Grant win the election?*

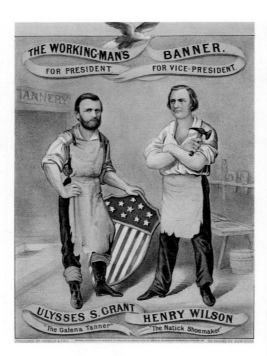

THE WORKING-MAN'S BANNER.
FOR PRESIDENT. FOR VICE-PRESIDENT.

ULYSSES S. GRANT   HENRY WILSON
"The Galena Tanner"   "The Natick Shoemaker"

policies. The Radicals, however, were publicly humiliated by their defeat, lost the support of Republican moderates in Congress, and turned many people in the North against Radical Reconstruction.

With Johnson no longer an obstacle, the Radical Republicans sought a candidate in the 1868 presidential election who could sweep the country and keep them in power. They found such a person in General Grant. Grant had been a Democrat before the war and shared Lincoln's and Johnson's lenient attitude toward the South. But he allied with the Radicals after his failed appointment as Johnson's secretary of war. The Democrats chose Horatio Seymour, former governor of New York, and their platform condemned Radical Republican actions.

Although Grant won handily, 214 to 80, in the electoral college, a small shift in the popular vote in key states would have given Seymour the election. Grant won only because he was supported by the carpetbag governments of the South and because three Southern states had not yet been readmitted to the Union. Throughout Grant's two administrations, troops remained in the South. By keeping the South under military rule, the Republicans hoped to keep control of Congress and the presidency.

SUMMARY

Differences over how Reconstruction should be carried out soon divided the government. Radical Republicans tried to consolidate their power by limiting the power of the President, culminating in charges of impeachment against President Johnson. With the President no longer an obstacle, the Radicals were able to implement their version of Reconstruction. Then by selecting Civil War hero Ulysses S. Grant as their candidate, and with the support of carpetbag governments, the radicals gained control of the White House in the presidential election of 1868.

CHECKING FOR UNDERSTANDING

1. **Identify** Radical Republicans, Andrew Johnson, Fourteenth Amendment, Fifteenth Amendment, Tenure of Office Act
2. **Define** pocket veto, amnesty, mandate
3. **List** two objections the Radicals had to Lincoln's Reconstruction plans.
4. **Explain** the purpose of the black codes.
5. **Summarize** the changes in policy made under Radical Reconstruction.

THINKING CRITICALLY

6. **Determining Cause and Effect** The 1866 congressional elections served as a contest between President Johnson and the Radical Republicans for control of Reconstruction. How do congressional elections during a President's term of office act as a barometer of presidential policies and popularity?

CONNECTIONS: HISTORY AND ECONOMICS

7. **Analyzing Motives** The black codes restricted the opportunities and freedoms of blacks. What economic motives do you think the black codes served for Southern whites?

★ ★ ★ ★ ★ ★ ★ ★ ★ ★ ★ ★ ★ ★ ★ ★ ★ ★

Critical Thinking Skills

Making Predictions

The big game of the year is this Friday. Since the other school's team has lost two in a row, and it is rumored that their quarterback may not be able to play, you decide the score will be 24-0, in your team's favor. Your decision is actually a prediction.

Explanation

A *prediction* is a foretelling of something before it happens. When you predict something, you are stating what you believe will happen in the future. Good predictions are based on present conditions as well as what has happened in the past.

In the example you know the opposing football team's present condition—that its quarterback might not be able to play. You also know the past—that the opposing team has lost two games in a row. Based on these two facts, you are able to make an intelligent prediction.

Asking the questions that follow can help you predict the possible results of any historical event:

a. What related conditions existed prior to the event being studied?

b. What caused the conditions?

c. What was the event supposed to accomplish?

d. Based on the answers to these questions, what is your prediction about what will happen as a result of the event?

Freed African Americans line up to cast their first ballot.

Example

Note how the questions have been applied in predicting the results of the passage of the Fourteenth Amendment:

a. What conditions existed prior to the passing of the Fourteenth Amendment?
• *Blacks were considered by many to be inferior to whites.*
• *Blacks were denied rights guaranteed to whites.*
• *Many people spoke out against the institution of slavery.*
• *The Civil War had freed the slaves, although they were without equal rights.*

b. What caused these conditions?
• *the firm belief of many people that blacks were inferior.*
• *the belief by many that blacks should be considered equal.*

c. What was the event supposed to accomplish?
• *The Fourteenth Amendment was written and passed to ensure that all persons born and naturalized in the United States would have all the rights due them under the Constitution.*

d. Predict what will happen as a result of the passage of the Fourteenth Amendment.
• *Passage of the Fourteenth Amendment will cause conflict, unrest, and confusion.*
• *Equality for African Americans will have to come gradually.*

Practice

For further practice in making predictions, apply these questions and make a prediction about the success of Lincoln's plan for Reconstruction had he lived to carry out his program.

Restoring Southern Power

It was in 1876, thirty years ago...There was a condition bordering on anarchy... Life ceased to be worth having on the terms under which we were living, and in desperation we determined to take the government away from blacks.

—BENJAMIN R. TILLMAN
South Carolina, speech in the United States Senate, 1906

Section Focus

Reconstruction left a mixed legacy. It allowed the South to begin rebuilding its economy, but proved to be of only temporary help to black Southerners. As political and civil rights were restored to former Confederates, they were increasingly denied to blacks.

Objectives

After studying this section, you should be able to:
- Describe Southern resistance to Reconstruction.
- Discuss political and economic change in the South after Reconstruction.

White Southerners at first put up little resistance to Radical Reconstruction. Weary from the war, they were busy with the business of keeping alive amid general poverty. But there were many "unreconstructed rebels" who were not inclined to follow General Lee's advice to "unite in the restoration of the country and the re-establishment of peace and harmony."

Unable to strike openly at the federal government, opponents of Reconstruction organized secret resistance societies. The largest of these groups was the Ku Klux Klan. Started in Tennessee in 1866, the Klan spread throughout the former Confederacy. Hooded, white-robed Klan members rode in bands at night and threatened carpetbaggers, teachers in black schools, and black people themselves. Using beatings, murder, and other violence to back up their threats, Klansmen broke up Republican meetings, tried to drive Freedmen's Bureau officials out of their communities, and tried to keep freed slaves from voting.

Although by 1872 it had been greatly suppressed by federal troops, the Klan and similar organizations contributed to the establishment of Southern governments opposed to the Radicals. Democrats, often called "Redeemers" or "Conservatives," gained control of one Southern state after another, until by 1876 only South Carolina, Florida, and Louisiana did not have governments controlled by white Democrats, many of whom were former Confederates.

One reason for these Democratic successes in the South was that Northerners were becoming weary of Radical Reconstruction. In 1872 a group called the Liberal Republicans, including some of the most prominent people in the Republican Party, opposed the Radicals and refused to support Grant for re-election because they considered him unfit for the presidency. The Liberal Republicans joined with the Democrats to nominate newspaper publisher Horace Greeley for President. Although Grant won re-election, the Radical's power was weakened, and Grant's administration loosened its controls over the South. As fewer troops were sent to protect black voters during Southern elections, white political power was restored.

The Compromise of 1877

The presidential election of 1876 brought the end of Radical Reconstruction. In the campaign the Republicans "waved the bloody shirt," the label applied to stirring up bitter memories of the war.

Connections

HISTORY AND ECONOMICS

GROWTH OF SOUTHERN MANUFACTURING

Many factors pushed the postwar South toward industrialization. Most important, however, was the surplus labor supply. Widows, orphans, and displaced former slaves needed work, and agriculture could not employ them all. This meant there

Pig iron factory in Alabama

was a large pool of cheap labor. In addition, Northerners and Europeans invested capital in fledgling Southern industry, as did a number of Southerners themselves.

Two industries that made spectacular advances in the postwar South were textile and tobacco processing. Cotton mills sprang up in the major cotton-growing areas of the South. By 1900 there were 400 mills in operation. The postwar demand for a new product—cigarettes—and the invention of the cigarette-rolling machine in 1880 were the catalysts that fueled the development of the tobacco-processing industry.

Other industries based on agriculture or minerals also developed such as steel manufacturing and making cottonseed oil. Despite gains in industrialization, the South remained primarily rural and agricultural until industrial advances developed in the middle of the twentieth century.

★ ★ ★ ★ ★ ★ ★ ★ ★

MAKING THE ECONOMICS CONNECTION

1. What factors led to the development of industry in the postwar South?

2 What southern cities of the 1900s are noted as industrial-centers?

LINKING PAST AND PRESENT

3. Why was the region's economy primarily agricultural until the mid-1900s?

★ ★ ★ ★ ★ ★ ★ ★ ★

Democrats countered by attacking the excesses of Radical Reconstruction and the corruption they claimed was rampant in the Grant administration.

On election day, Democratic candidate Samuel J. Tilden, governor of New York, polled 250,000 more popular votes than the Republican, Ohio's governor Rutherford B. Hayes. Tilden was a vote short of a majority in the electoral college, but 20 electoral votes were disputed. One of these electoral votes was from Oregon, and was challenged on a technicality. The other 19 involved disputed results from the three Southern states still under carpetbag rule—Florida, South Carolina, and Louisiana—where charges of massive voting fraud flew. Republicans complained that Democrats prevented blacks from voting, and Democrats accused Republicans of using federal troops to raise its vote totals. These three states each filed two sets of election returns, one for Tilden and another for Hayes.

Because the Constitution did not provide for settling such a dispute, Congress appointed a commission of five members each from the House, the Senate, and the Supreme Court to settle the matter. Tilden needed only one of the disputed electoral votes to become President, but Hayes needed all of them. Voting strictly along party lines, the commission awarded all 20 disputed electoral votes to Hayes. Congress accepted the verdict on March 2, 1877, two days before the inauguration.

The Democrats were outraged at the commission's decisions, and they were determined not to be defrauded. There were threats of civil war and talk of blocking Hayes's inauguration. But the Republicans were just as determined to keep control of the presidency, and they began to talk about a compromise. After negotiations between party leaders, the Democrats agreed to accept the election results and the Republicans agreed to several demands. Democrats were assured

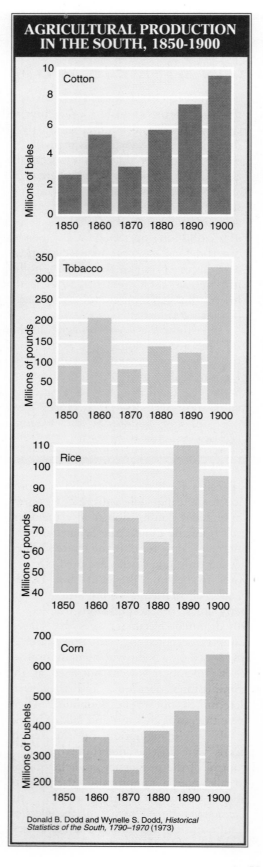

AGRICULTURAL PRODUCTION IN THE SOUTH, 1850-1900

Cotton (Millions of bales)

Tobacco (Millions of pounds)

Rice (Millions of pounds)

Corn (Millions of bushels)

Donald B. Dodd and Wynelle S. Dodd, *Historical Statistics of the South, 1790–1970* (1973)

that a Southerner would become postmaster general, an important position because of the many federal jobs it controlled. Republicans also promised federal funds for internal improvements in the South. Most importantly, Republicans agreed to withdraw the remaining federal troops from the South. Without soldiers to protect them, the three remaining carpetbag governments collapsed and Reconstruction officially came to an end.

After Reconstruction

In many ways, the South after Reconstruction was similar to the South before the Civil War. As white Southern Democrats returned to power, blacks lost many of their civil rights.

For years, in the North as well as the South, **segregation,** or the practice of separating people on the basis of their race, had been an accepted way of life. Even before the Civil War, custom in the North had separated black and white travelers on railroads, stagecoaches, and steamboats, and in hotels. Such segregation also existed in Northern schools, churches, hospitals, and cemeteries. After Reconstruction, however, the South began to pass "Jim Crow laws" that added legality to the practice of segregation.

Where possible, blacks protested segregation. Black protests helped to integrate the streetcar lines of Washington, D.C., Richmond, Virginia, and Charleston, South Carolina. In 1875 Congress passed a Civil Rights Act requiring that all people have equal access to public places and transportation facilities. But in 1883 the Supreme Court ruled that the Act was unconstitutional, and by the 1890s Jim Crow laws were common throughout the South.

Despite the South's return to white supremacy, by the late 1870s there was increasing talk of a "New South." An alliance between powerful white Southerners—many from the old planter families—and Northern financiers brought about the economic rebuilding of the South. Northern capital helped to build railroads, and by 1890 the South had twice the railroad mileage that it had in 1860.

Better transportation encouraged the industrialization of the South. A growing iron and steel industry developed around Birmingham, Alabama, and in North Carolina tobacco processing became big business. Cotton mills appeared in countless small towns throughout the South. But far from populous Northern markets, and paying high freight rates, Southern industries faced serious problems. To compete and make a profit, Southern factory owners generally paid lower wages than in the North.

With these developments in transportation and industry, and with the spread of sharecropping in agriculture, the South's economy gradually revived. By 1870, the South was producing as much cotton as it had in 1860, and by 1890 its cotton yield had doubled. By 1900 Southern industrial production was four times what it had been in 1860.

In many ways, Reconstruction aided the South. But it also caused much bitterness in that section, helping to create the "Solid South"—a voting bloc, dominated by the Democrats, that did not break up for a century. Reconstruction also provided only limited and temporary help to Southern blacks, whose rights it professed to defend. As time passed, abolitionist idealism declined, and many Radicals proved more interested in black votes than in the welfare of black Americans. Congress closed the Freedmen's Bureau after only five years, and it made no long-range plans to provide what the freed slaves needed most—land and education. As the black codes revealed, without federal protection, for many blacks emancipation merely meant a new kind of slavery—continued attachment to the white power structure as sharecroppers and tenant farmers.

Although immediate efforts to improve the lives of Southern blacks failed, the Fourteenth and Fifteenth amendments wrote into the Constitution the principle of equality for all people. For many years these amendments remained almost a dead letter, but in the 1900s they provided the legal basis and, in part, the inspiration for movements to obtain for black Americans their full rights as citizens.

★ ★ ★ ★ ★ ★ ★ ★ ★ ★ ★ ★ ★ ★ ★ ★ ★

Section Three Review

★ ★ ★ ★ ★ ★ ★ ★ ★ ★ ★ ★ ★ ★ ★ ★ ★

SUMMARY

The emergence of the Ku Klux Klan was an indication of the simmering resentment many southern whites held toward Radical Reconstruction policies and African Americans. Democrats steadily regained control of Southern governments as support for Radical Reconstruction policies waned. The results of Reconstruction were mixed. The South began slowly to rebuild. There were few substantial economic gains for blacks, although the Fourteenth and Fifteenth amendments established the principle of equality for all people.

CHECKING FOR UNDERSTANDING

1. **Identify** Ku Klux Klan, Compromise of 1877, "Solid South"

2. **Define** segregation

3. **Describe** the tactics used by the Ku Klux Klan.

4. **Explain** two important concessions that were made in the Compromise of 1877.

5. **List** two major reasons why the Southern economy eventually improved after the war.

THINKING CRITICALLY

6. **Distinguishing Fact from Opinion** Describe the images of the South created by motion pictures and novels. What facts from the era refute these images?

LINKING PAST AND PRESENT

7. **Analyzing Cause and Effect** Historians have noticed that membership in organizations such as the Ku Klux Klan increases during times of rapid social change and conflict. Membership in the Ku Klux Klan and other racist organizations has surged once again. Make a list of events and changes that you see in present-day society that might explain why this increase has occurred.

★ ★ ★ ★ ★ ★ ★ ★ ★ ★ ★ ★ ★ ★ ★ ★ ★

★ Chapter 16 Review ★

★ Summary

After the Civil War, blacks and whites set out to rebuild the South. Economically and politically, however, African Americans were thwarted by segregation and black codes. The Radical Republicans' version of Reconstruction, advocating voting rights for blacks and harsher treatment of former Confederates, was set in motion when the Radical Republicans gained control of Congress. Reconstruction governments were often handicapped by corruption. Eventually white southerners regained control of southern government. Although Reconstruction was only partially effective for blacks, a degree of cooperation was achieved between the North and South.

★ Using Vocabulary

The terms that follow can be related to one another in some way. Create a classification system that demonstrates how these words are related. First, write *Reconstruction* as your main heading. Under the main heading create several smaller categories such as *Treatment of Blacks, Legislation,* or *Farming.* Challenge yourself to see how many different classifications you can devise.

tenant farming	sharecropping
segregation	black codes
amnesty	carpetbaggers
mandate	concessions
impeach	

★ Reviewing Facts

1. **Cite** two reasons why tenant farming and sharecropping were used in the South.
2. **List** three services provided by the Freedmen's Bureau.
3. **Specify** two differences between the Reconstruction plans of Presidents Lincoln and Johnson and the Radical Republicans.
4. **Explain** how black codes prevented blacks from achieving equality.
5. **List** three motives of the Radical Republicans.
6. **Name** three sectors of the southern economy that improved after the Civil War.

7. **List** the long-term successes and failures of Reconstruction for southern blacks.

★ Understanding Concepts

ADAPTATION

1. Explain how tenant farming and sharecropping were a means for southern landowners to adjust to new conditions after the Civil War.
2. Explain why freedom did not automatically lead to equality for blacks after the Civil War.

POWER AND AUTHORITY

3. What are the significant reasons that explain how the power of the Radical Republicans first grew and later diminished?
4. What factors led to the rise of the Ku Klux Klan? What feelings and beliefs did the Ku Klux Klan appeal to among southerners?

★ Thinking Critically

1. **Evaluating Roles**   Contrast the roles of the federal government and the state governments in relation to blacks after the Civil War.
2. **Analyzing a Comparison**   Was southern society during Reconstruction similar to South African society under apartheid? Explain.
3. **Recognizing Bias**   Although many outward actions were taken to help freed blacks achieve equality after the Civil War, their political and economic status did not improve much. Explain why laws and policies were not enough to achieve equality for blacks.
4. **Identifying Central Issues**   The 1860s were a time of radical change. Summarize the string of events that caused so much political and social turbulence during the 1860s.

★ Writing About History

COMPARISON

Refer to the description of how to write a comparison essay in the History Writer's Handbook in the Appendix of this book. Your teacher will give you more specific instructions on the essay's length and the assignment's due date.

Imagine that you are a newly freed African American person living in the South during Reconstruction. Thanks to a school run by the Freedmen's Bureau, you have learned to read and write. You decide you will write a letter to a long lost relative living in the North describing the changes that have taken place in your life. In your letter compare your life before the Civil War to life during Reconstruction. Include information about your work, your way of life, and your relations with whites.

★ Learning Cooperatively

You belong to a group analyzing Reconstruction policies. Each member of your group will assume one of these roles: a Southern landowner, a Northern carpetbagger, and a black sharecropper. Your goal is to write two Reconstruction laws that are acceptable to all. Write one law on voting rights for blacks, and a second law on the treatment of former Confederate soldiers.

★ Mastering Skills

DETECTING BIAS

Almost everyone has certain opinions, ideas, or beliefs about particular topics or subjects. For this reason, written material is not always objective, free from the influence of a writer's or speaker's personal views or emotions. Sometimes, even if a writer or speaker does not intend it to happen, what he or she writes or says shows bias, a set idea or opinion about something or someone. Bias may be in favor of or against an idea or person.

As you read in this chapter, Lincoln had one view about how the South should be treated after the war, while the Radical Republicans had a different view. Northern and southern leaders often expressed opposite points of views in their speeches and writings.

Example   As a student of history, you need to develop a method to critically examine historical sources and detect bias in materials from the past. Asking the questions that follow will help you learn how to detect bias.

• *When and why was the document written?* Before reading a document determine, if possible, its date, its authorship, and the historical circumstances surrounding it.

• *Are certain phrases used in order to have emotional impact?* Speakers sometimes persuade their audiences by presenting statements of fact. Other times they stir their listeners' emotions by using emotion-packed phrases.

• *Does the writer or speaker tend to show one group as good and the other group as evil?* A person's bias is often evident if he or she tries to show that a group is either completely wrong or completely right.

Practice   The following excerpt is from President Lincoln's Second Inaugural Address (1865). Compare it to what one of the Radical Republicans, Colonel Robert Ingersoll, had to say about Democrats (see page 484). Then answer the questions.

With malice toward none, with charity for all, with firmness in the right as God gives us to see the right, let us strive on to finish the work we are in, to bind up the nation's wounds, to care for him who shall have borne the battle and for his widow and his orphan, to do all which may achieve and cherish a just and lasting peace among ourselves and with all nations.

1. How can knowing about Lincoln's Reconstruction plans help you understand his message in his inaugural address?

2. What effect did Lincoln want to create in the minds of his listeners?

3. What is the difference in bias between Ingersoll's remarks and Lincoln's address? What words and phrases did Ingersoll use to create an emotional impact?

Look, for example, at these two statements:

By the end of Reconstruction, the South was once more a part of the Union.

The once-proud and unwilling states of the South had, by the end of Reconstruction, been forced back into the Union.

Each of the statements seems to be saying roughly the same thing. But if you keep in mind the definition of bias, the difference between the two statements becomes clear. The first statement presents a fact—the Southern states were once again united with the other states. The second statement, however, reflects the writer's personal feelings. In addition, this statement may make you view the "facts" in a different light than you would have if the writer had not biased your view.

★ ★ ★ Unit 5 Digest ★ ★ ★

While the United States was moving to become more democratic, Americans were moving in other directions as well. Driven by a desire to expand United States borders, Americans were pushing westward. Americans were also moving apart ideologically with the slavery issue the main source of dissension. This powerful issue led to a conflict that would ultimately divide the nation in war.

Chapter 13
Manifest Destiny

The American drive to the Pacific was caused by several factors, including the habitual desire of Americans to move onto new land, the mistaken belief that the plains were unsuitable for farming, commercial interests concerning East Asian trade, and patriotism. Initially, the push westward met with little resistance from the Indians, Mexico, and Britain, but ultimately conflict did arise.

In Texas, disputes between American settlers and the Mexican government led to several conflicts. In 1836 Texas became independent and the Rio Grande was accepted as the boundary line separating Texas and Mexico. In 1846 the United States and Mexico clashed over the southern boundary of Texas and war broke out. The Treaty of Guadalupe Hidalgo, which ended the Mexican War, granted the United States full title to Texas with the Rio Grande as a boundary, California, and what was then New Mexico territory.

The war with Mexico preempted a war with Britain over the Oregon boundary. Although Americans shouted "Fifty-four forty or fight!", this dispute was settled peacefully by compromise between the United States and British government, with both agreeing to the 49th parallel.

Manifest destiny also moved American interests to other parts of the globe. Americans sought to acquire Cuba, but after several unsuccessful attempts abandoned their efforts. Americans did, however, succeed in laying the groundwork for a canal across the Isthmus of Panama. In East Asia, Americans opened up China and Japan for trade.

Chapter 14
Compromise and Conflict

The Mexican War and the Treaty of Guadelupe Hidalgo brought into the open the slavery issue. Once the United States acquired New Mexico and California, the nation's leaders realized that a decision had to be made concerning slavery in the territories. This issue became acute after the discovery of gold in California led to California's application for statehood as a free state. This touched off a bitter debate, which was settled by the Compromise of 1850. Unfortunately, this turned out to be only a truce.

By 1850 the United States was booming economically—new inventions; further development of established industries; increased agricultural productivity; increased labor force from immigration; and great advances in transportation, which tied together the North and the Midwest.

Many of these developments, however, benefited only the North. The South's feelings of isolation were intensified by its reliance on slavery, which was also causing tensions throughout the nation. Tensions increased after the passage of the Kansas-Nebraska Act. The rush among settlers from both slave and free states to populate the Kansas Territory culminated in bloodshed known as "bleeding Kansas." The nation was further torn apart by the *Dred Scott* decision.

The slavery issue was kept alive with the Lincoln-Douglas debates of 1858 in which Douglas admitted that territorial legislatures could practically nullify the *Dred Scott* decision, and John Brown's raid on Harpers Ferry. In the election of 1860, slavery was the key issue, with Republican Lincoln, viewed as an abolitionist, emerging victorious. In response to Lincoln's victory, most of the southern states seceded from the Union.

Chapter 15
The Civil War

War broke out in 1861 with the South's attack on Fort Sumter. The attack sparked patriotism on both sides, and thousands joined the ranks of their respective armies. The North and the South each had advantages. The North had superior resources and an established federal government, whereas the South had intense nationalism and better generals.

Part of the northern strategy was to blockade southern ports. This tactic was successful and reduced southern trade dramatically. The South, though, gained momentum, crushing Union troops at both the first and second battles of Bull Run. In the West, they were less successful, losing several key battles to General Grant and later to General Sherman.

Behind the scenes, both sides faced difficulties recruiting volunteers and resorted to conscription. The South also faced production and supply difficulties. In addition, the South had trouble financing the war, and Confederate money eventually became worthless.

As the war progressed, Lincoln turned the war into an abolitionist crusade. Thus, the Union was now fighting to end human bondage. The progression of the war also saw Grant finally face the brilliant Confederate general, Robert E. Lee. Grant emerged victorious, and Lee and his army agreed to lay down their arms at Appomattox Court House on April 9, 1865. The war had finally ended.

Chapter 16
Reconstruction

The Civil War had left the South in disarray, with the land, government, and transportation system in ruin. Both the rich and the poor were affected, with many poor blacks and whites resorting to tenant farming and sharecropping. Freedom, however, strengthened black family ties. For many, it also meant leaving the plantation and heading for the larger cities where they sought the protection and aid of the Freedmen's Bureau. The freed blacks, though, were soon subjected to restrictive black codes.

Two questions remaining after the war were how to deal with the defeated South and what rights should the newly freed blacks have. Lincoln had favored a generous policy for readmitting the defeated states, but many Radicals strongly opposed this plan. Lincoln did not address the freed slave issue. Andrew Johnson, Lincoln's successor, tried to implement his predecessor's plan but failure to try to overturn the black codes and conflicts with Congress ultimately gave the Radical Republicans the chance to enact their own version of Reconstruction.

The Radicals were motivated primarily by a desire to punish the South and keep the Republican party in power, although many cared about the plight of the freedmen. One of their first acts was to pass Reconstruction laws that put the South under military rule and established stringent requirements for readmission to the Union. Once in power, some of the leaders of the new state governments were accused of graft and corruption. Although this was to an extent true, these "carpetbag" governments encouraged industrial development and social improvements.

Radical Reconstruction met with several opponents. Andrew Johnson, still in conflict with the Radicals, was impeached under the Radical Republicans, turning many people against Radical Reconstruction. The Ku Klux Klan, also against Reconstruction, openly used violence against freed slaves.

Reconstruction ended after the disputed Tilden-Hayes election of 1876. Following this election, there was a new alliance between wealthy southerners and northern financiers intent on building a "New South." Although the South's economy gradually revived, the region lagged behind other areas of the country for decades.

SYNTHESIZING UNIT THEMES

RELATING IDEAS

1. How did the spirit of manifest destiny affect the role of the United States in world affairs?

IDENTIFYING TRENDS

2. How did the status of blacks change after the Civil War?

MAKING COMPARISONS

3. How did the ideas of the Radical Republicans differ from those of Lincoln and Johnson?

★ Unit 5 Review ★

★ Analyzing Unit Themes

CIVIL RIGHTS AND LIBERTIES

1. Compare the legal and social status of African Americans before and after the Civil War.
2. How did southern states continue to manipulate and deny African Americans their freedom after the Civil War? Explain the role of the federal government in attaining equality for blacks during Reconstruction.

CONFLICT AND COOPERATION

3. Was a compromise on the slavery issue ever a feasible tactic? Why or why not?

CULTURAL DIVERSITY

4. How were cultural differences between Northerners and Southerners a factor that caused the Civil War? Did the war have any effect on these differences?

U.S. ROLE IN WORLD AFFAIRS

5. In the mid-1800s the United States was willing to use force to acquire territory. Give examples to support this generalization.
6. By the time the Civil War began, the United States was increasingly becoming part of a global economy. How did this interdependence between nations affect the outcome of the Civil War?

★ Reviewing Chronology

Study the unit time line on pages 390-391, then answer the questions that follow.

1. What two similar events occurred both inside and outside the United States during this period?
2. Would it be correct to say that *Uncle Tom's Cabin* was an immediate cause of the Civil War? Why or why not?

★ Linking Past and Present

In 1989 a book entitled the *Encyclopedia of Southern Culture* was published. It had taken 10 years, 800 writers, and 1,600 pages to complete the project. One conclusion that emerged from the publication of this book was that, perhaps more than any other region in the United States, the South continues to maintain a unique and strong cultural identity.

Based on the information just read, answer the questions that follow.

1. **Making Comparisons** Compare the regional differences that divided the United States in the Civil War era to those in American society today.
2. **Analyzing Trends** Do cultural differences in the United States today act as a unifying or a divisive force for society? Support your answer with details.

★ Demonstrating Citizenship

Promoting Interests Government agencies can be used to promote the values and interests of a particular group of people. Evaluate the effectiveness of the Freedmen's Bureau in helping blacks during Reconstruction. Explain how a lack of support from the President and white Southerners thwarted the efforts of this agency. Why is support from leaders and the general population for a particular agency an important factor in determining its usefulness?

★ Interpreting Illustrations

The Civil War was one of the first times the new invention of photography was used to document history. Before this time, historical events had only been recorded by artists who often sketched pictures.

Study the photograph shown above, and answer the questions that follow.

1. What impact do you think the use of photographs had on the average American citizen's perception of war?

2. Do you think the use of photographs offered an objective way to depict information? Explain your answer.

★ Thinking Globally

1. Comparing Cultures At the time of the Civil War, Americans knew very little about the African continent. Africa at this time had hundreds of different ethnic groups, each with its own language and customs. How did Americans' ignorance about African culture affect their attitudes toward African Americans?

2. Applying Concepts Many people in Europe, after reading and hearing about the American Civil War, argued that anarchy and rebellion were the result of a government that allowed such a great degree of popular representation and freedom. People on both sides of the Atlantic Ocean considered the war to be a test of democratic ideas. Evaluate the Civil War from the European perspective. What do you think Europeans learned about democracy from watching the Civil War?

★ Relating Geography and History

MOVEMENT: MIGRATION

One way to gain information about groups of people is to study their reasons for moving from one place to another. In the first part of the nineteenth century, many Americans migrated westward.

Answer the questions that follow.

1. What ideas and beliefs encouraged and motivated many people in the United States to migrate to the West?

2. What was the effect of this migration on native peoples such as Indians and Mexicans?

3. Why was this migration one cause of the Civil War?

★ Practicing Skills

CLASSIFYING INFORMATION

Refer to the skills lesson on Classifying Information on page 425 to help you practice this skill.

Classify the following items, indicating what major category each could fit under and whether it should be classified under "North" or "South."

Abraham Lincoln	industrial capability
Antietam	Jefferson Davis
blockade enemy ports	military tradition
Bull Run	Richmond
Chancellorsville	Robert E. Lee
defend own territory	smaller population
early defeats	"Stonewall" Jackson
Fredericksburg	Ulysses S. Grant
George McClellan	Vicksburg
George Pickett	Washington, D.C.
Gettysburg	William T. Sherman

MAKING PREDICTIONS

Suppose developments in the 1840s and 1850s had turned out differently. What consequences might such developments have had for later history? Study the following fictitious "events." For each event, make a prediction about its consequences and explain the reason for your prediction.

1. The Wilmot Proviso, which provides that the new territories acquired in the Mexican War will be closed off to slavery, passes both houses of Congress and becomes law.

2. Congress debates the Compromise of 1850 but is unable to reach agreement on the issue of slavery in the territories.

3. Angered over the Fugitive Slave Act of 1850, Harriet Beecher Stowe writes a vivid antislavery novel, *Uncle Tom's Cabin,* but she is unable to find a publisher for her book and, dejected and depressed, she moves to France.

4. Congress organizes the Kansas and Nebraska territories and decides to allow slavery there, thus repealing the Missouri Compromise.

5. The Supreme Court rules that because Dred Scott had been taken as a slave into free territory and lived there for a period of years, he is now a free man.

UNIT 6

The Emergence of Modern America: 1860-1900

…There is in all the past nothing to compare with the rapid changes now going on in the civilized world…. The snail's pace of crawling ages has suddenly become the headlong rush of the locomotive….

—HENRY GEORGE, *Social Problems,* 1883

SETTING THE SCENE

Time

Late nineteenth century

Mood

This was an age of optimism, coupled with a belief in the certainty of human progress. As pioneers continued to spread across the continent and immigrants flocked to industrial centers, Americans adapted to the rapidly changing environment in which they found themselves. Political corruption, social problems, and widespread agrarian unrest seemed overwhelming. Ultimately, faith in the political process led to needed reforms and to an overall improvement in the quality of life.

Themes

- Geography and Environment
- Conflict and Cooperation
- Influence of Technology
- Cultural Diversity

Key Events

- First transcontinental railroad
- Interstate Commerce Act
- Civil Service reform
- American Federation of Labor formed
- Sherman Antitrust Act
- Battle at Wounded Knee
- Populist Party formed
- Pullman strike

Major Issues

- Transcontinental railroads allow the rapid settlement of the Great Plains.
- A wealth of natural resources and abundant labor makes the United States a major industrial power.
- The swift growth of industry creates a demand for new labor unions.
- The alliance between government and big business leads to widespread political corruption.
- Agrarian unrest promotes new political movements that seek to regulate commerce.

◀ Capital and Labor in Accord, *printed cotton textile from Cocheo Manufacturing Company, Dover, New Hampshire, 1886*

501

Global Perspectives

By 1860 the entire world had become a marketplace. People became increasingly aware that what happened in other countries affected their own political, economic, and social life. New industrial technology and improved systems of transportation and communication brought nations closer together.

As Europe, in general, and England, in particular, became more and more urbanized, less food was raised on farms. Europe found itself importing food and raw materials and exporting manufactured goods. In the mid-1890s, when the European wheat crop fell by 30 percent, American farmers felt the impact. The

THE WORLD

	ASIA AND OCEANIA	AFRICA	EUROPE	SOUTH AMERICA	NORTH AND CENTRAL AMERICA
1860					
		1867 Diamond fields discovered in South Africa	1870 Germany unifies under Bismarck ▲		
1875		1874 British adventurer Henry Stanley explores the Congo			
			1882 Germany, Austria, and Italy form the Triple Alliance		
1890				1889 Brazil becomes a republic ▲	
	1894 Sino-Japanese War begins ▲				1895 Cubans revolt against Spanish rule
	1900 Boxer rebellion	1899 Boer War ▲			
1905					

demand for American wheat increased, and so did the prices that farmers received for it.

The United States also felt the impact of other events in Europe and elsewhere. In many areas, there was a new sense of nationalism. In Italy, Giuseppe Garibaldi worked to unite the nation. In 1871 his goal was achieved. In Germany Otto von Bismarck, the prime minister of Prussia, vowed that he would unite the German states. German victory over France in a brief war in 1870 helped achieve this goal. In Southern Africa British rule was solidified in a war against the Dutch Boers.

Political, industrial, and economic factors combined to attract millions of immigrants to American shores. Between 1880 and 1890, about 100,000 "new" immigrants arrived each year. Some established Americans, however, were not pleased that the country was becoming a "melting pot."

THE UNITED STATES

	PACIFIC AND NORTHWEST	SOUTHWEST	MIDWEST	SOUTHEAST	ATLANTIC NORTHEAST
1860		1860 The Pony Express is established			
	1869 First transcontinental rail route is completed			1870 H.R. Revels of Mississippi becomes the first black in Congress	
1875					1878 First electric light company is established
	1876 Sioux Indians defeat Custer at Little Big Horn ▼		1884 First steel-skeleton construction is begun, making it possible to build skyscrapers ▲		
1890					1892 Ellis Island becomes a receiving station for immigrants ◄
1905					

AMERICAN LITERARY HERITAGE

The Civil War shattered the illusions of many Americans, including writers. They had little use for the idealism of antebellum books. This postwar generation of writers depicted events and characters in the hard, cold light of reality.

Two masters of the new realism were Mark Twain and Hamlin Garland. In the first of the following selections, Twain applies a light touch to his account of a journey to Carson City with two miners. In the second selection, Garland paints a stark picture of farming in the late 1800s.

As you read, determine what each author is implying about human nature.

Mark Twain

Hamlin Garland

from *Roughing It*

The snow lay so deep on the ground that there was no sign of a road perceptible, and the snowfall was so thick that we could not see more than a hundred yards ahead, else we could have guided our course by the mountain ranges. The case looked dubious, but Ollendorff said his instinct was as sensitive as any compass, and that he could "strike a bee-line" for Carson City and never diverge from it. He said that if he were to straggle a single point out of the true line his instinct would assail him like an outraged conscience. Consequently we dropped into his wake happy and content. For half an hour we poked along warily enough, but at the end of that time we came upon a fresh trail, and Ollendorff shouted proudly:

"I knew I was as dead certain as a compass, boys! Here we are, right in somebody's tracks that will hunt the way for us without any trouble. Let's hurry up and join company with the party."

So we put the horses into as much of a trot as the deep snow would allow, and before long it was evident that we were gaining on our predecessors, for the tracks grew more distinct. We hurried along and at the end of an hour the tracks looked still newer and fresher—but what surprised us was, that the *number* of travelers in advance of us seemed to steadily increase. We wondered how so large a party came to be traveling at such a time and in such a solitude. Somebody suggested that it must be a company of soldiers from the fort, and so we accepted that solution and jogged along a little faster still, for they could not be far off now. But the tracks still multiplied, and we began to think the platoon of soldiers was miraculously expanding into a regiment—Ballou said they had already increased to five hundred! Presently he stopped his horse and said:

"Boys, these are our own tracks, and we've actually been circussing round and round in a circle for more than two hours, out here in the blind desert! By George this is perfectly hydraulic!"...

All agreed that a campfire was what would come nearest to saving us, now, and so we set about building it. We could find no matches....This was distressing, but it paled before a greater horror—the horses were gone! I had been appointed to hold the bridles, but in my absorbing anxiety...I had unconsciously dropped them and the released animals had walked off in the storm....

We were miserable enough, before; we felt still more forlorn, now....At this critical moment Mr. Ballou fished four matches from the rubbish of an overlooked pocket. To have found four gold bars would have seemed poor and cheap good luck compared to this. One cannot think how good a match looks under such circumstances— or how lovable and precious, and sacredly beautiful to the eye. This time we gathered sticks with high hopes; and when Mr. Ballou prepared to light the first match, there was an amount of interest centered upon him that pages of writing could not describe. The match burned hopefully a moment, and then went out. It could not have carried more regret with it if it had been a human life. The next match simply flashed and died. The wind puffed the third one out just as it was on the imminent verge of success. We gathered together closer than ever, and developed a solicitude that was rapt and painful, as Mr. Ballou scratched our last hope on his leg. It lit, burned blue and sickly, and then budded into a robust flame. Shading it with his hands, the old gentleman bent gradually down and every

heart went with him....The flame touched the sticks at last, took gradual hold upon them—hesitated—took a stronger hold—hesitated again—held its breath five heartbreaking seconds, then gave a sort of human gasp and went out.

Nobody said a word for several minutes. It was a solemn sort of silence; even the wind put on a stealthy, sinister quiet, and made no more noise than the falling flakes of snow. Finally a sad-voiced conversation began, and it was soon apparent that in each of our hearts lay the conviction that this was our last night with the living. I had so hoped that I was the only one who felt so....We put our arms about each other's necks and awaited the warning drowsiness that precedes death by freezing....

Then came a white upheaval at my side, and a voice said, with bitterness:

"Will some gentleman be so good as to kick me behind?"

It was Ballou—at least it was a tousled snow image in a sitting posture, with Ballou's voice.

I rose up, and there in the gray dawn, not fifteen steps from us, were the frame buildings of a stage station and under a shed stood our still saddled and bridled horses!

An arched snowdrift broke up, now, and Ollendorff emerged from it, and the three of us sat and stared at the houses without speaking a word. We really had nothing to say. We were like the profane man who could not "do the subject justice," the whole situation was so painfully ridiculous and humiliating that words were tame and we did not know where to commence anyhow.

A Forty-niner

from *Under the Lion's Paw*

askins worked like a fiend, and his wife, like the heroic woman that she was, bore all uncomplainingly the most terrible burdens. They rose early and toiled without intermission till the darkness fell on the plain, then tumbled into bed, every bone and muscle aching with fatigue, to rise with the sun next morning to the same round of the same ferocity of labor.

The eldest boy drove a team all through the spring, ploughing and seeding, milked the cows, and did chores innumerable, in most ways taking the place of a man.

An infinitely pathetic but common figure—this boy on the American farm, where there is no law against child labor. To see him in his coarse clothing, his huge boots, and his ragged cap, as he staggered with a pail of water from the well, or trudged in the cold and cheerless dawn out into the frosty field behind his team, gave the city-bred visitor a sharp pang of sympathetic pain. Yet Haskins loved his boy, and would have saved him from this if he could, but he could not.

By June the first year the result of such Herculean' toil began to show on the farm. The yard was cleaned up and sown to grass, the garden ploughed and planted, and the house mended.

Council had given them four of his cows.

"Take 'em an' run 'em on shares. I don't want 'o milk s'many. Ike's away s'much now. Sat'dys an' Sund'ys, I can't stand the bother anyhow."

Other men, seeing the confidence of Council in the newcomer, had sold him tools on time, and as he was really an able farmer, he soon had round him many evidences of his care and thrift. At the advice of Council he had taken the farm for three years, with the privilege of re-renting or buying at the end of the term.

A Veteran in a New Field *by Winslow Homer, 1865*

"It's a good bargain, an' y' want 'o nail it," said Council. "If you have any kind of a crop, you c'n pay y'r debts, an' keep seed an' bread."

The new hope which now sprang up in the heart of Haskins and his wife grew great almost as a pain by the time the wide field of wheat began to wave and rustle and swirl in the winds of July....

"'M, yes; 'm, yes; first-rate," said Butler, as his eye took in the neat garden, the pig-pen, and the well-filled barnyard. "You're gitt'n quite a stock around yeh. Done well eh?"

Haskins was showing Butler around the place. He had not seen it for a year, having spent the year in Washington and Boston with Ashley, his brother-in-law, who had been elected to Congress.

"Yes, I've laid out a good deal of money durin' the last three years. I've paid out three hundred dollars f'r fencin'."

"Um—h'm! I see, I see," said Butler, while Haskins went on:

"The kitchen there cost two hundred; the barn ain't cost much in money, but I've put a lot o'time on it. I've dug a new well, and I—"

"Yes, yes, I see. You've done well. Stock worth a thousand dollars," said Butler, picking his teeth with a straw... "I suppose you've kind o' calc'lated on stayin' here three years more?"

"Well, yes. Fact is, I think I c'n buy the farm this fall, if you'll give me a reasonable show."

"Um—m! What do you call a reasonable show?"

"Well, say a quarter down and three years' time."

Butler looked at the huge stacks of wheat, which filled the yard, over which the chickens were fluttering and crawling, catching grasshoppers, and out of which the crickets were singing innumerably. He smiled in a peculiar way as he said, "Oh, I won't be hard on yeh. But what did you expect to pay f'r the place?"

"Why, about what you offered it for before, two thousand five hundred, or pos-sibly three thousand dollars," he added quickly as he saw the owner shake his head.

"This farm is worth five thousand and five hundred dollars," said Butler, in a careless and decided voice.

"What!" almost shrieked the astounded Haskins. "What's that? Five thousand? Why, that's double what you offered it for three years ago."

"Of course, and it's worth it. It was all run down then; now it's in good shape. You've laid out fifteen hundred dollars in improvements, according to your own story."

"But you had nothin' t' do about that. It's my work an' my money."

"You bet it was; but it's my land."

"But what's to pay me for all my—"

"Ain't you had the use of 'em?" replied Butler, smiling calmly into his face.

Haskins was like a man struck on the head with a sandbag; he couldn't think; he stammered as he tried to say; "But—I never'd git the use—You'd rob me! More'n that you agreed—you promised that I could buy or rent at the end of three years at —"

"That's all right. But I didn't say I'd let you carry off the improvements, nor that I'd go on renting the farm at two-fifty. The land is doubled in value, it don't matter how; it don't enter into the ques-tion; an' now you can pay me five hun-dred dollars a year rent, or take it on your own terms at fifty-five hundred, or—git out"....

"It's stealin'.... You take three thou-sand dollars of my money—the work o' my hands and my wife's." He broke down at this point.

"But I don't take it," said Butler, cool-ly. "All you've got to do is to go on jest as you've been a-doin', or give me a thou-sand dollars down, and a mortgage at ten per cent on the rest."

Haskins sat down blindly on a bundle of oats near by, and with staring eyes and drooping head went over the situation. He was under the lion's paw. He felt a horrible numbness in his heart and limbs. He was hid in a mist, and there was no path out.

INTERPRETING LITERATURE

1. Were the men in *Roughing It* experienced western travelers? Explain.

2. Why does the narrator in the Twain selection find the group's situation humiliating?

3. Why is the phrase "the lion's paw" significant?

MAKING COMPARISONS
4. Which of the writers shows greater cynicism about the values that Americans held before the war?

CHAPTER 17
Opening the Trans-Mississippi West

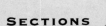

SETTING THE SCENE

Historical Focus

The settlement of the far West frontier was filled with hardships and tragedy as well as adventure. For native Americans, the slaughter of the buffalo and gradual expansion of white settlement meant the end of their way of life. For miners, ranchers, and farmers, life on the Great Plains meant long hours of work, a harsh climate, and isolation. Still, by 1890 when the Census Department declared the frontier closed, the vast region had been transformed into a land of farms, ranches, mining camps, and towns.

Concepts to Understand

- Why national **expansion** developed in the Great Plains region.
- How **conflict** between the Plains Indians and white settlers led to the destruction of Indian society.

People to Know

James J. Hill, John Chivington, Chief Joseph, Edna Ferber

Places to Locate

Promontory Point, Wounded Knee, Chisholm Trail

Terms to Identify

nomadic, Dawes Act, long drive, vigilance committees, "Westerns," Homestead Act, meridian, commodities

Guided Reading

As you read this chapter, seek the answers to the following questions.

1. What was the role of the railroads in the settlement of Great Plains?
2. How did life on the Great Plains measure up to settlers' expectations?

SPANNING THE DECADES

POLITICAL	1862 *Homestead Act is passed*	1864 *Sand Creek massacre in Colorado*	1869 *Union Pacific and Central Pacific railroads link; first transcontinental railroad*	1874 *Discovery of gold in the Black Hills of South Dakota*
1860			**1870**	
CULTURAL	1861 *The Pony Express gives way to the transcontinental telegraph*	1866 *First major "long drive" of Texas longhorns to Missouri*	1872 *Yellowstone National Park is created in Wyoming Territory*	1876 *Mark Twain publishes* Tom Sawyer

The Last of the Buffalo *by Albert Bierstadt, c. 1889*

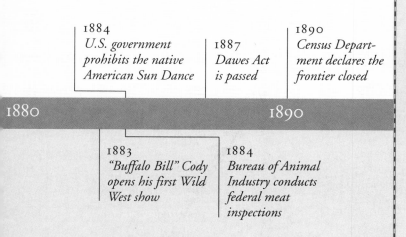

1884
U.S. government
prohibits the native
American Sun Dance

1887
Dawes Act
is passed

1890
Census Depart-
ment declares the
frontier closed

1880

1890

1883
"Buffalo Bill" Cody
opens his first Wild
West show

1884
Bureau of Animal
Industry conducts
federal meat
inspections

...The western country is rapidly filling up. A steady stream of immigration is following the railroad lines and then spreading right and left. The vacant places still existing are either worthless or will soon be exposed to the same invasion....What is to become of the Indians?...

—CARL SCHURZ
Secretary of the Interior, 1881

SECTION ONE

The Plains Indians Era

SETTING THE SCENE

When you first came we were very many, and you were few; now you are many, and we are getting very few, and we are poor.... Look at me. I am poor and naked, but I am the Chief of the Nation.

—RED CLOUD
Chief of the Teton Sioux, speech at Cooper Union, New York, July 16, 1870

Section Focus

The steady push of settlement across North America slowed when it reached the Mississippi River, fanned out along the rich river bottoms, then skipped over a thousand miles of treeless expanse before resuming again at the Pacific Coast. For a few years the United States government reserved most of the vast interior of the country to the native Americans because it believed these "Great Plains" to be too dry for farming. When whites began to infringe on these territories, they met determined resistance from the Plains Indians.

Objectives

After studying this section, you should be able to:
• Describe the Plains Indians' way of life.
• Give three reasons the Plains Indians' way of life came to an end.

The United States government assigned Major Stephen H. Long the exploration of the region beyond the Mississippi River in 1820. In his report, Long used the term "Great American Desert" to describe the territory—a term that soon appeared on all the maps of the West. Believing the land to be completely desolate, many who ventured to California and Oregon completely avoided it, choosing to travel by clipper ship around Cape Horn at the tip of South America. Some who attempted to cross the "desert" by wagon train lost hope and life in what Mark Twain called "one prodigious graveyard."

Nomadic Life Ends

The territory that early European explorers believed to be a desert was home to countless species of wildlife. Hundreds of millions of jack rabbits and "prairie dogs," millions of wolves and coyotes, and an estimated 12 to 15 million American bison, usually called buffalo, roamed the Great Plains.

The region was also home to many different native American nations. Some, like the Omaha and the Osage nations, lived in communities as farmers and hunters. Most of the Indians, however, including the Sioux [SOO], the Comanches [kuh MAN cheez], and the Blackfeet, were **nomadic** peoples, roaming vast distances, following their main source of food: the great herds of buffalo that lived on the plains.

For generations the nomadic people of the plains had only dogs to haul their possessions as they traveled from one hunting area to another. In the 1600s, horses, either traded or stolen from Spanish settlers in the Southwest, changed the Plains Indians' way of life. By the mid-1750s, almost every Plains Indian rode on horseback. Horses became a vital part of their social, economic, and political life. Comanches were perhaps the best riders, but the Sioux, Cheyenne [shy AN], Pawnee, Blackfoot, and Crow nations were nearly as skilled. In the deserts of the region that would become the states of Arizona and New Mexico, Apaches [uh PACH ees] and Navajos [NA vuh HOHS] captured horses to sell to northern Indians.

The horse made the Plains Indians much more effective hunters than they had been on foot. It became easier to

Examining Fine Art *Covered with wolf skins, George Catlin, the artist, and an Indian hunter get a close look at the buffalo, whose poor eyesight made it an easy prey. Why did the elimination of the buffalo destroy the Plains Indians' way of life?*

follow the buffalo, the Indians' source of food, skins for clothing and shelter, and bones for tools. The buffalo hunt not only yielded life's necessities, it provided sport, ritual, worship, and training for war. Fighting from horseback, the Indian warriors were better able to resist the encroachments of settlers and railroads. Captain Randolph B. Marcy's admiration for the Indians' skill is apparent in the following description:

It is when mounted that the prairie warrior exhibits himself to the best advantage.... his skill in various manoeuvers which he makes available in battle—such as throwing himself entirely upon one side of his horse and discharging his arrows with great rapidity toward the opposite side from beneath the animal's neck while he is at full speed—is truly astonishing.

Plains Indian nations often limited their alliances with other groups. Some, such as the Cheyenne and Arapaho [uh RAP uh HOH] established close friendships. But others, such as the Lipan [LIHP ahn] Apaches and the Utes [YOOTS], competed with one another for the same hunting lands or control of the same horse herds and sometimes became lasting enemies.

Railroads Open the West

A Dakota newspaper editor wrote, "Without the railroad it would have required a century to accomplish what has been done in five years." What was "accomplished" was the killing of nearly all the buffalo and other prairie life, the destruction of the Plains Indians' way of life, and the removal of any surviving Indians to reservations.

Railroad-building in the West began at a furious pace during the Civil War. The most dramatic achievement was the completion of the first transcontinental line in 1869. Discussion of this project started when gold was discovered in California in 1848. During the 1850s at least 10 routes were surveyed, and the Gadsden Purchase was acquired from Mexico principally because the Gila River valley provided the easiest route across the western plateau. Congress wanted to finance this huge project, but sectional rivalry caused delays. The South preferred that the eastern terminal be located at New Orleans; the North argued for St. Louis or Chicago. In 1862, with Southern representation temporarily withdrawn from Congress, the government passed an act to encourage the building of a Pacific Railroad. The Union Pacific Company was to build west from Omaha, while the Central Pacific Company was to run lines east from Sacramento. The federal government loaned money to both companies at the

Linking Across Time

INDIAN TREATIES

In the nineteenth century, the United States negotiated hundreds of treaties with various Indian nations across the continent. These were usually enforced very selectively, if at all. Provisions that benefitted the tribes were neglected or ignored. Those that benefitted miners, ranchers, or settlers were enforced.

In the last half of the twentieth century, many Indian groups have gone to court seeking to redress grievances caused by uneven enforcement of treaties. The courts have given several favorable settlements to native Americans.

rate of $16,000, $32,000, or $48,000 per mile, according to the terrain. Each company also received land grants along the right-of-way averaging 640 acres per mile.

Construction proceeded rapidly as the two lines raced to get more government money and land. At the height of the competition, the Union Pacific builders employed 10,000 workers. Irish immigrant crews working for the Union Pacific and Chinese immigrants working for the Central Pacific sometimes laid as much as 10 miles of track a day—a remarkable feat because the digging and grading were done by hand. The Central Pacific had a difficult time in the Sierra Nevada ranges with snow that sometimes collected in drifts 60 feet deep. Its heavy equipment was carried from the East 19,000 miles around Cape Horn to California by a fleet of 30 ships.

On May 10, 1869, the "wedding of the rails" took place at Promontory Point, Utah. The whole country celebrated as a transcontinental telegraph reported the blow of a silver sledge hammer driving a golden spike to complete the railroad. A magnetic ball dropped from a pole on the top of the Capitol in Washington, D.C.; in Chicago a seven-mile procession paraded through the streets; in small towns citizens rang church bells.

The first transcontinental line was soon followed by others—the Northern Pacific; the Atchison, Topeka, and Santa Fe; the Southern Pacific; and the Great Northern. Beginning in 1879, James J. Hill built the Great Northern, connecting the state of Minnesota and the Washington Territory, without government help. By encouraging settlement as soon as the rails were laid, Hill assured that his line would have customers. He offered free transportation from eastern ports, credit, farm machinery, and even gave farmers free advice on how to improve crops. Hill's careful construction of the Great Northern kept maintenance costs down and enabled him to charge lower rates. As a result, his railroad became the leading carrier in the Northwest.

The railroads played a major role in the extermination of the buffalo. Formerly ranging eastward as far as Pennsylvania and the Carolinas, the buffalo's natural habitat was the Great Plains where they migrated north and south with the seasons. The Union Pacific Railroad effectively cut the huge herds in half. At first buffalo hunting supplied meat for railroad workers, but later it became "sport" for city vacationers to shoot the animals from train windows. In 1871 it was discovered that buffalo leather could be sold at a profit. Professional hunters killed millions for their hides. Train loads of bones were shipped east to make fertilizer or charcoal. By 1886 only a few hundred buffalo were left, deep in the Canadian woods.

Examining Illustrations *Chinese immigrants to America built snowsheds to keep the rails clear of avalanches in the Sierra Nevadas. How was construction of the transcontinental railroad financed?*

Plains Wars

To protect their lands and to stop the waste of the buffalo, Plains Indians had to fight. For two and one-half centuries they had maintained their way of life against Spanish, English, French, and American invaders. The last battles against overwhelming forces proved futile. The military effort to remove the Indians from the plains was relentless with the United States spending an estimated million dollars for each adult male Indian killed.

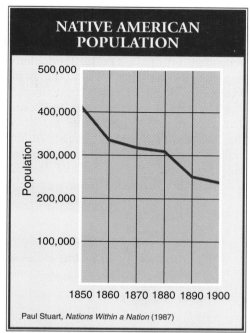

NATIVE AMERICAN POPULATION

Paul Stuart, *Nations Within a Nation* (1987)

Examining Graphs *Census figures show a declining native American population before 1900. The United States army fought the Plains Indians from 1869 to 1890. In what ten-year period did this fighting take its heaviest toll?*

The first concentrated fighting broke out in Colorado, just after the Civil War started in the East. Government officials tried to force the Arapaho and Cheyenne from an area that had been granted to them "forever" ten years earlier. Warfare continued for three years until Black Kettle, the Cheyenne Chief, was trapped at Sand Creek in eastern Colorado by Colonel John Chivington. The militia ignored Black Kettle's repeated attempts to surrender and killed men, women, and children.

In 1862 the Santee Sioux of Minnesota attacked a group of white settlers who had moved into their hunting lands. After the militia defeated them, the Sioux were forced to move to Indian reservations in the Dakota Territory. A short time later, the Oglala [oh LGAH lah] Sioux became enraged at the territorial government's plans to build a road through their sacred lands. Led by Red Cloud, they successfully resisted for several years. In the end, however, the Sioux lost their land to miners searching for gold in the Black Hills.

After the bloody war with the Sioux, humanitarians in the East called for a change of government policies. The United States divided responsibility for the native Americans between the Department of the Interior and the War Department. The Department of the Interior first was to placate Indians with gifts and to establish reservations; the War Department was to make war on those who resisted.

In 1867 the federal government sent a peace commission to meet with representatives of several nations, including the Comanches, Kiowas [KY uh WOHS], Cheyenne, and Arapaho. This effort to end the constant warfare produced agreements that stipulated the Indians were to live on two major reservations on the Great Plains,

Life of the Times

INDIAN SCHOOLS

In the 1870s and 1880s, the federal government passed legislation and instituted policies designed to assimilate native Americans into white society. Education figured prominently in the plan for assimilation. If Indian children were removed from their parents and traditional cultures, the thinking went, they would more readily absorb the skills, knowledge, and values of white society.

Most of the 106 Indian day and boarding schools operated by the federal government in 1881 were on or adjacent to reservation land. However, white educators believed that native American children would learn more and be assimilated more quickly if they attended nonreservation boarding schools. Native American parents showed reluctance to whites who came to recruit their children for boarding school. For example, parents were particularly reluctant to send their daughters away from home. They understood that it would change the children's values. One mother of an especially bright 10 year-old girl refused to let her daughter go off to an industrial training school without her. Education and civilization, the mother explained, would make the child regard her mother as a savage. In the end, this mother was allowed to accompany her child to school.

one in Oklahoma and one in the Dakota Territory. Not all nations were involved, however, so conflicts between the Indians and the army continued.

With the discovery of gold in the Dakota Territory in 1874, miners flooded into Sioux and Cheyenne lands. Two years later the Sioux, led by chiefs Sitting Bull and Crazy Horse, attacked the miners and settlers. The conflict came to a climax in June 1876 at the Little Bighorn River, where a large group of Cheyenne and Sioux were camped. General George Custer attacked, but the Indians killed Custer and all of his troops at the Battle of the Little Big Horn. The Sioux victory meant only a brief reprieve. In 1881 they surrendered for a final time to the United States Army.

The final clash between the army and the Indians occurred at Wounded Knee, South Dakota, in December of 1890, where more than 190 unarmed Indians were killed. With this tragic encounter, the wars came to an end.

Although Plains Indian nations fought hundreds of battles from 1860 to 1890, their cause was doomed because they were dependent on the buffalo for food, clothing, fuel, and shelter. When the herds were wiped out, resistance became impossible. In spite of some victories and heroic deeds, such as the 1,500-mile march of the Nez Percés (NEHZ PUHRS) under Chief Joseph in 1877 to avoid capture, the result was inevitable. Chief Joseph's speech at his surrender summarized the hopelessness of the Indian cause:

———— ✧ ————

Our chiefs are killed…. The little children are freezing to death. My people…
have no blankets, no food…. Hear me, my chiefs; I am tired; my heart is sick and sad. From where the sun now stands, I will fight no more forever.

———— ✧ ————

Examining Fine Art
Kicking Bear painted this description of the Battle of the Little Big Horn. Sitting Bull, Rain-in-the Face, Crazy Horse, and the artist are standing in the center. What did the Sioux victory mean?

UNIT 6 THE EMERGENCE OF MODERN AMERICA: 1860-1900

Examining Fine Art The Song of the Talking Wire *(detail) by Henry Earney contrasts two civilizations. The telegraph eliminated the Indians' advantage of surprise attacks. What eventually destroyed all Indian resistance?*

In 1887, three years before Wounded Knee, Congress passed the Dawes Act, which broke up Indian nations, even on the reservations. The Dawes Act gave each family 160 acres to cultivate. After a probation period of 25 years, an Indian was granted ownership of the land and United States citizenship.

The Dawes Act was the result of humanitarian opposition to the U. S. Army's extermination policy. In 1881 Helen Hunt Jackson had written *A Century of Dishonor,* a book that criticized the government policy toward native Americans. Unfortunately, the new legislation did more harm than good. Plains Indians were nomadic peoples whose way of life was based on the buffalo hunt. They did not understand the fine points of land ownership, knew little about farming, and were demoralized by reservation life. Between 1887 and 1943, native Americans lost to real estate speculations and dishonest government agents an estimated 86 million acres of the 138 million acres that had been set aside for them.

★ ★ ★ ★ ★ ★ ★ ★ ★ ★ ★ ★ ★ ★ ★ ★ ★

Section One Review

★ ★ ★ ★ ★ ★ ★ ★ ★ ★ ★ ★ ★ ★ ★ ★ ★

SUMMARY

With the completion of the first transcontinental railroad line, settlement of the plains accelerated, followed by further removal of native Americans from their lands. Settlement also brought unrestrained slaughter of the buffalo—on which nomadic Plains Indians depended for food and shelter. The Plains Indians responded by attacking settlers. After years of bloodshed, the United States army forced survivors onto reservations. The Plains Indians' way of life was destroyed.

CHECKING FOR UNDERSTANDING

1. **Identify** Sioux, Promontory Point, James J. Hill, Sitting Bull, Little Big Horn, Wounded Knee

2. **Define** nomadic

3. **Contrast** the lifestyles of the Osage and the Omaha with the Sioux and the Comanches.

4. **Explain** how the expansion of the railroads benefited some people at the expense of others.

5. **Enumerate** the events that eventually brought an end to the Plains Indians' way of life.

THINKING CRITICALLY

6. **Formulating Hypotheses** Why did the United States government fight unrelenting wars against Plains Indians in spite of the high cost in both money and lives?

LINKING PAST AND PRESENT

7. **Making Comparisons** Following a major oil spill in 1989, Alaskan salmon fishers received compensation from Exxon Oil Company for the damage done to their salmon breeding grounds. What similarities and differences do you see between this and the slaughter of the buffalo?

★ ★ ★ ★ ★ ★ ★ ★ ★ ★ ★ ★ ★ ★ ★ ★ ★

Ranching and Mining

*O bury me not on the lone prairie
Where the wild coyotes will howl o'er me
In a narrow grave just six by three;
O bury me not on the lone prairie!*

—"THE DYING COWBOY"
A prairie song, late 1800s

Section Focus

The image of the "Old West" that inspired romantic tales for over a century is based on the realities of two industries: cattle ranching and mining. The removal of the buffalo and the Indians from the plains, as well as the opening of eastern markets by the railroad, introduced the great days of the cattle ranchers. Discoveries of more gold and silver in the western mountains lured thousands of fortune-seekers to the mining towns.

Objectives

After studying this section, you should be able to:
• Explain the role of the environment in the rise and fall of the long drive.
• Identify the realities behind the myths of the "Old West."

The open-range cattle industry started in Spanish Texas. The Spanish brought the techniques of herding on horseback, roping, and the roundup to the Americas. From the Spanish, too, came the distinctive dress and equipment of the cowhand. The cattle in Texas were mainly Spanish in origin, although some were brought by American and French settlers to Texas when it was part of Mexico.

The Cattle Kingdom

After the Texas revolution in 1836, **mavericks,** or unbranded cattle, multiplied on the open range. An estimated 330,000 head of cattle in 1850 grew to between 3 and 4 million head by 1860. There were so many that they could be bought for as little as $3 or $4 a head in Texas. After the Civil War, opportunity developed for great profit in the cattle industry as growing cities of the North provided huge markets for meat. There were, however, no direct railroad lines from Texas to the North. The result was the **long drive.** As the spring of 1866 turned the grasslands green, cowhands drove herds of steers to railroad shipping centers in Missouri and Kansas. The routes of the long drives became known as trails—such as the Chisholm Trail from near San Antonio to Abilene, a station on the Kansas Pacific Railroad.

Examining Illustrations *After the Civil War many blacks took demanding jobs as cowhands driving cattle north. Why were cattle worth more in Chicago than in Texas?*

Examining Fine Art *Charles Russell lived among the cowhands he painted.* Cowboy Camp During the Roundup *is full of color and motion. Cowhands received about $25 to $30 pay per month and all the adventure they wanted.* What were the dimensions of the Cattle Kingdom in 1885?

A single herd might number 2,500 and be attended by 8 to 10 cowhands, a trail boss, and wranglers to care for the horses. The life of a cowhand on the trail demanded discipline, endurance, and courage, but it paid well to those who survived. More than 30,000 cowhands may have ridden the trails to deliver cattle from Texas to the North. Several thousand of these were African Americans, free to earn their first wages after the Civil War.

Life in the cattle towns was exciting, but many cowhands told exaggerated tales of daring that multiplied as dime novels—books of stories that sold for a dime—spread the myths of the "Wild West" in eastern towns and cities. A typical tale was *The Life and Adventures of Nat Love: Better Known in the Cattle Country as "Deadwood Dick"—By Himself.* Love was an authentic black cowboy whose story became part of the romance of the West.

For the investor, the profits obtained from a successful cattle drive were enormous. As the buffalo were cleared from the plains, the Cattle Kingdom expanded northward until, by 1885, it covered an area half as large as Europe, extending from Texas to Montana. From the East, even from Great Britain and France, people with cash to invest and a taste for adventure put their money in cattle.

Although offering vast profits, the industry was beset by difficulties. Steers could go blind from drought, drown in flash floods, die in stampedes, or get infected by the dreaded Texas fever. They might be stolen by rustlers or shot by angry homesteaders trying to protect their crops. The open-range cattle industry collapsed even more rapidly than it had risen. Too many animals were put on the ranges, and overgrazing resulted. Overproduction drove prices down. Sheepherders and homesteaders competed with the cattle ranchers for land.

Nature helped to end the long drives. The cold winter of 1885 and 1886 was followed by a summer so dry that the grass withered and streams disappeared. In the following winter, 1886 and 1887, terrible blizzards covered the ground with snow so deep that the cattle could not paw down to grass. Next came an

Linking Across Time

AMERICAN COWBOYS

The cowboy hero is one of America's unique contributions to literature. This character has taken on many roles. He is a loner and totally self-sufficient. He has a strong code of honor and is incorruptible. He avenges injustice and rights wrongs singlehandedly; the law simply gets in his way. He first appeared as a sole pioneer on the frontier, Natty Bumppo. He then developed into a "real" cowboy. Numerous television series from "Gunsmoke" to "Bonanza" extolled his virtues. In the movies he was played by Tom Mix, John Wayne, and Clint Eastwood. Today he is Rambo, or perhaps James Bond. But even with an English accent, he is all-American.

unprecedented cold spell, with temperatures ranging as low as -60°F. "When spring finally came," wrote historian Ray Allen Billington:

Cattlemen saw a sight they spent the rest of their lives trying to forget. Carcass piled upon carcass in every ravine, gaunt skeletons staggering about on frozen feet, trees stripped bare of their bark....

The cattle industry survived this terrible blow, but the day of the open range was over. From then on herds were raised on fenced-in ranches, English Herefords replaced longhorns, and the cowhand became a ranchhand.

The Mining Frontier

The discovery of gold in California was just the beginning of prospecting in the West. Inspired fortune seekers moved to California, then spread east into the Great Basin and Rocky Mountain regions. A gold strike in Colorado in 1858 set off a stampede to the region the next year:

The first breath of spring started the hordes westward. Steamboats crowded to the rails poured throngs of immigrants ashore at every Missouri River town.... All through April, May, and June they left the jumping-off places in a regular parade of Conestoga wagons, hand carts, men on horseback, men on foot—each with "Pike's Peak or Bust" crudely printed on their packs and wagon canvas.... By the end of June more than 100,000 "fifty-niners" were in the Pike's Peak country.

The Colorado strike was followed by many other finds; gold in the Black Hills of Dakota, copper in Montana, and silver in many places. The Comstock Lode at Virginia City, Nevada, yielded about $300 million worth of silver ore between 1859 and 1877. These discoveries attracted swarms of fortune seekers, and new mining towns appeared overnight.

Human life was cheap in these communities of tents and crude dwellings, with their rows of saloons and gambling houses.

Examining Illustrations *These miners in the Auburn Ravine, like so many others, were lured to the West by rumors of easy fortunes. Most miners stayed to take up other occupations. How many "fifty-niners" went to Pikes Peak?*

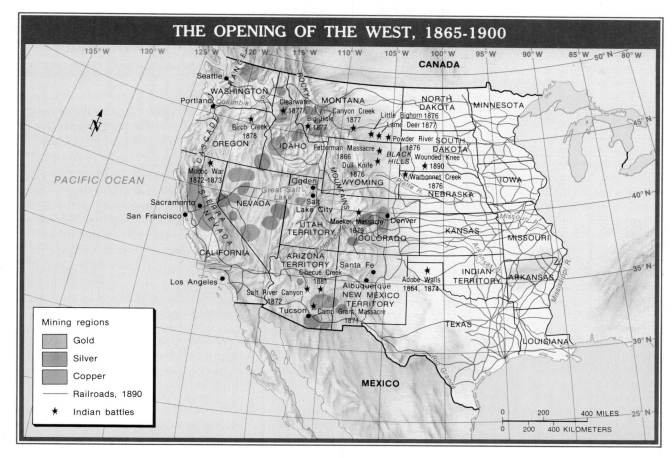

THE OPENING OF THE WEST, 1865-1900

Mining regions
- Gold
- Silver
- Copper
- Railroads, 1890
- ★ Indian battles

Examining Maps *Although 35 years of settlement had changed the face of the West, by 1900 much of this territory remained unsettled. The 27 percent of the nation's population that lived there remained concentrated in larger towns such as San Francisco, Los Angeles, and Denver. The population was growing rapidly, however. Between the end of the Civil War and the turn of the twentieth century, nearly every state in the West had been touched by railroad building, precious metals mining, and battles with Indians. In what area were most of these battles concentrated?*

There was a vital need for law enforcement agencies to settle disputes over mining claims and to punish or prevent crime. Self-appointed volunteers called **vigilance committees,** sometimes provided law and order. Other times mass meetings drew up their own rules and elected their own officials. Soon the different communities of a region such as Colorado or Nevada would band together and demand territorial status or statehood. Usually the actual grant of statehood came with the arrival of homesteaders and miners, because cattle raisers were too nomadic to provide stable government.

The "Wild West" captured the imagination of Americans immediately. Dime novels and popular ballads spread the adventures of Wild Bill Hickok, Billy the Kid, and Jesse James. A Wild West Show became part of Barnum and Bailey's circus; and Annie Oakley, the sharpshooter, appeared on **vaudeville,** or live variety show, stages everywhere. The Wild West period lasted little more than 30 years, yet its fascination has continued in storybooks and comics, western songs and costumes, and **"Westerns"**—movies produced by Hollywood and shown at the movie theater or on television.

The romance of the Wild West conceals some of the truth. The conquest of the Plains and the Rockies by the invading cattle ranchers, miners, and homesteaders destroyed natural resources, wildlife, and human beings. Charles Marion Russell, a frontier artist gave this sobering message in a speech to "forward-looking citizens" in Helena, Montana:

I have been called a pioneer.... a pioneer is a man who comes to a virgin country, traps off all the fur, kills off all the wild meat, cuts down all the trees, grazes off all the grass, plows the roots up, and strings ten million miles of wire. A pioneer destroys things and calls it civilization. I wish to God this country was just like it was when I first saw it and that none of you folks were here at all.

AMERICAN PORTRAITS

CHARLES M. RUSSELL
1864-1926

Born in St. Louis, Charles Russell much preferred to watch the fur traders and men who worked along the Mississippi River than to attend school.

In 1880, at the age of 16, Russell set out for Montana to work as a cowhand and to observe native American life. He began to paint life as he saw it, creating realistic scenes of the untamed West: cowhands riding bucking broncos, Indians hunting buffalo, and outlaws holding up stagecoaches. Little realizing the value of his paintings, he often gave them away. By the early 1890s, however, Russell was able to stop cowpunching and devote himself solely to art. By 1920 Russell's portrayals of cowboys and Indians commanded high prices, and he was recognized as one of the finest artists of the American West.

★★★★★★★★★★★★★★★★★★★★★

Section Two Review

★★★★★★★★★★★★★★★★★★★★★

SUMMARY

Due to demand for beef in the growing cities and the abundance of inexpensive longhorns, a huge and profitable Cattle Kingdom developed rapidly as an open range industry. It collapsed even more rapidly as a result of overgrazing, falling prices due to overproduction, and several seasons of unfavorable weather. Meanwhile, the opportunities created by precious metal discoveries drew settlers ever farther west. In spite of its destruction of life and resources, the Old West inspired romantic myths perpetuated by stories, songs, clothing, and films.

CHECKING FOR UNDERSTANDING

1. **Identify** Chisholm Trail, Nat Love, Cattle Kingdom, Comstock Lode, Annie Oakley

2. **Define** mavericks, long drive, vigilance committees, "Westerns"

3. **Summarize** the rise and fall of the open-range cattle industry.

4. **Locate** the precious metal mines that attracted people to the West.

5. **Examine** the realities of life that inspired the romanticized myths of the "Old West."

THINKING CRITICALLY

6. **Predicting Outcomes** Had the open range system continued, what conflicts could have developed as the farmers settled the plains?

CONNECTIONS: HISTORY AND GEOGRAPHY

7. **Recognizing Human-Environmental Interaction** Throughout history people have adapted themselves to features of the environment in which they live. Point out how the Plains Indians and people in the cattle industry adapted to the terrain and the climate of the Great Plains.

★★★★★★★★★★★★★★★★★★★★★

Farming Moves West

We see the farmer with pleasure and respect.... Put him on a new planet and he would know where to begin; yet there is no arrogance in his bearing, but a perfect gentleness.

—RALPH WALDO EMERSON
"Farming," 1870

Section Focus

For years the Great Plains resisted settlement. The most fundamental reason for farmers' unwillingness to venture into the great ocean of grass was not the Plains Indians; it was the totally new environment. Three forces worked to overcome the farmers' hesitation: new agricultural technology, the western expansion of the railroads, and European immigration.

Objectives

After studying this section, you should be able to:
- List three factors that made farming the Plains possible.
- Summarize the problems faced by Plains farmers.

In 1862 Congress passed the Homestead Act, enabling a head of a family to acquire a 160-acre farm for $10. To ensure that the land went to actual settlers, the act required that the owner must reside on or cultivate the land for five years. The act was passed as a result of nearly half a century of agitation by western farmers and eastern laborers. But the Homestead Act did not work out as planned. Through fraud, speculators rather than actual settlers gained possession of much land. The law required that a would-be homesteader put up a home and cultivate the land. Speculators paid relatives or employees to lay down a few logs as a "foundation" and scatter a few grains of corn. After five years they collected title to a large tract. A more important reason for the ineffectiveness of the Homestead Act was that much of the most desirable land near the railroad lines was usually controlled by the railroad companies themselves.

Farming the Great Plains

Before the plains could be settled, farmers had to be convinced that they could overcome the disadvantages of the dry environment. In the East a farmer could get water from a stream or by digging a well 10 to 20 feet deep. In the plains few streams ran all year-round, and underground water was 30 to 300 feet down. The American farmer had always depended on trees for fuel, buildings, and fences. On the plains, trees were found only in the bottomlands near rivers.

Some of the difficulties of farming the plains were overcome by technology from the Industrial Revolution. Cheap iron and steel made possible the iron-encased drilled well and the cast-iron windmill. Joseph Glidden sold his first barbed-wire in 1874, making up for the lack of wooden fence rails.

Improved agricultural machinery cut the cost of raising crops. The reaper, in general use by 1865, was followed by the mechanical binder, which tied the grain into sheaves as fast as it was cut. By the 1880s two people and a team of horses could harvest and bind 20 acres of wheat a day. The steam-driven threshing machine also came into general use. In addition to solving technical problems, the Industrial Revolution created a vast new urban population and expanded the market for food, both in America and Europe.

The ineffectiveness of the Homestead Act provided Westerners with a grievance but did not interfere with settlement. Although railroads sometimes discouraged the acquisition of free land, they actively promoted

would easily find husbands. "When a daughter of the East is once beyond the Missouri," said one railroad advertisement, "she rarely recrosses it except on a bridal tour."

To offset the myth of the "Great American Desert," a new myth was created. Some "experts" said that rainfall on the Great Plains would increase with the planting of trees or with simple cultivation; a Nebraska promoter summed it up in the catchy epigram, "Rain follows the plow."

As the plains were opened, the production of wheat, centering in Minnesota, the Dakotas, Kansas, and Nebraska, quadrupled. Wisconsin, too far from the market to send fresh dairy products, used its surplus milk for cheese production. Near every great city, truck gardens provided fresh vegetables.

Sod House Reality

The life of a Great Plains farmer seldom approached the railroad agents' glowing prophecies. The climate that was supposed to cure all known diseases turned out to be severe. In the summer the temperature might go over 100°F for days at a time. In winter there were periods of extreme cold, and terrible blizzards drove the snow through every chink in doors and windows. Families could be stranded in sod houses for many days. Prairie fires were a constant danger in the spring and fall. Sometimes huge swarms of grasshoppers appeared, as if from nowhere, to eat everything green, choke wells to the brim, break the branches off fruit trees by their weight, and even devour tool handles.

Worst of all disasters was drought. The normal rainfall of the plains region was markedly less than that of the wooded East, dropping from about 30 to 40 inches along the 98th **meridian,** or line of longitude, to as little as 10 inches just east of the Rockies.

The greatest push westward into the Great Plains took place in the early 1880s, during a cycle of wet years that offered false promises of abundant crops. In the late 1880s, drought returned to drive thousands back east in despair. William Allen White, editor of the Emporia

the sale of their own. They did not charge high prices because they wanted settlers to get the land into production. In fact the most important factor in promoting settlement was the railroad. A spectator of the Dakota boom of the early 1880s wrote:

*You may stand ankle deep in the short grass
of uninhabited wilderness; next month
a mixed train will glide over the waste and
stop at some point where the railroad
has decided to locate a town. Men, women,
and children will jump out of the
cars, and their chattels [personal property]
will tumble out after them. From that
moment the building begins.*

Land-grant railroads had "Bureaus of Immigration" to persuade farmers to settle along their lines. They maintained offices in the principal European cities and agents in eastern seaports to meet immigrants as they left the boat. Steamship companies and western states advertised the region as so healthy that it cured all known diseases. The industrious person could expect to become wealthy; an $8,000 investment, it was claimed, might soon result in a steady income of $11,000 per year—an enormous sum considering that a 160-acre farm was homesteaded for $10. The West was pictured as a place where unmarried women

Connections

HISTORY AND GEOGRAPHY

THE GREAT AMERICAN DESERT

To Americans accustomed to well-watered, timbered lands east of the Mississippi River, the Great Plains seemed a vast and forbidding desert. The 100th meridian marked the line west of which annual rainfall was less than 20 inches. Farther west the annual rainfall was even less. Aquifers—strata of water-bearing rock—

Homestead of Harriet Conn, c. 1890 Thomas County, Kansas

lay much farther below the surface than they did in the East, making hand-dug wells impractical.

The general aridity of the Great Plains region caused explorers to label the area a desert. Major Stephen Long, leading an army expedition to explore the Great Plains in 1819, stated that ". . . it is almost wholly unfit for cultivation. . . . The scarcity of wood and water, almost uniformly prevalent, will prove an insuperable obstacle in the way of settling the country." Long prepared a map, labeled the region the Great American Desert, and influenced Americans' perception of the plains for decades. Almost every map published between 1820 and 1860 used Long's label. Americans' misconception about the plains delayed settlement until new technology-drilling machines and the windmill-tapped deep aquifers. Until the water runs out, technology has conquered geography.

★ ★ ★ ★ ★ ★ ★ ★ ★ ★ ★

MAKING THE GEOGRAPHY CONNECTION

1. The absence of what resources led people to think of the Great Plains as a desert?

2. How would settlers adapt to the environment?

LINKING PAST AND PRESENT

3. How might the "mining" of aquifers affect people on the Great Plains today?

★ ★ ★ ★ ★ ★ ★ ★ ★ ★ ★

Gazette, described a family he saw returning from western Kansas:

―――≈∞≈―――

There came through Emporia yesterday two old-fashioned mover wagons headed east. The stock in the caravan would invoice four horses, very poor and very tired, one mule more disheartened than the horses, and one sad-eyed dog.... These movers ...had seen it stop raining for months at a time. They had heard the fury of the winter wind as it came whining across the short burned grass.... They have tossed through hot nights, wild with worry, and have arisen only to find their worst nightmares grazing in reality on the brown stubble in front of their sun-warped doors.

―――≈∞≈―――

In spite of all the difficulties, most settlers managed to adjust to their physical environment. Water from deep wells enabled them to plant gardens and trees around their homes. Railroads brought lumber and brick for houses to replace sod huts and coal to replace cornstalks or hay as fuel.

Plains farmers faced a second problem at least as frustrating as the weather. They were in the grip of economic forces beyond their control. Formerly, out of necessity as subsistence farmers, they produced almost everything they needed. The independent farmer was admired in literature and melodramas, especially when contrasted with unhappy factory hands, the idle rich, or "city slickers." With the opening of great urban markets, however, farmers tended to specialize. Some farmers grew a single cash crop, such as wheat or corn; others might specialize in dairy production or cattle raising. Their incomes went up, but so did their expenses. Large-scale farming required agricultural machinery. The need to buy clothing and food made farmers less independent.

A farmer's prosperity, perhaps even the ownership of the farm, might depend on the unpredictable price of grain in an international market. Farmers also became dependent on the railroad, which carried their crops to market, on the commission merchant who marketed it, and on the owners of grain elevators who stored it. Farmers who raised hogs or beef cattle were in a similar situation; they had little bargaining power and were forced to take whatever the meat packers paid.

Farming on the plains demanded large investments of money to drill wells, put up windmills, enclose fields in barbed wire, and buy machinery. Because few farmers could pay with cash, they had to borrow by mortgaging their land. Then, to pay interest on the mortgages, they were forced to concentrate more than ever on raising cash crops. If prices dropped or a lean year came, they could not meet their payments and lost their land. By 1900 about one-third of the farms in the corn and wheat areas were cultivated by tenants.

Not surprisingly, farmers protested. Even though they fed the cities, and supplied the **commodities,** or economic goods that paid for European investments, the wealth they created seemed to be siphoned off to others. Their attitude was expressed by a Nebraska newspaper:

There are three great crops raised in Nebraska. One is a crop of corn, one a crop of freight rates, and one a crop of interest.
One is produced by farmers, who sweat and toil, from the land.
The other two are produced by men who sit in their offices and behind their bank counters and farm the farmers.

For women, life on the plains often meant solitude and drudgery. "Born and scrubbed, suffered and died," is the epitaph given a woman in one of Hamlin

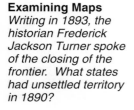

Examining Maps
Writing in 1893, the historian Frederick Jackson Turner spoke of the closing of the frontier. What states had unsettled territory in 1890?

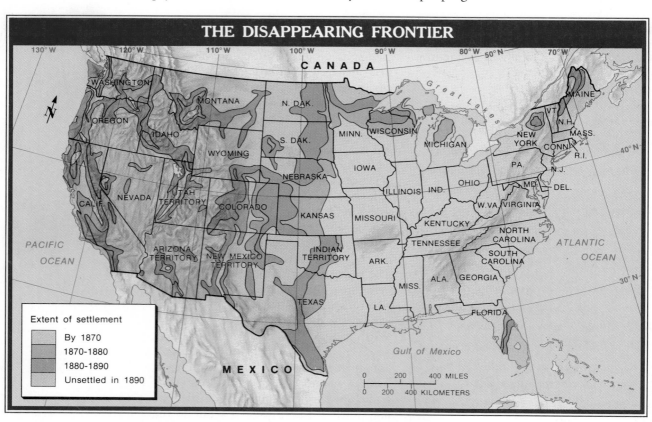

THE DISAPPEARING FRONTIER

CANADA

WASHINGTON
OREGON
IDAHO
MONTANA
N. DAK.
S. DAK.
WYOMING
NEVADA
UTAH TERRITORY
CALIF.
COLORADO
NEBRASKA
KANSAS
ARIZONA TERRITORY
NEW MEXICO TERRITORY
INDIAN TERRITORY
TEXAS
MINN.
WISCONSIN
IOWA
MISSOURI
ILLINOIS IND.
MICHIGAN
OHIO
KENTUCKY
TENNESSEE
ARK.
MISS.
ALA.
GEORGIA
LA.
FLORIDA
NEW YORK
PA.
N.J.
MD. DEL.
W.VA. VIRGINIA
NORTH CAROLINA
SOUTH CAROLINA
MAINE
VT.
N.H.
MASS.
CONN.
R.I.

Great Lakes

PACIFIC OCEAN
ATLANTIC OCEAN
Gulf of Mexico
MEXICO

Extent of settlement
By 1870
1870-1880
1880-1890
Unsettled in 1890

0   200   400 MILES
0   200   400 KILOMETERS

Garland's poems. Yet the settlement of the West owed much to the endless toil of frontier women. A character in Edna Ferber's novel *Cimarron* pays this tribute:

You can't read the history of the United States... without learning the great story of those thousands of unnamed women... women in mud-caked boots and calico dresses and sunbonnets, crossing the prairie and the desert and the mountains enduring hardship and privation. Good women with a terrible and rigid goodness that comes of work and self-denial. Nothing picturesque or romantic about them, I suppose... no, their story's never really been told. But it's there just the same. And if it's ever told straight, you'll know it's the sunbonnet and not the sombrero that's settled this country.

Women have written some of the best accounts of plains life, such as Ferber's *Cimarron* and *My Antonia* by Willa Cather. While not minimizing the sufferings of pioneering, these novels reveal how much easier life became after the sod house days were past. Willa Cather described Black Hawk, Nebraska, the locale of *My Antonia*:

...[A] clean, well-planted little prairie town, with white fences, and good green yards about the dwellings, wide, dusty streets, and shapely little trees growing along the wooden sidewalks.

Cather mentioned a prominent building in Black Hawk—a new brick high school. As soon as farm communities had the funds, they established churches and schools. The Morrill Act helped states to establish universities. These were open to women as well as men; women had gained a new position of equality.

Examining Illustrations
Colorado women brand a steer on the family ranch in 1890. What new equality did the Morrill Act provide?

Farmers, however, were losing status. For years they had been held up as the most admirable and the happiest of people. A member of Congress supporting free homesteads in 1851 had said:

The life of a farmer is peculiarly favorable to virtue; and both individuals and communities are generally happy in proportion as they are virtuous.... His life does not impose excessive toil, and yet it discourages idleness. The farmer lives in rustic plenty, remote from the contagion of popular vices, and enjoys, in their greatest fruition, the blessings of health and contentment.

By the 1880s power and prestige had shifted from the rural areas to the cities. "Captains of industry" won the admiration of the public and urban America regarded country people not as the backbone of the nation, but as unsophisticated and backward.

In 1890 the Census Bureau reported that settlement had been so rapid "that there can hardly be said to be a frontier line." In reality, much land was still unoccupied, and new settlement continued at a brisk pace into the twentieth century, but the news that the frontier was closing encouraged prophets of doom, who saw the end of an era. They believed that the existence of unoccupied land at the frontier had provided a "safety-valve of social discontent," the idea that Americans could always make a fresh start.

Plains Literature

The farmers' struggle produced a literature quite unlike the romance of the Wild West. Cowhands and miners were usually young and their lives were adventurous. Homesteaders, on the other hand, took on long-term responsibilities; they invested in tools and land, and started to raise a family. When misfortune struck, patience was their virtue. Because of these differences, literature about farming the plains was realistic, sometimes bitter. This can be seen in the stories of Hamlin Garland, who was born on a Wisconsin farm in 1860. Garland's family moved west three times during his boyhood. In books such as *Main-Travelled Roads* and *A Son of the Middle Border,* he told "a tale of toil that's never done." Although describing moments of joy such as harvest time, or of beauty as when the spring touched the plains, Garland refused to say that "butter was always golden and biscuits invariably light and flaky." "I will not lie," he wrote, "even to be a patriot. A proper proportion of the sweat, flies, heat, dirt, and drudgery shall go in."

The railroads enticed so many immigrants from Scandinavia to the wheat country that by 1890, 400 Minnesota towns bore Scandinavian names. Letters written to relatives back home described the wonders of the new land. "Here it is not asked," wrote one, "what or who was your father, but the question is, what are you?" Another wrote of the pleasure of eating white bread every day and pork three times a week. But they told of troubles too: Indian raids, prairie fires, locusts, and loneliness. Such struggles provide the subject of one of the greatest novels of the Great Plains, O.E. Rölvaag's *Giants in the Earth,* written in Norwegian. It describes the heroic efforts of Per and Beret Hansa to establish a farm in South Dakota. The farm is built, but the human cost is terrible: Beret goes slowly mad, and Per dies in a blizzard.

The Great Plains had offered the individual family a chance to be independent in the farming business. By the 1880s, however, it was apparent to most farmers that to survive they would have to unite.

★ Section Three Review ★

SUMMARY

In 1862 the Homestead Act made farms more available. Railroads later encouraged the settlement of the plains, not only by making settlement practical, but by actively promoting it to ensure customers on their lines. Settlers began to farm once profitable farming of the Great Plains was made possible by new technology. Unfortunately the technology was expensive, forcing farmers to mortgage their farms and to specialize in single cash crops. This left them vulnerable to price fluctuations as well as to the harsh environment. Many farmers still failed financially, though, in spite of backbreaking toil by both men and women.

CHECKING FOR UNDERSTANDING

1. **Identify** Homestead Act, Morrill Act, Willa Cather, Hamlin Garland

2. **Define** meridian, commodities

3. **Describe** the changes that made the West profitable for farmers.

4. **List** the problems the environment created for the Plains farmers.

5. **Explain** the role of the railroads in settling the Great Plains.

THINKING CRITICALLY

6. **Analyzing Transfer of Risk**   In the 1800s farmers began to sell "futures," that is, to contract months in advance to sell a crop to a grain merchant for a certain price. What are the advantages and disadvantages to the farmer of selling crops this way? What are the problems to the grain merchant?

CONNECTIONS: HISTORY AND TECHNOLOGY

7. **Relating Problem and Solution** What geographic features of the Great Plains created needs for new agricultural technology? How did technology answer these needs?

Map and Graph Skills

Analyzing Map Data

You can sometimes tell how good a new movie is by looking at the lines of people waiting to see it. If the lines are long, chances are the movie is good. Very short lines or none at all may tell you the movie is only fair to poor. Although not always accurate, this kind of data can be used to judge how good a movie might be.

Likewise one way to tell how good agriculture will be in an area is to look at the amount of rainfall it receives. Analyzing data on rainfall helps you judge whether an area's agricultural potential is good, fair, or poor. The plains farmers had no way of doing this as accurate records of rainfall on the Great Plains did not then exist.

that collect data about rainfall. This data can be separated and organized so that it provides a

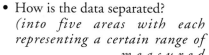

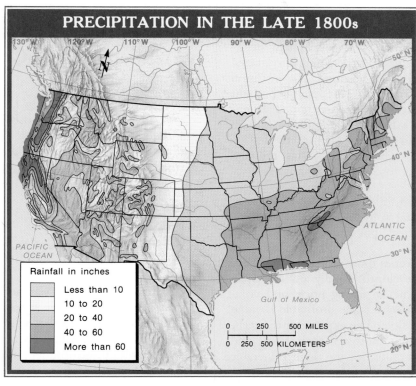

PRECIPITATION IN THE LATE 1800s

PACIFIC OCEAN

ATLANTIC OCEAN

Gulf of Mexico

Rainfall in inches

Less than 10
10 to 20
20 to 40
40 to 60
More than 60

0   250   500 MILES
0 250 500 KILOMETERS

comparison of different amounts and different geographic areas. This gives a basis by which to judge the agricultural potential of different areas.

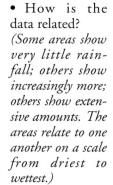

• How is the data separated? *(into five areas with each representing a certain range of measured rainfall)*

• How is the data related? *(Some areas show very little rainfall; others show increasingly more; others show extensive amounts. The areas relate to one another on a scale from driest to wettest.)*

• What judgments can you make? *(Agricultural potential was best in the eastern, southern, and western coastal areas and poorest in the western plains and mountain areas. As one went from east to west, agricultural potential went from good to fair to poor. Farming on the plains was difficult because of the small amount of rain, especially as one traveled farther west.)*

Explanation

Analysis is the process of separating data into its various parts and seeing how they relate to one another. Once you have analyzed data, you can then make better judgments based on it. For example, instruments exist today

Example

Analyze the data on the climate map of the United States by answering the following questions:

• What data is shown on the map? *(the amount of rainfall in inches that fell over all of the United States during the late 1800s)*

Practice

For further practice in analyzing map data, answer the same questions while studying the map showing the various climates of the United States in the Appendix of this book.

★ Chapter 17 Review ★

★ Summary

Settlers moving west had avoided the Great Plains for decades, convinced that the area was a vast desert. For years the federal government had debated the need for a transcontinental railroad. Americans celebrated the completion of this line in 1869. When other railroads crossed the Plains in the decades following the Civil War, the myth of a "Great American Desert" began to disappear. The government determined to open the Plains to settlers and encouraged families to "homestead" large acreages. The intrusion of railroads and settlement of the plains brought wars with native Americans. The unrestrained slaughter of the buffalo—on which nomadic Plains Indians depended for food and supplies—helped to destroy an entire way of life. The United States military, after years of bloodshed, forced survivors onto reservations.

Settlement accelerated following the completion of the first transcontinental railroad. Railroads not only made settlement practical, but they promoted it to ensure customers.

Precious metal discoveries drew settlers to the West. A Cattle Kingdom developed rapidly on the open range, then collapsed due to falling prices and unfavorable weather. Technology made profitable farming of the Great Plains possible. The expense of the technology forced farmers to mortgage their farms and specialize in single cash crops, leaving them vulnerable to price fluctuations as well as the harsh environment.

★ Using Vocabulary

Explain why each of these terms is used in a chapter about opening the West.

nomadic	**mavericks**
long drive	**vigilance committees**
Westerns	**meridian**
commodities	

★ Reviewing Facts

1. **Describe** the lives of the nomadic Plains Indians.
2. **Give** reasons why the Plains Indians' way of life came to an end.

3. **List** the factors that drew settlers to the West.
4. **Contrast** the open-range cattle industry with the system that replaced it.
5. **Specify** the changes that made farming attractive on the Great Plains.
6. **Discuss** the hardships faced in settling the Old West.

★ Understanding Concepts

EXPANSION

1. During the 1700s and early 1800s, most expansion took place east of the Mississippi. What changes and developments accelerated expansion west of the Mississippi?
2. What part did railroads play in the westward expansion?

CONFLICT

3. Explain the conflicts between native Americans and settlers. What groups today might oppose unrestrained development and fencing of wilderness areas?
4. Conflict on the Plains was not confined to Indian wars. Open-range cattle ranchers often came into conflict with sheepherders and homesteaders. How might the interests of an open-range cattle industry conflict with those of other settlers?

★ Thinking Critically

1. **Assessing Changes** How did the change from a nomadic to a reservation lifestyle affect native Americans?
2. **Linking Past and Present** The English Channel tunnel is due to be completed in 1993. How does this tunnel's completion compare in its importance to the British with the completion of transcontinental railroad to Americans?
3. **Correcting Stereotypes** Imagine that you have been asked to direct the making of a Western film. What ideas would you recommend to correct some false notions about the Old West?
4. **Recognizing Effects** How did the railroads benefit from encouraging farmers and immigrants to settle near their rail lines?

★ Chapter 17 Review ★

★ Writing About History

NARRATION

Refer to the description of how to write a narrative essay in the History Writer's Handbook in the Appendix of this book. Your teacher will give you more specific instructions on the essay's length and the assignment's due date.

In the 1870s railroads greatly improved travel by shortening travel time and smoothing the ride. Nevertheless, people who ventured on long journeys by train faced some difficulties. Crossing the Plains was still an adventure because the area was sparsely settled and government was just beginning to establish control and order. Write a day's entry in the diary of a seventeen-year-old traveling west by rail in 1870. Include details about the geographic features, the hardships, and the traveler's reactions.

★ Learning Cooperatively

Your group will research either the details of life during the days of the open-range cattle industry or the same details as depicted in Westerns. Divide the research assignments so that each group member is responsible for a different aspect of real life or life in a Western.

The group that researches Westerns will find rental video tapes of Westerns produced since the 1940s very helpful. The group that researches real life during the open-range cattle industry should also find library materials that give an accurate account. Two good sources are *Cowboys of the Wild West* by Russell Freedman and *The Day of the Cattleman* by Earnest Staples Osgood. Your teacher may have other suggestions.

After each group has completed its research and written notes, then the groups should create two dramatizations of an event during a roundup or a long drive. Remember that the long drive usually culminated in a railroad town such as Abilene, Dodge City, or Sedalia, where cowhands sold their cattle to buyers from the larger cities. The first dramatization should depict the event as it may have been shown in a Western, and the second should present it as it would have happened in real life. Each should last from four to six minutes. Create both realistic and romanticized characters and dialogue. After rehearsing, present your dramatizations to the class.

★ Mastering Skills

IDENTIFYING THE VALUES OF A CULTURE

When you buy a popular brand of jeans or tennis shoes, you are expressing a value of modern American culture, that of having the right material possessions. In Jon Hassler's novel, *North of Hope,* a value of sharing is demonstrated when Chippewa Indians in northern Minnesota pass a ladder from one family to another, regardless of ownership. This example shows that the Chippewa do not place the same value on material possessions as do most white Americans.

Each culture has its own set of values, or customs and beliefs. The values of any culture are expressed in its art, religion, and politics and are reflected in its everyday life. Each individual living in a culture learns its values as a normal part of life. It may be difficult for a person to identify many of his or her own cultural values unless they are contrasted with those of another culture. For this and other reasons, it is helpful to learn the values of differing cultures through study.

Example   Two methods can be used to identify the values of a culture. One is to examine sources such as a textbook. Note the practices of the people of the culture. From these, you can determine important values. For example, you read in your textbook about Per and Beret Hansa, characters from a Norwegian novel who attempted to establish a farm in South Dakota in the late 1800s. From this account, you can determine that Norwegian settlers valued land ownership, farming, and hard work.

The other method of identifying cultural values is to examine the source for the expression of a belief or idea and then check for evidence that supports it. For example, your textbook states that "human life was cheap" among fortune seekers in the mining towns of the West. To check this, you could read to find out whether the miners' actions demonstrated a disregard for life. Since your textbook states that there was a "vital need for law enforcement," you may conclude that the belief is correct.

Practice   For further practice in this skill, reread Chapter 17 and find library resources on the nomadic Plains Indians. While these groups did not see themselves as one entity, their cultures and values were actually very similar. Using the two methods described, determine and list the major values of the Plains Indians.

CHAPTER 18
The Rise of Industrial America

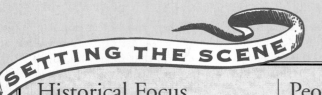

SETTING THE SCENE

Historical Focus

The United States developed into a great industrial power in the latter decades of the nineteenth century. By 1900 U.S. industrial production was the first in the world. This remarkable economic growth was the result of many factors—cheap labor, abundant raw materials, new technology—but also of new forms of business organization. The empires of industrialists such as Andrew Carnegie epitomized this new business spirit.

Concepts to Understand

- Why business leaders believed that **individual initiative** benefited all of society.
- How lack of **government restriction** helped large companies but hurt small ones.

People to Know

Thomas Edison, Horatio Alger, John D. Rockefeller, Ida Tarbell

Places to Locate

Cleveland

Terms to Identify

entrepreneurs, railroad consolidation, corporation, trusts, rebate, philanthropy, Sherman Antitrust Act

Guided Reading

As you read this chapter, seek the answers to the following questions.

1. What factors caused American industry to grow so rapidly?
2. How were Andrew Carnegie and John D. Rockefeller able to become industrial giants?

SPANNING THE DECADES

POLITICAL	1881 *James Garfield inaugurated as 20th President*	1884 *Congress established the Federal Bureau of Labor*	1887 *Tenure of Office Act repealed*

1870   1880

CULTURAL	1873 *Andrew Carnegie begins to build his steel company*	1876 *Alexander Graham Bell invents the telephone*	1879 *Thomas Edison invents the first practical electric light*	1882 *Standard Oil Trust formed* 1883 *Standardized time zones adopted by U.S. and Canadian railways*

The Gun Foundry *by John Ferguson Weir, ca. 1875*

1890
Sherman
Antitrust
Act passed

1893
Colorado grants
women the right
to vote

1890

1900

1901
U.S. Steel Corporation
formed; first company
capitalized at over one
billion dollars

*...I ascribe the success of the
Standard [Oil Company] to its consistent
policy to make the volume of its
business large through the merits and
cheapness of its products. It has spared
no expense in finding, securing, and
utilizing the best and cheapest methods
of manufacture....*

—JOHN D. ROCKEFELLER
Testimony before the U.S. Industrial
Commission, 1899

Industrialization Takes Hold

SETTING THE SCENE

...[T]he close of the war with our resources unimpaired gives an elevation, a scope to the ideas of leading capitalists, far higher than anything ever undertaken in this country before. They talk of millions [of dollars] as confidently as formerly of thousands.

—JOHN SHERMAN
U.S. Senator, in a letter to General William T. Sherman, 1865

Section Focus

The tremendous industrial growth that occurred in the United States after the Civil War resulted from foundations that had been laid over the previous half-century. As settlement reached beyond the Mississippi River, agriculture flourished in the South and Midwest, and manufacturing increased in the Northeast. A transportation network spread people, products, and information across the nation. Yet greater growth was ahead.

Objectives

After studying this section, you should be able to:
- Identify and explain the factors that encouraged industrial growth.
- Discuss the railroad's role in the growth of industry.

Unlike the South, the North emerged virtually undamaged by the Civil War, its railroads and factories intact. Furthermore, the war and Reconstruction eliminated Southern planters as rivals to Northern industrialists for political power, allowing industrial growth to proceed at an even greater pace. Although interrupted by depressions in 1873 to 1878, 1882 to 1884, and 1893 to 1896, America's industrial production doubled every 12 to 14 years. By the 1880s the United States had overtaken Great Britain as the world's industrial leader.

Although historians differ over the relative importance of the reasons for industrial growth after the Civil War, they generally agree that several factors combined to support its rapid development.

Natural and Human Resources

The United States contained tremendous deposits of the natural resources upon which industry depended—coal, iron ore, and petroleum. Before the war, these deposits had scarcely been touched. By the 1860s, however, methods for extracting and utilizing these resources were well developed.

Mineral resources were abundant in several regions of the country. The amount of coal mined in the United States more than doubled in every decade between 1840 and 1890. By the 1870s, vast deposits throughout the Appalachians from Pennsylvania to Alabama were being mined. Completion of the Soo Canal between Lake Superior and Lake Huron in 1855 allowed ships to move iron ore mined from large deposits in Michigan and Wisconsin to iron and steel mills on the lower Great Lakes.

The American oil industry got its start in 1859 in western Pennsylvania when the first successful well was drilled. By 1900 oil fields extended as far west as Texas. Production had risen from 2,000 barrels per year in 1859 to 64 million barrels per year in 1900.

The human resources available to American industry were as important as the mineral resources. European capitalists sometimes had difficulty recruiting labor for new industries. Children of working class families often were raised to follow traditional occupations, and in the European countryside peasants frequently were reluctant to leave their home villages. In the United States, however, labor was more mobile. Workers came to new jobs in cities the way pioneers moved to new lands.

Between 1860 and 1890, America's population more than doubled, rising from 31 million to nearly 75 million. The flood of immigration that had begun in the 1840s continued, contributing to this growth. Pulled by opportunities in America—and pushed out by the lack of them at home—14 million immigrants arrived between 1860 and 1900, more than twice the number of the previous 40 years. Many of these immigrants were adult males, eager to find employment. These newcomers enlarged the labor pools that gathered wherever jobs were available, which helped keep industrial wages low.

Public Policies and Private Investment

American industry developed within a free enterprise system. Whereas European governments exerted controls over manufacturing and trade, Americans embraced a philosophy of *laissez-faire,* which comes from the French phrase meaning "let alone." As a result, American industries developed with few government restraints.

Some government policies actually encouraged industrialization. American **entrepreneurs,** or business organizers, sought and received special favors from Congress. Liberal immigration laws insured a steady supply of cheap labor. High protective tariffs encouraged American industries and raised manufacturers' profits by keeping out foreign goods. The federal government sold public lands containing vast mineral resources for a small proportion of their true values and assumed about one-third of the cost of building western railroads. It gave railroads grants of money totaling more than

$700 million and gave them public lands throughout the West equaling the size of Texas.

In the United States, business attracted and held people of high ability and ambition. While European entrepreneurs often retired when they acquired enough money to buy their way into the upper class, Americans regarded money-making itself as a worthwhile goal. "Such opportunities for making money," wrote Thomas Mellon, a Pittsburgh judge who became a banker, "never existed before in all my former experience."

The money to be made in American manufacturing and transportation attracted private investors. The savings of New Englanders—accumulated from the West

Life of the Times

WORKING-CLASS TENEMENTS

Working-class incomes varied greatly during the late nineteenth century. For example, in 1889 a carpenter earned $686 annually; a laborer, $384; and a young girl in a silk mill, only $130. The carpenter ate meat or eggs, hotcakes, butter, and cake for breakfast. The laborer and silk worker had only bread and butter for two meals out of three. The carpenter lived in a comfortable, spacious house. Most working-class people like the laborer and the silk worker crowded together in tenements designed to house as many families as possible.

Living conditions in tenements were primitive. Beds often consisted of boxes filled with straw. Few buildings had indoor plumbing, and in those that did, several families shared a bathroom. Living areas were cramped.

Rags, bones, and other garbage piled up outside, freezing in winter and reeking in summer. Disease festered in the pervasive dirt and vermin.

Working-class men and women developed a community life as vibrant as their physical surroundings were bleak. Frequently this life was based on ethnic ties. Irish Americans gathered in taverns and parish churches. Jewish Americans organized Hebrew schools and Yiddish-speaking literary groups. Most immigrant groups and African Americans developed social clubs, storefront churches, and mutual-aid societies.

Indies and China trade, from clippers and whalers, from textile mills and shoe manufactures—helped build hundreds of factories and thousands of miles of railroad track. An equally important source of private capital was Europe, especially Great Britain. By 1900 British investors owned $2.5 billion in American railroad securities—more than twice the national debt of the United States.

Science and Technology

A flood of important inventions helped increase America's productive capacity and improved the network of transportation and communications that was vital to the nation's industrial growth. As American universities, influenced by German education, extended their activities beyond teaching, they became important centers of scientific research.

The American public knew little of the university professors who extended the boundaries of science. But it was greatly impressed with inventors like C. Latham Sholes, a Wisconsin printer whose idea for a typewriter in 1868 revolutionized business communications.

Equally inventive was Alexander Graham Bell, an immigrant from Scotland. Bell's profession was teaching children to speak. He applied his speech training to developing the principles upon which the telephone is based before he knew enough about electricity to build one. In 1876 he sent the first telephone communication to his laboratory assistant in the next room, "Mr. Watson, come here; I want you." A year later he demonstrated the commercial value of his invention by sitting in Boston and talking with Watson in New York—and the Bell Telephone Company was founded. By 1886 more than 250,000 phones were in use, mostly in businesses—creating jobs for thousands of women as switchboard operators in offices throughout the United States. By 1900 rates had been lowered, and telephones began to appear in American homes.

Examining Photographs *The telephone made business communications quick and personal. Telephone operator was the first American occupation considered to be strictly "women's work." Which person in this photograph is likely the manager? Why?*

UNIT 6 THE EMERGENCE OF MODERN AMERICA: 1860-1900

Examining Artifacts *After Edison's improvements, the first typewriters were produced in 1874 by E. Remington and Sons, a gun manufacturer. The first model printed only in capital letters. How did typewriters benefit business?*

Perhaps even more famous than Bell was Thomas Alva Edison, who has been erroneously given credit for inventing the electric light, the phonograph, and moving pictures. Edison actually made few original discoveries. Instead, he was a great innovator who put the inventions of others to practical use. For example, Edison's redesign of Sholes's typewriter permitted people to type faster than they could write. His improvement of Bell's telephone allowed voices to be transmitted longer distances. His work on improving the telegraph led to one of his few actual inventions, the phonograph. The laboratory he founded in 1876 at Menlo Park, New Jersey, and staffed with highly skilled technicians, was the forerunner of today's industrial research laboratories.

The incandescent electric light had been demonstrated in Britain in 1840. But it was Edison who, in 1879, developed cheap methods of supplying power and wire, as well as filaments that lasted more than just a few minutes. The incandescent bulb lighted America's cities and made industrial production possible 24 hours a day.

As technology exploded, its effect was felt almost everywhere in the United States. During the Civil War, soldiers in the Union army had received some rations in cans, an innovation that demonstrated the value of canned food. After the war the canning industry improved its methods, and by 1900 machines had been designed to make, fill, and seal cans. A large variety of canned foods, not always available as fresh produce, began to appear on the shelves of the nation's stores.

America's textile industry had long depended on machines to turn fibers into cloth. In 1893 the invention of the Northrup automatic loom led to the manufacture of cloth at an even faster rate. Bobbins, which had previously been changed by hand while the loom was stopped, were now changed automatically without stopping the loom.

Great changes also occurred in the clothing industry. Standard sizes, developed from measurements taken of Union soldiers during the Civil War, were used

Examining Illustrations *In the 1850s a Yale University professor developed a process to convert oil into kerosene to light lamps. Soon oil fields such as this one were pumping so much oil that by 1861 the price of a barrel dropped from $16 to 49 cents. In what other ways did technology contribute to industrial growth?*

in the manufacture of ready-made clothes sold in the nation's new department stores and by mail order. Power-driven sewing machines and cloth cutters rapidly moved the clothing business from small tailor shops to large factories.

Similar changes took place in shoe-making. New processes and inventions made **economies of scale** possible in the shoe industry. In other words, large factories could mass produce shoes more cheaply and efficiently than smaller companies and could pass these savings on to their customers in the form of lower prices. By the turn of the century, local cobblers had nearly disappeared. Prices of many other products also dropped as the United States became an industrial nation.

Much of the nation's phenomenal industrial growth was made possible by earlier advances in specific industries. For example, the Bessemer process revolutionized

American steelmaking in the 1870s. As steel was increasingly used for products such as machines, rails, and building beams, industry in general began to expand. The boom in the oil industry, along with the development of oil-lubricated machine tools—metal lathes, punches, and drill presses used to make other machines—brought tremendous growth in the country's industrial capability.

New technology also stimulated the growth of the railroad industry. Steel produced by the Bessemer process enabled the railroad companies to replace iron rails and expand their operations because steel held up better and carried heavier loads. The Westinghouse air brake allowed the cars and locomotives to stop simultaneously—another factor making longer trains and heavier loads possible. Kerosene lamps, and later electric lights, provided better headlights for nighttime travel.

Examining Maps *After the first transcontinental railroad was completed in 1869, travel time from the Atlantic Ocean to the Pacific Ocean was reduced from a month to a week. More track was laid in the 1880s than in all the years between 1828 and 1870. Why did transportation improvements encourage industrial growth?*

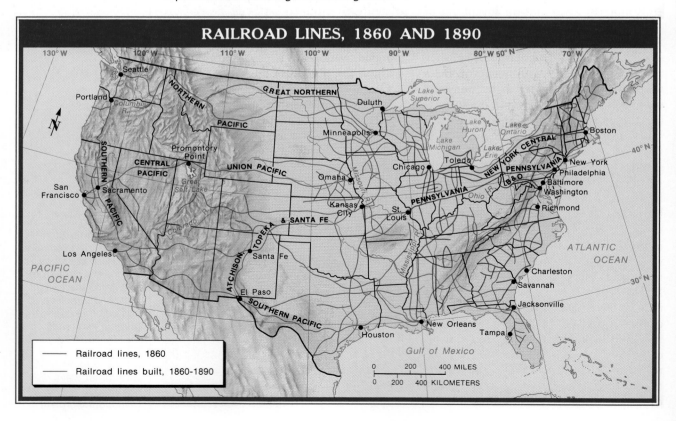

RAILROAD LINES, 1860 AND 1890

Railroad lines, 1860
Railroad lines built, 1860-1890

Connections

HISTORY AND GEOGRAPHY

STANDARD TIME ZONES

Throughout most of the nineteenth century, few Americans could agree on the time of day because every community determined its own time by the position of the sun. When it was noon in New York City, for example, it was 11:55 A.M. in Philadelphia and 11:47 A.M. in Washington, D.C. Railways, however, required a single standard of time for scheduling

Grand passenger station, Chicago

and routing. In huge countries such as the United States, more than a single time zone was required. In 1883 American and Canadian railroads established standardized time zones.

In 1884 delegates from 27 nations met in Washington, D.C., and divided the earth into 24 time zones. The base time zone was established with the prime meridian (0° longitude) as its midpoint. This zone extended about $7\frac{1}{2}$ degrees on either side of the prime meridian. Since the prime meridian ran through Greenwich in Britain, the time in the base zone became known as Greenwich time.

The time zones are not equally divided in 15-degree intervals. The zones deviate considerably to suit the needs of the people living within them. The International Date Line, which runs through the Pacific Ocean at roughly 180 degrees longitude, is the point where one loses a day if traveling east or gains a day if traveling west.

MAKING THE GEOGRAPHY CONNECTION

1. Why did standardized time zones become necessary in the 1800s?

LINKING PAST AND PRESENT

2. If time zones were being set up today, do you think the base zone would be in Britain? Why or why not?

Railroad Building

Perhaps no other single factor was more responsible for the growth of American industry than the expansion of the nation's railroads. At the end of the Civil War, there were 35,000 miles of railroad track in the United States, of various gauges, or widths between the two rails. By the mid-1870s the amount of track had doubled and by 1890 more than doubled again. In 1900 passenger and freight trains steamed along almost 200,000 miles of rails in the United States. This was more than 40 percent of the world's track and more than all the track in Europe and Russia combined. By then track also was laid according to a standard gauge—4 feet, $8\frac{1}{2}$ inches–wide—so that freight could move from line to line without having to unload it from one car and reload it onto another. This standardized railroad network bound all sections of the country into one market and one nation.

Trains could carry bulky products long distances quickly and cheaply, making it possible for businesses to sell their goods across the continent. In 1860 railroads carried less than half as much freight as inland waterways. By 1890 railroads carried five times as much.

Railroads were not only the biggest shippers of industrial products; they were also American industry's best customers. In the mid-1880s, for example, rails were the single most important product of American steel companies. In addition, construction and operation of railroads required huge amounts of coal to power locomotives, lumber for ties and cars, iron for bridges, and petroleum products to lubricate moving parts.

The consolidation of smaller lines in the Midwest, East, and South was as important to the nation's development as the building of great railroads to span the West. Railroad building east of the Mississippi River generally was intended to

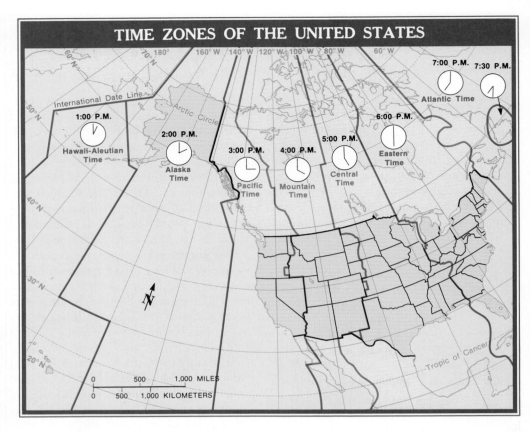

TIME ZONES OF THE UNITED STATES

Linking Across Time

RAILROADS

Cars, trucks, and airplanes have made railroads less profitable in this century. But rising fuel costs and ecological concerns have revived interest in trains, especially for mass transit. Commuter rail lines can carry 70 times as many people as highways, yet cost one-tenth as much to build and use only 1 percent of the fuel. Pollution-plagued southern California plans a rail system that will cover 150 miles and carry 500,000 passengers a day.

promote specific cities or to serve local needs. As a result, hundreds of unconnected small lines existed after the Civil War, with tracks of varying gauges. The South, for example, had more than 400 railroads averaging less than 40 miles each. The challenge facing eastern capitalists was to create a single rail transportation system from this maze of small companies.

Railroad consolidation proceeded rapidly from the end of the Civil War to the turn of the century. More than two-thirds of the nation's railroads were absorbed by the other one-third. In the 1880s about 400 railroads became controlled by other lines. By 1890 the Pennsylvania Railroad was a consolidation of 73 smaller companies with more than 5,000 miles of track. The Southern Railway had pieced together companies with 8,500 miles of lines. Eventually most rail traffic was controlled by 7 giant systems with terminals in major cities and scores of branches reaching into the countryside.

In gaining and using such power, many railroad builders and consolidators became tough, ruthless, and unethical competitors

who amassed huge fortunes in the course of their activities. Railroad consolidator Jay Gould sold small lines that he owned to large railroads that he controlled at prices far above the small railroads' actual worth. When railroad builder Collis Huntington remarked "It takes money to fix things," he meant bribing government officials, not repairing equipment! In describing his industry, railroad executive Charles Francis Adams, Jr., observed:

Honesty and good faith are scarcely regarded. Certainly they are not tolerated at all if they interfere with a man's getting his "share of the business." Gradually this demoralizing spirit of low cunning has pervaded the entire system. Its moral tone is deplorably low....That healthy mutual confidence...between man and man does not exist in the American railroad service taken as a whole.

One of the most famous, and most successful, railroad consolidators was Cornelius Vanderbilt, a tough former boat captain who built the New York Central system. Vanderbilt liked to be called "the Commodore" because he got his start as owner of a Staten Island ferry. By the mid-1850s, he had built the largest steamboat fleet in America. Yet the Commodore saw that the future of transportation was in railroads. So at age 73 he merged 3 short New York railroads he had purchased to form the New York Central, running from New York City to Buffalo. Within 4 years Vanderbilt extended his control over lines all the way to Chicago. In addition to bringing many lines under one management, Vanderbilt made great improvements in service. He was one of the first to use the Westinghouse air brake and the very first to lay a four-track main line—two tracks for freight and two for passenger traffic.

In accomplishing his goals, Vanderbilt, like most other railroad tycoons, was a combination of shrewd speculator, ruthless competitor, and visionary. In business deals the Commodore often showed little respect for either law or the public interest. He was one of the first to practice "insider trading," rigging the stock market to force prices up or down as he pleased and driving other companies into bankruptcy in the process.

Yet Vanderbilt, and other entrepreneurs who made the railroad America's first national business, provided great benefits, too. Standard-gauge track was universally accepted and standard time zones were established to simplify scheduling. The big systems were able to improve equipment, to shift cars from one section of the country to another according to seasonal needs, and to speed long-distance transportation. They made railroad operation so much more efficient that the average rate per mile for a ton of freight dropped from 2 cents in 1860 to three-fourths of a cent in 1900. The railroad executives also showed entrepreneurs how to organize and operate large companies across great distances, an example that was successfully followed in other industries.

Section One Review

SUMMARY

Following the Civil War, abundant resources, a large and mobile labor force, immigration, protective tariffs, government policy favorable to business, and private and foreign investment combined to produce an explosion of industrial growth. By the 1880s, the United States had become the world's leading industrial nation. Technological advances in manufacturing equipment, communications, and transportation fueled a further acceleration of growth. In particular, the railroads facilitated industrial expansion, both as transporters of goods and as heavy buyers of industrial products.

CHECKING FOR UNDERSTANDING

1. **Identify** Alexander Graham Bell, Thomas Alva Edison, Cornelius Vanderbilt

2. **Define** entrepreneurs

3. **List** reasons for the growth of American industry.

4. **Describe** how specific technology accelerated the growth of industry.

5. **Explain** the contribution of the railroad in the growth of industry.

THINKING CRITICALLY

6. **Applying Ideas** "This standardized railroad network bound all sections of the country into one market and one nation." Name some standardizing influences that exist in the United States today.

CONNECTIONS: HISTORY AND GEOGRAPHY

7. **Relating Place and Transportation** What physical characteristics and settlement patterns of the United States might make the railroad more important in late-nineteenth-century America than in a European country such as France or Germany?

The Growth of Big Business

SETTING THE SCENE

[Consolidation] has revolutionized the way of doing business all over the world. The time was ripe for it. It had to come, though all we saw at the moment was the need to save ourselves from wasteful conditions.... The day of combination is here to stay. Individualism has gone, never to return.

—JOHN D. ROCKEFELLER
American industrialist, 1839-1937

Section Focus

As railroads gave industrialists access to raw materials and markets, great opportunities developed for business expansion. The result was "Big Business." By 1900 several major industries were dominated by gigantic companies that owned scores of plants, sold products nationwide, and had hundreds of millions of dollars in capital and credit behind them.

Objectives

After studying this section, you should be able to:
- Discuss the methods big business used to become successful.
- Explain why incorporation encouraged business growth.

The railroads were America's first "Big Business." Founding a major railroad consumed larger sums of money than any previous American enterprise. The investment required was so great that no one individual could make it. Instead, a large railroad line was organized as a **corporation**—a company formed by a group of investors who each receive a share of ownership in proportion to the amount they invested. Investors also enjoyed the protection of limited liability; that is, they risked only the amount of their investment, even if the corporation went bankrupt and could not pay its bills. This business structure allowed entrepreneurs in many industries to raise the money they needed to launch or expand companies as opportunities arose.

Benefits of Big Business

Big business enjoyed many advantages. Large companies could manufacture enough products to meet the demands of a national market. They produced better products at lower cost than their smaller competitors through the economics of scale that resulted from using the newest processes and combining operations formerly performed by separate companies. High salaries were offered in order to get expert managers. At the same time, they increased efficiency by establishing separate departments for specialized functions such as purchasing, production, research, distribution, and sales.

In conducting their operations, big companies organized work to gain maximum production from their employees. A steel company engineer, Frederick W. Taylor, developed a system to study and time workers and to make changes so their jobs could be performed more efficiently. Such studies even included counting the steps a worker took in moving from one place to another on the job and determining what size shovels were best for shoveling coal, rice, and iron ore!

The advantages of big business were shown dramatically by the development of large meat-packing companies. In the past, fresh meat was slaughtered locally, and every town had at least one slaughterhouse. When the refrigerated railroad car made it possible to ship fresh meat over long distances, huge companies such as Swift and Armour appeared, selling their products throughout the country. The big packers were so highly organized and efficient that they could sell meat at a loss and make their profit from the rest of the carcass. Chicago humorist Finley Peter Dunne, writing under the name of the fictional Irish saloon-keeper "Mr. Dooley," hardly exaggerated when he noted:

A cow goes lowin' softly into Armour's an' comes out glue, gelatin, fertylizer, celooloid, joolry, sofy cushions, hair restorer, washin' sody, soap, lithrachoor an' bed springs so quick that while aft she's still cow, for'ard she may be anything fr'm buttons to pannyma hats.

Because of their efficiency, organization, and size, large businesses were frequently in a position to take advantage of their competitors and sometimes of the public. Big companies could demand volume discounts from shippers. They could sell their products in an area at a loss until local competitors were forced to shut down or sell out. If a large company succeeded in getting a monopoly in its industry, it could raise consumer prices and pay less to suppliers of raw materials. Economist David Wells recognized these trends in 1889:

…the smaller flour mills in the United States are being crushed, or forced into consolidation with the larger companies, the latter being able, from dealing in such immense quantities, to buy their wheat more economically, obtain lower rates of freight, and, by contracting ahead, keep constantly running.…And what has been thus affirmed…might be equally affirmed of a great variety of other leading commodities.

Big business in the late nineteenth century resulted from the vision of people who recognized great opportunities for wealth and were willing to take risks to get it. The companies they organized, American Tobacco, General Electric, and United Fruit, for example, came to dominate their industries and sold products not just nationwide, but to the entire world.

In attaining success, however, many entrepreneurs showed few scruples in driving competitors out of business, evading the law, bribing officials, destroying labor unions, and devastating the environment. They commonly sold products at below their cost until local businesses were forced to close down or sell out. The American public, therefore, had

AMERICAN PORTRAITS

GUSTAVUS SWIFT
1839-1903

At 16, Gustavus Swift borrowed $25, bought a cow, slaughtered it, and sold the beef at a $10 profit. From that point on, Swift devoted his life to making money from meat.

Swift first opened several butcher shops. With a talent for buying only the best cattle, he next moved to Chicago—capital of the cattle market—and went into business shipping livestock by rail to Eastern cities. He soon realized, however, that he could make more money butchering the animals in Chicago and shipping the meat. At first, to prevent spoilage, Swift could ship only during winter months. But then he hired an engineer who developed a refrigerated railroad car that made it possible to ship year-round. As hungry workers swelled the size of eastern cities, Swift & Co. made great profits by shipping huge quantities of meat to feed them.

Examining Illustrations *Mass production of consumer goods, such as blue jeans, combined with transportation improvements inspired entrepreneurs to print merchandise catalogs and open mail-order stores. Why were big businesses able to sell for less than local companies?*

business's efficiency, its lower prices, and the jobs it created. Success in business became a best-selling theme in popular fiction. Horatio Alger became wealthy himself when he wrote novels like *Mark the Match Boy, Tattered Tom,* and over 100 others—all "rags-to-riches" stories of young men who became successful in business because of hard work and lucky breaks.

The Role of Corporations

American law allowed the formation of business corporations, and conditions in the United States encouraged their existence. As a business form, the corporation offered a number of advantages over a partnership or a sole proprietor. The corporation had a permanence that lasted beyond the lives of its owners or stockholders. So company managers could confidently plan far into the future.

mixed feelings about big business. Americans worried about the corrupting influence of wealth and power. Yet others admitted that they benefited from big

Examining Political Cartoons *In this 1888 cartoon big business is portrayed as a hydra—a many-headed monster from Greek mythology—that is threatening the nation. Each head on the hydra represents a trust. The cartoonist is calling for laws, represented by the club, to give the government the power to destroy the monster. Why did some Americans oppose big business?*

By selling stocks and bonds, a corporation could raise the capital, or investment money, for its operations. Small amounts of capital, from many individual investors could be pooled into the huge sums needed to start or expand a large company. In that way no one investor would have to take a big financial risk. To reduce risk even more, investors could spread it out by purchasing stock in several corporations. One specialized form of corporation, the **holding company,** became very popular. Holding companies manufactured no products and had no customers. They existed only to own stock in other corporations. Through holding companies, wealthy capitalists could own controlling interests in many businesses.

Other companies were organized into **trusts.** A trust was formed when several companies gave control of their operations to a single board of trustees. The shareholders of each individual company continued to own it and keep its profits, but management of all companies in the trust was in the same hands. Through holding companies and trusts, entrepreneurs formed the huge business combinations that dominated the late nineteenth century.

Business consolidation—that is, combining companies into one unit—took various forms. Sometimes companies were consolidated by **horizontal integration,** in which several firms engaged in the same kind of business were joined together. If a horizontal combination became large enough, it could achieve a monopoly of that industry.

Companies also were consolidated by **vertical integration,** which joined businesses engaged in different but related activities. A vertical combination might include, for example, under the same ownership individual companies that provided raw materials; transported those raw materials to factories; manufactured a product from those raw materials, and distributed and sold the finished product.

A horizontal combination, once established, was able to expand vertically because of the control its size gave it over both suppliers and distributors. And a vertical combination could become so efficient that it expanded horizontally by buying its competitors, forcing them into trusts, or driving them out of business.

Section Two Review

SUMMARY

Corporate structure allowed the growth of big business. By combining management in trusts or holding companies, or in horizontal or vertical business combinations, these colossal corporations further extended their control. The efficiency, organization, size, and resources of a big business gave it tremendous advantages over smaller operations. Big businesses frequently used these advantages to destroy smaller competitors and to smash labor unions. Moreover, big business leaders broke laws and devastated the environment. Yet the public reaped the benefits of lower prices and more jobs.

CHECKING FOR UNDERSTANDING

1. **Identify** Frederick W. Taylor, Horatio Alger

2. **Define** corporation, horizontal integration, vertical integration

3. **Describe** the practices that made big business both successful and objectionable.

4. **List** the various ways businesses can be organized.

5. **Explain** why the corporation was a successful business structure for promoting business growth.

THINKING CRITICALLY

6. **Evaluating Change** How might the shift to the prevalence of big business work to the advantage or disadvantage of a consumer? a worker? an owner of a small business?

CONNECTIONS: HISTORY AND ECONOMICS

7. **Predicting Effects** All business organizations operate on the premise of earning a profit. How could organizing a trust lead to unfair business practices?

Captains of Industry

Two pounds of ironstone mined upon Lake Superior and transported nine hundred miles to Pittsburgh; one pound and one-half of coal, mined and manufactured into coke, and transported to Pittsburgh; one half-pound of lime, mined and transported to Pittsburgh; a small amount of manganese mined in Virginia and brought to Pittsburgh—and these four pounds of materials manufactured into one pound of steel, for which the consumer pays one cent.

—ANDREW CARNEGIE
American industrialist, 1835-1919

Section Focus

Two industries illustrate big business growth, each dominated by a man as ruthless as he was efficient. Rising from poverty to attain enormous wealth and power, John D. Rockefeller and Andrew Carnegie represented to many the American Dream.

Objectives

After studying this section, you should be able to:
• Compare the methods used by Carnegie and Rockefeller to achieve success.
• Explain social Darwinism and the Gospel of Wealth.

Although giant combinations arose to control the beef, flour, whiskey, tobacco, lead, and sugar industries, as well as many others, by 1900 the American economy ran on oil, and its backbone was steel. No industrialists exemplified the principles of doing "big business" in late-nineteenth-century America more than the entrepreneurs who dominated these two basic industries—John D. Rockefeller in oil and Andrew Carnegie in steel.

Rockefeller and the Standard Oil Trust

The most successful example of horizontal consolidation was the Standard Oil Trust, which gained a near-monopoly of oil refineries and pipelines. The guiding genius behind Standard Oil was John D. Rockefeller, who during his 98 years, from 1839 to 1937, amassed what was at the time the world's largest fortune—almost $1 billion.

Rockefeller went to work at age 16 as a bookkeeper in a wholesale commission and produce company in Cleveland, Ohio. Dominated by the idea that he was "bound to be rich," he saved $800 in 3 years, on a salary of $15 per week. At 19 he left his job and opened his own commission house. In only 4 years he increased his capital to about $100,000. Then in 1865, at age 23, he put all his money into a new and growing industry—petroleum refining.

Until the 1850s, petroleum, then called "rock oil," had been used only as a patent medicine. In 1855 scientists discovered that petroleum, when refined into kerosene, was better than whale oil in lamps and made a much better lubricant than animal fat.

The first oil well, drilled in 1859, set off a stampede to western Pennsylvania much like the California gold rush of 1849. Land values jumped from a few dollars an acre to hundreds of dollars a square foot, new towns appeared overnight, and the demand for kerosene spread worldwide. In spite of the Civil War, the petroleum industry grew so fast that by 1865, oil products had risen to fourth place among American exports.

Drilling for oil was always a big gamble, and Rockefeller realized oil refining was a much safer investment. But the entire oil business was highly disorganized. Fortunes were made and lost overnight as the price of oil fluctuated wildly. Rockefeller believed these unstable conditions resulted from competition among thousands of small producers and hundreds of small refiners.

By 1870 Rockefeller's firm, the Standard Oil Company of Ohio, with capital stock of $1 million, was the largest of 26 refineries in Cleveland, processing 2 or 3 percent of the crude oil produced in the United States. Over the next 9 years, Rockefeller gained control of more than 90 percent of the nation's refining business and brought order to a chaotic industry. But to achieve stability and efficiency in the oil business, Rockefeller used methods so shrewdly brutal that when they were revealed he became one of the most hated men in America.

One of Standard Oil's major weapons was the **rebate,** or discount, on freight charges. In 1872 the company offered to give certain railroads all its shipping business if those railroads secretly agreed to charge Standard Oil 25 to 50 percent less than they charged its competitors. In return for its business, these railroads also promised to tell Rockefeller the destination of all his competitors' shipments. This

Examining Photographs
Although he was a ruthless businessman, John D. Rockefeller always carried dimes in his pockets to give to small children he encountered on the street. What changes did he bring to the oil industry?

information gave him valuable insights into his rivals' business dealings. These secret arrangements gave Standard Oil such an advantage over other Cleveland

Examining Graphs *Although the growth of the oil industry after the Civil War was phenomenal, the growth of steel started later and was nearly 30 times greater. What benefits did the success of these industries bring to the nation?*

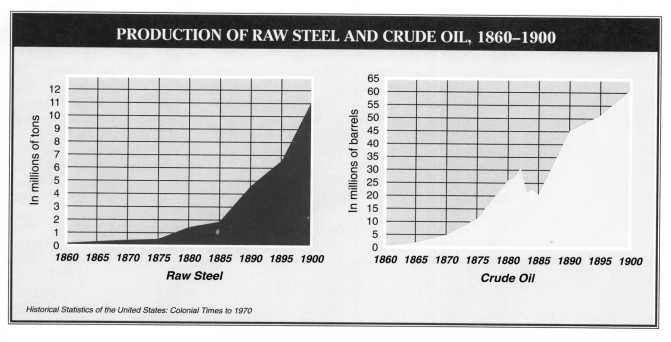

PRODUCTION OF RAW STEEL AND CRUDE OIL, 1860–1900

Raw Steel

Crude Oil

Historical Statistics of the United States: Colonial Times to 1970

Much like Standard Oil, the Organization of Petroleum Exporting Countries (OPEC) tries to maintain stability in the oil industry to ensure profits. Since 1970, OPEC has controlled approximately one-third to one-half of the world's oil supply. In 1991 member nations included Algeria, Ecuador, Gabon, Indonesia, Iran, Iraq, Kuwait, Libya, Nigeria, Qatar, Saudi Arabia, United Arab Emirates, and Venezuela.

refineries that within three months all but five were forced to sell out to Rockefeller. Once it controlled oil refining in Cleveland, Standard Oil moved rapidly toward a nationwide monopoly by allying with the strongest companies throughout the industry. In 1880 a committee of the New York legislature reported on the extent of Standard Oil's domination of the oil business:

It owns and controls the pipe lines of the producing regions that connect with the railroads. It controls both ends of these roads. It ships 95 per cent of all oil....
It dictates terms and rates to the railroads. It has bought out and frozen out refiners all over the country. By means of the superior facilities for transportation which it thus possessed, it could overbid [its competitors for crude oil] in the producing regions and undersell [its competitors] in the markets of the world.

By a secret agreement that became known as the Standard Oil Trust, Rockefeller moved in 1882 to consolidate his control of the oil industry further by combining 40 companies under a single management. Controlling interest in the stock of these companies was turned over to 9 trustees headed by Rockefeller.

Once in control of most of the refining and transportation of oil in the United States, Standard Oil expanded vertically. It gained control of oil fields to have an independent supply source, and it marketed natural gas. At the other end of the production process, Standard Oil moved into the distribution of petroleum products, both in the United States and overseas. Eventually Standard Oil controlled a fleet of ocean-going tankers and door-to-door delivery wagons in Europe. It even manufactured and sold cooking stoves to increase the demand for kerosene!

Standard Oil's spectacular success led others to establish horizontal combinations of companies in industries as varied as whiskey, bituminous coal, and rope. The purpose of these combinations was mainly to prevent overproduction and to keep prices up. But it was difficult to control an entire industry and to keep new firms out of the market. Such efforts to obtain monopolies were greatly resented by small business people and consumers. Vertical combinations, on the other hand, were not monopolistic. The savings that resulted from the economies they brought to production were passed on to consumers in lower prices. Vertical combination thus became a common form of business organization that is still seen today in such giant organizations as General Motors and American Telephone and Telegraph.

Although Rockefeller's rivals in the oil industry were painfully aware of his ruthless methods, it was a young investigative journalist who exposed them to the public. In 1903, in a series of brilliant articles in *McClure's Magazine,* Ida Tarbell revealed Rockefeller's secret deals and high-pressure tactics. She explained how companies controlled by Standard Oil continued to do business under their former names. She documented how, to conceal his control of these companies, Rockefeller appointed "dummy directors," who were sometimes employees such as errand-runners or secretaries.

Rockefeller, a devout churchgoer and Sunday school teacher, did not think that his actions in what he called "systematizing" the oil industry were wrong. He pointed out that what he had done to destroy his competitors had not been illegal when he first did it. Rebates, for example, were granted by railroads to big shippers in many other industries. When buying out his competitors, Rockefeller offered to pay them in either cash or Standard Oil stock, advising them to take the stock. Those who took his advice became rich.

Much of Rockefeller's advantage over competitors came from his passion for efficiency and his hatred of waste. Standard Oil continuously improved its product. The company had few labor troubles because it paid its workers well. It tried to protect their jobs in times of depression and was one of the first companies to pay old-age pensions.

Andrew Carnegie, Master of Steel

The most remarkable example of the creation of a vertical combination was the giant steel corporation built by Andrew Carnegie. Coming to Pittsburgh from Scotland at the age of 13, Carnegie went to work in a cotton factory, where he earned $1.20 for working a 72-hour week. He saw an opportunity to grow with the railroad, however, and in 1853 he went to work as a clerk and telegraph operator for the Pennsylvania Railroad. His ability, energy, and ambition were so great that at age 23 he became superintendent of the railroad's western division.

While working for the railroad, Carnegie wisely invested his earnings in iron companies. As the railroads grew, Carnegie foresaw his opportunity for personal success in the increasing demand for rails, bridges, and locomotives. By age 30, when he left the railroad to manage an iron bridge company, his investments were producing an annual income of nearly $50,000.

After seven years making iron bridges, Carnegie again looked at the future and saw it was in steel. He decided to "put all his eggs in one basket and watch the basket." In 1873 he formed a group of investors to build the largest and most modern steel mill in the world near Pittsburgh. Carnegie was the first person in the United States to use two new ways of making steel—the Bessemer process and

Examining Photographs *This portrait of a young Andrew Carnegie was taken at about the time that he was getting started in the steel business. What caused Carnegie to believe the future was in iron and steel?*

the open-hearth process. These processes enabled him to produce steel so cheaply that it could now be used for rails and construction girders, as well as for cutlery and precision machines.

Between 1866 and 1876, the production of American steel jumped from 20,000 to 600,000 tons; by 1897 it had skyrocketed to more than 7 million tons. Almost overnight Carnegie changed the character of the industry. Previously iron and steel had been manufactured at hundreds of small furnaces all over the country. But Bessemer converters and open-hearth furnaces required heavy investments of capital, and huge amounts of coke and ore to keep them going. Small

Examining Illustrations *Carnegie Steel Company's Homestead plant near Pittsburgh was one of many built in the late 1800s. What advantage did Carnegie's use of technology give him over his competitors?*

547

companies were soon forced out of business by big ones.

Fewer than 20 years after putting all his eggs in one basket, Carnegie was the greatest steelmaker in the world. One reason for his phenomenal success was that he took the guesswork out of making steel by getting the best technical and scientific experts he could find. Carnegie liked to boast that he "was smart enough to surround himself with men far cleverer than himself." For example, his managers were able to determine almost to the penny what it cost to produce a ton of steel. With this knowledge, Carnegie could set prices below his competitors and still make a profit. His chemists found uses for by-products previously considered to be industrial waste, and they discovered how to use low-grade ores formerly considered worthless.

Seeking out the ablest people in the industry, Carnegie bought their loyalty by making them partners. Equally alert for ability inside his companies, he rapidly promoted exceptional employees. Common laborers in his mills fared less well, however, as he drove wages down and hours up. In 1892, with his partner, Henry C. Frick, he crushed the steelworkers' union, so that the 12-hour day remained standard in the industry for many years.

During the three major depressions of the late 1800s, while other steel companies closed down and laid off employees, Carnegie expanded. He rebuilt his factories to be even more efficient and acquired his

Examining Fine Art The Hatch Family *by American artist Jonathan Eastman Johnson portrays a family in fine clothing enjoying a comfortable afternoon in their home. Note that parents, children, and grandchildren live in the household—a typical arrangement for the times among the rich as well as the poor. This family was painted, and the family on page 549 was photographed. What clue does that provide about the economic status of each family?*

Examining Photographs *This large working-class household is crowded into a small tenement apartment. Compare the clothing and surroundings in this photograph with the scene on the previous page. What explanation would the philosophy of social Darwinism offer to account for such differences?*

weakened competitors. "So many of my friends needed money that they begged me to repay them," Carnegie explained. "I did so and bought out five or six of them. That was what gave me my leading interest in this steel business." Carnegie "gambled on the future of America," as he put it, "and won."

In his constant effort to be more efficient, Carnegie combined all the processes required for making steel into one great vertical combination. In addition to blast furnaces and steel mills, Carnegie Steel Company controlled: rich iron ore deposits near Lake Superior, fleets of ships to carry the ore over the Great Lakes, a railroad to carry the ore from the Lake Erie region to Pittsburgh, coal mines in Pennsylvania to fire the blast furnaces, and factories for producing finished steel products such as wire.

Social Darwinism and the Gospel of Wealth

Andrew Carnegie was making $25 million a year, at a time when there was no income tax. His workers, on the other hand, earned $8 or $9 a week. He made steel so cheaply and competed so mercilessly that remaining steel companies faced bankruptcy. Carnegie and most other great industrialists found justification for these actions and their consequences in a philosophy known as **social Darwinism,** which applied the biological theories of naturalist Charles Darwin to human society. Darwin believed that in nature a competition exists in which only the fittest—the strongest, most clever, most efficient—plants and animals survive. The weak individuals die out, and each species thereby remains strong and healthy. Philosophers such as Yale professor William Graham Sumner argued that this competition also operated in human society, and that industrialists like Rockefeller and Carnegie had succeeded because of their rare talents. "The millionaires are a product of natural selection," Sumner wrote. "They get high wages and live in luxury, but the bargain is a good one for society."

Andrew Carnegie and John D. Rockefeller both believed wholeheartedly in the philosophy of social Darwinism. Carnegie called it a method better than elections for selecting leaders. "By a process of pitiless testing we discover who are the strong and who are the weak," he wrote. "To the strong we give power in the form of the autocratic control of industry and of wealth." Rockefeller told his Sunday school class that his business practices merely demonstrated "the survival of the fittest....a law of nature and a law of God."

But for Carnegie the achievement of great power and wealth was not enough. He looked beyond success to question whether those who profited from society owed anything to it in return. His answer was what he called his "Gospel of Wealth." Writing in the *North American Review* in 1889, Carnegie maintained that a wealthy person should:

---

*...consider all surplus revenues
which come to him simply as trust funds,
which he is called upon to administer...
in a manner which, in his judgment,
is best calculated to produce the most
beneficial results for the
community....becoming the mere agent
and trustee for his poorer brethren,
bringing to their service his superior
wisdom, experience, and ability to
administer, doing for them better
than they would or
could do for themselves.*

Business people should invest their wealth not as charity to the poor, but "to help those who will help themselves," he wrote, "to provide part of the means by which those who desire to improve may do so."

Carnegie practiced what he preached. In 1901 he sold his steel properties to the newly formed United States Steel Corporation for $250 million and withdrew from business to devote the rest of his life to **philanthropy,** that is, to actions benefiting society. By the time he died, in 1919, he had donated $350 million—mostly to building public libraries, improving education, and promoting research. Rockefeller also returned much of his fortune to society in gifts that totaled more than $500 million.

Sherman Antitrust Act

In 1881 *Atlantic Monthly* published an article entitled "The Story of a Great Monopoly," by Henry Demarest Lloyd, telling how the Standard Oil Company had monopolized the oil-refining business. It caused such a sensation that the magazine had to print three times as many copies as usual. Throughout the next decade, as it was revealed that industry after industry was in danger of being monopolized, demands for federal regulation came from many different groups—small businesses, farmers, consumers, and laborers.

Officials of the great corporations began to have concerns about growing public cries for reform. Henry O. Havemeyer, head of the American Sugar Refining Company, which controlled a trust producing more than 90 percent of the nation's sugar, urged that manufacturers of products in general use should submit to some federal regulation. In the election of 1888, both political parties promised action, and in 1890, with only one dissenting vote, Congress passed the Sherman Antitrust Act.

The Sherman Act wrote into federal law a traditional principle of English common law—that private monopolies and artificial restrictions on trade were wrong. In the words of the act:

Every contract, combination, in the form of trust or otherwise, or conspiracy, in restraint of trade or commerce among the several states or with foreign nations, is hereby declared to be illegal.

For a number of reasons the Sherman Act had little effect on preventing business consolidation. It was not strictly enforced and was so loosely worded that its meaning was doubtful. Did the law mean, for example, that all mergers were unlawful, that all business transactions must be open and public, that any contract that permitted one company to take business from another was illegal?

Under the Constitution, the answers to such questions are left to the federal courts, which in the 1890s were probably more favorable to business interests than at any other time in American history. In the *United States v. E. C. Knight Company,* the Supreme Court in 1895 agreed that the American Sugar Refining Company was a trust and that it enjoyed a near monopoly in the manufacture of sugar. But the Court ruled that the company's activities did not violate the Sherman Act because manufacturing was not interstate commerce.

The Supreme Court's decision in the Knight case was followed by one of the greatest periods of business consolidation in American history. In 1890 there had been 24 trusts worth a total of $436 million. In 1900 there were 183 huge combinations with a total worth of over $3 billion. At the same time, big business simply turned away from trusts and toward holding companies in creating combinations.

In spite of its early failures, the Sherman Act was a very important law. It signaled to large corporations to be more aware of how their activities looked to the public. Corporate image and public relations became important business concerns. Later regulation of big business would depend on additional legislation, the interpretations of future courts, and on attitudes in the executive branch about enforcement.

Section Three Review

SUMMARY

Business growth was driven by the ambition of captains of industry such as Rockefeller and Carnegie. Beginning with nothing, both men built enormous industrial empires—Rockefeller in oil, and Carnegie in steel. They forced out competition and manipulated prices, using social Darwinism to justify their actions. Although the nation benefited from their efficiency and innovation, the public demanded restriction of big business. But the resulting Sherman Antitrust Act was ineffective because court rulings favored business.

CHECKING FOR UNDERSTANDING

1. **Identify** John D. Rockefeller, Standard Oil, Ida Tarbell, Andrew Carnegie, social Darwinism, Sherman Antitrust Act, Gospel of Wealth

2. **Define** philanthropy, rebate

3. **Compare** the methods used by Rockefeller and Carnegie to build their industrial empires, noting any differences between the two.

4. **Describe** how the theory of social Darwinism could be made to apply to business success.

5. **Explain** why the Sherman Antitrust Act failed to control big business.

THINKING CRITICALLY

6. **Judging Actions** Would the United States have been better off with or without industrial giants such as Rockefeller and Carnegie?

LINKING PAST AND PRESENT

7. **Determining Causes** Rockefeller and Carnegie were among "the rich and famous" people and were considered "celebrities" of their day. With whom could you compare them today? What do you think accounts for the influence and power exercised by famous people?

★ Chapter 18 Review ★

★ Summary

Following the Civil War, abundant resources, a large and mobile labor force, immigration, protective tariffs, technological advances, government policy favorable to business, and private and foreign investment combined to produce an explosion of industrial growth—which was further accelerated by growth of railroads. Corporate structure, combining management in trusts or holding companies, and horizontal or vertical business combinations created big business—with all the advantages of efficiency, organization, size, and resources. Though the public enjoyed lower prices and employment opportunities, leaders of big business used their advantages to force smaller competitors out and smash labor unions. Rockefeller and Carnegie, in the oil and steel industries respectively, exemplified in their operations the best and the worst in big business. In response to public demand for restriction of big business, Congress passed the Sherman Antitrust Act.

★ Using Vocabulary

Use the listed vocabulary words to complete the sentences that follow. You will use all but one of the words. Write an original sentence using the remaining word.

entrepreneurs	horizontal integration
rebates	vertical integration
corporations	

1. Businesses organized as _____ can raise capital from a number of investors.
2. When governments practice *laissez-faire* policies, _____ can run businesses with very little government regulation.
3. Carnegie and Rockefeller consolidated a number of businesses using both _____ and _____.

★ Reviewing Facts

1. **Enumerate** the factors that boosted industrial growth in the United States.
2. **State** the roles played by the railroad in the growth of American industry.
3. **Identify** the strategies that big business used to become successful.
4. **List** all the types of business organization, big and small, that companies could form.
5. **Summarize** the common elements in the strategies of Rockefeller, Carnegie, and Vanderbilt.
6. **Describe** the provisions of the Sherman Antitrust Act and its effects.
7. **Cite** some industries that big business controlled.

★ Understanding Concepts

INDIVIDUAL INITIATIVE

1. Cite examples of individuals and how they used their initiative to accelerate or shape industrial growth in America.
2. In what ways did Vanderbilt's individual initiative benefit other business owners and the country as a whole?

GOVERNMENT RESTRICTION

3. Would a social Darwinist support or oppose *laissez-faire* government policies? Explain why.
4. Lack of government restriction benefited some businesses and hurt others. Which types of businesses benefited, and which might have been more successful with some protection?

★ Thinking Critically

1. **Analyzing a Causal Chain**   Explain how the following factors can be both a cause and an effect of industrial growth: (a) immigration, (b) investment of foreign capital, (c) growth of railroads.
2. **Judging Effects**   Discuss how a big company manufacturing products in both quantity and quality benefits the consumer and the company.

★ Writing About History

CAUSE AND EFFECT

Refer to the description of how to write a cause-and-effect essay in the History Writer's Handbook in the Appendix of this book. Your teacher will give you more specific instructions on the essay's length and the assignment's due date.

Imagine you are a nineteenth-century writer who hopes to publish a collection of true rags-to-riches stories. Write a brief biography of a nineteenth-century captain of industry who began with little and built an industrial empire. Choose an entrepreneur from this chapter or conduct research about another from the same period.

Focus on what you believe to be the causes of your subject's success. Write about the traits and experiences that influenced the person's growth. What decisions were the key to success? What risks did the entrepreneur take, and what were the results of those risks? Were there mistakes and failures along the road to success? What may have contributed to this person's ability to rebound from failures?

The "gospel of success" preached that almost anyone who tried hard enough could achieve results similar to those of the captains of industry. Summarize your research in a paragraph that expresses whether or not you believe this to be true.

★ Learning Cooperatively

Work with a partner to research the history of the Bell telephone system from the parent company's formation to its breakup into smaller companies in recent years. Then discuss between yourselves what were the company's contributions to the nation and why the system was broken up by the government. Present your findings to the class, with one partner explaining Bell's contributions and the other explaining why it was broken up. Compare your findings with those presented by other class pairs.

★ Mastering Skills

MAKING COMPARISONS

To *compare* means to examine data in order to identify similarities and/or differences. You can compare things that are very different or that are very much alike.

Example   No matter what you are comparing, there are some questions that you can ask yourself to help you make an effective comparison. The following questions enable you to compare Andrew Carnegie and John D. Rockefeller.

- What are the subjects to be compared? *(Carnegie and Rockefeller)*
- What areas do the subjects have enough in common that a comparison is possible? *(personal success, use of business combinations, values and beliefs, practice of philanthropy)*
- Which area do I want to compare? *(personal success)*
- What similarities do the subjects have in this area? *(both men started out in low-paying jobs; both saved their money and invested it wisely; both eventually amassed huge personal fortunes)*
- What differences do the subjects have in this area? *(Rockefeller's success was in oil, Carnegie's success came in steel)*

Practice   You already know that graphs can be used to compare information and to see how things change over time. The questions above can help you in comparing graphs. The graph below shows the production of bituminous coal from 1860 to 1900.

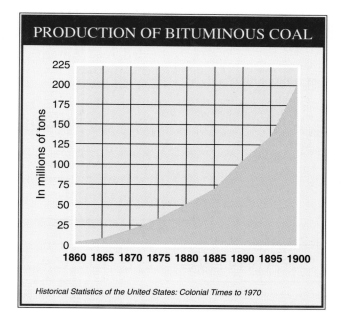

PRODUCTION OF BITUMINOUS COAL

In millions of tons

225 200 175 150 125 100 75 50 25 0

1860 1865 1870 1875 1880 1885 1890 1895 1900

Historical Statistics of the United States: Colonial Times to 1970

Compare the graph above to the graphs of raw steel and crude oil production found on page 545.

1. What are the three subjects you can compare by using these graphs? What is the time period?
2. Compare the production trends each graph shows. For example, are the increases (or decreases) rapid or gradual?
3. Why is it easier to compare this kind of information using graphs than if the information was just written out?

CHAPTER 19
Labor, Immigrants, and Urban Life

SETTING THE SCENE

Historical Focus

One factor behind supporting industrialization in the late nineteenth century was the abundant labor supply. For workers, poor pay and working conditions led to a renewed interest in labor unions. Efforts by unions such as the Knights of Labor to improve conditions, however, were only modestly successful. The union movement was also influenced by the influx of millions of immigrants. These new arrivals crowded into America's cities and brought with them the cultural heritage of their old world.

Concepts to Understand

- How **unity** among workers led to a new interest and growth in unions.
- How **conflict** between workers and employees resulted in unrest and strikes.

People to Know

Terence V. Powderly, Samuel Gompers, Eugene V. Debs, Jacob Riis, Jane Addams, Louis Sullivan

Places to Locate

Pullman, Milwaukee

Terms to Identify

script, business cycle, blacklists, collective bargaining, injunction, arbitration,

Guided Reading

As you read this chapter, seek the answers to the following questions.

1. What difficulties did labor unions experience in the late 1800s?
2. What were the major factors behind the migration to American cities?

SPANNING THE DECADES

POLITICAL

1872
Victoria Claflin Woodhull, first woman presidential candidate, nominated

1877
Railroad strike against the B&O Railroad is put down by Federal troops

1886
Haymarket Square Riot takes place in Chicago

1870   1880

CULTURAL

1871
52 persons dead after New York City riot between Irish Catholics and Protestants

1876
Central Park opens in New York City

1880
First Salvation Army mission is opened in Philadelphia

1883
Brooklyn Bridge in New York City is completed

Hester Street *by George Luks, 1905*

1892
Steelworkers strike against Carnegie's Homestead mill in Pennsylvania ends

1894
Strike against the Pullman railroad car company ends

1890

1900

1893
Columbian Exposition opens in Chicago

...*A strike gives...evidence that we shall not go down further in the economic and social scale. And it is a warning that labor has more rights than it now enjoys, and a determination that it is going to secure them—if not today, some other day...*

—SAMUEL GOMPERS
President of the American Federation of Labor, 1894

The Workers' Plight

A few years ago a skilled workman could make up three dozen pairs of sleeve buttons per day. Now, by the aid of the most improved machinery, a boy can make up 9,000 pairs or 250 times as many.... When he set up 36 pairs a day, he received $2.50 or $3 for it. Now the boy, who does as much as 250 men could then, receives less than 90 cents for it.

—JOSIAH STRONG
Congregational minister, 1893

Section Focus

The new industrial age brought many problems for workers. They toiled long hours for low wages, earning from $9 to $20 a week, depending on their skills. In an attempt to improve working conditions, workers began to organize. In spite of rapid growth after the Civil War, unions encountered many difficulties.

Objectives

After studying this section, you should be able to:
• Describe the difficult conditions under which people worked during the late 1800s.
• Explain the obstacles faced by labor unions during this period.

With the growth of industry, the number of factory workers rose from about 900,000 in 1860 to more than 3.2 million in 1890. Industrialization affected many aspects of workers' lives—where they worked and lived, the size of the work force, and the nature of work itself. Many workers were forced to make the transition from skilled to semiskilled or unskilled labor. The experience and skill of such artisans as carpenters, silversmiths, and furniture makers no longer gave them any advantage over the unskilled. It took little training to tend a machine.

Problems in the Workplace

With machines taking the place of human skills, work became monotonous. Workers concentrated on highly specific, repetitive tasks and could take little pride in the fruits of their labor. As factories increased the efficiency of production, more and more people worked for fewer and fewer employers. The workers began to feel like "cogs in a wheel." Machines were designed to work at a given pace, and the workers had to keep up.

Low wages and long hours posed additional burdens for industrial workers. Workdays of 10 to 14 hours were common. Although **real wages**—wages adjusted for inflation—rose more than 10 percent between 1870 and 1900, the average income remained inadequate. Most industrial workers earned between $400 and $500 a year during the 1890s; $600 was the minimum annual income needed to maintain a decent standard of living.

In some industries workers were required to live in **company towns**, built and run by the companies. The best known was the town of Pullman, Illinois, where every citizen worked for the Pullman Palace Car Company. The usual practice was for companies to deduct from the workers' pay money for rent and advances to the company store, as well as medical and fuel fees. Some companies paid their workers in **scrip**, or company money, that could only be redeemed at the company store.

Added to workers' other problems was the fact that factory work was unhealthful as well as dangerous. Miners breathed coal dust all day. Factory workers breathed sawdust, stone dust, cotton dust, or toxic fumes. Heavy machines, grouped together on shop and mill floors for the sake of efficiency, caused an appallingly high injury rate among workers. An 1884 government report described working conditions for women in a small factory in Boston:

The work is dangerous…[they] are liable to get their fingers jammed under the bench, or caught in the die when it comes down to press the parts of the buttons together. A man (although not a surgeon) is provided to dress wounds three times for each individual without charge; afterwards, the person injured must pay all expenses. There are 35 machines in use, and accidents are of very frequent occurrence.

Children, some as young as six, were regularly employed as factory workers. Throughout the 1800s there were some efforts to restrict child labor but state laws were usually worded in such a way that they could be easily evaded both by employers and by parents who needed the income. In 1885 in New Jersey, there were 340,000 children of school age. About 90,000 of them did not attend school; most worked full-time jobs. Industrial work was neither less difficult nor less dangerous for children than it was for adults. As a Pennsylvania newspaper, the *Luzerne Union*, reported in January 1876:

During the past week, nearly one boy a day has been killed, and the public has become so familiar with these calamities that no attention is given them after the first announcement through a newspaper or friend.

Always looming was the threat of pay cuts or layoffs. Workers were vulnerable to the **business cycle**—a recurring sequence

Examining Photographs *Young boys often worked as coal sorters in mines for low wages and under dangerous conditions. Why were early efforts to restrict child labor unsuccessful?*

of change in business activity. Beginning with a period of prosperity, business activity declines until a low point, or depression, is reached. A period of recovery follows when business conditions become more active. A period of prosperity is again reached. The cycle is then repeated.

In the late 1800s, business went through many such cycles. During slack periods, employers kept their costs down by reducing wages or laying off workers. Millions of people lost their jobs or had

In 1955, the AFL merged with the CIO (Congress of Industrial Organizations). The union retained its skilled labor, while extending membership to semiskilled and unskilled workers as well. Today, union members also include white-collar and college-educated members: teachers, musicians, retail workers, and radio and television artists. The AFL-CIO is the most powerful labor organization in America, boasting more than 17 million members— 78% of the nation's organized workers.

their wages slashed during depressions of 1873, 1882, and 1893. Workers looked to labor unions for protection.

The Revival of Labor Unions

The growth of labor unions during the early 1800s had been halting and sporadic, but conditions during the Civil War spurred the revival of unionism. With hundreds of thousands of workers serving in the army, unions were in a strong position to demand better pay. During the war, the number of local unions rose dramatically. To strengthen local unions, labor also began to organize on a national scale.

In spite of rapid growth during the Civil War and afterward, labor unions faced serious difficulties, including the mobility and diversity of the American labor force. Workers who did not "stay hitched," but moved from job to job were difficult to organize. The constant influx of large numbers of immigrants—averaging more than one-third of a million a year between 1870 and 1900—also presented a problem. Differences in language, religion, and customs among the immigrants made it hard to unite them into an effective union.

Another problem was that different labor leaders had different goals. Some leaders envisioned uniting all workers into one large union in order to promote widespread reforms. Others believed that unions should be organized by particular crafts or industries, and work only for short-term benefits.

Unions also faced strong opposition from employers. Workers were often required to take oaths swearing they would not join a union. If found to have been involved in union activity, a worker would be fired and often could not get another job because of **blacklists**, or records kept by employers of "troublemakers." Once blacklisted, a laborer could get a job only by changing residence, trade, or even name. Another way employers retaliated against union organizing in a workplace was the **lockout**— whereby the factory was shut down—or by firing union members and hiring **scabs**, or replacement workers. In any lockout or strike, the odds favored employers. Few unions had enough money to support their members through the long period of unemployment caused by a strike.

Labor unions also had to fight public opinion. Many Americans viewed fixing

Examining Photographs
Union leaders hoped to improve conditions for workers such as these immigrants in a New York City tenement sweatshop. What were the difficulties that unions encountered in organizing immigrants?

Examining Illustrations *The Railroad Strike of 1877 resulted in the most violent upheaval in the history of American labor. In several places, such as the city of Baltimore (shown here), there were clashes between troops and strikers. How did the strike originate?*

wages and hours by **collective bargaining** between workers and employers as violating the right of an individual to deal personally with the employer. Only infrequently did public opinion condemn employers when labor disputes resulted in violence. This happened during the Homestead lockout in 1892, when the Carnegie Steel Company hired a private army of 300 Pinkerton detectives armed with repeating rifles. Generally, however, labor unions were held responsible when disorder occurred.

Another problem for unions was that law enforcement agencies usually sided with the employers. Employers suffered no penalties for lockouts and blacklists. Union strikes and boycotts, on the other hand, were judged to be "conspiracies in restraint of trade," for which labor leaders might be jailed or fined. Contracts between employers and unions were not usually enforceable by law. When violence occurred, or was even threatened, the police—and sometimes armed troops—were sent to the aid of employers.

Railroad Strike of 1877

Despite these obstacles, labor unions survived—sometimes just barely. Union membership fluctuated according to business conditions. Following the panic of 1873, 5,000 businesses closed, causing widespread unemployment and homelessness. Union membership dropped from more than 300,000 to 50,000. Three million workers were unemployed. At this time there were no unemployment or relief benefits available from either the state or federal government. Tramps and hobos roamed the countryside; workers' rallies to demand relief were suppressed by mounted police.

The hard times of the 1870s reached a climax in the railroad strike of 1877, which shook the nation as no labor conflict in its history had done before. It began when four Eastern railroads cut workers' wages. To protest the cuts, the workers went on strike. As other railroads cut wages, the strike spread to Chicago and beyond.

In city after city, strikers seized and sometimes destroyed railroad property. In Pittsburgh alone the Pennsylvania Railroad lost 2,000 cars, 25 locomotives, 2 roundhouses, and a railroad station. At the height of the strike, more than one-half of the freight on the nation's 76,000 miles of track had stopped running. Troops and workers clashed in the streets of Martinsburg, West Virginia, as well as Pittsburgh and Baltimore. Although the clashes were usually spontaneous, newspapers viewed them collectively as:

...an insurrection, a revolution, an attempt of Communists and vagabonds to coerce society, and endeavour to undermine American institutions.

This reaction was indicative of the extent to which a smoothly running railroad system had become central to the economic health of the nation. In several cities order was restored only after President Rutherford B. Hayes had sent in federal troops. But Hayes himself was troubled. He felt railroad officials had brought on the crisis by their own ruthless actions. The President confided in his diary, "Shall the railroads govern the country or shall the people govern the railroads?"

When the railroad strike was over, more than 100 persons were dead, 1,000 had been jailed, and 100,000 workers had gone on strike. In addition, there was such fear of violent revolution that state militia were reorganized. National guard armories were built in many large cities as fortresses, where troops could hold out against strikers if necessary. Union leaders learned from the strike that they were not united or strong enough to defeat the powerful combination of business and government.

SUMMARY

As industrialization took hold, workers faced unhealthful conditions at unskilled, repetitive tasks for low wages. Moreover, they suffered unemployment during declines in the business cycle. Labor organizers were hampered by the diversity of the workers, differing goals of organizers, public opinion, decreasing membership during hard economic times, and opposition from employers. Law enforcement agencies generally supported employers against the unions, breaking up strikes with troops and police. Even so, workers showed their strength during the railroad strike of 1877, nearly bringing the nation's railway system to a standstill. More importantly, union supporters realized that they needed to strive for a greater sense of unity and purpose if labor organizations were to survive.

CHECKING FOR UNDERSTANDING

1. **Identify** Panic of 1873
2. **Define** real wages, company towns, scrip, business cycle, blacklists, lockout, collective bargaining
3. **Discuss** the hardships facing industrial workers during the late 1800s.
4. **Describe** the obstacles labor organizers faced in creating unions.
5. **Give examples** of problems unions faced once they were organized.

THINKING CRITICALLY

6. **Weighing Options** Imagine that you are an industrial worker in 1870. List the advantages and disadvantages of joining a union.

CONNECTIONS: HISTORY AND ECONOMICS

7. **Analyzing Relationships** Explain how economic hard times make things difficult for employers which in turn make things difficult for workers.

Study and Writing Skills

Summarizing

Imagine that you have received an expensive camera for your birthday. The instructions are complicated, with at least 12 pages describing how to adjust it for certain shots. The more you read, the more confused you become. Finally, you discover a *summary* of the main steps, and your confusion disappears.

Explanation

Summarizing is the process of recapping main ideas by bringing together the major points and excluding the minor ones. Knowing how to summarize is a useful skill for students who have to answer essay questions, take notes, and write research papers.

Example

Read the following material carefully. Then study the two steps to summarizing information that follow.

During the late 1800s, the United States, like other modernized nations, was experiencing societal changes brought on by the shift from an agriculture-based economy to one based on industrial production. American life up to this time had been based on a rugged self-determinism, a belief that one should take care of one's self and family. This was largely done through owning and farming land.

Ironworkers at the Corns Rolling Mills in Massillon, Ohio

The growth of industry lured many people to the cities, and into jobs which required a new set of values. Often a man did not so much work for his family as he did for his boss. Further, working conditions and pay were often a source of discontent. Labor unions began to organize, and although their intent was to lend support to exploited employees, it often made workers feel they were helpless to take care of themselves.

a. Locate and list in order of appearance the main ideas expressed in the material:

- America experienced a shift from an agriculture-based economy to an industrial-based economy.
- This change required a shift away from self-determinism.
- Men at city jobs worked to please a boss, not their families; yet they were unhappy with working conditions and pay.
- Labor unions made workers feel they were helpless to take care of themselves.

b. Summarize by rewriting the main ideas in your own words:

The shift from agriculture to industry caused many to feel they were not as self-reliant as they had been in the past. Now they worked to please a boss, even though they were unhappy with pay and working conditions. Even labor unions caused people to feel they were too reliant on the union and not enough on themselves.

Practice

For practice in this skill, read the material under the subhead "Urbanization" in Section 4 of this chapter. Then following the guidelines suggested in the example, list the main ideas of the material and write a short summary of the material presented there.

The Rise of New Unions

I am a workingman…and in every nerve, in every fibre, in every aspiration, I am on the side which will advance the interests of my fellow workingmen.

—SAMUEL GOMPERS
President of the American Federation of Labor, 1906

Section Focus

Individually, workers were powerless to change hazardous working conditions, low pay, and long hours. When little was done to improve their lot, workers in growing numbers came to accept the idea of forming new, better organized unions. Two important organizations were the Knights of Labor and the American Federation of Labor.

Objectives

After studying this section, you should be able to:
- Identify two of the strongest labor unions of the late 1800s.
- Evaluate the gains labor unions achieved during this period.

As industrialization was an urban phenomenon, so, too, were unions. Those states with the highest percentage of workers in industry had the greatest urban populations. It was in these industrial areas of the North and the Midwest that a score of new labor organizations were established in the late 1860s. By far the most influential was the Noble Order of the Knights of Labor. Founded in 1869, the Knights of Labor attempted to bring all laboring people—skilled and unskilled, black and white, men and women, white-collar and blue-collar—into one big union.

The Knights of Labor and the AFL Unions

At the head of the Knights of Labor was Terence V. Powderly, an immigrant who rose from a railway switchtender to mayor of Scranton, Pennsylvania. An eloquent speaker and tireless organizer, Powderly had great hopes for the Knights:

We seek and intend to enlist the services of men of every society, or every party, and every religion, and every nation in the crusade we have inaugurated against those twin monsters, tyranny and monopoly.

Powderly persuaded the Knights to support equal pay for women, temperance, the abolition of child labor, and above all, the establishment of cooperatively owned industrial plants. A man of peace, he opposed strikes and wished to submit labor disputes to **arbitration**, that is, a process whereby an impartial third party helps workers and management reach an agreement.

Membership in the Knights grew rapidly in the early 1880s—especially after the striking Knights won against Jay Gould's Wabash Railway. Membership in the Knights soared from 100,000 in 1885 to 700,000 in less than a year. Conservative newspapers feared that Powderly, the "labor czar," would become stronger than the President.

The Knights of Labor, however, were soon swamped with troubles. The union had wasted its funds in unsuccessful attempts to set up cooperative businesses. Moreover, the effort to unite different kinds of labor into one big union had failed. Workers in different crafts and industries often had little in common with one another and little interest in working for the same goals.

Membership in the Knights of Labor was open to men and women of all races. Here, Frank Farrell (left) introduces Terence Powderly, the founder of the union, at the Knights' tenth annual convention. What aims did the union strive to achieve for its members?

The decline of the Knights was hastened by the Haymarket Square riot in Chicago on May 4, 1886. This event followed a peaceful meeting of some 3,000 workers who gathered together to protest the shooting of striking McCormick Harvester Company workers by the police. As the meeting was breaking up, someone threw a bomb into a group of police officers. Seven persons were killed and more than 60 were injured. Although the identity of the bomb-thrower was never established, 8 anarchist leaders were arrested and found guilty of taking part in the crime. Four were later executed for murder. Although the Knights of Labor could in no way be held responsible for the Haymarket affair, it became identified with radicals and violence. From then on, the Knights of Labor declined as rapidly as it had grown.

In 1886, the year the Knights of Labor began to decline, the American Federation of Labor was organized. In its principles as well as its structure, the AFL differed greatly from the Knights. While the Knights had accepted a large number of unskilled workers, the AFL accepted only skilled workers. This policy indicated the reluctance of the AFL to accept women, African Americans and immigrants—the majority of whom were unskilled—into their union. Another difference was that the AFL organized workers into separate unions, each covering a particular craft.

Each union managed its own affairs with only occasional help from the national organization. The AFL's fees were relatively high, in order to restrict membership, build up strike funds, and provide benefits to members and their families in cases of sickness, unemployment, or death.

The AFL might never have enjoyed the success it did were it not for Samuel Gompers, its president for 37 years. Born

Examining Illustrations *On the night of May 4, 1886, a crowd gathered in Chicago's Haymarket Square to protest police violence. As the meeting was breaking up, a bomb was thrown into a group of police and the police fired into the crowd. What effect did the Haymarket Affair have on the labor movement?*

in London, Gompers brought to the United States some of the ideas of British trade unions, the best established in the world. Gompers, who prided himself on being practical, was interested only in day-to-day gains of AFL members—higher wages, shorter hours, and benefits for disabled workers.

So effective was the organization and leadership of the AFL that when hard times hit again in 1893, its member unions not only survived but thrived. Between 1890 and 1900, when other labor organizations lost members, AFL membership rose from 190,000 to 500,000.

The Pullman Strike of 1894

To address the needs of unskilled and semiskilled labor—and yet avoid the "one big union" approach favored by the Knights—a new type of labor organization developed. This was the **industrial union,** in which all classes of workers in a single industry are joined together. Among those who saw the advantages of an industrial union was Eugene V. Debs, an officer of the Brotherhood of Locomotive Firemen, one of several railway unions. He felt that the separation of

railway workers into different unions weakened their power. Conductors and engineers, the "aristocracy of labor," looked down on less skilled and lower paid workers, and the unskilled had no organization at all. Debs, therefore, started a new organization in 1893—the American Railway Union. This union included all types of railroad workers—from conductors, firemen, and engineers to telegraph operators and station clerks. By 1894 the union was powerful enough to force James J. Hill, the owner of the Great Northern Railway, to restore wage cuts to his employees.

Hardly had the Great Northern strike ended than the Pullman strike began in Pullman, Illinois, the company town built by George M. Pullman for his workers. Losing profit because of a reduced demand for its railroad cars, the Pullman Palace Car Company laid off two-thirds of its employees and cut the wages of the rest. It did not, however, reduce either the dividends it paid to stockholders or the rents charged to workers in the town. When a delegation of workers met with Pullman to protest the pay cuts, they were fired. At noon the following day, 10,000 Pullman workers walked off the job.

The American Railway Union took up the Pullman workers' cause. Debs' first move was to propose that the dispute be referred to arbitration. Pullman, however, replied, "There is nothing to arbitrate." Realizing that negotiating with Pullman was futile, the union called for members to refuse to work on any train that included a Pullman car. Railway workers answered the union's call. Within 5 days 100,000 railroad workers had walked off the job. Railway traffic west of Chicago was almost paralyzed. Debs warned his followers not to interfere with the mail and appealed to them to be "orderly and law-abiding." A few mail trains were delayed, but there were few disturbances.

Then President Grover Cleveland stepped in. Over the protests of the mayor of Chicago and the governor of Illinois, who claimed they had matters in hand, the President sent federal troops to guard mail trains. Cleveland adamantly defended the decision:

...if it takes every dollar in the Treasury and every soldier in the United States army to deliver a postal card in Chicago, that postal card should be delivered.

Immediately, rioting broke out as angry mobs, sympathetic to the strikers, taunted the soldiers. Members of the American Railway Union kept out of trouble, but nevertheless received the blame. Even before the troops had arrived, the federal government obtained an **injunction**, or court order, forbidding the union to continue the strike. Debs refused to obey the injunction and was imprisoned. Even outside labor circles there was strong feeling that putting Debs in jail was an unfair extension of judicial power. The Springfield *Republican,* noted that:

If Debs has been violating the law, let him be indicted, tried by a jury, and punished. Let him not be made the victim of an untenable court order and deprived of his liberty entirely within the discretion of a judge.

Without Debs' leadership, the Pullman strike collapsed and with it, the American Railway Union. From that point on, employers used the injunction as a means of breaking up strikes.

Although labor unions lost more disputes than they won, and most workers remained unorganized (only 4 percent of American workers belonged to unions in 1900), workers made some gains in the late 1800s. Federal and state legislation reflected the growing political influence of labor. Wages began to increase slowly, and the workday was shortened. Moreover, nearly every state passed laws regulating working conditions and requiring minimum standards of health and safety.

SUMMARY

The Knights of Labor attempted, with only limited success, to bring all skilled and unskilled workers, into one big union. The American Federation of Labor, an association of separate unions, was more successful but excluded unskilled labor. The industrial union included all classes of workers in a given industry. One such union, the American Railway Union, forced the Great Northern Railway to restore wage cuts. Subsequently, however, the union collapsed following the arrest of its leader in the Pullman strike. In spite of the unions' difficulties, workers made some short-term gains.

CHECKING FOR UNDERSTANDING

1. **Identify** Knights of Labor, American Federation of Labor, Terence V. Powderly, Samuel Gompers, Eugene Debs, Haymarket Square

2. **Define** arbitration, industrial union, injunction

3. **Summarize** the difficulties faced by the Knights of Labor and the American Railway Union.

4. **Examine** the achievements of labor unions during the late 1800s.

5. **Compare** the Great Northern strike and the Pullman strike.

THINKING CRITICALLY

6. **Supporting an Opinion** Do you agree with Debs that an industrial union was more powerful than separate unions of craft workers? Why or why not?

CONNECTIONS: HISTORY AND GOVERNMENT

7. **Interpreting a Quotation** Read President Cleveland's explanation for calling in troops during the Pullman strike. How does it explain the federal government's involvement?

Changing Patterns of Immigration

SETTING THE SCENE

I was thrilled with the realization of what this freedom of education meant. A little girl from across the alley came and offered to conduct us to school.... We knew the word school. We understood....This incident impressed me more than anything I had heard in advance of the freedom of education in America.

—MARY ANTIN
Russian immigrant, 1894

Section Focus

Between 1860 and 1900 almost 14 million people came to America. Another 14.5 million came between 1900 and 1915. Even more significant than the increase in numbers was the changing character of immigration during these years. The vast majority no longer came from northern and western Europe but from southern and eastern Europe.

Objectives

After studying this section, you should be able to:
• Identify the reasons that immigrants came to the United States.
• Distinguish between the "old" and the "new" immigration.

The 13 colonies had been settled mainly by English settlers. Other settlers from Holland, Sweden, France, Scotland, Ireland and Germany came later. After 1815, however, increasing numbers of immigrants started to arrive from Ireland. During these early years, a total of only about 400,000 immigrants had come to America. Beginning in the 1850s and continuing after the Civil War, immigration rose sharply.

The "Old Immigration"

During the period of "Old Immigration," which started in the 1830s and reached a high point in the 1840s, there was a great wave of immigration to America's shores. Between 1840 and 1850, an additional 1.5 million newcomers journeyed to the United States. Nearly one-half were from Ireland, which was suffering from a potato famine. Between 1846 and 1860, about 1.5 million Irish immigrated to America settling in New York and Boston, which functioned as ports of entry into the United States.

In the 1840s large numbers of Germans also began to come to America. Some left their homeland because of crop failures. Others came to escape political persecution after the failure of the Revolution of 1848. Still others were German Jews seeking religious freedom. Large numbers of German immigrants settled on farms and in cities in the Midwest—areas that were rapidly growing and had job opportunities. The Germans gave a distinctive flavor to such cities as Cincinnati, Milwaukee, and St. Louis. Then, in the 1850s, after the Gold Rush, Chinese immigrants began to come to the Pacific Coast. Many were hired to help build the railroads. About 100,000 Chinese had settled in the far West by the mid-1870s.

During the colonial period, most immigrants were readily accepted. Workers were badly needed in all the colonies. In the 1840s and 1850s, however, some native-born Americans began to resent the newcomers, especially the Irish and German immigrants. The Irish in particular suffered discrimination. Some Americans resented them because they dressed and sounded "different" and because they were Catholics.

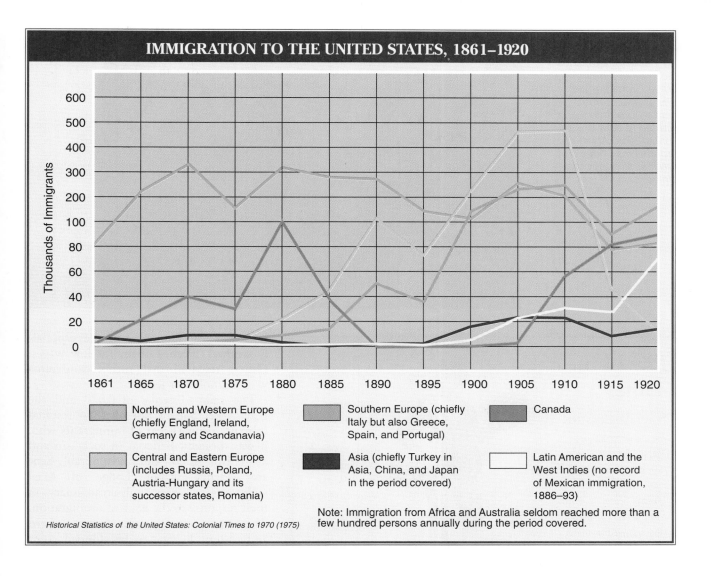

IMMIGRATION TO THE UNITED STATES, 1861–1920

Thousands of Immigrants

Legend:
- Northern and Western Europe (chiefly England, Ireland, Germany and Scandanavia)
- Southern Europe (chiefly Italy but also Greece, Spain, and Portugal)
- Canada
- Central and Eastern Europe (includes Russia, Poland, Austria-Hungary and its successor states, Romania)
- Asia (chiefly Turkey in Asia, China, and Japan in the period covered)
- Latin American and the West Indies (no record of Mexican immigration, 1886–93)

Historical Statistics of the United States: Colonial Times to 1970 (1975)

Note: Immigration from Africa and Australia seldom reached more than a few hundred persons annually during the period covered.

The "New Immigration"

Until the 1880s most newcomers had come from the nations of western Europe. After 1885, however, large numbers came from nations of southern and eastern Europe. The new immigrants were from Italy, Russia, and Poland, as well as from the nations of the Austro-Hungarian Empire. These newcomers were for the most part poor. They hoped to find a better life in America. In part, it was their labor that made the rapid industrialization of the United States possible. For many Jews, Poles, and Czechs immigrating to the United States was the only way for them to escape persecution in their homeland. One Jewish immigrant noted that

"the only hope for the Jews in Russia is to become Jews out of Russia."

The new immigrants flocked to the cities. There they lived together in ethnically homogeneous neighborhoods such as "Little Italy" or the Jewish "Lower East Side" in New York City. There they practiced the ways of life they were used to and spoke their native languages. They recreated the churches, synagogues, clubs, and newspapers of their homeland and adapted them to their new environment.

This huge influx of immigrants created special social problems. Because immigrants lived in their own neighborhoods, practiced their own customs, and spoke their own languages, many Americans wondered if they could ever be assimilated

Examining Graphs
Beginning in the late 1800s, immigration from central, eastern, and southern Europe began to increase. In what year did immigration from those regions surpass the total from northern and western Europe?

**Examining
Photographs**
*An inspector examines
the eyes of a newly
arrived immigrant at
Ellis Island. Some
native-born Americans
wanted to slow or stop
immigration. At what
groups was Lodge's
proposed literacy test
aimed?*

Life of the Times

ITALIAN CUISINE

*Between 1890 and
1910 about 2.7 mil-
lion southern Italians
immigrated to the
United States. Coming
from farms in Italy,
they settled primarily in
the cities on America's
east coast. By 1920
New York City had
become home to more
Italians than there were
living in Venice,
Genoa, and Florence
combined. Italian-
Americans adjusted to
many changes in their
adopted country, and
they adapted their
cooking to substitute
some more readily
available ingredients.
These Italian dishes
became a lasting con-
tribution to American
culture.*

Pasta was
enjoyed by
everyone,
sometimes sev-
eral times a
week. Maca-
roni, manicot-
ti, spaghetti,
and lasagna
were first intro-
duced to
Americans by
the little shops
nestled among
the blocks of
tenements.
Often macaroni or some other form of noo-
dles could be seen drying in the windows.

Italian bakery ovens produced the first
pizzas, which had been a strictly Neapolitan
item back in Italy. Opening in 1905,
"G Lombardi" on Spring Street in New
York's Little Italy became the first known
pizzeria in the United States. Deep-dish,
Chicago-style pizza, cooked in a black skillet,
did not come along until 1943, when it was
created by Ike Sewell and Ric Riccardo at
Pizzeria Uno in Chicago. After World War II,
the pizza industry boomed in the United
States. Within 10 years there were few cities
that did not have at least one pizzeria.

into American life. Some people, especially workers, blamed them for low wages.
Others resented that many immigrants
were Catholics or Jews.

The railroad strike of 1877 and the
Haymarket Square riot of 1886 resulted
in many people's fear of immigrants who,
it was thought, believed in socialism and
anarchism. A few politicians, notably Senator Henry Cabot Lodge of Massachusetts, were strongly reactionary in
their response to the issue of immigration.
They wanted immigration from southern
and eastern Europe to be stopped completely. In 1896 Lodge argued for a bill
that would exclude all prospective immigrants who could not read or write 25
words of the United States Constitution
in some language. Lodge concluded that
such a test would:

———————

*...bear most heavily
upon the Italians, Russians, Poles,
Hungarians, Greeks,
and Asiatics...races most affected
by the test are those whose
emigration has...swelled rapidly....and
who are most alien to the great
body of he United States.*

———————

Examining Photographs *During the late 1800s, "new" immigrants poured into the United States, braving the long and difficult journey to start a new life. Why did many people perceive these newcomers as a threat?*

Linking Across Time

MODERN IMMIGRANTS

Today the flow of immigrants to America is higher than in any decade since 1900-1910. Six hundred thousand immigrants arrive yearly. Like those of the late 1800s and early 1900s, today's immigrants also come to escape oppression or to make a better life for themselves and their children. Unlike their predecessors contemporary immigrants come from Asia, the Caribbean, and Latin America.

In the late 1800s, hostility toward many of the new racial and ethnic groups coming into the new country grew. The differences in the customs, dress, and language of the new arrivals created a basic distrust of the foreign born by many native-born Americans. Some historians believe that this reaction was a response to the rapid changes occurring in America because of industrialization. For those native-born Americans who were uncertain and disturbed by social change, immigrants became easy targets of hostility.

Some Americans formed groups to counter what they considered the immigrant threat. One of these groups, the American Protective Association, was founded in 1887 to protest the large number of Catholic immigrants. In some parts of the country, local laws were passed that prohibited immigrants from holding certain kinds of jobs and denied them other rights. Jewish immigrants, for

example, were denied admission to some universities. In addition, the immigrants faced actual physical attacks.

The anti-immigration movement was not limited to groups such as the American Protective Association. Some well-known scholars of the time were susceptible to these feelings as well. Historian and future-President Woodrow Wilson and frontier historian Frederick Jackson Turner lamented the lessening flow of immigration from northern Europe and the rise in numbers of "inferior stocks" coming to America. One writer considered the new immigration a plot by European governments to "unload the sweepings of their jails and asylums."

Anti-immigration sentiment was not limited to newcomers from Europe, however. The Chinese, too, suffered discrimination on the Pacific Coast. Discovery of gold in 1849 and the subsequent demand for cheap labor first brought the Chinese to

Examining Political Cartoons *This anti-immigration cartoon, drawn by F. Victor Gillom in 1890, has the Statue of Liberty threatening to go back to France if the United States becomes an "immigrant dumping site." Which racial and ethnic groups encountered the strongest hostility?*

California. Many found work in the gold fields or on the construction of the Central Pacific Railroad. By 1852 there were some 25,000 Chinese men, women, and children living on the Pacific Coast and thereafter they came at the rate of 4,000 a year. By the end of the 1870s, there were almost 75,000 Chinese in California alone. Their willingness to work for low wages prompted a violent anti-Chinese movement among the white workers of California. Such feelings intensified during hard economic times. During the depression that followed the panic of 1873, unemployed workers in California attacked the Chinese. Some Americans began to demand that Chinese immigrants be excluded from the United States.

In 1879 Congress forbade the importing of foreign workers under contract—a law aimed primarily at the Chinese. Then, in 1882, Congress, responding to pressure from the western states, suspended nearly all immigration from China for 10 years.

SUMMARY

Beginning in the 1830s, immigrants from northern and western Europe poured into the United States, driven by crop failures, persecution, or hopes for a better life. In the 1880s, immigrants began arriving from southern and eastern Europe. Their labor made rapid industrialization possible, but some Americans blamed immigrants for keeping wages low. They tended to cluster in ethnic neighborhoods, maintaining their own language and customs. Ethnic and religious tensions developed, erupting into violence when Chinese workers were attacked by unemployed workers following the Panic of 1877. The Chinese became the first targets of anti-immigration legislation.

CHECKING FOR UNDERSTANDING

1. **Identify** Henry Cabot Lodge
2. **Explain** why people migrated from Europe to the United States.
3. **Differentiate** the "Old Immigration" from the "New Immigration."
4. **Explain** why some Americans feared and disliked immigrant groups.
5. **Identify** two attempts to decrease immigration to the United States.

THINKING CRITICALLY

6. **Understanding Bias** Throughout history, people suffering hardship have found "scapegoats" on whom to blame their troubles. Explain why immigrants were chosen as scapegoats by native-born residents during the 1800s.

CONNECTIONS: HISTORY AND RELIGION

7. **Recognizing Causes** How did religious prejudice in the United States create problems for some immigrants? Was religious prejudice any worse in other parts of the world?

★★★★★★★★★★★★★★★★★★★

City Life and Problems

I looked about the narrow street of squeezed-in stores and houses, ragged clothes ...ash-cans and garbage cans cluttering the sidewalks.... "Where are the green fields and open spaces in America?"

—ANZIA YEZIERSKA
A Jewish girl who emigrated
from Poland, 1901

Section Focus

With the rise of industrialism, the landscape of the nation changed. Railroads crisscrossed the continent. Where farms once stood, factories spewed forth black smoke. Thousands of Americans left the nation's farms hoping to make their fortunes in the city. Millions of immigrants came to better their lives and share in the benefits of the new industrial age.

Objectives

After studying this section, you should be able to:
- Identify the factors that led to the growth of cities during the late 1800s.
- List the problems resulting from an increase in the urban population.

All over the nation—but especially in the Northeast—cities were growing rapidly. This urban growth was a result of industrialization. In 1840, one out of every 12 Americans lived in a city with a population of more than 8,000. By 1900, however, one out of every three Americans lived in a large city. Why were so many people attracted to the cities? One reason was that rising new industries held out the promise of jobs and opportunity. Where else could immigrants—or other Americans for that matter—fulfill the "rags to riches" dream of making a fortune overnight? The cities of the 1890s held the promise of excitement and activity in contrast to the isolation of rural farm life. There were bright lights, running water, modern plumbing, museums, libraries, theaters, shops, convenient transportation, and countless things to do and see. City people found in the noises, the crowds, the excitements a charm they were unable to resist.

Urbanization

Between 1860 and 1900 American urban areas grew twice as fast as the total population. Chicago, which in the 1830s had been a frontier town with a few hundred residents, became a vast metropolis of almost 2 million people. New York became the second-largest city in the world. The day dreaded by Thomas Jefferson—when Americans would abandon farm life—was clearly on the way.

The new industrial cities were essentially the product of the mines, the factories, the steamships, and the railroads. New cities appeared, or old ones mushroomed, near coal and iron deposits (Birmingham and Pittsburgh), near sources of water power (Lowell and Lawrence, Massachusetts), shipping centers (Baltimore and New York City), and at railroad centers (Omaha and Chicago).

Once established, cities seemed to generate their own growth. To serve industry, such facilities as banks, insurance companies, docks, and warehouses were developed. These, in turn, attracted more industry and workers. Immigrants, lacking the agricultural skill or money to buy a farm, could often find employment only in urban industrialized areas. In the big cities, too, immigrants often had relatives who spoke their native language and preserved their customs.

But an even greater number of people who flocked to the big cities came from America's rural areas. They came not only from the rocky hillsides of New Hampshire and Vermont but even from rich lands in Iowa and Illinois.

Problems of City Life

Although the modern industrial city offered many people the opportunity for a higher standard of living than they had had before, it also confronted them with an unfamiliar and often unattractive environment. The new cities were built with less concern for the comforts of the inhabitants than for the profits of builders and real-estate speculators. People poured into the cities faster than housing could be built to accommodate them. Many had no choice but to live in tenements, poorly constructed five- or six-story buildings that housed many families. Many of the rooms had no windows and were often dark, narrow, and airless.

As more and more people were crowded together and the buildings began to deteriorate, city slums developed. Lacking proper sanitation, tenements became foul-smelling and vermin-infested. Typhoid and other epidemic diseases often spread rapidly.

Other city services besides housing were inadequate. There was a shortage of police and firefighters. City water was impure and the sewers were often clogged. Garbage collection was sporadic. In addition, there were no attempts at city planning. Little was done to provide for open spaces, parks and playgrounds, or to take advantage of rivers and other natural features. The few open spaces were more often than not used as garbage dumps or simply left vacant, where a scanty growth of grass and weeds competed with cinders and tin cans.

Rivers and harbors were polluted by sewage and factory wastes, and the air was made foul by smoke from thousands of chimneys. In many ways the new environment seemed a sort of prison, cutting off people from sun, air, and natural beauty.

The growth of cities created many practical and social problems. There was, for example, a demand for new sources of water, as wells and brooks provided too scanty a supply and were often polluted. New York City, the first of the major cities to meet this problem head-on, built the Croton Aqueduct 25 miles outside the city limits.

Another issue that had to be addressed was transportation. Cities had become so large in area that a more efficient means of inter-city transportation had to be developed. This was accomplished by the horse car, and later by the elevated railway, trolley car, and subway. The demand for space in preferred localities such as Wall Street in New York or the Loop in Chicago resulted in the creation of huge

AMERICAN PORTRAITS

JANE ADDAMS
1860-1935

By the time the guns of World War I began blazing in 1914, Jane Addams was already famous as the founder of Hull House—the settlement house that served Chicago's immigrants and urban poor.

But by then peace had become her passion. In 1915 Addams urged European leaders to find a way to end the mounting carnage. When the United States entered the war, she was labeled unpatriotic for holding true to her pacifist ideals. After the war ended in 1918, Addams worked to assure no repetition of the "war to end all wars." She was elected president of the Women's International League for Peace and Freedom in 1915 and held that office until 1929. Her devotion to world peace was recognized in 1931, when she was named corecipient with educator Nicholas Murray Butler of the Nobel Peace Prize.

**Examining
Illustrations**
*In city tenements
poverty and over-
crowding brought on
many social problems.
This watercolor shows
Baxter Street in New
York City during the
late 1800s. What prob-
lems did residents of
tenements in the
nation's larger cities
face?*

skyscrapers, which, in turn, added a verti-cal dimension to transportation—in the form of the elevator.

An unexpected problem of urban life, however, was the increase in crime. Until the rise of the city, there had naturally been occasional violence and theft, but never on a scale demanding an organized police force. There had been nothing resembling modern police until the for-mation of the Metropolitan Police of Lon-don, known as "bobbies," about 1830. But because the problems experienced by growing urban centers were new, old solu-tions could not be relied upon. Indeed, sometimes it seemed as if the answers were as varied as the problems. Some peo-ple looked back to an earlier morality. Especially pious people sought to enforce the Puritan Sabbath as a means of regen-erating the city. As a result, restaurants and amusement places were closed, and there were even efforts to forbid the run-ning of trains and streetcars.

Such reactions, however, seemed out of touch with the realities of life in factories, shops, and slums. One of those who did face these realities was Jacob A. Riis (REES), a Danish-American police reporter for New York newspapers. In the course of his work, Riis had seen again and again the connection between slums and human degradation. In 1890 he focused public attention on the ill-effects of slum-living in a best-selling book, *How the Other Half Lives.* By appealing to pub-lic conscience, Riis secured legislation that reduced the worst slum conditions, along with other measures that improved the lives of city dwellers, such as playgrounds for schools. Among his close friends was a rising young Republican politician, Theodore Roosevelt, whom he "educated" by taking him into tenements, sweat-shops, and jails.

The year before *How the Other Half Lives* was published, Jane Addams found-ed in a Chicago slum, the most famous settlement house in the United States, Hull House. About this neighborhood, Addams wrote:

*[T]he streets were inexpressibly dirty…the
street lighting bad.…Many
houses have no water save the faucet in the
back yard; there are no fire escapes…*

Addams, a deeply religious woman, was inspired by a passionate desire to put her faith to work. Modeling her endeavor on

Connections

HISTORY AND ENVIRONMENT

URBAN POLLUTION AND PUBLIC HEALTH

Citizens who complain about air pollution, poor water quality, and inadequate garbage disposal in modern cities might feel at home if transported to the New York City of 1866. A report on the sanitary conditions of the city in that year identified the following problems.

(1) filthy streets; (2) neglected garbage and domestic refuse; (3) obstructed and faulty sewers and drains; (4) neglected privies and stables; (5) cattle pens and large stables in the more populous districts; (6) neglected and filthy markets; (7) slaughter-houses and hide and fat depots in close proximity to populous streets; (8) droves of cattle and swine in crowded streets; (9) swill-milk stables…; (10) bone-boiling, fat-melting…within the city limits; (11)…offensive exhalations…in gas manufacture…; (12)…dumping grounds and manure-yards in vicinity of populous streets; (13)…management of refuse and junk materials…; (14) overcrowding of… public conveyances…; (15) the neglect of dead animals in the streets and gutters of the city.

Traffic jam on Broadway, 1869

★★★★★★★★★★

MAKING THE ENVIRONMENT CONNECTION

1. Categorize the pollution problems under air, soil, and water.

2. Why do you think the speed of urban growth contributes to environmental problems?

LINKING PAST AND PRESENT

3. Which of these problems are unlikely to occur in modern cities?

★★★★★★★★★★

Toynbee Hall, a settlement house in England, Jane Addams was determined to improve the life of the "other half." Hull House soon had activities as varied as an art gallery and a gymnasium, as well as hot lunches for factory workers and classes in English. Above all, Addams was interested in helping children, believing that "a fence at the top of a precipice is better than an ambulance at the bottom." To that end, Addams surrounded herself with young people glad to enlist in a war against human suffering.

Religious conviction and the desire to serve humanity were also the motivating forces behind the founding of other settlement houses, including the Henry Street Settlement in New York City, the Santa Maria Institute in Cincinnati, and South End House in Boston. In addition to providing immediate services to neighborhood people, settlement houses were schools where hundreds of men and women learned social responsibility.

Many of these people later entered politics and helped to promote reform legislation, either as lobbyists or as officeholders. "Graduates" of Hull House, for example, were instrumental in securing the first playgrounds in Chicago, better garbage collection, and the first Illinois factory inspection law. Frances Perkins, trained in a New York settlement house, embarked on a political career that led to her appointment as Secretary of Labor, the first woman in the President's cabinet.

Beautifying the City

Among the indictments against sprawling industrial cities were their ugliness and their lack of provision for rest and recreation. Architects and landscape designers were among those who sought remedies. In 1876 New York City opened Central Park, designed by Frederick L. Olmsted and Calvert Vaux, as "a great breathing space for the toiling masses." Olmsted was the first person to use the term *landscape architect* as the name for this kind of work. He also designed Prospect Park in Brooklyn.

Many other cities followed New York's example. In 1892 and 1893 Chicago celebrated the 400th anniversary of European arrival in America by putting on a great World's Fair. The fairgrounds were designed by Olmsted, who turned "a rough, tangled stretch of bog and dune" along Lake Michigan into a gleaming "White City," with buildings in the classical style surrounded by lagoons and landscaped grassy areas.

The Chicago Columbian Exposition revealed that American architecture was emerging from the period of ignorance and bad taste into which it had fallen earlier in the 1800s. The best American architects now thoroughly understood European styles and adapted them for modern use. The firm of McKim, Mead, and White used the Italian Renaissance style in their design for the Boston Public Library. Henry Richardson adapted Romanesque style in his design for churches, libraries, warehouses, and even department stores. Two notable examples of his style are Trinity Church in Boston and the Marshall Field's department store in Chicago.

The Transportation Building at the Chicago Exposition, designed by Louis Sullivan, did not, however, imitate earlier styles. Sullivan preached a new concept: "Form follows function." By that he meant that the architect should create designs that reveal a building's purpose and method of construction. Sullivan was one of the first architects to design skyscrapers. His influence, both directly and later through the work of his pupil Frank Lloyd Wright, reached worldwide.

Examining Fine Art *As the United States became a nation of cities, public services expanded to serve the needs of the people. Paved roads, electric street lights, and streetcars improved transportation as shown in this W. Louis Sonntag watercolor of New York City's Bowery in 1895. What did critics say about the appearance of cities?*

The finest example of a structure in which form expressed function was the Brooklyn Bridge. Completed in 1883, 16 years after it was begun, it was the largest suspension bridge in the world at that time. Hung from great steel cables with a span half again as long as that of any previous bridge, it was designed and constructed by two German-Americans, John Roebling and his son Washington Roebling. During the project John was killed on the job. His son continued directing the work until he himself was injured. The work was then taken over by John's wife, who with her son's direction, completed the project.

Examining Photographs *Before 1880 buildings rarely were higher than five stories. Skyscrapers such as the Flatiron Building in New York transformed America's cities. What did architects mean by "form follows function"?*

For those who wished to continue their education, American cities provided opportunities that had never existed before. Perhaps the most important agencies promoting adult education were improved public libraries. In 1876 the American Library Association was founded to encourage "the best reading for the largest number at the least expense." By 1900, the public libraries, which receive support from taxes, revenues, and private donations, came to be recognized as "no less important than the schoolhouse in the system of popular education."

To meet the needs of the hundreds of thousands of workers in the nation's industrial cities, new means of **merchandising,** or the buying and selling of goods, were created. One striking example was the department store. Stores such as A. T. Stewart and John Wanamaker were retail centers where nearly all kinds of goods were sold in one location. These stores had an enormous appeal to people of all classes, particularly women. Here the working class could mix freely with those who were better off, and be, at least for a short time, on an equal footing with them. As a result, the downtown areas of cities became centers where women came to shop. Merchants who wanted this new business were active in making sure that the areas were kept clean and attractive. New streets, sidewalks, and buildings were constructed.

Despite some setbacks, achievements were made solving some of the problems facing major cities. The availability of electricity enabled shops and factories to remain open after dark and thus stimulated urban nightlife as well. And municipal governments and private organizations made gains in their efforts to solve some of the public-health problems that accompanied the rapid growth of the cities.

Throughout the late 1800s city governments turned their efforts toward providing the services needed for their citizens. Steps were taken to reduce crime and to improve recreational opportunities and living conditions. Methods of identifying criminals, such as the use of photographs, were improved. Electric street lights added a large measure of safety on city streets.

Many parks were built, usually toward the edges of already congested cities. Public utilities provided electricity, clean water, and sewage services for many urban areas. By 1898 approximately 350 communities had built public owned electric light companies, and by 1900 more than 3,500 public waterworks had been constructed nationwide.

The need for better communication accompanied the growth for better urbanization and industrialization. As a result the use of the telephone spread rapidly. Within a few years after the telephone was invented in 1876, telephone exchanges were established in more than 80 cities. Within 20 years, nearly 800,000 telephones were in use throughout the United States, twice as many as were in use in Europe. The impact of the telephone upon American life was enormous, linking many of the urban and rural areas of the nation almost instantly.

Despite these changes for the better, many reformers felt that this was only a start and that it was essential to find solutions for problems before they occurred. More and more reformers urged government to deal with the causes of social and economic problems. Jacqueline Shaw Lowell, the founder of the New York Charity Organization Society, expressed this attitude when she noted:

[There are] five hundred thousand wage earners in this city, 200,000 of them women, and 75,000 of those working under dreadful conditions.…
If the working people had all they ought to have, we should not have the paupers and the criminals.…
It is better to save them before they go under than to spend your life…taking care of them afterwards.

Section Four Review

SUMMARY

Cities offered jobs, conveniences, educational and cultural facilities, and entertainment. However, as they grew, the air became fouled and water became polluted. People crowded into tenements, which quickly became slums that bred disease and crime. Settlement houses attempted to improve the lives of the urban poor and pressed for legislation to improve city conditions. City governments and private organizations increasingly turned their efforts to providing services needed for their citizens. Architects and landscape designers created tasteful buildings and relaxing parks. Still, cities provided a backdrop against which poverty contrasted sharply with the indulgences of the idle rich.

CHECKING FOR UNDERSTANDING

1. **Identify** Jacob A. Riis, Jane Addams, Louis Sullivan

2. **Define** merchandising

3. **List** the factors that led to the growth of cities during the late 1800s.

4. **Summarize** the problems that developed as population in urban areas grew.

5. **Describe** the efforts made to improve life and conditions in the cities.

CRITICAL THINKING

6. **Understanding Analogies**   How does Jane Addams's theory that "a fence at the top of a precipice is better than an ambulance at the bottom" explain her focus on children?

LINKING PAST AND PRESENT

7. **Proposing Solutions**   Cities today see an ever increasing number of people affected by poverty. Many have lost their homes. Can you suggest any as-yet-untried solutions to these urban problems?

★ Chapter 19 Review ★

★ Summary

Workers faced long hours, unsafe and unhealthy working conditions, and low wages. Unionizing was hampered by employers, the public, and workers themselves. Even so, workers made their presence felt during a violent railroad strike in 1877.

Two early labor unions were the Knights of Labor, one big union, and the American federation of Labor, an association of separate unions. These were followed by the American Railway Union, which took in all railroad industry-related workers. Despite difficulties in gaining their objectives, union activities eventually won some concessions in wages, hours, and conditions for their members.

Immigration from Northern and Western Europe gave way to new arrivals from Southern and Eastern Europe in the later 1800s. As always, immigrants were driven by old fears and new hopes. Although contributing much to America's rapid industrialization, the tendency of the newer immigrants to keep to themselves created tensions with native-born Americans.

Cities became a place to live and work for more people. However, the attractions of jobs and conveniences were soon outweighed by the drawbacks of slums, crime, and pollution. Gradually, efforts were made to improve living conditions, recreational opportunities, and the appearance of cities, although poverty only became more visible.

★ Using Vocabulary

Use the following terms in sentences or short paragraphs. Relate them by using two or more of the terms in each sentence or paragraph.

real wages	company towns
business cycle	blacklists
lockout	collective bargaining
arbitration	industrial union
injunction	tenements

★ Reviewing Facts

1. **Discuss** the hardships and problems that plagued industrial workers in the late 1800s.

2. **Report** on the problems facing labor unions in the late 1800s.
3. **Summarize** the achievements of labor unions during the late 1800s.
4. **List** the reasons why people immigrated to the United States.
5. **Cite** reasons for the growth of cities during the late 1800s.
6. **Identify** the problems created by growth in urban populations.
7. **Describe** efforts to improve nineteenth-century city life.

★ Understanding Concepts

UNITY

1. Read the quotation by Terrence Powderly on page 562. How did Powderly envision such a unified force as being capable of confronting big business?
2. How could unions, by creating unity among workers, balance a business monopoly?

CONFLICT

3. How did conflicting goals among workers hamper efforts to organize the Knights of Labor? How did later unions overcome this problem?
4. With what groups did labor unions have conflict once they were organized? What were some of the reasons for the conflict?

★ Thinking Critically

1. **Understanding Stereotypes** What stereotypes of labor unions were created because of the actions of a few union members or nonunion strikers? How did they work against the efforts of organized labor?
2. **Understanding Effects** Explain how technology and industrialization created wealth among business owners. How did the same technology and industrialization create poverty among workers?
3. **Judging Relevance** How did economic hard times in other countries work to the advantage of United States industry? What problems did hard times cause in the United States?
4. **Supporting a Viewpoint** Thomas Jefferson had dreaded the day when most citizens would shift

from farms to the cities. In what way did city life during the later 1800s suggest that his dread was justified?

★ Writing About History

DESCRIPTION

Refer to the description of how to write a descriptive paragraph or essay in the History Writer's Handbook in the Appendix of this book. Your teacher will give you more specific instructions on the description's length and the assignment's due date.

Imagine you are a reporter assigned to cover the railroad strike of 1877. Write an article describing the scene of the strike as you arrive. Include enough sensory details so that your readers can share your experience and sense the mood and emotions of the strikers and onlookers.

★ Learning Cooperatively

Work with a partner to research a major strike that occurred within the last five years. Find information on the workers' grievances and the company's position in the strike. Use this information to take turns as a union representative and a company representative questioning each other during an arbitration meeting.

★ Mastering Skills

RECOGNIZING STEREOTYPES

Students who get good grades are often stereotyped as "brains." Girls can be stereotyped both as helpless and as caretakers. Scandinavian Americans are stereotyped as lacking a sense of humor. Likewise, Italians are stereotypically members of the Mafia.

A stereotype is a way of thinking about a person or group of people that follows a fixed pattern and does not allow for individual differences. Stereotyping is harmful because it portrays people as having only one trait and lacking in the depth that "real" people have. Also most stereotypes are negative and can lead to prejudice and discrimination.

Example Two methods can be used to help you recognize stereotypes in written material. One is to examine your sources and note the practices of the author or characters in them. From these practices, you can determine whether or not their views are stereotypic.

For example, your text states that "Conductors and engineers, the 'aristocracy of labor,' looked down on less skilled and lower paid workers." The less skilled workers were often recent immigrants who did not speak English well or understand local customs. However, they were stereotyped as being coarse, less intelligent, and unable to do the more skilled jobs.

The other method of recognizing stereotypes is to examine your source for the expression of a stereotype. A good way to check this is to look for absolutes (use of the word all): "All Irish immigrants are drunkards", or "All librarians are stuffy and boring."

Practice Read the examples below and, using the methods described above, decide whether or not they include stereotyping. Give reasons for your decisions.

1. The following is a fictional statement by an American factory owner: "I would never hire a union member. All union members are troublemakers. Once they join the union, they are no longer dependable workers."

2. The following is a statement by a citizen who voted against President John F. Kennedy in the 1960 election: "The U.S. should never have a Catholic as its president. All Catholics are puppets of the Pope."

3. The following statement is from a speech by Martin Luther King, African-American civil-rights leader during the 1950s and 1960s: "The marvelous new militancy (among African Americans) must not lead us to a distrust of all white people, for many of our white brothers. . .have come to realize that their destiny is tied up with our destiny. . . . .This offense we share. . .must be carried forth by a biracial army. We cannot walk alone."

4. The following statement is from a speech delivered by labor leader Samuel Gompers on May 1, 1890, concerning the eight-hour work day: "Is it not a fact that we find laborers in England and the United States, where the hours are eight, nine and ten hours a day—do we not find that the employers and laborers are more successful? Don't we find them selling articles cheaper? We do not need to trust the modern moralist to tell us those things. In all industries where the hours of labor are long, there you will find the least development of the power of invention. How can you expect a man to work 10 or 12 or 14 hours at his calling and then devote any time to the invention of a machine or discovery of a new principle or force?"

CHAPTER 20
The Gilded Age

SETTING THE SCENE

Historical Focus

American political life reached a low point between 1865 and 1900. Corruption in the form of graft and bribery became almost routine in local, state, and national government. Both political parties came under the influence of lobbyists and other special interests. Neither party was ready for change, although the assassination of President Garfield prompted civil service reform. Overall, the culture of the Gilded Age reflected a preoccupation with wealth and the partnership between business and politics.

Concepts to Understand

- How the spoils system and lobbyists fostered **corruption** in government.
- How **public protest** by a free press worked to end political corruption.

People to Know

William Tweed, Thomas Nast, Jay Gould, Samuel Clemens, Joseph Pulitzer

Places to Locate

New York City, Montana

Terms to Identify

graft, kickback, lobbyists, riders, antebellum, realism, expatriates, yellow journalism

Guided Reading

As you read this chapter, seek the answers to the following questions.

1. What were the major forms of political corruption?
2. What new forms of leisure pastimes and amusements attracted the interest of Americans before 1900?

SPANNING THE DECADES

POLITICAL		1872 *Crédit Mobilier scheme uncovered*	1880 *James Garfield elected President*	1883 *Pendleton Act passed*	1884 *Grover Cleveland elected President*
	1870		**1880**		
CULTURAL		1873 *One of the first schools of nursing opens at Bellevue Hospital in New York*	1876 *National Baseball League formed*	1883 *Joseph Pulitzer buys the New York* World	

Fairman Roger's Four-in-Hand *by Thomas Eakins, 1879*

1890
*McKinley Tariff
passed*

1890   1900

1890
*Reporter Nelly Bly
circles globe by
train and steamship
in 72 days*

1895
Stephen Crane publishes
The Red Badge of
Courage

*…There's an honest graft, and I'm an
example of how it works. I might sum up
the whole thing by saying: "I seen my
opportunities and I took 'em." … Ain't it
perfectly honest to charge a good price and
make a profit on my investment and
foresight? …*

—George Washington Plunkitt
New York City politician, 1905

A Tarnished Image

SETTING THE SCENE

What tells in holdin' your grip on your district is to go right down among the poor families and help them in the different ways they need help. If a family is burned out I don't ask whether they are Republicans or Democrats, I just get quarters for them...and fix them up till they get things runnin' again...

—GEORGE W. PLUNKITT
New York City politician, 1905

Section Focus

The voters of this postwar era swarmed to the polls, at the rate of 80 percent of all those eligible. The grass-roots level was a far more active center for political activity than nationally. Indeed, the voting public practiced their right out of necessity—with thousands of jobs handed out to political allies and votes bartered for ordinary needs of citizens, political participation became a matter of survival.

Objectives

After studying this section, you should be able to:

- Identify the major causes of increased political corruption in the post-Civil War era.
- Give examples of corruption at local, state, and national levels.

The Gilded Age was a phrase coined by two authors of the period—Mark Twain and Charles Dudley Warner—in a novel about the corrupt years of the Grant administration. They saw this era as a time when politicians were irresponsible, loyalties were shallow, and money was tainted.

In this post-Civil War period, the most ambitious and talented people were no longer attracted to politics but to business. Indeed, politics itself became something of a business. The goal of political entrepreneurs was to achieve power and position through political office. Quite often politicians were also able to line their pockets with money as a result. Corruption appeared to flourish at every level of government.

Political Machines

Some of the most outrageous examples of **graft**, or thievery in office, were those at the grass-roots level of city government. A major factor that contributed to corrupt city government was the rapid growth of cities. In 1840 there were only 131 cities in the United States; by 1880 there were 939. In addition, cities often doubled, tripled, or even quadrupled in size within a single decade. Services for these large populations had to be expanded at a rate that had never been experienced before. Providing increased police and fire protection, water supplies, and sewage disposal was a daunting task for what often were untrained and ill-paid city officials. At the same time, businesses were eager to get lucrative contracts for paving streets and building new schools. The result was an alliance between business and politics that fostered corruption.

The usual democratic restraints on abuses of power did not work well in the cities of this era. Large portions of the population of cities were immigrants who had little or no experience with democratic government. Many were accustomed to corruption in government. Both poor immigrants and native-born residents alike had little time to worry about abstract notions of government. They worked from dawn to dusk just to keep food on the table. Those more well-off, who might have gone into politics, were busy making money in business and real estate. As a result, almost every major city was dominated by a **political machine**—a party-linked political organization that maintained power by controlling votes, controlling the courts, and controlling the police as well.

The strength of a political machine came from the bottom up, not from the top down. Local politicians took care of the needs of their voters. They often provided groceries to families who were needy, organized free celebrations on important national holidays, attended ethnic religious and social events, and even helped get people out of jail. In this way politicians earned the loyalty of their neighborhood citizens. When election time came around, the votes were always there, keeping the helpful politicians in power.

The most notorious city machine was the "Tweed Ring" in New York City. In 1868 "Boss" William M. Tweed gained control of New York's Democratic machine, known locally by the name of its central meeting place—"Tammany Hall." For the next 3 years, he and his underlings managed to steal millions of dollars of city funds. The usual way this was done involved a process known as the "kickback." A **kickback** was an arrangement whereby contractors would pad, or increase, the amount of their bills for city work, and pay or "kickback" a percentage of that amount to politicians in the ring. In one example, a county courthouse that should have cost taxpayers $250,000 actually cost $11 million. One plasterer was paid almost $3 million for 9 months' work.

In 1871 *The New York Times* published evidence of Tweed's rampant greed. At the same time, Thomas Nast, a brilliant political cartoonist, ridiculed Tweed in his cartoons for *Harper's Weekly*. Nast's cartoons found their mark and were devastating. Tweed was driven to complain: "I don't care a straw for your newspaper articles: my people don't know how to read, but they can't help seeing them…pictures." Tweed and his cronies were ultimately convicted of criminal conduct and driven from office.

In spite of Tweed's removal, Tammany Hall continued to be an active influence in New York politics. This was true because local machine leaders drew their power from the local neighborhoods that they served 24 hours a day. A good deal of the graft, however, was used to help needy residents of the neighborhood **wards,** or small administrative divisions of a city. As Henry Adams, grandson of John Quincy Adams, described it:

…The Tammany district leader…keeps watch not only on the men but also on the women and children; knows their needs, their likes and dislikes, their troubles and their hopes.…Is it any wonder that scandals do not permanently disable Tammany and that it speedily recovers from what seems to be crushing defeat?

Occasionally city graft became so flagrant that voters were driven to "throw the rascals out" and put in a reform administration. Such movements often failed. Reform candidates focused on economy and honest administration but failed to understand the reasons why the political machines commandeered so much loyalty and met with such success.

Widespread Corruption

Politics at the state level was nearly as corrupt as in the cities. In many states big business stood to gain or lose tremendous amounts of money as a result of legislative votes on various matters, ranging from tax rates to internal improvements. Accordingly, companies spent large sums to influence legislators' votes.

In pre-Civil War times, businesspeople influenced politicians by writing letters and inviting them to expensive dinners. After the war the demands on government increased to the point that the amount of money spent by state governments was

By the time of the Gilded Age, the pool of citizens eligible to vote had expanded considerably. In the early days of the Republic, only white, male, property owners over age 21 could vote. By the 1850s, property— and in some states religious— restrictions had disappeared and most white adult males could vote. In 1870 the Fifteenth Amendment gave African American males the franchise. With the addition of women voters in 1920 and 18-year-old voters in 1971, the voter pool had reached its contemporary constituency: all American citizens 18 years and older.

quite huge, and the stakes for those seeking state contracts were quite high. Businesses now began to employ **lobbyists**—people paid to represent a company or special interest group. Sometimes they tried to influence votes by offering money in the form of campaign contributions. If it was unclear who would win a race, contributions were given to both parties. Such payments were regarded by legislators and lobbyists alike as "insurance" against unfavorable legislation.

At other times money was offered in the form of outright bribes. When Jay Gould controlled the Erie Railroad, he was reported to have spent $500,000 in bribes during a single session of the New York state legislature. Of the relations between the Standard Oil Company and the government of Pennsylvania, one observer wrote, "The Standard has done everything with the Pennsylvania legislature except to refine it."

In general there was more corruption in state and local politics than in national politics. Nonetheless, corruption did exist. By far the worst misconduct in the federal government occurred during the administration of President Grant.

Grant had been a great general, but he was a poor President. Although he was personally honest, he seemed unable to distinguish decent people from the dishonest. Dazzled by wealth, he fell under the sway of the financial speculators James J. Fisk and Jay Gould, who reaped millions of dollars from their relationship with the President. Members of Grant's family, personal staff, and Cabinet peddled influence and jobs in return for cash. At one time Grant's brother managed to hold four jobs by farming out the duties to other men.

In 1872 the scandals spread to Congress as well. A New York newspaper revealed that officers of the Union Pacific Railroad had formed their own construction company called the Crédit Mobilier. The contracts this company received enabled the railroad officers to reap enormous personal profits. To forestall investigation, the company distributed shares of stock "where it would do the most good." Grant's Vice President and several prominent members of Congress turned out to have accepted these thinly disguised bribes.

When the graft in his administration was finally uncovered, Grant declared that

Examining Political Cartoons *Powerful trusts dominate the United States Senate in this 1889 cartoon by Joseph Keppler. The people's entrance to the Senate chambers (upper left) is shown bolted shut. How did the trusts influence senators?*

THE BOSSES OF THE SENATE.

he would "let no guilty man escape." Later, however, he protected many accused of wrongdoing from both investigation and punishment.

Postwar Political Parties

In *The American Commonwealth,* British author James Bryce found it difficult to explain the positions Democrats and Republicans took on major issues such as the tariff and railroad regulation. He wrote:

Neither party has, as a party, anything to say on these issues; neither party has any clean-cut principles....All has been lost except office or the hope of it.

One reason that parties seemed so similar was that their strength was evenly divided. At every level, from wards to **townships,** or smaller divisions of a county broken up into local government districts, political parties were popular, and democratic participation was high. They did not avoid any of the issues; rather, they were split internally on most of them. In the Northeast, for example, with its strong banking system, both parties favored the gold standard. In the Midwest both parties favored increasing the amount of money in circulation. Republicans in the Midwest were protariff, while southern Democrats were antitariff. Both parties in the Northeast were divided on the tariff issue.

The humorist "Mr. Dooley," created by Finley Peter Dunne, described a hypothetical candidate for President as someone who was pulled in different directions by such varied positions and needed to be all things to all people:

Wanted: a good, active Dimmycrat, sthrong iv lung an' limb; must be…a sympathizer with th' crushed an' down throdden people but not be anny means hostile to vested inthrests; must advocate sthrikes, gover'mint be injunction, free silver, sound money, greenbacks, a single tax, a tariff f'r rivinoo…at home in Wall sthreet an' th' stock yards, in th' parlors iv th' r-rich an' th' kitchens iv th' poor.

Examining Photographs *The Statue of Liberty torch, displayed in Philadelphia in 1876, symbolized freedom to new immigrants. Which political party were new immigrants likely to join?*

Examining Graphs
The Republicans dominated the presidency and often controlled Congress between 1860 and 1900. In which presidential elections did the Republicans win over 50 percent of the popular vote?

Although fairly evenly matched in strength, the two parties were hardly identical. Though both parties received support from people in every walk of life, each had a distinctive base of support. The Republicans' base of support was a coalition of western farmers and merchants, who benefited from Republicans' internal improvements and liberal land policies, and Eastern businesspeople, who benefited from high tariffs and national banks. As a group, the Republicans tended to be Protestants of old-immigrant stock—Presbyterians, Congregationalists, Methodists, or Baptists. The great problem of the Republican party was to keep together its eastern and western wings, which were likely to break into open warfare over such issues as greenbacks, free silver, tariffs, and banking.

The Republicans' "patron saint" was Abraham Lincoln, whose birthday they honored with banquets and oratory. As the party that had led during the Civil War, they had great prestige in the North and West. "The party that saved the nation must rule it," they proclaimed.

While critics attacked the Republicans for keeping alive war hatreds by "waving the bloody shirt," appeals to the memory of the Civil War were much more than that. Republican strength came from genuine devotion to the idea of the United States as a nation rather than as a federation of states. Many Republicans continued to be inspired by the party's early idealism. They felt that government existed to advance the public good.

Democrats, too, looked back to the Civil War. From the end of radical Reconstruction until well into the twentieth century, southern states formed the solid

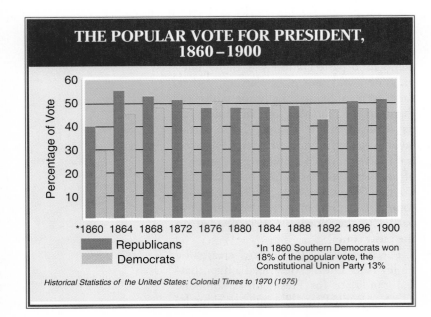

THE POPULAR VOTE FOR PRESIDENT, 1860–1900

Percentage of Vote

*1860 1864 1868 1872 1876 1880 1884 1888 1892 1896 1900

■ Republicans
□ Democrats

*In 1860 Southern Democrats won 18% of the popular vote, the Constitutional Union Party 13%

Historical Statistics of the United States: Colonial Times to 1970 (1975)

South, never wavering in its allegiance to the Democrats. But the Democrats could not have remained a national party with only southern support. The party depended on an alliance between white southerners and northern city machines. As in Thomas Jefferson's day, Democrats tended to get the support of recent immigrants, many of whom were Catholics or liturgical Protestants, such as Lutherans or Episcopalians whose religious and cultural background was quite different from that of evangelical Protestants, such as Methodists and Baptists, who formed the core of the Republican party. The Democrats had allies among western farmers, especially when prices for their crops were low, and among certain groups of businesspeople and owners of import companies who favored a lower tariff.

The Democratic party had two "patron saints"—Jefferson and Andrew Jackson. Like these leaders, the Democrats claimed to represent the interests of ordinary Americans. The Democrats took issue with the Republican view of the United States as a nation. "This is no nation," said one Democrat. "We are free and independent states." In contrast to the Republicans' view that the federal government should take an active role in helping the needy and shaping national growth, the Democrats wanted to keep the federal government on a skimpy allowance and a short leash. "That government governs best which governs least" remained their motto, and it appealed to many Americans.

The Democrats were so used to being out of office, according to the humorist Dooley, that when writing their platform they forgot how to say "we commend" but automatically began to "denounce and deplore." During the entire period from 1865 to 1900, Democrats held the presidency for only two terms. Although they usually lost the White House, the Democrats were seldom far out of the running. Democratic candidates often got almost as many popular votes as their victorious opponents, and it was rare that the Republicans did not have to deal with Democrats in control of at least one house of Congress.

★ ★ ★ ★ ★ ★ ★ ★ ★ ★ ★ ★ ★ ★ ★ ★ ★

Section One Review

★ ★ ★ ★ ★ ★ ★ ★ ★ ★ ★ ★ ★ ★ ★ ★ ★

SUMMARY

In a society dominated by business interests, an uninformed and indifferent electorate ignored the corruption that pervaded all levels of government. Corruption was worst at local levels, where party political machines held power. The Grant administration, too, was shaken when it was discovered that high-ranking officials, including the Vice President and members of Congress, had accepted bribes. Though supporters of the Democratic and Republican parties differed greatly, their strength was almost evenly divided.

CHECKING FOR UNDERSTANDING

1. **Identify** William M. Tweed, Thomas Nast, Finley Peter Dunne

2. **Define** graft, political machine, kickback, ward, lobbyists, township

3. **Examine** the causes of increased political corruption.

4. **Cite** examples of corruption that occurred in government.

5. **Distinguish** those groups of people who supported the Republican and Democratic parties.

6. **State** how the Republicans and Democrats viewed the role of the federal government.

THINKING CRITICALLY

7. **Interpreting Satire** In his description of the ideal campaign candidate on page 586, what was Mr. Dooley expressing about politicians?

LINKING PAST AND PRESENT

8. **Contrasting Attitudes** Much attention today is focused on campaign contributions, gifts to officeholders, lobbyists' activities, speaking fees for legislators, and other perceived conflicts of interest. How does this contrast with the post-Civil War political climate?

★ ★ ★ ★ ★ ★ ★ ★ ★ ★ ★ ★ ★ ★ ★ ★ ★

Interpreting Primary Sources

POLITICAL CARTOON

Who Stole the People's Money?
'Twas Him

Political Corruption

None of William "Boss" Tweed's critics leveled more scathing attacks at his notorious Tammany Hall machine than Thomas Nast, a cartoonist for *Harper's Weekly*. *Harper's* magazine pioneered the use of illustrations and cartoons to comment on significant political issues of the day. Under Nast's pen, Tweed and his cronies were depicted as vultures, jailed criminals, and smiling deceivers.

Tweed was well aware of the political damage that Nast's cartoons could do to him and the Tammany Hall political machine. He ordered his men to stop Nast from drawing his cartoons. Tweed cared little what the papers wrote about him because his constituents could not read. But they could see and understand the message of the cartoons.

In an effort to get Nast out of the way, Tweed ordered his men to offer the cartoonist $500,000 to "study art" in Europe. Nast, whose annual income was a relatively small $5,000, negotiated the offer up to half a million dollars before he refused it. Applying his artistic talents to political corruption, Nast helped drive Tweed out of office.

In this cartoon, "Who Stole the People's Money?" the answer is "'Twas Him." Tweed appears as the heavyset man in the left foreground of the cartoon.

On Tweed's right a man holds a hat labeled "chairs," a reference to the $179,000 New York City paid for 40 chairs and 3 tables. Other contractors and cheats—their names on their coats—complete the circle.

Nast is also credited with creating the elephant and donkey symbols of the Republican and Democratic parties.

EXAMINING THE PRIMARY SOURCE

1. What label identifies the group in the circle?

2. What does clothing show in this cartoon?

3. How does the cartoon visually answer the question posed in its title, "Who Stole the People's Money?"

THINKING CRITICALLY

4. What statement does Nast make in his cartoon about the extent of political corruption in New York City?

5. Describe a recent instance in which government leaders were, like the Tammany Ring, accused of "stealing the people's money."

Calls for Good Government

Our government by the people has in large degree become...government by the strong and unscrupulous...In our national Senate, sovereign members of the Union are supposed to be represented; but what are more truly represented are railroad kings and great moneyed interests.

—HENRY GEORGE

American social reformer,
Social Problems, 1883

Section Focus

During the 1870s and 1880s, social reformers like Henry George tried to raise the alarm that official corruption threatened democracy in the United States. If reformers wanted rebellion, they were disappointed; but through their efforts, a slow and steady movement away from the abuses of the Grant administration began to occur. And the first hopeful sign was the election of Rutherford B. Hayes in 1876.

Objectives

After studying this section, you should be able to:

- Identify the reforms made during the 1870s and 1880s.
- Describe the tariff controversy.

Before the administration of Rutherford B. Hayes, one of the common practices had been **patronage** — the assumed right of elected officials to control political appointments to unelected positions. Moreover, the federal government was the epitome of apathy and astonishingly idle.

With the election of Hayes, the tone of national politics began to change.

Civil Service Reforms

After his inauguration in 1877, Hayes named Carl Schurz, owner of a German-language newspaper in St. Louis, Missouri, and U.S. Senator from Missouri, to take charge of the Department of the Interior, which had previously been the scene of some of the worst examples of patronage. The practice was soon curbed. Hayes also forbade the practice of "shaking down" federal workers—forcing them to make campaign contributions.

Hayes also defied congressional leaders by preventing important appointments favored by individual members of Congress. In addition, he refused to sign otherwise acceptable legislation if Congress had attached **riders**–irrelevant amendments–of which he disapproved. Through his actions, Hayes not only cut down on corruption but began to restore the balance of power between Congress and the presidency.

Examining Illustrations *President Garfield was shot only four months after his inauguration by a frustrated patronage seeker, Charles J. Guiteau. In this engraving, Guiteau attempts to flee while James G. Blaine, secretary of state, supports Garfield. After Garfield's death, who became President?*

Hayes' reforms brought him enemies among the Stalwarts, a group of Republican machine politicians who strongly opposed civil service reform. After Hayes declined to run for a second term, the party became divided between the Stalwarts, who wanted to nominate Grant for a third term, and the "Halfbreeds," who opposed Grant. After a prolonged deadlock at the National Convention, the Republicans nominated dark horse James A. Garfield, a former Union general.

To blunt the old charge of disloyalty in wartime, the Democrats nominated General Winfield S. Hancock, a Union hero of the battle of Gettysburg. The intellectual level of the ensuing campaign may be judged by the following excerpt from the speech of a Republican orator:

I belong to a party that believes in good crops; that is glad when a fellow finds a gold mine; that rejoices when there are forty bushels of wheat to the acre...The Democratic party is a party of famine; it is a good friend of an early frost; it believes in the Colorado beetle and in the weevil.

Despite such inflammatory rhetoric, Garfield narrowly won the election.

Under Hayes and Garfield, government was cleaner than it had been during the Grant administration, but the spoils system remained a constant source of inefficiency and sometimes of graft. Disputes over patronage poisoned the relationship between the President and Congress.

Still, there was little momentum for reform. In July 1881, however, as President Garfield entered the Washington, D.C., railroad station, he was shot by a disappointed office seeker. The unbalanced man cried, "I am a Stalwart and Arthur is President." Garfield clung to life for two months, but in September Vice President Chester A. Arthur, a New York Stalwart, did indeed succeed to the presidency.

Garfield's assassination excited public opinion against the spoils system. In 1883 Congress responded to public pressure, passing the Pendleton Act, which has been called (with some exaggeration) "the Magna Carta of civil service reform." This law allowed the President to decree which federal jobs would be filled according to rules laid down by a bipartisan Civil Service Commission. Candidates competed for these jobs through examinations, and appointments could be made only from the list of those who

AMERICAN PORTRAITS

SUSAN B. ANTHONY
1820-1906

From her Quaker upbringing, Susan B. Anthony learned that men and women were equal before God. She spent most of her 86 years trying to convince others of that equality.

After teaching school for several years, Anthony returned home to help run the family farm. While living in her father's house, she began to focus on the great reform movements of the day. Anthony first joined a temperance group and experienced gender discrimination firsthand when she was refused permission to speak at a temperance rally. Realizing that as long as women were propertyless and voteless they would also be powerless, Anthony began devoting her considerable energies to securing equal rights for women. Throughout the four decades from the end of the Civil War to her death, she was the nation's foremost crusader for women's right to vote.

took the exams. Once appointed, a civil service official could not be removed for political reasons.

Although President Arthur was a veteran of machine politics, he supported the Pendleton Act, placing 14,000 jobs (about one-tenth of the total) under the control of the civil service. The federal government had finally begun a shift away from the spoils system.

Cleveland in Office

The major theme of the presidential election of 1884 was honesty in politics. The Republican nominee, Representative James G. Blaine, was a man of great ability and personal charm, but his reputation was clouded by charges that he had taken money in return for helping a railroad. As a result, some independent reformers in the Republican party, called "Mugwumps," refused to support him. The Democrats won Mugwump support by nominating Grover Cleveland, who earned a reputation for stubborn integrity as mayor of Buffalo and governor of New York.

The campaign of 1884 was a negative one, focusing less on issues and more on character assassination. Blaine was portrayed as a "tattooed man" with railroad stocks and bonds indelibly engraved on his skin. Cleveland was attacked on the grounds that he had hired a substitute to fight for him in the Civil War and that he had fathered an illegitimate child. Republicans chanted:

Ma! Ma! Where's my pa?
Gone to the White House,
Ha! Ha! Ha!

To which the Democrats countered:

Blaine, Blaine, James G. Blaine,
The continental liar from the
State of Maine.

Cleveland won the election by an extremely narrow margin, becoming the first Democratic President since 1856. The balloting in New York was close. Had about 600 voters switched to Blaine, he would have won the state—and the presidency. The Republicans retained control of the Senate, but the Democrats gained a majority in the House of Representatives.

Unskillful in political maneuvering, Cleveland often met defeat in his dealings with Congress. Nevertheless, his devotion to the public good did much to restore the prestige of the presidency. Cleveland's first problem was to deal with the Democratic officeseekers who swarmed to Washington seeking the fruits of his victory. If he were to make appointments on merit alone, he would split his party wide open. If he were to give in to the spoils system, he would lose the support of the Mugwumps and other reformers who had played a decisive part in electing him. As a compromise, Cleveland appointed many "deserving Democrats" to office among the two-thirds of federal offices that changed hands after his election. He also made every effort to see that the new appointees were qualified for their jobs.

Cleveland entered office with a weak understanding of most national issues but worked intensely at the job. Few Presidents have put in more study to determine what course of action to follow. His Republican predecessors, for example, had signed hundreds of private bills giving pensions to veterans unable to qualify under regular laws. Examining such bills with care, Cleveland found many of them fraudulent. One veteran, for example, asked for a pension for an injury he had suffered while *intending* to enlist. Cleveland disapproved of so many private pension bills that his vetoes totaled more than those of all previous Presidents.

Cleveland worked to improve government efficiency and integrity. He supported the Presidential Succession Act, which established a line of succession to the presidency in the event of the death of the Vice President. He also won repeal of the Tenure of Office Act, which strengthened the independence of the

Linking Across Time

DEMOCRATS AND REPUBLICANS

Grover Cleveland was the first Democratic President elected in 28 years. The Democratic party had been in existence since Thomas Jefferson's time, but had undergone several name changes: from Republican, to Democratic-Republican, to Democrat. From 1801 to 1861, 9 of the 13 Presidents were Democrats. From 1861 to 1913, 10 of the 12 Presidents were Republicans.

Today's Republican party emerged in the 1850s to oppose the extension of slavery. The first Republican President, Abraham Lincoln, began his first term of office in 1861.

Examining Illustrations *The political cartoon on the left, "The Amazing Growth of the Pension Pig" satirizes the huge funds voted in "pork-barrel" legislation during 1877 to benefit Civil War veterans. Unlike Cleveland before him, President Benjamin Harrison, shown on the right, favored attempts to freely spend the mounting treasury surplus. How long did it take the "Billion-Dollar Congress" to convert the surplus into a deficit?*

President. Interested in the preservation of public lands, Cleveland reclaimed government land from private companies that had not lived up to the terms of their land grants.

Tariffs and the Election of 1888

The public question that Cleveland studied most seriously was the tariff. During the Civil War, duties had been raised from an average of 19 percent in 1861 to more than 40 percent in 1865. The high rates, which benefited manufacturers, were constantly attacked by farmers, consumers, shippers, and importers.

These **free-traders** argued that a protective tariff was unfair government interference with the normal laws of supply and demand. Tariffs, they said, were subsidies paid to manufacturers out of the pockets of consumers.

Protectionists, on the other hand, defended the tariff as a means of nurturing fledgling industries in the United States. They argued that tariffs kept wages high by shielding them from competition with cheap foreign labor. Previous bills to lower the tariff had been defeated.

Shortly after he took office, Cleveland was asked to give his opinion on the tariff question. "You know I really don't know anything about it," he said. But true to form, Cleveland investigated the problem thoroughly. His studies convinced him that the existing tariff was responsible for the treasury's large surplus. Cleveland argued that the surplus was a sign of over-taxation. He proposed a reduction of the tariff—not because he was a free-trader, but because he was in favor of limited government. Excess money in the treasury, he said, was not good for the economy; it was a temptation to Congress, which was apt to spend it wastefully. The President's dramatic effort to lower the tariff was blocked by House Republicans.

The tariff then became the major issue in the presidential election of 1888.

Openly avowing protection for the first time, the Republicans collected a record-breaking campaign fund. "Put all the manufacturers of Pennsylvania under the fire," said a Republican campaign manager, "and fry that fat out of them." The Republicans revived Henry Clay's name for the protective tariff, calling their economic program the "American system." Renominating Cleveland, the Democrats campaigned against unnecessary taxation. As in 1880 and 1884, the result was extremely close. Although he got fewer popular votes than Cleveland, the Republican candidate, Benjamin Harrison, won a majority in the electoral college.

The new President was a quiet, reserved man, whom one observer called a "human iceberg." Harrison was, in fact, too reserved to make a good Gilded Age politician. Still, he had an able legal mind

and a distinguished career as attorney in Indiana. He was elected to the Senate in 1881.

Harrison had fought under Sherman at Atlanta and was not shy about "waving the bloody shirt" for votes. An ardent protectionist, he was conservative in fiscal policy and liberal when it came to veterans' pensions.

Once in office, the Republicans promptly disposed of the treasury surplus by spending it, and it was the last time in history that the government held one. Within two years the "Billion-Dollar Congress" had created a deficit, mostly through handouts to special-interest groups. The number of Civil War pensioners increased by more than half—many of them the same ones who Cleveland had turned down.

Moving on to the election-winning tariff issue, the Republicans passed the McKinley Tariff of 1890, which was the

Examining Illustrations *The 1888 Democratic nominees for President and Vice President are shown in this campaign poster. The Cleveland and Thurman ticket received more popular votes than their Republican opposition but failed to win the presidential election. How could this happen?*

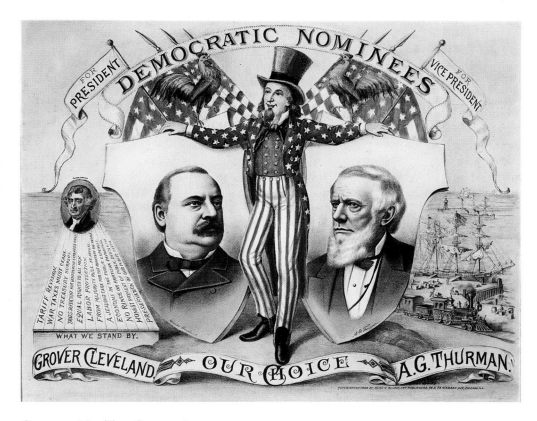

highest in the country's history. It dried up revenue by levying rates so high that some foreign products were kept out of the country entirely. Nearly every foreign product that competed with American-made products were heavily taxed, including food, clothing, furniture, and tools. Western silver states supported the tariff in exchange for the passage of the Sherman Silver Purchase Act, which authorized the federal government to buy up 4.5 million ounces of silver a month.

Millions were spent on the improvement of harbors and waterways, coastal defenses, federal buildings, and naval expansion. In addition to these measures, Congress passed the Sherman Antitrust Act and provided for admission to the Union of North and South Dakota, Montana, Washington, Idaho, and Wyoming.

The Republicans' position on protective tariffs, which had helped them win the presidency in 1888, hurt them two years later. Because there was little competition in the market, prices for the most part were falling; thus debts were harder to repay.

In addition, Republicans were hurt nationally by local Republicans in such states as Wisconsin and Massachusetts, who supported compulsory public school attendance where instruction was in English. Many Catholic and Lutheran immigrant families resided in these states and wanted public funding for their parochial schools in which students were taught in their language. Republicans also pushed Prohibition at the grassroots level. Democrats used these issues, together with that of a backfiring tariff, to attack the Republicans. The congressional elections of 1890 resulted in a Democratic landslide. By 1892 the Republicans' position was even worse. Disspiritedly, they renominated Harrison, and the Democrats nominated Grover Cleveland again. Popular discontent with the Republicans was so high that, for the first time since before the Civil War, Democrats won not only the White House but both houses of Congress.

Section Two Review

SUMMARY

Presidents Hayes, Garfield, and Cleveland worked for reform of civil service and sought to restore a balance of power between the presidency and Congress. Cleveland, a Democrat, gained the office when Republican reformers refused to support a candidate charged with corruption. While in office, Cleveland unsuccessfully opposed high tariffs, free-traders being outnumbered by protectionists. After Cleveland's election loss to Harrison, Republican spending quickly turned a treasury surplus into a deficit. Sentiment shifted in the next election when voters rejected Harrison and returned the presidency to Cleveland.

CHECKING FOR UNDERSTANDING

1. **Identify** Rutherford B. Hayes, James Garfield, Chester Arthur, Grover Cleveland, McKinley Tariff

2. **Define** riders, free-traders, protectionists

3. **Describe** political reforms made during the 1870s and 1880s.

4. **Explain** the controversy over raising or lowering the tariff.

5. **Contrast** the condition of the treasury during Cleveland's and Harrison's administrations, noting what caused the change.

THINKING CRITICALLY

6. **Evaluating Reforms** How could the civil service system limit the patronage system and cut down on corruption?

CONNECTIONS: HISTORY AND GOVERNMENT

7. **Evaluating Alternatives** Why do some people feel that limiting congressional terms of office would be an effective reform? Explain why you agree or disagree.

Cultural Life

> ...[C]lose to [the water's] edge, the [Washington] Monument...towers out of the mud....It has the aspect of a factory chimney with the top broken off...tradition says that the spirit of Washington often comes down and sits on [the decaying scaffolding] to enjoy this tribute of respect which the nation has reared as the symbol of its unappeasable gratitude.
>
> —MARK TWAIN AND CHARLES DUDLEY WARNER
> *The Gilded Age,* 1873

Section Focus

The Civil War was a turning point not only in the political life of the nation but in its cultural life as well. The period after the war was a time of rapid change. Some satirized the values of post-Civil War society, as in Twain and Warner's description of a poorly maintained Washington Monument. Others celebrated the country's emergence as an industrial giant.

Objectives

After studying this section, you should be able to:
- Discuss developments in literature, art, and higher education.
- Describe how various leisure activities expanded.

The United States was quickly becoming an urban, industrialized society. It needed citizens who could understand complex political and economic questions, and it needed literate workers and managers who could staff its offices, shops, and factories. In the late nineteenth century, the nation reformed its educational system.

Education

By 1900 many states had or were working toward compulsory school attendance. In cities, graded schools replaced one-room school houses. The school year, which had traditionally been squeezed in between fall harvest and spring planting, was lengthened. Many cities also introduced free secondary education, and the number of public high schools increased from a few hundred in 1860 to more than 2,500 in 1890. Yet there was still great room for improvement: in 1900 the average child in the United States received only 5 years of schooling.

The most far-reaching development in education in the latter half of the nineteenth century was the expansion of higher education. At mid-century most colleges and universities in the United States had poor equipment, scanty libraries, and ill-trained, overworked faculties. Their fixed curriculum, which emphasized ancient Greek and Roman thought, included no training in modern languages, history, or science. There were no first-rate graduate schools in law, medicine, or the liberal arts, and no American scientific school deserved to be mentioned in the same breath with the best in Europe.

By 1900 these weaknesses had been vigorously attacked. Responding to the need for more practical education, colleges in the United States reformed their curricula. Courses in the social and natural sciences were made available, and the elective system, first introduced at Harvard, made it possible for students to choose an individual course of study. Young scholars from the United States trained in the world's best universities—in Germany—brought back higher standards of scholarship and scientific research. Existing private universities were greatly expanded, and new ones were founded—most with the aid of wealthy businesspeople who supported the trend toward making education more useful. More than two dozen new schools were devoted specifically to technical training. The Massachusetts Institute of Technology and others like it supplied industry with highly trained engineers, metallurgists, and chemists. Also during this period the first graduate schools of business, such as the Wharton School of Finance, were established.

Along with the growth of privately endowed universities and technical schools came an expansion of state universities. Such institutions owed a great deal to the Morrill Act of 1862, which gave public lands to each state as a grant to finance the endowment of colleges. While the main goal of these schools was to extend knowledge of "agriculture and the mechanic arts," they were funded to teach science and classical studies as well. In addition to such southwestern universities as the University of California and Texas A&M, most of the large state universities of the Midwest began as land-grant colleges.

Universities in the Midwest also played an important role in opening higher education to women for the first time. In the pre-Civil War era, women had been admitted to Oberlin and Antioch colleges in Ohio. After the war, coeducation became common west of the Appalachians.

In the more conservative East, women founded private colleges of their own, such as Mount Holyoke, Vassar, Smith, Radcliffe, and Bryn Mawr. These colleges shared the same educational goals as all-male institutions.

The adult public also cried out for more learning. Beginning in 1874 as a summer program to train Sunday school teachers, the Chautauqua (shuh TAW kwuh) Institute in western New York sparked a movement that provided the masses with instruction in such subjects as literature, economics, science, and government through summer school instruction and correspondence school.

Literature

United States writers responded to the post-Civil War era in different ways. One popular school of postwar writers looked backward, striving to capture the romance of vanishing rural traditions. A center of such "local-color" writing was the South. Civil War and Reconstruction had swept away an entire way of life there, leaving poverty and destruction in its wake. In the 1870s and 1880s, southern local colorists wrote nostalgically about **antebellum,** or prewar, manners, customs, and institutions. Through their work they created a myth of an aristocratic order that appealed to people the world over.

The movement was not confined to the South, however. Local colorists also wrote of vanishing ways of life in the small towns and fishing villages of New England, on the farms of the Midwest, on the ranches of the plains, and in the mining camps and boomtowns of the Wild West.

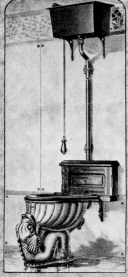

Examining Fine Art *Winslow Homer's* Snap the Whip, *1872, captures the joy of a school recess. Homer became famous for his vivid use of color and attention to detail. What European artistic styles did he reject?*

One of America's greatest writers was a local colorist named Samuel Clemens, who wrote under the name of Mark Twain. Twain wrote vivid and hilarious stories about his travels in the West. His most enduring works—*The Adventures of Tom Sawyer* and *The Adventures of Huckleberry Finn*—are tales of his boyhood home on the Mississippi River. Twain's books were not only acclaimed by critics but loved by the public. He combined shrewd observation and irreverent wit. His writing bridged the gap between popular and highbrow literature, between ordinary local-color writing and **realism,** a European-influenced movement that strove for accurate representation without idealization.

Realist writers wanted to get away from the emotional preoccupations of the romantic movement and the pretty, sentimental themes of popular literature. Realist writers set out to take a close look at real people's lives and problems. One of the leading realists, William Dean Howells, declared that novels should "speak the dialect, the language, that most Americans know." In *The Rise of Silas Lapham,* Howells depicted a crude, but likeable bumpkin—the new American millionaire. In *The Red Badge of Courage,* often called the first modern war novel, Stephen Crane depicted a Union soldier's fear and cowardice under fire. Other realists undertook to expose the seamy underside of urban life. Critics of realism argued that realistic fiction was not uplifting, that its subject matter was often ordinary or even ugly, and that its characters' misdeeds were not always suitably punished.

Art and Architecture

Realism was also an important force in American painting during the Gilded Age. Rejecting the classicism and romanticism of the first half of the century, realist painters portrayed ordinary people in

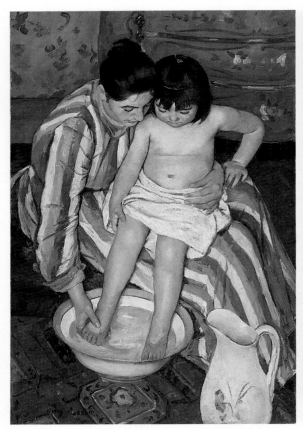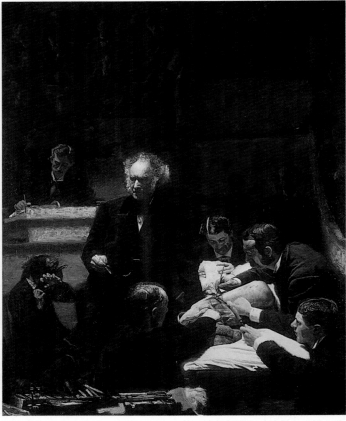

Examining Fine Art *Mary Cassatt's* La Toilette, *1892, on the left, is one of many paintings she did of mothers and children. Thomas Eakins'* The Gross Clinic, 1875, *on the right, depicts a moment when the famous surgeon Dr. Gross paused during an operation to lecture to medical students. What subjects did realist artists seek to portray?*

everyday activities. Winslow Homer, for example, moved from painting scenes of battle in the Civil War to subjects such as a schoolyard full of boys playing a rowdy game, a hunter and his dogs, or sailors at sea. Of another great realist painter Walt Whitman said:

I never knew of but one artist, and that's Tom Eakins, who could resist the temptation to see what they thought ought to be rather than what is.

Some of America's greatest painters, however, became **expatriates**—people who choose to live outside their native country. John Singer Sargent lived in England and became a brilliant portraitist of Europe's upper classes. James Abbott McNeill Whistler, creator of "Whistler's Mother," and Mary Cassatt also chose to live in Europe. Cassatt, in particular, was influenced by a style of painting called Impressionism. Impressionists tried to capture the play of light, color, and pattern as they made immediate *impressions* on the senses.

The architecture of the Gilded Age was heavy and ornate. It is often called "Victorian," after Queen Victoria of Great Britain, who reigned from 1837 to 1901. On the outside, fashionable Victorian houses were festooned with turrets, towers, porches, and gables. The development of better woodworking machines made it possible to add elaborate "gingerbread" decorations to roofs and porches of houses. The interior decor was similarly ornamented. Rooms were crowded with dark, thickly carved furniture, plush carpeting, heavy curtains, and countless knickknacks on ornate shelves. Some dismissed Victorian style as vulgar and ostentatious—a symbol of the greed that characterized the Gilded Age. Others have celebrated the gaudiness as a symbol of the period's vitality and exuberance.

Yellow Press and the Dime Novel

The Industrial Revolution brought some Americans unaccustomed leisure time. As machines took over the work of more and more hands, the time required to produce a shirt, a bucket, a pin, or a table was reduced to a small fraction of what it had been. Hours of work, although still long by the standards of the twentieth century, were gradually reduced. As leisure time increased, new forms of entertainment developed.

One was a new form of journalism. In the late 1800s, improvements in paper-making and printing made it possible to produce newspapers far more cheaply than ever before. At the same time there was such increased demand for advertising space that newspapers could make their profits entirely from advertisers, selling copies below cost in order to attract the greatest number of readers. The new penny-newspapers strove to amuse readers as much as to inform them. Their intended audience was not the educated middle and upper classes but clerks, laborers, and housewives.

The pioneer among the penny newspapers was the *New York World,* purchased by Joseph Pulitzer in 1883. In 15 years its circulation rose from 15,000 to more than 1 million. Pulitzer, dedicating his paper "to the cause of the people rather than the purse-proud potentates," attacked unfair employers and grafting politicians with vigor. But the real source of Pulitzer's success was not politics but sensationalism. He was one of the first to use "scare headlines" like "Baptized in Blood" and "Death Rides the Rails." He

also introduced the colored Sunday supplement and the serialized comic strip. From the yellow ink he used in his comics came the term **"yellow journalism,"** which critics applied to the subject matter and style of the *World* and all its imitators. If he could not find news, Pulitzer made it. Once he sent a young woman, Nelly Bly, to travel around the globe in less time than it took the hero of Jules Verne's popular novel, *Around the World in Eighty Days.*

Another form of reading matter produced for a mass market was the dime

Examining Political Cartoons *Currier and Ives produced this cartoon in 1875 with the caption "The Ladder of Fortune." Industry and morality brought solid rewards, such as "Riches," while idle schemes led to poverty and ruin. Why were some moralists against dime novels?*

Connections

HISTORY AND TECHNOLOGY

IMPROVEMENTS IN PRINTING

During the late 1800s, improvements in printing led to the inexpensive mass production of newspapers, magazines, and books. In 1863 American inventor William A. Bullock produced the first

Newsboy photograph by Lewis Hine, c.1890

web-fed press. This press printed on huge rolls of paper rather than single sheets. Printer Richard March Hoe perfected the continuous-roll press in 1871. This device made it possible to produce up to 12,000 full newspapers an hour.

In 1886 linotype typesetting machines cut the time required to set type to a fraction of that required to set it by hand. The linotype operator sat at a keyboard. When the operator touched a letter on the keyboard, a lead mold was placed in line with other letters. Each complete line of type was molded onto a single slug, and the slugs were made into printing plates. The linotype allowed text to be assembled much faster into columns and pages.

Improved printing technology led to rapid growth of the publishing industry. It also led to increased competition among newspaper publishers to get out the "latest edition."

★ ★ ★ ★ ★ ★ ★ ★ ★ ★

MAKING THE TECHNOLOGY CONNECTION

1. What is a linotype machine?

2. How did improved methods of printing and typesetting affect the publishing industry?

LINKING PAST AND PRESENT

3. How is most publishing done today?

★ ★ ★ ★ ★ ★ ★ ★ ★ ★

novel, which was designed especially to interest boys. These were adventure stories, most often set in the Wild West, where heroes such as Mustang Sam and Deadwood Dick fought cattle rustlers and outlaws. Dime novels also portrayed the worlds of business and crime in such works as *Jay Gould's Office Boy* and *The Terrible Mystery of Car 206.* Moralists suspected that these early paperbacks would corrupt the young, and they were often hidden from the eyes of alarmed parents. Defenders pointed out, however, that because dime novels were not the work of realists, no bad deed ever went unpunished; no good boy went without his just reward.

Magazines were another important source of information and leisure reading in the late 1800s. New kinds of specialized publications appeared. Women's magazines such as *Ladies' Home Journal* were highly popular.

Sports and Entertainment

As work became less strenuous, many looked for leisure activities that involved physical exercise. Golf, croquet, and lawn tennis—all imported from Great Britain, were popular sports with the middle and upper classes. College students brought in still other British sports, including rowing, track, and rugby (from which the American game of football was derived).

Baseball, however, was a truly American invention—its earliest form was played before the Civil War. College and club teams sprang up all over the country in the late 1800s. The first team to turn professional was the Cincinnati Red Stockings in 1869; in 1876 the National League was organized. A British visitor observed that football and baseball games

Examining Illustrations
Baseball promoters enclosed fields and built stadiums for professional teams. What city had the first professional baseball team?

excited "an interest greater than any other public events except the presidential election...." Professional baseball found a ready audience and loyal fans in crowded urban areas where working-class people had little money to spend on entertainment.

The amusement that for a time outstripped all others was bicycling. After the modern safety bicycle was substituted for the dangerous "high wheeler," bicycling became a craze. There were hundreds of bicycle clubs; special trains carried cyclists into the country on Sundays; special bicycle paths were built in parks and suburbs. There was even demand for a transcontinental bicycle route.

The nation's cities became centers of cultural life. Circuses and vaudeville shows enjoyed great popularity. For more sophisticated tastes, large cities boasted opera companies and symphony orchestras, theatres, and museums of fine art.

SUMMARY

By 1900 most states had made school attendance compulsory, and many were supporting state universities. In addition, higher education opened to women, and universities began to offer scientific, technical, business, and agricultural courses of study. Local-color, realist, and impressionist styles emerged in literature and fine art. Yellow journalism and dime novels were born for the benefit of the working-class laborers. Indeed, a host of leisure-time activities became popular—including sports such as baseball and bicycling, theaters, and museums.

CHECKING FOR UNDERSTANDING

1. **Identify** Mark Twain, Stephen Crane, James Abbott McNeill Whistler, Joseph Pulitzer, Thomas Eakins

2. **Define** antebellum, realism, expatriates, yellow journalism

3. **List** advances in education.

4. **Characterize** the local-color and realist styles of literature.

5. **Describe** realist paintings.

6. **Give examples** of how Americans entertained themselves.

THINKING CRITICALLY

7. **Supporting Opinions** Argue for or against compulsory education in a democratic society. Support your opinion with facts or arguments that show how your position supports democratic goals.

CONNECTIONS:
HISTORY AND LITERATURE

8. **Distinguishing Literary Genre** What features set dime novels apart from the realism that predominated in literature? How did the purpose and audience of dime novels explain their lack of realism?

★ Chapter 20 Review ★

★ Summary

Following the Civil War, corruption pervaded all levels of government in the form of graft, bribes, kickbacks, and influence-peddling. Corruption was worst in city governments dominated by political machines, but it even flourished among the associates of President Grant. Subsequently, Presidents Hayes, Garfield, Arthur, and Cleveland sought to limit the patronage system, strengthen civil service, and balance the power between the President and Congress. The Democratic and Republican parties were about equal in strength, although their supporters differed significantly. The tariff became an increasingly important issue as well, resulting in the passage of the country's highest tariff ever in 1890.

By 1900 most states had made school attendance compulsory, and many supported state universities. Moreover, universities began to expand courses of study. Local-color, realist, and impressionist styles emerged in literature and the fine arts. Leisure time gave birth to yellow journalism and dime novels, and impetus to the growth of professional and amateur sports, theatres, and museums.

★ Using Vocabulary

Each of the following terms has one of the following connotations: *political, economic,* or *cultural.* Classify each term under its respective connotation. Write a sentence that explains the connection between the term and its connotation.

antebellum	political machine
expatriates	protectionists
free traders	realism
graft	riders
kickback	yellow journalism

★ Reviewing Facts

1. **Explain** the increase in political corruption following the Civil War.
2. **Describe** types of corruption that took place in government.
3. **Name** the Presidents who introduced reform or resisted corruption in government.

4. **List** some political reforms made during the 1870s and 1880s.
5. **Point out** why some were in favor of higher tariffs and others were opposed.
6. **Discuss** changes in higher education during the later 1800s.
7. **Define** the styles that were used in writing, painting, and architecture, and literature during the post-Civil War period.
8. **Relate** how shortened work hours affected American lifestyles.

★ Understanding Concepts

CORRUPTION

1. How might patronage and the spoils system have allowed for more corruption in government?
2. What legitimate purposes do lobbyists serve? What restrictions should be placed on them to avoid wrongdoing?

PUBLIC PROTEST

3. What events described in this chapter suggest that a free press can inspire public protest of corruption in government? Can you think of recent examples of the press doing so?
4. Why did Presidents after Grant become more sensitive to public demands for reform?

★ Thinking Critically

1. **Examining Causes** Throughout most of the country's history, government workers and officeholders have earned substantially less than people in business with comparable ability and responsibility. How can this imbalance favor corruption in government?
2. **Weighing Benefits** Explain how the reform of civil service under the Pendleton Act was supposed to make for a better federal government.
3. **Linking Past and Present** What businesses today depend on people having leisure time? Would all these businesses be absent if work hours had not been shortened? Explain.
4. **Extending Concepts** In what types of periodicals do you find yellow journalism today? What kinds of stories do they emphasize? Who might be offended by their contents?

★ Chapter 20 Review ★

★ Writing About History

DEFINITION

Refer to the description of how to write a definition essay in the History Writer's Handbook in the Appendix of this book. Your teacher will give you more specific instructions on the essay's length and the assignment's due date.

Imagine that you are an art critic attending the first showing of a group of American realist painters. Write a definition of realism that would be appropriate to include in an art review. To help your readers understand realism, use examples and comments about how this style contrasts with other schools of painting.

★ Learning Cooperatively

Work with a partner to act out an interview between a newspaper reporter and a local political boss or machine politician. Decide which role each of you will assume. The reporter should review information on corrupt government practices as were presented in the chapter. The politician should review information on party machines. The reporter should prepare a list of questions to ask the politician. The politician should prepare a list of answers to questions that he or she feels may be asked. After the interview, both of you should list what were the most pertinent points brought out in the interview. Compare your findings with those of other groups.

★ Mastering Skills

MAKING GENERALIZATIONS

If you say, "We have a great football team," you are making a *generalization,* or general statement about your team. If you go on to say that your team was last year's top-ranked team and has not lost a game this season, you have provided evidence to support your generalization. In many fields of study, such as history, it often is necessary to put together bits and pieces of information in order to arrive at a complete picture; for example, an understanding of what life was like during the Gilded Age. Just as you put together pieces of a jigsaw puzzle, you can put together pieces of written information to arrive at a general statement—a generalization.

In some cases, authors will provide both the generalizations and the supporting statements. In other cases, only supporting statements are given, and you will need to make the generalizations on your own. When doing this, make sure that the supporting statements are directly related to the topic. Otherwise, your generalizations may be incorrect.

Example   In the following examples, a series of supporting statements are given. From these statements a generalization is made.

Example A:

- President Rutherford B. Hayes put a reformer, Carl Schurz, in charge of the Department of the Interior.
- Hayes forbade the practice of "shaking down" federal workers for campaign contributions.
- Hayes defied congressional leaders in important appointments and in refusing to allow riders.

(Generalization: *Hayes cut down on corruption in government.*)

Example B:

- Presidential candidate Grover Cleveland was attacked for hiring a substitute to fight for him during the Civil War.
- Candidate James G. Blaine was portrayed as a "tattooed man," with railroad stocks and bonds "engraved" on his skin.
- Cleveland was accused of fathering an illegitimate child.

(Generalization: *The presidential campaign of 1884 was a negative one, focusing less on issues and more on character assassination.*)

Practice   Make a generalization based on the following statements:

1. By 1900 all but two states outside the South had made school attendance compulsory.
2. In cities, graded schools replaced one-room school houses, greatly improving the quality of education.
3. The school year, which traditionally was squeezed between fall harvesting and spring planting, was lengthened.
4. Many cities introduced free secondary education, and the number of public high schools increased to more than 6,000.

CHAPTER 21
Politics, Protest, and Populism

SETTING THE SCENE

SECTIONS

1

Agrarian Unrest

2

Rise and Fall of Populism

3

Other Forces for Reform

Historical Focus

In the late nineteenth century, most Americans continued to live on the farm. By the 1880s, however, agriculture was in crisis. Farmers blamed their difficulties on abuses by the railroads, greedy bankers, and eastern industrialists. Farmers began to band together to fight these problems, which in turn led to the creation of a new political party, the Populists. Populism shared some goals with a larger movement aimed at redistribing the wealth and political power in the United States.

Concepts to Understand

- Why **economic inequity** developed between farmers and urban workers.
- Why many reformers believed that **social change** would result in a more just and equitable society.

People to Know

Mary E. Lease, Mark Hanna, William McKinley, William Jennings Bryan, Susan B. Anthony, Henry George

Places to Locate

Kansas, Omaha

Terms to Identify

pooling, inflation, deflation, gold standard, Southern Alliance, proletariat, single-tax

Guided Reading

As you read this chapter, seek the answers to the following questions.
1. What were some of the problems that American farmers faced in the 1880s?
2. What were the major goals of the Populist party?

SPANNING THE DECADES

POLITICAL

1877
Munn v. Illinois

1878
Bland-Allison
Act passed

1887
Interstate
Commerce
Act passed

1870   1880

CULTURAL

1874
National Women's
Christian Temp-
erance Union formed
in Cleveland

1879
Henry George
publishes
Progress and
Poverty

1881
Clara Barton
founds the
American Red
Cross

1888
Edward Bellamy
publishes Looking
Backward

Electioneering in Country Town *by E. L. Henry, 1913*

The universal depression of agriculture…the dwindling of agricultural communities, would seem to indicate that the cultivators of the soil are being exploited for the benefit of manufacturers, and that cities are appropriating the largest part of the profit.…

—HENRY J. FLETCHER
Sociologist, from *Forum*, August 1895

Agrarian Unrest

SETTING THE SCENE

The farmers of the United States are up in arms. They are the bone and sinew of the nation; they produce the largest share of wealth but they are getting...the smallest share for themselves.

—WASHINGTON GLADDEN
Protestant pastor and social reformer, 1890

Section Focus

During the late nineteenth century, the majority of people in the United States still lived in rural areas, but the balance was rapidly shifting. The country's attention was on the future—on booming industry and bustling cities. While much of America prospered, farmers were struggling. As conditions grew worse, they organized to protest their exclusion from the table of plenty.

Objectives

After studying this section, you should be able to:
• Identify the problems farmers faced during the late 1800s.
• Discuss the rise and fall of the Grange.
• Analyze the impact of the Interstate Commerce Act.

There appeared, as if from nowhere, a plague of grasshoppers that destroyed not only the wheat but the morale of farmers on the Great Plains. They ate anything green, choked wells to the brim, broke the branches off fruit trees by their weight, and even devoured harnesses and tool handles. They came in clouds that darkened the sun and covered the ground. The Norwegian-American writer, Ole Rolvaag, described the coming of the grasshoppers in his novel *Giants in the Earth:*

*They actually hurt me as they flew against
my face and hands. The wagon...
was literally filled with them.
The road was seething....
I saw Father standing almost in despair.
So thick were the grasshoppers in the
cornfield of which both of us had
been so proud, that not a spot of green was
left to be seen. And within two hours...
not a leaf was left....*

The Plight of the Farmers

But grasshoppers were only one of the hazards of life on the plains. There was always the threat of prairie fires, dust storms, and, worst of all, drought, which combined with hot winds and temperatures over 100°F to bake crops in the ground and cake farmers' faces with the salt of their sweat.

Farm prices began to decline in the 1880s; the price of wheat fell from 91 cents a bushel in 1883 to 69 cents in 1886. This decline was largely the result of overproduction of crops. New inventions, such as steam-powered harvesting and threshing machines, improved crop yields, and more efficient techniques greatly increased farm production. As prices declined, farmers had to borrow more and more money. Costs of the new farm machinery that assisted with large harvests were high. So were the costs of shipping crops to market. The more farm prices fell, consequently, the harder it became for farmers to pay back the principal and interest on their loans. Farmers believed that the government was the tool of the industrialists and the bankers and that politicians were ignoring the interests of the farmers.

Farmers' economic problems were largely the result of the new industrial economy that was emerging. Industrialization had created complex new problems that few people understood. For their problems farmers blamed the railroads, the distributors of farm goods, industrialists, bankers, and the shortage in the money supply. They wanted the government to regulate railroads and to put more money into circulation.

Railroad Abuses

Railroads opened vast stretches of the West to settlement, making it possible for farmers to get their crops to markets and to get manufactured goods from the East. Soon, however, many farmers began to view railroad companies as their enemies. Indeed, the railroads were guilty of a number of abuses of the public interest. Railroad companies spent millions of dollars in bribes to state legislators and other public officials in exchange for special favors such as land grants, cash subsidies, pro-railroad laws, and tax exemptions. But they often evaded laws designed to make them provide services in return for the benefits they were granted.

Railroad financing was marked by a common abuse called "stock watering," the practice of increasing the number of shares of a company without adding to the company's assets. For example, when Jay Gould and James J. Fisk gained control of the Erie Railroad in 1868, they issued $71 million of stock on property worth $20 million. They made money by selling this "watered stock" to the public, who did not know of the stock's actual lower value. Such action cheated all the stockholders. It also hurt the public because the railroads that had raised the value of their stock had to keep their rates high to pay dividends.

In a day when trucks and highways were not yet dreamed of, railroads often enjoyed a natural monopoly, that is, in certain places there was no competition for services. In some areas there was only one railroad line and no other possible means of transportation. Railroads took advantage of this situation by charging more for short

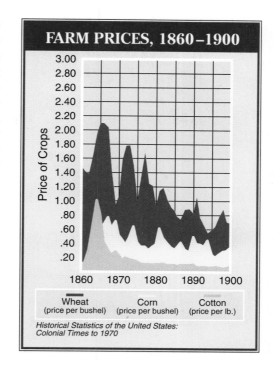

FARM PRICES, 1860–1900

Wheat (price per bushel) Corn (price per bushel) Cotton (price per lb.)

Historical Statistics of the United States: Colonial Times to 1970

Examining Graphs
Farm prices peaked during the Civil War. What crop declined the most by 1900?

hauls where they had a monopoly than for long hauls where they faced competition from other railroad lines. Thus, it cost shippers more to send goods from Poughkeepsie, New York, to New York City, than to send goods from Chicago to New York.

Sometimes competing railroad lines made agreements to keep rates high, a practice known as **pooling**. That is, several companies that operated in an area joined in a decision to fix rates and divide the profits according to a prearranged formula. This often resulted in extremely high freight rates.

The Grange

Feelings against railroad abuses ran high all over the country, but were especially strong in the West where there was almost no competition from other forms of transportation. This was because railroads had been favored by huge government subsidies in the form of land. Business owners and workers in the cities as well as farmers resented the railroads. It was a nationwide farm organization however, that began a movement against the unfair practices of the railroads. This organization tried to end railroad abuses with laws passed by state legislatures.

Linking Across Time

FARMING TODAY

Today's high-tech farm equipment has increased farm efficiency over 1960 levels almost as dramatically as the steam-powered equipment of the 1900s advanced farm productivity over its 1860 level.

Today's tractors pull 30-foot-wide plows that can till as much ground in an hour as 1960 models could in a day. But even though farm production is greater than ever, high equipment prices and slim profit margins mean that only 60,000 of 2.2 million farmers could be considered wealthy.

mills, factories, banks, insurance companies, grain elevators, and **cooperatives**, or non-profit stores owned by the farmers themselves. The local Granges involved themselves in local and national politics and pressed for state laws to help farmers.

By 1874 the Grange had 1.5 million members in states throughout the Midwest, South, and West. Its solidarity met with such success that several states passed "Granger laws" that fixed maximum freight and passenger rates, forbade railroads to discriminate between places or shippers, and attempted to regulate monopolies of such farmer necessities as grain elevators and warehouses.

Examining Illustrations *The Grange served to unite farmers against the forces that they believed were preventing their reaping the fruits of their hard labor. It had some success in pushing through state legislatures laws controlling railroad rates. What brought a temporary end to this legislation?*

The Patrons of Husbandry, commonly called the Grange, was the first national farm organization. It was founded in 1867 by Oliver Hudson Kelley. At first, the main purpose of the Grange was to relieve the isolation and loneliness in the lives of farm families by having social activities. And recognizing the importance of women on the farm, the Grange was the first fraternal organization to admit women on an equal basis.

The panic of 1873, however, turned the Grange into a reform lobby. As crop prices fell and interest rates rose, farmers began to talk about how to solve their common problems. Local Grange organizations pooled farmers' resources to set up

AMERICAN PORTRAITS

WILLA CATHER
1873-1947

Life on the prairie was a memorable experience for a young girl in the 1880s and 1890s. The beauty of the land and the hardy determination of the pioneers lasted long in the memory of Willa Cather. Born in Virginia in 1873, Willa moved with her family to a farm near Red Cloud, Nebraska, at the age of nine. The next eight years would provide the reflections for several novels, written years later.

Cather tried her hand at writing while teaching school in Pittsburgh in 1901 and then became an editor for *McClure's Magazine.* But her real success did not begin until she started writing about life on the plains. Many of her famous novels, such as *O Pioneers!* (1913), tell of the tough, yet sensitive nature of the immigrants who matched their determination against the demanding and lonely life on a plains farm.

Private businesses protested loudly against the Granger laws. Their main argument was that government should not interfere with private enterprise. "Can't I do what I want with my own?" demanded Cornelius Vanderbilt. Railroad lawyers argued that Granger laws were unconstitutional because the Fourteenth Amendment forbade a state to "deprive any person of life, liberty, or property, without due process of law." They viewed a railroad corporation as a legal "person" that should not be deprived of its property by being forced to lower its rates.

Defenders of the Granger laws said railroads that had accepted generous aid from federal and local governments should not claim to be devotees of *laissez-faire* capitalism. Further, they argued that *laissez-faire* rules did not apply to natural monopolies because there was no competition to keep prices down. The Grangers maintained that government must regulate railroads and other such monopolies in order to protect the public.

In 1877 the Supreme Court decided in favor of the Granger laws in the case of *Munn v. Illinois*. The Court stated that common carriers, such as railroads, and public utilities, such as grain elevators, "stand in the very gateway of commerce" and "take toll of all who pass." Therefore, these carriers must exercise "a sort of public office" and "submit to being controlled by the public for the common good."

In spite of such Court decisions, the Granger laws were unsuccessful. The railroads fought the laws by cutting services or threatening to lay no more track until the acts were repealed. Moreover, in the late 1870s, membership in the Grange declined and so did its political activity. The main cause of the Grange's collapse was its venture into business activities. The Grange set up plow and reaper factories, grain elevators, packing plants, and banks. Bitterly opposed by private companies and often not well run, these Granger businesses usually failed. Their collapse discredited the Grange, and by 1880 its membership was less than one-fourth of what it had been in 1874.

The remaining Granger laws were dealt a mortal blow by the Supreme Court in 1886. In the Wabash Railway decision, the Supreme Court held that the states could only control railroad traffic within each state's own borders. They did not have the power to regulate railroad traffic that crossed state borders. Because most railroad traffic crossed state boundaries, the Wabash Railway decision effectively wiped out state regulation of railroad rates.

Interstate Commerce Act

The Supreme Court's ruling in the Wabash decision made it clear that regulation would have to come at the national level. In 1887 Congress passed the first federal law to regulate interstate commerce.

Examining Illustrations *Most farmers ordered their household goods through catalogs such as this. What form of natural monopoly delivered these goods?*

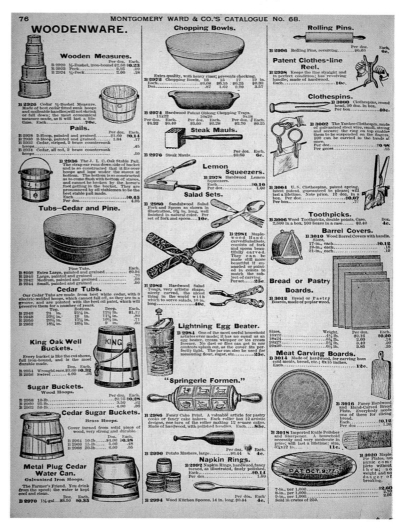

Examining Illustrations *This cartoon expressed the view that most people were not aware of the danger of railroad monopolies. What was the duty of the Grange?*

The Interstate Commerce Act declared that railroad charges must be "reasonable and just"; it forbade pooling, rebates, and higher rates for short rather than long hauls. The companies were required to publish rates, give advance notice of all changes, and make annual financial reports to the federal government. Violations of these provisions were punishable by fines of up to $5,000 for each offense. Enforcement of the law was placed under the Interstate Commerce Commission (ICC), a five-member panel appointed by the President.

As far as its immediate purpose was concerned, the Interstate Commerce Act was a failure. The ICC, lacking power to set rates, could only make recommendations or bring suits in the federal courts. Of 16 such cases that reached the Supreme Court, the Court held for the railroads in 15. In retrospect, though, the Interstate Commerce Act was a very important law. It established the precedent that the federal government might control large-scale private enterprise if the public good seemed to require it. It also provided a model for regulatory commissions today.

Rise and Fall of Populism

There is something radically wrong in our industry. There is a screw loose....The railroads have never been so prosperous and yet agriculture languishes. The banks have never done a better or more profitable business, and yet agriculture languishes....Towns and cities flourish and boom and yet agriculture languishes....

—*FARM JOURNAL,*
North Carolina, 1887

Section Focus

After the collapse of the Granger movement, farmers in the South and West began to form new organizations to promote their interests. In the 1890s these Farmers' Alliances grew into a new national political party. American farmers prepared to do battle to maintain their political power against the growing influence of industry.

Objectives

After studying this section, you should be able to:
- Explain the motivations of the groups that supported greenbacks and free silver.
- Describe the campaign and results of the election of 1896.
- Discuss the purposes and achievements of the Populist movement.

"In God we trusted, in Kansas we busted," and "Going home to Mother"—so read signs on the wagons of "busted" farm families returning east during the hard times of the 1880s. Discontent in rural areas grew

to new heights. Farm prices continued to fall, money was in short supply, and more and more people were losing their land to creditors. Many blamed their problems not only on the drought that was baking crops in the ground summer after summer but on human forces as well: greedy bankers, industrialists, and railroad companies that were accused of controlling government policies and bleeding rural areas dry. Like the Grangers, these men and women believed that farmers were the backbone of the country both economically and morally. Once again they turned to politics to solve the problems caused by rapid economic change. The Farmers' Alliances, which spawned the Populist Party, succeeded beyond the dreams of the Grangers.

Greenbacks and Free Silver

If there was anything that farmers in the late nineteenth century demanded more strongly than the regulation of natural monopolies or the reduction of the marketers' profits, it was "cheap money." The value of money, like that of any other commodity, changes according to the supply. If the number of dollars in circulation increases while there is no increase in the amount of goods and services for sale, the dollar buys *less,* and prices go up. This situation is called **inflation.** On the other hand, if the number of dollars in circulation decreases while there is no decrease in the amount of goods and services for sale, the dollar buys *more,* and prices go down. This situation is called **deflation.** In the three decades after the Civil War, the production of agricultural staples, such as wheat and cotton, nearly quadrupled while the supply of money increased very little. Thus, the prices received by farmers dropped by nearly two-thirds.

A period of deflation lasted for nearly 30 years. In 1865, with the value of currency inflated by the wartime issuance of United States notes, or greenbacks, there was $10.6 in circulation for every person in the country. By 1895 per capita circulation had sunk to $4.5. This was partly the result of a movement toward adoption of the **gold standard** in many nations. A country that adopted the gold standard made all its currency convertible into gold.

Formerly most countries had been on a bimetallic standard whereby the government coined both gold and silver and established the official value of each. In spite of official "mint prices" for gold and silver, their relative value often changed sharply.

The difficulty with the gold standard in the late nineteenth century was that world production of gold did not increase as fast as world production of goods. This restricted the currency supply and drove prices down. Deflation was hard on farmers, who borrowed money more heavily than ever before. This resulted in thousands of farm owners losing their land.

As soon as greenbacks began to be called in during the late 1860s and prices began to drop, farmers started to demand inflation. They protested that bankers and bondholders had lent 50-cent dollars during the war; they now wanted to be repaid in 100-cent dollars. Western delegates to the Democratic Convention of 1868 even forced an inflationist plank into the party platform. In the midterm election of 1878, a Greenback party polled more than 1 million votes, electing 15 members of Congress.

The Greenback movement declined after the mid-1870s as inflationists turned to free silver. Ever since the gold rush of 1849 had lowered the price of gold, silver miners had sold their silver commercially rather than selling it to the Treasury. In 1873 Congress, unaware of the potential of new silver mines, decided to stop coining silver money and adopted the gold standard. Six years later, after building up a gold reserve, the federal government resumed specie, or coin, payments. These events caused a howl of protest from western silver miners because new mines, especially the famous Comstock Lode, produced a flood of silver that would no longer be coined. Denouncing what they called "the Crime of '73," silver miners demanded a policy of free silver, meaning that the government should coin all silver brought to the mint. They were joined by farmers of the West and South who expected that free silver would mean a cheaper dollar and higher prices.

The strength of the silver movement was shown by the Bland-Allison Act of 1878, which was passed over President Hayes's veto. This law required that the treasury buy from $2 million to $4 million worth of silver a month and issue currency against it. Although adding to the money supply, the Bland-Allison Act did not halt deflation. The increase in business far exceeded that in currency.

The Populist Movement

The election of 1892 was notable because for the first time since 1860, a **third party**, a minor political party, won electoral votes. The new organization, the People's, or Populist party, was principally an expression of farmers' grievances. Ever since the Civil War, federal policies had favored industry over agriculture and the city over the country. In spite of clamor for a cheaper dollar, the United States remained on the gold standard—to the

Examining Photographs *Mary E. Lease of Kansas was an often-quoted Populist leader. Like many Populists, she sharply criticized the economic system. What did Populists believe about banking?*

advantage of creditors—and farm prices went steadily down—to the advantage of urban consumers. The protective tariff raised the price of the goods farmers bought, to the advantage of manufacturers, but American agricultural staples were sold overseas in an unprotected market. Legislation that favored agrarian, or farming, interests proved ineffective. State and federal regulation of railroads had been frustrated by adverse judicial decisions. The Homestead Act offered free farms to settlers, but the greater part of the public lands actually went to railroads and speculators. When drought hit the Great Plains region in the late 1880s, the farmers were in a rebellious mood. "Those who could submit quietly to such outrage," said a western editor, "must be either more or less than men." In the West in general, economic distress was widespread; after the depression of 1893, feelings became so bitter that many citizens feared a revolution.

The Populist party originated from two great farmers' organizations, which were formed after the decline of the Grange—the Southern Alliance, which covered the cotton and tobacco belt, and the Northern Alliance, especially strong in the Plains region. Although the two alliances failed to merge, they made similar demands—free silver, more paper money, cheaper credit, government ownership of railroads, and the restoration of railroad bounty lands to the federal government. After several congressional election successes and conferences in Cincinnati in 1891 and St. Louis in February 1892, a new political party was formed. The People's party held a national convention in Omaha in July 1892. Although mostly from farm organizations, delegates also represented the Knights of Labor and followers of social reformers Henry George and Edward Bellamy.

Following the custom of the time, the convention nominated for President a Civil War veteran, James B. Weaver. There was nothing customary, however, about the platform. Instead of the usual resounding double talk, the Populists made clear their position and presented specific demands.

The Omaha Platform

The preamble of the Omaha platform expressed indignation at the existing political and economic conditions, which were, it claimed, bringing the nation "to the verge of moral, political, and material ruin." It condemned political corruption, newspapers dominated by business interests, the mortgage burden, and the condition of labor. The influence of social reformers was seen in the statements that "the land is concentrating in the hands of the capitalists" and that governmental injustice breeds "two great classes—tramps and millionaires." Turning to money and banking, the Populists characterized worldwide adoption of the gold standard as "a vast conspiracy against mankind...organized on two continents."

The following was perhaps the most zealously radical statement in the preamble of the Omaha platform:

We believe that the powers of government—in other words, of the people—should be expanded ...
as rapidly and as far
as the good sense of an intelligent people and the teachings
of experience
shall justify.

The Omaha platform revealed that it was the agriculturalists rather than organized labor who dominated the Populist party. The demands of organized labor, were given a subordinate position. Excluded from the platform proper, labor's demands were placed among a miscellaneous list of resolutions that were given the title "Expression of Sentiments."

The Omaha platform now seems less radical in perspective than it did at the time. The Populists proposed not to overthrow the capitalist system but simply to change the rules. They aimed to achieve

Connections
HISTORY AND MUSIC

FOLK SONGS OF PROTEST

Songs of protest are threaded throughout American History. In 1777, Americans marched to battle at Saratoga singing "Yankee Doodle." During the 1960s protesters marched for civil rights singing "We Shall Overcome." In the 1890s, too, Populists sang a protest song against bankers called "The Kansas Fool."

Farmers baling hay

THE KANSAS FOOL

We have the land to raise the wheat
And everything that's good to eat;
And when we had no bonds or debt,
We were a jolly, happy set.

With abundant crops raised everywhere,
'Tis a mystery, I do declare,
Why, farmers all should fume and fret,
And why we are so deep in debt.

* * * * *

The bankers followed us out west,
And did in mortgages invest;
They looked ahead and shrewdly planned,
and soon they'll have our Kansas land.

CHORUS
Oh Kansas fools! Poor Kansas Fools!
The banker makes of you a tool;
I look across the fertile plain,
Big crops—made so by gentle rain;
But twelve-cent corn gives me alarm,
And makes me want to sell my farm.

★ ★ ★ ★ ★ ★ ★ ★ ★ ★

MAKING THE MUSIC CONNECTION

1. What complaints do farmers make in this song?

2. How does this protest song reflect the fears and concerns of farmers that organized interests were acting against them?

LINKING PAST AND PRESENT

3. Describe the complaints found in a current protest song.

★ ★ ★ ★ ★ ★ ★ ★ ★ ★

---

their ends not through revolution but through the orderly process of free elections. The Populist platform reveals an important function of third parties in the United States—to bring to public attention measures that the major parties later adopt as their own.

The Populists' enthusiasm as they entered the campaign of 1892 had a religious tone. They adapted revival meeting hymns as party songs. Huge rallies were addressed not only by men but also by "women with skins tanned to parchment by the hot winds, with bony hands of toil, and clad in faded calico." The balloting revealed the distinct character of various regions in the People's party. All of its 22 electoral votes came from states lying west of the Mississippi River. In the South sympathy with Populist aims was widespread, but there was fear that the new party might divide the Democratic vote and let the Republicans back into power. Southern Democrats with Populist

principles—"Popocrats"—nonetheless helped elect their own party's candidate, Grover Cleveland.

Cleveland's Second Term

Cleveland's second term proved difficult. Inheriting a treasury deficit from the Harrison administration, he had scarcely taken office when the panic of 1893 burst upon the country. Although Cleveland could not have prevented this disaster, he was blamed for it. Furthermore, he managed to antagonize almost every element in his party. Above all, he antagonized farmers by defending the gold standard. Fearful that the Sherman Silver Purchase Act would flood the U.S. Treasury with so much silver that it could not be redeemed in gold, he called a special session of Congress in 1893 and forced repeal of the law. Because most western and southern Democrats opposed him, he was able to do this only with Republican support. Even after federal buying of silver ceased, the gold standard was endangered because it was difficult for the government to keep an adequate gold reserve in the treasury. To obtain the precious metal, the Treasury Department sold United States bonds.

In one transaction J. Pierpont Morgan, the most powerful banker on Wall Street, obtained federal bonds so far below their market value that he and the bankers associated with him made $1.5 million. Western fury at the Morgan bond transaction was unbounded. The gold standard was bad enough, but to pay bankers to preserve it seemed to them almost treasonable. More and more, western Democrats turned against the President, became "Popocrats," and demanded that the Democrats favor free silver.

The President faced other problems. Never popular with "machine" politicians, he angered them further by putting 120,000 civil service jobs on the merit system. Cleveland also infuriated workers by using troops in the 1894 Pullman strike.

The President's hope of lowering the prohibitive duties of the McKinley Tariff faded when a few Democratic senators joined the Republicans in tacking 633 amendments on a new tariff bill, thereby keeping rates almost at former levels. Cleveland let the resulting Wilson-Gorman Tariff of 1894 become a law without his signature, but he denounced the action of the rebellious senators as "a piece of party perfidy and dishonor."

Meanwhile the Republicans had become, more than ever, identified with business interests. A dominant figure in the party was Mark Hanna, an Ohio businessman-politician. Big, bluff, and low-browed, Hanna became, perhaps unjustly, a symbol of the alliance between corporate wealth and politics. Anti-Republican cartoons habitually portrayed him in a suit covered with dollar signs. In 1896 Hanna used his great organizing talents to secure the Republican nomination for his friend William McKinley, on a platform pledging high tariffs and maintenance of the gold standard.

Republicans in 1896 boasted that they could "nominate a rag-baby or a yellow dog and elect it" because of divisions among their opponents. The Democratic national convention opened with such a bitter fight between Gold Democrats and Silver Democrats that it was almost impossible to keep a semblance of order. Then, with dramatic suddenness, the party found a leader in a rather obscure presidential candidate, William Jennings Bryan of Nebraska. Bryan combined a romantic devotion to free silver with a

Examining Political Cartoons The New York Journal *identified Republican "boss" Mark Hanna as the New Guardian of Wall Street. Whose nomination did Hanna help to secure in 1896?*

personality, voice, and presence, which made him literally a spellbinder, especially when he spoke the following:

You come to us and tell us that the great cities are in favor of the gold standard. We reply that the great cities rest upon our broad and fertile plains. Burn down your cities and leave our farms, and your cities will spring up again as if by magic; but destroy our farms, and the grass will grow in the streets of every city in the country.

In his famous concluding words, Bryan used images that seemed to identify the gold standard with evil itself:

You shall not press down upon the brow of labor this crown of thorns—you shall not crucify mankind upon a cross of gold!

Examining Political Cartoons *The British magazine* Puck *shows candidate Bryan as a puppet being controlled by the silver-mine owners. Besides the mine owners, who supported free silver?*

Examining Maps *William Jennings Bryan made the election of 1896 a referendum on the unlimited coinage of silver. The map shows how the nation divided geographically in the election. Why was Bryan's main support in the South and West?*

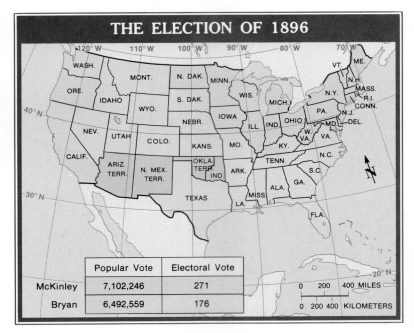

	Popular Vote	Electoral Vote
McKinley	7,102,246	271
Bryan	6,492,559	176

This speech contained hardly a single fact-based argument for a bimetallic standard. It was so charged with emotion that it made free silver a crusade—with Bryan as its standard bearer. Although only 36 years old, he received the Democratic nomination. Most Populists also agreed to support Bryan.

Breaking with tradition, which held that political campaigning was beneath the dignity of one who aspired to the presidency, Bryan traveled the country in search of support. He covered 18,000 miles on the most strenuous speaking tour a candidate had ever made.

In spite of all his efforts, Bryan's cause was doomed. Most large Democratic newspapers abandoned him; the Gold Democrats deserted the Democratic party and ran a separate candidate. Collecting an immense campaign fund, Hanna hired thousands of speakers and issued millions of pamphlets aimed at countering the free silver arguments. McKinley, depicted as "the advance agent of prosperity," was helped by the fact that prices of grain and

Examining Illustrations *William McKinley and the Republican party favored high tariffs as a means to protect the growing American industry. What appeals to traditional American values are made in this poster?*

cotton rose as Election Day approached. The most serious weakness in Bryan's campaign was that free silver was a poor issue on which to base an entire campaign. No one knew what the result of free coinage of silver would be; it would not have ended fluctuation in the value of money, and it might have caused a business panic.

The Republicans won the election of 1896 by a decisive margin, carrying all the thickly populated states of the Northeast and Midwest. It was a victory for industry over agriculture, the city over the country, the North and East over the West and South.

After their defeat in the election of 1896—some say after their decision to endorse the Democratic candidate—the Populists ceased to be a force in American politics. Though many at the time felt that all of these efforts had ended in dismal failure, those who lived long enough saw most of the planks of their party's platform signed into law.

SUMMARY

The Populist party pressed for inflationary policies that favored the farmer. To this end they protested the gold standard and supported free silver. In addition, they opposed national banks and proposed nationalization of railroad and telegraph lines. Populists entered the campaign of 1892 with the full support of farmers and some support of laborers. In 1896 they supported the Democratic party's narrow focus on free silver, which split the Democrats and gave the Republicans an easy victory.

CHECKING FOR UNDERSTANDING

1. **Identify** Populist party, Mark Hanna, William McKinley, William Jennings Bryan
2. **Define** inflation, deflation, gold standard, third party
3. **Analyze** the causes of more rapid price declines on farm crops than on many other goods and services.
4. **Summarize** what farmers wanted in terms of prices and credit.
5. **List** two objectives of the Populist party.
6. **Outline** the candidates, the basis of their support, and the issues in the 1896 election campaign.

THINKING CRITICALLY

7. **Recognizing Common Goals** The alliance between laborers and farmers was hampered by each group's different interests. What did the two groups have in common that encouraged such an alliance?

CONNECTIONS: HISTORY AND ECONOMICS

8. **Analyzing Policy** Why did the gold standard prevent the money supply from growing as fast as the production of goods and services? How did this contribute to a drop in prices?

★ ★ ★ ★ ★ ★ ★ ★ ★ ★ ★ ★ ★ ★ ★ ★ ★ ★

Linking Across Time

MINOR POLITICAL PARTIES

The Republican and Democratic parties dominate the two-party system, yet the United States has a long history of political parties that have risen to challenge the major parties. The Republican party was itself a third party in 1856; four years later it captured the White House. And at the turn of the century, the Populists seriously threatened the two-party monopoly. The Populist party had an impact on politics and government far beyond its showing in national elections. Most importantly, minor parties have served as vehicles for reform by taking clear-cut stands on controversial issues and proposing bold and original solutions. The table below shows some of the Populist proposals that were adopted and are still in use today.

A list of all the minor party proposals that were eventually adopted would be a long and impressive one. Minor parties, for instance, pushed for an end to slavery, voting rights for women, and child and labor regulation long before the major parties did. Still, it is fair to ask why no minor party has risen to the level of the Democrats and Republicans. One reason is that many of the ideas proposed by minor parties were viewed as radical in their day. They often were accepted years later, but usually long after the party has dissolved. Another reason is that once a minor party's idea gains strong support from the people, one or both of the major parties adopts it for their own. When this happens, the minor party is almost sure to lose its identity.

1891 political cartoon, Party of Patches

★ ★ ★ ★ ★ ★ ★ ★ ★ ★ ★

MAKING CONNECTIONS

1. What, in your opinion, was the Populists' purpose in introducing the initiative and the referendum?

ANALYZING IDEAS

2. What issues might be the basis for a minor party today?

★ ★ ★ ★ ★ ★ ★ ★ ★ ★ ★

POPULIST PROPOSALS

PROPOSAL	FIRST ADOPTED	STATUS TODAY
Federal Income Tax	16th Amendment, 1913	accounts for one-half of monies collected at all levels of government
Direct Election of U.S. Senators	17th Amendment, 1913	standard method for all senatorial elections
Secret Ballot	late 1890s	standard practice in all elections
Primary Elections	Wisconsin, 1903	used to settle virtually all contests for majority-party nominations for state and congressional offices and for many local offices
Initiative and Referendum	South Dakota, 1898	hundreds of cities and about one-half of the states have passed laws permitting citizens to introduce legislation and vote on proposed laws

Other Forces for Reform

...[R]eason and right feeling on any public subject has a better chance of being favorably listened to...than at any previous time in American history. This great benefit will probably not last...and all depends on making the utmost use of it.

—JOHN STUART MILL
British reformer, speech to the American Social Science Association, 1870

Section Focus

Though the Gilded Age is often thought of as a period of greed, corruption, and self-centered individualism, it was also a period of reform. Like the Populists, whose strength lay mainly in the West, reformers in other areas of the country were trying to call attention to problems in need of solutions.

Objectives

After studying this section, you should be able to:
• Trace women's involvement in the temperance and suffrage movements.
• Discuss the political ideas of Karl Marx and Henry George.

R eforms of the Civil War and Reconstruction periods encouraged people in the United States to look to government as the agent of social change. In the years of its unquestioned dominance, the Republican party had freed slaves, imposed a new way of life on the South, and opened the West to settlement. After the war, reformers who were dissatisfied with various aspects of life in the Gilded Age also looked to the government for action.

Temperance and Women's Rights

The period after the Civil War was not just a time of industrial progress, urban growth, and agrarian and labor discontent. Like the Jacksonian period, it also produced "a fertility of projects for the salvation of the world"—reforms designed to cure the ills of the new industrial society of the United States. Several reform movements that had begun earlier continued to reach toward their goals. Supporters of Prohibition, for example, formed a national political party in 1869; from 1872 on they ran a presidential candidate. The temperance movement had never been more active.

Most effective were two national organizations that waged a ceaseless campaign against the evils of liquor and the saloon: the Anti-Saloon League and the Women's Christian Temperance Union (WCTU). The WCTU revealed that women were

Examining Illustrations *The West led the way in granting women suffrage. These women voted in Cheyenne, Wyoming, in 1888. What other reform movement was reaching toward its goals before 1900?*

learning the techniques of large-scale organization. Frances Willard, the head of the WCTU, made her group an effective force for causes other than temperance, such as prison reform and protective labor laws. Because women were far more likely than men to favor temperance, temperance advocates usually favored women's suffrage.

The women's suffrage movement had its beginnings in the antebellum period; its first leaders were female abolitionists, like Elizabeth Cady Stanton, who decided to put the antislavery cause ahead of their own. After the war women's suffrage was championed with renewed vigor. Opponents of women's suffrage argued that women's interests were represented by their male relatives and spouses and that politics was a dirty business that would degrade "the fairer sex." Wendell Phillips, a former abolitionist, argued for the suffragist cause as follows:

―――――⬦⬦⬦―――――

One of two things is true: either a woman is like a man—and if she is then a ballot based on brains belongs to her as well as to him; or she is different, and then man does not know how to vote for her as well as she herself does.

―――――⬦⬦⬦―――――

In 1878 Susan B. Anthony of the National Woman Suffrage Association (NWSA) persuaded a sympathetic senator to propose the first women's suffrage amendment to the Constitution. It was voted down many times in the next 40 years. These defeats reflected the opinion of the majority. Most people in the United States, male and female, thought women's suffrage was an outlandish idea.

At the state level, suffragists had better success. By 1900 about half of the states allowed women to vote on school issues, where their special knowledge of children was presumed to be a benefit. On the frontier, where women shared the hardships and dangers equally with men, support for women's suffrage was more widespread. By 1900, 4 states—Colorado, Wyoming, Utah, and Idaho—had granted women the right to vote. It would take 20 more years for all the women of the United States to win this right.

Women workers especially suffered exploitation during the new industrial age. By 1900 almost 5 million women were employed in the United States. It was not uncommon for women to work in "sweat shops" for 10 to 14 hours a day, often for less than $4 a week. Most unions, however, refused to accept women as members. One exception was the International Ladies' Garment Workers Union, which had women leaders as well as women members. In 1903 a group of women formed the

Life of the Times

BOARDINGHOUSES

Beginning in the 1830s, farm girls moved to Lowell, Massachusetts, to work in the textile mills there. The mill owners set up boardinghouses with strict curfews and comfortable if sparse accommodations for the girls. Young workers in other towns generally boarded with families who took them in to help pay the rent. Later in the century, immigrant workers often boarded with other immigrants who had lived in the same village in the old country and had preceded them to America.

The practice of boarding offended the sensibilities of some middle-class reformers. They complained that boarding weakened the family unit and helped spread disease. But many immigrants had a different point of view. They knew that all boardinghouses were not the same. In some tenements, as many as ten immigrants slept in a room.

But other boardinghouses were like the establishment of one immigrant woman who thought she would own her own home in America. Having difficulty just making ends meet shortly after she arrived in the United States, she cooked for four boarders. Initially she resented having to share her home, prepare meals, and attend to the needs of people she did not even know. However, the woman's attitude changed. She began to enjoy providing a home for new immigrants who otherwise would have no place to stay.

Examining Photographs *In the early 1900s, the professions were largely reserved for men, while typing and secretarial jobs were thought to be women's work. How many women were employed by 1900?*

National Women's Trade Union League to campaign for better working conditions.

National Women's Trade Union League to campaign for better working conditions.

Socialism

Wherever industrialism appeared, there were people driven toward extreme solutions for the problems it created. Something seemed wrong with a system that produced both the idle rich, who lived in mansions, and the unemployed poor, who lived in slums. Some were impelled toward socialism. Eugene V. Debs, for example, became a lifelong convert to socialism because of unjust treatment after his imprisonment in an Illinois jail during the Pullman strike. Declaring that in a democracy workers could gain control of the government and use it to change the free enterprise system, he organized the American Socialist party.

Unlike Debs, Socialists in the early 1800s did not attempt to change the economic system by gaining control of the government. While early European Socialists believed private property to be incompatible with the emerging industrial

system, they tried to effect change by experimenting with cooperative communities. Robert Owen brought his idea of cooperative control of industry from England to New Harmony, Indiana, in 1825. Such socialist communities reached their peak in America in the 1840s.

Examining Photographs *Karl Marx saw all of history as a struggle between classes. What did he predict would be the last conflict?*

Socialists of the late nineteenth century, however, were dedicated to changing the entire social and political system, partly because of the influence of Karl Marx. Marx had been a student at the University of Berlin during the emergence of a new philosophical and literary movement that questioned established values. Searching for meaning in history, Marx finally wrote his economic philosophy in *The Communist Manifesto* in 1847 and *Das Kapital,* the first volume published in 1867. Marx, who wrote with force and buttressed his opinions with great learning, predicted that capitalism was doomed. Fewer and fewer capitalists, he said, would control all wealth, while the mass of the people would be pushed into the ranks of the proletariat (people without property). Eventually the proletarians, preferring the risk of death at the barricades in violent revolution to slow starvation in the poor conditions of factories and slums, would rise and overthrow their masters. History, said Marx, had seen continual class struggles, but the conflict between industrial workers and capitalists would be the last. When the workers eventually took control of society, Marx believed they would establish a classless society. Using the slogan "Workers of the world, unite!" Marx called on workers everywhere to join his crusade.

Marxist socialism enlisted many workers in the industrial countries of Europe to its cause. In the United States, however, it gained only a small following, mostly among intellectuals and immigrant groups in big cities.

Henry George and the Single Tax

Another writer with a proposal for re-making society was Henry George, whose major work, *Progress and Poverty,* was published in 1879. George attacked the central problem posed by the socialists: Why should the advance of the industrial revolution, with more and more machinery for producing wealth, apparently result in more poverty? George said the problem was that ownership of land—the source of

all wealth—was being concentrated in the hands of speculators. These speculators did not put the land to use. They merely waited for it to increase in value, meanwhile charging high rents that drove down wages and business profits. George criticized the growing gap between rich and poor:

We need not look far from the palace to find the hovel. When people can charter special steamboats to take them to watering places …build marble stables for their horses and give dinner parties which cost…a thousand dollars a head, we may know that there are poor girls on the streets…[facing] starvation.

A believer in private property, George did not propose socialism as a remedy. Instead, he urged what he called the "single tax" on land values. The rate of the single tax would be based not on existing value but on *potential* value if the land were used efficiently. Thus there would be no profit in keeping land out of use and waiting for it to increase in worth; owners would either have to develop it themselves or sell it to someone else who would do so. George argued that this would cause prosperity by promoting maximum productivity and by plowing the profits of the land monopoly back into society. George's ideas had great appeal to the people of the United States who were dismayed over the growth of monopolies and who had begun to realize that the frontier was closing. Single-tax clubs and magazines spread his ideas. Although the single-tax idea was too radical a change to be accepted completely, it influenced methods of taxation both in this country and abroad.

Dissenting Voices

Another widely read book, *The Theory of the Leisure Class,* was published in 1899 by Thorstein Veblen. The son of Norwegian immigrants, Veblen was influenced by Populism in his early days in Wisconsin. Attending Yale and Johns Hopkins University, he became interested in the social sciences, especially economics. His appreciation for science led him to write with the cool detachment of an observer, not a fiery revolutionary. While he believed in the evolutionary process of natural selection, Veblen argued that the "leisure class," those who had great wealth, was not an example of the most fit. In fact, he said the leisure class hindered progress and evolution. Veblen believed that, like the dinosaur, the leisure class would disappear.

Veblen used the phrase "conspicuous consumption" to describe the life of the upper class. These were the people who wasted vast resources just for show. The phrase had deep meaning because the contrast between wealth and poverty was not hidden in the United States. The mansions that lined the streets of cities like New York and Chicago were within a few blocks of immigrant ghettos. However, Veblen's vision of a community of equals governed by an elite group of social planners was judged impractical by most Americans of his time.

Probably the reason why radical formulas for altering society did not gain wide support was that Americans were, on the whole, too prosperous to want change. Even those at the bottom often felt they had bettered their position from an earlier time. A New England farm boy might prefer drawing wages of a dollar a day for a 60-hour week in a factory to working from dawn to dark trying to make a living from a rocky farm. An immigrant might be living with his or her family in a single room and working in a windowless sweatshop, but for the first time in his life he was wearing shoes. Even the poorest workers believed that, in time, they would also be able to "get ahead" and become property owners. If they destroyed property rights, what would happen to the American dream?

Furthermore, the United States was so large and had so many different interests that no one idea attained universal appeal. People in the United States, wanting to promote their interests, worked habitually through political parties. These parties tried to appeal to as many groups as possible.

SUMMARY

Following the Civil War, reform movements aimed to cure the ills of the new industrial society. Women began to press for voting and working rights. Because most unions excluded women, they formed their own. Temperance advocates formed the Prohibition party and began to sponsor presidential candidates. Some people turned to socialism as the answer to the problems of industrialization. Karl Marx wrote of classless socialist societies free of private ownership, capitalism, economic inequities, and exploitation. Dissenters such as Thorstein Veblen and Henry George attracted a reading audience, but most Americans resisted change.

CHECKING FOR UNDERSTANDING

1. **Identify** Susan B. Anthony, Eugene V. Debs

2. **Discuss** the goals and methods of the temperance movement.

3. **Describe** the movements to gain voting rights for women.

4. **Compare** the solutions proposed by Karl Marx, Thorstein Veblen, and Henry George.

THINKING CRITICALLY

5. **Arguing an Opinion** Women fought for the right to vote but had success in only 4 states by 1900. What arguments would you propose to justify allowing women the right to vote in the late 1800s?

GLOBAL PERSPECTIVES

6. **Analyzing Ideology** Marxist theory developed a following in industrial countries of Europe but never really took hold in the United States. Describe three conditions in the American experience that probably made socialism an unpopular idea.

★ ★ ★ ★ ★ ★ ★ ★ ★ ★ ★ ★ ★ ★ ★ ★ ★ ★

★ Chapter 21 Review ★

★ Summary

By the 1880s hardship had replaced the prosperity that farm families enjoyed after the Civil War. American farmers now faced hard times because of their own overproduction of crops. Economic factors caused farm prices to drop sharply. Overburdened with debt and at the mercy of the elements, many lost their farms.

Farmers sought solutions to their social and economic problems through the Granger Laws and the Populist party. These were successful in bringing attention to a number of political reforms later adopted by the Democratic and Republican parties. Among the most important reform efforts was the passage of the Interstate Commerce Act in 1887.

Attempts to regulate such monopolies as the railroads failed when new laws were not strictly enforced. Other attempted reforms included voting and working rights for women and socialist proposals to improve industrial society.

★ Using Vocabulary

Use each of the following terms in a statement that might have been made by each of the following people:

Railroad owner: **pooling**

Farmer: **cooperatives**

Banker: **inflation**

★ Reviewing Facts

1. **Summarize** the factors that created financial hardships for farmers in the late 1800s.
2. **List** three purposes of the Granger laws.
3. **Specify** what the Interstate Commerce Act required of the railroads.
4. **Explain** why deflation hurt the farmers.
5. **Describe** the gold standard and its effect on money supply.
6. **State** the reforms the Populists demanded in their platform.
7. **Compare** Karl Marx's solution to poverty with Henry George's.

★ Understanding Concepts

ECONOMIC INEQUITY

1. In the farmers' view, what groups enriched themselves at the farmers' expense?
2. Read the quote from the farm journal editorial at the beginning of Section Two. On what factors did the farmers blame the inequities described?

SOCIAL CHANGE

3. What groups of people might be expected to support extreme solutions for social problems? What groups would likely oppose such solutions? Why did most Americans vote for more moderate candidates in the late 1900s?
4. What did the Populist party, the Grange, and the followers of Marx, George, and Veblen have in common?

★ Thinking Critically

1. **Understanding Cause and Effect** Explain how new agricultural technology helped the farmers. How did it hurt some farmers financially?
2. **Linking Past and Present** Today banks and lending institutions offer variable-rate loans with an interest rate that varies as prices rise and fall. What problem is this intended to solve?
3. **Proposing Strategy** Assume you are William Jennings Bryan's campaign manager in the 1896 election. Draw up a plan of recommendations to improve Bryan's chances of success.
4. **Contrasting Ideas** How did Marxist theory of reform contrast with the methods used or envisioned by the other reform proposals discussed in this chapter?

★ Writing About History

COMPARISON

Refer to the description of how to write a comparison essay in the History Writer's Handbook in the Appendix of this book. Your teacher will give you more specific instructions on the essay's length and the assignment's due date.

Assume you are a European tourist attending a rally at which the Populists describe their platform. Write a letter to a Marxist friend in Europe, comparing and contrasting the Populist approach at reform with the Marxist formula. You may wish to research additional details about Marx's theory.

★ Learning Cooperatively

You will be part of a discussion between four people meeting in a Great Plains town in the year 1886. Divide the following roles among yourselves: a farmer, a banker, a railroad owner, and a politician. The purpose of this meeting is to discuss the problems of the farmer. Review Section One to gain background information on your role. The farmer will begin the meeting by stating his or her main concerns. The other members should discuss ways to answer the farmer's problems, although each individual should be prepared to argue why they cannot agree to a recommended change. End the meeting by having all members agree on two recommendations for helping the farmer.

★ Mastering Skills

IDENTIFYING UNSTATED ASSUMPTIONS

Suppose you receive a phone call from a salesperson offering you a free carpet cleaning, but your residence has hardwood floors. The salesperson made an *unstated assumption,* that is, assumed or took for granted that your residence is carpeted.

There are many kinds of unstated assumptions. Sometimes an author makes an unstated assumption regarding what the reader knows. Assuming that the reader understands or has knowledge of certain information, the author may move on to make a point—one that is unclear to the reader because of the unstated assumption. Another kind of unstated assumption made by an author may be a result of the author's own lack of information. In this case a reader may become aware that an author has made an assumption that is not true. This type of unstated assumption is usually discovered only by informed readers or those who have a special interest in the subject.

While it may be very difficult for you to identify **incorrect** assumptions made by the author of a history textbook, it is a valuable skill to learn to identify unstated assumptions made by historical figures or groups. For example, the farmers in the late 1800s

who distrusted banks made the unstated assumption that a better alternative to banks could be found.

To identify an unstated assumption, follow these guidelines.

- First read the statement to determine its meaning.
- Review the context of the statement. Who is the speaker? What special focus may this person or group have?
- Study the content of the statement. What are the historical facts upon which the speaker relies? What facts are not included in the statement?
- Use the answers to these questions to identify the missing idea or information that the author takes for granted—the unstated assumption.

Example   Following is a list of statements that were made by an identified historical figure or group. An unstated assumption follows each statement.

- *The farmers…produce the largest share of wealth, but they are getting … the smallest share for themselves.* —Washington Gladden, Protestant pastor and social reformer; assumption: Each group should receive on the basis of what it produces.

- *We believe that the powers of government—in other words of the people—should be expanded.…* Omaha Populist platform; assumption: If the government had greater power, it could solve people's problems.

- *Burn down your cities and leave our farms, and your cities will spring up again as if by magic.…* William Jennings Bryan, Democratic and Populist presidential candidate; assumption: Cities depend upon farms for their existence.

Practice   Read the statements below, each of which contains at least one unstated assumption. Follow the guidelines above to identify the unstated assumptions. Look on the page noted for each item to find the name of the speaker.

1._____: *Workers of the world, unite!* (p. 622)

2._____: *Can't I do what I want with my own?* (p. 609)

3._____: *The bankers followed us out west, and did in mortgages invest; They looked ahead and shrewdly planned, and soon they'll have our Kansas land.* (p. 614)

4._____: *Those who could submit quietly to such outrage must be either more or less than men.* (p. 613)

★ ★ ★ Unit 6 Digest ★ ★ ★

During the second half of the 1800s, the landscape of America changed. The Plains frontier was settled, and the rise of industry brought unparalleled growth to the economy. America ceased to be a rural nation of small farms and became an industrial nation of cities and city dwellers. It was, according to writer Mark Twain, a Gilded Age, bright and attractive on the surface but corrupt underneath.

Chapter 17
Opening the Trans-Mississippi West

In the early 1860s, many Indian nations lived on the Great Plains with the buffalo herds that provided their food. Settlers from the East believed early explorers' descriptions of the area as a "Great American Desert." The federal government reserved this vast area for the Indians. Then, beginning in 1869, transcontinental railway lines opened the West. The discovery of gold and other minerals and the promise of wealth from cattle also lured many people. Before long, the once-desolate region blossomed into a land of farms, towns, mining communities, ranches, and open ranges.

Native Americans fought the intrusion of the railroads and the settlers, but their cause was doomed. Their way of life was disappearing. White hunters had slaughtered the buffalo almost to extinction, and farmers, miners, and ranchers had taken much of their land. In 1890 at Wounded Knee, their resistance came to an end. The American "old West" frontier was gone.

The Homestead Act made land in the West easy to obtain and the railroads actively promoted settlement. Pioneer farmers poured onto the plains by the thousands and, with the aid of new technology, overcame the harsh realities of the region. Many farmers failed, in part, because they were heavily mortgaged and grew only a single cash crop.

Chapter 18
The Rise of Industrial America

The key to the growth of the American economy was industrialization. The United States had all the necessary ingredients for industry to grow—abundant natural and human resources, investment money, a growing transportation system, a free enterprise economic system with few government restrictions, and new inventions and technology.

By 1900 huge companies dominated the economy. One business after another consolidated. The efficiency of business combinations resulted in cheaper production, higher quality, and lower prices that drove smaller competitors out of business. Corporations, monopolies, and trusts became the norm. John D. Rockefeller and the oil industry and Andrew Carnegie and the steel industry typified "big business." Industrial leaders used social Darwinism to explain and justify their actions and rise to wealth and power. The Sherman Antitrust Act, passed in 1890, did little to stop the consolidations.

Chapter 19
Labor, Immigrants, and Urban Life

With industrialization the work force grew and workers' lives changed. Gone was the personal relationship between workers and employers. Hours were long, wages low, and work places hazardous. Machines had taken over many traditional tasks. Unable to improve their lot individually, workers turned to labor unions.

Opposed by the big corporations, management, and to a certain extent, government, the unions resorted to strikes. But even major strikes, like the 1894 Pullman railroad strike, failed to win significant gains for the workers.

An important influence on the efforts of labor were the large numbers of immigrants who provided unskilled labor for urban industries. The United States had always been a nation of immigrants, but the nature of immigration changed during the late 1800s. The "new immigration" consisted primarily of southern and eastern European and Chinese immigrants rather than northern and western Europeans. The immigrants flocked to the cities, where they created their own ethnic communities. Their unfamiliar languages and customs and willingness to take any available job aroused anti-immigration sentiment.

Along with the influx of immigrants from other countries, rural Americans also migrated to the cities. As a result, cities across the nation grew in size. A new way of life evolved in this urban environment. While new opportunities emerged in education and some other areas, human and technical problems plagued the cities.

Chapter 20
The Gilded Age

With industrialization and urbanization came political corruption. Scandals arose at every level of government. Political machines dominated almost all major cities. Graft was common, and at the state level, businesses bought favors from legislators. Scandals even touched the President and Congress.

Government in general lacked leadership. Under Presidents Hayes and Garfield, reform efforts met with limited success. Less graft occurred, but patronage and the spoils system still prevailed. Civil service reform finally came in 1883 with passage of the Pendleton Act. The tariff and the currency question, however, continued to provoke controversy.

In addition to these reforms, the society and culture changed as well. Education expanded and improved. Local-color writers like Mark Twain described their locales with realism and detail. Sports events became a favorite leisure-time activity as did vaudeville, penny-newspapers, and dime novels.

Chapter 21
Politics, Protest, and Populism

The prosperity of the Gilded Age did not extend to farmers. Burdened with high costs, low incomes, and heavy debt, they blamed their plight on unfair railroad practices, greedy banks, and the federal government's monetary policy.

To solve the farmers' problems, they organized into groups such as the Grange and the farmers' alliances. Ultimately these groups turned to politics. One of their major concerns was the railroads. The farmers' calls for reform led to the passage of Granger laws in some states and prompted passage of the Interstate Commerce Act of 1887.

The farmers wanted to raise prices for their produce by putting more "cheap money" into circulation. They joined with labor and other reform groups to form a new national political party—the Populist party—and made paper money and "free silver" a campaign issue in the 1892 presidential election. The Omaha Platform of the Populist party clearly reflected the interests of the farmer.

The Populist party had some successes, and eventually some of its reform ideas were adopted by the two major parties. But the Populist movement itself died soon after William Jennings Bryan lost the 1896 presidential election. Republican victory made that election a triumph of industry over agriculture.

Farmers were not the only ones seeking reform. The temperance movement had never been more active—nor had women. Women's suffrage became a popularly debated issue across the country. Some women, like Susan B. Anthony believed that it would take a constitutional amendment to improve their position in society. At the same time, writers like Karl Marx proposed socialism as an economic remedy, while Henry George favored a "single tax" on land values. However, Americans on the whole were not interested in or actively resisted instituting such radical change.

RELATING IDEAS

1. In what ways did technology influence American life and society between 1860 and 1900?

IDENTIFYING TRENDS

2. What changes took place in American business in the decades before 1900?

MAKING COMPARISONS

3. Compare the American landscape and environment in 1860 and 1900.

★ Unit 6 Review ★

★ Analyzing Unit Themes

GEOGRAPHY AND ENVIRONMENT

1. What geographic and environmental features created hardships for those who settled and farmed the West?

CONFLICT AND COOPERATION

2. How did the settlement of the West affect native Americans? the nation as a whole? How might cooperation have resolved the many conflicts?

3. What groups united against a commonly perceived opponent in order to better their lives?

INFLUENCE OF TECHNOLOGY

4. Name some inventions of the late 1800s and tell how they made rapid industrialization possible.

CULTURAL DIVERSITY

5. What ethnic groups played a role in the settlement of the West and in industrialization?

★ Reviewing Chronology

Study the unit time line on pages 502-503, then answer the questions that follow.

1. The United States became politically unified in 1776. How long after was it before the country became unified by rail?

2. In 1870 Germany became a unified nation. How many years later did Germany become one of the members of the Triple Alliance?

★ Linking Past and Present

- 1989 Speaker of the House of Representatives forced to resign over unethical practices.
- 1990 five U.S. Senators accused of exercising undue influence on behalf of an savings and loan bank president who gave them political contributions.

1. **Making Comparisons** How does the corruption and questionable ethics of the Gilded Age contrast with recent problems in the legislative branch of government?

2. **Making Judgments** In your opinion, is ethical personal behavior equally as important in government leaders as their professional behavior? Explain your answer.

★ Demonstrating Citizenship

Assessing Involvement A citizen's interest in an issue may depend on how it affects him or her personally. For example, a citizen may be both a taxpayer who does not want taxes raised for a clean air program and an urban resident who does not want to breathe polluted air. In this exercise decide what issues each type of citizen is likely to favor. You may list more than one issue for each citizen, and some issues will be shared among citizens. Explain your logic for each choice.

Citizens	Issues
1. a manufacturer	a. high wages
2. a farmer	b. low wages
3. a commercial businessperson	c. high food prices
	d. low food prices
4. a government worker	e. high tariffs
5. an unemployed worker	f. low tariffs
	g. large government budget
6. a consumer	h. small government budget

★ Interpreting Illustrations

Jerked Down *by Charles Russell*

Examine the painting above, then answer the questions that follow.

1. What are the cowboys in this painting attempting to do?

2. What image of the West do you think Russell conveys?

3. Cowboys and Plains Indians have been depicted in fiction and popular culture as enemies. What might they have had in common?

4. By the 1890s the long drives were over, and the nation had become increasingly industrialized and urbanized. Why do you think cowboy adventures continued to be told in dime novels?

★ Thinking Globally

1. Making Comparisons In East Africa during the 1800s an epidemic killed 95 percent of the cattle. What similar incident occurred in the United States during the late 1800s? How did the two incidents differ?

2. Making Comparisons In 1871 diamonds discovered in South Africa drew thousands of fortune seekers and created a booming mining town. European investors became wealthy from mines worked by South African natives, who were harshly treated. What similar event occurred in the United States in the late 1800s? How were the South African and American situations different? How were they similar?

★ Relating Geography and History

MOVEMENT: TRANSPORTATION

In the 1800s settlers moved west and established farms, towns, and cattle ranches. Settlement and development accelerated rapidly after the building of the railroads.

Answer the questions that follow.

1. What geographic features attracted people to move west?

2. Why did the building of the railroad accelerate the movement of people to the West?

★ Practicing Skills

ANALYZING MAP DATA

Refer to the skills lesson on Analyzing Map Data on page 527 to help you practice this map and graph skill.

Study the election map of 1896 on page 616. Then answer the questions that follow.

1. What data is shown on the map?

2. How is the data separated?

3. How is the data related?

4. What judgments can you make?

SUMMARIZING

Refer to the skills lesson on Summarizing on page 561 to help you practice this study and writing skill.

Read the following material carefully.

Big business enjoyed many advantages. Big companies could manufacture enough products to meet the demands of a national market. They produced better products at lower cost than their smaller competitors by using the newest processes and by combining operations formerly carried on by separate companies. They paid high salaries to executives to get expert managers. At the same time, they increased efficiency by establishing separate departments for specialized functions such as purchasing, production, research, distribution, and sales.

By using its efficiency, organization, and size, big business was frequently in a position to take advantage of its competitors and sometimes of the public. Big companies could demand volume discounts from shippers. They could sell their products in an area at a loss until local competitors were forced to shut down or sell out. If a big company succeeded in getting a monopoly in its industry, it could raise consumer prices and pay less to suppliers of raw materials.

Big business resulted from the vision of people who recognized great opportunities for wealth and were willing to take risks to get it. In attaining success, however, many entrepreneurs showed few scruples in driving competitors out of business, evading the law, bribing officials, destroying labor unions, and devastating the environment. The American public, therefore, had mixed feelings about big business. Some worried about the corrupting influences of wealth and power. Yet others admitted that they benefited from the efficiency of big business, its lower prices, and the jobs it created.

List the main ideas expressed in the material. Then summarize by rewriting the main ideas in your own words.

UNIT 7

Entering a New Century: 1880-1914

...We must so conduct ourselves that every big nation and every little nation that behaves itself shall never have to think of us with fear, and shall have confidence not only in our justice but in our courtesy....

—THEODORE ROOSEVELT
Outlook, 1914

SETTING THE SCENE

Time

Late nineteenth and early twentieth centuries

Mood

In an age of optimism and idealism, two important changes took place in the way Americans thought about their country. United States foreign policy shifted away from isolationism and the nation became a major power in international affairs. Americans also took a look at their political institutions and concluded that change was necessary. Progressive-minded reformers sought a more democratic government while working to end a host of social ills.

Themes

- American Democracy
- Economic Development
- The Individual and Family Life
- U.S. Role in World Affairs

Key Events

- Purchase of Alaska and annexation of Hawaii
- Spanish-American War
- Building of the Panama Canal
- States institute direct primary, initiative, and referendum
- Formation of the National Association for the Advancement of Colored People
- Income taxes enacted
- "Bull Moose" party formed
- Federal Reserve System created
- Federal Trade Commission established

Major Issues

- Commercial interests and war with Spain leads to the acquisition of a colonial empire.
- Muckraking literature inspires a new generation of reformers who seek to correct social inequities.
- Reform-minded Presidents extend democracy and protect Americans from big business.

◄ Cliff Dwellers *(detail) by George Wesley Bellows, 1913, the Los Angeles County Museum of Art, Los Angeles County Funds*

Global Perspectives

In 1898 an explosion on the United States battleship *Maine* in the harbor at Havana, Cuba, resulted in a war that dramatically altered the place of the nation in world affairs. Victory in the Spanish-American War brought with it an American empire that stretched from islands in the Caribbean to the Philippines off the coast of Asia.

Conflict broke out in other areas of the world as well. In 1894 Japan and China went to war over Korea. The Japanese were victorious and annexed Korea. Ten years later, Japan became involved in a war with Russia. The Russo-Japanese

THE WORLD

	ASIA AND OCEANIA	AFRICA	EUROPE	SOUTH AMERICA	NORTH AND CENTRAL AMERICA
1885					
				● 1889 *Brazil becomes a republic*	
	● 1894 *Sino-Japanese war begins*		● 1893 *New Zealand becomes first nation to grant women suffrage*		
1900					● 1898 *Battleship* Maine *explodes; Spanish-American war begins*
	● 1904 *Russo-Japanese war begins* ▼	● 1908 *Belgium establishes control over the Congo* ▲			
1915					● 1914 *Panama Canal opens* ▲

War ended with a Japanese victory that greatly enhanced its prestige as a world power.

In southern Africa the British and the African Dutch became embroiled in the Boer War, which lasted for three years. The settlement of this conflict in 1902 laid the basis for the South African policy of apartheid, or racial segregation.

Also at this time, the United States strengthened its influence in Central America. In 1903 a revolt in Panama City against Colombia led to the formation of an independent republic. Panama gave the United States exclusive rights to build a canal through a 10-mile wide zone through its territory, connecting the Atlantic and Pacific oceans. Construction on the canal, which opened in 1914, was soon underway. The year 1914 also marked the start of World War I in Europe, a war that would eventually involve the United States and reshape world affairs.

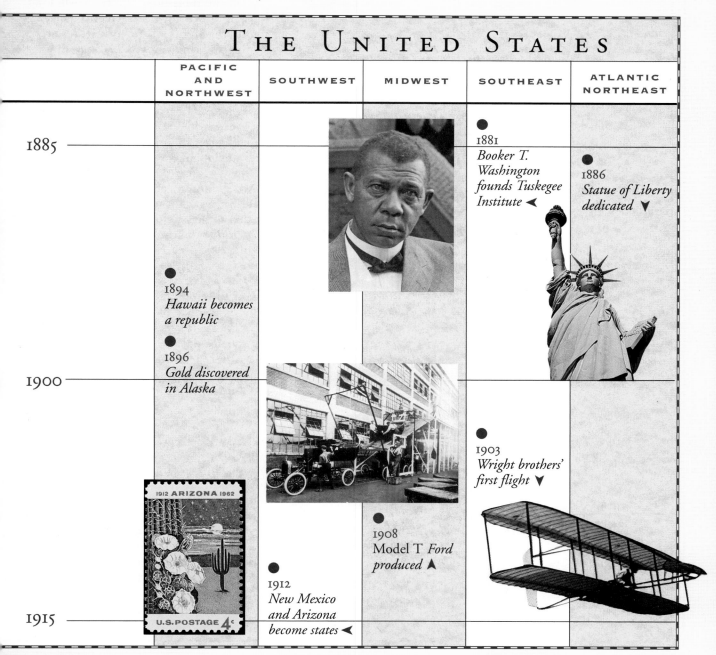

THE UNITED STATES

PACIFIC AND NORTHWEST	SOUTHWEST	MIDWEST	SOUTHEAST	ATLANTIC NORTHEAST

1885

● 1881
Booker T. Washington founds Tuskegee Institute ◄

● 1886
Statue of Liberty dedicated ▼

● 1894
Hawaii becomes a republic

● 1896
Gold discovered in Alaska

1900

● 1903
Wright brothers' first flight ▼

● 1908
Model T Ford produced ▲

1912 ARIZONA 1962
U.S. POSTAGE 4c

● 1912
New Mexico and Arizona become states ◄

1915

AMERICAN LITERARY HERITAGE

A major literary development in the late nineteenth century was naturalism, which developed out of realist fiction. Naturalist writers carried the vivid detail of realism a step further by depicting environmental factors. Characters seem to be caught in a web of circumstances and events that they can not control or do not understand.

Theodore Dreiser was a master of the naturalist style. In his first novel, Sister Carrie, *published in 1900, he describes the compelling attraction as well as the cold indifference of life in growing cities such as Chicago and New York.*

Theodore Dreiser

from *Sister Carrie*

Minnie's flat, as the one-floor resident apartments were then being called, was in a part of West Van Buren Street inhabited by families of labourers and clerks, men who had come, and were still coming, with the rush of population pouring in at the rate of 50,000 a year. It was on the third floor, the front windows looking down into the street, where, at night, the lights of grocery stores were shining and children were playing. To Carrie, the sound of the little bells upon the horse-cars, as they tinkled in and out of hearing, was as pleasing as it was novel. She gazed into the lighted street when Minnie brought her into the front room, and wondered at the sounds, the movement, the murmur of the vast city which stretched for miles and miles in every direction.

Mrs. Hanson, after the first greetings were over, gave Carrie the baby and proceeded to get supper. Her husband asked a few questions and sat down to read the evening paper. He was a silent man, American born, of a Swede father, and now employed as a cleaner of refrigerator cars at the stock-yards. To him the presence or absence of his wife's sister was a matter of indifference. Her personal appearance did not affect him one way or the other. His one observation to the point was concerning the chances of work in Chicago.

"It's a big place," he said. "You can get in somewhere in a few days. Everybody does."

It had been tacitly understood beforehand that she was to get work and pay her board. He was of a clean, saving disposition, and had already paid a number of monthly installments on two lots far out on the West Side. His ambition was some day to build a house on them.

In the interval which marked the preparation of the meal Carrie found time to study the flat. She had some slight gift of observation and that sense, so rich in every women—intuition.

She felt the drag of a lean and narrow life. The walls of the rooms were discordantly papered. The floors were covered with matting and the hall laid with a thin rag carpet. One could see that the furniture was of that poor, hurriedly patched together quality sold by the installment houses.

She sat with Minnie, in the kitchen, holding the baby until it began to cry. Then she walked and sang to it, until Hanson, disturbed in his reading, came and took it. A pleasant side to his nature came out here. He was patient. One could see that he was very much wrapped up in his offspring.

"Now, now," he said, walking. "There, there," and there was a certain Swedish accent noticeable in his voice.

"You'll want to see the city first, won't you?" said Minnie, when they were eating. "Well, we'll go out Sunday and see Lincoln Park."

Carrie noticed that Hanson had said nothing to this. He seemed to be thinking of something else.

"Well," she said, "I think I'll look around tomorrow. I've got Friday and Saturday, and it won't be any trouble. Which way is the business part?"

Minnie began to explain, but her husband took this part of the conversation to himself.

"It's that way," he said, pointing east. "That's east." Then he went off into the longest speech he had yet indulged in, concerning the lay of Chicago. "You'd better look in those big manufacturing houses along Franklin Street and just the other side of the river," he concluded. "Lots of girls work there. You could get home easy, too. It isn't very far."

Carrie nodded and asked her sister about the neighborhood. The latter talked in a subdued tone, telling the little she knew about it, while Hanson concerned himself with the baby. Finally he jumped up and handed the child to his wife.

"I've got to get up early in the morning, so I'll go to bed," and off he went, disappearing into the dark little bedroom off the hall, for the night.

"He works way down at the stock-yards," explained Minnie, "so he's got to get up at half-past five."

"What time do you get up to get breakfast?" asked Carrie.

"At about twenty minutes of five."

Together they finished the labour of the day, Carrie washing the dishes while Minnie undressed the baby and put it to bed. Minnie's manner was one of trained industry, and Carrie could see that it was a steady round of toil with her.

She began to see that her relations with Drouet would have to be abandoned. He could not come here. She read from the manner of Hanson, in the subdued air of Minnie, and, indeed, the whole atmosphere of the flat, a settled opposition to anything save a conservative round to toil. If Hanson sat every evening in the front room and read his paper, if he went to bed at nine, and Minnie a little later, what would they expect of her? She saw that she would first need to get work and establish herself on a paying basis before she could think of having company of any

Working girls leaving a shoe factory, 1895

sort. Her little flirtation with Drouet seemed now an extraordinary thing.

"No," she said to herself, "he can't come here."

She asked Minnie for ink and paper, which were upon the mantel in the dining-room, and when the latter had gone to bed at ten, got out Drouet's card and wrote him. "I cannot have you call on me here. You will have to wait until you hear from me again. My sister's place is so small."

Birdseye view of the business district of Chicago

She troubled herself over what else to put in the letter. She wanted to make some reference to their relations upon the train, but was too timid. She concluded by thanking him for his kindness in a crude way, then puzzled over the formality of signing her name, and finally decided upon the severe, winding up with a "Very truly," which she subsequently changed to "Sincerely." She sealed and addressed the letter, and going in the front room, the alcove of which contained her bed, drew the one small rocking-chair up to the open window, and sat looking out upon the night and streets in silent wonder. Finally, wearied by her own reflections, she began to grow dull in her chair, and feeling the need of sleep, arranged her clothing for the night and went to bed.

When she awoke at eight the next morning, Hanson had gone. Her sister was busy in the dining-room, which was also the sitting-room, sewing. She worked, after dressing, to arrange a little breakfast for herself, and then advised with Minnie

as to which way to look. The latter had changed considerably since Carrie had seen her. She was now a thin, though rugged, woman of twenty-seven, with ideas of life coloured by her husband's, and fast hardening into narrower conceptions of pleasure and duty than had ever been hers in a thoroughly circumscribed youth. She had invited Carrie, not because she longed for her presence, but because the latter was dissatisfied at home, and could probably get work and pay her board here. She was pleased to see her in a way but reflected her husband's point of view in the matter of work. Anything was good enough so long as it paid—say, five dollars a week to begin with. A shop girl was the destiny prefigured for the newcomer. She would get in one of the great shops and do well enough until—well, until something happened. Neither of them knew exactly what. They did not figure on promotion. They did not exactly count on marriage. Things would go on, though, in a dim kind of way until the better thing would eventuate, and Carried would be rewarded for coming and toiling in the city. It was under such auspicious circumstances that she started out this morning to look for work.

Before following her in her round of seeking, let us look at the sphere in which her future was to lie. In 1889 Chicago had the peculiar qualifications of growth which made such adventuresome pilgrimages even on the part of young girls plausible.

Its many and growing commercial opportunities gave it widespread fame, which made of it a giant magnet, drawing to itself, from all quarters, the hopeful and the hopeless—those who had their fortune yet to make and those whose fortunes and affairs had reached a disastrous climax elsewhere. It was a city of over 500,000, with the ambition, the daring, the activity of a metropolis of a million. Its streets and houses were already scattered over an area of seventy-five square miles. Its population was not so much thriving upon established commerce as upon the industries which prepared for the arrival of others. The sound of the hammer engaged upon the erection of new structures was everywhere heard. Great industries were moving in. The huge railroad corporations which had long before recognised the prospects of the place had seized upon vast tracts of land for transfer and shipping purposes. Streetcar lines had been extended far out into the open country in anticipation of rapid growth....

In the central portion was the vast wholesale and shopping district, to which the uninformed seeker for work usually drifted. It was a characteristic of Chicago then, and one not generally shared by other cities, that individual firms of any pretension occupied individual buildings. The presence of ample ground made this possible. It gave an imposing appearance to most of the wholesale houses, whose offices were upon the ground floor and in plain view of the street. The large plates of window glass, now so common, were then rapidly coming into use, and gave to the ground floor offices a distinguished and prosperous look. The casual wanderer could see as he passed a polished array of office fixtures, much frosted glass, clerks hard at work, and genteel business men in "nobby" suits and clean linen lounging about or sitting in groups. Polished brass or nickel signs at the square stone entrances announced the firm and the nature of the business in rather neat and reserved terms. The entire metropolitan center possessed a high and mighty air calculated to overawe and abash the common applicant, and to make the gulf between poverty and success seem both wide and deep.

Into this important commercial region the timid Carrie went. She walked east along Van Buren Street through a region of lessening importance, until it deteriorated into a mass of shanties and coalyards, and finally verged upon the river. She walked bravely forward, led by an honest desire to find employment and delayed at every step by the interest of the unfolding scene, and a sense of helplessness amid so much evidence of power and force which she did not understand. These vast buildings, what were they? These strange energies and huge interests, for what purposes were they there? She could have understood the meaning of a little stonecutter's yard at Columbia City, carving little pieces of marble for individual use, but when the yards of some huge stone corporation came into view, filled with spur tracks and flat cars, transpierced by docks from the river and traversed overhead by immense trundling cranes of wood and steel, it lost all significance in her little world.

It was so with the vast railroad yards, with the crowded array of vessels she saw at the river, and the huge factories over the way, lining the water's edge. Through the open windows she could see the figures of men and women in working aprons, moving busily about. The great streets were wall-lined mysteries to her; the vast offices, strange mazes which concerned far-off individuals of importance. She could only think of people connected with them as counting money, dressing magnificently, and riding in carriages. What they dealt in, how they laboured, to what end it all came, she had only the vaguest conception. It was all wonderful, all vast, all far removed, and she sank in spirit inwardly and fluttered feebly at the heart as she thought of entering any one of these mighty concerns and asking for something to do—something that she could do—anything.

INTERPRETING LITERATURE

1. Why has Carrie come to live with her sister?

2. What kind of attitude about life in the city at this time does Hanson exemplify?

3. What are some circumstances over which Carrie has no control?

4. Do large cities today hold the attraction that they held for Carrie and other ambitious men and women at the turn of the century? Why or why not?

CHAPTER 22
Imperialism

SETTING THE SCENE

Historical Focus

Foreign policy before the late nineteenth century had been dominated by two ideas. The first was President Washington's isolationist warning against entering into "entangling alliances." The second was President Monroe's warning to Europe against interference in the Americas. War with Spain, however, resulted in a more aggressive foreign policy and the acquisition of overseas colonies. Suddenly, the United States had become a major world power.

Concepts to Understand

- How increased U.S. **economic and political** power led to the acquisition of an overseas empire.
- How **confrontation** with Spain resulted in war over Cuba.

People to Know

John Hay, William McKinley, Theodore Roosevelt, George Dewey, Walter Reed

Places to Locate

Hawaii, Cuba, Philippines, Puerto Rico, China, Panama Canal

Terms to Identify

imperialism, isolationism, arbitration, "yellow press," protectorate, corollary

Guided Reading

As you read this chapter, seek the answers to the following questions.

1. Why did Americans move away from a policy of isolationism?
2. What problems and responsibilities did victory in the Spanish-American War bring the United States?

SPANNING THE DECADES

				1898	1899
			1893	*Spanish American War;*	*John Hay*
		1882	*Queen Liliuokalani*	*Spain cedes Guam,*	*initiates the*
POLITICAL		*Chinese Exclusion*	*of Hawaii is*	*Puerto Rico, and the*	*Open Door*
		Act is passed	*overthrown*	*Philippines*	*policy*

1880			1890	

	1880	1890	1891	1893	1897
	"General" William	*Alfred T. Mahan*	*University*	*World's*	*Library of*
CULTURAL	*Booth organizes the*	*publishes* The	*of Chicago*	*Columbian*	*Congress*
	Salvation Army	*Influence of Sea*	*founded*	*Exposition is*	*completed*
		Power on History		*held in Chicago*	

The Return of the Conquerors *by Edward Moran, 1898*

1900
Boxer Rebellion
in China

1904
*Roosevelt
Corollary to the
Monroe Doctrine
announced*

1905
*Roosevelt arbitrates
Russo-Japanese war*

1900   **1910**

1903
The Great Train
Robbery *motion picture
produced; first to have a
fully developed plot*

1910
21 percent of
the work force
is women

*...Our foreign policy should be at all
times firm, vigorous and dignified,
and all our interests in the western
hemisphere should be carefully
watched and guarded.*

—REPUBLICAN PARTY PLATFORM, 1896

America Looks Abroad

...The burning question is whether the American people will accept the gifts of events; whether they will rise as lifts their destiny; whether they will proceed upon the lines of national development....

—ALBERT J. BEVERIDGE
Senator from Indiana, in a campaign speech, 1898

Section Focus

Beginning in the 1500s, European nations built vast colonial empires. By the mid-1800s, however, many of these colonies had won their independence. The Industrial Revolution pushed several nations into new empire-building. Germany, France, Belgium, Portugal, and Japan joined the race for colonies. The United States had grown entirely by expansion on the North American continent. Would the race for empire tempt a once-colonial people to seek colonies of their own?

Objectives

After studying this section, you should be able to:

• Discuss the emergence of the United States from isolationism.
• Cite two examples of arbitration averting war.

European colonialism was motivated by trade and adventure, power and profit, idealism and national patriotism. These nations also believed they had a "civilizing mission" toward nonwhite populations. The Industrial Revolution generated a need for markets for manufactured goods and new sources of raw materials. **Imperialism**—the policy of establishing colonies and building empires—answered these needs. New weapons made the subjection of native people easier. Steamships and ocean cables required coaling stations and cable bases; they also tightened control over distant colonies.

Isolationism, or separation from the political affairs of other countries, was a policy established early in United States history. George Washington, in his farewell address, had warned against entangling alliances. Later the Monroe Doctrine emphasized the United States' desire to keep the Americas separate from Europe. While Washington had recognized that the United States was too weak to participate in European struggles, James Monroe's policy was meant to prevent what he saw as the corrupting influence of European affairs on the Americas. Another factor affecting American foreign policy was the Declaration of Independence—based on the idea that people had the right to govern themselves. This key principle argued against any United States colonial ventures.

By the 1890s, however, the United States was faced with the opportunity of building a colonial empire. Expansion on the continent was complete, but a Cuban revolt against Spain provided the nation with a timely circumstance with which it could expand beyond its natural border—"the gifts of events" to which Beveridge referred. The urge to imperialism, practiced by Europe, proved infectious. The United States, like Europe, began to expand its influence onto islands in the Caribbean and South Pacific areas.

Securing an American Continent

The United States challenged a French expansion effort in 1861. Ignoring the Monroe Doctrine and taking advantage of the United States' divisiveness and its Civil War, the French emperor Napoleon III overthrew the Republic of Mexico. He

Examining Illustrations *Fort Yukon, one of the principal Russian outposts in Alaska, was not very well developed in 1867. When Tsar Alexander I proclaimed Russian commercial ambitions in Alaska in 1821, President James Monroe responded that the American continents were not open to future colonization by European powers. The purchase of Alaska was in keeping with the Monroe Doctrine. Why then were Americans not eager to make this purchase?*

hoped to establish a French empire in the Western Hemisphere.

The French venture began when Mexico's reform government under Benito Juarez (HWAHR uhz) stopped payment of its foreign debts. French, Spanish, and British troops entered the country. The debts were collected and Spain and Britain left, but the French remained and quickly occupied Mexico City. In 1864 Napoleon III installed Austrian prince Maximilian as Mexico's emperor.

The United States protested and, after the Civil War, sent nearly 50,000 troops to the border at the Rio Grande. Napoleon's forces withdrew. The Mexicans promptly defeated Maximilian's army and executed Maximilian. The United States had proved willing to back the Monroe Doctrine with force if necessary.

The purchase of Alaska removed another North American territory from European control. Secretary of State William E. Seward was among those Americans who believed in manifest destiny. He envisioned a future United States empire and wanted to expand by annexing Canada, Hawaii, and several Caribbean islands. Although he did not achieve this, Seward had one great success: the purchase of Alaska in 1867. This undeveloped territory, twice the size of Texas, was inhabited by only about 20,000 people. Although Alaska was held by Russia, the tsar saw little value in a territory so unproductive and so far away.

In 1867 the Russian minister to the United States informed Seward that the tsar wanted to sell Alaska. In a few hours, the eager secretary of state arranged a treaty in which the United States would buy Alaska for $7.2 million—less than two cents an acre. Americans knew little of Alaska and could not anticipate the discovery of gold in 1899 or other valuable resources later. Newspapers called it "Seward's icebox." After four months of selling the idea to Congress, the transaction was completed. Charges of bribery to get the deal through, however, further soured the public's attitude toward Alaska and expansion in general for the next 30 years.

Economic Empire-building

At one time the United States had little need to look beyond its own borders for growth. Raw materials were abundant, and the home market was immense. By the 1890s, the country had developed into a great industrial nation, able to compete with European producers.

James G. Blaine, secretary of state under Presidents Garfield and Harrison, wanted to open up new markets not by taking on colonies, but by increasing American trade through **reciprocity**—the

Connections

HISTORY AND TECHNOLOGY

COALING STATIONS AND COLONIES

Captain Alfred Mahan believed that for a country to become a major sea power, its ships needed remote sources of supplies that could not be carried for an entire voyage. While commercial shipping required these supply stations, an armed navy needed them even more. The supplies, according to Mahan, were "first, fuel; second, ammunition; last of all, food."

Fuel became essential to shipping as nations switched from sail to steam power at the turn of the century. No ship could steam away from its home port for any great distance without refueling. A fleet that wanted to trade or fight very far beyond its home waters needed coaling stations in distant lands.

Mahan did not favor unchecked expansionism. Too many supply and fueling bases in foreign lands, he warned, could drain the resources of the parent country and could become "a source of weakness, multiplying exposed points, and entailing division of force."

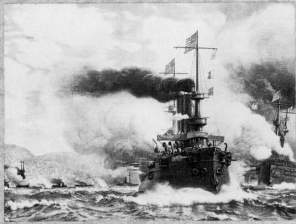

Battle of Santiago de Cuba *by James G. Tyler, 1898*

★★★★★★★★★★★

MAKING THE TECHNOLOGY CONNECTION

1. What supplies did coaling stations provide?

2. How did new technology influence American foreign policy?

LINKING PAST AND PRESENT

3. In what areas of the world does the United States have refueling stations today?

★★★★★★★★★★★

mutual lowering of tariff barriers. He tried, without much success, to include reciprocity provisions in the McKinley Tariff of 1890. He was able to chair a Pan-American Congress in Washington, D.C., in 1889. The goal of the group, which later became the Pan-American Union, was to promote economic cooperation and trade between the Americas. Success was limited, however, because the United States intervened, often forcibly, in Latin American affairs.

The United States also intervened in, and only temporarily resisted, the temptation to annex Hawaii. American missionaries and traders first ventured to Hawaii in the early 1800s. American sugar growers followed. By the 1890s Hawaii was closely connected to the United States through commerce and the many Americans living there. While many nationalities lived in Hawaii, native Hawaiian rulers were controlled by the American business community until the Hawaiian Queen Liliuokalani (lee LEE OO oh KAH LAH nee) came into power in 1891. She was determined to return control to her own people. In response, some American business leaders, with the help of marines from the cruiser *Boston*, took over the government, raised the American flag, and requested that the United States annex the islands.

The American minister to Hawaii wrote the Department of State: "The Hawaiian pear is now fully ripe, and this is the golden hour for the United States to pluck it." President Cleveland disagreed. He decided that the use of American troops to overthrow the Hawaiian government was a violation of "national honesty." Despite criticism for lowering the Stars and Stripes and "turning back the hands of civilization," Cleveland withdrew American soldiers from Hawaii. He also tried, but failed, to oust the revolutionary provisional government and put Liliuokalani back on her throne. Although Americans in

Examining Illustrations *Queen Liliuokalani succeeded her brother, King Kalakuaua, in 1891. Her determination to end white rule in Hawaii aroused American business leaders. How did President Cleveland respond?*

Hawaii continued to control the islands, annexation was postponed until 1898.

Challenging Great Britain

After the Civil War, the United States appeared ready to take a position among the powers of the world, even if it meant challenging Great Britain. Twice the United States forced Britain to submit to arbitration, or the settlement of a dispute by an impartial group. In the first case, in 1868, Charles Sumner, head of the Senate Foreign Relations Committee, claimed that Great Britain owed the United States more than $2 million in damages for allowing Confederate ships to use British ports during the Civil War. If the British would not pay, Senator Sumner declared, the United States should take British-controlled Canada.

In 1871 Secretary of State Hamilton Fish cooled the situation by arranging for arbitration. Britain did not want to risk war in Canada and feared that a hostile United States might supply Britain's enemies with warships. The United States backed down on its demand for "indirect" damages and agreed to refer the matter to an international arbitration commission. In the resulting Treaty of Washington, the United States was awarded $15.5 million, which Britain promptly paid.

The martial spirit in America raised the threat of war with Great Britain again in 1895. President Cleveland requested that the British put a long-standing Venezuela-British Guiana boundary dispute to arbitration. In July 1895, Secretary of State Richard Olney wrote the British government that their refusal to arbitrate was a violation of the Monroe Doctrine. He warned:

The United States is practically sovereign on this continent and its fiat is law upon the subjects to which it confines its interposition.

After waiting several months, Britain's foreign minister answered that the Monroe Doctrine had no standing in international law and did not apply to the Venezuelan situation.

Aware of the possibility that his actions might lead to war, Cleveland asked the Congress for authorization to appoint a commission to determine the boundary without consulting Britain. Americans responded with excitement over Cleveland's bold move, but Britain thought it "monstrous and insulting." For a few days, war seemed imminent. Britain's fleet was made ready to sail, and American coastal defenses were strengthened. Once again some Americans began to talk of invading Canada.

Fortunately, events made the British government willing to back down. Early in January 1896, Britain's attention was diverted from Venezuela by a dispute with Germany involving South Africa. Seeking to improve relations with the United States,

Linking Across Time

HAWAII'S STRATEGIC IMPORTANCE

Hawaii's strategic position—just a "hop, skip and a jump" from American shores—made the islands highly attractive to the United States. The government expanded its coaling stop at Pearl Harbor into a naval base that proved invaluable in World War II. Attacked by the Japanese on December 7, 1941, the harbor and naval base sustained crippling casualties: 18 ships, 200 planes, and 3,700 troops. The United States rebuilt the harbor, however, and ran the victorious Pacific campaign from Pearl Harbor Naval Base.

Britain agreed to arbitration. In the end, both sides gained. The boundary settlement turned out in Britain's favor and a new era of Anglo-American understanding emerged.

The Venezuelan crisis called attention to the fact that the United States had only three modern battleships to pit against Britain's huge fleet. The crisis also popularized the writing of an American naval officer, Captain Alfred T. Mahan.

Although Mahan's best-known work, *The Influence of Sea Power on History, 1660-1783,* was published in 1890, it had been delivered as a series of lectures at the new Naval War College in 1886. Mahan believed that as America developed its industrial strength, the nation should look outward. Great nations of the past had built up foreign markets, expanded their merchant fleets, constructed navies to protect their commerce, and planted colonies in distant territories. Mahan argued that a modern nation needed sea power in order to become great. A country that neglected its navy was courting disaster.

At first Mahan had more influence abroad than in his own country. Kaiser (Emperor) Wilhelm II of Germany studied his books and instructed German naval officers to read them. In Great Britain Mahan was showered with honors. Mahan influenced rising American leaders such as Senator Henry Cabot Lodge and Theodore Roosevelt and helped to shape United States naval policy.

While American commercial interests searched for overseas markets, those who favored naval power worked hard to build the United States navy in the 1880s. Congress established a Naval Advisory Board in 1881—a group that pressed for ever larger naval appropriations. In 1883 Congress gave the secretary of the navy authority to construct 1 more cruiser and 3 battleships. By adding 3 heavier and more powerful ships in 1890 and by voting for 13 new ships in 1895, Congress made it clear that it intended to have a navy capable of matching any enemy on the high seas. The United States moved from twelfth to third place among naval powers by 1900. Its new ships built before 1898 were soon tested in war with Spain.

★ ★ ★ ★ ★ ★ ★ ★ ★ ★ ★ ★ ★ ★ ★ ★ ★

Section One Review

★ ★ ★ ★ ★ ★ ★ ★ ★ ★ ★ ★ ★ ★ ★ ★ ★

SUMMARY

The United States increased its influence in the world community from 1861 to 1900. The acquisition of Alaska, new trading ties with Hawaii and Latin America, and a strong stand against Great Britain in the Venezuela boundary dispute enhanced the stature of the United States among more established countries.

CHECKING FOR UNDERSTANDING

1. **Identify** Maximilian, William Seward, Queen Liliuokalani, Charles Sumner

2. **Define** imperialism, isolationism, reciprocity

3. **Cite** the isolationist aspects of Washington's Farewell Address and the Monroe Doctrine.

4. **Show** how the French challenged the Monroe Doctrine in 1861.

5. **State** the goal of the Pan-American Union.

6. **Describe** two instances of confrontation with Great Britain that were settled by arbitration.

THINKING CRITICALLY

7. **Understanding Cause and Effect** How did publication of *The Influence of Sea Power on History* lead to increasing the American navy?

GLOBAL PERSPECTIVES

8. Study the following international political events for 1893. In what way are all related to the concept of imperialism?

- Hawaii proclaimed a republic; annexed by treaty in February; treaty withdrawn in March.
- France establishes protectorate over Laos.
- British occupy Bulawayo, South Africa.

★ ★ ★ ★ ★ ★ ★ ★ ★ ★ ★ ★ ★ ★ ★ ★ ★

The Spanish-American War

SETTING THE SCENE

…it would be everything for us to take firm action on behalf of the wretched Cubans. It would be a splendid thing for the Navy, too.

—THEODORE ROOSEVELT
Assistant Secretary of the Navy, to Henry Cabot Lodge, 1897

Section Focus

The plight of Cuba captured the attention and sympathy of the American people. Struggling for freedom under Spanish rule for years, they had gained only greater repression. When a new revolution took place in 1895, Americans were moved by two main impulses to intervene. Many humanitarians urged American support for the repressed Cuban people, while others saw the revolt as an opportunity to expand the American empire.

Objectives

After studying this section, you should be able to:
• List the events that led to the Spanish-American War.
• Explain the reason for the involvement of the Philippines in the war.

Americans were outraged when they found that the Spanish Governor-General Valeriano Weyler had ordered Cuban men, women, and children into "reconcentration camps." Weyler, unable to tell civilians from rebels, had set up the camps where 200,000, an estimated one-eighth of the population, died of illness and starvation. Some leaders of the Cuban independence movement were naturalized American citizens who had returned to work in Cuba. When captured by Spanish authorities, they demanded protection by the United States.

Not all sentiment supported the Cubans, however. American business interests had invested more than $30 million in Cuba—mostly in sugar plantations—and wanted the revolt to end. Some plantation owners, doubting the capacity of the Cubans for self-government, favored the restoration of Spanish rule. The force of public opinion, however, caused many in the business community to change their minds.

Although President Cleveland preserved strict neutrality in the Cuban struggle, he warned that if "the useless sacrifice of human life" went on, the United States might have to abandon the policy of "patient waiting."

"Remember the *Maine*"

President McKinley, who came into office in the middle of the conflict, was also committed to maintaining neutrality. He even offered to buy Cuba to "avert this terrible calamity" but was rejected. A peaceful solution seemed possible when Spain recalled General Weyler and offered Cuba a measure of local self-government. Assistant Secretary of the Navy Theodore Roosevelt was impatient with McKinley's negotiation with Spain and described the President as having "no more backbone than a chocolate eclair." William Randolph Hearst's *New York Journal* and Joseph Pulitzer's *New York World* fanned public anger with exaggerated and sometimes fabricated stories of Spanish atrocities in Cuba. This "yellow journalism" helped sell papers, but it also encouraged war. Public sentiment in favor of war was growing when, on February 9, 1898, the *Journal* printed a private letter written by Enrique Dupuy de Lôme, the Spanish ambassador to the United States, in which he called McKinley "weak and a bidder for the admiration of the crowd...." Less stinging, perhaps, than Roosevelt's comment, it was a national insult coming from a foreigner. The ambassador resigned, but the damage to United States-Spanish relations was done.

Six days later the United States battleship *Maine,* at anchor off the Cuban capital, Havana, exploded. Two hundred sixty crewmembers were killed. United States naval experts declared that the explosion came from outside the ship. Spanish experts replied that there were no mines.

The "yellow press" in 1898 expressed no indecision. Papers promptly blamed Spain and even printed diagrams showing just how the deed was done. "Remember the *Maine!*" became the battle cry around the country.

Examining Illustrations *Journalism in this Hearst newspaper dated February 17, 1898, fired American anger against Spain. The subhead included, "Men Tell Thrilling Stories of Being Blown into the Air Amid a Mass of Shattered Steel...." Who destroyed the Maine?*

AMERICAN PORTRAITS

JOSEPH PULITZER
1847-1911

After emigrating from Hungary, Joseph Pulitzer made publishing history—and a personal fortune—by creating a new form of newspaper journalism.

As a soldier during the Civil War, Pulitzer noted how Americans loved to read newspapers. After the war, he bought and merged two St. Louis newspapers. Circulation soared as he filled his paper with scandals and attacks on big business. He later bought two New York papers, bringing to them the same successful recipe—sensationalism and controversy. He won a mass audience by running comic strips and covering fashions and sports. After retiring, he saw his papers engage in "yellow journalism" to compete with William Randolph Hearst's flag-waving newspapers. Pulitzer took back control and returned his newspapers to their flamboyant investigative style.

Congress responded to a torrent of public indignation against Spain by allocating $50 million for war preparations. McKinley, meanwhile, demanded that Spain give Cuba independence. Although at the last moment Spain claimed it was trying to comply, McKinley nevertheless delivered a warlike message to Congress. Congress demanded that Spain evacuate the island. When no reply to this ultimatum was received, Congress declared war on April 25.

While expansionists were excited about the prospects of gaining Cuba, humanitarian forces in Congress attached the Teller Amendment to the declaration of war. In it Congress pledged "to leave the government and control of the Island to the people" as soon as peace was established there.

"A Splendid Little War"

While the army prepared to invade Cuba, the conflict, called by Secretary of State John Hay a "splendid little war," began in the Pacific. Although the McKinley administration had no thought of expanding the territories of the United States, some officials believed that this was a prime opportunity to do so. One such person was Theodore Roosevelt. When John D. Long, secretary of the navy, was out of his Washington office, Roosevelt took charge. On February 25, 1898, he ordered on his own authority a Pacific squadron stationed in Hong Kong to sail for the Philippine Islands, a Spanish colony for 300 years, if war broke out. Commodore George Dewey, commander of the United States fleet, would try to prevent a Spanish fleet in Manila Bay from going to sea. As soon as war was declared, Dewey's fleet set sail; it penetrated Manila Bay on May 1 and rapidly destroyed the weaker Spanish fleet. The quick victory surprised the President, and an army of occupation was hastily organized to sail from San Francisco to the Philippines.

A native Filipino, Emilio Aguinaldo (AHG ee NAHL DOH), had led an uprising against Spanish rule of the Philippines in 1896. Aguinaldo was exiled in Hong Kong where Dewey met him and provided supplies so he could lead a revolt against the Spanish forces that remained in the islands. By the time the American army arrived in the Philippines, Aguinaldo's forces controlled all the territory except the city of Manila. When the Spanish surrendered and turned the Philippines over to the United States army, it left unanswered the question of who would rule the islands after the war.

When war was first declared, McKinley had called for 200,000 volunteers to supplement the regular army, which numbered only 28,000. The War Department proved to be utterly inefficient—a substantial problem when it

Examining Maps *American troops sailed from Tampa, Florida, to the south coast of Cuba in June 1898. Admiral Dewey had already sailed from Hong Kong to Manila. Why was Dewey able to engage the Spanish in the Philippines so quickly?*

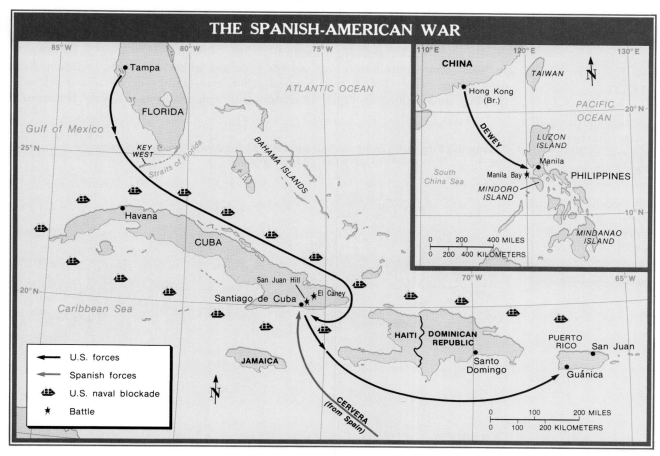

THE SPANISH-AMERICAN WAR

Linking Across Time

BLACKS IN THE MILITARY

The 24th was one of 4 units of African American soldiers to serve in Cuba. African Americans have swelled the ranks in every war: 5,000 in the Continental Army; almost 200,000 in the Union army; 400,000 in World War I, and more than 1 million in World War II. Until 1941, however, less than 1 percent were promoted to officer rank. In 1940 Benjamin O. Davis broke a military race barrier to become the first black brigadier general. In 1954 the Army demolished segregated military units and ruled that more African Americans be allowed to serve in combat units.

Examining Illustrations *Many American soldiers died in hospital tents like this one. What was the cause of most deaths?*

came time to organize 17,000 volunteers and regulars into an expeditionary force. Nevertheless, the troops were declared ready to sail from Tampa, Florida, to Cuba by the middle of June. To fight a war in the tropics, they were issued heavy woolen uniforms left over from the Indian wars; their ammunition was out-of-date; there were almost no medical supplies; and rations included inedible meat that the soldiers nicknamed "embalmed beef."

After landing on the south coast of Cuba, the Americans advanced on the city of Santiago. The martial spirit inspired excess bravado. One regiment was called the "Rough Riders"—an assortment of college athletes, cowboys, miners, and law officers—led by Theodore Roosevelt, who had resigned from the Navy Department

Examining Fine Art Charge of San Juan Hill, *by Frederic Remington depicts the bravado of the Rough Riders. Where were the "Riders" horses?*

in order to join the fight. On foot because their horses were still in Florida, they recklessly charged up San Juan Hill, heedless of casualties. By securing the heights overlooking Santiago, they helped capture the city.

The Rough Riders were not alone in this attack. Among the other regiments was the all-black 10th Cavalry Regiment. Many African Americans had responded to the call for soldiers both because they identified with the Cubans' struggle for freedom and because they hoped it would improve their own lot. At least four of these black soldiers were awarded the Congressional Medal of Honor.

At the outbreak of hostilities, an American squadron of new battleships under Admiral William T. Sampson was given the task of intercepting a Spanish squadron under Admiral Pascual Cervera (pahs KWAHL suhr VAIR uh). Knowing that Cervera had left the Cape Verde Islands off the west coast of Africa in April, Americans feared he would attack the undefended Atlantic coast of the United States. They canceled hotel reservations at seaside resorts and prepared for defense, but Cervera headed directly for Santiago harbor.

Sampson's superior force found the Spanish fleet at Santiago and immediately blockaded the harbor. Once the American army took the heights overlooking Santiago, Cervera had the choice of surrendering or trying to break the blockade. On July 3, knowing that he had little hope of victory, Cervera ordered his ships out of Santiago harbor. In the ensuing battle, all the Spanish vessels were sunk, while only one American was killed and one wounded. Effective Spanish resistance in Cuba ceased with the surrender of Santiago two weeks later. American troops immediately went on to occupy another Spanish possession, the island of Puerto Rico. On August 12 Spain and the United States agreed to an armistice.

The "splendid little war" cost 5,000 American lives, mostly due to disease and food poisoning. The flag of the United States, an emerging world power, flew over distant islands. Had American isolationism ended?

SUMMARY

The Spanish-American War, though short-lived, demonstrated a number of principles that were to become part of the American tradition. The United States established its willingness to become involved in conflict to help oppressed people and to protect its own self-interests, even though American life and security were not threatened. The war also demonstrated the power of the media to influence public opinion. A big difference between this and later conflicts was that the United States emerged a clear-cut winner with little loss of life, a matter of great national pride.

CHECKING FOR UNDERSTANDING

1. **Identify** William Randolph Hearst, Joseph Pulitzer, Dupuy de Lôme, the *Maine*, Theodore Roosevelt, Rough Riders

2. **List** the key events leading to war with Spain over Cuba.

3. **Describe** the unique character of the 10th Cavalry Regiment and their contribution to the war in Cuba.

4. **State** the importance of the naval battle between Admiral William T. Sampson and Admiral Pascual Cervera.

THINKING CRITICALLY

5. **Making Judgments** How did the United States justify going to war with Spain given previous American policy of noninvolvement in foreign affairs?

LINKING PAST AND PRESENT

6. **Making Comparisons** In a democracy the press is important because it influences people, who in turn, influence the government. Compare the role of the press in bringing about the Spanish-American War and the role of the media in influencing American intervention in the Persian Gulf in 1990.

The United States Becomes a World Power

Take up the White Man's burden—
Send forth the best ye breed—
Go, bind your sons to exile
To serve your captives' need....

—RUDYARD KIPLING
"White Man's Burden," 1899

Section Focus

After the Spanish-American War ended, the United States was confronted by a host of questions and responsibilities. Congress debated what to do about the Philippine Islands. Commercial and industrial interests argued for annexation, but how could colonialism be reconciled with the principles of the Declaration of Independence? If acquired, how should the new territories be governed?

Objectives

After studying this section, you should be able to:
• Explain why the Philippine Islands were the most difficult of the new colonies to govern.
• Discuss the constitutional difficulties involved in colonization.

The Spanish-American War and the prospect of expanding in the Pacific brought a change of policy toward the Hawaiian Islands. Cleveland had resisted a move to annex them in 1893, and in 1897 the Senate had turned down an annexation treaty presented by McKinley. But Hawaii, the halfway point between California and the Philippines, would be valuable as a naval base. In July 1898, before the war ended, the Hawaiian Islands were annexed by a joint resolution of Congress.

The Philippines

The armistice left Americans in control of the Spanish-owned Philippine Islands. The debate over whether or not to acquire and annex the Philippines was a stormy one. Several leading Democrats, including former President Grover Cleveland, were opposed. Many influential private citizens agreed with them. Prominent Republicans such as Speaker of the House Thomas B. Reed and several senators fought annexation as a violation of American tradition.

Senator Henry Cabot Lodge spoke for those who wanted a larger American role in world affairs. Business interests thought of new markets and fields of investment. Public opinion was excited by the prospect of acquiring an empire. Patriotism merged with belief in social Darwinism, or the belief in the "survival of the fittest." If the United States was the most fit to govern the Philippines, why should it haul down the Stars and Stripes and allow Japan or Germany or some other power to step in and take them?

For others, like Reverend Josiah Strong, there was a sense of mission based on racial and religious bias. Strong, in his book *Our Country,* blended social Darwinism with his interest in spreading Christianity. He felt the nationality groups were in a competition from which Anglo-Saxons were destined to emerge victorious.

Examining Illustrations *Fighting between the U.S. army and Filipinos broke out in 1899. Guerrilla bands occupied the mountains outside Manila. Scattered resistance continued even after Emilio Aguinaldo (left), the Filipino leader, was captured. Why did the United States encounter difficult problems in trying to govern the Philippines?*

McKinley, a deeply religious man, wrestled with the problem, then reported that through prayer he had decided to:

...[E]ducate the Filipinos, and uplift and
civilize and Christianize them,
and by God's grace, do the very best we
could by them, as our fellow men
for whom Christ died.

Actually, Catholic missions had been started in the Philippines in the 1500s.

McKinley instructed his peace commissioners to ask for all of the Philippine Islands. When Spain resisted, the United States offered to pay $20 million for them. In the treaty, signed December 10, 1898, Spain gave up control over Cuba and surrendered Puerto Rico, the Pacific island of Guam, and the Philippine Islands.

The United States encountered very difficult problems in trying to govern the Philippines. The 7,100 islands had 7.5 million people, who were divided into 43 ethnic groups, speaking 87 different languages and dialects. The Filipinos ranged from people living in the forests to highly literate city-dwellers. Filipino patriots had helped the American forces capture the islands. Once it became clear that the United States intended to annex the Philippines, however, a new uprising broke out—this time against the Americans. More than 60,000 troops—four times the number sent to Cuba—and three years of fighting were required to suppress the Filipino patriots.

At the conclusion of the fighting, Andrew Carnegie commented to a friend in the government:

You seem to have finished your work
of civilizing the Filipinos; it is thought
about 8,000 of them have been
completely civilized and sent to heaven.
I hope you like it.

Many Americans were distressed to find their country at war with an independence movement. Mark Twain suggested that Old Glory should have its white stripes painted black and its stars replaced with skull and crossbones.

Even before the Filipino uprising was put down, President McKinley declared

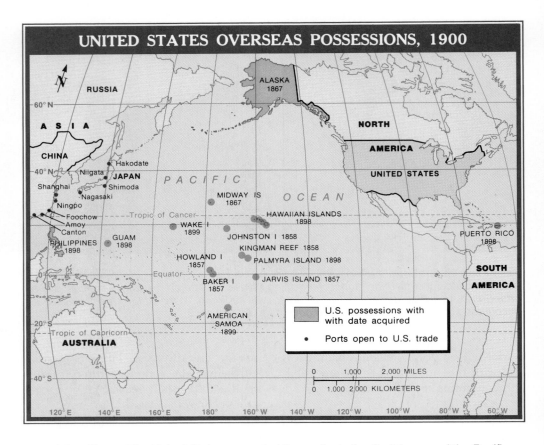

UNITED STATES OVERSEAS POSSESSIONS, 1900

Examining Maps *The United States expanded its empire in the Caribbean and the Pacific from the 1850s to 1900. Many of the acquisitions were the result of the Spanish-American War. Locate Puerto Rico, Guam, and the Philippines. Which of these is farthest from the continental United States?*

that American policy toward the islands would be for the good of the Filipinos. "The Philippines are ours," said the President, "not to exploit but to develop, to civilize, to educate, to train in the science of self-government." The President sent two commissions to investigate the conditions in the Philippines and set up a civil government.

Resentment against American rule in the Philippines was somewhat relieved in 1901 when Theodore Roosevelt, now President, appointed William Howard Taft as the first civilian governor. Genuinely devoted to the interests of the island people, Taft started a program to prepare the Filipinos for self-government, and public schools were established. The United States bought out large foreign landowners and passed laws to keep property in the hands of the Filipinos. Taft did not believe that the

Philippines would be ready for independence for many years, though. In 1907 an elective legislature was established, and in 1916 the United States promised the Philippines eventual independence. That independence was finally granted in 1946.

Problems of an Overseas Empire

The new possessions posed constitutional problems summarized in the question, "Does the Constitution follow the flag?" Congress, according to the Constitution, may not set tariff duties on goods carried within the United States. Did this mean that no duties would be laid on goods from American colonies? Did constitutional guarantees of civil rights extend to the people of the new colonies who knew nothing of American justice?

The Supreme Court decided that the Constitution did not cover overseas possessions. Puerto Rico, the court ruled, was a dependency; therefore Congress could set tariffs on its products. Other decisions determined that inhabitants of dependencies enjoyed full civil rights only if granted them by congressional legislation.

According to the Teller Amendment, the United States pledged to withdraw from Cuba when order was restored. After three years of civil war, however, the island was in terrible condition. The United States Army remained in Cuba to set up a republican government, oversee Cuban finances, and establish public health and sanitation programs. In 1901, to protect its interests in Cuba, the United States Congress added the Platt Amendment to an army bill. This Amendment, which governed the relations between Cuba and the United States for 33 years, provided that: (1) Cuba should not make any treaty with another nation that weakened its independence; (2) Cuba should allow the United States the right to buy or lease naval stations; (3) Cuba's public debt should not exceed its capacity to pay; and (4) the United States should have the right to intervene to protect Cuban independence and keep order. These conditions, written into Cuba's constitution and into a treaty with the United States, made Cuba an American **protectorate**—a nation or region controlled by a stronger state. The attitude that Cuba was part of "the white man's burden" was reflected in an editorial by William Allen White in Kansas's *Emporia Gazette:*

Only Anglo-Saxons can govern themselves. The Cubans will need despotic government for many years to restrain anarchy until Cuba is filled with Yankees.

For almost four years, Cuba was under military rule directed by General Leonard Wood. The greatest achievement of Wood's administration was the suppression of yellow fever. An American medical team under Dr. Walter Reed proved the theory of a Cuban physician, Carlos J. Finlay: that yellow fever was transmitted by the stegomyia mosquito. American doctors and volunteers allowed themselves to be bitten by mosquitoes, and some of them died as martyrs to medical progress. Major William C. Gorgas, an army doctor, carried on a campaign to eliminate mosquitoes from Havana. By 1901, for the first time in centuries, there was no yellow fever in the Cuban capital.

Life of the Times

IMPERIAL FRUITS

Tropical fruits, such as lemons and oranges, first came to North America in the 1500s by way of the Spanish explorers and missionaries in Florida. But more exotic tropical fruits were unavailable to the average person until the late nineteenth century. Only wealthy and influential Americans and Europeans could afford these rare delicacies. One such person was Benjamin Disraeli, the English prime minister, who proclaimed, "There is nothing so delicious as a banana."

Tropical fruits like bananas, coconuts, and pineapples appeared on the breakfast tables of ordinary Americans for the first time when steamships reduced travel time from the tropics. Foods such as bananas, which easily rotted, could be transported expeditiously by steamship from the Caribbean islands to the United States. The imperialistic impulse that brought the United States distant colonies also inspired business entrepreneurs to build plantations. In 1899 Lorenzo Dow Baker and Minor Keith founded the United Fruit Company; their goal was to own and operate banana plantations in Central America. Baker and Keith realized enormous profits and indirectly helped coin the term, "banana republics" for Costa Rica, Guatemala, and Nicaragua— where American corporations often influenced United States policy.

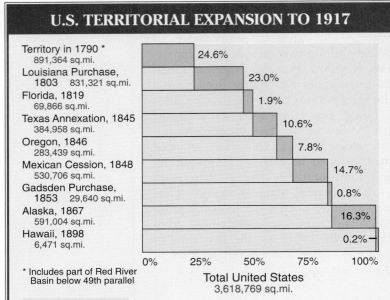

U.S. TERRITORIAL EXPANSION TO 1917

Territory		%
Territory in 1790 * 891,364 sq.mi.		24.6%
Louisiana Purchase, 1803 831,321 sq.mi.		23.0%
Florida, 1819 69,866 sq.mi.		1.9%
Texas Annexation, 1845 384,958 sq.mi.		10.6%
Oregon, 1846 283,439 sq.mi.		7.8%
Mexican Cession, 1848 530,706 sq.mi.		14.7%
Gadsden Purchase, 1853 29,640 sq.mi.		0.8%
Alaska, 1867 591,004 sq.mi.		16.3%
Hawaii, 1898 6,471 sq.mi.		0.2%

0%   25%   50%   75%   100%

* Includes part of Red River
Basin below 49th parallel

Total United States
3,618,769 sq.mi.

Other Acquisitions

- Acquired following Guano Act of 1856: Howard, Baker, and Jarvis Islands (1857), Johnston I. (1858), Swan Is. (1863) returned to Honduras in 1972, Navassa (1865).
- Midway Is. (1867); Wake I. (1898); Guam (1898).
- Puerto Rico (1898) Commonwealth since 1952; American Samoa (1898); Philippines (1898) granted independence in 1946.
- Palmyra (1912); Virgin Is. (1917).

Statistical Abstract of the United States 1990; Webster's New Geographical Dictionary

Examining Graphs *By war, by purchase, and by negotiation, United States territorial expansion proceeded at a steady pace from 1790 to 1898. What was the longest single period of time between two major acquisitions?*

The United States had made no prior commitment to withdraw from Puerto Rico as it had done in Cuba. That island's cultural ties with Spain and Latin America through the Roman Catholic Church, the Spanish language, and other traditions had existed for nearly 300 years. Yet, the United States chose to keep the island as its territory.

After a brief period of military rule, Congress gradually allowed Puerto Rico a degree of self-government. The Puerto Rican people demanded either independence or complete self-rule under the American flag. In 1917 they were granted territorial status and made citizens of the United States.

SUMMARY

The acquisition of overseas possessions raised serious questions regarding rights and self-government. Influenced by social Darwinism and the "white man's burden" philosophy, the administration decided these matters in the economic and political interests of the United States. A Supreme Court ruling that the Constitution does not necessarily follow the flag gave Congress the power to determine the rights and privileges of the new territories. Many prominent Americans protested the country's imperialist ventures.

CHECKING FOR UNDERSTANDING

1. **Identify** William Gorgas, Walter Reed, "white man's burden," Platt Amendment

2. **Define** social Darwinism, protectorate

3. **List** reasons why the United States wanted to annex Hawaii.

4. **Describe** conditions within the country that made the Philippines difficult to govern.

5. **Explain** ways in which the President and Congress resolved the annexation difficulties in the Philippines.

THINKING CRITICALLY

6. **Making Decisions**   Analyze the reasoning of the Supreme Court on constitutional guarantees for overseas possessions. Do you agree with their conclusions? Explain.

CONNECTIONS:
HISTORY AND SCIENCE

7. **Analyzing Relationships**   Between 1898 and 1904, the American army carried out a campaign to eliminate yellow fever from Cuba and the Canal Zone. Explain how this effort relates to political and military actions in Latin America and the Caribbean countries.

Politics of Imperialism

It is not necessary to own people in order to trade with them....We do not own Japan or China, but we trade with their people. We have not absorbed the republics of Central and South America, but we trade with them. Trade cannot be permanently profitable unless it is voluntary.

—WILLIAM JENNINGS BRYAN
Democratic presidential nominee, from his acceptance speech, 1900

Section Focus

The year 1898 was a turning point in United States history. As a result of the Spanish-American War, the country had expanded into the Caribbean and extended its frontier 6,000 miles across the Pacific to the Philippines. America's attention now turned toward East Asia. Some felt the events of 1898 marked a deviation from American principles. Others thought they were part of the United States' destiny.

Objectives

After studying this section, you should be able to:

- Discuss the goals and results of the "Open Door" policy in China.
- Explain the reasons for McKinley's change in viewpoint on American isolationism.

merican expansion into the Pacific brought closer contact with Pacific Rim nations, particularly China. Several European countries, along with Japan, were fiercely competing for trading rights in China. The United States entered a new and complex arena of international politics, more dangerous than any it had experienced before.

The problems that arose in East Asia, along with moral questions about America's adventure into imperialism, soon became political issues. In the presidential election of 1900, Democratic candidate William Jennings Bryan led the nationwide debate against imperialism.

China and the Open Door

At the close of the nineteenth century, it looked as though China, like Africa, would be **partitioned,** or divided among stronger powers. Though China had a great cultural heritage, its power as a nation had declined during the 1800s. In 1895 Japan easily defeated China and annexed Formosa (Taiwan) and the Pescadores Islands. In 1898 and 1899, Russia, Germany, France, and Great Britain forced China to lease its ports, some of them for 99 years. Each "leasehold" was expected to become the center of a **sphere of influence**—an area where a European nation controlled economic development.

Although American missionaries had remained in China, Chinese-American trade had slowed since the great days of the tea clippers. By 1898 only 2 percent of China's trade was with the United States, partly as a result of other nations' spheres of influence. The acquisition of the Philippines revived American interest in business opportunities in China. Manila, some people predicted, would become as important a center for commerce with China as the great British port of Hong Kong.

The United States and Great Britain, in order to ensure open avenues of trade with China, decided to oppose the parceling out of Chinese territory. The United States feared that it would not be able to benefit from its possession of Manila if it did not increase its share of trade with China. Great Britain, controlling 80 percent of the trade, feared that some of its profits would be diverted to other countries. Early in 1898 the British government proposed a joint declaration with the United States in favor of the "Open Door"—with the goal of preserving equal trading opportunities in China for all foreign nations. At that time the United States was cool to the idea, but its annexation of the Philippines changed the American attitude.

John Hay, secretary of state, thought that the days of American isolationism must end. Having defended the acquisition of an overseas empire, he agreed with Great Britain on the policy of an Open Door in China. In September 1899, Hay sent notes to countries with leaseholds in China asking that they keep the ports open to vessels of all nations on equal terms, set equal tariffs on imports, and charge equal railroad rates within their spheres of influence.

Because none of the nations wished to state publicly that it intended to discriminate against the trade of other countries, none disputed these points. Hay immediately announced that the Open Door had been "guaranteed." He was credited in the United States with having achieved a great diplomatic victory.

The results of the Open Door notes were less important than they seemed. The polite but evasive replies of leaseholding countries hardly amounted to a guarantee. Furthermore, the notes did not affect exclusive rights to build railroads and exploit natural resources. Hay's well-publicized actions were a serious move into international politics, however, and achieved the goal of popularizing McKinley's expansionist aims.

Boxer Rebellion

While foreign countries debated who could control what in China, Chinese secret societies were organizing to oust foreign control. One of these, the Righteous and Harmonious Band, was called the Boxers by westerners, because of the physical exercises they practiced.

When a falsified story was printed in several American newspapers suggesting that westerners were negotiating the dismantling of a Chinese monument, the Boxer Rebellion, a violent uprising, broke out. With secret aid from the Chinese government, the Boxers intended to wipe out "foreign

devils" and their Christian converts. They killed more than 200 foreigners, mostly missionaries and their families. For 7 weeks the Boxers laid siege to foreign embassies in Beijing where 900 diplomats and their families held out. These people were finally rescued by a joint military expedition to which the United States contributed 2,500 troops.

During this crisis Hay worked to prevent full-scale retaliation and war against China and to persuade the leaseholding powers not to use the Boxer Rebellion as an excuse to partition the country. In July 1900, he sent a second set of Open Door notes. This time he declared that the policy of the United States was to seek ways to "preserve Chinese territorial and administrative entity."

Hay did not ask for a commitment and gave no guarantee that the United States would back the policy with force. But he used his influence to decrease the amount China was forced to pay as punishment. Of the $333 million that China paid, $25 million was awarded to the United States. This was more than enough to satisfy all Americans who claimed to have suffered in the rebellion. As a gesture of good will toward China, the United States returned $17 million. The Chinese government used the money to educate Chinese youths at American universities.

The Election of 1900

Imperialism became an issue in the presidential election of 1900. In October 1899, an anti-imperialist congress met in Chicago. The delegates denounced the attempt to subdue the Philippines as "open disloyalty to the distinctive principles of our government." They quoted what Abraham Lincoln said about slavery:

When the white man governs himself,
that is self-government,
but when he governs himself and
also governs another man,
that is more than self-government—
that is despotism.

In 1900 William Jennings Bryan, again the Democratic candidate, attempted to make imperialism the paramount issue of the presidential campaign. He weakened his case, however, by continuing to demand free silver, which had become a dead issue.

The Republicans renominated McKinley for President. Theodore Roosevelt, who had become governor of New York, received the nomination for Vice President. As much as possible, the Republicans avoided discussion of imperialism, a question on which they themselves were divided. Adopting the slogan "the full dinner pail," they claimed credit for the country's prosperity during McKinley's administration and predicted a depression if Bryan were elected. The result was an even greater Republican victory than that in 1896.

Six months after his second inauguration, McKinley revealed an awareness of the United States' new position in the world. Previously considered the "high priest of protective tariffs," he announced a change of heart, saying:

Isolation is no longer possible or desirable. God and man have linked the nations together. No nation can longer be indifferent to any other....

McKinley went on to explain that America's diversity of products and its efficiency in producing them had so increased that there was an urgent need for more markets. He proposed reciprocity treaties with foreign nations, providing for mutual lowering of tariffs.

McKinley did not live to put his new policy into effect. The day after delivering his speech he was shot by an **anarchist,** one who opposes all forms of government. Vice President Roosevelt was immediately summoned to Buffalo where the President lay dying. But the Vice President, on a camping trip deep in the Adirondack wilderness, was unable to reach McKinley before he died.

Just short of 43 years old, Roosevelt became the youngest President. The Rough Rider, whom the Republican party had hoped to bury in the obscurity of the vice-presidency, would now guide the nation.

★ ★ ★ ★ ★ ★ ★ ★ ★ ★ ★ ★ ★ ★ ★ ★ ★ ★ ★

Section Four Review

★ ★ ★ ★ ★ ★ ★ ★ ★ ★ ★ ★ ★ ★ ★ ★ ★ ★ ★

SUMMARY

By the end of the nineteenth century, Americans were caught in a dilemma. Tied to the old notions of isolation, they were anxious to capitalize on the increased productivity resulting from industrialization. New markets in East Asia, Latin America, and the Caribbean were inviting. The call of commercial ventures ended isolationism—a change further justified by the need to Christianize less fortunate populations.

CHECKING FOR UNDERSTANDING

1. **Identify** Open Door, John Hay, Boxer Rebellion, William Jennings Bryan

2. **Define** sphere of influence

3. **Cite** reasons why Britain and the United States opposed parceling out Chinese territory to stronger powers.

4. **Explain** why Hay's Open Door notes were less important than they seemed.

5. **Describe** the causes of the Boxer Rebellion. What was the outcome?

6. **State** three groups to whom McKinley's rationale for abandoning isolationism appealed in 1900.

THINKING CRITICALLY

7. **Recognizing Stereotypes** Although the United States did not have specific spheres of influence in China, many Chinese regarded Americans as "Yankee imperialists." What actions justified this view? How did Hay attempt to dispel the image?

GLOBAL PERSPECTIVES

8. **Central Issues** At the same time McKinley was retreating from isolationism, Britain was annexing much of South Africa and Nigeria; Japan was seeking concessions in Korea; and Germany secured the Baghdad Railroad contract. How are all these events related?

★ ★ ★ ★ ★ ★ ★ ★ ★ ★ ★ ★ ★ ★ ★ ★ ★ ★ ★

Interpreting Primary Sources

DECLINED WITH THANKS

Anti-Imperialism Politics

McKinley tailors an expanding Uncle Sam

As Democratic presidential candidate in 1900, William Jennings Bryan became a leading advocate of the anti-imperialist cause. The following passage illustrates the major arguments of the anti-imperialists.

From William Jennings Bryan's speech to the Democratic National Convention, 1900—

The principal arguments... advanced by those who enter upon a defense of imperialism are:

First—That we must improve the present opportunity to become a world power and enter into international politics.

Second—That our commercial interests in the Philippine Islands and in the Orient make it necessary for us to hold the islands permanently.

Third—That the spread of the Christian religion will be facilitated by a colonial policy.

Fourth—That there is no honorable retreat from the position which the nation has taken....

It is sufficient answer to the first argument to say that for more than a century this nation has been a world power. For ten decades it has been the most potent influence in the world....

It is not necessary to own people in order to trade with them.... We do not own Japan or China, but we trade with their people....

The religious argument varies... from a passive belief that Providence delivered the Filipinos into our hands, for their good and our glory, to the exultation of the minister who said that we ought to "thrash the natives (Filipinos) until they understand who we are," and that "every bullet sent, every cannon shot and every flag waved means righteousness."

...If true Christianity consists in carrying out in our daily lives the teachings of Christ, who will say that we are commanded to civilize with dynamite and proselyte with the sword?

EXAMINING THE PRIMARY SOURCE

1. Identify the sentences that introduce Bryan's answers to the four arguments he cites as commonly advanced by imperialists.

2. What evidence does Bryan give to refute the argument that commercial interests of the United States necessitate permanent control of the Philippines?

THINKING CRITICALLY

3. Compare Bryan's description of the imperialists' attitude toward Filipinos with the attitude of those who embraced manifest destiny toward native Americans.

4. Does Bryan's proposal for resolving the Philippine question differ significantly from that of the imperialists? Explain your answer.

Theodore Roosevelt and Foreign Affairs

I am not as sure as you are that the only virtue we need exercise is patience. I think it is well worth considering whether we had better warn those cat-rabbits that great though our patience has been, it can be exhausted.

—THEODORE ROOSEVELT
President of the United States,
in a letter, 1903

Section Focus

Americans expected President Roosevelt to adopt an aggressive foreign policy. Roosevelt was resolved that the United States should be a great power. In the Western Hemisphere, he enlarged the scope of the Monroe Doctrine and secured United States domination of the Caribbean. In the Pacific and East Asia, he attempted to keep a balance of power and restrain first Russian, then Japanese, ambitions. He was the first President to interest himself in the peace of Europe.

Objectives

After studying this section, you should be able to:
- Give examples of Roosevelt's "Big Stick" diplomacy.
- Discuss America's concerns over the Russo-Japanese War.

President Roosevelt had a genius for the dramatic gesture. He told young men, "Don't flinch, don't foul, hit the line hard!" His actions were sometimes impulsive, sometimes unwise, but he firmly believed that power imposed responsibility. One of Roosevelt's mottoes in foreign policy was a West African saying, "Speak softly and carry a big stick." The "Big Stick" was most in evidence in the Caribbean. The acquisition of Puerto Rico and the establishment of a protectorate over Cuba gave the United States a new interest in this region. The acquisition of the Panama Canal Zone showed the nation's willingness to do whatever was necessary to further its interests in the area.

The Panama Canal

Roosevelt's most dramatic and debated action in the Caribbean was his acquisition of the Panama Canal Zone in 1903. Roosevelt and others believed that in addition to saving time for commercial shipping, a canal would answer the strategic need to shuttle warships between the Atlantic and the Pacific oceans. This was clearly demonstrated during the Spanish-American War. The battleship *Oregon,* ordered from Puget Sound to Cuba, was forced to steam 14,000 miles around Cape Horn—3 times as far as if there had been a canal.

In the 1880s a French company had made a vain and costly effort to cut through Panama. Early in the 1890s, an American company started to dig a canal through Nicaragua, but soon abandoned the attempt. In 1901 Britain, which also had an interest in the canal, agreed that the United States could build, control, and fortify a canal, providing ships of all nations were charged equal tolls.

Immediately, Secretary of State John Hay offered Colombia, which controlled Panama, $10 million and the yearly rent of $250,000 for the right to construct the canal and control a narrow strip of land on

either side. However, feeling that the price was too low and fearful of losing control of Panama, the Colombian senate unanimously refused to ratify the agreement.

Roosevelt was furious. He considered seizing Panama but settled for letting it be known privately that he would not mind if Panama revolted. On November 3, 1903, a revolution (financed by French canal company agents who wanted to recover their investments) broke out on the isthmus, and an independent Republic of Panama was proclaimed. Although the United States had previously agreed to uphold Colombia's sovereignty, a cruiser was sent to assist the revolutionaries. On November 6 the United States recognized Panama's independence. Less than two weeks later the United States and Panama signed a treaty not only allowing the canal, but enlarging the Canal Zone.

Roosevelt defended his Big Stick diplomacy in Panama on the ground that he advanced "the needs of collective civilization" by speeding up the building of an interocean canal. But he also said, "I took the canal zone and let Congress debate." His action was widely condemned in the United States as unjustifiable aggression. In Latin America it aroused dislike and distrust of the United States, the "Colossus of the North."

The engineering difficulties involved in cutting through the Isthmus of Panama were enormous, and were compounded by the tremendous health problems encountered in the tropics. In 1885 an Englishman wrote of Panama:

THE PANAMA CANAL

Caribbean Sea

Colón
Cristóbal

Madden Lake

Gatun Locks

Chagres R.

Gatun Lake

Culebra Cut

Pedro Miguel Locks

Miraflores Locks

Panamá

Balboa

PANAMA

9° N

□ Canal Zone
‖ Canal route
— Railroad
⸗ Locks

PACIFIC OCEAN

0   5   10 MILES
0   5   10 KILOMETERS

N

80° W

In all the world there is not perhaps now concentrated in any so much foul disease....The Isthmus is a damp, tropical jungle, intensely hot, swarming with mosquitoes...the home, even as Nature made it, of yellow fever, typhus, and dysentery.

George W. Goethals, a colonel in the Corps of Engineers, directed the engineering feat that completed the canal in 1914. Dr. William C. Gorgas, who had cleaned up Havana, reduced the health threats in Panama.

The Big Stick

Roosevelt, like Cleveland, defended Venezuela from possible European aggression, strengthening the Monroe Doctrine. By 1902 Venezuela owed money to citizens of several European countries. Cipriano Castro, the Venezuelan dictator-president, refused either to pay the debts or submit them to arbitration. Roosevelt, who had little sympathy for Castro, said the Monroe Doctrine did not protect Latin American nations against punishment for misbehavior but only against loss of territory.

After consultation with the American State Department, Great Britain and Germany, Venezuela's two principal creditors, blockaded Venezuelan ports to force payment. Although there was no threat of annexing territory, the blockade was very unpopular in the United States because it was perceived as a violation of the Monroe Doctrine. Feeling was intensified when Venezuelan gunboats were sunk and Venezuelan ports bombarded. Public anger moved Roosevelt to press for an end of the blockade and the submission of the dispute to arbitration.

Although both parties agreed to arbitration, Great Britain was quicker to respond than Germany. This added to Roosevelt's

Examining Illustrations *Work on the Panama Canal began in 1904 and lasted 10 years. What difficulties were encountered?*

distrust of the rising German empire, which had the best army in the world and was building a modern navy. He wrote his friend Senator Henry Cabot Lodge that the Germans might take some step "which will make us either put up or shut up on the Monroe Doctrine."

In 1903 Argentine foreign minister Luis Drago urged that forcibly collecting debts from bankrupt countries be made a violation of international law. The Drago Doctrine posed a problem for the United States. If the United States opposed Drago and allowed foreign nations to block the coasts and bombard the cities of defaulting Latin American nations, the door was left open to further aggression. If, however, the United States outlawed forcible collection of debts, it might be pushed into defending financial dishonesty. The President's reply to the Drago Doctrine became known as the Roosevelt **Corollary**, or addition, to the Monroe Doctrine. Whenever an American republic was guilty of "chronic wrongdoing," said Roosevelt, the United States might have to intervene itself.

The Roosevelt Corollary was first applied in the Dominican Republic. In 1905 the United States assumed the responsibility of collecting Dominican customs. The United States Marine Corps collected the duties and divided them to support the Dominican government and to pay European debts.

Many Latin Americans resented the interference of the United States. To charges of imperialism, Roosevelt replied that the United States had no more desire for Dominican territory than "a gorged boa constrictor might have to swallow a porcupine wrong-end-to." Still, the United States retained control over the finances of the Dominican Republic until 1941.

Roosevelt's successor, President William Howard Taft, continued Roosevelt's policies, but with a shift of emphasis. Taft's secretary of state, Philander C. Knox, promoted American business interests abroad, with the slogan, "Every diplomat a salesman." In Latin America this "dollar diplomacy" resulted in increased sales of United States goods—including warships—and in efforts to increase American investments there.

Although Taft described his brand of diplomacy as "substituting dollars for bullets," in Nicaragua he used both. In 1912 marines were sent to Nicaragua to install a government acceptable to the United States, to force acceptance of a loan from New York bankers, and to put the customs office under the control of a former United States colonel. Knox declared that the United States wished only to exercise "a measure of benevolent supervision." But the economic imperialism and armed intervention that he fostered increased the unpopularity of the United States in Latin America.

Balance of Power in East Asia

Roosevelt realized that the position of the United States in East Asia was weak. He called the Philippines the "Achilles heel" of American defense; they were easily vulnerable to attack by Japan. In China the United States lacked sufficient military power to enforce Hay's Open Door notes of 1899 and 1900. Equal trading opportunities in China and the preservation of China's territorial integrity lay in maintaining a "balance of power" among the nations with ambitions in East Asia. "The Open Door Policy," wrote Roosevelt, "completely disappears as soon as a powerful nation determines to disregard it...."

China's two closest neighbors, Japan and Russia, were especially threatening. The Japanese had first opened trade with western nations when Commodore Matthew Perry impressed them with a show of naval strength in 1853. From that point on, the Japanese moved quickly to establish an elected parliament, speed industrial development, and build a strong military establishment. Japan believed its manifest destiny was to expand onto the Asian mainland. In 1893 Japan established a protectorate over the independent kingdom of Korea and obtained Formosa and other islands off China's northeast coast.

Japan had designs on the resource-rich Chinese province of Manchuria, in which Russia was already established. The Russians hoped to move into Korea. This clash of interest led to the Russo-Japanese War in 1904.

American opinion was at first overwhelmingly pro-Japanese. The Russian tsarist government was unpopular because of its tyranny and persecution. America regarded the Japanese with an almost paternal air because of Commodore Perry's exploits and admired their rapid westernization.

To the astonishment of the world, Japan won victories over Russia both on land and sea. By the summer of 1905, however, both countries were ready to make peace—Japan, because it was nearing the end of its resources; Russia, because of fear of revolution at home. The Japanese secretly asked Roosevelt if he would serve as go-between. After consulting the tsar, Roosevelt formally offered to help make peace. Both nations accepted the President's proposals and sent diplomats to a peace conference in Portsmouth, New Hampshire, in August 1905.

The President induced Japan to give up claims for a money **indemnity,** or payment for damages, and Russia to give up the southern half of the island of Sakhalin (SAK uh LEEN). Japan also took over Russian interests in southern Manchuria.

Although Roosevelt was awarded the Nobel Peace Prize for bringing hostilities to an end, the Treaty of Portsmouth had unhappy results. By siding with Russia on the indemnity question, he caused such ill feeling in Japan that anti-peace riots broke out in Tokyo.

The war itself altered the balance of power in East Asia. Now it was no longer Russian expansion that was most to be feared, but Japanese. Roosevelt himself believed that there was potential danger of war. Both Americans and Europeans were alarmed that the "yellow race" might overwhelm the "white race." This idea of a "yellow peril" was played up by sensation-seeking newspapers. Resentment against Japanese immigrants led to the segregation of Japanese children in California's public schools.

In a complicated series of maneuvers, Roosevelt attempted to soothe Japanese anger, satisfy their ambition, save the Philippines from aggression, and show the Japanese that he was not afraid of them. The President persuaded California to stop discriminating against Japanese children. Japan in turn agreed to halt the emigration of laborers to America. This compromise, arranged in 1907 and 1908, was known as the Gentlemen's Agreement. To check Japanese expansion toward the Philippines, Roosevelt recognized Japan as dominant in Korea and Manchuria. At the same time, he attempted to impress Japan with American naval power by sending an American fleet to Tokyo during its voyage around the world in 1908.

The resolution of the Russo-Japanese War was an example of Roosevelt's efforts to use arbitration rather than war to settle controversies. Although his bluster and statements of bravado made him appear ready to lead the nation to war over minor incidents, Roosevelt's actions were usually milder than his words. While he upgraded America's military power, he believed that the United States had an obligation as a leader of an interdependent world to act responsibly and to show restraint.

Section Five Review

SUMMARY

The personality and Big Stick policy of Theodore Roosevelt dominated the period from 1900 to 1908. He extended American influence over Venezuela and Argentina. Through the Roosevelt Corollary, he had occasion to exercise police power in the Dominican Republic and the Canal Zone. He even exerted influence in the imperial activities of Russia and Japan as peacemaker in the Russo-Japanese War. William H. Taft was so impressed with Roosevelt's successes that he sent dollars and bullets to stabilize conditions in American spheres of influence.

CHECKING FOR UNDERSTANDING

1. **Identify** Big Stick diplomacy, Drago Doctrine, dollar diplomacy, Gentlemen's Agreement, Colossus of the North

2. **Define** Roosevelt Corollary, indemnity

3. **Describe** the dilemma the Drago Doctrine presented to the United States.

4. **Show** how Theodore Roosevelt used the Big Stick policy in Panama.

5. **Cite** the difficulties involved in building the Panama Canal.

6. **Indicate** how Theodore Roosevelt acted as peacemaker in the Russo-Japanese War.

THINKING CRITICALLY

7. **Understanding Cause and Effect** Explain how Taft's dollar diplomacy in Nicaragua led to ill-feeling against the United States throughout Latin America.

LINKING PAST AND PRESENT

8. **Making Comparisons** Historically, the United States has had a keen interest in Latin America. Compare the Big Stick diplomacy of Theodore Roosevelt with the foreign policies of Presidents Bush and Reagan.

★ Chapter 22 Review ★

★ Summary

The acquisition of overseas possessions and extension of American political and economic influence in Latin America, the Caribbean, and the Far East brought an end to American isolationism. Annexing these territories brought the problem of governance. After much deliberation the Supreme Court settled the issue: the Constitution did not follow the flag. Goods from U.S. protectorates could be taxed, unlike products exempted from tariffs by the interstate commerce clause. Congress could determine the extent of citizenship privileges to be granted.

United States intervention in foreign countries was accomplished with the use or show of force—sanctioned by Roosevelt's Big Stick diplomacy. A war was fought with Spain to liberate Cuba. Confrontations with Great Britain and Germany in Venezuela led to the Roosevelt Corollary sanctioning American involvement in Latin American affairs when the situation warranted. This policy was justified by the popular theory of social Darwinism and acceptance of the "white man's burden" to rule over the disadvantaged.

Big Stick diplomacy, effective in Latin America where the United States was in a position to back up threats with force, was not practical in the Pacific and East Asia. There a combination of diplomacy and dollars allowed this country to engage in trade on an equal basis with other nations.

★ Using Vocabulary

Assume that you are a reporter for an antiadministration newspaper covering the Latin American situation in 1903. Write a feature article describing Theodore Roosevelt's policies using the following vocabulary terms.

imperialism	protectorate
isolationism	sphere of influence
reciprocity	corollary
social Darwinism	

★ Reviewing Facts

1. **State** three reasons why the United States abandoned isolationist policies after the Civil War.
2. **Explain** how confrontation with Great Britain in 1895-1896 led to strengthening the American navy.
3. **Describe** the position of the President and press regarding war with Spain over Cuba. Why did McKinley change his mind?
4. **List** three reasons America went to war over Cuba. Which was most important?
5. **Discuss** why Hawaii had fewer difficulties accepting its position as a United States possession than Puerto Rico or the Philippines.
6. **Cite** the reasons for the Supreme Court decision that the Constitution did not follow the flag.
7. **Show** why Americans favored an Open Door Policy in China.
8. **Indicate** why the United States needed to build the Panama Canal.

★ Understanding Concepts

ECONOMIC AND POLITICAL POWER

1. How did the use of the Big Stick in Latin America increase American wealth and political power?
2. In what ways were economic and political power related to the concept of social Darwinism?

CONFRONTATION

3. How did a show of force with Great Britain and Germany enhance the American position in Latin America?
4. Why was the United States unable to avoid military confrontation in Cuba?

★ Thinking Critically

1. **Recognizing Stereotypes**   How did adherence to social Darwinism cause the United States to stereotype people who lived in countries under their possession? In what ways did stereotyped thinking influence political and economic policies toward these territories?
2. **Linking Past and Present**   Compare the actions and power of Congress in declaring war on Cuba in 1898 with the actions and power of Congress in their attempts to conduct military operations in the Persian Gulf in 1990 and 1991.
3. **Understanding Cause and Effect**   Explain how sending the American fleet on a world tour

influenced perceptions of American power in East Asia.

4. **Making Judgments** If you had been President during the Cuban crisis, how would you have handled public opinion, the press, and the insult of the Spanish ambassador? What actions would you have taken to resolve the situation?

★ Writing About History

ARGUMENTATION

Refer to the description of how to write an argumentation essay in the History Writer's Handbook in the Appendix of this book. Your teacher will give you more specific instructions on the essay's length and the assignment's due date.

Write a headline and article for a Hearst newspaper urging war with Spain over Cuba. Remember, the article is designed to stir up public opinion in favor of conflict. Take into account: national honor; persecuted people wanting freedom; business interests in Cuba; the superior economy and government of the United States; and the strategic position of Cuba.

★ Learning Cooperatively

Organize into three groups representing diplomats charged with negotiating the conclusion to the Russo-Japanese War. Consider:

• What points are on the table for negotiation?

• What does each team hope to gain?

• What is each willing to concede in order to reach its objectives?

• What is the conclusion of the negotiations?

• What is the special role of the United States in the proceedings?

★ Mastering Skills

WRITING A ROUGH DRAFT OF A RESEARCH REPORT

After you have prepared note cards on your selected topic, you are ready to begin writing your research report. Remember as you write that you are making a *rough draft*, or first copy, and that you will have opportunity to make changes when you finalize your report.

Example   You may find that making an outline, if you have not made one, will be helpful at this point. Good planning before you begin writing will help your report flow more smoothly. Include in your outline all subheads that you will put in your report. The following is an outline of the first section with subsection headings from Chapter 22 of your text:

Chapter title: Imperialism
Section 1: America Looks Abroad
          Securing an American Continent
          Economic Empire-Building
          Challenging Great Britain

Begin your report with a paragraph that states its theme. Then follow your outline, using the information on your notecards to craft paragraphs. Place your cards in the order you will address them as you write. Begin each paragraph with a topic sentence that states the main idea. Make sure that each subsequent sentence supports this idea.

Since you should be using more than one source, you may find conflicting information. In this case, recheck your sources to make sure your note cards are accurate. Also check the copyright of your sources; you may have used a source that is no longer current. If you are still faced with conflicting information, check other sources for agreement.

When beginning to write the draft from your note cards, it is important to write in your own words. This is difficult if you write directly from the cards, one sentence at a time. Try reading several sentences from a note card, thinking about what they mean, and phrasing several sentences that are clear to you. Quoting material from a source should be done only if the quote is essential to carry the meaning or if the quote makes the point better.

As you write the draft, be sure that each time you refer to or quote directly from a source, you prepare a footnote based on the information listed on your bibliography note cards.

When you have covered all of the main ideas in your outline, write a final paragraph that summarizes what you have learned, and/or expresses any conclusions you may have reached.

Practice   Use material in this chapter and in three other sources to prepare a rough draft of a report on the Panama Canal. Only one of your three sources can be an encyclopedia.

CULTURAL KALEIDOSCOPE

Circa 1900

As America evolved into a world power at the turn of the twentieth century, it also began to look differently at itself. The frontier was nearly gone and in its place, from 1880 to 1914, booming industrial expansion and a celebration of grass roots became hallmarks of American culture.

Literature

REALISM, REGIONALISM, AND NATURALISM

Post-Civil-War prosperity on the one hand and urban blight and farm problems on the other led Americans to rethink their optimism. Realism replaced romanticism in fiction. Heading the movement to "tell it like it is" was William Dean Howells.

Mark Twain's writing combined realism and regionalism, a style that accentuated local color. Other noted regionalists were Kate Chopin and Sarah Orne Jewett.

Naturalism, seen in the works of Jack London and Stephen Crane, stressed the role of nature as a force in all human affairs.

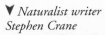

➤ *Regionalist writer Sarah Orne Jewett*

▼ *Naturalist writer Stephen Crane*

▲ *1901 cartoon showing America adjusting her new hat— World Power*

➤ *Crane's classic Civil War novel, considered by most as his finest literary achievement*

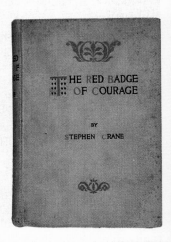

The Arts

PAINTING

Realism influenced visual artists as well. Painter Thomas Eakins (AY kuhnz), a leader of the movement, so shocked the public with his depiction of a bloody surgical procedure that early viewers dubbed him "The Butcher."

Recognition came late to Eakins' most gifted pupil, Henry Tanner, who painted scenes of African-American life in the South. In 1891 Tanner moved to Europe to escape racial prejudice.

PHOTOGRAPHY

Nor was realism confined to painting. Champions of "pictorial" photography Alfred Stieglitz and Peter H. Emerson captured slices of everyday American life in their pioneering works in the genre. Like regional writers and musicians, they focused on the "grass roots" of America.

COLOSSAL SCULPTURE

The year was 1886. Unveiled in New York Harbor was the colossal statue *Liberty Enlightening the World,* more popularly known as the "Statue of Liberty." The work, which stands 151 feet and 1 inch, was a gift of the French government and had to be dismantled and shipped to the United States in 214 wooden crates.

THE BLUES AND RAGTIME

It had grown up among black slaves as a strain of simple, plaintive melody. By 1900 the "Blues" had blossomed— with help from New Orleans jazz greats "Buddy" Bolden, "Bunk" Johnson, and "Ma" Rainey— into a full-fledged musical form. Ragtime, another all-American music form, got its start in the piano stylings of Texas-born Scott Joplin.

➤Unveiling of the Statue of Liberty *by Edward Moran*

▼The Steerage *(1907) from Camera Work, No.36, 1911. Collection, The Museum of Modern Art, New York, Gift of Alfred Stieglitz.*

➤*Musician Scott Joplin*

Entertainment and Recreation

THE PHONOGRAPH

By the early years of the twentieth century, the phonograph was weaving its spell on families all over America. Credit for the magic belonged equally to Thomas Edison, undisputed father of recorded sound, and German immigrant Emile Berliner, whose variant, the gramophone, introduced the grooved wax-covered platter.

SYMPHONY ORCHESTRAS

Music lovers who preferred live performances had, by the second decade of the 1900s, half a dozen major symphony orchestras to choose from. A concert-goer on a musical tour of the six cities would take in the New York Philharmonic and the Boston, Chicago, Pittsburgh, Philadelphia, and Baltimore Symphony Orchestras.

PROFESSIONAL SPORTS

By the 1880s, "Play ball!" echoed through ball parks in nine cities across the country, all of them home to major league baseball teams.

Football, a variation on the British game of rugby, came into its own as a professional sport in 1895. Basketball was played as a professional sport just a few years after it was invented in 1891.

PUBLISHING

Fed up with his wife's taunts over the inadequacy of the women's section of his *Tribune and Farmer,* publisher Cyrus Curtis defied her to do better. Louisa Kanpp did just that. By 1883 the supplement was in such hot demand it was accorded independent magazine status, as well as its own title: *Ladies' Home Journal.*

◄ Thomas Edison in his laboratory, *photographed by Edward Steichen, 1906*

▼ *Nipper and Gramophone*

▼ *Boston Symphony Orchestra*

▼ *1916 football poster*

Technology

TRANSPORTATION

New sources of power—electricity and the internal combustion engine—moved Americans from here to there in record time. On September 1, 1897, the nation's first subway began service in Boston. The project cost $4,369,000.

Henry Ford, meanwhile, was busy cranking out interchangeable parts for his mass-produced Model Ts, making "a car in every garage" a reality for Americans.

Model T, designed in 1908 ▼

◄ *Thomas Edison invented the incandescent lamp in 1879. Two years later, African American inventor Lewis Howard Latimer developed a method of making carbon filaments for incandescent lamps.*

SKYSCRAPERS AND AIRPLANES

Building design took a previously unexplored direction—up, thanks to the invention of the elevator by Elisha Otis. In 1890 one of the world's first skyscrapers, the nine-story Wainwright Building, went up in St. Louis.

A decade later humans touched the sky literally with the first airplane flight by Orville Wright near Kitty Hawk, North Carolina.

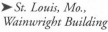

➤ *St. Louis, Mo., Wainwright Building*

FREEZING FOOD

Mindful of the ever-quickening pace of life, an enterprising wildlife expert named Clarence Birdseye set to work perfecting a technique for quick-freezing fresh vegetables. The method, which remains in use to this day, netted its inventor, the founder of General Foods Company, a cool $1 million.

▲ *Trademark of Birds Eye frozen food*

ANALYZING CULTURE

1. Give examples of realism and interest in grass roots in several areas of culture.
2. Which aspects of culture reflect a new restlessness and desire for speed?

CHAPTER 23
The Progressive Era

SECTIONS

1

Sources of
Progressivism

2

Progressive
Reforms

3

Limits of
Progressivism

SETTING THE SCENE

Historical Focus

In the late 1800s, the Grangers and Populists had sought to resist corrupt government and unfair business practices. By 1900 their stalled efforts were given fresh life by a new group of reformers—the progressives. These optimistic, largely urban, and middle class reformers were confident in their ability to improve government and the quality of life. Their reforms were based in traditional democratic values, but also in the new philosophy of pragmatism and study of the social sciences.

Concepts to Understand

- How **values and beliefs** shaped the program of the Progressive Era.
- Why **reform** efforts were successful in correcting the worst abuses of big business and government.

People to Know

Edward Bellamy, Florence Kelley, William James, John Dewey, Booker T. Washington, W. E. B. Du Bois

Places to Locate

Galveston, Wisconsin

Terms to Identify

Wobblies, social gospel, muckrakers, pragmatism, direct primary, initiative, referendum, recall

Guided Reading

As you read this chapter, seek the answers to the following questions.
1. What types of reform did progressive leaders advocate?
2. What were the limitations of progressivism?

SPANNING THE DECADES

POLITICAL	1890 *Sherman Silver Purchase Act passes*	1896 *Plessy v. Ferguson*	1902 *Oregon adopts the initiative and referendum*	1903 *First direct primary election in Wisconsin*	1906 *Pure Food and Drug Act is passed*

1890   **1900**

CULTURAL	1890 *Census shows population of the United States at 63 million*	1897 *The first subway system is completed in Boston*	1904 *Ida Tarbell publishes* History of the Standard Oil Company	1906 *Upton Sinclair publishes* The Jungle	1909 *National Association for the Advancement of Colored People (NAACP) is formed*

New York *by George Wesley Bellows, 1911*

1913
*Sixteenth and
Seventeenth
amendments
are ratified*

1917
*United States
declares war
on Germany*

1910   1920

1911
*Pulitzer Prizes
are established*

*…Do we Americans really want good
government? Do we know it when we see it?
Are we capable of that sustained good
citizenship which alone can make a
democracy a success?…*

—LINCOLN STEFFENS
The Shame of the Cities, 1903

Sources of Progressivism

SETTING THE SCENE

The poor we shall have always with us, but the slum we need not have. These two do not rightfully belong together. Their present partnership is at once poverty's worst hardship and our worst blunder.

—JACOB RIIS
American journalist, in *The Battle With the Slum*, 1902

Section Focus

The 1900s presented the United States with many challenges and opportunities for change. As city populations exploded with immigrants and rural Americans attracted by jobs, squalid slums and worker discontent also grew. As a result, a variety of politically moderate, middle-class reformers worked to protect, preserve, and improve American society in the face of threats of radical change.

Objectives

After studying this section, you should be able to:
- Discuss the role of the muckrakers in promoting social change.
- Explain how methods used in business and education influenced social reform.

Despite widespread social, political, and economic change in the late 1800s, the Gilded Age produced no broad effort to improve society. Populism was a large movement, but it was farm-based and did not attract urban workers to its goals.

The labor movement was also large, but involved itself primarily with issues related to workers' jobs, wages, and working conditions. Not until the 1890s did Americans begin to show widespread concern about the direction in which their society was moving.

Alternate periods of prosperity and depression accompanied industrialization in the late nineteenth century. Economic contractions shook the United States in the mid-1870s and in the mid-1880s. But the depression that followed the panic of 1893 was the worst the nation had yet seen. As the split between rich and poor became too wide to ignore, Americans of all classes began to ask hard questions about the nation's political and economic systems, and they saw much that alarmed them.

Inequality in America

Millions of American laborers worked long hours for low wages in the late 1800s. Wages of industrial workers averaged $10 to $12 for a 60- to 80-hour week. One of every 5 women worked, frequently for as little as $6 to $8 a week, and children received even less. If workers were injured in industrial accidents, laid off when business slowed, or became unemployed for any reason at all, their income completely stopped. At the other end of the scale were the immensely rich, people who owned huge yachts, palatial estates, private railroad cars, and summer retreats covering thousands of acres. In 1900, when Andrew Carnegie earned $25 million from his steel company, the average worker made $500.

While 20 percent of the nation's families lived in comfort, 80 percent barely subsisted. A 1904 study estimated that 10 million Americans—12 percent of the nation's population—were "underfed, underclothed, and poorly housed." Relief for the poor was of little help because it was local, unsystematic, and largely dependent on private charity.

It was not just the disparity of wealth that was alarming but also the distribution of political power. Not only did wealthy industrialists seem beyond the reach of government, they appeared to dominate it. At every level of government, Americans could see what newspaper editor William Allen White called "the alliance between government and business to the benefit of business." With such vast wealth and power at the top of society and such grinding poverty at the bottom, many Americans feared revolution.

Some Americans turned to socialism as the answer. Edward Bellamy's 1887 novel *Looking Backward 2000-1887* made socialism seem an attractive alternative to the existing industrial society. His book tells the story of a nineteenth-century person in the United States who awakens from a prolonged, hypnotic trance to find himself alive in a socialist paradise in the year 2000. All business has been merged into one big trust run by the people themselves; and there is work and leisure for all, without a trace of poverty or crime. Bellamy's vision of a socialist utopia made such an impact that his book sold one million copies, and numerous Nationalist Clubs were founded to advance his ideas. Bellamy had no real program for action, however, and his following eventually drifted toward other reform movements. Bellamy's influence, however, was reinforced by other socialist writers. Socialist ideas were widely circulated by popular authors such as Jack London and Upton Sinclair. Influential Protestant theologian Walter Rauschenbusch, in his widely read 1907 book, *Christianity and the Social Crisis,* condemned capitalism:

The force of the religious spirit should be bent toward asserting the supremacy of life over property. Property exists to maintain and develop life. It is unchristian to regard human life as a mere instrument for the production of wealth.

Popular labor leader Eugene V. Debs also lost faith in capitalism after being jailed during the Pullman Strike of 1894. Declaring that in a democracy workers

WEEKLY WAGES IN THE WOOLEN INDUSTRY, 1890 & 1900

Occupation and Location	Men		Women	
	1890	1900	1890	1900
New England	Median weekly rates in dollars			
Bobbin hands, doffers, and filling and roving carriers..........................	4.50	5.00	3.00	4.00
Dresser tenders and beamers.................	12.00	8.00	6.00	6.50
General hands, helpers, and laborers..................	6.50	7.00	5.00	5.50
Loom fixers....................	12.50	13.50	—	—
Overseers and foreman.	19.50	19.50	—	—
Spinners.......................	7.50	9.50	5.50	6.00
Weavers.......................	7.50	9.00	6.50	7.50
All Occupations.............	7.50	8.00	6.50	6.50
Middle States				
All Occupations.............	7.50	9.00	5.00	5.00
Southern States				
All Occupations.............	6.50	6.50	3.50	3.50
Central States				
All Occupations.............	8.50	8.00	4.00	4.00
Pacific States				
All Occupations.............	9.50	9.50	5.00	5.00
All Sections				
All Occupations for workers under 16......	3.00	3.50	3.00	3.50

Twelfth Census of the United States, 1900 *Special Reports: Employees and Wages (1903)*

could gain control of the government and use it to change the free enterprise system, he organized the American Socialist party.

Opposed to Debs and other moderates, were radical socialists like Daniel De Leon, who preached that democratic reform was useless. "We Socialists are not reformers; we are Revolutionists," he declared. "We care nothing for forms. We want a change of the inside of the mechanism of society...." De Leon argued that even labor unions were traitors to the working class because they compromised with the industrialists. He proposed to organize all workers into new industrial unions that would eventually take over American business.

Debs and De Leon briefly cooperated in 1905 in founding such a labor union, the Industrial Workers of the World, or "Wobblies." Debs soon withdrew, however, and the IWW rejected De Leon in favor of more radical leaders who preached murder and sabotage.

Examining Tables
Note the differences in pay rates for skilled and unskilled labor and for men and women doing the same jobs. Also note regional variations in pay and the lower wages of children. Why are no rates shown for female supervisors?

The Preamble of the IWW's Constitution declared:

The working class and the employing class have nothing in common. There can be no peace so long as hunger and want are found among millions of working people and the few, who make up the employing class have all the good things in life....It is the historic mission of the working class to do away with capitalism.

Wherever the IWW existed, there was confrontation, strikes, sabotage, and often violence. The IWW remained strong, however, until after World War I, when it disintegrated as Americans rejected radical politics.

Most socialists were more moderate than the Wobblies, however, and the socialist movement gained strength throughout the early 1900s. At its height in 1912, Debs polled nearly 1 million votes as the Socialist party candidate for President. Although this was less than 10

Examining Photographs *Unionized garment workers strike in New York City in 1909 for higher wages and shorter hours. What did more-radical labor unions think the goal of the labor movement should be?*

percent of the total votes cast, the socialist movement had an importance greater than its numbers indicated. Other more moderate reformers, called "progressives," owed much of their success to a growing public feeling that the only way to save the capitalist system was to improve it.

Progressive Leadership

The Progressive Era occupied the first 15 years of the twentieth century. Although the reforms of this period are sometimes called the Progressive Movement, that label can be misleading. Unlike the Populists, the progressives were not a political party. Although a Progressive party was formed in 1912, progressives also were found in both Republican and Democratic parties. Nor were progressives united by a geographic section or by an occupation. Instead, they were a broad and largely unorganized group of reformers who often worked independently, each seeking solutions to a specific social, economic, or political problem. Some were local reformers, while others worked for

Examining Illustrations *In this powerful radical statement titled* From the Depths, *the artist depicts society's poor and oppressed breaking through class barriers to threaten the rich. What conditions made some Americans fear a revolution?*

change at state or national levels. The reforms progressives advocated sometimes even conflicted. In spite of their differences, what the progressives shared was their desire to improve society.

Also unlike the Populists, the progressives were generally not the victims of existing conditions. They were mostly urban middle-class professional men and women who worked as journalists, social workers, educators, and clergy. Although they were not suffering themselves, they sympathized with the victims of what they saw as injustice.

Progressives among Catholic priests, Jewish rabbis, and Protestant ministers began to preach a new **social gospel** that religious organizations should work to improve society as well as to meet the spiritual needs of their congregations. In 1908 the National Council of the Churches of Christ, representing 32 denominations, was founded and pledged to support a program of social reform. In every large city the Salvation Army, a religious group devoted to helping the needy, provided food, lodging, and hope for the despairing and poor. Like the settlement houses of the late 1800s, urban churches began to consider the whole person by providing recreational facilitites, adult-education classes, nurseries for children of working women, and counseling for unemployment and alcoholism.

The settlement-house movement, which women continued to lead, expanded into broader areas of reform such as slum clearance and legislation to limit working hours and outlaw child labor. Florence Kelley left Jane Addams and Hull House in Chicago and founded the National Consumers League, where she organized boycotts of goods produced by children or by workers in unsafe or unhealthful conditions. Another former Hull House social worker, Julia Lathrop, became the first head of the federal Children's Bureau, created in the Department of Labor in 1912 and now part of Health and Human Services. Other female progressives included Carrie Chapman Catt, widely known for her work in the women's suffrage movement. Elizabeth Platt Decker headed the General Federation of Women's Clubs, which attracted nearly 1 million women in the early 1900s to promote the arts, education, and community health.

Ironically, progressive reformers owed a great debt to the big businesses that so many of them detested. Unlike Populists, who believed that common people could solve society's problems, progressives put their faith in experts. Although critical of the methods and power of business leaders, progressives admired their ability to run large companies smoothly and efficiently. Progressives were confident that just like the trained managers, scientists,

AMERICAN PORTRAITS

IDA TARBELL
1857-1944

After teaching school briefly, Ida Tarbell made her career as a writer and editor. She wrote hundreds of articles and many books, but her reputation as a "muckraker" rests on one book, *The History of the Standard Oil Company,* initially published as articles in *McClure's Magazine.*

Her interest in Standard Oil was deeply personal. Her father had claimed that the company forced him out of the oil tank business and had caused his partner to commit suicide. *McClure's* asked her to write about Standard because of her knowledge of the oil business and because of her flair for writing. For two years she researched Standard Oil's practices. Her revelations created such a popular furor that Standard Oil was investigated and eventually broken up by the Supreme Court for violating federal antitrust laws.

Linking Across Time

WOMEN AND THE SUPREME COURT

Since the early 1900s, the Supreme Court has strengthened and expanded the rights of working women. In 1971 the Court ruled that unequal treatment of women based on their gender violates the Fourteenth Amendment and is therefore unconstitutional. A 1986 ruling declared that sexual harassment in the workplace violates the 1964 Civil Rights Act. This ruling also makes companies liable for such behavior by any employee and allows women the right to seek trial-by-jury and punitive damages for harassment.

and efficiency experts who solved business problems, expert reformers could analyze and solve problems that kept society from running smoothly.

Educators and Investigators

In the mid-1800s, most American colleges were small, church-supported institutions whose concern was less with knowledge than with shaping the character of their students. Graduates who wanted to pursue further studies often went to Germany, where universities awarded an advanced degree, the Ph.D. These students brought back to America a learning style that emphasized questioning and research instead of memorizing facts. They pioneered changes in American colleges.

Coupled with educational reform was a new way of thinking known as **pragmatism**, an approach to problem-solving that was popularized by Harvard philosopher

William James. Pragmatists questioned the absolute truth of science. They believed that scientific laws stated only what was *probably* true and that ideas must be tested to see if they worked.

By the late 1800s many American colleges offered courses in social work, economics, political science, and sociology and granted advanced degrees. Professors such as social scientist Richard Ely at the University of Wisconsin taught students to solve problems pragmatically. At Johns Hopkins University, historian Henry Adams taught students how to do research and told them, "By the instrumentality of scholars great improvement of society is to be made." American colleges thus provided a core of reformers to study society and change it.

Pragmatist John Dewey, who taught at the University of Chicago, argued that the value of government actions should be measured by the good they do. Harvard Law School professor Oliver Wendell Holmes, Jr., was a pragmatist. In his book

Examining Photographs *In 1903 S. S. McClure, editor and publisher of one of the nation's most popular magazines, decided that the press had a responsibility to expose wrongdoing in society. The investigative reporting of journalists like Ida Tarbell, Ray Stannard Baker, and Lincoln Steffens (below) made them frequent contributors. Why did President Roosevelt call such reporters "muckrakers"?*

The Common Law, he wrote that law should not be an absolute set of principles but a tool to meet the needs of society. When Holmes was appointed to the Supreme Court in 1902, his ideas began to influence its decisions.

Other more popular writers played a major role in investigating and exposing a variety of social problems. President Theodore Roosevelt compared these writers to a character in John Bunyan's book, *The Pilgrim's Progress,* who constantly looked downward and raked filth, and he labeled them "muckrakers."

Most muckrakers were journalists who wrote for popular magazines like *McClure's Magazine, Cosmopolitan,* and *Collier's.* Although similar to the "yellow journalism" of the period, these articles were not written to boost sales but because the writers were deeply disturbed by the conditions they uncovered. For example, in 1902 Lincoln Steffens wrote a series of articles for *McClure's Magazine* that described shocking graft and corruption in city governments across the nation. He was followed in the same magazine by Ida Tarbell, who exposed the corrupt business practices of the Standard Oil Company. In 1906 David Phillips shocked the nation with a series in *Cosmopolitan* about links between big business and 75 United States senators.

Other muckrakers revealed the results of their investigations in books. In 1906 John Spargo's *Bitter Cry of the Children* documented abuses of child labor, and two years later, Ray Stannard Baker's *Following the Color Line* revealed the long pattern of discrimination against blacks in both North and South. Still other muckrakers were novelists who used fiction to criticize existing social conditions. In *The Octopus,* Frank Norris told how railroads dominated wheat farmers in a rich western valley. Booth Tarkington's *The Gentleman from Indiana* recounted an honest man's struggle with a political boss and with organized crime.

Despite their revelations of society's ills, most muckrakers were not activists. They merely identified problems and argued for reform but counted on others to accomplish it.

Section One Review

SUMMARY

Concerned about the direction society was taking in the early 1900s and fearful of radical remedies, middle class men and women from all professions became part of a widespread effort to bring about reforms. These reformers helped the needy, founded settlement houses, crusaded for better working conditions, and called for child-labor reform. Attorneys and judges reexamined the law to make it relevant to existing conditions. Writers exposed graft, corruption, and deplorable living and working conditions. Educators and social scientists developed new ways to investigate and solve problems. Conscientious politicians passed laws to reform business and government.

CHECKING FOR UNDERSTANDING

1. **Identify** *Looking Backward,* Ida Tarbell, John Dewey, Oliver Wendell Holmes, muckrakers

2. **Define** social gospel, pragmatism

3. **Describe** the inequities in society in the late 1800s.

4. **Compare** the moderate socialism of Eugene Debs with the radical views of Daniel De Leon.

5. **Explain** the debt that the progressives owed to big business.

6. **List** five social problems exposed by the muckrakers.

THINKING CRITICALLY

7. **Understanding Cause and Effect** What relationship does the thinking of philosophy professor William James have to progressive reform?

CONNECTIONS: HISTORY AND RELIGION

8. **Determining Consequences** What changes in organized religion resulted from the spread of the social gospel?

SECTION TWO

Progressive Reforms

> *The time is for action and political organization. Better cast a vote than write a book. I am inclined to think that these people organizing charities and setting germs of self-betterment to sprout on a large or small scale are the important people.*

—JOHN JAY CHAPMAN
Letter to his fiancée

Section Focus

Progressive reforms affected many areas of American life, among them government, consumer's rights, and education. People began to speak out against children working in mines, mills, and factories, and for women's suffrage and temperance. Although early accomplishments were mainly local changes, later reforms occurred at state and national levels as reform gained ever wider appeal.

Objectives

After studying this section, you should be able to:

- Explain how reforms strengthened democracy.
- Describe the advances made in protecting adult and child workers.

I t is fitting that the earliest evidence of progressive activism dealt with cities. Being primarily city residents, progressives were viewed as moderate in political opinion and representative of the increasing importance of the nation's urban centers.

What is perceived as the initial progressive reform came even before the muckrakers began to write. This reform was inspired not by a book or a magazine article but by a natural disaster.

Reforms in Government

In 1900 a hurricane roared in from the Gulf of Mexico and devastated the coastal city of Galveston, Texas. When the political machine that controlled city government proved incapable of responding to the disaster, local reformers and business leaders convinced the state legislature to allow them to take control. In April 1901, the mayor and city council were replaced by five commissioners chosen in a nonpartisan election. Four of the commissioners were local business leaders who applied their management experience to running the city, and it quickly recovered. Reformers in other cities, dissatisfied with their corrupt bosses and inefficient political machines, were impressed. Galveston's experience demonstrated the benefits of running a city like a business, dividing government into departments and placing each under the charge of an expert commissioner.

From the commission plan developed another progressive reform—the city-manager plan. In this reform an elected city council hired a professional manager to run city government, much like the directors of a business would hire a superintendent to run a factory. Early city managers often were engineers, because much of the business of running a modern city—such as sewage disposal, water supply, and paving streets—was technical in nature. By 1915 more than 400 cities had adopted commission or city-manager plans.

Even in cities where progressives could not reshape government, reform mayors fought powerful combinations of political bosses, unethical business leaders, and corrupt city officials. Mayors such as Tom Johnson in Cleveland, Samuel "Golden Rule" Jones in Toledo, and Hazen Pingree in Detroit gained national attention. All three left successful businesses to battle corruption in city government and to force streetcar lines, electric companies, and other utilities to behave in the public interest.

At the state level, political reform was first achieved in Wisconsin. Robert La Follette, after twice failing to become Republican candidate for governor, finally was elected in 1900. He used his office to attack the tradition of party nominating conventions. Because party bosses controlled the selection of convention delegates, they also controlled the selection of election candidates. From his own experience, La Follette knew that reformers had little chance of being chosen to run for office. In 1903 he pressured the state legislature to require that each party hold a **direct primary,** a preliminary election in which voters choose candidates for the general election. This reform took the nomination of party candidates from the bosses and their political machines and gave it to the people.

To reduce the control that big business and the party bosses had over state legislators, La Follette introduced three other reforms. The **initiative** allowed a group of citizens to introduce legislation and required the legislature to vote on it. The **referendum** allowed proposed legislation to be submitted to the voters for approval, and the **recall** allowed voters to remove an elected official from office by holding a special election. Although none of these ideas originated in Wisconsin, La Follette's great success in achieving them there gave the state a reputation as "the laboratory of democracy," and progressives in other states copied Wisconsin's reforms.

It was difficult to argue that the people should have a greater voice in government without including women, especially because they were increasingly holding jobs in factories, business offices, and schools, as well as taking prominent roles in reform movements. In addition, some progressives believed that if women gained the right to vote, their influence would help push through other reforms.

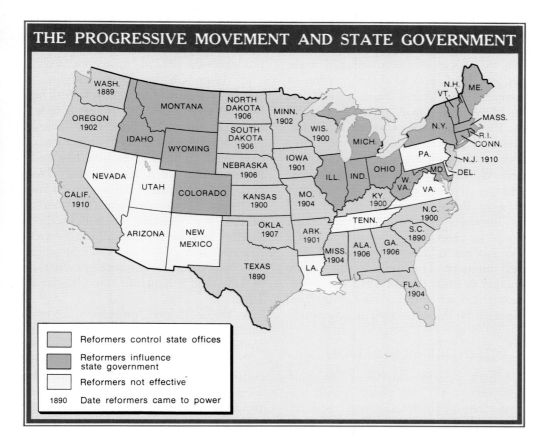

THE PROGRESSIVE MOVEMENT AND STATE GOVERNMENT

WASH. 1889
OREGON 1902
MONTANA
IDAHO
WYOMING
NORTH DAKOTA 1906
SOUTH DAKOTA 1906
MINN. 1902
WIS. 1900
MICH.
N.H.
VT.
ME.
N.Y.
MASS.
R.I.
CONN.
NEVADA
UTAH
COLORADO
NEBRASKA 1906
IOWA 1901
ILL.
IND.
OHIO
PA.
N.J. 1910
DEL.
CALIF. 1910
ARIZONA
NEW MEXICO
KANSAS 1900
MO. 1904
KY. 1900
W. VA.
MD.
VA.
OKLA. 1907
ARK. 1901
TENN.
N.C. 1900
S.C. 1890
TEXAS 1890
MISS. 1904
LA.
ALA. 1906
GA. 1906
FLA. 1904

Reformers control state offices
Reformers influence state government
Reformers not effective
1890 Date reformers came to power

Examining Maps
Although they achieved notable success at the state level, in most industrial states progressive reformers were unable to completely break the power of the bosses and political machines. Why was Wisconsin called the "laboratory of democracy"?

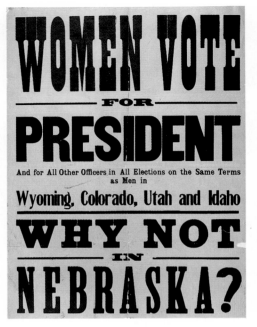

Examining Photographs *Women parade for the right to vote in New York. In Nebraska a poster appeals for the same cause. Which region of the nation was first to grant women's suffrage?*

By 1914, 11 western states had granted women full suffrage. In the East, women promoted their cause by holding parades and circulating petitions. Many women believed, however, that a constitutional amendment would be needed to gain the vote nationwide.

The most significant political reform that the progressives accomplished at the national level was the direct election of senators. The United States Senate had long been known as a "millionaires' club." In 1905 muckraker Charles E. Russell described senators as nothing more than "butlers for industrialists." Because they were chosen by their state legislatures, senators were shielded from direct public pressure. Progressive reformers felt that if its members were elected, the Senate would be more responsive to the public will and less influenced by powerful business interests. The call for this reform became so great that in 1913 the Seventeenth Amendment to the Constitution provided for direct election of senators.

Consumer Protection

A basic principle that American business inherited from Great Britain was *caveat emptor,* or "let the buyer beware." This meant that people who purchased worthless life insurance, bread made with sawdust, or colored water labeled as medicine had only themselves to blame for not being more careful. Progressives argued that consumers had no way of knowing when meat was prepared under unsanitary conditions, children's cough syrup was dosed with opium, or other products were similarly misrepresented.

In 1905 Charles Evans Hughes, a lawyer who worked for the New York legislature, investigated the insurance industry. He uncovered bribery of elected officials and huge salaries insurance executives paid to themselves and to family members they hired. Consequently, New York—and later other states—passed laws to regulate insurance companies and to protect the interests of policyholders. Hughes used his reputation as a progressive reformer, gained from this investigation, to become the governor of New York in 1907 and a Supreme Court justice in 1910.

At the local level, protection for consumers often came in the form of city zoning laws. The laws regulated how land and buildings could be used. Building codes prohibited some of the worst features of tenements by setting minimum requirements for light and air, fire escapes, room size, and sanitation.

Passage of pure food and drug laws demonstrated the effectiveness of the muckrakers in influencing consumer protection. Articles in *Collier's* about harmful medicines in 1906 convinced the chief chemist of the Department of Agriculture to perform experiments on himself and then to call for regulation. Even more sensational was the publication in 1906 of Upton Sinclair's best-selling book, *The Jungle*, a fact-based novel that portrayed horribly unsanitary conditions in slaughterhouses:

There would come all the way back from Europe old sausage that had been rejected, and that was moldy and white—it would be doused with borax and glycerine, and dumped into the hoppers, and made over again for home consumption. There would be meat that had tumbled out on the floor, in the dirt and sawdust, where workers had tramped and spit uncounted billions of [tuberculosis] germs. There would be meat stored in great piles in rooms; and the water from leaky roofs would drip over it, and thousands of rats would race about on it.

Examining Photographs *Factory workers make sausage in 1906. What does the Food and Drug Administration do?*

An outraged President Theodore Roosevelt demanded reform, and Congress responded with legislation. The Pure Food and Drug Act established a government agency, the Food and Drug Administration, to protect consumers from unsafe medicines and foods. The Meat Inspection Act was passed on the same day in 1906. These laws regulated the content and inspection of food, prohibited the use of addictive drugs in non-prescription medicines, and required accurate labels on food and drug products. Because the Constitution gave Congress control only over interstate commerce, state governments followed with similar legislation to regulate food and drugs that did not cross state lines.

Protecting Workers

"I aimed at the public's heart," Upton Sinclair complained, "and by accident I hit it in the stomach." Sinclair did not intend *The Jungle* to focus public attention on impure food. Instead he wanted to expose the terrible working conditions in slaughterhouses. One of the grim realities of industrialization was the frequency of industrial accidents.

Until the twentieth century, workers who suffered industrial accidents had little protection. Employers argued that industrial accidents were not caused by unsafe conditions but by carelessness, and they often fired employees who were seriously disabled. The few injured workers who could afford to hire lawyers and sue their employers found that neither judges nor legal precedent were on their side. And with no income, they seldom had enough money to afford medical treatment or to get through a long period of recovery.

Impressed by what Germany and New Zealand were doing about this problem, progressives joined labor union leaders to pressure state legislatures for workers'-compensation laws. These laws established insurance funds into which employers made payments. Workers who were injured by industrial accidents were paid from the fund. Maryland was first to pass such legislation in 1902, and by 1911

Linking Across Time

A PROGRESSIVE LEGACY

The Progressives' concern with protection against harmful substances was echoed in 1972 when DDT was banned. Although an effective pesticide, DDT was found to endanger other animal wildlife. In addition, it appeared to be contaminating the food people eat.

10 of the states had workers'-compensation laws on the books. Workers'-compensation laws not only helped injured workers, they improved working conditions for all workers because employers with low accident rates paid lower insurance premiums. Related progressive legislation established state agencies to inspect factories, limited workers' hours, and attempted to end crowded, unsanitary work environments.

Many progressives involved in labor reform were especially interested in improving working conditions for women. By 1900 about 20 percent of all workers were women, and progressive reformers believed women workers needed special protection. In 1903 Oregon passed a law limiting female factory workers to a 10-hour day. Employers challenged the law as violating a woman's civil right to work as long as she chose, and in 1908 the case was appealed to the Supreme Court.

To defend the law in *Muller v. Oregon,* progressive attorney Louis D. Brandeis presented research data gathered by his sister-in-law, Josephine Goldmark, and by Florence Kelley, both of the National Consumers League. The data convinced the Court that long working hours damaged women's health, and the Oregon law was upheld. After the *Muller* decision, several other states quickly passed similar laws.

Muller v. Oregon was a revolutionary legal decision. For the first time, the Court looked beyond legal principles and precedents and applied pragmatism to the law. The Court began to weigh what was best for society when it decided cases. In so doing, it took the first step in becoming an instrument of social reform.

Probably the most emotional progressive labor reform was the campaign against child labor. Although children typically worked on family farms, urban children found factory work monotonous and conditions often unhealthy or dangerous. Children were often treated like adult workers. One foreman stated that his child workers "don't have many accidents, once in a while a finger is mashed or a foot, but it does not amount to anything."

Reformers established a National Child Labor Committee in 1904 to campaign for the abolition of child labor. Muckraker John Spargo's 1906 book, *The Bitter Cry of the Children,* presented detailed evidence of the conditions of child labor in America. He told of anthracite coal mines, where thousands of "breaker boys" were hired at age 9 or 10 to pick slag out of coal and were paid 60 cents for a 10-hour day. He described how the work permanently bent their backs and often crippled their hands. He revealed that in textile mills more than one-eighth of the employees were less than 16 years old, and that some children entered cotton factories at age 7 or 8. Spargo reported that:

During the long weary nights many children have to be kept awake by having cold water dashed on their faces, and when morning comes they throw themselves upon their beds—often still warm from the bodies of their brothers and sisters— without taking off their clothing....[Do not] judge the ages of working children by their physical appearance, for they are usually behind other children...as much as two or three years.

Examining Photographs *A major concern of reformers was protecting children. How was child labor reform achieved?*

Public opinion was so stirred by such information that by 1914 all but one state set a minimum age for employment, and many established other limits on child labor as well. At the federal level, the newly established Children's Bureau had few powers, but it investigated and published information that helped the campaign to improve the well-being of child workers.

Varieties of Reform

In addition to reforming labor practices, many progressives insisted that business be regulated in ways to protect the public interest. Because of their great influence and power, large corporations commonly got tax breaks from state legislatures. In Wisconsin, for example, Governor La Follette determined that railroads paid less than half the property taxes of other businesses, and he obtained reform laws to tax railroads more equally. In addition, he established a commission of experts—many from the University of Wisconsin—to regulate the operation of railroads in the state. Other states followed Wisconsin's lead.

On the federal level, Congress began to tax corporate profits in 1909. Although the Supreme Court in 1895 had declared an income tax unconstitutional, in 1913 the Sixteenth Amendment empowered the federal government to levy such a tax.

The Progressive Era also was a time when reformers called for regulation of public utilities such as street-car lines, waterworks, and electric-light companies. Many states set up public service commissions with the power to control the rates charged by public utilities. Some city reformers, doubtful that regulation could force utility companies to act in the public interest, called for city governments to buy them out and run the utilities directly. By 1915, for example, all but 1 of the 36 largest cities owned or operated their own waterworks.

Progressive reform expressed itself in many other ways. It resulted in playgrounds and dental clinics for children. The Boy Scouts, Campfire Girls, and Girl Scouts were founded during this period.

Private charities multiplied and broadened their social usefulness. The Rockefeller Foundation, for example, led a campaign to eradicate hookworm, which was causing serious health problems in rural areas of the South. Juvenile courts and reform schools were established to care for young lawbreakers. Progressives began to show concern about America's natural resources. State and federal governments passed conservation laws and set aside public recreation areas.

The reform impulse also resulted in great progress in education. Many states passed laws requiring children to attend school, and the number of high schools more than doubled between 1900 and 1920. The school year was lengthened

Life of the Times

BOY SCOUTS

While many progressive reformers focused on social issues, such as worker protection, tax reform, and temperance, others concentrated on keeping the nation's youth under control. Without farm chores to command their full attention, urban boys were becoming, to their parents' dismay, an unsupervised leisure class.

"BE PREPARED"

"DO A GOOD TURN DAILY"

Organizations such as the Boy Scouts of America (BSA) arose to provide supervised activities that stressed old-fashioned values and sheltered adolescents from the lures of the city. Scouts hiked in the school year, camped in the summer, and attended weekly meetings packed with instruction, drills, and games. Scouting channeled adolescent energy into the wholesome pursuit of specialized merit badges, acquired by passing tests on woodcraft, reconnaissance, and citizenship skills.

The Boy Scouts of America was designed, in part, to reinforce what were perceived at the time to be traditional American male values. BSA executives and scoutmasters strongly opposed girl scouting and were reluctant to involve the Boy Scouts in service projects on which Boy and Girl Scouts worked as equals.

and the curriculum enriched by courses in music, art, home economics, and industrial arts. The pragmatism of philosopher John Dewey influenced schools to revise their traditional curriculum and offer studies relevant to the needs of modern society.

Among the most controversial progressive reforms was the campaign for family planning. Margaret Sanger, a nurse who worked with poor residents of New York's Lower East Side, came to believe that high birth rates, poverty, and infant mortality were related. In 1914 she began a movement to educate women about family planning. Although Sanger faced strong opposition, and was twice arrested for violating obscenity laws, her organization endured to become the Planned Parenthood Federation.

Some progressives saw temperance as another reform to protect women and children, arguing that money spent for alcohol deprived families of necessities, and that drunken men sometimes beat their wives and children. Others supported it because of the well-known connection between saloonkeepers and corrupt city politicians. Temperance also had the support of many business leaders, who believed that alcohol use among their employees increased absenteeism, decreased efficiency and productivity, and contributed to industrial accidents.

Long at the forefront of the temperance movement was the Woman's Christian Temperance Union (WCTU), founded in 1874. By 1890, it already had 150,000 members. The WCTU was typical of many progressive organizations. While its main focus was a crusade against the use of alcohol, it spoke out on a variety of issues and supported other changes such as women's suffrage, prison reform, and world peace.

Like so many progressive reforms, temperance was first accomplished at the local level. By 1914 nearly half the people of the United States lived in areas where the sale of alcohol was illegal, and 12 states had passed statewide Prohibition laws. In 1919 Prohibition became nationwide when the Eighteenth Amendment was added to the Constitution.

★★★★★★★★★★★★★★★★★★★

Section Two Review

★★★★★★★★★★★★★★★★★★★

SUMMARY

Although some progressive reforms were national in scope, most occurred at the state and local levels. The power of political bosses was reduced by reforming the structure of city governments and through primary elections. Other political reforms also gave voters a more direct voice in government at all levels. Legislation protected consumers from poor products and workers from horrible working conditions and disabling injuries. Although court decisions did not always reflect the reform spirit, a wide variety of reforms were accomplished in government, the economy, and society.

CHECKING FOR UNDERSTANDING

1. **Identify** Galveston, Seventeenth Amendment, Charles Evans Hughes, Upton Sinclair, *Muller v. Oregon*, John Spargo, WCTU

2. **Define** direct primary, initiative, referendum, recall

3. **Describe** the commission plan as a form of city government.

4. **Discuss** five reforms that involved voters in government more directly.

5. **Explain** how Upton Sinclair's novel, *The Jungle*, contributed to consumer protection.

6. **List** the problems workers faced and the reforms that remedied them.

THINKING CRITICALLY

7. **Understanding Cause and Effect** Explain why progressive reforms strengthened the cause of women's suffrage.

LINKING PAST AND PRESENT

8. **Comparing Trends** In the 1980s groups such as Mothers Against Drunk Driving were formed. Compare the temperance movement with such modern groups.

★★★★★★★★★★★★★★★★★★★

Linking Across Time

THE ORIGINS OF MODERN GOVERNMENT

Although the United States government is the nation's largest civilian employer, it has not always been so. "Big government" is a development that has accompanied the government's growing role in society.

Through the eighteenth and nineteenth centuries, Americans subscribed to the adage that the best government was the least government. For more than 100 years, government planning generally was limited to tariff policy. Social programs did not exist. As a result, government was small in size and limited in function.

But beginning in the Progressive Era, reformers planted the seeds of a new concept—that government was responsible for maintaining a stable, smoothly functioning, and just society. This goal could be achieved, they believed, through planning and control by expert managers. In this belief, government bureaucracy—and "big government"—was born.

Before the Progressive Era government generally reacted to social problems by passing legislation directed at specific conditions—the Sherman Antitrust Act of 1890, for example. But after 1900, areas of concern were increasingly managed by "bureaucrats"—unelected officials who provided daily oversight in their specialties. Government grew rapidly as new executive agencies arose to fulfill this regulatory function. The Department of Commerce, created in 1903, pro-

vided President Theodore Roosevelt the business experts he needed to battle the trusts, as this 1904 cartoon depicts. In his progressive

Theodore Roosevelt about to battle the trusts.

campaign for President in 1912, Woodrow Wilson summarized the new approach to government by saying "America stands for a government responsive to the interests of all." This theme was echoed in 1913 when a new Department of Labor began to promote worker welfare.

The progressive ideal of the relationship between government and society inspired President Franklin

Roosevelt's New Deal programs aimed at achieving recovery from the Depression of the 1930s. New agencies like the Social Security Administration involved government in social planning by providing for aged, dependent, and disabled Americans.

The progressive spirit was extended again in the 1960s as President Lyndon Johnson's Great Society established the Equal Employment Opportunity Commission, the War on Poverty, and many other government protections and programs.

Today, of more than 90 independent executive agencies and commissions, about two-thirds are involved in some way in regulating society or in protecting its members. All but one of these agencies were created during or after the Progressive Era.

Partly because of the progressives nearly a century ago, government began to take on more and more functions, and the "hands-off" government of the late 1800s began to change to the "hands-on" government of today.

★ ★ ★ ★ ★ ★ ★ ★ ★ ★

MAKING CONNECTIONS

1. What did the progressives see as the government's role in society?

2. What evidence can you see in American government today of a progressive legacy?

★ ★ ★ ★ ★ ★ ★ ★ ★ ★

Limits of Progressivism

SETTING THE SCENE

...[A]n American, a Negro, two souls, two thoughts, two unreconciled strivings....The history of the American Negro is the history of this strife....He would not bleach the Negro soul in a flood of white Americanism. ...He simply wishes to make it possible for a man to be both a Negro and an American, without being cursed and spat upon.

—W.E.B. DU BOIS
Civil rights leader and
professor at Atlanta University, 1897

Section Focus

While progressivism resulted in many lasting changes, reform had its limits. Much progressive reform was based on traditional American attitudes about race, sex, and nationalism. When public attention turned to world affairs, and the progressive spirit began to wane, not all Americans had shared equally in the benefits of reform.

Objectives

After studying this section, you should be able to:
- Describe progressive attitudes about immigrants and racial minorities.
- Explain why black leadership changed.

The achievements of progressive reform at the national level were less far-reaching than its successes at local and state levels. It was more difficult to create nationwide demands for reform than to organize effective campaigns on a smaller scale. The federal government also was more difficult to prod into action. The Senate, chosen by boss-dominated state legislatures until 1913, was a highly conservative body. In the House of Representatives, powerful figures such as committee heads and the speaker usually resisted change.

The Supreme Court became somewhat less conservative than it was in the 1890s, as progressives Oliver Wendell Holmes (1902), Charles Evans Hughes (1910), and Louis D. Brandeis (1916) were appointed to the Court. Yet the majority of justices seldom were willing to extend federal power into new areas. The Court demonstrated this reluctance when it declared unconstitutional a federal law providing workers' compensation for railroad workers in 1908 and a federal child labor law in 1918. Partly because of the attitude of the courts, many of the evils described by the muckrakers—child labor, city corruption, and industrial accidents, for example—were considered outside the constitutional sphere of the federal government's powers, making national reform of these conditions nearly impossible.

The benefits of progressivism were spread unevenly in other ways, too. Many middle-class progressives feared labor unions almost as much as they did trusts. So although progressives worked with labor leaders to improve working conditions, few objected when businesses organized effectively to prevent unions in their plants—often with cooperation from local courts and police. Therefore, wage gains during the Progressive Era came only among skilled workers. The earning power of unskilled workers—the largest part of the labor force—actually dropped because prices increased more rapidly than their rates of pay.

Reformers and Immigrants

Among the many factors that held down the wages of unskilled workers was the continuing flood of immigrants

Examining Photographs

Progressives believed in compulsory public education to keep children out of factories and to provide them with proper values. Why did many states require high school students to study American history?

to the United States, averaging one million a year during the Progressive Era—largely from southern and eastern Europe. This "New Immigration" caused widespread alarm, as immigrant men and women competed for unskilled jobs in American mines, mills, and factories. In addition, the newcomers seemed to have more difficulty fitting in to established American culture than the "old immigrants" from northern and western Europe. Pressure from labor-union leaders and such organizations as the Immigration Restriction League persuaded Congress in 1897, 1913, and 1915 to enact laws requiring all immigrants to pass literacy tests. All three laws were vetoed, but such a law passed over President Woodrow Wilson's veto in 1917.

Many progressives feared the socialist ideas that immigrants brought from Europe. As middle-class reformers, progressives wanted to change capitalism, not abolish it. Many also worried about preserving existing values and culture. Therefore, many progressive reforms weakened the political strength of immigrant numbers and instilled in newcomers what reformers thought were proper American values.

Examining Photographs

Many businesses organized English classes for their employees and held them in the plant so that workers could attend at the end of their shift. Why would employers consider learning English important?

Connections

HISTORY AND RELIGION

REFORM JUDAISM

By 1880 about 250,000 Jews lived in America, most were of German ancestry. Influenced by liberal Protestantism and the social gospel of reformers, many Jews began to adapt their religious customs and rituals to the American way of life. For example, they adopted a congregation structure similar to that of American Christians. Like their liberal Christian counterparts, Reform Jews supported such progressive social reforms as child-labor laws and collective bargaining. Attorney and later Supreme Court justice Louis D. Brandeis, for example, was an ardent champion of progressive causes.

The Jews of the West
The Metropolitan Years

A poster celebrating Jewish contributions to America

After 1880 Jewish immigrants flooded into America, many escaping persecution in Russia. Reform Jews helped these newcomers make their way in the United States. The help was given partly because of their belief in social reform and partly because they feared these poor, old-fashioned Yiddish-speaking Jews would create an anti-Jewish reaction among American Christians. The Russian Jews were Orthodox—observing traditional Jewish beliefs and rituals. In turn, Orthodox Jews reintroduced the Reform Jews to a number of customs and rituals discarded by their parents.

MAKING THE RELIGION CONNECTION

1. In what ways were Reform Jews influenced by the American way of life?

2. For what reasons did Reform Jews help Russian Jewish immigrants?

LINKING PAST AND PRESENT

3. How have American Jews helped recent Russian Jewish immigrants?

In calling for reform of city government, one writer complained about:

[T]he mass of ignorant voters, who now help the vicious bosses to govern our cities....A colony of Italians, Scandinavians, Germans, or Irish, preserving their national language and their national ideas, and living as foreigners among us is very difficult to reach, but their votes count just as much as the votes of the most highly educated men among us.

When progressives reformed government by defeating political bosses and machines, they also destroyed the system that provided immigrant groups with a political voice, political jobs, and political power.

As reformers obtained child labor laws and compulsory school attendance laws, they forced immigrant children out of factories and into classrooms. Many states made the study of American history a required course in public schools during the Progressive Era. Educator John Dewey advised that it was essential to teach students to be good citizens.

Immigrant groups opposed many progressive reforms. Many poor immigrants needed their children to work to aid the family income. Those from countries where drinking wine or beer was acceptable behavior objected to attempts to force temperance on them. Many immigrant women resisted the efforts of settlement-house social workers to teach them about "proper" diet, hygiene, or child care.

Progressives and Race

The most conspicuous limit to progressivism was its attitudes about race. Like the majority of Americans at that time, most progressives believed that nonwhite races were inferior. Therefore, reformers did not object to the segregation of Japanese Americans in San Francisco schools in 1906, nor did they oppose sharp cuts in Japanese immigration to the United States that began in 1907.

In addition, progressives generally accepted widespread discrimination against African Americans. Although many progressives sympathized with their plight, most reformers agreed with Theodore Roosevelt, who stated that blacks "as a race and in the mass are altogether inferior to the whites."

Few progressives objected to the Jim Crow laws that southern states had passed after Reconstruction to restore segregation. In 1896, when the Supreme Court ruled in *Plessy v. Ferguson* that segregation was constitutional as long as separate facilities were equal, no progressive campaign was launched for reform. While southern whites were lynching black people and barring them from voting or holding public office, progressives were crusading for primary elections, direct election of senators, and other reforms to spread democracy. Like most whites, progressives generally accepted the South's Jim Crow system, partly due to indifference, and partly because northern blacks also were restricted to low-paying jobs, segregation, and inferior social status.

These circumstances help explain a shift in black leadership during the Progressive Era. At the turn of the century the most influential black leader was Booker T. Washington. A former slave, Washington founded Alabama's Tuskegee Institute in 1881 to train African Americans in 30 trades. Washington argued that equality would be achieved not through campaigns for reform, but when blacks gained the education and skills to become valuable members of their communities. In 1895 he spelled out this view:

Examining Photographs *To blend immigrants into American society, settlement house social workers organized recreational activities, visited immigrants' homes, conducted homemaking and parenting classes, and worked with individual families. What attitude did progressives have about immigrant cultures?*

...[T]he agitation of questions of social equality is the extremist folly... progress in the enjoyment of all the privileges that will come to us must be the result of severe and constant struggle rather than of artificial forcing. No race that has anything to contribute to the markets of the world is long in any degree ostracized.

Yet as the great changes in society that accompanied progressive reform largely bypassed African Americans, a new black leadership arose that rejected Washington's approach to achieving equality. The most prominent new black leader was W. E. B. Du Bois, a Harvard-educated history professor at Atlanta University. Du Bois rejected Washington's emphasis on job skills and argued that suffrage was the way to end white supremacy, stop the lynching of blacks, and gain better schools. In 1905 Du Bois and 28 other black leaders met at Niagara Falls to demand full political rights and responsibilities for African Americans as well as an end to racial discrimination. This call eventually resulted in the founding of the National Association for the Advancement of Colored People (NAACP) in 1909. "The power of the ballot we need in sheer self-defense," he said, "else what shall save us from a second slavery?"

Despite the failure of most progressives to be concerned about such questions, progressive reform helped change American society in many ways. Although they excluded large groups from their efforts, the progressives expanded democracy, reformed education, and improved the quality of life for millions of men, women, and children. Except for two amendments to the Constitution in 1919 and 1920, progressivism in America ended as the United States entered World War I. Americans turned from reforming their own society to a crusade to "make the world safe for democracy."

Section Three Review

SUMMARY

The progressives' reasons for advocating reform were as varied as the reforms themselves. While all progressives wanted "progress" for society, they disagreed over what that meant. For some progressives, improving society meant limiting the political power of immigrants and eliminating customs and behaviors that reformers thought were un-American. In addition, progressives generally agreed with the racial attitudes of most Americans in the early 1900s. Asian Americans and African Americans were bypassed by progressive reform. Black leaders founded organizations such as the NAACP, however, and worked to reform society.

CHECKING FOR UNDERSTANDING

1. **Identify** Booker T. Washington, W.E.B. Du Bois, *Plessy v. Ferguson*
2. **Cite** the threats posed by new immigrants from eastern Europe.
3. **Describe** how some progressive reforms limited the political power of immigrants.
4. **Explain** why some immigrants resisted progressive reforms.
5. **Discuss** the status of African Americans during the Progressive Era.

THINKING CRITICALLY

6. **Making Comparisons** Compare the methods of Booker T. Washington and W.E.B. Du Bois for increasing African Americans' participation in society.

GLOBAL PERSPECTIVES

7. **Comparing Attitudes** In the 1980s many immigrants came to the United States from Asia, Mexico, and Central America. Compare American attitudes toward those immigrants with the attitudes toward immigrants of the 1900s.

Critical Thinking Skills

Recognizing Fallacies in a Line of Reasoning

Suppose you heard the following statements: "When our football team played on artificial turf, we lost by 20 points. That artificial turf must have been too slippery to play on." Couldn't there be other reasons the team lost? The statement that you heard is an example of a fallacy in a line of reasoning.

Explanation

A fallacy in a line of reasoning is an error in thinking something out. The fallacy may be an unsupported argument or a mistaken conclusion. In the above example, it was a fact that your team played on artificial turf. It was also a fact that your team was defeated by 20 points. But to say that it lost because the artificial turf was too slippery is a fallacy. The other team won while playing on the same turf, so there must have been other reasons your team lost. More facts are needed to explain it.

To determine whether there is a fallacy in a line of reasoning, ask the following questions:

• Is there any connection between the facts and the conclusion? If not, the statement contains a fallacy. If there is a connection, go on to the next question.

• Is there only a loose connection between the facts and the conclusion? If there is, go on to the next question.

• Are there enough facts given to reach the conclusion, or is additional information needed? If more facts are needed, the statement contains a fallacy.

A group of immigrant women sew clothing by hand, Ridge Street in New York City in 1908

Example

The following examples each contain a statement of fact and a conclusion. Read the statements, and note how the three steps have been applied:

In the early 1900s, the managers of women workers were almost always men. This was because women lacked the ability to direct others. *(There is a loose connection between the fact that men were managers and the conclusion that women did not have the ability. But more facts are needed to support that ability was the reason. What roles did lack of educational opportunities for women and biases of male bosses play? The conclusion that women did not have*

management ability is not supported. The reasoning contains a fallacy.)

In the late 1800s immigrants lived in the poorer sections of American cities. This indicates that they did not care about how they lived. *(There is a loose connection between the fact and the concluding statement, but more information is needed to explain why immigrants lived in the poorer sections of American cities. In reality, immigrants held the least desirable low-paying jobs and often did not have the educational opportunities that would have given them the skills needed to perform the higher-paying jobs. So the claim that they did not care about how they lived is not supported.)*

Practice

For practice in this skill, read the following sentences, and determine if a fallacy exists. If so, explain why a fallacy is present.

1. The Constitution did not contain provisions against child-labor, so the government was powerless to do anything about it.

2. The muckrakers published many books and articles, so the entire public became more aware of social injustices.

3. It was difficult to operate a democratic government and not allow women to vote, so many western states granted women full suffrage by 1914.

★ Chapter 23 Review ★

★ Summary

Beginning about 1900 a large, loosely organized group of urban middle-class professionals—including journalists, social workers, educators, ministers, and socially conscious politicians—became concerned about the need for social change in the United States. Influenced by German education and American pragmatism, these reformers—called "progressives"—were the first to thoroughly investigate a variety of social problems that they felt were unjust and undemocratic. Progressives were concerned that if society's problems were not solved, democracy and capitalism might be threatened. The growing popularity of socialism in the early 1900s seemed to confirm their fears.

Progressives believed that the methods developed to manage big businesses in the late 1800s could be applied to running the country. Their goal was an efficient, smoothly functioning nation where each social problem could be managed by experts trained in that area. The many areas in which the progressives focused their efforts included the following: reform of the political system, business regulation, consumer protection, immigrants, tax reform, protection of women and children, labor reform, education, and temperance. Journalists called *muckrakers* brought many of these problem areas to public attention, and most Americans supported calls for change. Reform occurred first at local and state levels. Many went on to be national in scope.

While progressives had the nation's best interests at heart, some reforms came at the expense of immigrant and racial minorities. Reformers tried to extinguish immigrant cultures and they neglected African Americans almost completely.

With America's entrance into World War I, the progressive reform fervor slackened. Instead, people turned their attention to world affairs.

★ Using Vocabulary

Imagine that you are a muckraker who is investigating the need for reform in your city. Use the following vocabulary words to write an article summarizing the corruption and stating your recommendations.

social gospel	referendum
recall	pragmatism
direct primary	initiative

★ Reviewing Facts

1. **Discuss** the role of the muckrakers in promoting social change.
2. **Describe** the inequalities that existed between the upper and lower classes of society.
3. **List** the improvements in city government achieved through progressive reform efforts.
4. **Explain** why reform was more successful at state and local levels than at the national level.
5. **State** the connection between progressive reform and big business management methods.
6. **Identify** reforms that improved the lives of industrial workers.
7. **Indicate** the importance of the socialist movement in early twentieth-century reform.
8. **Discuss** why progressives were not considered to be radical reformers.

★ Understanding Concepts

REFORM

1. To what extent did reform in government extend democracy in the Progressive Era?
2. What changes did labor reforms bring to other areas of society in the early 1900s?

VALUES AND BELIEFS

3. Describe the values of the people who preached the social gospel and pioneered social programs.
4. How did progressives' values and beliefs about immigrant cultures influence their reform activities?

★ Thinking Critically

1. **Understanding Cause and Effect** To what extent were progressive reformers inspired by the Populists? Consider the membership, goals, and approach to problem-solving of each reform group.
2. **Making Comparisons** Compare the commission plan of government to the city-manager plan and explain how each expressed the progressive approach to government.
3. **Interpreting Points of View** Assume you were a recent immigrant to the United States. Explain how you might feel about the progressive reformers.

What reforms would you feel strongest about? Why?

★ Writing About History

CLASSIFICATION

Refer to the description on writing a classification essay in the History Writer's Handbook in the Appendix of this book. Your teacher will give you more specific instructions on the essay's length and the assignment's due date.

Use classification to organize all the progressive reforms discussed in this chapter and to write an essay on how progressive reform changed American society.

★ Learning Cooperatively

Working in a group of three, organize a debate among candidates for governor during the early 1900s. Select one student to be a socialist follower of Eugene Debs, another to be a socialist follower of Daniel De Leon, and the third student to be a progressive reform candidate. Candidates should each prepare a statement expressing their views regarding reform, what they will do once elected, and why voters should support them. After completing their statements, students should exchange them with the other group members so that each candidate can prepare a rebuttal statement to the other candidates' positions. Each group should be prepared to present their statements and rebuttals to the class if called on to do so by the teacher.

★ Mastering Skills

IDENTIFYING AMBIGUOUS OR EQUIVOCAL STATEMENTS

What might your first reaction be if someone said to you, "With that neon jacket, anyone can spot you from a mile away"? Chances are that you would take the comment to mean that the color of your jacket makes you stand out in a crowd. On second thought, however, you might decide that the comment was not meant as a compliment but as a criticism of your jacket.

Situations such as the one described above are not uncommon. They often happen because someone has made an ambiguous or equivocal statement. An *ambiguous statement* is a statement that is unclear or misleading by accident. An *equivocal statement* is a statement that is unclear or misleading on purpose. Both can be interpreted in a variety of ways and can be confusing, twisted, or contradictory.

To identify an ambiguous or equivocal statement ask yourself the following questions:

• Is the statement unclear and or not understandable?

• If the statement is clear, can it be interpreted or understood in more than one way?

If your answer is "yes" to both questions, you have identified an ambiguous or equivocal statement.

Example Look at the following statements and the comments in italics accompanying them:

1. "O kings, lords and rulers of us all, listen to our plea!" *(This statement is clear but can be interpreted in more than one way. Are kings being called lords and rulers, or are three different kinds of leaders being addressed?)*

2. The spirit of progressive reform resulted in dental clinics and playgrounds for children. *(This statement is unclear. Were the dental clinics for children, too, or only the playgrounds?)*

On first reading, the statements above may have seemed perfectly clear. However, after reading the questions that follow each of them, you can see why some people would consider them ambiguous or equivocal.

Practice Read the following passage carefully, checking each statement to determine if it really is clear and understandable. Identify those statements that are ambiguous or equivocal:

John Dewey was a well-known philosopher and educator. He believed that ideas are plans of action that serve their purpose by solving problems. His influence has been great in the United States in public education and in other nations.

Dewey was born in Burlington, Vermont, and received a Ph.D. from Johns Hopkins University in 1884. He became a professor of philosophy in 1888 at the University of Minnesota. Until his retirement he was a professor at the University of Michigan, Columbia University, and at the University of Chicago, where he served as head of the philosophy department.

CHAPTER 24
White House Reformers

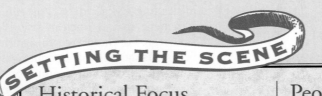

SETTING THE SCENE

Historical Focus

From 1900 to 1917, progressive reforms at the national level were aided by three strong-minded Presidents, Theodore Roosevelt, William Howard Taft, and Woodrow Wilson. These Presidents had different political philosophies, leadership styles, and personal temperaments. Such differences sometimes led to bitter controversies, as in the election of 1912. Yet, each worked to control big business, gain protection for workers, and protect the American people from social ills.

Concepts to Understand

- How **interests and positions** of the Progressives were translated into federal legislation.
- How business practices worked to limit **economic competition**.

People to Know

John Mitchell, William Howard Taft, Gifford Pinchot, Woodrow Wilson

Places to Locate

New Jersey, Wall Street

Terms to Identify

Hepburn Act, Bull Moose party, Underwood Tariff, income taxes, Federal Reserve System, price-cutting

Guided Reading

As you read this chapter, seek the answers to the following questions.

1. In what ways was Roosevelt successful or disappointing as a progressive leader?
2. What progressive reforms did Wilson achieve as President?

SPANNING THE DECADES

POLITICAL

1901
Theodore Roosevelt becomes President

1902
Roosevelt uses his office to help settle the coal strike

1906
Pure Food and Drug Act passed

1908
William Howard Taft elected President

1900   **1905**

CULTURAL

1902
First Rose Bowl football game

1903
Orville Wright flies first heavier-than-air airplane

1906
San Francisco earthquake causes extensive damage

1907
Electric washing machine invented

The Grand Canyon of Yellowstone *by Thomas Moran, 1893-1901*

1912
*Progressive
Party
is formed*

1913
*Federal Reserve
System created*

1910

1915

1908
*First Model T Ford
automobile produced*

1913
*Congress designates
Mother's Day as the
second Sunday in May*

*…We are face to face with our destiny
and we must meet it with a high and
resolute courage. For us is the life of action,
of strenuous performance of duty;
let us live in the harness, striving mightily;
let us rather run the risk of wearing out
than rusting out….*

—THEODORE ROOSEVELT
Campaign Speech, New York City,
October 5, 1898

Roosevelt's Progressive Domestic Policies

SETTING THE SCENE

...We must treat each man on his worth and merits....We must see that each is given a square deal, because he is entitled to no more and should receive no less....

—THEODORE ROOSEVELT
Address at the New York State Fair, 1903

Section Focus

From the time Theodore Roosevelt succeeded William McKinley as President, leaders of industry feared that he would use the power of his office to break up existing trusts. And with Roosevelt's first speeches, their worst fears were realized. The President made it clear that he intended to carry out his pledge of a "square deal."

Objectives

After studying this section, you should be able to:

- Explain why Theodore Roosevelt became known as a "trust buster."
- Identify the series of events that led to settlement of the 1902 coal strike.
- Examine Roosevelt's efforts for conservation of wilderness areas.
- Discuss Roosevelt's legacy to the United States.

W hen Theodore Roosevelt received the Republican vice-presidential nomination in 1900, the powerful Republican leader Mark Hanna warned that there would be only one life between "that cowboy" and the White House.

When the election resulted in a Republican victory, Hanna turned to McKinley and said, "Now it is up to you to live." But McKinley would not live. After McKinley's assassination in 1901, Theodore Roosevelt—the "cowboy," the reformer, the progressive—did indeed become President of the United States.

The Trust Buster

After McKinley's death, Roosevelt had promised America that he would "continue absolutely unbroken the policy of President McKinley." Not having become President by election, though, Roosevelt felt he did not have the authority to push a general program of reform through Congress. Even members of his own party urged him to "go slow."

During this time, however, industries were merging at an all-time high rate. This was especially evident with the formation of the United States Steel Corporation, which produced more than half of America's steel, and the Northern Securities Company, which tried to attain a monopoly of northwestern railroads. This rash of mergers prompted Roosevelt to urge Congress to pass legislation regulating big business.

When Congress did not respond, Roosevelt went to the American people, making a series of speeches to garner support for his program. The response was overwhelming—every day Roosevelt's popularity grew. And government leaders responded by beginning a series of moves designed to limit the trusts. First, the attorney general took Northern Securities to court. In 1904 the Supreme Court overturned previous court decisions and ruled that Northern Securities had violated

the Sherman Act. This decision resulted in the dissolution of Northern Securities.

Roosevelt was not opposed to all trusts, however. He also understood that trust-busting suits were not the most effective means of regulating business; they did not prevent monopolies but only tried to break them up after they had already been formed. But Roosevelt was less interested in the economic effects of carrying out antimonopoly laws than he was in using them to force even the most powerful businesspeople to obey the law.

Still, Roosevelt's reputation as a "trust buster" grew. When he thought that a trust damaged the public or worked outside the law, he acted quickly. At one time, J. Pierpont Morgan, the brilliant billionaire financier who helped construct both the United States Steel and the Northern Securities trusts, asked Roosevelt, "Are you going to attack my other interests?" Roosevelt responded, "Certainly not, unless we find out that in any case they have done something we regard as wrong."

Eventually, Congress followed Roosevelt's lead regarding the regulation of trusts and, in 1903, passed the Expedition Act, which gave Federal antitrust suits precedence on the dockets of circuit courts. A few days later, an act of Congress also established the Department of Commerce and Labor, empowered to investigate corporations involved in interstate commerce. In addition, the Department of Justice started more trust-busting suits against corporations than they had at any time during the three previous administrations. And in most of these cases, the government won.

The Coal Strike of 1902

One of the most prolonged strikes in United States history started in May 1902, when nearly 150,000 workers walked out of the anthracite mines of eastern Pennsylvania. Terrible conditions precipitated this strike: low wages and frequent layoffs were common for the anthracite miners, whose earnings averaged less than $300 per year. Living in cheaply built company towns, the cash-poor miners were forced to trade at company stores that charged exorbitant prices. Such conditions drew widespread public support for the strikers.

John Mitchell, a worker who had started working in the mines at the age of 12, represented the miners as a member of the United Mine Workers. He asked mine operators to consider allowing three men, two of them clergy, to determine whether miners' wages were adequate. But George F. Baer, principal spokesperson for the mine employers, refused Mitchell's suggestion, saying that "anthracite mining is a business and not a religious, sentimental, or academic proposition." Baer further alienated a public already sympathetic to the plight of the workers when he refused to listen to the miners' complaints, to submit to arbitration, or to recognize the United Mine Workers as the true representative of the mine workers. This attitude and the strong conviction behind the miners' position caused the strike to drag on, through the summer and into the fall, with no prospect of settlement. Appeals for action poured in to the President.

Roosevelt had no power, either by law or by precedent, to force the mine operators and miners to come to an agreement. Yet he resolved to use whatever influence he had to end the strike. Early in October, Roosevelt invited representatives of the operators to meet Mitchell at the White House. Nothing was accomplished in this stormy session, but public opinion soured even more toward the employers.

Faced with this deadlock, Roosevelt considered a legally questionable seizure of the mines by federal troops. But before he decided on such drastic action, a compromise was reached. After a conference between Elihu Root, the President's representative, and J. Pierpont Morgan, whose banking firm indirectly controlled most of the anthracite mines, Morgan was able to put enough pressure on the operators to force them to back down. Morgan's action was apparently prompted by concern that if Americans did not have coal for the

Examining Photographs *Coal miners at Shenandoah, Pennsylvania, demonstrate to win better pay and working conditions during the 1902 coal strike. How was the strike settled?*

Connections

THE CONSERVATION MOVEMENT

By the beginning of the twentieth century it was becoming clear that the natural resources Americans had long taken for granted were—in fact—in danger of being used up. Theodore Roosevelt, a champion of conservation, made an effective case for the wise and scientific use of natural resources to people of all ages.

Theodore Roosevelt and John Muir at Yosemite National Park

To the Society of American Foresters in 1903, Roosevelt said, "First and foremost, you can never afford to forget for one moment what is the object of forest policy....Your attention should be directed not to the preservation of the forests as an end in itself, but as the means for preserving and increasing the prosperity of the nation."

His 1907 Arbor Day message to school children said in part, "Within your lifetime the nation's need for trees will become serious....You will want what nature once so bountifully supplied and man so thoughtlessly destroyed; and because of that want you will reproach us, not for what we have used, but for what we have wasted...."

MAKING THE ENVIRONMENT CONNECTION

1. What did Roosevelt suggest was the object of forest policy?

2. How did Roosevelt's conservation program relate to the Square Deal?

LINKING PAST AND PRESENT

3. Why has forest conservation received renewed emphasis in recent years?

winter, United States businesses would also suffer. Roosevelt's action in using the prestige of his office and his personal influence with Morgan to settle the strike was recognized in this country and abroad as an important precedent. The London *Times* commented:

The President has done a very big and entirely new thing. We are witnessing not merely the ending of the coal strike, but the definite entry of a powerful government on a novel sphere of operation.

Efforts at Conservation

Even before Theodore Roosevelt became President, the nation was adopting a policy of conservation. In 1872 an act of Congress created Yellowstone National Park, and the 1890s saw the establishment of four more national parks. In 1891 Benjamin Harrison's administration enacted the Forest Reserve Act, empowering Presidents to set aside land for national forests. But it was not until after Theodore Roosevelt took office that "conservation" became a household word.

Roosevelt's efforts to preserve the nation's natural resources stemmed from a deep commitment to conservation, born of a love for America's wilderness. Before this time, great forests had been felled without thought of erosion or future timber needs; grasslands turned barren from overgrazing and overplanting; and the indiscriminate slaughter of wildlife had resulted in the extinction of many species, such as the passenger pigeon.

Roosevelt's beliefs made conservation popular. He stimulated public interest in the subject by writing, and by taking publicized holiday trips to the West, by constantly pushing for better conservation

a national conference on conservation at the White House. This conference resulted in the creation of more than 40 state conservation commissions as well as a National Conservation Commission, which began an inventory of the nation's natural resources.

Wisconsin senator Robert La Follette, though often critical of Roosevelt, paid tribute to the "high statesmanship" the President showed in advancing the idea of conservation. La Follette predicted that future historians would conclude that Roosevelt's greatest achievement was not the Square Deal, but the preservation of the nation's natural resources for the benefit of all.

Further Regulation

After being elected to a full term in 1904, Roosevelt felt confident enough to respond to the growing public clamor for stricter regulation of the railroads. The Interstate Commerce Commission, lacking authority to set rates or to examine railroads' financial records, had only limited success in controlling the unfair practices and political influence of these powerful businesses. In defense of government controls, newspaper editor William Allen White spoke for many when he wrote:

The railroads cannot name senators, pack state conventions, run legislatures, and boss politics generally... and then successfully maintain that they are private carriers doing a private business.

Some well-known figures, among them William Jennings Bryan, proposed that the railroads be owned and operated by the government. Thinking such a step would lead to disaster, Roosevelt instead called for tighter regulation.

The result was the Hepburn Act of 1906, which strengthened the Interstate Commerce Act of 1887 in several ways. It

Examining Photographs
Roosevelt and his conservationist friend John Muir ride in Yosemite National Park. How much land did Roosevelt add to the national forests?

laws. Roosevelt also used the power and prestige of the presidency to promote the cause.

From the beginning of his presidency, Roosevelt encouraged legislation aimed at preserving the nation's natural resources. The Newlands Act of 1902, supported by Roosevelt, provided federal aid to irrigation projects in arid states. He also enforced laws against the illegal occupation of public lands. Using the Forest Reserve Act, Roosevelt more than tripled the amount of land previously set aside for national forests.

Roosevelt also enlisted states' aid in the conservation effort. In May 1908 he called abolished the "free pass" that railroads granted to politicians and other influential people such as newspaper editors. It widened the jurisdiction of the Interstate Commerce Commission to include express companies, pipelines, ferries, and sleeping-car companies. Railroad corporations were restrained from operating other businesses. And most important of all, the Interstate Commerce Commission was granted power to fix rates, although its decisions could be appealed to the courts.

After reading Upton Sinclair's 1906 novel, *The Jungle,* Roosevelt urged legislation to address the abuses in the food and meat-packing industries. The Meat Inspection Act of 1906 gave government the right to inspect meats sold in interstate commerce and the right to enforce cleaner conditions in meat-packing plants.

Assessing Roosevelt's Progressive Policies

In spite of Roosevelt's many accomplishments, Congress offered much resistance to his ideas. Legislative achievement under Roosevelt's leadership was so unimpressive that some critics accused Roosevelt of producing "more noise than accomplishment." Often the President could persuade Congress to act only when he had overwhelming public opinion behind him.

In addition, although Roosevelt favored revision of the tariff, he failed to effect a revision, regarding the issue as "political dynamite." He did use the issue to his advantage, however, occasionally threatening to bring it up unless congressional leaders supported other legislative measures. Roosevelt also never seriously supported long-overdue efforts to make the banking system more stable and the currency system more flexible.

Although he accomplished less than he seemed to promise, Roosevelt restored the people's faith in the power of the federal government to serve their interests. Through his Square Deal philosophy, he promoted the idea that the cure for the evils of unrestrained individualism was not socialism but moderate reform.

★ ★ ★ ★ ★ ★ ★ ★ ★ ★ ★ ★ ★ ★ ★ ★ ★ ★

Section One Review

★ ★ ★ ★ ★ ★ ★ ★ ★ ★ ★ ★ ★ ★ ★ ★ ★ ★

SUMMARY

During Theodore Roosevelt's presidency, legislation was passed regulating railroads, supporting union efforts to get higher wages and better working conditions, and reclaiming wilderness land for national forests. Labeled a "trust-buster," Roosevelt was concerned with the regulation of big business and forcing powerful owners to obey the law. Although Roosevelt never exerted strong leadership over Congress, he was very popular with the American people and restored their faith in the power of the federal government to protect their interests. Perhaps his biggest failure as a leader was that he inspired loyalty to himself rather than to his ideals and policies.

CHECKING FOR UNDERSTANDING

1. **Identify** J. Pierpont Morgan, Expedition Act, Forest Reserve Act, Hepburn Act, Square Deal

2. **Describe** how the *Northern Securities* case led to Roosevelt's attempt to regulate trusts.

3. **Explain** why Roosevelt preferred regulation to trust busting.

4. **List** the reasons for and outcome of the 1902 coal strike.

5. **State** how Roosevelt influenced the solution of the 1902 coal strike.

6. **Summarize** Roosevelt's progressive accomplishments.

THINKING CRITICALLY

7. **Understanding Cause and Effect** Analyze how Roosevelt's conservation policies grew out of his love for the American wilderness.

LINKING PAST AND PRESENT

8. **Making Comparisons** Compare current attempts to stop air pollution, clean up oceans, and preserve forests with Roosevelt's conservation efforts.

★ ★ ★ ★ ★ ★ ★ ★ ★ ★ ★ ★ ★ ★ ★ ★ ★ ★

The Taft Presidency

SETTING THE SCENE

I do not know that I have had harder luck than other Presidents, but I do know that thus far I have succeeded far less than have others. I have been conscientiously trying to carry out [Theodore Roosevelt's] policies but my method of doing so has not worked smoothly.

—WILLIAM HOWARD TAFT
President of the United States, 1910

Section Focus

In 1908 Theodore Roosevelt declined to run for reelection, accepting the custom that limited Presidents to two terms. He had enough influence, however, to choose his successor, William Howard Taft. Although Taft was a supporter of Roosevelt's progressive policies, his presidency led not only to a split between him and Roosevelt but also to a division of the Republican party itself.

Objectives

After studying this section, you should be able to:
- Explain the impact of the Payne-Aldrich Tariff.
- Examine the public reaction to the Ballinger-Pinchot controversy.
- Describe the reactions of Roosevelt and the public to Taft's leadership.

Although a distinguished public servant, having served as a federal judge, as governor of the Philippines, and as Roosevelt's secretary of war, Taft was a reluctant President. His true ambition lay in the judicial,

not the executive branch of government. Remarking on the snow, sleet, and rain that pelted the people coming to the inauguration, Taft said with sorrow, "Even the elements do protest."

Taft in Difficulty

Taft began his term as President by addressing the tariff issue, largely ignored during Roosevelt's eight-year tenure. Since passage of the Dingley Tariff of 1897, prices had advanced more rapidly than wages, and many blamed the resulting high cost of living on unduly high tariff rates. Some, including Taft, also believed that high rates encouraged monopoly.

Congress met in March 1909, and within less than a month the House of Representatives passed a measure, introduced by Sereno Payne of New York, that provided for substantial reductions in the tariff without abandoning the principle of protection. Under the leadership of conservative Senator Nelson W. Aldrich of Rhode Island, however, more than 800 amendments were tacked onto the House bill. Many of these amendments were designed to conceal higher rates, such as changing a duty on certain small articles from so much "per hundred-weight" to so much "per hundred."

When Aldrich attempted to railroad the amended bill through the Senate, he was met with resistance in his own party. Several Republican senators, nicknamed the "Insurgents," used their privilege of unlimited debate to reveal the way Aldrich and his allies were carrying out the demands of high-tariff lobbyists instead of the people. Too late, Taft attempted to persuade the Old Guard leaders to reduce the rates, but they made only slight concessions before the bill received Senate approval. By the time the bill reached Taft's desk, the Payne-Aldrich Tariff contained high duties on iron ore, coal, and hides and increases on other materials. The bill however, allowed for a corporation tax, established a tariff commission to make a scientific study of rates, and provided for some flexibility in rates at the discretion of the President. For these reasons, and because he feared a split

Examining Political Cartoons *In this cartoon, a frowning Roosevelt sees that Taft, his chosen successor, has been "dozing" while Square Deal measures in Congress became tied up in knots. Why did Taft dismiss Roosevelt's Chief Forester, Gifford Pinchot?*

between the Old Guard and the Insurgents in his own party, Taft signed the bill, despite its weaknesses.

The public saw Taft's action as a betrayal of his campaign promise. On a speaking tour in the Midwest, Taft argued that the bill fulfilled the Republican platform, adding:

If the country…wishes the manufacturers all over the country to go out of business, and to have cheaper prices at the expense of the sacrifice of many of our manufacturing interests, then it ought to…put the Democratic party in power….

Despite his efforts, there continued to be widespread dissatisfaction with the tariff and with Taft for supporting it.

Another blow was dealt to Taft's popularity when a conflict developed between Taft's Secretary of the Interior, Richard A. Ballinger, and the chief forester, Gifford Pinchot. Ballinger reopened for private purchase certain lands in Montana, Wyoming, and Alaska that had been withdrawn while Roosevelt was President. Pinchot, a well-known conservationist, protested these actions and publicly accused Ballinger of fraud. Taft, convinced of Ballinger's innocence—later confirmed by a congressional investigating committee—dismissed Pinchot for insubordination. But the public viewed Taft's action as a move against the conservation effort begun by Roosevelt, and Taft's popularity plummeted. Even though Ballinger was exonerated of the charges, he eventually resigned his post.

Immediately following the Ballinger-Pinchot controversy came an outbreak of insurgent Republicanism in the House of Representatives, which took the form of an attack on the Old Guard Speaker of the House, Joseph G. "Uncle Joe" Cannon. The speaker had come to enjoy a power over legislation greater in some ways than that of the President. He appointed all committees, he decided what bills should be referred to which committees, and by almost absolute control over debate he could push some measures through without discussion and see that others never reached the floor.

The conservative Cannon used the powers of this office to hold up progressive

Linking Across Time

PRESIDENT TAFT'S POLITICAL HEIRS

In 1990 William H. Taft's great-grandson, Robert A. Taft III, was elected Ohio's secretary of state. By entering politics, Taft III not only followed in his great-grandfather's footsteps but also those of his father, Robert A. Taft, Jr. He had followed his father, Robert A. Taft, into the United States Senate. Like their predecessor William, the three succeeding Tafts have all been Republicans.

legislation. He also cooperated with Aldrich during the tariff debacle in 1909. And Cannon had long been an opponent of conservation.

Finally, in March 1910, a coalition of Democrats and Republican Insurgents forced a change in the rules of the House that stripped the speaker of much of his power. This attack on Cannon hurt Taft, who in order to keep party harmony aligned himself with the speaker. Thus, by signing the Payne-Aldrich Tariff, by supporting Ballinger against Pinchot, and by backing Cannon, Taft gave the impression that he had "sold the Square Deal down the river." Popular indignation was so great that the congressional elections of 1910 resulted in a sweeping Democratic

Examining Photographs *As Speaker of the House of Representatives, Republican Joseph Cannon exercised great influence over his colleagues. Why were his powers reduced?*

victory, with Democrats taking the majority in the House and Democrats and Republican Insurgents wresting control of the Senate from the Old Guard.

Roosevelt Proclaims "New Nationalism"

During his retirement Roosevelt tried hard to maintain faith in the man he had chosen as his successor. But he found public opinion toward Taft had worsened. In spite of Roosevelt's intention to remain out of politics, Taft's disappointing performance as President soon drew Roosevelt back into the political arena.

Roosevelt aligned himself with the insurgents in the Republican party, who had started to call themselves "Progressive Republicans," or simply "Progressives." In a speech at Osawatomie, Kansas, during the congressional election of 1910, Roosevelt spoke of what he called the "New Nationalism." His words reflect the Progressive outlook:

Life of the Times

ELDERLY IN GREENWICH VILLAGE

Although Progressive leaders used the power of government to improve society, not all Americans benefited from reform efforts. Not until the 1920s and 1930s were state and federal pension systems established to meet the needs of aging citizens. Only a few companies had retirement plans. Growing old for many in the early 1900s meant a life of poverty or near-poverty and dependence for many Americans.

The aged poor showed imagination and ingenuity in making ends meet. For example, a survey of elderly residents of New York's Greenwich Village in 1914 showed seventy-four-year-old Mrs. S. working as a janitress in exchange for free rooms and seventy-five-year-old Miss F. subletting one of her three rooms to cover $10.00 of her $16.00 monthly rent. Seventy-year-old Mrs. N. took in sewing and washing.

Even when entirely dependent on charity, many aged people managed to find or create opportunities for recreation. Miss M., financially supported by her church, lived "in proud isolation, scorning her neighbors," and repeated poetry that she learned as a child in Canada. "I used to go to lectures at [the public] school," she said, "but the only lectures they have now are *economical,* and I have enough of that at home, and I don't like it!"

UNIT 7 ENTERING A NEW CENTURY: 1880-1914

> *The man who wrongly holds that every human right is secondary to his profit must now give way to the advocate of human welfare....*

In his New Nationalism speech, Roosevelt outlined a much more radical program of action than he had ever proposed as President. He favored both state and federal legislation to actively promote human welfare, including laws to protect women and children in the labor force and workers' compensation for those injured on the job. Attacking the courts for declaring certain progressive legislation unconstitutional, Roosevelt suggested that state judges be subject to recall and that Supreme Court decisions be reversible by popular vote. By taking such stands, Roosevelt established his position as the natural leader of the Progressive Republicans.

Taft's Successes

Despite Taft's political problems, his administration experienced several successes. Although it was Roosevelt who was nicknamed the "trust buster," Taft actually prosecuted twice as many antitrust cases in four years as his predecessor had in seven. Taft established the Tariff Board to investigate tariff rates, and under his leadership a federal budget began to take shape. Taft also supported the Sixteenth Amendment, giving Congress power to collect **income taxes** or taxes on the income of individuals and companies, and the Seventeenth Amendment, calling for direct election of United States senators. And his administration saw the admittance of New Mexico and Arizona to the United States.

Taft genuinely supported Roosevelt's Square Deal policies, but unlike Roosevelt, who claimed an executive right to do anything not forbidden, Taft's judicial background allowed him to use "only those powers expressly authorized by law." Taft also lacked his predecessor's gift for dramatizing issues and enlisting public support. In the end, however, Taft's administration would be remembered for its failures rather than its achievements.

Section Two Review

SUMMARY

Taft was a reluctant President. Despite his judicial and administrative ability, people viewed Taft's handling of the tariff issue, the Ballinger-Pinchot controversy, and his support for Speaker Cannon as an abandonment of the Square Deal. His low public opinion in 1910 resulted in the election of a Democratic House and an "Insurgent" Republican takeover of the Senate. Dismayed at Taft's leadership, Theodore Roosevelt returned to politics. In a speech in which he outlined the New Nationalism, Roosevelt established himself again as the leader of the progressive Republicans. Despite Taft's problems, his administration experienced several successes.

CHECKING FOR UNDERSTANDING

1. **Identify** Payne-Aldrich Tariff, Richard Ballinger, Joseph Cannon, New Nationalism, "Insurgent" Senators

2. **Define** income taxes

3. **List** the reasons the public thought Taft was destroying the Square Deal.

4. **Explain** Theodore Roosevelt's return to national politics with the New Nationalism program.

5. **Describe** the changes in the Constitution during Taft's administration.

THINKING CRITICALLY

6. **Making Judgments** Analyze how Taft's leadership led to increasing the power and authority of the federal government.

LINKING THE PAST AND PRESENT

7. **Synthesizing Information** Jimmy Carter and William Howard Taft were one-term twentieth century Presidents. Although they were from different parties, how were their administrations similar?

The Election of 1912

A presidential campaign may easily degenerate into a more personal contest and so lose its real dignity. There is no indispensable man.

—WOODROW WILSON
Speech to the Democratic Convention, 1912

Section Focus

With his 1910 New Nationalism speech, Theodore Roosevelt returned to the political arena. As the election of 1912 approached, he remained convinced that Taft was unfit for another term as President. Despite his no-third-term pledge of 1904, it was not in Roosevelt's nature to sit on the sidelines. Thus the great question in American politics as the campaign began was whether Roosevelt would run again for the presidency.

Objectives

After studying this section, you should be able to:
• Relate the events that led to the formation of the Progressive party.
• Explain how a split in the Republican party helped lead to Woodrow Wilson's election in 1912.

Senator Robert La Follette, a man of great ability and a leader of the recently formed National Progressive Republican League, had the support of many Progressive Republicans for the 1912 presidential nomination. When La Follette suffered a temporary nervous collapse, however, Progressives turned to Roosevelt. Explaining that his no-third-

term pledge referred to a third *consecutive* term, Roosevelt declared himself a candidate against Taft for the Republican nomination. Now began a heated, emotional battle for control of the Republican party.

Roosevelt Challenges Taft

The struggle for control of the Republican party reached its climax at the national convention in June. Conservatives rallied behind Taft, as did many former supporters of the Square Deal who thought Roosevelt too radical or who disliked his running for a third term. Except for some devoted followers of La Follette, the Progressive Republicans lined up for Roosevelt.

The Taft forces, however, had the immense advantage of controlling the party machinery. Of 254 convention seats disputed by Taft and Roosevelt, the convention's Credentials Committee gave 235 to Taft. When Taft received the nomination on the first ballot, Roosevelt charged the Republican party leaders with stealing the nomination. He stood ready, he said, to carry on the battle for progressive principles outside the party.

Progressive Party Forms

In August a convention met in Chicago to found a new political party—the Progressive party. The delegates were a curious mixture—college professors, social

Examining Political Cartoons *Contemplative American voters must judge which "pumpkin" would be best for their country. Who are the 1912 presidential candidates?*

workers, newspaper editors, former Rough Riders, wealthy people motivated by social conscience, and some professional politicians. Senator Albert J. Beveridge, who had followed Roosevelt out of the Republican party, called on the new party to work for a nobler America.

The Progressives, said Beveridge, stood for "social brotherhood" as opposed to "savage individualism," for a "representative government that represents the people," as opposed to invisible government controlled by corrupt bosses and the "robber interest."

Examining Photographs *In contrast with Roosevelt or Taft, Woodrow Wilson was relatively new to politics when he received the Democratic nomination in 1912. In speeches he was able to impress listeners with his sincerity and eloquence. What was Wilson's political background?*

The Progressive platform demanded reforms such as a more direct democracy through such means as the initiative and referendum, for conservation of natural resources for the general welfare, for woman suffrage, and for labor reforms such as the prohibition of child labor and "minimum wage standards for working women...and the establishment of an eight-hour day for women and young persons...." In addition, Progressives called for revision of the currency system and the introduction of an inheritance tax.

The party nominated Theodore Roosevelt for the presidency and immediately acquired a party symbol when the former President announced that he felt "as strong as a bull moose." But the Bull Moose party would not succeed in its bid to put Roosevelt back into the presidency. All that Roosevelt accomplished by bolting from the Republican party was to give control of it to the Old Guard, thus ensuring the election of a Democratic President.

Woodrow Wilson and the New Freedom

When the Democratic convention met at Baltimore in June 1912, there was discord between the progressive wing, to which William Jennings Bryan belonged, and the conservative wing, whose delegates represented city political machines. Although disclaiming any desire for a fourth nomination, Bryan was influential in seeing that the Democratic platform was as progressive as that of the Bull Moose party itself. After a protracted struggle, Woodrow Wilson, who had won national fame as a reform governor of New Jersey, received the nomination on the 46th ballot, partly through the help of Bryan.

In the ensuing campaign Taft was not active, privately expressing the opinion that Wilson was sure to win. The real battle took place between Roosevelt and Wilson. Both men supported progressivism, although under different labels. Wilson countered Roosevelt's New Nationalism with what he called the "New Freedom." Although there appeared to be little distinction between the philosophies of the two candidates, they did in fact differ. Roosevelt's New Nationalism accepted big business as a fact of life and proposed a more powerful federal government and a strong executive to keep it under control. Wilson's New Freedom viewed monopolies as absolute evils, the antithesis of free competition. He also advocated the use of federal power to insure more equality of opportunity.

The contrast between Wilson and Roosevelt was striking. Roosevelt had long been the best known political figure in the country. Wilson, a former university president and college professor, had been active in politics for only three years. Roosevelt, the former Rough Rider, was thought of by the public as a fighter in a war on privilege. While Roosevelt enjoyed mixing with all sorts of people, Wilson was aloof. Although Wilson lacked his rival's magnetism, he was a persuasive speaker, and he knew how to touch people's conscience and appeal to their reason.

The results of the election fulfilled Taft's prediction of victory for Wilson. Although he won the presidency, Wilson actually had fewer popular votes than Roosevelt and Taft combined. But because of the split in the Republican vote—and also a surprisingly strong Socialist party vote—Wilson carried 40 of the 48 states, with a total of 435 electoral votes; his opponents together received only 96. So, for the first time since Grover Cleveland's election in 1892, a Democrat became President of the United States.

★ ★ ★ ★ ★ ★ ★ ★ ★ ★ ★ ★ ★ ★ ★ ★ ★ ★

Section Three Review

★ ★ ★ ★ ★ ★ ★ ★ ★ ★ ★ ★ ★ ★ ★ ★ ★ ★

SUMMARY

During the presidential election of 1912, the Republican party was divided between progressives and Old Guards. Taft's nomination by the Republican convention prompted Theodore Roosevelt to help form the Progressive party. Based on human-welfare principles, this new national party attracted reformers, educators, literary figures, and philanthropists. Their platform was similar to that of the Democrats and the election became a battle between Theodore Roosevelt's New Nationalism and Woodrow Wilson's New Freedom. With the Republican vote split between Taft and Roosevelt, Wilson won the election.

CHECKING FOR UNDERSTANDING

1. **Identify** Bull Moose party, New Freedom

2. **Explain** why Roosevelt left the Republicans and helped form the Progressive party.

3. **List** Progressive party ideals.

4. **Describe** the Progressive party platform.

5. **Summarize** the popular and electoral votes in the 1912 election.

THINKING CRITICALLY

6. **Recognizing Stereotypes** Analyze whether supporters of the Progressive party were radical reformers or dreamers.

GLOBAL PERSPECTIVES

7. **Drawing Conclusions** While Roosevelt and Wilson campaigned for human welfare, there were widespread strikes in Great Britain; Lenin planned a communist revolution in Russia; and Sun Yat-sen worked in China for reforms in commerce and industry, agriculture, and education. What connection do you see among these events?

★ ★ ★ ★ ★ ★ ★ ★ ★ ★ ★ ★ ★ ★ ★ ★ ★ ★

Map and Graph Skills

Supporting Generalizations

You tell a transfer student that all the students in a particular physical education class are in above-average condition. You have made a generalization. When the transfer student asks how you can make that claim, you reply that each student in that class has to pass a rigorous stamina test. You have supported your generalization.

Explanation

A generalization is a statement that offers a general characteristic rather than a specific one. Your statement about the physical condition of the students was a general characteristic of a particular physical education class.

In order to support it, you could have shown the transfer student results of the stamina test indicating which students were allowed to take the physical education class. This would have supported your generalization. In this case, a generalization can be recognized as a fact.

Sometimes when making a point or offering an interpretation, an author may make a generalization and then give supporting statements. At other times, however, you may be given only a generalization without supporting statements, or supporting statements without a generalization. In such cases you will need to use your understanding of the content and thought processes to supply what's missing—either the generalization or the supporting statement.

As a historian, it is important to back up generalizations with supporting statements or evidence. Here are guidelines for making supporting statements.

- They must relate directly to the generalization.

- They must be logical.

- They must be based on fact.

THE ELECTION OF 1912

	Popular Vote	Electoral Vote
Wilson	6,296,547	435
Roosevelt	4,118,571	88
Taft	3,486,720	8

Example

Study the map of the election of 1912, noting how the two guidelines have been applied to the following generalizations:

- The southern states had a great influence on the election of the Democratic candidate, Woodrow Wilson.
Supporting statement:
The election map shows that all electoral votes from the southern states went to Woodrow Wilson. *(This statement relates directly to the generalization, is logical, and is based on fact.)*

- The citizens who voted preferred Woodrow Wilson.
Supporting statement:
Woodrow Wilson won the election of 1912. *(This statement relates directly to the generalization and is logical, but it is not based on fact. The majority of citizens who voted did not vote for Wilson.)*

- The western states did not support any one candidate.
Supporting statement:
California, Nevada, and Utah each gave their electoral votes to a different candidate. *(This statement relates directly to the generalization, is logical, and is supported by fact.)*

Practice

For further practice in supporting generalizations, write a supporting statement for the following generalizations. Use information you have learned from this chapter.

1. Theodore Roosevelt, although popular with the public, had difficulty getting "Square Deal" measures through Congress.

2. William Howard Taft continued Roosevelt's reform program, but the public lost confidence in his presidential leadership.

President Wilson's Progressivism

SETTING THE SCENE

There has been something crude and heartless and unfeeling in our haste to succeed and be great....There can be no equality of opportunity... if men and women and children are not shielded...from the consequences of great industrial and social processes....

—WOODROW WILSON
First Inaugural Address, 1913

Section Focus

Before becoming President, Woodrow Wilson had held only one political office, as governor of New Jersey from 1910 to 1912. In those two years, however, he had successfully worked for an elaborate program of progressive laws. Wilson began his first presidential term determined to obtain major social reform at the federal level.

Objectives

After studying this section, you should be able to:
- Explain why Wilson had congressional support for his programs.
- List the accomplishments of Wilson's domestic program, including legislation on tariffs and on trusts.

T he new President entered office with several handicaps. He was a minority President, chosen by only 42 percent of the voters. With no experience in national politics, he knew few Democratic party leaders. In addition, the Democratic party at the time was comprised of a loose alliance of local interests not expected to work well together. Long out of office, the Democrats lacked people with experience in government at the federal level.

Wilson and Congress

Although inexperienced in national politics, Wilson enjoyed certain advantages upon entering office. The 1912 election results sent Congress a clear message that most Americans demanded progressive legislation. If the Democrats did not support the President in the creation of this legislation, warned a member of Congress, they would be "turned into the wilderness for 40 years more." However, no prominent Democratic leaders opposed Wilson, as Republicans Cannon and Aldrich had thwarted Taft. On the contrary, Wilson enjoyed the loyal support of most Democrats—including Bryan, the most influential man in the party, whom Wilson appointed secretary of state.

In his first inaugural address, Wilson stated his goals—not, he said, Democratic or Republican goals but goals for all the nation. After calling for reform of tariffs and banking, equality of business opportunity, improvements in agriculture, and conservation of natural resources, he concluded:

This is not a day of triumph. It is a day of dedication. Here muster not the forces of party, but the forces of humanity....I summon all honest men, all patriotic, all forward-looking men to my side. God helping me, I will not fail them, if they will but counsel and sustain me!

Examining Photographs *After receiving the Republican nomination, Taft did not campaign hard, leaving the main contest between Roosevelt and Wilson. President-elect Wilson and Taft are shown here on inauguration day, 1913. What goals did Wilson set forth in his inaugural address?*

The Underwood Tariff

The President lost no time in embarking on his program of reform. Like Taft, Wilson at once called Congress into special session. Appearing in person before Congress—the first President to do so in 100 years—he delivered a special message on the tariff. This short speech made headlines nationwide and illustrated Wilson's long-standing belief that the President's greatest power lay in focusing public attention on important issues.

Wilson's message charged that high tariffs had:

...built up a set of privileges and exemptions from competition behind which it was easy...to organize monopoly; until...nothing is obliged to stand the tests of efficiency and economy....

Lower rates, he claimed, would help businesses by putting them under "constant necessity to be efficient, economical,

and enterprising...." Opening the American market to foreign products would at the same time open foreign markets to American goods. Wilson warned, however, against undue haste, making it clear that he did not favor removing protective duties entirely.

The House of Representatives soon passed a bill, sponsored by Alabama Representative Oscar W. Underwood, embodying the President's recommendations. The real fight occurred in the Senate, where previous attempts to lower the tariff had foundered, and where the Democrats had only a six-vote majority. Lobbyists swarmed to Washington, pressuring senators to alter the bill. But before senatorial opposition could crystallize, Wilson again appealed to the people. He denounced the "insidious" lobbyists and asked an aroused public to insist that Congress put an end to "this unbearable situation." The President then held personal conferences with Democratic senators and wrote letters to those threatening to oppose him. Under such varied and unrelenting pressure from the executive office, the Senate voted to accept the House bill with little change.

The Underwood Tariff Act represented the first substantial drop in import duties since 1857. It attempted to fix duties at a level where costs of production in the United States and abroad would be equalized, thus lowering the duty paid on almost 1,000 articles. It removed protection entirely from industries that already competed successfully with foreign producers.

A most important section of the Underwood Tariff Act was the provision for levying an income tax, now legalized by the Sixteenth Amendment. Originally introduced merely to make up for losses in revenue created by lower tariffs, the income tax became the federal government's chief source of revenue in a very short time.

The Federal Reserve Act

As the tariff debate reached a crescendo, Wilson appeared before Congress to introduce the second major item in his reform program: a revision of the banking and currency system. The purpose of the revision was to provide businesses with cheaper and more available credit. Like the tariff message, Wilson's speech was so brief that many influential newspapers published the entire text.

In 1907 a sharp panic had revealed serious weaknesses in the American banking and currency system. There were runs on banks, many of which closed or stopped lending as a result. In 1908 Congress set up the National Monetary Commission, headed by conservative Senator Aldrich, to investigate the situation and propose change. After four years of study, the Aldrich Commission reported that the financial organization of the United States was flawed in four respects.

First, American banking lacked stability in times of crisis. Banks did not keep enough money on reserve to cover sudden withdrawals, and there was not enough cooperation between banks.

Second, America's currency was inflexible. The amount of money in circulation was based on the amount of gold and silver in the treasury, plus the bonds held by the national banks. The present system provided no way to increase or decrease the supply of money according to the investment needs of the country.

Third, there was no central control of banking practices. In other modern, industrialized countries, central banks, such as the Bank of England and the Bank of France, directed banking policy. Nothing similar had existed in this nation since Andrew Jackson had destroyed the second Bank of the United States.

Finally, the commission found that too much bank capital was concentrated in New York City and on Wall Street. Meanwhile, other parts of the country, especially isolated rural districts, often suffered from a lack of adequate banking facilities and credit.

Although few questioned the list of ills in the banking and currency system, government leaders disputed the cure. Bankers favored a great central bank, privately controlled, like the first and second Banks of the United States. But many progressives, especially Bryan, called for strict federal control of banking and credit. It was Wilson's difficult task to select a plan that would work and at the same time win support from both bankers and Bryan's followers.

Examining Graphs *Tariff duties on imports had been high throughout the second half of the nineteenth century, up through the Taft administration. Tariffs were favored by business because they limited competition from foreign-made goods. Looking at the duties collected, why was there a sharp reduction in the percentage of the total value of imports between 1910 and 1915?*

U.S. IMPORTS AND TARIFF DUTIES, 1880–1920

	VALUE OF IMPORTS (Millions of dollars)			DUTIES COLLECTED	
Year	Total	Free	Dutiable	(Millions of dollars)	(Percent of total value of imports)
1880	$ 628	$ 208	$ 420	$ 183	29.1%
1885	$ 579	$ 192	$ 387	$ 178	30.8%
1890	$ 766	$ 258	$ 508	$ 227	29.6%
1895	$ 731	$ 377	$ 354	$ 149	20.4%
1900	$ 831	$ 367	$ 464	$ 229	27.6%
1905	$1,087	$ 517	$ 570	$ 258	23.8%
1910	$1,547	$ 761	$ 786	$ 327	21.1%
1915	$1,648	$1,033	$ 616	$ 206	12.5%
1920	$5,102	$3,116	$1,986	$ 326	6.4%

Historical Statistics of the United States: Colonial Times to 1970

The plan Wilson finally chose was called the Federal Reserve Act. Again, under constant pressure from the President, Congress finally passed the law in December 1913. The Federal Reserve Act promptly became one of the most important and useful pieces of legislation in United States history.

The new system provided for 12 Federal Reserve Banks situated throughout the country. All national banks were required to join them, and other banks could join if they wished. The Federal Reserve did not deal directly with individuals but instead serviced member banks. These "banks for bankers" concentrated reserves, so they could provide support to individual banks in times of temporary difficulty such as a "run." They also provided for local investment needs and made it easier to move funds from one part of the country to another.

The Federal Reserve Act provided a compromise between private and public control. The Federal Reserve Banks themselves were privately owned, a majority of their directors being elected by the member banks. Overall control of the Federal Reserve Banks, however, remained in the hands of a Federal Reserve Board, whose seven members were appointed by the President, subject to approval by the Senate, for 14-year terms. Thus the center of the nation's financial power moved from Wall Street to Washington, D.C.

Before passage of the Federal Reserve Act, local banks frequently lacked funds to make sound loans to businesspeople and farmers. For want of adequate funds, stores and factories closed, and crops rotted. The Federal Reserve Act greatly

Examining Maps *The Federal Reserve System divided the nation into 12 districts, each served a single "bank for bankers." This arrangement made the country's bank system more responsive to local need and less dominated by financial brokers on Wall Street. By what criteria do you think the 12 districts and the Federal Reserve Bank cities were chosen?*

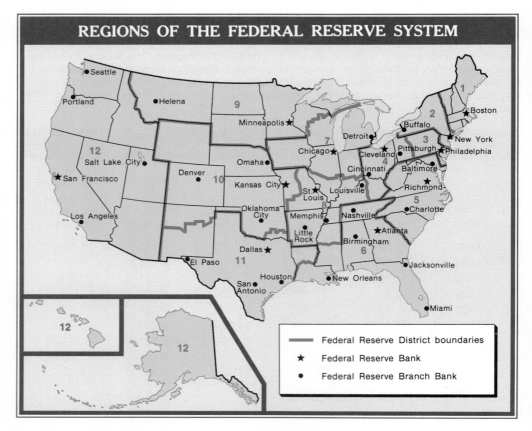

REGIONS OF THE FEDERAL RESERVE SYSTEM

Federal Reserve District boundaries
★ Federal Reserve Bank
● Federal Reserve Branch Bank

Examining Photographs *The Tuskegee Institute in Alabama offered educational opportunities in trade skills and professions for African Americans. Most Progressives, however, believed in segregating the races and were blind to the need for black advancement. Why did black leaders, such as Booker T. Washington and W.E.B. Du Bois, repudiate Wilson after 1912?*

Linking Across Time

THE FEDERAL RESERVE SYSTEM

When the Federal Reserve System, or Fed, was established in 1913, its powers were more limited than today. In its early days, the Fed served as the nation's central bank. It cleared the checks of member banks and regulated banking activities. Since the United States went off the gold standard in 1933, the Fed has served as watchdog over the nation's money supply. By controlling the supply of money the Fed seeks to keep the economy from expanding too fast, or slipping into a recession.

improved this situation by providing for a new form of "flexible" currency known as Federal Reserve notes. The new money went into circulation when local banks needing cash brought businesspeople's promissory notes to Federal Reserve Banks. In return, the Federal Reserve Bank issued Federal Reserve notes, assessing the member bank a small fee called a **rediscount.** When a Federal Reserve Bank bought promissory notes, it could print and issue more paper money, using those notes as part of the security, or collateral, thereby protecting the value of the currency. Then, when the notes were paid and the money came back to the Bank, the currency was retired.

The Federal Reserve Banks also controlled the amount of money in circulation by raising or lowering the rediscount rate, or the rate at which they charged for rediscounting. Raising the rate discouraged banks from lending and so "contracted" the currency; lowering the rate encouraged lending and "expanded" the currency. Thus currency and credit in any

Federal Reserve district expanded or contracted according to the economic needs of that region.

On the whole, the Federal Reserve Act made the banking system responsive to the needs of a great industrial nation. It succeeded in its first great test, during World War I, when it assisted industrial expansion and helped the federal government finance the war effort.

Wilson Regulates Trusts

Shortly after signing the Federal Reserve Act, Wilson asked Congress to pass an antitrust law more effective than the Sherman Antitrust Act. Denying any desire to interfere with legitimate business activities, his message to Congress proposed various methods of preventing the "indefensible and intolerable" abuses of private monopoly.

Late in 1914, Congress responded to Wilson's requests by passing two laws. The first, the Federal Trade Commission Act, established a Federal Trade Commission to investigate and regulate business practices. The commission had power to order companies to "cease and desist" from unfair conduct. In actual practice, though, Wilson's appointees to the commission failed to take strong actions against trusts.

In October 1914, less than a month after passage of the Federal Trade Commission Act, Congress passed the Clayton Antitrust Act. This act forbade several practices that destroyed competition or prevented new businesses from being developed. These practices included: ruinous **price-cutting,** whereby a large company deliberately sold goods at a loss to drive weaker competitors out of business; "tying" of contracts, whereby a purchaser of goods from a particular company had to agree not to trade with its competitors; intercorporate investment, whereby a company bought part ownership in a rival concern; **"interlocking" directorates** between large corporations and banks, whereby the same people acted as directors in many different companies.

The Clayton Act also contained two sections favorable to trade unions. As noted earlier, the Sherman Act, by forbidding conspiracies, had proven more effective against labor unions than against business monopolies. To discourage such use of antitrust laws, the Clayton Act stated that "nothing in the antitrust laws shall be construed to forbid the existence and operation of labor...organizations."

In addition, ever since the jailing of Eugene V. Debs for contempt of court in the 1894 Pullman strike, labor unions had protested the use of court injunctions forbidding strikes and boycotts. The Clayton Act forbade federal courts to issue injunctions against peaceful strikes, picketing, boycotts, or union meetings.

The Clayton Antitrust Act lost most of its effectiveness because of loose wording and unfavorable interpretations by the federal courts. The protection of labor unions from suits under the Sherman Act was limited to unions pursuing their "legitimate" purposes—and it was the courts that defined the word *legitimate*. Injunctions might still be issued when "necessary to prevent irreparable damage to property or to a property right," which again left a large loophole for conservative judges.

W.E.B. DU BOIS
1868-1963

The first African American to receive a Harvard Ph.D., W.E.B. Du Bois was a distinguished educator who refused to accept racial inequality. Du Bois initiated the Niagara Movement in 1905 to fight against racial discrimination against black Americans in the United States.

For 24 years, Du Bois served as editor of the NAACP's journal, *Crisis,* using it as a tool to assert demands for racial justice and equality. Between 1910 and 1930, his influence shaped not only the NAACP but a generation of black intellectuals and activists. In 1919 he organized the first Pan-African Congress, which promoted the idea that all people of African descent throughout the world should work together to combat discrimination. *Pan-Africanism* is still strong today among nations in Africa, where Du Bois moved in 1961.

Other Accomplishments of Wilson

The Clayton Act completed the legislative program that Wilson had originally promoted. But Wilson did not stop there. Additional legislation passed during his first term included the establishment of 12 regional Federal Farm Loan Banks, endowed with public funds in order to provide loans for agriculture. A Federal

Highways Act, designed to help farmers get their produce to market, allotted federal funds to states for road construction and development. Wilson also supported the Keating-Owen Child Labor Act, which prohibited the employment of children under age 14 in factories producing goods for interstate commerce. The Adamson Act, passed under threat of a nationwide tie-up in transportation, established an eight-hour day for railroad workers.

Under Wilson's directed eye, so much constructive legislation had been passed so quickly. Wilson supplied a skillful and dynamic leadership, sometimes keeping Congress in session throughout the hot summer months. Chauncey Depew, a noted conservative Republican, said that for a man regarded as a mere theorist, Wilson had accomplished "the most astonishing practical results."

The reforms Wilson achieved did not have "practical results" for black Americans, however, as the President brought Jim Crow to Washington. The nation's capital had been desegregated since Reconstruction, but Wilson, a native Virginian, strongly believed in separating the races. Therefore his administration segregated drinking fountains, rest rooms, and lunch counters in government office buildings and assigned jobs according to race. A number of prominent black leaders like W.E.B. Du Bois, who had supported Wilson in 1912, turned against him. Black newspaper editor William Monroe Trotter blamed Wilson's New Freedom for a "new slavery for your Afro-American fellow citizens." Yet the President merely reflected the racial blindness of many other progressive reformers.

Wilson's efforts during the beginning of his first term focused almost exclusively on domestic matters. In fact, foreign affairs did not even receive mention in his first inaugural address. But by the end of his term, world events overshadowed these domestic achievements, and soon Wilson's role as architect and promoter of progressive legislation was all but forgotten. It was obscured by growing tensions in foreign affairs that resulted in tragedy for him and for the world.

Section Four Review

SUMMARY

The election of Woodrow Wilson brought in new reform legislation that focused on curbing anti-competition practices of big business, improving working conditions, helping farmers, lowering the tariff, and revising the bank and currency systems. Wilson's exercise of federal intervention and regulation was a blend of early Federalist and Democratic ideals—respect for the rights of the common people through federal control. The Underwood Tariff was the first significant drop in import duties since 1857. Wilson's domestic programs were enormously popular, and he put the country on a sound financial footing.

CHECKING FOR UNDERSTANDING

1. **Identify** Underwood Tariff, Federal Reserve Board, Federal Trade Commission, Clayton Antitrust Act

2. **Define** interlocking directorate

3. **Explain** how the Federal Reserve System works.

4. **Describe** the provisions of the Clayton Antitrust Act that limited the power of monopolies.

5. **Show** how the Keating-Owen Child Act and the Adamson Act improved the condition of American labor.

THINKING CRITICALLY

6. **Making Judgments** Evaluate the effect of Wilson's antitrust legislation and the creation of the Federal Reserve System on the economy of the nation.

CONNECTIONS: HISTORY AND ECONOMICS

7. **Identifying Central Issues** Compare the economic programs of Wilson and Alexander Hamilton. How did Wilson draw on Hamilton even though Hamilton acted in the interests of business and Wilson was opposed to many big-business practices?

★ Summary

Theodore Roosevelt, William H. Taft, and Woodrow Wilson were reform Presidents. They sought to improve the welfare of the average American citizen, regulate big-business practices, and conserve the nation's natural resources. Roosevelt and Taft worked within the framework of the Republican party, which recognized the need for big business but sought federal controls. Wilson, a Democrat, believed monopolies were inherently wrong and wanted to eliminate them.

Roosevelt's greatest achievement lay in the area of conservation. During Taft's presidency the Constitution was strengthened with passage of the 16th Amendment (providing for an income tax) and the 17th Amendment (allowing direct election of senators). Taft had been Roosevelt's chosen successor but political difficulties caused many progressives to turn against him. Roosevelt, after a brief retirement, decided to reenter national politics. When he failed to win the Republican nomination in 1912, he helped form the Progressive party. The election quickly became a contest between Roosevelt and the Democratic nominee, Woodrow Wilson. With the Republican vote split, Wilson won. Wilson was most successful in achieving a progressive legislative program. He implemented a reform of banking and currency practices, secured passage of a labor reform bill, brought about tariff reduction, and engineered legislation regulating trusts.

★ Using Vocabulary

Write a paragraph describing Wilson's New Freedom program using the following terms:

progressivism	**labor**
antitrust	**monopolies**
free competition	**income tax**

★ Reviewing Facts

1. **Describe** the progressive beliefs of Theodore Roosevelt.
2. **Identify** the sources of support for Roosevelt's Square Deal and New Nationalism.
3. **Explain** the failure of William Howard Taft as an administrator.

4. **Cite** two important achievements of William Howard Taft's administration.
5. **Compare** the progressivism of Woodrow Wilson and Theodore Roosevelt based on their respective programs.
6. **Explain** how Woodrow Wilson won the presidential election of 1912.
7. **Tell** how Wilson was able to get his progressive program through Congress.
8. **Describe** the improvements in labor brought about by the Keating-Owen Child Labor Act and the Adamson Act.
9. **State** the reason for including an income tax provision in the Underwood Tariff bill.

★ Understanding Concepts

INTERESTS AND POSITIONS

1. Describe the conflicting interests in the Coal Strike of 1902. How was the conflict resolved?
2. Show how Taft's policies seemed to go against the Roosevelt's Square Deal.

ECONOMIC COMPETITION

3. In what way did big-business practices in the early 1900s inhibit economic competition?
4. How does economic competition operate in the best interests of the consumer?

★ Thinking Critically

1. **Linking Past and Present** Compare Theodore Roosevelt's approach to conservation of natural resources with those of Ronald Reagan and George Bush.
2. **Recognizing Stereotypes** How does the stereotype of the Republican party in the 1990s—big business bias, state responsibility for welfare programs, strong defense—apply to Theodore Roosevelt and William H. Taft?
3. **Understanding Cause and Effect** Analyze the change in the American banking policy that brought about the Federal Reserve System.
4. **Making Judgments** Evaluate Taft's performance as President as seen by the public and by his legislative record.

★ Chapter 24 Review ★

★ Writing About History

ARGUMENTATION

Refer to the description of how to write an argumentation essay in the History Writer's Handbook in the Appendix of this book. Your teacher will give you more specific instructions on the length of the examples and the assignment's due date.

Imagine you are a campaign manager for Theodore Roosevelt, William Howard Taft, and Woodrow Wilson during the election of 1912. From your knowledge of American history and the presidential elections of 1900, 1904, and 1908, you are aware that speeches and campaign slogans are excellent ways to communicate the views of candidates. Write a campaign speech with slogans for Roosevelt, Taft, and Wilson that reflect the views of each and their party.

★ Learning Cooperatively

Organize the class into three debate groups. Each group will then choose one of the following three topics:

(1) the Ballinger/Pinchot controversy over protecting wilderness areas

(2) the Payne/Aldrich debate over protective tariffs

(3) the mine workers/mine owners dispute in the Coal Strike of 1902

You will work within your group to research and prepare arguments on both sides of the issue. Conduct the class debates when each group has completed their preparation.

★ Mastering Skills

RECOGNIZING PROPAGANDA

Many people think propaganda is an activity of dishonest persons who seek to persuade others for a selfish purpose. But propaganda can be used in both positive and negative ways. Nearly everyone—advertisers, editors, entertainers, teachers, political leaders, preachers, parents, friends—and even yourself—uses propaganda to influence the opinions of others.

Propaganda is a persuasion tactic used to influence people to believe certain ideas, or to follow certain courses of action. It does this by linking an idea with a common symbol that elicits a powerful emotion or attitude. To determine whether or not a statement contains propaganda, apply these guidelines:

- Is the purpose of the message to persuade? If so, state the purpose.

- Does it use a tactic such as name calling, speaking in generalities, testimonials, card stacking (listing only the good facts), transferring a reputation, urging others to hop on the band wagon, and/or appearing to belong to the common people? If so, identify the tactic.

- Does it associate its idea to symbols that many people feel strongly about? Such symbols can be positive ones that refer to patriotism, beauty, justice, health, security, education, or negative ones such as prejudice, murder, hatred, or greed. If so, list the symbols and tell what powerful emotions or attitudes they elicit.

Example These guidelines may be used to determine whether or not the following statement by President Theodore Roosevelt contains propaganda:

A man who is good enough to shed his blood for his country is good enough to be given a square deal afterward. More than that no man is entitled to, and less than that no man should have.

- The purpose of this statement is to persuade the public to look favorably on Roosevelt's progressive ideas.

- It uses a tactic of transferring the positive reputation of a soldier ("good enough to shed his blood") to the common citizen.

- Soldiers serve as a symbol that elicits feelings of respect and admiration for those who risk their lives for their country. The phrase "square deal" symbolizes an attitude of justice.

Practice Read the following statements which reflect ideas of President Roosevelt, and apply the three steps listed above:

1. The great corporations known as trusts are like wolves gobbling up the wealth of the nation and keeping the common people in a state not much different from slaves.

2. I would rather retire from public office and enjoy a hunting trip to Africa than run for a third term.

3. During the holidays I will enjoy a camping trip to the wilderness areas of Wyoming. These scenic lands must be set aside as natural resources to preserve the country's heritage for future generations.

★ ★ ★ Unit 7 Digest ★ ★ ★

The United States had changed greatly during the late 1800s. At the start of the twentieth century, the nation felt strong and confident. Its people sought to expand their borders and to solve their pressing domestic problems.

Chapter 22
Imperialism

In the last decades of the nineteenth century, Americans reassessed and abandoned their traditional isolationist policy. Following the Civil War, Alaska was purchased and a show of American force prompted the French to leave Mexico. Because of growing industrial power, trade and contacts with Latin America also increased. In the Pacific, American interest in Hawaii led to its annexation in 1898. Controversies developed with Britain over shipping loss claims dating from the Civil War and the Venezuela-British Guiana boundary. Both issues were resolved peacefully.

In 1898 the United States went to war, not with Britain but with Spain. Americans sympathized with an independence movement in Cuba seeking to overthrow Spanish control. Yellow Journalism created a reading public that welcomed intervention. Thus when the *Maine*—an American battleship anchored in Havana's harbor—exploded, the United States declared war on Spain. The Spanish American War was over in six months.

As a result of the war, the United States gained a colonial empire and with it the challenge of governing overseas territories—Puerto Rico, Guam, and the Philippines. In the Philippines, several years were spent suppressing a nationalist uprising. Questions soon arose over whether native people living in colonial possessions were entitled to the same civil rights as American citizens. Eventually the Supreme Court of the United States ruled that the Constitution did not cover overseas possessions.

As the United States expanded into the Pacific, Americans were anxious to renew trade opportunities with the Chinese. To protect any potential trade between the two countries, Secretary of State John Hay asked the Chinese in 1899 to grant an "open door" trade policy. This accomplished little but it popularized American expansionist aims in China. United States soldiers also helped rescue foreign diplomats from China during the Boxer Rebellion in 1899, and Secretary Hay worked to prevent full-scale retaliation against China for encouraging the rebellion.

President Theodore Roosevelt strengthened American involvement in world affairs. He defended Venezuela from possible European aggression and he issued the Roosevelt Corollary, a statement that attempted to justify United States intervention in Latin America. In addition, Roosevelt negotiated an end to the Russo-Japanese War. Perhaps most important, Roosevelt allowed American warships to prevent Colombia from putting down an insurrection in Panama City. This action allowed Panamanians to establish the Republic of Panama. Roosevelt quickly negotiated a treaty for the rights to build a canal across Panama.

Chapter 23
The Progressive Era

On the domestic front, urbanization and immigration contributed to the spread of slums and to the exploitation of workers. Progressive reformers sought to remedy these conditions. Progressives included academics, religious leaders, and writers known as muckrakers.

Progressive political reforms on the national level included women's suffrage and the direct election of senators. Progressive accomplishments in state and local politics were even more impressive. They included the direct primary, in which voters choose candidates directly; and the initiative, referendum, and recall, which gave voters a direct voice in legislation and the power to remove an elected official. Other state successes were corrupt-practice laws that regulated campaign spending, and the commission and city-manager systems of city government.

Many progressive reforms sought to improve human welfare. These included laws prohibiting child labor, worker's compensation insurance, the regulation of public utilities, and tax reform. Laws were also passed protecting consumers from tainted foods, mislabeled products, and substandard housing. In addition, the progressive spirit in local government helped to bring about health clinics, new playgrounds, and public recreation areas. The Boy Scouts, Girl Scouts, and Campfire Girls were organized to provide wholesome activites for youth.

But Progressive reform also had limits. For example, Progressives were satisfied with the regulation of capitalism. Socialists such as Eugene V. Debs, however, were outspoken in their efforts to modify or replace capitalism. Many Progressives were also critical of the flood of new immigrants from southern and eastern Europe. There were calls for restrictions on immigration and a 1917 law required all immigrants pass a literacy test.

Progressives also generally ignored the problems of African Americans. Increasingly, blacks found themselves legally segregated and denied their full civil rights. But many blacks refused to settle for an inferior position in society. As a result, black leadership shifted. Conservative Booker T. Washington was succeeded by W.E.B. Du Bois.

Chapter 24
White House Reformers

Roosevelt supported the progressive movement with his domestic goal to give everyone a "square deal." He soon became known as a "trust buster" because he broke up trusts such as the U.S. Steel Corporation and the National Securities Company. Roosevelt also helped settle the coal strike of 1902, in which Americans sympathized with the poorly treated miners. Furthermore, Roosevelt supported stricter railroad regulation by strengthening the Interstate Commerce Commission. Conservation was another of Roosevelt's major concerns. He tripled the amount of land set aside for national forests.

William Howard Taft was Roosevelt's chosen successor as President. He prosecuted twice as many trusts in four years as Roosevelt had in seven. Taft also created the Tariff Board to investigate duties. He supported the Sixteenth Amendment, giving Congress power to collect income taxes, and the Seventeenth Amendment, calling for the direct election of senators.

Yet Taft lost popularity when he raised tariff rates by signing the Payne-Aldrich Tariff; sided with Secretary of the Interior Ballenger against chief forester Pinchot; and backed conservative House Speaker Joseph Cannon in a leadership struggle within the House. Americans thought Taft had abandoned the "square deal." Roosevelt, fearful that progressive reforms would be lost, returned to politics.

In 1912 Roosevelt lost the Republican nomination to Taft, but he then formed the Progressive party and ran as their candidate. His "new nationalism" proposed a more powerful federal government and a strong executive. Roosevelt also accepted big business as a fact of life. Democrat Woodrow Wilson's "new freedom," on the other hand, viewed monopolies as absolute evils. Republicans split their votes between Taft and Roosevelt, allowing Wilson to win the election.

One of Wilson's first acts as President was to help pass the Underwood Tariff Act, which lowered import duties and introduced a federal income tax. Wilson also pushed through the Federal Reserve Act, which overhauled the nation's banking and currency system. In addition, he persuaded Congress to pass two bills that regulated trusts—the Federal Trade Commission Act and the Clayton Antitrust Act. Other Wilson accomplishments included laws that helped farmers, protected children in the work force, and established an eight-hour day for railroad workers.

SYNTHESIZING UNIT THEMES

RELATING IDEAS

1. How did Roosevelt's "square deal" help to carry out the progressives' ideals of equality and a better life for everyone?

IDENTIFYING TRENDS

2. How did American foreign policy change around 1900? Give examples of this change.

MAKING COMPARISONS

3. Compare the accomplishments of Roosevelt and Wilson in regulating big business.

★ Unit 7 Review ★

★ Analyzing Unit Themes

ECONOMIC DEVELOPMENT

1. How did the opening of new markets in East Asia and the acquisition of territories create economic growth in the United States?

AMERICAN DEMOCRACY

2. Why was the United States ready to extend its democratic principles into Latin America, the Caribbean, the Pacific, and East Asia?

3. In what ways did reforms in government help the middle class and hinder African Americans?

THE INDIVIDUAL AND FAMILY LIFE

4. In what ways did social and political reforms improve the quality of life for many Americans?

U. S. ROLE IN WORLD AFFAIRS

5. How did Roosevelt's role resolving the Russo-Japanese War show that the United States had become a world leader?

★ Reviewing Chronology

Create a time line of at least six events between 1865 and 1900 that illustrate the end of American isolationism.

★ Linking Past and Present

- 1990   President Bush and his advisers established the New Paradigm, an antipoverty program calling for ownership of public housing to be turned over to tenants, and a policy of substituting job training or jobs in place of welfare payments.

- 1990   Conservative Republicans and liberal Democrats gave little support to the New Paradigm.

Study the information above, then answer the questions that follow.

1. Making Comparisons   How was the New Paradigm of George Bush similar to the New Nationalism of Theodore Roosevelt?

2. Making Judgments   In your opinion, is it possible for an antipoverty program to work without a political base and large infusions of government money? Explain your answer.

★ Demonstrating Citizenship

Making Judgments   Muckrakers of the early 1900s played a major role in investigating and exposing a variety of social problems. Do you believe that investigating social problems should be a prime responsibility of today's media? Why or why not?

★ Interpreting Illustrations

Study the photograph of the children sleeping in the doorway of this New York City tenement in the 1880s, then answer the questions that follow.

1. What does it show about how some Americans lived at that time?

2. This photograph is one of many taken by Danish-American journalist Jacob Riis. For what purpose do you think he took these photographs?

3. Describe reform legislation that you might have proposed to address this problem.

★ Thinking Globally

1. Making Comparisons   In the late nineteenth century, the Parliament of Great Britain implemented many social reforms to help the working classes, including minimum wage laws, laws limiting working hours, and safer working conditions in factories. Compare these reforms and the way they were achieved with the reforms brought about by American socialists and progressives in the same period. What did the reform movements in the United States and Great Britain have in common?

2. **Analyzing Motives** In 1885 European imperialist powers met in Berlin to set the ground rules for partitioning Africa. They agreed that if a nation formally announced its claim and occupied the territory, that territory would be recognized as the nation's possession, or colony. Before this meeting, nations only had to point to longstanding claims. How does this new policy compare with the Roosevelt Corollary of the Monroe Doctrine?

★ Relating Geography and History

LOCATION: RELATIVE LOCATION

The Suez Canal in Egypt, opened in 1869, linked the Mediterranean and Red seas. The Panama Canal in Central America, opened in 1914, linked the Atlantic and Pacific oceans.

Answer the questions that follow.

1. Locate the site of each canal on a map. Explain why the two canals were located where they were.

2. Explain how each canal's relative location was critical to Great Britain and the United States.

★ Practicing Skills

RECOGNIZING FALLACIES IN A LINE OF REASONING

Refer to the skills lesson on Recognizing Fallacies in a Line of Reasoning on page 691 to help you practice this critical thinking skill.

Read the following statements to determine if a fallacy exists. If so, explain why a fallacy is present.

1. The United States purchased Alaska at a bargain rate of $7.2 million—meaning that the United States accepted Alaska from Russia as a favor.

2. President Cleveland refused to annex Hawaii, which showed that sometimes ethical reasons won out over political reasons in foreign policy.

3. American business interests in Hawaii and Cuba concentrated on economic affairs, which left them little time or interest in both islands' political affairs.

4. Newspapers constantly exaggerated reports of Spanish atrocities in Cuba, so that it was only a matter of time before the United States would go to war with Spain over Cuba.

5. Considering the poor quality of medical supplies and food rations, it was little wonder that 5,000 American soldiers died in the Spanish-American War.

6. Americans remembered well their own struggle for independence against Great Britain, so it came as a surprise to learn that American troops were suppressing Filipinos fighting for independence.

7. Because Puerto Rico's culture was Spanish and Catholic, it was unusual that its inhabitants were granted United States citizenship.

8. When William Jennings Bryan, the anti-imperialist candidate, lost the election of 1900, it proved that more Americans favored an overseas empire than opposed it.

9. Roosevelt's perceived need of an interocean canal allowed the United States to ride roughshod over Latin American sensibilities.

SUPPORTING GENERALIZATIONS

Refer to the skills lesson on Supporting Generalizations on page 710 to help you practice this map and graph skill.

Study the map of United States overseas possessions in 1900 on page 652. Use the map to write a supporting statement for each of the following generalizations.

1. United States overseas possessions actually amounted to very little land area.

2. As the United States entered the twentieth century, its attention had turned from an exclusive focus on Europe and the Atlantic to a growing awareness of Asia and the Pacific.

3. The acquisition of overseas territories was a benefit to United States trade with Asian countries such as China and Japan.

4. Acquiring a "Pacific empire" did not mean that the United States became a military threat to expand into China, Japan, and Russia.

UNIT 8
Conflict, Confidence, and Collapse: 1914-1932

…Our country has resources sufficient to provide in abundance for everybody. But it cannot confer a disproportionate share upon anybody. There is work here to keep amply employed every dollar of capital and every hand of honest toil.…

—CALVIN COOLIDGE
Memorial Day Address, 1923

SETTING THE SCENE

Time

Early twentieth century

Mood

Prior to 1914 the United States had become a world power at the same time that it experienced the optimism of progressive reforms. The reform spirit dwindled, however, as the nation drifted toward the conflict of World War I. Once the war ended, the national mood was no longer progress and optimism but "normalcy" and isolation. During the postwar decade of the 1920s, Americans elected conservative Republican leaders who promised prosperity and a job for every worker.

Themes

- Conflict and Cooperation
- Influence of Technology
- The Individual and Family Life
- U.S. Role in World Affairs

Key Events

- World War I begins in Europe
- Germany resumes unrestricted submarine warfare
- Congress declares war on Germany
- The Senate rejects the Treaty of Versailles and the League of Nations
- Teapot Dome oil scandal
- Stock market crash
- Bonus Army marches on Washington

Major Issues

- Violation of neutral rights leads the United States to declare war on Germany.
- Despite Wilson's leadership, an isolationist mood defeats the Versailles treaty and the League of Nations.
- Prosperity of the 1920s fails to reach African Americans and farmers.
- Widespread depression and human misery after the crash prompts the federal government to provide direct relief.

◄ *Detail of* Transients Cooking Their Meal in the Snow Near a Coal Chute, DeKalb, Illinois; *oil on canvas by J. Porter, 1975, from a photograph taken by Ivan E. Prall in 1938*

Global Perspectives

At the turn of the century, the industrialized countries of Europe —France, Germany, Great Britain, Italy, Austria-Hungary, and Russia—were the most powerful in the world. A strong sense of nationalism resulted in an intense rivalry among them. Some, like Great Britain, controlled huge empires in Asia and Africa. All built up their military, turning Europe into an armed camp.

As each nation sought more power and control, a system of alliances heightened tensions. As a result, in 1914 war exploded in Europe. People were drawn into a global struggle unlike any they had ever known or imagined.

THE WORLD

	ASIA AND OCEANIA	AFRICA	EUROPE	SOUTH AMERICA	NORTH AND CENTRAL AMERICA
1910					
			1914 *World War I begins* ▶		1912 *U.S. marines land in Nicaragua*
			1917 *Russian Revolution*		1916 *U.S. marines land in Dominican Republic; Mexico warns U.S. not to invade*
1920			1919 *Treaty of Versailles*		
		1922 *Egypt becomes independent* ▲	1922 *Mussolini and his Fascists march on Rome* ▼	1925 *New Chilean Constitution calls for direct election of president by voters*	
1930	1928 *Chiang Kai-shek and his Kuomintang army win control of China*				
1940					

Governments were toppled, and new leaders with different political philosophies took control. In 1917 in Russia, the centuries-old reign of the tsars came to an end as Bolsheviks led by V.I. Lenin took control. In eastern Europe the Austro-Hungarian Empire broke apart into new nations, such as Czechoslovakia and Yugoslavia.

At first the United States tried to stay neutral when war broke out, but in 1917 the United States entered the conflict.

President Wilson sought a fair and just peace with his Fourteen Points and a proposal for a League of Nations. But the United States turned down the Treaty of Versailles that ended the war and refused to join the League.

During the 1920s, the country sought to "return to normalcy." People looked with hope toward a time of peace and prosperity. Instead the nation slid into its worst economic collapse—one that reverberated around the world.

THE UNITED STATES

	PACIFIC AND NORTHWEST	SOUTHWEST	MIDWEST	SOUTHEAST	ATLANTIC NORTHEAST

1910

U.S. COURT DECISION

INDICTMENT OF FALL, DOHENY AND SINCLAIR

TEAPOT DOME

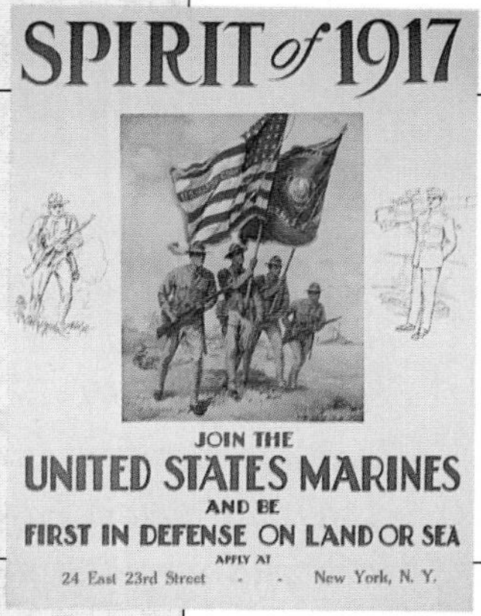

SPIRIT of 1917

JOIN THE
UNITED STATES MARINES
AND BE
FIRST IN DEFENSE ON LAND OR SEA
24 East 23rd Street — New York, N.Y.

1920

1917 *U.S. declares war on Germany and Austria-Hungary* ◄

1923 *Teapot Dome oil scandal* ▲

1920 *Prohibition begins nationwide* ▼

1925 *Scopes "Monkey" trial captures national attention*

1930

1929 *Stock Market crashes, triggering the Great Depression*

1940

AMERICAN LITERARY HERITAGE

After World War I, divergent movements in American literature grew up in New York's Harlem and Greenwich Village and in the nation's heartland. Three poets who typify these movements are Edna St. Vincent Millay, Langston Hughes, and Carl Sandburg.

In the first two of the following selections, Millay captures the tireless energy of youth. In the selections by Hughes, the poet uses rhythms of the jazz age to reflect his African American pride. Sandburg celebrates jazz and recreates the flavor of the tall tale, while displaying his affection for American slang.

As you read, notice how the three poets differ in their view of American life during the "Roaring Twenties."

EDNA ST. VINCENT MILLAY

Recuerdo

We were very tired, we were
    very merry—
We had gone back and forth
    all night on the ferry.
It was bare and bright, and smelled like a
    stable-
But we looked into a fire, we leaned across
    a table,
We lay on a hill-top underneath the
    moon;
And the whistles kept blowing, and the
    dawn came soon.

We were very tired, we were very merry—
We had gone back and forth all night on
    the ferry;
And you ate an apple, and I ate a pear,
From a dozen of each we had bought
    somewhere;
And the sky went wan, and the wind
    came cold,
And the sun rose dripping, a bucketful of
    gold.

We were very tired, we were very merry,
We had gone back and forth all night on
    the ferry.
We hailed, "Good-morrow, mother!" to a
    shawl-covered head,
And bought a morning paper, which
    neither of us read;
And she wept, "God bless you!" for the
    apples and the pears,
And we gave her all our money but our
    subway fares.

Edna St. Vincent Millay

Langston Hughes

Carl Sandburg

Midnight Oil

Cut if you will,
with Sleep's dull knife,
Each day to half its length,
my friend,—
The years that Time
takes off *my* life,
He'll take from off
the other end!

Harlem

What happens to a dream deferred?
Does it dry up
like a raisin in the sun?
Or fester like a sore—
And then run?
Does it stink like rotten meat?
Or crust and sugar over—

like a syrupy sweet?
Maybe it just sags
like a heavy load.

Or does it explode?

LANGSTON HUGHES
Dream Boogie

Ain't you heard
The boogie-woogie
    rumble
Of a dream deferred?

Listen closely:
You'll hear their feet
Beating out and beating out a—

*You think
It's a happy beat?*
Listen to it closely:
Ain't you heard
something underneath
like a—

What did I say?

Sure,
I'm happy!
Take it away!

*Hey, pop!
Re-bop!
Mop!*

Y-e-a-h!

Life *magazine cover, July 1, 1926*

Dream Variations

To fling my arms wide
In some place of the sun.
To whirl and to dance
Till the white day is done.
Then rest at cool evening
Beneath a tall tree
While night comes on gently,
Dark like me—
That is my dream!

To fling my arms wide
In the face of the sun,
Dance! Whirl! Whirl!
Till the quick day is done.
Rest at pale evening…
A tall, slim tree…
Night coming tenderly
Black like me.

I, Too, Sing America

I, too, sing America.

I am the darker brother.
They send me to eat in the kitchen
When company comes,
But I laugh,
And eat well,
And grow strong.

Tomorrow,
I'll sit at the table
When company comes.
Nobody'll dare
Say to me,
"Eat in the kitchen,"
Then.

Besides,
They'll see how beautiful I am
And be ashamed—

I, too, am America.

CARL SANDBURG

Jazz Fantasia

rum on your drums, batter
on your banjoes,
sob on the long cool
winding saxophones.
Go to it, O jazzmen.

Sling your knuckles on the bottoms of the
happy
tin pans, let your trombones ooze, and go
husha-
husha-hush with the slippery sandpaper.

Moan like an autumn wind high in the
lonesome treetops, moan soft
like you wanted somebody terrible, cry
like a racing car slipping
away from a motorcycle cop, bang-bang!
you jazzmen, bang
altogether drums, traps, banjoes, horns,
tin cans—make two people
fight on the top of a stairway and scratch
each other's eyes in a
clinch tumbling down the stairs…

from *The People, Yes*

They have yarns
Of a skyscraper so tall they had to put
hinges
On the two top stories so to let the moon
go by,
Of one corn crop in Missouri when the
roots
Went so deep and drew off so much water
The Mississippi riverbed that year was
dry,
Of pancakes so thin they only had one
side,
Of "a fog so thick we shingled the barn
and six feet out on the fog,"
Of Pecos Pete straddling a cyclone in
Texas and riding it to the west coast
where "it rained out under him,"
Of the man who drove a swarm of bees
across the Rocky Mountains and the
Desert "and didn't lose a bee,"

Of a mountain railroad curve where the
engineer in his cab can touch the
caboose and spit in the conductor's
eye,...
Of the herd of cattle in California getting
lost in a giant redwood tree that had
hollowed out,
Of the man who killed a snake by putting
its tail in its mouth so it swallowed
itself,
Of railroad trains whizzing along so fast
they reach the station before the
whistle,
Of pigs so thin the farmer had to tie knots
in their tails to keep them from
crawling through the cracks in their
pens,

Of Paul Bunyan's big blue ox, Babe,
measuring between the eyes forty-two
ax-handles and a plug of Star tobacco
exactly,
Of John Henry's hammer and the curve of
its swing and his singing of it as "a
rainbow round my shoulder."
"Do tell!"
"I want to know!"
"You don"t say so!"
"For the land's sake!"
"Gosh all fish-hooks!"
"Tell me some more.
I don't believe a word you say
but I love to listen
to your sweet harmonica
to your chin-music...."

INTERPRETING
LITERATURE

1. What period of
time is covered in
the three stanzas of
"Recuerdo"?

2. How many
speakers are there
in "Dream
Boogie"? What
device is used to
set them apart?

3. Who does
"They" refer to in
the opening line of
The People, Yes?

4. What differences
and similarities in
voice can you find
among the authors
of these selections?

IDENTIFYING
VIEWPOINTS

5. What views of
American life in
the 1920s do Mil-
lay, Hughes, and
Sandburg embody?

Babe, the Blue Ox

CHAPTER 25
World War I

SETTING THE SCENE

Historical Focus

When Europe went to war in 1914, the United States sought to stay out of the conflict. Both sides disregarded American neutrality. Germany's use of unrestricted submarine warfare and economic ties to Great Britain eventually led the United States into the bloody struggle. Mobilization called for many sacrifices by the American people. The Senate, however, rejected Wilson's proposed peace settlement, and wartime fervor led to intolerance.

Concepts to Understand

- How **conflict** became evident in American society during and after World War I.
- How Wilson's idealism and American economic **interests** led to controversy over foreign policy.

People to Know

Victoriano Huerta, John J. Pershing, George Creel, A. Mitchell Palmer

Places to Locate

Veracruz, Château Thierry, St. Mihiel

Terms to Identify

contraband, Sussex Pledge, Bolshevik, armistice, Fourteen Points, covenant, deport

Guided Reading

As you read this chapter, seek the answers to the following questions.

1. Why did the United States declare war on the German Empire in 1917?
2. Why was President Wilson unsuccessful in achieving U.S. membership in the League of Nations?

SPANNING THE DECADES

POLITICAL	1914￼ *World War I begins when Austria-Hungary declares war on Serbia*	1916￼ *Pershing expedition in Mexico*	1916￼ *Sussex pledge; Germany agrees to restrict submarine warfare*	1917￼ *United States declares war on Germany*

1914 **1916**

CULTURAL		1915￼ *First transcontinental telephone hookup*	*D. W. Griffith's cinema masterpiece Birth of a Nation is released*	1917￼ *Temperance movement leads to prohibition laws in 29 states*

American Troops Arriving in Paris, France *by J. F. Boucher, 1918*

1918	1919	1920
Wilson proclaims his Fourteen Points	*Versailles peace conference is held*	*Nineteenth Amendment is ratified*

1918   **1920**

1918	1919
Daylight savings time first adopted	*Sherwood Anderson publishes* Winesburg, Ohio

...There is one thing the American People always rise to and extend their hand to, that is, the truth of justice and of liberty and of peace. We have accepted that truth and we are going to be led by it....

—WOODROW WILSON
Speech in Colorado, 1919

733

Prelude to War

There is such a thing as a man being too proud to fight. There is such a thing as a nation being so right that it does not need to convince others by force that it is right.

—WOODROW WILSON
Responding to the sinking of
the *Lusitania,* 1915

Section Focus

On the day he took office, President Woodrow Wilson remarked to a friend that it would be an irony of fate if his administration had to deal mainly with foreign affairs. But Wilson's administration soon was confronted with difficult and complex foreign problems that involved the fate of the world.

Objectives

After studying this section, you should be able to:
- Describe Wilson's foreign policy toward Latin American nations.
- Identify the causes of World War I.
- Explain why the United States had difficulty remaining neutral during the war.

President Wilson's focus on domestic issues was demonstrated in his first inaugural address in 1913. He was comfortable with and very well-informed on matters such as the tariff and banking. Wilson's advisers in these fields were capable of solving problems when they surfaced. But in foreign affairs neither Wilson nor his advisers was experienced. His secretary of state, William Jennings Bryan, had no diplomatic training. However, circumstances catapulted this President, a former college professor, into an international spotlight where his political and ethical ideals would be witnessed in other parts of the world.

Wilson's Moral Diplomacy

As President, Wilson resolved to "strike a new note in international affairs" and to see that "sheer honesty and even unselfishness...should prevail over nationalistic self-seeking in American foreign policy." However, as events during Wilson's presidency would demonstrate, other forces were at work at home and abroad that frustrated his hope to lead the world by moral example. In fact, Wilson's first international crisis was awaiting him when he took office in March 1913.

For nearly 30 years, Mexico had been ruled by a dictator, Porfirio Díaz (pawr FEE rih oh DEE AHS), who brought stability to that nation and encouraged foreign investment in Mexico's economic development. When Díaz was overthrown in 1911 by a combination of unhappy peasants and middle-class reformers, Mexico entered a period of political chaos. Francisco Madero (frahn SEES koh mah DAY ROH) came to power, and investors in Mexico feared that the new president would confiscate all property owned by foreigners. Businesspeople and foreign diplomats, with the knowledge of the U.S. ambassador to Mexico, plotted with units of the Mexican army to overthrow Madero. Shortly before Wilson took office, General Victoriano Huerta (veek toh ree AH noh WEHR tah) seized power in Mexico, and Madero was murdered— presumably on Huerta's orders.

American capitalists, who had more than $1 billion invested in Mexico, supported Huerta in the belief that he would support business interests. Because foreign investors controlled most Mexican industry and commerce, other countries with large Mexican investments lost little time in recognizing the new ruler. But repulsed by Huerta's brutality, Wilson decided to support "the submerged 85 percent" of the Mexican people who were "struggling toward liberty," and he refused to recognize the new government. Wilson was convinced that without United States support "the unspeakable Huerta" would soon be overthrown. In the meantime, he said that the situation inside Mexico "was no affair of ours." Wilson tried to prevent arms from reaching Huerta, however, and permitted Americans to arm his enemies.

Because Huerta remained in power, Wilson decided to teach the Mexicans "to elect good men," and he looked for a reason to directly intervene. In April 1914, American sailors on shore in the city of Tampico (tahm PEE KOH) clashed with Mexican authorities. Seeing a chance to overthrow Huerta, Wilson sent marines to seize the Mexican port of Veracruz (VEHR uh KROOZ). Although Wilson expected the Mexican people to welcome his action, anti-American riots broke out in Mexico and throughout Latin America. The President's intervention also was condemned in the European press.

Shocked by world reaction, Wilson accepted an offer from the ABC powers (Argentina, Brazil, and Chile) to mediate the dispute. The ABC powers supported Wilson by recommending that Huerta go into exile. Venustiano Carranza (vay noos TYAH noh kuh RAN zuh), a candidate favored by the United States, was installed as Mexico's president.

Examining Political Cartoons *Symbols in this cartoon illustrate the conflict between Wilson and Huerta. What does Huerta's huge sword represent?*

Examining Photographs *Americans saw Pancho Villa as a bandit; to Mexico's poor, he was a democratic savior. What action did Wilson take against Villa?*

Yet trouble continued between the United States and Mexico. Mexican forces opposed to Carranza conducted raids into the United States. Led by Pancho Villa (PAHN choh VEE yah), guerrillas burned the town of Columbus, New Mexico, and killed 18 Americans. Wilson responded by sending 6,000 U.S. troops under General John J. Pershing across the border to find and capture Villa. The year-long expedition not only failed to capture the guerrillas but resulted in a clash with the Mexican army. Tensions did not ease until January 1917, when Wilson's growing concern over the war raging in Europe caused him to recall Pershing's troops.

Wilson's Mexican policy did not win the United States any friends. The British ridiculed the President's attempt to "shoot the Mexicans into self-government." Latin Americans regarded his "moral imperialism" as no improvement on Theodore Roosevelt's Big Stick diplomacy.

In the Caribbean, Wilson followed Roosevelt's example by ordering marines in Nicaragua, Haiti, and the Dominican Republic to preserve order and set up governments viewed by Americans as more stable than those in control. In 1917 the

United States expanded its naval power in the Caribbean by purchasing Denmark's strategically valuable Virgin Islands.

War in Europe

While Wilson was dealing with the situation in Mexico and problems in the Caribbean, Europe began one of the bloodiest wars in its history. Although Europeans had experienced almost 50 years of general peace, the tensions that developed during that period were ignited by a single event that plunged the entire continent into war. The rivalries that exploded in 1914 resulted from decades of European nationalism and imperialism.

In the late 1800s, as Europe became industrialized and nations sought to establish or expand overseas empires, tensions arose among colonizing nations. As France sought to expand in Africa, for example, it risked war with Italy over Tunis, with Britain over the Sudan and Egypt, and with Germany over Morocco.

Within Europe itself, nationalism also heightened rivalries and tension. Much of central and eastern Europe was ruled by empires that included several nationality groups, each with its own language. Many of these groups wanted to form independent nations by joining with similar groups in other nations. In Austria-Hungary, for example, seven Slavic groups—Czechs, Serbs, Croatians, Poles, Ukrainians, Slovaks, and Slovenes—resented being ruled by the Germans and Magyars (Hungarians). They wanted to join other Slavic peoples to form a South Slav, or Yugoslav (YOO goh SLAHV), nation in the Balkans.

The Balkans were an area of Slavic peoples in southeastern Europe that for decades had been fought over by three major powers—Russia, Austria-Hungary, and the Ottoman Empire (Turkey and its provinces). In 1908 Austria-Hungary annexed Bosnia and Herzegovina (HERT suh goh VEE nah), two Balkan territories once ruled by the Turks. Serbia, a Balkan nation on Austria-Hungary's border, felt that the annexation reduced its hopes for Slavic unification and called on Russia, its historic protector, for help. The Russians, weakened from their defeat by Japan in 1905 and wanting the Balkans for themselves, did nothing. This was the situation when Archduke Franz Ferdinand, heir to the throne of Austria-Hungary, visited Bosnia in the summer of 1914.

This instability in Europe—and the complex rivalries of the European nations at home and overseas—led to a great arms race as each country sought to defend itself. The arms race not only generated more mistrust but also helped military leaders achieve more power and influence in European governments.

Seeking additional protection, the European nations entered into alliances with one another for mutual self-defense. The Triple Alliance drew together Germany, Austria-Hungary, and Italy. Fearing isolation in Europe, France and Russia agreed to help each other in the event either became involved in war with Germany or Austria-Hungary. France also arranged a separate partnership with Great Britain known as the Entente Cordiale (AHN TAHNT KAWRD YAHL), meaning "cordial understanding." After

Examining Maps
National boundaries in Europe before World War I were quite different from what they are today. Several present-day nations did not exist less than 100 years ago. Find two regions on the map that are now nations, and two nations that no longer exist.

EUROPE IN 1914

Allies
Central Powers
Neutral nations

Russia's defeat in 1905 reduced Britain's fear of Russian power, all three nations came together to form the Triple Entente.

These two great alliances—the Triple Alliance and the Triple Entente—attracted weaker countries that sought protection. This alliance system meant that any international incident could easily involve all of Europe in conflict. For years Europe had been preparing for war, but hoping to avoid it. Tensions were high in June 1914, when the assassination of Archduke Ferdinand in Bosnia by Slavic nationalist Gavrilo Princip provided the incident that ignited Europe into war. One of the conspirators in the plot to kill the Archduke witnessed the event:

<hr />

As [Franz Ferdinand's] car came abreast, [Princip] stepped forward from the curb, drew his automatic pistol from his coat, and fired two shots. The first struck the wife of the Archduke, the Archduchess Sofia, in the abdomen. She was an expectant mother. She died instantly. The second bullet struck the Archduke close to the heart. He uttered only one word: "Sofia"—a call to his stricken wife. Then his head fell back and he collapsed. He died almost instantly.

<hr />

Although the assassin was a Bosnian college student, Serbia, which was the center of Slavic nationalism, was blamed. Austria-Hungary wanted to use the incident to punish Serbia and to expand its influence in the Balkans, but it was afraid that Serbia's ally, Russia, would resist this action. Germany, wanting to weaken Russia in Europe, urged Austria-Hungary to be harsh with the Serbians. In spite of the fact that Serbia agreed to most of its demands, Austria-Hungary declared war on Serbia anyway on July 28, 1914.

One month after the assassination, war exploded in Europe. To protect its status as a European power, Russia felt it had to

defend Serbia. Believing that Germany would aid Austria-Hungary, Russian armies mobilized along the borders of both nations. Germany demanded that Russia halt its threatening acts and that France pledge neutrality in the event of a war between Russia and Germany. Both Russia and France rejected Germany's demands. On August 1 Germany declared war on Russia; on August 3 it declared war on France.

Great Britain still hoped to avoid war, but when the German army crossed neutral Belgium on its way to invade France, Belgium appealed to Britain for help. As the German army marched through Brussels, an eyewitness reported:

<hr />

For seven hours the army passed in such solid columns that not once might a taxicab or trolley car pass through the city. Like a river of steel it flowed, grey and ghostlike. Then, as dusk came and as thousands…of iron boots continued to tramp forward, they struck tiny sparks from the stones….

<hr />

Responding to the invasion of Belgium, Great Britain declared war on Germany. Europe was thus divided into two warring camps. Those fighting for the Triple Entente were called the Allies. Italy—which switched sides in 1915, France, Russia, and Great Britain formed the backbone of the Allies. What remained of

Examining Photographs
Austria's Archduke Ferdinand made a goodwill visit in June 1914 to the Slavic minority in his empire's territory of Bosnia. What unrest existed in the territory?

the Triple Alliance—Germany and Austria-Hungary—joined with the Ottoman Empire and Bulgaria to form the Central Powers.

United States Neutrality

As war consumed Europe, Americans were hopeful that the protection offered by the vast Atlantic Ocean would keep them out of the conflict. President Wilson stated that this was "a war with which we had nothing to do." Besides issuing a proclamation of neutrality, he called on Americans to be "impartial in thought as well as in action."

Despite the official neutrality of the United States, America could not help but take sides. The massive immigration of various European nationality groups to the United States over the previous half-century gave many Americans roots that influenced their opinions about the war. Many of the 8 million German Americans were sympathetic to their homeland. Many Irish Americans, seething from a long history of British domination of Ireland, also hoped for a German victory. In general, however, the common heritage shared by the United States and Britain, and America's historic links with France, put American public opinion on the side of the Allies. In addition, American support of the Allies was promoted through propaganda. Both sides used it, but German propaganda was clumsy and unconvincing. British propaganda, on the other hand, was extremely skillful, especially in accusing the Germans of wholesale atrocities in Belgium.

But Wilson found that America's neutrality did not protect it from either the Allies or the Central Powers. The British were the first to violate international law when they imposed a tight blockade on the Central Powers. They planted mines in the North Sea, forced neutral ships into British ports for inspection, opened American mail, and redefined **contraband,** or prohibited materials, so that not even food could be shipped to Germany. The British blockade was so effective that trade between the United States and the Central Powers shrank to less than 1 percent of its prewar level.

At the same time, exports from the United States to the Allies nearly quadrupled, as American war materials and food helped to keep the Allies going. The American economy experienced enormous prosperity as a result of this trade. Ties between the United States and the Allies became even closer when the U.S. government allowed the Allies to borrow $2 billion. In addition, the

American public purchased another $2 billion in British and French war bonds.

To retaliate against the British blockade, cut off Britain's war supplies, and starve Britain into submission, the Germans relied on a new weapon—the submarine. The "U-boat" broke long-established rules of warfare. International law required that unarmed ships not be sunk without providing for the safety of passengers and crews. Yet U-boats continually sank unarmed ships.

The 1915 sinking of the British passenger liner *Lusitania* illustrated the full horror of submarine warfare. As a result of this incident, nearly 1,200 passengers drowned—including 128 Americans. Some Americans felt that this act was grounds for war. But others thought that people who traveled on ships of warring nations did so at their own risk, especially when Germany had taken out newspaper ads warning Americans not to travel on the *Lusitania*. In addition, recent evidence indicates that the ship was secretly carrying ammunition for the Allies.

Wilson steered a middle course on the issue of the U-boats. He refused to take extreme measures against Germany, saying that the United States was "too proud to fight." But he sent several diplomatic notes to Germany insisting that its government safeguard the lives of noncombatants in the war zones. Late in March 1916, Wilson's policy was tested when a U-boat torpedoed the French passenger ship *Sussex,* injuring several Americans on board. Although Wilson's closest advisers favored breaking off diplomatic relations with Germany immediately, the President chose to issue one last warning. He demanded that the German government abandon its methods of submarine warfare or risk war with the United States. Germany did not want to strengthen the Allies by drawing the United States into the war. So it offered to compensate Americans injured on the *Sussex* and promised with certain conditions to sink no more merchant ships without warning. The Sussex Pledge, as it was called, met the foreign-policy goals of both Germany and the President by keeping the United States out of war a little longer.

Section One Review

SUMMARY

The Wilson administration attempted to implement a foreign policy based on morality and honesty. These goals were tested in Mexico when Victoriano Huerta forced his way to power. Tensions continued when the United States sent troops into Mexico. In Europe the assassination of the heir to the throne of Austria-Hungary inflamed nationalist feelings, and a system of alliances brought war. Willing or not, eventually the United States found itself economically and politically involved in the conflict.

CHECKING FOR UNDERSTANDING

1. **Identify** Victoriano Huerta, Pancho Villa, Austria-Hungary, Serbia, Triple Alliance, Triple Entente, *Lusitania,* U-boat

2. **Define** contraband

3. **Describe** Wilson's philosophy and approach to foreign policy.

4. **Cite** two causes of World War I.

5. **Explain** the role of nationalism as a cause of World War I.

6. **Describe** two trends that made American neutrality difficult.

THINKING CRITICALLY

7. **Evaluating Tactics**   Can German U-boat attacks on the *Lusitania* and *Sussex* be justified? Explain your position.

GLOBAL PERSPECTIVES

8. **Making Predictions**   Many Americans considered the war in Europe to be far removed from American affairs. Some Americans feel that way about world events today. What problems would an American President encounter in trying to stay neutral if a war broke out between Britain and Ireland? Use data from the section to support your prediction.

America Enters the War

Property can be paid for; the lives of peaceful and innocent people cannot be. The present German submarine warfare against commerce is a warfare against mankind.

—WOODROW WILSON
War message to Congress, April 1917

Section Focus

In the presidential election of 1916, the Democrats again chose Woodrow Wilson as their candidate. This time the campaign focused on Wilson's diplomatic skills, using the slogan "He kept us out of war." But Americans gave his policies a less-than-ringing endorsement. When the election votes were counted, Wilson won, but it was one of the closest races in United States history.

Objectives

After studying this section, you should be able to:
- Identify the events that led the United States to enter World War I.
- Describe the role of the United States in helping the Allies to achieve victory over the Central Powers.

Following his reelection, Wilson devoted his energies to finding a peaceful solution to the war. The President realized the only sure way to keep Americans out of the European conflict was to end this terrible war altogether.

A quick victory eluded both sides, as defensive weapons proved superior to offensive tactics. The war was especially gruesome. The use of poison gas and such other new weapons as the tank and the machine gun, along with enormous casualty lists, ended the optimism that had pervaded Western Europe before the war.

"Peace Without Victory"

On December 18, 1916, Wilson asked the warring nations to state their peace terms. As a neutral party, he hoped to negotiate a settlement, but both sides responded with terms that their opponents would not accept. In spite of these replies, Wilson addressed the Senate on January 22, 1917, calling for "peace without victory." "A victor's peace," he argued, "would leave a sting, a resentment, a bitter memory upon which terms of peace would rest only as upon quicksand. Only a peace between equals can last."

The Germans soon dashed Wilson's hope of mediating an end to the war. German losses on the battlefield and the shortages caused by the British blockade forced Germany to resume unrestricted submarine warfare. German naval commanders claimed they could starve Britain into submission in five months if the German government gave U-boats permission to sink ships on sight. The Germans felt that even if this violation of their Sussex Pledge drew the United States into the war, the Americans could not raise an army and transport it to Europe in time to prevent the Allies from collapsing. Therefore, Germany decided to risk American involvement and, on January 31, 1917, announced that all vessels in waters near Great Britain, France, and Italy would be sunk without warning.

On February 3, 1917, Wilson responded to this threat by breaking off diplomatic relations with Germany. When goods piled up in American ports because ships feared to sail, he asked Congress for the power to arm U.S. merchant ships. This measure passed the House of Representatives easily, but an 11-person filibuster blocked the bill on the Senate floor. The President refused to be stopped by the effort of this "little group of willful men." Finding the authority in an 1819 law, Wilson armed the merchant ships.

Meanwhile, other events caused the nation's antagonism toward Germany to mount. The British government revealed that it had intercepted a cable from the German foreign minister, Arthur Zimmermann, to the German ambassador in Mexico. Zimmermann instructed the Ambassador to arrange an alliance between Mexico and Germany in the event that the United States entered the war. To encourage Mexico's cooperation, Germany promised that Mexico would regain Texas, Arizona, and New Mexico upon a German victory. American newspapers published the Zimmermann Note, outraging the public. Then, between March 12 and March 19, four American merchant ships were sunk without warning. Two days later Wilson called a special session of Congress to consider "grave questions of national policy."

On April 2, 1917, Wilson appeared before Congress with a heavy heart. In one of the most eloquent speeches ever delivered in the Capitol, the President asked the members of Congress to declare war on Germany:

It is a fearful thing to lead
this great, peaceful people into war, into the
most terrible and disastrous of all
wars, civilization itself seeming to be in the
balance. But the right is more precious
than peace, and we shall fight for
the things which we have always carried
nearest our hearts—for democracy,
for the right of…free peoples as shall bring
peace and safety to all nations and
make the world itself at last free. To such a
task we dedicate our lives and our
fortunes, everything we have….the day
has come when America is privileged
to spend her blood and her might for the
principles that gave her birth
and happiness and the peace
which she has treasured. God helping her,
she can do no other.

In his war message, the President insisted that the United States' quarrel was only with the "military masters" of Germany, and he expressed friendship for the German people. Maintaining that the United States had "no selfish ends to serve," Wilson stated that the people of the United States would be fighting to make the world "safe for democracy" and to promote "peace and safety to all nations." Four days after Wilson's message, Congress, after a spirited debate, declared war on Germany by an overwhelming margin.

Raising an Army

When the United States entered the war, the Allies seemed in danger of defeat. U-boats were sinking ships at a rate that threatened to wipe out the entire merchant tonnage of the world; the British Isles had only a two-month supply of food with no relief in sight. Late in 1917 the Italians suffered a severe defeat at the village of Caporetto. Russia's military effort slackened and then ceased after the overthrow of the tsar and the Bolshevik, or communist, revolution. In March 1918, Russia signed the Treaty of Brest-Litovsk, surrendering to Germany immense areas of land including the Ukraine. With one of the richest grain-growing areas in the world now in its possession, Germany hoped to relieve the severe food shortages caused by the tightening blockade. Russia's withdrawal from the conflict also freed German armies to fight on the western front—the area along the French-German border where the war had been stalemated for nearly four years.

The Allies did not expect the United States to participate in combat, because in the spring of 1917 American forces numbered only 200,000. In addition, the army possessed only 1,500 machine guns, 55 obsolete airplanes, and no heavy artillery at all.

Although these numbers looked discouraging, the United States mobilized rapidly. Supported by his able secretary of war, Newton D. Baker, Wilson called for a draft, which he said was based on the democratic principle of "a universal obligation to serve." Because conscription had

PRESIDENTIAL MEDIATION

Woodrow Wilson's offer of mediation in 1916 was not without precedent. Theodore Roosevelt had mediated an end to the Russo-Japanese War and an end to the crisis in Morocco between France and Germany. Both disputes were marginal to the European powers, however. Roosevelt's real aim had been to secure a place for the United States in world politics. The aim of Wilson's mediation offer was just the opposite of Roosevelt's, though. Wilson wanted to keep the U. S. out of world politics by ending the war before America was pulled into it.

Examining Illustrations *Although this poster was intended to attract male recruits, more than 300 women enlisted in the Marines and 11,000 in the Navy. How else were troops raised?*

morale of the Allies. A British nurse described her first sight of American soldiers:

I was leaving quarters to go back to my ward, when I had to wait to let a large contingent of troops march past....though the sight of soldiers marching was now too familiar to arouse curiosity, an unusual quality of bold vigour in their swift stride caused me to stare at them with puzzled interest.
They looked larger than ordinary men; their tall, straight figures were in vivid contrast to the undersized armies of pale recruits to which we had become accustomed....
The coming of relief made me realize how long and how intolerable had been the tension, and with the knowledge that we were not, after all, defeated, I found myself beginning to cry.

Examining Illustrations *World War I produced this classic poster, which has been used ever since. What percent of American troops went to Europe?*

not been necessary since the Civil War, some Americans, including representatives in Congress, opposed a draft. But the President's will prevailed, and on May 18, 1917, Congress passed the Selective Service Act. This act required all men between the ages of 21 and 30 to register for military service. In June nearly 10 million young men signed up. The draft eventually extended to all men between 18 and 45 and resulted in the induction of 2.8 million men into the armed forces. Another 2 million men and women volunteered for military service.

Twelve weeks after war had been declared, the first United States soldiers landed in France. On July 4, symbolically recalling the American-French partnership during the American Revolution, Colonel Charles E. Stanton stood at the tomb of France's great war hero, Marquis de Lafayette, and said, "Lafayette, we are here." More than 2 million American soldiers comprising 42 infantry divisions reached France before the war ended. This vast new reservoir of military strength was an important factor in the Allied victory. It lowered German morale and raised the

THE WORLD AT WAR: WORLD WAR I

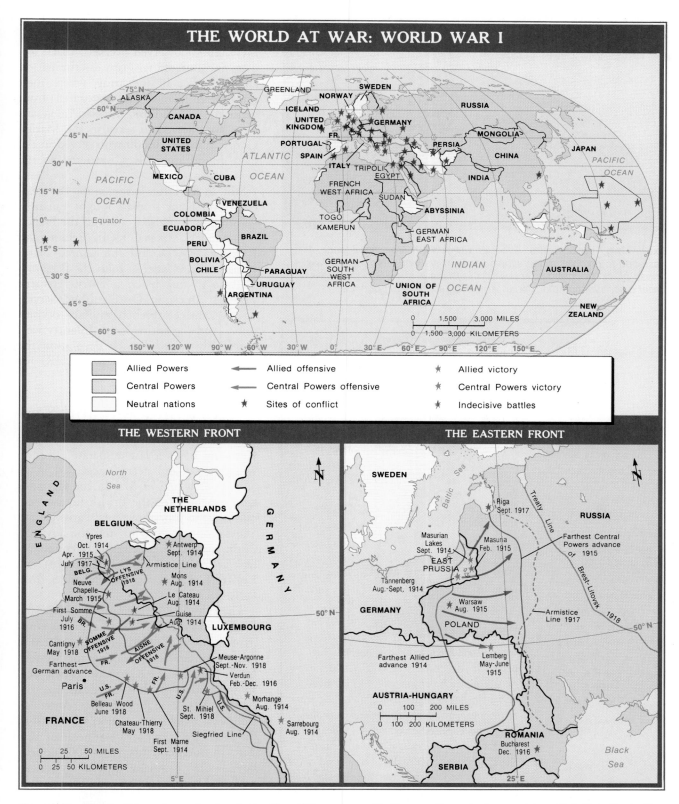

THE WESTERN FRONT

THE EASTERN FRONT

Legend:
- Allied Powers
- Central Powers
- Neutral nations
- Allied offensive
- Central Powers offensive
- ★ Sites of conflict
- ★ Allied victory
- ★ Central Powers victory
- ★ Indecisive battles

Examining Maps *Although most action in the Great War occurred in Europe, it was truly a world conflict. Note the battles outside Europe, the intercontinental alliances, and Europe's division of Africa. Why were so many battles fought in the Middle East?*

Examining Photographs *Although few African Americans were assigned to combat, those allowed to fight distinguished themselves. These black "doughboys" received the Distinguished Service Cross. What discrimination did African American soldiers experience?*

Among those drafted to serve in the war were some 370,000 African Americans; of these, 200,000 served overseas. Black soldiers encountered rampant discrimination and prejudice in the army, where their units were completely segregated from white units. In addition, black Americans were not allowed to serve in the Marine Corps, and the 10,000 who served in the navy found themselves restricted to the lower ranks.

Still, in the bitter battles along the western front, black soldiers fought valiantly, winning high praise from both the French commander, Marshal Henri Pétain (ahn REE pay TAN), and the United States commander, General John J. Pershing. Soldiers in one black infantry regiment won 21 American Distinguished Service Crosses and 68 French military decorations. And the entire 369th Infantry won the highly prized French decoration the *Croix de Guerre* (kwahd ih GEHR) for gallantry in battle.

Victory on Land and Sea

In the spring and early summer of 1918, Germany made a last desperate effort to win the war and nearly succeeded in its attempt. Starting in March, the Germans almost penetrated the British lines; a second drive in June threatened Paris. United States troops helped to stop the advance, distinguishing themselves in a counterattack at Château-Thierry (SHAH TOH TEE EHREE), a town less than 50 miles from Paris.

The tide turned in mid-July as Marshal Ferdinand Foch (FAWSH), supreme commander of the Allied armies, ordered a great counteroffensive along the western front close to the German border. Pershing, leader of the American Expeditionary Force, requested that American troops be assigned a section of the front for themselves—an area southeast of Verdun. In mid-September 550,000 "doughboys"—the nickname given American soldiers—won an overwhelming victory at St. Mihiel (san mee yehl). Then an even larger force drove toward the key city of Sedan, breaking through well-defended portions of the German lines.

Examining Photographs *Both sides dug in on the Western Front and attacked each other for months with no victor. These German troops in trenches await an Allied attack. How did U.S. forces affect this stalemate?*

By early November, the Allies were poised to advance onto German soil. Realizing the war was lost, the Germans signed an **armistice,** or temporary stop to the fighting, on November 11, 1918.

American naval forces joined the British in waging war against Germany's deadly U-boats. The invention of the depth charge, an underwater explosive, provided the Allies with a new weapon, but its effective use demanded hundreds of patrol vessels to watch for U-boats and protect Allied ships by convoying, or escorting, them out of dangerous areas. So, in addition to 79 destroyers, the United States supplied 128 small "sub-chasers" plus a variety of former yachts, tugs, and fishing boats—"almost any craft which could carry a wireless, a gun, and depth charges was boldly sent to sea." By the end of 1917, the number of U-boat casualties was slashed in half and few troop transports were sunk. In 1918 the United States Navy took the principal role in laying mines across the North Sea, which prevented U-boats from reaching the Atlantic Ocean and isolated those already at sea from ports and supplies.

★ ★ ★ ★ ★ ★ ★ ★ ★ ★ ★ ★ ★ ★ ★ ★ ★

Section Two Review

★ ★ ★ ★ ★ ★ ★ ★ ★ ★ ★ ★ ★ ★ ★ ★ ★

SUMMARY

Because of Germany's decision to resume submarine warfare, Wilson led the United States into the war. The United States set to work building up its military and began to draft men into the army. Soon American troops were helping the Allies turn the tide against Germany on land. At sea, British and American navies, with the newly invented depth charge, cut losses from U-boats in half.

CHECKING FOR UNDERSTANDING

1. **Identify** Zimmermann Note, Selective Service Act, John Pershing, doughboys

2. **Define** armistice

3. **Explain** the meaning of the phrases "peace without victory" and "Lafayette, we are here."

4. **Summarize** the events that brought the United States into the war.

5. **List** three ways the United States helped the Allies achieve victory.

6. **Describe** the experiences of African-American soldiers in World War I.

7. **Cite** Allied success on land and sea.

THINKING CRITICALLY

8. **Assessing Outcomes** Would Germany have won if the United States had not entered the war? Assess the importance of American participation in the Allies' war effort.

CONNECTIONS: HISTORY AND TECHNOLOGY

9. **Drawing Inferences** World War I utilized industrial technology to build weapons deadlier than any before. These included the automatic machine gun, poison gas, tanks, blimps, and U-boats. What effect do you think technology had on military strategy from that point on? How do you think such technology might affect public opinion about war in general? Explain your answers.

★ ★ ★ ★ ★ ★ ★ ★ ★ ★ ★ ★ ★ ★ ★ ★ ★

SECTION THREE

War on the Home Front

SETTING THE SCENE

Every single person in this democracy has the opportunity of the centuries to take part in the greatest adventure for democracy ever known.... Your right to your own life, to liberty, and to the pursuit of happiness is worth your service, your cooperation, your devotion.

—*INDEPENDENT* MAGAZINE
In article titled "America's Food Problem", 1917

Section Focus

In order to raise and equip vast armies, increase the size of the navy eleven-fold, and keep munitions and food flowing to the Allies, massive reorganization of American business, industry, and agriculture was needed. Victory in World War I was due, in large part, to the great efforts and sacrifices made on the home front.

Objectives

After studying this section, you should be able to:
• Explain how the war was financed.
• Describe how public opinion was shaped by the government.
• Discuss the goals of Wilson's Fourteen Points.

The United States found itself ill-equipped for battle when it entered World War I. The most immediate domestic concern that Congress faced was to keep the United States and Allied armies supplied by gearing U.S. industry to the war machine. In addition, the federal government needed to raise money to pay for the war and to mobilize the American people to support the war effort. To accomplish these goals, Wilson and Congress applied the Progressive Era's ideals of efficiency, control, and conformity in society to the war effort at home.

Mobilizing the Economy

The government's solution to the problem of supplying the troops was to place most industries under the control of federal agencies. The most important of these—the War Industries Board—handled purchasing for both the Allies and the United States. Under the leadership of Bernard Baruch, a Wall Street stockbroker, the War Industries Board attempted "to operate the whole United States as a single factory dominated by one management." Enlisting the most able businesspeople in America to direct the war effort, the government received the cooperation of business to convert factories to war production. Federal officials determined how raw materials would be allocated and what prices should be fixed.

The Fuel Administration was in charge of boosting coal and oil production, while encouraging people to conserve. The agency introduced such conservation methods as daylight savings time and shortened workweeks for nonwar-related factories. The Railroad Administration took charge of the railroads and ran them as a single system. The War Labor Board worked to prevent labor disputes.

Labor unions generally supported the war effort, however, hoping that cooperation would result in goodwill from the government and big business. Union leaders correctly saw in the war opportunities for higher pay, better working conditions, and the right to organize and bargain collectively. Membership in labor unions doubled during the war, and with government support they won concessions, such as the 8-hour day that industries had long opposed.

Wartime also meant increased opportunities for American women. Millions of jobs given up by men who volunteered or were drafted were filled by women. For the first time, women were welcomed in

746 UNIT 8 CONFLICT, CONFIDENCE, AND COLLAPSE: 1914-1932

many occupations previously open only to men. Women workers became an essential part of the nation's war effort in war industries and defense plants.

Despite the progress toward social and economic equality the war offered them, many women wondered how the United States could be fighting to save democracy and still deny them the vote at home. Activists for women's suffrage continued to work during the war.

African Americans might well have asked similar questions because southern states continued to deny them the right to vote. In addition, black soldiers fighting in Europe encountered far less discrimination from Europeans than they experienced in their own country.

Nevertheless, the war offered new opportunities for blacks at home. Job opportunities and high wages during the war pulled 500,000 African Americans from southern farms to northern factories. Most were offered only unskilled or semiskilled jobs, but by war's end, more than 100,000 blacks held jobs as skilled workers or factory supervisors. Although discrimination against black workers led to race riots in 26

northern cities in 1919, African Americans in the North made significant economic gains during the war. As a result, black migration northward continued after the war ended. One African American wrote a letter to a Chicago newspaper explaining this "great migration." Blacks, he said were:

...compelled to go where there is better wages and sociable conditions, believe me... many places here in [Alabama] the only thing that a black man gets is a peck of meal and from 3 to 4 lbs. of bacon per week, and he is treated as a slave.

The war had a great impact on the lives of all American civilians. Using the slogan "Food Will Win the War—Don't Waste It," the Food Administration, directed by Herbert Hoover, supervised efforts to reduce food consumption. Families were encouraged to "Hooverize" by "serving just enough" and by having Wheatless Mondays and Meatless

Tuesdays. Citizens were also encouraged to plant "victory gardens" to raise their own vegetables. To increase wheat production, the federally financed Grain Corporation guaranteed farmers first $2.00, then $2.26 per bushel. In 1918 it bought the entire American wheat crop. The combined efforts of the Food Administration and the American public were tremendously successful.

The Great War was costly beyond all expectation. By its end the United States government was spending about $44 million a day, or a total of about $33 billion. Of that amount, $10 billion went to the Allies as loans. The government raised about one-third of the money to finance the war through taxation. Income taxes were increased, although only wealthier families paid income taxes at that time. Corporations also paid higher taxes, including an "excess profits" tax, designed to return war profits to the government. The government also levied excise duties on items as varied as theater tickets, chewing gum, and phonograph records.

The government borrowed the rest of the money—more than $20 billion—from the American people by selling four issues of Liberty Bonds and a postwar issue of Victory Bonds. Posters, rallies, and "Liberty Loan sermons" encouraged

FOOD WILL WIN THE WAR
You came here seeking Freedom
You must now help to preserve it
WHEAT is needed for the allies
Waste nothing
UNITED STATES FOOD ADMINISTRATION

Examining Illustrations *The controls that characterized progressive reform were applied to the war effort. How did government increase food supplies?*

people to buy the bonds. Purchasing bonds became an act of patriotism. Even children were urged to use their pennies to buy War Savings Stamps. Boy Scouts sold the stamps under the slogan "Every Scout to Save a Soldier." Twenty-one million people—more than one-fifth of the nation's population—subscribed to the Fourth Liberty Loan.

Controlling Public Opinion

Because the success of the war effort depended heavily on voluntary civilian cooperation, the government wanted to make sure that Americans understood and supported the nation's war aims. It established the Committee on Public Information under the leadership of journalist and author George Creel to "sell" the war to America. Creel described his job as "the world's greatest adventure in advertising." He recruited advertising people, commercial artists, authors, songwriters, entertainers, public speakers, and motion-picture

Examining Photographs *With American and British flags flying, this huge rally was one of many held to encourage Americans to support the war by purchasing war bonds. How does their name, "Liberty Bonds," reflect the nation's reasons for war as Wilson defined them?*

companies to help him. Millions of pamphlets were distributed explaining the causes and aims of the war. Thousands of "four-minute men" spoke at movie theaters and public gatherings in support of the war effort. Although this flood of propaganda reinforced Wilson's image of the war as a moral crusade, it also helped promote widespread intolerance.

To prevent spying and resistance to the war effort, Congress passed the Espionage and Sedition acts. The severe penalties imposed by these laws effectively silenced most opposition to the war. Loyalty Leagues, organized by Creel, encouraged Americans to spy on their neighbors and to report those who might be "disloyal." Thousands of people were imprisoned, sometimes for opinions expressed in private conversations. People were arrested for criticizing the President, for questioning the American form of government, for criticizing the army or even military uniforms. Socialist leader Eugene Debs was arrested and sentenced to 10 years in prison for merely telling an audience to "resist militarism, wherever found." People were even jailed for criticizing the Red Cross and the YMCA.

Although war fever was responsible for the vigorous enforcement of these laws, the courts generally upheld the principle behind them. During the war about 3,000 cases involving convictions under the Espionage and Sedition acts were heard on appeal in federal courts. After the war, some of these cases reached the Supreme Court. In the landmark case *Schenck v. United States* (1919), Justice Oliver Wendell Holmes, Jr., writing for a unanimous Court, stated:

When a nation is at war,
many things that might be said in
time of peace are such a hindrance to
its effort that their utterance
will not be endured so long as [soldiers]
fight and that no Court
could regard them as protected by any
constitutional right....

The Court refused, however, to support punishment when no "clear and present danger" of hurting the United States existed or when the accused was jailed for unpopular political beliefs.

War fever was also to blame for the mistreatment and persecution of German Americans. Despite Wilson's insistence that Americans were "the sincere friends of the German people," anti-German sentiment ran high. Many school systems banned the teaching of the German language, and orchestras stopped performing the music of Beethoven, Schubert, and Wagner.

AMERICAN PORTRAITS

GEORGE M. COHAN
1878-1942

By the time he wrote "Over There"—the most popular song of World War I—George M. Cohan was already a star. At the age of 14, he was creating songs and skits for his family's vaudeville act. By his early 20s, he was writing, producing, and starring in hit Broadway shows.

Claiming that he had been born on the 4th of July (actually July 3), Cohan discovered early in his career that he could excite crowds with such patriotic appeals as his "I'm a Yankee Doodle Dandy." When American troops left for France in 1917, he quickly penned "Over There," touching the chord of nationalistic fervor sweeping the country. His song became America's war anthem. In 1940 Congress awarded Cohan a Medal of Honor for "Over There" and "You're a Grand Old Flag," another patriotic song.

Examining Photographs *This scene showing alleged German military brutality is from "Hearts of the World" by America's best known silent filmmaker, D. W. Griffith. It was part of a government effort to shape public opinion about the war. What government agency was responsible for the propaganda campaign?*

Sauerkraut was renamed "Liberty cabbage," Frankfurters were "Liberty sausage," and German measles became "Liberty measles."

While the war was foremost in the President's mind, Wilson never ceased to think ahead to the peace that would follow. In January 1918, Wilson went before Congress to present his goals and objectives for a lasting peace. With his Fourteen Points (see Appendix), the President hoped to establish a new world order.

The Fourteen Points were based on "the principle of justice to all peoples and nationalities." The President proposed to eliminate the general causes of war through disarmament, freedom of the seas, and open diplomacy instead of secret agreements. Wilson also addressed the right of peoples to live under a government of their own choosing. Finally, he proposed an international peacekeeping organization.

Although Wilson's words appealed to a world weary of war, the other Allied leaders were not particularly supportive of the Fourteen Points. They had designs on German territory and a desire to see Germany punished for starting the war. A formidable challenge lay ahead for President Wilson if he were to see his dream of a lasting peace realized.

★ ★ ★ ★ ★ ★ ★ ★ ★ ★ ★ ★ ★ ★ ★ ★ ★

Section Three Review

★ ★ ★ ★ ★ ★ ★ ★ ★ ★ ★ ★ ★ ★ ★ ★ ★

SUMMARY

The war drastically changed life in America. Besides the cost in lives, the war was a financial drain, financed by increased taxation and borrowing. The government took control of the nation's economy, waged a propaganda campaign to instill public support for the war, and passed laws to suppress opposition to the war effort. Wilson kept his sights on ending the war by actively promoting his peace plan.

CHECKING FOR UNDERSTANDING

1. **Identify** Bernard Baruch, George Creel, War Industries Board, Liberty Bonds, Espionage and Sedition Acts, Fourteen Points

2. **Describe** three ways that Americans at home supported the war effort.

3. **List** the two ways the government raised money for the war.

4. **Explain** how the government shaped public opinion and suppressed opposition to the war.

5. **Summarize** the Fourteen Points.

THINKING CRITICALLY

6. **Defending an Opinion** Was government action to suppress opposition to the war justified? List the pros and cons of this issue, including the legality of such actions. Based on this list, formulate your own opinion and use facts to defend it.

LINKING PAST AND PRESENT

7. **Making Comparisons** Today's United Nations is an outgrowth of Wilson's dream for an international peacekeeping organization. Compare world tensions in 1914 to those that exist today in areas such as the Middle East and Latin America. Compare the need for an international peacekeeping organization today to the need in the early 1900s.

★ ★ ★ ★ ★ ★ ★ ★ ★ ★ ★ ★ ★ ★ ★ ★ ★

Linking Across Time

SUPPRESSING DISSENT

In 1780 Seagoe Potter, a British Loyalist, was tried and convicted of treason in a court in Delaware. For his dissent against the American Revolution the jury sentenced Potter to be tortured and hanged. A nation that had been founded on the fundamental right to disagree was itself stifling dissent. Although the American government no longer brutalizes dissenters, it has often suppressed those who disagree with its actions or policies, particularly during wartime.

Seagoe Potter was not the only colonist to remain loyal to Britain during the Revolution. Perhaps one-third of the population retained their ties to King George and Parliament—some openly, some secretly. Although about 100,000 Loyalists emigrated, as many as 400,000 remained in America. Some Loyalists actively aided British armies. To the revolutionaries, their presence and opposition constituted a danger to the security of the nation. Loyalists were denounced in the press, reviled in the streets, tarred and feathered in barnyards, and sometimes, like Potter, tortured and hanged.

During the Civil War, dissenters who opposed Abraham Lincoln's attempt to force the South back into the Union resisted the draft system. Union troops forcefully suppressed rioting dissenters in New York City and an uprising in the coal-mining region of Pennsylvania. Others supported the war but opposed the methods Lincoln used to wage it, particularly his suspension of the writ of habeas corpus. The Emancipation Proclamation, which for modern Americans defines the moral purpose of the war, caused widespread dissent at the time it was issued. Many officers of volunteer regiments protested by resigning, and thousands of enlisted men deserted.

Junior Red Cross parading for patriotism, St. Paul, Minnesota

During World War I, President Wilson called for all citizens who opposed the war to be silenced. German Americans were perceived to be treasonous dissenters simply because of their nationality. They were spied on by their neighbors, coerced into buying war bonds, and forbidden to speak German in public or on the telephone. The campaign of suppression was almost totally baseless. German Americans, about 8 percent of the population, were overwhelmingly loyal to the United States.

There was loud antiwar dissent before the United States entered World War II. But after Japan bombed Pearl Harbor, Americans united behind the war effort. This time Japanese Americans became the target of suspicion. As with German Americans in World War I, the threat was perceived rather than real. However, most Japanese Americans lost their businesses and homes and were detained in "internment camps," for most of the war.

Dissenters during the Vietnam war questioned the morality of involvement in another country's fight for democracy instead of using American resources to fight poverty and civil rights violations at home. The government used the courts, the FBI, and even the Internal Revenue Service to investigate and harass leading dissenters. But as antiwar rallies grew to hundreds of thousands of people, public opinion increasingly influenced American withdrawal from that conflict.

Although some dissent arose after American forces were sent to the Persian Gulf to fight Iraq in 1991, antiwar protests were countered by rallies of equal size in support of the war.

MAKING CONNECTIONS

1. Why is the right to dissent vital in a democracy?

2. Why might the government treat dissent more severely in times of war?

3. In your opinion, when does dissent become treason?

SECTION FOUR

After the War

SETTING THE SCENE

*American soldiers and American sailors
....went to die for the great cause of freedom and of civilization....We have done
splendid work....we do not require to be
told by foreign nations when we shall do
work which freedom and civilization
require.*

—HENRY CABOT LODGE
Speech to the Senate, 1919

Section Focus

As Kaiser Wilhelm abdicated the German throne and fled, Germany signed an
armistice. Now the Allies faced the task of
constructing a framework for peace. Wilson still had support at home and enjoyed
great popularity abroad. The opportunity
to carry out his peace plan seemed at hand.
But his political blunders and the demands
of Allied leaders doomed his chances.

Objectives

After studying this section, you should
be able to:
• Describe the outcome of the Versailles
Peace Conference.
• Explain why the Senate rejected the
Treaty of Versailles.
• Identify domestic problems that arose
after the war.

Midterm elections in the United States in November 1918
showed a changing attitude
toward Wilson and his poli-
cies. Realizing that Democrats faced heavy
losses in the elections, the President
appealed to voters to show support for his
peace program by returning Democrats to
Congress. Instead, voters elected Republican majorities in both houses. Shortly
after the election, Wilson announced his
intention to head the American delegation
to the peace conference. His decision was
not received well by those who thought
that as President his place was at home.
Wilson faltered again when he failed to
include any prominent Republicans in the
American delegation to the conference.

The Peace Plan Opposed

The peace conference opened at the
palace of Versailles in January 1919, but
most of the sessions took place in Paris.
Delegates from 27 nations attended. The
proceedings, however, were dominated by
the leaders of the three most powerful
nations—the United States' Wilson,
Britain's prime minister David Lloyd
George, and France's premier Georges
Clemenceau (KLEM uhn SOH). With Vit-
torio Orlando, the Italian premier, these
men became known as "the Big Four."
Because their meetings were held in
secret, Wilson was robbed of an effective
weapon—direct appeal to public opinion.
Secrecy also seemed to violate the Fourteen Points, which pledged "open
covenants openly arrived at." Nevertheless, the President scored an immediate
triumph by forcing plans for a League of
Nations into the peace treaty. In mid-
February the **covenant**, or charter, of the
League, written by Wilson himself, was
accepted by the conference.

During Wilson's absence his political
influence in the United States weakened
alarmingly. The likelihood that Wilson's
peace program would fail became evident
when 39 Republican senators and sena-
tors-elect—far more than enough to prevent ratification of a treaty—signed a
statement opposing the League of
Nations. Instead of trying to repair the
rift, however, Wilson publicly denounced
the "narrow, selfish, provincial purposes"
of his opponents and insisted that the
League be part of the peace treaty. At the
peace table, he tried to appease his critics
at home by calling for changes designed
to protect American interests. But to
accept such changes, the Allies required

Wilson to make further concessions in their favor.

Despite Wilson's hopes, it was a victor's peace. In the Middle East, the Ottoman Empire lost territory. In Europe, Austria-Hungary was split up. But the greatest humiliation was reserved for the Germans. Germany lost territory and was stripped of its colonies. In addition, Germany was required to pay for damage it had done in Europe and to repay what the Allies had spent to fight the war. Although many of the Fourteen Points were ignored, Wilson trusted the League of Nations to right injustices after the postwar desire for revenge subsided.

The peace settlement complete, in July 1919, President Wilson came home to face his foes. Although he hoped Americans would support the treaty, they criticized it from all sides. Some thought it too soft, and others found it too harsh. Several nationality groups, including German Americans, considered it unfair to their native lands. Fear grew that the League of Nations would be the kind of "entangling alliance" that Washington, Jefferson, and Monroe warned against. In Congress a small group of senators branded the League a "treacherous and treasonable scheme," while a much larger group wanted the Senate to ratify the treaty but

Examining Maps *The outcome of World War I brought great changes in Europe and the Middle East as new nations and colonies were created. Much of the instability that has plagued the Middle East originated with the borders the Allies drew there in 1919. What territory on this map is now the state of Israel?*

with amendments that would preserve the nation's freedom to act independently.

Instead of compromising, Wilson insisted that the Senate ratify the treaty without changes. Convinced that he could defeat his opposition by appealing to public opinion, Wilson went directly to the people. Starting in Ohio in September, he traveled 8,000 miles and made 37 major speeches in less than a month on behalf of the treaty. Almost everywhere his reception was warm; he seemed to be regaining popular support. Had his strength held out, he might have won the battle. But the physical strain proved too great for the President. He collapsed in Colorado on September 25 and was forced to abandon his speaking tour. Shortly after returning to the White House, Wilson suffered a stroke that paralyzed one side of his body and impaired his speech. He was bedridden for months, isolated from even his closest advisers.

Examining Fine Art *This 1919 painting of the treaty-signing ceremony is by John Christen Johansen. Who played major roles in treaty negotiations?*

Connections

HISTORY AND GEOGRAPHY

CHANGING THE MAP OF EUROPE

Part of President Wilson's peace program following World War I called for self-determination of nations. Before the war Europe was a complex mosaic, or pattern, of distinct ethnic groups. Many of these groups lived within the borders of nations dominated by other ethnic groups. Wilson believed that national boundaries should be drawn to give each ethnic population its own nation.

Other powers at the Versailles Peace Conference, however, had their own plans. Allied leaders wanted to weaken the Central Powers by dividing their land. Some Allies also wanted their enemies' territory for themselves. Wilson's secretary of state, Robert Lansing, noted that the boundaries created after the war were artificial and did not follow ethnic population patterns. Lansing stated that they would last only as long as dissatisfied nations were too weak to change them. He believed that when one nation became confident of its strength and began to seek to remedy these boundaries, a new war would take place. Twenty years later that became the case.

Wilson with Allied leaders at Versailles

MAKING THE GEOGRAPHY CONNECTION

1. How did Wilson think national boundaries should be determined in Europe after World War I?

LINKING PAST AND PRESENT

2. How did the desire for autonomy among ethnic groups affect the Soviet Union in the 1990s?

With the President silenced, in November 1919, and again in March 1920, the Senate refused to ratify the Versailles Treaty. Instead, the United States negotiated a separate peace treaty with each of the Central Powers in 1921.

America's Postwar Problems

The fate of the treaty was only one of a number of problems the United States faced in the years after World War I. Demobilizing the armed forces, returning to a peacetime economy, and coping with fears of espionage presented the country with serious challenges.

The United States began to demobilize as soon as the hostilities ended. Within a short time, the army was reduced to less than 500,000, and economic controls were lifted. The businesspeople left Washington, and industry converted to peacetime production. With Wilson preoccupied with the peace treaty and later incapacitated, the nation received little overall direction. Industry enjoyed a brief postwar boom, resulting from the increased demand for consumer goods that had been scarce during the war. But government spending during the war brought inflation that nearly doubled the cost of living by 1919, and prices rose to a point where many consumers could not afford to pay for new items. Consequently, after 1920 business activity slowed. Farmers were especially hard-hit. The slackening of wartime demands for food and the end of government price guarantees caused agricultural prices to plummet. Many farmers who took advantage of high wartime crop prices and went into debt to expand their farms now faced bankruptcy.

High prices also contributed to labor unrest after the war, and when the War Labor Board disbanded, the truce between employers and organized labor ended. A record number—3,600—strikes occurred in 1919, most meeting with little success. But 4 of them—the Seattle General Strike, the Boston Police Strike, the steel strike, and the coal strike—were highly disruptive and had effects that lasted well into the 1920s.

In January 1919, only 2 months after the armistice, 35,000 shipyard workers from Seattle, Washington, went on strike in an attempt to gain an increase in their wages. The next month union workers in all Seattle industries walked off their jobs in support of the shipyard strikers. Many city residents viewed the strike as revolutionary. They responded by hoarding food and fuel and by purchasing guns. Seattle's mayor blamed the situation on dangerous radicals and after 5 days used the state militia to break the strike.

In September 1919, another major city was hit by labor unrest as Boston's police force went on strike for better wages and working conditions. Looters soon were in the streets, smashing windows and stealing goods. When the mayor was unable to restore order, Massachusetts governor Calvin Coolidge called out the state guard. A new police force was hired, and Coolidge received national acclaim for his view that "There is no right to strike against the public safety by anybody, anywhere, anytime."

Later that month more than 350,000 steelworkers went on strike across the nation, demanding better wages, an 8-hour rather than a 12-hour day, and the right to join a union. Two-thirds of the strikers were immigrants. Most of the office workers and supervisors, who refused to join the strike, were American-born. The steel companies blamed the strike on labor radicals who told "these foreigners…that if they would join the union they would get Americans' jobs." When the companies hired replacement workers, violence broke out, and federal troops were called in to protect them. After 4 months, the strikers gave up with no gains.

While the steel strike was underway, 450,000 coal miners walked off their jobs nationwide. Overworked and underpaid, the strikers demanded a 60 percent pay increase and a 30-hour week. Since at the time coal was the nation's major energy source, the government responded quickly. Obtaining a court order, it forced the strikers back to work. Eventually, however, coal miners won a large pay increase to an average of $7.50 a day.

Many Americans had long suspected a link between labor unrest and political radicalism. The strikes of 1919 helped fuel a larger "Red Scare" than the United States experienced after the war. When the Bolsheviks seized power in Russia in 1917, they called on workers everywhere to revolt. In 1919 communism seemed to have great appeal among the poverty-stricken peoples of wartorn Europe. Although the overwhelming majority of American labor leaders were not allied with the communists, nervertheless, many Americans suspected them of planning revolution.

The same laws used to quiet opposition and suppress civil liberties during the war were now turned against radicals. Immigrants—especially those with Russian names—came under suspicion. Attorney General A. Mitchell Palmer rounded up 6,000 immigrants that the government suspected of being communists and **deported**—expelled from the country— nearly 600 of them. Some of the immigrants deported had become American citizens, and some were deported without trials.

Accompanying the Red Scare was a wave of racism. Racial tensions rose as white soldiers returning from Europe found themselves competing for jobs and housing with blacks who had come north during the war. During the summer of 1919, race riots broke out in many northern cities. The worst of these was in Chicago, where nearly 40 people were killed and more than 500 injured. One journalist described the scene:

During this wild week mobs of whites pursued and beat and killed [blacks]. Other mobs of [blacks] pursued and beat and killed whites.... Armed bands in motor trucks dashed wildly up and down the streets, firing into houses....if rain had not come, it is doubtful if the armed forces could have stemmed the emotional tide that was inflaming Chicago's citizens.

Few cities in the United States escaped racial violence in the early 1920s. Even after the Red Scare died down, racial intolerance lived on in organizations such as the Ku Klux Klan, which spread from the South to become a powerful national force during the decade.

Wilson's Legacy

Despite a lack of presidential leadership as Wilson's second term drew to a close, Congress and the states implemented important laws. In 1920 Congress passed the Esch-Cummins Act, which turned the operation of railroads back to their owners. This statute gave the Interstate Commerce Commission almost complete power to fix rates as well as to regulate railroad financing, but the commission was now less concerned with restraining railroad companies as it was with helping them.

World War I helped to add two amendments to the Constitution—both the culmination of century-old reform movements. Prohibition, which had made great gains before the war, made even greater advances during the war. "Hooverizing" put the country in the mood to sacrifice, and war needs compelled the government to forbid the use of grain to manufacture liquor. By January 1919, two-thirds of the states had ratified the Eighteenth Amendment,

Examining Maps *Before the Nineteenth Amendment was ratified, half the states had granted full or partial women's suffrage. But state laws could change, so suffragists continued to push for an amendment. What effect did the war have on the movement?*

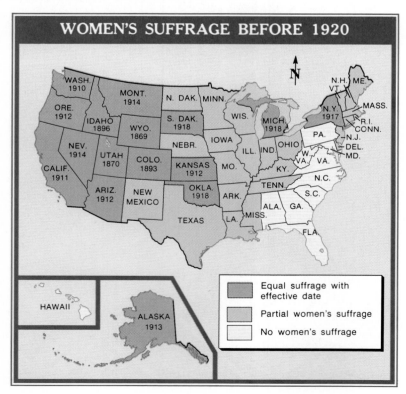

WOMEN'S SUFFRAGE BEFORE 1920

WASH. 1910
ORE. 1912
MONT. 1914
N. DAK.
MINN.
N.H.
VT.
ME.
MASS.
N.Y. 1917
R.I.
CONN.
IDAHO 1896
WYO. 1869
S. DAK. 1918
WIS.
MICH. 1918
PA.
N.J.
DEL.
MD.
NEV. 1914
UTAH 1870
COLO. 1893
NEBR.
IOWA
ILL.
IND.
OHIO
W. VA.
VA.
CALIF. 1911
KANSAS 1912
MO.
KY.
N.C.
ARIZ. 1912
NEW MEXICO
OKLA. 1918
ARK.
TENN.
S.C.
ALA.
GA.
TEXAS
LA.
MISS.
FLA.

HAWAII
ALASKA 1913

Equal suffrage with effective date
Partial women's suffrage
No women's suffrage

prohibiting "the manufacture, sale, or transportation" of intoxicating beverages.

The war also advanced the cause of women's rights. It was difficult to deny demands that women be allowed to vote after they had performed traditionally male jobs in factories and fields and served with courage and devotion behind the lines in Europe. On the eve of the 1920 presidential election, after decades of struggle, women gained suffrage when the Nineteenth Amendment was ratified.

Wilson's final year and a half in office left the country virtually leaderless. The President had recovered sufficiently to transact routine business. But his attention and energies still were focused on getting the United States into the League of Nations. Retaining a belief that the American people would not retreat from world leadership, he urged that the election of 1920 be a "great and solemn referendum" on the League issue.

But the 1920 election saw Wilson's party and the League repudiated at the polls. The country wanted to turn its back to world responsibilities. In 1923, shortly before he died, Wilson warned:

---

*I can predict with absolute
certainty that within another generation
there will be another world
war if the nations of the world do not
concert the method by which
to prevent it.*

Few people listened to Wilson's warning, however. Most Americans wanted to put their memories of war, suffering, and sacrifice behind them. The return of prosperity by 1923 caused Americans to view the future with optimism and confidence. The war to end all wars was over. The United States had done its part in making the world "safe for democracy." Americans turned their backs on Europe. It was time to start enjoying the peace.

★ ★ ★ ★ ★ ★ ★ ★ ★ ★ ★ ★ ★ ★ ★ ★ ★ ★ ★

Section Four Review

★ ★ ★ ★ ★ ★ ★ ★ ★ ★ ★ ★ ★ ★ ★ ★ ★ ★ ★

SUMMARY

Wilson's chances to achieve peace on his terms were damaged when he snubbed his Republican opposition and spent too much time in Europe. His attempts to write many of his Fourteen Points into the peace treaty were thwarted by France and Great Britain who were more interested in repayment and revenge. Although some of Wilson's points were accepted in altered forms, the treaty faced opposition at home. In response, Wilson toured the United States promoting the treaty until his health failed. In addition, the nation's peacetime economy was hampered by a rising cost of living, labor unrest, and lower crop prices. Yet reform continued as Prohibition and women's suffrage were enacted by amendments to the Constitution.

CHECKING FOR UNDERSTANDING

1. **Identify** Treaty of Versailles, League of Nations, Eighteenth Amendment, Nineteenth Amendment

2. **Define** covenant, deported

3. **List** the provisions of the Versailles Treaty.

4. **Describe** the economic problems of the United States after the war.

5. **Summarize** the reasons that the Red Scare occurred.

6. **Explain** why the war helped the cause of women's suffrage.

THINKING CRITICALLY

7. **Analyzing Motives** Explain why "peace without victory" was so difficult to achieve at Versailles.

GLOBAL PERSPECTIVES

8. **Identifying Assumptions** How did the Senate's rejection of the Treaty of Versailles reflect changing American attitudes about participation in world affairs?

★ ★ ★ ★ ★ ★ ★ ★ ★ ★ ★ ★ ★ ★ ★ ★ ★ ★ ★

★ Chapter 25 Review ★

★ Summary

Wilson's principles of morality and honesty in conducting foreign policy were soon tested over Victoriano Huerta's rule in Mexico, Pancho Villa's raid on the United States, and pressure from American business to actively support pro-American governments in Latin America. When longstanding tensions in Europe erupted in war in 1914, however, the United States attempted to maintain neutrality.

Although several factors made American neutrality increasingly difficult, Germany's policies regarding submarine warfare brought the United States into the conflict in 1917. Because of unprecedented government controls, the nation mobilized for war at an astonishing pace. Within months an army was drafted and sent to fight in Europe. To finance the war effort, the government sold bonds and borrowed money. To maintain popular support, public opinion was carefully controlled. With the help of American troops and supplies, the Allies broke the deadlock that existed on the western front and turned the tide against Germany. On November 11, 1918, the German army surrendered and signed an armistice to end the fighting. President Wilson set to work advancing his plan for peace, but Congress rejected the Treaty of Versailles and refused to enter the League of Nations.

After the war the nation struggled with a sagging economy, while fear of communism made unions and immigrants unpopular in the eyes of many Americans. The mood was right for the Eighteenth Amendment to the Constitution, prohibiting the manufacture and sale of alcohol. Acknowledging the contribution made by women during the war, the Nineteenth Amendment extended them voting rights.

★ Using Vocabulary

Imagine that you have kept a diary of events of World War I. Write headlines of three diary entries using each of the following terms in a headline.

covenant   **contraband**

armistice

★ Reviewing Facts

1. **Discuss** Wilson's foreign policy views and how they related to his actions in Latin America.

2. **State** how nationalism and alliances created the conditions that led to World War I.

3. **Identify** two reasons the United States declared war on Germany.

4. **Cite** changes in economic and political policies that were imposed in the United States during World War I.

5. **List** two actions taken by the American military that helped win the war.

6. **Describe** the terms of the Versailles Treaty.

7. **Explain** why Wilson was frustrated with Congress after the war.

8. **Summarize** the social difficulties confronting the United States after the war.

★ Understanding Concepts

CONFLICT

1. Identify the two types of nationalism that existed in Europe and explain why each was a factor in causing World War I.

2. Explain how Wilson's ideals influenced his actions and made compromise nearly impossible.

INTERESTS

3. Explain how economic and political interests in the United States were factors in its inability to remain neutral in World War I.

4. Analyze how competing interests made the adoption of Wilson's Fourteen Points difficult.

★ Thinking Critically

1. **Comparing Actions** Did Wilson's actions in Latin America reflect his principles of honesty and morality? Make a list of similarities and differences in his ideals and his actions.

2. **Evaluating Foreign Policy** Consider the United States' neutrality policy before entering the war. Evaluate the feasibility of this policy. Consider the events that forced the United States to abandon neutrality and enter the war.

3. **Expressing Viewpoints** After America's entrance into World War I the government worked to control public attitudes about the war. In your opinion, was it necessary for the government to take such

★ Chapter 25 Review ★

actions? Explain your viewpoint.

4. **Analyzing Effects** How did World War I change society's perception of women in the United States? Explain the effect of women's wartime experiences on their social and political status during the war and after.

★ Writing About History

COMPARISON

Refer to the description of how to write a comparison essay in the History Writer's Handbook in the Appendix of this book. Your teacher will give you more specific instructions on the essay's length and the assignment's due date.

Write an essay to compare Wilson's ideals with the realities he faced in world politics. Before you begin writing, make two lists: one of Wilson's foreign policy goals and another of his actions. Use these lists to help you write.

★ Learning Cooperatively

Work with a partner to write two newspaper editorials on the United States government's methods of controlling public opinion during World War I—one supporting the government's policies and the other opposing them. Before writing, collaborate on a list of pros and cons about the government's activities, including the Espionage and Sedition Acts and the Committee on Public Information. Then each of you should take opposite positions and write an editorial. When you have finished, exchange your editorials. After reading your partner's work, write a "letter to the editor" as a rebuttal to his or her position.

★ Mastering Skills

ANALYZING GRAPHIC DATA

Numerical or statistical information can be presented in many ways. Graphs are often used to help you understand and use such complex material. For example, some graphs show how something changes over time. By comparing two such graphs, you can also determine similarities and differences between related kinds of information.

To successfully analyze complex information, you must first break it into smaller parts that you can examine more easily. By analyzing the information presented in the bar graph below, you can obtain a clearer understanding of American military support for its Allies in Europe.

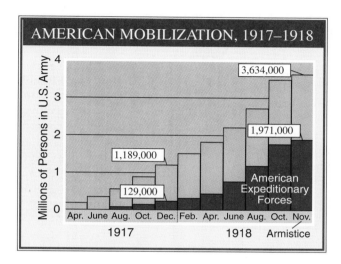

AMERICAN MOBILIZATION, 1917–1918

The graph provides information about the United States Army between April 1917 and November 1918. In analyzing its detail you can see that one set of bars shows the growth in total size of the American army from the time the United States entered the war until the armistice was signed. The other set of bars shows how many of those troops were sent to fight in Europe.

Practice Use your analysis of the graph above in answering the following questions to better understand American involvement in the war:

1. When the United States declared war, fewer than 250,000 soldiers were ready to fight. When was the first month that the United States had 1 million troops in the army? By what month were there 1 million American soldiers in Europe?

2. Between what months was there the greatest increase in the size of the American army?

3. About what percentage of the United States Army was in Europe by the end of 1917? by the armistice a year later?

4. After reading about America's mobilization to fight the war in the chapter, what information does this graph provide about the efficiency of that effort?

CHAPTER 26
The Decade of Normalcy

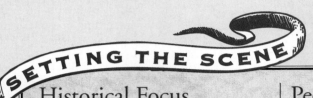

Historical Focus

The decade that followed the World War I differed considerably from the Progressive years that came before it. Voters turned to conservative leaders who promised to turn the country away from European affairs and inward to "normalcy." For many Americans this shift meant preserving the values of rural America and enjoying prosperity. For others it meant a fascination with a dazzling new assortment of consumer goods, entertainment, and changing fashions.

Concepts to Understand

- Why shifts in government policies and increased production resulted in **economic change**.
- How **social change** affected the arts, the role of women, and minorities.

People to Know

Warren G. Harding, Calvin Coolidge, Andrew Mellon, Henry Ford, Mary McLeod Bethune

Places to Locate

Japan, Teapot Dome, Nicaragua

Terms to Identify

normalcy, Prohibition, welfare capitalism, Harlem Renaissance

Guided Reading

As you read this chapter, seek the answers to the following questions.

1. In what ways did the United States involvement in international relations change following World War I?
2. What signs of social tension were evident in the 1920s?

SPANNING THE DECADES

POLITICAL	1920 *Warren Harding is elected*	1921 *Washington Conference is held*	1923 *Calvin Coolidge becomes President after Harding's death*	1926 *United States intervention in Nicaragua*

1920 **1924**

CULTURAL	1920 *First commercial radio broadcast is aired*	1922 *Lincoln Memorial is dedicated in Washington, D.C.* *Sinclair Lewis publishes* Babbitt	1925 *John Scopes trial over teaching evolution in Dayton, Tennessee*	1927 *First "talking" motion picture,* The Jazz Singer, *is released*

Traveling Carnival, Santa Fe *by John Sloan, 1924*

1928
*Kellogg-Briand Pact
is negotiated*

1928   1932

1929
*Chicago mobsters murder
seven rival gang members
in the St. Valentine's Day
Massacre*

*…If a man saves $15 a week and invests
in good common stocks…at the end of
twenty years he will have at least $80,000
and an income from investments of
$400 per month. He will be rich.…I am
firm in my belief that anyone not only can
be rich but ought to be rich.…*

—JOHN J. RASKOB
Chairman of the Board,
General Motors Corporation, 1929

The Harding Years

America's present need is not heroics but healing, not nostrums but normalcy, not revolution but restoration....

—WARREN G. HARDING
Speech to the Boston Home Market Club, May 1920

Section Focus

The internationalism of Woodrow Wilson was reversed in the United States during the 1920s under the administrations of the next three Presidents—all Republicans. The party's slogan "America First" hailed the country's unparalleled prosperity, characterized by remarkable achievements in the field of business.

Objectives

After reading this section, you should be able to:
• Describe the accomplishments of the Washington Conference.
• Explain the provisions of the National Origins Act.
• Describe the scandals in the Harding administration.

The end of the war created new problems for the United States. After the dismantling of the War Industries Board, business lost the profitable military contracts of the war years. Four million recently demobilized service men and women needed work. In 1920 and 1921, unemployment soared, as did prices. Labor unrest was reflected in the United States Steel strike and the Boston police strike of 1919.

Americans had to face the coming decade, as noted novelist F. Scott Fitzgerald stated, with "all wars fought, all faiths shattered."

The Election of 1920

Several prominent candidates sought the Republican nomination in 1920, but after a convention deadlock, the prize went to a dark horse, Ohio senator Warren G. Harding. Many saw in Harding a welcome contrast to Woodrow Wilson. While Wilson was intellectual and restrained, Harding was affable and easy-going. Wilson favored government regulation of business; Harding wanted to leave it alone. As *Harper's* magazine editor Frederick Lewis Allen explained:

Wilson thought in terms of the whole world; Harding was for America first....Wilson wanted America to exert itself nobly; Harding wanted to give it a rest.

Harding's running mate was Massachusetts governor Calvin Coolidge. To oppose Harding, the Democrats chose Ohio governor James M. Cox, a loyal Wilson supporter. Cox's running mate was Franklin D. Roosevelt, who, like his distant cousin, Theodore, had served as assistant secretary of the Navy. Cox needed to win votes away from the Republicans, the majority party at the time. The strategy chosen by Cox was as Wilson desired—to campaign for the League of Nations, in the hopes of turning the election into a referendum on this issue.

The Republicans, however, would not debate the League, partly because they were divided on the issue. Harding said he favored "a society of free nations" to keep peace. Most prominent Republicans took this to mean that Harding supported their decision to join the League, but anti-League Republicans seemed certain that Harding opposed it. Thus, as journalist Walter Lippmann pointed out, Harding received support from "men and women who thought a Republican victory would kill the League, plus those who thought it was the most practical way to procure the League."

The election was an overwhelming Republican victory. "It was not a landslide," said Wilson's secretary, Joseph P. Tumulty, "it was an earthquake." Harding carried every northern and western state and even broke the solid South by carrying Tennessee. A key to the election results may be found in the President's reassuring slogan—"a return to normalcy"—coined by Harding during his campaign. It suggested a return to "the good old days," to the conditions that prevailed before the shocks of World War I. After the war, according to Frederick Lewis Allen, the nation was tired of fighting:

Sick of Wilson and his talk of America's duty to humanity, [Americans] hoped for a chance to pursue their private affairs without governmental interference, and to forget about public affairs. There might be no such word in the dictionary as normalcy, *but normalcy was what they wanted.*

Postwar Foreign Policy

After his election, Harding announced that the League issue was "dead as slavery." His administration, he said, would not lead the United States into the League of Nations "by the side door, back door, or cellar door." The United States was too powerful, too economically interconnected, and too widely involved in world affairs to retreat into isolationism, however, and participated actively in many League conferences.

One international problem that demanded a solution, for example was $10.3 billion in Allied war debts owed to the United States for food and war materials. The debtor nations had difficulty meeting their payments. They argued that high American tariffs had closed the U.S. market to their imports and slowed their economic recovery. Furthermore, debtor

nations argued, because the United States had lost fewer people in the war than the other Allies, it should be willing to pay more of the financial cost. The United States government, however, took the position that it could not ask American taxpayers to assume the Allies' war debts; that the Allies had gained territory and **reparations,** or payments for damages, as a result of the victory while the United States had claimed no reward; and that to cancel these debts would destroy faith in international agreements. This long dispute resulted in hard feelings on both sides of the Atlantic Ocean.

Eventually the United States made agreements with 17 of the 20 debtor nations, reducing the debts by 30 to 80 percent. Most of the money the Allies paid actually came from Germany. To pay its reparations, Germany obtained private bank loans from other countries—especially the United States.

Although the Harding administration wanted to keep out of European affairs, it cooperated with major European powers and Japan to negotiate a series of treaties addressing important issues in the Pacific

Examining Political Cartoons *By showing the League of Nations agreement trying to replace the Constitution in ruling the nation, this artist expressed concern that joining the League would deprive the United States of the freedom to set its own policies. What role did the 1920 election play in resolving this issue?*

region and east Asia. An international conference, meeting in Washington, D.C., in 1921, attempted to produce the first major disarmament agreement in modern history.

At the time the Harding administration called the Washington Conference, the United States, Great Britain, and Japan were experiencing costly and competitive naval buildups that originated during the war. There was also friction in east Asia, caused mainly by conflicts over commercial rights in China and by western suspicion of Japan's recent territorial gains. After World War I, Japan had acquired all of Germany's Pacific islands north of the equator as well as the Chinese port of Kiaochow (jee OW JOH). Japan also treated the rest of the Chinese province of Shantung as its own. To further increase tensions, the United States and Japan were disputing possession of the tiny island of Yap, a key cable communications station between Guam and the Philippines—both United States possessions.

In the hope of resolving these problems, the administration invited eight nations to the conference. These nations included the principal naval powers of the world, those with Pacific possessions, and those with an economic stake in China. The negotiations, which lasted from November 1921 to February 1922, led to three important treaties.

The Four-Power Treaty was signed by the United States, Great Britain, France, and Japan. It ended an Anglo-Japanese alliance, replacing it with an agreement by the four great powers to respect one another's Pacific holdings. In case of disagreements between the four powers or a threat from another nation, the signers also agreed to confer with one another "fully and frankly."

Under the Five-Power Treaty, the 5 naval powers of the United States, Great Britain, Japan, France, and Italy agreed to freeze their navies at 1921 levels and thus avoid the financial strain of further naval buildups. The signers further agreed to halt the building of large warships for 10 years; some ships under construction would even be scrapped. The treaty also included an agreement by the United States and Great Britain not to build new fortifications or naval bases in the western Pacific. This provision gave Japan control of nearby waters in exchange for agreeing to remain at inferior naval strength.

The Nine-Power Treaty signed by the United States, France, Great Britain, Japan, Italy, Belgium, China, the Netherlands, and Portugal put the "Open Door" China policies of John Hay into a treaty. The signers agreed to preserve equal commercial rights in China and to refrain from "taking advantage of conditions in China to seek special rights or privileges." Following this policy, Japan soon withdrew from the province of Shantung.

The immediate results of the Washington Conference were encouraging. Powerful nations, hoping to avoid future large-scale wars, had peacefully agreed to arms limitations. By lessening tensions in east Asia, the conference made war there less likely. In retrospect, though, these diplomatic accomplishments did not further long-term peace.

One failure of the conference was that it reached no agreements limiting military forces on land. Moreover, the treaties had notable shortcomings. Under the Five-Power Treaty, naval powers could still build unlimited numbers of smaller combat vessels, such as submarines and destroyers. In addition, the Four-Power Treaty did not commit the signers to active military defense of their allies; indeed, such a commitment might have been unacceptable to the United States. And the Nine-Power Treaty made no provision for enforcement of the Open Door Policy. Nonetheless, the conference gave Americans some reason to look forward to a period of peace and recovery.

Business Normalcy

From the start, Harding's handling of domestic problems made it apparent that normalcy meant a general retreat from government regulation of business. "We want less government in business and more business in government," Harding declared. Although the federal government actively aided businesses by levying protective tariffs, promoting foreign trade, and breaking strikes, its policy in other matters was *laissez-faire*. There was little effort to enforce the antitrust laws that regulated business mergers. Regulatory agencies such as the Interstate Commerce Commission and the Federal Trade Commission consisted largely of members who were unsympathetic to policies restricting private enterprise. The ineffectiveness of these agencies reflected the dominant feeling of the time.

The new trend was immediately seen in the tariff laws. In 1922 Congress passed the Fordney-McCumber Act, raising import duties to high levels. This protected agriculture as well as certain young industries, such as rayon, china, and the optical-glass and chemical products for which the United States seized patents from Germany during the war. The Fordney-McCumber Act was designed to be "flexible"; it therefore authorized the President to raise or lower duties by as much as 50 percent. The President could do this on the recommendation of the Tariff Commission, set up in 1916 to study costs of production at home and overseas. In practice, this provision meant that rates often went still higher.

In putting more business into government, the Republican administrations introduced more accountability into federal finances. Because World War I had raised the national debt from less than $10 per person to over $200, the Harding and Coolidge administrations attempted to lower this burden by making the government more fiscally responsible. In 1921 Congress created the Bureau of the Budget in the Treasury Department. Until this time, income and outgo had never been coordinated. The efforts of the Bureau of the Budget to introduce savings were especially supported by Coolidge, who felt so strongly about curbing the nation's expenditures that he devoted serious attention to routine federal purchases such as lead pencils and typewriter ribbons. After the Washington Conference, there was no threat of war on the horizon, and even military expenditures were greatly lowered.

Andrew Mellon, secretary of the treasury from 1921 to 1932 and an immensely wealthy man in his own right, believed that heavy taxes on excess profits "penalized success" and discouraged investment in productive enterprise. At Mellon's insistence, Congress abolished the wartime excise and excess profits taxes and reduced tax rates on incomes by nearly two-thirds. Even with these cuts, the nation's tremendous prosperity produced enough tax revenue to reduce the national debt by $8 billion between 1921 and 1929.

Labor and Labor Unions

In 1927 Andre Siegfried, a French sociologist, wrote, "A worker is far better paid in America than anywhere else in the world." Between 1921 and 1928, the average annual wage rose from $1,227 to $1,384.

But new manufacturing caused **technological unemployment**—jobs lost when occupations become obsolete. Although people replaced by machines usually found

Examining Graphs *Except for a drop resulting from the labor unrest that followed World War I, earnings rose steadily throughout the 1920s. How did this trend affect unions?*

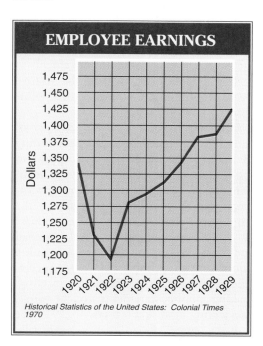

EMPLOYEE EARNINGS

Historical Statistics of the United States: Colonial Times 1970

jobs elsewhere, the transition was sometimes difficult. Not only were they often forced to leave home to find employment, but they also frequently lost the benefit of long years spent learning a particular skill. The introduction of juke boxes and sound films, to cite an extreme example, caused widespread unemployment among musicians. And although the assembly line lowered the costs of production, many laborers could not stand the monotony and nervous tension caused by working at a speed set by the machine. This was particularly true of middle-aged workers, for whom "old at 40" became a bitter slogan.

The "prosperity decade" saw labor unions decline in number and strength. Even the American Federation of Labor, one of the largest workers' organizations, had difficulty holding its members in the face of the antiunion activities of employers' associations. Employers joined to promote the **open shop**—or a shop where workers did not have to join a union. Labeled the "American Plan," in practice the open shop meant a shop closed to union members. To further reduce the power of unions, companies promoted **welfare capitalism**, a system to make employees feel more a part of the business by enabling them to buy shares of stock, by instituting profitsharing, and by providing such fringe benefits as medical care, retirement pensions, and recreational facilities. Moreover, wages and working conditions improved somewhat for many during the 1920s. With some improvement in their standards of living and the relative weakness of unions, striking seemed pointless to many workers.

Although Herbert Hoover, secretary of commerce, persuaded President Harding to make a successful personal appeal to the leaders of the steel industry to abandon the 12-hour day, the federal government was usually on the side of the employers. Thus Attorney General Harry M. Daugherty helped to break railroad and coal strikes in 1922 by obtaining injunctions that prohibited every conceivable union activity, including picketing, making public statements to the press, and jeering at strikebreakers. In 1919 the Indiana State Guard—and eventually

federal troops—protected strikebreakers at United States Steel. In addition, the Supreme Court continually whittled away at the protections that unions thought they had secured by the Clayton Act of 1914. Once again, injunctions were freely used to stop strikes and boycotts.

Restricting Immigration

In the decade before World War I, approximately 1 million persons a year came to live in the United States, over two-thirds of these from countries in southern and eastern Europe, such as Italy, Spain, Poland, Hungary, and Greece. Living standards in those countries were low and educational opportunities limited. To slow down this tide of immigration, Congress passed in 1917 an act requiring a literacy test, designed to exclude large numbers of immigrants.

The act, however, had little effect. New immigrants congregated in such cities as New York and Chicago, where opportunities for employment were greatest. Here immigrants formed homogenous ethnic communities—every major city had its own "Little Italy," "Little Poland," "Little Greece," and so forth. But this in turn gave rise to the charge that the new immigrants resisted "Americanization." Established immigrants resented the new immigrants' increasing political power. Even more, they feared that the newcomers, most of whom were Catholic, would overthrow traditional Protestant values. Conservative labor unions were angered by the willingness of poor immigrants to work for very low wages. Employers, who had previously favored unrestricted immigration as a means of hiring cheap labor, now came to fear that the new immigrants were radicals who would fight for a communist revolution.

During and after World War I, feeling against "hyphenated-Americans" was stimulated by anti-German hysteria, by the "Red scare," and by the sinister Ku Klux Klan. When immigrants began to pour into the United States, fleeing their war-torn countries in the hopes of finding a mythical land of wealth and opportunity, Congress took quick action. In 1921

Harding signed the Emergency Quota Act, which severely cut the number of people admitted to the United States. According to this act, only 3 percent of the total number of people in any national group already living in the United States in 1910 would be admitted during a single year. Three years later the National Origins Act made restriction a permanent policy. This 1924 law temporarily reduced the quota still further, setting it at 2 percent of those residing in this country in 1890. It also provided that after 1927 a total of only 150,000 immigrants would be admitted to the United States per year, their nationalities apportioned on the basis of the 1920 census. This meant that more than 85 percent of the new immigrants would be from Europe—mainly from Great Britain, Ireland, Germany, and Scandinavia.

The intention of the National Origins Act was clearly to discriminate against certain nationalities and races. This became even more apparent when immigrants from Asia and Africa were assigned either very small quotas or barred entirely. In fact, Japanese immigration was completely

Examining Photographs *Members of the Ku Klux Klan parade down Pennsylvania Avenue in Washington, D.C. The KKK spread from the South to gain national power in the 1920s. How did the Klan as well as many other Americans react to increased immigration after World War I?*

excluded, even though the Gentlemen's Agreements of 1907 and 1908 between Japan and Theodore Roosevelt had been faithfully observed. Secretary of State

Examining Graphs *The effect of the 1924 National Origins Act on Asian immigration is shown on this graph. What changes did the law cause in European immigration, and how did it accomplish those changes?*

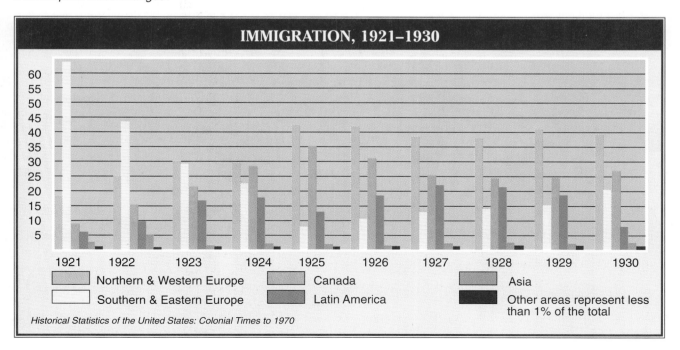

IMMIGRATION, 1921–1930

Northern & Western Europe   Canada   Asia
Southern & Eastern Europe   Latin America   Other areas represent less than 1% of the total

Historical Statistics of the United States: Colonial Times to 1970

day of public mourning and national humiliation in Japan. The incident discredited moderate Japanese politicians who sought to cooperate with the United States and advanced the cause of reactionary militarists in Japan who were planning to usurp power and lead their nation on a course of military conquest and war.

An event that for many came to symbolize mistrust of immigrants in the United States was the trial of Nicola Sacco and Bartolomeo Vanzetti. These two Italian immigrants and anarchists were accused in 1921 of killing two men during a robbery in Massachusetts. They were convicted, but many thought they never received a fair trial. It was believed that the trial judge was prejudiced against the defendants because of their ethnic backgrounds and political beliefs. For years attempts were made to obtain a retrial, but in 1927 Sacco and Vanzetti were executed. In his final statement in court, Vanzetti continued to maintain his innocence of the crime, saying:

Hughes wrote that Japanese exclusion undid all the good accomplished by the Washington Conference. The Japanese regarded the law as a national insult, and the day it went into effect was declared a

…[M]y conviction is that I have suffered for things that I am guilty of. I am suffering because I am a radical and indeed I am a radical; I have suffered because I was an Italian and indeed I am an Italian….

The question of the guilt or innocence of Sacco and Vanzetti has never been answered with certainty, but their trial made many people think critically about the American justice system.

Scandals Among Harding's Advisers

Although President Harding was personally honest, there was more corruption in his administration than in any previous one. Harding's poker-playing friends, known as "the Ohio Gang," used their ties to the President and the attorney general to sell government appointments, pardons, and immunity from prosecution. Harding's choice for head of the Veterans' Bureau, for example, arranged fraudulent contracts that sold supplies from veterans' hospitals at a cost to the taxpayers of about $250 million.

The worst scandal, however, involved Harding's secretary of the interior, Albert B. Fall, who secretly leased to private interests oil lands, which had been set aside for the navy, at Teapot Dome, Wyoming, and Elk Hills, California. In return, Fall received bribes totaling more than $300,000. Eventually the Senate investigated the Teapot Dome scandal, and Secretary Fall went to prison.

When Harding learned what was going on, he complained privately that he had been betrayed. He said that he had no troubles with his enemies, but his friends—they were a different story: "They're the ones that keep me walking the floor nights!" In the summer of 1923, Harding traveled to Alaska, deeply concerned and depressed over the scandals in his administration. On his return from Alaska, Harding became severely ill with what may have been food poisoning, pneumonia, or a heart attack. He died on August 2, shortly before news of the scandals broke to the public.

★ ★ ★ ★ ★ ★ ★ ★ ★ ★ ★ ★ ★ ★ ★ ★ ★

Section One Review

★ ★ ★ ★ ★ ★ ★ ★ ★ ★ ★ ★ ★ ★ ★ ★ ★

SUMMARY

President Harding's easy, comfortable style matched America's mood in 1920. In an attempt to maintain world peace and order, the Harding administration negotiated the Allies' war debts and concluded the Washington Conference treaties. But Harding's administration was marred by scandal. Business returned to prewar conditions, but the nation reacted to the war by restricting immigration and by discriminating against racial and ethnic minorities.

CHECKING FOR UNDERSTANDING

1. **Identify** Fordney-McCumber Tariff, Washington Conference, National Origins Act

2. **Define** reparations, open shop, technological unemployment, welfare capitalism

3. **Cite** two foreign policy problems the United States faced after the war.

4. **Summarize** the treaties negotiated at the Washington Conference.

5. **Explain** the main provisions of the National Origins Act.

6. **Describe** the scandals of President Harding's administration.

THINKING CRITICALLY

7. **Analyzing Changes** Explain why the election of Harding fit America's mood and why this mood had changed since 1917.

GLOBAL PERSPECTIVES

8. **Demonstrating Reasoned Judgment** One major effect of World War I was the decline of Europe's dominance due to its heavy indebtedness from the war. Write a short paragraph to evaluate the pros and cons of demanding the payment of war debts from Allies. Include in your analysis the desire among nations for peace and cooperation.

★ ★ ★ ★ ★ ★ ★ ★ ★ ★ ★ ★ ★ ★ ★ ★ ★

Map and Graph Skills

Interpreting Graphic Data

"A picture is worth a thousand words." How many times have you heard that expression? Often it is true. A political cartoonist, for example, can reduce a wordy newspaper column into a clever illustration that says the same thing in a more concise and interesting way. Another way to present information pictorially is in the form of a graph.

Explanation

When historical information involves numbers and statistics, it is often presented as a graph. Graphs frequently have an advantage over printed text because they make organizing and comparing detailed or complex information much easier. Graphic data can be presented in the form of circle graphs, bar graphs, or line graphs. All three forms organize and show information visually rather than verbally. That is why graphs, just like political cartoons, catch your eye and hold your attention.

Use the following guidelines to interpret data presented as a graph:

a. What is the purpose of the graph? How does the data it presents relate to any printed material that accompanies it?

b. What does each part of the graph represent? What does each color, line, or bar represent? Are there labels? If two or more graphs are shown, observe the labels for each.

c. What significant changes or other relationships does the graph show? What generalizations can be made about these changes or relationships?

Example

The circle graphs on this page provide immigration data. Apply the guidelines to interpret the data shown on them.

a. What is the purpose of this graph?

• Each graph compares the geographic distribution of immigrants who came to the United States during three different years. Related written material in the chapter notes anti-immigrant sentiments in the 1920s. It also details a change in immigration policy after 1927 to restrict Asian immigrants and those from eastern and southern Europe.

b. What does each part of the graph represent?

• Each colored section on these graphs shows the percentage of immigrants who came to the

United States from a specific area of the world in 1921, 1925, and 1930.

c. What significant changes or other relationships does the graph show?

• The proportion of immigrants from eastern and southern Europe was reduced from 41 percent in 1921 to only 4 percent in 1925, while at the same time

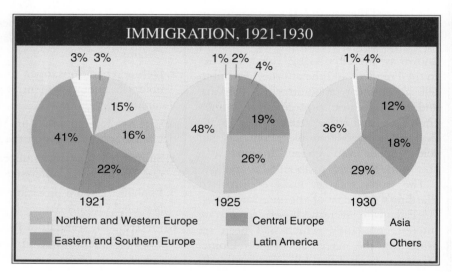

IMMIGRATION, 1921-1930

1921: 3%, 3%, 15%, 16%, 22%, 41%
1925: 1%, 2%, 4%, 19%, 26%, 48%
1930: 1%, 4%, 12%, 18%, 29%, 36%

Northern and Western Europe   Central Europe   Asia
Eastern and Southern Europe   Latin America   Others

Latin American immigration increased from 15 percent to 48 percent. The percentage of immigrants from northern, western, and central Europe remained fairly constant throughout the 1920s.

Practice

For further practice, apply the guidelines to the bar graph on page 767 showing additional data about immigration.

The Coolidge Era

SETTING THE SCENE

The chief business of the American people is business. The man who builds a factory builds a temple. The man who works there worships there.

—CALVIN COOLIDGE
Speech to the American Society
of Newspaper Editors, January 1925

Section Focus

When awakened to hear that Harding's death had made him President, Vice President Coolidge was off at his boyhood home in Vermont. His father, a justice of the peace, administered the oath of office in the flickering light of a kerosene lamp. This homey scene typified the small-town values of the new President—values he would come to depend on throughout the course of his presidency, and which many Americans still shared.

Objectives

After studying this section, you should be able to:
- Discuss the changes to industry Henry Ford introduced.
- Outline the problems of farmers during the 1920s and the government's response to them.
- Describe the purpose of the Kellogg-Briand Pact.

Coolidge had many of the traits often associated with rural small-town America. He was intensely conservative, cautious, and given to few words. In occasional public speeches and magazine articles, he preached the old-fashioned virtues of honesty, thrift, and hard work. His philosophy of government was simple: economy and *laissez-faire*. To take as little action as possible was with Coolidge almost a principle of life; he once said, "Four-fifths of all our troubles in this life would disappear if we would only sit down and keep still." As President, Coolidge was reputed to sleep 10 hours every night and take a nap every afternoon.

By 1924 the scandals of the Harding administration had surfaced, thus presenting the Democratic party with a ready-made issue for the presidential campaign. But the Democrats threw away their chances for victory at their national convention. The party was deeply divided over two issues: Prohibition—which the rural regions favored and the cities opposed—and more importantly, the Ku Klux Klan. This secret society, which took its name and ritual from the southern organization of Reconstruction times, resembled the Know-Nothings of the 1850s in that it was designed to intimidate African Americans, Catholics, Jews, immigrants, and "foreign ideas" such as the League of Nations. By the mid-1920s the Klan had become a major force in politics, despite its willingness to use terror and violence to carry out its goals.

At the 1924 Democratic convention, the rivals for the nomination were William G. McAdoo of California—who favored Prohibition and was generally supported by the West and South—and Governor Alfred E. Smith of New York—a Roman Catholic and opponent of Prohibition whose following came mostly from urban areas of the Northeast. Smith's supporters wanted an outright condemnation of the Ku Klux Klan, which southern and western delegates blocked. The two candidates were deadlocked for so long that the cowboy-humorist Will Rogers suggested that the eventual nominee might be born at the convention. By the time a compromise candidate—John W. Davis of West Virginia—was nominated on the one-hundred-and-third ballot, the Democrats had lost all chance of winning the election.

The Republicans campaigned on the slogan "Keep cool with Coolidge"; the way to keep business thriving, they said, was not to "rock the boat" but to keep in power the party that favored business. This strategy was successful. In an election that attracted only half the eligible voters to the polls, Coolidge won easily. The Democrats carried only the states of the solid South—a traditional Democratic stronghold.

The Growth of Big Business

During the 1920s many Americans went almost dizzy with prosperity. As business boomed and wages rose, former

WILL ROGERS
1879-1935

Part native American, Will Rogers grew up in Indian Territory and became a cowboy while in his teens. He landed jobs with Wild West shows, where he would mix in a few jokes while doing his rope-twirling act. Aiming good-natured barbs at famous people, he became known as the "cowboy philosopher."

By 1920 Will Rogers was a star of both stage and screen. Starting in 1926, his daily newspaper column spread his humorous views of life and politics throughout the nation. Claiming "I don't make jokes—I just watch the government and report the facts," he always poked fun in a lighthearted way and was never hostile; one of his favorite sayings was "I never met a man I didn't like." By the late 1920s audiences were listening to his commentary on radio. To Americans, Rogers had become a national treasure.

luxuries became necessities. A combination of increased leisure time for both men and women, new gadgets, new amusements, and more money to spend resulted in something approaching glorification of wealth and of the material comforts that went with it.

The outstanding symbol of the new age was the automobile. In the early twentieth century, when the manufacture of automobiles in the United States was just beginning, driving cars was a sport for the well-off, like racing yachts. By 1930, however, with about 27 million automobiles registered, it was possible for the nation's entire population to be on the highway at one time.

Henry Ford almost single-handedly changed the automobile from a toy of the wealthy to a necessity for all. Ford's famous "Model T"—affectionately known as the "Tin Lizzie"—was so simple to operate that anyone could learn to drive, and so cheap that most families could afford it. Ford applied many of the familiar techniques of successful industrialists, such as the use of standardized parts and the formation of a vertical organization to combine different operations and eliminate "middlemen." But Ford's greatest achievement was the assembly line, which divided operations into such simple tasks that most of the work could be done by unskilled labor. Furthermore, by bringing the parts to the workers, assembly lines sped up production so fast that Ford could boast that:

...[R]aw iron ore at the docks at eight Monday morning could be marketed as a complete Ford car on Wednesday noon, allowing 15 hours for shipment.

Ford's economies so reduced costs that an American automobile, which sold for an average price of $2,123 in 1907, could be bought for as little as $290 in 1924. And while reducing costs, he staved off unionization by nearly doubling wages, in 1914, to $5 a day. Other employers

resented Ford because his pay scale was so high that it caused discontent among their own workers. It was Ford's belief that mass production methods and low prices would produce an immense market for goods. This turned out to be correct, but the very simplicity of the formula spawned imitators, and by the mid-1920s other great trusts, notably General Motors and Chrysler, were competing successfully with Ford.

The impact of the automobile on life in the United States was revolutionary. Although small businesses generally continued to decline, new fields for small enterprises—garages, gas stations, diners, and tourist homes appeared. Draft animals disappeared from farms as tractors took their places. The isolation of rural areas lessened, as cars put towns within easy reach of many farmers, and put the country within reach of city dwellers. Workers could commute to their jobs. Whole families became more mobile. Sunday drives became so popular that one wit remarked, "If all the cars in America were placed end to end, it would be Sunday."

It seemed that Americans had discovered a magic formula for producing wealth and fulfilling human wants on a scale never before thought possible. Its ingredients were mass production, standardized products, and a nationwide market. This formula tended to favor big businesses over small, because only big businesses could set up assembly lines, do the research necessary for constant development of new products, and afford nationwide advertising. It was natural then that the 1920s should see much concentration of industry. Mergers and holding companies helped to concentrate

Examining Graphs   *A drop in auto sales occurred in 1927, when Ford stopped producing the Model T. Six months later his new Model A came out. What factors spurred auto sales?*

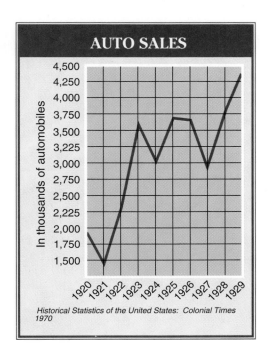

AUTO SALES

In thousands of automobiles

4,500
4,250
4,000
3,750
3,500
3,225
3,000
2,750
2,500
2,225
2,000
1,750
1,500

1920 1921 1922 1923 1924 1925 1926 1927 1928 1929

Historical Statistics of the United States: Colonial Times 1970

industry by reducing competition. The chain store soon became a familiar sight on Main Street, capturing one-fourth of the grocery business by 1929.

Whereas many Americans had formerly regarded big business as an enemy, they now relied on it both to supply cheap products and to create new opportunities for wealth. The stock market provided striking evidence of this when, for the first time in history, some members of the general public began to buy securities. The prices of shares of stock, especially those connected with new industries, mounted to dizzying heights. More and more purchasers "invested in the future."

With wealthier Americans speculating in the stock market, money to run business came from more and more diverse sources. Business, on the other hand, was becoming more and more concentrated. One device used by businesspeople to concentrate financial power was the "pyramiding" of holding companies, whereby it was possible—with a relatively small outlay of capital—for businesspeople to gain control of immense industrial properties. Another legal method promoters used to gain the use of other people's money without surrendering control was the issuance of nonvoting preferred stock. Both of these devices led to such flagrant abuses that they were later forbidden by law.

The Plight of Agriculture

Farmers were the one great economic group that did not share in the Coolidge prosperity. The average income for farmers in 1929 was less than one-third of the average income for the rest of the country. Technological advances led to greater production, which caused a slump in farm prices even while farmers' costs mounted. As one account puts it:

———

Freight rates, wages, taxes, farm implements, and the like, all of which went into the farmers' cost of production, remained high or came down via the stairway, while farm prices took the elevator.

———

Examining Photographs In this park in St. Louis, Missouri, drivers out for a Sunday ride create a huge traffic jam. By 1929 one in every five Americans owned a car. What changes did the popularity of the automobile bring to American life?

Farm prices took a disastrous slide in 1920 and 1921 and did not recover. Wheat went from almost $2.50 a bushel to less than $1.50. The foreign market dwindled because the United States had changed from a debtor to a creditor nation. Before World War I, foreign investments in the United States exceeded American investment abroad; the principal means of making up this unfavorable credit balance was for the United States to export agricultural staples, such as wheat and cotton. During the war the balance shifted the other way, principally because of United States loans to the Allies. With the return of peace, countries owing the United States money preferred not to buy its products. Great Britain, for example, often bought wheat from Argentina or Canada rather than from the United States, especially after the Fordney-McCumber Tariff reduced the American market for British goods.

The domestic market also diminished. The use of new fabrics such as rayon lessened the demand for cotton; the substitution of tractors and trucks for draft animals reduced the need for fodder. Faced with decreasing demands for the traditional staples, farmers might have been expected to shift to other products—but that was easier said than done. A Southern tenant farmer usually had no skill at anything but raising cotton. A Dakota wheat farmer usually lacked the capital and the knowledge to change, say, to dairy farming, which in any case was not well suited to that region. Moreover, credit and marketing facilities were geared to the existing staple crops of each region. Many farmers had borrowed heavily during the war to buy new land at inflated prices. The only obvious way to pay off the debt was to raise more crops. But more crops meant unsaleable surpluses; unsaleable surpluses meant low prices. And low prices made the debt burden even heavier.

Early in Harding's administration, members of Congress from the Midwest and plains states formed what was known as the Farm Bloc. It included about 25 Senators and 100 Representatives from both parties. Strong enough to hold a balance of power in Congress, the Farm Bloc was able to force through several laws favoring farmers. The Capper-Volstead Act of 1922 made farm cooperatives free of antitrust laws; the Intermediate Credits Act of 1923 set up federal banks to make loans to aid farm cooperatives.

But none of the laws dealt with the farmers' major problem: surpluses they could not sell. If wheat farmers were to benefit from the 42-cent a bushel protective tariff, which eliminated foreign competition, they somehow had to limit the amount of wheat they themselves put on that market.

The Farm Bloc supported the McNary-Haugen bill. Senator Charles McNary of Oregon and Representative Gilbert Haugen of Iowa presented the bill to Congress every year from 1924 to 1928. This bill proposed that the federal government buy crop surpluses and sell them abroad, while protecting the U.S. market with a high tariff. This would immediately raise the domestic price. Whatever losses the government suffered would be covered by an equalization fee—a tax charged against producers. Supporters of the McNary-Haugen bill claimed that it would help farmers as the tariff helped manufacturers. They claimed it would raise farm incomes by as much as one-third.

Twice the bill passed Congress, but both times President Coolidge vetoed it. The idea would not work, he insisted, and furthermore, a "healthy economic condition is best maintained through a free play of competition." Thus, farmers failed in their effort to obtain protections similar to those many businesses received at the time.

Foreign Affairs

During the 1920s both Republican Presidents worked to promote world peace through individual agreements rather than through membership in the League of Nations, which they perceived as an entangling alliance. During Coolidge's administration, France and the United States took the lead in promoting a treaty that attempted to "outlaw war." Called the Kellogg-Briand Pact after the American secretary of state and the French foreign minister who proposed it, the treaty was eventually ratified by 64 nations, each solemnly agreeing to abandon war "as an instrument of national policy" and to settle disputes by peaceful means. The treaty was hailed as a great victory for peace. The Pact, often called the Pact of Paris, was signed by most nations only under certain conditions. The primary condition of most was to retain the right to defend themselves against acts of aggression. The United States, for example, also stated that the pact did not overrule the principles of the Monroe Doctrine.

A serious weakness of the pact was no means of enforcement. No provisions were set down in the pact in the event there were acts of aggression among signer nations.

Although the United States generally participated in talks and treaties with European and Asian nations during this period, its manner toward Latin America remained protective. The Harding and Coolidge administrations—following the Roosevelt Corollary to the Monroe Doctrine—occasionally sent troops to "preserve order" in Caribbean countries. They became increasingly aware, however, that the Latin American people acutely resented such intervention. Although not willing to give up the right to intervene, Secretary of State Charles Evans Hughes believed troops should be sent to Latin America only to promote political stability, not to assist American investors. Accordingly, in the mid-1920s, U.S. marines withdrew from the Dominican Republic and Nicaragua, where they had been sent in the previous decade to maintain order. But in 1926 a revolt broke out in Nicaragua against President Adolfo Diaz, who had gained power with the help of American financial interests. Coolidge sent more than 5,000 marines to assist Diaz, arousing a storm of protest both within this country and without. The rebels, led by César Augusto Sandino, continued fighting until 1933.

★ ★ ★ ★ ★ ★ ★ ★ ★ ★ ★ ★ ★ ★ ★ ★ ★

Section Two Review

★ ★ ★ ★ ★ ★ ★ ★ ★ ★ ★ ★ ★ ★ ★ ★ ★

SUMMARY

After Harding's death, Coolidge continued Harding's probusiness economic policies. The automobile industry symbolized the American public's postwar spending spree that was spurred by higher wages, mass production, and standardized products. The economy boomed, but membership in labor unions declined and prices for farm products dropped. The Kellogg-Briand Pact symbolized the world's efforts to solve international problems without war. United States intervention, however, continued in Latin America's affairs.

CHECKING FOR UNDERSTANDING

1. **Identify** Henry Ford, assembly line, McNary-Haugen Bill, Farm Bloc

2. **Explain** Henry Ford's manufacturing process and why it made automobiles less costly.

3. **List** three ways that the automobile changed American life.

4. **Summarize** the farmers' situation in the 1920s and how government reacted to their economic condition.

5. **Discuss** the purpose and effectiveness of the Kellogg-Briand Pact.

THINKING CRITICALLY

6. **Supporting an Opinion** Would you agree with the opinion that Coolidge did not regard farming in the same way he viewed big business? Supply facts to support your opinion.

CONNECTIONS: HISTORY AND ECONOMICS

7. **Analyzing a Quotation** Reread the quotation from Calvin Coolidge in "Setting the Scene" on page 771. Write two opinions on his statement: one from the perspective of a union worker and the other from a businessowner's point of view.

★ ★ ★ ★ ★ ★ ★ ★ ★ ★ ★ ★ ★ ★ ★ ★ ★

The "Roaring Twenties"

SETTING THE SCENE

[Today's woman] is shameless, selfish, and honest, but at the same time she considers these three attributes virtues. Why not? She takes a man's point of view as her mother never could, and when she loses she is not afraid to admit defeat....

— *THE NEW YORK TIMES*
July 16, 1922

Section Focus

The 1920s saw striking changes in American society. Radio and film, the new entertainments, became immensely popular. The arts flowered. "Coolidge prosperity" provided more leisure time and more spending money for new gadgets. The availability of credit helped many to buy more than they could afford. Women adopted new standards of behavior that would never have been acceptable before. To many, however, these changes suggested a loss of important traditional values.

Objectives

After studying this section, you should be able to:
- Describe changes in women's lives during the 1920s.
- Outline developments in the arts and education during this period.

From a Long Island airfield on May 20, 1927, a small plane called the *Spirit of St. Louis* took off for France. Twenty-five-year-old Charles Lindbergh set off to make the first nonstop solo flight across the

Atlantic. Thirty-three and one-half hours later, Lindbergh landed near Paris. Huge crowds greeted him. An American naval vessel brought him home, and even greater crowds welcomed him back to the United States. "Lucky Lindy," as he was called, became a hero of the age.

President Coolidge called him "a boy representing the best traditions of his country." In an era when the ideals and heroes of history were questioned, when politics was riddled with graft, and when machines seemed to be replacing people, Lindbergh helped people restore some confidence in themselves. He proved that Americans were still capable of pioneering, even in the machine age. Quiet, courageous, and self-reliant, Lindbergh showed that not all the old values of life had disappeared, despite the changing priorities of modern society. As writer F. Scott Fitzgerald said of Lindbergh:

A young Minnesotan who seemed to have nothing to do with his generation did a heroic thing, and for a moment people set down their glasses in country clubs and speakeasies and thought of their old dreams.

Radio and Motion Pictures

Advertising and the increased demand for goods were especially stimulated by the spread of a new invention—the radio. In November 1920, station KDKA in Pittsburgh broadcast the news of Harding's landslide victory in one of the first commercial broadcasts in history. By 1927 the Federal Radio Commission was established to regulate broadcasting stations—already numbering close to 700. The sales of radio equipment skyrocketed from $12.2 million in 1921 to $842.5 million in 1929. NBC and CBS, the first nationwide radio networks, sold advertising time to finance their operations and hired popular entertainers to appear on

The young motion-picture industry also mushroomed. The first feature-length film appeared in 1915. By 1929 there were about 100 million paid admissions to movie theaters every week—proof that moviegoing had gained respectability. During the 1920s the motion-picture industry moved from New York to southern California. Mary Pickford, Charlie Chaplin, Douglas Fairbanks, Gloria Swanson, and Clara Bow were among the first stars of the silent screen. In 1927 Warner Brothers introduced "talking" pictures, which made the movies more popular than ever.

Together, radio and motion pictures helped to make the 1920s a "golden age of sports." By listening to sportscasters and watching newsreels, it was possible for the general public to enjoy sporting events all over the nation. Well-established sports such as football, boxing, and baseball reached new heights of popularity, and traditionally upper-class sports such as golf, tennis, and polo gained new followers. Notre Dame's famous football backfield, the "Four Horsemen," were better known than the cabinet members. Baseball star Babe Ruth became a national hero. Enthusiasm for the Jack Dempsey-Gene Tunney boxing match in 1927 reached such a frenzy that one department store sold $90,000 worth of radios in the two weeks before the event.

their shows. Secretary of Commerce Herbert Hoover opposed advertising, which he thought would "kill broadcasting." The public, however, which had few choices for entertainment, continued to enjoy radio; products that were advertised nationwide gained a great advantage over local products.

New Directions in Society

The rapid changes caused by the progress of technology in the 1920s did cause some serious problems, however. Automobiles, though they offered an exciting new freedom of movement, also killed as many Americans in 1928 and 1929 as had lost their lives in battle during World War I. Cities lost some of their attractiveness as automobiles enabled people and businesses to move to the suburbs. The easily available "canned entertainment" provided by radio and motion pictures seemed to discourage Americans from creating their own amusements.

Unfortunately, during the 1920s crime became big business. Gangsters such as Al

ONE perfected feature—the MOTOR DRIVEN BRUSH—is alone worth to you the entire price of the Electric SWEEPER-VAC. This efficient, soft brush (motor driven) revolves 1350 times per minute. It gets ALL lint, threads, hairs and embedded dirt, and, with Powerful Suction, draws them into the dust bag. Ask your dealer for the "Electric SWEEPER-VAC" (don't accept a substitute.) Give it a thorough test on your own rugs.

Pneuvac Company — 166 Fremont Street — Worcester, Mass.

Electric
SWEEPER-VAC
With Motor Driven Brush

Capone and Dutch Schultz consolidated the illegal liquor trade on many of the same principles used to consolidate the automobile and steel industries. The Prohibition Bureau, set up to enforce the law against the distilling and sale of liquor, was understaffed, underpaid, graft-ridden, and ineffective. Although liquor consumption dropped substantially during Prohibition, illegal drinking by millions created an illegitimate billion-dollar industry. The entrepreneurs in this illegal business became wealthy enough to buy beautiful homes in Florida, steel-plated limousines, and fabulous jewels, such as Capone's eleven-and-a-half carat diamond ring. Some gangsters became powerful enough to corrupt and even take over local governments.

Rural America, with its traditional values and churchgoing ways, tended to support Prohibition, but the cities generally opposed it. The customary diets of several urban ethnic groups included liquor, and many city dwellers resisted Prohibition as the work of religious crusaders. Regardless, Prohibition was never fully enforced. Many people supported Prohibition publicly while privately continuing to drink, prompting humorist Will Rogers to note that some folks would vote dry "as long as [they] can stagger to the polls."

Despite the success of the illegal liquor trade, Prohibition actually gained in popularity during the 1920s. In 1928 voters elected more supporters of Prohibition to Congress than ever before, as well as a "dry" President, Herbert Hoover. The popularity of Prohibition was a sign of continuing faith in the possibility of achieving a better life, of a longing for the ideals that had eroded in the horrors of World War I. Traditional standards of behavior were changing as Americans left

the villages for the cities and the farms for the factories. To many, Prohibition seemed a way to halt this change in values.

Women in the 1920s

The 1920s saw women express greater personal freedom. A dramatic new woman of the 1920s—the "flapper"—demanded the same freedom enjoyed by men. She sometimes smoked cigarettes and drank liquor and dressed in a way her mother and grandmother would not have believed possible. While most women in the 1920s were not flappers, this new young woman demonstrated how modern women's behavior was changing.

American family life was also changing. Couples had fewer children because of increased knowledge about family planning, divorce rates increased, and more women than ever before sought employment outside the home.

Having achieved the right to vote, women sought financial independence as well. Many young single women became salesclerks in department stores, secretaries, or telephone operators, for example. In 1920, 25 percent of women workers were in clerical and sales work. Eventually the employees in those particular jobs became almost exclusively female. Graduates of women's colleges began to seek jobs in business rather than in more traditional jobs such as teaching. But many women, especially married women who had to work to support families, were confined to jobs with long hours, poor conditions, and low wages. Women who worked outside the home suffered severe discrimination, often receiving only 50 to 60 percent of a man's wages for the same work. And women continued to meet with difficulty when trying to enter prestigious professions such as science and law.

Examining Illustrations *Activists like Mary McLeod Bethune failed to get a federal law against the lynching of blacks. What attitudes might explain why such incidents increased in the 1920s?*

Holeproof Hosiery

One of the clearest indicators of emerging feminism was in women's fashions. Skirts that only years before had rested at the ankles were raised to the knee. Dark cotton stockings were replaced by flesh-colored silk ones. Long hair that was once pulled back and formed into a bun was cut close to the head with a single curl at each ear. Camisole knickers came to symbolize the new equality between the sexes.

Women revolutionized fashion during the 1920s as a display of their desire for greater status in society and as a response to society's changing standards of prosperity, independence, and beauty. A modern woman needed to look modern—different. The "modern" look involved not just clothing and coordinated accessories, but an updated "face." Cosmetics sales soared as women copied the look of Hollywood movie stars. The average American woman used about one pound of face powder and eight rouge compacts yearly.

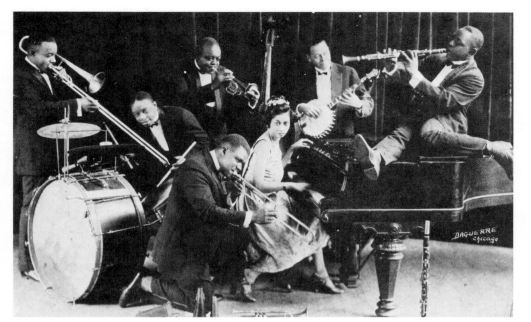

Individual women, however, made great contributions in many fields—often under difficult circumstances. Amelia Earhart learned to fly planes and became the first woman to complete a solo flight across the Atlantic. Dorothy Thompson became a famous journalist. Mary McLeod Bethune—though a black woman born into poverty—founded her own college, founded the National Council of Negro Women, and served as a government consultant.

Most Americans—both men and women—continued to believe that a married woman's place was in the home. Thus, in spite of a spirit of independence, most women continued to be bound by the belief that their role was different from that of men, that they were to be mothers and homemakers. With new electric technology, the nature of being a homemaker changed. New household appliances, such as refrigerators and vacuum cleaners, commercial laundries, and canned food made hard, time-consuming domestic duties much easier. Many who stayed at home and became mothers, particularly in middle-class families, managed motherhood by listening to child-rearing experts who promoted regularly scheduled feedings for children and regimented routines for such children's extra-curricular activities as music lessons and clubs.

Cultural Achievements

American literature thrived in the 1920s. Some writers, such as the novelist Willa Cather and the poet Robert Frost, tried to recapture the spirit and traditions of rural America; others, such as poet Carl Sandburg, examined what was happening in America's cities. In Eugene O'Neill, the United States produced its finest playwright. O'Neill found material in many aspects of American life—from the rage of a worker in the hold of a steamship in *The Hairy Ape,* to family tension in a decaying New England town in *Desire Under the Elms.* Ernest Hemingway, who had driven an ambulance on the Italian front during World War I, wrote about the meaningless violence of war in *A Farewell to Arms.* His fiction created a new literary style characterized by direct, simple, spare prose. The poet T. S. Eliot saw a world filled with "hollow men" and, in *The Wasteland,* one that would end "not with a bang but a whimper."

Postwar disillusionment was often manifested as criticism of American life. Henry Ford said that "history is bunk," and a school of "debunking" historians reexamined the past and reevaluated more accurately the facts behind the myths of many American heroes. Many American writers did the same. In his novels *Main*

Connections

HISTORY AND TECHNOLOGY

HOUSEHOLD TECHNOLOGY

"…the wise woman," proclaimed a 1920s electric company ad, "delegates to electricity all that electricity can do." Inventions such as electric irons, vacuum cleaners, and washing machines changed the lives of urban middle-class housewives

A 1920s appliance store

in the 1920s. But these devices only changed the way women spent their time, not how much time they spent.

One study revealed that upper middle-class homemakers employed only half as many full-time servants as their mothers had. These women did work their mothers had hired others to do. Although some women found that laborsaving devices gave them more leisure time, others said that the dirt and soot caused by automobile traffic and nearby factories made their homes dirtier than those of the previous generation. Most of the women surveyed said they spent less time on housework than their mothers, but other demands had increased. "So many things our mothers didn't know about, we feel that we ought to do for our children," said one woman.

> **MAKING THE TECHNOLOGY CONNECTION**
>
> **1.** What laborsaving devices aided housewives in the 1920s?
>
> **2.** How did laborsaving devices affect American homemakers?
>
> **LINKING PAST AND PRESENT**
>
> **3.** What technologies of today have changed the way people spend their time?

Street and *Babbitt*, Sinclair Lewis depicted the absurdities of life in small-town America. H. L. Mencken mocked the "vast… herd of good-natured animals" who made up most of the machine-age society. Mencken saw no hope for improvement. "If I am convinced of anything," he wrote, "it is that Doing Good is in bad taste."

Achievements in American literature were matched in the arts. The new city skyscrapers and suburban homes expanded the opportunities of architects like Frank Lloyd Wright, who achieved worldwide fame for his bold use of new materials and for architectural designs free of traditional influence. In jazz, which started with black Dixieland bands in New Orleans, America produced a new form of music. At first seen as corrupting the morals of young people, jazz was soon accepted as an important art form. In the fine arts, the American scene was brilliantly portrayed by such painters as Reginald

Marsh, Thomas Hart Benton, George Bellows, and Edward Hopper. In photography, Alfred Stieglitz achieved an international reputation.

Changes and Challenges in Education

A significant amount of the new wealth of the 1920s went into education, both through taxes for new public schools and through private donations to colleges and universities. The introduction of the school bus made possible the gradual replacement of bare, one-room country schoolhouses with large, well-equipped central schools. High school was no longer the privilege of the well-off, but was also attended by the children of farmers and workers—although graduation from high school remained the exception rather than the rule. Both high school and college enrollment increased steadily.

Examining Photographs *Opposing attorneys Clarence Darrow (left) and William Jennings Bryan pose during the famous Scopes trial. Scopes was later freed on appeal, but the trial proved too much for Bryan, who died a week after it ended. What basic clash of values in 1920s' society did the trial illustrate?*

A philosophy of education, long championed by John Dewey, emphasized learning through direct experience and experiment rather than through memorization. Greater emphasis was placed on science, which Dewey viewed as a way of using both thought and activity to investigate nature.

Some religious groups found these new educational theories threatening and were able to gain laws in some states to prevent the teaching of evolution in public schools. This set the stage for a battle between science and religion. It came in 1925, at the trial of John T. Scopes, a teacher in Dayton, Tennessee, who was willing to be arrested for teaching evolution to his high-school class. The American Civil Liberties Union (ACLU) had raised money to test the new anti-evolution law in Tennessee and had asked Scopes if he would volunteer for the cause. The famous attorney Clarence Darrow defended Scopes, while William Jennings Bryan aided the prosecution for the anti-evolution forces. After a sensational trial, Scopes was convicted, but Bryan, who took the witness stand as an expert on the Bible, was made to look foolish through Darrow's penetrating questioning. The Scopes case symbolized the tensions of the 1920s, as some Americans tried to resist the tide of social change and preserve older values and beliefs.

The Harlem Renaissance

World War I had been a liberating experience for many African Americans. This was especially true of those who went abroad. For the first time they were freed from the second-class citizenship they suffered in the United States. But the prejudice and discrimination that awaited them at home helped to create among blacks a spirit of pride and protest, forging a new unity and a new African American:

. . . who had pride in heritage and self and who, through poetry, music, dance, and the theater, was able to create works of beauty out of travail and sufferings, as well as out of the more humorous facts of life.

A striking outcome of this new spirit among black Americans was the "Harlem Renaissance." In New York City, the intellectual capital of the United States, a number of highly talented black people rose to fame. Some were in the performing arts, including actors Charles Gilpin and Richard B. Harrison, singers Roland Hayes and Ethel Waters, dancer Bill Robinson, and singer-actor Paul Robeson. Others were scholars, including sociologist E. Franklin Frazier and economist Abram L. Harris. Still others were writers, such as poets Countee Cullen and Langston Hughes and novelists Jessie H. Fauset, Zora Neale Hurston, and Walter White.

Musical revues, small nightclubs with singing and dancing, drew many whites to Harlem during this period. Here they mixed with blacks for the first time, enjoying the entertainment but never seeing the real lives of ordinary African Americans. White interest in black expression in art, literature, and music produced a feeling among some blacks in Harlem that the race problem had been solved. Langston Hughes had a different perception of white interest in black culture when he wrote in *The Big Sea:*

---

*I was there. I had a swell time while
it lasted. But I thought it wouldn't last
long. For how could a large and
enthusiastic number of people be crazy
about [blacks] forever?*

More influential than the intellectuals and artists among African Americans themselves was a dynamic leader from Jamaica, Marcus Garvey. A spokesman for "Negro Nationalism," which exalted black culture and traditions, Garvey formed the Universal Negro Improvement Association, which soon boasted a million members. Garvey told his followers they would never find justice in America and proposed to lead them to Africa. People were not interested, but Garvey stimulated the pride of blacks in their history and heritage.

SUMMARY

Prosperity gave Americans more leisure time, and they spent much of it listening to radio, traveling in automobiles, and watching motion pictures. Rapid social changes made some Americans anxious, however, especially as crime rates soared. Although women in the 1920s gained some personal and economic freedom, their roles in society continued to be separate from those of men. American literature and art blossomed, highlighted by the Harlem Renaissance.

CHECKING FOR UNDERSTANDING

1. **Identify** Amelia Earhart, Mary McLeod Bethune, John T. Scopes

2. **List** three ways that radio and motion pictures changed the nature of entertainment in America.

3. **Cite** the factors that resulted in increased crime in the 1920s.

4. **Summarize** changes in women's personal and economic status during the 1920s.

5. **Describe** three cultural achievements of the 1920s.

6. **Discuss** the significance of the Harlem Renaissance.

THINKING CRITICALLY

7. **Evaluating Achievements** How are the advances made by women in the 1920s significant to the lives of American women today?

CONNECTIONS: HISTORY AND TECHNOLOGY

8. **Making Comparisons** Compare the impact of the new entertainment technologies of the 1920s with the effect of television, compact disc and tape players, videocassette recorders, video games, and other modern machines. In which era do you think new technology played a larger role in people's lives? Explain.

★ ★ ★ ★ ★ ★ ★ ★ ★ ★ ★ ★ ★ ★ ★ ★ ★ ★

Interpreting Primary Sources

Harlem Renaissance

Just as Americans had become interested in the theater, movies, and literature, many developed an interest in art in the 1920s. While some Americans were pleased with the outpouring of creativity as painters broke away from past traditions to explore new ways of portraying the world, others were shocked. African Americans, in particular, began to express their unique identity and heritage through art.

Although the outpouring of literature, art, and music known as the Harlem Renaissance involved only a handful of artists and writers, the power of their work brought international attention and acclaim to Harlem in the 1920s and 1930s. The visual artists associated with the Harlem Renaissance were a diverse group of people. Some, such as Edwin A. Harleston and Laura Wheeler Waring, painted in a style that was virtually indistinguishable from that of their white European and American peers. Others, such as Lois Mailou Jones and Aaron Douglas, used African design motifs to shape a distinctively African-American art.

Aaron Douglas, the best-known visual artist of the Harlem Renaissance, was perhaps also the one most influenced by African design. He developed his style of geometric symbolism as a painter of murals on public buildings. The painting shown here, *The Creation,* shows several elements characteristic of Douglas's style: a figure that represents not a particular person but all humankind; subtle, barely differentiated shades of purple and gray; and shapes such as circles, arches, and waves. Douglas believed that art can be a bridge between different cultures and peoples. He asserts this belief through his paintings, which describe human experience in a streamlined visual language that people of different times, places, genders, and races can easily understand.

In addition to his creative talent, Douglas inspired the Harlem Renaissance by actively searching out and training other African-American artists. His efforts were rewarded in January 1928 when the first all-black art show in the United States was held in New York City. Many of the exhibitors became eminent in American art.

Aaron Douglas became a professor of art at Fisk University in Nashville, Tennessee. Other exhibitors at the 1928 show later joined the faculties of Howard University, Atlanta University, and other black colleges. Still others opened art studios in cities such as Philadelphia and Chicago, to spread the spirit of the Harlem Renaissance well beyond New York.

The Creation *by Aaron Douglas*

EXAMINING THE PRIMARY SOURCE

1. Identify one shape, besides the circle, in the painting. What might it stand for?

2. Suggest what the circles represent.

3. What might the hand and figure symbolize?

THINKING CRITICALLY

4. What emotions may the figure in the painting be experiencing? Explain your viewpoint.

5. What foods, clothes, or celebrations reflect the origins of several groups of Americans?

★ Chapter 26 Review ★

★ Summary

President Harding's promise of a return to normalcy in 1920 struck a responsive chord among Americans who longed for peace, prosperity, and a return to simpler times. To establish peace, Harding negotiated a number of treaties with other nations to limit arms and to avoid future conflicts. Domestically, Harding put the United States on a course that stressed *laissez-faire* economics and the stimulation of business through high tariffs and low taxes. After Harding's death, his successor, Calvin Coolidge, continued the same probusiness economic programs.

Economic changes produced social changes. American industry produced an endless array of goods, including automobiles, that were eagerly snapped up by increasingly well-paid workers. Equally exciting was a burst of creativity in art and literature, typified by the Harlem Renaissance. Women pushed for more personal freedom and for a share in the prosperity. Not everyone shared equally, however. Farmers suffered due to slumping prices caused by overproduction. Union membership declined, and would-be immigrants encountered new barriers that barred their entry into the United States.

★ Using Vocabulary

Imagine that you are the chairperson of a large industrial company in the 1920s. Write a letter to the President using the terms below:

welfare capitalism   open shop

★ Reviewing Facts

1. **State** two reasons Harding was elected President in 1920.
2. **Summarize** the foreign policy actions of Harding and Coolidge.
3. **List** three ways that Harding and Coolidge helped stimulate business in America.
4. **Explain** why the Congress enacted the Emergency Quota Act and the National Origins Act.
5. **Discuss** how Henry Ford's innovations contributed to the growth of the economy.
6. **Describe** ways farmers were affected by tariffs and improved technology.

7. **Cite** evidence that the 1920s changed the arts and the lives of women and African Americans.

★ Understanding Concepts

ECONOMIC CHANGE

1. Explain why urban dwellers of all economic levels would support the economic changes of the 1920s. How did the rich, middle class, and poor stand to benefit?
2. Why did union membership decline during the 1920s? Speculate on the effect of an economic downturn on union membership.

SOCIAL CHANGE

3. Art, literature, and music thrived in the 1920s. What changes in society do you think inspired artists, writers, and musicians?
4. Explain why the 1920s was a period of both advances and setbacks for women and African Americans.

★ Thinking Critically

1. **Evaluating Foreign Policy**   What was the overriding goal of the treaties negotiated during the Harding and Coolidge terms? Would the United States have been better served by simply joining the League of Nations? Explain your position.
2. **Drawing Conclusions**   Explain how changes in business and manufacturing during the 1920s sparked a revolution in social customs, arts, and entertainment.
3. **Making Inferences**   Although this was a prosperous era, there were scandals in politics and organized crime increased. Explain how the new prosperity and Prohibition may have worked to make corruption more tempting.

★ Writing About History

NARRATION

Refer to the description of how to write a narrative essay in the History Writer's Handbook in the Appendix of this book. Your teacher will give you more specific instruction on the essay's length and the assignment's due date.

★ Chapter 26 Review ★

As you have read, radio became a phenomenon in the 1920s. During this time, most radio programs were broadcast "live" by actors and actresses in sound studios. Choose a topic from Chapter 26 and write an imaginary news report that could be narrated over radio. Remember that a radio broadcast must vividly describe details. When you have finished writing, reread your narrative and imagine you are the listener. Rewrite any parts that are unclear or do not adequately convey the sights, sounds, and feelings of the topic.

★ Learning Cooperatively

Work in groups of four to evaluate the changes that took place in the 1920s. One member of each group should assume one of the following roles: business-owner, farmer, African American, flapper. The goal of your group is to write four paragraphs that discuss the changes from these four perspectives. Have each group member read the paragraph describing the changes which affected him or her. Refer to the History Writer's Handbook for help in writing a paragraph.

★ Mastering Skills

DISTINGUISHING BETWEEN WARRANTED AND UNWARRANTED CLAIMS

When you make a claim, you are stating something as a fact. When you *warrant,* or guarantee, what you say to someone, you are assuring that person of the dependability and truth of what you have said. Therefore, when you make a *warranted claim,* you are stating something as a fact that has a basis in truth and can be proven. An *unwarranted claim,* on the other hand, is a statement that lacks any proof or facts to support it.

Thus, to determine if a claim is warranted or unwarranted, you have to look for supporting proof. Even if a claim appears to be true, if no evidence is presented to back it up, it must be considered unwarranted, and you would be correct to question it. In each case, you must ask yourself, "What evidence is presented to prove the truth of this statement?"

When you study history you need to determine if claims are warranted or unwarranted. The following guidelines will help you:

- Identify the claim that the speaker or writer is trying to make.

- Ask yourself, "What evidence is presented to prove the truth of this claim?"
- Realize that any claim that cannot be supported with evidence is an unwarranted claim.

Example   Study and analyze the two paragraphs that follow, and note how the guidelines have been applied.

When married women of the 1920s sought employment outside of the home, their troubles soon began and American family life would never be the same. Divorce rates increased, women smoked and drank in public, and wore dresses with hemlines above the knees. If they all had remained at home and followed their traditional roles, their circumstances would not have been so difficult.

(While it may be true that some women's behavior changed during the 1920s, the last statement is an assumption that cannot be proved by any facts. As a result, it is an unwarranted claim.)

Most married women who worked in the 1920s did so because they had to and then they suffered severe discrimination. They often worked as maids, or in garment and canning factories for long hours in bad conditions for low wages. They also received only 50 to 60 percent of a man's wages, even for the same work. In addition, women were barred from many jobs that were thought to be unsuitable for them.

(The claim that working women in the 1920s were discriminated against is supported by the statements that follow it. Therefore, the claim made at the beginning of the passage is a warranted claim.)

Practice   Think about what you have read in the chapter about the cultural achievements in the 1920s and then decide if the following claims are warranted or unwarranted. Cite evidence for those claims you consider warranted.

1. Ernest Hemingway could write accurately about the destruction and violence of war because he witnessed it first hand.

2. One reason historians deflated the image of many American heroes was because of postwar disillusionment with American society.

3. Jazz would not have survived if young people had not liked it first.

Chapter 27

The Depression Begins

Setting the Scene

Sections

1 The Stock Market Crashes

2 Hoover's Policies

3 The Depression Worsens

Historical Focus

Most Americans believed that the election of Herbert Hoover as President in 1928 would continue a decade of prosperity. This optimism quickly disappeared. A prolonged slump in agriculture, industrial overproduction, high tariffs, and the stock market crash, all contributed to the worst economic Depression in the nation's history. By 1932 millions of Americans were out of work. When Hoover's best efforts to revive the economy proved unsuccessful, the nation turned to a new President.

Concepts to Understand

- Why **economic change** from prosperity to depression was triggered by the stock market crash.
- How **political policy** changed as a result of the depression.

People to Know

Herbert Hoover, Alfred E. Smith, Harry L. Stimson, Franklin D. Roosevelt

Places to Locate

Manchuria

Terms to Identify

armories, speculation, on margin, installment buying, Hoover-Stimson Doctrine, Bonus Army

Guided Reading

As you read this chapter, seek the answers to the following questions.

1. How did President Hoover try to lift the country out of depression?
2. Why was Hoover's political leadership not more successful?

Spanning the Decades

	1928	1929	1930
Political		1929 *Stock market crash*	1930 *Hawley-Smoot Tariff is passed*
Cultural	1928 *First color motion pictures demonstrated by George Eastman*	1929 *Ernest Hemingway publishes* A Farewell to Arms	1930 *Sinclair Lewis is the first American to win Nobel Prize for Literature*

Employment Agency by Isaac Soyer, 1937. Oil on canvas 34 ¼ x 45 inches. Collection of Whitney Museum of American Art. Purchase 37.44

1932
Reconstruction Finance Corporation established

Bonus Army marches on Washington

Franklin D. Roosevelt elected President

1931   1932   1933

1931
"Star-Spangled Banner" becomes official U.S. national anthem

1932
Amelia Earhart is first woman to fly solo across the Atlantic

…Just knowing that for once in the time of the country they was a man to stand up and speak for him [the common worker], a man that could make what he felt so plain nobody could doubt he meant it, has made a lot of us feel a sight better even when they wasn't much to eat in our homes.

—GEORGE DOBBIN
in *These Are Our Lives,* 1939

The Stock Market Crashes

SETTING THE SCENE

...[T]he crowds about the ticker tape, like friends around the bedside of a stricken friend, reflected in their faces the story the tape was telling. There were no smiles. There were no tears either. Just the camaraderie of fellow-sufferers. Everybody wanted to tell his neighbor how much he had lost.

—*THE NEW YORK TIMES*
October 10, 1929

Section Focus

When Calvin Coolidge declared, "I do not choose to run in 1928," he cleared the way for Herbert Hoover to head the Republican ticket. Many people believed that electing Hoover President would help continue the prosperity. With the great stock market crash of 1929, however, and the chain of economic problems that followed, this optimism disappeared.

Objectives

After studying this section, you should be able to:

• Explain how Hoover's philosophy affected his economic policy.
• Explain the major causes of the Great Depression.

H erbert Hoover easily won the Republican nomination in 1928. A successful geologist, he had spent eight years as Secretary of Commerce in the Harding and Coolidge administrations. The Democrats chose Alfred E. Smith, four-time governor of New York. Their race for the presidency was marked by the influence of a new invention—the radio. This important political tool, however, helped Hoover more than Smith.

Although Smith had more personal sparkle, many listeners were repelled by his New York accent and witty off-the-cuff remarks. Hoover, on the other hand, sounded dignified and presented himself as a typical Iowa farmboy.

The Election of 1928

The most visible issue in the election campaign was Prohibition. Both candidates vowed to continue enforcing Prohibition, which Hoover dubbed "a great social and economic experiment, noble in motive and far-reaching in purpose." Smith candidly admitted that he occasionally broke the law by drinking a little wine. The Prohibition issue, however, masked other important differences between the candidates. Hoover represented rural, agrarian interests; Smith represented urban, industrial interests. The candidates' personal views on Prohibition brought to light their religious differences. Simply put, Hoover was a "dry" Quaker and Smith was a "wet" Roman Catholic.

Religion was at the core of a smear campaign against Smith's Catholicism. Wild tales circulated alleging that Catholics had turned certain Washington church sites into **armories**, or storehouses for guns. Some believed that the White House under Smith would become a branch of the Vatican. Although Hoover was embarrassed by these accusations and tried to squash them, they certainly hurt Smith's candidacy, especially in rural Protestant areas.

Late in the campaign, Hoover made a speech to offer his ideas on the proper relationship of government to business. Government, Hoover claimed, should be "an umpire instead of a player in the economic game." To be sure, government had a part to play—conservation of natural resources, scientific research, and flood control were places where Hoover

Examining Illustrations *Campaign posters often depict major differences between candidates in an election. The posters of Herbert Hoover and Alfred E. Smith contrast the stiff formality of Hoover with the smiling, more easy-going Smith. What was the most visible issue of the 1928 campaign?*

believed government could make useful contributions. But personal liberty depended on economic freedom. To involve government in business, Hoover warned, would undermine "the very instincts which carry our people forward to progress." He reminded his listeners that:

Our experiment in human welfare has yielded a degree of well-being unparalleled in the world.... We are nearer to the ideal of abolition of poverty and fear from the lives of men and women than ever before in any land.

Indeed, prosperity was the campaign issue that proved most damaging to the Democrats. The almost uninterrupted prosperity the country had enjoyed during the 1920s was associated in the minds of many voters with the Republican party. Republican campaign slogans such as "two cars in every garage" meant that the Democrats never really had a chance of winning the election.

Hoover won an impressive victory in the electoral college with a vote of 444 to 87. His appeal to rural Protestant voters even broke the Democrat's traditional hold on the solid South, resulting in a Republican win in 5 southern states. Although Smith lost the election, he won twice as many votes as had the Democratic candidate in 1924. More importantly, Hoover became the first presidential winner to lose in the nation's 12 largest cities. A shift in the rural-urban balance of political power in America was in the wind.

Hoover in the White House

When he took office in March 1929, Herbert Hoover still radiated optimism. In his inaugural address, he predicted that the United States would soon be "in sight of the day when poverty will be banished from this nation." Hoover did not believe the federal government should let economic events run their course but rather that it should help people to help themselves. He appointed commissions to investigate problems as diverse as housing, retirement pensions, unemployment insurance, child welfare, and conservation. One commission in particular, headed by former Attorney General George W. Wickersham, devoted 2 years to investigating Prohibition. The 11 members of the commission disagreed among themselves on whether Prohibition should continue. Most felt that the "noble experiment" was ineffective and promoted crime, yet the commission as a whole recommended that Prohibition be continued. Their report was satirized by the humorist Franklin P. Adams:

Prohibition is an awful flop.
We like it.
It can't stop what it's meant to stop.
We like it.
It's left a trail of graft and slime,
It don't prohibit worth a dime,
It's filled our land with vice and crime,
Nevertheless, we're for it.

The plight of farmers was an issue that demanded more immediate action. In their 1928 campaign platforms, both Democrats and Republicans had promised relief for the nation's growing agricultural problem. In April 1929, Hoover called Congress into special session to pass farming legislation. Members of Congress from farm states demanded that the federal government buy surplus farm products and sell them abroad. Hoover opposed this on the grounds that "no government agency should engage in buying and selling and price-fixing of products." Instead the President proposed that the federal government help farmers use their own organizations to market produce more efficiently and adjust supply to demand. Following this recommendation, Congress passed the Agricultural Marketing Act of 1929, which created a Federal Farm Board with $500 million at its disposal to help existing farm organizations and to form new ones. The Farm Board established national cooperatives—such as the National Livestock Marketing Association and the American Cotton Cooperative Association and then loaned these organizations money to help keep prices stable. But it was too little, too late. Farmers were soon worse off than ever, as America and the rest of the world plunged into the worst depression in history.

The Crash of 1929

The market value of **securities,** or stocks and bonds, on the New York Stock Exchange more than tripled between 1925 and 1929—from $27 billion to $87 billion. In the summer of 1929, for example, a share of American Telephone and Telegraph rose from $209 to $303. During the same period, a share of General Motors rose from $268 to $391 and by September 2 rose even higher—to $452 per share. As prices rose, more and more people began speculating. **Speculation** is engaging in a risky business venture on the chance a quick or sizeable profit can be made. People bought shares they thought would rise in price quickly, and after prices went up they would sell the stocks for a profit.

To maximize the potential profits on their investments, speculators commonly

Examining Photographs *Panic hit the stock market as people frantically tried to sell. What effect did speculation have on the stock market in 1929?*

TWO CENTS | In Greater | THREE CENTS | FOUR CENTS Elsewhere
New York | Within 200 Miles | Except 7th and 8th Postal Zones

STOCK PRICES SLUMP $14,000,000,000 IN NATION-WIDE STAMPEDE TO UNLOAD; BANKERS TO SUPPORT MARKET TODAY

Sixteen Leading Issues Down $2,893,520,108;
Tel. & Tel. and Steel Among Heaviest Losers

A shrinkage of $2,893,520,108 in the open market value of the shares of sixteen representative companies resulted from yesterday's sweeping decline on the New York Stock Exchange.

American Telephone and Telegraph was the heaviest loser, $448,905,162 having been lopped off of its total value. United States Steel common, traditional bellwether of the stock market, made its greatest nose-dive in recent years by falling from a high of 202½ to a low of 185. In a feeble last-minute rally it snapped back to 186, at which it closed, showing a net loss of 17½ points. This represented for the 8,131,055 shares of common stock outstanding a total loss in value of $142,293,446.

In the following table are shown the day's net depreciation in the outstanding shares of the sixteen companies referred to:

PREMIER ISSUES HARD HIT

Unexpected Torrent of Liquidation Again Rocks Markets.

DAY'S SALES 9,212,800

Nearly 3,000,000 Shares Are

Connections

HISTORY AND ECONOMICS

THE STOCK MARKET

"Sooner or later," said economist Roger Babson on September 5, 1929, "a crash is coming...factories will be shut down...men will be thrown out of work...the result will be a serious business depression." But most analysts assured Americans that the stock market was healthy and thriving.

Outside the New York Stock Exchange, October 24, 1929

A stock exchange is an organized system for buying and selling shares, or blocks of investments, in corporations. In the late 1920s, the value of stocks on the New York Exchange climbed to dizzying heights. To take advantage of the boom, investors borrowed money to buy stocks, a practice known as buying on margin.

The boom could last only as long as investors added money to the pool. By 1929, everyone with money to invest had bought into the market, and it ran out of new customers. Prices stopped rising. People sold shares to pay the interest on their loans. As shares were sold, prices fell. Panicked investors tried to minimize their losses.

On October 29, less than two months after Babson's prediction, the market crashed. But the crash was a symptom not a cause of the Great Depression.

★ ★ ★ ★ ★ ★ ★ ★ ★ ★ ★

MAKING THE ECONOMICS CONNECTION

1. What series of events occur when the stock market crashes?

2. Why did people begin selling shares of stock in the fall of 1929?

LINKING PAST AND PRESENT

3. Compare the 1929 stock market crash with the savings and loan crisis of the 1980s.

★ ★ ★ ★ ★ ★ ★ ★ ★ ★ ★

bought stock **on margin.** To buy stock in this way one made a small cash down payment and borrowed the rest from a stockbroker. For example, if one had $2,000, rather than paying cash for 10 shares of stock at $200 per share, one could buy 100 shares on margin. The purchaser simply put down 10 percent of the price (or $20 per share), and borrowed the other $18,000 from a broker, who would then hold the shares of stock as collateral for the loan. Brokers loaned billions of dollars, which the borrower was obliged to repay on demand. But few borrowers were worried. So long as prices continued to rise, investors could sell the stock later, repay the loan, and reap the profit.

Some bankers, brokers, and economists were concerned, however, because they knew the stock for many companies was greatly overpriced in comparison to the earnings and profits the companies were making. Yet most investors were swept

along on the tide of the day's optimism. Even President Coolidge abandoned his usual cautious silence to say that he saw nothing wrong with the great increase in brokers' loans. Meanwhile, the market continued its dizzying climb. By the end of 1929, brokers' loans to those who had bought on margin exceeded $7 billion. The Federal Reserve Board tried to restore stability to the market by advising banks not to loan money for buying stocks on margin, but few banks listened.

In September 1929, the market started to waver as some professional speculators sensed danger and began to pull out, and prices slipped. Late in October real disaster struck. On Thursday, October 24, almost 13 million shares of stocks were traded so frantically the ticker couldn't keep up. As stocks' values dropped below the amounts borrowed to purchase them, brokers demanded that investors repay their loans. If they could not, the brokers offered the stock for sale.

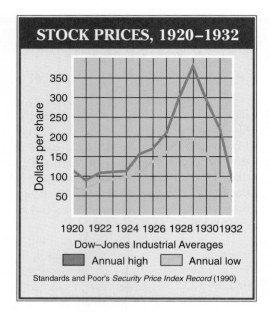

STOCK PRICES, 1920–1932

Dollars per share

350
300
250
200
150
100
50

1920 1922 1924 1926 1928 1930 1932
Dow–Jones Industrial Averages

Annual high   Annual low

Standards and Poor's *Security Price Index Record* (1990)

Causes of the Depression

The collapse of the stock market was only a prelude to a catastrophic economic decline from which the United States did not recover for 12 years. The causes of the Great Depression were so complex that economists have debated the issue ever since. Most agree, however, that over-production was a factor. Laborsaving machinery had greatly increased the production capacity of the nation's industry, which was now able to produce far more goods than the American population could consume. For a time, consumer purchasing power was bolstered by **installment buying**—an agreement whereby a purchaser made a down payment and paid the rest of the cost in periodic regular installments, to which an interest charge was added. By the late 1920s, most consumers who could afford high-cost items such as refrigerators, cars, or stoves had bought them on an installment plan. Consumer spending began to decrease.

Recognizing what was going on, over the next few days, investment bankers such as J.P. Morgan, tried desperately to shore up market prices by purchasing as many shares as they could. But it was not enough to stabilize an overvalued market. On October 29—Black Tuesday—the bottom fell out. Some 16 million shares were sold, causing such a collapse that by mid-November the average price of securities had been cut nearly in half. This cost investors about $30 billion, a sum that represented almost one-third of the value of all goods and services produced in the United States in 1929. Put another way, the loss was equal to the total wages of all Americans that year.

About 1.5 million Americans had been actively involved in purchasing stock. Many investors lost their entire life savings. The country would soon feel the effects of the crash.

Ultimately, it was the failure of the banks that hit people the hardest. Banks loaned money to brokerage houses, which in turn either bought stock themselves or loaned money to investors for speculative stock purchases. When loan payments were not forthcoming, many banks went bankrupt. In the aftermath, millions of people who had never bought stock but had trustingly kept their money in savings accounts lost everything as the banks were forced to close their doors.

Examining Cartoons *"Sold Out," which was published in late October, depicts the desolation felt when Wall Street collapsed. How many Americans purchased stocks in 1929?*

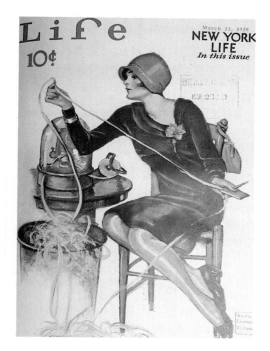

Examining Illustrations *The cover of* Life *magazine depicts a woman reading a stock market ticker tape. One cause of the Depression was overspeculation. What were the other causes?*

From January to September 1929, for example, the number of automobile purchases dropped by one-third.

Another cause of the Depression was underconsumption. In the 1920s the rich got richer much faster than the rest of the people. Some 30,000 families at the top of the economic pyramid had as much income as did the 11 million families at the bottom. Though production increased, employment stood still, and workers' wages went up at a far slower rate than executive salaries or corporation profits. In 1929 more than two-thirds of the nation's families were earning less than $2,500 per year, a sum said to be the minimum income for a decent quality of life. About one-fifth of the nation lived in dire poverty. Thus there was insufficient purchasing power to support the nation's mass-production industries.

A prolonged slump in agriculture, which affected the economic life of the entire country was another factor. Farmers were heavily indebted to banks, which held mortgages on farmlands throughout the nation. The declining value of farms made it harder for farmers to get credit. Banks that had invested heavily in farm mortgages were in danger of failing.

In addition, huge farm surpluses produced a drop in farm prices so great that farmers often spent more money growing and marketing their products than they received in selling them. The resulting loss in farmers' purchasing power further reduced the consumption of manufactured goods—a condition that only added to the problem of underconsumption.

The Great Depression was not solely a result of economic practices. Many of the economic policies of the Harding and Coolidge administrations during the 1920s set the stage for problems by the end of the decade. Policies such as the prohibitively high Fordney-McCumber tariff, combined with the Republican administrations' insistence on collecting war debts, interfered with world trade and destroyed foreign markets for American products, especially in agriculture. The Mellon tax policies, which aided the

Examining Tables *Statistical tables can give answers to questions about what happened to the American economy during the Crash of 1929 and the Depression. Study each column heading, noting the years that show the greatest change. What was the worst year of the Great Depression for both business and labor?*

	GNP, STOCK VALUES, AND UNEMPLOYMENT, 1920–1932		
Year	**Gross National Product (in billions)**	**Stock Values, New York Stock Exchange (in billions)**	**Unemployment (Percent)**
1920	$140.0	$5.5	5.2
1921	127.8	4.7	11.7
1922	148.0	5.7	6.7
1923	165.9	5.9	2.4
1924	165.5	5.9	5.0
1925	179.4	7.6	3.2
1926	190.0	8.6	1.8
1927	189.8	10.5	3.3
1928	190.9	13.7	4.2
1929	203.6	17.9	3.2
1930	183.5	14.4	8.7
1931	169.3	7.5	15.9
1932	144.2	3.8	23.6

upper class, contributed to the uneven distribution of wealth. Failure to curb or discourage the stock market's early on boom made the ultimate crash more severe.

Once started, the Great Depression took on a momentum of its own that helped to create a vicious downward spiral. Individuals with mortgages on their homes, who had bought cars and other goods on credit, and who had purchased stocks on margin, "lost their shirts." They stopped buying, for example, luxuries like radios, causing radio manufacturers to close down plants or run them only part-time. Thousands of workers were laid off as orders were canceled for copper, wood cabinets, and glass radio tubes. Montana copper miners, Minnesota lumberjacks, and Ohio glassworkers in turn lost their jobs. Because these jobless workers could not meet mortgage payments or repay loans, they lost their property. Banks that had lent them money failed, wiping out their depositors' savings. Such chain reactions closed down more and more factories, drove more and more firms into bankruptcy, and put more and more Americans out of work.

Russell Hunter, a brass worker in the Naugatuck Valley region of Connecticut, known as the "Brass Valley," describes what the early years of Depression were like:

During Hoover's time, we went on short time. After a while, when things really were bad, in 1932, we were working sometimes five hours a week, one day a week. That was tough, trying to raise a family. Nobody lost their jobs completely. They shared [the work] to give everybody something to do. Still , you had to go on welfare. People got by by going on the welfare. At that time, people were losing their homes, automobiles....

Thus, the suddenness and violence of the stock market crash helped to change the mood of the country from one of optimism to one of fear.

★ ★ ★ ★ ★ ★ ★ ★ ★ ★ ★ ★ ★ ★ ★ ★ ★

Section One Review

★ ★ ★ ★ ★ ★ ★ ★ ★ ★ ★ ★ ★ ★ ★ ★ ★

SUMMARY

Aided by a campaign based on prosperity Herbert Hoover easily won the 1928 presidential election. During the campaign, Hoover stressed his belief that the role of government was to referee the booming American economy, but not to restrict it. But there were some troubling economic signs, including a continuing slump in farm prices and Americans' willingness to accumulate debt. On October 29, 1929, the stock market crashed, signaling an end to prosperity.

CHECKING FOR UNDERSTANDING

1. **Identify** Wickersham Commission, Agricultural Marketing Act

2. **Define** armories, securities, speculation, on margin, installment buying

3. **State** four reasons Herbert Hoover won the 1928 election.

4. **Summarize** the three ideas Hoover thought created prosperity and some practical examples of these ideas at work.

5. **Explain** how speculation caused the stock market to rise.

6. **List** four causes of the Great Depression.

THINKING CRITICALLY

7. **Synthesizing Ideas** Who was to blame for stock market speculation and the problems it caused—stock brokers, banks, speculators, or the government? Explain your answer.

LINKING PAST AND PRESENT

8. **Making Comparsons** Today's economists are undecided on the possibility of another Great Depression. There are some similarities between today's economy and events in 1929. Do you think another Great Depression could happen?

★ ★ ★ ★ ★ ★ ★ ★ ★ ★ ★ ★ ★ ★ ★ ★ ★

Hoover's Policies

SETTING THE SCENE

No country is more loved by its people. I have an abiding faith in their capacity, integrity, and high purpose. I have no fears for the future of our country. It is bright with hope.

—HERBERT HOOVER
Inaugural Address, 1929

Section Focus

Before 1929 the federal government had responded to economic depressions by considering different monetary or tariff policies. During the Great Depression, however, the government was forced to seek more vigorous remedies for the nation's vast economic problems. Failing to succeed, however, in domestic policies, President Herbert Hoover made peace the cornerstone of his administration.

Objectives

After studying this section, you should be able to:

• List the ways in which Hoover tried to end the Depression.
• Describe the change in United States policy toward Latin America under Hoover.
• Describe the Hoover-Stimson Doctrine and evaluate its effectiveness as a foreign policy.

No sooner had the stock market collapsed than President Hoover asked leaders of industry, finance, and labor to come to the White House. He asked labor leaders to abandon wage demands, industry leaders to keep employment high, and bankers to continue lending. Hoover and other leaders tried to restore public confidence by issuing optimistic statements. But their rosy predictions were contradicted by worsening conditions, and the phrase "prosperity is just around the corner" became a joke. The Republican campaign slogan "Two cars in every garage" had become "Two families in every garage."

Domestic Concerns Loom

In dealing with Congress and the public, Hoover was limited by his inflexible views. A man of great ability and possessed of a sincere desire to serve the nation, he lacked practical political experience. Even with such skills, his position would have been difficult. Republican party leaders never gave him their wholehearted support, and members of the Farm Bloc were in open revolt. As a result of the midterm elections of 1930, the Democrats made gains in the Senate and won control of the House of Representatives. This shift in power led to a Congress hostile to Hoover's policies during the last two years of his administration.

Like President Taft in 1909, Hoover was unable to control Congress on the tariff issue. The Hawley-Smoot Tariff started in the House as a protection for farmers, but by the time it passed the Senate it had turned into the highest protective tariff in peacetime history. It raised the average duty on raw agricultural materials and other items above the Fordney-McCumber Act levels.

By the time the Hawley-Smoot bill reached the President's desk in 1930, more than a thousand leading economists had signed a letter urging him to veto it. They argued that it would help inefficient producers, raise consumer prices, reduce foreign markets, and cause ill will toward the United States in other countries. This opinion was voiced by many conservative newspapers, by the American Bankers Association, and even by a number of manufacturers. Now Hoover faced a dilemma. If he used his veto power, he

Examining Photographs *"Work is what I want" gives the feeling of what it was like to be out of work during the Depression. How did Hoover feel about providing direct aid to the unemployed?*

Farmers' income was cut by more than half between 1929 and 1932; their burden of debt became unbearable. During this crisis, the Farm Board tried to maintain the price of wheat and cotton by buying up the surplus of these crops. The Farm Board also attempted—without success—to persuade farmers to plant less, in order to reduce the amount of farm produce grown and thus to prevent further surplus crops. The immense quantities of wheat and cotton held by the government actually drove prices down, however, because buyers feared that the government would sell these surpluses as soon as prices rose. Finally, in 1931, the Farm Board acknowledged defeat and stopped its purchases. Immediately prices dropped even lower. By 1932 farmers were receiving only 38 cents a bushel for wheat that in 1929 had sold at $1.04. Even Hoover's relatives in Iowa suffered from the depressed farm economy. Harry Terrell, a farmer who lived in the same neighborhood as President Hoover in Iowa, described conditions in the following way:

Examining Graphs *American agriculture suffered as indicated by the steep decline in farm prices in the 1920s. How successful were the Farm Board's policies to alleviate this crisis?*

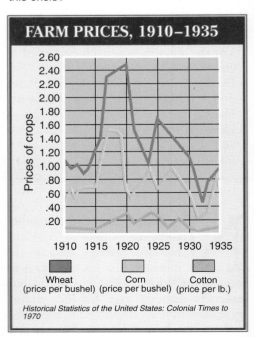

FARM PRICES, 1910–1935

Prices of crops

2.60		
2.40		
2.20		
2.00		
1.80		
1.60		
1.40		
1.20		
1.00		
.80		
.60		
.40		
.20		

1910 1915 1920 1925 1930 1935

Wheat (price per bushel)   Corn (price per bushel)   Cotton (price per lb.)

Historical Statistics of the United States: Colonial Times to 1970

would isolate himself politically by breaking with the Republican values he held so strongly. Furthermore, he would abandon the one feature of the bill he had fought so hard for—a revised Tariff Commission with the authority to raise and lower rates. He therefore signed the bill in spite of the warnings.

Within a year, 25 nations retaliated with laws to restrict purchases of American goods, causing foreign trade with the United States to drop rapidly. Some American corporations managed to avoid international barriers by establishing factories overseas. Ironically, an act designed to promote American economic recovery instead created employment overseas.

American farmers, beleaguered throughout the 1920s, were hit even harder.

Hoover's Strong Resolve

Hoover was deeply affected by all the misery and poverty around him. But as a staunch believer in private enterprise, he feared direct government hand-outs would destroy personal initiative. Hoover therefore offered government help to banks and businesses in the hope that restored financial health at the top of the economic pyramid would eventually trickle down to relieve unemployment at the bottom. Keeping his attitude positive and his resolve strong, Hoover sought to inspire confidence in a people ravaged by hopelessness and despair: "Ninety percent of our difficulty in depression is caused by fear."

In 1932, after Hoover's initial resistance, Congress established the Reconstruction Finance Corporation (RFC). With $2 billion in resources, the RFC made loans to hard-pressed railroads, insurance companies, banks, and even state and local governments—but not to individuals. The RFC favored projects that were "self-liquidating"; that is, projects designed to pay their way so the government would eventually get back its money. Thus projects such as toll bridges and dams that would produce electric power were favored over those which could have been socially useful but brought in no revenue, such as playgrounds, schools, and city halls.

There was a point beyond which Hoover refused to use the power and resources of the federal government. He feared that too much reliance on federal action would result in the very "paternalism" and "state socialism" he had warned against in the 1928 campaign. He opposed direct federal relief for the unemployed on the grounds that it would weaken the self-respect of those who received it, undercut the efforts of private charity, and that it would destroy the tradition of local responsibility for the unfortunate. Hoover, therefore, vetoed the Garner-Wagner bill in 1932, which would have given direct aid to the unemployed. He also vetoed the Norris bill, which would have put the government in the business of producing and selling electricity in the Tennessee Valley—thus setting up a direct competition with private companies.

Efforts for Peace

The desire for world peace was strong during these hard times, partly because preparation for war was costly, and partly because few had forgotten the horrors of World War I.

As a Quaker and a pacifist, Herbert Hoover believed that war was morally wrong; as administrator of Belgian relief between 1914 and 1917, he saw the devastation of World War I firsthand. Hoover was committed to world peace. As he stated in 1928:

I think I may say that I have witnessed as much of the horror and suffering of war as any other American. From it I have derived a deep passion for peace. Our foreign policy has one primary objective, and that is peace.

Hoover's peace efforts were aided by his many years spent overseas. The most widely traveled man ever to occupy the White House, he had visited every continent and knew many foreign leaders personally.

As secretary of commerce, Hoover had come to understand that Latin America's resentment and distrust of the United States inhibited American trade with that region. To allay this ill will, he used the time between his election in November

1928 and his inauguration in March 1929 to make a goodwill tour of 10 Latin American countries. In his speeches, published in English, Spanish, and Portuguese, Hoover stressed that the United States wished to be a friend to its neighbors in Latin America. Many expressed doubts about how effective Hoover's efforts would be. Commenting on Hoover's trip, one Cuban journal printed this statement:

If Mr. Hoover wants to conquer the immediate sympathy of Latin America, he should at once announce a change in the policy of his country, declaring that the Monroe Doctrine does not mean that the American continent is only for the United States....

But Hoover's Latin American policies reflected a sincere desire to improve relations. In addition to successfully arbitrating a long-standing boundary dispute between Chile and Peru, Hoover abandoned military intervention in Latin American countries. The Clark Memorandum, written by Undersecretary of State J. Reuben Clark, argued the position that the Roosevelt Corollary to the Monroe Doctrine had no historical basis. Clark wrote, "The Monroe Doctrine states a case of the United States v. Europe, not of the United States v. Latin America." In other words, the Monroe Doctrine could no longer be used to justify American intervention in Latin America.

In accordance with this principle, Hoover withdrew troops from Nicaragua and refused to intervene in the affairs of Latin American states that, because of political chaos, had repudiated their debts to the United States. While this nonintervention policy helped to convince many Latin Americans that the United States had no aggressive intentions, it won Hoover little goodwill. The Hawley-Smoot Tariff had hurt Latin America's economy, and the region's underlying resentment of the wealth and power of the United States did not disappear. Nonetheless, Hoover had laid the basis for the "Good Neighbor" policy that Franklin Delano Roosevelt would develop during his administration.

Disarmament and Moratorium

Hoover strongly favored disarmament, not only because of his personal beliefs but also because military spending and increased taxes depleted valuable resources. Shortly after taking office, Hoover made arrangements for a new conference in London on naval disarmament. Its goal would be to extend the limits on battleships that had been set in the Five-Power Treaty signed in 1921-1922.

After four months of talks, the London Naval Conference of 1930 produced a treaty fixing ratios for the submarines, cruisers, and destroyers of the United States, British, and Japanese navies. Italy refused to sign. France, fearing aggression by Germany and Italy, said that it favored disarmament only if other powers would agree to give France assurance of protection. In the end, France chose not to sign.

Ever since 1927, a disarmament conference hosted by the League of Nations had

Examining Photographs
Hoover said his Latin American visit was of "one good neighbor to another." Why were Hoover's efforts unsuccessful?

Examining Photographs

Japanese soldiers celebrate victory over the Chinese in the port of Hankow, China. What was the American response to the Japanese invasion?

been meeting at Geneva. Its work was hampered by the activities of lobbyists for arms manufacturers and by mutual mistrust among the delegates. For five years it had gotten nowhere, focusing on such trivial issues as the influence of fog on war. In 1932 President Hoover proposed to the Geneva Conference that the nations of the world either entirely abandon aggressive weapons or cut existing arms by one-third. No action resulted. With Adolf Hitler's rise to power in Germany, however, and Japanese invasions into China, disarmament now seemed like an invitation to aggression. Hoover's proposal could have succeeded only if the United States had been willing to join an alliance of nations committed to "collective security," whereby members would all agree to come to the aid of any member nation who was threatened with aggression.

By 1931 Germany was in the throes of a serious depression. Germans could not continue paying war reparations to the Allies without defaulting on their debts to American private investors. Hoover, like Harding and Coolidge before him, believed that reparations were "a European problem." But heavy war debts and rising unemployment caused great discontent among the German people and led directly to the rapid growth of two antidemocratic parties—the Communist party and the Nazi party.

The Allies were unlikely to cancel German reparation payments, which they used to pay off their own war debts to the United States. To address the problem in 1931, Hoover proposed an international moratorium that suspended, for one year, all war-debt payments to the United States. Hoover's aim was to protect United States investments in Germany and to save the German Republic from collapse, as well as to stimulate international trade. Secretary of State Henry L. Stimson urged that war debts and reparations be canceled completely, but Hoover refused. To do so would have been a highly unpopular measure and would have worsened Hoover's already poor relations with Congress.

The Hoover-Stimson Doctrine

In September 1931, Japan seized China's rich province of Manchuria. Taking advantage of the civil war in China and the weak condition of the western nations, Japanese armies speedily overran Manchuria. This action was in direct violation of the Nine-Power Treaty of 1922, which guaranteed China's sovereignty, and the Kellogg-Briand Pact, which outlawed wars of aggression. It also breached the Charter of the League of Nations, to which both China and Japan belonged.

China appealed to the League of Nations, which turned to the United States for help. President Hoover, however, refused to consider either economic or military action. Instead, he sent a United States army officer to serve on a League commission to investigate Japanese actions in Manchuria. Secretary Stimson proclaimed in 1932 that the United States would refuse to recognize the legality of any territorial arrangement that violated the Kellogg-Briand Pact. The Hoover-Stimson Doctrine, designed to enlist world opinion against aggressor nations, did nothing to aid China and served only to irritate the Japanese.

Although the nonrecognition policy had been worked out by Hoover and Stimson together, it meant different things to each of them. Stimson wanted the policy to act as a warning, which later might be backed up by economic or military aid. But according to Hoover, the statement itself was enough. The United States, he said, did not exist to police the world. Economic sanctions might lead to war, he said, and Japanese aggression in Asia did not "imperil the freedom of the American people." Nor were the British and French governments willing to apply sanctions. The failure of western nations to take action only encouraged Japanese expansion into China and Southeast Asia.

The American public was not prepared to support any interventionist effort that could potentially involve the United States in war once again. This feeling was evident in 1931 when Congress overwhelmingly overrode Hoover's veto and voted to give independence to the Philippines within 10 years. This measure pleased Filipino leaders; it also pleased the United States business community, who wanted to keep Filipino products out of America. But a major reason for passage of the bill was that the American people no longer wanted to defend the islands, upholding the American anti-imperialist past.

Section Two Review

SUMMARY

The Great Depression deepened and Hoover's signature on the Hawley-Smoot Tariff Act hurt American business. American farmers were hard hit during the depression when crop prices fell so low that farmers could not make a living. Hoover, torn between helping people with direct aid and his belief in free enterprise, compromised by helping banks and businesses.

Hoover also sought to maintain world peace during the Depression. He established a good neighbor policy toward Latin America and proposed a one-year moratorium on German war reparations.

CHECKING FOR UNDERSTANDING

1. **Identify** Hawley-Smoot Tariff, Reconstruction Finance Corporation, Clark Memorandum, Naval Conference, Hoover-Stimson Doctrine

2. **Summarize** why Hoover disapproved of relief programs and direct involvement in business and give examples of actions he took based on this reasoning.

3. **List** three actions Hoover took to promote ties with Latin America.

THINKING CRITICALLY

4. **Predicting Consequences** What message did the United States and its allies send to leaders such as Adolf Hitler by not taking action against Japan?

CONNECTIONS: HISTORY AND RELIGION

5. **Analyzing Ideas** In the late 1600s, Quakers settled in the present-day state of Pennsylvania, in part, so they could practice their pacifistic beliefs. Write a short paragraph analyzing the difficulty of maintaining these beliefs in the twentieth century and how they might have affected the policies of Herbert Hoover, a Quaker.

Study and Writing Skills

Writing a Persuasive Argument

The last time your school had an election, whether it was for class president or the homecoming queen, how did you decide who to vote for? Was it because of popularity or because that person presented a very persuasive argument?

Explanation

A persuasive argument is one in which the reader or listener is urged to do something or believe in the same thing as does the writer or speaker.

The following guidelines will help you organize and write a persuasive argument:

a. Before writing, research the topic. What are the facts, and how do people feel about this subject? This will aid you in determining what arguments to use.

b. Tailor your argument to your audience. Exactly who are you trying to persuade? Keep in mind that many people will share your point of view if they see some benefit for themselves.

c. Support your argument with solid facts and examples. Use only those which are most likely to cause the reader to share your viewpoint.

d. Save the most persuasive arguments for last, then end your paper by summarizing your points.

Example

Imagine that the following is a paper that you wrote as Herbert Hoover defending his war debt moratorium. Note how the above guidelines were applied:

President Herbert Hoover

I am writing to you, the people of France, as you continue to heal the wounds inflicted by the Great War. My heart and thoughts are with you. Look around you. In what condition is Europe? There is depression, unemployment, and debt. Germany, for all its past offenses, is teetering on the brink of collapse. Europe, like America, is fighting the effects of this demoralizing depression. International trade is at dangerously low levels, and the spectre of debt hangs over all of us like a shadow. The time has come to close the gap between how we feel about that Great War, and what we know to be the just and proper way to revive our ailing economies. Let us consider our children's future, and not so much our temporary feelings of outrage for a war that is over. Abide with me in my decision to place a one year, international moratorium on all war debts. It is time to let go of the past, and resurrect the quality of life that has been obscured by this spectre of debt.

After reading this, it should be clear to Hoover's audience that:

a. Hoover researched the topic. He cited world conditions, international trade, and debt.

b. He knew that France would be in opposition, since it was France that was most in favor of demanding payments from Germany. Hoover therefore tailored this paper for the French people.

c. Hoover used facts about the low levels of trade and the political and economic problems of Germany. His remark about America's suffering made the point that all countries were linked by common interests and needs.

d. He mentioned the future of the world's children as perhaps the most persuasive argument, making the reader realize that feelings of revenge could affect the world for years to come. Then he summarized the argument with an appeal to let go of the past and to restore the quality of life that had been lost.

Practice

For practice in this skill, write a persuasive argument against the Hawley-Smoot tariff. Determine your audience before you begin writing.

The Depression Worsens

SETTING THE SCENE

We thought American business was the Rock of Gibraltar. We were the prosperous nation and nothing could stop us now.... Suddenly the big dream exploded. The impact was unbelievable.

—E.Y. HARBURG
Songwriter interviewed in *Hard Times*, 1978

Section Focus

Between Election Day in November 1932 and Inauguration Day in March 1933, the nation's economy hit rock bottom. National income had dropped from $81 billion to $41 billion. Over 25 percent of the nation's workers were unemployed, and many others worked only part-time. Thousands of businesses were bankrupt, thousands of banks had closed, and farmers were in revolt.

Objectives

After studying this section, you should be able to:

• Compare the condition of workers and farmers in the early 1930s.
• Discuss the mood of the country as the election of 1932 approached.

The Depression was uneven in its impact. While many people lost their jobs, the majority of Americans did not. Instead many found their hours reduced. The few who kept their jobs and did not have their hours or wages cut, actually were better off because prices declined. But for most Americans the mood was gloomy—and for good reason. In 1932, over 30,000 companies closed. In just 2 months in 1931 over 800 banks failed, wiping out the life savings of thousands of depositors.

Want in the Land of Plenty

As the Depression deepened, fear and despair replaced the buoyant optimism of the 1920s. "I'm afraid, every man is afraid," steel industrialist Charles M. Schwab admitted. "I don't know, we don't know, whether the values we have are going to be real next month or not."

Loss of confidence affected all sorts of people. Some who lost their jobs suffered such emotional effects that they became unemployable. "My father spent two years painting his father's house," one man later remembered. "He painted it twice. It gave him something to do."

Business leaders hesitated to build new factories or to bring out new products. Frightened bankers became unwilling to lend money, even to borrowers with good character and ample collateral. On the stock market, security prices dropped dramatically. Stock in Radio Corporation of America (RCA), for example, dropped from $101 per share in 1929 to $2.50 in 1932.

One of the great ironies of the Depression was that starvation existed in the midst of plenty. The productive capacity of farmers did not slacken. On the contrary, farmers' problems resulted, in part, from their ability to grow more food than they were able to sell. Already in a depression throughout most of the 1920s, the collapse of the farm economy after 1929 wreaked havoc on rural America. Despite Hoover's programs, grain prices dropped so low that farmers heated their homes by shoveling their crops into their furnaces. They protested low agricultural prices by declaring "farmers' holidays" and tried to prevent food shipments to cities. In Iowa, farmers blockaded highways and dumped milk trucks in an attempt to make milk scarce and raise its price. In Oregon, they slaughtered sheep because mutton prices were lower than what it cost to ship the animals to market. Meanwhile, in America's cities people picked through garbage looking for scraps of meat.

Virginia Durr, an Alabama activist for tenant farmers' rights, described the suffering when she said, "Have you ever seen a child with rickets shaking, as with palsy? No proteins, no milk. And the companies pouring milk into the gutters....People with nothing to eat and they killed the pigs."

The Human Cost of the Depression

Although business leaders promised Hoover that they would not cut wages of remaining workers, as the Depression deepened, their situation changed. In October 1931, United States Steel Corporation cut salaries and wages by 10 percent, and employers in other industries soon followed. By 1933 salaries had decreased 40 percent and hourly wages by 60 percent. The average family's income fell from $2,300 in 1929 to $1,600 in 1932. More layoffs followed the wage cuts. In 1930, 4 million workers were unemployed; by 1933 the num-

Examining Photographs Life *photographer Margaret Bourke-White took this famous photograph at a relief station in Louisville, Kentucky. Contrast the message on the billboard with the line of people waiting for food.*

ber of jobless Americans more than tripled.

In cities throughout the country breadlines and soup kitchens appeared on sidewalks as local governments and private charities struggled to feed the poor. In some cases the lines stretched for blocks as people waited for their only good meal each day.

As unemployment grew, Hoover's Reconstruction Finance Corporation began to loan money to state governments for relief. But these and other relief funds proved woefully inadequate. Toledo, Ohio, for example, could only spend 2 cents for each relief meal it served. New York City provided only $2.39 per week to each family on relief. But in many other cities, after private charity was exhausted, there was nothing.

Throughout the nation, families who could not pay their rent or make their mortgage payments were evicted from their homes. Some moved in with relatives if they could. The less fortunate ended up in makeshift communities dubbed "Hoovervilles" on the outskirts of cities. One woman later remembered Oklahoma City's Hooverville:

Here were all these people living in rusted-out car bodies. I mean that was their home. There were people living in shacks made of orange crates. One family with a whole lot of kids living in a piano box. This wasn't just a little section, this was maybe ten miles wide and ten miles long. People living in what ever they could junk together.

People who were even less fortunate slept in doorways or on park benches. Desperate men grubbed in garbage cans to feed their families. Nearly every street corner had its apple seller. So many apples were available because of a surplus of the fruit in the Pacific Northwest. To reduce the surplus, the International Apple Shippers Association set up a system for unemployed people to sell the apples. A person could get a credit for $1.75 for a crate of 100-to-120 apples, then turn around and sell the apples for 5 cents each, making a small profit. However, as more and more people tried to make money this way, apple vendors reacted by raising the price to $2.25 a crate. Unless a person sold more than half a crate, he or she made no profit.

Other jobless Americans banded together in hunger riots, smashing into grocery stores and grabbing whatever food they could carry. Begging increased dramatically, and "Brother, Can You Spare a Dime" became a bitter testimony to veterans who remembered fighting a war to protect American values and to make the world safe for democracy:

Once in khaki suits,
Gee we looked swell,
Full of that Yankee Doodle-de-dum
Half a million boots went
sloggin' through Hell,
I was the kid with the drum.
Say don't you remember,
they called me Al—
It was Al all of the time.
Say don't you remember
I'm your pal—
Buddy, can you spare a dime?

The Bonus Army

In May 1932, some 1,500 unemployed army veterans marched on Washington, D.C., to demand early payment of the bonus Congress had promised to pay them in 1945. Within sight of the White House, some set up a Hooverville in an area across the Potomac River known as Anacostia Flats. Others occupied abandoned buildings in the area. As they daily demonstrated in front of the White House and the Capitol, their numbers increased to more than 20,000.

The government tried to keep the protesters peaceful. President Hoover supported their right to express their views and even provided them with army tents, cots, and field kitchens. When Congress rejected their demands, most of the veterans left Washington. But about 2,000 refused to leave. After a clash between the veterans and the local police, Hoover called in the army. General Douglas MacArthur, commander of the troops, carried out the President's orders to clear the veterans from federal buildings. Using tanks, machine guns, and tear gas, his troops drove the veterans out of Washington and burned their camp. Historian Frederick Lewis Allen described the sudden chaos that resulted:

AMERICAN PORTRAITS

DOROTHEA LANGE
1895-1965

By the time she finished high school, Dorothea Lange had chosen her career. She wanted to be a photographer—even though she had never used a camera.

After taking a photography course, Lange journeyed from New York to San Francisco, where she ran a portrait business for 10 years. Then the Depression struck. Lange became a documentary photographer, her compassion showing clearly in her photos. By the mid-1930s, she was documenting the life of California's migrant laborers, work that earned her a position with the Farm Security Administration (FSA). Her FSA photos revealed poverty's brutal effects on rural Americans. Lange later traveled through the dustbowl states, capturing people's suffering in a book called *An American Exodus, A Record of Human Erosion.*

Cavalrymen were riding into the crowd, infantrymen were throwing tear-gas bombs, women and children were being trampled and choking from the gas;...[People] were running wildly, pell-mell across uneven ground, screaming as they stumbled and fell.

The troops moved slowly on, scattering before them veterans and homegoing government clerks alike....That evening, the Washington sky glowed with fire. Even after midnight the troops were still on their way with bayonets and tear-gas bombs.

Examining Photographs *In 1932, the Bonus Army gathered in Washington, D. C., to demand that Congress vote early bonuses for World War I veterans. What was Hoover's response to these demands?*

Many Americans blamed Hoover for the use of brutal and excessive force against the veterans. He seemed more than ever an inflexible leader.

Fear of Revolution

During this time of bewilderment and despair, fear of revolution started to spread. Lloyds of London, a British insurance company, began to write policies for riot insurance in the United States. Looking for scapegoats, Americans blamed the Depression on the very people they had admired and willingly followed a few years earlier—industrialists and bankers. Public outrage increased when a Senate investigation charged that some of the nation's wealthiest were trying to get away without paying taxes on their huge incomes. Others were accused of using unscrupulous business practices to increase their wealth in the midst of such widespread poverty and suffering.

The unrest in society offered hope to both Socialists and Communists, who preached that the Depression marked the end of capitalism, which would soon be replaced by a system that distributed goods more fairly. Both groups proposed that government control the means of production and distribution. Both promised that a planned economy would result in greater abundance for all. "Folks are restless," observed Mississippi governor Theodore Bilbo, "communism is gaining a foothold....In fact, I'm getting a little pink myself."

But such radical alternatives were weakened because Socialists and Communists bitterly opposed each other, and destroyed each other's credibility. The Socialists proposed to gain their power by persuasion and the ballot box. The Communist party, however, held that capitalism could not be overthrown without violent revolution— what Earl Browder, the general secretary of the party, called the "omelet theory." Just as it was impossible to make an omelet without breaking eggs, Browder explained, it was impossible to make a revolution without breaking heads.

Fears of a revolution in the United States proved to be unfounded, however. Although many Americans were suffering, angry, and wanted a change, protest movements tended to be splintered. No single leader emerged to galvanize them or act as a unifying force. Most Americans clung to their democratic traditions and expressed their anger at the ballot box.

The Election of 1932

As the presidential election of 1932 approached, the Democrats sensed victory for the first time since 1916. The Democratic national convention rejected Al Smith's bid for renomination and instead chose New York governor Franklin D. Roosevelt as their candidate. In 1928, while Smith was losing the presidential election, Roosevelt had won New York's race for governor and in the process proved himself to be a remarkable vote-getter. In 1930 he had been reelected by a huge majority.

The Democratic platform of 1932—the briefest in U.S. political history—urged the repeal of Prohibition and made general proposals for reform and recovery.

The Democrats' most effective asset, however, was Roosevelt himself. Setting the tone for what became a whirlwind campaign, he flew by plane to the Democratic convention to become the first candidate to accept a presidential nomination in person. In his acceptance address, he pledged "a new deal for the American people." In later speeches, however, he was vague and described the "New Deal" in broad terms only. But it remained clear that Roosevelt intended to take action that would help "the forgotten man at the bottom of the economic pyramid."

The Republicans, meanwhile, gloomily renominated Hoover, who suffered the problem of having to defend his policies in the midst of a terrible Depression. He maintained that hard times were the result of economic collapse abroad—for which his administration could not be held responsible—and that without his relief measures the disaster might have been

Linking Across Time

"INSIDER" PUBLIC ANGER

In 1990 public anger ran high against unscrupulous speculators, much as it had in the 1930s. During the 1980s, Wall Street moguls had manipulated stocks to make huge fortunes. In 1986 Ivan Boesky, first of these "raiders," was fined $100 million and sentenced to three years in prison. In 1990 Michael Milken, convicted of similar crimes, received a ten-year sentence, a $600,000 fine, and 5400 hours of public service. Analysts believed the sentence reflected growing public anger at such practices.

Examining Photographs *The American people looked upon the election of 1932 with optimism. What did Roosevelt pledge during his acceptance speech at the Democratic Convention?*

worse. But Hoover flatly rejected Roosevelt's position that government had "a positive duty to see that no citizen shall starve." "You cannot," warned Hoover, "extend the mastery of government over the daily life of a people without somewhere making it master of people's souls and thoughts."

On Election Day, the Republican victories of the 1920s were completely reversed as Roosevelt carried 42 of the 48 states. This landslide revealed not only a widespread willingness to blame the Republicans for the Depression but also a desire to use government as an agency for human welfare. Yet even at the bottom of the worst depression in history, few Americans favored the overthrow of capitalism, either by violent or peaceful means. The election results revealed that the Socialists polled 900,000 votes and the Communists only 100,000. This meant that their combined share was a little more than 2 percent of the total vote.

In the time between Roosevelt's election in November and his inauguration in March, the Twentieth Amendment was added to the Constitution, changing the date of the presidential inauguration from March 4 to January 20. Had this amendment gone into effect sooner, it would have been better for the country. But for four months, the nation was virtually leaderless, as it had been in the months before Lincoln took office in 1861. Even though Hoover had been repudiated, the new President—Franklin Delano Roosevelt—was without power to act.

During this short time, the entire banking system disintegrated, and the economy ground almost to a standstill. Although thousands of smaller banks had already failed, most of the larger banks seemed to be able to hold firm during

Examining Fine Art Home Relief Station, *by Louis Ribak, describes the frustration felt by the American people during the Depression years. What did the election of 1932 reveal about American public opinion concerning the Hoover administration and its response during the most difficult years of the Depression?*

Mar. 4, 1933 · THE · Price 15 cents

THE NEW YORKER

peter Arno

Examining Illustrations *During the ride to Roosevelt's inauguration, Hoover was silent and glum while Roosevelt seemed confident in his ability to meet the crisis in America. What happened to the American economy between Election Day 1932 and inauguration day 1933?*

this time. Despite Roosevelt's promise that upon becoming President he would take action to rescue the nation from the Depression, in early 1933 the entire country was seized by a banking panic. Having lost faith in the nation's economy, thousands of depositors withdrew their money from banks and hoarded cash and gold. Given such a situation, even the most stable banks were bound to stop payments eventually because there was not enough gold in circulation to cover all deposits. As the situation deteriorated, state governors issued proclamations closing the banks of their states until confidence could be restored. By March 4—the day Roosevelt would take the oath of office—almost every private bank in the country was closed or placed under restriction by state regulation. The people of the nation waited anxiously to see what the new President would do.

Section Three Review

SUMMARY

The Depression did not affect everyone equally—those with little to begin with were hurt the most. World War I veterans marched on Washington to demand their military bonuses early. Farmers were producing more food than ever, but could not sell it for a profit. The mood of many Americans turned to anger. The threat of revolution spurred the hopes of socialists and communists. Instead of revolution, Americans turned to the ballot box, and Democrat Franklin Delano Roosevelt was elected President in 1932.

CHECKING FOR UNDERSTANDING

1. **Identify** bonus army, General Douglas MacArthur.

2. **Describe** the mood of the country as the Depression worsened.

3. **Explain** why farmers destroyed crops and livestock even though people were hungry.

4. **Explain** why Americans never really feared revolution during the Great Depression.

5. **Contrast** the message delivered by Roosevelt in 1932 with the one delivered by Hoover.

THINKING CRITICALLY

6. **Identifying Problems** The banking crisis was caused partly by public fear and panic. Do you think this crisis reflected the public's lack of confidence in government and Hoover?

LINKING PAST AND PRESENT

7. **Contrasting Candidates** Compare the campaign philosophies of Hoover and Roosevelt. Which of these candidates do you think would be elected today? Contrast today's economy with the Great Depression to explain your answer.

★ Chapter 27 Review ★

★ Summary

The stock market crash that began on October 29, 1929, ended the era of prosperity that had ushered Herbert Hoover into office. Hoover's leadership philosophy, which emphasized self-government, individual freedom, and equality of opportunity, was challenged by the crisis. The many effects of the Depression were self-generating and created a chain reaction of negative consequences.

Hoover's actions to end the Depression were ineffective. His inability to stop passage of the Hawley-Smoot Tariff Act hurt American businesses instead of helping them. American farmers continued to suffer from plunging prices for their products. Hoover continued to oppose direct federal relief, but he did give aid to banks and businesses in hopes that it would ease unemployment. In foreign policy, Hoover navigated a course to maintain world peace and avoid conflict. He abandoned military intervention in Latin America and pushed unsuccessfully for worldwide disarmament. The practicality of America's isolationism was challenged by the Japanese invasion of Manchuria in 1931.

Despite Hoover's hopes for an economic lift, the Depression worsened. Some believed that revolution was imminent. The socialist and communist parties hoped that capitalism was dying. Instead of revolution, however, Americans went to the ballot box and elected Franklin D. Roosevelt.

★ Using Vocabulary

Imagine that you must write a handbook on tips for investing in the stock market. Write an entry about speculation that explains the pros and cons. Use these terms.

speculation	**on margin**
securities	**installment buying**

★ Reviewing Facts

1. **Explain** how overproduction or underconsumption was one cause of the Great Depression.
2. **Describe** the effects of the Hawley-Smoot tariff.
3. **Summarize** Hoover's actions to combat the Depression and the philosophy behind the actions.

4. **List** two defeats Hoover had in foreign policy.
5. **Cite** reasons for the rise of communism and socialism during the Depression.
6. **State** three reasons Franklin Roosevelt won the election of 1932.
7. **Discuss** the banking crisis of 1933 and relate it to the overall mood of Americans.

★ Understanding Concepts

ECONOMIC CHANGE

1. Was America's appetite for money and consumer goods a cause of the Great Depression? Explain how activities such as stock market speculation and installment buying contributed to the crisis.
2. How did economic changes affect American faith and beliefs about the United States? Why do you think some Americans feared a revolution? Explain the increased activity among the socialists and communists in America.

POLITICAL POLICY

3. Explain why Hoover's political beliefs were popular while the economy was doing well, but increasingly unpopular during the Depression.
4. Do you think Franklin Roosevelt, using the platform he proposed in 1932, would have won the 1928 presidential election? Explain your answer.

★ Thinking Critically

1. **Contrasting Ideas** Explain the difference between *laissez-faire* economics and Hoover's beliefs about government in the economy.
2. **Recognizing Ideologies** Imagine that you are a political opponent of President Hoover. Write a criticism of his "trickle down" economic philosophy. In your writing, address how this philosophy might create the impression that Hoover favored the wealthy over the poor.
3. **Analyzing Choices** Explain why the Hoover-Stimson Doctrine was ineffective. Make a list of reasons why Americans might have been unwilling to go to war in the early 1930s.
4. **Identifying Assumptions** Compare the Democratic and Republican platforms in the election of

1932. What assumptions did the Republicans make about what American voters were thinking?

★ Writing About History

CAUSE AND EFFECT

Refer to the description of how to write a cause-and-effect essay in the History Writer's Handbook in the Appendix of this book. Your teacher will give you more specific instruction on the essay's length and the assignment's due date.

Write an essay on how the Great Depression might have affected a young person your age. Before you begin writing, make a list of the worries, fears, and hardships the Depression caused. Use this list to write an essay on the effect these factors might have had on an individual your age. Include how the Great Depression would have affected your ideas about careers and school, your self-esteem and way of life, and your hopes for the future.

★ Learning Cooperatively

Work in groups of three to analyze the causes of the Great Depression. Assign each group member two of the causes listed on pages 794-796 of your text. Have each group member make a list of economic and social effects that might have resulted from his or her cause. For example, if your subject is underconsumption, explain how this factor affected store owners, manufacturers, and consumers. When you have finished your individual lists, create a master list entitled, "How the Great Depression Changed America."

★ Mastering Skills

TESTING HYPOTHESES

At one time or another, you may have read a statement and wondered about what you read. Then you may have begun to form explanations about the material, explanations that you may or may not have been able to prove. What you did was to *hypothesize*. You formed one or more *hypotheses,* assumptions that offer a possible answer or answers to a problem or provide a possible explanation for an observation. Hypotheses are only preliminary explanations. They must be accepted, rejected, or modified as the problem is investigated. Each hypothesis must be tested against the information gathered. Hypotheses that are supported by evidence can be accepted as explanations of the problem.

Example   The steps in the following example will help you hypothesize:

• Read these statements.

The Communists made much of the fact that there was no unemployment in Russia. What the defenders of Russian Communism did not tell, however, was the terrible price in human suffering. In 1931, for instance, several million farmers in the Ukraine were allowed to starve to death because they refused to give up their land and livestock to the government.

• Ask yourself what the statement is actually saying. To do this, put the statement in your own words. For example:

While Communism appeared to be doing well because many people had jobs, the fact was that many more people were actually suffering because of it.

• Determine what you might logically assume from these facts. For example, two hypotheses might be:

The price people paid for communism in Russia during the '30s was giving up their belongings.

People might have been employed but they did not have jobs of their own choosing because the government controlled everything.

• Test each hypothesis to determine whether or not it is correct or true. Often, this can be done by asking yourself questions that relate to your hypothesis and then researching the answers.

• Finally, based on your research, determine which hypothesis, if any, provides an explanation for or supports the statements in step 1.

Practice   Using the steps above and what you have read in the chapter, test the following hypotheses and determine if they can be supported.

1. Due to the public's fear about Catholics having power in the White House, Herbert Hoover won the election in 1928.

2. The Depression was a result of people's greed.

3. The stock market crash of 1929 did not happen overnight but rather was years in the making.

4. Hoover would have taken action to alleviate the problems of the Depression had it not been for his philosophy of government.

★ ★ ★ Unit 8 Digest ★ ★ ★

In 1913 the main defender of American ideals was President Woodrow Wilson, who took office opposing war, imperialism, and "big stick" diplomacy. But within a short time, Wilson and the nation were caught up in World War I—one of the bloodiest struggles in history. The war changed nearly everything—politics, the economy, and moral standards. Americans went from isolationism to worldwide involvement and from an economic boom to the depths of depression.

Chapter 25
World War I

Wilson, an idealist who believed in friendship and fair play, sought to change the direction of American foreign policy. He wanted the United States to stop using military force and economic pressure. However, he ended up imitating his Republican predecessors by sending American troops to shore up Caribbean governments he supported. And when Wilson rejected the new Mexican government because its leader had the previous president murdered, Latin Americans resented his "moral imperialism" as much as Roosevelt's "Big Stick."

When war erupted in Europe in 1914 after years of European nationalism and imperialism, the United States declared neutrality. But eventually British and French propaganda and American business interests persuaded Americans to side with the allies. Furthermore, the German use of unrestricted submarine warfare endangered American lives and cargo and strained to the breaking point Wilson's efforts to keep the United States neutral.

Reelected by a narrow margin in 1916, Wilson continued to press for peace. But warring countries were cool to his arguments for "peace without victory." An apparent conspiracy between Mexico and Germany against the United States and the sinking of four American merchant ships ended American neutrality. Congress declared war on Germany in April 1917.

Unprepared for war, Americans mobilized with incredible speed. The production of armaments became a priority, and government agencies such as the War Industries Board reorganized the economy to supply them. The draft was reinstated and a Committee on Public Information produced propaganda to influence public opinion to support the war. The government raised vast amounts of money for the war effort through taxes and the selling of bonds. Meanwhile, intolerance toward German Americans and all things German became rampant.

American troops—and new forms of weaponry—tipped the balance of the war in favor of the allies, and an armistice was signed in November 1918. Wilson pushed hard for his Fourteen Points—a plan for preserving the hard-won peace. But the allies rejected most of Wilson's peace plan, and the Senate turned down the Treaty of Versailles because of disagreements over the League of Nations. Afterwards, the United States experienced economic and social unrest, punctuated by strikes and race riots.

Chapter 26
The Decade of Normalcy

By the 1920s, Americans wanted to get on with their lives, forget about public affairs, and stay out of wars. Warren G. Harding understood this when he promised "normalcy," a return to the values and practices of the past. But the United States was now too enmeshed in world affairs to return to isolationism. The government sought to improve relations with Japan and Latin America and negotiated a series of important treaties with nations worldwide. Americans also won major diplomatic victories by leading disarmament talks and by promoting the 1928 Kellogg-Briand Pact—an attempt to outlaw international war that many nations eventually signed.

President Harding, his successor Calvin Coolidge, and the Republican party believed in "less government in business and more business in government." So the government eased its restrictions on business and looked after business interests. These policies seemed to work because many urban Americans experienced unparalleled prosperity during the 1920s. For the first time, the average person began to buy shares in businesses and to "invest in the future." The growth of new industries such as home appliances and automobile-making fueled the economic boom. The growing prosperity was a key factor in the decline of labor unions' numbers and strength.

The automobile affected more than the economy; it seemed to change the American way of life. It helped shift homes, shops, and factories from the inner cities to the suburbs. Some people claimed that the automobile even contributed to the relaxation of moral standards.

Other major social changes and cultural achievements took place during the 1920s. Prohibition brought on a crime wave. The success of radio and radio advertising increased the demand for consumer goods. The first "talkie" stimulated Americans' taste for the styles and morals shown in the movies. Along with their newly won suffrage, American women demanded economic opportunity. And in the art of the "Harlem Rennaissance," African Americans reflected a new spirit of pride and protest.

After World War I, however, feelings against immigrants fueled by a postwar hysteria "Red scare," led Congress to seriously restrict all immigration into the United States.

Chapter 27
The Depression Begins

Herbert Hoover slid into the presidency in 1928 full of optimism. In foreign policy, Hoover made peace efforts a priority and practiced a "good neighbor" policy with Latin American republics. An advocate of disarmament, he proposed an international moratorium that suspended all war-debt payments to the United States. In domestic policy, he assured Americans that as long as business thrived, the country would prosper.

But prosperity did not last. Farmers were already experiencing a depression. Government relief to farmers proved ineffective. At the same time, the stock market was booming. Stock prices rose, and people began speculating. Often investors paid only a small percentage of the total cost of the stock and borrowed the rest. Then a panic of selling started, requiring investors to repay the money they had borrowed. Many, however, could not. On Black Tuesday, October 29, 1929, the stock market crashed, losing much of its value. This touched off a business and ecomonic decline from which the country did not recover for more than a decade. The Great Depression had begun, caused not only by stock-market speculation but also by the effects of World War I, the depressed condition of agriculture, overproduction or underconsumption, and unwise government policies. Soon the Depression had spread worldwide.

By the end of the 1920s, thousands of Americans were jobless, and farmers lost the land they bought during the boom time of World War I. The government searched for remedies. Hoover thought the Hawley-Smoot tariff would stimulate consumption of domestic goods. Instead the higher tariff caused foreign markets to curtail their American imports, hurting business even further. Hoover offered to help banks and businesses but opposed direct federal relief to the unemployed because he feared that government handouts would destroy Americans' drive to work. As a result, unemployed people blamed the President for their continuing financial troubles.

The American economy had hit rock bottom by the 1932 presidential election. Signs of instability and rebellion appeared everywhere. Angry and restless, Americans expressed their eagerness for change in leadership in the voting booth. Democrat Franklin D. Roosevelt won the presidency by a wide margin.

SYNTHESIZING UNIT THEMES

RELATING IDEAS

1. How did American foreign policy change under Presidents Wilson, Harding, and Hoover?

IDENTIFYING TRENDS

2. What factors contributed to the boom and bust of the American economy between 1914 and 1932?

MAKING COMPARISONS

3. Compare American society before and after World War I.

★ Unit 8 Review ★

★ Analyzing Unit Themes

CONFLICT AND COOPERATION

1. Explain why Americans felt so willing to cooperate with their government during World War I but felt in conflict with it during the Depression? What accounted for these changes in attitude toward the government? Give examples of ways people cooperated with the government and ways they engaged in conflict.

INFLUENCE OF TECHNOLOGY

2. How did technological innovation alter the lives of Americans in both war and peace? What was one important technology that revolutionized both?

THE INDIVIDUAL AND FAMILY LIFE

3. Trace the social changes covered in the unit from war to peace, from prosperity to depression. Think about other social changes during the era. How do you think all these changes affected families—for better and for worse?

U. S. ROLE IN WORLD AFFAIRS

4. In what specific ways did the United States' role in world affairs change during this era?

5. How did Americans feel about their nation's involvement in war during this time? Why?

★ Reviewing Chronology

Study the unit time line on pages 726-727, then answer the questions that follow.

1. How soon after the start of World War I did the United States enter the war?

2. How would you characterize the 1920s for the world? for the United States?

★ Linking Past and Present

In the late 1980s and 1990s, some economists noted economic factors similar to those in the 1920s and 1930s. These factors included a period of economic growth, a stock-market crash, bank failures, a slump in agriculture, industrial innovation, and a call for high tariffs.

1. **Making Predictions** Research recent news magazines such as *Newsweek, U.S. News and World Report, TIME,* or *Business Week* for a summary report on the present state of the economy. Compare the factors listed above and the information in the report with the description of the economy prior to the Depression in your text. List any similarities and differences between the two time periods. Predict whether or not another depression could occur.

2. **Making Comparisons** Compare the economic policies of Hoover and Coolidge. How do you think their policies would be viewed by Americans today? Support your answer with information about each President's economic policies.

★ Demonstrating Citizenship

Making Decisions In the years during World War I and the Great Depression, the United States government made several controversial decisions that affected American citizens. Answer the questions that follow to evaluate two of these actions.

1. Is it the role of government to control public opinion through propaganda, as the United States did during World War I? Explain your answer.

2. Was President Hoover justified in his refusal to give direct aid to victims of the Great Depression? Explain your answer.

★ Interpreting Illustrations

Revolutionists *by José Clemente Orozco*

Study the mural shown above, then answer the questions that follow.

1. What themes are illustrated?
2. What was happening in Mexico in the early 1900s that may have inspired this work?
3. Why would a wall mural be a good way to spread a message?

★ Thinking Globally

1. **Analyzing Motives** During the 1920s and 1930s American and European oil companies discovered vast deposits of oil in the Middle East. Soon these companies were making large sums of money exporting the oil to meet the demands of the industrializing world. Explain what developments and inventions from this time created an increasing appetite for oil.

2. **Comparing Cultures** If you went to a jazz club in Paris or a movie theater in Rome in the 1920s, it was likely that you would see and hear American musicians and actors. The burst of American culture during the 1920s influenced the entire world. Some American jazz musicians were more acclaimed in Europe than in their homeland. Though many countries in the 1920s produced movies, 90 percent of all films shown in the world were produced on the lots of movie studios in Los Angeles, California. How would the experiences of World War I help to create this exchange of cultures between the United States and Europe? What in American culture appealed to audiences in Europe?

★ Relating Geography and History

REGIONS: BOUNDARIES

Geographical regions can be defined in many ways. The most common way to define a region is a political boundary. For example, nations and states have political boundaries. You could also create your own classification for regions. Answer the questions below to demonstrate both of these methods.

1. Compare a map of Europe before World War I to a map of Europe after World War I. Make a list of national boundaries that were changed during the conflict.

2. Use your imagination to make a list of factors other than political boundaries that could be used as criteria to create regional maps. Remember that regions are defined as areas with any unifying factor, such as language.

★ Practicing Skills

COMPARING GRAPHIC DATA

Refer to the skills lesson on Interpreting Graphic Data on page 770 to help you practice this map and graph skill.

Refer to the graph on page 794 to answer the following questions.

1. What kind of graph is shown here?
2. What is the title of the graph?
3. What is the purpose of the graph?
4. What do the numbers along the vertical grid represent?
5. What do the numbers along the horizontal grid represent?
6. In what year were stock prices the highest?
7. In what year were stock prices the lowest?
8. What do the two lines along the grid represent?
9. What significant changes does the graph show?
10. What general conclusion can you draw from interpreting this graph?

WRITING PERSUASIVE ARGUMENTS

Refer to the skills lesson on Writing a Persuasive Argument on page 803 to help you practice this study and writing skill.

Imagine that you are an American citizen living at the time of World War I. You have relatives who are old enough to be drafted and who might be sent to fight in Europe if the United States declares war. Use information from Chapter 25 to write a persuasive argument on one of the following topics:

1. Why the United States should/should not go to war in 1917.
2. Why African Americans should/should not enlist in the military to serve during World War I.
3. Why citizens should/should not be opposed to the Espionage and Sedition acts.
4. Why the United States should/should not join the League of Nations.

UNIT 9
Times of Crisis: 1932-1960

…Today the guns are silent. A great tragedy has ended. A great victory has been won. The skies no longer rain death—the seas bear only commerce—men everywhere walk upright in the sunlight. The entire world lies quietly at peace. The holy mission has been completed.…

—DOUGLAS MACARTHUR
Radio broadcast, 1945

SETTING THE SCENE

Time

Mid-twentieth century

Mood

The period beginning with the 1930s and ending in 1960 was very difficult. The carefree atmosphere and isolationism of the 1920s gradually had given way to a sobering reality—a great depression endangered the nation's economic system, and military dictatorships threatened its national security. Americans committed themselves to economic recovery and fighting the Axis Powers in World War II. After the war, the United States sought to contain the spread of communism.

Themes

- American Democracy
- Civil Rights and Liberties
- Conflict and Cooperation
- U.S. Role in World Affairs

Key Events

- New Deal legislation
- Dust Bowl
- Japanese attack Pearl Harbor
- Surrender of Germany and Japan
- United Nations charter
- Cold War
- Truman doctrine
- North Atlantic Treaty Organization
- Korean War
- Polio vaccine
- Suez Crisis
- Castro controls Cuba

Major Issues

- New Deal programs attempt to relieve economic hardships and pull the United States out of the Great Depression.
- Aid to the Allies and the Japanese attack on Pearl Harbor pulls the United States into World War II.
- The desire to contain communism leads the United States to assume a more active role in world affairs.

CHAPTERS

28
The New Deal

29
World War II

30
The Cold War

31
Search for Stability

◄ Interchange *by Wayne Thiebaud, 1979*

Global Perspectives

As the world was held in the grip of economic disaster in the early 1930s, a World Economic Conference in London failed to recommend solutions. The depression worsened. With more people feeling the sting, some began to question their form of government.

Seizing the opportunity, dictatorial leaders, promising national glory and economic prosperity, rose to power. Benito Mussolini seized power in Italy; in Germany, Adolf Hitler; and in Spain, Francisco Franco. In the Soviet Union, the Communists held firm under Joseph Stalin. In China Mao Zedong and his communist

THE WORLD

	ASIA AND OCEANIA	AFRICA	EUROPE	SOUTH AMERICA	NORTH AND CENTRAL AMERICA
1930					
			● 1934 *Hitler becomes* Der Führer *of Germany* ▲		
			● 1939 *World War II begins in Europe*	● 1938 *Venezuela becomes the third largest oil-producing nation in the world*	
1940					
	● 1945 *Atomic bombs devastate Hiroshima and Nagasaki* ▲				
1950	● 1948 *The modern nation of Israel is created* ➤				
		● 1956 *Suez Canal Crisis*	● 1956 *Revolts in Poland and Hungary*		● 1959 *Fidel Castro takes over Cuba*
1960					

followers fought the Nationalists for control of the country.

Increasing world tensions led to vast military buildups. When Germany attacked Poland in 1939, global war again broke out. This conflict was far more devastating than previous wars as countries from all corners of the globe—Europe to Asia to Latin America—took sides. A new weapon, the atomic bomb, was dropped on Hiroshima and Nagasaki in Japan, and the havoc it reaped shocked the world.

The war ended with the defeat of Germany, Italy, and Japan and, as a result, the world balance of power shifted. Two "superpowers" emerged as the most powerful nations—the United States, which had fought to preserve democracy, and the Soviet Union, which wanted to spread communism worldwide. A cold war of confrontation threatened for decades to erupt into a full-scale "hot" war. The bitter rivalry between these two nations affected almost every other nation in the world.

THE UNITED STATES

	PACIFIC AND NORTHWEST	SOUTHWEST	MIDWEST	SOUTHEAST	ATLANTIC NORTHEAST
1930					**1933** Newly inaugurated President Roosevelt launches New Deal ◄
		1937 Parts of the Southwest and the Great Plains become a Dust Bowl			
1940	**1941** Japanese surprise attack on Pearl Harbor brings the United States into World War II ▼				**1946** United Nations headquarters is established in New York ◄
1950					**1953** McCarthyism stirs national interest
			1955 AFL-CIO merge to form one union	**1958** First successful launch of a U.S. satellite	
1960					

AMERICAN LITERARY HERITAGE

When the economy collapsed in 1929, millions of American lives collapsed with it. People everywhere lost their jobs and homes. And in the nation's Dust Bowl, sharecroppers had to leave the lands that their families had worked for generations.

In The Grapes of Wrath, *John Steinbeck chronicles the hardships of the Joads, an Oklahoma farm family whose plight resembles that of the downtrodden everywhere.*

As you read the excerpt from Steinbeck's novel, look for statements that reveal the beliefs, concerns, and attitudes of tenant farmers during the 1930s.

John Steinbeck

from
The Grapes of Wrath

he owners of the land came onto the land, or more often a spokesman for the owners came. They came in closed cars, and they felt the dry earth with their fingers, and sometimes they drove big earth augers into the ground for soil tests. The tenants, from their sun-beaten dooryards, watched uneasily when the closed cars drove along the fields. And at last the owner men drove into the dooryards and sat in their cars to talk out of the windows. The tenant men stood beside the cars for a while, and then squatted on their hams and found sticks with which to mark the dust.

In the open doors the women stood looking out, and behind them the children—corn-headed children, with wide eyes, one barefoot on top of the other bare foot, and the toes working. The women and the children watched their men talking to the owner men. They were silent.

Some of the owner men were kind because they hated what they had to do, and some of them were angry because the hated to be cruel, and some of them were cold because they had long ago found that one could not be an owner unless one were cold. And all of them were caught in something larger than themselves. Some of them hated the mathematics that drove them, and some were afraid, and some worshiped the mathematics because it provided a refuge from thought and from feeling. If a bank or a finance company owned the land, the owner man said, The Bank—or the Company—needs-wants-insists-must have-as though the Bank or the Company were a monster, with thought and feeling, which had ensnared them. These last would take no responsibility for the banks or the companies because they were men and slaves, while the banks were machines and masters all at the same time. Some of the owner men were a little proud to be slaves to such cold and powerful masters. The owner men sat in the cars and explained. You know the land is poor. You've scrabbled at it long enough, God knows.

The squatting tenant men nodded and wondered and drew figures in the dust, and yes, they knew, God knows. If the dust only wouldn't fly. If the top would only stay on the soil, it might not be so bad.

The owner men went on leading to their point: You know the land's getting poorer. You know what cotton does to the land; robs it, sucks all the blood out of it.

The squatters nodded—they knew, God knew. If they could only rotate the crops they might pump blood back into the land.

Well, it's too late. And the owner men explained the workings and the thinkings of the monster that was stronger than they were. A man can hold land if he can just eat and pay taxes; he can do that.

Yes, he can do that until his crops fail one day and he has to borrow money from the bank.

But—you see, a bank or a company can't do that, because those creatures don't breathe air, don't eat side-meat. They breathe profits; they eat the interest on money. If they don't get it, they die the way you die without air, without side-meat. It is a sad thing, but it is so. It is just so.

The squatting men raised their eyes to understand. Can't we just hang on? Maybe the next year will be a good year. God knows how much cotton next year. And with all the wars—God knows what price cotton will bring. Don't they make explosives out of cotton? And uniforms? Get enough wars and cotton'll hit the ceiling. Next year, maybe. They looked up questioningly.

We can't depend on it. The bank—the monster has to have profits all the time. It can't wait. It'll die. No, Taxes go on. When the monster stops growing, it dies. It can't stay one size.

Soft fingers began to tap the sill of the car window, and hard fingers tightened on the restless drawing sticks. In the doorways of the sun-beaten tenant houses, women sighed and then shifted feet so that the one that had been down was now on top, and the toes working. Dogs came sniffing near the owners cars and wetted on all four tires one after another. And chickens lay in the sunny dust and fluffed their feathers to get the cleansing dust down to the skin. In the little sties the pigs grunted inquiringly over the muddy remnants of the slops.

The squatting men looked down again. What do you want us to do? We can't take less share of the crop—we're half starved now. The kids are hungry all the time. We got no clothes, torn an' ragged. If all the neighbors weren't the same, we'd be ashamed to go to meeting.

And at last the owner men came to the point. The tenant system won't work any more. One man on a tractor can take the place of twelve or fourteen families. Pay him a wage and take all the crop. We have

Hoe Culture
photographed by
Dorothea Lange in
Alabama, 1937

to do it. We don't like to do it. But the monster's sick. Something's happened to the monster.

But you'll kill the land with cotton.

We know. We've got to take cotton quick before the land dies. Then we'll sell the land. Lots of families in the East would like to own a piece of land.

The tenant men looked up alarmed. But what'll happen to us? How'll we eat?

You'll have to get off the land. The plows'll go through the dooryard.

And now the squatting men stood up angrily. Grampa took up the land, and he

died on it. Even if it's no good, it's still ours. That's what makes it ours—being born on it, working it, dying on it. That makes ownership, not a paper with numbers on it.

We're sorry. It's not us. It's the monster. The bank isn't like a man.

Yes, but the bank is only made of men.

No, you're wrong there—quite wrong there. The bank is something else than men. It happens that every man in a bank hates what the bank does, and yet the bank does it. The bank is something more than men, I tell you. It's the monster.

The Dust Bowl by Alexander Hogue, 1933

had to kill the Indians and drive them away. An Pa was born here, and he killed weeds and snakes. Then a bad year came and he had to borrow a little money. An' we was born here. There in the door—our children born here. And Pa had to borrow money. The bank owned the land then, but we stayed and we got a little bit of what we raised.

We know the—all that. It's not us, it's the bank. A bank isn't like a man. Or an owner with fifty thousand acres, he isn't like a man either. That's the monster.

Sure, cried the tenant men, but it's our land. We measured it and broke it up. We were born on it, and we got killed on it,

Men made it, but they can't control it.

The tenants cried, Grampa killed Indians, Pa killed snakes for the land. Maybe we can kill banks—they're worse than Indians and snakes. Maybe we got to fight to keep our land, like Pa and Grampa did.

And now the owner men grew angry. You'll have to go.

But it's ours, the tenant men cried. We—

No. The bank, the monster owns it. You'll have to go.

We'll get our guns, like Grampa when the Indians came. What then?

Well—first the sheriff, and then the troops. You'll be stealing if you try to stay, you'll be murderers if you kill to stay. The monster isn't men, but it can make men do what it wants.

But if we go, where'll we go? How'll we go? We got no money.

We're sorry, said the owner men. The bank, the fifty-thousand-acre owner can't be responsible. You're on land that isn't yours. Once over the line maybe you can pick cotton in the fall. Maybe you can go on relief. Why don't you go on west to California? There's work there, and it never gets cold. Why, you can reach out anywhere and pick an orange. Why, there's always some kind of crop to work in. Why don't you go there? And the owner men started their cars and rolled away.

The tenant men squatted down on their hams again to mark the dust with a stick, to figure, to wonder. Their sunburned faces were dark, and their sun-whipped eyes were light. The women moved cautiously out of the doorways toward their men, and the children crept behind the women, cautiously, ready to run. The bigger boys squatted beside their fathers, because that made them men. After a time the women asked, What did he want?

And the men looked up for a second, and the smolder of pain was in their eyes. We got to get off. A tractor and a superintendent. Like factories.

Where'll we go? the women asked.

We don't know. We don't know.

And the women went quickly, quietly back into the houses and herded the children ahead of them. They knew that a man so hurt and so perplexed may turn in anger, even on people he loves. They left the men alone to figure and to wonder in the dust.

After a time perhaps the tenant man looked about—at the pump put in ten year ago, with a goose-neck handle and iron flowers on the spout, at the chopping block where a thousand chickens had been killed, at the hand plow lying in the shed, and the patent crib hanging in the rafters over it.

The children crowded about the women in the houses. What we going to do, Ma? Where we going to go?

The women said, We don't know, yet. Go out and play. But don't go near your father. He might whale you if you go near him. And the women went on with the work, but all the time they watched the men squatting in the dust—perplexed and figuring.

The tractors came over the roads and into the fields, great crawlers moving like insects, having the incredible strength of insects. They crawled over the ground, laying the track and rolling on it and picking it up. Diesel tractors, puttering while they stood idle; they thundered when they moved, and then settled down to a droning roar. Snub-nosed monsters, raising the dust and sticking their snouts into it, straight down the country, across the country, through fences, through dooryards, in and out of gullies in straight lines. They did not run on the ground, but on their own roadbeds. They ignored hills and gulches, water courses, fences, and houses.

The man sitting in the iron seat did not look like a man; gloved, goggled, rubber dust mask over nose and mouth, he was part of the monster, a robot in the seat. The thunder of cylinders sounded through the country, became one with the air and the earth, so that earth and air muttered in sympathetic vibration. The driver could not control it—straight across the country it went, cutting through a dozen farms and straight back. A twitch in the controls could swerve it, but the driver's hands could not twitch because the monster that built the tractor, the monster that sent the tractor out, had somehow got into the driver's hands, into his brain and muscle, had goggled him and muzzled him—goggled his mind, muzzled his speech, goggled his perception, muzzled his protest. He could not see the land as it was, he could not smell the land as it smelled; his feet did not stamp the clods or feel the warmth and power of the earth....

He loved the land no more than the bank loved the land.

INTERPRETING LITERATURE

1. Locate passages where the tenant men are beseeching, protesting, or resigned.

2. What is the "monster"? Do you think this is an apt metaphor? Why or why not?

EVALUATING VIEWPOINTS

3. Steinbeck clearly sides with the tenant farmers. What arguments could be made for the banks and the owners? Which viewpoint do you favor?

The New Deal

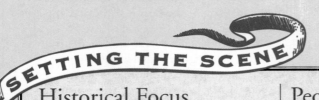

SETTING THE SCENE

Historical Focus

When Franklin D. Roosevelt took the oath of office, Congress and the American people were eager to follow the President's leadership. Within months, laws were passed to provide relief, recovery, and reform of the economic system. Two years later, however, millions of Americans were still unemployed, and the New Deal came under increasing criticism. Throughout Roosevelt's second term, many programs were reshaped to permanently change the way government relates to its citizens.

Concepts to Understand

- Why the **political leadership** of Roosevelt was effective at bringing about New Deal reforms.
- How New Deal **economic reform** differed from previous government policies.

People to Know

Eleanor Roosevelt, Frances Perkins, Harry L. Hopkins, Huey Long, Charles Coughlin, Francis Townsend

Places to Locate

Tennessee Valley, Grand Coulee Dam

Terms to Identify

brain trust, pump priming, dole, craft union, industrial union

Guided Reading

As you read this chapter, seek the answers to the following questions.

1. How did New Deal legislation attempt to end the depression?
2. What were the long-term effects of New Deal programs on American society?

SPANNING THE DECADES

POLITICAL	1933 *Repeal of Prohibition*	1933 *"Hundred Days" begins after Roosevelt's inauguration*	1934 *Securities and Exchange Commission is established*	1935 *Social Security Act is passed*
	1932		**1934**	
CULTURAL	1932 *American speed skaters and bobsledders earn medals in the Winter Olympics*		1934 *Severe drought in the Great Plains creates a "dust bowl"*	1935 *Robert and Helen Lynd publish* Middletown

Norris Dam *by Paul Sample, 1935*

	1937 *Roosevelt attempts to pack the Supreme Court*	1938 *Fair Labor Standards Act passed*
1936 *Roosevelt is reelected*		

1936   **1938**

1936 *Tornadoes kill more than 400 southerners in 5 states*	1937 *German dirigible* Hindenburg *explodes at Lakehurst, New Jersey*	1938 *Radio broadcast,* The War of the Worlds, *causes panic*

I pledge you—I pledge myself to a new deal for the American people. Let us all here assembled constitute ourselves prophets of a new order of competence and courage. This is more than a political campaign; it is a call to arms....

—FRANKLIN D. ROOSEVELT
Democratic nomination
acceptance speech, 1932

Roosevelt Takes Charge

SETTING THE SCENE

First of all let me assert my firm belief that the only thing we have to fear is fear itself—nameless, unreasoning, unjustified terror which paralyzes needed efforts to convert retreat into advance.

—FRANKLIN ROOSEVELT
First Inaugural Address, March 1933

Section Focus

President Roosevelt's inaugural address attempted to lift the clouds of gloom and fear that had hovered over the country since the stock market crash. At last, a new President promised action against the Depression. Congress and the American public—some in eager anticipation and others out of desperation—were ready to follow the President's lead.

Objectives

After studying this section, you should be able to:
- Identify the traits that made Franklin Roosevelt an effective leader.
- Describe how Roosevelt garnered ideas and support for his New Deal.

Within his inaugural address Franklin D. Roosevelt made the same promises about the nation's recovery that Herbert Hoover and his advisers had been saying since 1929. Roosevelt promised that the nation "will endure as it has endured, will revive and will prosper." Unlike Hoover, however, the new President reflected the popular mood of the nation by blaming bankers, "the unscrupulous moneychangers," for allowing starvation in the midst of plenty. The nation was in a kind of war, he said, and strong presidential leadership was needed. If Congress failed to act quickly, Roosevelt promised to ask for executive authority "as great as the power that would be given to me if we were in fact invaded by a foreign foe."

A Master Politician

Before taking office, Roosevelt displayed little evidence of the leadership he would offer in his 12 years in the White House. His outstanding attribute was his name, which his cousin Theodore Roosevelt had made well known in American politics. The only son of wealthy parents, FDR, as his friends called him, attended the best schools.

At the time of his election, Roosevelt had been in politics for more than 20 years, yet his views on many issues were unknown. Nor did many Americans realize that he had overcome a serious physical handicap.

In 1921, at age 39, Roosevelt was stricken with polio. Fighting back against the crippling disease, he regained the use of his hands and arms, but he remained paralyzed from the waist down. His painful recovery toughened him and, at the same time, gave him genuine sympathy for the less fortunate. Playwright Robert Sherwood, a close associate, described his toughness and compassion:

I tried continually to study him, to try to look beyond his charming and amusing and warmly affectionate surface into his heavily forested interior. But I never understood what was going on in there....He could be a ruthless politician, but he was the champion of friends and associates who for him were political liabilities...and of causes which apparently competent observers assured him would be political suicide.

Both friends and foes agreed that, despite his complexity, Roosevelt was master of the art of politics. Few Presidents had such varied political training—at local, state, and federal levels—in elected and appointed offices. Elected to the New York legislature in 1910, at the height of the Progressive Era, Roosevelt learned about local government. As assistant secretary of the Navy during World War I, he had an insider's view as the Wilson administration organized the federal government to wage war. As governor of New York when the stock market crashed, FDR dealt with many of the same problems he would face as President.

Perhaps Roosevelt's greatest strength as a politician was his warm and understanding approach to people. Although Hoover had withdrawn to the isolation of the White House as the Depression settled in, Roosevelt reached out by radio to the American people in a series of "fireside chats." These were informal talks in which the President calmly but confidently explained in simple terms the nation's problems and how the New Deal planned to defeat the Depression. Millions of radio listeners felt that the President was talking directly to them. After a fireside chat, Roosevelt sometimes received as many as 50,000 letters a day.

Roosevelt also knew how to use the press better than his predecessor. Hoover had avoided reporters and refused to answer questions unless they were written out in advance. In contrast, FDR allowed reporters to barrage him with questions during frequent press conferences. This approach made him popular with the press—important shapers of public opinion—and focused public attention on Washington and his New Deal programs. "Gone is the fortress that was the White House," wrote one reporter after Roosevelt took office.

A product of the Progressive Era, FDR retained the progressives' approach to solving society's problems. As President he was a pragmatist and an experimenter. He sometimes asked three or four people with conflicting opinions to do the same job. FDR compared himself to a quarterback on a football team who called a play, and

Examining Photographs *President Franklin Roosevelt, First Lady Eleanor, and their son James posed for this photograph shortly after FDR's Inauguration on March 4, 1933. What personal qualities did Roosevelt bring to the presidency?*

if it did not work tried another. Action, he felt, was better than inaction. Most Americans, desperate for relief from the effects of the Depression, agreed with him. Humorist Will Rogers observed:

The whole country is with him.
Even if what he does is wrong, they
are with him. Just so he does something.
If he burned down the Capitol,
we would cheer and say, "Well,
at least we got a fire started anyhow."

Examining Photographs *Frances Perkins, appointed secretary of labor by Roosevelt, is shown here greeting steelworkers. A long-time advocate of minimum wage and maximum hour laws, child-labor restrictions, and other progressive reforms, she was one of only two cabinet members to serve throughout Roosevelt's four terms. What was unique about her appointment?*

Roosevelt also had trust in the ability of experts to plan for society. Even before receiving the Democratic nomination for President, he gathered a group of professors from Columbia University to advise him. This group of economists, political scientists, and attorneys was nicknamed the "brain trust" by the press. After Roosevelt became President, the brain trust stayed on to help him plan New Deal recovery programs. In selecting his cabinet, FDR named people who presented a variety of viewpoints and ideas—northerners and southerners, liberals and conservatives. He named Republican Harold Ickes as secretary of the interior, and for secretary of agriculture he chose Henry A. Wallace, whose father had the job under Harding. For secretary of labor Roosevelt named the first woman cabinet officer, former child labor reformer Frances Perkins. Other women held important positions in almost every New Deal agency. Like Secretary Perkins, many of these women had been social workers. Now the President was calling upon them to administer the federal government's social and relief programs.

Outside the brain trust, the adviser that Roosevelt relied on most was his wife, Eleanor. Because of his paralysis, FDR moved with difficulty in a wheelchair or with heavy braces on his legs. As a result, he asked Eleanor to assume a significant role in his administration. The President called her his "eyes and ears" outside the White House. During the first year of the New Deal, she traveled extensively to attend political rallies, tour factories, visit coal mines, and contact many people that FDR might not otherwise have met. At cabinet meetings, the President would report, "My missus says that people are working for wages well below the

AMERICAN PORTRAITS

ELEANOR ROOSEVELT
1884-1962

Eleanor Roosevelt did not herself hold public office until she was a 61-year-old widow. But as First Lady she fought tenaciously for social justice and added a sense of compassion to the New Deal.

Although painfully shy as a young girl, Eleanor Roosevelt emerged as a vibrant public personality during the 1920s when her husband, FDR, was recovering from polio. She did all she could to keep his name in the public mind. After Roosevelt's election, she spoke for people who otherwise would have been ignored—women, the underprivileged, and African Americans. Sensitive to racial injustice, she spoke up so strongly for civil rights that she won black support for the New Deal. Eleanor Roosevelt later worked for global human rights in the United Nations.

minimum…in the town she visited last week." Eleanor Roosevelt shared Franklin's concern for the victims of the Depression—close friends thought that her concern was even deeper than his—and that decisive government action was needed to conquer society's ills.

The Hundred Days

President Roosevelt fulfilled his promise to provide "action now." On Sunday, March 5, 1933, the day after his inauguration, he called a special session of Congress. On Monday he used an old law still on the books to suspend the nation's banking activity. Many Americans had lost faith in banks after the crash, withdrew their money, and kept it at home. Banks needed depositors' funds to make loans that would help recovery, but, in many areas, the loss of deposits was so great that banks had to close their doors. After a week in office, the President went on the radio with his first fireside chat. He explained that only healthy banks would be allowed to reopen. He assured Americans that it would be "safer to keep money in a reopened bank than under the mattress." The next day most banks began to do business again, and in a few days deposits exceeded withdrawals. As the President's calm assurances restored public confidence in the nation's financial system, the bank crisis ended.

That first week was just the beginning of feverish activity. In the "Hundred Days" between March 9 and June 16, 1933, Congress passed 15 major bills, more than had ever been enacted in such a short time. Most were bills that the President submitted and that Congress passed with little debate. Seldom had a

Linking Across Time

NEW DEAL PRECEDENTS

The substance, style, and organization of the New Deal followed distinctly American precedents. The program had its roots in such late-1800s progressive legislation as railroad regulation and antitrust acts. President Roosevelt's activist style was modeled after that of his cousin, Theodore Roosevelt.

Much as Wilson's administration worked to fight World War I, the New Deal was mobilized to fight the Great Depression. Many top New Dealers, including FDR, had been officials in the Wilson administration.

Examining Photographs *Afraid for the safety of their savings, panicked depositors line up outside a bank. Such "runs"—when all depositors tried to withdraw their money at the same time—usually caused those banks to fail, making their depositors' fears come true. How did Roosevelt handle the bank crisis?*

President enjoyed such overwhelming support. As Anne O'Hare McCormick reported in *The New York Times Magazine* in May 1933:

In his present temper the American is not in the least afraid of experiments.... But he wants action, the immediate action promised by Mr. Roosevelt in his inaugural address and no lobby ever exerted so much pressure on Congress as the people are bringing to bear...we have never had a President as powerful as Mr. Roosevelt is at this moment.

Roosevelt took office with no clear idea of how to solve the nation's economic crisis. "There's nothing to do," he said, "but meet each day's troubles as they come." The New Deal, therefore, was not a carefully worked out reform plan. Instead, it was a series of measures quickly drawn up to attack the Depression in many ways at once. Some laws were in response to special demands from specific groups in society. Some were even passed against the President's wishes, but he signed them to head off something that he might like even less, or to avoid holding up other legislation. However, New Deal programs had three general purposes: recovery from the Depression, relief for its victims, and reform of the economic system. Much legislation reflected all three goals.

From 1933 to early 1935, the dominant purposes were recovery and relief. During the "First New Deal," as this phase was called, the President and his advisers thought that a series of temporary measures could get the economy moving again and then recovery would come on its own momentum. Therefore, little additional legislation followed the Hundred Days of the First New Deal. The administration merely implemented the laws Congress had created and waited for recovery to occur.

SUMMARY

President Roosevelt attempted to deal with the Depression on two levels. On a psychological level, he offered the positive image of an energetic, caring leader who would get the economy moving. His fireside chats and easy manner with the press reinforced this perception. On a more practical level, he immediately addressed the banking crisis and quickly implemented a number of government programs to attack the causes of the Depression. These approaches inspired confidence and led people to believe that the government was acting at last.

CHECKING FOR UNDERSTANDING

1. **Identify** FDR, fireside chats, brain trust, Frances Perkins, the Hundred Days

2. **Cite** the political experience that prepared Roosevelt to lead the nation out of the Depression.

3. **Describe** the personal characteristics that gained Roosevelt the confidence and trust of Americans.

4. **Explain** Roosevelt's approach to solving problems.

5. **Discuss** the role women played in the Roosevelt administration.

6. **List** the three general approaches that New Deal programs took in attacking the Depression.

THINKING CRITICALLY

7. **Making Comparisons** Compare Roosevelt's style in managing the crisis to Hoover's approach. Why did the public support Roosevelt?

CONNECTIONS: HISTORY AND ECONOMICS

8. **Interpreting Primary Sources** Explain Roosevelt's statement about the Depression that "the only thing we have to fear is fear itself."

★ ★ ★ ★ ★ ★ ★ ★ ★ ★ ★ ★ ★ ★ ★ ★ ★ ★

Reform, Relief, and Recovery

The country needs and, unless I mistake its temper, the country demands bold, persistent experimentation. It is common sense to take a method and try it. If it fails, admit it frankly and try another. But above all, try something.

—FRANKLIN ROOSEVELT
Campaign speech in Atlanta,
May 22, 1932

Section Focus

Many of the laws passed during the Hundred Days were popularly known by their initials—AAA, NRA, TVA, and CCC. People jokingly called them the New Deal's "alphabet soup," yet the programs gave the nation a sense of hope. Many were intended as stopgap measures, but their effects are still felt.

Objectives

After studying this section, you should be able to:

- Give examples of how Roosevelt's policies helped and hurt the rural poor.
- Compare the effectiveness of measures aimed at farmers and city workers.

Both Hoover and Roosevelt believed that prosperity would return with a little help to spark the economy. So, like Hoover, FDR sought the help of the business community and spoke of an alliance of "business and banking, agriculture and industry, and labor and capital." But he differed from Hoover in the amount and variety of legislation he proposed and in his willingness to call on the full powers of the federal government to solve national problems. He also rejected Hoover's belief in "rugged individualism" and used government to help people.

Financial Reform

In June 1933 Congress passed the Glass-Steagall Act. This law prohibited banks from investing in the stock market and created a Federal Deposit Insurance Corporation (FDIC) to insure depositors' savings. Although the program was opposed by the American Bankers' Association as "unscientific, unjust, and dangerous," federal insurance made people feel confident that their money would be safe in banks.

Congress also responded to the demand that the government prevent stock market fraud. The Federal Securities Act of 1933 required companies that issued or marketed stocks and bonds to provide complete and truthful information to purchasers. Congress followed this act in 1934 with the Securities and Exchange Commission (SEC) to regulate the stock market.

When Roosevelt took office, he faced strong pressure to inflate the currency. A number of senators and representatives wanted to stimulate recovery by putting into circulation billions of dollars in new paper money. But Roosevelt rejected inflation and took a conservative approach in his early efforts to achieve recovery. During the campaign he had promised efficiency and economy in government, and he was reluctant to create budget deficits. He realized, however, that to keep relief agencies from closing and millions of Americans from starving, **deficit spending** was necessary. In other words, the federal government's annual spending would exceed its income.

Help for the Jobless

From balancing the budget, the New Deal moved to **pump priming**—pouring government money into the economy through loans and federal spending in the hope of stimulating recovery. Roosevelt called for government to give money directly to people who would spend it.

THE FEDERAL BUDGET AND DEFICIT, 1932–1940

	Federal Receipts (in billions of dollars)	Federal Deficit (in billions of dollars)	Gross Federal Debt (in billions of dollars)	Per Capita Federal Debt (total dollar amt.)
1940	6.9	−1.3	43.0	325
1939	5.0	−2.2	40.4	309
1938	5.6	−2.1	37.2	286
1937	5.0	−.4	36.4	283
1936	4.0	−3.6	33.8	264
1935	3.7	−2.6	28.7	226
1934	3.0	−2.9	27.1	214
1933	2.0	−1.3	22.5	179
1932	1.9	−1.5	19.5	156

Historical Statistics of the United States: Colonial Times to 1970

Examining Tables *As the nation recovered from the Depression, the government's income increased. But it never equaled federal spending during the 1930s. Why did the government spend more than it earned?*

Increased spending would increase demand for consumer goods, New Dealers claimed, which would stimulate production and create jobs.

By 1933, 12 million to 15 million Americans—1 of every 4 workers—was unemployed, and many were on the verge of starvation. At first Roosevelt, like Hoover, thought that local agencies should handle relief until industry and agriculture recovered enough to provide jobs. It soon became clear, however, that states, cities, and local charities had exhausted their resources. So in May 1933 Congress established a Federal Emergency Relief Administration (FERA), the first of several New Deal relief agencies. FERA made outright grants to states and municipalities to distribute as they chose. They generally provided a **dole**—direct gifts of money, food, and clothing. Although the dole was the cheapest and quickest form of relief, its critics were concerned that people who received handouts would lose their self-respect and job skills, making them even more unemployable in the future. So once the federal government had met the need for emergency relief, New Dealers searched for alternatives to the dole.

The Public Works Administration (PWA), created in June 1933, offered jobs instead of handouts. Under the direction of Secretary of the Interior Harold Ickes, the program provided jobs on construction projects—improving highways and building dams, sewer systems, waterworks, schools, and other government buildings. Although the PWA generally worked through private contractors rather than employing workers outright, Ickes broke down long-standing racial barriers in the construction trades by insisting that contractors hire blacks. However, the PWA grew slowly, and some time passed before it had an impact on employment.

In the autumn of 1933, Harry Hopkins, a former social worker appointed by Roosevelt to head the FERA, convinced the President that large-scale work relief was needed. Hopkins won approval for a Civil Works Administration (CWA) to hire jobless persons and put them to work. During the winter of 1933-1934, the CWA employed 4 million people—300,000 of them women. Under Hopkins's direction, the CWA built or improved 1,000 airports, 500,000 miles of roads, 40,000 school buildings, and 3,500 parks, playgrounds, and playing fields. But the cost of all the projects and employees was tremendous—$1 billion in just five months. In the spring of 1934, Roosevelt gave in to fierce criticism from conservatives and cancelled the program.

The most generally admired New Deal relief agency reflected Franklin Roosevelt's concern for conservation. The Civilian

Examining Photographs *Unemployment was a major problem during the Depression. Many New Deal programs were aimed at putting people to work. Why were jobs important to economic recovery?*

Conservation Corps (CCC), established in March 1933, offered outdoor work to unemployed single men, 18 to 25 years old, at $30 per month, $22 of which went back to their families. By midsummer the CCC had established 1,500 camps, including separate camps for black CCC workers. During its existence, the CCC put 3 million young men to work planting trees, fighting forest fires, building reservoirs, and stopping soil erosion. The CCC took better care of its young workers than their families could. As one CCC worker observed:

This is better clothes than I ever had at home, before I got to the CCC. You see, at home they was so many of us, we couldn't have much clothes to wear and in the summer time we jist didn't wear no shoes, and no shirts much, nor nothing else much.

Examining Photographs
CCC workers plant seedlings. What else did the CCC do?

The average CCC worker returned home after six months to a year, better nourished and with greater self-respect.

One early New Deal program combined emergency relief and pump priming

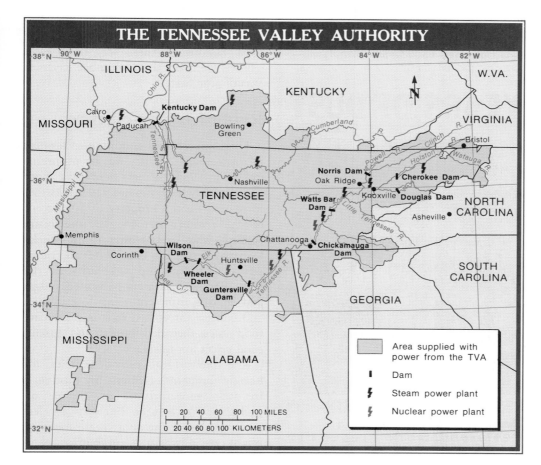

THE TENNESSEE VALLEY AUTHORITY

Area supplied with power from the TVA

I Dam

⚡ Steam power plant

⚡ Nuclear power plant

Examining Maps
Covering a huge region, the Tennessee Valley Authority was one of the most ambitious New Deal programs. Today its lakes are heavily used recreational sites that pump millions of tourist dollars annually into the region's economy. What benefits did TVA bring to the area in the 1930s?

with long-term economic and social planning. In May 1933, after Roosevelt's prodding, Congress established the Tennessee Valley Authority (TVA), designed to promote the development of a seven-state region drained by the Tennessee and Cumberland rivers.

Before the TVA, the natural resources of the Tennessee Valley had long been exploited. Forests were leveled, and heavy rainfalls caused erosion and disastrous floods. Poor farmers attempted to work worn-out land, and many of the people in the Tennessee Valley were on relief.

Employing as many as 40,000 workers at a time, the TVA built 20 dams for flood control and improved 5 others. The TVA also moved farmers from marginal lands, reforested millions of acres, built power plants and fertilizer factories, and even started new towns. But the most notable change was the immense amount of cheap electricity that the TVA produced. Its increased availability improved agriculture, allowing farmers to install refrigerators, milking machines, and other equipment. Cheap power also brought industry and jobs to the valley.

Despite its obvious benefits, the TVA was one of Roosevelt's most controversial programs. Critics charged that it favored one small section by using government funds that could support programs nationwide. But above all, the TVA was attacked by the power companies. One goal of the TVA was to provide a basis to determine fair electricity rates all over the country. But private power companies argued that to use the TVA for this purpose was unfair because the government charged large parts of the cost of electricity production to the cost of flood control and navigation. For the federal government to take over the production of private power, they argued was unfair and communistic.

Although the power companies were powerful enough to prevent any more regional authorities like TVA, the New Deal did build other power plants. The most famous of these was the Grand Coulee Dam on the Columbia River in Washington State.

Relief for Agriculture

The impoverished condition of farmers in the Tennessee Valley was by no means unique in 1933. Farmers were in an angry mood everywhere. Since 1929 banks had foreclosed on the property of 10 percent of the nation's farmers. In **foreclosure** actions, when a borrower cannot make loan payments, the bank seizes the property that was put up as security for the loan. Bands of farmers prevented judges and sheriffs from enforcing foreclosures, and farmers threatened to stop producing food unless their debt burden and agricultural prices improved.

The New Deal provided relief for heavily indebted farmers by placing a five-year **moratorium,** or freeze, on mortgage foreclosures. But New Dealers recognized that the root of the farmers' plight was low agricultural prices, and

Examining Artifacts *This poster by famous graphic artist Ben Shahn promotes a New Deal agency founded in 1935 to resettle poor farmers on good land and provide them with equipment for a new start. But due to inadequate funding, the program aided less than 4,500 families. What problems did farmers face?*

YEARS OF DUST

RESETTLEMENT ADMINISTRATION
Rescues Victims
Restores Land to Proper Use

that this situation was related to a problem that had plagued farmers since the end of World War I—overproduction. Roosevelt proposed an unusual approach: stop agricultural surpluses by paying farmers to *not* produce crops. In May 1933, Congress passed the Agricultural Adjustment Act (AAA), under which the government paid farmers who reduced production of basic crops like cotton, wheat, tobacco, hogs, and corn. Funds for these payments came from a tax levied on flour mills, slaughterhouses, and other food processors. These processors passed this cost on to consumers.

In 1933 cotton farmers plowed under a quarter of their acreage, and hog producers killed 6 million piglets instead of fattening them for market. In 1934 and 1935, farmers withdrew 10 million acres from production and received more than $1 billion in benefit payments. Surpluses were greatly reduced by 1936, and total farm income rose by more than 50 percent.

The AAA did not relieve the suffering of all farmers. Large commercial farmers, who concentrated on one crop, benefited more than smaller farmers who raised several. The crop reduction program actually hurt some people. In the West and Southwest,

Examining Photographs *A homeless farm family was the subject of photographer Dorothea Lange. What farm programs did the New Deal offer?*

Examining Photographs *Evicted sharecroppers set up camp in southeast Missouri, near the Arkansas border. Why did many sharecroppers and tenant farmers lose their farms?*

Mexican migrant workers suffered when growers raised less produce and so hired fewer pickers. Tenant farmers and sharecroppers—black and white alike—were forced off the land they worked as owners took it out of production. About 150,000 white tenants and almost 195,000 black tenants left farming during the 1930s. To stop this trend, the New Deal created the Farm Security Administration to give loans to help tenants purchase land. But only 3,400 black farmers received any of this money. Landless farmers joined other urban and rural migrants who wandered the country in search of jobs.

In 1934 and 1935 a terrible disaster struck the Great Plains and added to the number of farmers on the move. The origins of the disaster arose during World War I, when high crop prices tempted farmers to grow wheat and cotton on what traditionally had been grazing lands. Plows broke up the deep, tough sod that had prevented erosion and conserved moisture in this semiarid region. When the years from 1933 and 1935 were unusually dry, the area began to turn to desert. Dust storms carried away so much

Connections

HISTORY AND ENVIRONMENT

THE DUST BOWL

As the entire nation struggled to cope with the Depression, farmers in Kansas, Oklahoma, and Texas suffered from the scourges of drought and dust. From the 1890s to the 1920s, grasslands in this part of the Great Plains were put to the plow, and when rain fell, they were bountiful. But in the 1930s, the rains

A farm in the Dust Bowl

failed. As crops withered, leaving bare dirt exposed, the region's high winds lifted the fine topsoil to create dust storms called "dusters."

Large-scale mechanized farming on the plains after 1900 exposed huge areas of soil. Farmers eager to maximize yields overtilled the soil and burned wheat stubble to kill weeds. These poor soil-conservation practices and the long drought created a dust bowl on the plains throughout most of the 1930s, as millions of tons of airborne powdery topsoil buried crops and killed livestock.

The dust bowl took its toll on people too. People sat helpless while their farms blew away. They sometimes lost their way and died in the thick storms while only yards from their houses. Thousands of families abandoned their land and became migrant farm workers. Those who stayed on their land were encouraged to plant crops that conserve the soil.

MAKING THE ENVIRONMENT CONNECTION

1. How did humans change the natural environment on the Great Plains in the early twentieth century?

2. How was a dust bowl created in this region?

LINKING PAST AND PRESENT

3. What soil-conservation practices are used today?

---

topsoil that a haze obscured the sun, sometimes as far away as the Atlantic coast. Between 1934 and 1939, nearly 350,000 farm families left what came to be called the "Dust Bowl."

To take care of immediate distress, Congress provided the farmers in the Dust Bowl with funds for new seed and livestock. For long-term solutions, the Department of Agriculture helped farmers plant millions of trees in shelter belts to cut wind velocity and help retain moisture. The government also encouraged farmers to return the land to grazing. Yet there was much criticism of New Deal farm policies. Many farmers did not like being told what to raise or how much to plant. To others, decreasing food supplies when people were hungry seemed immoral. However, the New Deal provided more direct assistance to farmers than to any other group, and saved thousands of farm families from poverty and despair.

In addition, as *Collier's* magazine reported in a 1934 article:

[The farmer's] morale has been strengthened not just with money but by the conviction that at last he is considered by Washington to be as important—perhaps even more important—than the capitalist and at last government is being administered in his interests.

Industrial Relief

In 1933 the condition of American industry was as desperate as the situation in agriculture. So in June 1933 the New Deal tried to help industry with the National Industrial Recovery Act (NIRA), which Roosevelt hailed as probably "the

LABOR UNION MEMBERSHIP, 1900–1940

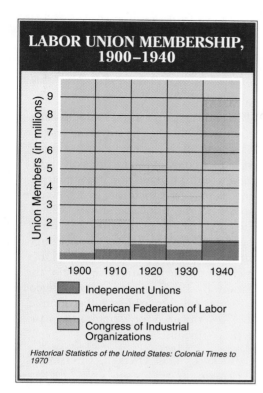

Union Members (in millions)

9
8
7
6
5
4
3
2
1

1900 1910 1920 1930 1940

◼ Independent Unions
◻ American Federation of Labor
◻ Congress of Industrial Organizations

Historical Statistics of the United States: Colonial Times to 1970

Examining Graphs *New Deal laws let workers join unions. Membership jumped when the CIO left the AFL in 1936 and formed industrial unions. How did the NRA help workers?*

most important and far-reaching law ever passed by an American Congress." It proposed a partnership of business, labor, and government to attack a variety of problems resulting from the Depression.

Roosevelt's advisers believed that industry, like agriculture, suffered from overproduction. To control production, the NIRA provided that representatives of labor and of management from competing companies draw up "codes of fair competition" in each industry. These codes set the prices of products to eliminate discount selling. They shortened workers' hours in order to create more jobs, and they established minimum-wage levels. To spread production among as many firms as possible, factories were limited to two shifts a day. To direct this complex program, the act created the National Recovery Administration (NRA).

The government's power to enforce the codes was very limited, so the NRA used

the power of public opinion to enlist the cooperation of American business. Those that signed code agreements were given signs to display with blue eagles and the words "We Do Our Part" on them. Consumers were encouraged to purchase goods only from businesses that displayed the Blue Eagle. Despite a temporary revival of the business economy, the NIRA never worked out as planned. Prices rose faster than wages. Businesses complained that large companies wrote the codes to favor themselves and to put small competitors out of business.

Probably no group suffered more during the Depression than people who worked for hourly wages. By 1933 one-third of

Examining Fine Art *Depression painter Joe Jones emphasized working people in his art. In* We Demand, *he concentrated on the efforts of workers to organize and protest to improve their wages and conditions of employment. What problems did industrial workers face in the 1930s?*

these workers were unemployed. The earnings of the rest had shrunk as their hourly rates or work hours were cut. The average laborer earned $375 in 1933, nearly half as much as in 1929. Women earned as little as $3 a week. Even outside the labor movement, the idea spread that the best way to restore workers' wages and purchasing power was to strengthen labor unions. And under Section 7a of the NIRA, every NRA code guaranteed workers the right to organize unions and to bargain collectively with their employers.

As a result, Section 7a encouraged a revival of unionism, and between May and October 1933, American Federation of Labor (AFL) membership jumped by about a million workers. After this initial success, however, the effort to enlist new members stalled. The AFL was not greatly interested in organizing the mass-production industries such as steel and automobiles. In addition, employers generally opposed labor unions in their plants. In some cases they avoided organization while technically complying with Section 7a by forming their own "company unions," which lacked real power, of course, because they were controlled by the employers.

In 1934 a wave of strikes swept the nation as workers demanded the right to organize for improved wages and job security. Many of these strikes became violent, and most resulted in defeat for the workers, as police generally sided with employers. Although sympathetic to organized labor, the only way the NRA could punish a company was to take away its Blue Eagle symbol. Workers began to demand stronger labor laws.

In November 1934, Americans showed they approved of FDR's efforts by returning overwhelming Democratic majorities to Congress. But as the nation entered 1935—the New Deal's third year and the Depression's fifth—American spirits noticeably sagged. Despite the New Deal, farm prices and industrial wages were well below 1929 levels, and workers remained unemployed and poor. To many Americans, the New Deal was taking too long and accomplishing too little. FDR and his advisers clearly saw that they must find other means to restore prosperity.

SUMMARY

To end the Depression, Franklin Roosevelt was willing to try anything and see what worked. He offered jobs and direct relief to victims of the Depression and tried to enlist cooperation among business, labor, and agriculture to achieve economic reform. But labor unions lacked the power to secure improvements for workers, and management would not give up control. Farm income continued to trail behind the income of the rest of the nation. By 1935, as Roosevelt's emergency measures failed to achieve full economic recovery, the need for a long-range plan became obvious.

CHECKING FOR UNDERSTANDING

1. **Identify** FDIC, FERA, PWA, CCC, AAA, NRA, Section 7a

2. **Define** deficit spending, pump priming, dole, foreclosure, moratorium

3. **List** three programs designed to create jobs by employing workers on projects to benefit the nation.

4. **State** the positive and negative effects of New Deal farm programs.

5. **Explain** Roosevelt's theory that giving money directly to people would stimulate economic recovery.

THINKING CRITICALLY

6. **Making Judgments** During widespread unemployment, is government money better used as a dole or for more expensive work-relief programs? Why?

GLOBAL PERSPECTIVES

7. **Making Comparisons** In Germany during the Depression, Adolf Hitler employed workers in building projects and military enterprises. He placed controls on wages and prices and outlawed unions. Compare his strategies with Roosevelt's.

★ ★ ★ ★ ★ ★ ★ ★ ★ ★ ★ ★ ★ ★ ★ ★ ★ ★ ★

Linking Across Time

THE AGRICULTURE BUSINESS

Thomas Jefferson wrote that "Those who labor in the earth are the chosen people of God, if ever He had a chosen people." The years from 1865 to 1900 seemed to support this idyllic view, showing the largest increase in the number of farms of any period in United States history.

Technological advances, the rise of agricultural education, and the application of business practices to production and marketing, however, changed farming dramatically. These changes led to an increase in farm production—and the beginning of a problem that plagues the American farmer to this day. Efficiency increased production, resulting in falling prices. But goods that farmers buy have not fallen in price as fast as those they sell. This disparity has been the root of much of the difficulties.

The shift from local self-sufficient farms to specialized business farming began in the mid-1800s. The most successful farms became large cash-crop operations that depended heavily on machinery. Specialization made the farmer dependent on weather conditions, markets, transportation, and financial institutions that were stable. When times were good, farmers borrowed for machinery, increased cultivation, and hoped for good weather. Many who borrowed heavily lost their land when crop failures or low farm prices lowered their income.

When their problems became widespread, farmers joined cooperatives and turned to government for help. In farm crises before the 1930s, the federal government always left competition and the free enterprise system intact among farm businesses. The Great Depression of the 1930s, however, triggered actions that altered the face of agriculture. Farmers, long thought of as free and independent, became largely dependent on government assistance. The Agricultural Adjustment Act of 1933, for example, offered farmers payments to reduce production.

The period since World War II has seen almost continuous battles over how much government control should be exercised over farm production. The farmers' own efficiency sometimes works against the government's solution. When production is slowed by one method, such as limiting acreage planted, farmers turn to technology to pull ahead again. They improve their farming methods to make those fewer acres yield more than before.

Nor have price supports, another New Deal remnant, been the answer. Under this program, if market prices for certain crops fall below a guaranteed price, the government buys them. An immensely expensive program, it reaches few small farmers.

Government efforts to preserve the independent farmer continue. But with each farm crisis, large agribusinesses gradually replace smaller farms.

FARM INCOME BY SIZE OF FARM, 1985

SALES CLASS	FARMS		GROSS CASH INCOME	
	Number in Thousands	Percent of Total	Millions of Dollars	Percent of Total
Under $40,000	1,638	72	16,064	10.3
$40,000 to $99,999	323	14	24,468	15.7
$100,000 to $249,999	221	10	39,383	25.2
$250,000 to $499,999	66	3	25,987	16.6
$500,000 and over	27	1	50,266	32.2

U.S. Department of Agriculture

MAKING CONNECTIONS

1. Why do many farmers react to production controls by increasing production?
2. Why do government farm programs often become a source of political debates?
3. What does the information in the table indicate has happened to Jefferson's vision of America as a nation of small farmers?

The Second New Deal

I'm for the poor man—all poor men. Black and white, they all gotta have a chance...."Every Man a King"*—that's my slogan.*

—HUEY LONG
United States senator from Louisiana

Section Focus

Some of Roosevelt's critics planted seeds of dissatisfaction with the New Deal by appealing to the jobless, the displaced, the underpaid, and the elderly. These victims of the Depression were fertile ground for the radical ideas floating about in 1935. FDR recognized that the New Deal must be reassessed and redirected. Yet even after strong voter support in the 1936 presidential election, Roosevelt faced continued opposition to any extension of the New Deal.

Objectives

After studying this section, you should be able to:
- List the special interest groups that challenged Roosevelt.
- Outline the steps that Roosevelt's Second New Deal took to achieve permanent reform.
- Identify the events that led to the end of the New Deal.

For the 10 million unemployed Americans in 1935, "Every Man a King" was an appealing fantasy but a far cry from their reality. They received just enough relief to keep themselves and their families alive. Their miserable dole seemed hardly worth the humiliation it caused. Millions of elderly Americans faced a similar stark reality, without savings, without adequate medical care, and without hope.

Attacks on the New Deal

The radical critics of the New Deal posed a greater threat to the Roosevelt administration than the Republican party. Every week Father Charles E. Coughlin, the "Radio Priest" whose broadcasts reached 40 million listeners, bitterly attacked Roosevelt. Originally a New Deal supporter, Coughlin became impatient with its moderate reforms. The priest accused the President of being too timid and of turning the New Deal into a "raw deal." His political organization, the National Union for Social Justice, called for such socialistic measures as heavy taxes on the wealthy and a guaranteed income for everyone.

An even more dangerous rival to Roosevelt was Huey Long, senator from Louisiana. With the backing of the rural poor, he became extremely powerful in his home state and used it as a base on which to build national popularity. With his folksy, humorous manner, Long knew how to win audiences. He proposed confiscating the property of the rich and giving every family a home, $2,000 a year, and a free college education for their children. His followers organized hundreds of "Share–Our–Wealth" clubs.

Less colorful than Father Coughlin or Senator Long but just as threatening, was Dr. Francis Townsend. A former public health official, Townsend was shocked by the plight of older Americans who were no longer able to compete for jobs. He proposed a plan that he claimed would provide relief for the elderly and at the same time stimulate economic recovery, calling for the federal government to pay all Americans over age 60 a pension of $200 per month. Recipients would be required to spend their entire pension check within 30 days. Townsend claimed that this plan not only would end the suffering of older Americans but the money they pumped into the economy would

Examining Photographs *Father Charles Coughlin (far left) reached millions of listeners before the Catholic church made him stop his radio broadcasts. Until his assassination, Senator Huey Long (right) was equally popular. What did these radicals have in common?*

increase consumption and create jobs. The pensions could be financed by a national sales tax on consumer goods, Townsend argued. His innovative plan attracted millions of devoted advocates.

Roosevelt's annual address to Congress in January 1935 answered his attackers.

He admitted that "we have not weeded out the overprivileged and we have not effectively lifted up the underprivileged." The President announced a "Second New Deal" to put recovery on a new course. This new phase showed greater concern for the less fortunate and abandoned

Examining Political Cartoons *Some Americans thought the New Deal was too restrictive to free enterprise. This cartoonist shows Uncle Sam tied down by New Deal agencies and laws, much as Gulliver was bound by the Lilliputians in the famous book,* Gulliver's Travels. *Why might critics have thought this way?*

The political groups supporting the New Deal also changed. In the election of 1932, Roosevelt had received support from many groups, including the business community. He had played down partisanship to gain the support of moderate and progressive Republicans. Now he devoted his energies to achieving his goals through the Democratic party alone. To strengthen it, he attempted to form a **coalition**, or combination, of separate groups whose members could be counted on to vote for Democrats. To the traditional source of Democratic political power—the South and northern urban political machines—Roosevelt attempted to add labor unions, farmers, and blacks. Many of the Second New Deal's programs were intended to appeal to these groups.

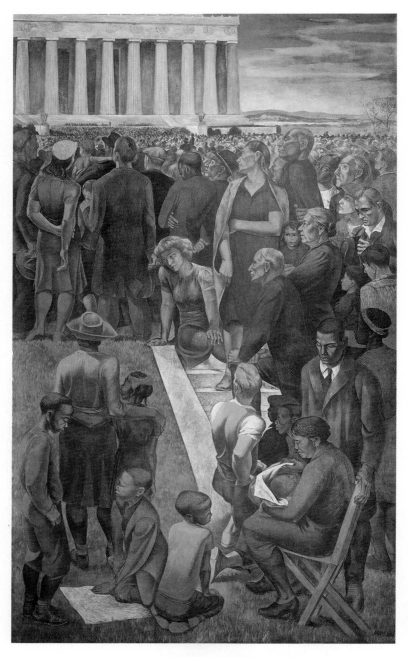

Examining Fine Art *WPA artists painted murals in many government offices. Mitchell Jamieson's mural of black opera singer Marian Anderson's famous concert before an integrated audience of 73,000 at the Lincoln Memorial is in the offices of the United States Department of the Interior in Washington, D.C. What political favor did Roosevelt want from African Americans?*

efforts to enlist the support of business. In government finance, attempts to balance the budget were abandoned.

Work Relief and Social Security

The most immediate result of the New Deal's shift in attitude was the President's demand for large-scale work relief. Responding to Roosevelt's request, Congress appropriated funds in April 1935 for "work relief and to increase employment by providing useful projects." An immense new agency, the Works Progress Administration (WPA) was set up under the direction of Harry Hopkins to provide a chance for all people to use their skills to earn an income. In addition to work relief projects such as building roads and schools, the WPA employed writers, teachers, librarians, actors, musicians, and artists. A "junior WPA," the National Youth Administration (NYA), helped high school and college students stay in school by giving them part-time work, such as typing and library cataloguing. Existing work-relief programs were expanded. The Reconstruction Finance Corporation lent large sums to businesses and to local governments. The Civilian Conservation Corps increased the number it employed. The Public Works Administration finally rolled into high gear and provided hundreds of thousands of jobs.

The unemployable needed help during the Depression as much as the unemployed. Persons with no source of support and no ability to earn an income had no place to go. To remedy this problem, Congress in 1935 passed the Social Security Act. Under this program, the federal government financed state unemployment insurance plans through payroll taxes paid by employers. Federal grants to states provided care for dependent mothers and children. The core of the program was retirement benefits, paid for by taxes on workers and employers, that people could collect when they stopped working at age 65.

The Social Security Act had flaws. For example, the act did not protect some groups who needed it most, such as farm workers and domestic help. Since 65 percent of all black employees in the 1930s fell into these two categories, the act neglected blacks the most. Yet the Social Security Act was a landmark in reforming society. It set the policy that an industrial society was responsible for those who, through no fault of their own, are unable to work.

Business and Labor

Several pieces of legislation passed during the Second New Deal demonstrated Roosevelt's efforts to appeal to the political coalition he was forming. Early in the New Deal, taxes remained at levels set in the 1920s. Now Congress passed tax increases on the incomes of wealthy Americans, inheritance taxes on the property of deceased persons, and higher taxes on corporations. Although the law was attacked as communistic, Roosevelt was more interested, some felt, in heading off the various "share-the-wealth" schemes than he was in actually redistributing the nation's wealth.

Next to the Social Security Act, the most important and lasting legislation of the Second New Deal was the National Labor Relations Act, also called the Wagner Act, passed in July 1935, after the Supreme Court declared the National Industrial Recovery Act unconstitutional. The Wagner Act set up a National Labor Relations Board (NLRB), which could hold secret elections in factories to find out whether workers wanted to unionize. The board could arbitrate grievances, reinstate workers fired for supporting unions, and order employers to stop antiunion activities.

The Wagner Act stimulated a burst of labor union activity. But the AFL was ill-equipped in both philosophy and structure to organize workers in mass-production industries such as radio, steel, automobiles, and textiles. The AFL was a federation of **craft unions**—unions where all members had the same skill. But in mass-production industries, workers from many crafts or skills often worked in a single plant. To have several unions undermined unity. So some labor leaders proposed that factory workers be organized in an **industrial union**—a union to which all workers in a single industry belong, regardless of the job they perform. When the AFL rejected this approach, these leaders abandoned it to form the Congress of Industrial Organizations (CIO).

"If I went to work in a factory, the first thing I'd do would be to JOIN A UNION," read the slogan signed by President Roosevelt on union recruiting posters, as the CIO moved into industries that the AFL had long neglected. By 1936 the CIO had signed up enough steel workers to threaten a nationwide strike. Instead, in March 1937 the nation's largest steel producer, the United States Steel Corporation, recognized the union as bargaining agent for its workers, established a 40-hour work week, and increased wages. Just beginning to recover from the Depression, the company was not willing to risk a major strike. The smaller producers did not follow this lead, however, and bloody strikes broke out around the country. But by 1941, the steelworkers' union had contracts with the entire industry.

Meanwhile, the CIO moved into the automobile industry, where management discouraged worker unity by exploiting racial and religious tensions among blacks, southern whites, and Catholic ethnic groups. Although hourly wages in the industry were high, seasonal layoffs reduced the average worker's annual earnings to less than $1,000. Workers also

Linking Across Time

AMERICAN LABOR LAWS

The gradual reversal of government attitudes toward labor unions was completed in 1935.

The Sherman Anti-Trust Act of 1890 had declared illegal any "combination in restraint of trade." Courts consistently used this provision to break strikes and outlaw other activities of labor unions.

The Clayton Act of 1914 aided labor by exempting unions from the anti-trust laws. Section 7a of the National Industrial Recovery Act of 1933 legally recognized the right of workers to organize unions, and the National Labor Relations Act of 1935 established rules to enforce this guarantee.

resented the "speed-ups" that occurred when management increased the rate at which cars moved along the assembly line.

The CIO did not want to challenge the auto industry until the struggle with the steel companies had ended. But autoworkers were impatient for change and they took matters into their own hands, using a strike strategy called the "sitdown strike." Rather than walking off their jobs, strikers remained in the factory. The company could not hire new workers to continue production nor could it remove the strikers by force without risking violence to the factory. One striker later remembered:

We were nervous. We didn't know we could do it. Those machines had been kept going as long as we could remember. When we finally pulled the switch and there was some quiet, I finally remembered something....that I was a human being, that I could stop those machines....

The sitdown strike was not originated by the autoworkers, nor was it unique to them. The radical International Workers of the World first used the technique against General Electric in 1906. But in the late 1930s factory workers, taxi drivers, maids, secretaries, and sales clerks sat down at their jobs to protest their pay and working conditions.

Union success in the auto, steel, and other industries swelled the ranks of organized labor during the Second New Deal. The CIO grew especially rapidly because it was willing to organize women workers, whom the AFL had ignored. From less than 3 million in 1933, union membership more than tripled by 1939. Organized labor showed its appreciation for the Wagner Act and other New Deal programs by giving political support to the Democrats.

The 1936 Election

The Democrats renominated Roosevelt for President in 1936, and they enthusiastically endorsed the New Deal. The business community, however, contributed to his 1936 campaign only about one-fifth as much as it contributed in 1932, and many newspapers turned against FDR. The Republican nominee, Kansas governor Alfred M. Landon, denounced Roosevelt for endangering the "American system of free enterprise." He labeled social security as "unjust, unworkable, stupidly drafted, and wastefully financed," and attacked many other New Deal programs.

Four years of New Deal programs, however, had forged a new political coalition for the Democrats. Farmers, labor

Life of the Times

SITDOWN STRIKES

Passage of the Wagner Act boosted workers' morale and inspired imaginative techniques to bring reluctant managers to the negotiating table. Chief among their strategies was the sitdown strike. On December 30, 1936, the UAW members of General Motors' Fisher Body plant in Flint, Michigan, sat down at their work stations. Meanwhile, workers at other General Motors plants followed suit or struck in more traditional ways: picketing factories, seizing plants by force, and jeering at scabs—workers sent to take their places.

General Motors strike veteran Bob Stinson described how workers managed to get food and keep in touch with their families during the sitdown: "The soup kitchen was outside the plant. The women handled all the cooking, outside of one chef who came from New York. He had anywhere from 10 to 20 women washing dishes and peeling potatoes in the strike kitchen. Mostly stews, pretty good meals. They were put in containers and hoisted up through the window....

We had a ladies' auxiliary. They'd visit the homes of the guys that was in the plant. They would find out if there was any shortage of coal or food. Then they'd maneuver around amongst themselves until they found some place to get a ton of coal."

Since the strikers were not going to starve, GM decided to freeze them out. It turned off the heat in the plant. But after six weeks, when the strikers still refused to give in, General Motors signed a contract with the UAW.

unions, retirees, and many ethnic groups supported Roosevelt and his programs. Black voters abandoned an allegiance to the Republican party that dated back to Reconstruction to support the party of Roosevelt. FDR's New Deal had not offered special programs for African Americans, but it had not tried to exclude them either. Black workers, who often were the first fired when hard times hit, owed much to New Deal relief programs, and they showed their gratitude at the polls. On Election Day, Roosevelt won in a landslide, and Democrats elected huge majorities to the House and Senate.

The New Deal and the Supreme Court

Before he could continue the New Deal in his second term, Roosevelt believed he had to eliminate opposition on the Supreme Court. During 1935 and 1936 the Court struck down New Deal programs, including the NIRA and AAA. Never before had the Court declared so much legislation unconstitutional. Roosevelt and his supporters believed that "9 old men" on the Court, 7 of whom had been appointed by Republican Presidents, were interfering with the New Deal's attempts at recovery. Laws that helped millions of people, passed by large majorities in Congress, were being rejected by the Court, often by margins of 5 to 4.

Roosevelt considered his landslide reelection to be a mandate to curb the Supreme Court. In February 1937 the President presented legislation allowing him to appoint an additional justice to the Supreme Court for each justice over 70 years of age. Although the Court's size would increase from 9 to 15, Roosevelt argued that it needed "an infusion of younger blood." The "court-packing" bill caused a furor even in the President's own party. Many Americans were alarmed by the threat it posed to the system of checks and balances. Enough Democrats joined the Republicans in Congress to defeat Roosevelt's proposal. Although he suffered a major setback and lost many supporters, the President claimed that he had "lost the

battle but won the war." While debate on the "court-packing" bill raged in Congress, in two 5 to 4 decisions, the Court upheld the constitutionality of the two major laws of the Second New Deal—the Social Security Act and the Wagner Act.

Later New Deal Measures

By 1937 the economy had recovered nearly to 1929 levels, although widespread unemployment still remained. Roosevelt's financial advisers urged a cutback in spending and a balanced federal budget. So Federal Reserve banks tightened credit, and the WPA cut the number of its employees in half. The economy quickly slumped into a **recession,** a mild downturn in the business cycle, that critics called a "Roosevelt Depression." Huge crop surpluses collapsed agricultural prices, and industrial production dropped by a one-third, almost to 1932 levels. The President blamed the slump on businesses that, he claimed, failed to reinvest profits in production and on monopolies that kept prices artificially high. To meet the economic crisis, the President again expanded the work-relief programs of the WPA and stepped up military spending. People went back to work and prices rose. But the recession proved that hard times were not yet over.

Examining Political Cartoons *Although Roosevelt was overwhelmingly reelected in 1936, most people reacted negatively in 1937 to his attempt to "pack" the Supreme Court. In this cartoon, what does the donkey's reaction symbolize?*

In 1938 Congress passed a number of New Deal measures that carried out earlier policies. A Fair Labor Standards Act abolished child labor and placed a ceiling on hours and a floor under wages, at least for workers in businesses classified as "interstate commerce." A new Farm Security Administration promoted the well-being of impoverished farmers. A new AAA attempted to cope with surpluses by paying farmers not only to produce less but also to improve the soil and to control erosion. In addition, a food-stamp plan helped to distribute farm surplus among those on relief.

These were some of the last New Deal programs. In the fall of 1937, when Roosevelt called a special session of Congress not one of his proposals was enacted. Both in 1937 and in 1938 Congress rejected the President's request to reorganize the executive branch. These defeats were largely the result of a coalition of Republicans and conservative southern Democrats who increasingly opposed the President in Congress. Roosevelt tried to weaken this coalition by supporting liberal Democrats against incumbents in the 1938 primary. Montana senator James Murray spoke for many Democrats in Congress:

There was a time when I would have bled and died for him, but in view of the way he has been acting I don't want to have any more dealings with him…

Roosevelt's attempted "purge" of his own party ended in defeat. In most cases, the conservative Democrats won. In the November election the Republicans staged a modest comeback, picking up seats in both houses of Congress. The coalition of Republicans and Southern Democrats was growing powerful and could block further extension of the New Deal.

Roosevelt accepted the judgment of the voters in the 1938 election. In January 1939 he announced that he would propose no further New Deal programs. Instead, he turned his attention to the growing threat of war in Europe.

★ ★ ★ ★ ★ ★ ★ ★ ★ ★ ★ ★ ★ ★ ★ ★ ★

Section Three Review

★ ★ ★ ★ ★ ★ ★ ★ ★ ★ ★ ★ ★ ★ ★ ★ ★

SUMMARY

Faced with mounting criticism, Roosevelt abandoned business support, moved away from conservative policies, and searched for long-term economic solutions. Social security provided benefits for the poor and the elderly, and the National Labor Relations Act increased labor unions' power. Political support from farm and labor groups gave Roosevelt a solid base within the Democratic party. But his plan to gain control of the Supreme Court angered his supporters and marked the beginning of the end for the New Deal.

CHECKING FOR UNDERSTANDING

1. **Identify** Father Coughlin, Huey Long, WPA, NLRB, CIO, court-packing

2. **Define** coalition, craft union, industrial union, recession

3. **Explain** Dr. Townsend's recovery plan.

4. **Describe** steps the New Deal took toward reform after 1935.

5. **Cite** the purpose and provisions of the Social Security Act.

6. **Explain** why Congress rejected Roosevelt's plan to reorganize the Supreme Court.

THINKING CRITICALLY

7. **Contrasting Ideas** How did the second New Deal differ from the first in its objectives, support base, and program focus? Which was more successful?

LINKING PAST AND PRESENT

8. **Examining Change** Membership in labor unions increased dramatically in the 1930s. In recent years, however, union membership has fallen again. Compare the economic and political climates of each era and suggest possible explanations for this change.

★ ★ ★ ★ ★ ★ ★ ★ ★ ★ ★ ★ ★ ★ ★ ★ ★

The Impact of the New Deal

We Americans of today—all of us—we are characters in the living book of democracy. But we are also its author. It falls upon us now to say whether the chapters that are to come will tell a story of retreat or a story of continued advance.

—FRANKLIN ROOSEVELT
Final national address of the campaign, 1940

Section Focus

Just as Roosevelt's "fireside chats" over the radio directly reached the American people, his New Deal programs directly touched their lives. From relief for the poor to wages and working conditions, along with regulation of the nation's economy and financial markets, programs affected society at every level. The New Deal involved the federal government in American life to an extent unprecedented in the nation's history.

Objectives

After studying this section, you should be able to:
• Identify changes that the New Deal caused in American society.
• Evaluate the effects of the New Deal on life today.

Sociologists Robert and Helen Lynd in 1929 published a study of values, behaviors, and everyday life in the 1920s in a typical American city that they called "Middletown." (It really was Muncie, Indiana.) In 1935 they returned to "Middletown" for a follow-up study and found that the Depression and the New Deal had profoundly affected the families living in that community.

The New Deal and Society

During the Depression, both births and divorces decreased as people could not afford either event. Older people moved in with working relatives. Many families rented rooms to boarders or moved to smaller and less expensive homes. Housewives took in laundry and sewing to help support their families. Sales of prepared food declined, and many people canned foods at home.

Competition among adults for jobs resulted in stronger child labor laws, and the number of working children declined during the 1930s. Consequently, the number of high school and college students rose. The number of elementary school students, however, declined because of the lower birth rate.

In Middletown, the Lynds noted that the community traditionally had expected a husband to support his family. But when a man lost his job and could not find another, family roles often were reversed, "with the woman taking a job for whatever money she could earn and the man caring for the household and children." There were, however, strong social pressures against working women. They were accused of taking jobs from men, and businesses often refused to hire married women.

Most women who worked outside the home, with the exception of farm and domestic workers, benefited from the New Deal. Women's wages rose and working conditions improved. The greatest direct assistance to women came from the Women's Division of the WPA. It employed between 300,000 and 400,000 women, some in traditionally female white-collar jobs such as teacher, nurse, and librarian. But most worked on canning and sewing projects. Their pay was low, but it often made the difference between food and famine, as in this sharecropper's family:

*Last year my wife…got herself a
job with the government and she's
making 21 dollars a month, working
at the sewing room. This just about
takes care of everything.*

The New Deal and Minorities

As the poorest of the poor, blacks often fell through the cracks of broad legislation such as the AAA and the Social Security Act. For example, although the AAA gave money to rural landowners, in the South 80 percent of all black farmers owned no land. In addition, Roosevelt offered no civil rights program and did little to challenge the segregation that continued to exist throughout the nation, and he tolerated job discrimination. Even some government agencies refused to hire African Americans. Those that did, such as the CCC and armed forces, segregated blacks and whites. In addition, African Americans received lower wages than white workers and were not assigned to certain jobs.

Nevertheless, Roosevelt appointed more African Americans to government posts than any President before him. Although most black officials filled secondary posts, they influenced the President as an unofficial "black cabinet." Heading the black cabinet was Mary McLeod Bethune, director of the Negro Affairs Division of the National Youth Administration. A personal friend of Eleanor Roosevelt, she often expressed the black cabinet's concerns to the First Lady, who then carried them to FDR.

Examining Photographs *Most blacks did not directly benefit from the New Deal. Although African Americans in the North contributed heavily to Roosevelt's election victories, he did not protest the poll taxes in the South that prevented poor blacks and whites from voting. What explanations are there for his stand?*

One concern of blacks in and out of government during the Depression was an increase in lynching and other acts of mob violence against African Americans. One piece of civil rights legislation that Roosevelt did support was a 1934 federal antilynching bill that held local sheriffs accountable for the frequent lynchings of blacks in the South. But he never made the bill a legislative priority, so it never reached the House floor and it finally died in the Senate in 1938.

One reason New Deal programs for African Americans were so limited was the opposition of powerful congressional committee heads who were from the South. So Roosevelt accepted NRA codes, for example, that permitted a lower minimum wage in the South than in the rest of the nation. FDR felt that if he pushed these southern legislators too strongly, he would lose their support.

In general, the federal government responded more favorably to white ethnic groups. During the 1930s the federal Office of Education sponsored a radio

Examining Artifacts *Comic strip hero Little Orphan Annie became a radio star complete with a fan club book. What cartoon character was popular?*

Examining Photographs *Clark Gable and Vivien Leigh starred in the movie of the 1930s' best selling novel,* Gone With the Wind. *The film was a big hit because people got nearly 4 hours of entertainment for just 10 to 25 cents. What other mass entertainment medium was popular in the 1930s?*

series called "Americans All...Immigrants All." The show celebrated the cultural vitality of a democracy made up of people from many lands. It also indicated the Democrats' awareness of the political power that ethnic groups could exercise if they were organized. Immigrants and their children made up 40 percent of the white population at that time. They tended to vote in groups and could swing elections, especially in large urban areas. Americans of Irish, Italian, and Polish descent became major partners in the New Deal coalition. Because of the Depression, however, immigration declined in the 1930s. In fact, more people emigrated from the United States during the 1930s than immigrated to it.

Popular Culture

The 1930s were somber years compared to the fads and frivolity of the 1920s. Literature and the arts generally turned to more realistic themes about poverty and human suffering. Grim times provided powerful themes for American authors such as John Dos Passos, whose trilogy of novels called *U.S.A.* focused on fictional characters who lost their ideals and became hardened by society. Erskine Caldwell's popular novel, *Tobacco Road,* portrayed the hard and cruel lives of a tenant farm family in Georgia. But perhaps the most powerful novel of the era was John Steinbeck's *Grapes of Wrath,* the story of a family who left their Oklahoma farm in the Dust Bowl and headed to the migrant labor camps of California.

But there was also much escapism in popular culture, as people turned to entertainment when things became grim. The best-selling book of the decade was Margaret Mitchell's *Gone with the Wind.* Although set in the South during the Civil War and Reconstruction, it offered a hopeful account of Scarlett O'Hara's efforts to rebuild her life and had much

Examining Fine Art *This WPA mural,* Prairie Poets, *is a testament to the legacy of the New Deal. It is on display at the Franklin D. Roosevelt presidential library in Hyde Park, New York. How did the New Deal change the relationship between Americans and their government?*

meaning for readers who had gone through the Crash and the Depression.

As "talkies"—films with sound—became common during the 1930s, about 85 million people escaped the realities of the Depression for a few hours each week at the movie theater. There they watched movies that were often about the lives of happy and successful people. In many popular movies, the poor girl married the millionaire's son or a wealthy woman fell in love with a struggling young man. Continued improvements in sound technology ushered in the era of musicals, and audiences delighted at the dance routines of Fred Astaire and Ginger Rogers. Cartoon characters, such as Mickey Mouse, made audiences laugh, and as color-film technology spread, full-length animated features like Walt Disney's *Snow White and the Seven Dwarfs,* provided more fantasy and escape.

At home families could listen to network radio programs broadcast coast-to-coast. "Amos 'n Andy" became the first popular national radio show. Although white actors portrayed black characters and employed racial stereotypes, their weekly stories about surviving hard times attracted huge audiences. Daytime radio offered "soap operas," where characters suffered through daily crises. At night comedy, adventure, and musical variety programs dominated the airwaves. And the performances of Arturo Toscanini conducting the NBC Symphony of the Air brought classical music for the first time to millions of radio listeners.

Just as books, movies, and the radio provided Americans with an emotional outlet from the realities of the Depression, the automobile made them feel that they could physically escape their problems. Americans' love affair with cars, which began during the prosperity of the 1920s, continued throughout the poverty-stricken 1930s. The number of automobiles increased from 26 million in 1933 to 32 million by 1940. During the depths of the Depression, almost half the families in the United States owned a car, even though many could not afford to buy gasoline.

Yet despite the expense, many Americans continued to drive their cars during the 1930s. By late in the decade, thanks to government work projects, a maze of paved highways crisscrossed the nation. Large numbers of people took off down these two-lane roads, some searching for employment and others pioneering what became an American institution—the family vacation by car.

In the arts, as in so many other areas of society, the New Deal played a role. The WPA helped unemployed actors, artists, writers, and musicians. The Federal Theatre Project sponsored performances of Shakespeare as well as children's plays. Some 6,500 writers put together state and regional guidebooks and recorded life stories of former slaves, immigrants, and American Indians. The Federal Arts Project had artists paint murals and sculptors create statues, many of which still can be viewed today. Photographers like Dorothea Lange and artists like Ben Shahn documented people's lives during the Depression. Arts projects were among the most controversial New Deal programs, however. Critics called them socialistic. In 1939 Congress cut off funds for the theater project, and the other arts programs were discontinued as employment rose during World War II.

To many people who lived through it, the New Deal seemed to have changed American society. Yet it was not the revolutionary assault on capitalism that some of its critics charged. The New Deal changed the lives of farmers through crop subsidies and rural electrification. It changed the lives of industrial workers by strengthening labor unions and expanding collective bargaining. It provided social security and welfare programs for the aged, the unemployed, and dependent children. In so doing, it turned a government that previously had responded more to business groups into a government open to labor, farmers, and other interests.

Yet the New Deal did not adopt national planning of the economy, as some of Roosevelt's advisers had expected. Rather than government owning industry, the New Deal emphasized federal regulation of private enterprise. Rather than overturning capitalism, New Dealers believed that they had helped to save it.

SUMMARY

To many who lived through it, the New Deal seemed to bring radical change. But as time has passed, Americans can see that basic values remained intact in the 1930s: people were still committed to the work ethic, free enterprise, and the capitalist system. The New Deal had made government more responsive to the needs of ordinary citizens. Roosevelt's programs also fed Americans' cultural appetites by supporting arts and theater projects. A wide variety of literature also developed.

CHECKING FOR UNDERSTANDING

1. **Identify** black cabinet, John Steinbeck, Margaret Mitchell, soap operas, Federal Arts Project

2. **Summarize** the impact of the New Deal on African Americans.

3. **Describe** the social and cultural changes in American society that occurred during the Depression.

4. **Discuss** popular forms of entertainment in the 1930s.

5. **Explain** how the effects of the New Deal are felt today.

THINKING CRITICALLY

6. **Seeing Relationships**   Analyze how the Depression influenced themes in American art and literature during the 1930s.

LINKING PAST AND PRESENT

7. **Contrasting Political Climates**   The Roosevelts sponsored programs to help African Americans, but avoided politically dangerous equal rights legislation. Recent Presidents who have opposed civil rights legislation have been widely criticized. What can you infer from this contrast about differences between values prevailing today and values in the 1930s?

★ ★ ★ ★ ★ ★ ★ ★ ★ ★ ★ ★ ★ ★ ★ ★ ★ ★ ★

★ Chapter 28 Review ★

★ Summary

Franklin Delano Roosevelt's active and positive approach to fighting the Depression focused on relief, reform, and recovery in a series of measures known collectively as the New Deal. He attempted to restore purchasing power with programs financed by deficit spending, offering relief and work to the poor and jobless. He attempted to bring more order and planning to the economy through increasing government intervention in banking, business, labor, and agriculture. Lasting gains were made in conservation, conditions of labor, and assistance programs such as Social Security. In implementing reform, Roosevelt worked within the capitalist system to restore hope and dignity, and to improve the quality of life for Americans. In so doing, he established the principle that government had a responsibility for the nation's economic health and for the well-being of its people.

★ Using Vocabulary

Write sentences about Roosevelt's New Deal using these vocabulary words.

deficit spending	**pump priming**
dole	**foreclosure**
moratorium	**recession**

★ Reviewing Facts

1. **Explain** the purpose of the bank holiday in the first 100 Days.
2. **Compare** the purposes of New Deal legislation before and after 1935.
3. **Cite** the means Roosevelt used to advocate, promote, and gain public support for his New Deal programs.
4. **Identify** specific New Deal programs that provided help to various types of needy people in society.
5. **Describe** Roosevelt's attempts to help farmers.
6. **Discuss** developments and achievements within organized labor movements during the 1930s and the role that the New Deal played in these developments.
7. **Specify** groups that did not fully share in the benefits of the New Deal.

8. **List** ways the New Deal supported the arts during the Depression.
9. **Explain** lasting effects of the New Deal.

★ Understanding Concepts

ECONOMIC REFORM

1. **Which** New Deal programs would you classify as achieving lasting economic reform? Explain your reasons for your choices.
2. **Explain** how "pump priming" works and how its use is intended to aid the nation's recovery in times of recession or depression.

POLITICAL LEADERSHIP

3. **Much** of the success of the New Deal relied on the charismatic personality and leadership of Franklin Roosevelt. Explain how he used these assets to gain support for his controversial and complicated New Deal policies.
4. **One** mark of a good leader is the ability to choose and utilize able administrators. Explain to what extent this was true of Franklin Roosevelt.

★ Thinking Critically

1. **Interpreting a Quotation** Review the quotation by Robert Sherwood on page 828. Explain whether or not Sherwood assessed Roosevelt's personality and character accurately.
2. **Finding Explanations** Though farmers received substantial assistance during the New Deal and have since, many farmers have continued to suffer economically. What problems inherent in farming could possibly account for this recurring difficulty?
3. **Assessing Causes and Effects** Why do you suppose Roosevelt abandoned his efforts to enlist the support of the business community for the New Deal reforms that he launched during his second term as President?
4. **Linking Past and Present** Refer to the quotation at the beginning of Section Four and reflect upon society today. Does the evolution of American society from the 1930s to today represent "a story of retreat or a story of continued advance"? Give your opinion and explain your reasons for holding it.

★ Writing About History

ARGUMENTATION

Refer to the description of how to write an argumentation essay in the History Writer's Handbook in the Appendix of this book. Your teacher will give you more specific instructions on the essay's length and the assignment's due date.

Assume the nation has entered a depression in the 1990s. As a member of Congress devoted to economic reform, write an argument proposing and supporting deficit spending to stimulate the economy and to finance expanded government assistance programs. Think about what reasons an economist might have to favor such programs. Also think carefully about the reasons why some of your constituents would favor such policies and why others would oppose them.

★ Cooperative Learning

Working in a group of three, assume roles of government officials during Roosevelt's term. One member should assume the role of a Roosevelt supporter in Congress and present an argument to Congress for enlarging the Supreme Court. The second member should assume the role of an anti-Roosevelt senator and address Congress, refuting the need to enlarge the court. The third member will listen to both arguments and decide which is the more effective. All group members should then be prepared to argue either position before the class if called upon by the teacher.

★ Mastering Skills

DETERMINING THE STRENGTH OF AN ARGUMENT

Perhaps you have listened to others as they try to persuade you to their point of view. Whether or not they are successful often depends on how strong an argument they are able to present.

You also have at times tried to convince others to come around to your way of thinking. The most successful way to do this is to present an *argument,* or series of reasons, that support your views. Again, your success may depend on how strong an argument you make.

Asking questions such as the following will help you determine the strength of an argument:

- Has the main point or theme of the argument been clearly stated?

- Do each of the reasons given in the argument truly relate to the issue under discussion?

- Are the reasons that form the basis of the argument presented in a logical order?

- Is any evidence given that supports the information offered in the argument?

Example The following statement presents an argument against the Social Security Act of 1935. Read the statement entirely before attempting to determine the strength of the argument it makes.

> *The Social Security Act of 1935 is seriously flawed. For example, it excludes some of the people who most need it, namely farm workers and domestic help. It also endorses racism, as 65 percent of all black workers fall into these categories.*
>
> *The act also does not do nearly enough to alleviate the problems faced by the unemployable people it covers. It is, as Father Coughlin and Huey Long have stated, merely "crumbs from the rich man's table." As such, this act meant to provide security for its citizens is in fact a disgrace to the nation. A more respectable and wide-reaching act is needed.*

Read the statement again, this time seeking an answer to each of the four guideline questions noted earlier. *(The main point of the argument is clearly presented in the statement's opening sentence. The reasons that follow all relate to the issue. They are presented in a logical order. Each sentence between the first and last sentences presents the reasons for the point or factual information that supports it, or both.)* The answer to all four guideline questions is "yes." The statement presents a strong argument.

Practice Keeping in mind that in a strong argument the main point or theme must be clearly stated, the reasons given must relate to the issue and be presented in a logical order, and evidence must be provided as support, evaluate the following argument that *supports* the Social Security Act of 1935.

> *The Social Security Act of 1935 has created one of the most vital social programs of the New Deal. The act establishes that government will protect old, young, and disabled Americans who are unable to provide for themselves. Nearly one of every four American workers remains unemployed. Jobs and income are necessary to recover from the Depression. Social Security is greatly needed.*

SECTIONS

1

World Affairs,
1933–1939

2

Moving Closer
to War

3

The United States
at War

4

War on the
Home Front

CHAPTER 29
World War II

SETTING THE SCENE

Historical Focus

The depression of the 1930s was worldwide. Italy and Germany turned to dictators who built up aggressive military forces. When a new war engulfed Europe, Roosevelt sought to aid the British. After Japan attacked Pearl Harbor in 1941, America entered the war directly. Initially, Allied prospects were bleak, but by 1944 the tide had turned. Victory in the Pacific, however, came only after the use of nuclear weapons.

Concepts to Understand

- Why **international alliances** were formed between Germany, Italy, and Japan.
- How the allies prevented Germany and Italy from winning the **military conflict** in Europe.

People to Know

Adolf Hitler, Winston Churchill, Wendell Willkie, Dwight D. Eisenhower, Chiang Kai-shek

Places to Locate

Pearl Harbor, Stalingrad, Hiroshima

Terms to Identify

fascism, totalitarian, appeasement, lend-lease, convoy, holocaust

Guided Reading

As you read this chapter, seek the answers to the following questions.

1. What events led the American people to abandon isolationism and neutrality?
2. Why was Roosevelt more successful than Wilson in helping to form a world peacekeeping body?

SPANNING THE DECADES

POLITICAL	**1933** *United States recognizes the government of the Soviet Union*		**1939** *Germany attacks Poland; war in Europe begins*

1930		1935	

CULTURAL	**1928** *First experimental television transmittals*		**1936** *Babe Ruth and Ty Cobb named to baseball's Hall of Fame*	**1939** *Classic films* Gone With the Wind *and* The Wizard of Oz *are released*

V-J Day—Crowds Cheering at Times Square *by Edward Dancig, 1947*

1940
Selective
Service
Act
passed

1941
Japanese attack
on Pearl Harbor

1944
Allied
invasion
at
Normandy

1945
Germany and
Japan surrender;
First use of
nuclear weapons

1940

1945

1940
Color television
is demonstrated
by the Columbia
Broadcasting System

1942
Sugar and
gasoline are
rationed

1945
Tennessee Williams's
play The Glass
Menagerie opens in
New York

...We are now in this war. We are all in it—all the way. Every single man, woman, and child is a partner in the most tremendous undertaking of our American history. We must share together the bad news and the good news, the defeats and the victories—the changing fortunes of war....

—FRANKLIN D. ROOSEVELT
Radio Address, 1941

World Affairs, 1933-1939

Those who cherish their freedom and recognize...the equal right of their neighbors to be free and live in peace must work together...in order that peace, justice and confidence may prevail in the world.

—FRANKLIN D. ROOSEVELT
Speech in Chicago, Illinois,
October 1937

Section Focus

Like President Woodrow Wilson, for whom he had worked during World War I, Franklin Roosevelt was greatly interested in world affairs. But when he entered the White House in 1933, recovery from the Depression kept most of his energy and attention focused on the United States. As Europe again moved toward war, however, the President experienced growing concern with events overseas.

Objectives

After studying this section, you should be able to:
• Discuss how the Depression influenced American foreign policy.
• Explain the reasons for Japan's aggression in Asia.

S haring his cousin Theodore's viewpoint, Franklin Roosevelt believed that the United States should play a leadership role in the world. For most of his first two terms, however, the President focused on domestic affairs. Events in Europe and Asia seemed distant when compared to the crisis of the Depression. In addition, the President recognized that Americans, pressed by hard times at home, cared little about the world at large. So although Roosevelt believed that German expansion posed a threat to the United States, he was cautious in his efforts to alert the nation to this danger. Only when dealing with affairs in the Western Hemisphere did Roosevelt act with his typical bold political style.

New Deal Foreign Policy

At his first inaugural in 1933, President Roosevelt pledged that the United States would be a "good neighbor" in the family of nations. The President and Secretary of State Cordell Hull worked to improve relations with the United States' southern neighbors. Later that year, at a Pan-American Conference at Montevideo, Uruguay, the United States agreed to a resolution that "no state has the right to intervene in the internal affairs of another." Roosevelt demonstrated his commitment to the Good Neighbor Policy by recalling American troops from Haiti and Nicaragua, where they had been protecting American property since the 1920s. When Cuba erupted in revolution in 1933, Roosevelt used diplomacy, not troops, to help restore order. When Mexico seized American-owned oil companies in 1938, Roosevelt resisted demands for military action and sought a peaceful settlement.

During Roosevelt's first years in office, the United States seemed less inclined to cooperate with Europe. The New Deal adopted a policy of economic isolation, and its recovery programs were attempts to solve agricultural and industrial production problems without considering the rest of the world. In 1933 delegates from more than 60 nations met in London to bring about cooperation in confronting world depression. Roosevelt wrecked the conference by rejecting proposals to peg the value of the dollar to any other currency. He feared that such a move would hurt his efforts to raise American farm prices.

Only when the United States had achieved some recovery from the Depression was the President willing to consider economic cooperation with other nations. Secretary of State Hull believed world prosperity and goodwill could be gained by reducing tariffs. At Hull's urging, Congress passed the Reciprocal Trade Agreements Act of 1934, allowing the State Department to make treaties with other countries to mutually lower import duties. Within 6 years, the United States had reached such agreements with more than a dozen nations, covering more than 60 percent of American trade.

Another change in foreign policy took place when the United States recognized the government of the Soviet Union. Since the Bolshevik revolution of 1917, the United States had refused to recognize the communist government. After their revolution, the Soviets tried to encourage communism throughout the world. By 1933, however, the USSR was beset by serious economic problems at home and seemed less of a threat. Much more threatening was the rising power of Japan, Russia's rival in Asia. The President hoped that a strong Soviet Union could slow Japanese expansion. In addition, Roosevelt saw the Soviets' need for food and industrial equipment as a market for American farmers and manufacturers. "The United States would probably recognize the Devil," Will Rogers

joked, "if it could sell him pitchforks." Recognition of the Soviet Union helped improve relations but did little to increase trade or to check Japanese militarism.

Aggression and Appeasement

Between 1872 and 1925, Japan's population nearly doubled, causing severe problems for that small island nation. To

Examining Photographs
President Roosevelt says hello to Uruguay with president Gabriel Terra in Montevideo. What changes did Roosevelt make in United States policy toward Latin America?

Examining Photographs
Japanese troops pass through the gate leading to the palace of the imperial Forbidden City as they occupy China's capital of Beijing in 1937. How did Roosevelt hope to slow Japan's aggression in Asia?

Linking Across Time

THE NEUTRALITY ACTS

By the mid-1930s, it was obvious that war in Europe was again on the way. The U.S. had twice been drawn into European wars, once in 1812 and again in 1917. The scenarios had been eerily similar in both cases: warring nations had forcibly interfered with neutral U.S. ships. Fearing that history would repeat itself, Congress passed the Neutrality Acts, forbidding any American action that could lead the United States into war.

provide more jobs, Japan rapidly industrialized. But to sustain this growth Japan needed larger markets for its products and more raw materials for its factories. To meet these needs and to ease overcrowding in the home islands, Japan pursued a policy of expansion in the Pacific.

During World War I, Japan supported the Allies, but used the war to violate the Open Door policy by increasing its influence in China. After the war Japan was bitter toward the West. The Washington Conference of 1921 cost Japan most of its gains in China and limited Japan's naval power. When the United States joined other western nations in 1924 in banning immigrants from Japan, its leaders looked to military solutions for their nation's problems.

In September 1931, Japanese troops invaded and occupied mineral-rich Manchuria in northeastern China. When the League of Nations demanded that Manchuria be returned to China, Japan ignored the order.

On March 5, 1933, the day after Roosevelt took office, the German parliament voted Adolf Hitler, the National Socialist (Nazi) leader, the power he needed to begin a program of conquest in central and eastern Europe. In Italy, dictator Benito Mussolini made similar plans to control the Mediterranean and to expand Italy's empire in Africa.

Mussolini and Hitler followed a new political doctrine known as **fascism** (FASH IHZ uhm), a form of government in which a dictator and supporters cooperate to seek more power for their nation at the expense of human rights. Each ruler established a **totalitarian** state—a nation that totally controls the life of its people. Like the Communists in Russia, the Fascists in Italy and the Nazis in Germany set up all-powerful official parties. Both whipped up support with huge patriotic rallies, parades, music, and appeals to national pride and racial hatred, and both used force to silence all opposition.

Examining Photographs *Italy's dictator Benito Mussolini, surrounded by bodyguards, gives the Fascist salute as he reviews his military forces in 1939. After Italy surrendered to Allied forces, Mussolini was captured and executed by the Italian people. What did Mussolini have in common with Adolf Hitler?*

Each dictator blamed his country's problems after World War I on undesirables in society. Mussolini accused Italy's Communists of causing strikes and social unrest. The Nazis blamed Germany's economic chaos on its Jewish population. They expelled Jews from the government and the universities, boycotted Jewish-owned stores, and destroyed synagogues. Both Hitler and Mussolini hinted that another war might be necessary to right the wrongs they felt had been done to their countries by the Treaty of Versailles.

The glorification of war by Italy, Germany, and Japan was not idle talk. In 1935 Mussolini attacked and took control of Ethiopia in Africa. In 1937 Japanese armies poured into the rest of China. In March 1938 Hitler marched into Austria. In 1936 General Francisco Franco rebelled against the republican government of Spain, and German and Italian tanks, bombers, and troops helped Franco win a bitter civil war that lasted until 1939.

The response of Great Britain and France was **appeasement**, a policy of giving aggressor nations what they wanted to avoid war. Like the Americans, the British and French were disillusioned by World War I and wanted peace. Appeasement reached its peak at the Munich Conference of September 1938 when British and French leaders allowed Hitler to annex part of Czechoslovakia in return for his promise to make no further territorial demands. British prime minister Neville Chamberlain returned from Germany to tell a jittery world that the Munich Pact meant "peace for our time." Winston Churchill, however, who soon would replace Chamberlain as prime minister, observed that "Britain and France had to choose between war and dishonor. They chose dishonor. They will have war."

The American people were also determined to avoid war. World War I had left the United States with a huge domestic debt and billions of dollars in foreign debts that could not be collected. To prevent being drawn into war again, Congress passed Neutrality Acts in 1935, 1936, and 1937. These laws barred the

Examining Photographs *In 1935 Adolf Hitler announced that he intended to ignore the Versailles Treaty and began to rearm Germany. In 1936 his army reoccupied the Rhineland on Germany's border with France. How did the Allies respond when Hitler began to act aggressively in Europe?*

transportation or sale of arms to warring nations and banned loans to nations at war outside the Western Hemisphere.

Roosevelt signed the Neutrality Acts without protest. But he would have preferred some freedom to distinguish between aggressors and victims. The President believed that Germany, Italy, and Japan were "bad neighbors" who were

Examining Photographs *Despite Roosevelt's public warnings that the United States could not remain isolated, the nation's mood was to avoid war. But when Japan invaded China in 1937, Roosevelt evaded the Neutrality Acts and allowed American arms to reach the Chinese on British ships bound for Hong Kong. What changes did Roosevelt want in the Neutrality Acts?*

bent on war. In a speech in October 1937, Roosevelt called for the abandonment of isolation:

[L]et no one imagine that America will escape....There is no escape through mere isolation or neutrality....
the epidemic of lawlessness is spreading. When an epidemic of physical disease starts to spread, the community...joins in a quarantine of the patients in order to protect the health of the community against the spread of the disease.

But American public opinion forced him to drop any idea of collective action against aggressor nations. "It's a terrible thing," Roosevelt remarked, "to look over your shoulder when you're trying to lead—and find no one there."

SUMMARY

Despite aggressive acts by Germany, Italy, and Japan, the United States and Europe were determined to avoid war. The Good Neighbor Policy extended this peaceful stance to Latin American relations. When war finally broke out in Europe, the United States declared neutrality and refused to deal with countries at war. Despite his reservations about isolationism, Roosevelt bowed to public opinion by signing the Neutrality Acts.

CHECKING FOR UNDERSTANDING

1. **Identify** Benito Mussolini, Munich Conference, Neutrality Acts
2. **Define** fascism, totalitarian, appeasement
3. **Describe** what influence the Depression may have had in shaping American foreign policy.
4. **Examine** Japan's objectives in its aggressive expansion in Asia.
5. **Explain** why democratic nations did nothing when Hitler and Mussolini began to seize territory in Europe and in North Africa.

THINKING CRITICALLY

6. **Evaluating Policy**   Should one country use military intervention in the internal affairs of another to protect private property owned by its citizens? Explain.

LINKING PAST AND PRESENT

7. **Contrasting Policy**   In 1990 President Bush, a combat pilot in World War II, sent military units to the Middle East in response to Iraq's annexation of Kuwait. How does his response contrast with that of his former commander in chief, Roosevelt, to Hitler's annexation of Czechoslovakian territory in 1938?

Moving Closer to War

I speak to you tonight because I believe that the American people are about to commit suicide. We are not planning to. We have no plan. Deafened by martial music, fine language, and large appropriations, we are drifting into war.

—ROBERT HUTCHINS
President of the University of Chicago, in a national radio address, January 1941

Section Focus

As war in Europe became a certainty, a great debate took place among Americans over what role the United States should play. Isolationists opposed any American involvement in European affairs and wanted the United States to act independently in the world. On the other side of the debate, internationalists believed that America's own security was linked to the success of Europe's struggle against Hitler.

Objectives

After studying this section, you should be able to:
- Discuss Germany's conquest of Europe.
- List the steps by which Roosevelt increased support to the Allies.

The most outspoken isolationists in Congress were progressive Republicans from the Midwest and West, who received support from many newspapers, most notably those in the William Randolph Hearst chain. On the radio, Roosevelt's New Deal critic, Father Charles Coughlin, also lined up with the isolationists. An America First Committee sponsored rallies around the country against the war. A frequent speaker was the popular pilot Charles Lindbergh who warned that "the only way our American life and ideals can be preserved is by staying out of this war." The internationalists were strongest in the Democratic party and generally represented states in the South and Northeast. They looked to President Roosevelt for leadership.

Europe at War Again

As Churchill had predicted, the Munich agreement failed to appease Hitler, who in March 1939 swallowed up the rest of Czechoslovakia and demanded territory in Poland. Britain and France pledged to defend Poland from Hitler, and they asked the Soviet Union to join in an alliance to contain Germany. But in August 1939, Soviet dictator Joseph Stalin signed a nonaggression pact with Germany. By removing the threat of war on two fronts, the pact cleared the way for Hitler to invade Poland. But Hitler still doubted that Britain and France would resist him.

Before dawn on September 1, 1939, German forces crossed into Poland in an attack so fast and brutal that a new word was coined—*blitzkrieg*, meaning "lightning war." This time Britain and France decided to fight, and on September 3 they declared war on Germany.

Roosevelt declared the United States' neutrality, but he added, "Even a neutral cannot be asked to close his mind or his conscience." Within weeks he asked Congress to lift the Neutrality Acts' arms embargo that prevented Britain and France from buying American weapons. Although Congress was flooded with telegrams urging it to "keep America out of the blood business," after weeks of debate, it agreed to sell arms to the Allies if they paid cash and carried the goods in their own ships.

After a lull in the fighting over the winter of 1939 and 1940, Hitler launched an invasion of Norway and Denmark. Next the German armies swept into the Netherlands and Belgium, where for the

Examining Photographs *As the trapped British and French armies awaited evacuation at Dunkirk, they were bombarded by German planes and artillery. The largest retreat in military history was accomplished by the British navy and private boats ranging from yachts to tugboats, all protected by the Royal Air Force. Huge amounts of equipment were left behind, but Britain's army was saved from total destruction. What effect did the fall of France have on American foreign policy?*

first time they met resistance from British and French troops. In May 1940, German forces defeated the Allied army and drove it to the sea at the French town of Dunkirk on the Belgian border. Cut off from retreat by land, the army was saved when 300,000 British and French troops were evacuated across the English Channel in a heroic nine-day rescue effort aided by 600 private boats.

In June 1940, Italy suddenly invaded France and declared war on Great Britain. Declaring that "the hand that held the dagger has struck it into the back of its neighbor," Roosevelt announced that, although the United States would not enter the war, it would extend as much aid as possible to the democracies. But on June 22 France surrendered, and Britain faced Hitler alone.

As the German air force bombed British airfields, factories, and cities to prepare the way for German armies to cross the English Channel, Britain found leadership in its new prime minister, Winston Churchill. Offering only "blood, toil, tears, and sweat," he pledged:

...we shall defend our island, whatever the cost may be. We shall fight on the beaches. We shall fight on the landing grounds. We shall fight on the fields and in the streets. We shall fight in the hills. We shall never surrender....until, in God's good time, the New World, with all its power and might, steps forth to the rescue and liberation of the Old.

America Abandons Neutrality

Prime Minister Churchill asked the United States for a loan of 50 destroyers to protect British shipping from German submarines. Recognizing that the isolationists in Congress would block approval of the loan, Roosevelt decided to act on his own. In September 1940, by executive order, he transferred 50 old World War I destroyers to Britain in return for the use of bases in Newfoundland and the Caribbean.

Meanwhile, for months London suffered bombing day and night by hundreds of German planes. The fighter pilots of the Royal Air Force, however, kept the Germans from gaining control of the skies over Britain and forced Hitler to abandon his invasion plans. "Never in the field of human conflict," said Churchill, "was so much owed by so many to so few."

The fall of France and the threat to Britain shook many Americans out of their belief that events outside the Western Hemisphere were none of their business. The possibility that Hitler and Mussolini might add the British and French fleets to their own made the Atlantic Ocean suddenly seem narrower, and Congress began to heed Roosevelt's warnings. It appropriated billions of dollars for defense and passed a Selective Service Act in September 1940, the first peacetime draft in American history, adding 800,000 men to the armed forces.

In the presidential election of 1940, the debate between internationalists and isolationists was carried on in both major parties. The Republicans nominated a newcomer to politics—Wendell Willkie, a Wall Street lawyer and utility company executive, best known for his criticism of the New Deal. For Democrats the question was whether Roosevelt would seek a third term, breaking the precedent set by George Washington. With the United States facing war in Europe and Asia, Roosevelt felt his experience was needed. He kept silent until the Democratic convention, then announced that he would accept the nomination.

At first, both candidates agreed on foreign-policy issues. Willkie attacked Roosevelt for breaking the two-term tradition, and he blamed the New Deal for failing to end unemployment. But when he began to slip in the polls, Willkie warned that Roosevelt's reelection would mean war. Roosevelt's promise to keep American troops out of war, Willkie said, was no better than his promise to balance the

Examining Photographs *The free world was surprised and horrified by the ease with which Germany smashed the British army. As its defeated troops returned home, Great Britain awaited a German invasion. Why did the invasion not take place?*

Examining Photographs *Londoners seek shelter in a subway station during a night of heavy bombing by the German* Luftwaffe *in September 1940. German pilots flew 1,000 missions per night over England and Scotland. How did Britain respond?*

budget. In November 1940, Roosevelt won reelection. With the world in crisis, most American voters did not want to gamble on a change in leadership.

Roosevelt's reelection encouraged him to find new ways to aid Britain. The British government was running out of money to pay for weapons, so the President proposed that the United States abandon its "cash and carry" policy. But not wanting to revive the old war-debts controversy, Roosevelt suggested that the United States merely lend goods to Britain, which the British could return or replace after the war. "Lend-lease" again stirred debate, but public opinion was shifting in Roosevelt's favor. A poll in January 1941 showed that 60 percent of Americans believed that it was more important to help Britain than to keep out of war. In March 1941, large majorities in both houses of Congress passed lend-lease, authorizing the President to send American supplies and weapons to other nations on any terms he thought would protect the security of the United States.

It was one thing to enact lend-lease, however, and another to get supplies across the Atlantic in time to help. When Hitler attacked Yugoslavia and Greece in the spring of 1941, the Nazis overran those countries before lend-lease aid could reach them. When Hitler's bombers failed to knock out Britain, he ordered his submarine fleet to starve that nation into submission. In trying to make sure that lend-lease supplies reached their destination, the United States was drawn step-by-step into the critical battle of the Atlantic. As German U-boats sank British and American supply ships almost daily, Roosevelt ordered the United States Navy to protect merchant shipping. By the fall of 1941, American and German warships were exchanging fire, and in October a German U-boat sank an American destroyer, killing more than 90 of its crew. Congress responded by revising the Neutrality Acts to allow merchant ships to be armed.

While German-American tensions were escalating in the Atlantic, in June 1941 Hitler, wanting Russia's vast wheat and oil supplies, suddenly attacked the Soviet Union. As German armies quickly advanced into the USSR, Stalin signed an alliance with Great Britain, and the United States offered lend-lease aid. American isolationists were outraged that Roosevelt would aid the Soviets. But Churchill knew that American aid to the Soviet Union would reduce German pressure on Britain. In supporting Roosevelt's decision, he remarked:

I have only one purpose,
the destruction of Hitler....
If Hitler invaded Hell
I would at least make a favorable reference
to the Devil in the House of Commons.

By the end of November 1941, very few Americans were preaching isolation. Most agreed with Roosevelt that the United States must be an "arsenal of democracy" to supply Great Britain and the Soviet Union against Hitler. In fact, about 15,000 Americans were already at war, most in British or Canadian uniforms.

Aggression in the Pacific

While the American public's attention was fixed on the Atlantic and Europe, events were taking place in the Pacific and Asia that would eventually plunge the United States into war. Already in China, Japan took advantage of the war in Europe to move against European colonies in Southeast Asia. This vast region contained the rice, rubber, tin, zinc, and oil needed for Japan's expanding industries. With France defeated, Britain on its knees, and the Soviets retreating in front of German armies, the United States was the only remaining obstacle to Japanese ambitions in the Pacific.

In September 1940, Japan allied with the Axis powers, Germany and Italy, and the United States responded by cutting off exports of scrap metal to Japan. As Japan continued its aggression in Asia, Roosevelt extended the embargo to include other products with possible military uses. In July 1941, he told the Japanese that the United States would help them find raw

Examining Fine Art *Even before the United States entered the war, Roosevelt and Churchill met to coordinate Allied strategy and to make peacetime plans. After the United States joined the Allies' war effort, the meetings were expanded to include Stalin. Out of this meeting off the North American coast in August 1941, plans emerged for the United Nations. How did Churchill feel about helping Stalin?*

Examining Photographs *Still hoping to avoid war, Secretary of State Cordell Hull emerges from meetings with Japanese diplomats. But Japan's leaders felt that American foreign policy was to weaken Japan in the Pacific. What secret decision did they make?*

materials if they abandoned their policy of conquest. When Japan rejected his proposal, the President halted all trade with Japan and ordered American forces in the Pacific to prepare for war.

In October 1941, Japan's moderate prime minister resigned and was replaced by General Hideki Tojo (hee deh kee TOH JOH), who favored war to eliminate American and British influence in Asia. By late November, as the United States continued to insist that Japan honor the Open Door, Japanese leaders decided that if the dispute did not quickly come to a favorable conclusion, they would attack. As negotiations deadlocked, Roosevelt realized that war was inevitable. The only uncertainty was where Japan's attack would come. On December 6, the President appealed for peace directly to Japan's Emperor Hirohito. American officials did not know that, on November 26, a Japanese fleet had put to sea, headed for the United States' main naval base in the Pacific—Pearl Harbor in Hawaii.

SUMMARY

The appeasement policies of Britain, France, and the United States allowed Hitler to take Czechoslovakia without a struggle. After signing a nonaggression treaty with the Soviet Union to avoid a two-front war, Hitler blitzed through Europe, conquering nations ill-prepared to resist. Then he turned and attacked the Soviet Union. These actions, and fear of what would happen if Britain fell, caused the United States to abandon neutrality and resume arms shipments and aid to the Allies. Japan's expansion in Asia also gave Roosevelt concern. While attempting to avoid war, he began an arms buildup and to increase the size of the military. When negotiations with Japan failed, Japanese forces attacked the United States fleet at Pearl Harbor.

CHECKING FOR UNDERSTANDING

1. **Identify** Winston Churchill, Selective Service Act, *blitzkrieg*, "lend-lease," Pearl Harbor

2. **Describe** why hostilities developed between the United States and Japan.

3. **Chronicle** Hitler's conquests in Europe in the order of their occurrence.

4. **Explain** the importance of the election of 1940.

THINKING CRITICALLY

5. **Citing Evidence** What actions and policies demonstrated that Congress and Roosevelt recognized the possibility that the United States would be drawn into war?

CONNECTIONS: HISTORY AND GEOGRAPHY

6. **Examining Relative Location** How did the United States' location encourage isolationism and hamper efforts to supply the Allies?

★ ★

The United States at War

Yesterday, December 7, 1941—a date which will live in infamy—the United States was suddenly and deliberately attacked by naval and air forces of the Empire of Japan....The people...well understand the implications to the very life and safety of our nation....No matter how long it may take us...the American people in their righteous might will win through to absolute victory....

—FRANKLIN ROOSEVELT
War Message to Congress, 1941

Section Focus

Three days after Congress declared war on Japan, Germany and Italy declared war on the United States. Americans now faced war in both Europe and Asia. But Japan's unprovoked attack had ended the public debate over foreign policy. The American people were now united in their determination to win the war.

Objectives

After studying this section, you should be able to:
- Discuss the course of the war in Europe and in Asia.
- Describe the Atlantic Charter and the agreements the Allies reached at the Yalta Conference.

On December 6, 1941, American officials intercepted a coded message from Japan to its embassy in Washington, D.C., indicating that Japan was about to break relations with the United States.

American authorities sent warnings to military commanders throughout the Pacific. But by the time the message reached Pearl Harbor, Japanese bombers were already attacking the American fleet there. Shortly after noon on Sunday, December 7, President Roosevelt received an urgent telephone call from the secretary of the navy. The secretary had just received a wire from Hawaii: "Air Raid on Pearl Harbor. This is no Drill."

In 2 hours, Japanese planes sank many vessels, including 5 battleships and 3 destroyers, and heavily damaged many others. The attack also destroyed about 250 airplanes and about 4,500 people were killed or wounded. Only the fleet's aircraft carriers, out of the harbor on maneuvers, escaped the devastation.

The World at War

However determined the American people were to defeat the Axis powers—Germany, Italy, and Japan—the immediate outlook was bleak. The destruction of the American fleet removed Japan's only obstacle in the Pacific. For six months the Japanese won victory after victory, capturing American bases at Guam and Wake Island, conquering Britain's colonies at Hong Kong and Singapore, and occupying the independent kingdom of Thailand. In April 1942, American forces that had been holding out on the peninsula of Bataan in the Philippines finally surrendered. Meanwhile, the Japanese conquered Burma and the East Indies.

The situation was equally bad in the West. Axis forces occupied nearly all of Europe, and Britain was besieged. In North Africa German General Erwin Rommel, "the Desert Fox," led an Italian-German force toward the Suez Canal, pushing the British back to the borders of Egypt. By summer 1942 the Germans had pushed deep into the Soviet Union, capturing the rich farmland of the Ukraine and threatening the cities of Stalingrad, Leningrad, and Moscow. Roosevelt and Churchill feared that if the Soviets were crushed, German armies might sweep through the Middle East and join with their Japanese allies in the British colony

Examining Photographs

Japan's surprise attack on Pearl Harbor severely damaged the U.S. Pacific Fleet. In addition, about 250 warplanes were destroyed and more than 2,400 Americans were killed. How did the attack affect American public opinion about isolation?

of India. Success or failure of the war in Europe depended on whether the Soviet Union could hold out until the United States and Britain could launch an offensive on the western front.

Even before Japan attacked Pearl Harbor, American strategists had decided that in the event of war, the United States would concentrate on defeating Hitler before dealing with Japan. Not only did the United States have closer ties with the countries occupied by Germany, but Germany seemed a greater threat to the Western Hemisphere, where Nazi sympathies were strong in several Latin American nations. Churchill agreed with this plan, observing that:

...[T]he defeat of Germany...
will leave Japan exposed to an
overwhelming force, whereas the defeat of
Japan would by no means bring the
World War to an end.

Meanwhile, German troops survived the Russian winter of 1941 to 1942 and launched a second attack on the Soviets. In the spring they moved toward the oil fields near the Caspian Sea, and by midsummer they were more than halfway to their goal. Stalin pleaded with Roosevelt and Churchill for an invasion of western Europe that would take some pressure off the Soviet Union. But Churchill told him that such a second front in Europe was a year away. Although thousands of British tanks and American trucks and hundreds of thousands of tons of American supplies were reaching the USSR, Soviet troops were left to face the Germans alone.

In September 1942, the Red Army made a desperate and heroic stand at Stalingrad. For four months, Soviet and German troops battled house-to-house for control of the city. Although the German invasion was halted, Stalingrad was reduced to rubble and the Soviets suffered more casualties defending it than the United States did in the entire war. Stalin never forgave Roosevelt and Churchill for allowing this to happen.

In November the Soviet army counter-attacked. Taking advantage of the Russian winter, the Red Army surrounded Hitler's freezing forces. In February 1943, the tattered remains of the invading German army, only one-third of its 330,000 men still alive, surrendered. Soviet troops then started an advance toward Germany, which ended in Berlin two years later.

While Soviet troops were fighting around Stalingrad, a British-American army landed in Morocco and Algeria in November 1942 to attack Axis forces in North Africa. General Rommel, defeated by the British in Egypt in October, was retreating toward this invading army. Now pressed on both sides, Axis troops were trapped in Tunisia, where they surrendered in May 1943.

Allied victories in North Africa cleared the way for an attack on what Churchill called "the soft underbelly" of Europe. In August 1943, British and American forces took Sicily, and in September they invaded the Italian mainland. After his defeat in Sicily, Mussolini was overthrown, and the new Italian government quickly surrendered. But German troops still occupied

Examining Maps *Churchill and Roosevelt delayed an attack in Europe to first fight in the Mediterranean. Some historians believe this was a plan to weaken Soviet power in postwar Europe. What reasoning might support such a theory?*

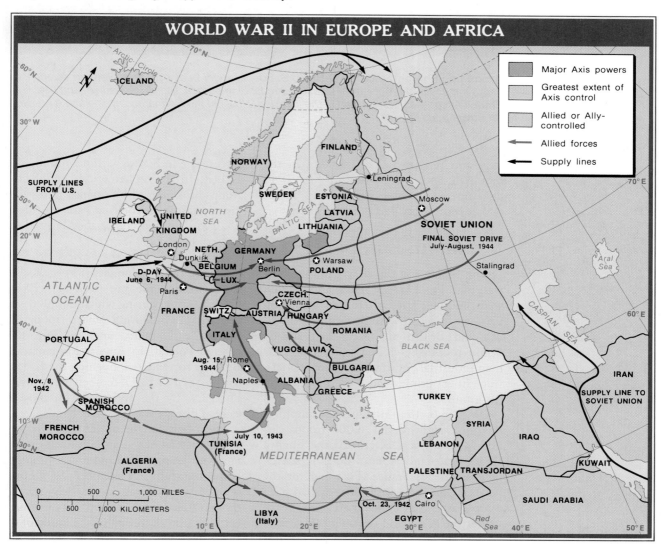

WORLD WAR II IN EUROPE AND AFRICA

Examining Photographs *On D-Day U.S. troops, under heavy fire from German defenders, storm the coast of France from Coast Guard landing barges. British, Canadian, and free French forces also participated in the invasion. How did the Normandy invasion take pressure off Soviet forces?*

Italy and put up fierce resistance in the mountainous terrain. Not until June 1944 did the Allies enter Rome. Axis forces remained in control of northern Italy.

Victory in Europe

One reason for the slow gains in Italy was that the United States and Britain were building strength for an attack on German forces in western Europe. American and British air forces had already begun round-the-clock bombing of German industrial and transportation centers. But Hitler's armies had to be defeated on the ground.

On June 6, 1944, the greatest amphibious force in history, 176,000 troops carried in 5,000 vessels, crossed the English Channel to land along a 60-mile stretch of coastline in France. Planning for the "D-Day" invasion at Normandy had been under way for more than two years. Under the command of American general Dwight D. Eisenhower, a million Allied

forces were in France within a month after D-Day. In August American and British troops broke out of Normandy and struck rapidly eastward, entering Paris on August 25, 1944. In September they crossed the western border of Germany.

At the same time, the Soviets closed in from the east. In January 1944, the Red Army freed Leningrad from an 890-day German siege, during which 800,000 residents died. By spring Soviet troops had freed the Ukraine, and in July they entered Poland. In August Romania and Bulgaria surrendered, opening the Balkans to the Soviets. In December they entered Hungary. By the end of 1944, most of eastern Europe was in Soviet hands.

The Nazis fought to the end. In June 1944, they launched an air attack on Britain with jet-propelled and rocket-propelled bomber aircraft. In December 1944, Hitler ordered a counterattack in Belgium. Although Allied lines "bulged," the Germans could not break through. The Battle of the Bulge was the last German offensive. In

March 1945, the Allies crossed the Rhine River and moved into the heart of Germany. Meanwhile, the Soviets pushed from the east, taking Berlin in April 1945. In April, Hitler committed suicide in his underground shelter in Berlin, and on May 7, 1945, German leaders agreed to an unconditional surrender. Franklin Roosevelt, who led the nation through the Depression and the war, however, did not witness this event. Only days before Hitler's suicide, the President died of a massive cerebral hemorrhage.

As they entered Germany, Allied armies discovered evidence of one of the most terrible acts of the war—the Nazi **holocaust,** or deliberate extermination of 6 million European Jews. As early as 1942, the United States government received reports that Hitler had ordered the murder of all Jews in German-occupied territories. At first officials would not believe that such stories were true. In 1944 Roosevelt responded to criticism within his own administration that the United States was passively accepting the murder of Jews. He created a War Refugee Board, but for 6 out of 10 Jews in Europe, action came too late. Not until Allied troops reached the Nazi death camps—at Auschwitz, Dachau, Buchenwald, and elsewhere—and found survivors and the gas chambers in which so many had died was the horrible truth fully realized.

War in the Pacific

Although Allied strategy was to first concentrate on defeating Hitler, the Japanese were not able to consolidate their gains in the Pacific before the tide of war began to turn. In May 1942, American warships defeated a Japanese fleet in the Battle of the Coral Sea. A month later a Japanese flotilla was turned back with heavy losses in the three-day Battle of Midway. Despite these defeats, Japan still held many heavily fortified Pacific islands. So the Allies adopted a military strategy called "island hopping"—to cut Japanese supply lines by capturing key islands and to use them as bases to attack other Japanese strongholds, especially the Philippines and eventually Japan itself.

In August 1942, Americans took the first step in the long and bloody road to Tokyo when marines landed on Guadalcanal in the Solomon Islands. The struggle for Guadalcanal was fought on the ground, at sea, and in the air, lasting six months. Not until 1943 did Japan's resistance there come to an end.

In attacking the United States, Japan had failed to realize the industrial power of America and its ability to mobilize that power rapidly. Of the 19 ships sunk at Pearl Harbor, 17 were returned to duty by December 1942, and new ships were constantly added. The Navy worked out new

Examining Photographs
American and Soviet armies meet at the Elbe River in central Germany in April 1945. How was the invasion of Germany carried out?

Examining Photographs
The condition of survivors in the Nazi death camps horrified the world. Why were the death camps created?

ways of fueling and repairing ships at sea, allowing fleets to stay at sea for long periods of time.

During 1943 and 1944, American forces "island-hopped" toward the Philippines and Japan. In October 1944, Allied forces under American general Douglas MacArthur landed in the Philippines. MacArthur's advance was matched by amphibious operations directed by Admiral Chester Nimitz against Japanese-held islands in the central Pacific.

In 1945 the last of Japan's island outposts fell with the taking of Iwo Jima (EE WOH JEE muh) in March and Okinawa (OH kuh NAH wuh) in June. Though Iwo Jima measures only a few square miles, American marines suffered more than 20,000 casualties in capturing it. Japan now began to use *kamikazes* (KAHM ih KAHZ eez), suicide pilots who flew bomb-laden planes into American ships. During the invasion of Okinawa, kamikazes scored 279 hits on United States vessels.

By the summer of 1945, after Germany was defeated, all Allied power was turned against Japan. The Soviet Union agreed to

Examining Maps *While a joint British-American force freed Southeast Asia from Japanese occupation, American forces recaptured strategic islands as they moved northward in "hops" of about 200 miles each toward the Philippines and Japan itself. What strategic importance does the map show for Iwo Jima and Okinawa?*

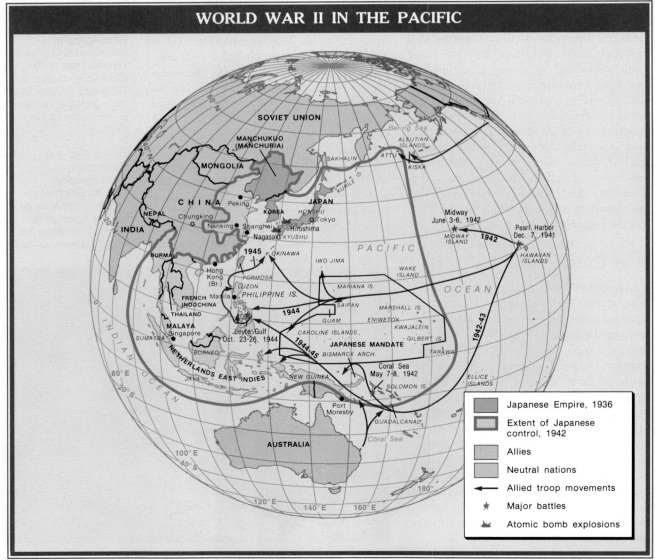

WORLD WAR II IN THE PACIFIC

UNIT 9 TIMES OF CRISIS: 1932-1960

Connections

HISTORY AND SCIENCE

THE ATOMIC BOMB

"We must not be the most hated and feared people in the world," a physicist wrote, urging President Truman not to use the atomic bombs that would kill some 150,000 mostly civilian Japanese.

Rumors that the Nazis might develop an atomic bomb spurred American and

Hiroshima

British efforts to build one. Scientist Albert Einstein wrote President Roosevelt urging that a major research program begin at once so that the nation would be the first with the bomb.

The secret project, later called the Manhattan Project, was carried out primarily at facilities in Oak Ridge, Tennessee, and, later, at Los Alamos, New Mexico. American physicist J. Robert Oppenheimer was the director and persuaded many top nuclear physicists to join the project.

President Truman did not know the bomb existed until a few weeks before his decision to use it. Although some historians disagree about why atomic bombs were dropped on Japan and about the ethical issues involved, President Truman believed the bombing was justified: "The dropping of the bombs stopped the war, saved millions of lives."

★★★★★★★★★★

MAKING THE SCIENCE CONNECTION

1. Why did the United States start the Manhattan Project?

LINKING PAST AND PRESENT

2. Given the present concerns about the dangers of nuclear war, do you think the U.S. was right to develop nuclear weapons? Why or why not?

★★★★★★★★★★

---

declare war on Japan and confront Japan's forces in Manchuria. But the conquest of the Japanese islands was left to the United States. America's long-range B-29 bombers had been bombing Japan from bases on recaptured Pacific islands since June 1944. In one raid alone in March 1945, more than 83,000 Tokyo civilians were incinerated by American napalm bombs. But despite such heavy casualties, Japan's military leaders rejected calls for unconditional surrender. American commanders worried that an invasion of Japan would meet heavy resistance and might cost a million lives.

The most terrible weapon the world had ever known removed the need to invade Japan or to count on the Soviets for help. Since early in the war, American scientists had secretly been developing an atomic bomb. First tested in New Mexico in July 1945, it gave Harry Truman, who became President after Roosevelt's death, another choice, and Soviet leader Stalin told Truman to "make good use of it."

After the Japanese government rejected Truman's final warning to surrender or risk "utter destruction," on August 6 an atomic bomb destroyed 60 percent of Hiroshima, a major Japanese industrial city. In announcing the bombing, Truman warned:

We are now prepared to obliterate more rapidly and completely every productive enterprise the Japanese have above ground in any city....if they do not now accept our terms they may expect a rain of ruin from the air, the like of which has never been seen on this earth.

When Japan still refused to surrender, a second bomb was dropped on the city of Nagasaki on August 9, causing almost as much destruction as the first. The two attacks took about 150,000 Japanese lives. When reports of the death and devastation reached Tokyo, the stunned emperor, telling his people that "the unendurable must be endured," asked for peace. The final surrender took place on September 2, 1945, on the battleship *Missouri* anchored in Tokyo Bay.

Wartime Diplomacy

The first planning for peace took place in August 1941 when Roosevelt and Churchill met on a ship off the coast of Newfoundland. At that meeting they issued the Atlantic Charter, a statement of principles on which depended "hopes for a better future for the world." Much like Wilson's Fourteen Points, the Atlantic Charter looked forward to a world where people would have the right to choose their form of government and where resources would be shared to provide a better life for all. Also like the Fourteen Points, it suggested a new world organization to keep the peace.

After Pearl Harbor, Roosevelt turned his attention to forming an alliance among the nations fighting against Hitler. On January 1, 1942, representatives of the 26 countries at war with the Axis met in Washington, D.C., and signed the Declaration of the United Nations. Members of this new group agreed to support the principles of the Atlantic Charter. They promised full economic and military support in the war, and they agreed not to make a separate peace.

In holding the great alliance together, Roosevelt and Churchill kept constantly in touch. Although they often did not agree on strategy, neither wavered in admiration for the other. Working closely with the other major Allies was more difficult. Japanese troops had pushed China's government deep into the interior, and Chinese leaders were unhappy that the war in Europe was the top priority. General Charles de Gaulle (di GOHL), leader of the French government in exile, disapproved of the United States' recognizing a government in south France that was friendly to the Nazis. But Roosevelt and Churchill did not make De Gaulle a full partner in their meetings because they were not sure whether he really represented France.

Cooperation with the Soviet Union proved the most difficult problem. Stalin had almost never been outside of his country and was suspicious of capitalist nations. Even so, the alliance between the United States and Great Britain and Soviet Union lasted until the end of the war. Germany could not be defeated without Soviet aid, and the Soviets depended on supplies from Britain and the United States.

Planning for War and Peace

Cooperation in plans for war and peace was worked out in a series of international conferences. At Casablanca, Morocco, in January 1943, Roosevelt and Churchill agreed to demand "unconditional surrender" from the Axis powers, assuring the Soviet Union that its western allies would not sign a separate peace treaty with Germany.

At Quebec, Canada, in August 1943, Roosevelt and Churchill agreed on peace terms for Italy, while their military advisers developed plans for the invasion of western Europe. At Cairo, Egypt, in November 1943, Roosevelt and Churchill met Chinese leader Chiang Kai-shek (jyahng ky SHEHK) and agreed that Japan should be stripped of its Pacific empire and Korea given independence. From Cairo Roosevelt and Churchill flew to Teheran, capital of Iran, to meet with Stalin. There they promised that the D-Day invasion of France would be launched the next year. In return Stalin agreed to begin a new offensive against Germany at the same time from the east. The three leaders also discussed the possibility of the Soviet Union declaring war on Japan.

In February 1945, Roosevelt, Churchill, and Stalin met for the last time at Yalta, in the Soviet Union. They agreed publicly that the United States, Britain, and the Soviet Union, along with France, should

Examining Photographs *Looking tired and drawn, Franklin Roosevelt (center) poses with Stalin (right) and Churchill during a break in their meetings at Yalta. Two months later, Roosevelt was dead. What agreements were reached at Yalta?*

occupy Germany after the war, but they promised the other peoples of Europe:

...[I]nterim governmental authorities broadly representative of all democratic elements and pledged to the earliest possible establishment through free elections of governments responsive to the will of the people.

They also agreed on a conference to be held at San Francisco in April 1945 to establish a world organization.

Secret agreements at Yalta covered the terms on which the Soviet Union should enter the war against Japan after Germany was defeated. The Soviets were promised Japanese territories, and that they could keep Outer Mongolia in China and obtain an ice-free naval port. In return, Stalin agreed to support the Nationalist government of Chiang Kai-shek instead of the Chinese Communists who were challenging Chiang for power.

Although the Yalta agreements later were attacked as a "sellout," at the time it seemed vital to keep the Soviet Union from making a separate peace with Germany when American and British forces were still fighting in the west. Even more important, the United States wanted Soviet support in the war against Japan. Before the atomic bomb was successfully tested, American military experts expected that defeating Japan would take another 18 months. American diplomats also suspected that Stalin's agreement to free elections in Eastern Europe was not sincere. But with Soviet troops already in those nations, Roosevelt felt that this loose agreement was the best he could do. He had faith in the future world organization and in his personal relationship with Stalin to solve any problems that might arise.

When he reported to Congress on his Yalta trip, Roosevelt looked tired and pale. He sat down to deliver his address rather than standing. Two months later, on April 12, 1945, the President died suddenly at Warm Springs, Georgia. The nation he led for more than 12 years was shocked, and newspapers that printed daily lists of soldiers and sailors who had died in action added the name: "Roosevelt, Franklin D., Commander in Chief."

Two weeks after Roosevelt's death, representatives of 50 nations met at San Francisco to make plans for a new world organization. But the talks at San Francisco were made more difficult by rising suspicions among the Allies. The Soviet Union was keeping a firm hand on Poland and seemed to be breaking its Yalta promises. Still, the meeting at San Francisco produced a charter for a United Nations (UN). The preamble of the UN Charter pledged all the countries signing it to "faith in fundamental human rights," to "justice and respect" for the terms of peace treaties, and to the goal of living together.

In July 1945, when the Senate ratified the Charter by a vote of 89 to 2, the United States became the first nation to join the UN. The first use of the atomic bomb 9 days later reinforced the belief of many Americans that war must not happen again. Trusting the new United Nations, in which they expected to take a full part, and not yet aware of its weaknesses, Americans hoped to return forever to the path of peace.

SUMMARY

After the bombing of Pearl Harbor, the United States entered a war that consumed it from 1941 to 1945. As Japan conquered Southeast Asia and strategic islands in the South Pacific, the Allies first concentrated on victory in Europe. While the Soviets made a heroic stand at Stalingrad, British and American forces were victorious in North Africa and Italy. When Allied forces invaded France and pushed east, the Soviets pushed west, and Germany was defeated. In the Pacific, an island-hopping campaign and two atomic bombs defeated Japan. Allied leaders met during the war to plan for peace, but distrust emerged between the Soviets and the other Allies.

CHECKING FOR UNDERSTANDING

1. **Identify** D-Day, Dwight Eisenhower, Harry Truman, Atlantic Charter, Yalta Conference

2. **Define** holocaust

3. **Summarize** the progression of the war in Asia, Europe, Africa, and the Pacific.

4. **List** the meetings held among Allied leaders between 1941 and 1945 and the resulting agreements.

THINKING CRITICALLY

5. **Anticipating Consequences** In a wartime alliance, what risk is carried by each nation that agrees not to make a separate peace? What is to be gained by such a commitment?

CONNECTIONS: HISTORY AND SCIENCE

6. **Considering Moral Responsibility** Some suggest that scientists should not use research to develop tools of destruction. Should scientists refuse to develop such weapons of mass destruction as nuclear weapons? Justify your answer.

★ ★ ★ ★ ★ ★ ★ ★ ★ ★ ★ ★ ★ ★ ★ ★ ★

War on the Home Front

Ships and planes, more ships and planes is the American battle cry of 1943. "Give us the tools for quick victory." That's the patriotic challenge to management and worker alike.

—FREDERICK CRAWFORD
Director of the United States Chamber of Commerce, in a speech, April 1943

Section Focus

To fight the Axis, the United States had to mobilize people and resources more quickly than ever before. By 1944 more than 11 million men and women were in uniform. As the number of industrial workers also rose to new heights, the war accomplished what the New Deal had never been able to—it ended the Depression's unemployment.

Objectives

After studying this section, you should be able to:
- Discuss efforts to mobilize the economy for war production.
- Explain the war's impact on women, blacks, and Japanese Americans.

Americans were amazed at the speed with which industry turned to making war materials. When in May 1940 President Roosevelt talked of producing 50,000 airplanes a year, some thought he was asking the impossible. Yet, by 1944 the number of planes produced annually had risen to about 100,000. Mass production was so effective in the ship industry the average time for building a freighter dropped from a year to less than 2 months. In 4 years American shipyards put to sea tonnage equal to the entire merchant fleet of all the other countries of the world.

The Production Battle

As in World War I, federal agencies took on the direction of private companies doing war work. After a Senate investigation revealed corruption and mismanagement among companies involved in war production, in January 1942 Roosevelt gave a War Production Board strong regulatory power. Its head, Donald Nelson, could seize vital materials, order industrial plants to convert to war production, and prohibit manufacture of products he considered unessential to the war effort.

Within weeks of Pearl Harbor, production of bicycles, beer cans, refrigerators, toothpaste tubes and more than 300 other items was cut back or banned. Automobile manufacturers were ordered to convert production to tanks and other war supplies. Entire new industries were created. Synthetic rubber, for example, became important when Japan's conquest of Southeast Asia cut off America's supply of natural rubber. By the end of 1942, nearly 33 percent of American production went to war materials, and by 1944 nearly 50 percent. Production of all goods nearly doubled, and America's production of war materials matched the total output of Germany, Italy, and Japan combined.

In May 1941, Roosevelt set up the Office of Scientific Research and Development to mobilize science and technology for the war effort. Among the many inventions that came from this agency were: DDT which controlled insects and made jungle fighting more tolerable; the bazooka, a weapon that enabled an infantry soldier to destroy a tank; and radar, which determined the position and speed of airplanes and ships.

To raise funds for the war effort, the government increased taxes and sold war bonds in amounts ranging from $25 to $10,000. In 1942 the government extended the income tax for the first time to include middle- and lower-income people. To make collection easier, the government in 1943 began to require that employers deduct taxes from workers' paychecks before they received them.

The war increased employment, and workers' earnings rose as war production brought longer work weeks and overtime. As people had more money to spend, and as the shift to war materials made consumer goods scarce, prices rose. To combat inflation, in 1942 Congress created the Office of Price Administration, which set price ceilings on consumer products and began to ration goods that were in short supply. By war's end 20 items—including sugar, meat, butter, coffee, gasoline, fuel oil, and shoes—required government-issued rationing coupons to be presented at the time of purchase. Despite attempts to hold down prices, however, the cost of living rose 29 percent during the war, leading to demands for higher wages.

To help prevent strikes, a National War Labor Board was established to settle labor disputes by mediation. Although this task was made easier by the no-strike pledges that both the AFL and the CIO made after Pearl Harbor, there were many small **wildcat strikes**—work stoppages without union approval—and a short national strike by 500,000 coal miners. Even though most labor unions kept their no-strike pledge, a 1943 act outlawed strikes against war industries.

The War and Social Change

The need for defense workers altered traditional patterns of society. As millions of men joined the armed services, more women than ever before entered the labor force. "If you can drive a car, you can run a machine," industries advertised. The government, newspapers, radio, and newsreels encouraged women to take factory jobs as a patriotic duty, and 5 million American women entered the work force during the war. "Rosie the Riveter," who first appeared in overalls in a Lockheed Aircraft poster, became a national symbol of the vital contribution women were making to the war effort.

More than ever before, women filled jobs that were not traditional for females. They worked on production lines, in steel mills, on the docks, and in other jobs that required heavy manual labor. Outside war industries, women also took over such traditionally male jobs as driving buses and trucks and working as train conductors, lumberjacks, and barbers. Most of these new workers were married and had children. Yet women still encountered resistance from male

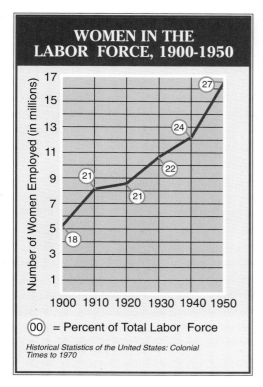

WOMEN IN THE LABOR FORCE, 1900-1950

Number of Women Employed (in millions)

1900 1910 1920 1930 1940 1950

(00) = Percent of Total Labor Force

Historical Statistics of the United States: Colonial Times to 1970

Examining Graphs *The number of women in the workforce skyrocketed during both world wars. But when soldiers returned to their peacetime jobs, female employment declined again. What decade had the greatest peacetime growth in female employment?*

workers. As one woman aircraft worker described:

The men really resented the women very much, and in the beginning it was a little bit rough....after a while they realized that it was essential that the women worked there, 'cause there wasn't enough men, and the women were doing a good job....However, I always felt that they thought it wasn't your place to be there.

To encourage women to work, the government offered job-training courses, and Congress appropriated funds for child-care centers, but even this was not enough to meet the need. Federal and state governments suspended laws that limited the hours women could work, and women's wages rose as the concept of equal pay for equal work spread. Although at first most women considered their new employment to be temporary, by war's end 80 percent said they wanted to keep their jobs. Employers, however, had promised to give jobs back to soldiers when the war ended. Within a year after the war was over, 2 million women had lost their jobs, and others moved out of higher-paying industrial jobs to lower-paying clerical ones. Yet more women remained in the work force after the war than were working before it.

The need for workers also speeded the shift of African Americans from farming to manufacturing. More blacks left the South and moved to cities in the Northeast, Midwest, and California to work in war industries. Some companies, such as the aircraft producers, hired few blacks before the war, but by 1945 thousands of black Americans had jobs in defense plants.

Between 1941 and 1945, one of every five Americans relocated to another part of the country. The movement of so many Americans to fill jobs in war industries created housing shortages, crowded schools, and heightened social tensions. Old-timers resented the newcomers, regardless of their race. In California there were prejudices against "Okies," white migrants from Oklahoma and Texas who arrived in the 1930s to look for work after losing their farms in the Dust Bowl. In many cities prejudices arose against newly arrived blacks. The police were needed to help black families move into public housing in Detroit, when angry mobs tried to block them. It took federal troops to break a strike of streetcar operators in Philadelphia, who protested against the promotion of black workers.

The federal government's response to racial discrimination during the war was uneven. In 1941 black labor leader A. Philip Randolph threatened to lead 100,000 protesters on Washington, D.C., to demand an end to discrimination in defense jobs and the armed forces. In order to stop the march, Roosevelt established the Fair Employment Practices Commission to promote minority hiring

Linking Across Time

AMERICAN PRODUCTION AND WAR IN EUROPE

American industry in World War II would not have been so productive had the American people not fully supported the war effort. Such support was in marked contrast to the detachment with which Americans traditionally viewed Europe's great conflicts.

Americans called for neutrality in 1803, as Napoleon swept through Europe, and again in 1914 when the Kaiser was on the march. Even as Hitler gobbled up the continent, Americans watched. But when Japan bombed Pearl Harbor, Americans felt threatened, and they channeled their fear into tremendous wartime efforts.

Examining Photographs *World War II offered increased job opportunities for women and for African Americans. The number of women who worked jumped from 27 percent to 37 percent. Although women's wages rose, they still averaged 60 percent less than men's wages. What happened to women's jobs when the war ended?*

in government offices and in companies that had war contracts. But while it opposed discrimination, the commission did not reject segregation. Even the military remained segregated, and although hundreds of thousands of African Americans served in uniform, in every capacity from cooks to fighter pilots, most served in all-black units.

The most significant racial discrimination of the war involved the removal of Japanese Americans from the West Coast. About 90 percent of all Japanese Americans, outside Hawaii, lived in California and the Pacific Northwest. Because of immigration restrictions after 1924, two-thirds had been born in the United States and were citizens by birth. Yet government officials were suspicious of their loyalty. When war broke out, residents of California, Oregon, and Washington feared that with the Pacific fleet at Pearl Harbor severely damaged, they were vulnerable to invasion at any time. Californians, in particular, were concerned that their neighbors of Japanese descent might engage in sabotage. Army General John DeWitt investigated and reported that:

The Japanese race is an enemy race and while many second and third generation Japanese born on United States soil have become "Americanized," the racial strains are undiluted....It, therefore, follows that along the vital Pacific Coast over 112,000 potential enemies of Japanese extraction are at large today.

Based on such reports, beginning in February 1942, the government moved 110,000 Japanese Americans to detention centers surrounded by barbed wire and patrolled by soldiers and confined them there for the duration of the war.

The order to evacuate Japanese Americans from the West Coast came quickly. Detainees had as little as 48 hours to make arrangements for their homes, businesses, and farms. Many had to sell their property at a loss or abandon it. Bargain hunters descended on them, taking advantage of their plight.

Arriving at one of 10 detention camps in isolated areas of Utah, Wyoming, Arizona, and other sparsely settled western states, they were put to work at menial low-paying jobs. Their military guards searched their quarters for "weapons," sometimes confiscating kitchen knives, scissors, and even knitting needles. Entire families lived out the war in a single room in army-style barracks furnished with cots and bare light bulbs. Since the authorities had no plans for running the camps, the detainees established their own camp governments, schools, and newspapers.

Almost immediately detainees appealed to the courts to protect their civil liberties. When the issue finally came before the Supreme Court in December 1944, in

Examining Photographs *Seattle residents look on as a group of the city's Japanese American population, under army escort, are put on trains to be shipped to camps for detention during the war. How did the Supreme Court rule on this action?*

Korematsu v. United States, the justices upheld the government's policy as necessary for national security.

Despite their unhappy experience, most Japanese Americans remained loyal to the United States. Thousands served in segregated military units. A Japanese-American army unit recruited from detention camps fought in the Italian campaign and was the army's most decorated unit in American military history. However, the government's policy toward Japanese Americans at home became a blot on the nation's war record.

CHARLES DREW
1904–1950

Born and raised in the segregated city of Washington, D.C., Charles Drew refused to let racial prejudice bar him from professional success. After graduating from Amherst College in Massachusetts, he earned his M.D. degree at Canada's McGill University.

In the 1930s Drew conducted pioneering research on blood plasma, and he established a model blood plasma bank. When the United States entered World War II, Drew was asked to head the military's blood plasma program. By collecting, storing, transporting, and transfusing donated blood plasma, this program saved the lives of countless wounded soldiers. But in 1942 Drew resigned when the military refused to accept blood donations from African Americans unless their blood was segregated from the blood of white donors and was given only to black soldiers.

SUMMARY

Although the cost was suffering, brutal devastation, and tragic loss of life abroad, World War II accomplished on the home front what the New Deal failed to achieve—an end to the Depression. Demand for war goods created new industries and stimulated existing business. Under orders from the War Production Board, many industrial plants converted to war production. The government responded to inflation with price ceilings, and to scarcity with rationing of specific consumer goods. Wartime productivity increased employment, wages, and opportunity for all workers, including African Americans and women. Japanese Americans, however, were gathered and detained for the duration of the war.

CHECKING FOR UNDERSTANDING

1. **Identify** War Production Board
2. **Define** wildcat strikes
3. **Explain** how the United States' productive capacity aided the Allies' war effort.
4. **Describe** the roles of women in aiding the war effort.
5. **Contrast** the war's effects on African Americans and on Japanese Americans.

THINKING CRITICALLY

6. **Formulating Hypotheses** Why were Japanese Americans detained during the war while Americans of German or Italian descent were not?

CONNECTIONS:
HISTORY AND ECONOMICS

7. **Applying Economics** A war economy often results in inflation as increased earnings and scarce goods pushed up prices and the cost of living. How did the United States curb inflation during World War II?

Interpreting Primary Sources

Who Is an American?

Peter Ota was 15 when he was interned in 1942. When he reached draft age, Ota was required to register for military service. He served in an armored division of the U.S. Army. In the following passage, Ota reflects on the effects of his internment on himself and his children.

From Studs Terkel, "The Good War," An Oral History of World War Two:

We came back to Los Angeles at the end of the war, believing that there was no other way but to be American. We were discouraged with our Japanese culture. My feeling at the time was, I had to prove myself. I don't know why I had to prove myself. Here I am, an ex-GI, born and raised here. Why do I have to prove myself? We all had this feeling. We had to prove that we were Americans, okay?

My mother and father sent me to a Japanese school teaching the culture. My wife and I did nothing with our children in that respect. We moved to a white community near Los Angeles. It was typical American suburb living. We became more American than Americans, very conservative. My wife and I, we talk about this. We thought this

Japanese Americans waiting for registration at the Santa Anita Reception Center, Los Angeles County, California

was the thing we had to do; to blend into the community and become part of white America.

My children were denied a lot of the history of what happened. If you think of all those forty years of silence, I think this stems from another Japanese characteristic: when shame is put on you, you try to hide it. We were put into camp, we became victims, it was our fault. We hide it.

My oldest daughter, Cathy, in her senior year at college, wanted to write a thesis about the camp experience. She asked if we knew people she might interview. Strange thing is, many people, even now,

didn't want to talk about it. Some of the people she did talk to broke down. Because this was the first time they had told this story. This is the same thing I did. When I first went into detail, it just broke me up. When it came out, I personally felt good about it. It was somethin' that was inside of me that I've wanted to say for a long time.

EXAMINING THE PRIMARY SOURCE

1. What effect did Ota's wartime experiences have on his feelings about Japanese culture?

2. How does Ota explain the long silence of Japanese Americans on the internment camps?

THINKING CRITICALLY

3. Compare Ota's upbringing with that of his children. Suggest reasons for the differences that you identify.

4. What, in your opinion, may have prompted Ota's daughter to write about the camp experience?

5. Was the United States' domestic policy of interning Japanese Americans inconsistent with its opposition to Hitler's racial policies? Explain your answer.

★ Summary

In the late 1930s, war clouds gathered in Europe and Asia. The territorial ambitions of the German-Italian Axis included the Mediterranean and all of Europe. Meanwhile, Japan expanded its holdings in Asia and the Pacific. European appeasement, American isolationism, and a Soviet-German nonaggression pact allowed the Axis to overrun Europe and North Africa. As Britain was left to struggle alone and Hitler turned on the Soviet Union, the United States supplied military equipment, but did not enter the war until Japan attacked Pearl Harbor. The tide turned against Germany when Russian defenses held at Stalingrad. An Allied invasion beginning in 1944 forced Hitler to fight a two-front war. As Allied and Soviet troops converged on Berlin, Germany surrendered. Allied troops then focused on the Pacific, where they retook strategic islands. Atomic bombs dropped on Hiroshima and Nagasaki finally ended the war.

At home, war production ended the Depression and enhanced employment opportunities for all workers, including women and African Americans. Japanese-Americans, however, spent the war in detention camps.

★ Using Vocabulary

Use each of the following words in a statement about the aggressor nations in World War II, the kind of warfare they conducted, and world response.

fascism	**totalitarian**
appeasement	**holocaust**

★ Reviewing Facts

1. **List** reasons for isolationist polices in the United States and appeasement in Europe.
2. **State** the reasons for Japan's territorial ambitions in Asia.
3. **Chronicle** the steps by which the United States progressed from neutrality to war.
4. **Discuss** the priorities and sequence of the Allies' military campaigns in World War II.
5. **Explain** the difficulties Roosevelt and Churchill faced in dealing with Chiang Kai-shek, de Gaulle, and Stalin.

6. **Describe** how World War II affected women and minorities in the United Sates.

★ Understanding Concepts

INTERNATIONAL ALLIANCES

1. How did World War II underscore the importance of an organization such as the United Nations?
2. Explain the importance to Hitler of the 1939 nonaggression treaty with the Soviet Union. Why do you suppose the Soviet Union signed it?

MILITARY CONFLICT

3. Analyze Hitler's strategy for war. After his early victories, where did he go wrong?
4. Why did *kamikaze* missions pose such a deadly threat to American forces? What does this strategy suggest about the values and patriotism of the Japanese?

★ Thinking Critically

1. **Evaluating Policy** The need to focus on economic problems at home was one reason that the United States initially avoided involvement in World War II. What subsequent developments suggest that this policy may have been self-defeating?
2. **Linking Past and Present** In 1990 the United Nations Security Council demanded that Iraq withdraw its forces from Kuwait and restore Kuwait's government. Had the United Nations existed in 1935, could it have prevented World War II? Explain your answer.
3. **Analyzing Trends** How did American leadership in creating the United Nations illustrate the dramatic change World War II had made in long-range United States foreign policy?
4. **Understanding Oppression of Minorities** Compare and contrast the actions taken against Japanese-Americans in the United States and Jews in Germany during World War II.

★ Writing About History

DESCRIPTION

Refer to the description of how to write an extended definition in the History Writer's Handbook in the Appendix of this book. Your teacher will give you more specific instructions on the essay's length and the assignment's due date.

Write an extended definition of neutrality. Begin with a formal definition, followed by examples of neutrality as demonstrated by the Neutrality Acts and United States foreign policy in the 1930s. Use comparison and contrast to expand on the definition by showing how later foreign policy began to depart from neutrality as defined.

★ Learning Cooperatively

As a class, create a courtroom with students role-playing a panel of judges, a three-member prosecution team, three defense attorneys, a jury, three defendants, and an audience. Put the following people on trial for crimes against humanity: Adolf Hitler—for beginning World War II and establishing the Nazi death camps; a German military officer—for carrying out orders to execute Jews in a death camp; General Hideki Tojo—for ordering *kamikaze* attacks against Allied forces.

★ Mastering Skills

RECOGNIZING ETHNOCENTRIC STATEMENTS

Some people believe that their own racial, ethnic, or cultural group is superior to any other. This leads them to judge the behavior and attitudes of others on the basis of their own values and standards. Such people believe that if something is right for them, it is also right for everyone else, even though others' values, standards, and culture might be completely different from their own. This attitude is known as *ethnocentrism*. Ethnocentrism may be found to some degree in almost every racial, ethnic, or cultural group.

Adolf Hitler carried ethnocentrism to a horrifying extreme. He believed that Aryans, or Germanic peoples, were a master race. Hitler based these beliefs, in part, on ancient German mythology that had absolutely no basis in facts. In his opinion, the Slavs, Latin peoples, and especially the Jews, were all inferior to Aryans. Hitler felt that if inferior ethnic groups were enslaved or exterminated, the Aryan race could rise to greatness.

Although ethnocentrism is not always as blatant as Hitler's, it is important to be able to detect ethnocentric statements when evaluating information about global issues or events. To recognize ethnocentric statements in written or spoken material, ask these questions:

- What is the writer's or speaker's own cultural, ethnic, or racial group, and about what group is he or she making statements?
- Are there words or phrases in the statements that appear to reflect the writer's or speaker's cultural values, behaviors, or beliefs? Such words or phrases often indicate ethnocentrism.
- Does the writer or speaker feel superior to another group? Statements that judge another group can be ethnocentric.
- Can the information in the statements be proved or verified? If not, the statements may very well be ethnocentric.
- By whose standards are the judgments being made? If they are by the standards of the speaker or writer, chances are that the statements are ethnocentric.

Example Read the following excerpt from *Mein Kampf* and ask the questions that will help you recognize ethnocentric statements.

"[N]ature does not desire the mating of weaker with stronger individuals, even less does she desire that a superior race should mingle their blood with that of an inferior race....[E]very mingling of Aryan blood with that of inferior peoples resulted in the downfall of the cultured people."

(Hitler was German and was making statements about other racial groups. Phrases like downfall of a cultured people *show that Hitler judged other cultures on the basis of his own. Words like* weaker/stronger *and* superior/inferior *evaluate without any proof or verification. Hitler's judgement clearly was based on his belief in the superiority of German culture.)*

Practice Read the following report by General John DeWitt after Japan's attack on Pearl Harbor and apply the guidelines to recognize ethnocentrism.

"The Japanese race is an enemy race, and while many second and third generation Japanese born on United States soil have become 'Americanized,' the racial strains are undiluted. To conclude otherwise is to expect that children born of white parents on Japanese soil...become loyal Japanese subjects, ready to fight and, if necessary, to die for Japan in a war against the nation of their parents."

CHAPTER 30
The Cold War

SETTING THE SCENE

Historical Focus

Within months after the end of World War II, the United States and the Soviet Union entered into a period of intense confrontation and rivalry. American leaders sought to maintain workable links with the Soviets while trying to check communism in Europe. Later this containment policy was applied to China, but it could not prevent the outbreak of war in Korea. At home, Americans sought to adjust to a peacetime economy.

Concepts to Understand

- Why the **political and economic power** of the United States and Soviet Union were set against each other.
- How effective presidential **leadership** resulted in aggressive foreign and domestic policies.

People to Know

Harry S Truman, George Kennan, George C. Marshall, Mao Zedong, Alger Hiss, Joseph McCarthy

Places to Locate

Greece, Turkey, Berlin, Korea

Terms to Identify

communism, "iron curtain," containment, Truman Doctrine, Marshall Plan, satellite nations, guerrilla

Guided Reading

As you read this chapter, seek the answers to the following questions.

1. In what ways did the United States seek to contain the Soviet Union?
2. What effect did the cold war have on Americans at home?

SPANNING THE DECADES

POLITICAL

1945
Harry Truman becomes President on death of Franklin Roosevelt

1946
Winston Churchill makes Iron Curtain speech

1947
Truman Doctrine announced

1944   1946

CULTURAL

1946
Mother Frances Xavier Cabrini is first U.S. citizen to be made a saint by the Roman Catholic Church

1947
Jackie Robinson becomes first African American to play for a major league baseball team

The Subway *by George Tooker, 1950. Egg tempera on composition board. 18½ x 36⅛ inches. Collection of Whitney Museum of America Art. Purchased with funds from the Juliana Force Purchase Awards. 50.23*

1948 Berlin Air lift	1949 NATO created	Communist forces take China	1950 North Korea invades South Korea

1948   **1950**

1948 Largest telescope in the world is dedicated at Mount Palomar Observatory	1950 National Council of Churches of Christ is formed, representing 30 denominations

...It is logical that the United States should do whatever it is able to assist in the return of normal economic health in the world.... Our policy is directed not against any country or doctrine but against hunger, poverty, desperation, and chaos....

—GEORGE C. MARSHALL
Harvard commencement address, 1947

Truman's Policy of Containment

SETTING THE SCENE

...[H]istory will remember my term of office as the years when the cold war began to overshadow our lives. I have had hardly a day in office that has not been dominated by this all-embracing struggle.

—HARRY S TRUMAN
President of the United States, 1945-1953

Section Focus

With the end of World War II, the Allies' goal of defeating Germany and Japan had been attained; its goal of establishing democratic governments throughout Europe, however, proved to be illusive. To Churchill and Truman, democracy meant political and economic systems like those in Great Britain and the United States. Western democracy was unacceptable to Stalin, who began to establish Soviet-style communism in Eastern Europe. The clash of intentions and ideals led to the division of Europe and much of the rest of the world.

Objectives

After studying this section, you should be able to:
• Describe the changes in Eastern Europe after World War II.
• List factors that made communism strong during the postwar period.

L ate in the afternoon of April 12, 1945, Vice President Harry S Truman was called to the White House. There Eleanor Roosevelt met him and said, "Harry, the President is dead." For a moment Truman could not

speak. Then he said, "Is there anything I can do for you?" Mrs. Roosevelt replied, "Is there anything we can do for *you?* For you are the one in trouble now." On the next day the new President told reporters that he felt as though the moon, the stars, and all the planets had fallen on him. He asked them to pray for him.

Harry S Truman seemed ill-prepared for the presidency. After working as a machine politician in Missouri, he had served two terms in the Senate. As Vice President he had met with President Roosevelt only three times since their inauguration in January. Roosevelt had not briefed Truman on major matters of foreign policy or on military strategy.

President Truman's policies from the beginning of his administration showed his determination and the high degree to which he was personally involved in handling both domestic and international affairs. On his desk he kept a sign: "The buck stops here." In times of great crisis, Truman showed an extraordinary capacity for quick, effective, yet restrained action.

East-West Suspicions

In 1945, during the first months of his administration, President Truman concentrated his attention on winning the war against Germany and Japan. Like Roosevelt, he supported the creation of the United Nations as a world peace-keeping organization. But Truman was much more suspicious than Roosevelt had been of the Soviet Union and its dictator, Joseph Stalin.

When the war ended, the alliance between the United States, Great Britain, and the Soviet Union unraveled. While there was a common enemy, Western democracies and Soviet leaders had overlooked their political, economic, and social differences. After the war, suspicions returned. Soviet expansion into Eastern Europe heightened American fears of **communism,** a system in which society as a whole, represented by the Communist party, owns and controls property and the means of production.

As fighting ended, Soviet troops occupied much of Eastern Europe. The Soviet leaders, who had promised free elections in these nations, did not follow through. In Hungary, where free elections were held in November 1945, communist candidates received only 17 percent of the vote. Unwilling to lose control, Stalin later suppressed elections in Hungary and in the other nations of Eastern Europe. Then, under elections supervised by Soviet troops, voters gave 90 percent of the vote to communist candidates in Poland. This pattern was repeated in all Soviet-occupied areas, helping to establish communist governments throughout Eastern Europe. Nations that were held under Soviet domination came to be called **satellite nations.**

To restore the devastated Soviet economy, the Soviets removed whole factories, transportation equipment, and machinery from the satellite nations. Stalin also ordered **purges,** or forced removals, of leaders of satellite nations who were deemed disloyal. Only Marshall Josip Tito (TEE toh) of Yugoslavia, whose troops drove the Germans out during World War II, was able to steer a neutral course between the Soviets and the western democracies.

The leaders of Western Europe and the United States watched with grave concern as the Soviet Union crushed all opposition in the nations of Eastern Europe after 1945. Former prime minister Winston Churchill identified the new threat in a speech in March 1946 at Fulton, Missouri. With President Truman on the platform, Churchill warned:

…[F]rom Stettin on the Baltic to Trieste on the Adriatic, an iron curtain has descended across the continent. Behind that line lie all the capitals of the ancient states of central and eastern Europe.

The phrase "iron curtain" would be used to describe Soviet policy in Europe from 1945 to 1989. The West, said Churchill, must meet this challenge with force, if needed, because the Communists had no respect for weakness. Truman and his advisers agreed that a "get tough" policy was their only choice.

Republicans in both houses of Congress, who opposed Truman on domestic measures, supported his foreign policy to oppose expansion of the Soviet Union. As a result, foreign policy became **bipartisan,** that is, supported by both parties.

The Strength of Communism

Following World War II, the United States began to withdraw troops from Europe, leaving the Soviet army as the most powerful military force in Europe. As a result of the invasion by Germany, the Soviet Union had lost 20 million people and suffered vast devastation of land, property, and industry. Feeling threatened by western powers, the Soviet Union wanted to create a **buffer,** or safety zone, on its western border. Soviet troops stationed there ensured that the nations of Eastern Europe would remain its allies.

The Communists promised to abolish poverty, privilege, and private property. They guaranteed productive work, shelter, education, health care, and a classless society in the new "people's democracies" of war-torn Eastern Europe.

Examining Photographs *Churchill and Truman appear together during Churchill's speech at Fulton, Missouri. What message did Churchill give to the American people?*

The Communists saw the world as divided between forces of progress and forces of oppression. Soviet rhetoric incited revolts in other impoverished nations, as people living in poverty listened eagerly to the Communists' plans. Communists began to organize resistance to governments they considered to be reactionary and imperialist. Sometimes they organized groups of **guerrilla** forces—armed bands that were not a part of a regular military unit—to foment civil war. After 1945, nationalists or antigovernment forces in poorer nations often turned to the Communist party for leadership.

Truman responded with a policy of **containment**—preventing the further spread of communism. This policy, first proposed by George Kennan, the State Department's leading specialist on the Soviet Union, was based on the belief that foreign policy goals of Soviet leaders included conquering other nations—not simply the securing of their own borders. Containment, however, did not win universal support. Indeed, it often caused bitter debate both in Congress and among American citizens.

Some who opposed the policy believed that it was too soft. Angry with the advance of communism, they called for a quick and decisive victory over the Soviet Union. Another view was expressed by Walter Lippmann, a newspaper columnist. Lippmann argued that Soviet troops remained in Eastern Europe to protect the Soviets' western border. He warned that the United States could not contain the Soviet Union everywhere. Such a policy, he said, would require the United States to defend all anticommunist governments—no matter how repressive, or unpopular they might be.

Lippmann published his newspaper columns on containment in a book called *The Cold War.* The title, a term coined by Lippmann to refer to a state of war that did not involve actual bloodshed, came to be used by everyone, including the President, to describe the icy rivalry that existed between the United States and the Soviet Union.

★ Section One Review ★

SUMMARY

The armed conflict that ended with the establishment of peace in 1945 was replaced by a different kind of warfare—the cold war. As Soviet troops established and protected communist governments in Baltic and Balkan states, Stalin dropped an "iron curtain" over Eastern Europe to exclude influences of capitalism and democracy. Truman responded with a containment policy that became a source of debate in the United States.

CHECKING FOR UNDERSTANDING

1. **Identify** cold war, George Kennan
2. **Define** communism, satellite nations, purges, bipartisan, buffer, guerrilla, containment
3. **Explain** the threat perceived by the Soviet Union and its response in Eastern Europe.
4. **Describe** the groups that supported communism and the basis of its appeal in the world.

THINKING CRITICALLY

5. **Arguing a Position** State whether you agree or disagree with Walter Lippmann's warnings about the containment policy as a post-war strategy, and then support your opinion.

LINKING PAST AND PRESENT

6. **Drawing Inferences** In 1945 Stalin dropped an iron curtain over Eastern Europe and established communism to assure distribution of wealth and a workers' society. In 1990 the peoples of Eastern Europe revolted against their communist governments and lifted the iron curtain. They demanded capitalist economies and democratic governments. What does this change suggest about the progress of these nations under communism?

Map and Graph Skills

Hypothesizing

A friend walks up and hands you a map, then leaves without saying anything. Your only explanation for her behavior is that perhaps she wants you to take a trip. Later she asks if you would like to visit any of the places on the map during the summer. In this case, it seems your explanation was right.

Explanation

Hypothesizing is the process of forming a tentative explanation based on available evidence. A hypothesis offers a possible answer to a problem, or an explanation for why a situation or condition exists. In the example, thinking that a friend wants you to take a trip is your hypothesis to explain why she handed you a map.

A hypothesis cannot be judged right or wrong until it is confirmed or disproved by additional evidence. In this case, your friend's later remark provided evidence to confirm your hypothesis.

In studying history, you can hypothesize on information taken from any number of sources: writing, photographs, maps, and graphs. The following guidelines will help you form hypotheses from historical maps:

a. Determine the situation that the map is showing, and write it as a statement.

b. Form some possible hypotheses that may explain the statement you have written.

c. Gather additional evidence about the situation, and test each hypothesis.

d. Accept or reject each hypothesis as an explanation for the situation.

Example

Look at the historical map below showing the Allied occupation of Berlin, and note how the above guidelines have been applied.

THE OCCUPATION OF BERLIN

a. State the situation shown.
- Berlin was divided and occupied by the Allies. The Soviets occupied East Berlin. West Berlin was divided into French, British, and American sectors.
  (*This is a statement of the situation based on a reading of the map.*)

b. Form hypotheses to explain the statement.
- Berlin was divided because the Allies wanted to keep the city for themselves.
  (*This is one hypothesis that might explain the statement.*)
- Berlin was divided among the Allies because the western nations did not want the Soviets to have control of it.
  (*This is another hypothesis.*)
- Berlin was divided so that its citizens would have self-government.
  (*A third hypothesis.*)
- Berlin was divided because the western Allies feared Soviet intentions in Europe.
  (*Yet another hypothesis.*)

c. Gather additional evidence to test the above hypotheses.
- Research additional information in this chapter, other textbooks, encyclopedias, and other sources.

d. Accept or reject each hypothesis based on the evidence gathered.
- The information from reading Chapter 30 and from additional research might indicate that the second hypothesis best explains the statement of the situation.

Practice

For further practice in hypothesizing, apply the above guidelines to the map of the election of 1948 on page 906.

The Cold War Begins in Europe

SETTING THE SCENE

...[T]he United States...must continue to regard the Soviet Union as a rival ...in the political arena.... It must continue to expect [that] Soviet policies will reflect... pressure toward the disruption and weakening of all rival influence and rival power.

—GEORGE F. KENNAN
Specialist on Soviet Affairs, 1947

Section Focus

To implement the policy of containment, the Truman administration provided massive economic aid to war-torn Western Europe, joining with these countries in the first peacetime alliance in United States history. In so doing, the United States shouldered a heavy economic and military commitment.

Objectives

After studying this section, you should be able to:
* Outline the foreign policy goals of the Truman administration.
* Explain how the United States became a world power after World War II.

T he cold war was like no other struggle that had ever engaged the United States. It required a constant state of military preparedness; it called for military support for countries believed to be in danger of a communist takeover. It had other economic costs, as both the United States and the Soviet Union tried to "buy" allies with gifts ranging from food to steel mills.

Aid to Europe

The policy of containment began in Europe. Great Britain, in financial trouble, was forced to notify United States officials early in 1947 that it would withdraw its soldiers from Greece and end aid to Turkey. United States diplomats in Greece warned that this could lead to a communist takeover. Already, they said, Soviet-supported guerrillas were controlling much of the country. It was feared that if Greece fell to the Communists, Turkey would be next.

President Truman decided that the United States must act. In March 1947 he told Congress that if the United States was not willing to give aid to Greece and Turkey to contain communism, democratic governments everywhere would be threatened. Truman's warning that the nation faced a crisis was clear:

*I believe that it must be the policy of the United States to support free peoples who are resisting attempted subjugation by armed minorities or outside pressures....
If we falter in our leadership, we may endanger the peace of the world—and we shall surely endanger the welfare of our own nation.*

Truman's policy, which became known as the Truman Doctrine, proposed that the United States provide military and economic support to Greece and Turkey. Immediately approved by Congress, the Truman Doctrine superseded the Monroe Doctrine, shifting the United States away

EUROPE AFTER WORLD WAR II

Zones of occupation

- British
- French
- American
- Russian
- Air corridors
- Iron Curtain
- Jointly occupied cities

Examining Maps *After being invaded twice in less than 30 years, the Soviets especially feared future German power. Thus after World War II the Allies agreed to divide and occupy Germany. What other nation was divided after the war?*

from peacetime isolationism toward assuming world responsibility.

Soon after the Truman Doctrine went into effect, the administration proposed a plan for economic aid to Europe. The situation in Europe was desperate in 1947. There were shortages of food, fuel, and raw materials, and European nations needed money to rebuild industries and transportation systems. The Truman administration realized that economic deprivation in France, Italy, and other Western European countries might lead to the election of communist governments. The nation's leaders were also concerned that Europe's faltering economy would affect United States markets and trigger a recession, at home.

In June 1947, Secretary of State George C. Marshall went beyond the Truman Doctrine to propose a massive recovery plan for European nations. Under the Marshall Plan, American aid in the form of money, supplies, and machinery would help to end Europe's "hunger, poverty, desperation, and chaos." The United States offered the Marshall Plan to all nations in Europe—including the Soviet Union. Believing that the plan would promote the interests of United States capitalism, the Soviets and Eastern European communist nations turned it down.

The nations of Western Europe, on the other hand, welcomed the offer. Drawing up detailed plans for restoring production and controlling inflation, they also agreed to change trade laws—tariffs and quotas that blocked the flow of commerce.

The Marshall Plan was an enormous success. During the Truman years, the United States gave more than $13 billion in loans and grants to the nations of

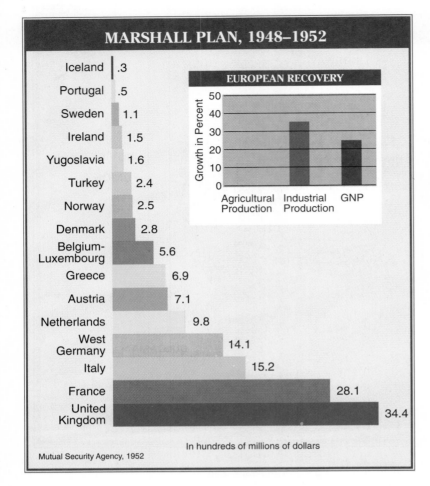

MARSHALL PLAN, 1948–1952

Country	Amount
Iceland	.3
Portugal	.5
Sweden	1.1
Ireland	1.5
Yugoslavia	1.6
Turkey	2.4
Norway	2.5
Denmark	2.8
Belgium-Luxembourg	5.6
Greece	6.9
Austria	7.1
Netherlands	9.8
West Germany	14.1
Italy	15.2
France	28.1
United Kingdom	34.4

In hundreds of millions of dollars

Mutual Security Agency, 1952

EUROPEAN RECOVERY

Growth in Percent (Agricultural Production, Industrial Production, GNP)

Examining Graphs
The Marshall Plan speeded the recovery of Western Europe. Why did no Eastern European nations receive aid?

Western Europe. To administer aid effectively, the 16 Western European nations formed the Organization for European Economic Cooperation. This organization marked the first step toward European economic unity.

The Berlin Airlift

At the end of the war, the Allies had decided on a joint occupation of Germany. The United States, Great Britain, France, and the Soviet Union each controlled a zone, or section, of Germany. They also each controlled a section of the capital city of Berlin, deep within the Soviet-controlled zone.

Failing to reach agreement with the Soviet Union, the Western powers in May 1949 announced plans to join their 3 sections of Germany to form an independent nation. The Soviet Union responded by closing off all traffic from West Germany

to Berlin. They thought that this move would force the West to back down from its control of West Berlin. President Truman saw this action as a test of Western determination. Instead of sending troops through the land corridor to Berlin and risking war, Truman ordered a massive "airlift" to supply Berlin's 2 million people. Night and day for more than 10 months, British and United States cargo planes carried food, medicine, clothing, raw materials, and even coal to Berlin. In May 1949, the Soviet Union finally lifted its blockade. Truman said:

When we refused to be forced out of Berlin, we demonstrated to the people of Europe that with their cooperation we would act, and act resolutely, when their freedom was threatened.

North Atlantic Treaty Organization

Believing that rebuilding their economies without rebuilding their military strength might invite Soviet aggression, five Western European states formed an alliance in March 1948. They then appealed to the United States, the world's only atomic power, to join their alliance.

Examining Photographs *Berlin children watch the airlift to the city. Why was the Berlin airlift necessary?*

alliance. With Senate approval, Truman immediately began talks to create a North Atlantic Treaty Organization (NATO), which formed in April 1949.

NATO linked into a military alliance the United States, Great Britain, Canada, Belgium, Italy, France, the Netherlands, Luxembourg, Iceland, Denmark, Norway, and Portugal. Shortly afterwards, Greece, Turkey, and West Germany also joined. NATO was based on the principle of **collective security,** an agreement by which "an armed attack against one or more of them in Europe or North America shall be considered an attack against all of them."

All the members of NATO agreed to increase their military strength. The United States provided most of the money, weapons, and troops, and was given the right to appoint the commander of NATO's forces. Truman appointed General Dwight D. Eisenhower, who exercised sole authority over the atomic weapons that the United States committed to the defense of NATO. The West relied on the atomic threat, since NATO had only 12 military divisions in Europe compared to 25 well-armed Soviet divisions.

In the midst of the Senate debate on how much military aid to supply NATO, Truman made an announcement that shocked and frightened the nation: In September 1949, the Soviet Union had exploded its first atomic bomb. Much sooner than military experts had expected, the United States had lost its nuclear monopoly. Faced with this new threat, Congress quickly passed the NATO appropriations bill. In 1955, the Soviet Union and the satellite countries of Eastern Europe countered NATO by establishing their own military alliance—the Warsaw Pact. The arms race had begun.

Within a few years, both the United States and the Soviet Union developed a new and more powerful weapon—the hydrogen bomb. Later, other nations, including Great Britain, France, and China also built nuclear weapons. Aboveground testing of these weapons continued during the next decade, spreading harmful radioactive fallout. The first nuclear test-ban treaty, banning aboveground testing of nuclear weapons, was finally signed in 1963.

SUMMARY

From 1945 to 1948, the United States proved an invaluable ally to Western European countries. The Truman Doctrine showed that Americans had no inclination to return to their traditional peacetime isolation. The United States initiated and provided the means to implement the Marshall Plan for European economic recovery; supported NATO, a military alliance to check communism in Western Europe; and staged the Berlin airlift to provide food, clothing, and medical supplies when the Soviets blockaded that divided city. The Soviet Union and its satellites in Eastern Europe countered with the Warsaw Pact. In addition, after 1949 the Soviet Union had the capability to produce and use atomic weapons.

CHECKING FOR UNDERSTANDING

1. **Identify** Truman Doctrine, George Marshall, Marshall Plan, NATO, Berlin airlift

2. **Summarize** the Truman administration's major foreign policy goals.

3. **Explain** the events and policies that established the United States as a world leader following World War II.

4. **Describe** the main provisions of the Marshall Plan.

THINKING CRITICALLY

5. **Analyzing Policies** How did exercising the Truman Doctrine in Greece nullify the Monroe Doctrine of 1823?

CONNECTIONS: HISTORY AND TECHNOLOGY

6. **Assessing Technological Impact** How did developments in nuclear technology shift the balance of power and influence foreign policy goals and strategies?

★ ★ ★ ★ ★ ★ ★ ★ ★ ★ ★ ★ ★ ★ ★ ★ ★ ★

SECTION THREE

The Cold War in Asia

SETTING THE SCENE

To the Pacific basin has come the vista of a new emancipated world.... Today, in Asia as well as in Europe, unshackled peoples are tasting the full sweetness of liberty....

—DOUGLAS MACARTHUR
U.S. Army general, as Japan signed surrender, September, 1945

Section Focus

In Asia the end of World War II brought peace only to the people of Japan. Under United States occupation, the Japanese renounced militarism, disbanded their army, democratized their society, and embarked on a program of economic development that brought them unprecedented prosperity. In contrast, the rest of Asia was caught up in the cold war. As tensions grew, the cold war escalated into a hot war with bloodshed and the dislocation of people.

Objectives

After studying this section, you should be able to:
• Cite the outcome of the United States occupation of Japan.
• Explain the political situation in China after the war.
• Explain why the United Nations waged a limited war in Korea.

A‌t the close of World War II, the aims of the United States in Asia were to restore peace, help Asian peoples to resist foreign rule, and restore Asian trade with the world. The United States felt it had a special commitment to the Philippines, Japan, and China. In the first two countries, American policies were largely successful. In the last, they suffered a severe defeat.

On July 4, 1946, the United States carried out its promise of independence for the Philippines. In return for special business rights and the lease of military bases, the United States gave the Philippine nation tariff concessions in American markets and $600 million to repair war damage. Later, when communist-led guerrilla groups revolted against the government, the United States sent money and weapons to put down the rebellion. Despite difficult economic and political problems, the Philippines made the transition from a colony to an independent democratic nation.

The Occupation of Japan

In July 1945, shortly before the United States dropped atomic bombs on Hiroshima and Nagasaki, the leaders of Great Britain, the United States, and the Soviet

Examining Photographs *Japan's Emperor visits General MacArthur, who had almost total authority over that occupied nation. What changes did MacArthur bring to Japan?*

Union met in Potsdam, outside Berlin. There they discussed how they would deal with Germany and Japan after the war ended.

The agreement regarding Japan provided that Japanese militarists should be punished and Japan disarmed, Japanese rule should be restricted to their home islands, and the Japanese should be reeducated so that a democratic Japanese nation could be formed. American troops would occupy Japan until these aims were accomplished. To carry out this Potsdam Declaration, General Douglas MacArthur was named Supreme Commander of the Allied Powers.

Under MacArthur's leadership, Japan's military was dismantled. A few militarists were tried and convicted of war crimes and hanged. Under American direction, a new constitution provided for elected representative government and women's suffrage. Most other aspects of Japanese culture remained intact. The emperor remained as a symbol of Japan's unity, but he was no longer to be looked upon as a god.

MacArthur encouraged economic opportunity and trade unionism, and he attempted to redistribute large rural tracts to landless Japanese. A reorganized school system taught democratic values. At first, the Allies had planned to make Japan pay reparations for war damages, but MacArthur realized that the Japanese lacked the resources to pay such compensation. Instead, Japan received nearly $2 billion in aid from the United States. The Japanese people accepted the new reforms. In a treaty signed in San Francisco in 1951, the country gained back its independence. Japan achieved a remarkable recovery, establishing itself as the leading economy of Asia.

Communist Triumph in China

Japan's surrender left China a divided nation. The Communists under Mao Zedong [MOW dzuh DOONG] controlled the north, the Nationalists led by Chiang Kai-shek held the southwest, and Japanese armies occupied the center. The United States helped the Nationalist armies of Chiang Kai-shek take back the land the Japanese had held. In planning for the peace, President Roosevelt had insisted to Churchill and Stalin that China be treated as a great power. As a result, China gained a permanent seat on the UN Security Council.

Since the early 1930s, a civil war between the nationalist government and the Communists had ravaged China. During World War II, both sides stopped fighting one another and fought the Japanese. In the war against Japan, Mao's Communists grew to be a strong guerrilla force. Through his promise of land reform, as well as military and political pressure, Mao's forces were able to extend their control over much of mainland China. The civil war of the 1930s had greatly weakened the Nationalists, and the Japanese controlled most of the cities that had been centers of nationalist support.

After Japan surrendered, the conflict between the Communists and the Nationalists again flared. To prevent the extension of communist power, Truman sent General George C. Marshall to China. Marshall was unsuccessful. As the Communists gained strength, Chiang asked Truman to send military aid. Marshall, now secretary of state, advised that it was more important to spend the limited

Linking Across Time

LEAVING THE PHILIPPINES

The United States long maintained bases in the Philippines. Late in 1990, at the request of the Philippine government, the United States agreed to remove its fighter aircraft from Clark Air Force Base by September 1991, and to close its other 3 air bases within 10 to 12 years. The Philippine government made its request on the grounds that U.S. military presence violated their national sovereignty. The agreement was cordial, and ties between the two nations remain strong.

Examining Photographs
Mao Zedong led communist forces in China's civil war. What was the United States policy toward China?

foreign aid resources of the United States on saving Western Europe from Stalin rather than on saving China from Mao. In addition, a fact-finder Truman sent to China reported no attempt to save it from the Communists could succeed because:

The only basis on which national Chinese resistance to Soviet aims can be revitalized is through the presently corrupt, reactionary and inefficient Chinese National government.

DOUGLAS MACARTHUR
1880-1964

Douglas MacArthur was born into a military family. His father won the Congressional Medal of Honor during the Civil War and later became the Army's top general. Following in his father's footsteps, MacArthur saw action during World War I and was twice wounded. By 1918 he had risen to the rank of general. When Japan attacked Pearl Harbor, MacArthur was stationed in the Philippines, where he led its defense. Ordered to retreat in 1942, he pledged: "I shall return." He kept his promise in 1944 by leading the liberation of the islands. After the war, as commander of occupation forces in Japan, he wrote its constitution. From July 1950 until Truman fired him in April 1951, MacArthur commanded UN forces in Korea. Some Republicans urged MacArthur to run for President, but he declined and retired.

Having already given Chiang's forces $2 billion in aid, the State Department judged that further help would not save the Nationalists from their own internal weaknesses. By the end of 1949 Mao Zedong's forces had forced Chiang's army off the mainland to Taiwan and a few other small islands.

Truman's China policy came under bitter political attack. American supporters of the Nationalists accused Truman of "writing off" Chiang and losing China to the Communists. Truman believed, however, that most Americans would not support the massive military intervention needed to save Chiang's government.

The United States recognized the nationalist government in Taiwan as the government of all of China and blocked attempts by Mao's government to gain a seat in the United Nations. To protest the exclusion of the Chinese communist government, the Soviet Union walked out of the United Nations Security Council and boycotted its proceedings. This action was to have a major impact on events in Korea.

War in Korea

The allied powers had promised Korea "freedom and independence" at the Cairo conference in 1943. When the Japanese surrendered, Soviet troops, who had only recently entered the war in the Pacific, occupied Korea north of the 38th parallel. Aided by Korean Communists, they set up a communist government. As with other Soviet satellite states, North Korea sealed itself from the outside world. A 1948 UN fact-finding commission was not allowed to travel north of the 38th parallel.

In the South the United States supported the government of Syngman Rhee (SING mehn REE) who was chosen in United Nations supervised elections. In 1948 the UN recognized the South Korean Republic as the lawful government of all Korea.

United States military and diplomatic experts advised that Korea should be viewed as outside the "defense perimeter" of the United States because of the great cost of defending it. The next year the

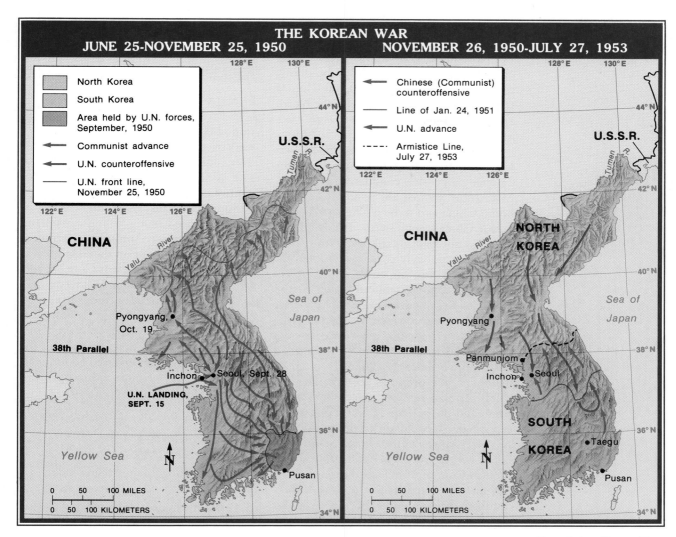

THE KOREAN WAR

JUNE 25–NOVEMBER 25, 1950

Legend:
- North Korea
- South Korea
- Area held by U.N. forces, September, 1950
- ← Communist advance
- ← U.N. counteroffensive
- — U.N. front line, November 25, 1950

CHINA · U.S.S.R. · Yalu River · Tumen R. · Sea of Japan · Pyongyang, Oct. 19 · 38th Parallel · Inchon · Seoul, Sept. 28 · U.N. LANDING, SEPT. 15 · Yellow Sea · Pusan

NOVEMBER 26, 1950–JULY 27, 1953

Legend:
- ← Chinese (Communist) counteroffensive
- — Line of Jan. 24, 1951
- ← U.N. advance
- --- Armistice Line, July 27, 1953

CHINA · U.S.S.R. · NORTH KOREA · Yalu River · Tumen R. · Sea of Japan · Pyongyang · 38th Parallel · Panmunjom · Inchon · Seoul · SOUTH KOREA · Taegu · Yellow Sea · Pusan

United States withdrew most of its troops from Korea. This move proved to be an invitation to communist aggression.

On June 25, 1950, North Korean troops invaded South Korea. Poorly armed, the South Koreans were no match for the North. The Truman administration was not sure whether North Korea was acting by itself or as the agent of the Soviet Union or China. The invasion, however, became a vital test for the UN. Calling an emergency meeting of the Security Council, the United States won a 9-to-0 vote to order North Korea to withdraw its troops. The Soviet Union, boycotting the UN because of its refusal to admit communist China, was not present for the vote. On June 27, 1950, as the invasion continued, the Security Council called on all UN members to aid South Korea.

President Truman quickly appointed General MacArthur to command all UN troops in Korea and instructed him to limit the fighting to South Korean territory below the 38th parallel. Truman also ordered United States military forces to Korea without asking Congress to declare war, claiming he was acting under his authority as commander in chief and under the United Nations Charter.

During the summer of 1950, North Korean troops pressed UN forces down the Korean peninsula until they had their backs to the water at Pusan (poo SAHN), a major port in South Korea. In the fall, however, General MacArthur planned a surprise landing midway up the peninsula at the South Korean port of Inchon. This landing gave the UN troops the offensive, and MacArthur was given authority by

Examining Maps *For three years UN troops and communist forces battled up and down the Korean peninsula. Which nation led the fight to protect South Korea?*

the UN Security Council to liberate North Korea and unite it with the South. By November, UN troops were as far north as the Yalu River Valley, bordering communist China, when 200,000 Chinese troops crossed the border to aid the North Koreans. MacArthur's troops were once again pushed back.

A major disagreement developed between General MacArthur and President Truman over the conduct of the war. MacArthur wanted the United States to bomb China and to help Chiang Kai-shek invade China from Taiwan. Truman, however, did not want to risk war with China. MacArthur publicly criticized Truman for limiting the war effort. In April 1951, Joseph Martin, Republican leader of the House of Representatives, released a letter he had received in which MacArthur criticized the President's reluctance to use Chiang Kai-shek's army in Korea and to bomb supply lines in China. In order to maintain authority as commander in chief, Truman removed MacArthur from command of the United States forces. He explained, "I could do nothing else and still be President of the United States."

The Senate Foreign Relations and Armed Services Committee opened hearings to determine the circumstances of MacArthur's dismissal. Two months of interrogations dispelled much of the controversy. Truman's decision emerged as acceptable to the country. The debate produced a more determined opposition to communist China, and American ships were sent to defend Taiwan. The United States continued to oppose communist China's admission to the United Nations.

Years of fighting had produced a stalemate in Korea. Presidential candidate Dwight Eisenhower in 1952 pledged to "go to Korea," to settle hostilities. The war continued until 1953, when a ceasefire was declared. Korea was left a divided country, much as it had been before the war began. The Korean struggle was costly for the United States, which lost more than 54,000 troops. But as a result, many neutral nations drew closer to the United States, and noncommunist ones began to arm for their own defense.

Section Three Review

SUMMARY

In East Asia, successful U.S. reconstruction policies in Japan and the Philippines were overshadowed by defeats in China. Truman decided it was more important to save Western Europe from Stalin than to continue support for Chiang Kai-shek's corrupt Nationalist government. Mao Zedong drove Chiang from the mainland and established a communist government. Chiang's government on the island of Taiwan continued to represent China in the United Nations, however. Following the withdrawal of American troops from South Korea, North Korean Communists invaded the South in an attempt to annex it. Under United Nations resolutions, the United States troops engaged communist forces in order to maintain South Korea's independence.

CHECKING FOR UNDERSTANDING

1. **Identify** Chiang Kai-shek, Mao Zedong, Douglas MacArthur

2. **Describe** how United States' policies toward Japan led to its recovery.

3. **Explain** why the United States' China policy failed.

4. **Summarize** the events that led to the Korean War.

5. **Restate** Truman's reasons for relieving MacArthur of his command.

THINKING CRITICALLY

6. **Choosing a Position** Explain the two positions represented by Truman and MacArthur in the debate over the Korean War. Which position would you have chosen? Justify your answer.

GLOBAL PERSPECTIVES

7. **Making Comparisons** Compare Mao's tactics in China with Stalin's actions in Eastern Europe during the same period. What was the common basis for their appeal?

Cold War America

SETTING THE SCENE

> *I think small business, the small farmer, the small corporation are the backbone of any free society, and when there are too many people on relief and too many people at the top who control the wealth of the country, then we must look out.*
>
> —HARRY S TRUMAN
> December 18, 1948

Section Focus

Life in cold-war America was marked by a search for security. Blacks and women sought to keep the gains they had made during the war, and many Americans struggled to maintain their standard of living in the face of postwar inflation. For some, security meant exposing the subversives they suspected were operating in society and at high levels of their government. In the face of mounting opposition, Truman attempted to pursue policies that addressed these concerns.

Objectives

After studying this section, you should be able to:
- Explain changes in the American labor force after the war.
- Describe the condition of African Americans during the 1940s.
- Evaluate the Truman presidency.

W orld War II brought great changes to the nation's economy. War industries solved the unemployment problem of the depression. In fact, with 16 million in the United States armed services, there was actually a shortage of workers in industry. The number of black workers in defense industries more than tripled. Six million women joined the labor force, a rise of nearly 60 percent. When the war ended in 1945, people were fearful of depression. In the past, when government spending for war materials stopped and soldiers returned home to look for jobs, unemployment spread. Even if the factories kept running, some newly hired black and women workers now feared that they would be replaced by returning soldiers.

Prosperity Continues

Fears of a depression proved groundless. After a slight drop in business activity, the number of Americans with jobs actually increased. Several factors contributed to the continuing prosperity. As the United States kept feeding not only its own people but millions of people overseas, farm income remained high. During the war, Americans, due to rationing and scarcity of consumer goods, had saved $30 billion. Now they spent their savings for postponed purchases. In addition, Congress stimulated postwar business by cutting wartime taxes nearly $6 billion. Instead of depression, consumer demand stimulated a sharp rise in prices, or inflation. Defense spending, which had dropped to $15 billion by 1949, escalated to $50 billion by 1953, pouring even more money into the economy. In addition, the Marshall Plan restored markets in Europe for American goods.

In some ways, the cold war economy of the 1950s resembled the wartime economy of the 1940s. The government's military spending continued to stimulate industrial production, while a portion of the labor force continued in military service.

Immediately following World War II, soldiers returning from service took the places of many women who were employed in factories. In the automobile plants the proportion of women on assembly lines dropped from 25 percent in 1944 to 7.5 percent in 1946. The head of the Women's Bureau, a federal agency set up to protect women's interests, stated that "women ought to be delighted to give up any job and return to their proper sphere in the kitchen." Federal and state aid to child-care centers in factories was stopped.

Yet, women did not entirely disappear from the work force. Continued prosperity created new job opportunities. By 1952 more than two million more women were employed than were employed in 1946. The kinds of work available to women were changing. This change was dramatically reflected in the experience of black women. Between 1940 and 1950 the percentage of black women employed as domestic servants dropped from 72 to 48 percent. The number of those working as farm laborers fell from 20 to 7 percent. At the same time, the percentage hired by factories rose from 7 to 18 percent.

The rise in female employment did not mean that women had gained economic equality, however. Women in industries earned less than two-thirds as much as men. They were limited in job assignments. During the 1940s the number of women in well-paid supervisory and professional positions actually declined. Only a very few women were accepted into professional schools where they could study law or medicine.

Gains for Blacks

As a group, African Americans benefited from the postwar economic boom. Many made the transition from farming to manufacturing, from rural areas to cities, from the South to other regions of the country. The number of black workers in white-collar, skilled, and supervisory jobs nearly tripled, increasing from about 300,000 to nearly 900,000. As opportunities for black Americans opened up fields such as law, nursing, and professional sports, average income of blacks—even adjusted for inflation—almost doubled.

Changing social attitudes of both whites and blacks helped these advances. The war against Germany and the cold war both played a part. The horrifying racism of the Nazis helped to make some Americans more sensitive to racism in their own country. They began to realize that not only African Americans, but also Asian Americans and Hispanic Americans had been treated unfairly and denied opportunity.

During this period, black Americans worked hard to gain civil rights. During the war, the membership of the National Association for the Advancement of Colored People (NAACP) rose from 100,000 to 351,000. The NAACP hired teams of able lawyers to bring a series of lawsuits to the federal courts to end violations of the constitutional rights of black citizens. Like women, however, black Americans fell short of gaining full equality in the 1940s.

In the North blacks often lived in crowded inner-city areas. African-American

---

Life of the Times

VETERANS RETURN

After World War II, thousands of military personnel came home. They poured off the troop ships and into the arms of families, wives, and girlfriends. When the celebrating was over, however, these former soldiers faced the task of rebuilding their lives and returning to their jobs or education.

As the nation adjusted to a peacetime economy, there was turmoil in the job market. Thousands of veterans hunted for jobs while wartime industries changed to peacetime production.

Many veterans decided to take advantage of the Servicemen's Readjustment Act of 1944. More popularly known as the G.I. Bill of Rights, this legislation assisted veterans in finding employment, education, and medical care. Many who went to college on G.I. Bill assistance were married men with young families. At most colleges and universities, housing was not sufficient for this increased enrollment. For some veterans the answer was a small mobile home or house trailer. During the late 1940s and early 1950s, many campuses included large trailer parks where "GIs" and their families lived. Lasting relationships developed from the strong sense of community in these parks, helping veterans adjust to civilian life.

Connections

BLACK MIGRATION

Black migration from the rural South to northern and western cities between 1910 and 1950 was one of the largest migrations in American history. African Americans migrated in search of greater economic opportunity and a better life, than the drought, boll weevils, racism,

A family moving north in the 1940s

and poverty they were accustomed to in the South. Much of the black migration took place during the two world wars.

During World War I, industrial agents traveled the South promising jobs with high wages and free transportation north. Soon the black population of cities such as Chicago, Cleveland, and Detroit swelled. Detroit alone saw an increase of over 600 percent.

In the 1940s rural southern blacks streamed into northern and western cities for two main reasons. First, around 1940 cotton farming became mechanized, far fewer workers were needed, and many blacks became jobless. Second, many saw great opportunity in wartime industries.

Although blacks' social and economic gains in the cities were limited by racial prejudice, they acquired a political voice. Their migration forever changed the face of American politics and society.

★ ★ ★ ★ ★ ★ ★ ★ ★ ★

MAKING THE GEOGRAPHY CONNECTION

1. Where did blacks migrate to from 1910 to 1950?

2. Why did they migrate from the rural South?

LINKING PAST AND PRESENT

3. Where did many people migrate to in the 1970s and 1980s?

★ ★ ★ ★ ★ ★ ★ ★ ★ ★

---

wages averaged about 60 percent of those paid to white workers. Black workers were still likely to be "last hired, first fired." In the South old patterns of segregation and racism remained. Black southerners resented that their children had to attend separate schools that were often ill-equipped and understaffed. They objected to Jim Crow laws that forced them to use segregated facilities. Even worse, most black southerners were denied the vote, either by custom or by law. Almost none held political office.

Inflation in the Postwar Years

Government spending on wartime military programs and for postwar domestic programs brought prosperity and inflation. During periods of inflation the amount of money in circulation increases and prices rise sharply as the demand for

goods exceeds the supply.

Because increased taxes were not sufficient to pay the costs of war, the federal government ran a large deficit during World War II. The national debt rose from $50 million to nearly $270 billion. The government borrowed much of this money from Federal Reserve Banks. Using the federal bonds that the government gave as security, the banks issued new money. As a result, there was four times as much money in circulation in 1945 as there was in 1938.

As inflation drove prices up, the purchasing power of paychecks decreased. When consumers could not buy as much, factories slowed production returning to a 40-hour week and employers stopped paying overtime. Workers, losing purchasing power, demanded pay raises and often went on strike. In 1946 there were nearly 5,000 strikes, in which nearly 4.6 million workers took part—a record that is unlikely to be surpassed. Some strikes hit industries basic to the national economy such as steel, transportation, and coal. When railroad workers went on strike, President Truman asked Congress for power to draft them into the army. Fortunately, however, the strike ended before this measure was necessary.

The Taft-Hartley Act

Union activities were a major issue in the congressional elections of 1946. The anxiety caused by the strikes in basic industries helped conservative anti-labor candidates. The Republicans showed new vigor as they ran on the slogan, "Had enough?" For the first time in 18 years, they gained control of both the Senate and the House.

An immediate result of this swing toward conservatism was the Taft-Hartley Act, passed over President Truman's veto in 1947. Intended to keep unions from abusing their power, the act outlawed practices such as the closed shop, which forced business owners to hire only union members; **jurisdictional strikes**, which forced businesses to recognize one union instead of another; **featherbedding**, which limited workers' output in order to create more jobs; and high fees charged to workers for joining a union. In addition,

unions were forbidden to use their money to support political campaigns.

The Taft-Hartley Act was a very controversial measure. Its supporters claimed the law held irresponsible unions in check the way the Wagner Act of 1935 restrained antiunion activities of employers. Labor leaders called the act a "slave labor" law. They claimed it erased many of the gains that unions had made since 1933. In addition, they deeply resented that union leaders had to swear they were not members of the Communist party.

Election of 1948

As the presidential election of 1948 drew near, the Democratic party was divided. Southern Democrats objected to Truman's civil-rights program, which included proposals to end racial, religious, and ethnic discrimination, to abolish immigration quotas, and to integrate the armed forces. Many white southerners left the Democratic party to form the "Dixiecrat" Party, which nominated South Carolina Governor Strom Thurmond for President. Other Democrats thought Truman was taking too hard a line against the Soviet Union. They supported the Progressive party ticket led by former Vice President Henry Wallace. Truman appeared certain to lose the election; he had lost the support of both the right wing and the left wing of his party. The Democrats renominated Truman only after party leaders failed to persuade General Eisenhower to accept the nomination.

The Republicans united behind their candidate for President, Governor Thomas E. Dewey of New York. Dewey was so confident that he would win that he avoided discussing issues and simply called on Americans to join him in building unity.

Far behind in the public-opinion polls, President Truman pursued an aggressive campaign. First, he called the Republican Congress back into special session and asked them to carry out the promises of the Republican party platform by passing civil rights and other progressive legislation. When they failed to act, Truman had his campaign theme: The "do-nothing, good

Examining Maps *The Democratic party split in 1948. Why did the Dixiecrat candidate take support from Truman in the South?*

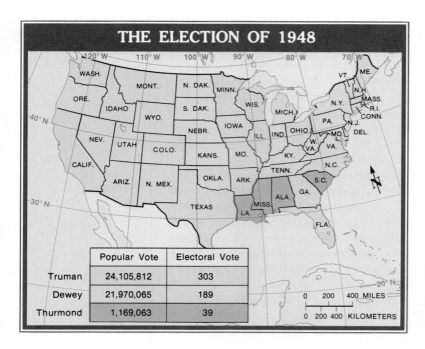

THE ELECTION OF 1948

	Popular Vote	Electoral Vote
Truman	24,105,812	303
Dewey	21,970,065	189
Thurmond	1,169,063	39

for nothing" Republican 80th Congress. Setting out on a "whistle stop" tour of the country by train, Truman covered 30,000 miles, giving some 350 speeches along the way.

Right up to Election Day, the pollsters predicted a Republican victory. But Truman won 2 million more votes than Dewey and piled up a 303 to 189 margin in the Electoral College. Truman had held together the New Deal coalition. He won labor support for his veto of the Taft-Hartley Act. He won support from black voters for his civil-rights proposals. He won the farmers' vote for his support of high-farm price supports. Not only did Truman defeat Dewey, but the Democrats regained their majority in Congress.

In his inaugural address in January 1949, Truman called for a Fair Deal, a return to and expansion of New Deal policies. The President asked for slum clearance, federal subsidies for public schools, government-backed medical insurance, aid to farmers, and higher minimum wages. Although the Democrats held a majority, the new Congress was still influenced by an alliance of Republicans and conservative southern Democrats. Together they blocked most of Truman's proposals.

In 1949 postwar prosperity slipped into a recession. Unemployment reached 7 percent of the labor force. But the recession lasted only a few months. A tax cut, passed in 1948, took effect making more money available. The New Deal's built-in stabilizers such as farm price supports and social security benefits helped to lessen the effect of the downturn. Beginning in 1950, the Korean War changed the economic picture sharply. Rearmament now competed with the demand for consumer goods. The war also fueled anticommunist sentiment at home.

Fear of Communists

The cold war and the Korean War heightened fear of communism in the United States. A communist spy ring, which had been sending atomic secrets to the Soviet Union, was uncovered in Canada. To Americans, this explained the

Soviets' success in developing an atomic bomb so early. Americans began to suspect that there might be other communist sympathizers and spies in the government, universities, press, and the arts—all working to undermine American democracy. In a period of international tensions, national insecurity led to a search for scapegoats.

The question arose: Should the rights of Communists be protected by the Constitution? In 1949, 11 members of the Communist party in the United States were convicted of conspiracy. The courts held that since the Communist party was organized to overthrow the United States government by force, its members were not entitled to protection by the free speech rights of the First Amendment. Although there were relatively very few Communist party members in the United States, the suspected communist conspiracy led to extensive precautions. Many people were forced to take loyalty oaths before being hired for jobs. Government officials were subjected to security checks.

During the postwar period, a tendency grew among many Americans to mistake criticism of American institutions with disloyalty. As judge Harold Medina told the jury that convicted the 11 Communists of conspiracy, taking away

Examining Photographs *The press was confident of a Dewey victory in 1948. The morning after the election Truman displays the front page that one newspaper printed for its early edition. What groups gave Truman support? Why?*

Examining Photographs *Senator McCarthy testified in sensational congressional hearings about Communists in America. When he produced no evidence, the Senate condemned him for his actions. What cold-war events stirred McCarthy and others?*

the right to criticize does not make a country stronger. Instead, allowing abuses of rights to go unchecked makes it weaker. In several rulings during this period, however, the Supreme Court found state loyalty oaths to be constitutional. The Court noted that the states had a constitutional right to assurance that an employee was not engaged in subversive activity.

The "loss" of China to the Communists and the stalemated Korean War helped to create this mood in the United States that was much like the "red scare" in the years following World War I. Critics of Truman accused the President of having lost China, alleging that his close advisers were Communists or communist tools. Senator Robert A. Taft, Republican leader in the Senate, claimed that the State Department was "riddled" with **subversives,** or individuals attempting to overthrow the government. Taft said that State Department officials had:

———— ❦ ————

…surrendered to every demand of the Soviet Union and promoted, at every opportunity, the communist cause in China.

———— ❦ ————

In 1948 the House Committee on Un-American Activities heard testimony from Whittaker Chambers, a magazine editor. Chambers admitted that he had been a communist spy in the 1930s and said that he had received secret documents from Alger Hiss, then a high-ranking State Department official. At first, few people believed Chambers's story. However, Richard M. Nixon, a young representative from California, pressed the case forward. Finally, Chambers produced several rolls of microfilm of secret documents he claimed to have received from Hiss. Hiss denied these charges. Though not convicted of spying, Hiss was found guilty of lying under oath.

Increased fears of communist subversion were fertile ground for more reckless voices. At a Lincoln's Day speech in February 1950, Senator Joseph R. McCarthy of Wisconsin accused the Democratic party of "twenty years of treason." McCarthy charged that Roosevelt had deliberately sacrificed the navy at Pearl Harbor and had "sold out" to the Soviet Union at Yalta. In addition, McCarthy claimed to have a list of "card-carrying Communists" in the State Department.

While McCarthy never produced the list, nor a shred of evidence to support his charges, he ruined the careers of many government officials. A growing atmosphere of hysteria inspired other "witch-hunts." Private groups used the communist label to drive liberal professors out of colleges. They made sure books they believed to be subversive were removed from schools. They had many broadcasters and entertainers barred from television and kept many actors from working on the stage and in films.

Years later a Senate committee determined that McCarthy's accusations and investigations had been groundless. The use of indiscriminate, unfounded political accusations to destroy or assassinate the character of one's opponent came, in time, to be known as McCarthyism.

Truman's Legacy

In 1952 President Truman, despite his remarkable victory of 1948, announced that he would not run for reelection. By the time Truman left office, he had become unpopular. The successful Soviet atomic bomb explosion, the defeat of the Nationalists in China, and the problems with carrying out the war in Korea, all contributed to charges that Truman was "soft on communism." Other Americans thought his loyalty program had hurt innocent people.

Instances of corruption in high places were also discovered—some of the President's closest aides had received valuable gifts in return for political favors. Although Truman was not personally involved, the "Truman scandals" gave the Republicans a ready-made issue for the 1952 elections.

The problems Truman and his advisers faced were new and complex. Congress was often suspicious or hostile, yet Truman got many of his programs enacted. Americans were tired of foreign involvements, yet he managed to keep the nation from retreating into isolationism. Truman's reputation as leader rose after he left the White House. Most of the Fair Deal measures he called for eventually became law. His policy of "containment" was continued by other Presidents. He set the United States a course of world responsibility that included aid for those in need and an unwavering defense of democracy everywhere.

★★★★★★★★★★★★★★★★

Section Four Review

★★★★★★★★★★★★★★★★

SUMMARY

Truman led America through the postwar years. Continued government spending brought inflation, but high employment as well. Women and African Americans remained in the labor force and enjoyed expanded, but not equal, opportunity. A shift in the national mood led to anti-labor legislation and a fear of communism. Political opportunists fanned the fear into a witch hunt that destroyed the lives and careers of innocent people. Truman's policies faced opposition from both the left and the right, and he ended his presidency under heavy public criticism.

CHECKING FOR UNDERSTANDING

1. **Identify** Taft-Hartley Act, Alger Hiss, Joseph McCarthy

2. **Define** jurisdictional strike, featherbedding, subversives

3. **List** reasons why economic growth continued after World War II.

4. **Describe** the contrasting trends for women in the labor market after World War II.

5. **Compare** gains made by African Americans in their struggle for equality with the limitations on their achievements.

6. **Describe** contrasting attitudes toward Truman's performance as President.

THINKING CRITICALLY

7. **Drawing Conclusions** Why was Senator McCarthy, with groundless accusations, able to generate mass hysteria about communism?

CONNECTIONS: HISTORY AND ECONOMICS

8. **Extending Ideas** Describe the postwar inflationary cycle in the United States. Based on information in this section, why do you think inflation often occurs during or after a war?

★★★★★★★★★★★★★★★★

★ Chapter 30 Review ★

★ Summary

The postwar years were marked by stunning successes and failures. In foreign policy, the United States exercised leadership in the economic and political reconstruction of Europe, Japan, and the Philippines. At home, the condition of African Americans and women improved because of government policies and increased job opportunities. The economy remained strong due to government spending, full employment, and consumer demand.

Communism spread in Europe and Asia, however, as the Soviets created a buffer of satellite states. An iron curtain dropped over Eastern Europe, and communist governments were established in China and North Korea. The troops that Truman sent to resist an attack on South Korea fought to a stalemate, while at home criticism mounted against the war.

Communism dominated Truman's last years in office, as anticommunist extremists created a hysteria that ruined many lives and careers. Thus at home as well as abroad, the cold war overshadowed the years after World War II.

★ Using Vocabulary

Using the following vocabulary, write a paragraph describing the Soviet establishment of an iron curtain and the development of cold war.

communism	**satellite nations**
containment	**subversives**
purges	**buffer**

★ Reviewing Facts

1. **Discuss** how and why the Soviets created a buffer of satellite states.
2. **Explain** why communism appealed to people in certain parts of the world.
3. **Summarize** arguments for and against containment and the Truman Doctrine.
4. **Cite** actions taken in the Philippines and Japan after World War II that led to successful economic recovery.
5. **Examine** the reasons for the charge that Truman was soft on communism.
6. **Detail** events leading to war in Korea.

7. **List** the advances made by African Americans during and after the War.
8. **Explain** how the Truman agenda for prosperity at home and abroad enabled him to win in 1948.

★ Understanding Concepts

POLITICAL AND ECONOMIC POWER

1. Explain how communism concentrates economic power in the hands of those who hold political power.
2. How did the United States use its position as the strongest and wealthiest nation in the world to shape economic recovery in Europe?

LEADERSHIP

3. Analyze the qualities that made President Truman an effective leader.
4. Compare the goals and leadership styles of Stalin and Mao Zedong.

★ Thinking Critically

1. **Applying Ideas** What does the term *cold war* mean and how does it apply to the post-World War II years?
2. **Applying Principles** How was the Truman Doctrine applied in assistance to Greece, by the Marshall Plan, and in creating NATO?
3. **Testing Conclusions** According to some experts, the United States failed to save China because of its loyalty to the Nationalists and its ignorance of China's true situation. Test this theory using information from the text.

★ Writing About History

COMPARISON

Refer to the description of how to write a comparison essay in the History Writer's Handbook in the Appendix of this book. Your teacher will give you more specific instructions on the essay's length and the assignment's due date.

Write an essay comparing the purposes and provisions of the Monroe Doctrine and the Truman Doctrine. Address such questions as: What were the foreign policy objectives that the United States tried to accomplish in each case? What commitment of resources was required to support each doctrine? Explain what the differences indicate about fundamental changes in foreign policy between 1823 and 1947.

★ Learning Cooperatively

In 1947 George Kennan, a member of the United States foreign service with expertise in Soviet affairs, explained the need for a firm American policy toward communism. Writing anonymously in *Foreign Affairs,* Kennan said that Soviet communism was like a "fluid stream which moves constantly, wherever it is permitted to move, toward a given goal." President Truman's policy of containment was based on this perception.

In 1967 Walter LaFeber wrote an alternate view in *America, Russia, and the Cold War, 1945-1966.* LaFeber saw the Soviet policy of creating a buffer of satellite states in Eastern Europe as primarily defensive—a result of their great losses of soldiers, civilians, and equipment in World War II. He explained that the United States was trying to "open the Soviet empire" by its cold war policies.

Working in groups of three, conduct a debate about the possible alternatives of United States foreign policy in Europe after World War II. One member should propose and support pulling troops out of Europe to lessen the Soviets' perceived need for a buffer of satellites. Another should support George Kennan's contention that the Soviets wanted to conquer other nations as well as secure their own borders, and only a heavy military presence in Europe would contain them. The third member should decide which position was best supported and write an opinion that examines the best points of each argument. All members should be prepared to argue either position in front of the class if called on by the teacher.

★ Mastering Skills

DETERMINING FACTUAL ACCURACY

If you compared a Soviet history textbook with an American history textbook, you would find that their accounts of the cold war would differ substantially. It is important to be aware that everything you read or hear is not necessarily *accurate*—correct or without error. It is also important to understand that everything presented as factual is not necessarily fact—something known for certain or that can be proven.

Asking the following questions will help you determine factual accuracy in written material:

- Does the source have reason to distort the truth?
- What evidence does the source give to support the "facts" presented?
- Do other sources agree or disagree with the information you are questioning?
- If sources disagree, which source is the most current? Which has the best reputation?

Example   These questions can used to determine the factual accuracy of the following passage:

Despite efforts to end discrimination in the South, African Americans did not gain full equality in the 1940s. Black children continued to attend separate, substandard schools. Blacks were required to sit in the back of buses and to use separate entrances and separate facilities in public buildings. Laws prevented southern blacks from voting.

Although the first sentence sounds like an opinion, it is factually accurate. The rest of the passage gives facts to support it. Other sources including state laws and newspapers from the 1940s, and this book, would confirm the factual accuracy of the passage.

Practice   Use the guidelines above to determine factual accuracy in the following statement about postwar American foreign policy. Consult your textbook and research other sources as needed.

China and Eastern Europe were lost to the Communists because President Truman was soft on communism. Truman refused to act when Stalin's troops invaded Eastern Europe after World War II to protect the communist governments that had previously seized power. Truman's refusal to offer the Marshall Plan to Eastern Europe allowed the communists to remain in control. If any elections ever had been held in those nations, the prosperous citizens would have thrown the Communists out.

In China, the proud and prosperous masses fully supported the Nationalists. If Truman had ever given any aid to the Nationalist forces, their honest and capable leaders would have quickly overwhelmed the Chinese Communists, who were weak and disorganized after World War II.

The heroic Senator Joseph McCarthy was right. The peoples of the world were sold out by the Communists in the American government who set foreign policy after World War II.

CHAPTER 31

Search for Stability

SETTING THE SCENE

SECTIONS

1 Eisenhower in the White House

2 The Straight Road Down the Middle

3 An Affluent Society

4 Eisenhower-Dulles Foreign Policy

5 The Cold War and Developing Nations

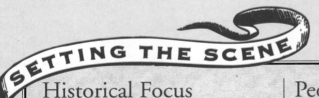

Historical Focus

A war hero, Dwight D. Eisenhower proved to be one of the most popular Presidents of modern times. Both his domestic and foreign policies were stable and consistent. At home, the nation was generally prosperous. In foreign policy, however, he continued Truman's efforts at containment. The Cold War expanded into the Middle East, Africa, and Latin America. Covert operations increased, and America troops were sent into Lebanon.

Concepts to Understand

- Why United States' **international leadership** led to the use of covert operations in other countries.
- How **economic growth** stimulated the economy during the 1950s.

People to Know

Richard M. Nixon, Adlai Stevenson, John Kenneth Galbraith, Jonas Salk, John Foster Dulles, Nikita Khrushchev

Places to Locate

Indochina, Hungary, Suez Canal

Terms to Identify

Bricker amendment, agribusinesses, affluent society, automation, "baby boom," Eisenhower Doctrine

Guided Reading

As you read this chapter, seek the answers to the following questions.

1. How did President Eisenhower view his role as President?
2. How did the lives of most Americans improve following World War II?

SPANNING THE DECADES

POLITICAL

- 1950 *McCarthy charges communist influence in government*
- 1952 *Eisenhower elected President*
- 1953 *Truce in the Korean War reached*
- 1954 *International Geneva Conference divides Vietnam*
- 1955 *Formation of the AFL-CIO*
- 1956 *Suez Canal crisis*

1950 — 1954

CULTURAL

- 1950 *Census shows 151.3 million Americans*
- 1952 *Ralph Ellison publishes* Invisible Man
- 1955 *Jonas Salk develops vaccine to prevent polio*
- 1957 *The musical* West Side Story *premieres in New York*

Snack Bar *by Isabel Bishop, 1954*

1959
Castro comes to power in Cuba

1960
Soviets shoot down a United States U-2 surveillance plane

1958

1962

1958
John Kenneth Galbraith publishes The Affluent Society

1960
There are more than 45 million television sets

…We do not fear this world of change…. Everywhere we see the seeds of the same growth that America itself has known. The American experiment has, for generations, fired the passions, and the courage of millions everywhere seeking freedom, equality, and opportunity….

—DWIGHT D. EISENHOWER
Second Inaugural Address, 1957

Eisenhower in the White House

SETTING THE SCENE

My job here, as I see it, is not to create friction, not to accentuate differences, but to bring people together so we can actually achieve progress.

—DWIGHT D. EISENHOWER
President of the United States, taken from *Firsthand Report of the Eisenhower Administration* by Sherman Adams, 1961

Section Focus

As the Truman presidency came to an end, the fear of communism preoccupied the nation. In Asia the United States was engaged in a long and frustrating war with the Communists. In other parts of the world, a dangerous cold war between communism and American interests grew increasingly heated. The nation was ready for new leadership to guide it through these troubling and uncertain times.

Objectives

After studying this section, you should be able to:
• Describe President Eisenhower's style of leadership.
• Explain how Senator Joseph McCarthy's influence came to an end.

After 7 years of the Truman administration and 20 years of Democratic leadership, the Republicans hoped that 1952 would be their year. They knew Americans were worried about the continuing war in Korea and the tense cold war in the rest of the world. Americans were also concerned with the frequent charges of communist infiltration in the government. President Truman's reputation was damaged by news reports that some of his officials had accepted bribes. These issues gave the Republicans their rallying cry for the election. They ran against "Korea, communism, and corruption." As their candidate, the Republicans picked one of the nation's most popular war heroes, Dwight D. Eisenhower—the five-star army general who led the Allied invasion of Europe during World War II.

"I Like Ike"

When asked to run for President in 1948, Eisenhower flatly refused. He believed that professional soldiers should stay out of politics. By 1952, however, Eisenhower became concerned that isolationists might regain the White House and agreed to run. He won the Republican nomination after a hotly contested race with Senator Robert A. Taft of Ohio. As his running mate, Eisenhower chose Richard M. Nixon, a 39-year-old senator from California who had made his reputation pursuing alleged communists in government.

The Democrats nominated Adlai Stevenson, the popular governor of Illinois, to run against Eisenhower. Stevenson was a thoughtful and eloquent liberal, but his campaign was burdened by the need to defend the actions of the Truman administration.

The Republicans adopted the slogan: "It's time for a change!" The warm and friendly Eisenhower, known as "Ike," promised to end the war in Korea and took a hard line against the corruption in government. "I like Ike" became the Republican rallying cry.

Examining Photographs *The 1952 Republican campaign slogan "I Like Ike" swept the nation. Why did Eisenhower at first refuse to run for the presidency?*

Eisenhower's promise to keep his administration "clean as a hound's tooth" was soon regarded with skepticism. After the campaign was underway, charges were disclosed that Richard Nixon had received gifts from California businesspeople totaling $18,000 while he was a senator. For a while, it looked as though Nixon might be dropped from the ticket. But in a nationwide speech broadcast on radio and television, he insisted the funds had been used for legitimate political purposes. He did admit that his family had kept one gift, a cocker spaniel puppy named "Checkers," and he added:

[Y]ou know, the kids love the dog. And I just want to say this right now that regardless about what they say about it, we're going to keep it.

The "Checkers speech" saved Nixon, who remained on the Republican ticket.

It is doubtful that Stevenson ever had a chance to win against the popular Eisenhower. If he did, he lost it two weeks before Election Day, when Eisenhower promised to make a trip to Korea if elected. When the votes were counted, the election was a landslide for Eisenhower. He won in excess of 6 million popular votes more than Stevenson and carried the electoral college by 442 to 89 votes. The Republicans also gained an 8-seat majority in the House. The Senate was evenly divided between Democrats and Republicans. Clearly, the Republican party was not as popular as its leader.

A New Style of Leadership

Although Eisenhower was a career soldier, he did not run the White House like an officer commanding an army. Instead, he acted as the chief administrator or leader of the White House team. His cabinet assumed new importance and acted as a genuine advisory board. For the first time in history, the cabinet had a full-time secretary, an agenda, and regularly kept minutes. Eisenhower made Sherman Adams, former governor of New Hampshire, his chief of staff. Adams wielded great power by controlling access to the President.

The advantages of Eisenhower's kind of administration were clear. If, for some

Examining Photographs *A war hero without experience in elective office, candidate Eisenhower was enthusiastically cheered by crowds everywhere. How great was his margin of victory over Stevenson?*

Linking
Across
Time

PRESIDENTIAL
ILLNESS OR
INCAPACITY

The problem of presidential incapacity was not new. William H. Harrison suffered from pneumonia for a month before his death in 1841. In 1881 James Garfield lingered for two months before he died from an assassin's bullet. In 1919 Woodrow Wilson suffered a paralyzing stroke that destroyed his part in upcoming treaty negotiations.

reason, the President was unable to lead, the government would not come to a standstill. Cabinet members could easily take over day-to-day operations. Indeed, Eisenhower suffered serious illnesses three times during his presidency, and each time the White House staff carried on with little difficulty. Critics of Eisenhower's style of leadership, however, claimed that the President was abdicating his responsibilities. At crucial times he seemed unaware of decisions made by his aides. Historians later described Eisenhower's management style as a "hidden-hand presidency."

Eisenhower hoped to establish good working relations with Congress, but members of his own party sometimes made this difficult. Still angry over the secret agreements that President Roosevelt had made with Stalin and Churchill at Yalta, Republican Senator John Bricker of Ohio introduced a law to limit presidential power. This law, known as the Bricker Amendment, required Senate ratification of all agreements made by the President with other nations. It also prohibited the President from making a treaty that conflicted with the laws of any state.

President Eisenhower believed that the Bricker Amendment would limit the President's power to deal effectively with other nations. It would also allow any state to disrupt United States foreign policy. Although a majority of Republicans in Congress supported the Bricker Amendment, the Eisenhower administration fought hard against it. In February 1954, the law was defeated by a single vote. Wearily, President Eisenhower commented:

If it is true that when you die the things that bothered you most are engraved on your skull, I am sure I'll have there the mud and dirt of France during the invasion and the name of Senator Bricker.

McCarthy's Influence Ends

Some Americans believed that the election of a Republican President would put an end to Senator Joseph McCarthy's charges that the government was filled with Communists. But McCarthy continued his crusade and subjected many government officials to a series of humiliating investigations.

For a time McCarthy succeeded in giving the impression that he was saving the country from communism. A public opinion poll taken in 1954 reported that 50 percent of the people favored him and 29 percent opposed him. Senators wary of McCarthy's influence with the voters were reluctant to oppose him.

Although the President privately disapproved of McCarthy and his methods, Eisenhower refused to "get down in the gutter" with McCarthy by attacking him publicly. The President believed that if he fought McCarthy, he would only give him more publicity. This tactic, however, deprived McCarthy's opponents in Congress of Eisenhower's leadership.

McCarthy's underhanded tactics were finally exposed to the public in 1954. In a series of televised hearings regarding possible communist subversion in the army, Americans had a chance to observe firsthand McCarthy's callous disregard of law and fairness. After the hearings ended, the Senate passed a resolution condemning McCarthy for his conduct. McCarthy's witch-hunt was over.

Presidential Disability

In September 1955, President Eisenhower suffered a heart attack. Although the President recovered rapidly, the nation's confidence was shaken. The stock market dropped more sharply than it had since 1929. Then, within the next two years, Eisenhower suffered two major illnesses.

The President's health focused attention on the question of presidential succession. It was true Eisenhower had kept the government running smoothly during his illnesses. But Americans wondered what would happen if the President remained ill. The Constitution provides that the Vice President should become President in the event that the President is unable to handle the duties of office. However, the Constitution does not say who is to decide whether the President is, or is not, able to serve.

The matter, not resolved for more than a decade, was finally addressed in 1967 after the states ratified the Twenty-fifth Amendment, which outlines procedures for times when the President is disabled. Moreover, it deals with the difficult situation when a President feels capable of continuing in office but is thought by others to be incapable.

The Election of 1956

In 1956 the Republicans renominated Eisenhower for the presidency. The Republicans claimed that the Eisenhower administration had brought peace and prosperity to the nation. Eisenhower had ended the war in Korea and avoided other world conflicts. "Everything is booming again except guns," they boasted. The Democrats, nominating Adlai Stevenson for a second time, capitalized on fear about the President's health. They played upon the public's concern that Vice President Nixon might become President.

On Election Day 1956, Eisenhower won by an even greater margin than he did in 1952. But again the President's popularity did not rub off on his party. Democrats won control of both the House of Representatives and the Senate.

In his second term, Eisenhower was more independent of his party than any other President in the twentieth century. Many conservative Republicans regarded Eisenhower as too liberal in domestic affairs and too interventionist in foreign affairs. However, "modern Republicans" supported the President. Eisenhower also found allies among the Democrats. His policies won support from the two Democratic leaders in Congress, House Speaker Sam Rayburn and Senate Majority Leader Lyndon Johnson. On domestic issues, a shaky alliance developed between "modern Republicans" and moderate-to-liberal Democrats.

★★★★★★★★★★★★★★★★★★★★

Section One Review

★★★★★★★★★★★★★★★★★★★★

SUMMARY

The election of Dwight Eisenhower in 1952 ushered in one of the most prosperous periods in American history. Eisenhower's leadership style and his willingness to work with moderate Democrats in Congress allowed implementation of his foreign and domestic programs despite conservative opposition. Concerns over presidential disability lingered and led to passage of the Twenty-fifth Amendment in 1967. With Stalin's death and the end of the Korean war, Senator McCarthy's anticommunist crusade lost much of its impact. McCarthy was eventually censured in the Senate for his tactics, which ended his political career.

CHECKING FOR UNDERSTANDING

1. **Identify** Adlai Stevenson, Richard Nixon, "Checkers," Bricker Amendment

2. **Account** for Eisenhower's election in 1952 and in 1956.

3. **Discuss** why Senator McCarthy's investigations came to an end.

4. **Explain** the need for an amendment concerning presidential succession.

5. **State** reasons for Eisenhower's appeal to moderate Democrats.

THINKING CRITICALLY

6. **Evaluating Performance** Describe Eisenhower's leadership style and discuss its advantages and disadvantages.

LINKING PAST AND PRESENT

7. **Finding Contrasts** In George Bush's 1988 election, presidential succession became an issue because many citizens lacked confidence in Dan Quayle, his running mate. What differences do you see in the reasons for public concern about presidential succession in 1955?

★★★★★★★★★★★★★★★★★★★★

Critical Thinking Skills

Discovering Symbolism in History

Neil Armstrong was the first person to walk on the moon. This accomplishment had a powerful impact on people all over the world. One reason this event had such an impact was that people saw his walking on the moon as a *symbol*—and attached extra meaning to it.

Explanation

A *symbol* is something used to represent or stand for something else, often an abstract idea, concept, or feeling. Symbols are all around us, even though we often do not recognize them as such. All words, for example, are symbols for objects or ideas.

A familiar symbol is the American flag, which stands for the United States and patriotic pride. Other familiar symbols are the color purple that stands for royalty, lions that stand for courage, and the skull and crossbones that symbolize death.

Armstrong's moon walk symbolizes human progress, the power of modern technology, and our neverending curiosity about the universe. The following guidelines will help you discover symbolism in history:

- Think about the event or condition being studied. What is the main activity in it?
- What overall condition led to this main activity?

- Who or what could be affected by this activity?
- What consequences could there be for those who are affected?
- What statement could be made that would demonstrate the symbolism, or meaning, of this event?

1950 political cartoon by Al Hirschfeld
© Al Hirschfeld. Drawing reproduced by special arrangement with Hirschfeld's exclusive representative, The Margo Feiden Galleries Ltd, New York

Example

Note how the guidelines have been followed in discovering what McCarthyism symbolizes:

1. The main event—Senator Joseph McCarthy claimed that certain government officials and other professional people were communist sympathizers, and thus possibly guilty of treason.

2. The overall condition—mistrust and suspicion between the United States and the Soviet Union during the period of cold war that followed World War II.

3. Those affected—hundreds of government officials, teachers, union leaders, actors, and even clergy who were labeled Communists, some without proof.

4. The consequences: innocent people were charged with treason, spying, and unpatriotic beliefs.

5. Possible statements of the symbolism in McCarthyism:
   a. McCarthyism symbolized a callous disregard for law and fairness.
   b. McCarthyism symbolized cold-war mistrust between two superpowers.
   c. McCarthyism symbolized a pervasive fear of communism.
   d. McCarthyism symbolized America's desire to safeguard its values and ideologies.
   e. McCarthyism symbolized fanaticism.

Practice

Read Section Three of this chapter and use the above guidelines to discover the symbolism in the Eisenhower Doctrine.

The Straight Road Down the Middle

In all those things which deal with people, be liberal, be human. In all those things which deal with people's money, or their economy, or their form of government, be conservative.

—DWIGHT D. EISENHOWER
From the Republican Platform, 1956

Section Focus

When the Republicans rallied voter support with the cry "It's time for a change" in 1952, they were referring to the country's economic policies. For the previous 20 years, Democratic administrations leaned toward the interests of labor. When Eisenhower accepted the presidential nomination, he promised that in economic matters he would "travel the straight road down the middle." As a result, the nation enjoyed an unprecedented period of prosperity and witnessed the rapid development of big business and agribusiness.

Objectives

After studying this section, you should be able to:
- Explain Eisenhower's economic policies.
- Discuss the plight of the small farmer in the 1950s.

Throughout both of his administrations, Eisenhower steered a course between conservatism and liberalism. Ike's middle course pleased most Americans. At the beginning of his administration it looked as though he might try to undo the New Deal. Like Hoover, Eisenhower believed that the role of government should be limited. Eisenhower advocated cutting the budget, reducing taxes, and ending government regulation of business. He condemned the Tennessee Valley Authority as "creeping socialism" and tried unsuccessfully to arrange for private industry to build new power plants in Tennessee, Alabama, and Kentucky.

Despite this conservative agenda, Eisenhower recognized that New Deal programs were strongly supported by most Americans. He wrote in a private letter:

Should any political party attempt to abolish Social Security, unemployment insurance, and eliminate labor laws and farm programs, you would not hear of that party again in our political history.

The debate during Eisenhower's presidency was not over ending such New Deal programs as Social Security or the minimum wage, but over how much larger to allow them to become. With President Eisenhower's encouragement, Congress extended Social Security to 7 million more people and increased benefits. Congress also extended unemployment compensation to 4 million more people. Eisenhower tried to persuade Congress to enact a health insurance program partly funded by the federal government, but Congress rejected the legislation.

Examining Photographs *George F. Meany, left, president of the American Federation of Labor, and Walter P. Reuther, right, president of the Congress of Industrial Organizations, shake hands on the merger of the two unions. How did the joining of these unions help organized labor?*

Business and Labor

Big business also had an ally in the White House. During the 1950s, 3,000 companies merged with the 500 largest corporations without any antitrust challenges by the government. The nation's 100 largest companies controlled more than 30 percent of all industrial production. Some corporations, such as General Motors and American Telephone and Telegraph, had annual budgets that were larger than those of many countries.

The American labor movement grew more slowly than big business, but it continued to gain strength. In 1955 the American Federation of Labor (AFL) and the Congress of Industrial Organizations (CIO) merged, forming the AFL-CIO. The merger increased the strength of organized labor and made it easier for workers to form local unions.

Organized labor tried hard to win pay increases for its members. During the 1950s, take-home pay and buying power rose sharply. Workers also enjoyed longer paid vacations. United Auto Workers president Walter Reuther observed that the labor movement was developing a "whole new middle class."

Organized labor was not very successful in its efforts to organize the lowest-paid factory workers and office workers. Often, these workers were women or minorities. The growth in AFL-CIO membership actually slowed by 1957. Union growth was also adversely affected by congressional

AMERICAN PORTRAITS

BETTY FRIEDAN
1921-

Betty Friedan (free DAN) was one of the first to analyze the lives of women. When she began her analysis, most women were homemakers or worked in low-paying jobs.

In 1957 she began a year-long study of her Smith College classmates. She discovered that many of these well-educated women were leading unhappy lives. With additional research it became clear to Friedan that American women were failing to find fulfillment in life. Instead, they were succumbing to "the feminine mystique"—a belief that they were supposed to ignore their talents and interests and live only for the achievements of her family.

In 1963 Friedan published *The Feminine Mystique,* a book that sparked the modern women's liberation movement. In 1966 she helped found the National Organization for Women (NOW) to lead the fight for equal rights.

investigations into corrupt union practices. The investigations revealed that strong-arm tactics were used by some unions to force employers into accepting the unions. The Teamsters' Union, accused of misappropriating funds, was expelled from the AFL-CIO. These revelations began to turn public opinion against unions.

Farm Problems

Despite the prosperity of the 1950s, it was a difficult time for many of the nation's farmers. Between 1948 and 1956, the farmers' share of the national income dropped from 9 to 4 percent. While the average American enjoyed a per capita income of $1,629, the farm population averaged $632 a year.

Eisenhower was reluctant to have the government continue to guarantee farmers set prices for their products. The heart of the issue, according to the administration, was:

[W]hether our farms are to continue to be operated by freemen. Or…to offset some very real and obvious problems that farmers now face, will government go in the opposite direction and subsidize agriculture in such a manner that it also takes control?

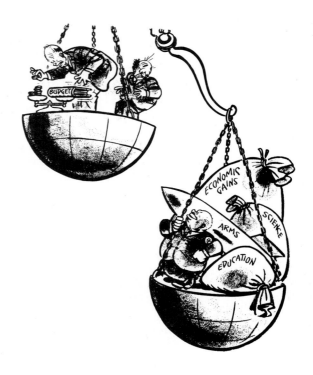

Examining Political Cartoons *This cartoon, with the caption "Got to Keep Things Balanced You Know," appeared in* The Washington Post *December 24, 1958. According to the cartoonist, what programs of the Eisenhower administration need to be "balanced" by adding to the budget?*

But without strong price supports from the government, the small family farmer faced economic ruin. Overproduction from better seeds, fertilizers, and mechanization kept farm prices low. Legislation

Examining Photographs *Heavy crop surpluses caused storage problems for farmers, shown by this wheat being temporarily stored on streets. Surpluses forced farm prices down. What was Eisenhower's view of price supports?*

reduced but did not end price supports or the farm surplus.

Many small farm families gave up and sold out to large farmowners who raised only a single crop and used the latest machinery and agricultural methods. Because of their efficiency, the large farmowners could cut their costs and still make a profit. More small farmers were unable to compete with the **agribusinesses,** or modern large-scale farms that covered 1,000 acres or more. By 1959 half of the nation's farmland belonged to 4 percent of the farmers.

There were other problems associated with America's changing agricultural patterns. Large farmowners hired seasonal workers to cultivate and harvest their crops. Many of the workers were Mexican Americans from California and the Southwest, but as many as 400,000 workers were Mexicans allowed into the United States on short-term visas. Unprotected by the National Labor Relations Act or federal minimum wage laws, these migrant workers labored long hours for little pay and endured terrible living conditions. Their children grew up with little, if any, education.

Prosperity and Recession

Much of the economic growth of the 1950s was due to a tremendous increase in consumer credit. Effective advertising enticed Americans to borrow more and more money to buy houses, cars, and consumer goods. This growing demand, in turn, encouraged industries to produce more goods and hire more people.

President Eisenhower worried that this rapid growth of the economy would lead to inflation, or rapidly rising prices. Because of this, he tried to hold down government spending, both for domestic and military projects. But in 1957 and 1958, his attempts to balance the budget set off a recession. Sales dropped and manufacturers laid off workers. Unemployment rose to 7.6 percent of the work force. Eisenhower resisted congressional pressure for a tax cut to stimulate the economy. Finally, late in 1958, boom times returned again.

★ ★ ★ ★ ★ ★ ★ ★ ★ ★ ★ ★ ★ ★ ★ ★ ★ ★

Section Two Review

★ ★ ★ ★ ★ ★ ★ ★ ★ ★ ★ ★ ★ ★ ★ ★ ★ ★

SUMMARY

During his administration, President Eisenhower steered a middle course between conservatism and liberalism. Although Eisenhower favored lower taxes, reduced government spending, and minimal government regulation, New Deal assistance programs continued to serve people in need. Businesses continued to prosper and hundreds of large business mergers went unchallenged. Production and profits increased, and workers benefited as labor unions gained in size and influence. Many of the nation's farmers, however, were left out of the economic upswing because of overproduction, which in turn brought lower prices. By 1959 small farms, unable to survive economically, were being replaced by agribusinesses.

CHECKING FOR UNDERSTANDING

1. **Identify** creeping socialism, AFL-CIO, migrant workers
2. **Define** agribusinesses
3. **Characterize** the economic philosophy and practice of Eisenhower.
4. **State** reasons why the growth of labor union membership had slowed by 1957.
5. **List** two problems connected with farming in the 1950s.

THINKING CRITICALLY

6. **Comparing Trends** Compare developments in business and agriculture during the 1950s, including the impact on workers and their families.

CONNECTIONS: HISTORY AND ENVIRONMENT

7. **Assessing Environmental Impact** From the growth of suburbs, what impact would you expect on wilderness and wildlife areas? availability of agricultural land? energy consumption? air quality? Explain.

★ ★ ★ ★ ★ ★ ★ ★ ★ ★ ★ ★ ★ ★ ★ ★ ★ ★

SECTION THREE

An Affluent Society

Wealth is not without its advantages and the case to the contrary, although it has often been made, has never proved widely persuasive.

—JOHN KENNETH GALBRAITH
United States economist,
from *The Affluent Society,* 1958

Section Focus

The economic growth of the 1950s brought great changes to the nation. For the first time, most Americans enjoyed a life of abundance. This prosperity greatly changed the way people lived. Advances in technology and medicine coupled with economic prosperity gave Americans great confidence in the future.

Objectives

After studying this section, you should be able to:
- Describe the effect of affluence on American life.
- Give examples of advances in medical technology.
- Explain the pressures of conformity in the 1950s.

After World War II, Americans were ready to settle down and enjoy a period of peace and prosperity. Industry responded to the demands of Americans by turning out huge quantities of new goods. New communities and housing developments were built as people moved from the cities to the suburbs. Americans were on the move, and they relied heavily on the

automobile for this new mobility. People anxiously awaited each year's new car models with their added gadgets and longer "tail fins." Highways stretched across the country carrying more and more traffic. A new suburban life-style evolved among middle-class Americans.

An Economy of Abundance

In 1958 economist John Kenneth Galbraith published *The Affluent Society,* in which he claimed that America's postwar prosperity was a new phenomenon. In the past, Galbraith said, all societies were based on an "economy of scarcity," that is, the productivity of the economy was limited by a lack of resources and overpopulation. But in the 1950s, the United States and a few other highly industrialized nations were experiencing what Galbraith called an "economy of abundance." Up-to-date technology enabled these nations to produce an endless variety and amount of goods and services for their people. The citizens of these countries were enjoying a standard of living never before thought possible. Poverty was disappearing, except within such groups as the unskilled, uneducated, and new immigrant population.

Some critics accused Galbraith of overstating the situation, but the facts and figures seemed to support it. Americans produced more than they could use, and this new wealth was being distributed throughout the population. During the 1920s the wealthiest 5 percent of the population received 35 percent of the country's income, but by 1960 this group received only 18 percent.

Life for most Americans was easier than ever before. They earned more money than they needed for such necessities as food and housing. With their surplus income, they purchased automobiles, household appliances, and other luxury items. The number of Americans owning their own homes went up from 40 to 60 percent between 1940 and 1960. Americans also had more free time as working hours were reduced and they were given holidays with pay.

CHAPTER 31 SEARCH FOR STABILITY

923

Income Distribution by Families, 1950–1960

Percent Distribution by Income Level	1950		1955		1960	
	Whites	Blacks and Others	Whites	Blacks and Others	Whites	Blacks and Others
More than $15,000	} 3.5	} .3	1.5	—	4.1	.6
$12,000–$14,999			2.0	.3	4.6	1.6
$10,000–$11,999			3.2	.3	6.6	2.7
$7,000–$9,999	6.1	1.6	14.0	3.1	21.3	8.7
$5,000–$6,999	15.1	3.4	23.3	10.6	24.5	15.4
$3,000–$4,999	35.7	17.8	30.3	28.3	19.9	24.5
Less than $3,000	39.4	76.9	25.7	57.3	19.2	46.5

Historical Statistics of the United States: Colonial Times to 1970

Examining Tables *During the 1950s the income for most Americans rose. In 1955 what percentage of white Americans earned less than $3,000?*

Examining Photographs
Early computers, such as this UNIVAC, occupied entire rooms and used vacuum tubes rather than microchips to process information. How did businesses first use computers?

Technological and Scientific Progress

The United States made spectacular leaps in the field of science. With more money to spend, an increase in the number of university-trained scientists, and a growing commitment to the future, the United States led the world in new technological developments. America's factories and industries began to use **automation**, the technique of operating a production system using mechanical or electronic devices. With automated production methods, goods could be produced more efficiently and quickly than with human workers.

During the 1950s the use of computers began to revolutionize American industry. Businesses used computers for many purposes. Computers took over bookkeeping functions such as billing and inventory control. They were also used for such things as making hotel reservations, sorting bank checks, guiding satellites, predicting election results, forecasting weather conditions, identifying fingerprints, and setting type for printing.

Automation and computers in the workplace caused many workers to lose their jobs. In the long run, however, computers and automation created more jobs than they eliminated. And the new jobs usually demanded a higher level of education.

Breakthroughs in medicine during the 1950s were also impressive. In April 1955, Americans learned of one of the most important discoveries in the history of medicine. After many years of research, United States scientist Dr. Jonas Salk had developed a vaccine for preventing the dreaded childhood disease known as polio. The Salk vaccine was proven effective after a huge test run on 1,830,000 school children. Within a few years, cases of polio nearly disappeared.

By 1960 other major illnesses, including pneumonia, tuberculosis, and diphtheria, were nearly wiped out. Life expectancy in the United States increased. While cancer and heart disease continued to be serious threats to the lives of Americans, researchers made important advances in diagnosing and treating these diseases.

From Cities to Suburbs

In the 1950s, the automobile changed the face of America. No longer did people have to live near their places of work. Those who lived and worked in the city could move to less-crowded places. This migration of city residents caused rapid growth of suburbs. In the years after World War II, cities became ringed by

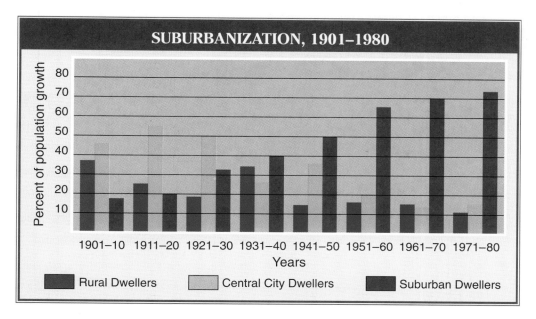

SUBURBANIZATION, 1901–1980

Percent of population growth

80
70
60
50
40
30
20
10

1901–10 1911–20 1921–30 1931–40 1941–50 1951–60 1961–70 1971–80

Years

■ Rural Dwellers □ Central City Dwellers ■ Suburban Dwellers

Examining Graphs *Many Americans moved to the suburbs during the 1950s. Between 1951 and 1960, what percentage of population growth was in the central cities?*

seemingly endless housing developments carved out of the less densely settled country land. Shopping centers with vast parking lots were built to serve the new suburban population. Businesses and factories also began relocating from the cities to the suburbs, where their workers now lived. The Highway Act of 1956 contributed to the growth of the suburbs by adding 41,000 miles to the interstate highway system.

Meanwhile, cities began to experience serious problems. To handle the flood of automobile traffic, new highways had to be built, often destroying whole urban neighborhoods. Those who were left behind to live in the cities often included poor people and the members of minority groups. With a declining population, cities faced growing financial problems. Taxes could no longer keep up with the demands for such services as public transportation, police protection, housing, and education.

Pressures to Conform

In the affluent 1950s, a new house in the suburbs, a larger television in the living room, and the newest model automobile in the garage represented the fulfillment of the "American Dream." For many young couples, the suburbs offered comfort, security, and a pleasant place to

raise their children. Yet it soon became clear that this new life-style had problems of its own.

Critics noted that a strong pressure to conform characterized American suburban life. Suburban neighborhoods were usually filled with people who were very much alike. They were generally typified as being young, with comfortable incomes, and having jobs in the service industries. Often

Examining Photographs *Lakewood Park, a planned community southeast of Los Angeles, was typical of new suburban areas in the 1950s. What advantages did suburban living offer?*

Connections

HISTORY AND MUSIC

ORIGINS OF ROCK AND ROLL

During the Eisenhower years, many teenagers rebelled against the pressure to conform by rejecting the mellow pop music favored by their parents. Teens preferred the heavily accented beats and repetitious lyrics of rock and roll.

Rock and roll developed in the mid-1950s. It was a derivation of the rhythm and blues that black musicians had created for black audiences years before. It also often had some elements of country music. In rock and roll, the tempo was quicker, the accented beats were moved, and electrically amplified instruments—mostly guitars—were used.

Because rock and roll was such a departure from the sentimental love songs of the past, it shocked and dismayed many parents. Teenagers, however, were sold. One of the first rock hits, recorded in 1955, was Bill Haley and the Comets' *Rock Around the Clock*, which sold 17 million copies. In 1956 Elvis Presley came on the rock scene. In his performances, he moved to the beat of the music. Presley set the musical style for a decade. The lyrics of most rock-and-roll music, however, remained about love.

Elvis Presley, rock and roll star of the 1950s

★★★★★★★★★★

MAKING THE MUSIC CONNECTION

1. How did rock-and-roll music evolve?

2. Why did rock and roll shock and dismay parents?

LINKING PAST AND PRESENT

3. What conflicts exist in rock and roll today?

★★★★★★★★★★

---

this conformity led to discrimination or ostracization of those who seemed "different." For example, in many suburbs racial and religious minorities were unable to buy homes. To some extent, the high cost of homes in the suburbs was responsible, but prejudice was an even more important factor. Often suburban residents refused to sell homes to minority families. And if minority families did move to the suburbs, others in the community made them feel unwelcome.

Many writers criticized the trend toward conformity in American life in the 1950s. Nonfiction works, such as David Reisman's *The Lonely Crowd* (1950), William H. Whyte's *The Organization Man* (1956), and Sloan Wilson's novel, *The Man in the Gray Flannel Suit* (1956), tried to explain the pressure to conform. Sometimes, as represented in *The Man in the Gray Flannel Suit,* these pressures were so subtly pervasive as to

make people feel they had little control over their own lives.

[I]t seemed as though all I could see was a lot of bright young men in gray flannel suits rushing around New York in a frantic parade to go nowhere. They seemed to be pursuing neither ideals nor happiness—they were pursuing a routine.... I thought I was on the sidelines watching that parade.... It was quite a shock to glance down and see that I too was wearing a gray flannel suit.

The pressures to conform in business were especially great. Employees who wanted to advance to better positions took care to adhere to the company's rules. This often meant being loyal to the corporation and being "one of the team." Outside work it meant having the "right" type of family life and belonging to the "right" clubs and religious groups. Social critics complained that Americans were in danger of losing their individualities.

Changes in Family Life

During the 1950s there were renewed social pressures on women to remain at home. Women's magazines ran articles such as "Should I Stop Work When We Marry?" and "The Business of Running a Home." The immensely popular *Pocket Book of Baby and Child Care* by Dr. Benjamin Spock said that raising children was more important and rewarding than the extra money or satisfaction that a woman might get from a job. Many women who had gone to college or had careers traded their aspirations and jobs for marriage and motherhood. The number of women who worked continued to rise, but women lost ground in the workplace. They were still paid less than men for doing the same work. They were also shut out of better jobs with higher salaries.

After World War II, more women dropped out of school and married at an early age. The nation's birthrate increased so rapidly that people refer to the period between 1945 and 1961 as the "baby boom." During the baby boom, more than 65 million children were born in the United States.

Parents in the prosperous 1950s wanted their children to have all the things that they had not been able to have during the Depression and war years. They gave their children an increasing amount of material goods and emphasized the benefits of living the "good life." Parents also allowed their children greater freedom than they themselves had known as youngsters. Critics pointed to this new "permissiveness" as the major cause of the rise in juvenile delinquency.

The Impact of Television

One of the symbols of the prosperity of the 1950s was the television set. In 1945 fewer than 1 in every 20,000 people had a television. But within a few years, televisions were everywhere, and they were almost as common as telephones.

Beginning with the election of 1952, television brought national politics into American living rooms. There were televised broadcasts of political party conventions, in which not only the public speeches but the goings-on in committee meetings were recorded. During the campaign, both parties spent millions on television advertising and broadcasts. Although television stirred greater interest in voting, it also posed disturbing questions. Would television give an unfair advantage to the candidate who used television most effectively and who could afford to buy the most air time?

Life of the Times

CHILDRAISING BY SPOCK

Millions of women, voluntarily and involuntarily, left their wartime jobs to make room for returning soldiers. Feminist writer Hurst complained that women were "retrogressing into . . . that thing known as The Home." Along with homemaking, motherhood became the major preoccupation of American women, and they threw themselves into pregnancy and mothering with a vengeance.

Just as women received training for the skilled positions they held during the war, they looked to experts for training in their renewed positions as mothers.

Dr. Benjamin Spock obliged them by publishing *Baby and Child Care* in 1946.

Spock urged flexibility in child care, but he also advised mothers to give undivided attention to their infants. "For [a baby's] spirit to grow naturally," Spock admonished, "he needs someone to dote on him. . . ." One mother, a homemaker and career woman, wrote Spock describing her anxiety because she might not be giving her son enough affection. She wondered whether she or her child needed more help.

Many experts on childhood concluded that Spock's methods led to a generation of permissive young people in the next decade who were used to getting their own way.

Examining Photographs *Watching television at home became a popular family leisure activity during the 1950s. Why were some people worried about the effect of watching television?*

Some critics also worried that television would have a negative effect on American culture. In 1953 George Gallup, one of the country's first pollsters, voiced concern that:

[O]ne of the real threats to America's future place in the world is a citizenry which daily elects to be entertained and not informed.

Supported by advertisers trying to reach the widest possible audience, television programs often appealed to the lowest common denominator of public taste. In order to avoid offending potential customers, advertisers would not buy time on programs that dealt with controversial issues. As a result, television furnished entertainment that was intended "to fix the attention but not engage the mind."

Yet the 1950s has been called the "Golden Age of Television." Many of the country's best writers, comedians, musicians, and actors flocked to the new medium. There they could reach an audience of millions.

SUMMARY

In the new "economy of abundance," economic growth resulted in increased employment and higher wages throughout the 1950s. Technology expanded the range of available products and revolutionized business with automation and computers. An even more dramatic change resulted from the automobile, which made possible an exodus of the affluent from cities to nearby suburbs. There the pressure to conform created communities that were similar to each other. As middle-class suburban life developed, women left the work force to raise families and the lines between black and white society became more divisive. Affluence and technology also perfected the electronic media of television. Television viewing brought politics and a wide range of entertainment into American homes.

CHECKING FOR UNDERSTANDING

1. **Identify** John K. Galbraith, Jonas Salk, Benjamin Spock, baby boom
2. **Define** automation
3. **Discuss** changes in American life as a result of abundance, affluence, and technology.
4. **List** ways in which early computers were used in the 1950s.
5. **Report** how minority groups were adversely affected by white suburban pressures to conform.

THINKING CRITICALLY

6. **Analyzing Results** Examine the ways television and the automobile changed the American lifestyle during the 1950s. How would your life be different without them?

CONNECTIONS: HISTORY AND MEDICINE

7. **Appreciating Medical Advances** What breakthroughs and advances in medicine reduced risks and increased life expectancy during the 1950s?

★ ★ ★ ★ ★ ★ ★ ★ ★ ★ ★ ★ ★ ★ ★ ★ ★ ★ ★

Eisenhower-Dulles Foreign Policy

SETTING THE SCENE

There is one solution and only one: that is for the free world to develop the will and organize the means against open aggression by Red armies, so that, if it occurred anywhere, we could and would strike back....

—JOHN FOSTER DULLES
Secretary of State,
from *Life* magazine, 1952

Section Focus

In the 1950s contented affluence at home contrasted sharply with political upheaval abroad. Communism and new nations emerging from former colonies were changing the international landscape. President Eisenhower and Secretary of State John Foster Dulles aggressively waged the biggest campaign against communism.

Objectives

After studying this section, you should be able to:
• Discuss Eisenhower's approach to foreign policy.
• Describe the Eisenhower Doctrine.

During the 1950s the Eisenhower administration labored to contain the spread of communism, particularly in newly independent nations in Asia and Africa. Eisenhower used diplomacy, military power, and covert activities to achieve these goals.

President Eisenhower's foreign policy was greatly influenced by his secretary of state, John Foster Dulles (DUHL uhs). After serving in the U.S. Senate in the late 1940s, Dulles had years of experience in high-level diplomacy, particularly with Asian nations. Secretary Dulles favored a vigorous foreign policy, denouncing Truman's "containment" policy as inadequate. Instead, he advocated "liberation" of Eastern European nations that were under Soviet domination:

If our policy is to stay where we are, we will be driven back. It is only by keeping alive the hope of liberation, by taking advantage of that wherever opportunity arises, that we will end this terrible peril which dominates the world....

Dulles threatened "massive retaliation" against communist aggression. "If you are scared to go to the brink [of nuclear war], you are lost," he said. Accordingly, the Department of Defense reduced the size of the regular army and increased its nuclear arsenal.

Eisenhower tempered Dulles's tough stance and took a more cautious approach. He insisted that "there is no alternative to peace." A nuclear war might well mean the end of civilization. Therefore, the Eisenhower administration continued Truman's policy of containment.

War and Peace in Asia

Carrying out his campaign promise, Eisenhower went to Korea in December 1952. Peace negotiations to end the Korean War, however, seemed to go nowhere. Exasperated, Eisenhower threatened the Communists with possible use of nuclear

Examining Photographs *Supported by American military aid, Ngo Dinh Diem was made South Vietnam's president following the 1954 Geneva peace conference. Why was the Diem regime unpopular?*

You have a row of dominoes set up and you knock over the first one, and what will happen to the last one is the certainty that it will go over very quickly.

Secretary Dulles favored giving military support to France. But when Eisenhower could get no support from the leaders of Congress or from other Western nations, he decided to stay out of the war. Dien Bien Phu fell in May 1954, and the French soon withdrew from Indochina.

At a conference in Geneva, Switzerland, in 1954, Vietnam was divided along the 17th parallel. North of that line, Ho Chi Minh's communist forces took control. To the south, a U.S.-supported government under Ngo Dinh Diem was set up. Diem's regime was dictatorial, inefficient, and unpopular. Communist-supported guerrillas began to fight against Diem's government. The United States provided most of the money for South Vietnam's defense. President Eisenhower had avoided war in Vietnam, but he had tied American prestige to the survival of Diem's unpopular government.

The Eisenhower Approach

When it came to solving foreign problems, Eisenhower preferred using diplomacy and **covert**, or secret, activities carried out by the Central Intelligence Agency (CIA). In 1953 Eisenhower became concerned when Iran's prime minister, Mohammed Mossadegh, seized control of the Anglo-American Oil Company. The President feared that Iran was aligning itself with the Soviet Union, which would endanger oil supplied to western nations. Under Eisenhower's orders, the CIA secretly funded a successful revolt by the young shah of Iran. Later Iran signed an agreement allowing United States, British, and French companies to share in Iranian oil production.

weapons. Finally in July 1953, after long and bloody fighting, the United Nations Command and the North Koreans reached a settlement. Korea was divided along a line close to the 38th parallel.

The United States then was faced with a new problem in Southeast Asia. After Japan surrendered Indochina in 1945, France tried to regain control of its colonies. The people of this region, however, wanted to rule themselves. Ho Chi Minh, a dedicated Communist, headed an independence movement called the Vietminh, whose goal was to drive the French from Vietnam, one of the regions of in Indochina. The United States stayed out of the fighting but supplied most of the weapons and supplies used by the French.

In 1954 the Vietminh surrounded French troops at the key fortress of Dien Bien Phu. The French asked the United States to bomb communist positions. Eisenhower believed that a French defeat might lead to communist domination of all of Southeast Asia. He explained:

In 1954 the CIA helped to remove another unfriendly government. The Guatemalan government of Colonel Jacobo Arbenz Guzman had seized property of the American-owned United Fruit Company. The United States learned that Guzman was getting weapons from communist nations. Concerned that Guatemala would become a communist foothold in Latin America, the Eisenhower administration funded a coup that overthrew the government.

In both Iran and Guatemala, the revolutions appeared to have been inspired from within the nation. Only later did people learn of the CIA's role.

Secretary Dulles believed the events in Vietnam, Iran, and Guatemala were evidence of the Soviet Union's intention to spread communism. He argued that newly emerging nations should choose sides in the worldwide struggle between communism and democracy. Many of the leaders of these nations disagreed with him.

In 1955 representatives from 29 Asian and African states met and signed an agreement calling for racial equality and self-determination for all people. Two

Examining Paintings *As Norman Rockwell's painting* After the Prom, 1957, *suggests, American youth were more concerned with social rather than international issues. What did Americans know about CIA covert operations abroad?*

thousand delegates, from countries containing more than half the world's population, saw themselves as the "Third World."

Examining Photographs *Shah Mohammad Reza Pahlavi came to power in Iran in 1953 with the help of secret American funds. He was later overthrown during the Iranian Revolution of 1979. Why did Eisenhower involve the CIA in Iran?*

Examining Photographs *After striking at Israel and closing the Suez Canal in 1956, Egypt was invaded by Britain, France, and Israel. The smoke stack and flag of a ship sunk by the Egyptians are visible in the canal, as British and French warships patrol nearby. What caused Britain, France, and Israel to withdraw?*

They declared their intention to remain independent of both the "First World"—the West—and the "Second World"—the Soviet Union.

The policy of neutralism was hotly debated in the United States. Some observers compared neutralism to isolationism and defended it as necessary for new and comparatively weak nations. Others attacked neutralism. Secretary Dulles took the position that no nation had the right to remain neutral in a conflict between "tyranny and freedom."

Middle East Powder Keg

During the 1950s the United States became drawn into the affairs of the Middle East. Before World War II, American businesses had begun to exploit the area's rich oil supplies. After the war, the United States became increasingly dependent on Mideast oil. Americans were anxious to protect this oil supply. Also many Americans were deeply interested in the survival of Israel, which was established in 1948 as a Jewish homeland.

The Middle East was considered by many to be a "powder keg ready to explode." Arab nations believed that Israel had been established on land belonging to the Palestinians. They threatened to destroy Israel. Moreover, deep divisions existed among the Arab nations. Poverty and discontent were widespread in the region. Finally, Soviet expansion posed a threat to Western oil supplies.

The first explosion came in 1956 in Egypt. Egypt's President Gamal Abdel Nasser was anxious to gain military superiority over the Jewish state. To get weapons, Egypt signed a commercial treaty with the Soviet Union, exchanging cotton—Egypt's major cash crop—for tanks and guns. The United States had tried to forge friendly relations with Egypt by offering to loan the nation money to build a giant dam across the Nile River. But Nasser's overtures toward the People's Republic of China and the

Soviet bloc forced Dulles to cancel the loan. Nasser responded by seizing the Suez Canal from the British and French in July 1956.

The British, French, and Israelis decided to attack Egypt and reclaim the Suez Canal, which provided a vital trade link between Europe, the Middle East, and Asia. Acting independently of the United States, the three nations invaded Egypt in October 1956.

The world seemed on the verge of another major war. During a heated debate in the United Nations, the United States voted with the Soviet Union to condemn the actions of Israel, Great Britain, and France. This pressure forced the three nations to agree to withdraw from Egypt.

The Suez crisis greatly embarrassed the United States. Three of its strongest allies had acted alone. The affair might have shattered the western alliance if Soviet action to crush the Hungarian revolution had not persuaded them to close ranks again.

The Eisenhower Doctrine

After the Suez crisis, the Soviets supported Egypt and offered to help build the Aswan Dam. President Eisenhower worried that the Soviets would gain new strength in the region. In January 1957, Eisenhower asked Congress to give him authority to use United States military forces to defend any Middle Eastern country that requested help against the forces of "international communism." Congress overwhelmingly approved the so-called Eisenhower Doctrine.

A year later the president of Lebanon asked Eisenhower to send troops to protect his government. He feared that Nasser and the Soviet Union might encourage a revolt in Lebanon. In July 1958, American soldiers landed on the beaches of Lebanon. American troops remained in Lebanon until new elections established a stronger government there. By sending troops to Lebanon, the United States showed that it intended to play a leading role in the Middle East.

***

Section Four Review

SUMMARY

In spite of the containment policy in the Far East, Communists gained control of portions of Korea and Indochina. American aid became critical to the survival of South Vietnam. Meanwhile, different methods were used to contain communism in the Middle East and Latin America. Covert CIA-backed activities led to the overthrow of governments thought to be friendly toward the Soviet Union. Following the Suez crisis, Eisenhower promised aid to Middle East countries resisting Soviet aggression. Many nations, however, alarmed at cold-war tensions, responded with calls for self-determination and neutrality in the East-West conflict.

CHECKING FOR UNDERSTANDING

1. **Identify** John Foster Dulles, Ho Chi Minh, Gamal Abdel Nasser

2. **Define** covert

3. **Describe** Eisenhower's foreign policy.

4. **Discuss** the provisions and the reason for the Eisenhower doctrine.

5. **Explain** American interests in the Middle East.

THINKING CRITICALLY

6. **Locating Evidence** What event described in this section supports the idea that the containment policy might result in supporting unpopular or repressive regimes?

GLOBAL PERSPECTIVES

7. **Predicting Reactions** Independence movements begun in the 1950s in Africa and Asia resulted in the independence of most former European colonies. How might economically developing countries, representing most of the world's people, view the continuing cold war?

The Cold War and Developing Nations

SETTING THE SCENE

No principle treasure that we hold... lies safely beyond the reach of this struggle....Freedom is pitted against slavery; lightness against the dark.

—DWIGHT D. EISENHOWER
First Inaugural Address, 1953

Section Focus

The Eisenhower years saw the spread of the cold war throughout the world. Fully aware of the dire consequences of nuclear war, Eisenhower attempted to manage international conflict through a series of cooperative alliances.

Objectives

After studying this section, you should be able to:
• Describe how the fear of nuclear war affected the cold war.
• Explain what Eisenhower meant by the "military-industrial complex."
• Discuss why American relations with Latin America were poor in the 1950s.

President Eisenhower and Secretary Dulles expanded the nation's network of alliances in order to contain communism. In Western Europe, the United States took a leading role in NATO. In Southeast Asia, the United States helped to create the Southeast Asian Treaty Organization (SEATO). In the Middle East, the United States counted on the cooperation of the Central Treaty Organization (CENTO), and in Latin America, the United States promoted the Organization of American States (OAS). However, these alliances were not always equal partnerships. Weaker members tended to be client states of the stronger members. The alliances also could do nothing to prevent internal revolutions from taking place.

The NATO Alliance

After President Eisenhower took office in 1953, he attempted to strengthen NATO under a unified command. But France was fearful of German resurgence and strongly opposed the plan. Western defenses were strengthened, however, when West Germany was allowed to rearm and join NATO.

In addition to the problem of coordinating military power, the NATO alliance faced other difficulties. Europeans had mixed feelings about the United States. European Socialists and Communists regarded the United States as a materialistic nation where workers were exploited in order to increase the profits of a few great trusts. Conservatives believed Europe was in danger of being Americanized. In Britain and France, many people blamed the United States for their nation's loss of power in the world. Despite these complaints, Soviet aggression persuaded Western Europe and the United States to maintain a common front.

Political uprisings in two of its satellites prompted the Soviet Union to reassert its control over Eastern Europe. In October 1956, anti-Soviet riots broke out in a number of Polish cities. The Soviet Union ultimately agreed to Polish demands for more freedoms. In Hungary, however, what began as peaceful protests ended with open fighting. When communist leaders attempted to put down the unrest, the Hungarian people turned against them.

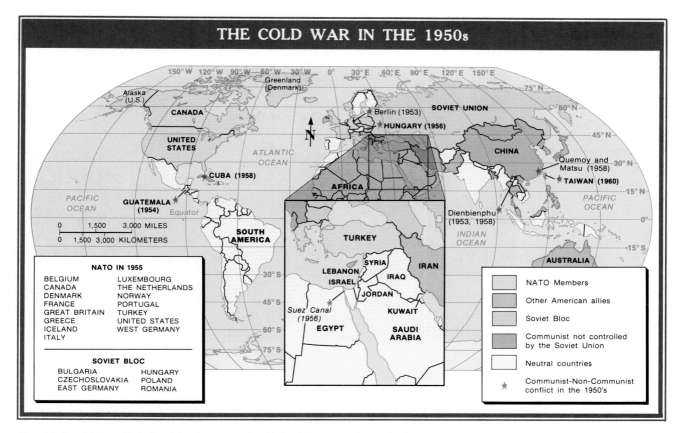

THE COLD WAR IN THE 1950s

NATO IN 1955

BELGIUM	LUXEMBOURG
CANADA	THE NETHERLANDS
DENMARK	NORWAY
FRANCE	PORTUGAL
GREAT BRITAIN	TURKEY
GREECE	UNITED STATES
ICELAND	WEST GERMANY
ITALY	

SOVIET BLOC

BULGARIA	HUNGARY
CZECHOSLOVAKIA	POLAND
EAST GERMANY	ROMANIA

NATO Members
Other American allies
Soviet Bloc
Communist not controlled by the Soviet Union
Neutral countries
★ Communist-Non-Communist conflict in the 1950's

Examining Maps *Relationships between the United States and the Soviet Union and China worsened in the 1950s as the cold war continued to spread. Confrontations took place in Latin America, Europe, Asia, and the Middle East. Name the trouble spots in Asia.*

On October 30, 1956, after less than a week of fighting, Budapest radio told the Hungarians: "You have won!" For five days jubilant Hungarians tasted freedom. Then suddenly, on November 4, Soviet tanks and troops rolled through Budapest and overwhelmed its defenders. In the United States there was much sympathy for the Hungarians, but little Eisenhower could do to help without risking war.

Trouble in Latin America

While the United States worried about communist gains in Europe, Asia, and Africa, it largely ignored the political situation in Latin America. There, the great poverty of the majority of the people and the concentration of land and power in the hands of a few created a breeding ground for political instability.

Latin Americans had good cause to believe they were "forgotten neighbors." They saw the United States pouring billions of dollars into remaking Europe's economy and strengthening weak governments in Asia. Yet Latin America received little United States foreign aid.

In 1958 Vice President Nixon made a goodwill visit to Latin America. In some of the countries he visited, Nixon faced hostile demonstrations. In Peru and Venezuela, mobs threw stones and beat sticks against Nixon's car. This shocking attack on the Vice President brought home to people of the United States their neglect of Latin America's problems.

Events in Cuba further soured United States-Latin American relations. In 1959 a resistance movement headed by Fidel Castro successfully forced the resignation of Cuba's corrupt dictator, Fulgencio Batista. Castro became a popular figure in the

*Fidel Castro overthrew
the government of dic-
tator Fulgencio Batista
and triumphantly
entered Havana in
1959. Why did the
United States cut off
diplomatic relations
with Cuba following the
revolution?*

United States, and there was hope that the two nations would establish friendly relations. But American enthusiasm for Castro quickly waned. The Cuban leader made friendly moves toward the Communists, denounced the United States, and seized private property. Castro also sought the military support of the Soviet Union. In response, President Eisenhower sharply cut the quota of sugar the United States imported from Cuba and eventually broke off relations with the Castro government.

Thaws in the Cold War

During the Eisenhower administration, the cold war spread to all continents. Yet there were signs that a "thaw" was possible. After Stalin's death in 1953, the Soviet people were allowed a little more freedom. The new premier, Nikita Khrushchev, denounced Stalin as a brutal tyrant. The Soviets now talked of peaceful coexistence and said that war in the atomic age would be so horrible that "the living will envy the dead."

In July 1955, Eisenhower met with the leaders of the Soviet Union, France, and Great Britain in Geneva, Switzerland. He made a strong plea for nuclear disarmament, saying that it would:

…ease the fears of war in the anxious hearts of people everywhere…. It would make [it] possible for every nation, great and small, developed and less developed, to advance the standards of living of its people….

The Geneva summit, however, settled nothing.

In 1958 tensions between the superpowers escalated once more, this time over the divided city of Berlin. The Soviets again threatened to cut off Western access to Berlin unless the West recognized the East German government. War seemed perilously close. When the crisis cooled down, both sides made new efforts to reduce world tensions. In 1959 Vice President Nixon and Premier Khrushchev exchanged visits. Khrushchev met with President Eisenhower at Camp David, where they made plans for a second summit meeting.

The new thaw was short-lived. Two weeks before the second summit meeting was to be held, in May 1960, an American U-2 surveillance plane was shot down over the Soviet Union. The CIA had sent it to spy on and photograph Soviet nuclear sites and missile bases. Khrushchev denounced Eisenhower as a prisoner of the "war mongers" and refused to take part in the upcoming meeting. Relations between East and West once again turned colder.

Eisenhower's Farewell Address

The U-2 incident and the failure of East-West negotiations brought Eisenhower's years in office to a frustrating close. After the death of Secretary Dulles in 1959, Eisenhower took over more of the direction of foreign policy himself. He traveled widely in Europe, Asia, the Middle East, and Latin America to promote "peace and goodwill" and a "better understanding of America." But Eisenhower was unable to lessen the tensions of the cold war and the threat of nuclear confrontation.

Still, Eisenhower remained a popular President, as near to a "father figure" as any President since George Washington. Like Washington, Eisenhower gave a farewell address. In it he warned against the overpowering influence of the military-industrial complex:

We must never let the weight of this combination [of the military and industry] endanger our liberties or democratic processes.... Only an alert and knowledgeable citizenry can compel the proper meshing of the huge industrial and military machinery of defense with our peaceful methods and goals, so that security and liberty may prosper together.

The President's message was all the more impressive because it came from a man who had spent most of his life as a professional soldier.

★★★★★★★★★★★★★★★★★★

Section Five Review

★★★★★★★★★★★★★★★★★★

SUMMARY

Cold-war tensions heightened during the late 1950s. The administration was unable to contain communism in Europe or Asia. Although the accession of Nikita Khrushchev in the Soviet Union raised hopes that there would be a thaw in the cold war, these hopes were soon dashed. In Eastern Europe restrictions tightened against the Hungarians following their 1956 uprising. Closer to home, Latin American countries became critical of the United States for neglecting their needs. In Cuba Fidel Castro led a successful revolution and established close ties with the Soviet Union. Eisenhower avoided war, but his years in office ended with the U-2 incident and discouraging East-West negotiations.

CHECKING FOR UNDERSTANDING

1. **Identify** SEATO, CENTO, OAS, Fulgencio Batista, Fidel Castro, U-2

2. **State** reasons why European attitudes toward the United States changed in the 1950s.

3. **Describe** how the Soviets dealt with challenges to their authority in Poland and Hungary.

4. **Explain** why Vice President Nixon received such a hostile reception in Latin America.

THINKING CRITICALLY

5. **Interpreting Ideas**   What do you think Eisenhower means by the phrase "industrial and military machinery" in his farewell address? Why might he fear its influence?

CONNECTIONS: HISTORY AND TECHNOLOGY

6. **Weighing Influence**   How did the existence and continuing development of nuclear weapons influence the cold war? What events illustrate the influence of these weapons?

★★★★★★★★★★★★★★★★★★

★ Chapter 31 Review ★

★ Summary

The slogan "I like Ike" echoed throughout the 1950s. Americans liked Eisenhower's optimism, style of government, and willingness to serve all segments of society. Even more, they liked the peace and prosperity that characterized his years in office.

Americans entered an age of affluence and found their lifestyles forever changed by television and the automobile. Many moved to the suburbs and imposed upon their neighbors a strong pressure to conform. Women left the work force to keep house and raise children.

The end of the Korean War in 1953 diminished the threat of communism. Television exposure of McCarthy's brutal tactics brought an end to McCarthyism. Meanwhile, Eisenhower continued to focus on containment of communism worldwide through diplomacy, aid, and covert operations. Although he avoided war, the cold war continued, and nuclear disarmament efforts failed.

★ Using Vocabulary

Use these vocabulary words in a statement about the influence of technology on business and agriculture.

agribusiness   **automation**

★ Reviewing Facts

1. **State** reasons why Americans elected Ike by overwhelming majorities in 1952 and 1956.
2. **Explain** the Eisenhower administration's dilemma regarding the farm problem.
3. **Show** how Eisenhower policies toward health and welfare programs and big business reflected his middle course economic policy.
4. **Identify** technological advances of the 1950s that contributed to the strength of the American economy.
5. **Describe** the effects of economic growth and affluence on American life.
6. **Cite** the differences between Dulles's and Eisenhower's approaches to foreign policy.
7. **Discuss** how the following groups were affected by the pressure to conform: (1) middle-class families, (2) African Americans, (3) women.

8. **Speculate** about the effects of the nuclear threat on the conduct of the cold war.

★ Understanding Concepts

INTERNATIONAL LEADERSHIP

1. If you were to examine Eisenhower's leadership style as commander of NATO forces, how would you expect it to differ from his international leadership style as President? Why?
2. What is your opinion of Eisenhower's use of covert operations to remove unfriendly foreign governments? Explain.

ECONOMIC GROWTH

3. What factors stimulated economic growth in the 1950s?
4. How did the growth of the television industry both reflect and stimulate economic growth?

★ Thinking Critically

1. **Applying Philosophy**   Read Eisenhower's words at the beginning of Section Two on page 919. Which of the following policies would be justified by Eisenhower's expressed philosophy? (a) civil rights legislation; (b) expanded government work-relief programs for minorities; (c) works of art produced at government expense; (d) laws protecting workers' rights; (e) government financial assistance to underpaid workers.

2. **Demonstrating Reasoned Judgement**   Find an example of Eisenhower's actions that supports both national security and global security. Did he take any steps in the interest of national security at the possible expense of global security? Support your answer.

3. **Locating Examples**   What lifestyle changes reflected the "economy of abundance" during the 1950s? Which have persisted to the present, even during economic recessions?

4. **Defending an Opinion**   Respond to Eisenhower's domino theory. Do you believe it justifies the containment policy? Defend your opinion.

5. **Assessing Outcomes**   Do you agree with Eisenhower that nuclear disarmament would allow each nation to "advance the standards of living of its people?" Why or why not?

★ Chapter 31 Review ★

★ Writing About History

DESCRIPTION

Refer to the description of how to write a descriptive essay in the History Writer's Handbook in the Appendix of this book. Your teacher will give you more specific instructions on the essay's length and the assignment's due date.

Imagine you are a journalist in 1961 when Eisenhower left office. Write a profile of Eisenhower for a popular publication, focusing on his personal traits, his leadership style, or both. For details, refer to biographies and reference books covering the history of the 1950s.

★ Learning Cooperatively

Working in a group of four, research life in the United States during the Eisenhower administration. Divide the research assignments so that different members are responsible for finding information about news events, movies, television shows, popular music, theater, art achievements, literary publications, advances in science and technology, sports events, and fashion trends for those years. Have members record their findings. Combine the reports to form a history of the Eisenhower years.

★ Mastering Skills

FINALIZING A RESEARCH REPORT

The last step when preparing a research paper is to check over your rough draft to make sure you have not made any errors or omissions. Ask yourself questions such as these:

- Will the reader understand it?
- Are more or better facts needed to support the thesis statement and main ideas?
- Do the main headings relate to the thesis statement? Does each subheading relate to the main heading?
- Does each paragraph have a main idea?
- Are there strong supporting statements for each main idea?
- Is the information presented in a logical order?
- Are the paragraphs indented; correct capitalization, grammar, and punctuation use; and all words spelled correctly?

- Are all direct references and quotes cited in footnotes or endnotes correctly?

Example   Read the following rough draft of a short report on migrant workers, and note the errors that were made:

Migrant workers *[indent paragraph]* are farm laborers who move into a region temporarily *[incorrect spelling]* to help harvest fruits and vegetables that must be picked by hand. Migrants usually work in several different areas during the year, although some become permanent residents and landowners. *[incorrect facts]* Because they move so frequently, the children of migrants seldom receive more than a few years of elementary education *[missing period]*

Mexican-American workers earn low wages but receive other benefits such as Social Security and disability insurance. *[Transition missing—are all migrants Mexican Americans? Other minorities? Also, check facts on pay and benefits]*. They typically live in substandard housing, lack sufficient food, and does not *[subject-verb agreement]* have access to satisfactory Health Care. *[capitalization]*

After the errors are found and corrected, the report should read like this:

Migrant workers are farm laborers who move into a region temporarily to help harvest fruits and vegetables by hand. Migrants usually work in several areas during the year, and they do not become permanent residents. Because they move so frequently, the children of migrants seldom receive more than a few years of elementary education.

Many migrant workers are Mexican Americans. Others may be native Americans, African Americans, or Mexicans who have temporary work visas. Migrant workers receive low wages, $7,000 to $10,000 per year. Because their work is considered temporary they are not eligible for Social Security, food stamps, or other benefits. Migrant laborers typically live in substandard housing, lack sufficient food, and do not have access to satisfactory health care.

Your final copy should also include a cover page indicating the title, your name, class, and date, as well as a bibliography of the sources used.

Practice   Use the material in this chapter and in two other sources to prepare a short report on either Jonas Salk or the impact of television on American culture.

★ ★ ★ Unit 9 Digest ★ ★ ★

Changes came rapidly during the 1930s and 1940s as Americans slid from a depression into a global war, and the nation's focus turned from domestic to foreign affairs. Out of the war came a new prosperity and a new sense of global responsibility. Suddenly the United States found itself a superpower protecting western democracy.

Chapter 28
The New Deal

Franklin Roosevelt came to office in 1932 ready to act immediately to ease the Depression. His New Deal program was a two-part program of emergency measures and long-range planning with three specific aims—recovery from the Depression, relief for victims of the Depression, and reform of the nation's economic system.

During Roosevelt's first 100 days in office, he drew up and Congress enacted an unprecedented number of new programs. These programs kept the economy from collapsing, provided relief for the unemployed, and helped the nation toward financial recovery.

In response to critics such as Huey E. Long, the second phase of the New Deal emphasized social reform rather than short-term emergency measures. The beneficiaries were farmers, workers, the poor, the unemployed, and the unemployable. Out of these efforts came large-scale public works programs and a social security system for the elderly. For labor, the passage of the Wagner Act guaranteed unions the right to collective bargaining.

Roosevelt won reelection in 1936 by a landslide, largely because of his popularity with organized labor, immigrants, and minorities. Labor unions in particular made great gains. The CIO emerged and successfully negotiated contracts with the steel and automobile industries.

In 1935 and 1936 the Supreme Court ruled that many key programs of the early New Deal were unconstitutional.

Roosevelt responded by attempting to increase, or "pack," the number of justices on the court. His effort failed and other setbacks in Congress slowed the pace of the New Deal. But by then its programs already had altered the role of government in American life. Aid to the needy and managing the economy were now government concerns.

Chapter 29
World War II

During Roosevelt's first and second administrations, the United States worked to improve relations with Europe and Latin America. The Good Neighbor Policy committed the United States to nonintervention in Latin America. In Europe, Roosevelt recognized the Soviet Union and sought to maintain neutrality with other nations. Aggressive, totalitarian governments, however, came to power in Germany and Italy. In the Pacific, Japan moved against China. When war in Europe broke out in 1939, the United States again declared its neutrality.

German victories, however, gradually prompted the United States to aid the allied powers of Britain, France, and the Soviet Union. With the world in a state of crisis, Roosevelt was reelected for an unprecedented third term in 1940. The following year, after Japanese planes bombed Pearl Harbor, the United States declared war on Japan and Germany.

For the second time in 25 years, the American economy converted to war production and transformed the nation's way of life. Women left home to serve in the armed forces and to work in offices and defense plants. African Americans also joined the armed forces and increasing numbers of blacks found work in factories. Japanese Americans, however, were placed in detention camps because the government questioned their loyalty.

By 1944 when an ailing Roosevelt was reelected to a fourth term, Germany and

Japan had suffered major defeats on all fronts. With Allied armies on the outskirts of Berlin and much of the nation in ruins, Germany surrendered in May 1945. Japan surrendered a few months later, but only after American planes had dropped atomic bombs on Hiroshima and Nagasaki. Before the war ended, the United States and 50 other countries formed the United Nations in hopes of maintaining international peace and cooperation.

Chapter 30
The Cold War

After World War II, the United States found itself the leader of the western democracies. The war-time alliance came apart when the Soviet Union drew an "iron curtain" between Eastern European nations they controlled and the rest of Europe. An intense cold war of words, rivalry, and confrontation soon developed between the West and the Soviet Union.

Western fear that communism would spread led to a policy of containment, or sending American aid or troops to help check Soviet aggression. The Marshall Plan also gave massive economic aid to war-torn Western Europe. A Soviet blockade of Berlin prompted the Berlin airlift, which provided tons of supplies to beleaguered residents. To guard against further Soviet aggression, the United States, Canada, and nations of Western Europe established the North Atlantic Treaty Organization (NATO), a peacetime alliance. European communist countries responded with the Warsaw Pact.

Meanwhile, the cold war spread to Asia. In 1949 Mao Zedong succeeded in establishing a communist government in China, despite American efforts to prevent it. In Korea, the country was divided between the noncommunist South and the communist North. Americans under the United Nations flag fought a "hot war" to stop a communist takeover of the peninsula.

At home the Truman administration pushed for economic and social reform. Inflation was rising and labor resorted to strikes to increase wages. The 1947 Taft-Hartley Act, however, prevented unions from abusing their power by outlawing the closed shop. Also, fear generated by the cold war led to a search by Senator Joseph McCarthy for Communists in the federal government.

In the early 1950s the country began a long period of economic prosperity. The growing economy created millions of new jobs. Two million more women had jobs in 1952 than in 1946. After World War II, the number of black supervisors and professionals tripled from what it was before the war. Encouraged by their role in the war and by their new economic strength, blacks began to lobby for their civil rights.

Chapter 31
Search for Stability

In 1953 anxiety about the cold war, concern about corruption, and frustration with the Korean War brought Dwight Eisenhower and a new style of leadership to the White House. Although friendly to corporations, Eisenhower also expanded New Deal programs such as social security, and raised the minimum wage. Despite inflation and a brief recession, businesses and working men and women prospered. Farmers, however, did not fare well. Even though New Deal price supports continued, small family farms could not compete with agribusinesses.

For many Americans, affluence came with economic growth. Prosperity, combined with technological and medical advances inspired a new confidence in the future. Automation, computers, and television changed work and leisure. A new way of life evolved for many Americans as they moved from the cities to the suburbs and commuted to work.

Meanwhile, communism and nationalism were on the rise in Southeast Asia, the Middle East, and Latin America. Under Eisenhower, America's cold-war containment policy continued through diplomacy, military and economic aid, and covert operations. His efforts to lessen tensions and reduce the Soviet nuclear threat, however, failed.

SYNTHESIZING UNIT THEMES

RELATING IDEAS

1. What major changes took place in American-Soviet relations and policy after World War II?

IDENTIFYING TRENDS

2. How did the position of women and blacks change during and after World War II?

MAKING COMPARISONS

3. Compare the roles that the United States played in world affairs during the 1930s, the 1940s, and the 1950s.

★ Analyzing Unit Themes

AMERICAN DEMOCRACY

1. How did the role of government in American democracy change during the Depression and the New Deal? What changes persist to the present?

2. How did fear of communism become a serious threat to American democracy during the Truman administration? What ended the threat during the Eisenhower administration?

CIVIL RIGHTS AND LIBERTIES

3. Describe the progress made by African Americans during the New Deal and World War II. What values introduced in the 1950s worked against them?

4. Throughout the 1930s and 1940s, women gained new employment opportunities and a recognized place in the work force. How do you account for the ground they lost in the 1950s?

CONFLICT AND COOPERATION

5. Explain the purposes of NATO and the Warsaw Pact.

6. How does the purpose of the United Nations differ from that of NATO, the Warsaw Pact, and alliances of World War II?

U. S. ROLE IN WORLD AFFAIRS

7. How did World War II and the Cold War permanently change United States foreign policy?

8. Describe United States efforts to contain the spread of communism worldwide from 1948-1960. What were the results of these efforts?

★ Reviewing Chronology

Study the unit time line on pages 820-821, then answer the questions that follow.

1. What subsequent events probably occurred as a direct result of Hitler's assuming power in 1934?

2. What world event later helped McCarthy win support for his crusade?

★ Linking Past and Present

1. **Applying Principles** When NATO was established in 1949, each country promised to come to the aid of the others in case of attack. In 1991 NATO dispatched three squadrons of German, Italian, and Belgian jet fighters to Turkey, a member of NATO, to strengthen its border with Iraq in case of war. How does this 1991 NATO action carry out the intent of the charter?

2. **Evaluating Performance** In November 1990, after failed attempts to reach a peaceful settlement and months of economic sanctions, the United Nations passed a resolution authorizing the use of force if Iraq had not ended its occupation of Kuwait by January 15, 1991. In the final days before the deadline, the United Nations Secretary General met personally with Saddam Hussein to persuade him to withdraw and avoid war. Hussein refused, the deadline passed, and the forces of member nations launched an air strike against Iraq. How did these actions align with the intent of the leaders who created the United Nations as a peacekeeping agency in 1945?

★ Demonstrating Citizenship

Assessing Involvement High-level decisions are often made without input from the people whose lives they affect. Examples include Truman's decision to send troops to Korea in 1950 and Bush's decision to send troops to the Persian Gulf in 1990. As a concerned citizen, how might you have responded to each of these decisions?

★ Interpreting Illustrations

Study the photograph above of Hungarian rebels with a captured Soviet tank in Budapest, November 2, 1956. Then answer the questions that follow.

1. What can you tell about the mood of the crowd standing around the square?

2. What might displaying the Hungarian flag from the tank in this setting mean?

3. Why was the Hungarian uprising unsuccessful?

★ Thinking Globally

Assessing Outcomes   Throughout the latter part of the twentieth century, conflict has existed over the presence of Israel in the Middle East and United States support of Israel's positions. Several wars have been fought between Israel and neighboring Arab countries. Palestinian refugees from these wars, many of whom live under Israeli administration in occupied territories, have used guerrilla tactics to publicize their plight. The Palestinian issue was even raised in attempts to resolve the conflict over Iraq's invasion of Kuwait. What events in the 1930s and 1940s led to the creation of Israel? How did Israel's presence contribute to the Suez crisis of 1956?

★ Relating Geography and History

RELATIONSHIPS WITHIN PLACES: HUMANS AND ENVIRONMENTS

Japan is a small island country lacking in natural resources. In 1940 Japan was short 65 million bushels of rice to feed its rapidly increasing population and lacked land to produce more. How did Japan's geographic situation influence its actions in 1940 and its postwar development?

★ Practicing Skills

HYPOTHESIZING

Refer to the skills lesson on Hypothesizing on page 893 to help you practice this critical thinking skill.

Each of the following statements is accompanied by two hypotheses. Indicate whether each hypothesis is correct or incorrect.

1. An heroic rescue effort evacuated 300,000 British and French troops from Dunkirk in 1940.
   a) German capture of those Allied forces could have ended World War II then and there.
   b) The rescue effort by so many private boats pointed up the determination of Allied citizens to resist Nazi Germany.

2. Stalin was told in 1942 that an Allied invasion of western Europe was at least a year away.
   a) The United States and Britain hoped to see Germany considerably weaken the Soviet Union.
   b) The United States and Britain felt unready to launch a massive invasion of Europe.

3. After the fall of Mussolini, German troops in Italy put up fierce resistance against the advancing Allies.
   a) The Germans fought fiercely to restore Mussolini to power in Italy.
   b) The Germans fought fiercely to defend against the Allies advancing on to Germany.

4. Toward the end of the war, it seemed vital that the United States and Britain keep the Soviet Union from making a separate peace with Germany.
   a) It would have allowed the Germans to concentrate all their forces against the Allies in western Europe.
   b) It would have resulted in the Soviet Union joining with Germany to attack the Allies.

5. The United States dropped atomic bombs on two Japanese cities, killing nearly 200,000 people.
   a) The bombings were intended to intimidate the Japanese before the Allies invaded Japan.
   b) The bombings were intended to warn the Soviets against interfering with American postwar interests in East Asia.

DISCOVERING SYMBOLISM IN HISTORY

Refer to the skills lesson on Discovering Symbolism in History on page 918 to help you practice this critical thinking skill.

Write a sentence in which you express the symbolism associated with each of the following items from World War II.

1. Munich

2. *Blitzkrieg*

3. Winston Churchill

4. Pearl Harbor

5. D-Day

6. Holocaust

7. Hiroshima

8. Berlin

UNIT 10

Redefining America's Role: 1954-Present

…What we are creating is a new multilayered global game in which not merely nations but corporations and trade unions, political, ethnic, and cultural groupings, transnational associations and supranational agencies are all players.…

—ALVIN TOFFLER
The Third Wave, 1980

SETTING THE SCENE

Time

Mid- to late twentieth century

Mood

American society from the mid-1950s to the present has been described as a roller-coaster. Americans were taken to new heights of optimism and confidence but lows of doubt and frustration as well. Americans became deeply troubled about economic instability, lack of honesty in government, and military involvement abroad. Yet many Americans continued to press for social reform and equal rights. In addition, growing awareness of new technology redefined the way Americans lived and worked.

Themes

- Civil Rights and Liberties
- Conflict and Cooperation
- Cultural Diversity
- U.S. Role in World Affairs

Key Events

- Desegregation in public schools
- Kennedy's assassination
- American withdrawal from Vietnam
- Watergate scandal
- United States bicentennial
- Camp David Peace Accords
- Persian Gulf War

Major Issues

- The growing civil rights movement opens the political process for thousands of Americans.
- Involvement in Vietnam polarizes Americans at home and tarnishes the nation's image abroad.
- Illegal activities by high-level government officials results in the Watergate scandal and the resignation of President Nixon.
- Democratic movements lead to the demise of the Communist party and the end of the Soviet Union.
- The United States and allies liberate Kuwait after Iraqi invasion.

◄ Glorious Lady Freedom *by Moneca Calvert, 1986*
From the permanent collection of The Museum of American Folk Art

Global Perspectives

The post-World War II era witnessed monumental political, social, and economic changes throughout the world. In Africa nationalist movements swept across the continent. By 1975 over 30 African nations had become newly independent from European rule.

In Eastern Europe, however, the Soviet Union strengthened its control. The massive Berlin Wall, erected by the East Germans in 1961, stood for nearly 30 years as a symbol of the division between East and West. Beginning with Poland in the late 1980s, democratic movements swept through Eastern Europe and the Soviet

THE WORLD

	ASIA AND OCEANIA	AFRICA	EUROPE	SOUTH AMERICA	NORTH AND CENTRAL AMERICA
1955	● 1954 *French are defeated in Vietnam*				● 1959 *St. Lawrence Seaway opens*
		● 1960 *"Year of Africa"— many countries become independent* ▲	● 1961 *Berlin Wall built*		
1970	● 1966 *Chinese Cultural Revolution begins in China*				
				● 1974 *Isabel Peron becomes President in Argentina* ▲	
	● 1979 *Shiite leader Ayatollah Khomeini led a revolt against the shah*			● 1982 *Argentina invades Falkland Islands*	● 1983 *American troops invade Grenada*
1985					
	● 1990 *Iraq invades Kuwait* ➤		● 1990 *Communism crumbles in Eastern Europe* ➤		● 1991 *Allied forces liberate Kuwait*
2000					

Union. After decades as two distinct nations, Germany was reunited in 1990.

China, too, underwent dramatic changes. Improved relations with the United States began in 1972, but China continues to be plagued by internal strife.

Political conflict dominated the Middle East. After nearly 30 years of hostilities, peace between Israel and Egypt was achieved in 1979. Throughout the 1970s and 1980s, civil war plagued Lebanon, while Iraq and Iran clashed for eight years.

After Iraq invaded Kuwait in 1990, allied forces led by the United States succeeded in liberating Kuwait in 1991.

The United States had also become involved in armed conflict in Asia. In the 1960s and 1970s, the Vietnam War claimed more than 57,000 American lives. Military action also took place in Grenada and Panama. Through its actions and leadership as the most powerful and prosperous nation in the free world, the United States continues to represent freedom.

THE UNITED STATES

	PACIFIC AND NORTHWEST	SOUTHWEST	MIDWEST	SOUTHEAST	ATLANTIC NORTHEAST
1955			1954 Brown v. Board of Education decision	1955 Rosa Parks; Montgomery bus strike	
	1959 Alaska and Hawaii become states ➤			1965 "Freedom March" from Selma to Montgomery	
1970		1966 First artificial heart implant in human ▼			
1985					1975 American military evacuate Saigon ◄
	1989 Exxon Valdez oil spill in Alaska	1990 Navaho nation elects its first president			1987 Worst Wall Street stock market plunge in history
2000					

from *Hunger of Memory*

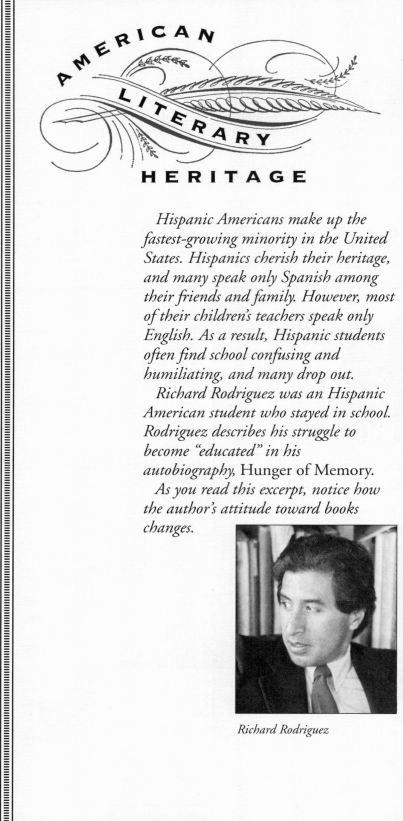
Hispanic Americans make up the fastest-growing minority in the United States. Hispanics cherish their heritage, and many speak only Spanish among their friends and family. However, most of their children's teachers speak only English. As a result, Hispanic students often find school confusing and humiliating, and many drop out.

Richard Rodriguez was an Hispanic American student who stayed in school. Rodriguez describes his struggle to become "educated" in his autobiography, Hunger of Memory.

As you read this excerpt, notice how the author's attitude toward books changes.

Richard Rodriguez

From an early age I knew that my mother and father could read and write both Spanish and English. I had observed my father making his way through what, I now suppose, must have been income tax forms. On other occasions I waited apprehensively while my mother read onion-paper letters airmailed from Mexico with news of a relative's illness or death. For both my parents, however, reading was something done out of necessity and as quickly as possible. Never did I see either of them read an entire book. Nor did I see them read for pleasure. Their reading consisted of work manuals, prayer books, newspapers, recipes....

In our house each school year would begin with my mother's careful instruction: "Don't write in your books so we can sell them at the end of the year." The remark was echoed in public by my teachers, but only in part: "Boys and girls don't write in your books. You must learn to treat them with great care and respect."

OPEN THE DOOR OF YOUR MIND WITH BOOKS, read the red and white poster over the nun's desk in early September. It soon was apparent to me that reading was the classroom's central activity. Each course had its own book. And the information gathered from a book was unquestioned. READ TO LEARN, the sign on the wall advised in December. I privately wondered: What was the connection between reading and learning? Did one learn something only by reading it? Was an idea only an idea if it could be written down? In June, CONSIDER BOOKS YOUR BEST FRIENDS. Friends? Reading was, at best, only a chore. I needed to look up whole paragraphs of words in a dictionary. Lines of type were dizzying, the eye having to move slowly across the page, then down, and across....The sentences of the first books I read were coolly impersonal. Toned hard. What bothered me most, however, was the isolation reading required. To console myself for the loneliness I'd feel when I read, I tried reading in a very soft voice. Until: "Who is doing all that talking to his neighbor?" Shortly after, remedial reading classes were arranged for me with a very old nun.

At the end of each school day, for nearly six months, I would meet with her in the tiny room that served as the school's library but was actually only a storeroom for used textbooks and a vast collection of *National Geographic*. Everything about our sessions pleased me: the smallness of the room; the noise of the janitor's broom hitting the edge of the long hallway outside the door; the green of the sun, lighting the wall; and the old woman's face blurred white with a beard. Most of the time we took turns. I began with my elementary text. Sentences of astonishing simplicity seemed to me lifeless and drab: "The boys ran from the rain....She wanted to sing....The kite rose in the blue." Then the old nun would read from her favorite books, usually biographies of early American presidents. Playfully she ran through complex sentences, calling the words alive with her voice, making it seem that the author somehow was speaking directly to me. I smiled just to listen to her. I sat there and sensed for the very first time some possibility of fellowship between a reader and a writer, a communication, never *intimate* like that I heard spoken words at home convey, but one nonetheless *personal*.

One day the nun concluded a session asking me why I was so reluctant to read by myself. I tried to explain; said something about the way written words made me feel all alone—almost, I wanted to add but didn't, as when I spoke to myself in a room just emptied of furniture. She studied my face as I spoke; she seemed to be watching more than listening. In an uneventful voice she replied that I had nothing to fear. Didn't I realize that reading would open up whole new worlds? A book could open doors for me. It could introduce me to people and show me places I never imagined existed. She gestured toward the bookshelves. (African women danced, and the shiny hubcaps of automobiles on the back covers of the *Geographic* gleamed in my mind.) I listened with respect. But her words were not very influential. I was thinking then of another consequence of literacy, one I was too shy to admit but nonetheless trusted. Books were going to make me "educated." That confidence enabled me, several months later, to overcome my fear of the silence.

In fourth grade I embarked upon a grandiose reading program. "Give me the names of important books," I would say to startled teachers. They soon found out that I had in mind "adult books." I ignored their suggestion of anything I suspected was written for children. (Not until I was in college, as a result, did I read *Huckleberry Finn* or *Alice's Adventures in Wonderland*.) Instead, I read *The Scarlet Letter* and Franklin's *Autobiography*. And whatever I read I read for extra credit. Each time I finished a book, I reported the achievement to a teacher and basked in the praise my effort earned. Despite my best efforts, however, there seemed to be more and more books I needed to read. At the library I would literally tremble as I came upon whole shelves of books I hadn't read. So I read and I read and I read: *Great Expectations;* all the short stories of Kipling; *The Babe Ruth Story;* the entire first volume of the *Encyclopedia Britannica (A-ANSTEY);* the *Iliad; Moby Dick; Gone with the Wind; The Good Earth; Ramona; Forever Amber; The Lives of the Saints; Crime and Punishment; The Pearl....* Librarians who initially frowned

around the house on Saturday mornings?) Always, "What do you see?..."

What *did* I see in my books? I had the idea that they were crucial for my academic success, though I couldn't have said exactly how or why. In the sixth grade I simply concluded that what gave a book its value was some major idea or theme it contained. If that core essence could be mined and memorized, I would become learned like my teachers. I decided to record in a notebook the themes of the

when I checked out the maximum ten books at a time started saving books they thought I might like. Teachers would say to the rest of the class, "I only wish the rest of you took reading as seriously as Richard obviously does."

But at home I would hear my mother wondering, "What do you see in books?" (Was reading a hobby like her knitting? Was so much reading even healthy for a boy? Was it the sign of "brains"? Or was it just a convenient excuse for not helping

books I read. After reading *Robinson Crusoe,* I wrote that the theme was "the value of learning to live by oneself." When I completed *Wuthering Heights,* I noted the danger of "Letting emotions get out of control." Rereading these brief moralistic appraisals usually left me disheartened. I couldn't believe that they were really the source of reading's value. But for many more years, they constituted the only means I had of describing to myself the educational value of books.

The Library *by Jacob Lawrence, 1960*

In spite of my earnestness, I found reading a pleasurable activity. I came to enjoy the lonely good company of books. Early on weekday mornings, I'd read in my bed. I'd feel a mysterious comfort then, reading in the dawn quiet—the blue-gray silence interrupted by the occasional churning of the refrigerator motor a few rooms away or the more distant sounds of a city bus beginning its run. On weekends I'd go to the public library to read, surrounded by old men and women. Or, if the weather was fine, I would take my books to the park and read in the shade of a tree. A warm summer evening was my favorite reading time. Neighbors would leave for vacation and I would water their lawns. I would sit through the twilight on the front porches or in backyards, reading to the cool, whirling sounds of the sprinklers.

I also had favorite writers. But often those writers I enjoyed most I was least able to value. When I read William Saroyan's *The Human Comedy,* I was immediately pleased by the narrator's warmth and the charm of his story. But as quickly I became suspicious. A book so enjoyable to read couldn't be very "important." Another summer I determined to read all the novels of Dickens. Reading his fat novels, I loved the feeling I got—after the first hundred pages—of being at home in a fictional world where I knew the names of characters and cared about what was going to happen to them. And it bothered me that I was forced away at the conclusion, when the fiction closed tight, like a fortuneteller's fist—the futures of all the major characters neatly resolved. I never knew how to take such feelings seriously, however. Nor did I suspect that these experiences could be part of a novel's meaning. Still, there were pleasures to sustain me after I'd finish my books. Carrying a volume back to the library, I would be pleased by its weight. I'd run my fingers along the edge of the pages and marvel at the breadth of my achievement. Around my room, growing stacks of paperback books reenforced my assurance.

I entered high school having read hundreds of books. My habit of reading made me a confident speaker and writer of English. Reading also enabled me to sense something of the shape, the major concerns, of Western thought…. In these various ways books brought me academic success as I hoped that they would. But I was not a good reader. Merely bookish, I lacked a point of view when I read. Rather, I read in order to acquire a point of view. I vacuumed books for epigrams, scraps of information, ideas, themes—anything to fill the hollow within me and make me feel educated. When one of my teachers suggested to his drowsy tenth-grade English class that a person could not have a "complicated idea" until he had read at least two thousand books, I heard the remark without detecting either its irony or its very complicated truth. I merely determined to compile a list of all of the books I had ever read. Harsh with myself, I included only once a title I might have read several times. (How, after all, could one read a book more than once?) And I included only those books over a hundred pages in length. (Could anything shorter be a book?)

There was yet another high-school list I compiled. One day I came across a newspaper article about the retirement of an English professor at a nearby state college. The article was accompanied by a list of the "hundred most important books of Western Civilization." "More than anything else in my life," the professor told the reporter with finality, "These books have made me all that I am." That was the kind of remark I couldn't ignore. I clipped out the list and kept it for the several months it took me to read all of the titles. Most books, of course, I barely understood. While reading Plato's *Republic,* for instance, I needed to keep looking at the book's jacket comments to remind myself what the text was about. Nevertheless…I looked at every word of the text. And by the time I reached the last word, relieved, I convinced myself that I had read *The Republic.* In a ceremony of pride, I solemnly crossed Plato off my list.

INTERPRETING LITERATURE

1. How did the writer's attitude toward reading change over time?

2. What benefits from reading do you think the writer especially appreciated because he was Hispanic American?

SYNTHESIZING IDEAS

3. Why do you think Rodriguez's parents viewed books differently from his teachers?

CHAPTER 32
New Frontiers

SETTING THE SCENE

Historical Focus

During the brief administration of John F. Kennedy, his leadership and the American people were repeatedly tested by staggering challenges at home and abroad. Domestically, these tests ranged from promoting racial integration and social justice to stimulating the economy. In foreign affairs, the tests included a failed invasion, a missile crisis, and signing of a treaty banning nuclear testing. The Kennedy years were a time of hope and fear, anguish and exhilaration.

Concepts to Understand

- Why efforts toward **civil rights** became an effective movement for change.
- How perceptions of the actions of the Soviet Union affected United States **foreign policy.**

People to Know

Rosa Parks, Martin Luther King, Jr., James Meredith, Fidel Castro, Robert Kennedy, Lyndon B. Johnson

Places to Locate

Montgomery, Little Rock, Bay of Pigs

Terms to Identify

New Frontier, Medicare, Peace Corps, Warren Commission

Guided Reading

As you read this chapter, seek the answers to the following questions.

1. What type of leadership did John F. Kennedy offer the nation?
2. What lessons did Kennedy learn from his handling of foreign policy?

SPANNING THE DECADES

POLITICAL	1954 Brown v. Board of Education	1955 *Montgomery Bus boycott begins*	1957 *Congress passes the first civil rights legislation since Reconstruction*	1961 *Peace Corps is established*

1954		1958	

CULTURAL	1954 *First mass inoculation of Salk polio vaccine*	1956 *John F. Kennedy publishes* Profiles in Courage		1961 *Baseball star Roger Maris hits 61 home runs*

Map *by Jasper Johns, 1961. Oil on canvas, 6'6" x 10'3". Museum of Modern Art, New York*

1962
Cuban
Missile
Crisis

1963
Kennedy is assassinated in Dallas; Lyndon Johnson becomes President

1965
Civil rights march at Selma

1962   1966

1962
John Steinbeck wins the Nobel Prize for Literature

1964
The Beatles appear on The Ed Sullivan Show

1964
Dr. Martin Luther King, Jr., wins the Nobel Peace Prize

...It should be clear by now that a nation can be no stronger abroad than she is at home. Only an America which practices what it preaches about equal rights and social justice, will be respected by those whose choice affects our future....

—JOHN F. KENNEDY,
undelivered speech, 1963

The Civil Rights Movement

In this state we are committed to segregation by custom and by law; we intend to maintain it. The settlement of differences over school attendance, public transportation and other public facilities must be made within these laws which reflect our way of life.

—GRAND JURY, on the Montgomery Boycott, 1956

Section Focus

Almost a century after passage of the Fourteenth and Fifteenth amendments, African Americans were still victims of discrimination and segregation. In the South these attitudes were entrenched not only in custom but also in law. The battle to obtain equal rights for blacks would have to be fought in the courts, in the news media, and in the consciences of the American people.

Objectives

After studying this section, you should be able to:
- Discuss the effects of the *Brown v. Board of Education* decision.
- Describe major events in the early civil rights movement.

Support for the civil rights movement spread rapidly during the 1950s and early 1960s. African Americans would no longer accept second-class citizenship nor the humiliating practice of forced segregation. They fought for equal opportunities in jobs, housing, and education. They fought against segregated schools, buses, and trains; they fought against separate facilities in restaurants, hotels, libraries, and hospitals. They won an important ally when the Supreme Court issued several decisions against racial discrimination. But the main force behind the civil rights movement came from citizens—black and white—who banded together in an effective protest movement.

Brown v. Board of Education

One of the Supreme Court's most significant rulings of the 1950s came in May 1954. Three years earlier, Linda Brown's parents had sued the school board of Topeka, Kansas, for not allowing their daughter to attend an all-white school, miles closer to their home than the segregated elementary school she was assigned to attend. The Supreme Court ruled in *Brown v. Board of Education of Topeka, Kansas,* that it was unconstitutional to separate schoolchildren by race. In the decision Chief Justice Earl Warren wrote:

Does segregation of children in public schools solely on the basis of race, even though the physical facilities and other "tangible" factors may be equal, deprive the children of the minority group of equal educational opportunities? We believe it does.

The *Brown* decision reversed the Court's decision in *Plessy v. Ferguson,* an 1896 ruling that had upheld the constitutionality of "separate but equal" public accommodations. *Plessy* had become the basis for Jim Crow laws and legal segregation in many states. In the *Brown* case, the Court did not set a deadline for ending segregation, but in 1955 ordered schools to desegregate with "all deliberate speed."

The Supreme Court's ruling in *Brown v. Board of Education* called for major changes in many states, especially those in the South. Some border states integrated their schools, but the South remained segregated. The governor of Virginia threatened to close the state's public schools and send white children to private schools. A group of 101 southern members of Congress signed a "Southern Manifesto," which called the Court's ruling "a clear abuse of judicial power" and pledged use of "all lawful means to bring about a reversal of this decision."

Boycotts and Demonstrations

The decisions of the Warren Court gave legal support to blacks' struggle for civil rights. But most civil rights battles, particularly in the South, were fought by brave men and women who broke down the barriers of segregation one by one. One of these was Rosa Parks, a black seamstress from Montgomery, Alabama. One day in December 1955,

Examining Photographs *Rosa Parks quietly took a seat in the front of the bus against law and custom. Why do you think she refused to give up her seat?*

Parks boarded a segregated bus in which all the seats allotted for blacks were filled; she took a seat in the front, which was reserved for white riders. Because she was too tired to stand, Parks refused to give up her seat. She was arrested and ordered to stand trial for disobeying the state's segregation laws.

Examining Photographs *Segregated public facilities such as rest rooms and drinking fountains were legal throughout much of the United States in the early 1950s. How did Martin Luther King, Jr., propose changing unjust laws?*

The arrest of Rosa Parks aroused anger in Montgomery's black community. Many of its leaders believed that now was the time to challenge Alabama's segregation laws. At a meeting held at the Dexter Avenue Baptist Church, a boycott of the city's buses was called. The 26-year-old minister of the church, Dr. Martin Luther King, Jr., was asked to lead the boycott.

On the day of Rosa Parks's trial, almost all of the black riders who usually took the buses boycotted them. Because a majority of the regular bus riders were black, the bus company lost much of its business. The boycott continued for almost a year.

Rosa Parks was convicted and fined $10. Dr. King and other black leaders were arrested for sponsoring an "illegal boycott." But in November 1956, the Supreme Court ruled that segregation in public transportation was illegal. The bus company ended its policy of segregation. The black citizens of Montgomery, assured of equal treatment, resumed riding the buses. The Montgomery bus boycott galvanized the civil rights movement, and in Martin Luther King, Jr., that movement found an inspiring leader.

Black churches and their ministers took the lead in organizing the civil rights movement. Dr. King, a Baptist minister, drew from his own faith and also from the nonviolent techniques of the great Indian leader Mohandas Gandhi. King told the people he led that they should disobey unjust laws, but at the same time he asked them to love their oppressors and never to use violence. He explained that public opinion not violence would force authorities to change unjust laws:

We who engage in nonviolent direct action are not the creators of tension. We merely bring to the surface the hidden tension that is already alive…. Injustice must be exposed, with all the tension its exposure creates, to the light of human conscience and the air of national opinion before it can be cured.

In 1957, to carry on this nonviolent struggle against discrimination in public places all over the South, King and other black Southern leaders from 10 states founded the Southern Christian Leadership Conference (SCLC).

The civil rights movement represented the work of many groups. Among them were such long-established black organizations as the National Association for the Advancement of Colored People (NAACP), which fought discrimination in many court cases, including *Brown v. Board of Education;* the National Urban League, which established community programs in cities to promote education

Life of the Times

SCHOOL DESEGREGATION

Melba Pattillo Beals was one of the African-American teenagers who integrated Little Rock's Central High School in the fall of 1957. Federal paratroopers escorted her and the other black students to protect them from the jeering crowds of parents and other townspeople outside the school. However, the troops could do little to protect the black teenagers from the other students once they started classes. Despite the danger, Beals felt proud to participate in what even then she saw as an historic happening.

In the following passage, Beals recalls some of her experiences at the formerly all-white school.

"I went in not through the side doors but up the front stairs, and there was a feeling of pride and hope that yes, this is the United States; yes, there is a reason I salute the flag….The troops were wonderful….[But] they couldn't be with us everywhere….We'd be showering in gym and someone would turn your shower onto scalding. You'd be walking out to the volleyball court and someone would break a bottle and trip you on the bottle…first you're in pain, then you're angry, then you try to fight back,… And then you just mellow out and you realize that survival is day-to-day and you start to grasp your own spirit, you start to grasp the depth of the human spirit and you start to understand your own ability to cope no matter what. That is the greatest lesson I learned."

and political power for minorities; and the Congress of Racial Equality (CORE), which worked for economic and political opportunities for African Americans. Dr. King remained at the forefront of the movement as it continued to grow in the 1960s. In 1964 he received the Nobel Peace Prize for his nonviolent leadership.

Eisenhower and Civil Rights

In May 1955, the Supreme Court had called for the implementation of integration "with all deliberate speed." The ruling needed the active support of President Eisenhower, but the President believed that the federal government should remain neutral concerning controversial issues that affected state and local governments. He remarked, "I don't believe you can change the hearts of men with laws and decisions."

In 1957 Congress passed the first civil rights law since Reconstruction. The act created a civil rights division within the Department of Justice and gave the government the power to seek court injunctions against those who denied any citizen's constitutional rights. A 1960 law empowered the Justice Department to go to court on behalf of citizens whose civil rights were violated.

Just a few months later, in September 1957, the state of Arkansas tested the federal government's policies on civil

Examining Photographs *Central High School in little Rock Arkansas, became the focus of court-ordered desegregation in 1957. After Govenor Faubus used the Arkansas national guard to prevent nine black students from attending, Eisenhower sent federal troops into Little Rock. How was the crisis resolved?*

The end of Reconstruction left African Americans economically, socially, and politically second-class citizens. The sharecropping system and "Jim Crow" segregation laws worked to deny them their rights as citizens. Black leaders began to work toward restoring their full civil rights in the early decades of the twentieth century, but the movement did not come into full flower until the 1950s. Backed by the federal government, Dr. Martin Luther King, Jr., and others then declared, "We shall overcome!"

rights. A federal court had ordered that nine black students be admitted to the all-white Central High School in Little Rock, Arkansas. The state's governor, Orval Faubus, defied federal authority and sent National Guard troops to prevent the students from attending.

President Eisenhower invited Governor Faubus to Newport, Rhode Island, to persuade him to obey the court order. The governor withdrew the troops, but without their protection the black students were exposed to an angry mob that threatened them with physical harm. Forced to act to maintain order, Eisenhower sent in 1,000 paratroopers and federalized 10,000 members of the Arkansas National Guard to surround the school so that the students could enter safely.

As Daisy Bates, then the president of the Arkansas NAACP, later remembered:

...the nine negro pupils marched solemnly through the doors of Central High School, surrounded by twenty-two soldiers. An Army helicopter circled overhead. Around the massive brick schoolhouse 350 paratroopers stood grimly at attention.... Within minutes a world that had been holding its breath learned that the nine pupils...had finally entered the "never-never-land."

Troops remained in Little Rock for the rest of the year, however, and Central High School was closed for the 1958-1959 academic year.

As the Eisenhower administration drew to a close, the nation remained racially divided. Custom and years of intimidation kept many African Americans from voting. Between 1957 and 1960, the Justice Department brought only 10 suits to secure voting rights for blacks. Only 25 percent of adult blacks voted in states of the deep South, and only 5 percent in Mississippi. The movement for civil rights was just beginning.

★ ★ ★ ★ ★ ★ ★ ★ ★ ★ ★ ★ ★ ★ ★ ★ ★

Section One Review

★ ★ ★ ★ ★ ★ ★ ★ ★ ★ ★ ★ ★ ★ ★ ★ ★

SUMMARY

In the 1950s black Americans used their growing voice and power to fight for an end to discrimination. Their efforts were aided by the Supreme Court's decision in *Brown v. Board of Education* that stated separation by race was inherently unequal. Conservatives thought that the Supreme Court had overstepped its bounds. Despite the *Brown* decision, most of the South desegregated slowly. Then, in 1955, Rosa Parks was arrested for refusing to give up her seat on a bus to a white rider. Black citizens in Montgomery boycotted the bus system, forcing the city to desegregate the buses. Perhaps just as important, the civil rights movement found among its ranks a powerful and inspiring leader: Martin Luther King, Jr.

CHECKING FOR UNDERSTANDING

1. **Identify** Earl Warren, *Brown v. Board of Education,* Rosa Parks, Montgomery, Martin Luther King, Jr., Southern Christian Leadership Conference

2. **Summarize** the tactics used in the Montgomery bus boycott.

3 **Explain** Martin Luther King's philosophy of nonviolence.

4 **Describe** why Eisenhower sent federal troops into Little Rock

THINKING CRITICALLY

5. **Analyzing a Viewpoint** How would you evaluate Eisenhower's stand on civil rights? Reread his quotation on page 957. Explain why many blacks in the South would not be content with this approach.

LINKING PAST AND PRESENT

6. **Supporting an Opinion** In the 1990s the struggle for the full civil rights for all Americans continues. In your opinion, what groups today experience discrimination? Explain.

★ ★ ★ ★ ★ ★ ★ ★ ★ ★ ★ ★ ★ ★ ★ ★ ★

Kennedy's New Frontier

Whatever the political affiliation of our next President…he must above all, be chief executive in every sense of the word. He must be prepared to exercise the fullest powers in his office—all that are specified and some that are not. The President is above at the top.

—JOHN F. KENNEDY
U.S. Senator, 1959

Section Focus

By the late 1950s, many people in the United States felt it was time to attack the nation's problems with new vigor. Despite the prosperity of the postwar years, poverty and racism were still prevalent. Eisenhower, the first President to be legally limited to two terms, would soon be leaving office. The people looked to his still-unchosen successor to provide strong, active leadership.

Objectives

After studying this section, you should be able to:
- Describe important legislation Kennedy proposed during his term of office.
- Describe advances made in civil rights during the Kennedy administration.

Washington, D.C., glittered during the Kennedy years. As never before, millions became familiar with the occupants of the White House: a young, energetic President, the cultured and glamorous First Lady, and the unusual sight of the Kennedy children playing under their father's desk. The public's enchantment with Kennedy was not shared by Congress, however. Many of Kennedy's most important legislative efforts would have to wait until after his death to become law.

The Election of 1960

In the 1960 presidential campaign, the Republicans chose Vice President Richard M. Nixon; and the Democrats chose Senator John F. Kennedy. The backgrounds of the two men presented striking contrasts. Kennedy was a Catholic from Massachusetts, the second-oldest son of a wealthy family. Nixon, born in California, was from a family in which his father was not financially successful, and his Quaker mother had struggled to keep the family together. Both candidates were young: Nixon was 47 years old, and Kennedy was 43. As his vice-presidential running mate Nixon chose U.N. Ambassador Henry Cabot Lodge. To win southern support, Kennedy chose the Texas Senator Lyndon B. Johnson as his running mate. Nixon and Kennedy were experienced legislators, both having served in the House of Representatives and in the Senate. Nixon had also served eight years as Eisenhower's Vice President.

The political differences between the candidates were small. Both were considered "Cold Warriors" who believed that communism (the Soviet Union, in particular), was the chief threat to the way of life in the United States. Senator Kennedy hoped to take advantage of Republican weaknesses and challenged Nixon to a series of televised debates. Nixon was the more skilled debator, and the majority of those people who listened to the debates on radio declared Nixon the winner. Yet, the millions more who watched on television thought a well-prepared, poised, and youthful Senator Kennedy won the debates. The debates were one of the earliest examples of the impact of television on United States politics.

Political observers wondered whether Kennedy's religion would be an obstacle to his election. No Catholic had ever been elected President, and some believed that

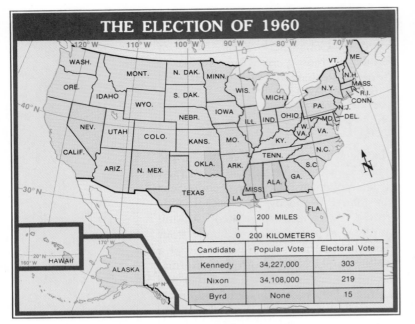

THE ELECTION OF 1960

Candidate	Popular Vote	Electoral Vote
Kennedy	34,227,000	303
Nixon	34,108,000	219
Byrd	None	15

Examining Maps *The popular vote for President in 1960 was the closest since 1888. Kennedy's popular margin was only about 120,000 out of more than 68 million votes cast. To what did Kennedy believe he owed his thin margin of victory?*

church and state. He declared he would resign, rather than violate either his conscience or the interests of the nation.

Kennedy carried the election by one of the narrowest margins in American history. He won the popular vote by 120,000 out of 68 million votes cast and the electoral college by 303 to 219. In several states a difference of only a few thousand votes would have swung the electoral votes the other way. Kennedy generally ran behind Democratic candidates in Congress, but he laid to rest the idea that a Roman Catholic could not be elected President. Analyzing his narrow victory, Kennedy concluded, "It was T.V. more than anything else that turned the tide."

The New Frontier

Kennedy devoted his inaugural address to defining the role of the United States in a divided world. The torch, he said, had been passed on to "a new generation," committed to the rights for which the United States had stood since the Revolution. He warned the communist world that the United States would remain strong. But he also urged both sides to renew the search for peace. He wanted

a Catholic could not make official decisions independent from the Roman Catholic Church. Kennedy answered by stressing his belief in the separation of

Examining Photographs
Outgoing President Eisenhower looks on as Kennedy delivers his inaugural address on a cold January 20, 1961. What was Kennedy's message to communist countries?

both to join forces against the common enemies of "tyranny, poverty, disease, and war itself." In ringing tones, he declared:

My fellow Americans, ask not what your country can do for you: Ask what you can do for your country. My fellow citizens of the world: Ask not what America can do for you, but what together we can do for the freedom of man.

The Kennedy administration became known as the "New Frontier." For the first time, the future of the United States lay in the hands of those born in the twentieth century. The President and his closest advisors were intelligent and tough-minded. They were sure of their ability to make the country and the world better places to live in.

In public the new President mixed idealism with realism and informality with dignity. Above all, Kennedy seemed to have the gift of leadership that inspired trust and devotion. Kennedy's qualities of leadership seemed to appeal not only to those in the United States but to people all over the world.

Kennedy's Economic Program

Essentially, Kennedy's New Frontier was a continuation of Roosevelt's New Deal and Truman's Fair Deal. Kennedy promised to stimulate the economy with tax cuts and increased federal spending.

When Kennedy became President, the nation's rate of economic growth was only 3 percent a year. Kennedy looked for ways to increase growth and create more jobs. In stimulating the economy, he chose not to rely on federal spending, which tends to cause inflation. Instead he sought to increase business production and efficiency. His administration also asked businesses to hold down prices and labor leaders to hold down requests for pay increases.

Prodded by Secretary of Labor Arthur Goldberg, labor unions in the steel industry agreed to reduce their demands for higher wages. Despite this agreement, several steel companies raised prices sharply in 1962. Kennedy denounced the steel company executives and threatened to have the Department of Defense buy cheaper steel from foreign companies. He also instructed the Justice Department to investigate whether the steel industry was guilty of price-fixing. The steel companies backed down and cut their prices. To achieve this victory, however, Kennedy had strained his relations with the nation's business leaders.

AMERICAN PORTRAITS

RACHEL CARSON
1907-1964

From her earliest days, Rachel Carson had two great loves: nature and books. At first, she planned to be a writer, but she switched majors from English to biology during her junior year of college. She combined her twin loves by becoming a science author.

An aquatic biologist by training, Rachel Carson wrote about the sea with great insight. But *Silent Spring,* her most important book, dealt with the environment. Long aware of the threat posed by careless use of toxic chemicals, she researched carefully and wrote movingly about how modern industry and agriculture were poisoning the planet. *Silent Spring* sparked a federal investigation that backed her conclusions and led to tougher laws regarding harmful chemicals. Rachel Carson died soon after publication of *Silent Spring,* unaware of the ecology movement that her work would inspire.

Connections

HISTORY AND SCIENCE

SPACE RACE

Americans were stunned by the news that the Soviets had put a satellite—*Sputnik I*—into orbit around the earth in October 1957. Physicist Edward Teller called the launch a Soviet victory in "a

Edwin E. Aldrin, Jr., lunar module pilot

battle more important and greater than Pearl Harbor." President Eisenhower told the panicked nation that only its pride, not its security, was damaged.

Americans, however, were threatened by what they considered Soviet technical superiority. In response, Congress passed the National Defense Education Act, which financed science and foreign-language programs in schools. In addition, the National Science foundation's curriculum-development budget was dramatically increased. Congress also created the National Aeronautics and Space Administration (NASA) in 1958. Huge sums of money were allocated to develop space technology and compete with the Soviets in space.

In 1961, the same year the Soviets put a cosmonaut into orbit, President Kennedy pledged America to landing a man on the moon by 1970. In July 1969, this goal was achieved.

★ ★ ★ ★ ★ ★ ★ ★ ★ ★

MAKING THE SCIENCE CONNECTION

1. How did Americans feel about the success of *Sputnik?*

2. What actions were taken in response to *Sputnik?*

LINKING PAST AND PRESENT

3. Why do you think the U.S. space program today has less support than it did in the 1960s?

★ ★ ★ ★ ★ ★ ★ ★ ★ ★

The country was generally prosperous during the Kennedy years. But there were areas of poverty, notably in the Appalachian Mountain region, in much of the South, and in the nation's inner cities. Kennedy supported the Area Redevelopment Act, designed to encourage industries to move into economically depressed areas. His Housing Act of 1961 called for $5 billion to be spent improving rundown homes and slum neighborhoods in the inner cities. And he achieved his aim of raising the national economic growth rate, which doubled during his administration.

Although the Democratic party enjoyed large majorities in both houses of Congress, Kennedy was unable to get Congress to pass much of his domestic program into law. Congress, dominated by a conservative coalition of Southern Democrats, rejected many New Frontier measures, just as they had done with Truman's Fair Deal.

When Kennedy proposed that the government recognize the problems of cities by creating a new Cabinet department for urban affairs, Congress voted down the proposal. Kennedy also asked for a national health insurance program, Medicare, to help older citizens pay their medical bills. The Senate defeated this bill, which was opposed by many doctors. The President called the Senate's action a "serious defeat for every American family."

Despite the power of the conservative coalition in Congress, Kennedy was able to win some legislative victories in his domestic program, including a bill for federal aid to public schools. Perhaps his most significant victory was increased funding for the National Aeronautics and Space Administration (NASA). Kennedy challenged the nation and NASA with the goal of putting an astronaut on the moon by 1970. There were those who objected to spending an estimated $20 billion for

Examining Photographs *Seven astronauts from NASA's Mercury project pose in 1961. What was Kennedy's goal in space exploration?*

manned space flights, but Kennedy saw space exploration as a challenge to the nation's prestige and a symbol of Cold War rivalry with the Soviet Union. He believed the United States must capture the lead that the Soviets had taken in space exploration when, in 1957, they had launched *Sputnik I,* the first space satellite to orbit the earth.

Kennedy and Civil Rights

In contrast to Eisenhower's cautious stand on civil rights, President Kennedy had promised vigorous support of the movement. Kennedy was aware of the support he needed from black voters to win the 1960 election. During the campaign he boldly declared that segregation in federal housing could be ended with "a stroke of the pen." But once in office, he moved slowly on civil rights. His slim victory over Nixon, coupled with the fear of losing southern Democratic support in Congress, made him act less forcefully than the words of his campaign had seemed to promise.

Kennedy's cautious attitude disappointed white liberals and black leaders. He waited until 1962 to sign an executive order ending segregation in government-owned housing. And although Kennedy appointed African Americans to his administration as well as to federal judicial positions, he also appointed some judges who supported segregation. Events in the South, however, soon forced Kennedy to take a more active role in civil rights.

In the spring of 1961, civil rights activists volunteered as "Freedom Riders" to ride chartered buses into segregated bus terminals throughout the South. In May bus loads of the Freedom Riders were attacked by mobs in the Alabama cities of Anniston and Birmingham; a bus was fire-bombed and riders were beaten and clubbed. As more and more Freedom Riders poured into southern cities, local police were unable or unwilling to protect them from angry racists. The President was forced to use federal marshals to restore order. The Justice Department also pressured the Interstate Commerce Commission to bring lawsuits against those terminals that refused to comply with regulations on desegregation.

Under Kennedy, from 1961 to 1963, the Department of Justice brought 6 times as many lawsuits to protect black voting rights as it did under Eisenhower, from 1958 to 1960. As a result, by 1964, the percentage of black citizens registered to vote in the deep South had risen from 25 to 40 percent, largely as a result of the work of the Freedom Riders.

In April 1963, during a demonstration led by Dr. King in Birmingham, Alabama, national television carried vivid pictures of police using fire hoses, clubs, and police dogs on demonstrators—among them women and children. Viewers were shocked by these outrageous actions, and Kennedy sent 3,000 troops to restore peace in the city. Then, in June he proposed a new civil rights bill that would outlaw segregation throughout the nation.

During Kennedy's administration, the Department of Justice brought numerous suits for desegregation of schools. In September 1962, James Meredith, a 29-year-old black Air Force veteran, sought entrance to the University of Mississippi. Although Meredith was backed by a court

Examining Photographs

The August 1963 March on Washington was the largest and most peaceful protest in the nation's history. What was the goal of the marchers?

order, Governor Ross Barnett declared, "Never! We will never surrender to the evil and illegal forces of tyranny." Kennedy immediately sent in marshals to enable Meredith to enter the university safely. When mobs at the university grew larger and uglier, President Kennedy sent in the Mississippi National Guard. Meredith was able to attend classes, but only after two people had been killed in a mob action. In 1963 Alabama Governor George Wallace tried to stop a black student from entering the University of Alabama. Once again the President sent marshals and the Alabama National Guard to the university campus.

The violence of such confrontations convinced Kennedy that federal legislation against segregation and discrimination was needed. He quickly proposed laws that would forbid segregation in stores, restaurants, hotels, and theaters and that would prohibit discrimination in employment. But progress on school desegregation was slow. Most black school children in the south continued to attend all-black schools.

The March on Washington

For the 100th anniversary of the Emancipation Proclamation, black leaders planned a "March on Washington for Jobs and Freedom." The march would press for passage of President Kennedy's proposed civil rights bill, which was then being debated in Congress. In August 1963, more than 200,000 demonstrators, both black and white, converged on the nation's capital. Led by priests, rabbis, ministers, and civic leaders, they sang hymns and spirituals as they gathered near the Lincoln Memorial. As one 15-year-old black girl described it:

There was this sense of hope for the future— the belief that this march was the big step in the right direction. It could be heard in the voices of the people singing and seen in the way they walked. It poured out into smiles.

At the Lincoln Memorial the marchers heard eloquent speeches, especially from Dr. Martin Luther King, Jr., who, in a famous address, described his dream of freedom and equality for all people:

I have a dream that one day this nation will rise up and live out the true meaning of its creed: 'We hold these truths to be self-evident; that all men are created equal' ...And when this happens, and when we allow freedom to ring, when we let it ring from every village and hamlet, from every state and every city, we will be able to speed up that day when all God's children...[will] join hands and sing in the words of the old...spiritual: 'Free at last, Free at last, Thank God Almighty, we are free at last.'

The leaders of the march then left to meet with Kennedy at the White House. It had been the largest and most peaceful protest in the nation's history. The March on Washington was a great victory for the civil rights movement. It not only awakened millions to the plight of blacks living in the South but also confirmed for Congress the widespread support for Kennedy's civil rights bill. Ironically, the bill, which did not pass until after Kennedy's death, was by then much stronger than the one he submitted to Congress.

But progress was slow. In 1963, 9 years after the *Brown* decision, only one-half of one percent of black public school children in the 11 former Confederate states were attending desegregated schools. Some southern communities desegregated public facilities only after boycotts and sit-ins. Others refused, however, and some even used violence to intimidate nonviolent protestors. As black homes and churches were bombed, and as some demonstrators were beaten and arrested, some African Americans began to abandon the nonviolent techniques of Dr. King. They chose to meet violence with violence.

Section Two Review

SUMMARY

After narrowly winning the 1960 election, President Kennedy put his energy, ideas, and charisma to work. Despite his popularity, many of Kennedy's programs, such as Medicare, were blocked by Congress. In civil rights, Kennedy was initially timid about alienating white southern Democrats, but events soon forced his hand. The President used federal courts and troops to enforce desegregation in the South. The efforts of the civil rights movement culminated in the March on Washington where 200,000 Americans gathered to demonstrate peacefully for racial harmony and justice.

CHECKING FOR UNDERSTANDING

1. **Identify** Richard M. Nixon, New Frontier, Housing Act of 1961, Freedom Riders, Birmingham, James Meredith, March on Washington

2. **Describe** the role of television in Kennedy's 1960 election victory.

3. **Characterize** the attitudes that described Kennedy's administration.

4. **List** three economic programs undertaken by President Kennedy.

5. **Explain** why many of Kennedy's domestic programs were not passed.

6. **Summarize** the advances and setbacks of the civil rights movement during Kennedy's presidency.

THINKING CRITICALLY

7. **Evaluating Events** The March on Washington is seen as one of the major events of the civil rights movement. Why was the march so effective?

CONNECTIONS: HISTORY AND TECHNOLOGY

8. **Analyzing Trends** Do you think television gives voters an accurate picture of presidential candidates? Use events from the 1960 presidential election to support your answer.

Foreign Policy Challenges

SETTING THE SCENE

I speak of peace because of the new face of war. Total war makes no sense in our age when great powers maintain large nuclear forces....It makes no sense in an age when a single nuclear weapon contains almost 10 times the explosive force delivered by all the Allied air forces in the Second World War.

—JOHN F. KENNEDY
Address at American University,
Washington, D.C., June 10, 1963

Section Focus

Kennedy entered office with little first-hand experience in international affairs. Yet he had to meet such challenges as the buildup of nuclear arms, anti-United States feeling in Latin America, and instability in economically developing nations in Africa and Asia. He achieved some triumphs; in other cases his inexperience led him into avoidable mistakes.

Objectives

After studying this section, you should be able to:
- Discuss Kennedy's responses to Soviet and international communism.
- Explain the purposes of the Alliance for Progress and the Peace Corps.

President Kennedy's basic aims in foreign policy were similar to those of Truman and Eisenhower. His major concern was the threat of communism, and he declared that he would not relax efforts to contain it. Yet he was more willing than his predecessors had been to reduce tensions if that could

be done without sacrificing U.S. interests. He showed greater tolerance for nationalism in the developing nations and more interest in helping those nations deal with economic and social problems.

Dealings with Latin America

In 1959 Fidel Castro had led a movement to overthrow Fulgencio Batista—the corrupt dictator then ruling Cuba—and had set up a new government. Castro soon established ties with the Soviet Union and began to adopt such Marxist-influenced policies as drastic land reforms and the seizing of foreign-owned businesses. As a result of such actions, the Eisenhower administration began to view Cuba as a threat to democracy in the Western Hemisphere. Eisenhower authorized the Central Intelligence Agency to train and arm Cuban exiles secretly for the overthrow of Castro.

The CIA believed that an invasion of Cuba by these exiles would touch off a popular uprising against Castro. Kennedy's military advisers approved the project. In office less than three months, trusting the experts, Kennedy agreed that the invasion should proceed.

On April 17, 1961, a force of 1,400 Cuban exiles came ashore at the Bay of Pigs on the south coast of Cuba. From the start the invasion went poorly. There was no popular uprising by the Cuban people. Within hours Castro's forces had the invaders surrounded.

The failed invasion hurt the prestige of the new Kennedy administration and strengthened Castro's position in the world. It also allowed Soviet leader Nikita Khrushchev to pose as the defender of Latin America against United States imperialism. Kennedy took the blame for the disaster himself and never again trusted military experts. Curiously, his rating in American public opinion polls went up. "The worse I do, the more popular I get," Kennedy observed wryly.

The Castro movement, known as "Fidelismo," threatened to spread to other countries in Latin America. Promoted by

Cuban agents, it often found support among the poverty-stricken and those seeking more political power. Kennedy announced a new economic program for Latin America—called the Alliance for Progress—that emphasized social reform and political freedom. Its purpose was to develop long-term economic growth among 19 Latin American nations, and thus make it less likely that poverty would drive these people to support communist-inspired revolutions. Over a 10-year period, the United States pledged $20 billion to help Latin American countries provide better schools, housing, and health care, as well as introduce fairer methods of taxation and redistribution of large landholdings to small farmers. Even though United States aid to Latin America quadrupled, the results were uneven. Communists regarded the Alliance as a front for U.S. imperialism, while wealthy Latin Americans saw it as a force for revolution and a threat to their property. In some countries—notably Chile, Colombia, Venezuela, and the Central American republics—the Alliance succeeded in promoting reform. In others, however, much of the money was diverted for the benefit of the military and the wealthy.

On October 22, 1962, President Kennedy went on television and made a chilling announcement. U-2 planes from the United States had taken photographs proving that the Soviet Union had placed long-range missiles on Cuba. These missiles, carrying nuclear weapons, posed a direct threat to the United States. Kennedy ordered a naval blockade to keep the Soviets from delivering any more missiles, and he demanded that the Soviets dismantle all their missile sites in Cuba. As Soviet ships approached, war seemed imminent.

Secretly, the Soviet Union offered to remove the missiles if the United States would promise never to invade Cuba. As the negotiations continued, Khrushchev added another demand: that the United States remove its own missiles from the Soviet border of Turkey. President Kennedy rejected this demand because it would weaken the NATO alliance. The President's brother, Attorney General

MISSILE ERECTOR

CABLE

MISSILE SHELTER TENT

TRACKED PRIME MOVERS

FUEL TANK TRAILERS

Examining Photographs
Defense Department photos such as this documented the presence of Soviet missiles in Cuba that were capable of reaching the United States. What was Kennedy's response?

Examining Fine Art *Norman Rockwell's* The Peace Corps in Ethiopia, 1966, *depicts a young American volunteer giving instruction on the use of a plow. Peace Corps volunteers worked in many developing countries around the world. In what kinds of projects were they involved?*

Robert Kennedy, suggested they ignore the new proposal and accept the Soviet Union's first offer.

After five agonizing days, when the world appeared on the brink of nuclear disaster, the Soviet ships turned back from the blockade. Soviet missiles were withdrawn from Cuba. President Kennedy won strong public support for his firm stand. Two years later Premier Khrushchev was removed from power. The Soviet Union then began a massive new buildup of its military strength.

The Peace Corps

Another program to help developing nations fight poverty and disease was the Peace Corps. When he established the Peace Corps in 1961, Kennedy declared:

Our own freedom, and the future of freedom around the world, depend...on their ability to build growing and independent nations where men can live in dignity, liberated from the bonds of hunger, ignorance, and poverty.

The Corps was made up of volunteers from the United States who wanted to help people in developing nations. After a period of rigorous training, Peace Corps volunteers went to countries that had asked for their assistance. There they lived among the people and helped them solve local problems. They laid out sewage systems in Bolivia, trained medical technicians in Chad, and built a model town in Pakistan. A high proportion of volunteers taught English and practical skills. In return they received only a living wage and a small vacation allowance. By late 1963 there were 11,000 Peace Corps volunteers serving in 40 countries.

Peace Corps volunteers in economically developing nations of Africa, Asia, and Latin America witnessed firsthand the problems and potential of newly independent nations that often lacked the necessary institutions to make the transition from colonial status to political and economic independence.

By 1961, 27 newly independent nations had been formed from European colonies in Africa. When boundary lines of the colonies were established by Europeans in the 1800s and early 1900s, ethnic and cultural organizations were not taken into account. Even decades later, it was difficult obtaining loyalty to the new nation-state.

In 1961 ethnic rivalries in the Congo, later renamed Zaire, broke out into civil war. When the mineral-rich province of Katanga attempted to secede because of tribal and regional differences, two Congolese leaders called for Soviet military aid. The United States, however, backed the efforts of the United Nations to arrange for a cease-fire. In 1963, after intervention by U.N. troops, the Congo

was reunited. Other attempts at superpower intervention were generally rebutted as most African nations developed a policy of nonalignment.

Challenges from the Soviet Union

Although holding to the containment policy, Kennedy sought means of relieving the tensions of the cold war. In his inaugural address he had said, "Let us never negotiate out of fear but let us never fear to negotiate." In June 1961, he met with Khrushchev in the Austrian capital, Vienna. The two men treated each other with wary politeness, but they could find no area of agreement. Khrushchev may have thought that he could intimidate Kennedy who had recently been embarrassed by the Bay of Pigs disaster. The Russian leader handed Kennedy a near-ultimatum on East Germany and Berlin. He insisted that the Western powers recognize the German puppet state and that the four-power occupation of Berlin, which was completely surrounded by East Germany, come to an end. When the President refused, the Communist answer was to build a wall through Berlin, blocking free movement between their section of Berlin and the rest of the city. This weakened the economy of West Berlin,

Linking Across Time

CONTAINMENT

With minor alterations, Presidents since 1947 have followed a similar policy toward the Soviet Union—containment. This policy was suggested by George Kennan, an American diplomat and Soviet authority. He proposed that the United States aggressively block Soviet expansion, but strive to avoid a third world war, until the Soviet system mellowed or was altered. The demise of communism in Eastern Europe in 1988 and 1989 has proven the wisdom of this policy.

Examining Photographs
The Berlin Wall dividing the East German and West German parts of the city was hastily constructed in August 1961. Why was the wall built?

which had drawn much of its labor from the Russian sector. The wall also prevented the flight of refugees seeking to escape the oppression of East Germany. Those attempting to escape were shot down by East German police.

In June 1963, Kennedy visited West Berlin. A vast, cheering crowd gathered to hear him at the city hall. The President told them:

Freedom has many difficulties and democracy is not perfect, but we have never had to put up a wall to keep our people in....All free men, wherever they may live, are citizens of Berlin, and therefore, as a free man I take pride in the words, "Ich bin ein [I am a] Berliner."

The Berlin Wall stood for nearly 30 years as a menacing symbol of the cold war division between East and West.

In 1961 the Soviet Union broke a three-year moratorium on testing nuclear weapons in the atmosphere. The Soviets exploded more than 40 bombs, one with 3,000 times the power of the bomb that destroyed Hiroshima. Kennedy attempted to persuade the Soviets to ban above-ground testing, because nuclear fallout pollutes the atmosphere of the whole world. But the Soviets would not agree to a method of inspection satisfactory to Americans. Not wanting the Soviet Union to gain nuclear superiority, the United States also resumed testing.

In 1963, after the Cuban missile crisis, both sides agreed that they must do something to reduce the risk of war. President Kennedy called on the Soviet Union to work with him toward world peace. It was not necessary for each side to "love his neighbor," Kennedy said, only that they tolerate each other and live together peacefully.

The inspection issue became less important as other means were found to monitor nuclear explosions from outside the Soviet Union. Consequently the United States gave up its demands for on-site inspection. In August 1963, the United States, the Soviet Union, and Great Britain signed a test-ban treaty that prohibited atomic tests in the atmosphere, in outer space, and underwater. The treaty, however, did not ban underground testing or reduce the total number of nuclear weapons. In September 1963, the Senate ratified the treaty by a vote of 80 to 19.

Trouble in Southeast Asia

During the Kennedy years, the Soviet Union lent its support to "wars of national liberation" in many economically developing nations. Truman and Eisenhower had countered by providing military aid and training troops for the established governments. When Kennedy took office in 1961, the Southeast Asian nation of Laos was in danger of falling to communist guerrilla forces. The CIA and the Joint Chiefs of Staff pressed for a strong defense of Laos, even the use of nuclear weapons. Kennedy, on the other hand, believed a diplomatic solution could be found. In the end Kennedy avoided war by striking a compromise with Khrushchev—first by agreeing to a cease-fire and then by establishing a neutral government. A formal agreement, stating that all sides accepted the neutrality of

Examining Photographs *While visiting Germany in 1963, President Kennedy told Berliners that all free people were citizens of their city. What did the Berlin Wall symbolize?*

Examining Political Cartoons
Kennedy tells Khrushchev in 1962, "Let's Get A Lock On This Thing." What agreement did they reach on nuclear testing?

Laos, was signed in Geneva in 1962. The Geneva agreement, however, did not resolve the situation and fighting between the Laos government and the guerrilla forces soon resumed.

Kennedy also inherited the problem of Vietnam, a former French colony in Southeast Asia, from previous administrations. In 1954 the country had been divided into North Vietnam, controlled by the communist government of Ho Chi Minh, and South Vietnam, controlled by a noncommunist government supported first by France and then by the United States. In the late 1950s the Vietcong—communist-trained guerrillas—began fighting to overthrow the U.S. backed government of Ngo Dinh Diem and to reunite South Vietnam with the North. Both Eisenhower and Kennedy responded by sending military aid and advisers to South Vietnam. By late 1963 Kennedy had increased the number of advisers to 16,000.

Kennedy's Vietnam policy was complicated because Diem was a corrupt and unpopular dictator, a French-educated, upper-middle class Catholic who ruled a largely Buddhist country. Middle- and lower-class Buddhists distrusted both Diem and the West. In his efforts to remain in power, Diem took increasingly harsh and undemocratic measures. Buddhists began to organize, putting out English-language newspapers and gaining television coverage of the Diem regime's abuses. Some Buddhist monks took the extreme step of setting themselves on fire, becoming martyrs as they dramatically expressed their protests.

President Kennedy warned Diem that he was losing control of the country. But Diem made no attempts at reform and finally, in November 1963, possibly with the knowledge of Kennedy officials, Diem was murdered by his own military staff. By the end of 1963, 160 American advisors had died in Vietnam.

Tragedy in Dallas

John F. Kennedy's years in office came to a sudden end on November 22, 1963, when he was assassinated while visiting Dallas, Texas. The sense of tragedy and grief that many felt was caught by a conversation between the newspaper columnist Mary McGrory and Daniel Moynihan, a member of Kennedy's staff. In response to McGrory's remark that "we'll never laugh again," Moynihan replied, "Heavens, Mary, we'll laugh again. It's just that we'll never be young again." It was this feeling of youth snuffed out, of promise unfulfilled, that made Kennedy's death seem peculiarly tragic to many.

The country and the world were deeply shocked and saddened at this loss. Americans everywhere grieved over the President's death. In Italy, people brought flowers to the gates of the American embassy in Rome. In India, crowds wept in the street of New Delhi. In Africa, President Sékou Touré of Guinea said, "I have lost my only true friend in the outside world."

The circumstances of Kennedy's death have not been explained to the satisfaction of all. His apparent assassin, Lee Harvey Oswald, was himself shot to death only two days after the assassination. This event led to speculation that Oswald was killed to protect others who may have helped plan the crime. In 1964 a national commission headed by Chief Justice

Examining Photographs *A weary Jacqueline Kennedy looks on as Vice President Lyndon Johnson takes the oath of office following her husband's assassination. Why do some people believe questions remain about the circumstances of Kennedy's death?*

Warren concluded that Oswald was indeed the assassin and that he acted alone. The commission's report did leave important questions unanswered, though, and theories still persist that Oswald acted as part of a conspiracy. None of those theories have gained wide acceptance, however.

Kennedy was succeeded in office by Vice President Lyndon B. Johnson. Johnson took the oath of office on the plane that carried Kennedy's body from Dallas back to Washington, D.C. From Kennedy, Johnson inherited both unsolved problems and unfulfilled promises. A major foreign policy challenge was Vietnam. Kennedy's intentions for further involvement there were unclear; Johnson, in any case, had to make his own decisions about that troubled area. In domestic policy, Kennedy's New Frontier program was stalled in Congress. Yet, only two years after his death, most of these programs became law. The public reaction to the young president's tragic death, combined with the political skills of Lyndon Johnson, made possible sweeping social reform.

Section Three Review

SUMMARY

In foreign policy Kennedy hoped to reduce cold-war tensions while helping developing nations. In Cuba the Bay of Pigs invasion and the missile crisis kept relationships tense. Elsewhere in Latin America, the Alliance for Progress had mixed results. The Peace Corps, a self-help development program, sent volunteers around the world. Meanwhile, relations with the Soviet Union were strained over Berlin. When Kennedy refused to negotiate on Soviet demands, the Communists built a wall dividing the city. Kennedy and Khrushchev did agree however, to a nuclear test-ban treaty. Kennedy also inherited the Indochina problem. He increased the number of military advisers in Vietnam, but his tragic death prevented him from finding a solution.

CHECK FOR UNDERSTANDING

1. **Identify** Bay of Pigs, Nikita Khrushchev, Alliance for Progress, Peace Corps, Berlin Wall

2. **Explain** why the Bay of Pigs invasion failed.

3. **Describe** why the Alliance for Progress met opposition in Latin America.

4. **State** two possible reasons why Khrushchev sent missiles to Cuba.

5. **Cite** two factors that motivated agreement to a nuclear test-ban treaty.

THINKING CRITICALLY

6. **Making Inferences** Besides an economic policy, the Alliance for Progress was an attempt to stop communism. Explain this aspect of the program.

LINKING PAST AND PRESENT

7. **Making Comparisons** During the Kennedy years, Berlin was a cold-war trouble spot. What events in 1990 ended cold-war rivalry in Germany?

Interpreting Primary Sources

Collage Art in the 1960s

The decade of the 1960s was a fresh period in American art when artists experimented with a variety of media, materials, techniques, and styles. Robert Rauschenberg mastered the technique of *collage,* a two-dimensional art form using a variety of images.

Rauschenberg came into prominence in the mid-1950s when he began to incorporate pieces of discarded cloth, wood, crumpled printed materials, and other manufactured objects, such as tin cans or bottles onto his canvases. He referred to these works as "combine paintings."

The bold drips and splatters of Rauschenberg's brushwork, as well as his use of geometric shapes and colors, reflect his debt to abstract expressionism, an artistic movement that came into vogue after World War II. Yet his works also point to the emergence of pop art in the 1960s, an artistic style that used commonplace subject matter from popular culture.

Rauschenberg's kaleidoscope-like works often reflect an interesting interplay between reality and art, everyday life and technological achievement. In addition, his collages often draw

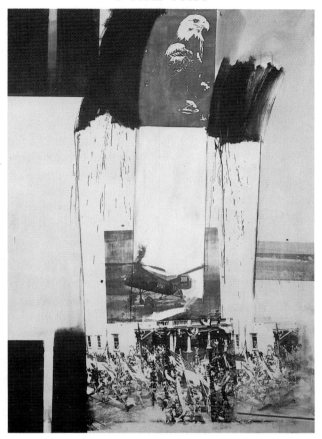

Kite, *1963*

on themes from significant events in American history.

In *Kite* Rauschenberg focuses attention on social unrest in the early 1960s. This is seen in the clash of troops and flags, and an army helicopter poised to either strike or bring assistance. Yet the images of the bald eagle and the military flag parade also stir feelings of patriotism and national pride.

When displayed in 1963, *Kite* may have reminded viewers of American troops in Little Rock or Birmingham, Korea or

Vietnam. The eagle, perhaps stained with blood, is positioned at the top of the collage where vertical paint thrusts resemble rocket blasts. This suggests American global power or the will to dominate outer space. The pale blue sky and white areas of the collage are spattered by ominous black markings. *Kite* is thus a statement of discord, a view of America filled with aggression and torn by turmoil.

EXAMINING THE PRIMARY SOURCE

1. Which of the images in the collage were probably mass-produced? How can you tell?

2. Describe an image that appears twice in this collage. Why do you think the artist repeated this image?

3. What mood does the pale blue and white areas of the canvas suggest?

THINKING CRITICALLY

4. Interpret the meaning of Rauschenberg's title *Kite.*

5. Why do you think the artist chose the major colors of this collage?

6. How does *Kite* capture the dynamic change of a nation?

★ Chapter 32 Review ★

★ Summary

In the 1950s, African Americans rebelled against second-class citizenship and segregation, aided by the Supreme Court decision in *Brown v. Board of Education*. In Montgomery, Alabama, Rosa Parks ignited a bus boycott by her refusal to give up her seat to a white rider. From the Montgomery boycott emerged a leader of the civil rights movement, Martin Luther King, Jr., who advocated nonviolent resistance to unjust laws. President Eisenhower sent federal troops to Little Rock, Arkansas, to protect black students.

In 1960 President Kennedy's vitality and charisma captivated Americans. In civil rights, events in the South forced him to send federal marshals to protect Freedom Riders and demonstrators. The March on Washington in 1963 demonstrated the growing and continuing power of this movement.

Kennedy also made his mark on foreign policy. The Peace Corps sent American volunteers around the world to help the peoples of developing nations. But the cold war continued. After evidence surfaced that the Soviets were building missile sites in Cuba, Kennedy blockaded Cuba and negotiated with the Soviets to have the sites dismantled. In Berlin, the Communists built a wall dividing the city after Kennedy refused to withdraw. In spite of these tensions, the United States, the Soviet Union, and Great Britain signed an agreement to limit the testing of nuclear weapons. Kennedy's assassination in late 1963 shocked and saddened the world.

★ Reviewing Facts

1. **List** two results of the Supreme Court's *Brown v. Board of Education* ruling.
2. **Cite** two results of the Montgomery bus boycott.
3. **Describe** Kennedy's presidential style.
4. **State** two legislative victories and two legislative setbacks for Kennedy.
5. **Name** three New Frontier programs.
6. **Arrange** in chronological order significant events in the civil rights movement that occurred between 1953 and 1963.
7. **Summarize** Kennedy's relations with Khrushchev.
8. **Explain** the foreign policy challenges that Kennedy faced in Southeast Asia.

★ Understanding Concepts

CIVIL RIGHTS

1. Explain the factors in American society that helped the civil rights movement grow.
2. Evaluate the importance of leadership to the civil rights movement in the 1950s and 1960s.

FOREIGN POLICY

3. In what way did Kennedy's foreign policy reflect his perception of communism and of Soviet Union foreign policy goals? Do you agree with his assessment of Soviet motives?
4. List events that occurred during the Kennedy years that demonstrated the growing interdependence of nations. How did world events affect Americans at home?

★ Thinking Critically

1. **Evaluating Tactics** Though Martin Luther King, Jr.'s, methods for change were nonviolent, they were not passive. What were some challenges faced by nonviolent civil rights demonstrators? Why was their nonviolence an effective tactic?
2. **Inferring Results** What lessons about military intervention do you think President Kennedy learned from the ill-fated Bay of Pigs invasion? How did the Alliance for Progress and the Peace Corps demonstrate an alternative to deter the spread of communism?

★ Writing About History

DESCRIPTION

Refer to the instructions on how to write a descriptive essay in the History Writer's Handbook in the Appendix of this book. Your teacher will give you more specific instructions on the essay's length and the assignment's due date.

Imagine that you are one of the first Freedom Riders on a bus traveling in the South during the spring of 1961. Describe your feelings and fears as you take part in this pioneering civil-rights tactic. Describe various incidents that occur along the highway and at stops at segregated bus terminals. Describe the human feelings of other blacks and whites accompanying you on the freedom rides.

★ Chapter 32 Review ★

★ Learning Cooperatively

Work with two other group members to explore the options facing President Kennedy during the Cuban missile crisis. Each of you should assume one of the following options: 1) Kennedy backs down and allows the missiles to be installed. 2) Kennedy invades Cuba to dismantle the missile sites. 3) Kennedy blockades Cuba. Write two potential consequences that might happen as a result of your option. Share these consequences with the two other group members. After each of you have shared your respective consequences, have the group rank them in order of their acceptability to Americans.

★ Mastering Skills

PREPARING NOTES AND A BIBLIOGRAPHY

A bibliography, or list of references used, must appear at the end of a research report. Notes—in either footnote form at the bottom of the page or endnotes at the conclusion of the report—are used to reference sources. It is essential that all direct quotes be cited in notes.

Your teacher or school may have style preference for noting sources and listing bibliography. Generally, all notes should be numbered consecutively. If they are to appear at the bottom of the page, they are separated from the main body by a line drawn partway across the page. The examples below are for either form.

Example For a book, give the author's name, then the full title, place of publication, publisher, and date, followed by the page number.

1. Diane Patrick, <u>Martin Luther King, Jr.</u> (New York: Franklin Watts, 1990), p. 17.

A note for a magazine article will look like this:

2. Martin Luther King, Jr., "Time for Freedom has Come," <u>New York Times Magazine</u> (Sept. 10, 1961), p. 25.

If the magazine or journal has a volume or issue number, the citation should read:

3. John H. Franklin, "Jim Crow Goes to School: The Genesis of Legal Segregation in Southern Schools," <u>South Atlantic Quarterly</u> 57 (1956), p. 225.

A note for a well-known reference book can be brief:

4. <u>Encyclopaedia Britannica</u>, 15th ed., "King, Martin L. Jr."

To refer to the same source again, use the author's last name, or the title if it is reference book, and page number. If the next note immediately follows one for that same source you may use *Ibid.* (from *ibidem*, meaning "in the same place").

5. Patrick, p. 29
6. Ibid., p. 30.

The form for bibliographies differs slightly from the form for notes. The list is arranged in alphabetical order, according to the author's last name. Notice that the author's name, title, and facts of publication are separated by periods and that page numbers for magazines or journals are included.

<u>Encyclopaedia Britannica</u>, vol. 10 Macropaedia, 15th ed. (1981). "King, Martin L. Jr."

Franklin, John H., "Jim Crow Goes to School: The Genesis of Legal Segregation in Southern Schools." <u>South Atlantic Quarterly</u> 57 (1956): pp. 225-235.

King, Jr., Martin Luther. "Time for Freedom has Come." <u>New York Times Magazine</u> (Sept. 10, 1961).

_____. <u>Stride Toward Freedom: The Montgomery Story</u>. New York: Harper & Row, 1958.

Washington, James Melvin, ed. <u>A Testament of Hope: The Essential Writings of Martin Luther King, Jr.</u> San Francisco: Harper & Row, 1986.

The dash under the King source indicates that the second work is also by King. The collection of King's writings is listed under the name of its editor.

Practice Prepare a bibliography, and note citations from five library sources—each for school desegregation in the 1950s and the Cuban missile crisis. Include books, periodicals, and reference works.

CHAPTER 33
The Vietnam Era

Historical Focus

President Lyndon Johnson used his experience to carry out programs initiated by President Kennedy. Great Society legislation fought unemployment, illiteracy, and racial discrimination. The cost of war in Vietnam and spending for social programs, however, strained the federal budget. The war became the focus of attention. With public division over the conduct of the war the nation's political system faltered.

Concepts to Understand

- How **social upheaval** affected national legislation, then led to political and cultural division.
- Why public opinion divided over the administration's conduct of the **war** in Vietnam.

People to Know

Hubert Humphrey, Dr. Martin Luther King, Jr., Ho Chi Minh, General William Westmoreland

Places to Locate

Selma, Alabama; Gulf of Tonkin

Terms to Identify

consensus, escalation, Vietcong, "hawks," "doves," Civil Rights Act

Guided Reading

As you read this chapter, seek the answers to the following questions.

1. What legislation addressed poverty and civil rights issues?
2. What events represented political turmoil during this period?

SPANNING THE DECADES

POLITICAL	1964 *Civil Rights Act is passed*	1965 *Voting Rights Act is passed*	1966 Miranda vs. Arizona *arrest rights case*	1967 *Thurgood Marshall becomes first African-American Supreme Court Justice*
	1964		**1966**	
CULTURAL	1964 *British spy movies with James Bond are popular*	1965 *"March for Freedom" begins in Selma, Alabama*	1966 Soul on Ice *states Black Panther aims*	1967 *Green Bay Packers win first Super Bowl, 35-10, over Kansas City Chiefs*

The Bridge—Vietnam 1966 *by Second Lieutenant Augustine Acuna, 1967*

1968
Robert Kennedy and Martin Luther King are assassinated

1969
Peace talks to end Vietnam war begin in Paris

1968   1970

1968
Cost of mailing a letter increased to 6 cents

1969
Woodstock draws 400,000 youth

1970
First Earth Day observed as millions protest pollution

The ultimate weakness of violence is that it is a descending spiral, begetting the very thing that it seeks to destroy. Instead of diminishing evil, it multiplies it.

—MARTIN LUTHER KING, JR.
Where Do We Go From Here, 1967

The Great Society

> *We have hate abroad in the world, hate internationally, hate domestically where a President is assassinated and then they [the haters] take the law into their own hands and kill the assassin....The roots of hate are poverty and disease and illiteracy, and they are broad in this land.*

—LYNDON BAINES JOHNSON
In a speech at the Governors' meeting, November 25, 1963

Section Focus

Lyndon Johnson was a big man, with great energy and ambition. Sharing the same goals as Kennedy, Johnson carried into legislation the former President's war on poverty and based his foreign policy on cold-war containment. As a former Senate leader, Johnson conceived and skillfully guided through Congress more significant domestic legislation than had been passed since the New Deal.

Objectives

After studying this section, you should be able to:
• Explain how Johnson's belief in consensus helped him win the 1964 election.
• Discuss Johnson's efforts to fight poverty.

Aided by the Kennedy cabinet and relying on his long experience in government, Lyndon Johnson quickly made the transition from Vice President to President. Five days after John F. Kennedy's

assassination, on November 27, 1963, Johnson appeared before a joint session of Congress. His words assured the nation's representatives that he intended to carry out Kennedy's programs:

> *...the ideas and ideals which [Kennedy] so nobly represented must and will be translated into effective action. John Kennedy's death commands what his life conveyed—that America must move forward.*

Elected to the House of Representatives in 1937 and the Senate in 1948, Johnson was at home in Congress. During the 1950s he was the powerful Democratic Majority Leader of the Senate. Although a southerner, Johnson had taken a moderate position on most issues and had been a leader in passing the Civil Rights Act of 1957.

As President, Johnson continued his effective policy of working through **consensus**, or general agreement. With skilled bargaining, compromising, and even verbal arm-twisting, Johnson reinforced his favorite Biblical quotation, "Come let us reason together." He took over the responsibilities of the chief executive with firmness and strength, determined to pursue the Democratic party's goals of social justice.

Civil Rights

National remorse over the assassination of President Kennedy assured passage of a civil rights bill. Johnson appealed for speedy action:

> *No memorial...could more eloquently honor President Kennedy's memory than the earliest possible passage of the civil rights bill for which he fought so long.*

Connections

HISTORY AND RELIGION

BLACK CHURCHES AND THE CIVIL RIGHTS MOVEMENT

African Americans in the South had long heard the message of the Christian scriptures that God is on the side of the oppressed. They concluded that if it was true in ancient Israel it could also be true in the American South. From the organization of the Montgomery bus boycott in 1955 until the March on Washington in

Dr. Martin Luther King, Jr.

1963, black churches played the central role in devising strategies and mobilizing volunteers for the civil rights movement. The message of the gospel became the message of the movement. The churches called for protest without retaliatory violence, for confrontation without conflict.

A number of leaders of the civil rights movement and the Southern Christian Leadership Conference were ministers. Some of them were arrested for taking part in demonstrations. Dr. Martin Luther King, Jr., himself was arrested repeatedly for demonstrating in Birmingham. When a group of Birmingham ministers criticized King for being an "outside agitator" he wrote from jail: "...just as the apostle Paul left his village of Tarsus and carried the gospel of Jesus Christ to the far corners of the Greco-Roman world, so am I compelled to carry the gospel of freedom beyond my own hometown."

MAKING THE RELIGION CONNECTION

1. How was the message of the gospel related to the civil rights movement?

2. Why were civil rights leaders sometimes jailed?

LINKING PAST AND PRESENT

3. How are black churches involved in politics today?

With the passage of the Civil Rights Act of 1964, Johnson eased the suspicions civil rights groups held about their southern President.

The strongest civil rights act since Reconstruction stated that all citizens should have equal access to such public facilities as parks and libraries and to such private businesses serving the public, as restaurants and theaters. It forbade discrimination in education and strengthened the right to vote. It also outlawed job discrimination because of race, sex, religion, or national origin. A few months after the act was signed into law, the Justice Department reported that southern states were generally complying with its terms. Most of the southern legislators who voted for the law were reelected in 1964.

Johnson himself won a landslide victory in the presidential election of 1964. His campaign plan offered something for everyone: business and labor, rich and poor,

Examining Photographs *Malcolm X, a bold and brilliant orator, preached a message of African American pride, discipline, and self-determination. What did the Civil Rights Act of 1964 provide?*

young and old, black and white. Known as "the Great Society," Johnson's domestic program was an effort to expand upon Kennedy's ideas as well as to make a contribution of his own. It was designed to fight poverty, discrimination, unemployment, pollution, and other social ills of America. At the same time, he pledged to provide major tax cuts for individuals and corporations. He also promised not to expand the war in Vietnam.

To offer voters "a choice, not an echo," Republicans selected an outspoken conservative, Barry Goldwater, to run against Johnson and his liberal running mate, Hubert Humphrey. The Arizona senator ran a determined, uncompromising campaign. His opposition to the Civil Rights Act of 1964 turned away black voters. His coolness to Social Security made older people fearful. His support of the open shop hurt him with organized labor. Above all, Goldwater's suggestion that military commanders should be allowed to decide for themselves whether or not to use nuclear weapons made many people nervous.

As predicted, Johnson's wide appeal won him more than 60 percent of the popular vote. Goldwater carried only his home state of Arizona and 5 southern states, where former "Dixiecrats" switched to the Republican party. The Great Society had won an overwhelming mandate.

War on Poverty

In the mid-1960s the United States had the highest standard of living in the world. But behind the Great Society program was a new awareness that many Americans did not share in the general prosperity. Contributing to this awareness was a book by Michael Harrington entitled *The Other America,* published in 1962. In response to economist John Kenneth Galbraith, who wrote in *The Affluent Society* that only "pockets" of poverty remained, Harrington claimed that as many as 40 million Americans—one-fourth of the population—were poor. He charged:

CESAR CHAVEZ
1927-

Born to Mexican-American migrant workers, Cesar Chavez picked crops in the Southwest as a child and young man. At age 25, he began organizing farm workers to win better pay and working conditions.

Early in the 1960s, Chavez founded a union for migrant farm workers and later merged it with another to form the first large-scale organization of farm workers. He then led a strike against grape growers. The strike drew national attention as Chavez borrowed tactics from the civil rights movement—marches and a 25-day fast. Yet the growers would not settle. The tide began to turn in 1968 when Chavez asked Americans to boycott grapes. Growers' profits tumbled as consumers sided with the workers. The strike lasted until 1970, when the growers finally agreed to settle.

The United States contains an underdeveloped nation, a culture poverty. Its inhabitants do not suffer the extreme poverty of the peasants of Asia...yet the mechanism of the misery is similar. They are beyond history, beyond progress, sunk in a paralyzing, maiming routine.

The public knew little of the great mass of human misery, said Harrington. The poor were hidden away in the slums of

The War on Poverty reached into Appalachia where poor soil and lack of education affected many lives. Why was Project Head Start established?

central cities, in rural areas—especially in Appalachia and the deep South—and on Indian reservations. Many of the poor were elderly people leading "lives of quiet desperation" in secluded rooms.

It was not possible for these people to "pull themselves up by their bootstraps," Harrington believed. Automation had done away with the jobs of many workers, and small farmers could no longer compete with agribusiness. Further, pensions and Social Security did not adequately cover medical expenses for older citizens.

Johnson announced his strategy in his first State of the Union Address on January 8, 1964: "This administration... declares unconditional war on poverty in America." A new Office of Economic Opportunity (OEO) aimed its billion-dollar budget at illiteracy, unemployment, and disease. The OEO-sponsored VISTA (Volunteers in Service to America) sent workers to improve conditions in poor neighborhoods. Job Corps provided training for the unskilled; Project Head Start helped poor children prepare for school.

The Elementary and Secondary Education Act of 1965 gave direct massive federal aid to public and parochial schools. A similar act provided college scholarships for needy students.

The Great Society's War on Poverty extended federal influence into areas that had traditionally been handled by local governments, private enterprise, or religious groups. In some cases OEO was granted power to overrule local governments.

The emphasis was not simply on relief but on helping poor people help themselves. For example, community action programs taught people to organize protests and put pressure on landlords, employers, and even government agencies to effect change.

After nearly 20 years of opposition by those who believed that the government should stay out of health care, Congress passed the Medicare Act. Medicare provided people over age 65 with hospital care. Medical centers were to be set up in areas where such facilities were lacking.

The act provided funds for medical schools to increase enrollments and reduce the shortage of doctors.

To many thousands of immigrants, the United States already represented a "great society"—a land of opportunity and freedom. The doors of this great society had opened wide to immigrants from northwestern Europe and nearly closed to others, because of a quota system established in 1924. Out of 157,000 immigrants admitted each year, Great Britain and Ireland were allotted 83,000; India, with a population of 450 million, and Andorra, with a population of 6,400, each were allotted 100. Presidents Truman, Eisenhower, and Kennedy had been unable to persuade Congress to change this system.

Standing beneath the Statue of Liberty, which welcomed immigrants to the country, Johnson signed the Immigration Act of 1965. The law replaced national quotas with global quotas and favored those with special skills. As a result, immigration to the United States from Asia and Latin America increased sharply.

Examining Maps *The Voting Rights Act of 1965 had a dramatic effect on registration of African-American voters. How did it influence elections?*

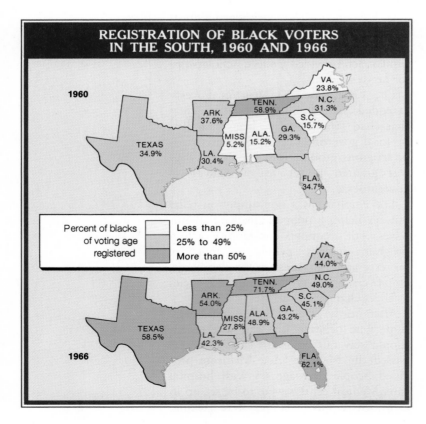

REGISTRATION OF BLACK VOTERS IN THE SOUTH, 1960 AND 1966

1960

VA. 23.8%
N.C. 31.3%
TENN. 58.9%
ARK. 37.6%
S.C. 15.7%
MISS 5.2%
ALA. 15.2%
GA. 29.3%
TEXAS 34.9%
LA. 30.4%
FLA. 34.7%

Percent of blacks of voting age registered
Less than 25%
25% to 49%
More than 50%

1966

VA. 44.0%
N.C. 49.0%
TENN. 71.7%
ARK. 54.0%
S.C. 45.1%
MISS 27.8%
ALA. 48.9%
GA. 43.2%
TEXAS 58.5%
LA. 42.3%
FLA. 62.1%

Voting Rights Act of 1965

In January 1965, Dr. Martin Luther King, Jr., organized a voter registration drive in Selma, Alabama. The county sheriff deputized whites and attacked groups of blacks with dogs and cattle prods as they tried to register. Then on March 7, Dr. King organized a "march for freedom" from Selma, Alabama, to the state capitol in Montgomery, 50 miles away. Although federal laws had already granted them the vote, many blacks in the South were deprived of their rights by violence and threats of violence and by unfair and unevenly applied eligibility tests. In Selma most of the blacks applying to vote were turned down. Dr. King wanted to dramatize this injustice through the march.

More than 25,000 people from all over the country joined in, more than 400 of them clergy. Police armed with billy clubs, bullwhips, and tear gas, and urged on by angry mobs, met the marchers. Many marchers were injured in the clash that followed and 2 white demonstrators were killed. The marchers reached Montgomery only after Johnson sent federal troops to provide protection.

National outrage over events in Selma helped speed the passage of the Voting Rights Act of 1965. It did away with such things as literacy tests in many southern states and provided for federal assistance in registering African Americans. Steps were also taken to eliminate the poll tax, forbidden by the Twenty-fourth Amendment, yet still used to keep the poor from voting. In a single year, more than 400,000 people, mostly blacks who had not previously voted, were registered.

As a result, black candidates began to win elections as state legislators, mayors, and members of Congress. Within 25 years, the number of African-American elected officials in the South rose from 100 to 5,000. Southern politicians who had championed desegregation appealed to black voters for support in their election campaigns.

John Lewis, the head of the Student Nonviolent Coordinating Committee (SNCC) and later a member of the House of Representatives said:

These elections signal a new level of maturation in American politics. They demonstrate the willingness of white voters to set aside racial differences, and they reflect the fact that many minorities have gained the broad political experience and skills to make them solid candidates for major office.

The Voting Rights Act of 1965 also helped other minorities. It set aside a New York state law requiring voters to be able to read English, enabling such groups as Puerto Ricans and Mexican Americans to vote.

Under Johnson's leadership Congress passed a great number of other important laws in a few months. "We did reach consensus," he concluded. "I think we did convince the vast majority of Americans that the time for procrastinating had passed."

His programs were well-received in part because people saw benefits for themselves. Some businesspeople, for example, benefited from the War on Poverty because of the increased purchasing power of poor people. Johnson's program also included subsidies to farmers.

Great Society programs required large sums of money. Federal spending for social purposes rose from $54 billion in 1964 to $98 billion in 1968. By 1967 American involvement in the Vietnam war was costing more than $20 billion a year. Federal budget problems and national inflation made Great Society spending an issue for debate.

At first, Johnson tried to finance the war with taxes, explaining that the nation could afford both guns and butter. New social programs and rising war costs made the federal deficits climb to $28 billion by 1968. The President realized that without additional taxes, either social or military programs would have to be cut. He asked Congress for a tax increase. Congress refused unless the President would cut the budget. Johnson chopped $6 billion out of proposed domestic spending, marking the end of the Great Society.

SUMMARY

After the assassination of John F. Kennedy, Americans found President Johnson's strong leadership reassuring. Johnson used his political skills to form a consensus and to continue the domestic programs begun by Kennedy. Johnson's first achievement was passage of the Civil Rights Act of 1964. After his election in 1964, Johnson set to work implementing his concept of the Great Society—a blueprint for the elimination of poverty and discrimination in America. Great Society programs offered training and opportunities to advance in American society. To end discrimination, Johnson backed the Voting Rights Act of 1965.

CHECKING FOR UNDERSTANDING

1. **Identify** Barry Goldwater, *The Other America,* Office of Economic Opportunity, Medicare Act

2. **Define** consensus

3. **Explain** the Great Society.

4. **List** four programs that were part of the War on Poverty.

5. **Describe** how blacks in the deep South were prevented from voting.

6. **Summarize** the effects of the Voting Rights Act of 1965 on black political power.

THINKING CRITICALLY

7. **Classifying Information** Do all Americans define poverty the same way? Make a list of guidelines that you would use to classify Americans who live in poverty.

LINKING PAST AND PRESENT

8. **Supporting an Opinion** In 1990, a Civil Rights Act was vetoed by President Bush because the bill contained hiring quotas. Compare Americans' attitudes toward civil rights today to their attitudes in the 1960s.

★ ★ ★ ★ ★ ★ ★ ★ ★ ★ ★ ★ ★ ★ ★ ★ ★ ★ ★

War in Vietnam

The Communist balance of power is still strong. The balance of power is still on the side of freedom. We are still the keystone in the arch of freedom, and I think we will continue to do as we have done in our past, our duty.

—JOHN F. KENNEDY
In a speech to the Fort Worth Chamber of Commerce, 1963

Section Focus

In his dealings with other countries, President Johnson relied on the advice of Kennedy's foreign policy advisers. He continued to honor the commitments of Eisenhower and Kennedy to South Vietnam, but the lack of success in a limited war in Vietnam soon divided the nation.

Objectives

After studying this section, you should be able to:
• Explain how the Gulf of Tonkin incident led to the escalation of the war in Vietnam.
• List reasons for opposition to the war.

During the 1964 campaign Johnson ran as the candidate of peace and restraint. "We seek no wider war," he repeatedly promised. "We don't want our American boys to do the fighting for Asian boys." At the same time, he did not want to appear weak or to allow a communist victory in Vietnam.

As the military situation in Vietnam continued to deteriorate, the war dominated the foreign policy of the administration. When Johnson entered the White House, South Vietnamese President Ngo Dinh Diem had just been assassinated. Within three months, another revolution took place in South Vietnam. This was followed by a series of governments, as one military faction after another gained power in South Vietnam.

The President faced disagreeable choices. He could admit defeat and pull out. If the "domino theory" was correct, the rest of Southeast Asia would fall to the Communists. He could continue limited support of South Vietnam's government, but the instability of that government would probably mean eventual defeat. Finally, he could actively enter the war and attack North Vietnam. This would mean the loss of lives and vast expense and also the possibility of war with The People's Republic of China.

By the summer of 1964 Johnson began to move cautiously toward the third alternative. In secrecy the United States began limited bombing of positions held by the **Vietcong,** or South Vietnamese communist guerrillas, and supported limited commando raids on North Vietnam's coast.

Escalation

Johnson reported that North Vietnamese torpedo boats fired on two American destroyers in the Gulf of Tonkin on August 2 and 4, 1964. Calling these attacks unprovoked, he asked Congress for authorization to bomb North Vietnam. On August 7 the Senate and House quickly passed the Gulf of Tonkin Resolution, authorizing the President to "take all necessary steps, including the use of armed force" to prevent further aggression. In effect, Congress, with only two dissenting votes, handed its war powers over to the President.

But Johnson had kept important information from Congress. The two American destroyers had been assisting the South Vietnamese military in conducting electronic spying on North Vietnam. It was unclear whether both ships had been attacked. Furthermore, Johnson did not reveal that a draft of the resolution had been prepared three months before the attack, in case such an event occurred.

President Johnson regarded the Gulf of Tonkin Resolution as a blanket approval of the war effort from Congress. At the suggestion of his military advisers, he ordered the bombing of bases in North Vietnam.

Until August 1964, the fighting in South Vietnam had been between South Vietnamese government troops and the Vietcong. After the Gulf of Tonkin incident, however, North Vietnam began sending its own troops to fight in the South. As the United States expanded its role, the civil war grew into a major conflict between American and communist forces.

In February 1965, after the Vietcong attacked an American base in South Vietnam, Johnson ordered an **escalation,** or military expansion, of the war. He ordered American planes to begin bombing targets in North Vietnam, and in April 1965, made the fateful decision that American ground forces should engage in combat.

In the Vietnam War the United States faced a far more difficult situation than it had in Korea. In Korea the United States fought as an agent of the United Nations, with widespread support from noncommunist countries. Now the United States stood almost alone in its military support of South Vietnam's government, and much of world opinion was hostile to American policy in Vietnam. The South Vietnamese Communists had strong support in rural areas and military aid from North Vietnam. Most noncommunist South Vietnamese were indifferent or opposed to their government, no matter what group happened to be in power.

Military operations turned into a "dirty, ruthless, wandering war" without a battlefront. The Vietcong guerrillas used hit-and-run tactics. Not as well equipped as the Americans, the Vietcong and North Vietnamese used ambushes, boobytraps, and small-scale attacks. They moved swiftly by night and by day hid in the jungles or in friendly villages. Using terrorism against civilians, the Vietcong controlled

much of the countryside. To counter such tactics, American troops adopted a "search-and-destroy" strategy. American forces tried to search out enemy troops, bomb their positions, destroy their supply lines, and force them out into the open for combat. By 1966 American planes had dropped nearly the same tonnage of bombs in Vietnam as had been dropped in the Pacific in World War II. Napalm, a jellied gasoline that explodes and splatters, clinging to whatever it touches, was sprayed from planes. In order to improve visibility, American planes sprayed chemical defoliants—Agent Orange for example—that stripped leaves from trees and shrubs, turning farmland and forest into wasteland. American troops burned villages believed to be hiding communist supporters.

Examining Maps
Throughout the war United States troops and the government of South Vietnam controlled the major cities. What strategy did the Vietcong use?

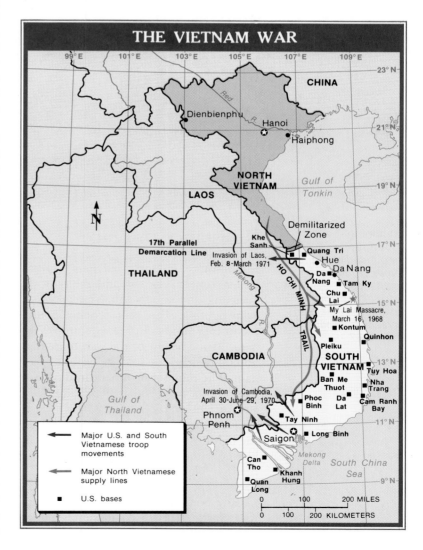

Examining Photographs
A wounded medic comes to the aid of another soldier. By how much did American casualties in Vietnam increase between 1966 and 1968?

Resistance to Peace

Johnson's military advisers greatly underestimated the will and ability of the Vietcong and the North Vietnamese to keep fighting. The United States poured increasing numbers of troops into Vietnam. At the height of the war, more than 500,000 American soldiers were in Vietnam. The number of American dead rose from 5,008 for 1966 to 9,377 for 1967 and 14,589 for 1968.

Once the United States had escalated the fighting, there seemed to be no way of leaving without damaging its international prestige. North Vietnam's leader, Ho Chi Minh, kept his forces in battle despite the massive bombing of his country, believing that North Vietnam could simply outlast the United States in the war.

With neither side willing to compromise, all peace attempts failed. In April 1965, Johnson offered to hold "unconditional discussions" with North Vietnam. He also promised a billion-dollar program to help rebuild South Vietnam. The American plan did not provide for Vietcong participation in the South Vietnamese government. North Vietnam put forward its own plan that was unsatisfactory to the United States. Between 1965 and 1967, American officials estimated that some 2,000 attempts were made to open direct negotiations, all unsuccessful. Other nations, including Great Britain, Poland, and the Soviet Union, offered plans to negotiate between the two sides. None succeeded.

Dominican Intervention

While Vietnam dominated Johnson's international concerns, in April 1965 the Dominican Republic in the Caribbean captured his attention. Rebels were trying to overthrow the rightist military government that controlled the island country. Fearing that the rebels were controlled by Communists, Johnson ordered 20,000 marines to the Dominican Republic. This was the first time the United States had openly sent troops to the Caribbean since 1926.

Many Latin Americans criticized this military action. They charged that fear of a communist takeover, similar to that of Cuba by Fidel Castro, was leading the United States to support reactionary governments whose oppressive policies drove people to revolt. Johnson answered these critics by describing the Dominican revolution as a violent action in which "some 1,500 innocent people were murdered and shot. . . ."

Senator J. William Fulbright, head of the Senate Foreign Relations Committee, concluded that the President had overreacted in sending troops. Fulbright criticized the President—his friend and fellow Democrat—for not being wholly truthful about the event. Nonetheless, most members of Congress continued to support the President. By a margin of 312 to 52, the House of Representatives voted in support

of sending American troops to prevent a communist takeover anywhere in Latin America. But the Dominican incident raised suspicions of a "credibility gap." Some suggested that the President's words were not to be trusted. If the President had exaggerated the truth about events in the Dominican Republic, then Fulbright and others thought that the details about the Vietnam War warranted closer examination.

Growing Opposition to War

As America moved deeper into the Vietnam War, opposition grew. The United States' reasons for fighting in Southeast Asia were questioned in newspapers and on television. Some university students and teachers held "teach-ins" to study and to protest against the expansion of the war. Members of Congress called for a negotiated end rather than a military solution to the war.

Beginning in January 1966, the Senate Foreign Relations Committee held "educational" hearings on Vietnam, calling in Secretary of State Dean Rusk and other policymakers to explain the administration's war program. The committee also listened to such critics of the war as George Kennan, who argued that Vietnam was not strategically important to the United States. Although he had helped create Truman's policy of "containment," Kennan said that it was not the business of the United States to solve the problems of other nations:

Our country should not be asked, and should not ask itself, to shoulder the main burden of determining the political realities in any other country, and particularly not in one remote from our shores, from our culture, and from the experience of our people.

The televised Senate hearings carried the senators' doubts about the war to millions of American homes. Perhaps even more influential was the nightly television news with video of the war—of soldiers fighting and dying, villages burning, children crying—that brought the grim reality of war into American homes.

Examining Photographs *Antiwar demonstrators protested loudly in marches such as this one on New York's Fifth Avenue. What did polls show about the opinion of the majority?*

Americans became divided into two groups. Those who supported the war were called "hawks" and those opposed "doves." Until 1968 public opinion polls showed that most Americans believed in the original commitment to South Vietnam and sided with the "hawks." But doubts continued to grow. Even Defense Secretary Robert McNamara began to question America's role in the war. In a letter to Johnson in May 1967, McNamara wrote:

The picture of the world's greatest superpower killing or seriously injuring 1000 noncombatants a week while trying to pound a tiny backward nation into submission on an issue whose merits are hotly disputed is not a pretty one. It could conceivably produce a costly distortion in the American national consciousness, and in the world image of the United States—especially if the damage to North Vietnam is complete enough to be "successful."

SUMMARY

In setting United States policy in Vietnam, President Johnson was torn between his wish to limit American involvement and his fear of a Communist victory. Passage of the Gulf of Tonkin Resolution gave Johnson the power to wage war on North Vietnam as he saw fit. American planes began bombing North Vietnam targets and in April, 1965, the President decided to engage American troops in combat. As American casualties mounted, there was growing opposition to the war. The President's decision to send troops into the Dominican Republic intensified the growing discontent with his leadership.

CHECKING FOR UNDERSTANDING

1. **Identify** Gulf of Tonkin Resolution, Ho Chi Minh, J. William Fulbright
2. **Define** Vietcong, escalation
3. **Summarize** America's policy choices in Vietnam.
4. **Explain** why a "credibility gap" was one result of United States intervention in the Dominican Republic.
5. **List** two reasons why some Americans began to oppose United States involvement in Vietnam.

THINKING CRITICALLY

6. **Expressing Problems Clearly** Some political analysts called Vietnam a "quagmire." Write two statements that explain the difficult choices the United States faced in Vietnam.

CONNECTIONS: HISTORY AND TECHNOLOGY

7. **Evaluating Policy** Searching for ways to end the war in Vietnam quickly, the United States turned to chemical herbicides designed to deny the enemy food and places to hide. What effect do you think this policy had on Vietnamese attitudes toward the war and the Americans?

SECTION THREE

Social Revolution

SETTING THE SCENE

Dear America you worry me. / Our friendship (& that's all it was) / is shaky. / I don't trust you / or your Dreams / or your Destiny / any more.

—ROBERT PETERSON
Poet, "Dear America," a poem of protest, 1966

Section Focus

The "credibility gap" widened as Americans scrutinized their government's policies. Large numbers of disillusioned young people demonstrated against America's involvement in Vietnam. African Americans found their situation unchanged in many ways: laws had not altered prejudice, and improvement in their economic status had practically ceased. Some began to talk less of racial integration and more of "black power." Lyndon Johnson, the master politician, could not prevent the collapse of his national consensus.

Objectives

After studying this section, you should be able to:
• List some of the factors responsible for discontent among African Americans.
• Describe the youth counterculture.

The Selma Freedom March that helped bring about the Voting Rights Act of 1965 was the last great triumph for Martin Luther King, Jr., and his vision of blacks and whites working together for equal rights.

Younger and more militant black leaders, impatient with Dr. King's insistence on nonviolence and integration, were breaking away from his leadership. They felt that African Americans must no longer wait for others to give them rights; they must seize their rights.

Black Revolution

Stokely Carmichael, head of the Student Nonviolent Coordinating Committee (SNCC) who later changed his name to Kwame Ture, introduced the slogan "black power." He and Charles Hamilton described the concept in the book *Black Power: the Politics of Liberation in America:*

It is a call for black people in this country to unite, to recognize their heritage, to build [a] sense of community. It is a call for black people to define their own goals, to lead their own organizations. It is a call to reject the racist institutions and values of this society.

Black power expressed itself in political action, but the deeper meaning of black power had to do with pride and leadership. Many members and leaders of the civil rights movement had been white liberals. Now groups like SNCC and the Congress of Racial Equality (CORE) moved whites out of leadership positions. African Americans began to reexamine their African heritage. Some took African names or wore "Afro" haircuts and African-style clothing. They demanded that schools adopt programs in African-American studies.

While some black leaders were leaning toward separatism, Dr. King and other civil rights leaders argued that to succeed, the black minority must continue to work with the white majority. But Dr. King did shift his demonstrations from the South to such northern cities as Chicago, where he protested against housing discrimination, unemployment, and urban poverty.

Linking Across Time

VIETNAM LEGACY

The Vietnam War caused controversy into the 1990s. Still unresolved was whether the American government would compensate war veterans who claimed that exposure to the jungle defoliant Agent Orange was to blame for their high cancer rate. In 1987 the government said that no such connection could be proven because it was impossible to assess a veteran's contact with the herbicide. In 1990 an opposing report said that records of troop movements could establish exposure to Agent Orange.

Examining Photographs *"Burn, baby, burn," became more than just a slogan of militant black-power groups in Detroit. Where were most of the riots of 1967?*

Northern black populations tended to be concentrated in the inner cities, where poverty was widespread and discontent was high.

Frustration over conditions led to a series of riots in many cities. Often occurring in the heat of summer, these riots were sometimes triggered by an incident between police and black citizens. When riots erupted, looting and burning sometimes broke out.

The first major riot took place in the Harlem section of New York City in July 1964. Other riots broke out that year in Philadelphia and Chicago. In August 1965, a riot in the black neighborhood of Watts in Los Angeles left 34 people dead, more than 3,000 arrested, and $20 million in property damaged. The summer of 1966 brought new disruptions in New York, Atlanta, Cleveland, Detroit, Chicago, San Francisco, and Los Angeles. Federal troops and National Guardsmen entered Detroit in July 1967, after much of the city was in flames. When the riot was over, 40 people had been killed and hundreds more were injured. Thousands were left homeless, and many businesses were in ashes.

Most of the riots took place outside the South, in parts of the country where African Americans supposedly enjoyed equal rights. Adam Clayton Powell, Jr., a black member of Congress from New York City, offered an explanation. In the South, he said, what blacks wanted was relatively easy for whites to give: the right to sit at a drugstore counter or in the front of a bus. In the North blacks had long been able to sit where they pleased. Now they wanted "a bigger piece of the pie"—better jobs, more money, better places to live. Some white jobholders and property owners felt threatened.

The President appointed a National Advisory Commission on Civil Disorders (the Kerner Commission) to look into the problem. The Kerner Commission laid responsibility for the ghettoes at the feet of white society:

White racism is essentially responsible for the explosive mixture which has been accumulating in our cities since the end of World War II....white society is deeply implicated in the ghetto. White institutions maintained it, and white society condones it.

Although African Americans suffered greater loss of life and property, the riots tended to harden white prejudices. The urgently requested commission report was quietly received and produced little change.

Student Protests

Much of the antiwar protests focused on the draft. While in 1966 alone 1.8 million students received deferments, reports showed unfair practices. A person with a limited education from a low-income family was far more likely to be sent to fight in Vietnam than someone with a good education from an upper-income family, and black soldiers made up a disproportionately large number of American soldiers fighting overseas.

As the war escalated, draft calls were sharply increased. With the increase in draft calls, more high school students

Examining Photographs *Young people often led war protests, because their lives were most likely to be affected by the war. How did some demonstrate their defiance of government?*

began to worry about their futures. Many of those facing the draft were uncertain why the war was being fought at all. They were deeply concerned by nightly television reports of the war's brutality and the growing list of American casualties.

In addition to student deferments, there were 171,000 **conscientious objectors,** or those who refused to fight or carry arms in battle for moral or religious reasons. An estimated 500,000 young men openly avoided the draft. Most of them simply did not report when called for induction. Others fled to Canada, Sweden, and other countries. About 3,000 young men went to prison rather than fight in a war they opposed.

Some antiwar protesters used tactics of civil disobedience and mass demonstrations that they had learned from the civil rights movement. Outside the White House, protesters chanted, "Hey! Hey! LBJ! How many kids did you kill today?" Some burned their draft cards to demonstrate their defiance of government policies. Many college students protested against military recruitment and training on campuses. They objected to the universities' cooperation in research projects with and stock ownership in corporations involved in military defense.

Like civil rights activists, young people began to think in terms of revolution—a revolution that affected not only

Life of the Times

WEDDINGS IN THE 1960s

During the 1960s not everyone under 21 was a hippie. Young people's lifestyles ran the gamut from the conventional to the bizarre. The weddings of the time mirrored this diversity. Many young people regarded the counter-culture of the hippies with disdain and modeled their celebrations after their parents' tastes—complete with morning coats, full-length gowns, and pictures of the couple in the society section of the local newspaper. Hippies, on the other hand, might wear Nehru jackets and jeans to their ceremonies in the park.

While marriages were not holding together as well as in the previous decade, some people opted for highly individualized weddings. A New Jersey couple was married in the roller skating rink where they first met. The bride and groom, their four attendants, and the town mayor who performed the ceremony all wore skates.

Traditionally White House weddings personified stolid respectability and decorum. But "extravagant" would be a more fitting description of Luci Johnson's wedding during the administration of Lyndon Johnson, her father. A 100-voice male choir sang at the ceremony, which took place at Immaculate Conception, the largest Roman Catholic church in the United States. Following the ceremony hundreds of guests attended the reception, a glorified Texas barbecue, which featured cold beef sirloin and a 300-pound cake.

government policies but every aspect of life. At the University of California at Berkeley, students demonstrated against the vast, impersonal, bureaucratic nature of the modern university. Many alienated youths rebelled against social pressures for personal achievement, material gain, and conformity. Instead they searched for meaning in various philosophies and religions. Some experimented with hallucinogenic drugs—those that induce hallucinations—attempting to achieve expanded awareness. They proclaimed their freedom of expression and individuality by long hair and unconventional clothing. A popular slogan taken from ever-present computer cards summed up their determination not to be caught up in the lockstep of society: "I am a Human Being; do not fold, spindle or mutilate."

In their rejection of their parents' values, the "hippies," or "flower children" as they were frequently called, were said to have established a **counterculture**—with values and practices that conflicted with established society. For many, their participation in the counterculture was reflected primarily in their choice of clothing and music; others left family and comfortable homes to live in **communes**—communities in which living quarters, food, and work were shared.

The counterculture was symbolized in an outdoor rock concert, the Woodstock festival, held in August 1969. More than 400,000 people attended what *Time* Magazine called "history's biggest happening." *Time* went on to say "it may well rank as one of the significant political and sociological events of the age."

Examining Photographs *A three-day rock music festival at Woodstock, New York, brought together young people from across the nation. Inclement weather and shortages of food and water did not bother the many "experience seekers" who had come mainly for the music. What were the visible reflections of the counterculture?*

While many who attended Woodstock were not involved in political activism, the event brought together isolated pockets of disaffected youth to demonstrate their numbers, their power, and their identity with each other. It was so strong a demonstration of the new youth culture that many began calling them "the Woodstock generation."

Conservative Backlash

Social frustration in the 1960s was not limited to African Americans, youth, or the political left. A growing number of Americans had also become angry over demonstrations, riots, soaring crime rates, welfare costs, inflation, and a war that seemed to be going nowhere. The sight of long-haired draft protesters outraged many Americans who did not hesitate to support their government in time of war. Many working-class Americans were offended by the actions of students they considered privileged. The deep anger these Americans felt soon developed into a backlash against the Great Society and the civil rights and antiwar movements.

Some white Americans believed that the civil rights movement had gone "too far." A number of homeowners feared that integration in their neighborhoods would decrease property values and lead to black domination there. Middle-income families often resented paying higher taxes to support antipoverty programs. Many families opposed the busing of their children away from neighborhood schools in order to achieve court-ordered racial balance in the classroom.

The political leader who gained most from the conservative backlash was Governor George Wallace of Alabama. Wallace had boosted his political career defending racial segregation. In the late 1960s Wallace built a national following on a program dedicated to ending school busing and restoring "law and order." Using these themes Wallace launched an independent presidential campaign in the election of 1968. The impressive popular support for Wallace was another sign that President Johnson's national consensus had fallen apart.

★★★★★★★★★★★★★★★★★★

Section Three Review

★★★★★★★★★★★★★★★★★★

SUMMARY

African Americans became disillusioned with American society and continuing discrimination. Increasingly, black leaders stressed a more militant stance that emphasized black pride, leadership, and African heritage. Tensions erupted in a series of riots throughout large American cities. Protests also broke out on college campuses, mainly over the war in Vietnam. A counterculture sprang up that encouraged alternative lifestyles. A backlash to the counterculture movement developed among conservative Americans who supported the government and increasingly felt besieged by the disorder and unrest of the 1960s.

CHECKING FOR UNDERSTANDING

1. **Identify** Stokely Carmichael, George Wallace, Kerner Commission, Watts, Woodstock

2. **Define** conscientious objector, counterculture, commune

3. **Summarize** the goals of the black power movement.

4. **Cite** two reasons for the summer riots during the 1960s.

5. **State** two reasons why Americans were opposed to the draft.

6. **Explain** how the conservative backlash developed.

THINKING CRITICALLY

7. **Identifying Central Issues**   Do you have the right to refuse to fight in a war? Explain why conservative Americans were unsympathetic to the antiwar movement in the 1960s.

CONNECTIONS: HISTORY AND MUSIC

8. **Making Comparisons**   Music united young Americans in the 1960s. Explain whether or not music continues to be a voice for social change today.

★★★★★★★★★★★★★★★★★★

Year of Disasters—1968

SETTING THE SCENE

At all levels of American life, people share similar fears, insecurities and gnawing doubts to such an intense degree that the country may be suffering from a kind of national nervous breakdown…a depression of the national spirit.

—*NEWSWEEK*, JANUARY 8, 1968

Section Focus

The United States was, *Newsweek* added, "divided and confused as never since the Great Depression." Not only had the credibility gap cut through Americans' confidence in their government but America's prestige around the world had reached a low point. Western Europeans demonstrated against America's actions in Vietnam. When the North Koreans seized an American naval vessel, the *Pueblo,* in January 1968, it marked the beginning of a year of disasters.

Objectives

After studying this section, you should be able to:
• List four major disasters of 1968.
• Explain why the Tet offensive was the turning point in the Vietnam War.

I srael won an impressive victory over three Arab nations in 1967. The fact that the United States provided Israel with continued support added significantly to cold-war differences with the Soviet Union. The speed of Israel's victory prevented a clash between the major powers. Nevertheless the Soviets continued to back and to arm Arab nations. Later in 1967 President Johnson met with Soviet Premier Aleksei Kosygin at Glassboro, New Jersey. They discussed their nations' views, but no end to the cold war seemed in sight.

In January 1968, North Korea captured the American naval vessel *Pueblo* and forced its captain to confess that his ship had been spying on North Korea. The United States seemed helpless to win release of the ship's crew. This event was just the first in a series of disasters that plagued the United States in 1968.

Tet and Retreat

At the end of 1967, General William Westmoreland, American commander in Vietnam, had assured the country that the end of that war was in sight. Vastly enlarged American forces expanded the "search-and-destroy" missions. American bombers destroyed North Vietnamese factories, roads, bridges, and cities. Secretary of State Dean Rusk said the enemy "was hurting very badly."

January 30, 1968, marked a turning point in the war. The supposedly exhausted communist guerrillas abruptly launched major offensive strikes. Early that morning a handful of Vietcong soldiers attacked the United States embassy compound in Saigon—the very center of the American presence in South Vietnam. Together, the Vietcong and the North Vietnamese then launched massive attacks on all American bases in South Vietnam and on most of South Vietnam's major cities and provincial capitals. Taken by surprise by the assault during the celebration of Tet, the Vietnamese lunar New Year, Americans and South Vietnamese sustained heavy losses. After fierce fighting, they finally drove back the communist offensive.

Militarily, the communists were defeated. Politically, however, they scored a victory. The American people were shocked that the enemy that was supposedly on the verge of defeat could launch such a large-scale attack. Television coverage of the attack and the destruction that followed shook the nation's confidence. When General Westmoreland requested an additional 209,000 troops for Vietnam—in addition to the 500,000 already there—it seemed like another admission that the United States could not win the war.

After Tet, one of the nation's most trusted television news broadcasters, Walter Cronkite, reported:

We have too often been disappointed by the optimism of the American leaders to have faith any longer in the silver linings....To say that we are closer to victory today is to believe, in the face of evidence, the optimists who have been wrong in the past. To suggest we are on the edge of defeat is to yield to unreasonable pessimism. To say that we are mired in stalemate seems the only realistic, yet unsatisfactory conclusion.

Hearing Cronkite's broadcast, President Johnson turned to his aides and said, "It's all over." He recognized that he had lost the battle for public opinion.

Indeed, public opinion polls now showed that the majority of Americans had turned against the President's handling of the war. Johnson had become so unpopular that he seldom appeared in public, for fear of hostile crowds. Politically, the nation became even further divided between "hawks" and "doves." The war had driven a wedge between the President and Congress, and it also had divided the Democratic party.

In November 1967, a little-known liberal senator from Minnesota, Eugene McCarthy, became the first "dove" to announce his candidacy against Johnson for the election in 1968. Initially, few people gave McCarthy much of a chance. But soon thousands of student volunteers went to work for his campaign. In the New Hampshire primary election in March 1968, with the slogan "Clean for Gene," students shaved their beards, cut their hair, wore conservative clothing, and campaigned door-to-door. McCarthy "shook every corner of the political landscape" by a near victory, winning more than 40 percent of the votes in this primary, which Johnson narrowly won. Four days later Senator Robert Kennedy, who also opposed the war, entered the presidential race.

At first Johnson had seemed ready to run for reelection. He called on the people to join him in a "total national effort to win the war, to win the peace, and to complete the job that must be done here at home." Polls, however, showed that many Americans no longer trusted his leadership.

On March 31, 1968, two weeks after Senator Kennedy announced his candidacy, a tired-looking Lyndon Johnson appeared on television and announced that he would halt nearly all bombing of North Vietnam. He offered to send special negotiators to hold peace talks with the North Vietnamese and the Vietcong. Then Johnson stunned the nation by announcing: "I shall not seek, and I will not accept, the nomination of my party for another term as your President."

A few days later, on April 3, North Vietnam accepted Johnson's offer to begin peace negotiations. It would be five long years of continued bitter struggle, however, before the United States left the war in Vietnam behind.

Examining Photographs
United States marines land near a military base in Vietnam. How many troops were in the war zone by 1968?

Whether the availability of guns is a cause of violence in America is a bigger issue now than in 1968. Although 225,000 people died from handguns in the 1980s, (four times as many as were killed in Vietnam) few gun-control measures were passed. A 1990 poll, however, showed that a large majority of gun owners favored a seven-day waiting period for handgun purchases and registration of semi-automatic weapons; and 50 percent favored registration of rifles and handguns.

Violence

In April 1968, Dr. Martin Luther King, Jr., was in Memphis, Tennessee, to support a strike of black sanitation workers. King was planning a National Poor People's Campaign to promote economic gains for African Americans and all poor people. There had been many threats against King's life in the past, but he had always dismissed them. King told a church meeting that night:

...I've been to the mountain top,
and I don't mind....I've looked over
and I've seen the Promised Land.
I may not get there with you,
but I want you to know tonight that
we as a people will get to the
Promised Land.

The next day, April 4, 1968, Martin Luther King, Jr., was killed by a sniper. Ironically, the murder of the great preacher of nonviolence set off a week of rioting, arson, and looting in 125 American cities.

It was as if King's death swept away the last bit of faith in a peaceful solution. "America," announced Stokely Carmichael, "must be burned down in order for us to survive." Rioting took place in Washington, D.C., just blocks from the White House. President Johnson ordered troops to enforce a curfew and protect government buildings.

Close on the heels of this assassination came another—that of Senator Robert Kennedy in June 1968. With Johnson withdrawn from the presidential race, it appeared that Kennedy was pulling out in front of candidates Senator Eugene McCarthy and Vice President Hubert Humphrey.

Kennedy's program and popularity seemed broad enough to rebuild the Democratic coalition shattered by Vietnam. Then on June 5, 1968, just after winning victory in the Democratic primary in California, Kennedy was assassinated by an Arab nationalist, angry at Kennedy for his support of Israel.

Some blamed the availability of handguns and rifles for the violence that seemed to be tearing the United States apart and killing some of its finest leaders. A commission to study the problem of violence in America concluded:

Examining Photographs *Jesse Jackson (left) and Ralph Abernathy (right) talk with Dr. Martin Luther King, Jr., (center) on the balcony where he was assassinated the following day. Why was the violence that followed King's death ironic?*

Examining Photographs *Robert Kennedy celebrates his victory in the California primary, just before being shot by Sirhan Sirhan. What two Democratic candidates remained in the race?*

Most assassinations have been the products of individual passion or derangement.... Political turmoil and violence have characterized the United States throughout its history.

Late in April of 1968, another form of violence jolted the public when hundreds of students seized buildings at Columbia University in New York City. The students protested the proposed building of a university gymnasium on public land in a nearby black neighborhood. They also opposed Columbia's weapons-research programs for the government and the presence of the student military organization, Reserve Officers Training Corps (ROTC). The takeover lasted for about a week. Continued police presence outside, however, provoked some students who then vandalized property and barricaded the streets. The riot that followed was marked by both police brutality and student retaliation.

The campus violence that erupted across the country was not limited to the United States. In the previous year, there had been student riots in Rio de Janeiro, London, Rome, Madrid, Warsaw, and Prague. Shortly after the Columbia outbreak, French students battled police in the streets of Paris. In Czechoslovakia in 1968, student protests triggered a rebellion leading to the overthrow of the repressive communist regime that had ruled their country since 1948. A new Czech premier restored freedom of speech and press, freer contact with the West, and a measure of democracy, but after a few months, 200,000 Soviet troops reinstated Soviet control.

Meanwhile, prospects for peace in Vietnam grew dim. Diplomats from the United States and North Vietnam met in Paris in May 1968, but they could not agree on terms. After a lull, the war continued. The number of American troops in Vietnam reached a new high.

The Election of 1968

The election of 1968 reflected the turmoil of the times. In August antiwar protesters gathered in large numbers in Chicago at the site of the Democratic National Convention. Reacting to the previous student uprisings and black riots in the cities, Chicago Mayor Daley, himself a Democrat, advised his police to "shoot to kill arsonists and shoot to maim looters." Senator Humphrey lost some support when he defended the mayor's efforts to control the riots.

Inside the convention, party members were torn by the Vietnam War issue. Finally the convention nominated Hubert Humphrey for President and Senator Edmund Muskie of Maine for Vice President. But from the start Humphrey's campaign was undermined by the violence in the streets. The sense of chaos in the American process deepened. The Democratic party itself underwent a change in leadership.

The splintering of the Democratic party made the Republican candidate, Richard M. Nixon, the front-runner in the election of 1968. Although defeated in his campaign for President in 1960 and for governor of California in 1962, Nixon had remained active in national politics. He had campaigned for many Republican candidates during the 1960s, and supporters said that he was now more relaxed

Examining Photographs *Local police in Chicago attempted to break up a crowd of antiwar demonstrators who had gathered outside the Democratic Convention. As the nation watched the nominating process, television also brought pictures of the violence on the streets, as police, armed with clubs, subdued hundreds of protesters. When the war issue split the Democratic party, the Republicans had an opportunity to recapture the White House. Whom did they nominate?*

and self-confident than ever. For his vice-presidential running mate, Nixon chose Spiro T. Agnew, governor of Maryland.

A third candidate, George Wallace, governor of Alabama, ran as an Independent in all 50 states. Wallace geared his campaign to those who felt threatened by the black power movement and by the social unrest and violence in the nation's cities. With General Curtis Lemay as his running mate, Wallace attacked "pointy headed" intellectuals and appealed to the blue collar workers. His stands against federally enforced equal rights attracted support in the South. Leaders of organized labor, however, campaigned hard for Humphrey and moved much of the blue collar vote back to the Democrats.

Public opinion polls gave Nixon a wide lead over Humphrey and Wallace. In his campaign, Nixon promised to unify the nation, return dignity to the presidency, stabilize American foreign policy, and lead a war against crime in the streets. He said he had a plan for ending the war in Vietnam, but he did not provide details.

At first Humphrey's support of President Johnson's Vietnam policies hurt his campaign. But after he called for a complete end to the bombing of North Vietnam, he began to move up in the polls. A week before the election, President Johnson helped Humphrey by announcing that the bombing of North Vietnam had halted and that a cease-fire would soon follow.

The popular vote in the presidential race was so close that it was not certain until the next day that Nixon had won. Johnson's decision, made on October 31, had come too late to change the election. The election day turnout was large—61 percent of the electorate participated. Nixon received 31.8 million votes, Humphrey had 31.3 million, and Wallace had 9.9 million. Nixon's narrow victories in a few key states gave him a comfortable electoral margin. In the electoral college Nixon won 301 votes to 191 votes for Humphrey and 46 votes for Wallace. Although the voters had elected a Republican President, they kept Democratic majorities in both the Senate and House of Representatives.

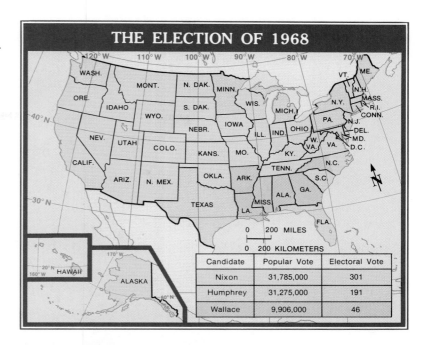

THE ELECTION OF 1968

Candidate	Popular Vote	Electoral Vote
Nixon	31,785,000	301
Humphrey	31,275,000	191
Wallace	9,906,000	46

Examining Maps *The results of the 1968 presidential election indicated a conservative backlash and a desire for stability. Taken together Nixon's and Wallace's popular vote totals greatly outweighed Humphrey's support. What campaign promises contributed to Nixon's victory?*

Speaking to reporters after his election, Nixon recalled seeing a young girl carrying a sign at one of his rallies that said: "Bring Us Together." This, he promised, would be his chief effort as President.

End of an Era

Lyndon Johnson left office in January 1969 a discouraged man. The American people had rejected Johnson's policies in Vietnam. Supporters of Nixon, he knew, were not sympathetic to the Great Society programs. The nation had become deeply divided.

The 1960s had begun as a time of youth, optimism, and confidence in the future and ended in war, riots, and violence. Three national heroes—President John F. Kennedy, Dr. Martin Luther King, Jr., and Senator Robert Kennedy—had been assassinated. Tens of thousands of young Americans had been killed or wounded in the most unpopular war the United States had ever fought. The New Frontier and the Great Society programs, designed to

Examining Photographs *The space race began in the early 1960s when President Kennedy launched a long-range program to land Americans on the moon. What significant event happened in 1968?*

make life better for the poor and the needy, had also become casualties of the war.

After the unhappy events in 1968, the year itself ended on an ironic note of hope and progress. Late in December 1968 the United States succeeded in sending the first astronauts into orbit around the moon. During one of the most difficult years in American history, the nation had scored a great technological achievement. The photographs sent back from space made planet Earth seem small, peaceful, and beautiful. It brought a new feeling to Americans that no matter how difficult, the problems they faced could be solved.

SUMMARY

1968 was a turbulent year for the United States. In January, North Vietnam staged the Tet offensive. Though it was turned back, Americans began to question whether or not the war could be won. Americans' faith in Johnson's leadership seriously eroded. In March, Johnson announced he would not run for reelection. The assassination of Dr. Martin Luther King, Jr., in April set off a week of rioting. In June, Robert Kennedy was also assassinated. At its August convention, the Democratic party split over the Vietnam War and lost the November election to Richard Nixon, who promised to reunify the American people.

CHECKING FOR UNDERSTANDING

1. **Identify** General William Westmoreland, Eugene McCarthy, Robert Kennedy, Richard Nixon
2. **Describe** how the Tet offensive was a turning point in the Vietnam War.
3. **Explain** why President Johnson did not run for reelection.
4. **List** three violent events that shook the nation in 1968.
5. **State** two reasons why Richard Nixon won the 1968 presidential election.

THINKING CRITICALLY

6. **Synthesizing Ideas** How did the war in Vietnam and violence at home affect Americans' confidence in President Johnson?

GLOBAL PERSPECTIVES

7. **Comparing Actions** In 1968, students in Paris took over entire sections of the city by barricading the streets. The students were joined by workers who staged national strikes for better working conditions. Explain why such a coalition between students and workers in America was unlikely.

★★★★★★★★★★★★★★★★★★★★★

Map and Graph Skills

Interpreting Military Maps

In your study of wars fought in American history, you have no doubt found it helpful to have maps included in the text that showed major battles and campaigns. Because wars involve movements and battles in many places, a military map is able to depict the areas where battles, movements, and strategy take place.

Explanation

A military map shows the areas controlled by opposing sides as well as the major battle sites, troop movements, military offensives, and battle victories within an area. Some military maps show the major military actions during the entire length or several years of war. Others may show the military actions during a particular battle or a specific period of time.

To interpret military maps, follow these guidelines:

a. Read the map title. This will indicate the location and time period covered on the map.

b. Read the map key. This will indicate what the symbols on the map represent. For example, areas under the control of a particular side may be represented by a color. Battle sites may be represented by crossed swords, a shell burst, or a star. Military movements and offensives may

be represented by solid or broken lines and arrows.

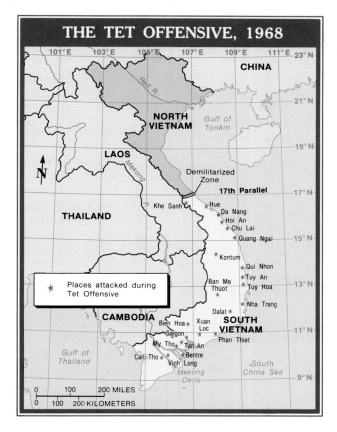

THE TET OFFENSIVE, 1968

Places attacked during Tet Offensive

c. Study the map itself. This will indicate the actual events or sequence of events that took place. Notice the geography of the area and try to determine how it would affect military strategy.

Example

Look at the military map of Southeast Asia on this page. Then follow the above guidelines.

a. The title indicates that the map covers a specific military action and

time period—the Tet offensive of 1968. The map shows the political boundaries of China, North Vietnam, South Vietnam Cambodia, Laos, and Thailand.

b. The map key indicates that the towns and cities shown were those attacked during the Tet offensive. No other symbols are indicated because the map is limited to a specific action and time.

c. The map itself indicates that the Tet offensive targeted towns and cities throughout South Vietnam. Although launched by the North Vietnamese, the offensive was not confined to areas close to the North Vietnam border, in the demilitarized zone, but struck deep into southern areas of South Vietnam, including Saigon. The text's reference to guerrilla tactics being launched against American bases, major cities, and provincial capitals explains and reinforces the wide range of targets on the map. North Vietnam used the Ho Chi Minh Trail through Laos and Cambodia to maintain a flow of military supplies into South Vietnam.

Practice

For further practice in interpreting military maps, apply the guidelines given above to the Vietnam War map on page 985.

★ Chapter 33 Review ★

★ Summary

Vowing to continue the work of John Kennedy, President Johnson set out to implement his domestic program known as the Great Society. It was designed to end poverty, discrimination, and other social ills of America. He also addressed the needs of people still living in poverty through government programs aimed at illiteracy, unemployment, and disease.

Johnson's domestic polices were played out against the backdrop of the Vietnam War, which increasingly took up resources and energy. Unable to end the war quickly, the United States found itself increasingly drawn into the conflict. As more soldiers died and the war dragged on, Americans began to question the wisdom of United States intervention. Demonstrations against the war took place across the country. Conservatives, who believed it was the duty of Americans to support their government, reacted to these events with anger and resentment.

Other unrest exploded in major cities as African Americans rioted against economic and social conditions. Growing opposition to the war led Johnson to abandon the race for the presidency. But Johnson's pledge to end the war was not enough to help Hubert Humphrey, the Democratic candidate, and Richard Nixon was elected in 1968.

★ Using Vocabulary

Each of the terms below has significance for the presidency of Lyndon Johnson. Use these terms in two sentences that explain pivotal moments during the Johnson years.

    consensus   **conscientious objectors**

    escalation

★ Reviewing Facts

1. **Identify** four achievements of the Johnson administration.
2. **State** two reasons why it was difficult for the United States to win the war in Vietnam.
3. **Explain** why Americans' support of the war in Vietnam eroded.
4. **List** two results of the black power movement.

5. **Describe** the military and political aspects of the Tet offensive.
6. **Name** four events that occurred in 1968 which damaged Americans' faith in their country.

★ Understanding Concepts

SOCIAL UPHEAVAL

1. Why was there so much turmoil in the 1960s? Explain how black power and counterculture movements represented desire for change.
2. Evaluate the effectiveness of violent versus nonviolent demonstrations. What were the results of nonviolent demonstrations in the early 1960s? Compare the results of the late 1960s riots to the goals of the black power movement. Use this information to formulate an opinion of the use of violence in demonstrations.

WAR

3. Explain how Americans' perceptions of communism influenced United States policy to support South Vietnam. Explain why some Americans believed it was critical to stop communism in South Vietnam and feared the repercussions if the United States failed to do so.
4. As you have read, the government in South Vietnam had little popular support. What effect do you think this lack of support had on the failure of the United States to achieve its military objectives in Vietnam? Explain your answer.

★ Thinking Critically

1. **Evaluating Achievements** President Johnson was able to get several landmark laws and programs enacted in only a few years. Explain how Johnson's efforts to form a consensus enabled him to do this. Predict the likelihood of maintaining this consensus for an extended period of time during the 1960s.
2. **Analyzing a Quotation** Reread the quotation by George Kennan on page 987 of your text. Explain why Kennan believed the United States should not intervene in Vietnam. Do you agree with Kennan? Do you believe that your answer would be different if the United States had been more successful in the war effort? Explain your answer.

3. Comparing Cultures Some Americans dismiss the counterculture movement of the 1960s as having no lasting effect. Others consider it as a unique expression of idealism and commitment to social values. What do you think? Explain whether or not you think this movement had any lasting effects on American society.

4. Analyzing Effects How was the violence that racked American society in 1968 perceived by conservative Americans? What effect do you think the violence had on the nomination of Hubert Humphrey and the election of Richard Nixon in 1968?

★ Writing About History

NARRATION

Refer to the description of how to write a narrative essay in the History Writer's Handbook in the Appendix of this book. Your teacher will give you more specific instructions on the essay's length and the assignment's due date.

Imagine that it is 1968 and you have just received a draft notice in the mail. Though you are legally obligated to join the military, many Americans at this time are refusing to be drafted. Write an essay explaining whether or not you will fight in the war. Before you begin writing, make a list of the reasons for and against going to fight. Use this list to explain both sides of the issue in your essay. Then write about your decision and the reasons for it.

★ Learning Cooperatively

Imagine it is 1968 and you are inside the Democratic convention hall in Chicago where Hubert Humphrey has just been nominated. Outside, protesters and police are clashing violently with one another and the nation seems to be coming apart from tension and unrest. You realize that millions of Americans are watching the convention coverage on live television. Your candidate, Hubert Humphrey will have this one opportunity to reach the American people at this critical moment. Work with a partner to write an acceptance speech for Hubert Humphrey. The purpose of the speech is to calm Americans' fears. Divide the writing chores this way: 1) what Humphrey will do to bring the nation back together, 2) what Humphrey will do about Vietnam. Collaborate on putting your best ideas on both into the speech. Present your speech to the class.

★ Mastering Skills

DETERMINING THE RELIABILITY OF A SOURCE

Suppose that you have been asked to write a report on the Vietnam War. Where would you obtain the information you need to begin writing? One basic ingredient needed to prepare an accurate report is supporting evidence from *reliable sources*—books, documents, or other records that supply dependable information. Because not all sources are reliable, when you research a topic you must determine the worth of your sources.

The following guidelines will help you to determine the reliability of your source:

- Evaluate the writers of the source by considering whether their background qualifies them to write on the topic.
- Consider the reputation of the publication or publisher of the source. Is the magazine, newspaper, or periodical generally reliable?
- Consult more than one source, comparing and contrasting the information presented in each.
- Ask yourself questions such as the following:

  Is this a primary source or a secondary source?

  Is the information supported by evidence?

  Is the information mostly facts (statements that can be verified) or opinions (something that someone believes or thinks is true)?

  Is the material objective in viewpoint?

Practice Using these guidelines and what you have read in the chapter, answer the following questions.

1. In writing a report on a subject that is still controversial, such as the Vietnam War, why is it especially important to use a variety of sources?

2. What special considerations might you have to take when determining the reliability of sources dealing with controversial subjects?

3. What advantage might there be to using a very recent source that deals with the Vietnam War compared to a newspaper article from that time?

CHAPTER 34
An Imperial Presidency

Historical Focus

Richard Nixon's election in 1968 seemed to promise a time of peace. As President, Nixon shifted social responsibility to the states and launched a new foreign policy by negotiating with top communist leaders. The withdrawal of troops from Vietnam seemed to assure Nixon's victory in the election of 1972. His reelection campaign, however, waged "dirty tricks" against the Democrats. The Watergate scandal eventually forced Nixon's resignation. President Ford worked to help heal the nation.

Concepts to Understand

- How **presidential power** is balanced by the other branches of federal government.
- How political isolation and **corruption** affected the presidency.

People to Know

Warren Burger, Henry Kissinger, Zhou En-lai, Betty Friedan, George McGovern

Places to Locate

Cambodia, Egypt, Vietnam

Terms to Identify

busing, balance of payments, OPEC, détente, summit, Pentagon Papers, ERA, executive privilege

Guided Reading

As you read this chapter, seek the answers to the following questions.

1. What were the foreign policy achievements of the Nixon administration?
2. What illegal activity caused Nixon to resign the presidency?

SPANNING THE DECADES

	1968	1969	1970	1971	1972
POLITICAL	1968 *Nixon elected President*	1969 *Gradual American withdrawal from Vietnam begins*	1970 *Riots at Kent State University*	1971 Pentagon Papers *are published*	1972 *Nixon visits Premier Zhou En-lai of China*
	1968		**1970**		**1972**
CULTURAL	1968 *Broadway musical* Hair *opens*	1969 *Neil Armstrong walks on the moon*		1971 *Amtrak passenger service begins*	1972 Ms. *magazine begins publication*

The White House *by H. Wrobel, 1945*

1974
*Watergate scan-
dal unfolds;
Nixon resigns*

1975
*140,000 Vietnamese
refugees are settled in
the United States*

1974   1976

1974
Happy Days *sitcom
premiers on ABC-TV*

1976
*Bicentennial
celebration of
the United States*

*... To that oath [to uphold and defend the
Constitution] I now add this sacred
commitment: I shall consecrate my
Office, my energies, and all the wisdom
I can summon to the cause of peace
among nations.*

—RICHARD NIXON
Inaugural Address, January 20, 1969

Nixon's Domestic Policy

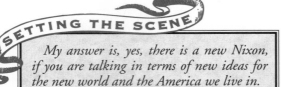

My answer is, yes, there is a new Nixon, if you are talking in terms of new ideas for the new world and the America we live in.

—RICHARD NIXON
Presidential campaign speech, 1968

Section Focus

While the "new Nixon" supported new ideas for solving the nation's economic problems, the specter of the "old Nixon" stalked the White House. Vestiges of the old Richard Nixon were seen in his attempts to change the direction of the Supreme Court. Neither Nixon's new policies nor his old, however, could curb the problems of inflation and high unemployment.

Objectives

After studying this section, you should be able to:
• Explain President Richard Nixon's southern strategy.
• Describe how Nixon tried to deal with the economic problems of the early 1970s.

To Americans and foreigners alike, the United States in the late 1960s had lost its direction. Not only was it losing the war in Vietnam, but its industries were losing their competitive edge. A sense of defeat and decay became apparent. Deep social, political, and racial divisions were threatening to tear society apart. Richard Nixon claimed that he had a "plan to end the war in Vietnam" and "bring Americans together." His promise of peace in

Vietnam and tranquility at home appealed to many in the United States. By a very narrow margin, Nixon was elected the thirty-seventh President of the United States.

Nixon's Political Career

Richard M. Nixon was the first President in modern times to be elected after having lost a previous bid for the presidency. After losing the 1962 California gubernatorial race, his political career seemed over. In the 1968 campaign, however, he changed his public image. The old Nixon had been intensely partisan and ruthless. When he had run for Congress from California in 1946, for example, he charged that his opponent had strong ties to communist organizations. The new Nixon, however, impressed observers as calm, broad-minded, and statesmanlike. He promised that his administration would be "open to new ideas, open to men and women of both parties, open to the critics as well as those who support us." "We want to bring America together," Nixon said.

Bringing the nation together proved difficult. With the Democrats in control of Congress, Nixon saw many of his domestic proposals rejected. The administration's failure in the domestic arena, however, was not a source of frustration for the President because his major interest was foreign policy.

One of Nixon's domestic successes was the **new federalism,** a partnership between the federal government and the state governments. The hallmark of the new federalism, Nixon declared, was that states and municipalities would assume greater responsibility for their own well-being. In a message to Congress, the President declared:

*I reject the patronizing idea that
government in Washington, D.C.,
is inevitably more wise and
more efficient than government
at the local or state level....The idea
that a bureaucratic elite in Washington
knows what is best for people...
is really a contention that people
cannot govern themselves.*

Following the President's lead, Congress passed a series of revenue-sharing bills that granted federal funds to local agencies to use as they saw fit.

Another domestic concern that Nixon addressed during the 1968 campaign was the permissive attitude toward the rights of those accused of crimes. Nixon criticized the record of the Supreme Court under Chief Justice Earl Warren. He denounced Supreme Court decisions that curtailed the powers of the police in the interrogation of suspects and that forbade the use of electronic "bugging" equipment for gathering evidence. Such decisions, Nixon maintained, violated "the first civil right of every American to be free of domestic violence." He promised to fill vacancies on the Supreme Court with judges who would not "weaken the peace forces as against the criminal forces."

Nixon eventually succeeded in his campaign to change the liberal thrust of the Court. When Chief Justice Warren resigned shortly after Nixon took office, the President nominated Warren Burger, a respected conservative judge, to take his place. He also placed three other conservative justices on the Court, including one from the South. The Burger Court, known as the Nixon Court by its critics, did not take away more rights of criminal suspects, but it did diminish the rights that had been affirmed by the Warren Court.

Nixon's appointment of a southern justice to the Supreme Court was only one part of a general "southern strategy," to lure southern voters away from the

Examining Photographs *The Supreme Court favored the use of busing as a constitutional way to desegregate the nation's schools, although many Americans disagreed. Southern leaders in particular thought the Supreme Court had overstepped its authority. What was President Nixon's position?*

Democrats. Another major part of that strategy was to reverse a Johnson administration policy that cut off federal funds from racially segregated school systems. Although this policy was affirmed in 1968 by the Supreme Court in *Greene v. County School Board*, Nixon ignored the Court's ruling and instructed the Justice Department to support school boards that were seeking to delay desegregation.

Contrary to Nixon's hopes, his appointments to the Supreme Court did not reverse the *Green* decision. Instead, the Court affirmed integration by means of **busing**—transporting of children to a school outside their residential area to achieve racial balance in that school. White Americans in the South and most other regions of the nation resisted busing, and Nixon denounced it, saying:

…[W]hile there may be some doubt as to whether segregated education is inferior, there is no doubt whatever …that education requiring excessive transportation for students is definitely inferior. I come down hard and unequivocally against busing for the purpose of racial balance.

The Nixon administration's open opposition to busing for desegregation intensified public controversy over the issue not only in the South but throughout the nation.

Nixon's Economic Policies

The Nixon administration inherited difficult economic problems. The combined costs of President Johnson's War on Poverty and the Vietnam War had produced a large federal budget deficit and mounting inflation. Between 1964 and 1969, the dollar lost one-fifth of its purchasing power.

After his inauguration, Nixon announced an economic plan that was based on reducing federal spending and curtailing the supply of money. By the end of 1970, however, it was apparent that the plan was not working. Restricting the supply of money drove interest rates up, and higher interest rates discouraged investment. Unemployment increased, and the stock market declined. The slowdown in business activity reduced federal revenues, and inflation accelerated. Meanwhile the costs of the Vietnam war mounted.

The weaknesses of the economy were reflected in a growing **balance of payments** deficit. The balance of payments is the difference between what a nation receives from foreign countries and what

Life of the Times

SHOPPING MALLS

A 1973 report on New Jersey's Cherry Hill Mall observed that the shopping mall had become to the suburb what main street once was to the small town—the focus of community life. The period between 1971 and 1975 was a heyday of mall construction. Cities and suburbs across the United States became home to enclosed malls featuring, under one roof, a fairly predictable array of small specialty stores for books, gifts, and shoes.

Large malls typically included major department stores as dependable "anchors" for sales and customers, as well as several popular restaurants. Some malls also had portable boutique stands that sold everything from perfume to wicker.

Mall managers were enormously successful in not only attracting shoppers, but also walkers, joggers, and vast crowds of teenagers just "hanging out." Malls became such popular gathering places in the early 1970s that a high school in Bethesda, Maryland, held its senior prom at one.

Despite the carefully controlled environment that malls maintain through regulated climate, piped-in music, security personnel, and squeaky cleanness, they did not escape the social upheaval of the 1970s. Several large malls became sites for Vietnam War protests.

Connections

HISTORY AND MATHEMATICS

THE METRIC SYSTEM

"…[T]he dinosaurs did not go away overnight," read an article in *National Geographic,* "nor will the older standards. The world has learned to live without dinosaurs. In time we'll all learn to live with metrics."

Metric-based robots assemble cars.

The Metric Act of 1975 committed the United States to a transition from the U.S. Customary system of measurement to Systeme International (SI)—the metric system. The metric system is based on units of ten and one hundred. Thus, 100 centimeters equal 1 meter.

Although many Americans believe metric conversion has failed, most major U.S. industries have switched, wholly or partially, to metrics. Companies that compete on the international market were forced to change because nearly every other industrial nation uses metrics.

Domestic consumer products have been slower to adopt SI. None of the laws authorizing use of SI have provided funds for public education. In addition, no target date has been set for 100 percent compliance, and no government agency has the power to enforce the use of the metric system.

MAKING THE MATHEMATICS CONNECTION

1. Why would the United States customary system of measurement be comparable to dinosaurs?

LINKING PAST AND PRESENT

2. What factors have made it difficult to establish international standards of measurement?

---

it spends overseas. Between 1970 and 1971, the nation's balance of payments deficit jumped from $4 billion to $22 billion.

The deficit was evidence that the United States had lost its dominance in world markets. Between 1950 and 1970, for example, the United States share of world automobile production dropped from 76 to 31 percent, and the same phenomenon was occurring in the textile, shoe, and electrical equipment industries.

A serious effect of the balance of payments deficit was that it weakened international faith in the value of the dollar. Because world trade depends on stable money and because the dollar was the major currency in the world, the dollar crisis threatened to disrupt international trade.

Thus, the Nixon administration found itself confronted with a recession, a dollar crisis, an expensive war in Southeast Asia

and a huge **trade deficit**, in which the value of imports was greater than exports. Nixon acted decisively. To combat inflation, in August 1971, he announced a 90-day freeze on prices and wages. To discourage imports, he placed an additional duty of 10 percent on all goods purchased from abroad. He also allowed the dollar to decline in value in relation to foreign currencies making it more expensive for Americans to buy goods from other countries. Therefore, goods made in the United States became cheaper than foreign-made goods, and that promoted exports. Although Nixon's policies brought some relief, inflation, chronic unemployment, and the loss of foreign markets remained a problem throughout his presidency. The measures also caused ill will in nations that depended on American markets for their products.

Another problem concerned energy. In the fall of 1973, Arab nations placed an embargo on crude oil shipments from the Middle East. The purpose of the embargo was to force the United States to stop supporting Israel in its struggle with the Arab states. Support for Israel did not change, but the embargo produced an energy crisis in America—and near panic. In some areas the price of petroleum shot up nearly 400 percent, and there were shortages of gasoline for cars and heating oil for homes, schools, and businesses.

Although the United States had about one-sixteenth of the world's population, Americans consumed about one-third of the world's energy. Most of this energy came from such nonrenewable resources as oil, gas, and coal. Coal reserves were abundant in America but supplied less than 20 percent of the nation's energy needs. By 1973, the United States was importing about 6 million barrels of oil each day, or about 36 percent of the oil needed to heat homes and to keep factories and automobiles running.

President Nixon announced a plan to make the country self-sufficient in energy by 1980. He called for higher taxes on imported oil and encouraged Americans to take conservation measures, such as lowering their thermostats. Congress passed a law requiring states to lower the speed limit on highways to 55 miles per hour to save gasoline and approved the construction of a pipeline in Alaska for the shipment of newly discovered oil to refineries. Congress provided some tax incentives to encourage energy research and put the nation on daylight saving time for two years.

After the Arab nations lifted the oil embargo in March 1974, most Americans forgot about the energy crisis. However fuel prices began a steep rise as the oil shortage continued. In the 1960s the major oil-exporting nations had formed the Organization of Petroleum Exporting Countries (OPEC). By 1970 OPEC had begun to raise prices, and over the next decade the cost of oil increased from less than $2 a barrel to more than $30 a barrel. The increases in the price of oil by the OPEC countries contributed to the problems that plagued the American economy throughout the 1970s.

Section One Review

SUMMARY

President Nixon came to the White House with the hope of bringing America together. A cornerstone of his domestic policy was a greater emphasis on local decision making and revenue sharing. To fulfill his promise of law and order, Nixon appointed conservative judges to the Supreme Court and replaced retiring Chief Justice Warren with Warren Burger. In the economy, Nixon faced tough challenges to balance the federal budget and control inflation. The United States' balance of payments deficit soared and it became increasingly evident that the United States no longer dominated world markets.

CHECKING FOR UNDERSTANDING

1. **Identify** Warren Burger, southern strategy
2. **Define** new federalism, busing, balance of payments, trade deficit
3. **Point out** how Nixon affected the criminal justice system.
4. **Describe** two features of Nixon's economic policies.
5. **Explain** how the declining United States economy affected world markets.

THINKING CRITICALLY

6. **Evaluating Policy** Write an evaluation of whether busing is an effective means of achieving school integration.

CONNECTIONS: HISTORY AND TECHNOLOGY

7. **Determining Cause and Effect** One major reason imports to the United States increased during the 1970s was the influx of compact European and Japanese automobiles which offered better gas mileage. How do you think these imports forced American car makers to change?

Critical Thinking Skills

Interpreting Point of View

As a member of the high school newspaper staff, Keisha spoke out for the right of the paper to print articles without being censored by the high school's administration. Two weeks later Keisha's brother was suspended from the basketball team because of his involvement in a fight that broke out after a home game. A school reporter then wrote a sharply critical article about student athletes who were "ruining the school's reputation." Keisha now tells her friends that articles like this should be cleared first with the school's principal. She has changed her point of view.

Explanation

A point of view is a person's opinion; it is affected by their role, their experiences, relationships, and beliefs. Students of history should learn to identify the points of view of historical figures and groups. Interpreting points of view helps students understand why people make certain decisions or behave in certain ways.

To interpret a person's point of view ask the following questions:

• What opinion is being expressed?

• What factors may have influenced the person or group to adopt this opinion?

• What arguments or evidence are used to support this point of view?

• What are the possible alternative points of view to this issue?

Vice President Spiro Agnew addresses the media

Example

Read the following quotation from a speech by Vice President Spiro Agnew, given in Des Moines, Iowa, in 1969:

…For millions of Americans, the networks are the sole source of national and world news.

…A raised eyebrow, an inflection of the voice, a caustic remark dropped in the middle of a broadcast can raise doubts in a million minds about the veracity of a public official …One Federal Communications Commissioner considers the powers of the networks equal to that of local, state, and Federal Governments all combined. Certainly it represents a concentration of power over American public opinion unknown in history.…Of the men who produce and direct the network news, the nation knows practically nothing.…The views of this fraternity do not…represent the views of America.

Applying the four questions above to this quotation, you can interpret Agnew's point of view:

a) His opinion is that the networks have too much power.

b) He is influenced because the networks do not show sympathy with his positions.

c) He supports his view by citing a member of the Commission who compares the influence of the networks to the power of government.

d) An alternative viewpoint is that the networks believe they have a duty to express views other than official government policy.

Practice

Use the four questions above to interpret President Nixon's point of view on the issue of busing on page 1008.

Secrecy, Surprise, and Summitry

SETTING THE SCENE

...So let us, in these next five days, start a long march together, not in lockstep, but on different roads leading to the same goal, the goal of building a world structure of peace and justice....

—RICHARD M. NIXON,
Banquet toast, Beijing, China,
February 1972

Section Focus

Nixon toasted the Chinese in Beijing and signed an arms-limitation agreement with the Soviets in Moscow. Also during his administration Nixon secretly plotted the bombing of Cambodia and the expansion of the war in Indochina. Later, through a policy of Vietnamization, he withdrew American troops. The foreign policy of the Nixon administration was one of secrecy and surprise.

Objectives

After studying this section, you should be able to:
• Explain why Nixon pursued détente.
• List the steps Nixon took to end American involvement in Vietnam.

Surprising both his supporters and his critics, Richard Nixon as President shed his long-held image as a "cold warrior." In the 1950s he looked for communists in the state department and talked tough to Khrushchev. As President he opened a dialogue with the communist leaders of China and entered into a series of agreements with the Soviet Union. Nixon even recognized the legitimacy of the communist regimes of Eastern Europe.

Nixon's Foreign Policy

Like Woodrow Wilson, President Nixon took almost sole charge of foreign policy. To help him handle foreign policy matters, Nixon appointed Henry A. Kissinger, a brilliant political scientist, as his national security adviser. Kissinger's job was to present the President with policy options in which the probable consequences of each policy were outlined. Kissinger also undertook secret missions abroad. In 1973 Nixon appointed Kissinger secretary of state.

Nixon, like Wilson, wanted to be remembered as a peacemaker. In his inaugural address he proclaimed:

After a period of confrontation, we are entering an era of negotiation.
Let all nations know that during this administration our lines of communication will be open. We seek an open world— open to ideas, open to the exchange of goods and people....

For Nixon, lines of communication were meant to reach friend and foe alike. To the communist leader of Romania, Nixon declared: "We seek normal relations with all countries, regardless of their domestic policies." Nixon proclaimed a policy of **détente,** or relaxation of tensions between the United States and the communist bloc. He maintained that it would be a "safer world and a better world if we have a strong, healthy United States, Europe, China, Russia, and Japan, each balancing the other."

To achieve this balance Nixon proposed a meeting between the United States and the Soviet Union to discuss strategic arms limitations. The SALT negotiations, as

Examining Photographs *President Nixon and Premier Brezhnev sign the SALT I agreement limiting nuclear weapons in 1972. What was Nixon's policy of détente?*

they were called, began in Helsinki, Finland, in 1969. Before the conclusion of SALT I in 1972 the two sides had agreed to ban biological warfare and limit the growth of nuclear weapons.

SALT culminated in the May 1972 Moscow **summit,** or diplomatic meeting, between the superpowers. In addition to signing the SALT agreement, Nixon and the Soviet leader, Leonid Brezhnev, also agreed to increase trade, exchange scientific information, and cooperate in preventing pollution.

President Nixon also sought improved relations with China. He began by lifting trade and travel restrictions. The President also withdrew the Seventh Fleet from defending Taiwan, an island which China claimed as its own.

The Chinese responded to Nixon's initiatives in a variety of ways, including inviting a ping-pong team from the United States to visit China. More importantly, the Chinese accepted Henry Kissinger's proposal that he visit Beijing to open discussions with Chinese leaders. During Kissinger's meeting with Chinese Premier Zhou En-lai (JOH EHN LYE), he arranged for President Nixon to visit China in February

1972. President Nixon's sensational announcement that he would visit Beijing foreshadowed the 1971 admission of the

"I'm not sure of the rules, but it looks like an interesting game."

Examining Political Cartoons *Mao, Brezhnev, and Nixon play a game of global politics. Nixon, a former "cold warrior," appears uncertain about his moves. Why would the Soviet leader be concerned about relations between the United States and China?*

DEMONSTRATION FOR DEMOCRACY

Twenty years after the People's Republic of China opened its door and let the West in, Chinese students demonstrated for democracy in Tiananmen Square, in Beijing, China. During the demonstrations, students erected a "Goddess of Democracy" statue symbolizing the students' desire for change and closely resembling the Statue of Liberty. The demonstrations lasted for seven weeks in May and June 1989, until government troops were finally sent in to crush them.

Examining Photographs *The Vietnam Memorial in Washington, D.C., was completed in 1982. It displays the names of more than 58,000 Americans who gave their lives during the Vietnam War. What was the policy of Vietnamization?*

government of the People's Republic of China to the United Nations.

During the course of Nixon's historic visit to China, the leaders of both nations agreed to establish "more normal" relations between their countries. President Nixon, Chairman Mao, and Premier Zhou recognized that détente could serve the interests of both countries.

Since the early 1960s, a rift had developed in the relationship between the communist governments of the Soviet Union and China, and troops of the two nations occasionally clashed along their border. Mao realized that détente with the United States could deter Soviet aggression, and Nixon believed that détente with China would encourage Brezhnev to be more accommodating. The Soviet leader would not want the United States to forge an alliance with China.

War in Vietnam and the Middle East

During the 1968 presidential campaign, Nixon declared that he had a plan for

ending the Vietnam War. After his inauguration he resumed peace negotiations with the North Vietnamese in Paris, but they produced no results.

The President was faced with a dilemma: if he continued U.S. involvement in the war, public opposition would increase. If he withdrew U.S. troops without a peace agreement, he would be the first President of the United States to have ever "lost a war." Like Lyndon Johnson, Richard Nixon did not seek that dubious distinction.

To make matters worse, in June 1971, *The New York Times* published a secret Department of Defense study of U.S. involvement in Vietnam. The *Pentagon Papers,* as they were called, documented that for two decades, four Presidents of the United States had escalated the nation's involvement in Indochina. Furthermore, despite America's increased involvement, the situation in Southeast Asia was not any closer to a resolution.

The *Pentagon Papers* were evidence of the growing power of the executive branch. They contained details of the decisions that were made by Presidents and their advisers without the consent of Congress. Equally important, they revealed how Presidents were drawn into a war they did not know how to win. The *Pentagon Papers* also showed how the various administrations acted to deceive Congress, the press, and the public about the true situation in Vietnam.

President Nixon was outraged over the "leaking" of the secret documents. He ordered the Justice Department to go to court to stop further publication of the papers. Nixon hoped the court would affirm the government's right to restrain publication in matters of national security, but the Supreme Court decided that the *Pentagon Papers* were not vital to national security.

The federal government then brought charges against Daniel Ellsberg, one of the authors of the *Pentagon Papers,* for leaking the documents to the press. President Nixon also authorized a group of people who were called "the Plumbers" to break into the office of Ellsberg's psychiatrist to collect information about him. When their activities came to light, the charges against Daniel Ellsberg were dropped.

President Nixon's response to the publication of the *Pentagon Papers* was a further sign that the credibility of his administration was eroding. Nixon himself, it was revealed, had ordered the secret bombing of North Vietnamese sanctuaries in Cambodia in 1969. In April 1970, Nixon, without consulting Congress, ordered an invasion of Cambodia to drive the North Vietnamese out of the country. Protests against the war now intensified.

To quiet opposition to the war, Nixon announced a policy of "Vietnamization." Vietnamization consisted of two steps: the phased withdrawal of U.S. troops from Vietnam; and their replacement by conscripts from Vietnam. Nixon hoped that Vietnamization, combined with the saturation bombing of North Vietnam, would allow the United States to withdraw from the war "with honor." But the *New York Times* called his bombing policy "diplomacy through terror," and the *Boston Globe* commented:

THE UNITED STATES IN VIETNAM, 1950–1975	
1950	**May 8** President Truman sends U.S. aid and advisers to French forces in Indochina
1954	**May 7** French defeated by Communists at Dien Bien Phu
	July 20–21 Geneva Conference provides cease-fire and divides Vietnam
1957	Vietcong begin attacks in South Vietnam
1960	**Dec. 20** Vietcong form National Front for the Liberation of South Vietnam
1961	**Nov. 16** President Kennedy increases number of U.S. advisers in Vietnam
1963	**Nov. 1** Ngo Dinh Diem assassinated
1964	**July 24** U.S. rejects French President de Gaulle's plan to neutralize all of Indochina
	Aug. 2–4 Gulf of Tonkin–N. Vietnam attacks a U.S. destroyer and U.S. retaliates
	Aug. 7 Gulf of Tonkin Resolution-Congress grants President Johnson authority to use force against aggression
1965	**Feb. 7–8** First U.S. bombing of North Vietnam
	March 2 Rolling Thunder bombing campaign begins against North Vietnam
	March 8–9 President Johnson sends 3,500 Marines (first combat troops) to join 23,500 U.S. advisers
1966	**March 2** U.S. forces number 215,000
	Dec. 31 U.S. forces number 389,000
1967	**May 19** First U.S. air strike against central Hanoi
1968	**Jan. 30–Feb. 24** Tet Offensive by Vietcong
	March 31 President Johnson announces cessation of bombing of N. Vietnam north of 20th parallel and that he will not seek reelection
	May 10 Paris Peace Talks begin between U.S. and N. Vietnam
1969	**January 25** First full session of Paris Peace Talks with Vietcong and S. Vietnam also represented
	March 16 My Lai massacre (revealed in November 1969)
	June 8 President Nixon announces the withdrawal of 25,000 U.S. troops from Vietnam
	Sept. 3 Death of Ho Chi Minh
	Oct. 15 Vietnam Moratorium Day—nationwide antiwar demonstrations across the U.S.
1970	**Feb. 20** Presidential adviser Henry A. Kissinger opens secret peace negotiations in Paris
	April 29 U.S. troops invade Cambodia
	May 4 Four antiwar students killed during demonstrations at Kent State University, Ohio
	Dec. 31 Senate votes to repeal Gulf of Tonkin Resolution
1971	**Nov. 12** President Nixon limits U.S. ground forces in Vietnam to a defensive role
1972	**April 15–20** Widespread antiwar demonstrations in U.S.
	June 17–22 Watergate break-in and arrests
	Aug. 12 Last U.S. ground combat troops leave Vietnam
	Dec. 18–30 Bombing of Hanoi and Haiphong resumed to break stalled peace negotiations
1973	**Jan. 27** Cease-fire in Vietnam agreed upon
	Feb. 12 N. Vietnam releases first U.S. prisoners of war
1974	**Aug. 9** President Nixon resigns
1975	**April 29–30** North Vietnamese capture Saigon. Ameri–can personnel evacuated. Vietnam War ends.

New York Times, April 30, 1985; An *Encyclopedia of World History,* 5th ed. (1972); Gorton Carruth, *What Happened When* (1989); James S. Olson, *Dictionary of the Vietnam War* (1988)

Examining Photographs *Secretary of
State Henry Kissinger meets with North Vietnamese negotiator Le Duc Tho in Paris for
peace talks. Why was it difficult to reach a
settlement?*

By the end of the war, the total tonnage of bombs dropped by the United States on Vietnam was more than twice that dropped by the United States on all targets in both World War II and the Korean War.

Finally, on January 23, 1973, representatives of the United States, South Vietnam, North Vietnam, and the Vietcong signed a cease-fire agreement, ending the military presence of the United States in Vietnam. The war, however, did not end for the people of Vietnam. Under the agreement, U.S. troops withdrew from South Vietnam, but North Vietnamese troops did not.

As the Vietnam War wound down, another war erupted, this time in the Middle East. On October 6, 1973, the Jewish holy day of Yom Kippur, Egyptian and Syrian troops launched surprise attacks against Israeli forces. Their objective was to recapture the territory Egypt and Syria had lost to Israel during the Six-Day War of 1967. Caught by surprise, the Israeli troops were initially pushed back, but they quickly regrouped and launched their own attack, pushing into Syria and across the Suez Canal into Egypt.

Israel appealed to the United States for help, and President Nixon responded with a massive airlift of $2 billion in military supplies. At the same time, the Soviet Union continued to supply Egypt and Syria. American aid to Israel angered the Arab countries, and quickly they retaliated by placing an embargo on the shipment of oil to the United States and other countries that supported Israel. The Arabs hoped to force Israel's friends into supporting a settlement that would require Israel to return the lands it had taken in 1967. Hardest hit by the embargo was Western Europe, which received 72 percent of its oil from the Middle East. Although the United States received only about 11 percent of its oil supply from the region, the embargo created an energy crisis during which the price of fuel for automobiles and home heating soared.

Even as the United States and the Soviet Union gave aid to the opposing sides, they worked through the United Nations Security Council to arrange a cease-fire. In late

"There Goes the 8:05"

Examining Political Cartoons *Kissinger, a political scientist as well as diplomat, became known for his "shuttle diplomacy." What did this involve?*

October, the nations of Israel, Egypt, and Syria, agreed to terms. By the end of 1973, a UN peacekeeping force had been sent to the Middle East to police the region.

After the conflict, Secretary of State Henry Kissinger worked with Israel and Egypt to reduce tensions in the Middle East. For the next two years, Kissinger engaged in shuttle diplomacy, flying back and forth between the capitals of the two nations in an effort to produce a lasting peace. Kissinger's efforts yielded two important results. Early in 1974 Golda Meir, the prime minister of Israel, and Anwar el-Sadat, the president of Egypt, agreed to reestablish diplomatic relations between their two countries. Then in September 1975, Israel and Egypt agreed to withdraw their forces from the cease-fire line and pledged not to attack each other. Although significant problems remained, a measure of peace had been achieved in the Middle East. For the United States, the war in the Middle East brought home the fact that Americans, who had become dependent on oil from the Middle East, risked being held hostage to the demands of the oil-producing nations.

★ ★ ★ ★ ★ ★ ★ ★ ★ ★ ★ ★ ★ ★ ★ ★ ★ ★

Section Two Review

★ ★ ★ ★ ★ ★ ★ ★ ★ ★ ★ ★ ★ ★ ★ ★ ★ ★

SUMMARY

President Nixon relished the challenges of foreign policy. Though once a fervent anticommunist, one of his chief foreign policy goals was to improve communications with communist nations through détente. At the Moscow summit, the SALT agreement reduced nuclear weapons between the United States and the Soviet Union. Nixon and Kissinger also set to work renewing relations with China. Nixon increased military involvement in Indochina while setting into motion a withdrawal of American troops and the negotiation of a cease-fire. In 1973 war in the Middle East led to an Arab oil embargo. This conflict was defused by Kissinger's shuttle diplomacy.

CHECKING FOR UNDERSTANDING

1. **Identify** Henry Kissinger, Leonid Brezhnev, Zhou En-lai, Daniel Ellsberg, SALT, *Pentagon Papers*, Vietnamization

2. **Define** détente, summit

3. **List** three steps taken during Nixon's presidency to end United States involvement in Vietnam.

4. **Describe** how Henry Kissinger's shuttle diplomacy helped to end war in the Middle East.

THINKING CRITICALLY

5. **Evaluating Foreign Policy**
   Evaluate the pros and cons of Nixon's use of secrecy in China and Vietnam.

LINKING PAST AND PRESENT

6. **Making Comparisons** In 1989 a prodemocracy student demonstration in China was brutally put down. Compare the difficulties the United States faced in dealing with China before détente and after the prodemocracy demonstration was crushed.

★ ★ ★ ★ ★ ★ ★ ★ ★ ★ ★ ★ ★ ★ ★ ★ ★ ★

Years of Protest and Change

SETTING THE SCENE

...[T]he more intense forms of protest do not last long. Protest has an ever-decreasing half-life.

—SAMUEL P. HUNTINGTON
Political scientist, *American Politics*, 1981

Section Focus

The Vietnam War led many people in the United States to question the wisdom of the nation's foreign policy and, with the close of the war, to take a closer look at issues of domestic concern. Discrimination against women, native Americans, and Spanish-speaking Americans became their next target for change.

Objectives

After studying this section, you should be able to:
• Describe the gains made by women and minorities.
• Explain why the Equal Rights Amendment was not ratified.

The 1960s and 1970s were times when young Americans became leaders in promoting social justice. They were determined to close up the gap between the realities of American life—discrimination, poverty, and other social inequities—and the nation's ideal of "liberty and justice for all."

Because for the first time in United States history youth was in the majority, their voices could not be ignored. These young people were dedicated to "self-realization" and social reform, and their organized protests exhibited their commitment to these goals. It was the Vietnam War that turned such impassioned protests into near rebellion.

Antiwar and Women's Rights Movements

The war in Vietnam generated heated and vocal opposition. At first the antiwar movement was centered on college campuses across the country, which was the source previously for many activists in the civil rights movement. Each escalation of the war prompted sit-ins, teach-ins, and demonstrations. And each escalation increased the number of protestors. By 1970 war protest had moved off campus to involve people from all walks of life in the antiwar movement.

While most antiwar protests were peaceful, a few had tragic outcomes. When President Nixon announced the invasion of Cambodia in May 1970, protests erupted on scores of campuses. At Kent State University in Ohio, rioting reached such an intensity that the National Guard was sent in. On May 4 a contingent of guardsmen, harassed by students, fired into the crowd, killing 4 students and wounding 10. On May 14, at Jackson State University in Mississippi, student protest was suppressed by the state police who fired randomly into a dormitory. Two students were killed, and 9 were wounded. These events precipitated a nationwide student strike. Hundreds of colleges and universities suspended classes or closed down completely.

Even though women constituted more than 50 percent of the population in the United States in the 1970s, their political, economic, legal, and social status resembled that of a disadvantaged minority. In 1977, for example, women held less than 5 percent of the elective offices in the United States. There were no women senators, Supreme Court justices, or mayors of major cities. Of the 435 members of the House of Representatives, only 18 were women. In her autobiography *Unbought, Unbossed,* Shirley Chisholm, the first black woman to serve in the House of Representatives, wrote:

When I decided to run for Congress, I knew I would encounter both anti-black and anti-feminist sentiments. What surprised me was the much greater virulence of the sex discrimination.

In 1976 the U.S. Department of Labor reported that full-time working men averaged 75 percent more pay than full-time working women. Such inequities, coupled with the success of blacks in the civil rights movement, contributed to the rebirth of the women's rights movement of the 1960s. The publication of *The Feminine Mystique,* by Betty Friedan, in 1963, inspired demands for change. Friedan rejected the notion that the destiny of women was only to be wives and mothers. She described how the media had created an image of women that was designed to imprison them in their households and bar serious consideration of them as competitors in the labor market.

In 1966 Betty Friedan joined with other women to establish the National Organization for Women (NOW). The organization's Statement of Purpose read:

SELECTED WOMEN'S OCCUPATIONS, 1979 & 1986

Occupation	Women as a percent of all full-time workers		Ratio of women's to men's earnings	
	1979	1986	1979	1986
Secretaries	98.8	99.2	.58	NA
Registered nurses	94.6	92.7	.82	NA
Nursing aides, orderlies	85.1	88.3	.72	.81
Bookkeepers	88.1	93.0	.66	.74
Cashiers	77.7	79.8	.71	.75
Computer operators	56.6	63.8	.69	.73
Computer programmers	28.0	39.7	.80	.81
Computer systems analysts	20.4	29.7	.79	.83
Accountants and auditors	34.0	44.7	.60	.72
Sales supervisors	22.4	26.6	.57	.55
Managers and administrators	22.1	28.9	.51	.61
Janitors and cleaners	15.3	21.0	.74	.69
Lawyers	10.4	15.2	.55	.63
Sales representatives	10.1	13.4	.62	.72
Electrical / electronic engineers	4.4	9.4	.75	NA
Automotive mechanics	0.9	0.6	.86	NA

Bureau of the Census, *Current Population Reports* (1987)

...[T]o take action to bring women into full participation in the mainstream of American society now, assuming all the privileges and responsibilities thereof in truly equal partnership with men.

Examining Tables
The earning power of women improved somewhat between 1979 and 1986. In what occupations do women continue to earn slightly more than half of what men receive?

Examining Photographs
The Equal Rights Amendment, submitted to the states in 1972 for ratification, aroused strong feelings among supporters and opponents. Who opposed its passage?

Among its early successes, NOW helped end separate classified ads for men and women and airline rules that required female flight attendants to retire at age 32. In the 1960s and 1970s, NOW and similar groups encouraged increasing numbers of women to enter professions; banks, realtors, and department stores began to grant loans, mortgages, leases, and credit that they long had denied to female applicants.

Following intense lobbying by women's groups, in 1972 Congress voted to submit the Equal Rights Amendment (ERA) to the states for ratification. This amendment stated that "equality of rights under the law shall not be denied or abridged by the United States or any state on account of sex."

Not all women supported ERA, however. Phyllis Schlafly, founder of STOP ERA, dismissed the women's rights movement as "a series of sharp-tongued, high-pitched, whining complaints by unmarried women." STOP ERA supporters contended that the ERA would force women to give up their traditional roles as wives and mothers, and that they would lose certain legal protections in the family and in the workplace. As a result of a vigorous campaign by STOP ERA and other groups, the Equal Rights Amendment failed to obtain the votes needed for ratification.

Changes for Minorities

By the 1970s Hispanic Americans had become the largest minority in the United States next to African Americans. Spanish-speaking people made up almost 8 percent of the population and were the largest minority group in several states. New York City alone contained about 2 million Spanish-speaking people. Part of Miami, Florida, became known as Little Havana because it was the home of hundreds of thousands of Cuban immigrants.

Mexican Americans made up the largest group of Hispanics. For years, many Mexican Americans labored as migrant farm workers, moving from place to place to harvest seasonal crops. They were not protected by federal minimum-wage laws, unemployment insurance, or social security. In 1965 Cesar Chavez organized a nationwide coalition that asked Americans to boycott California grapes picked by nonunion labor. After enduring five years of such persistent protest, most California grape growers relented and agreed to sign a contract with Chavez's union.

During the 1970s, inspired by the success of blacks in obtaining civil rights, Hispanic Americans began to organize. The League of United Latin American Citizens (LULAC) won suits in federal

AMERICAN PORTRAITS

RUSSELL MEANS
1939-

Russell Means, an Oglala Sioux, was born on a reservation in South Dakota. Raised in California, Means was taunted in high school by white classmates for being an Indian. During the 1960s he held a number of jobs and participated in Indian protests.

Excited by the newly formed American Indian Movement in 1968, Means joined the leadership of the organization. Militant Indians hailed him as a hero as he protested against government policies toward native Americans. The most serious protest took place at Wounded Knee, South Dakota. In 1973 Means and his followers seized Wounded Knee and held it for 71 days, demanding a review of 300 treaties between the U.S. government and Indian nations. The Indians surrendered only after the government promised to investigate their complaints.

courts to guarantee Hispanic Americans the right to serve on juries, to send their children to unsegregated schools, and to be taught in Spanish as well as in English. As their political strength grew, Hispanic Americans were elected to local and state offices as well as to Congress.

Native Americans also organized during the 1960s and 1970s. Their plight captured national attention when a 1966 study revealed that native Americans suffered from so much malnutrition and disease that their life expectancy was only 46 years. They had less formal education than any other minority group, and their family income was less than one-half the national average.

During the 1960s native Americans displayed a new militancy. In the state of Washington, men from more than 50 native American groups led a "fish-in." They deliberately broke game laws and risked imprisonment to protest the loss of their former fishing and hunting grounds.

Proclaiming "red power," the National Congress of American Indians demanded the end to federal control of native American affairs. "We simply want to run our lives our own way," said a young leader of the congress. "Our own way" meant the revitalization of their traditional cultures.

In 1973 a more militant group, the American Indian Movement (AIM), seized the reservation at Wounded Knee, South Dakota. They demanded that lands taken from native Americans in violation of federal treaties be returned. They also demanded that development programs on reservations be managed by Indian tribal government and not the federal Bureau of Indian Affairs. Although the seizure ended and native American support was low, federal policies toward native Americans began to change. The Pueblo of Taos, New Mexico, regained Blue Lake, a place sacred to their religious life. In 1975 a federal court declared that the Passamaquoddy and the Penobscot tribes had a valid claim to more than half the state of Maine and to $25 billion in damages and unpaid rents.

★ Section Three Review ★

SUMMARY

Inspired by the energy and organization of the civil rights and antiwar movements, efforts to empower other minority groups and women began. The antiwar movement peaked with the killings at Kent State and Jackson State. The women's rights movement fought for equal pay and questioned traditional roles for women. A conservative backlash, however, prevented passage of the Equal Rights Amendment. Hispanic Americans worked for better treatment and organized a migrant farm workers union. Native Americans organized and worked to reverse the economic and social decline in their community. They won battles in court for land rights and financial compensation.

CHECKING FOR UNDERSTANDING

1. **Identify** Shirley Chisholm, Betty Friedan, NOW, ERA, Phyllis Shlafly, STOP ERA, Cesar Chavez, LULAC, Russell Means, AIM

2. **List** three inequalities between men and women that existed in the 1970s.

3. **Cite** two ways that Hispanic Americans improved their economic and political status.

4. **State** two demands that were made by native American groups.

THINKING CRITICALLY

5. **Analyzing Point of View** Analyze the backlash to the women's rights movement in the 1970s. What stereotypes of women continue to exist today?

CONNECTIONS:
HISTORY AND ENVIRONMENT

6. **Making Comparisons** During the 1960s and 1970s, students took an active part in the civil rights and antiwar movements. How do the attitudes and actions of students in the 1990s compare?

Watergate and the Ford Administration

My fellow Americans, our long national nightmare is over. Our Constitution has worked....Here the people rule.

—GERALD FORD
President of the United States,
White House address, August 8, 1974

Section Focus

The public disclosure of Richard Nixon's involvement in the Watergate scandal culminated in his resignation from office. It also led Congress and the Supreme Court to reassert their constitutional powers. Although confidence in the government was shaken by Watergate, the bicentennial, or the 200th anniversary, of the American Revolution was cause for celebration.

Objectives

After studying this section, you should be able to:
- List the ways in which Congress sought to reassert its constitutional powers.
- Explain how the constitutional process solved the Watergate crisis.

I n 1974 it was discovered that Richard Nixon, who had been reelected in a landslide in 1972, had not only exceeded the powers of the presidency but had also abused the powers of his office and had betrayed his public trust. When he could no longer cover up his actions, the President was forced to resign from office. Two hundred years after the founding of the American Republic, the people of the United States could celebrate that the constitutional system of government worked.

The Watergate Scandal

Not surprisingly, the Republican party nominated President Nixon as its candidate in the election of 1972. Nixon ran against Senator George McGovern of South Dakota, who won the Democratic nomination with the support of a coalition of activists—young people, blacks, and women. Almost from the beginning, however, the McGovern campaign derailed itself. McGovern's running mate, Senator Thomas Eagleton, was forced to withdraw when it was disclosed that he had been hospitalized for depression. In addition, Democratic party regulars and labor union leaders were cool, if not hostile, toward the liberal McGovern's candidacy.

In contrast, President Nixon conducted a perfect campaign. The almost-complete withdrawal of U.S. troops from Vietnam defused the war issue, and the summits in Beijing and Moscow signaled an easing of cold-war tensions. Moreover, the President solidified his support among "middle Americans" by calling for law and order, by opposing busing, and by making continuous appeals to patriotism.

On Election Day the President received 61 percent of the popular vote and won every electoral vote except those of Massachusetts and the District of Columbia. It was later learned, however, that this tremendous victory was not entirely won fairly. During the campaign the President and his political advisers organized the Committee to Reelect the President (CREEP), and collected more than $50 million for Nixon's reelection campaign, some of which was illegally received. Some campaign contributions were used

THE PHILADELPHIA INQUIRER
AUTH

© 1973 by Chicago Tribune N.Y. News Synd. Inc.
World Rights Reserved

Examining Political Cartoons *In this 1973 cartoon, the White House is depicted as a huge tape recorder. How did the secret Nixon tape recordings lead to his resignation?*

Linking Across Time

THE NEWER NIXON

In the years since the Watergate scandal, former President Richard Nixon has worked hard to improve his image. Yet he had difficulty finding a location for the $21 million Nixon library. It was refused by Duke University, the University of California at Irvine, and the city of San Clemente, once the site of his "Western White House." The library found a place in Yorba Linda, California, opening in July 1990. Potentially a better gauge of Nixon's newer presidential image, 50,000 people attended the library's opening.

to finance "dirty tricks" against the Democrats. For example, a group of CREEP employees were caught "bugging" the offices of the Democratic National Committee in the Watergate building in Washington, D.C. Although the President's press secretary dismissed the break-in as a "third-rate burglary," this seemingly insignificant incident had serious consequences for the President.

Rumors began to circulate that the President himself had ordered the Watergate break-in. Stories were published in the *Washington Post* and other newspapers that linked key members of the White House staff and CREEP to the break-in. It was reported that key Nixon advisers had paid the Watergate burglars almost $1 million in "hush money" to plead guilty and say nothing else at their trials. To quiet the rumors, the President ordered his attorney general to appoint a special prosecutor, Harvard law professor Archibald Cox, to investigate the case.

At the same time, a special Senate committee began to hold televised hearings on the break-in and other abuses alleged to have been committed during the campaign of 1972. Starting in May 1973, millions of Americans watched in fascination as a parade of witnesses testified about illegal activities carried out by the White House staff and by CREEP. Perhaps the most startling was the discovery that the President tape-recorded most of the conversations he had in the Oval Office.

Following these revelations, federal grand juries indicted members of the Nixon administration for their illegal activities, including the unauthorized wiretapping, burglaries, illegal campaign contributions, and the bribing of witnesses. Eventually 25 people connected with the administration—including former Attorney General John Mitchell and two of Nixon's closest White House aides, H.R. Haldeman and John D. Erlichman—were convicted and served prison terms for Watergate-related crimes.

The President Resigns

Month after month President Nixon continued to deny any involvement in Watergate. Claiming **executive privilege**, or the principle that the President does not have to give information to other branches of government, Nixon refused to turn over the White House tapes to the special prosecutor. In October 1973, he offered to provide written summaries of the tapes. When the special prosecutor insisted on having the tapes, Nixon ordered the attorney general to remove Cox. Both the attorney general and his top assistant resigned rather than carry out the President's order. Finally Nixon found a Justice Department official who was willing to fire Cox. The dismissal of the special prosecutor became known as the "Saturday Night Massacre," and it provoked a wave of public protest as well as the first serious calls for Nixon's impeachment.

October 1973 proved to be a disastrous time for Richard Nixon for other reasons as well. His Vice President, Spiro Agnew, was forced to resign in disgrace. A grand jury found that Agnew, when governor of Maryland, had taken bribes from contractors who did business with the state. It was further revealed that Agnew continued to receive such payments while he was Vice President. Nixon nominated Gerald Ford, the Republican leader of the House of Representatives, as the new Vice President.

In an effort to quiet public outrage over the Saturday Night Massacre, Nixon appointed another special prosecutor in November 1973, and in April 1974, the President released written transcripts of 47 tape-recorded conversations. Even though the transcripts had been heavily edited, they seemed to indicate that the President had been involved in covering up the Watergate scandal. Nevertheless, the President still continued to proclaim his innocence:

If read with an open and fair mind and read together with the record of actions I took, these transcripts will show that what I have stated since the beginning to be the truth…my actions were directed toward finding the facts and seeing that justice was done, fairly and according to the law.

In July, the Supreme Court ruled that the President had to turn over the tapes themselves, not just their transcripts. A month later Nixon complied and handed over the tapes. One tape provided direct evidence that on June 23, 1972, only six days after the Watergate break-in, the President had ordered a cover-up. With this news, even the President's strongest supporters conceded that there was sufficient evidence to support impeachment. They advised Nixon that it seemed certain the House would impeach him and that the Senate would find him guilty. On August 8, 1974, Nixon announced

Examining Photographs *Following an announcement to the nation that he would resign, Nixon and his wife Pat depart the White House. Why did Nixon believe he might be impeached?*

on national television that he would resign. He also expressed hope that his departure would begin the process of healing the country.

The next day Gerald Ford was sworn in as the thirty-eighth President. President Ford appointed Nelson Rockefeller, former governor of New York, as his Vice President, making them the first unelected presidential team in the nation's history.

At first, President Ford inspired public confidence. He assured a joint session of Congress that his administration would be free of "illegal tappings, eavesdropping, buggings, or break-ins." The new President seemed to be a decent, candid, and trustworthy man.

A month after entering office, however, Ford damaged his public image by granting Richard Nixon an unconditional pardon for all crimes he committed or may have committed while in office. Ford insisted that he was acting not out of sympathy for Nixon, but in the public interest. He wanted to avoid the publicity and national division that a trial would create. Nevertheless, the pardon aroused fierce and widespread criticism of the new President.

Congress Reasserts Its Authority

When he took office, Gerald Ford promised to adopt a policy of "communication, conciliation, compromise, and cooperation" with Congress. He expected good relations with Congress, since he had served for 25 years as a representative and almost a decade as House Republican leader. Nevertheless, Ford was a conservative, and liberal Democrats controlled both houses of Congress. In addition, the new President confronted a Congress that was determined to reassert its authority over what some critics called the "imperial presidency."

Many members of Congress felt that the office of the President was becoming too powerful. Nixon, for example, had defied Congress by withholding funds Congress appropriated for programs that

Examining Photographs *Gerald Ford, assuring the nation that the Watergate "nightmare" was over, addresses Congress. What was Ford's relationship with Congress?*

he disliked. Nixon's claims of executive privilege also seemed to go beyond the bounds of the Constitution.

In the last year of the Nixon administration, as Watergate weakened the President, Congress attempted to regain some of its power. In November 1973, it passed the War Powers Act in spite of President Nixon's veto. This law required that the President report to Congress within 48 hours after sending combat troops abroad or after engaging in any military action. Unless Congress approved his action, the President had to withdraw all troops within 60 days. After the Watergate crisis, Congress passed the Congressional Budget and Impoundment Control Act of 1974, which allowed Congress to force the President to spend any appropriations that he attempted to **impound,** or withhold, unless he could justify his action to both houses.

In reviewing his difficult relationship with Congress, President Ford observed:

As a member of Congress for twenty-five years, I clearly understand the powers and obligations of the Senate and House under our Constitution. But as President for eighteen months, I also understand that Congress is trying to go too far in some areas.

One of the biggest problems facing the President and Congress was the economic recession. To Ford, inflation and the nation's dependence on foreign oil were the greatest threats to recovery. The Democratic Congress was more alarmed by the highest rates of unemployment and the lowest levels of productivity since the Great Depression of the 1930s.

Like Nixon, President Ford wanted to cut spending on social welfare programs and adopt an energy program. But Congress did not cooperate. Ford, in turn, prevented the enactment of liberal Democratic legislation by the use of the veto power.

In foreign policy Gerald Ford continued to pursue détente with the Soviets and the Chinese. He met with Leonid Brezhnev of

Examining Photographs In 1976 Americans were anxious to put the tragedy of the Vietnam War and Watergate affair behind them. A bicentennial spirit swept the nation as millions participated in parades, fireworks displays, and other activities, including a parade of tall ships in New York harbor. Following the parade the ships were opened to the public. How did President Ford begin the bicentennial ceremonies?

the Soviet Union in an effort to control the nuclear arms race. He also met with leaders of NATO and the Warsaw Pact to sign the Helsinki Accords in August 1975. Under the terms of the accords, the parties recognized the borders of the countries of Eastern Europe and committed themselves to respect and protect the human rights of their citizens.

In foreign policy, as in domestic affairs, Ford came into conflict with the Democratic-controlled Congress. In 1975 Congress refused President Ford's request for additional funds to aid South Vietnam and Cambodia in their continuing civil wars. As a result, the Cambodian government surrendered to the repressive Khmer Rouge forces on April 17. Twelve days later the North Vietnamese and the Vietcong overran Saigon and forced the government of South Vietnam to surrender. Communist regimes were now in control everywhere in Indochina, except Thailand, which remained an ally.

The Bicentennial

The nation's bicentennial began on a somber note with Cambodia and South Vietnam falling to the Communists. But President Ford headed for Boston to participate in the opening ceremonies of the celebration. There, the nation commemorated Paul Revere's famous ride and the historic battles at nearby Lexington and Concord.

As July 4, 1976, approached, most people in the United States caught the bicentennial spirit. Cities, towns, and villages held parades and concerts and displayed fireworks. A procession of Conestoga wagons traveled from the West to Valley Forge, Pennsylvania, and tall ships majestically sailed into New York Harbor on the Fourth of July.

As the bicentennial ended, the nation felt a new sense of hopefulness. It knew that the constitutional system of checks and balances had curbed the abuses of the imperial presidency. The people of the United States were proud of achievements such as the space program, and they began to regain their sense of confidence in themselves and in their country.

SUMMARY

Richard Nixon easily won the presidential election of 1972. Some of his campaign's tactics were illegal, however, including a break in of the Democratic party headquarters. Throughout Nixon's second term, evidence surfaced linking high officials in his administration to a campaign of illegal "dirty tricks." Finally, transcripts of secret White House tapes proved that Nixon had attempted a cover-up. Faced with impeachment, the President resigned and was succeeded by Gerald Ford. Congress reasserted its authority and stymied many of Ford's domestic policies. On a positive note, in 1976 Americans celebrated their nation's bicentennial.

CHECKING FOR UNDERSTANDING

1. **Identify** George McGovern, Archibald Cox, Gerald Ford, CREEP, War Powers Act, Helsinki Accords

2. **Define** executive privilege, impound

3. **List** three illegal activities for which the Nixon administration was indicted.

4. **Explain** why Nixon resigned.

5. **Summarize** actions Congress took to reassert its authority.

THINKING CRITICALLY

6. **Interpreting Viewpoints** Explain why many Americans, although dismayed by the Watergate scandal, felt proud of the way their government functioned during the crisis.

CONNECTIONS: HISTORY AND ECONOMICS

7. **Analyzing Relationships** The United States economy's dependence on Middle East oil became apparent during the 1970s. How does the price of oil affect the nation's economy? What steps could possibly be taken to help alleviate this problem?

★ ★ ★ ★ ★ ★ ★ ★ ★ ★ ★ ★ ★ ★ ★ ★ ★ ★ ★

★ Summary

Nixon's domestic agenda stressed state and local control and he made the Supreme Court more conservative. Inflation and a growing deficit, however, frustrated the economy. The growing trade deficit and falling dollar were indications of America's decline in world markets.

Nixon inaugurated a program of détente with communist nations, culminating in his historic trip to China. Despite growing opposition to the war in Vietnam, the war widened before Nixon decided on a policy of Vietnamization and a negotiated American withdrawal.

Though the war began to wind down, activism in America did not. The women's rights movement questioned women's traditional roles and fought for equality in the work place and in politics. Hispanic Americans also made important gains, including a successful boycott of nonunion-harvested crops. Native Americans, too, began new efforts for social and political change.

After Nixon's overwhelming reelection in 1972, few Americans could imagine that he would soon be forced to resign. Nixon's reelection committee authorized, and then tried to cover-up a break in of the Democratic party headquarters and other "dirty tricks." Although the President asserted his innocence, taped conversations in the White House proved he was involved. Facing certain impeachment, Nixon resigned and was succeeded by Gerald Ford. Ford continued Nixon's détente policy, though his domestic efforts were thwarted by Congress.

★ Using Vocabulary

Divide the terms below into one of two categories—*domestic policy* or *foreign policy*—based on your definition of each word.

new federalism	détente
balance of payments	summit
busing	impound
trade deficit	executive privilege

★ Reviewing Facts

1. **Explain** Nixon's southern strategy.

2. **Name** two factors that indicated a decrease in United States dominance of world markets.

3. **Characterize** Nixon's foreign policy.

4. **List** three foreign policy achievements of the Nixon administration.

5. **Describe** the goals of the women's rights movement.

6. **Summarize** advances made by native Americans.

7. **Chart** the sequence of events that led to Nixon's resignation.

★ Understanding Concepts

PRESIDENTIAL POWER

1. Why did President Nixon expand the war in Vietnam despite growing opposition to the war? Include in your answer an analysis of Nixon's responsiveness to public opinion.

2. What function did secrecy serve in the Nixon presidency? Why did some Americans and members of Congress resent this tactic?

CORRUPTION

3. How did Nixon use his office to circumvent the law? How do you think Nixon's attitude toward his office affected his illegal activities?

4. When President Nixon resigned over Watergate, some nations expressed astonishment that Americans would force their highest leader to step down over a "relatively small offense." Is it important for our nation to hold politicians accountable for their actions? Explain.

★ Thinking Critically

1. **Contrasting Policies** Contrast Nixon's different styles in domestic and foreign policy. What are some possible reasons Nixon was more effective in foreign affairs than in domestic affairs?

2. **Assessing Motives** Why did Nixon want a "strong, healthy United States, Europe, China, Russia, and Japan?" How does a balance of power maintain world peace? Compare this tactic with global dominance—which method do you think is more effective?

3. **Judging Opinions** Evaluate the reasoning used by the STOP ERA movement. Explain how

conflicting views on the role of women led to the defeat of the ERA.

4. **Drawing Conclusions** What are the lessons of the Watergate scandal? Would you agree that our system of government was vindicated by this affair? What long-term repercussions do you think Watergate had on American's views of government and politicians?

★ Writing About History

CAUSE AND EFFECT

Refer to the description of how to write a cause-and-effect essay in the History Writer's Handbook in the Appendix of this book. Your teacher will give you more specific instructions on the essay's length and the assignment's due date.

What caused the women's rights movement to organize effectively in the 1970s? What was the role of leaders such as Betty Friedan? Write an essay that traces the economic, social, and political causes of this movement. Conclude the essay by formulating your own opinion on what the goals of the women's rights movement should be during the next 10 years.

★ Learning Cooperatively

You will work in a group of with two others to analyze three activist movements of the 1970s: the anti-war movement, the women's rights movement, and the native American movement. The goal of your group is to find as many similarities between these three movements as you can. Each group member should choose one of these movements. First, work individually to make a list of the goals of each group and the method they used to attain them. Next, work with your partners to compile a master list of similarities between the three movements. Present your list to the class and discuss the findings.

★ Mastering Skills

INTERPRETING DEMOGRAPHIC DATA

Imagine that you are the president of a company that is about to introduce a line of products specifically designed for teenagers. Because your budget is limited, you can only send the products to the areas where you feel you will have the most success. What information would be helpful for you to make your decision?

You probably would need demographic information. *Demographics* is the data used to show the characteristics of human population for such things as size, growth, density, distribution, and vital statistics. The information can be presented a number of ways: in pie charts, bar graphs, and line graphs. One application of demographic data in the study of history or political science is to understand the relative voting strength of different ethnic groups. Candidates for political office need demographic information about their region in order to identify and target voter groups and to devise strategies that will attract those voters.

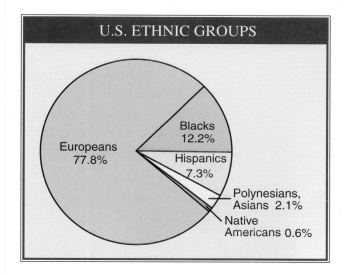

U.S. ETHNIC GROUPS

Europeans 77.8%
Blacks 12.2%
Hispanics 7.3%
Polynesians, Asians 2.1%
Native Americans 0.6%

Practice Study the pie chart above showing the racial background of United States citizens according to the 1980 census.

1. What does this chart suggest about the potential problems a small group such as native Americans would have affecting change through the political process?

2. By 1989 the African-American population had grown to 12.4 of the total population. Why might this demographic information be important to elected officials?

3. The Asian-American population doubled between 1980 and 1990. Hypothesize reasons why this rate of growth might be higher than that of other ethnic minorities.

CULTURAL KALEIDOSCOPE

Late 1900s

When American troops returned home at the close of World War II, few people suspected that the streets heroes paraded down would soon be overrun with civil unrest and violence.

Social activism, protests against unpopular foreign involvements, and high technology propelled American culture toward the twenty-first century.

◄ Untitled *by Andy Warhol, 1964*

The Arts

VISUAL ARTS

The decades since World War II have witnessed the arrival on the art scene of more new styles and approaches than in all the thousand years previous. Some, like the Abstract Expressionism of Helen Frankenthaler and Jackson Pollock, have rejected entirely the use of recognizable subject matter.

Others, like the Pop Art of Andy Warhol and Roy Lichtenstein, have satirized the crass commercialism rampant in late twentieth-century life.

MUSIC

Developments in music have paralleled those in painting and sculpture, as reflected in the harshly dissonant twelve-tone compositions of Roger Sessions and the "chance" orchestrations of experimentalist John Cage. Composer and conductor Leonard Bernstein, who remained active up until his death in 1990, did much with his televised Young People's Concerts to bridge the gap between so-called "classical" music and the casual listener.

▼ *Leonard Bernstein*

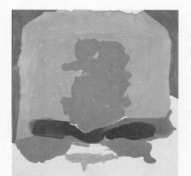

▲ Small's Paradise *by Helen Frankenthaler, 1964*

Literature

SOCIAL-CONSCIENCE PROSE

By the late 1960s, books designed to raise social consciousness had begun providing equality-starved Americans with food for thought. Ralph Ellison's award-winning tale of a young black man's quest for identity, *The Invisible Man,* had become required reading on college campuses. So had Betty Friedan's *The Feminine Mystique,* a book which helped elevate *feminism* to a household word.

➤ *Poster from film based on E.L. Doctorow's jazzy 1975 novel on early twentieth-century America*

FICTION

The literary mainstream of the last four decades has been characterized by a cluster of minimovements lumped together under the umbrella term *postmodernism.* One of the most provocative and controversial of these trends has been the judicious blending of fact and fiction typified in such "nonfiction novels" as Truman Capote's *In Cold Blood* and E. L. Doctorow's *Ragtime.*

➤ *Truman Capote*

GENEALOGY

One man's family history became the saga of black America, when Alex Haley published Roots in 1976. Its popularity widened when more than 100 million Americans watched at least one of eight segments in a television miniseries.

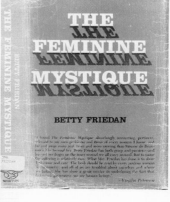

▼ The Feminine Mystique *by Betty Freidan, 1963*

Ralph Ellison ➤

Entertainment and Recreation

ELECTRONIC ENTERTAINMENT

Progress in electronics—in particular, the development of the integrated circuit, or "microchip"—has revolutionized home entertainment. The introduction in 1969 of the videocassette recorder allowed consumers to tune in to their favorite prime-time TV shows even when they could not be present at air time.

The more recent arrival on the market of the compact-disc player has threatened to render the phonograph obsolete, while entertainment-industry forecasters project that the home video-game system will remain the score to beat in sales through the year 2000.

POP MUSIC

Individually they were four young men from the streets of Liverpool, England. Together they were the Beatles, a musical and cultural phenomenon whose impact on young people of the 1960s was such that one of their LPs, *Sergeant Pepper's Lonely Hearts Club Band*, "went platinum" before it reached the stores.

The messages of "peace" and "love" that were the cornerstones of many Beatles hits also found notable expression in the enormously successful 1967 rock musical *Hair* and in the Woodstock Music and Art Fair, which drew in the summer of 1969 some half million "flower children" to a dairy farm in upstate New York.

FAST FOOD

It all started when a restaurant equipment manager named Ray Kroc persuaded two California restaurateurs, the McDonald brothers, to go national with their hamburger franchises. By the late 1980s the "hamburger wars" had escalated to a point where Burger King—one of the three top contenders for America's fast food dollar—needed to sell 108 million of its Whoppers just to cover its advertising budget!

► *Sign of success: McDonald's golden arches*

▲ *Making LP's obsolete: compact disc*

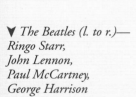

▼ *The Beatles (l. to r.)— Ringo Starr, John Lennon, Paul McCartney, George Harrison*

► *Video game's joy stick*

Technology

MEDICINE

Americans' chances of staying alive longer have improved markedly over the last four decades thanks to refinements in the transplanting of organs and microsurgery—the use of high-powered lenses and laser beams in the operating room. A space-age diagnostic tool, the nuclear magnetic resonating scanner, or NMR, uses a combination of radio waves and magnets to detect cancer, multiple sclerosis, and heart disease.

TO THE STARS

Advances in space exploration, beginning with the establishment of NASA in 1958, added terms like *moonwalk* and *moon rock* to the American vernacular. They also provided America and the world for the first time with a view of their home planet as a fragile blue-green orb standing alone in the black abyss of space.

In 1983 space went coed with the voyage of Sally Ride, the first female astronaut in the program.

ANALYZING CULTURE

1. Name three achievements of the late twentieth century that were related to social activism or the peace movement.

2. What areas of culture have been most affected by high technology? Give an example of an achievement or development in each area.

◄ *Sally Ride on six-day Challenger mission*

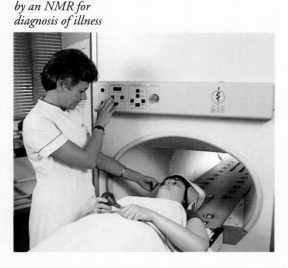

▼ *Patient scanned by an NMR for diagnosis of illness*

▼ *Earth as seen from Apollo 17, 1972*

CHAPTER 35
A Search for New Solutions

SETTING THE SCENE

Historical Focus

Jimmy Carter, an "outsider," won the election in 1976 partly because Americans distrusted government after Watergate and Vietnam. Runaway inflation and setbacks in trying to free American hostages in Iran helped defeat Carter in 1980. Ronald Reagan's election in 1980 marked the beginning of a period of Republican administrations with Democratic Congresses. Presidents Reagan and Bush attempted to control taxes and federal spending while maintaining American interests in a rapidly changing political world.

Concepts to Understand

- How Reagan's **political ideology** affected the nation's direction.
- How the **leadership** of Carter, Reagan, and Bush shaped events and policies.

People to Know

Ruhollah Khomeini, Geraldine Ferraro, Mikhail Gorbachev, Michael Dukakis, Jesse Jackson

Places to Locate

Afghanistan, Israel

Terms to Identify

Federal Reserve Board, federal deficit, *contras*, SDI, nuclear freeze, Gramm-Rudman Act

Guided Reading

As you read this chapter, seek the answers to the following questions.

1. What goals and principles underlay President Reagan's foreign policy?
2. What were the conservative domestic policies of Reagan and Bush?

SPANNING THE DECADES

POLITICAL

1978
Camp David Accords are signed

1979
Iran seizes 52 American hostages

1981
President Reagan is seriously wounded

1983
United States invades Grenada

1975   **1980**

CULTURAL

1979
Inflation reaches an unprecedented 13 percent

1980
United States boycotts Moscow Olympics

1982
Equal Rights Amendment defeated

1983
Sally Ride is first American woman in space

Statue of Liberty *by Kathy Jakobsen, 1985*

1986
Iran-Contra scandal

1987
Reagan, Gorbachev sign missile treaty

1990
Iraq invades oil-rich Kuwait

1985

1990

1985
"Live Aid" concert raises $70 million for the hungry in Africa

1989
Bicentennial of the Constitution

We are a nation that has a government—not the other way around. And this makes us special among the nations of the Earth. Our government has no power except that granted it by the people. It is time to check and reverse the growth of government which shows signs of having grown beyond the consent of the governed.

—RONALD REAGAN
Inaugural Address, January 20, 1981

Crisis of Confidence

Let our recent mistakes bring a resurgent commitment to the basic principles of our nation, for we know that if we despise our own government we have no future.

—JIMMY CARTER
Inaugural Address, January 1977

Section Focus

Americans felt a deep sense of pride and patriotism as they celebrated the Bicentennial in 1976. However, these feelings could not erase the painful memory of two of the most disillusioning events in United States history—the Vietnam War and the Watergate scandal. Americans were ready for new leadership to bolster the national mood and solve the difficult problems that loomed ahead.

Objectives

After studying this section, you should be able to:
- State reasons for the American public's crisis of confidence.
- Explain President Carter's call for a moral war on energy consumption.
- Describe President Carter's foreign policy.

As the 1976 elections approached, the United States was faced with the grim prospect of diminishing natural resources. The nation was no longer self-sufficient in its production of energy. At that time the United States imported more than half of its oil. Competition from Japan, Germany, and other countries threatened America's giant automobile and steel industries. With rising inflation and unemployment, the lifestyles of many Americans were severely affected. As the economy continued to shrink, the chances for women, African Americans, and other minority groups to achieve social and economic equality were jeopardized.

There were equally serious problems in foreign affairs. Political turmoil in economically developing nations upset the stability of world order. The Soviet Union pursued an increasingly aggressive foreign policy as the nuclear arms race continued. Was the United States government capable of meeting these challenges? Could a President with a fresh perspective renew the confidence of Americans in themselves and in their government?

The Election of 1976

Soon after Gerald Ford became President in 1974, he began to campaign for his election in 1976. The public regarded Ford as a warm, easy-going man of high integrity, but had doubts about his intellectual capabilities and competence as a leader. Ford was, as he himself admitted, "a Ford, not a Lincoln." From within the Republican party came a challenge from the conservatives, who rallied behind Ronald Reagan, former governor of California. Ford survived the challenge and won the Republican nomination, but only by a few votes.

The Democratic presidential primaries were relatively crowded with candidates, including a number of prominent senators and representatives. One of the candidates, however, James Earl Carter, Jr., or "Jimmy" Carter as he liked to be called, was something of a political outsider. A former governor of Georgia, Jimmy Carter had no previous experience in national government but nonetheless conducted a remarkable campaign. Starting two years before the election, Carter toured the nation meeting voters face to face. His informal, down-home style appealed to Americans tired of the "imperial presidency."

Jimmy Carter made a virtue of his inexperience in national affairs. He said:

*The people of this country want a fresh face,
not one associated with a long series
of mistakes at the White House and
Capitol Hill.*

To almost everyone's surprise, Carter won many of the primaries and secured the Democratic nomination for President.

During the presidential campaign, Jimmy Carter vowed to restore people's faith in the federal government by making it more open and efficient. He promised major new programs for energy development, tax reform, welfare reform, and national medical care. Carter had wide public appeal. Conservatives liked him because he promised to balance the budget. Liberals supported him because he insisted that he would not let unemployment rise as a means of lowering inflation.

Carter won a narrow victory over Ford, taking 51 percent of the popular vote and 297 electoral votes. Ford won 48 percent of the popular vote and 241 electoral votes. Carter won by combining the support of the old Democratic coalition of the industrial Northeast and the solid South (except for Virginia). For the first time since 1848, a candidate from the deep South had been elected President. And that candidate owed his margin of victory to black southern voters.

At his inauguration, Carter demonstrated his "plain folks" view of the presidency by walking from the Capitol to the White House rather than riding in a limousine. During his first months in office, he gave fireside chats, held phone conversations with ordinary citizens, and visited town meetings.

Energy and Economic Shocks

President Carter felt that the nation's increasing dependence on oil as an energy source was the country's most serious domestic problem. Experts warned that world supplies of oil, a non-renewable

GASOLINE CONSUMPTION AND PRICES, 1973–1980				
Year	Consumption (billions of gallons)	Cents per Gallon		
		Reg.	Prem.	No lead
1973	110.5	40	45	NA
1974	106.3	53	57	55
1975	109.0	57	61	60
1976	115.7	59	64	61
1977	119.6	62	67	66
1978	125.1	63	69	67
1979	122.1	86	92	90
1980	115.0	119	128	125

Statistical Abstract of the United States 1981

Examining Tables *Gasoline prices increased steadily beginning in 1973. In what years did prices affect consumption?*

resource, would soon be exhausted. Also, the oil-producing countries, which belonged to a cartel called the Organization of Petroleum Exporting Countries (OPEC), were setting prices at ever-higher levels. Rising oil prices added substantially to the price of consumer goods. In one of his first addresses to the nation, Carter rallied Americans to support a moral war against rising energy consumption. He declared:

*[The nation's] decision about energy
will test the character of the
American people and the ability of the
President and the Congress
to govern this nation. This difficult
decision will be the "moral equivalent
of war"— except that we
will be uniting our efforts to build
and not to destroy.*

Carter proposed a national energy program to conserve oil and to promote the use of coal, as well as such renewable energy sources as solar power. Although he persuaded Congress to create a Department of Energy, he was less successful in winning support for the rest of his program. The President asked Americans to make personal sacrifices to reduce their energy consumption. However, because he asked only for voluntary action, the public was confused about the seriousness of the crisis. When Carter later proposed stronger methods of restricting consumption, such as a 10 percent tax on all imported oil and emergency authority to impose gasoline rationing, Congress rejected them.

Carter did, however, convince Congress to lift controls on domestic oil production and to impose a "windfall profits" tax on the oil companies' huge earnings. When another fuel shortage occurred in the summer of 1979, Americans learned the value of smaller, more energy-efficient cars. Homeowners installed extra insulation to cut their heating and air-conditioning bills.

Sharp rises in the price of gasoline and oil contributed to **double-digit inflation**, rate increases of 10 percent or more. In 1979 the inflation rate reached an unprecedented 18 percent. By 1980 it cost more than $200 to purchase the same goods that $100 would have bought only 10 years earlier. At the same time, the Federal Reserve Board raised interest rates to all-time highs as a means of discouraging borrowing and bringing the economy under control. These policies helped reduce inflation but caused a severe business recession.

Governmental Disunity

The hope for change that had spurred Carter's election faded fast. Even though the Democrats held a majority in both the Senate and the House of Representatives, President Carter had a poor working relationship with Congress because he refused to play old-style politics. For example, in 1977, he announced that he would veto appropriations for a series of costly dams, canals, and other water projects. Such **pork-barrel legislation**, legislation that

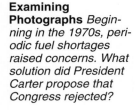

Examining Photographs *Beginning in the 1970s, periodic fuel shortages raised concerns. What solution did President Carter propose that Congress rejected?*

would benefit only a small part of the country, was common practice in Congress. Carter's move saved the nation millions of dollars, but it cost him valuable support from Congress. Congress, for example, rejected key parts of his energy program and blocked his proposals for tax and welfare reforms. Nonetheless, he was able to gain important legislative victories on such issues as civil service reform and airline deregulation.

Carter's inability to sell his political position on important issues puzzled many people. Unlike previous Democratic presidents who developed social programs such as the New Deal, the Fair Deal, the New Frontier, and the Great Society, Carter had no unifying theme that identified his administration. Instead, he followed a cautious middle course, promising to reduce government spending while endorsing expensive social programs. The President would not "choose up sides," as newspaper columnist James Reston observed. "Confronted with a series of ambiguous questions, he simply refused to give simple answers." As a result, the public was confused about Carter's goals. By 1979 his popular support had fallen dramatically. Public opinion polls showed that Carter's popularity had dropped lower than President Nixon's during the Watergate scandal.

The growing dissatisfaction Americans felt with the federal government soon included local and state governments. In California voters passed "Proposition 13," a measure that cut property taxes in half, resulting in cutbacks on funds to support schools, libraries, and other important services. This tax revolt soon spread to other states. There were, however, contradictions in this "antigovernment" mood. Polls showed that many Americans thought the government was spending too much money and should reduce taxes and balance the budget. Yet polls also showed that Americans believed the government was not doing enough to support health and educational programs and other pressing problems. Special-interest groups formed to promote their own particular needs and to compete against each other for ever smaller shares of government spending.

Morality in Foreign Policy

In contrast to his weak leadership at home, President Carter's foreign policy was bold and clearly defined. Carter had denounced past American foreign policy as "lacking moral principle." A man of strong religious beliefs, Carter argued that instead of relying on military and economic might, the United States must try to be "right and honest and truthful and decent" in its dealings with other nations.

In 1978 President Carter won Senate ratification of the Panama Canal treaties. Since 1903 the United States had controlled the Panama Canal. The treaties transferred control of the canal from the United States to Panama by the end of the century. The treaties removed a major symbol of United States interventionist policy and signaled a new approach to Latin American relations.

In his dealings with other nations, Carter expressed a "clear-cut preference for those societies which share with us an abiding respect for human rights." Accordingly his administration cut off military and economic support to several Latin American governments considered dictatorial and repressive. Most dramatically, Carter singled out the Soviet Union as a violator of human rights. He strongly condemned the Soviet practice of imprisoning people who protested against the government. He also pressed the Soviet Union to allow more of its Jewish citizens to emigrate. Soviet leaders claimed these actions violated the spirit of détente and constituted direct intervention by the United States in Soviet domestic affairs.

Relations between the United States and the Soviet Union suffered a further setback when Soviet troops invaded the Asian nation of Afghanistan late in 1979. In keeping with Carter's noninterventionist policy, however, the United States refrained from sending troops to the area. Instead, Carter imposed an embargo on the sale of grain to the Soviet Union and called for a boycott of the

Examining Photographs *In signing the Panama Canal treaties, President Carter completed the canal negotiations begun by Nixon's secretary of state, Henry Kissinger. What Carter foreign-policy objective did this help to accomplish?*

1980 Summer Olympic Games to be held in Moscow.

The Troubled Mideast

Carter's greatest foreign policy triumph and his greatest failure involved the Middle East. Since its early history, the region had been inflamed by deep political and religious conflicts. In recent years, the United States had shied away from becoming involved in the area. As Carter himself acknowledged:

[The Middle East] had long been a textbook for pessimism, a demonstration that diplomatic ingenuity was no match for intractable human conflicts.

Despite this, President Carter made a bold move to negotiate a peace treaty between Egypt and Israel, two nations that had been bitter enemies for 30 years. In

1978 Carter brought Egypt's President Anwar el-Sadat and Israel's Prime Minister Menachem Begin together at Camp David, the presidential retreat in Maryland. The two leaders talked for 14 days. More than once the discussions broke down, but Carter persisted until the leaders reached an agreement on September 17, 1978. In front of a joint session of Congress, with Sadat and Begin in the gallery, Carter announced that:

This is the first time that an Arab and an Israeli leader have signed a comprehensive framework for peace. It contains the seeds of a time when the Middle East, with all its vast potential, may be a land of human richness and fulfillment, rather than a land of bitterness and continued conflict.

The Camp David Accords, which were formally signed in 1979, established peace between Egypt and Israel. Most of the other Arab nations expressed strong opposition to the treaty because they felt Egypt should not have acted alone. Also the issue of the Israeli-occupied territories inhabited by Palestinians was yet to be solved. Still, an important first step toward peace in the Middle East had been taken.

Carter's success in negotiating peace between Egypt and Israel, however, could not make up for his failure to resolve the crisis with Iran in 1979. The United States had long supported the Shah of Iran. There were a number of practical considerations for U.S. support: Iran served as a major supplier of oil and as a reliable buffer against Soviet expansion in the Middle East. Iranians, however, had grown unhappy with the Shah's rule. The Shah had brought Western technology and reforms to his people with huge revenues from oil, but these changes only helped to widen the gap between the wealthy and the extremely poor in the nation. Islamic religious leaders objected to the Western reforms and customs that had been introduced into Iran, claiming that these customs were contrary to Islam-

Examining Photographs *President Carter joins Anwar el-Sadat (left) and Menachem Begin (right). What was the agreement?*

ic traditions. Huge protests were staged in Iran. In 1979 the Shah was forced to flee, and an Islamic republic was proclaimed.

The new regime, headed by the religious leader Ayatollah Ruhollah Khomeini, viewed the United States with deep

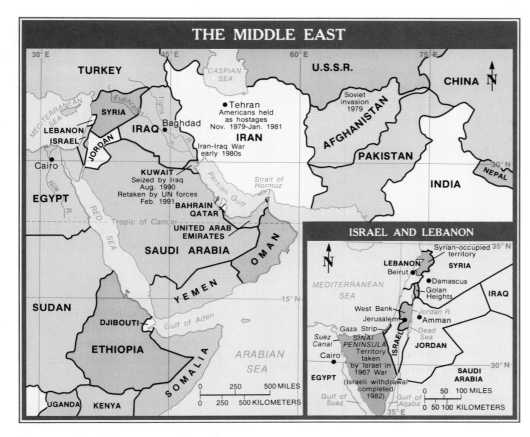

Examining Maps
Hopes for peace in the Middle East rest on shaky foundations. What five major events disturbed the peace between 1967 and 1991?

Examining Photographs *When the United States permitted the Shah to enter the country for medical treatment, Iranians protested by seizing American hostages. When were they released?*

distrust because of its ties with the Shah. Anti-American feelings were so strong among the Iranian revolutionaries that on November 4, 1979, militants stormed the American embassy in Teheran, the Iranian capital, and took hostage more than 50 Americans. The militants threatened to kill the hostages or try them as spies.

The Carter administration tried to negotiate for the freedom of the hostages, but was not successful. As pressure mounted to secure their release, Carter felt he had no other choice but to order a military rescue. One morning in late April 1980, Americans awoke to the shocking news that a mission to rescue the hostages had been attempted and failed. Eight members of the rescue team had died in the attempt. Despite this setback, Carter persisted in his efforts to free the hostages. Negotiations with Iran continued right up to President Carter's last day in office. Ironically, on January 20, 1981, the day of Ronald Reagan's inauguration, Iran released the Americans, ending their 444 days in captivity.

SUMMARY

American voters wanted a change in 1976 after Watergate and Vietnam. Their choice for President was Jimmy Carter, a new face in national politics. Carter put energy at the top of his priority list. To conserve oil and promote alternative energy sources, the President proposed a national energy program, created a Department of Energy, and placed a tax on oil profits. The price of oil, however, continued to rise and caused rapid inflation. In foreign policy, Carter emphasized respect for human rights. His greatest foreign policy achievement was negotiating the peace between Israel and Egypt. His greatest failure was his inability to free American hostages in Iran.

CHECKING FOR UNDERSTANDING

1. **Identify** Shah of Iran, Ayatollah Khomeini, Anwar el-Sadat, Menachem Begin, OPEC, Camp David Accords

2. **Define** double-digit inflation, pork-barrel legislation

3. **Name** one campaign promise Carter made that appealed to conservatives and one that appealed to liberals.

4. **List** three features of Carter's energy program.

5. **Summarize** Carter's successes and failures in the Middle East.

THINKING CRITICALLY

6. **Evaluating Leaders** Explain how Carter's inability to communicate a unifying theme hurt his support.

LINKING PAST AND PRESENT

7. **Making Comparisons** Has the United States developed alternative energy sources since Carter's administration? Compare the energy problems Carter faced to the ones the United States faces today.

★ ★ ★ ★ ★ ★ ★ ★ ★ ★ ★ ★ ★ ★ ★ ★ ★ ★

Linking Across Time

ECONOMIC EXPANSION AND FOREIGN AFFAIRS

Throughout American history, the nation's desire for economic expansion has affected its foreign affairs. New Englanders were the first Americans to engage heavily in commerce; their lack of rich interior farmland forced them to widen their horizons. Fishing schooners and rum distilleries built colonial fortunes and oriented New Englanders to the nearby sea.

Southern planters, meanwhile, depended on England to buy their tobacco, rice, and indigo and provide cloth, furniture, and other necessities. When England announced it would regulate colonial trade more strictly, the colonies rebelled.

In the War of 1812 the United States fought for the right of its ships to carry on trade at any port. Soon clipper ships developed a brisk trade, calling on ports from New Zealand to China. This commerce provided capital to expand American manufacturing.

With the end of the Mexican War, American business turned its attention to developing domestic trade. When the frontier ended, foreign markets regained their attractiveness.

Backed by British investment, American industrial production almost doubled between 1899 and 1917. As American financiers accumulated huge amounts of capital, they looked to developing

Coca Cola being distributed in Israel

nations for investment opportunities. Latin America, the Pacific, and East Asia attracted American business capital, and United States interests in those areas expanded.

Once American businesses made investments in these areas, they demanded protection from the United States government. The government used "dollar diplomacy" to force developing countries to accede to American wishes. When that failed, troops took charge. Many Presidents sent troops into one or another Latin American country to protect business interests. Troops were also sent to China in 1900 to safeguard trading opportunities. In the 1930s American interests in the East Asia conflicted with Japan's desire to control the natural resources of that region.

Following World War II, the

United States waged a propaganda war with communist bloc nations over the merits of free enterprise. Communist propaganda labeled the United States an imperialist nation and criticized American power and influence in developing countries. The United States responded by warning the world that communism sought to control people through repressive government. Both sides used economic and military aid to win support from developing countries.

By 1990 many communist countries realized their need to allow some free enterprise as they sought to respond to demands for change. The Soviets invited some American businesses to initiate ventures inside their country. The American free enterprise system appeared to have overcome one of its major foreign policy obstacles.

MAKING CONNECTIONS

1. How has the desire for economic expansion affected the foreign policy of the United States?

2. What economic developments signaled a change in relations between communist countries and the United States?

SECTION TWO

A Conservative Shift

In this present crisis, government is not the solution to our problem; government is the problem....

—RONALD REAGAN
Inaugural Address, January 20, 1981

Section Focus

As the 1980 elections approached, American dissatisfaction with the government was widespread. Economic conditions, the energy crisis, and President Carter's inability to free the hostages angered and frustrated many Americans. People once again seemed ready to make a dramatic change in their leadership.

Objectives

After studying this section, you should be able to:
• Explain the "conservative revolution" of 1980.
• Describe President Reagan's supply-side economic recovery plan.
• Compare President Carter's foreign policy with that of President Reagan.

As the 1980 presidential campaign got underway, the hostage crisis became a key issue in Carter's bid for reelection. For a while, Americans rallied behind their leader. During the Democratic party's primary elections, Carter continued to work for the captives' release instead of actively campaigning. This strategy helped Carter defeat a challenge to his renomination from Senator Edward Kennedy of Massachusetts. But Americans grew increasingly impatient with the situation. President Carter's failure to obtain the release of the hostages worked against him in the November election.

The Election of 1980

Republicans chose former California governor Ronald Reagan as their presidential candidate. Ironically, Reagan had been a New Deal Democrat when he was a young man. But during the 1950s, Reagan turned conservative in his thinking and began to serve the Republican party tirelessly.

Reagan's chief opponents in the primaries were two moderate Republicans: former United Nations Ambassador George Bush and Illinois Representative John Anderson. After his nomination, Reagan picked Bush as his running mate. Anderson decided to run for President as an independent candidate, hoping to appeal to voters who were unhappy with Reagan and Carter.

The Republicans adopted a conservative platform calling for reductions in taxes and government spending in order to restore the nation's economic prosperity. The party did endorse, however, higher defense spending to strengthen the role of the United States in world affairs.

Throughout the campaign, Reagan hammered at Carter's lack of leadership and the nation's weak economy. He promised voters economic growth and development instead of the economic sacrifices and restraints that Carter advocated. Carter responded by picturing Reagan as unsympathetic to the needs of the poor and minority groups. He also argued that Reagan's defense policies were a threat to world peace.

On Election Day Ronald Reagan claimed victory with 51 percent of the popular vote. Carter won 41 percent, while Anderson and other candidates of minor parties split the rest of the vote. After 4 years in office, Jimmy Carter bore the burden of the public's widespread disappointment with government. Little more than one-half of those registered to vote exercised their right, a statistic that clearly reflected the nation's apathy toward government.

Connections

HISTORY AND RELIGION

TELEVANGELISM

"It's not listed in the Bible," said Jim Bakker in 1979, "but my...specific calling from God is to be a television talk-show

Televangelist Jimmy Swaggart

host." Bakker became one of the most successful ministers of the *electronic church*—a term coined by mainstream clergy to describe television evangelism.

Televangelists combined revivalist techniques and satellite television to launch a moral crusade for conservative values and against such issues as the Equal Rights Amendment, sex education in public schools, pornography, and drugs. Contributions by viewers supported broadcasts, colleges, missions, retirement homes, and hospitals. Bakker's multimillion dollar PTL Club built a theme park.

In the late 1980s, scandal rocked Bakker's and Jimmy Swaggart's organizations. Bakker went to prison, and many televangelists lost money and credibility. The Christian Broadcasting Network's Pat Robertson, however, had enthusiastic support in the 1988 Republican presidential primaries.

MAKING THE RELIGION CONNECTION

1. Why are religious broadcasts popular?

2. How is religious broadcasting financed?

LINKING PAST AND PRESENT

3. Should commercial TV stations broadcast religious programs?

In the 1980 election, groups that had traditionally voted Democratic broke with their party and voted for Reagan in remarkable numbers. The coalition that elected Reagan included former liberals, blue-collar workers, southerners, the elderly, and others who had become disenchanted with Democratic leadership. It also included fundamentalist Christian groups that opposed abortion and favored school prayer, and anti-feminists who placed more emphasis on women's roles as wives and mothers than on the issue of equal rights.

The 1980 election was proof of a significant shift among Americans in their political convictions. Evidence enough was the fact that Reagan was one of the more conservative Presidents in decades. The conservative tide that elected Reagan also carried many other Republican candidates into office. For the first time in 28 years, Republicans took control of the Senate. Democrats held their majority in

their majority in the House of Representatives but by a very slim margin.

Examining Photographs
President Reagan promised to "get the government off the backs of the people." What practical step to this end did he propose?

Cutting Taxes and Spending

Throughout his campaign President Reagan had focused on the state of the nation's economy. After his inauguration he acted boldly and quickly to change federal economic policy. In February 1981, he told Americans:

Since 1960 our government has spent $5.1 trillion. Our debt has grown by $648 billion. Prices have exploded by 178 percent....[We] know we must act and act now. We must not be timid....

President Reagan proposed deep cuts in federal taxes. He predicted that income tax reductions, especially for wealthy Americans, would encourage new investment in business. Similarly, cuts in corporate taxes would spur business to expand production and hire more workers. Reagan's beliefs were based on an economic theory called **supply-side economics**, which claims that the economy can best be stimulated by increasing the supply of goods rather than the demand.

Reagan's economic views, which came to be called "Reaganomics," included, in addition to cutting taxes, a reduction in government spending. Reagan proposed cutbacks that would end federal job-training programs and reduce spending on programs such as Medicare, food stamps, and education. Critics of the President's program predicted that it would cause great suffering for the poor. Reagan denied this, claiming that there would always be a "safety net" of government aid for truly needy Americans.

Although the President faced opposition to his proposals, he had personal qualities that helped to promote his position: a great ability to communicate with his audience and a sense of humor. In March 1981, when he was shot and seriously wounded by a deranged young man, his aides visited the President in the hospital. They assured him that the business of government was continuing as usual. "What makes you think I'd be happy about that?" Reagan quipped.

Together with his shrewd handling of Congress, Reagan's popularity enabled him to win major legislative victories in his first year in office. The Republican Senate adopted his tax and spending programs, which included $39 billion in tax cuts and a 25 percent cut in income taxes over a 3-year period. In the House, Reagan appealed to a group of conservative Democrats, mostly from the South, known as "boll weevils." They voted for the President's programs, giving him a narrow but complete victory.

Examining Graphs *While the work force grew every year, unemployment reduced the total number of workers during recession. What year showed the largest gain in employment?*

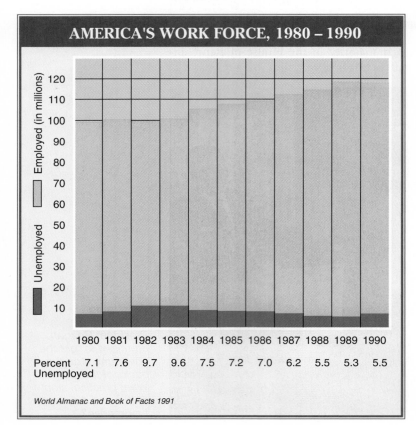

AMERICA'S WORK FORCE, 1980 – 1990

	1980	1981	1982	1983	1984	1985	1986	1987	1988	1989	1990
Percent Unemployed	7.1	7.6	9.7	9.6	7.5	7.2	7.0	6.2	5.5	5.3	5.5

World Almanac and Book of Facts 1991

Recession and Recovery

The economy revived more slowly than Reagan hoped, however. Spending cuts, together with high interest rates, brought inflation down, but the cure was not painless. A severe economic downturn occurred in 1982. Business bankruptcies, factory closings, and farm foreclosures increased at alarming rates. Unemployment swelled, and by the end of 1982 more than 11 million Americans—more than 10 percent of the workforce—were jobless. Blaming President Reagan's economic programs for the recession, Democrats won back many seats in the congressional elections.

By 1983 the economy began to turn around. The Federal Reserve Board lowered interest rates, making it easier for businesses and individuals to borrow money. And the inflation rate dropped just as a 25-percent cut in income taxes was putting more money in the hands of consumers. Feeling new confidence in the economy, Americans made purchases they had put off during the recession. Sales of every type of goods and services shot upward, and industries hired back workers who had been laid off during the recession. During 1983 unemployment declined but did not disappear. Levels of unemployment were still high by postwar standards. By 1988, however, at the end of Reagan's second term, unemployment dropped to a 14-year low of 5.5 percent.

President Reagan went before Congress in January 1984 to hail the recovery:

...America is back—standing tall, looking to the 80s with courage, confidence, and hope....Send away the hand-wringers and doubting Thomases.

But he warned that government needed to bring down its mounting deficits.

Reagan's policy was to cut taxes while increasing defense spending. Congress, however, controlled by Democrats, refused to make the deeper cuts in the social programs Reagan requested. The result was the most unbalanced budget in American history. By 1984 the **federal deficit,** the difference between the amount of money the government took in and what it spent, was nearing $200 billion a year. Critics argued that the deficit would undermine much of the social legislation begun under the Roosevelt, Truman, and Johnson administrations.

Although huge federal deficits have no immediate impact on the economy, their long-range effects are devastating. When government spends more money than it collects, it has to borrow money to make up the difference. The more it borrows, the more interest it owes on its debts. In 1984 the interest alone on the federal debt amounted to $153.8 billion, an increase of more than $55 billion from Reagan's first year in office.

Reagan's Foreign Policy

Reagan believed that the Soviet Union and its allies were a serious threat to the United States. He was determined that the United States be viewed as a strong power capable of countering Soviet influence everywhere.

The President was particularly concerned about the spread of communism in Central America. The proximity of this region to the United States made it strategically important. Half of America's foreign trade and two-thirds of its oil shipments went through the Panama Canal and the Caribbean. American banks and businesses had millions of dollars invested in the region.

Reagan saw Soviet influence in Nicaragua. He also believed that the Soviets were supporting guerrilla movements in El Salvador. He blamed Carter's human-rights policies for undermining the established government in Nicaragua, led by Anastasio Somoza who had been deposed by left-wing revolutionaries. Reagan reversed Carter's policy by restoring military aid to the government in El Salvador and by supporting the *contras,* guerrillas who fought against the pro-communist government in Nicaragua. Fearing that the United States was entering into a secret war, Congress enacted

Linking Across Time

GERALDINE FERRARO'S HOPES FOR A WOMAN PRESIDENT

A 1990 magazine interview reported Geraldine Ferraro's belief that, by running for Vice President in 1984, she would make it easier for future women candidates. Said Ferraro in the same interview, "We have a real shot at having a woman President in this…decade." Ferraro advised women who aspire to the office to work hard and take risks. To gain the right experience, a woman should first be a U.S. Senator or a state governor, Ferraro believes.

Examining Photographs *In 1983 Grenada's leftist leaders invited Cuba to build an airstrip on the island. Grenada's leaders said the airstrip was to promote tourism. But President Reagan, concerned about its potential military value and about the safety of American students, sent in troops. Where is Grenada located?*

legislation barring the use of military aid to overthrow Nicaragua's government.

In October 1983, Reagan took direct military action in the Caribbean. Concerned about the fate of 800 American medical students during a coup in the small island nation of Grenada, he dispatched troops to rescue the Americans and establish an anticommunist government. Reagan's action won widespread approval at home, despite international protests.

President Reagan was less successful with his Middle East initiatives. In 1982 when he sent a force of marines to help keep the peace in the war-torn nation of Lebanon, the United States found itself caught in the middle of a complicated and bloody civil war. Lebanese groups supported by Syria believed that the United States had taken sides and was not a neutral peacekeeper. Early one morning in October 1983, a truck loaded with explosives was driven straight at the marine barracks. The barracks were demolished, and 241 marines were killed. Recognizing

that the United States could neither retaliate effectively nor keep the peace, President Reagan withdrew all American armed forces from Lebanon. The withdrawal was a serious blow to U.S. prestige in the Middle East.

As the 1984 elections neared, Reagan was enjoying considerable popularity. The nation was at peace, and the economy had made a healthy recovery from the recession of 1982. These factors, combined with the President's image as a strong leader, made Ronald Reagan and Vice President Bush a formidable team. The Democrats nominated a traditional liberal, former Vice President Walter Mondale. Mondale broke precedent by choosing the first woman candidate of a major party to run for Vice President, Representative Geraldine Ferraro of New York.

From the start, public opinion polls showed the President far ahead of his challenger, who never overcame Reagan's advantage. Mondale claimed that Reagan's tax and budget cuts benefited only the

Examining Photographs *Walter Mondale chose House member Geraldine Ferraro as vice-presidential candidate in 1984. What office had Mondale held earlier?*

wealthy. Republicans countered that their economic program had aided all Americans by sharply reducing inflation. Seeking a solution to the rising federal budget deficit, Mondale proposed raising taxes, always an unpopular political step. Reagan declared his firm opposition to any tax increases. Reagan continued to insist that economic expansion and deeper government spending cuts would reduce the deficit. While Mondale tried to convince voters that the very policies Reagan wanted to continue were responsible for the deficit, the President ran on his record. "America is presented with the clearest political choice of half a century," he said, between "their government of pessimism, fear, and limits, or ours of hope, confidence and growth."

In November Americans gave President Reagan an overwhelming vote of confidence. Winning 59 percent of the popular vote, he gained 525 electoral votes to Mondale's 13, the biggest electoral margin in history. Reagan began his second term confident in his policies.

★ ★ ★ ★ ★ ★ ★ ★ ★ ★ ★ ★ ★ ★ ★ ★ ★

Section Two Review

★ ★ ★ ★ ★ ★ ★ ★ ★ ★ ★ ★ ★ ★ ★ ★ ★

SUMMARY

In the presidential election of 1980, discontented voters elected conservative Ronald Reagan. Reagan quickly set to work lowering taxes and cutting government spending. After a period of unemployment and recession, the economy started to revive. Lower interest rates and taxes gave Americans more to spend and unemployment fell. In foreign policy, Reagan fought communism vigorously, especially in Latin America where he rallied support for Contra rebels in Nicaragua. In the Middle East, however, 241 marines died on a peacekeeping mission in Lebanon. Reagan's overwhelming victory in the 1984 election demonstrated strong support for his policies.

CHECKING FOR UNDERSTANDING

1. **Identify** John Anderson, Walter Mondale, Geraldine Ferraro, Contras, Grenada, Lebanon

2. **Define** supply-side economics, federal deficit

3. **List** three measures Reagan took to restore the economy.

4. **Explain** two trends that indicated the economy was recovering in 1983.

5. **Summarize** Reagan's foreign policy goals.

THINKING CRITICALLY

6. **Making Inferences** Reagan was called the "Teflon President" because criticisms of him never stuck. List some factors that contributed to Reagan's popularity.

CONNECTIONS: HISTORY AND ECONOMICS

7. **Identifying Assumptions** What assumptions did Reagan make about what American consumers and business leaders would do with money gained from tax cuts?

★ ★ ★ ★ ★ ★ ★ ★ ★ ★ ★ ★ ★ ★ ★ ★ ★

Confidence Restored

SETTING THE SCENE

A new breeze is blowing—and a nation refreshed by freedom stands ready to push on. There's new ground to be broken and new action to be taken.

—GEORGE BUSH
Inaugural Address, January 1989

Section Focus

Since the reelection of President Ronald Reagan in 1984, Americans have seen new reasons for confidence in the nation's future, together with new challenges for democracy to meet. These challenges faced Americans at home and abroad.

Objectives

After studying this section, you should be able to:

- Explain the impact of the defense budget on the national deficit.
- Define *glasnost* and explain its importance in easing relations with the Soviet Union.
- Describe challenges facing the nation in the 1980s.

Ronald Reagan enjoyed immense popularity as he began his second term in office. Political and financial scandals, however, soon began to plague Reagan's administration. Americans were forced to recognize the enormity of the national deficit and its effects on the nation's future generations. And, although relations with the Soviet Union had greatly improved and the threat of nuclear war diminished, the previous world order was upset. Conflict erupted in the Middle East, and the United States became directly involved.

A Strong Defense

Reagan strongly supported America's space program, both as a means of restoring the nation's self-confidence and as a means of strengthening its defenses. Americans took pride in their successes in space exploration, and the launch of reusable space shuttles marked a new era in the space program. Astronauts, scientists, and even two members of Congress orbited the Earth in the shuttles, carrying out scientific studies and launching communications, weather, and military-surveillance satellites.

Reagan had a special interest in the military aspects of the space program. In 1983 he had announced a new research project to create a shield to intercept and destroy nuclear ballistic missiles—the Strategic Defense Initiative (SDI), or "Star Wars" as it was popularly known. Opponents of the program believed that SDI's uncertain technology could never provide a leak-proof umbrella to stop missile attacks. They feared that SDI might stimulate new nuclear competition between the superpowers. Reagan and other supporters of the program, however, believed it would improve chances of nuclear disarmament.

At the same time that he was promoting Star Wars, Reagan was spending huge sums of money for the military. More than $1 trillion was spent for new bombers, submarines, and missiles and to improve the training of ground troops. Many aspects of his program, including placing new nuclear missiles in Europe, basing intercontinental missiles in western states, and developing expensive new B-2 "stealth" bombers, caused a great deal of controversy.

The spread of nuclear weapons raised new fears of war. In response, a large antinuclear movement grew in Europe and the United States. The movement supported proposals for a **nuclear freeze,** an agreement that would require the

United States and the Soviet Union to stop the testing, production, and deployment of nuclear weapons. One group, the National Conference of Catholic Bishops, declared:

———○◇◇○———

We do not perceive any situation in which the deliberate initiation of nuclear warfare, on however restrictive a scale, can be morally justified.

———○◇◇○———

But the Reagan administration continued to oppose a nuclear freeze, arguing that a freeze would only perpetuate the Soviet's nuclear superiority. The United States put forward its own proposals for mutual reductions, but Soviet leaders rejected these proposals.

Relations with the Soviet Union

Relations between the United States and the Soviet Union began to improve after March 1985 when Mikhail Gorbachev became Soviet Premier. Gorbachev faced grave domestic crises. His country's economy was in shambles and various ethnic groups within the Soviet Union were demanding independence. Gorbachev responded by introducing a new openness, or **glasnost**, in Soviet society, and a political and economic restructuring, called **perestroika.**

In an effort to relax international tensions and to protect his domestic reforms, Gorbachev made dramatic offers to reduce nuclear missiles and weapons. He even offered a proposal whereby they could be completely eliminated. In 1986 Reagan and Gorbachev met in Reykjavík,

Iceland, to discuss reductions in nuclear arms, but the two sides could not come to an agreement on the issue of the SDI. However, when they met again in December 1987 in Washington, D.C., they signed a treaty calling for the removal of all intermediate-range nuclear missiles from Europe. This was the first agreement that eliminated an entire class of nuclear weapons.

Changes within the Soviet Union affected all aspects of international relations. Admitting that their intervention in Afghanistan had been "morally wrong," the Soviets withdrew their troops. The Soviet Union released political prisoners, allowed freer emigration of Soviet Jews, and held elections in which challengers often defeated Communist party candidates. The Soviets also sought more trade with the United States.

The spirit of *glasnost* and *perestroika* spread to Soviet bloc countries in Eastern Europe. The world witnessed a dramatic shift toward democratic reform in Poland and Hungary. At last the cold war seemed to be ending.

Hands-Off Presidency

The Reagan administration credited its strong defense program with convincing the Soviets to agree to reduce their nuclear arsenal. But the costly defense buildup had produced a huge rise in federal deficits. As deficits increased, a greater share of the tax revenues went to pay the interest on the national debt. This left less money available for new programs in education, environment, and public housing. Congress responded in December 1985 by passing the Gramm-Rudman Act, which put greater pressure on Congress and the President to reach budget agreements. If they were unable to reduce the annual deficit to certain limits, the act set automatic across-the-board federal spending cuts.

Reagan, however, steadfastly refused to increase income taxes as a way of

Examining Graphs *The federal budget was over $1 trillion in 1990, while yearly budget deficits had pushed the gross national debt to nearly $3 trillion. Between 1950 and 1975 which grew faster the federal budget or the national debt? Since 1975 which has grown faster?*

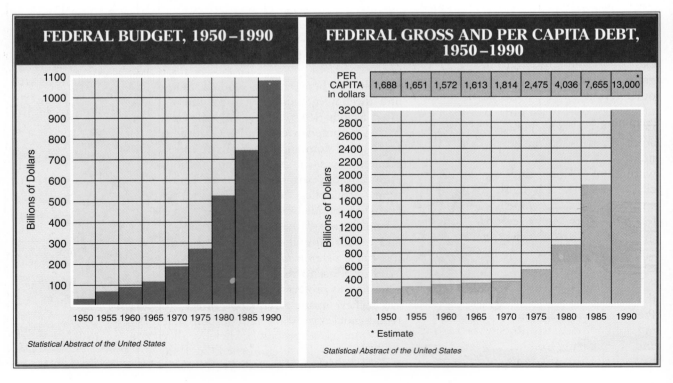

FEDERAL BUDGET, 1950–1990

Statistical Abstract of the United States

FEDERAL GROSS AND PER CAPITA DEBT, 1950–1990

| PER CAPITA in dollars | 1,688 | 1,651 | 1,572 | 1,613 | 1,814 | 2,475 | 4,036 | 7,655 | 13,000* |

* Estimate

Statistical Abstract of the United States

addressing the deficit. In an impassioned speech to the nation, Reagan explained:

The first American Revolution was sparked by an unshakable conviction: Taxation without representation is tyranny. Two centuries later a second American Revolution...is gathering force...born of popular resentment against a tax system that is unwise, unwanted and unfair.

Reagan's economic goals were helped by the great drop in oil prices that occurred in 1986. Fear of inflation lessened as interest rates dropped. Nonetheless, the deficit reached $2.3 trillion by 1988. Many critics charged that Reagan was passing the problem on to future generations rather than dealing with hard choices.

President Reagan's strong conservative beliefs shaped the programs of his administration. His skills as a speaker enabled him to explain his policies and goals to the public effectively. Within his administrative methods, however, he adopted a "hands-off" attitude toward the day-to-day operations of the presidency. Cabinet secretaries received little direction from Reagan on how to proceed or what policies to promote. Reagan delegated far greater responsibility to his staff than any other recent President had. This detachment allowed his subordinates to function on their own. Some, unfortunately, acted for personal gain. As a result, a number of financial scandals broke out within the Reagan administration. Officials were convicted of using their influence with the government in exchange for money or other rewards. Congress investigated irregularities in programs ranging from military purchasing to federal housing subsidies.

In 1986 the Iran-contra scandal shook the Reagan administration. Several of the President's national security aides, including John Poindexter, Robert McFarlane, and Lieutenant Colonel Oliver North, had schemed to sell arms to the Iranians

to win the release of American hostages in the Middle East. Furthermore, they had diverted the profits from these arms sales to the antigovernment contra forces in Nicaragua, a violation of a Congressional ban on such financing. Critics charged that an undercover foreign policy was being carried out without Congress's consent. Defenders maintained that the executive branch was forced to take these measures because of congressional interference with the President's authority to conduct foreign policy.

A special commission was set up to study the Iran-contra case. Although the commission cleared the President of direct blame, it found fault with Reagan for allowing aides to make policy decisions without his knowledge. A number

Life of the Times

PHYSICAL FITNESS

Ronald Reagan was one of the oldest Presidents and one of the fittest. He kept trim by riding horses and chopping wood. Thanks in part to Reagan's example, the late 1970s health craze continued into the 1980s. This trend generated social situations for which no rules had been prescribed. In Miss Manners' Guidebook to Excruciatingly Correct Behavior, syndicated columnist Judith Martin, a.k.a. "Miss Manners," applied traditional principles of gracious living to quandaries that might arise on the jogging track.

Miss Manners told joggers how and where to jog in a mannerly way. She also defined correct jogging attire as "a sports costume that clearly looks like a sports costume." In response to a question about whether a gentleman walker should yield the right of way to a lady jogger who emerges "at full tilt" on a narrow path, Miss Manners advises that "In all traffic situations, the first to yield should be the first who has realized that there is about to be a collision."

Miss Manners offered guidance to proper and gracious behavior for almost any conceivable social situation. She always designed her advice to help people get what they wanted in a polite but assertive way. For example, she advised a jogger who was saddled with a slower partner to "tell [your partner] before you start where you intend to finish and then go at your own pace, meeting him there."

of high-level administration officials were criticized, including Attorney General Edwin Meese and CIA Director William Casey.

The Iran-contra scandal helped Democrats win back a Senate majority in 1986. The effect of the voters' decision at the polls was to produce a divided government—with the presidency held by one party and control of Congress held by another—as a way of keeping power in check. Democratic majorities in Congress acted as a brake on the Reagan administration.

In 1987 Supreme Court Justice Lewis F. Powell, a moderate who often held the deciding vote in such controversial cases as abortion and minority rights, retired. Reagan was quick to nominate a conservative judge to fill the vacancy, but he met with much resistance from the Democratic Senate. After long and controversial hearings, the Senate rejected the nomination. Eight months later, Reagan's nomination of Anthony M. Kennedy, a conservative with more moderate views, was approved. During his presidency, Reagan had appointed two other conservatives to the Supreme Court—Justices Sandra Day O'Connor in 1981 and Antonin Scalia in 1986—each one young enough to have influence long into the future.

The Reagan Legacy

The oldest person ever to be elected to the presidency, Ronald Reagan was a President with enormous popular appeal. The 525 electoral votes he received in 1984 were the most ever received by a candidate. Reagan, however, left a contradictory legacy. Although he had campaigned to limit government, he left behind enormous federal deficits that would restrict future government actions. Reagan's conservative revolution stopped the expansion of liberal social welfare programs that had gone on since the New Deal, but actually ended few of them. Reagan—working together with both Democratic and Republican members of Congress—helped preserve and strengthen a number of social programs. Social security was strengthened, and Medicare for the elderly was expanded to protect them against "catastrophic" illness.

Reagan was not as reactionary as people thought. Comparing himself to Franklin D. Roosevelt, he said, "Like F.D.R., may I say I'm not trying to destroy what's best in our system of humane, free government. I'm doing everything I can to save it." Like Roosevelt, Reagan had a contagious optimism that helped to restore the confidence of many Americans in themselves, their economy, and their government.

Spurred on by low unemployment and a strong economy, Reagan received some of the highest popularity ratings any President has ever enjoyed.

AMERICAN PORTRAITS

JESSE JACKSON
1941-

Born in segregated Greenville, South Carolina, Jesse Jackson became involved in civil rights activities while a college student. He went on to join Dr. Martin Luther King, Jr.'s, protest marches in Selma, Alabama. Later, Jackson was selected to head Operation Breadbasket, a program designed to promote the hiring of more blacks by major businesses. After Dr. King was killed, Jesse Jackson emerged as the best-known black leader in America.

In 1971 Jackson launched his own organization: People United to Save Humanity (PUSH). Supported by a "rainbow coalition" he unsuccessfully sought the 1984 Democratic presidential nomination. When he ran again in 1988, he finished a strong second in the primaries, proving that an African American could be a serious presidential contender.

Election of 1988

The Twenty-second Amendment barred Ronald Reagan from seeking a third term as President. Republican candidates fought a spirited battle to inherit the presidency, but Vice President George Bush finally secured the nomination. Bush picked a young, little-known Indiana Senator—J. Danforth Quayle—as his running mate.

There was also tough competition for the Democratic nomination. The final contenders were Massachusetts Governor Michael Dukakis and the Reverend Jesse Jackson. Jackson, who appealed to a "rainbow coalition" of minorities and reformers, ran a far stronger race than anyone had expected for a black candidate. Dukakis, however, won the nomination. He chose veteran Texas Senator Lloyd Bentsen to run with him as Vice President.

Early in the campaign, Dukakis led Bush in the public polls. Then Bush's campaign unleashed a string of negative television advertisements that portrayed Dukakis as unpatriotic and sympathetic to criminals. Dukakis responded weakly to these ads and lost his lead. The candidates attacked each other. Bush identified Dukakis as a "card-carrying liberal," while Dukakis labeled Bush as a poor leader. Saying "read my lips," Bush pledged not to raise taxes and promised the nation that he would follow Reagan's economic policies. Bush also urged Americans to follow a new spirit of public service and volunteerism. In the election Bush won a resounding victory, taking 40 of the 50 states. Bush, with nearly 49 million votes, received 7 million more than his opponent. The final tally showed Bush with 426 electoral votes to 112 for Dukakis.

The campaign of 1988 offered evidence that slick television commercials based on slogans had replaced discussion of real issues. Emotional appeals often replaced thoughtful debate. It became clear that money available for television commercials was a crucial factor in running a successful political campaign. Incumbents with the largest campaign contributions usually won.

★ Section Three Review ★

SUMMARY

President Reagan began his second term intent on keeping the United States strong. The military buildup added to social spending sent the federal deficit soaring. In foreign affairs changing conditions in the Soviet Union eased strained relations with the United States. Reagan's "hands off" leadership hurt him in the Iran-contra scandal. He left office a popular President but with a mixed legacy that included a huge federal deficit. Promising to continue Reagan's policies, Republican George Bush captured the party's nomination in 1988. Although the Democratic candidate, Governor Michael Dukakis of Massachusetts, led early in the campaign, Bush won a resounding victory.

CHECKING FOR UNDERSTANDING

1. **Identify** Strategic Defense Initiative, Mikhail Gorbachev, George Bush, Dan Quayle, Jesse Jackson, Michael Dukakis, Gramm-Rudman Act

2. **Define** nuclear freeze, *glasnost, perestroika*

3. **List** three controversial weapons proposals of the Reagan administration.

4. **State** two reasons why George Bush won the election of 1988.

THINKING CRITICALLY

5. **Evaluating Policies** Consider whether technology such as the SDI will help prevent nuclear war.

GLOBAL PERSPECTIVES

6. **Assessing Cause and Effect** Did Reagan's arms buildup contribute to the Soviet Union's retreat from a policy of world domination, or are these changes a result of *glasnost* and a deteriorating Soviet economy? Explain and support your answer.

★ Chapter 35 Review ★

★ Summary

In 1976 American voters elected Jimmy Carter President. Domestically, Carter focused on solving the energy crisis, but double-digit inflation, poor relations with Congress, and a perception of indecisiveness cut away his support. In foreign policy, Carter emphasized human rights. He relinquished United States control of the Panama Canal and imposed a grain embargo on the Soviet Union for its invasion of Afghanistan. In the Middle East, Carter negotiated an accord between Israel and Egypt, but was unable to free American hostages from Iran.

President Reagan, in what was termed by some a "conservative revolution," enjoyed broad-based support, a reflection of discontent with Democratic leadership. He cut taxes and reduced federal spending. After a plunge that created high unemployment, the economy rebounded, although the federal deficit continued to grow. Reagan sent military aid to El Salvador and supported anticommunist rebels in Nicaragua. The death of 241 marines in Lebanon forced the President to withdraw the troops.

After an overwhelming victory in the 1984 elections, Reagan continued to build up the military. This buildup, however, was a drain on the federal budget. Mikhail Gorbachev ushered in a new era in Soviet relations in 1985. A crumbling economy and ethnic strife paved the way for a more open Soviet society. Reagan and Gorbachev held talks that reduced tensions. The Iran-Contra scandal tainted Reagan's final years in office. Vowing to follow Reagan's economic policies, George Bush won the 1988 presidential election. Bush overcame an initial image as a weak leader and acted decisively in foreign affairs in Panama and the Middle East. Domestically, however, problems with the economy and drugs continued to plague American society.

★ Using Vocabulary

Write three headings: *Carter, Reagan,* and *Bush.* Classify each of the following terms under the headings to which they are related. Some terms belong in more than one category.

supply-side economics	**nuclear freeze**
glasnost	*perestroika*
double-digit inflation	**federal deficit**

★ Reviewing Facts

1. **Explain** how Carter's election was partly a result of Watergate.
2. **Summarize** Carter's foreign policy philosophy.
3. **Describe** why Reagan appealed to Americans.
4. **List** one negative and one positive effect of Reagan's economic policies.
5. **Summarize** Reagan's legacy as President.
6. **State** two promises made by George Bush during his campaign for President.

★ Understanding Concepts

LEADERSHIP

1. Analyze Jimmy Carter's inability to articulate goals and themes during his presidency. Explain how this may have affected Carter's popular support compared to Reagan's.
2. How did Reagan's detached management style fail to prevent scandal and corruption? Explain whether you believe a President should be blamed for the actions of his staff.

POLITICAL IDEOLOGY

3. Evaluate Carter's stand on human rights and the role it played in his foreign policy. Based on your evaluation, formulate your own opinion on the role of human rights versus anticommunism in foreign policy.
4. In the 1988 election, candidates shied away from the label "liberal" because they feared it would be detrimental to their campaign. Explain why Reagan's presidency brought new support for conservative political ideas.

★ Thinking Critically

1. **Assessing Programs**   The United States has had difficulty implementing an energy policy. Evaluate Carter's energy program. Explain why it was only partially successful. Suggest possible solutions to the energy problem.
2. **Evaluating Results**   Weigh the successes and failures of Reagan's years in office. In your opinion, did Reagan's actions make revolutionary changes in American government and society? Explain.

3. **Linking Past and Present** Americans have been critical of Gorbachev's use of Soviet troops in his nation's rebellious republics. Yet Lincoln used similar force against the South in the Civil War. Compare the circumstances and state your opinion of Gorbachev's policy.

★ Writing About History

CLASSIFICATION

Refer to the description of how to write a classification essay in the History Writer's Handbook in the Appendix of this book. Your teacher will give you more specific instructions on the essay's length and the assignment's due date.

Write an essay on the changing relations between the United States and the Soviet Union during the administrations of Carter, Reagan, and Bush. Before you begin writing, divide your information into two classifications: 1) events, policies, and actions that eased tensions between the United States and the Soviet Union, and 2) events, policies, and actions that kept the two nations apart. Weave this information throughout your essay to explain the changing relationship between the two countries. Conclude your writing with predictions on future relations between these two nations.

★ Cooperative Learning Activity

Since the 1930s the United States has had deficit, or unbalanced, federal budgets most of the time. This policy of deficit spending led to increasingly large budgets and a growing national debt. The United States entered World War II with a national debt of about $40 billion. The government emerged from the war owing nearly $259 billion. By 1992 the national debt reached nearly $4 trillion.

Organize into four groups to research and analyze the two ways to reduce the federal deficit. Two groups will research and present arguments for and against raising taxes. The two other groups will research and present arguments for and against reduced government spending. You will have one class period to prepare your arguments. Select a representative from your group to report your arguments to the class. The members of the class should evaluate the arguments and decide which method would be best.

★ Mastering Skills

IDENTIFYING TRENDS

Trends can be identified by studying historical statistics or by examining past events to see if they show a pattern or direction.

When they are interpreted correctly, graphs that chart trends over a period of time lend useful information. There are several questions that help to understand the material on such graphs.

- What definite patterns or directions can be seen on the graph?

- Does the information extend over a significant period of time so that trends can be clearly determined?

- What could be some underlying causes of the trends shown on the graph?

- What additional information would make the graph more helpful in identifying trends?

Practice Study the graph on this page showing the value of United States exports and imports from 1965 to 1990. Apply the four questions above to the information on the graph.

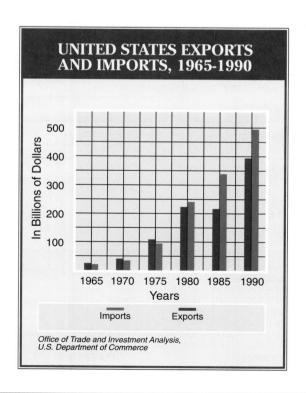

UNITED STATES EXPORTS AND IMPORTS, 1965-1990

In Billions of Dollars

Years

Imports   Exports

Office of Trade and Investment Analysis, U.S. Department of Commerce

CHAPTER 36
Toward a New Century

SETTING THE SCENE

Historical Focus

As 1992 dawned the Soviet Union no longer existed, the cold war had ended, and a new world order was emerging. During the period of the Soviet collapse, many pressing concerns emerged. The United States waged war on Iraq. On the domestic side, Americans were troubled by economic recession and the environment.

Concepts to Understand

- How **reform and change** altered world trade, technology, and political leadership.
- How Americans are dealing with the **challenges** they face.

People to Know

George Bush, Mikhail Gorbachev, Boris Yeltsin, Lech Walesa, Vaclav Havel, Saddam Hussein, Anita Hill, Bill Clinton, Carol Moseley Braun, Nelson Mandela

Places to Locate

Latvia, Moldova, Kuwait, Iraq

Terms to Identify

Commonwealth of Independent States, unification, Operation Desert Storm, trade deficit, AIDS, apartheid

Guided Reading

As you read this chapter, seek the answers to the following questions.

1. What important changes took place in the Soviet Union and Eastern Europe in the late 1980s and early 1990s?
2. What important economic, environmental, and public health issues face Americans?

SPANNING THE DECADES

POLITICAL	1986 *Congress grants amnesty to illegal aliens*	1987 *Trade deficit reaches $157 billion*	1988 *Federal revenue exceeds $1 trillion*	1989 *Democratic revolts in China, Eastern Europe*
	1986		1988	
CULTURAL	1986 Challenger *explodes killing seven astronauts*	1987 *Gene-altered bacteria for agriculture tested*	1988 *Office of Human Genome Research Established*	1989 *Scientists estimate 5-10 million people infected with AIDS*

Bill and Hillary Clinton and Al and Tipper Gore on election night, 1992

1990
Iraq invades Kuwait

1991
War in Persian Gulf
ends with ceasefire

1993
Bill Clinton is
inaugurated as
President

1990   1993

1990
Texas schools substitute
videodiscs for some
science textbooks

1993
Demographers project
Hispanics will become the
largest minority group by 2010

*The Cold War is over and the arms race
that turned our planet into a nuclear
arsenal begins to wind down.... To be sure
globalization will create new and
unforeseen problems but it will also create
tremendous opportunities.*

—MARIO VARGAS LLOSA, Writer
Speech, May 17, 1992

After the Cold War

![SETTING THE SCENE]

We again stand at history's precipice.... now the Western nations and the former Soviet republics stand as awkward climbers on a steep mountain. Held together by a common rope.... Surely we must strengthen the rope, not sever it.

—JAMES A. BAKER
Secretary of State
December 12, 1991

Section Focus

The Soviet Union's rigid central control had stifled the economy and a gigantic military buildup had impoverished the nation. Realizing that change was necessary, President Mikhail Gorbachev tried to save the Soviet system through reform and decontrol. His efforts to hold the union together failed. As the old Soviet empire crumbled, the ethnically diverse republics moved toward independence.

Objectives

After studying this section, you should be able to:
• list the events that led to the end of the Soviet Union.
• discuss the moves toward democracy throughout Eastern Europe.

Throughout the cold war decades, Americans and Soviets had lived under the threat of nuclear war, as each side built nuclear arsenals that included long-range missiles capable of massive destruction.

After the 1962 Cuban missile crisis, when war between the United States and the Soviet Union seemed imminent, tensions slowly diminished. The United States worked toward détente with the USSR and recognized the People's Republic of China. Still, both sides maintained mighty military arsenals and viewed almost all disputes around the world in terms of the East-West struggle.

Then with surprising suddenness, democratic movements erupted throughout the Soviet Union's Eastern European satellites. Popular demands for political, social, and economic reform toppled one communist government after another throughout Eastern Europe, until even the Soviet Union split into independent republics. Without a Soviet adversary, the United States faced the challenge of building what President George Bush called "a new world order."

A Tidal Wave of Change

George Bush came to the presidency with ample experience in foreign policy. He had been Ambassador to the United Nations, Ambassador to China, Director of the CIA, and Vice President. This training served Bush well, for he was immediately confronted with a tidal wave of change around the world. Much of this change resulted from the rapid democratization of the Soviet bloc. The disintegration of the Soviet Union, and the Soviet bloc, saw a rise of nationalism, and the outbreak of civil war throughout the Balkans and the Caucasus. In both regions, old ethnic rivalries that communist regimes had long suppressed now reignited into bloody conflict.

In the Soviet Union, the economy had grown stagnant and even declined after years of centralized political and economic control by the Soviet Communist party. After Mikhail Gorbachev became General Secretary in 1985, he set forth proposals to loosen economic controls. Following Gorbachev's lead, the Communist party changed the structure of the Soviet system, including a shift of some power to local organizations and limited terms for elected government and party officials.

These tentative steps toward democracy made the Soviet people demand even greater freedom.

The Soviet Union's new liberal policies also incited demands for change in Eastern Europe. In 1989 the people of the satellite nations of Poland, Hungary, Czechoslovakia, Bulgaria, and Romania overthrew their communist rulers. Polish citizens led the way by voting to remove the Communist party from power, and people from other Eastern European nations forced their governments to allow democratic elections. Most dramatic of all was the tearing down of the Berlin Wall that divided Germany and that had symbolized the "Iron Curtain" that divided Europe. As the wall came down, the Soviet Union agreed to the reunification of East and West Germany.

Then the 74-year-old Soviet experiment itself was swept away. Just as the Soviet republics were about to sign a new union agreement in August 1991, a group of hard-line Communists and other conservative forces proclaimed a new government in the old communist tradition. The plotters detained Gorbachev at his vacation resort in Crimea. They failed, however, to take into account Boris Yeltsin, the recently elected president of the Russian Republic. Appearing before crowds gathered in front of the Russian parliament building, President Yeltsin called for nonviolent resistance and urged military officials not to carry out the coup leaders' orders. In response to Yeltsin's appeal, Moscow citizens barricaded the parliament building. Tens of thousands of unarmed protestors defied the coup-ordered curfew and stood guard in the rain to protect Yeltsin and his aides in the parliament building. Inside, Yeltsin supporters frantically used fax machines and photocopiers to print makeshift newspapers for distribution.

The coup had faltered from the beginning and collapsed within days. When Gorbachev returned to Moscow, everything had changed. Yeltsin, not Gorbachev, was now in charge. Three days later, Gorbachev resigned as head of the Communist party and urged that the party be abolished. Even this dramatic act

could not stem the tide of change. First, the three Baltic republics of Latvia, Estonia, and Lithuania won their freedom, and then the remaining 12 republics demanded independence. By year's end, 11 had joined in a Commonwealth of Independent States (CIS). On December 25, 1991, Gorbachev resigned, saying: "We are living in a new world." His resignation marked the end of what was left of the Soviet Union. The communist red flag with its hammer and sickle no longer flew over the Kremlin; in its place flew the tri-color Russian flag. The United States quickly recognized Russia and other former Soviet republics.

For the United States, the greatest remaining worry was what would become of the former Soviet Union's large stockpile of nuclear weapons—some 27,000 missiles. About 70 percent of these were in Russia, but the rest had been deployed in Ukraine and other republics. Then, in 1992 the republics agreed to transfer strategic nuclear forces to Russia. The CIS pledged to carry out nuclear disarmament treaties that the Soviet Union had signed.

Economic reform proved far more problematic than disarmament, largely because the new CIS republics faced a severe economic crisis as they converted to a free-market economy. The Soviet economy was already in a depression. Productivity had declined and shortages of fuel, medical supplies, food, and housing left many people in need. Yeltsin moved to

Examining Photographs In November 1989 the Berlin Wall, which had separated the two Germanys since 1961, was opened. On the first weekend after the wall was opened, 3 million visitors crossed from East Berlin to visit West Berlin. What had the Berlin Wall symbolized?

Examining Photographs *Supporters of Russian president Boris Yeltsin carry a giant Russian flag to Red Square as the city celebrates the collapse of the August 1991 coup. In what ways did the United States try to help the new Commonwealth of Independent States?*

unfreeze prices and to privatize industry. When price controls were relaxed, however, prices shot up. Russia sought financial aid from the West to help it through this crisis. Although the United States offered agricultural credits and humanitarian aid, rising federal deficits and an economic recession hindered the United States' ability to help its old adversary.

Nationalism Reawakened

Having long called for the freedom of "captive nations," the United States felt a moral duty to support the transformation from dictatorship to democracy in Eastern Europe and the former Soviet Union, and to protect the stability of the new governments. At the same time, the United States and Western Europe sought to avoid being drawn into the ethnic rivalries and renewed nationalism that emerged.

The Warsaw Pact, which linked Eastern Europe in a military alliance with the Soviet Union, was terminated in July 1991 and Soviet troops began withdrawing from Eastern Europe. The West debated the future role of NATO because the biggest remaining challenges were economic rather than military.

In 1989 the United States Congress passed the Support for Eastern European Democracy Act (SEED), authorizing $1 billion in aid to the new democracies and encouraging greater trade and private investments there. Congress also established a "Gift for Democracy" that provided advisers, computer equipment, and other assistance to democratic parliaments in Poland and other Eastern European nations. As symbols of the new relationship, presidents Lech Walesa of Poland, Vaclav Havel of Czechoslovakia, and Boris Yeltsin of Russia addressed joint sessions of Congress to report on the progress of their democratic revolutions.

Eastern Europe had great need for help. Their attempts to shift from state-controlled economies to market-based economies caused many hardships. Like the Soviet Union, the new governments of Eastern Europe began lifting state controls at a time when their economies were already in sharp decline. Industrial production fell, prices rose, and unemployment spread.

Hardships caused discontent to rise and old ethnic rivalries to flare. Many in the West feared for the survival of Eastern Europe's new freedom. A strong nationalist movement in the province of Slovakia threatened to divide Czechoslovakia. Conflicts rose between Russian-speaking and Romanian-speaking people in Moldova. Romanians clashed with Hungarian minorities. In the Caucasus, old feuds emerged between Armenia and Azerbaijan. "The world was supposed to be a better place after the Cold War," lamented David Anderson, the former U.S. Ambassador to Yugoslavia.

Most disturbing was the fierce civil war that broke out between different ethnic groups in Yugoslavia. For years Yugoslavia had been held together by a common loyalty to its own brand of communism. As communist ideology began to wane, however, the different regions of Yugoslavia plunged into Europe's first large-scale civil war since 1945. Fighting took place between Christians and Muslims in Serbia, Croatia, and Bosnia. The United Nations charged Serbia with aggression, imposed trade sanctions, and supported UN peacekeeping troops. As the conflict escalated, and reports of concentration camps surfaced, pressure increased for the United States and European nations to intervene. President Bush felt reluctant, however, to send American troops.

While Eastern Europe fragmented, Western Europe debated unification. In 1991 representatives from the 12 nations of the European Community met in Maastricht, in the Netherlands, and took the first crucial steps toward economic and political union. They approved 2 treaties that would move Western Europe toward a common currency, end trade barriers between their nations, and pave the way for common defense, foreign, and economic policies. In addition, the new Eastern European governments sought entry into the European Community. The desire to create a unified region capable of competing in the global markets fueled this drive for union.

Are We Friends?

In February 1992, President Bush and Russian President Boris Yeltsin met at Camp David, Maryland. As the meeting ended, Yeltsin said:

Mr. President, I have one more question before we get up from the table. I don't understand who we are—are we friends? Are we enemies? Are we competitors? Are we partners? What are we?"

Bush replied, "We are partners who are standing at the beginning of the creation of a union." Bush declared that the meeting marked a "new relationship . . . based on trust, based on a commitment to economic and political freedom." Both leaders pledged a drastic reduction in the number of nuclear warheads and missiles, as a tangible sign of the new world order.

★ ★ ★ ★ ★ ★ ★ ★ ★ ★ ★ ★ ★ ★ ★ ★ ★ ★ ★

Section One Review

★ ★ ★ ★ ★ ★ ★ ★ ★ ★ ★ ★ ★ ★ ★ ★ ★ ★ ★

SUMMARY

The late 1980s and early 1990s were years of astonishing change. Soviet leader Mikhail Gorbachev and his followers unleashed a series of reforms in the country and the surrounding communist bloc nations. As demands for even more reform resounded throughout the Soviet Union and its Eastern European satellites, democratic movements erupted throughout the Soviet empire. One communist government after another toppled, until even the Soviet Union split into independent republics. The United States offered some economic and humanitarian aid to help the people of the former Soviet Union meet their needs, but its ability to do more was hampered by its own economic woes.

CHECKING FOR UNDERSTANDING

1. **Identify** Boris Yeltsin, Commonwealth of Independent States, Vaclav Havel, Serbia

2. **Describe** how changes in Soviet policies led to demands for change in Eastern Europe.

3. **Explain** how power in the Commonwealth of Independent States shifted from Gorbachev to Yeltsin.

4. **Discuss** how the United States responded to the growth of democratic movements in previously communist-controlled nations.

THINKING CRITICALLY

5. **Identifying Central Issues** What were the primary reasons for conflict in Yugoslavia?

GLOBAL PERSPECTIVES

6. **Evaluating International Relationships** Throughout the twentieth century, the United States has played a major role in global affairs. In what ways is the nation's role changing? In what ways should it change?

★ ★ ★ ★ ★ ★ ★ ★ ★ ★ ★ ★ ★ ★ ★ ★ ★ ★ ★

The Persian Gulf War

SETTING THE SCENE

.... [W]e have a real chance at this new world order, an order in which a credible United Nations can use its peacekeeping role to fulfill the promise and vision of the U.N.'s founders. We have no argument with the people of Iraq. Indeed, for the innocents caught in this conflict, I pray for their safety.

—PRESIDENT GEORGE BUSH
January 16, 1991

Section Focus

In August 1990, Iraq invaded Kuwait. Many nations joined the United States and President Bush in denouncing the invasion. Iraq's President Saddam Hussein refused to withdraw his forces despite several efforts to negotiate with him and economic sanctions against his country.

Objectives

After studying this section, you should be able to:
- list the events that led to conflict between Iraq and coalition forces.
- discuss the results of the conflict.

The end of the cold war caused Americans to contemplate reaping a "peace dividend"—funds from reduced military spending could be used to confront domestic problems. But world events quickly diminished such optimism. Americans realized that they could not shrink from their responsibilities as the most powerful military power in the world. Faced with a series of foreign-policy challenges, President Bush acted decisively. When a United States grand jury indicted Panama's dictator Manuel Noriega for drug trafficking, Bush took steps to remove him from power. At first the United States supported Panamanians who wanted to overthrow Noriega. When their attempt failed, the President ordered an invasion of Panama. Noriega surrendered to American troops on January 3, 1990, and was taken to the United States where he stood trial and was later convicted. Soon after, when Iraq invaded Kuwait, President Bush had an opportunity to demonstrate what he intended for America's role in the post-cold war world.

Crisis in the Middle East

The world was stunned on August 2, 1990, when Iraq invaded its oil-rich neighbor Kuwait. Calling the Iraqi move "naked agression," President Bush acted quickly. He imposed economic sanctions, froze $20 billion of Iraqi money in American banks, and banned imports of Iraqi oil. Only hours after the invasion, the United Nations passed a resolution condemning Iraq and demanding that it withdraw its forces. The United Nations also called for all nations to halt trade with Iraq immediately.

Many leaders feared, however, that these actions were not enough to force Iraq's president, Saddam Hussein, to withdraw his troops from Kuwait or prevent an invasion of Saudi Arabia.

Bush obtained assistance from more than 25 countries around the world, including Middle Eastern and European nations, and assembled a huge array of power against Iraq in a military coalition called "Operation Desert Shield." The President also gained support for these actions from the United Nations, which authorized military action to restore Kuwait's independence. For almost 6 months, coalition troops, planes, and ships took no action. The world hoped that sanctions and diplomacy as well as the threat of force would be enough to prevent the fifth major conflict in the region in less than 25 years.

George Bush was by no means the first American President to encounter the complex issues that plagued the Middle East. The area's vast oil reserves had long made its stability vital to the United States and to other industrial nations.

In part, the crisis in Kuwait was another consequence of the long-standing ethnic and religious conflicts in the region. More directly, the conflict resulted from policies by the United States and other oil-dependent nations to keep any Middle Eastern nation or leader from becoming too strong. The United States, for example, had long supported Israel against Arab nations who wanted to return Israeli land to Palestinian control. Yet a balance of power in the region was crucial. So the United States also developed ties with Israel's moderate Arab neighbors, Egypt and Jordan, and pressed Israel to solve the Palestinian issue.

Ironically, it was this same desire to maintain the balance of power that led the United States and its allies to arm the dictator they now opposed in Kuwait. Con-cerned about growing Iranian power, the United States aided Hussein when he went to war against Iran in 1980. To finance his 8-year war with Iran, Hussein borrowed billions of dollars from his rich neighbors, Kuwait and Saudi Arabia. Along with these leaders, Hussein feared the spread of Iran's Islamic fundamental-ism and military power. After the war ended in 1988, the Saudis and Kuwaitis wanted repayment from Iraq. Hussein charged that during the war Kuwait had drilled Iraqi oil and that its oil policies were wrecking Iraq's economy. In addition to a change in Kuwaiti oil policies, Hus-sein demanded $27 billion in reparations. When negotiations broke down, 100,000 soldiers that Hussein had amassed on Iraq's southern border poured into Kuwait. In just 12 hours, the tiny nation fell, giving Hussein control of 20 percent of the world's oil reserves.

Exactly 24 weeks later, after repeated warnings, negotiation attempts, and a naval blockade failed to resolve the crisis, President Bush implemented the UN

Examining Photographs *Break-fast customers in an Illinois cafe search the morning paper on Jan-uary 17, 1991, for details about the air campaign against Iraq. Why did the United States go to war?*

Examining Photographs *From the top of a captured Iraqi tank, Kuwaiti citizens celebrate the liberation of their country in February 1991. Why did Iraq invade and annex Kuwait?*

resolution authorizing force to restore Kuwait's sovereignty. After obtaining congressional approval, on the evening of January 16, 1991, Bush ordered massive air strikes against Iraq. The President announced that Operation Desert Shield had become Operation Desert Storm. He rejected calls for further delay:

The world could wait no longer. . . . While the world waited, Saddam Hussein met every overture of peace with open contempt. While the world prayed for peace, Saddam Hussein prepared for war.

In the following weeks, United States air and sea forces, aided by coalition allies, unleashed the high-tech weapons of President Reagan's 1980s arms buildup. Aided by hundreds of sea-launched missiles, coalition pilots flew more than 2,000 bombing missions a day against military centers, airfields, and bridges in Iraq and Kuwait. Overwhelmed by the power of the weapons arrayed against it, Iraq's response to the coalition's air assault was surprisingly ineffective. Attempting to weaken Arab support for the coalition by drawing Israel into the war, Hussein launched unsuccessful missile attacks on Israel. Partly in response to pleas from the United States, the Israelis did not retaliate.

As the bombing continued, so did diplomatic efforts to end the conflict. Soviet diplomats reached an agreement on

Iraqi withdrawal, but Iraq attached conditions that were not acceptable to the coalition. Concerned that a negotiated settlement might allow Iraq's military to remain intact, Bush set a deadline for Hussein's forces to unconditionally withdraw from Kuwait.

On February 23 at 8 P.M., only hours after the deadline passed, a lightning-swift coalition ground assault began. Under the command of General Norman Schwarzkopf, the high-tech armored invasion of Kuwait and Iraq devastated Iraqi forces, softened by 4 weeks of pounding by air. Just 100 hours after the ground offensive began, Allied forces had freed the Kuwaiti people and crushed the Iraqi army. "Kuwait is liberated," Bush told the American people as he announced the end of offensive operations. "America and the world have kept their word."

President Bush called off the offensive short of occupying Iraq. Bush wanted Saddam Hussein removed from power, but not at the price of splintering Iraq and leaving it at the mercy of Iran, Syria, and Turkey. Nor did he want to expose American troops to the dangers of invading and subduing Iraq. The United States and the United Nations sought instead to dismantle Iraq's capability to make nuclear and chemical weapons.

In the aftermath of the war, the United States helped rebuild Kuwait. It took 9 months to extinguish the 732 oil well fires set by fleeing Iraqi troops. Fire fighters from the United States, Britain, Hungary, China, and the Soviet Union battled the blazes so that Kuwait could once again begin pumping and exporting oil. Meanwhile the United States waited to see if Kuwait's ruler would keep his pledge to restore the parliament and allow for more democratic participation in the Kuwaiti government.

Although the war reduced the Iraqi threat to Middle East security, questions remained about the prospects for long-term stability in the region. In the wake of the war, the United States pressed hard for a settlement of the larger Arab-Israeli conflict. Secretary of State James Baker urged Israel to halt settlement of its occupied territories, and pressed Syria, Jordan, and other nations to negotiate with Israel to achieve some form of Palestinian self-rule.

Rethinking America's Military Role

The Persian Gulf War raised questions about America's military role in the world. Should the United States police the world or should it rely more on collective security arrangements through the United Nations? How large a military force could it afford? The collapse of the Soviet Union left the United States as the last military superpower. The emergence of Germany and Japan as new economic superpowers suggested, however, that financial power might replace military might in the new world order.

In the decades since World War II, the United States carried an overwhelming share of the Free World's military burden. As the federal deficits grew to enormous amounts in the 1980s and 1990s, the United States planned cuts in defense spending. The Pentagon planned a "drawdown" that would bring troops home from overseas bases in Europe and Asia. Defense Secretary Richard Cheney called for a "decade of development, more than of production." Although President Bush called for cuts in defense spending, Congress demanded even greater reductions. Military cutbacks and base closings, however, hurt many American cities and towns, from San Diego, California, to Caribou, Maine. Reduction in defense spending also caused job layoffs in military weapons production.

Some experts warned that the United States should not let its guard down too quickly. They pointed out that Cuba, North Korea, Vietnam, and the People's Republic of China remained communist nations. Although China had instituted some free-market programs, its Communist party leadership opposed calls for democracy. The party leadership used military force to massacre pro-democracy demonstrators in Beijing's Tiananmen Square in 1989. Similarly, tense relations in the Middle East, the Caucasus, and the Balkans compelled the United States to retain a strong military force.

Section Two Review

SUMMARY

When Iraq invaded Kuwait in August 1990, the United States and many other nations reacted quickly and decisively. Within days of the invasion, the United States announced it would send land, air, and naval forces to Saudi Arabia. Coalition forces set up a blockade that prevented Iraq from exporting oil and importing arms. The United Nations set a deadline of January 15, 1991, for Iraq to withdraw its troops. When Saddam Hussein refused to meet the deadline, United States-led air units launched a devastating series of attacks on Iraqi defenses. The coalition's massive ground attacks that followed forced Iraq to withdraw its forces from Kuwait.

CHECKING FOR UNDERSTANDING

1. **Identify** Kuwait, Saddam Hussein, Operation Desert Storm, Norman Schwarzkopf, James Baker, Tiananmen Square

2. **Discuss** the actions that the United States and the United Nations took to force Iraq to restore Kuwait's independence.

3. **Explain** why the United States resorted to force against Iraq.

4. **List** two reasons the United States stopped short of conquering Iraq.

THINKING CRITICALLY

5. **Making Comparisons** What are the economic advantages of cutting defense spending? What are the disadvantages?

GLOBAL PERSPECTIVES

6. **Identifying Cause and Effect** Did the United States arms buildup contribute to the Soviet Union's retreat from a policy of world domination, or were these changes a result of *glasnost* and a deteriorating economy? Explain and support your answer.

America in a Global Economy

SETTING THE SCENE

The engine driving the world toward higher growth will be the same force that has improved the human condition since the beginning of time: technology.
—AMERICA IN THE GLOBAL '90S
Austin H. Kiplinger and
Knight A. Kiplinger

Section Focus

While the general standard of living in America remained high in the early 1990s, poverty and homelessness spread. Americans continued to buy more than they sold in world markets, resulting in trade deficits. Despite its economic problems, the United States remained a land of opportunity that attracted new immigrants from all regions of the globe.

Objectives

After studying this section, you should be able to:
* Explain changes in the United States' balance of trade.
* Identify three major problems facing the United States and the world.

The United States had long based its economic prosperity on selling its industrial and agricultural goods abroad. Beginning in the 1970s, however, Americans experienced annual **trade deficits,** as they pur-chased far more from foreign nations than they sold in foreign markets. The trade deficit reached a new high of almost $152 billion in 1987. Foreign investors used their excess dollars to buy American companies. This investment moved the United States from a **creditor nation,** or lending nation, to a **debtor nation,** or borrowing one. An increasing number of Americans were employed by foreign-owned companies. From hotels along Waikiki Beach in Hawaii to Rockefeller Center in New York City, foreign-owned buildings dotted the American skyline. By the 1990s, favorable exchange rates and improved productivity and competitiveness helped American exports rise again. The United States achieved trading surpluses with most countries, with the notable exception of Japan.

The International Economy

While foreign investment in the United States grew, so did American investment in other countries. American investment overseas grew at a rate even faster than its two largest competitors—Japan and Great Britain. American **multinational corporations**—companies that expand into other countries—often built factories in developing nations where they paid workers less than workers in the United States earned. While imports from multinationals added to what was counted as the trade deficit, these same foreign branches of American corporations sold hundreds of billions of dollars of goods overseas.

A major global difficulty of the 1980s and 1990s was debt. Developing nations, especially in Latin America and Africa, borrowed more than they could repay. The resulting debt crisis cost the United States and other trading countries billions of dollars in lost exports.

To make themselves more competitive in the global economy, American manufacturers "downsized." They closed some plants and modernized others. Many manufacturers replaced workers with computer-operated machinery. In the automobile industry, for example, computerized robots took the place of some assembly-line workers. Displaced workers sought retraining, or took lower-paying jobs. Job opportunities shifted from blue-collar industries to white-collar high-technology companies and service work that required more education and training. In American businesses, the number of professionals, managers, technicians, and clerical and sales personnel all increased at a greater rate than industrial labor.

One of the most striking changes in the new service-industry jobs was the large increase in working women. Women took the largest share of the 12 million new service-industry jobs created during the 1980s. By the early 1990s, women workers held about 45 percent of all jobs, a substantial increase in the number of women working outside the home. Women also made inroads into managerial positions and the professions, in education, law, and medicine. Yet for the most part, women's salaries remained below men's, leading to calls for equal pay. Working women also asked employers to provide day-care centers for their children. Some companies responded to these personal needs, providing flexible hours, counseling, and family-related personal leave.

On the international front, the economic and political collapse of the Soviet Union removed the United States' largest military rival. Increasingly, however, the United States faced economic competition from Japan and the European Community. In 1992 the United States, Canada, and Mexico negotiated the North American Free Trade Agreement, making North America the world's largest free trade area. The agreement offered American manufacturers an opportunity to open factories in Mexico, where wages were lower. At the same time Mexican and Canadian markets would be open to more American products and services. President Bush promised that the agreement would create jobs and economic growth in all three counties. Labor unions protested, claiming that lowering trade barriers might mean the loss of American manufacturing jobs to Mexico. Environmentalists point-

ed out that Mexican industry operated under much less stringent regulations against pollution.

Immigration

World economic and political troubles brought a new tide of immigration to the United States. New immigration laws in 1965 had abolished the national quota system, leading to shifts in the pattern of immigration. Immigration from Europe declined, while immigration from Latin America and Asia increased dramatically.

Life of the Times

THE NEXT CENTURY

In 1992 former President Ronald Reagan noted, "While I take inspiration from the past, like most Americans, I live for the future." It has always been compelling to think about the future: What are our hopes, visions, and fears? Will science and technology advance the horizons of medicine, learning, and other fields? What new challenges and problems will arise?

What will life be like in the twenty-first century? Although no one knows for sure, analysts and scientists have offered some intriguing possibilities. Students and office workers will still toil before computers, although these new machines will respond to commands that are spoken and written as well as typed. People may wear telephones like jewelry with miniature speakers concealed behind the ears. Perhaps, too, the span of life will be greatly extended. Some experts believe that, if research on aging is successful, it is not out of the realm of possibility that some people alive today could live to be 150 or even 200 years old. In the not-too-distant future, drugs to raise human intelligence may be available.

Perhaps all—or none—of these predictions will be realized. Yet even if only some of these come true, a host of new issues arise. If drugs that boost intelligence appear, should they go to those who can afford to pay what the manufacturer charges or should the government distribute the drugs for the improvement of society?

The new immigration created special challenges for American schools. For many newcomers, English was their second language. In some school districts in the Southwest, Florida, and New York, a majority of students spoke Spanish. Schools struggled to create a balance between teaching students basic subjects in languages they understood and teaching them English.

Many of the new immigrants were refugees. Some were fleeing political persecution in such nations as Vietnam and Cuba. Others had come to escape the hardships of war-torn El Salvador and Nicaragua. Still others fled for a combination of these reasons, as did thousands of Haitians, who left both the political repression and dire poverty in their homeland and tried to sail to America in small boats.

The total of legal and illegal immigrants to the United States during the 1980s probably reached more than 1 million a year—the greatest number since the early 1900s. Many of the newcomers took low-paying jobs that most Americans would not perform.

The United States sought to stem the tide of illegal immigration without shutting the doors that had been open for generations. In 1986 Congress passed an alien amnesty act to enable immigrants who had entered the country illegally to become naturalized citizens. Those who applied and qualified were entitled to government benefits and protection. As former President Reagan pointed out in a speech in Japan:

We get new energy every year from the waves of immigrants who seek to make their lives and fortunes in our country. . . . Try convincing them that America's best days are behind her.

Examining Photographs *A Haitian woman carries her infant child from a United States Coast Guard vessel at Guantanamao Bay Naval Base. Why were many refugees forced to leave their homelands?*

Global Issues

Threats to the environment and public health caused controversy in the 1980s and 1990s. A debate arose between those who advocated environmental protection and those who favored greater development of natural resources. Environmentalists worried about such problems as acid rain, caused by gases emitted in the burning of fossil fuels. They saw acid rain kill fish, damage crops, and strip forests. On the other side, developers warned that strict laws against acid rain meant higher costs and loss of jobs.

In the early 1980s, James Watt, the Reagan administration's first Secretary of the Interior, proposed to increase offshore oil drilling and to open wilderness areas to oil and gas exploration. Watt believed these programs would help fill the nation's energy needs and reduce dependence on foreign suppliers, but environmentalists were outraged. Eventually, Watt's controversial stands and steadily escalating criticism forced his resignation.

Connections

HISTORY AND ENVIRONMENT

ENVIRONMENTAL ISSUES OF THE TWENTY-FIRST CENTURY

The industrialized world has purchased prosperity at the expense of the environment. The conflict between economic growth and environmental protection may well become the central issue of the next century.

Arctic ecology research team

The disappearing ozone layer—part of the upper atmosphere—is linked to the widespread use of chlorofluorocarbons (CFCs), commonly found in such products as aerosols and foam packaging. Ozone depletion may cause an increase in skin cancer. Another concern is global warming caused by high levels of carbon dioxide and other gases that trap heat from the sun in the atmosphere and cause a greenhouse effect. The destruction of rain forests, which absorb carbon dioxide and release oxygen, compounds the problem. Many scientists believe that global warming could cause polar ice caps to melt, raising ocean levels and flooding coastal cities.

Disposal of wastes, especially toxic and nuclear materials, will also be a continuing issue. The United States alone produces 40 million tons of toxic wastes annually.

★ ★ ★ ★ ★ ★ ★ ★ ★ ★

MAKING THE ENVIRONMENT CONNECTION

1. What is the cause of global warming?

2. How do you think future technology will affect environmental problems?

LINKING PAST AND PRESENT

3. What can individuals do to slow down the destruction of the environment?

★ ★ ★ ★ ★ ★ ★ ★ ★ ★

Concern about the environment heightened in 1989 when a tanker accident in Alaska caused the biggest oil spill in history. All sides seemed to recognize that human survival depended upon the fate of the earth's environment. Speaking for those who believed that more drastic actions were necessary, Douglas Olesen, president of an Ohio research institute, said:

So far we've focused. . . on eliminating waste only to the very end of the production line. . . . To cut waste at its source, maybe we'll have to change the way we make products. Maybe we'll even have to change the products themselves.

In 1990 Congress and President Bush reached agreement on tougher standards for automobile exhaust and other clean air hazards. But as the United States slipped into economic recession, President Bush chose to emphasize jobs over environmental protection. Vice President Quayle chaired a "Council on Competitiveness" that eliminated many regulations on business, even those that set environmental standards. Over the objections of the Environmental Protection Agency, President Bush sided with the Council and relaxed federal air pollution regulations. In 1992 the United States stood alone at the world environmental conference in Brazil, by refusing to sign a treaty to reduce global warming. The President feared implementing the treaty could hurt the American economy.

Public health was also a global issue as many nations faced epidemics of AIDS and drug abuse. AIDS (Acquired Immune Deficiency Syndrome), a blood-borne and sexually transmitted disease, is caused by a virus known as HIV. According to World Health Organization projections for the mid-to-late 1990s, there will be about 6 million new cases of AIDS and 15-20 million HIV-infected adults. Its spread in the United States, primarily among homosexual men and drug-users, led to 20,000 deaths a year during the early 1990s, including infants to which the disease was passed from their pregnant mothers. Led by former Surgeon General C. Everett Koop, the federal government launched a program to educate Americans on the dangers of AIDS. It encouraged voluntary behavioral changes that would reduce the spread of the disease.

The government also launched a war against the sale and use of illegal drugs. Troubled over the smuggling of cocaine from South America and the crime wave connected with drug selling, the Bush administration established an Office of National Drug Control Policy. The government attacked the supply of drugs by trying to halt drug smuggling and to prosecute drug sellers. It also attacked the demand by putting greater legal and social pressure on drug users.

The rising cost of medical care made health a political issue in the 1990s. An estimated 34 million Americans—most of them children and young adults—had no health insurance. Millions of others were inadequately insured. This raised two important questions: should people be able to get adequate health care regardless of their ability to pay for it? And should the federal government support some form of national health insurance? Although the recession and federal deficits made the financing of such a plan difficult, both President Bush and Democratic leaders in Congress proposed national health programs. Democrats favored a "play or pay" plan that would require employers to provide medical insurance to their employees or pay a tax to finance a government insurance program. Bush opposed national health insurance and instead proposed tax credits to help poor people pay their medical insurance premiums. He also proposed that the government help the chronically ill find insurance coverage. Political differences between the President and Congress stalled adoption of either plan.

Section Three Review

SUMMARY

Through most of the 1980s and early 1990s, the United States' trade deficit grew as foreign investments in American business and property increased. Other economic problems included the threat of loan defaults in Latin America and instability caused by underproduction in many areas of the world. Migration patterns to the United States changed. Immigration from Europe decreased, and immigration from Latin America and Asia increased. Important and long-standing global issues remained, including the environment, the spread of AIDS, and drug abuse.

CHECKING FOR UNDERSTANDING

1. **Identify** James Watt, C. Everett Koop, AIDS, acid rain, Office of National Drug Control Policy

2. **Define** trade deficit, creditor nation, debtor nation, multinational corporation

3. **Cite** two factors that contribute to the United States' trade deficit.

4. **List** two reasons for increased immigration to the United States.

5. **Contrast** Reagan's and Bush's environmental policies.

THINKING CRITICALLY

6. **Evaluating Tactics** Do you think the government's efforts should be focused on stopping the flow of drugs from other countries or on reducing the demand for drugs in this county? Explain your answer.

CONNECTIONS:
HISTORY AND ECONOMICS

7. **Making Judgments** Weigh the pros and cons of American companies moving factories to foreign countries in order to take advantage of lower wages. Consider in your evaluation the needs of business to be competitive and the needs of American workers.

A Changing World

SETTING THE SCENE

Surely, the same old struggle for dominance can be found in this new order....But the quest is no longer for geopolitical power...but for standard of living: the ability of a nation to provide its citizens security, comfort, opportunity, progress, and dreams.
—MICHAEL WOLF
Where We Stand, 1991

Section Focus

Despite efforts to invigorate the economy, the United States faced its worst recession since the early 1980s. In addition to solving economic woes, Americans sought answers to problems in education and with the environment and public health.

Objectives

After studying this section, you should be able to:
- discuss the reasons for discord between the legislative and executive branches.
- identify the economic problems facing the nation during the early 1990s.

Unlike foreign affairs, where President Bush acted decisively to meet the challenges of the new world order, he was accused of wavering leadership in domestic affairs. Bush took office promising to work towards a "kinder and gentler" nation. As President he first adopted an easygoing approach to the Democratic majorities in Congress in the hope that the two arms of government could work more closely together. This approach did not work. The legislative agendas of Congress and the White House were so different that compromise was difficult. President Bush complained that he extended his hand to the congressional leaders "—and they bit it."

Divided Government

When George Bush was elected President, he faced large opposition party majorities in both houses of Congress. Neither Bush nor the Democratic leaders showed much willingness to give in to the other. Congress ignored or drastically changed many of the President's proposals. The President, in turn, vetoed many bills, knowing that the Democrats lacked the two-thirds vote needed to override his vetoes. The executive and legislative branches of the government became gridlocked over such issues as reducing the federal deficit, reforming campaign financing, improving public education, and reinvigorating the economy. Each side blamed the other for the gridlock, and public approval ratings for both the President and Congress fell sharply.

High federal deficits forced President Bush to break his campaign pledge of "no new taxes." When budget deficits rose to record levels of more than $300 billion, Bush conceded that some revenue increases would be necessary to cut the deficit. In 1990, after weeks of tense negotiations with congressional leaders, the Bush administration emerged with an agreement to make deep cuts in Medicare and military spending, while raising gasoline, tobacco, and other user taxes. Strong opposition to the plan emerged from the public and from conservative Republicans in Congress, causing the first budget compromise to be defeated. After further wrangling, a new tax bill was enacted. Criticism of this accord from conservatives later caused the President to admit that he had made a mistake.

The budget crisis strengthened the perception that the President's domestic programs lacked direction. Although President

Bush declared a "War on Drugs," the administration's programs could not stem the rising tide of drug-related crimes. Bush had also pledged to be the "Education President" and improve the environment. Yet the deficits left little funding available for new programs. The recession forced states to make deep cuts in educational spending, and the Bush administration increasingly opposed environmental protection regulations that might cut jobs.

A Persistent Recession

The Reagan era had promised national economic growth and celebrated the accumulation of personal wealth. At the end of the 1980s, such popular books as Tom Wolfe's novel, *The Bonfire of the Vanities,* and Kevin Phillips' study, *The Politics of Rich and Poor,* prompted Americans to reconsider their preoccupation with money and luxury. Tax cuts and deregulation of business had spurred economic activity, but much of it proved to be nonproductive. Instead of creating savings, it produced debt. Instead of healthy investments and industrial productivity, much of the new wealth went into everything from yachts and expensive imported cars to real estate and the construction of endless office complexes and shopping malls.

During the early 1990s the national economy grew more slowly than at any time since the end of World War II. Among other factors, sharply rising oil prices following Iraq's invasion of Kuwait threw the American economy into a recession that spread to every region of the country. State governments, already hard hit by cutbacks in federal aid to the states, faced a dilemma: raise taxes or cut services. Unable to decide on either unpopular course, California reached a budget deadlock that forced it to issue "IOUs" to its creditors. Voters expressed their anger at governors who raised taxes. At the same time, however, citizens did not want their basic services, such as state education and health programs, cut.

The recession persisted longer than expected, partly because of consumer and corporate debts incurred during the 1980s. Deregulation had allowed banks and savings and loans to lend money more freely. Corporations funded mergers with "junk bonds" that placed high interest rates on the repayment of debt. Consumers ran up large debts on credit cards and home mortgages. In like manner, the federal government spent far more than it received in tax revenue. Eventually, these debts limited the ability of consumers, corporations, and the government to spend and invest. Rather than add to the economy through new purchases, consumers needed to pay off old debts. Companies that financed expansion through "junk bonds" had higher debts and fewer resources for investment. With business no longer expanding, vast new office space went vacant. Banks that had loaned money to construct the office buildings were not being repaid and had to cut back on new loans or close down altogether. Federal and state governments spent an ever-larger share of their tax revenues just on paying the interest on their debts.

Banks and savings and loans failed at rates unseen since the Great Depression. Well-known airlines went out of business. Famous department stores filed for bankruptcy. Automobile manufacturers and other industries announced plant closings and major layoffs of workers. As consumer confidence sank, President Bush expressed his frustration with the growing mood of pessimism. He pointed out that stock prices were high, inflation was low, and that unemployment had been worse in previous recessions. Still, people felt insecure and feared that their standard of living could decline.

Assuring the nation that recovery was just around the corner, President Bush asked Congress to cut the tax on **capital gains**—profits made on investments—to stimulate investment. Democrats charged that capital gains cuts benefited only the wealthy. Democrats urged instead that the government raise taxes on the wealthy to permit tax cuts for the middle class. Because neither side could move without the other, the continued gridlock between the President and Congress hampered efforts to deal with the recession.

To deal with federal deficits, the President favored constitutional amendments requiring a balanced budget and a **line-item veto** (permitting the President to veto a single portion of an appropriations bill without vetoing the entire bill). His opponents viewed a balanced budget amendment as too restrictive on govern-

ment's ability to act, and the line-item veto as weakening Congress's "power of the purse." Repeatedly, the amendments failed to gain passage.

By mid-1992 almost 10 million American workers were unemployed. Another 6 million workers were **underemployed**—holding part-time jobs while looking for full-time work. As unemployment rose, many people migrated from one state to another in search of jobs, and some found themselves among the ranks of the homeless. Homeless people included battered women, runaway children, alcoholics, drug abusers, deinstitutionalized mental patients, and people lacking family support. Homelessness reflected rising rents, lower wages for unskilled workers, and the urgent need for low-cost housing programs. Estimates of the number of homeless people in American cities ranged as high as 3 million.

The recession, poverty, and homelessness hit particularly hard at African Americans living in inner cities. Racial tensions ignited after four white police officers in Los Angeles were acquitted of beating an African American man, despite a video-

Examining Photographs *The failure of many savings and loan institutions in the late 1980s and early 1990s caused Americans to worry about the safety of their money. What were major causes of the financial crisis?*

Examining Photographs *The Senate delayed the confirmation of Clarence Thomas to the Supreme Court when University of Oklahoma law professor Anita Hill accused Thomas of sexual misconduct. What was the outcome of the confirmation hearing?*

tape taken of the beating. Los Angeles erupted into days of arson, looting, and rioting that claimed more lives than had the 1965 riots in Watts. Conservatives blamed the Los Angeles riots on welfare programs that weakened the family and individual initiative, while liberals blamed the government's general neglect of inner cities during the Reagan-Bush years.

Election of 1992

After victory in the Persian Gulf War, President Bush's reelection seemed assured. Several leading Democrats declined to run against him. The lengthening recession, however, raised new doubts about Bush's leadership, causing new challengers to enter the race. At the same time, public opinion turned against all **incumbents**—those holding office—and Washington "insiders."

Voters blamed incumbents for the recession, budget deficits, and government gridlock. Revelations that many members of the House of Representatives had repeatedly bounced checks at the House bank outraged many citizens. An unusually large number of representatives decided not to run for reelection or were defeated in primary elections. Further angered when members of Congress voted to raise their own salaries, many political leaders and citizens took action. As a result, the states ratified a 202-year-old amendment to the Constitution in 1992. Originally proposed by James Madison, the Twenty-seventh Amendment forbids any congressional pay raise from taking effect until after the next election, giving the voters a chance to act.

Many of the candidates seeking office in 1992 were women. Some of them ran in reaction to the furor surrounding one of President Bush's Supreme Court appointees—Clarence Thomas. When Bush had nominated Thomas in 1991, one of the justice's former coworkers, law professor Anita Hill, testified before the Senate Judiciary Committee that Thomas had sexually harassed her. Thomas adamantly denied the charge. Constituents flooded the capital with phone calls and telegrams expressing their opinion. The Senate narrowly confirmed Thomas to the Supreme Court, but many Americans were angry. Noting the absence of any women on the Senate Judiciary Committee, and that only 2 of the 100 senators were women, they argued that "2 percent is not enough." Building on the rising discontent, more women ran for the Senate and other political office. As "outsiders" in politics, women candidates drew support from both women and men who were fed up with the status quo and demanded change.

In the 1992 presidential race, President Bush faced a challenge from his own party, when former White House aide and political commentator Pat Buchanan ran against the President in the Republican primaries. The staunchly conservative Buchanan attacked Bush for breaking his pledge of "no new taxes." Although he garnered as much as 30 percent of the vote in some primaries, Buchanan was never able to defeat Bush. Nevertheless, Buchanan's strong showing demonstrated the weakness of the President's support among conservatives. The leading Democratic candidates included former Massachusetts Senator Paul Tsongas, who advocated reducing the federal deficit, former California governor Jerry Brown, who called for sweeping reforms in campaign spending, and Arkansas governor Bill Clinton, who advocated relief for middle-class taxpayers. Early in the primaries, the press raised questions about Clinton's character and his failure to serve in the military during the Vietnam War. Yet after Clinton won impressive victories in the southern state primaries and in such pivotal industrial states as Illinois and New York, he emerged as the front-runner.

A third-party challenge appeared when Texas billionaire H. Ross Perot promised to run as an independent if volunteers could collect enough petitions to get his name on all 50 state ballots. The outpouring of volunteers again showed the public's unhappiness with the 2 major parties and a widespread demand for change.

After years of division, the Democrats united at their convention to nominate Governor Clinton for President and Tennessee Senator Albert Gore, Jr., for Vice President. Anticipating a Republican campaign theme of "family values," both Clinton and Gore talked of the personal hardships and tragedies they had overcome. The Republican convention adopted a hard-line platform designed to hold the support of their conservative wing but offered little to moderates in the party, particularly on abortion rights. To solidify his reelection bid, President Bush asked Secretary of State James Baker to return to the White House as chief of staff and to help manage his campaign. Together they pledged a campaign that stressed America's need to be safe and strong both at home and abroad, integrating military and diplomatic strength with economic security. "The key to America's growth, expansion, and innovation," said Baker, "has always been America's openness to trade, to investment, to ideas, and to people."

Bill Clinton agreed with President Bush on many areas of foreign policy and had supported the Persian Gulf War. Clinton, however, charged that Bush lacked "a vision of our role in this new era." In Clinton's view, Bush too often had sided "with familiar tyrants rather than those who would overthrow them—with the old geography of repression rather than a new map of freedom." Bush's supporters responded by stressing Bush's leadership during the end of the cold war, a time of "historic changes that have made the world and country much safer."

Linking foreign policy with domestic issues, Clinton painted the recession as the President's "most glaring foreign policy failure." He pledged to revive the

Examining Photographs *The three major presidential candidates, Bill Clinton, H. Ross Perot, and the incumbent, George Bush, met in a series of televised debates during the 1992 campaign. Why did many voters turn against incumbents?*

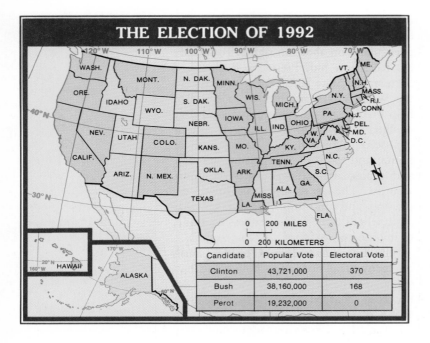

THE ELECTION OF 1992

Candidate	Popular Vote	Electoral Vote
Clinton	43,721,000	370
Bush	38,160,000	168
Perot	19,232,000	0

Examining Maps *Bill Clinton's victory in the 1992 presidential election placed a Democrat in the White House for the first time in 12 years. How many electoral votes did Clinton receive?*

by H. Ross Perot. Clinton received less than a majority—43 percent. Bush captured 38 percent and Perot, 19 percent—the highest for any third-party candidate since 1912.

Although Republicans gained seats in the House of Representatives for the first time since 1984, the Democrats retained control of both houses of Congress. Voters defeated 24 incumbents in House races and 3 running for reelection to the Senate. Even more significant, voters elected a record number of racial and ethnic minorities. Among those elected to the House were Jay Kim, the first Korean American, and Nydia Velazquez, the first Puerto Rican woman. Ben Nighthorse Campbell was the first Native American in the Senate in more than 60 years. Four women won election to the Senate, bringing the total to six in all. New Senators included Carol Moseley Braun of Illinois, the first African American woman Senator, and Barbara Boxer and Dianne Feinstein of California.

economy, so that the United States could continue "to play our proper role as leader of the world." Clinton called for better planning for conversion of defense production to civilian production, while Bush charged that Clinton would cut defense spending too severely.

Clinton Wins

The recession dominated the campaign. Clinton took credit for winning passage of "sweeping economic and educational reforms" as governor of Arkansas. President Bush told voters, that having set the world in order during his first term, he intended to set about rebuilding the nation. Blaming the Democrats' long control of Congress for the gridlock in government, Bush called for the election of a Republican Congress.

About 104 million Americans—the highest total ever—voted in the 1992 presidential election. Garnering 370 of the 538 electoral votes, Clinton rode to victory by winning states in the Midwest, South, and Far West that have voted for the Republican candidate in the last several elections. Clinton's popular vote margin was slimmer due to a strong showing

AMERICAN PORTRAITS

JAY KIM
(1939-

Voters elected a record number of women and minorities to Congress in 1992. Among the newcomers was Jay Kim, the first Korean American elected to the House of Representatives.

The House was not Kim's first foray into politics. Active at the local level, he served as mayor of Diamond Bar, California. After members of Congress voted themselves a pay raise—a move Kim adamantly opposed—he decided to run for a House seat. Kim defeated five opponents in the Republican primary and then won a solid victory in the general election.

Operation Restore Hope

By late 1992 anarchy ruled the east African nation of Somalia, plagued by a civil war for more than 3 years. Gangs of rival clans battled for power while civilians starved. In December 1992, President George Bush, acting in concert with the UN, sent more than 28,000 American troops to pacify the troubled land and provide food to the starving people. At first the Americans, along with French, Canadian, and other international forces, encountered no opposition, but the threat of violence loomed. Despite the uncertainty of the mission, President-elect Clinton praised Bush for "taking the lead in this important humanitarian effort."

The Triumph of Democracy

The collapse of the Soviet Union and emergence of democracies in Russia and Eastern Europe made it clear that the ideals of the American Revolution remain valid. A worker participating in the general strike that precipitated democracy in Czechoslovakia began his speech by quoting the Declaration of Independence. Nelson Mandela, long imprisoned in South Africa because of his opposition to **apartheid**—or racial segregation—told a joint session of Congress, "We could not have known of your Declaration of Independence and not elected to join in the struggle to guarantee the people life, liberty and the pursuit of happiness."

A Chinese sudent in Tiananmen Square invoked a goal expressed by Abraham Lincoln more than a century earlier. When asked why she would wish to go out and "argue with a tank," she said, "Government of the people, by the people, and for the people." Americans continue to take hope today like Lincoln in 1863:

[T]hat this nation, under God, shall have a new birth of freedom; and that government of the people, by the people, for the people, shall not perish from the earth.

SUMMARY

President Bush's decisive actions in the Persian Gulf War drew enthusiastic support. In sharp contrast, government was stymied in solving the economic woes plaguing the nation. Differences between the Bush administration and the Democratic-controlled Congress grew so acute that both sides had trouble compromising on taxes, the deficit, and economic planning. As the 1992 election drew near, the President faced challenges from within his own party as well as from Democratic and independent candidates. Voters elected the Democratic candidate, Bill Clinton, as the new President.

CHECKING FOR UNDERSTANDING

1. **Identify** Clarence Thomas, Anita Hill, Pat Buchanan, Bill Clinton, Nelson Mandela

2. **Define** capital gains, line-item veto, underemployed, incumbent, apartheid

3. **List** three issues over which Congress and President Bush disagreed.

4. **Discuss** the reason for the decision to raise taxes.

5. **Discuss** the details of the Twenty-seventh Amendment.

THINKING CRITICALLY

6. **Identifying Alternatives** In your opinion, should Presidents concentrate more on domestic issues than on foreign policy? Explain your answer.

CONNECTIONS: HISTORY AND GOVERNMENT

7. **Demonstrating Reasoned Judgment** Many Presidents have had to work with a Congress dominated by the opposition party. How is the process of governing affected if Congress and the President are from different political parties? What attributes are necessary to avoid a deadlock?

★ ★ ★ ★ ★ ★ ★ ★ ★ ★ ★ ★ ★ ★ ★ ★

★ Chapter 36 Review ★

★ Summary

Long plagued by an inefficient economy, the Soviet people hoped for a better standard of living. Mikhail Gorbachev's restructuring of the Soviet Union's economic and political systems led to demands for even greater change. The Soviet reform movement was also embraced by other Eastern European nations. Finally, the Soviet Union itself crumbled. Some of the former Soviet republics entered the new Commonwealth of Independent States. The rapidly changing face of Eastern Europe created challenges and opportunities for American foreign policymakers.

United States leaders faced another challenge, this time in the Middle East, when Iraq invaded and occupied Kuwait in August 1990. After nearly 6 months of negotiations and economic pressure, Iraqi leader Saddam Hussein showed no signs of removing his troops from Kuwait. Finally, in January 1991, forces from a coalition of more than 25 nations defeated Iraqi forces in the Persian Gulf War and liberated Kuwait.

Beginning in the 1970s, the United States experienced a new problem—a trade deficit. The American people and government and business leaders pondered ways to deal with the deficit and other economic and social problems that troubled the nation. These included the job market, salaries, environmental concerns, AIDS, drug abuse, and medical care.

Federal government attempts to address these problems produced few long-lasting solutions. Partisan politics played a role in the deadlock. The Bush administration and the Democratic-controlled Congress often were at odds and found it difficult to compromise.

★ Using Vocabulary

Assume that you are a magazine reporter covering the state of the economy today. Write an article detailing your findings, using the following vocabulary terms:

trade deficit	creditor nation
capital gains	debtor nation
multinational corporations	

★ Reviewing Facts

1. **Discuss** how Mikhail Gorbachev tried to revive the Soviet economy.

2. **Identify** the Commonwealth of Independent States.

3. **State** the problems that faced the Soviet Union and Eastern Europe in changing from state-controlled to market-controlled economies.

4. **Describe** the problems between Kuwait and Iraq.

5. **Describe** the tactics President Bush used to try to force Iraq to withdraw from Kuwait.

6. **Discuss** the problems American workers faced in the 1980s and 1990s.

7. **Summarize** what the North American Free Trade Agreement is expected to do.

8. **Describe** how the United States tried to stop illegal immigration.

9. **Compare** the different tax cuts offered by President Bush and by Democratic leaders.

10. **Identify** two reasons for the anti-incumbent mood of the nation during the early 1990s.

11. **Discuss** the significance of the presidential and congressional election of 1992.

★ Understanding Concepts

REFORM AND CHANGE

1. How does the role of the United States government in the economy today compare to its role in the early 1900s?

2. How did the countries of Eastern Europe respond to the changes made by the Soviet Union under Gorbachev?

CHALLENGES

1. What conflicts have prevented the United States from implementing a clear and consistent energy policy?

2. Why is it difficult for the United States government to reduce spending or raise taxes to balance the budget?

★ Thinking Critically

1. **Demonstrating Reasoned Judgment** Do you think there might be growing resentment against immigrants during difficult economic times? Why or why not?

2. **Synthesizing Information** Are any of the problems the United States faces in the last decade of the twentieth century truly "new"? Explain.

3. **Making Comparisons** Are economic problems, defense problems, or environmental problems the most critical issues facing the world today? Explain your answer.

★ Writing About History

ARGUMENTATION

Refer to the description of how to write an argumentation essay in the History Writer's Handbook in the Appendix of this book. Your teacher will give you more specific instructions on the essay's length and the assignment's due date.

Write an argument that supports or an argument that opposes free trade between nations. State the controversy or problem clearly and give your position or your solution to the problem. Gather relevant facts and statistics that support your position and refute opposing positions.

★ Learning Cooperatively

When Iraq invaded Kuwait in August 1990, Americans compared the actions of Iraqi leader Saddam Hussein to Hitler's aggression before World War II. Many Arabs, however, supported Hussein. Work with a partner and imagine that you each represent your nation in a debate before the United Nations General Assembly. First decide who will represent the United States and who will be the Iraqi delegate. Then prepare a statement that explains your nation's viewpoint and justifies its actions. Exchange statements with your partner and write a rebuttal to each other's point of view.

★ Mastering Skills

DEVELOPING A GLOBAL POINT OF VIEW

Americans who travel to other countries are surprised to find that people there often have points of view quite different from their own. This is because points of view in every culture are affected by the values of that culture, which are the result of its religious beliefs, history, economic conditions, or even the propaganda of its leaders. Mass communications are making various points of view better known in the world, but that may not change long-established differences among peoples.

In an interdependent world, it is vital to understand these different points of view—to develop a broad perspective, or a global point of view. This may not change one's personal values, but it helps each person to understand the values of persons in other cultures and the reasons for any differences in point of view.

To develop a global point of view, follow these guidelines:

- Become informed by talking with others, listening to news broadcasts, and by reading newspapers, magazines, and books.

- In your listening and reading identify individuals or groups from other nations who express points of view different from those you hold.

- Consider why each person or group may hold its point of view.

Example Read the following statement made by Soviet Foreign Minister Eduard Shevardnadze to the Soviet Congress of People's Deputies in December 1990, after Iraq seized Kuwait, and see how the guidelines have been followed.

"[W]e have no moral right to reconcile ourselves to aggression and the annexation of a small defenseless country....charges are made that the Foreign Minister plans to land troops in the Persian Gulf....Nobody is going to send...even a single representative of the Soviet armed forces there."

(As foreign minister, Shevardnadze was stating his government's official point of view. The Soviet Union condemned Iraq's aggression but did not commit troops against Iraq. Internal problems in the Soviet Union and a concern about its future relations with Iraq affected the Soviet point of view. The United Nations supported the use of force against Iraq, but each nation acted in its own perceived interests. Some responded militarily. A few supported Iraq's leader, Saddam Hussein.)

Practice Select a news article from a recent foreign newspaper. Apply these guidelines to the point of view presented.

★ ★ ★ Unit 10 Digest ★ ★

During the second half of the twentieth century, the United States adjusted to a complex and changing world. The nation made progress toward solving difficult social, economic, and political problems at home and abroad.

Chapter 32
New Frontiers

In the 1950s African Americans renewed their fight for full equality and an end to segregation and discrimination. A quiet pioneer of the civil rights movement was Rosa Parks, who in 1956 refused to give her seat on a Montgomery bus to a white man. Dr. Martin Luther King, Jr., emerged as the leader of a nonviolent protest against unjust segregation laws.

In 1961 the presidency passed from Dwight D. Eisenhower to John F. Kennedy. Kennedy wanted to stimulate the economy and to improve life for the poor but he moved cautiously on civil-rights legislation.

Foreign policy, however, soon became Kennedy's major concern. Like his predecessors, he wanted to contain communism. In Cuba Kennedy approved of a secret invasion attempt, which failed. When the Soviet Union then placed missiles in Cuba, Kennedy's resolve in avoiding nuclear war earned him respect worldwide. He also created the Peace Corps, a program that has sent thousands of volunteers to work in developing countries.

Berlin, Laos, and Vietnam also became trouble spots. In Berlin the Communists built a wall dividing the city when the United States and its allies refused to withdraw. Kennedy, however, was able to negotiate a test-ban treaty with the Soviets. In Indochina, Kennedy increased the number of American military advisers to help counter the communist threat. Kennedy was assassinated by Lee Harvey Oswald before many of his goals could be realized.

Chapter 33
The Vietnam Era

Lyndon B. Johnson, Kennedy's successor, vowed to carry out Kennedy's ideals. He persuaded Congress to pass the 1964 Civil Rights Act, the strongest act of its kind since Reconstruction, and the 1965 Voting Rights Act, which did away with literacy tests to qualify voters. Johnson also waged a "war on poverty" that helped poor people help themselves.

Johnson was less successful in foreign affairs. The 1964 Gulf of Tonkin Resolution permitted the number of troops in Vietnam to escalate.

As the war raged abroad, however, social unrest brewed at home. Many African Americans, dissatisfied with the slow progress of civil rights, proclaimed "black power." Students, too, became more militant in their antiwar protests. Many youth rebelled against the draft and pressures for social conformity. They dropped out, forming a "counter culture."

Social turmoil intensified during 1968. In Vietnam, the Tet offensive demonstrated that the Americans were far from victory. At home assassins murdered Dr. Martin Luther King, Jr., and Robert F. Kennedy—John Kennedy's brother and a presidential hopeful. Violence marred college campuses and the Democratic convention. Republican candidate Richard Nixon, promising to "bring the nation together," was elected President.

Chapter 34
An Imperial Presidency

Richard Nixon had great success in foreign policy. He and Soviet leaders discussed the Arab-Israeli conflict and strategic arms limitations. These negotiations culminated in the Moscow summit between Nixon and Soviet Premier Brezhnev. Nixon also visited and established more open relations with China.

The Vietnam War, however, eroded Nixon's credibility at home. He expanded the war into neighboring Cambodia and Laos to stop enemy lines of supply. This effort failed while antiwar protests increased. Finally, Nixon opted for "Vietnamization," the withdrawal of American troops and replacing them with Vietnamese soldiers.

At home, the war was not the only issue on American minds. Although an equal rights amendment failed, many women began to examine their traditional roles as wives and mothers. Migrant farm workers, many of whom were Mexican Americans, organized for better wages and benefits. American Indians also displayed a new urgency in demanding their rights.

Along with a new social awareness, the presidency was changed as well. When Nixon was reelected in 1972 with 61 percent of the vote, few suspected he would be forced out of office. Soon, however, evidence surfaced of illegal tactics used by his reelection campaign and his personal involvement in a cover-up of the Watergate break-in. Nixon resigned rather than face impeachment charges. Gerald Ford then assumed the presidency with a promise to restore integrity to the office.

Chapter 35
A Search
for New Solutions

After Vietnam and Watergate, Americans wanted a change in leadership. Outsider Jimmy Carter barely defeated Gerald Ford in the 1976 election. Carter's domestic policy focused on the energy problem. Poor relations with Congress, however, caused his efforts to falter.

Carter's weak leadership at home contrasted sharply with his bold initiatives in foreign policy. He won Senate ratification of a new Panama Canal treaty and took a tough stand against countries that violated human rights. His greatest triumph was negotiation of a peace treaty between Israel and Egypt. Elsewhere, however, Iran seized American hostages and Carter was unable to secure their release.

Republican Ronald Reagan soundly defeated Carter in the 1980 election. Reagan's administration was very popular. He cut taxes and dramatically reduced government spending on social programs. Americans blamed the President for a brief economic downturn but also credited him with the recovery that followed.

During Reagan's second term, he strengthened the space program, increased defense spending, and improved relations with the Soviet Union. His hands-off administrative style, however, led to financial mismanagement and an arms-for-hostage scandal.

George Bush succeeded Reagan as President. His domestic policies differed only slightly from the Reagan years. In 1990, however, he sent American troops to the Middle East to liberate Kuwait, an oil-rich country taken over by Iraq.

Chapter 36
Toward a New Century

In an extremely short period of time during 1991, the Soviet Union was swept away by the unforeseen series of events. While the Soviet Union no longer existed, profound changes heralded an uncertain future in Eastern Europe. The world faced another crisis in the Middle East when Iraqi troops invaded Kuwait in August 1990. The following January the United States and coalition forces launched an attack that reduced Iraq's military capabilities and liberated Kuwait.

Global economic issues included the debt crisis in developing nations and emerging market economies in countries long under communist control. The economy was a major reason for increased immigration to the United States. Environmentalists struggled with opponents who favored greater use of natural resources. Public health issues, such as the AIDS epidemic and drug abuse, continue to take their toll and also demand attention. After 12 years of Republican rule, voters elected Democrat Bill Clinton in 1992.

SYNTHESIZING UNIT THEMES

RELATING IDEAS

1. What political, social, and economic issues concerned Americans during the 1960s and 1970s?

IDENTIFYING TRENDS

2. How has technology changed Americans as they approach the twenty-first century?

MAKING COMPARISONS

3. Compare the foreign policy successes and failures of Richard Nixon and Jimmy Carter.

★ Analyzing Unit Themes

CIVIL RIGHTS AND LIBERTIES

1. How have the goals of the civil rights movement evolved over the past 40 years? Give examples of an event for each goal.

2. In the 1950s most women worked in the home. By the 1990s more than half worked outside the home. What information supports whether or not women's rights kept pace with their changing economic role?

CONFLICT AND COOPERATION

3. Which events during the past four decades helped create a spirit of cooperation between the United States and the Soviet Union? Which events represented low points in their relations?

4. The Cuban missile crisis, the Vietnam War, and American support of the Nicaraguan *contras* are events from different eras. Explain how each event represented similarities in foreign policy.

CULTURAL DIVERSITY

5. How have immigration and increased global interdependence contributed to a more culturally diverse and sensitive American society?

U.S. ROLE IN WORLD AFFAIRS

6. Why has the United States' relationship with foreign countries become more interdependent during the past four decades?

★ Reviewing Chronology

Arrange the following items in chronological order.

a. Americans taken hostage in Iran
b. Arab oil embargo
c. *Brown v. Board of Education*
d. Cuban missile crisis
e. Gulf of Tonkin Resolution
f. Kennedy elected president
g. March on Washington
h. Nixon's visit to China
i. Operation Desert Storm
j. Strategic Defense Initiative
k. Tet offensive
l. Watts riot

★ Linking Past and Present

Making Comparisons   In 1990 East and West Germany were reunified, the Berlin Wall came down, and democratic governments blossomed in Eastern Europe. Compare these events to those that created the cold war. Would you say the cold war is definitely over? Why?

★ Demonstrating Citizenship

Acquiring and Using Information   In some communities citizens can "plug in" to local government, using computers to send letters to and ask questions directly of their city-government representatives. How can such technology make for better citizen involvement? Make a list of questions you would like answered. How would you assess the impact of technology on elections and the democratic process in general?

★ Interpreting Illustrations

Sunrise by David Em, 1985. Represented by Spieckerman Associates, San Francisco.

The picture above was created with the help of a computer. In the 1990s computers are used increasingly in photography, animated film, and fine art.

Study the picture, then answer the questions that follow.

1. How does computer generated or assisted art differ from traditional artistic methods?

2. Do you think artists from the past would be critical of the use of computers to make art? Explain your answer.

★ Unit 10 Review ★

★ Thinking Globally

1. Predicting Outcomes In 1992 western European countries will become a single economic entity—the European Community. This confederation will become one of the most powerful trading blocs in the world. What ramifications do you believe this development will have on the United States' economy?

2. Analyzing Trends Computers and telecommunications make it possible for students around the globe to interact with each other, thereby creating a "global classroom." For example, using an international computer network, students in Japan and the United States could work together on a cooperative research project. What benefits do you see from learning in a "global classroom"?

★ Relating Geography and History

REGIONS: GLOBALIZATION

Communication and transportation networks have brought once-distant regions closer together, allowing people to interact quickly and easily. At one time, regions were separated by oceans, mountains, and deserts, which were also barriers to communication and interaction. These barriers have fallen to telephone networks and communication satellites. Regions still exist, but the world has taken on a more global dimension.

Answer the questions that follow.

1. Explain how advances in telecommunications technology and information processing have changed the way humans interact worldwide.

2. Describe how increased global interaction affected regional democratic movements in Eastern Europe and China.

★ Practicing Skills

INTERPRETING MILITARY MAPS

Refer to the skills lesson on Interpreting Military Maps on page 1001 to help you practice this map skill.

Draw your own military map showing the area of conflict between Iraq and the United States-led coalition allies during 1991. Use newsmagazines from 1991 as reference. Show as much of the region as you need to illustrate the various military maneuvers that took place. Include a map key to explain symbols and other information on the map.

When you have completed your military map, answer the questions that follow.

1. What countries are shown on the map?

2. What time period is covered?

3. Who controls which areas?

4. What offensives are shown?

5. What sequence of events took place?

INTERPRETING POINT OF VIEW

Refer to the skills lesson on Interpreting Point of View on page 1011 to help you practice this critical thinking skill.

Below is an excerpt from a recent speech by J. Richard Munro, Co-Chairman of Time Warner, Inc. Read the excerpt, and answer the questions from page 1011.

…Outside the U.S. there are very influential people who want America to stop exporting so many media and entertainment products.…A growing protectionist sentiment threatens to add new restrictions to those already in place.

…Last year, the European Economic Community decided that, starting in 1993, at least 51 percent of all television programming in member nations must be of European origin.

…The explanation that's given for this new and improved protectionism is almost always the same: American cultural imperialism. For some it's become a kind of mantra, conjuring up images of a colossus busy imposing its culture on one people after another.

…it is precisely because of this insistent distortion of what is really occurring that we must be clear about a few fundamentals.

First, American culture is not an imperialistic export being shoved down the throats of unwilling colonists.

…We require no nation, province or individual to buy our magazines, watch our TV programs, attend our movies, or listen to our records.

…Yet those who perceive that the world's old ways are being overthrown aren't hallucinating.…Culturally and economically, we are being drawn together as never before.

But if there is a culprit in this, it isn't America. It's technology.

Appendix

Atlas Key

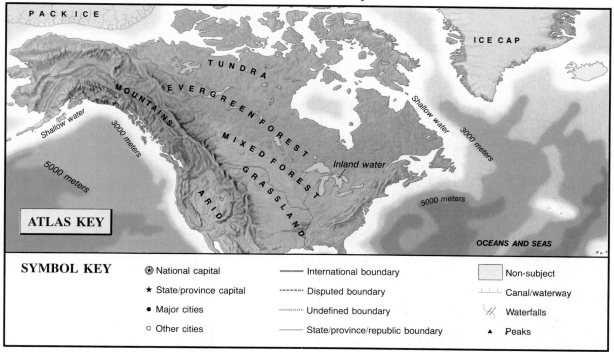

SYMBOL KEY			
⊛ National capital	—— International boundary	▭ Non-subject
★ State/province capital	┈┈┈ Disputed boundary	┴┴┴ Canal/waterway
● Major cities	┈┈┈ Undefined boundary	⤫ Waterfalls
○ Other cities	—— State/province/republic boundary	▲ Peaks

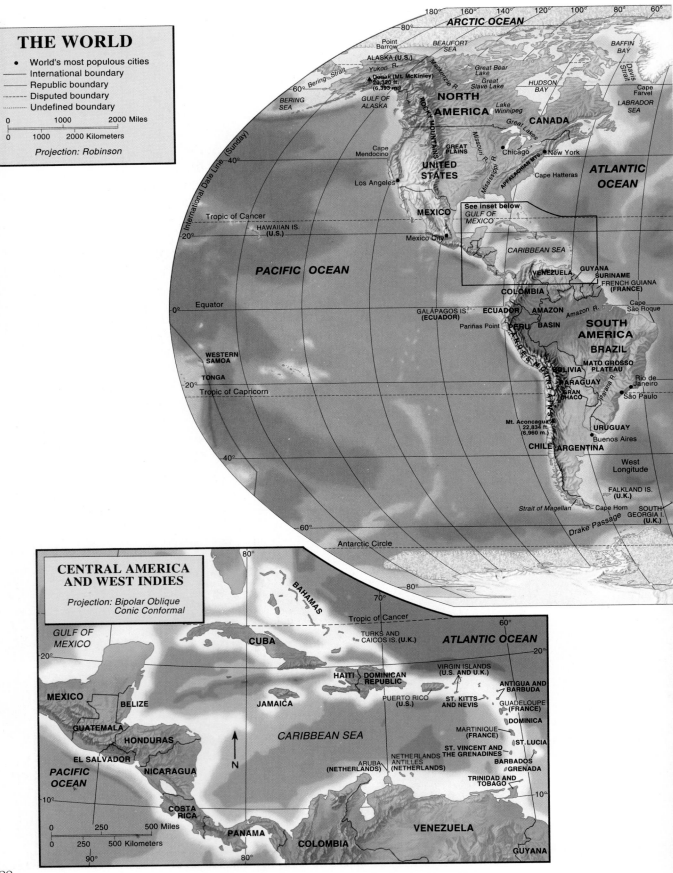

THE WORLD

- • World's most populous cities
- International boundary
- Republic boundary
- Disputed boundary
- Undefined boundary

0 1000 2000 Miles
0 1000 2000 Kilometers

Projection: Robinson

ARCTIC OCEAN

BEAUFORT SEA

BAFFIN BAY

Point Barrow

ALASKA (U.S.)

Yukon R.

Denali (Mt. McKinley)
20,320 ft.
(6,393 m.)

Bering Strait

BERING SEA

GULF OF ALASKA

Mackenzie R.

Great Bear Lake

Great Slave Lake

HUDSON BAY

Cape Farvel

Davis Strait

LABRADOR SEA

NORTH AMERICA

CANADA

Lake Winnipeg

Great Lakes

ROCKY MOUNTAINS

GREAT PLAINS

Missouri R.

Mississippi R.

Chicago

New York

APPALACHIAN MTS.

UNITED STATES

Los Angeles

Cape Mendocino

Cape Hatteras

ATLANTIC OCEAN

MEXICO

See inset below
GULF OF MEXICO

Tropic of Cancer

HAWAIIAN IS.
(U.S.)

Mexico City

CARIBBEAN SEA

VENEZUELA

GUYANA

SURINAME

FRENCH GUIANA
(FRANCE)

COLOMBIA

PACIFIC OCEAN

Equator

GALÁPAGOS IS.
(ECUADOR)

ECUADOR

AMAZON

Amazon R.

Cape São Roque

Pariñas Point

PERU

BASIN

SOUTH AMERICA

BRAZIL

WESTERN SAMOA

MATO GROSSO PLATEAU

TONGA

BOLIVIA

Rio de Janeiro

PARAGUAY

Paraná R.

São Paulo

GRAN CHACO

Tropic of Capricorn

Mt. Aconcagua
22,834 ft.
(6,960 m.)

URUGUAY

ANDES MOUNTAINS

Buenos Aires

CHILE ARGENTINA

West Longitude

FALKLAND IS.
(U.K.)

Strait of Magellan

Cape Horn

SOUTH GEORGIA I.
(U.K.)

Drake Passage

Antarctic Circle

International Date Line (Sunday)

CENTRAL AMERICA AND WEST INDIES

Projection: Bipolar Oblique Conic Conformal

GULF OF MEXICO

BAHAMAS

Tropic of Cancer

CUBA

TURKS AND CAICOS IS. (U.K.)

ATLANTIC OCEAN

MEXICO

BELIZE

HAITI

DOMINICAN REPUBLIC

VIRGIN ISLANDS
(U.S. AND U.K.)

ANTIGUA AND BARBUDA

JAMAICA

PUERTO RICO
(U.S.)

ST. KITTS AND NEVIS

GUADELOUPE
(FRANCE)

GUATEMALA

DOMINICA

HONDURAS

CARIBBEAN SEA

MARTINIQUE
(FRANCE)

ST. LUCIA

EL SALVADOR

N

ST. VINCENT AND THE GRENADINES

BARBADOS

NICARAGUA

ARUBA
(NETHERLANDS)

NETHERLANDS ANTILLES
(NETHERLANDS)

GRENADA

PACIFIC OCEAN

TRINIDAD AND TOBAGO

COSTA RICA

0 250 500 Miles
0 250 500 Kilometers

PANAMA

VENEZUELA

COLOMBIA

GUYANA

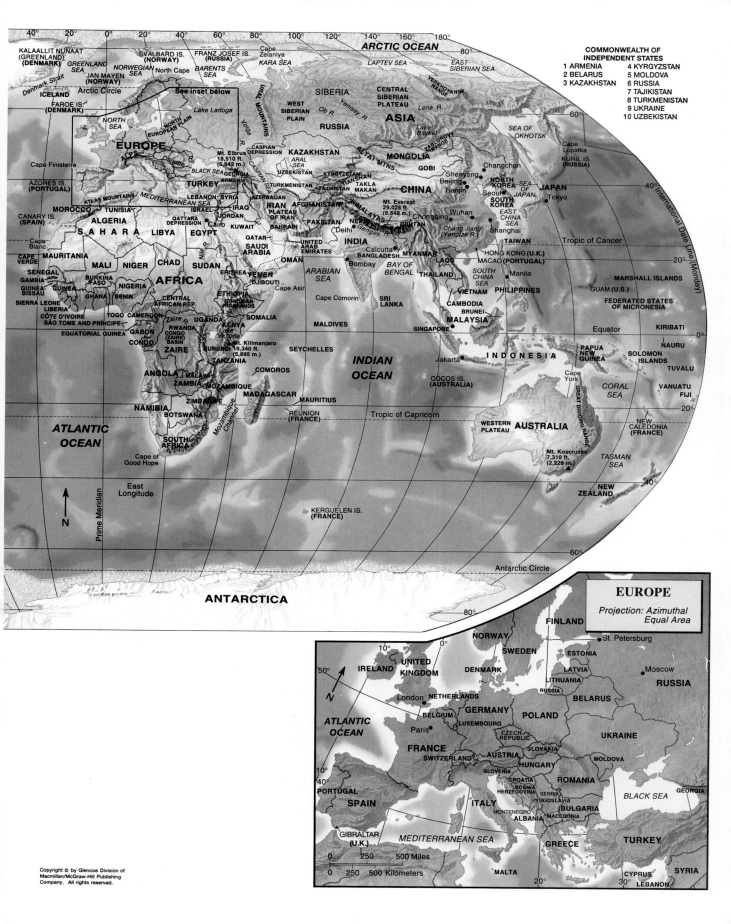

ARCTIC OCEAN

40° 20° 0° 20° 40° 60° 80° 100° 120° 140° 160° 180°

KALAALLIT NUNAAT
(GREENLAND)
(DENMARK)
GREENLAND

Denmark Strait
ICELAND
Arctic Circle
FAROE IS.
(DENMARK)

NORTH
SEA

EUROPE
ALPS
Cape Finisterre
BLACK SEA
AZORES IS.
(PORTUGAL)
TURKEY
ATLAS MOUNTAINS
MEDITERRANEAN SEA
CANARY IS.
(SPAIN)
MOROCCO TUNISIA

SVALBARD IS.
(NORWAY)
North Cape
NORWEGIAN
SEA

FRANZ JOSEF IS.
(RUSSIA)
BARENTS
SEA

Cape
Zelaniya
KARA SEA

See inset below

URAL MOUNTAINS
NORTH
EUROPEAN
PLAIN
Lake Ladoga
Volga
CASPIAN
DEPRESSION
Danube
Mt. Elbrus
18,510 ft.
(5,642 m.)
ARMENIA
GEORGIA
LEBANON SYRIA
ISRAEL IRAQ
JORDAN
CAIRO KUWAIT
QATTARA
DEPRESSION

LAPTEV SEA

SIBERIA

WEST
SIBERIAN
PLAIN
Ob R.

CENTRAL
SIBERIAN
PLATEAU
Yenisey R.
Lena R.

EAST
SIBERIAN
SEA

VERKHOYANSK
RANGE

80°

60°

RUSSIA

ASIA
Lake
Baykal
YABLONOVY
RANGE

SEA OF
OKHOTSK

Cape
Lopatka
KURIL IS.
(RUSSIA)

KAZAKHSTAN
ARAL
SEA
UZBEKISTAN
CASPIAN SEA
AZERBAIJAN
TURKMENISTAN
KYRGYZSTAN
TIANSHAN
TAJIKISTAN
TAKLA
MAKAN

ALTAI MTNS.

MONGOLIA
GOBI

Changchun
Shenyang
Beijing
Tianjin

NORTH
KOREA
Seoul
SOUTH
KOREA

SEA
OF
JAPAN

JAPAN
Tokyo

40°

COMMONWEALTH OF
INDEPENDENT STATES
1 ARMENIA   4 KYRGYZSTAN
2 BELARUS   5 MOLDOVA
3 KAZAKHSTAN 6 RUSSIA
              7 TAJIKISTAN
              8 TURKMENISTAN
              9 UKRAINE
             10 UZBEKISTAN

IRAN
PLATEAU
OF IRAN
AFGHANISTAN
HIMALAYAS
Mt. Everest
29,028 ft.
(8,848 m.)
PAKISTAN
NEPAL
Ganges
BHUTAN

CHINA
Chongqing
Wuhan
Chang Jiang
(Yangtze R.)
Shanghai

EAST
CHINA
SEA

International Date Line

ALGERIA LIBYA EGYPT
SAHARA
Nile
SAUDI
ARABIA
BAHRAIN
QATAR
UNITED
ARAB
EMIRATES
OMAN
Delhi
INDIA
Bombay

Calcutta
BANGLADESH
MYANMAR
LAOS
THAILAND
VIETNAM
CAMBODIA

TAIWAN
HONG KONG (U.K.)
MACAO (PORTUGAL)

Tropic of Cancer

20°

CAPE
VERDE
MAURITANIA
MALI NIGER CHAD SUDAN
ERITREA
YEMEN
DJIBOUTI
Cape Asir
ARABIAN
SEA
BAY OF
BENGAL
SRI
LANKA

SOUTH
CHINA
SEA
Manila

MARSHALL ISLANDS

GUAM (U.S.)
FEDERATED STATES
OF MICRONESIA

SENEGAL
GAMBIA
GUINEA-
BISSAU
SIERRA LEONE
LIBERIA
CÔTE D'IVOIRE
SÃO TOME AND PRÍNCIPE
GUINEA
BURKINA
FASO
GHANA
TOGO
BENIN
NIGERIA
CAMEROON
CENTRAL
AFRICAN REP.
ETHIOPIA
ETHIOPIAN
HIGHLANDS
SOMALIA

AFRICA

Cape Comorin

MALDIVES

SINGAPORE

PHILIPPINES

BRUNEI
MALAYSIA

Equator
KIRIBATI

0°

EQUATORIAL GUINEA
GABON
CONGO
Zaire
RWANDA
CONGO
(ZAIRE)
BASIN
BURUNDI
ZAIRE
UGANDA
Lake
Victoria
KENYA
Mt. Kilimanjaro
19,340 ft.
(5,895 m.)
TANZANIA

SEYCHELLES

INDONESIA

Jakarta

PAPUA
NEW
GUINEA

SOLOMON
ISLANDS

NAURU

TUVALU

ANGOLA
MALAWI
ZAMBIA
MOZAMBIQUE
ZIMBABWE
COMOROS

MADAGASCAR

MAURITIUS

COCOS IS.
(AUSTRALIA)

Cape
York

GREAT DIVIDING RANGE

CORAL
SEA

VANUATU
FIJI

20°

NAMIBIA
BOTSWANA
Mozambique Channel
RÉUNION
(FRANCE)

Tropic of Capricorn
WESTERN
PLATEAU
AUSTRALIA

NEW
CALEDONIA
(FRANCE)

ATLANTIC
OCEAN

SOUTH
AFRICA
Cape of
Good Hope

East
Longitude

INDIAN
OCEAN

Mt. Kosciusko
7,310 ft.
(2,228 m.)

TASMAN
SEA

N

Prime Meridian

KERGUELEN IS.
(FRANCE)

NEW
ZEALAND

40°

60°

Antarctic Circle

ANTARCTICA

80°

EUROPE
Projection: Azimuthal
Equal Area

FINLAND
NORWAY
SWEDEN
St. Petersburg
ESTONIA
LATVIA
LITHUANIA
RUSSIA
Moscow
RUSSIA
BELARUS

IRELAND
UNITED
KINGDOM
DENMARK
London
NETHERLANDS
BELGIUM
LUXEMBOURG
GERMANY
POLAND
UKRAINE

ATLANTIC
OCEAN

Paris
FRANCE
SWITZERLAND
CZECH
REPUBLIC
AUSTRIA
SLOVAKIA
HUNGARY
SLOVENIA
CROATIA
BOSNIA-
HERZEGOVINA
MOLDOVA
ROMANIA
SERBIA
YUGOSLAVIA
GEORGIA

PORTUGAL
SPAIN
GIBRALTAR
(U.K.)
ITALY
MONTENEGRO
ALBANIA
MACEDONIA
BULGARIA
BLACK SEA

MEDITERRANEAN SEA
GREECE
TURKEY

0 250 500 Miles
0 250 500 Kilometers

MALTA
CYPRUS
SYRIA
LEBANON

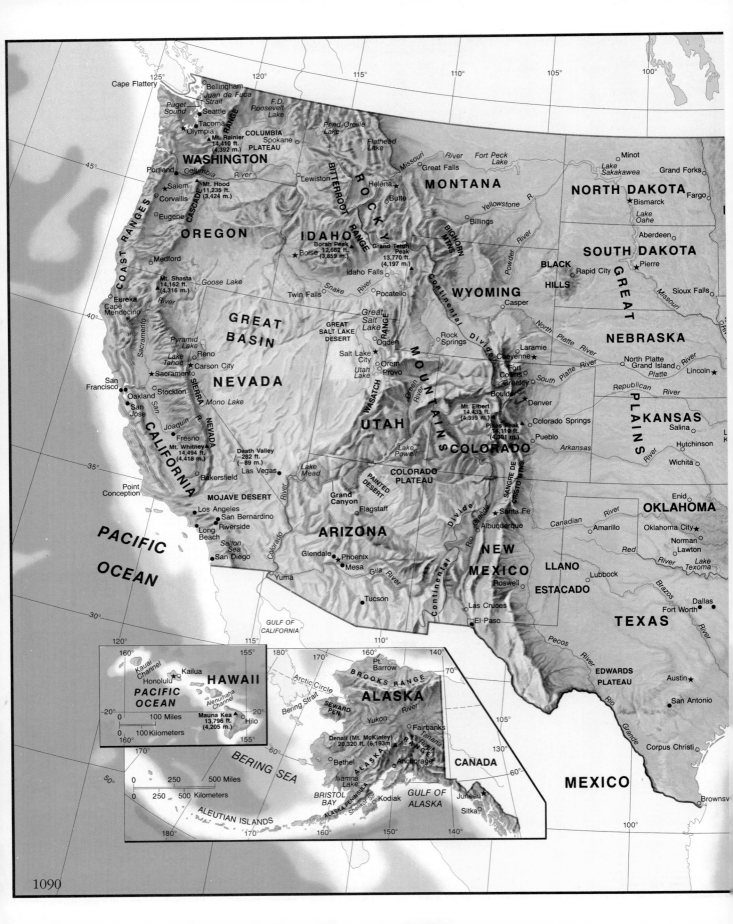

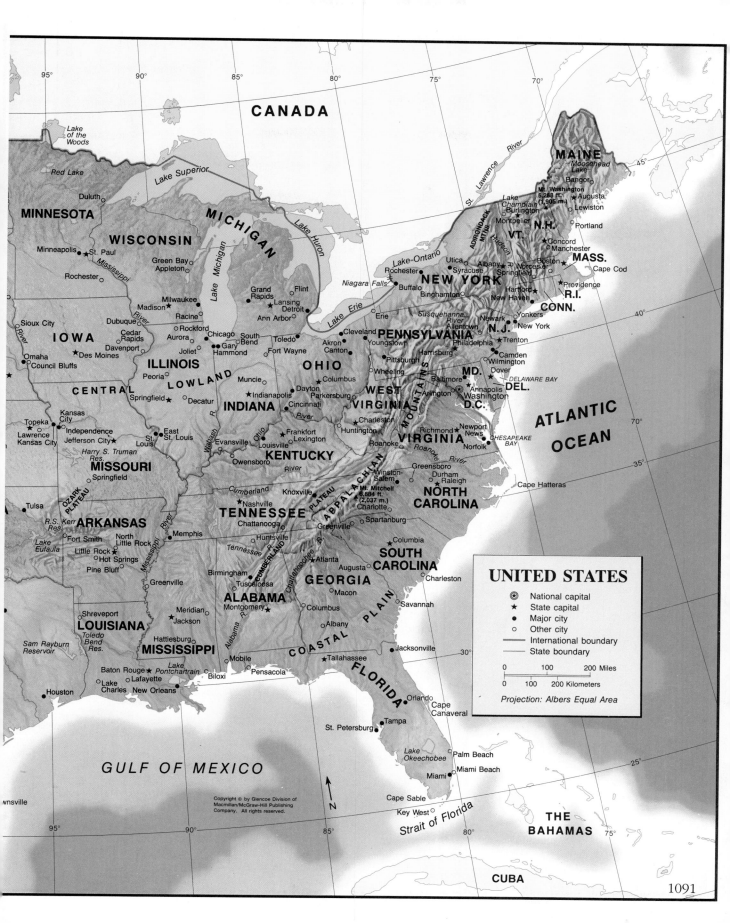

95°　90°　85°　80°　75°　70°

CANADA

Lake of the Woods

Red Lake

Lake Superior

Duluth

MINNESOTA

MICHIGAN

WISCONSIN

Minneapolis　St. Paul

Rochester

Mississippi River

Green Bay
Appleton

Madison

Milwaukee

Racine

Grand Rapids

Flint

Lansing

Detroit

Ann Arbor

Lake Michigan

Lake Huron

St. Lawrence River

MAINE

Moosehead Lake

Bangor

Mt. Washington
6,288 ft.
(1,905 m.)

Augusta

Lewiston

Lake Champlain

Burlington

Montpelier

N.H.

VT.

Concord

Manchester

Portland

Albany

Boston

MASS.

Cape Cod

Worcester

Springfield

Providence

R.I.

Hartford

CONN.

New Haven

Yonkers

New York

ADIRONDACK MTNS.

Hudson

Lake-Ontario

Rochester

Utica

Syracuse

NEW YORK

Binghamton

Niagara Falls

Buffalo

Lake Erie

Erie

Sioux City

IOWA

Dubuque

Cedar Rapids

Davenport

Des Moines

Omaha

Council Bluffs

Rockford

Chicago

Aurora

Joliet

Gary

Hammond

South Bend

Fort Wayne

Toledo

ILLINOIS

Peoria

CENTRAL

LOWLAND

Springfield

Decatur

Muncie

Indianapolis

INDIANA

Dayton

Cincinnati

Columbus

OHIO

Akron

Canton

Cleveland

Youngstown

Pittsburgh

Wheeling

PENNSYLVANIA

Harrisburg

Philadelphia

Trenton

N.J.

Newark

Allentown

Camden

Wilmington

Dover

DELAWARE BAY

MD.

DEL.

Baltimore

Annapolis

Washington

D.C.

Arlington

Kansas City

Topeka

Lawrence

Kansas City

Independence

Jefferson City

St. Louis

East St. Louis

MISSOURI

Springfield

Harry S. Truman Res.

Wabash R.

Evansville

Louisville

Frankfort

Lexington

KENTUCKY

Owensboro

Ohio River

Charleston

WEST VIRGINIA

Parkersburg

Huntington

MOUNTAINS

Richmond

Newport News

Roanoke

VIRGINIA

Norfolk

CHESAPEAKE BAY

ATLANTIC OCEAN

Tulsa

R.S. Kerr Res.

ARKANSAS

Fort Smith

Lake Eufaula

North Little Rock

Little Rock

Hot Springs

Pine Bluff

OZARK PLATEAU

Memphis

Nashville

Chattanooga

Knoxville

TENNESSEE

Huntsville

Tennessee River

Cumberland River

APPALACHIAN

PLATEAU

Mt. Mitchell
6,684 ft.
(2,037 m.)

Winston-Salem

Greensboro

Durham

Raleigh

Greenville

Spartanburg

Charlotte

NORTH CAROLINA

Roanoke River

Cape Hatteras

Shreveport

LOUISIANA

Toledo Bend Res.

Meridian

Jackson

MISSISSIPPI

Hattiesburg

Birmingham

Tuscaloosa

Montgomery

ALABAMA

Alabama River

Columbus

Macon

GEORGIA

Atlanta

Augusta

Columbia

SOUTH CAROLINA

Chattahoochee

CUMBERLAND

Charleston

Savannah

COASTAL

PLAIN

Sam Rayburn Reservoir

Houston

Lake Charles

New Orleans

Lake Pontchartrain

Baton Rouge

Lafayette

Biloxi

Mobile

Pensacola

Tallahassee

Jacksonville

FLORIDA

GULF OF MEXICO

Orlando

Cape Canaveral

St. Petersburg

Tampa

Lake Okeechobee

Palm Beach

Miami Beach

Miami

Cape Sable

Key West

Strait of Florida

THE BAHAMAS

CUBA

Greenville

Greenville

UNITED STATES

⊛ National capital
★ State capital
● Major city
○ Other city
— International boundary
— State boundary

0　　100　　200 Miles
0　　100　　200 Kilometers

Projection: Albers Equal Area

Copyright © by Glencoe Division of
Macmillan/McGraw-Hill Publishing
Company. All rights reserved.

N

45°

40°

70°

35°

30°

25°

75°

wnsville

1091

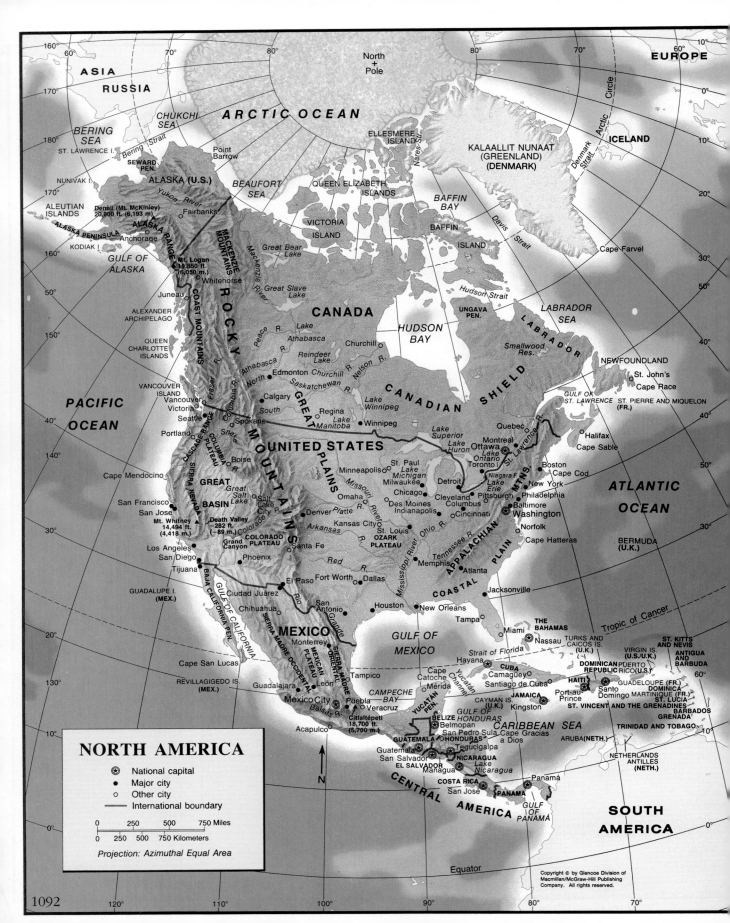

NORTH AMERICA

⊛ National capital
● Major city
○ Other city
— International boundary

```
0    250    500    750 Miles
0  250  500  750 Kilometers
```

Projection: Azimuthal Equal Area

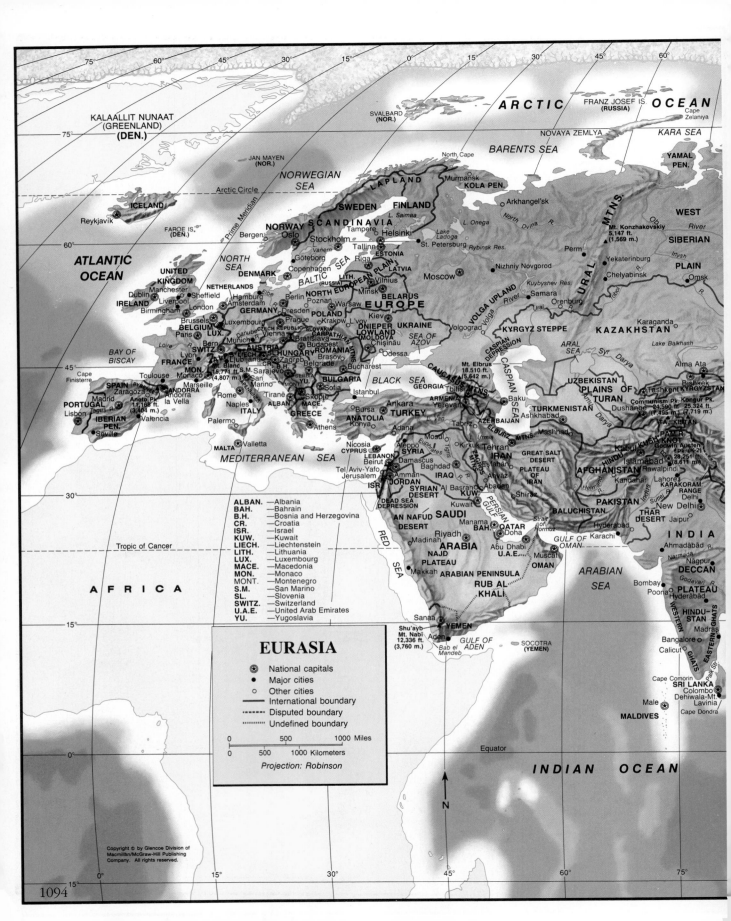

EURASIA

- ⊛ National capitals
- ● Major cities
- ○ Other cities
- —— International boundary
- ----- Disputed boundary
- ·········· Undefined boundary

0	500	1000 Miles
0	500	1000 Kilometers

Projection: Robinson

ALBAN.	—Albania
BAH.	—Bahrain
B.H.	—Bosnia and Herzegovina
CR.	—Croatia
ISR.	—Israel
KUW.	—Kuwait
LIECH.	—Liechtenstein
LITH.	—Lithuania
LUX.	—Luxembourg
MACE.	—Macedonia
MON.	—Monaco
MONT.	—Montenegro
S.M.	—San Marino
SL.	—Slovenia
SWITZ.	—Switzerland
U.A.E.	—United Arab Emirates
YU.	—Yugoslavia

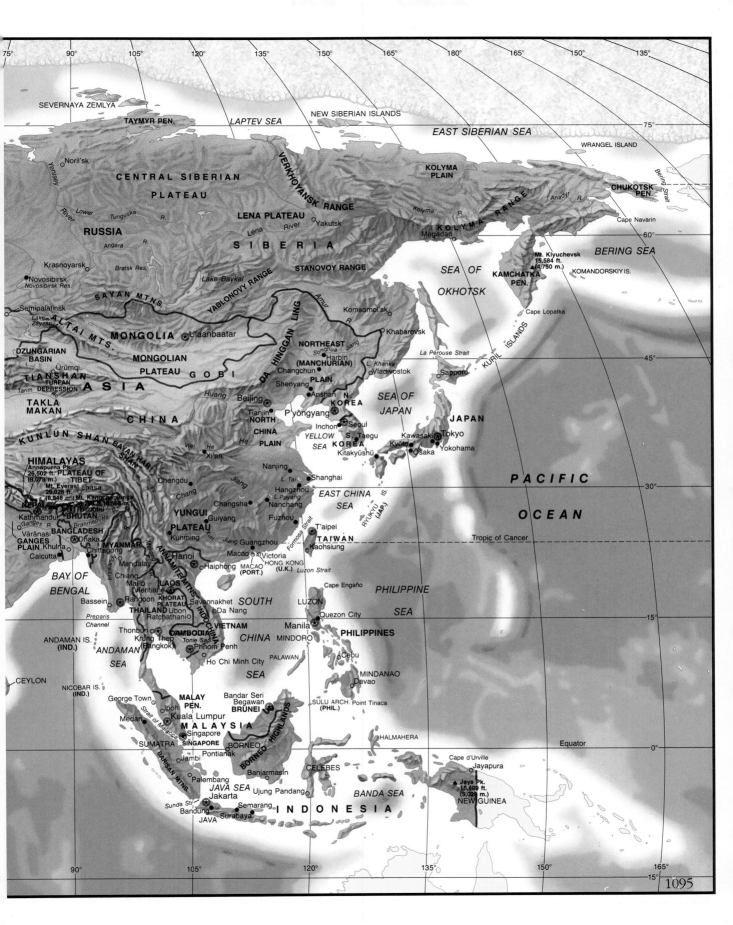

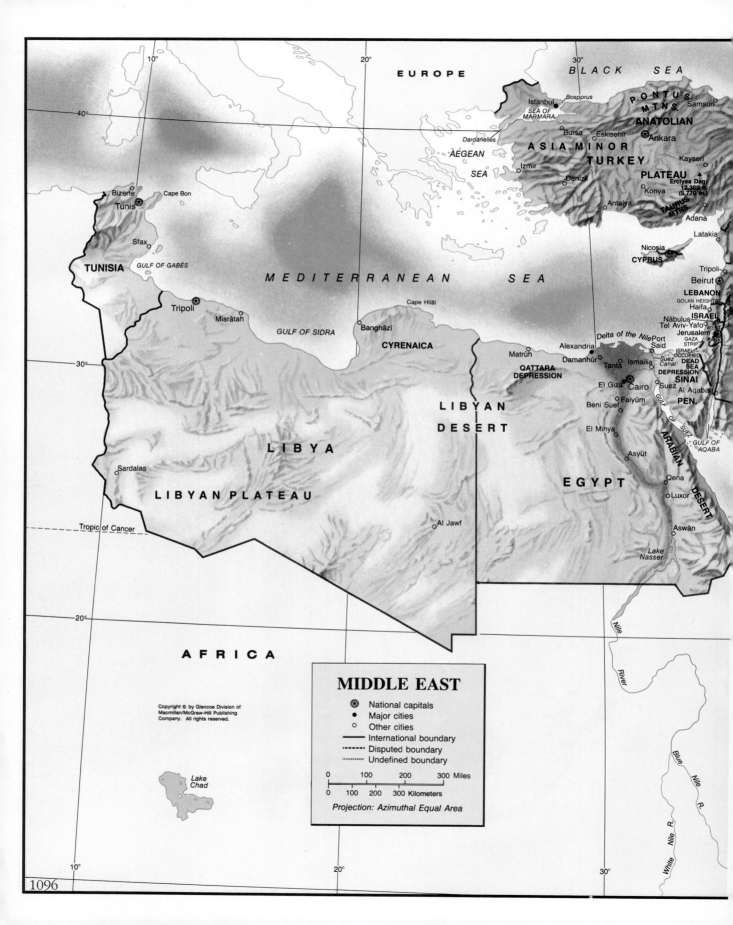

EUROPE

BLACK SEA

PONTUS MTNS.
Istanbul Bosporus Samsun
SEA OF
MARMARA
ANATOLIAN
Dardanelles Bursa Eskisehir Ankara
ASIA MINOR
AEGEAN   TURKEY   Kayseri
SEA   Izmir   PLATEAU   Erciyes Dagi
Denizli   Konya   12,369 ft.
(3,770 m.)
Antalya   TAURUS MTNS.
Adana

Bizerte
Tunis   Cape Bon   Latakia
Nicosia
Sfax   CYPRUS   Tripoli
TUNISIA   GULF OF GABÈS   Beirut
LEBANON
M E D I T E R R A N E A N   S E A   GOLAN HEIGHTS
Haifa
ISRAEL
Tripoli   Nābulus WEST
Misrātah   GULF OF SIDRA   Cape Hilāl   Tel Aviv-Yafo BANK
Banghāzī   Delta of the Nile Port Jerusalem
Alexandria   Said GAZA
CYRENAICA   Matrūh   Damanhūr Tanta STRIP
QATTARA   Ismailia Suez DEAD
DEPRESSION   El Giza Cairo Canal SEA
Beni Suef Faiyūm Suez DEPRESSION
LIBYAN   El Minya   Al Aqabah SINAI
DESERT   PEN.
Asyūt ARABIAN GULF OF
AQABA
L I B Y A   EGYPT   Qena DESERT
Sardalas   Luxor
LIBYAN PLATEAU
Aswān
Tropic of Cancer
Al Jawf   Lake
Nasser

A F R I C A

Copyright © by Glencoe Division of
Macmillan/McGraw-Hill Publishing
Company. All rights reserved.

Nile
Lake
Chad

River

MIDDLE EAST

⊛ National capitals
● Major cities
○ Other cities
── International boundary
----- Disputed boundary
········ Undefined boundary

0   100   200   300 Miles
0   100   200   300 Kilometers
Projection: Azimuthal Equal Area

Nile R.

Blue
Nile
R.

White
Nile R.

1096

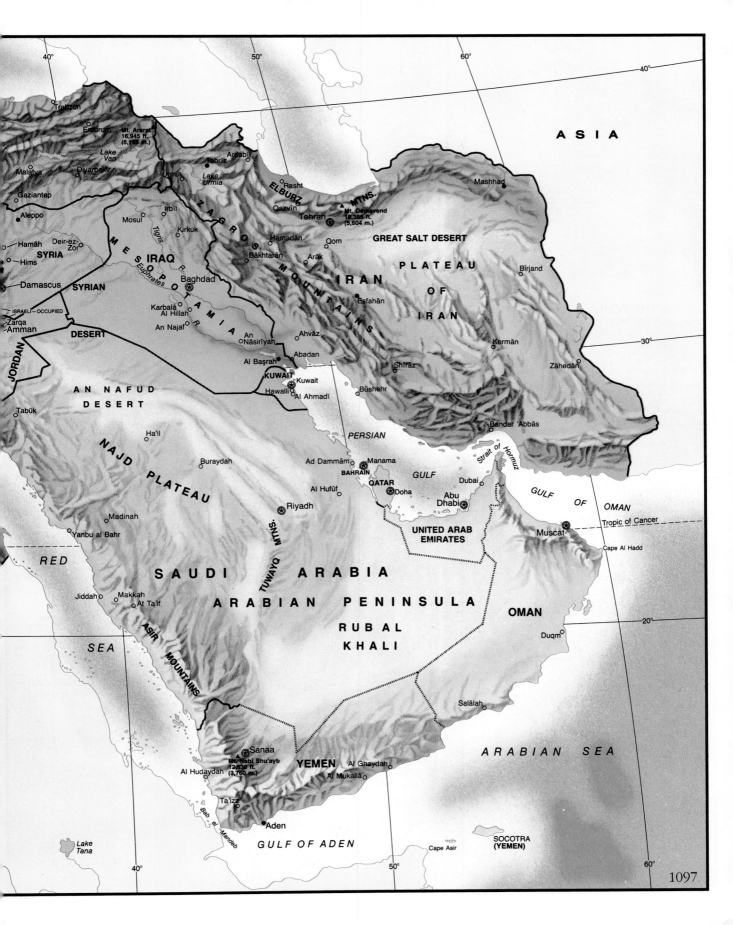

ASIA

Trabzon

Erzurum
Mt. Ararat
16,945 ft.
(5,165 m.)

Lake
Van

Ardabīl

Malatya
Diyarbakır

Urmia
Lake
Urmia

Tabrīz

Rasht

Mashhad

Gaziantep

Aleppo

Irbīl

Mosul

Tigris R.

Kirkuk

Qazvīn

Hamadān

Tehran
Mt. Demavend
18,386 ft.
(5,604 m.)

ELBURZ MTNS.

GREAT SALT DESERT

Bīrjand

Hamāh

SYRIA

Deir-ez-
Zor

Euphrates R.

Baghdad

Bākhtarān

Qom

Arāk

Esfahān

PLATEAU

OF

IRAN

Hims

Damascus

SYRIAN

Karbalā'
Al Hillah

An Najaf

Ahvāz

Kermān

ISRAELI—OCCUPIED

Zarqa
Amman

DESERT

An
Nāsirīyah

Abadan

Shīrāz

Zāhedān

JORDAN

Al Baṣrah

KUWAIT

Hawalli
Al Ahmadī

Kuwait

Būshehr

Bandar 'Abbās

Tabūk

AN NAFUD
DESERT

PERSIAN

Strait of Hormuz

Ha'il

GULF

GULF

OF

OMAN

NAJD PLATEAU

Buraydah

Ad Dammām
Manama
BAHRAIN

QATAR
Doha

Dubai

Abu
Dhabi

Muscat

Tropic of Cancer

Madinah

Al Hufūf

UNITED ARAB
EMIRATES

Cape Al Hadd

Yanbu al Bahr

Riyadh

TUWAYQ MTNS.

RED

SAUDI

ARABIA

OMAN

Jiddah
Makkah
At Ta'if

ARABIAN PENINSULA

RUB AL
KHALI

Duqm

SEA

ĀSĪR MOUNTAINS

Salālah

ARABIAN SEA

Sanaa
Mt. Nabi Shu'ayb
12,336 ft.
(3,760 m.)

Al Ghaydah

Al Hudaydah

YEMEN

Al Mukallā

Ta'izz

Bab el Mandeb

Aden

GULF OF ADEN

Cape Asir

SOCOTRA
(YEMEN)

Lake
Tana

40°

50°

60°

1097

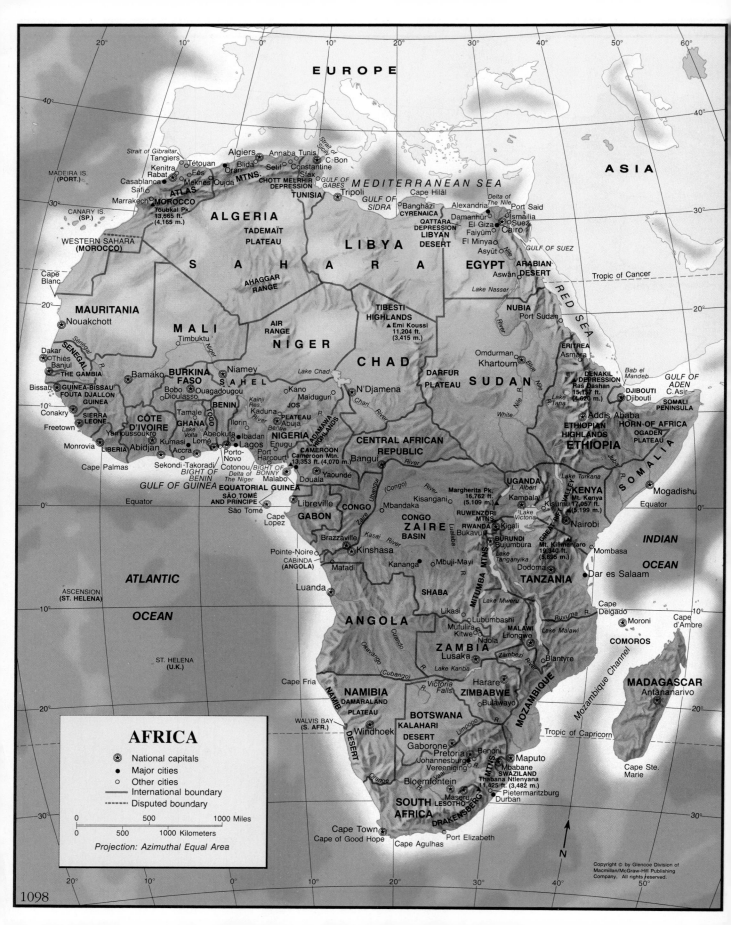

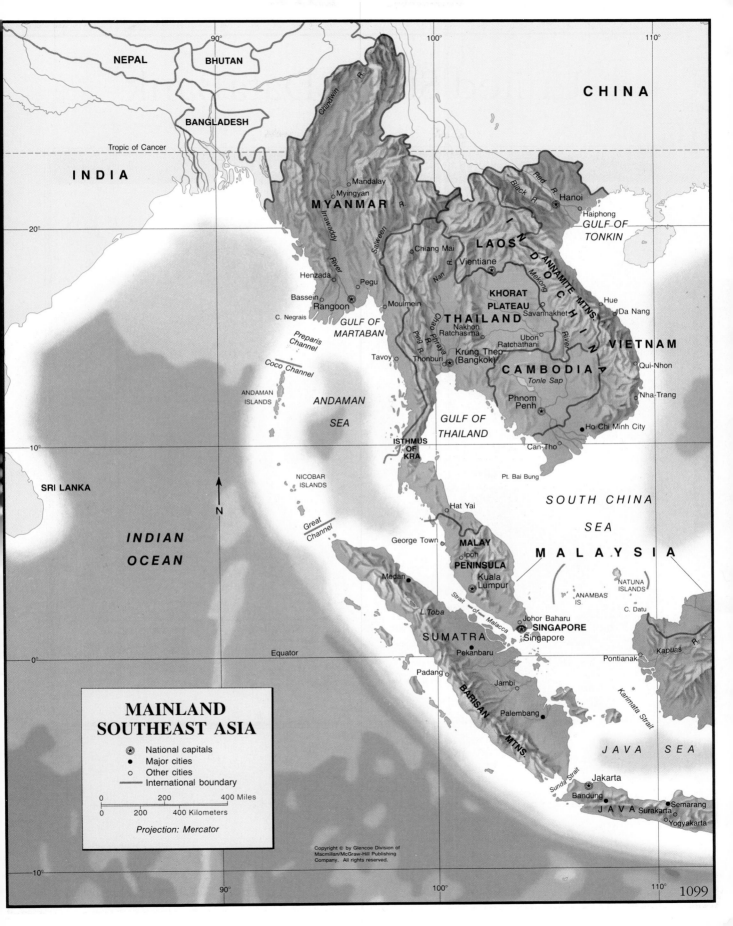

MAINLAND SOUTHEAST ASIA

National capitals ✯

• *Major cities*

○ *Other cities*

── *International boundary*

| 0 | 200 | 400 Miles |
| 0 | 200 | 400 Kilometers |

Projection: Mercator

NEPAL

BHUTAN

BANGLADESH

CHINA

Tropic of Cancer

INDIA

MYANMAR

Mandalay ○
Myingyan ○

Chindwin R.

Irrawaddy River

Salween R.

Henzada ○

Bassein ○
Pegu ○
Rangoon ✯

C. Negrais

Chiang Mai ○

Nan R.

Vientiane ✯

LAOS

Red R.

Black R.

Hanoi ✯

Haiphong ○

GULF OF
TONKIN

I
N
D
O
C
H
I
N
A

ANNAMITE MTNS.

Hue ○

Da Nang ○

KHORAT
PLATEAU

Savannakhet ○

Mekong River

Moulmein ○

GULF OF
MARTABAN

Preparis
Channel

Coco Channel

ANDAMAN
ISLANDS

ANDAMAN
SEA

Tavoy ○

THAILAND

Chao
Phraya
R.

Ping R.

Nakhon
Ratchasima ○

Krung Thep
(Bangkok) ✯
Thonburi

Ubon
Ratchathani ○

VIETNAM

Qui-Nhon ○

CAMBODIA

Tonle Sap

Phnom
Penh ✯

Nha-Trang ○

GULF OF
THAILAND

ISTHMUS
OF
KRA

Can-Tho ○

Ho Chi Minh City ●

Pt. Bai Bung

SRI LANKA

INDIAN
OCEAN

N

NICOBAR
ISLANDS

Great
Channel

Equator

Hat Yai ○

George Town ○

MALAY
PENINSULA

Ipoh ○

Kuala
Lumpur ✯

Medan ●

L. Toba

SOUTH CHINA

SEA

MALAYSIA

NATUNA
ISLANDS

ANAMBAS
IS.

C. Datu

Strait of Malacca

SUMATRA

Pekanbaru ●

Johor Baharu ○

SINGAPORE ✯
Singapore ○

Pontianak ○

Kapuas R.

Karimata Strait

Padang ○

Jambi ○

BARISAN

Palembang ●

MTNS.

JAVA SEA

Sunda Strait

Jakarta ✯

Bandung ●

J A V A

Surakarta ○

Semarang ●

Yogyakarta ○

United States DataBank

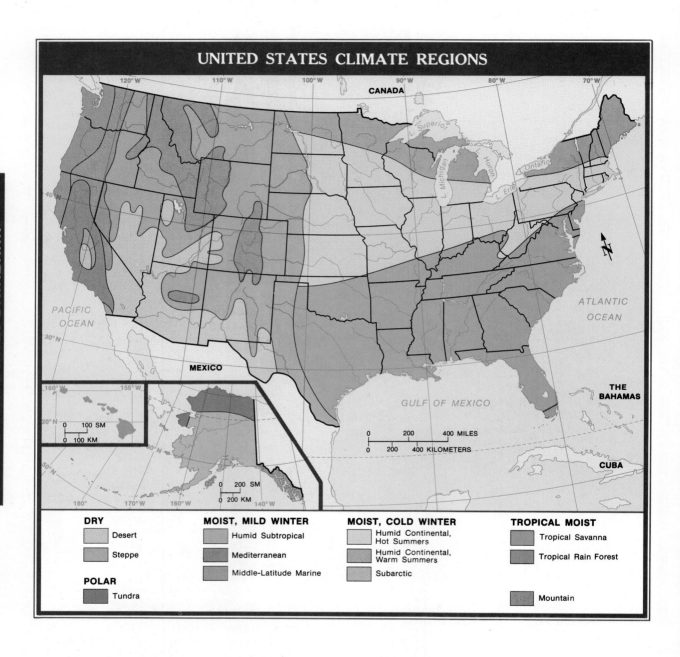

UNITED STATES CLIMATE REGIONS

CANADA

PACIFIC OCEAN

MEXICO

GULF OF MEXICO

ATLANTIC OCEAN

THE BAHAMAS

CUBA

DRY
- Desert
- Steppe

POLAR
- Tundra

MOIST, MILD WINTER
- Humid Subtropical
- Mediterranean
- Middle-Latitude Marine

MOIST, COLD WINTER
- Humid Continental, Hot Summers
- Humid Continental, Warm Summers
- Subarctic

TROPICAL MOIST
- Tropical Savanna
- Tropical Rain Forest
- Mountain

POPULATION OF THE UNITED STATES

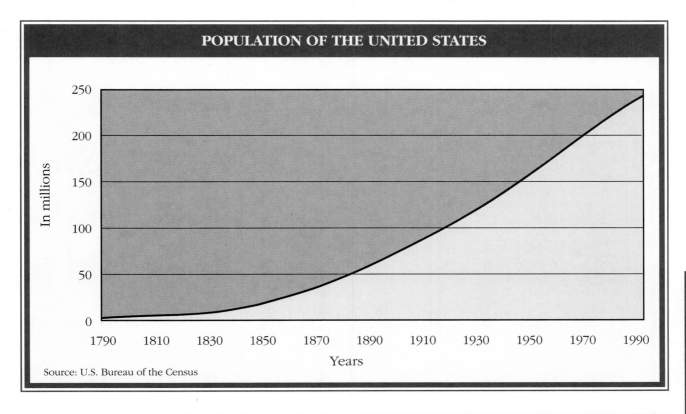

Source: U.S. Bureau of the Census

POPULATION DISTRIBUTION BY AGE, 1990

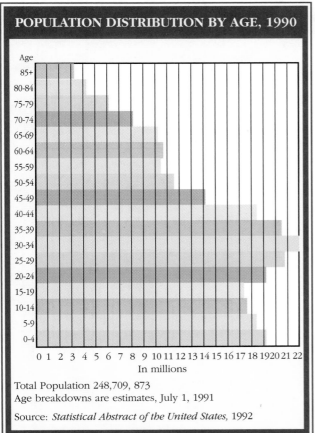

Total Population 248,709, 873
Age breakdowns are estimates, July 1, 1991

Source: *Statistical Abstract of the United States,* 1992

MAJOR RELIGIONS IN THE UNITED STATES

Roman Catholic Church 57,020
Southern Baptist Convention...........................14,908
United Methodist Church...................................8,979
National Baptist Convention..............................8,169
Muslims...6,000
Jews...5,944
Evangelical Lutheran Church............................5,239
Church of Jesus Christ of
   Latter-day Saints (Mormon)...........................4,175
Church of God in Christ (Pentecostal)..............3,710
Presbyterian Church (U.S.A.)............................2,886
National Baptist Convention of America...........2,669
Lutheran Church (Missouri Synod) 2,609
Episcopal Church 2,433
African Methodist Episcopal Church................2,210
Assemblies of God 2,138
Greek Orthodox Archdiocese of
   North and South America 1,950
United Church of Christ......................................1,626
Churches of Christ..1,626
American Baptist Churches in the U.S.A...........1,550
African Methodist Episcopal Zion Church 1,220
Christian Churches and Churches of Christ......1,071
Christian Church (Disciples of Christ)...............1,052
Orthodox Church in America 1,000

In thousands

Source: *Statistical Abstract of the United States,* 1992; Time
(November 19, 1990)

POLITICAL PARTIES IN POWER

George Washington, 1789-1797

John Adams, 1797-1801

Thomas Jefferson, 1801-1809

James Madison, 1809-1817

James Monroe, 1817-1825

John Quincy Adams, 1825-1829

Andrew Jackson, 1829-1837

Martin Van Buren, 1837-1841

William H. Harrison/John Tyler, 1841-1845

James K. Polk, 1845-1849

Zachary Taylor/Millard Fillmore, 1849-1853

Franklin Pierce, 1853-1857

James Buchanan, 1857-1861

Abraham Lincoln, 1861-1865

Andrew Johnson, 1865-1869

Ulysses S. Grant, 1869-1877

Rutherford B. Hayes, 1877-1881

James A. Garfield/Chester A. Arthur, 1881-85

Grover Cleveland, 1885-1889

Benjamin Harrison, 1889-1893

Grover Cleveland, 1893-1897

William McKinley, 1897-1901

Theodore Roosevelt, 1901-1909

William H. Taft, 1909-1913

Woodrow Wilson, 1913-1921

Warren G. Harding, 1921-1923

Calvin Coolidge, 1923-1929

Herbert C. Hoover, 1929-1933

Franklin D. Roosevelt, 1933-1945

Harry S Truman, 1945-1953

Dwight D. Eisenhower, 1953-1961

John F. Kennedy, 1961-1963

Lyndon B. Johnson, 1963-1969

Richard M. Nixon, 1969-1974

Gerald R. Ford, 1974-1977

Jimmy Carter, 1977-1981

Ronald Reagan, 1981-1989

George Bush, 1989-1993

Bill Clinton, 1993-

☐ Federalist ☐ Whig
☐ Democratic Republican ☐ Republican
☐ Democratic

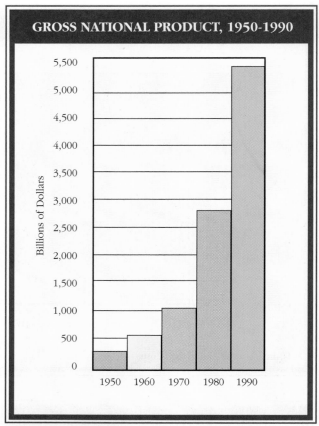

GROSS NATIONAL PRODUCT, 1950-1990

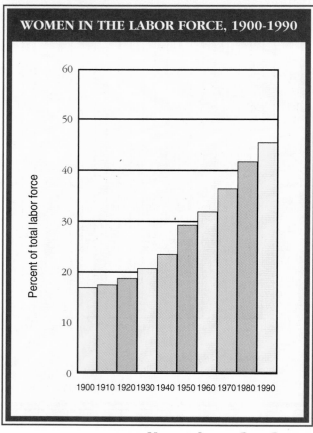

WOMEN IN THE LABOR FORCE, 1900-1990

THE UNITED STATES

STATE*	YEAR ADMITTED	POPULATION (1990)	AREA (sq mi)	CAPITAL	LARGEST CITY	HOUSE REP. (1990)**
1. Delaware	1787	666,168	2,057	Dover	Wilmington	1
2. Pennsylvania	1787	11,881,643	45,333	Harrisburg	Philadelphia	21
3. New Jersey	1787	7,730,188	7,836	Trenton	Newark	13
4. Georgia	1788	6,478,216	58,876	Atlanta	Atlanta	11
5. Connecticut	1788	3,287,116	5,009	Hartford	Bridgeport	6
6. Massachusetts	1788	6,016,425	8,257	Boston	Boston	10
7. Maryland	1788	4,781,468	10,577	Annapolis	Baltimore	8
8. South Carolina	1788	3,486,703	31,055	Columbia	Columbia	6
9. New Hampshire	1788	1,109,252	9,304	Concord	Manchester	2
10. Virginia	1788	6,187,358	40,817	Richmond	Virginia Beach	11
11. New York	1788	17,990,455	49,576	Albany	New York	31
12. North Carolina	1789	6,628,637	52,586	Raleigh	Charlotte	12
13. Rhode Island	1790	1,003,464	1,214	Providence	Providence	2
14. Vermont	1791	562,758	9,609	Montpelier	Burlington	1
15. Kentucky	1792	3,685,296	40,395	Frankfort	Louisville	6
16. Tennessee	1796	4,877,185	42,244	Nashville	Memphis	9
17. Ohio	1803	10,847,115	41,222	Columbus	Columbus	19
18. Louisiana	1812	4,219,973	48,523	Baton Rouge	New Orleans	7
19. Indiana	1816	5,544,159	36,291	Indianapolis	Indianapolis	10
20. Mississippi	1817	2,573,216	47,716	Jackson	Jackson	5
21. Illinois	1818	11,430,602	56,400	Springfield	Chicago	20
22. Alabama	1819	4,040,587	51,609	Montgomery	Birmingham	7
23. Maine	1820	1,227,928	33,215	Augusta	Portland	2
24. Missouri	1821	5,117,073	69,686	Jefferson City	Kansas City	9
25. Arkansas	1836	2,350,725	53,104	Little Rock	Little Rock	4
26. Michigan	1837	9,295,297	58,216	Lansing	Detroit	16
27. Florida	1845	12,937,926	58,560	Tallahassee	Jacksonville	23
28. Texas	1845	16,986,510	267,339	Austin	Houston	30
29. Iowa	1846	2,776,755	56,290	Des Moines	Des Moines	5
30. Wisconsin	1848	4,891,769	56,154	Madison	Milwaukee	9
31. California	1850	29,760,021	158,693	Sacramento	Los Angeles	52
32. Minnesota	1858	4,375,099	84,068	St. Paul	Minneapolis	8
33. Oregon	1859	2,853,733	96,981	Salem	Portland	5
34. Kansas	1861	2,477,574	82,264	Topeka	Wichita	4
35. West Virginia	1863	1,793,477	24,181	Charleston	Charleston	3
36. Nevada	1864	1,201,833	110,540	Carson City	Las Vegas	2
37. Nebraska	1867	1,578,385	77,227	Lincoln	Omaha	3
38. Colorado	1876	3,294,394	104,247	Denver	Denver	6
39. North Dakota	1889	638,800	70,665	Bismarck	Fargo	1
40. South Dakota	1889	696,004	77,047	Pierre	Sioux Falls	1
41. Montana	1889	799,065	147,138	Helena	Billings	1
42. Washington	1889	4,887,941	68,192	Olympia	Seattle	9
43. Idaho	1890	1,006,749	83,557	Boise	Boise	2
44. Wyoming	1890	455,975	97,914	Cheyenne	Cheyenne	1
45. Utah	1896	1,727,784	84,916	Salt Lake City	Salt Lake City	3
46. Oklahoma	1907	3,145,585	69,919	Oklahoma City	Oklahoma City	6
47. New Mexico	1912	1,515,069	121,666	Santa Fe	Albuquerque	3
48. Arizona	1912	3,665,228	113,909	Phoenix	Phoenix	6
49. Alaska	1959	550,043	586,412	Juneau	Anchorage	1
50. Hawaii	1959	1,108,229	6,450	Honolulu	Honolulu	2
District of Columbia (Washington, D.C.)	—	606,900	68	—	—	—
United States of America	—	248,709,873	3,615,124	Washington, D.C.	New York	435

* Numbers denote the order in which states were admitted.
** Number of members in House of Representatives

Presidents of the United States

George Washington
1789-1797

Born: 1732
Died: 1799
Born in: Virginia
Elected from: Virginia
Age when elected: 56
Occupations: Planter, Soldier
Party: None
Vice President: John Adams

1

John Adams
1797-1801

Born: 1735
Died: 1826
Born in: Massachusetts
Elected from: Massachusetts
Age when elected: 61
Occupation: Lawyer
Party: Federalist
Vice President: Thomas Jefferson

2

Thomas Jefferson
1801-1809

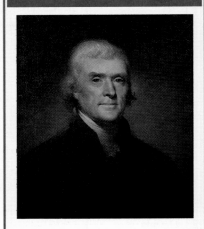

Born: 1743
Died: 1826
Born in: Virginia
Elected from: Virginia
Age when elected: 57
Occupations: Planter, Lawyer
Party: Republican**
Vice Presidents: Aaron Burr,
George Clinton

3

James Madison
1809-1817

Born: 1751
Died: 1836
Born in: Virginia
Elected from: Virginia
Age when elected: 57
Occupation: Politician
Party: Republican**
Vice Presidents: George Clinton,
Elbridge Gerry

4

James Monroe
1817-1825

Born: 1758
Died: 1831
Born in: Virginia
Elected from: Virginia
Age when elected: 58
Occupations: Politician, Lawyer
Party: Republican**
Vice President: Daniel D.
Tompkins

5

** The Republican party during this period developed into today's Democratic party. Today's Republican party originated in 1854.

John Quincy Adams
1825-1829

Most of the Presidents are portrayed in this section by their official White House portrait.

Born: 1767
Died: 1848
Born in: Massachusetts
Elected from: Massachusetts
Age when elected: 57
Occupation: Lawyer
Party: Republican**
Vice President: John C. Calhoun

6

Andrew Jackson
1829-1837

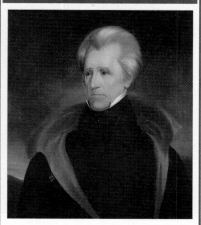

Born: 1767
Died: 1845
Born in: South Carolina
Elected from: Tennessee
Age when elected: 61
Occupation: Lawyer
Party: Democratic
Vice Presidents: John C. Calhoun, Martin Van Buren

7

Martin Van Buren
1837-1841

Born: 1782
Died: 1862
Born in: New York
Elected from: New York
Age when elected: 54
Occupation: Lawyer
Party: Democratic
Vice President: Richard M. Johnson

8

William H. Harrison
1841

Born: 1773
Died: 1841
Born in: Virginia
Elected from: Ohio
Age when elected: 67
Occupation: Soldier
Party: Whig
Vice President: John Tyler

9

John Tyler
1841-1845

Born: 1790
Died: 1862
Born in: Virginia
Elected as V. P. from: Virginia
Assumed presidency upon Harrison's death
Age when became President: 51
Occupation: Lawyer
Party: Whig
Vice President: None

10

PRESIDENTS

James K. Polk
1845-1849

Born: 1795
Died: 1849
Born in: North Carolina
Elected from: Tennessee
Age when elected: 49
Occupation: Lawyer
Party: Democratic
Vice President: George M. Dallas

11

Zachary Taylor
1849-1850

Born: 1784
Died: 1850
Born in: Virginia
Elected from: Louisiana
Age when elected: 63
Occupation: Soldier
Party: Whig
Vice President: Millard Fillmore

12

Millard Fillmore
1850-1853

Born: 1800
Died: 1874
Born in: New York
Elected as V.P. from: New York
Assumed presidency upon Taylor's death
Age when became President: 50
Occupation: Lawyer
Party: Whig
Vice President: None

13

Franklin Pierce
1853-1857

Born: 1804
Died: 1869
Born in: New Hampshire
Elected from: New Hampshire
Age when elected: 47
Occupation: Lawyer
Party: Democratic
Vice President: William R. King

14

James Buchanan
1857-1861

Born: 1791
Died: 1868
Born in: Pennsylvania
Elected from: Pennsylvania
Age when elected: 65
Occupation: Lawyer
Party: Democratic
Vice President: John G. Breckinridge

15

PRESIDENTS OF THE UNITED STATES

Abraham Lincoln
1861-1865

Born: 1809   **16**
Died: 1865
Born in: Kentucky
Elected from: Illinois
Age when elected: 51
Occupation: Lawyer
Party: Republican
Vice Presidents: Hannibal
   Hamlin, Andrew Johnson

Andrew Johnson
1865-1869

Born: 1808   **17**
Died: 1875
Born in: North Carolina
Elected as V.P. from: Tennessee
Age when became President: 56
Assumed presidency upon
Lincoln's death
Occupations: Tailor, Politician
Party: Republican
Vice President: None

Ulysses S. Grant
1869-1877

Born: 1822   **18**
Died: 1885
Born in: Ohio
Elected from: Illinois
Age when elected: 46
Occupations: Farmer, Soldier
Party: Republican
Vice Presidents: Schuyler Colfax,
   Henry Wilson

Rutherford B. Hayes
1877-1881

Born: 1822   **19**
Died: 1893
Born in: Ohio
Elected from: Ohio
Age when elected: 54
Occupation: Lawyer
Party: Republican
Vice President: William A.
   Wheeler

James A. Garfield
1881

Born: 1831   **20**
Died: 1881
Born in: Ohio
Elected from: Ohio
Age when elected: 49
Occupations: Lawyer, Politician
Party: Republican
Vice President: Chester A. Arthur

Chester A. Arthur
1881-1885

Born: 1830
Died: 1886
Born in: Vermont
Elected as V.P. from: New York
Assumed presidency upon
Garfield's death
Age when became President: 50
Occupation: Lawyer
Party: Republican
Vice President: None

21

Grover Cleveland
1885-1889   1893-1897

Born: 1837
Died: 1908
Born in: New Jersey
Elected from: New York
Age when elected: 47; 55
Occupation: Lawyer
Party: Democratic
Vice Presidents: Thomas A.
   Hendricks, Adlai E. Stevenson

22, 24

Benjamin Harrison
1889-1893

Born: 1833
Died: 1901
Born in: Ohio
Elected from: Indiana
Age when elected: 55
Occupation: Lawyer
Party: Republican
Vice President: Levi P. Morton

23

William McKinley
1897-1901

Born: 1843
Died: 1901
Born in: Ohio
Elected from: Ohio
Age when elected: 53
Occupation: Lawyer
Party: Republican
Vice Presidents: Garret Hobart,
   Theodore Roosevelt

25

Theodore Roosevelt
1901-1909

Born: 1858
Died: 1919
Born in: New York
Elected as V.P. from: New York
Assumed presidency upon
McKinley's death
Age when became President: 42
Occupations: Author, Politician
Party: Republican
Vice President: Charles W. Fairbanks

26

William H. Taft
1909-1913

27

Born: 1857
Died: 1930
Born in: Ohio
Elected from: Ohio
Age when elected: 51
Occupation: Lawyer
Party: Republican
Vice President: James S. Sherman

Woodrow Wilson
1913-1921

28

Born: 1856
Died: 1924
Born in: Virginia
Elected from: New Jersey
Age when elected: 55
Occupation: College Professor
Party: Democratic
Vice President: Thomas R.
   Marshall

Warren G. Harding
1921-1923

29

Born: 1865
Died: 1923
Born in: Ohio
Elected from: Ohio
Age when elected: 55
Occupations: Newspaper Editor,
   Publisher
Party: Republican
Vice President: Calvin Coolidge

Calvin Coolidge
1923-1929

30

Born: 1872
Died: 1933
Born in: Vermont
Elected as V.P. from: Massachusetts
Assumed presidency upon
Harding's death
Age when became President: 51
Occupation: Lawyer
Party: Republican
Vice President: Charles G. Dawes

Herbert C. Hoover
1929-1933

31

Born: 1874
Died: 1964
Born in: Iowa
Elected from: California
Age when elected: 54
Occupation: Geologist
Party: Republican
Vice President: Charles Curtis

Franklin D. Roosevelt
1933-1945

Born: 1882   **32**
Died: 1945
Born in: New York
Elected from: New York
Age when elected: 50
Occupation: Lawyer
Party: Democratic
Vice Presidents: John N. Garner,
   Henry A. Wallace, Harry S Truman

Harry S Truman
1945-1953

Born: 1884   **33**
Died: 1972
Born in: Missouri
Elected as V.P. from: Missouri
Assumed presidency upon
Roosevelt's death
Age when became President: 60
Occupation: Businessman
Party: Democratic
Vice President: Alben W. Barkley

Dwight D. Eisenhower
1953-1961

Born: 1890   **34**
Died: 1969
Born in: Texas
Elected from: New York
Age when elected: 62
Occupation: Soldier
Party: Republican
Vice President: Richard M. Nixon

John F. Kennedy
1961-1963

Born: 1917   **35**
Died: 1963
Born in: Massachusetts
Elected from: Massachusetts
Age when elected: 43
Occupations: Author, Politician
Party: Democratic
Vice President: Lyndon B. Johnson

Lyndon B. Johnson
1963-1969

Born: 1908   **36**
Died: 1973
Born in: Texas
Elected as V.P. from: Texas
Assumed presidency upon
Kennedy's death
Age when became President: 55
Occupations: Teacher, Politician
Party: Democratic
Vice President: Hubert H. Humphrey

Richard M. Nixon
1969-1974

Born: 1913 **37**
Born in: California
Elected from: New York
Age when elected: 55
Occupations: Lawyer, Politician
Party: Republican
Vice Presidents: Spiro T. Agnew,
  Gerald R. Ford

Gerald R. Ford
1974-1977

Born: 1913 **38**
Born in: Nebraska
Appointed by Nixon as V.P. upon
Agnew's resignation; assumed
presidency upon Nixon's resignation
Age when became President: 61
Occupations: Lawyer, Politician
Party: Republican
Vice President: Nelson R.
  Rockefeller

Jimmy Carter
1977-1981

Born: 1924 **39**
Born in: Georgia
Elected from: Georgia
Age when elected: 52
Occupations: Businessman,
  Politician
Party: Democratic
Vice President: Walter F. Mondale

Ronald Reagan
1981-1989

Born: 1911 **40**
Born in: Illinois
Elected from: California
Age when elected: 69
Occupations: Actor, Politician
Party: Republican
Vice President: George H.W. Bush

George H.W. Bush
1989-1993

Born: 1924 **41**
Born in: Massachusetts
Elected from: Texas
Age when elected: 64
Occupations: Businessman,
  Politician
Party: Republican
Vice President: J. Danforth Quayle

William J. Clinton
1993-

Born: 1946 **42**
Born in: Arkansas
Elected from: Arkansas
Age when elected: 46
Occupations: Lawyer, Politician
Party: Democratic
Vice President: Albert Gore, Jr.

Documents of America's Heritage

THE MAGNA CARTA

The Magna Carta, signed by King John in 1215, marked a decisive step forward in the development of constitutional government in England. Later, it became a model for colonists who carried the Magna Carta's guarantees of legal and political rights to America.

1. That the English church shall be free, and shall have her rights entire, and her liberties inviolate;. . .

2. We also have granted to all the freemen of our kingdom, for us and for our heirs forever, all the underwritten liberties, to be had and holden by them and their heirs, of us and our heirs forever. . . .

39. No freeman shall be taken or imprisoned, or diseased, or outlawed, or banished, or in any way destroyed, nor will we pass upon him, nor will we send upon him, unless by the lawful judgment of his peers, or by the law of the land.

40. We will sell to no man, we will not deny to any man, either justice or right.

41. All merchants shall have safe and secure conduct to go out of, and to come into, England, and to stay there and to pass as well by land as by water, for buying and selling by the ancient and allowed customs, without any unjust tolls, except in time of war, or when they are of any nation at war with us. . . .

42. It shall be lawful, for the time to come, for any one to go out of our kingdom and return safely and securely by land or by water, saving his allegiance to us (unless in time of war, by some short space, for the common benefit of the realm).

60. All the aforesaid customs and liberties, which we have granted to be holden in our kingdom, as much as it belongs to us, all people of our kingdom, as well clergy as laity, shall observe, as far as they are concerned, towards their dependents.

63. . . . It is also sworn, as well on our part as on the part of the barons, that all the things aforesaid shall be observed in good faith, and without evil duplicity. Given under our hand, in the presence of the witnesses above named, and many others, in the meadow called Runnymede, between Windsor and Staines, the 15th day of June, in the 17th year of our reign.

THE MAYFLOWER COMPACT

On November 21, 1620, 41 colonists aboard the Mayflower *drafted this agreement. The Mayflower Compact was the first plan of self-government ever put in force in the English colonies.*

In ye name of God Amen. We whose names are underwritten, the loyall subjects of our dread soveraigne Lord King James, by ye grace of God, of Great Britaine, Franc, & Ireland king, defender of ye faith, &c. Haveing undertaken, for ye glorie of God, and advancemente of ye Christian faith and honour of our king & countrie, a voyage to plant ye first colonie in ye Northerne parts of Virginia, doe by these presents solemnly & mutualy in ye presence of God, and one of another, covenant, & combine ourselves togeather into a Civill body politick; for our better ordering, & preservation & furtherance of ye ends aforesaid; and by vertue hereof to enacte, constitute, and frame such just & equall Lawes, ordinances, Acts, constitutions, & offices, from time to time, as shall be thought most meete & convenient for ye generall good of ye colonie: unto which we promise all due submission and obedience. In witnes whereof we have hereunder subscribed our names at Cap-Codd ye -11- of November, in ye year of ye raigne of our soveraigne Lord King James of England, France, & Ireland ye eighteenth, and of Scotland ye fiftie fourth. Ano Dom. 1620.

WASHINGTON'S FAREWELL ADDRESS

At the end of his second term as President, George Washington spoke of the dangers facing the young nation. He warned against the dangers of political parties and sectionalism, and advised the nation against permanent alliances with other nations.

Citizens by birth or choice of a common country, that country has a right to concentrate your affections. The name of American, which belongs to you, in your national capacity, must always exalt the just pride of patriotism more than any appellation derived from local discriminations. With slight shades of difference, you have the same religion, manners, habits, and political principles. You have in a common cause fought and triumphed together. . . .

In contemplating the causes which may disturb our Union, it occurs as matter of serious concern that any ground should have been furnished for characterizing parties by geographical discriminations: Northern and Southern; Atlantic and Western. . . .

No alliances, however strict between the parts, can be an adequate substitute. They must inevitably experience the infractions and interruptions which all alliances in all times have experienced. . . .

The basis of our political systems is the right of the people to make and to alter their constitutions of government. But the constitution which at any time exists, till changed by an explicit and authentic act of the whole people, is sacredly obligatory upon all. . . .

The great rule of conduct for us, in regard to foreign nations, is in extending our commercial relations to have with them as little political connection as possible. So far as we have already formed engagements, let them be fulfilled with perfect good faith. . . .

Relying on its kindness in this as in other things, and actuated by that fervent love toward it which is so natural to a man who views in it the native soil of himself and his progenitors for several generations, I anticipate with pleasing expectations that retreat in which I promise myself to realize, without alloy, the sweet enjoyment of partaking, in the midst of my fellow citizens, the benign influence of good laws under a free government, the ever favorite object of my heart, and the happy reward, as I trust, of our mutual cares, labors, and dangers.

THE STAR-SPANGLED BANNER

During the British bombardment of Fort McHenry during the War of 1812, a young Baltimore lawyer named Francis Scott Key was inspired to write the words to "The Star-Spangled Banner." Although it became popular immediately, it was not until 1931 that Congress officially declared "The Star-Spangled Banner" as our national anthem.

O! say can you see, by the dawn's early light,
What so proudly we hail'd at the twilight's last
  gleaming,
Whose broad stripes and bright stars through
  the perilous fight,
O'er the ramparts we watched, were so gallantly
  streaming?
And the Rockets' red glare, the Bombs bursting
  in air,
Gave proof through the night that our Flag was
  still there;
O! say, does that star-spangled banner yet wave
O'er the Land of the free and the home of the
  brave!

On the shore, dimly seen through the mists of
  the deep,
Where the foe's haughty host in dread silence
  reposes,
What is that, which the breeze o'er the towering
  steep,
As it fitfully blows, half conceals, half discloses?
Now it catches the gleam of the morning's first
  beam,
In full glory reflected, now shines on the
  stream.
'Tis the star-spangled banner; O! long may it
  wave
O'er the land of the free and the home of the
  brave.

THE MONROE DOCTRINE

In an 1823 address to Congress, President James Monroe proclaimed what has become known as the Monroe Doctrine. The doctrine was designed to end European influence in the Western Hemisphere. In addition, it showed the world the American spirit of strength and unity, and became a cornerstone of United States foreign policy.

A precise knowledge of our relations with foreign powers as respects our negotiations and transactions with each is thought to be particularly necessary. . . .

In the discussions to which this interest has given rise . . . the occasion has been judged proper for asserting, as a principle in which the rights and interests of the United States are involved, that the American continents, by the free and independent condition which they have assumed and maintain, are henceforth not to be considered as subjects for future colonization by any European powers. . . .

The citizens of the United States cherish sentiments the most friendly in favor of the liberty and happiness of their fellowmen on that side of the Atlantic. In the wars of the European powers in matters relating to themselves we have never taken any part, nor does it comport with our policy so to do. It is only when our rights are invaded or seriously menaced that we resent injuries or make preparation for our defense.

With the movements in this hemisphere we are of necessity more immediately connected, and by causes which must be obvious to all enlightened and impartial observers. The political system of the allied powers is essentially different in this respect from that of America. This difference proceeds from that which exists in their respective governments; and to the defense of our own, which has been achieved by the loss of so much blood and treasure, and matured by the wisdom of their most enlightened citizens, and under which we have enjoyed unexampled felicity, this whole nation is devoted. We owe it, therefore, to candor and to the amicable relations existing between the United States and those powers to declare that we should consider any attempt on their part to extend their system to any portion of this hemisphere as dangerous to our peace and safety.

With the existing colonies or dependencies of any European power we have not interfered and shall not interfere. But with the governments who have declared their independence and maintained it, and whose independence we have, on great consideration and on just principles, acknowledged, we could not view any interposition for the purpose of oppressing them, or controlling in any other manner their destiny, by any European power in any other light than as the manifestation of any unfriendly disposition toward the United States. In the war between those new governments and Spain we declared our neutrality at the time of their recognition, and to this we have adhered, and shall continue to adhere, provided no change shall occur which, in the judgment of the competent authorities of this government, shall make a corresponding change on the part of the United States indispensable to their security.

Our policy in regard to Europe, which was adopted at an early stage of the wars which have so long agitated that quarter of the globe, nevertheless remains the same, which is not to interfere in the internal concerns of any of its powers; to consider the government de facto as the legitimate government for us; to cultivate friendly relations with it, and to preserve those relations by a frank, firm, and manly policy, meeting in all instances the just claims of every power, submitting to injuries from none. But in regard to those continents, circumstances are eminently and conspicuously different. It is impossible that the allied powers should extend their political system to any portion of either continent without endangering our peace and happiness; nor can anyone believe that our southern brethren, if left to themselves, would adopt it of their own accord.

It is equally impossible, therefore, that we should behold such interposition in any form with indifference. If we look to the comparative strength and resources of Spain and those new governments, and their distance from each other, it must be obvious that she can never subdue them. It is still the true policy of the United States to leave the parties to themselves, in the hope that other powers will pursue the same course.

THE SENECA FALLS DECLARATION

One of the first documents to express the desire for equal rights for women is the Declaration of Sentiments and Resolutions, issued in 1848 at the Seneca Falls Convention in New York. Led by Lucretia Mott and Elizabeth Cady Stanton, the delegates adopted a set of resolutions that called for woman suffrage and opportunities in employment and education.

When, in the course of human events, it becomes necessary for one portion of the family of man to assume among the people of the earth a position different from that which they have hitherto occupied, but one to which the laws of nature and of nature's God entitle them, a decent respect to the opinions of mankind requires that they should declare the causes that impel them to such a course.

We hold these truths to be self-evident: that all men and women are created equal; that they are endowed by their Creator with certain inalienable rights; that among these are life, liberty, and the pursuit of happiness; that to secure these rights governments are instituted, deriving their just powers from the consent of the governed. Whenever any form of government becomes destructive of these ends, it is the right of those who suffer from it to refuse allegiance to it, and to insist upon the institution of a new government, laying its foundation on such principles, and organizing its powers in such form, as to them shall seem most likely to effect their safety and happiness. Prudence, indeed, will dictate that governments long established should not be changed for light and transient causes;. . . But when a long train of abuses and usurpations, pursuing invariably the same object, evinces a design to reduce them under absolute despotism, it is their duty to throw off such government and to provide new guards for their future security. . . .

The history of mankind is a history of repeated injuries and usurpations on the part of man toward woman, having in direct object the establishment of an absolute tyranny over her. To prove this, let facts be submitted to a candid world.

He has never permitted her to exercise her inalienable right to the elective franchise.

He has compelled her to submit to laws in the formation of which she had no voice. . . .

He has made her, if married, in the eye of the law, civilly dead.

He has taken from her all right in property, even to the wages she earns. . . .

He has endeavored, in every way that he could, to destroy her confidence in her own powers, to lessen her self-respect, and to make her willing to lead a dependent and abject life.

Now, in view of the entire disfranchisement of one-half the people of this country, their social and religious degradation, in view of the unjust laws above mentioned, and because women do feel themselves aggrieved, oppressed, and fraudulently deprived of their most sacred rights, we insist that they have immediate admission to all the rights and privileges which belong to them as citizens of the United States. . . .

Resolved, that woman is man's equal, was intended to be so by the Creator, and the highest good of the race demands that she should be recognized as such.

Resolved, that the women of this country ought to be enlightened in regard to the laws under which they live, that they may no longer publish their degradation by declaring themselves satisfied with their present position, nor their ignorance, by asserting that they have all the rights they want. . . .

Resolved, that it is the duty of the women of this country to secure to themselves their sacred right to the elective franchise. . . .

Resolved, therefore, that, being invested by the Creator with the same capabilities and the same consciousness of responsibility for their exercise, it is demonstrably the right and duty of woman, equally with man, to promote every righteous cause by every righteous means; and especially in regard to the great subjects of morals and religion, it is self-evidently her right to participate with her brother in teaching them, both in private and in public, by writing and by speaking, by any instrumentalities proper to be used, and in any assemblies proper to be held; and this being a self-evident truth growing out of the divinely implanted principles of human nature, any custom or authority adverse to it, whether modern or wearing the hoary sanction of antiquity, is to be regarded as a self-evident falsehood, and at war with mankind.

THE EMANCIPATION PROCLAMATION

On January 1, 1863, President Abraham Lincoln issued the Emancipation Proclamation, which freed all slaves in states under Confederate control. The Proclamation was a significant step toward the Thirteenth Amendment (1865) that ended slavery in all of the United States.

Whereas on the 22d day of September, A.D. 1862, a proclamation was issued by the President of the United States, containing among other things, the following, to wit: That on the 1st day of January, in the year of our Lord 1863, all persons held as slaves within any state or designated part of a state, the people whereof shall then be in rebellion against the United States, shall be then, thenceforward, and forever free; and the executive government of the United States, including the military and naval authority thereof, will recognize and maintain the freedom of such persons and will do no act or acts to repress such persons, or any of them, in any efforts they may make for their actual freedom.

That the executive will, on the 1st day of January aforesaid, by proclamation, designate the states and parts of states, if any, in which the people thereof, respectively, shall then be in rebellion against the United States; and the fact that any state or the people thereof shall on that day be in good faith represented in the Congress of the United States by members chosen thereto at elections wherein a majority of the qualified voters of such states shall have participated shall, in the absence of strong countervailing testimony, be deemed conclusive evidence that such state and the people thereof are not then in rebellion against the United States.

Now, therefore, I, Abraham Lincoln, President of the United States, by virtue of the power in me vested as commander in chief of the Army and Navy of the United States in time of actual armed rebellion against the authority and government of the United States, and as a fit and necessary war measure for suppressing said rebellion, do, on this 1st day of January, in the year of our Lord 1863, and in accordance with my purpose so to do, publicly proclaimed for the full period of 100 days from the day first above mentioned, order and designate as the states and parts of states wherein the people thereof, respectively, are this day in rebellion against the United States the following, to wit:

Arkansas, Texas, Louisiana (except the parishes of St. Bernard, Plaquemines, Jefferson, St. John, St. Charles, St. James, Ascension, Assumption, Terrebonne, Lafourche, St. Mary, St. Martin, and Orleans, including the city of New Orleans), Mississippi, Alabama, Florida, Georgia, South Carolina, North Carolina, and Virginia (except the forty-eight counties designated as West Virginia, and also the counties of Berkeley, Accomac, Northampton, Elizabeth City, York, Princess Anne, and Norfolk, including the cities of Norfolk and Portsmouth), and which excepted parts are for the present left precisely as if their proclamation were not issued.

And, by virtue of the power and for the purpose aforesaid, I do order and declare that all persons held as slaves within said designated states and parts of states are, and henceforward shall be, free; and that the executive government of the United States, including the military and naval authorities thereof, will recognize and maintain the freedom of said persons.

And I hereby enjoin upon the people so declared to be free to abstain from all violence, unless in necessary self-defense; and I recommend to them that, in all cases when allowed, they labor faithfully for reasonable wages.

And I further declare and make known that such persons of suitable condition will be received into the armed service of the United States to garrison forts, positions, stations, and other places, and to man vessels of all sorts in said service.

And upon this act, sincerely believed to be an act of justice, warranted by the constitution upon military necessity, I invoke the considerate judgment of mankind and the gracious favor of Almighty God.

DOCUMENTS

THE GETTYSBURG ADDRESS

On November 19, 1863, President Abraham Lincoln gave a short speech at the dedication of a national cemetery on the battlefield of Gettysburg. His simple yet eloquent words expressed his hopes for a nation divided by civil war.

Four score and seven years ago our fathers brought forth on this continent a new nation, conceived in liberty, and dedicated to the proposition that all men are created equal.

Now we are engaged in a great civil war, testing whether that nation or any nation so conceived and so dedicated can long endure. We are met on a great battlefield of that war. We have come to dedicate a portion of that field as a final resting place for those who here gave their lives that that nation might live. It is altogether fitting and proper that we should do this.

But, in a larger sense, we can not dedicate—we can not consecrate—we can not hallow—this ground. The brave men, living and dead, who struggled here have consecrated it far beyond our poor power to add or detract. The world will little note nor long remember what we say here, but it can never forget what they did here. It is for us, the living, rather, to be dedicated here to the unfinished work which they who fought here have thus far so nobly advanced.

It is rather for us to be here dedicated to the great task remaining before us—that from these honored dead we take increased devotion to that cause for which they gave the last full measure of devotion; that we here highly resolve that these dead shall not have died in vain; that this nation, under God, shall have a new birth of freedom; and that government of the people, by the people, and for the people, shall not perish from the earth.

I WILL FIGHT NO MORE

In 1877 the Nez Perce Indians fought the government's attempt to move them to a smaller reservation. After a remarkable attempt to escape to Canada, Chief Joseph realized that resistance was hopeless and advised his people to surrender.

Tell General Howard I know his heart. What he told me before I have in my heart. I am tired of fighting. Our chiefs are killed. Looking Glass is dead. It is the young men who say yes or no. He who led the young men is dead. It is cold and we have no blankets. The little children are freezing to death. My people, some of them have run away to the hills and have no blankets, no food; no one knows where they are—perhaps freezing to death. I want to have time to look for my children and see how many I can find. Maybe I shall find them among the dead. Hear me my chiefs. I am tired; my heart is sick and sad. From where the sun now stand, I will fight no more forever.

THE PLEDGE OF ALLEGIANCE

In 1892 the nation celebrated the 400th anniversary of Columbus's landing in America. In connection with this celebration, Francis Bellamy, a magazine editor, wrote and published the Pledge of Allegiance.

I pledge allegiance to the Flag of the United States of America and to the Republic for which it stands, one Nation under God, indivisible, with liberty and justice for all.

THE FOURTEEN POINTS

On January 8, 1918, President Woodrow Wilson went before Congress to offer a statement of aims called the Fourteen Points. Wilson's plan called for freedom of the seas in peace and war, an end to secret alliances, and equal trading rights for all countries. The excerpt that follows is taken from the President's message.

It will be our wish and purpose that the processes of peace, when they are begun, shall be absolutely open and that they shall involve and permit henceforth no secret understandings of any kind. The day of conquest and aggrandizement is gone by; so is also the day of secret covenants entered into in the interest of particular governments and likely at some unlooked-for moment to upset the peace of the world. It is this happy fact, now clear to the view of every public man whose thoughts do not still linger in an age that is dead and gone, which makes it possible for every nation whose purposes are consistent with justice and the peace of the world to avow now or at any other time the objects it has in view. We entered this war because violations of right had occurred which touched us to the quick and made the life of our own people impossible unless they were corrected and the world secured once for all against their recurrence. What we demand in this war, therefore, is nothing peculiar to ourselves. It is that the world be made fit and safe to live in; and particularly that it be made safe for every peace-loving nation which, like our own, wishes to live its own life, determine its own institutions, be assured of justice and fair dealings by the other peoples of the world, as against force and selfish aggression. All the peoples of the world are in effect partners in this interest, and for our own part we see very clearly that unless justice be done to others it will not be done to us.

The program of the world's peace, therefore, is our program, and that program, the only possible program, as we see it, is this:

I. Open covenants of peace, openly arrived at, after which there shall be no private international understandings of any kind, but diplomacy shall proceed always frankly and in the public view.

II. Absolute freedom of navigation upon the seas, outside territorial waters, alike in peace and in war, except as the seas may be closed in whole or in part by international action for the enforcement of international covenants.

III. The removal, so far as possible, of all economic barriers and the establishment of an equality of trade conditions among all the nations consenting to the peace and associating themselves for its maintenance.

IV. Adequate guarantees given and taken that national armaments will be reduced to the lowest point consistent with domestic safety.

V. Free, open-minded, and absolutely impartial adjustment of all colonial claims, based upon a strict observance of the principle that in determining all such questions of sovereignty the interests of the population concerned must have equal weight with the equitable claims of the Government whose title is to be determined. . . .

XIV. A general association of nations must be formed under specific covenants for the purpose of affording mutual guarantees of political independence and territorial integrity to great and small states alike.

In regard to these essential rectifications of wrong and assertions of right, we feel ourselves to be intimate partners of all the governments and peoples associated together against the imperialists. We cannot be separated in interest or divided in purpose. We stand together until the end. . . .

We have spoken, now, surely, in terms too concrete to admit of any further doubt or question. An evident principle runs through the whole program I have outlined. It is the principle of justice to all peoples and nationalities, and their right to live on equal terms of liberty and safety with one another, whether they be strong or weak. Unless the principle be made its foundation, no part of the structure of international justice can stand. The people of the United States could act upon no other principle, and to the vindication of this principle they are ready to devote their lives, their honor, and everything that they possess. The moral climax of this, the culminating and final war for human liberty, has come, and they are ready to put their own strength, their own highest purpose, their own integrity and devotion to the test.

FRANKLIN ROOSEVELT'S FIRST INAUGURAL ADDRESS

The New Deal was launched March 4, 1933, the day that Franklin Roosevelt became President. At a time when the nation was in the depths of the Great Depression, the address showed a great sense of leadership and encouraged the American people.

I am certain that my fellow Americans expect that on my induction into the presidency I will address them with a candor and a decision which the present situation of our nation [impels]. This is preeminently the time to speak the truth, the whole truth, frankly and boldly. Nor need we shrink from honestly facing conditions in our country today. This great Nation will endure as it has endured, will revive and will prosper. So, first of all, let me assert my firm belief that the only thing we have to fear is fear itself—nameless, unreasoning, unjustified terror which paralyzes needed efforts to convert retreat into advance. In every dark hour of our national life a leadership of frankness and vigor has met with that understanding and support of the people themselves which is essential to victory. I am convinced that you will again give that support leadership in these critical days.

In such a spirit on my part and on yours we face our common difficulties. They concern, thank God, only material things. Values have shrunken to fantastic levels; taxes have risen; our ability to pay has fallen; government of all kinds is faced by serious curtailment of income; the means of exchange are frozen in the currents of trade; the withered leaves of industrial enterprise lie on every side; farmers find no markets for their produce the savings of many years in thousands of families are gone.

More important, a host of unemployed citizens face the grim problem of existence, and an equally great number toil with little return. Only a foolish optimist can deny the dark realities of the moment.

Yet our distress comes from no failure of substance. We are stricken by no plague of locusts. Compared with the perils which our [ancestors] conquered because they believed and were not afraid, we have still much to be thankful for. Nature still offers her bounty, and human efforts have multiplied it. Plenty is at our doorstep, but a generous use of it languishes in the very sight of the supply. Primarily this is because the rulers of the exchange of mankind's goods have failed, through their own stubbornness and their own incompetence,. . .

True they have tried, but their efforts have been cast in the pattern of an outworn tradition. Faced by failure of credit, they have proposed only the lending of more money. Stripped of the lure of profit by which to induce our people to follow their false leadership, they have resorted to exhortations, pleading tearfully for restored confidence. They know only the rules of a generation of self-seekers. They have no vision, and when there is no vision the people perish.

The money changers have fled from their high seats in the temple of our civilization. We may now restore that temple to the ancient truths. The measure of the restoration lies in the extent to which we apply social values more noble than mere monetary profit.

Happiness lies not in the mere possession of money; it lies in the joy of achievement, in the thrill of creative effort. The joy and moral stimulation of work no longer must be forgotten in the made chase of the evanecent [fleeting] profits. These dark days will be worth all they cost us if they teach us that our true destiny is not to be ministered unto but to minister to ourselves and to our fellow men.

Recognition of the falsity of material wealth as the standard of success goes hand in hand with the abandonment of the false belief that public office and high political position are to be valued only by the standards of pride of place and personal profit; and there must be an end to a conduct in banking and in business which too often has given to a sacred trust the likeness of callous and selfish wrongdoing. Small wonder that confidence languishes, for it thrives only on honesty, on honor, on the sacredness of obligations, on faithful protection, on unselfish performance; without them it cannot live.

Restoration calls, however, not for changes in ethics alone. This nation asks for action, and action now.

BROWN V. BOARD OF EDUCATION

On May 17, 1954, the Supreme Court ruled in Brown v. Board of Education *that racial segregation in public schools was unconstitutional. This decision provided the legal basis for court challenges to segregation in every aspect of American life.*

The plaintiffs contend that segregated public schools are not "equal" and cannot be made "equal," and that hence they are deprived of the equal protection of the laws. Because of the obvious importance of the question presented, the Court took jurisdiction. . . .

Our decision . . . cannot turn on merely a comparison of these tangible factors in the Negro and white schools involved in each of the cases. We must look instead to the effect of segregation itself on public education.

In approaching this problem, we cannot turn the clock back to 1868 when the Amendment was adopted, or even to 1896 when *Plessy v. Ferguson* was written. We must consider public education in the light of its full development and its present place in American life throughout the nation. Only in this way can it be determined if segregation in public schools deprives these plaintiffs of the equal protection of the laws.

Today, education is perhaps the most important function of state and local governments. Compulsory school attendance laws and the great expenditures for education both demonstrate our recognition of the importance of education to our democratic society. It is required in the performance of our most basic public responsibilities, even service in the armed forces. It is the very foundation of good citizenship. Today it is a principal instrument in awakening the child to cultural values, in preparing him for later professional training, and in helping him to adjust normally to his environment. In these days, it is doubtful that any child may reasonably be expected to succeed in life if he is denied the opportunity of an education. Such an opportunity, where the state has undertaken to provide it, is a right which must be made available to all on equal terms.

We come then to the question presented: Does segregation of children in public schools solely on the basis of race, even though the physical facilities and other "tangible" factors may be equal, deprive the children of the minority group of equal educational opportunities? We believe that it does.

In *Sweatt v. Painter,* . . .in finding that a segregated law school for Negroes could not provide them equal educational opportunities, this Court relied in large part on "those qualities which are incapable of objective measurement but which make for greatness in a law school." In *McLaurin v. Oklahoma State Regents,* . . .the Court, in requiring that a Negro admitted to a white graduate school be treated like all other students, again resorted to intangible considerations: " . . .his ability to study, to engage in discussions and exchange views with other students, and, in general, to learn his profession." Such considerations apply with added force to children in grade and high schools. To separate them from others of similar age and qualifications solely because of their race generates a feeling of inferiority as to their status in the community that may affect their hearts and minds in a way unlikely ever to be undone. The effect of this separation on their educational opportunities was well stated by a finding in the Kansas case by a court which nevertheless felt compelled to rule against the Negro plaintiffs:

"Segregation of white and colored children in public schools has a detrimental effect upon the colored children. The impact is greater when it has the sanction of the law; for the policy of separating the races is usually interpreted as denoting the inferiority of the Negro group. A sense of inferiority affects the motivation of a child to learn. Segregation with the sanction of law, therefore, has a tendency to retard the educational and mental development of Negro children and to deprive them of some of the benefits they would receive in a racially integrated school system."

. . . .We conclude that in the field of public education the doctrine of "separate but equal" has no place. Separate educational facilities are inherently unequal. Therefore, we hold that the plaintiffs and others similarly situated for whom the actions have been brought are, by reason of the segregation complained of, deprived of the equal protection of the laws guaranteed by the Fourteenth Amendment. . . .

JOHN F. KENNEDY'S INAUGURAL ADDRESS

President Kennedy's inaugural address on January 20, 1961, set the tone for his administration. In his address Kennedy stirred the nation by calling for "a grand and global alliance" to fight tyranny, poverty, disease, and war.

We observe today not a victory of party but a celebration of freedom—symbolizing an end as well as a beginning—signifying renewal as well as change. For I have sworn before you and Almighty God the same solemn oath our forebears prescribed nearly a century and three-quarters ago.

The world is very different now. For man holds in his mortal hands the power to abolish all forms of human poverty and all forms of human life. And yet the same revolutionary beliefs for which our forebears fought are still at issue around the globe—the belief that the rights of man come not from the generosity of the state but from the hand of God.

We dare not forget today that we are the heirs of that first revolution. Let the word go forth from this time and place, to friend and foe alike, that the torch has been passed to a new generation of Americans born in this century, tempered by war, disciplined by a hard and bitter peace, proud of our ancient heritage—and unwilling to witness or permit the slow undoing of those human rights to which this nation has always been committed, and to which we are committed today at home and around the world.

Let every nation know, whether it wishes us well or ill, that we shall pay any price, bear any burden, meet any hardship, support any friend, oppose any foe to assure the survival and the success of liberty.

This much we pledge—and more.

To those old allies whose cultural and spiritual origins we share, we pledge the loyalty of faithful friends. United, there is little we cannot do in a host of cooperative ventures. Divided, there is little we can do . . .

Let us never negotiate out of fear. But let us never fear to negotiate. . . . Let both sides explore what problems unite us instead of belaboring those problems which divide us. . . . Let both sides seek to invoke the wonders of science instead of its terrors. Together let us explore the stars, conquer the deserts, eradicate disease, tap the ocean depths, and encourage the arts and commerce.

All this will not be finished in the first 100 days. Nor will it be finished in the first 1,000 days, not in the life of this administration, nor even perhaps in our lifetime on this planet. But let us begin.

In your hands, my fellow citizens, more than mine, will rest the final success or failure of our course. Since this country was founded, each generation of Americans has been summoned to give testimony to its national loyalty. . . .

Now the trumpet summons us again—not as a call to bear arms, though arms we need—not as a call to battle, though embattled we are—but a call to bear the burden of a long twilight struggle, year in and year out, "rejoicing in hope, patient in tribulation"—a struggle against the common enemies of man: tyranny, poverty, disease, and war itself.

In the long history of the world, only a few generations have been granted the role of defending freedom in its hour of maximum danger. I do not shrink from this responsibility—I welcome it. I do not believe that any of us would exchange places with any other people or any other generation. The energy, the faith, the devotion which we bring to this endeavor will light our country and all who serve it—and the glow from that fire can truly light the world. And so, my fellow Americans—ask not what your country can do for you—ask what you can do for your country.

My fellow citizens of the world—ask not what American will do for you but what together we can do for the freedom of man.

Finally, whether you are citizens of America or citizens of the world, ask of us here the same high standards of strength and sacrifice which we ask of you. With a good conscience our only sure reward, with history the final judge of our deeds, let us go forth to lead the land we love, asking His blessing and His help, but knowing that here on earth God's work must truly be our own.

I HAVE A DREAM

On August 28, 1963, while Congress debated wide-ranging civil rights legislation, Martin Luther King, Jr., led more than 200,000 people on a march on Washington. On the steps of the Lincoln Memorial he gave a stirring speech in which he eloquently spoke of his dreams for African Americans and for the United States.

Five score years ago, a great American, in whose symbolic shadow we stand, signed the Emancipation Proclamation. This momentous decree came as a great beacon light to millions of Negro slaves who had been seared in the flames of withering injustice. It came as a joyous daybreak to end the long night of captivity.

But one hundred years later, we must face the tragic fact that the Negro is still not free. One hundred years later, the life of the Negro is still sadly crippled by the manacles of segregation and the chains of discrimination. One hundred years later, the Negro lives on a lonely island of poverty in the midst of a vast ocean of material prosperity. One hundred years later, the Negro is still languished in the corners of American society and finds himself an exile in his own land. . . .

Now is the time to make real the promises of democracy. . . . *Now* is the time to open the doors of opportunity to all of God's children. . . .

There are those who are asking the devotees of civil rights, "when will you be satisfied?"

We can never be satisfied as long as the Negro is the victim of the unspeakable horrors of police brutality. . . .We cannot be satisfied as long as the Negro's basic mobility is from a smaller ghetto to a larger one. We can never be satisfied as long as a Negro in Mississippi cannot vote and a Negro in New York believes he has nothing for which to vote. . . .

I say to you today, my friends, that in spite of the difficulties and frustrations of the moment I still have a dream. It is a dream deeply rooted in the American dream.

I have a dream that one day this nation will rise up and live out the true meaning of its creed, "We hold these truths to be self-evident, that all men are created equal."

I have a dream that one day on the red hills of Georgia the sons of former slaves and the sons of former slaveowners will be able to sit down together at the table of brotherhood.

I have a dream that one day even the state of Mississippi, a desert state sweltering with the heat of injustice and oppression, will be transformed into an oasis of freedom and justice.

I have a dream that my four little children will one day live in a nation where they will not be judged by the color of their skin, but by the content of their character.

I have a dream today.

I have a dream that one day the state of Alabama, whose governor's lips are presently dripping with the words of interposition and nullification, will be transformed into a situation where little black boys and black girls will be able to join hands with little white boys and white girls and walk together as sisters and brothers.

I have a dream today.

I have a dream that one day every valley shall be exalted, every hill and mountain shall be made low, the rough places will be made plain, and the crooked places will be made straight, and the glory of the Lord shall be revealed, and all flesh shall see it together.

This is our hope. This is the faith with which I return to the South. With this faith we will be able to hew out of the mountain of despair a stone of hope. With this faith we will be able to transform the jangling discords of our nation into a beautiful symphony of brotherhood.

With this faith we will be able to work together, to pray together, to struggle together, to go jail together, to stand up for freedom together, knowing that we will be free one day.

This will be the day when all of God's children will be able to sing with new meaning. "My country 'tis of thee, sweet land of liberty, of thee I sing. Land where my fathers died, land of the Pilgrims' pride, from every mountainside, let freedom ring." When we let freedom ring, when we let it ring from every village and every hamlet, from every state and every city, we will be able to speed up that day when all of God's children, black men and white men, Jews and Gentiles, Protestants and Catholics, will be able to join hands and sing in the words of the old Negro spiritual: "Free at last! Free at last! Thank God Almighty, we are free at last!"

SOCIAL REFORMS IN RUSSIA

On June 17, 1992, Boris Yeltsin, the president of the Russian Federation, spoke before a joint meeting of the United States Congress. In his address, he envisioned a new relationship between Americans and the people of the former Soviet Union.

. . . For many years our two nations were the two poles, the two opposites. They wanted to make us implacable enemies. That affected the destinies of the world in a most tragic way.

The world was shaken by the storms of confrontation. It was close to exploding, close to perishing beyond salvation.

That evil scenario is becoming a thing of the past. Reason begins to triumph over madness. We have left behind the period when America and Russia looked at each other through gunsights, ready to pull the trigger at any time . . . .

The world can sigh in relief. The idol of communism, which spread everywhere social strife, animosity, and unparalleled brutality which instilled fear in humanity, has collapsed. It has collapsed, never to rise again.

I am here to assure you, we shall not let it rise again in our land. . . .

There is no people on this Earth who could be harmed by the air of freedom. There are no exceptions to that rule.

Liberty sets the mind free, fosters independence, and unorthodox thinking and ideas. But it does not offer instant prosperity or happiness and wealth to everyone. . . .

The experience of the past decades has taught us, communism has no human face. Freedom and communism are incompatible.

You will recall August 1991, when for 3 days, Russia was under the dark cloud of dictatorship. I addressed the Muscovites who were defending the White House of Russia. I addressed all the people of Russia. I addressed them standing on top of the tank, whose crew had disobeyed criminal orders.

I will be candid with you—at that moment I feared, but had no fear for myself. I feared for the future of democracy in Russia and throughout the world, because I was aware what could happen if we failed to win.

Citizens of Russia upheld their freedom and did not allow the continuation of the 75 years of nightmare. . . .

We realize our great responsibility for the success of our changes, not only toward the people of Russia, but also toward the citizens of America and of the entire world. Today the freedom of America is being upheld in Russia. Should the reforms fail, it will cost hundreds of billions to offset that failure. . . .

History is giving us a chance to fulfill President Wilson's dream; namely, to make the world safe for democracy.

More than 30 years ago, President Kennedy addressed these words to humanity:

"My fellow citizens of the world, ask not what America can do for you, but what together, we can do for the freedom of man."

I believe that his inspired call for working together toward a democratic world is addressed above all to our two peoples, to the people of America and to the people of Russia.

Partnership and friendship of our two largest democracies in strenghtening democracy is indeed a great goal.

Joining the world community, we wish to preserve our identity, our own image and history, promote culture, and strengthen moral standards of our people. . . .

At the same time, Russia does not aspire to change the world in its own image. It is the fundamental principle of the new Russia to be generous and to share experience, moral values, and emotional warmth, rather than to impose and coerce.

It is the tradition of the Russian people to repay kindness with kindness. This is the bedrock of the Russian lifestyle, the underlying truths revealed by the great Russian culture.

Free and democratic Russia will remain committed to this tenet.

Today free and democratic Russia is extending its hand of friendship to the people of America. Acting on the will of the people of Russia, I am inviting you, and through you the people of the United States to join us in partnership in the quest for freedom and justice in the 21st century. . . .

I would like now to conclude my statement with the words from a song by Irving Berlin, an American of Russian descent:

"God bless America," to which I will add, "and Russia."

History Writer's Handbook

WRITING PARAGRAPHS

Writing is a process used to convey ideas. This process has three phases: prewriting, writing, and revising. Each of these phases involves different activities. To use the writing process effectively, you must engage in the various activities of each phase without taking shortcuts. By going through the following process, you will write paragraphs that convey your ideas effectively, cohesively, and coherently.

Phase 1: Prewriting

- *Identify your audience and purpose.*

  Your basic aim in writing is to communicate ideas and information to an individual or a group of people. Therefore, when you write, you should always predetermine your specific audience. In history and other social studies classes, your audience will usually be your teacher and your classmates—persons whom you know and who share an interest in the subject you are writing about and in what you have to say about it.

  Determining your purpose for writing is as important as determining your audience. A paragraph you write to a friend to explain how you won $100, for example, will be far different from a paragraph you write to persuade your neighbors to donate money in support of a new recycling program. Brief descriptions with examples of 8 purposes of writing follow on pages 1125-1129. This part of the History Writer's Handbook will assist you in choosing and executing the proper kind of writing for your specific purpose.

  For example, read the model paragraph in the box below. The writer's audience is his or her teacher and fellow students; the writer's purpose is to inform them of the effects that the coal strike's settlement had.

  Keep your audience and purpose firmly in mind as you organize and write your paragraph(s). You will find it helpful to jot this information down and remind yourself of it as you write.

- *Decide on a topic and topic sentence.*

  You are often given an assignment to write about a broad subject. You must decide on a **topic,** a narrow, limited aspect of the subject that will be specific enough to be covered in a single paragraph. For example, the writer of the paragraph below was asked to write about the 1902 coal strike. He or she narrowed this subject to the topic of the effects of the coal-strike settlement.

WRITING PARAGRAPHS

Topic Sentence
Settlement of the coal strike was a partial success for everyone.

Supporting Details
Roosevelt was praised for settling the strike.

Roosevelt didn't send in federal troops.

Mineowners didn't have to recognize the mineworkers' union.

Mineworkers won a 10-percent pay increase and a nine-hour work day.

The public could stop worrying about lack of fuel in the coming cold winter.

Big business won because public resentment against business stopped growing.

Everyone got a square deal.

First Draft
Settlement of the coal strike was a partial success for everyone. Mineworkers won a 10-percent increase and a nine-hour work day. Mineowners also did not have to recognize a mineworker's union. Rooesevelt was praised for settling the strike without sending in troops. Big business won because public resentment against business stopped growing. The public could stop worrying about lack of fuel for the coming cold winter. Everyone got a square deal.

Revised Paragraph
The coal-strike settlement could be described as a "square deal for everyone." Mineworkers won a 10-percent pay increase and a nine-hour work day but not the recognition of their union. Mineowners won because they were not forced to recognize the mineworkers' union. Big businesses also won because the settlement successfully stopped the rising tide of public resentment against them. In addition, President Roosevelt earned praise for his part in settling the strike without sending in troops. Even the public benefited, because it could at last stop worrying about a possible fuel shortage.

Write a **topic sentence** that tells the main idea you want to convey about your topic. You may need to draft several versions of the topic sentence or change it during the drafting and revising process. Note the transformation of the topic sentence in the model below.

- *Develop your topic.*

  Brainstorm, bringing to mind everything you know or can recall about your topic. List these related ideas and supporting details as each comes to mind. You may first list these as words or phrases, but when your list is complete, write a sentence for every item. Then review the sentences to decide whether they genuinely contribute to your purpose. You can then follow the development of ideas into sentences below.

Phase 2: Writing

- *Organize your sentences.*

  The purpose for your paragraph generally determines the best way to organize your ideas. Your purpose for writing social studies paragraphs can be to describe something, to tell what happened, to explain, inform, compare, persuade, or to provide definitions and/or examples. Recall your purpose, then arrange your sentences according to the writing pattern best suited to achieving that purpose. Refer to the rest of this History Writer's Handbook for help in deciding on a purpose and selecting the most appropriate pattern for that purpose. Notice that the pattern used in the model paragraph is classification.

- *Connect your sentences.*

  Write your sentences in order adding transitions and cue words to show relationships between ideas. To see how cues can clarify a writer's purpose, examine the chart on cue words for historical reasoning in the skill lesson on page 251.

Phase 3: Revising and Editing

- *Revising and Editing*

  Expand and improve your sentences, varying their structure and length, adding modifiers, and revising word choices. Cut sentences that do not contribute to the main idea or that disrupt the flow of your paragraph.

  Finally copyedit your paragraph. Remember that you want to convey your ideas effectively, and that poor punctuation, capitalization, and misspellings will hamper that purpose. Check to be sure that the proper words are capitalized, that you have used commas and periods correctly, and that there are no misspellings in your paragraph.

WRITING FOR DIFFERENT PURPOSES

The purpose for your writing largely determines how and what you write. Your approach, your style, even your word choices are influenced by the purpose. In social studies such purposes can be to relate a series of events, describe something, make comparisons, persuade, provide examples or definitions, or to explain a cause and its effects. Learning to write narration, descriptions, comparisons, persuasions, examples, definitions, and cause-and-effect essays will help you to accomplish these goals.

Narration

To tell the story of an event or a series of events, you use narrative writing. Effective narrative writing is carefully organized: events are usually arranged in chronological order. To further clarify the relationships between events, transitional words and phrases are used. Effective narrative writing also limits details to those that are essential and contribute directly to the story. Notice the effectiveness of the narration in the following paragraphs from a diary of a pioneer woman of the late 1800s.

Mother had brought some medicine along. She hung the bag containing the medicine from a nail on the side-board of the wagon. . . . My little sister, Salita Jane wanted to tast (sic) it, but I told her she couldn't have it. She didn't say anything but as soon as we had gone she got the bottle and drank it all. Presently she came to the campfire where Mother was cooking supper and said she felt awfully sleepy. Mother told her to run away and not bother her, so she went to where the beds were spread and lay down. When Mother called her for supper she didn't come. Mother saw she was asleep, so she didn't disturb her. When Mother tried to awake her later she couldn't arouse her. Lettie had drunk the whole bottle of laudanum. It was too late to save her life. . . . Father took walnut boards and made a coffin for Salita and we buried her there by the roadside in the desert. . . .

Three days after my little sister Lettie drank the laudanum and died we stopped for a few hours, and my sister Olivia was born. We were so late that the men of the party decided we could not tarry a day, so we had to press on . . . After a great hardship . . . we faintly made our way through . . . to Oregon it was late in the year and the winter rains had started. We had been eight months on the road instead of five, we were out of food, and our cattle were nearly worn out. . . .

The writer related the events in chronological order, using *temporal* (time) words and phrases for additional clarity—*as soon as, when, later, too late, three days after, a few hours, finally.* Notice too that there are no unnecessary details. The writer included only those that are essential to explain the harshness of her particular pioneer experience.

Description

Use descriptive writing to convey an experience as concretely and vividly as possible. Descriptive writing incorporates sensory details and/or figures of speech. *Sensory details* are those that appeal to the senses, making an object or experience concrete for the reader by describing how something looks, feels, tastes, smells, and sounds. *Figures of speech,* such as simile and metaphor, compare unfamiliar objects or events to those that are familiar so that the reader can visualize the object or event exactly.

The key to effective descriptive writing is not *how many* sensory details and figures of speech you use, but rather the *kind* you use. Effective sensory details employ specific adjectives and adverbs and strong, active verbs that command the reader to see what you have seen, hear what you have heard, smell, taste, and felt as you have. Effective similes and metaphors use events and objects so familiar that they not only create a "vision" *for* the reader but a distinct impression *in* the reader.

The first paragraph that follows is a basic paragraph on a dust storm in the 1930s. The second paragraph shows how you can expand the basic paragraph's sentences to convey this experience more vividly and concretely. Think about all of the senses to which these words and phrases appeal. Also look for the similes and metaphors and notice how they help you to "see" and "feel" what it was like to be in this dust storm.

Basic Paragraph

On Sunday, April 14, 1935, people on the Great Plains of the United States experienced a dust storm. The blowing dust formed clouds that extended over 1,000 feet into the air and several miles wide. Birds flew to escape the choking dust. Motorists had to stop because they were unable to see through the dust. The dust piled up on railroad lines, where it stayed until snow plows cleared it away. The removal of the dust from the railroad took the plows several days.

Expanded Paragraph

On Sunday, April 14, 1935, one of the biggest dust storms of this century swept over the Great Plains of the United States. Huge black clouds of dust, more than 1,000 feet high, formed a wall miles wide. Birds flew frantically to escape suffocation in the turbulent storm. Motorists were stranded for hours along the highway, totally blinded by the impenetrable cloud. Dust from the "black blizzard" piled up on railroad lines, and it took snow plows several days to clear off the tracks.

The addition of half a dozen specific adjectives and adverbs—*biggest, huge, black, frantically, turbulent, totally blinded, impenetrable*—and two strong verbs—*swept over, were stranded*—produce an immediacy of experience that almost forces the reader into the storm. The final metaphor "black blizzard" compares the unfamiliar dust storm with the more familiar snowstorm, amplifying the physical description of the storm into an experience that engages not only the senses but the emotions as well.

Choice descriptive details can also recreate compelling positive experiences, as the following nineteenth-century love letter illustrates.

We have had snow-storms for several days together, and at this moment a snow-plow is at work opening a path to the churches. The death-like stillness of night and winter extends over meadow and valley, only a few cows wander about, like ghosts, over the snowy tracts, to pluck a scanty meal from the twigs of the trees that are not yet buried in the snow.

Close thine eyes, slumber, my beloved one, while I watch over thee. Thou shalt one day look upon night and winter and own that their power is not so fearful. Love, that geyser of the soul, can melt the ice and snow of the most frozen regions: wherever its warm springs well up there glows a southern climate.

Notice how *specific* the descriptive words are: *death-like stillness, scanty meal, most frozen regions*. The verbs are strong and active as well: *extends, wander, pluck, buried, slumber, melt, well up, glows*. The final touch that creates the impression is the vivid simile *Love, that geyser of the soul*, which compares an emotion to a physical object known for its heated force.

Comparison

Use the comparison writing pattern if your purpose is to explain how two things or events are alike or different. As long as you can find one likeness and one difference, a comparison can be made. So that your comparison will be as precise as possible, focus on items or events that are within the same *kind* or *class*. For example, you can compare Chryslers and Cadillacs because they share many common features—features that you can pinpoint.

When you have determined the related items, brainstorm the *specific* points you want to compare. Then organize your material so that your explanation of the likenesses and/or differences is as clear as possible. The most common pattern for a comparison paragraph compares specific points from the least important significant point to the most important point.

The following paragraphs compare the progressive reformers of the early twentieth century with the Populist reformers of the late nineteenth century.

Like the Populists of the 1880s and 1890s, progressives feared the concentration of power in the hands of the wealthy few. While hard-working immigrants could not afford to provide for their hungry and ill children, financiers like J.P. Morgan became millionaires by manipulating ownership of the companies for which these immigrants toiled. Through campaign contributions and bribes, trusts bought influence with lawmakers. Progressives wanted reforms to protect the public interest.

Unlike the Populists, who usually lived in rural areas, the progressives generally lived in cities. By the 1890s, cities faced crippling problems: housing shortages, political corruption, and spiraling crime rates. . . .

Progressives were also unlike Populists in their greater faith in experts. While Populists emphasized the wisdom of average people, progressives focused on the ability of knowledgeable experts to analyze and solve problems. . . . Progressives believed that trained experts could

analyze and conquer crime, alcoholism, and political corruption. Many progressives praised businessowners for their expertise in solving the problems of producing and distributing goods, and in running a store or a factory efficiently. Though fearing the power of large businesses, progressives often respected the methods business used to become effective.

The first paragraph compares specific likenesses of the Populists and progressives; the second and third paragraphs contrast specific differences between the two kinds of reformers. Reading these paragraphs, notice how the orderly, very specific comparison explains both the progressive and Populist reformers.

There are two other comparison arrangements in addition to the *alternating* (point by point) pattern shown. The *block* pattern explains all the characteristics of the first item or event, then explains all the characteristics of the second item or event in a corresponding paragraph. The *mixed* comparison pattern explains likenesses and differences in the same paragraph. Likenesses can be explained first, then differences, or vice versa.

Cause and Effect

Cause-and-effect writing combines characteristics of narrative with comparison writing. Like narration, cause-and-effect tells *what happened*. Like comparison writing, cause-and-effect explains *why* something happened or the *results* of what happened.

When you are relating the event (telling *what happened*), arrange your information chronologically, as you do for a narration. To explain the *cause* (why) or the *effect* (result) of the event, do so in the same point-by-point pattern as you would a comparison paragraph. You may also want to use transition words such as *because, as a result of, the effects of, due to*.

The following paragraphs illustrate cause-and-effect writing.

The consequences of the 1936 election were plain the day after the polls closed. The Democratic party had been reconstituted. No longer was it a sectional party with outposts here and there in the North and West. It was fully national, and it was that way because Roosevelt had put together and solidified a remarkable coalition of voters, including labor, blacks, ethnic groups, religious minorities, the poor, large numbers of farmers, and many men in small business. The New Deal coalition also swept up

HISTORY WRITER'S HANDBOOK

legions of women, youth intellectuals, and city folk . . . , along with many professionals and large blocs of civil servants.

More significantly, the election of 1936 confirmed that big government was here to stay, that Americans would now look more often to Washington for the solution of their problems instead of to themselves. . . .

One other major result was that Americans, by remaining committed to the Democratic and Republican parties, perpetuated at a time of economic crisis and political unsettledness not only the two-party system but also the concept of deciding national differences at the polls.

The first sentence presents the event: the 1936 election. Then begins the explanation of the results of *effects* of that election as well as the explanations of *why* (causes) those results came about. One *result* (effect) of the election was the reconstitution of the Democratic Party *because* (cause) Roosevelt had been able to get many kinds of voters on his side. Another *result* (effect) of the election was the confirmation that Americans wanted big government *because* (cause) so many Republicans had shifted to support a bigger role for the federal government.

Argumentation

Argumentation is a kind of formal writing you can use when your goal is to persuade, or convince, someone to accept your point of view on a controversial subject. Argumentation is logical, appealing to the reader's intellect. To best achieve this logical appeal in written argumentation, follow these steps:

- State the controversy or problem clearly.
- Give your position on the controversy or your solution to the problem.
- Present the evidence (relevant facts and statistics) you have gathered to support your position.
- Refute any opposing positions or solutions by presenting evidence that negates them.
- Conclude your argumentation by summing up your positive evidence and restate your position. Note the elements of argumentation in these closing paragraphs to a book on United States-Mexico relations.

The argument of this book is that the tensions, conflicts, and misperceptions which have always characterized the United States-Mexican relationship are rooted in history, asymmetry, and changes in each of the countries and in the

relationship. These, in turn, have led to policy mistakes and misconceptions. But the fact that the basic structure of the relationship changes so slowly does not mean that nothing can be done to improve it. These proposals will not transform the relationship, but perhaps the awareness that can emerge from our exchange will yield a synthesis that might permit some modest and positive changes.

A number of steps can be taken to improve the broader context of mutual understanding, beginning with improvements in both the amount and the quality of press coverage of the other country. . . . A second area would be improve the amount and quality of teaching and research. . . .

As our children grow on both sides of the border, they might relate as poorly as present and past generations have. But we hope they will understand each other better. We end this book without illusions but with hopes. Cooperation between the United States and Mexico will always be difficult but never impossible.

The first three sentences state both the writer's position and the problem. The next three sentences refer to the relevant facts and statistics presented as support in the body of the book, and propose solutions. The final paragraph presents a short summation and a restatement of the writer's position.

Classification

Classification is the writing method that organizes information about a complex whole into smaller, more useful categories. Many social studies texts and chapters are written in the classification mode. The chapter titles will identify the subject; for example, "The Civil War." Information about the subject is then categorized and treated in small, understandable sections: *The outbreak of War, The War on the Battlefield, Behind the Lines, Ending the War.*

Using classification writing in paragraphs often involves enumeration, or listing. All the items listed in any one category or classification should share a quality or characteristic. Determining categories, of course, will depend on your subject and topic.

The following paragraph demonstrates how the classification approach can simplify a complex whole by categorizing.

Who were the "invisible poor" of the mid-1950s? Almost half were children under the age of eighteen. *At least a third worked on farms or lived in depressed rural areas. Some were African and Hispanic Americans, facing long-standing racial and ethnic prejudice and discrimination. The poor also included jobless Appalachian whites, who moved to the cities because of lack of opportunity in the hills, and native Americans, who lived both in the cities and on reservations. There were the growing number of elderly Americans not covered by social security or receiving pensions.*

To better understand the complex group of mid-1950s poor people, the writer classifies, or categorizes, them into six subcategories. She then briefly enumerates the causes that force them to share a common characteristic—poverty.

Definition

In completing a writing assignment for history class, you may need to define terms you use in your essay. Define any terms that you think might be unfamiliar to your audience. Your definition can be a single synonym, several words or phrases, or several sentences. It is best, though, to keep the length as short as possible so as not to intrude on the flow and cohesion of the entire paragraph. Remember also to use words and terms appropriate and understandable to your audience.

Note how both of the definitions in the following sentences clarify unfamiliar terms without hampering the flow of thought.

At this time, dozens of publications appeared spreading the ideas of abolitionism, the movement to end slavery. Most of these papers called for a gradual end to slavery, believing that the slow pace would bring emancipation—freedom—to African Americans.

Some terms may require a more lengthy definition, particularly if the term has a complex connotation. Such an *extended definition* may employ other types of writing, such as description or classification. The following extended definition uses both.

Crummell defined civilization as: the clarity of the mind from the dominion of false heathen ideas, . . . the conscious impress of individualism and personal responsibility, . . . the recognition of the body, with its desires and appetites and passions as a sacred gift, and as under the law of divine obligation, . . . the honor and freedom of womanhood, allied with the duty of family development, . . . the sense of social progress in society, . . . the entrance of new impulses in the actions and policy of the tribe or

nation, . . . an elevated use of material things and a higher range of common industrial activities, . . . and the earliest possible introduction of letters, and books, and reading. . . .

Because the word *civilization* encompasses so many ideas and connotations, the writer feels it necessary to enumerate all the things the word means to him. His audience will then understand what he means by the term whenever they encounter it in the remainder of his argument.

Examples

Use examples in a paragraph to explain, illustrate, or amplify your main idea. Brainstorm a number of possible examples, then select those that illustrate your idea most accurately. Also choose those that you think your audience will find convincing. One or more examples can often clarify a main point so well that no other kind of explanation is necessary.

Notice how the examples in the following paragraphs illustrate and clarify the writer's topic sentence.

It was Madison . . . who tightened the constitutional language, substituting the imperative "shall" for the flaccid "ought" and "ought nots" of the state proposals, thus completing the process begun by John Adams in the Massachusetts Declaration of Rights. We can see Madison's contribution in this respect in the following sequence:

BILL OF RIGHTS, 1689: "That excessive bail ought not to be required, nor excessive fines imposed, nor cruel and unusual punishments inflicted."

VIRGINIA DECLARATION OF RIGHTS, 1776: "That excessive bail ought not to be required, nor excessive fines imposed, nor cruel and unusual punishments inflicted."

AMENDMENT PROPOSED BY MADISON, JUNE 8, 1789: "Excessive bail shall not be required, for excessive fines imposed, nor cruel and unusual punishments inflicted."

Madison's amendments were based on the understanding that . . . the situation called for flat commands. . . . It was Madison who toughened the old flaccid exhortations into imperative law.

All three examples that the writer provides accurately illustrate his or her main point concerning Madison's contribution to constitutional language. Note, too, that by providing strong examples, the writer does not need to say much more to prove his point.

Gazetteer

The gazetteer is a geographical dictionary that lists political divisions, natural features, and other places and locations. Following each entry is a description, its latitude and longitude, and page references that indicate where each entry may be found in this text. Pages noted in italic indicate that the entry is on a map.

A

Afghanistan country in south central Asia (33° N/63° E) 1039, *1094*

Africa continent of the eastern hemisphere south of the Mediterranean Sea and adjoining Asia on its northeastern border (10° N/22°E) 22, *1098*

Alabama state in the southeastern United States; 22nd state to enter the union (32°45'N/87°30'W) 238, 265

Alaska state in the United States, located in northwestern North America; territory purchased from Russia in 1867 (64°N/150°W) 10, *652*

Albany capital of New York located in the Hudson Valley; site where Albany Congress proposed first formal plan to unite the 13 colonies (40°45'N/73°45'W) 51, *137*

Allegheny River river in western Pennsylvania uniting with the Monongahela River at Pittsburgh to form the Ohio River (40° N/82°W) 98, *99*

Andes Mountains mountain system extending along western coast of South America (13°S/75°W) 12, *1093*

Antarctica continent located around the South Pole (80°15'S/127°E) 78, *1088*

Antietam Civil War battle site in western Maryland (39°45'N/77°30'W) 454, *455*

Appalachian Mountains chief mountain system in eastern North America extending from Quebec and New Brunswick to central Alabama (37°N/82°W) 101, *102*

Appomattox Court House site in central Virginia where Confederate forces surrendered ending the Civil War (37°N/77°W) 471, *473*

Arctic Ocean ocean in the northernmost part of the world (85°N/170°E) 89, *1094*

Arizona state in the southwestern United States; 48th state to enter the union (34°N/113°W) 15, *1090*

Arkansas state in the south central United States; acquired as part of Louisiana Purchase (34°45'N/93°45'W) 265, *291*

Aroostook Valley fertile farming region in Maine (47° N/68°W) 399

Asia continent of the eastern hemisphere forming a single landmass with Europe (50°N/100°E) 10, *1094-1095*

Atlanta capital of Georgia located in the northwest central part of the state (33°45'N/84°30'W) *433*, 468

Atlantic Ocean ocean separating North and South America from Europe and Africa (5°S/25°W) 14, *39*

Australia continent and country southeast of Asia (25°S/125°E) *1089*

B

Baltimore city on the Chesapeake Bay in central Maryland (39°15'N/76°45'W) 57, 272

Barbary Coast north coast of Africa between Morocco and Tunisia (36°45'N/3°E) 156, *277*

Baton Rouge capital of Louisiana located on the Mississippi River in the southeastern part of the state (30°30'N/91°15'W) 142, *1091*

Bay of Pigs site of 1961 invasion of Cuba (22°N/79°W) 966

Beijing capital of China located in the northeastern part of the country (40°N/116°30'E) 656, *1095*

Berlin city in east central Germany; former national capital divided into sectors after World War II; city reunited in 1989 (52°31'N/13°30'E) *1094*

Black Hills mountains in southwestern South Dakota; site of conflict between Sioux Indians and white settlers during 1870s (44°15'N/103°45'W) 513, *519*

Boston capital of Massachusetts located in the eastern part of the state; founded by English Puritans in 1630 (42°15'N/71°W) *57*, 64

Brazil country in eastern South America (9°S/53°W) 38, *1093*

C

California state in the western United States; attracted thousands of miners during gold rush of 1849 (38°15'N/121°15'W) 399, *438*

Cambodia country in Southeast Asia bordering Gulf of Siam; offical name Democratic Kampuchea (12° N/105°E) *1095*

Canada country in northern North America (50°N/100°W) 10, *1092*

Charleston city in South Carolina on the Atlantic coast; original name Charles Town (32°45'N/80°W) 62, *73*

Château-Thierry World War I battle site in France (49°N/3°15'E) *743*, 744

Chautauqua Lake lake in western New York State (42°15'N/79°45'W) 596

Chesapeake Bay inlet of the Atlantic Ocean in Virginia and Maryland (37°N/76°W) *59*, 143

Chicago largest city in Illinois; located in northeastern part of the state along Lake Michigan (41°45'N/87°30'W) *291*, 325

China country in eastern Asia; mainland (People's Republic of China) under communist control since 1949 (36°45'N/93°E) 23, *1095*

Chisholm Trail pioneer cattle trail from Texas to Kansas (34°N/98°W) 516

Cincinnati city in southern Ohio on the Ohio River; grew as result of increasing steamship traffic during the mid-1800s (39°15'N/84°30'W) 237, *291*

Cleveland city in northern Ohio on Lake Erie (41°30'N/81°45'W) *291*, 545

Colorado state in the western United States (39°30'N/107°W) 15, *519*

Columbia River river flowing through southwest Canada and northwestern United States into the Pacific Ocean (46°15'N/124°W) *264*, 403

Concord village northwest of Boston, Massachusetts; site of early battle of the American Revolution on April 19, 1775 (42 N/71 W) 111, *115*

Connecticut state in the northeastern United States; one of the original 13 states (41°45'N/73°15'W) *57*, 66

Cuba country in the West Indies, North America (22°N/79°W) 37, *647*

Czechoslovakia country in central Europe (49°30'N/16°E) 861, *1094*

D

Delaware state in the northeastern United States; one of the original 13 states (38°45'N/75°30'W) 66, *274*

Detroit city in southeastern Michigan; site of significant battles during the French and Indian War and the War of 1812; center of automobile industry (42°15'N/82°15'W) *274*, 325

Dust Bowl area of the Great Plains where the drought of the 1930s turned the soil to dust (37°N/98°W) 837

E

Egypt country in northeastern Africa (27°N/30°E) 26, *935*

England division of the United Kingdom of Great Britain and Northern Ireland (56°30'N/1°45'W) 20, *1094*

Erie Canal waterway connecting the Hudson River with Lake Erie through New York State (43°N/76°W) *291*, 293

Erie, Lake one of the Great Lakes between Canada and the United States (42°15'N/81°30'W) *57*, 272

Europe continent of the northern part of the eastern hemisphere between Asia and the Atlantic Ocean (50°N/15°E) 16, *1094*

F

Florida state in the southeastern United States (30°30'N/84°45'W) 100, *301*

Fort Duquesne French fort on the site of Pittsburgh, Pennsylvania (40°30'N/80°W) 98, *99*

Fort Sumter Union fort during the Civil War located on island near Charleston, South Carolina; site of first military engagement of Civil War (32°45'N/80°W) 448

France country in western Europe (49°45'N/0°45'E) 19, *736*

Fredericksburg city and Civil War battle site in northeast Virginia (38°15'N/77°30'W) 454, *455*

Freeport city in northern Illinois; site of 1858 Lincoln-Douglas debate (42°15'N/89°30'W) 436

G

Galveston city on the Gulf of Mexico coast in Texas; created nation's first commission form of city government (29°15'N/95°W) 678

Georgia state in the southeastern United States (32°45'N/83°45'W) 62, *274*

Germany country in central Europe; divided after World War II into East Germany and West Germany; unified in 1989 (50°N/10°E) 38, *736*

Gettysburg city and Civil War battle site in south central Pennsylvania; site where Lincoln delivered the Gettysburg Address (39°45'N/77°15'W) 455, *455*

Great Basin interior drainage area in Nevada (40°15'N/117°15'W) 518, *1092*

Great Britain commonwealth comprising England, Scotland, and Wales (56°30'N/1°45'W) 97

Great Lakes chain of five lakes, Superior, Erie, Michigan, Ontario, and Huron, in central North America (45°N/87°W) 99, 297

Great Plains flat grassland in the central United States (45°N/104°W) 10, *1090*

Great Salt Lake lake in northern Utah with no outlet and strongly saline waters (41°15'N/112°45'W) *264*, 404

Greece country in southeastern Europe (39°N/21°30'E) 23, *736*

Guadalcanal island in the Solomons east of Australia (9°45'S/158°45'E) 873, *874*

Guam United States possession in the western Pacific Ocean (14°N/143°15'E) *652*, 869

H

Harlem northern section of Manhattan in New York City; cultural center of African Americans in the early- and mid-1900s (40°45'N/74°W) 784

Harpers Ferry town in northern West Virginia on the Potomac River (39°15'N/77°45'W) 437

Hartford capital of Connecticut located on the Connecticut River in the central part of the state (41°45'N/72°45'W) 67

Hawaii state in the United States located in the Pacific Ocean (20°N/157°W) 641, *652*

Hiroshima city in southern Japan; site of first military use of atomic bomb, August 6, 1945 (34°15'N/132°30'E) *874*, 875

Hispaniola island in the West Indies in North America, where Haiti and the Dominican Republic are located (17°30'N/73°15'W) 37, *50*

Hong Kong British colony along the southern coast of China in Asia (21°45'N/115°E) 416, *1095*

Hudson Bay large bay in northern Canada 60°N/86°W) *1092*

Hudson River river flowing through New York State into the Atlantic Ocean at New York City (52°45'N/74°W) 51, *57*

Hungary country in central Europe (47°N/20°E) 934, *935*

Huron, Lake one of the Great Lakes between the United States and Canada in North America (45°15'N/82°45'W) *99*

I

Idaho state in the northwestern United States; ranks among top states in silver production (44°N/115°15'W) *519*, *594*

Illinois state in the north central United States; one of the states formed in the Northwest Territory (40°30'N/90°45'W) *144*, *291*

India country in southern Asia (23°N/77°30'E) 24, *1095*

Indian Territory land reserved by the United States government for native Americans, now the state of Oklahoma (36°N/98°15'W) *346*, *464*

Indiana state in the north central United States; one of the states formed in the Northwest Territory (39°45'N/86°45'W) *144*, *291*

Indochina region in Southeast Asia (17°15'N/105°15'E) *930*, *1095*

Iowa state in the north central United States acquired as part of the Louisiana Purchase (42°N/94° 15'W) *433*

Iran country of the Middle East in southwestern Asia (31°15'N/53°30'E) *930*, *1041*

Iraq country of the Middle East in southwestern Asia (32°N/42°30'E) *1041*

Israel country of the Middle East in southwestern Asia along the Mediterranean Sea (32°45'N/34°E) *932*, *1041*

Italy country in southern Europe along the Mediterranean Sea (44°N/11°15'E) 19, *736*

J

Jamestown first permanent English settlement in North America; located in southeastern Virginia (37°15'N/76°45'W) 56, 57

Japan island country in eastern Asia (36°30'N/133°30'E) 26, *1095*

K

Kansas state in the central United States; fighting over slavery issue in 1850s gave territory the name *Bleeding Kansas* (38°30'N/98°45'W) 433, *438*

Kentucky state in the south central United States; border state that sided with the Union during the Civil War (37°30'N/87°30'W) 104, *274*

Kings Mountain Revolutionary War battle site in northern South Carolina (35°15'N/81°15'W) 143, *143*

Korea peninsula in eastern Asia between China, the Soviet Union, and the Sea of Japan, on which are located the countries of North and South Korea (38°15'N/127°30'E) 662, *901*

Kuwait country of the Middle East in southwestern Asia between Iraq and Saudi Arabia (29°N/47°45'E) *1041*

L

Lebanon country in southwest Asia along the Mediterranean Sea (34°N/34°E) 933, *1041*

Lexington Revolutionary War battle site in eastern Massachusetts; site of first clash between colonists and British, April 19, 1775 (42°26'N/71°13'W) 111, *115*

Little Rock capital of Arkansas located in the center of the state; site of 1957 conflict over public school integration (34°45'N/92°15'W) *433*, 958

London capital of United Kingdom located in the southeastern part of England (51°30'N/0°15'W) *29*, 56

Los Angeles city along the Pacific coast in southern California; industrial, financial, and trade center of western United States (34°N/118°15'W) *404*, 410

Louisiana state in the south central United States (30°45'N/92°45'W) *291*, 323

Louisiana Territory region of west central United States between the Mississippi River and the Rocky Mountains purchased from France in 1803 (40°N/95°W) 100, *264*

M

Maine state in the northeastern United States; 23rd state to enter the Union (45°30'N/69°45'W) 67

Maryland state in the eastern United States; one of the original 13 states (39°15'N/76°30'W) 61, *274*

Massachusetts state in the northeastern United States; one of the original 13 states (42°15'N/72°30'W) *57*, 64

Mediterranean Sea sea between Europe and Africa (36°15'N/13°30'E) 28, *895*

Mexico country in North America south of the United States (23°45'N/104°W) 12, *1092*

Mexico, Gulf of gulf south of the United States and east of Mexico in North America (25°15'N/93°45'W) 12, *50*

Michigan state in the north central United States; one of the states formed in the Northwest Territory (45°N/85°W) 152, *291*

Michigan, Lake one of the five Great Lakes located in the north central United States (43°15'N/87°15'W) 49, *99*

Midway Islands United States possession in the central Pacific Ocean; site of Battle of Midway, June 1942 (28°N/177°W) 873, *874*

Milwaukee city in eastern Wisconsin along Lake Michigan (43°N/88°W) 325, *1091*

Minnesota state in the north central United States; fur trade, good soil, and lumber attracted early settlers (46°15'N/96°15'W) *433*, 512

Mississippi state in the southeastern United States; became English territory after French and Indian War (32°30'N/89°45'W) 324, *438*

Mississippi River river flowing through the United States from Minnesota to the Gulf of Mexico; explored by French in 1600s (29°N/89°W) 15, *264*

Missouri state in the south central United States; petition for statehood resulted in sectional conflict and the Missouri Compromise (40°45'N/93°W) *291, 330*

Missouri River river flowing through the United States from the Rocky Mountains to the Mississippi River near St. Louis (38°45'N/90°15'W) *291, 347*

Montana state in the northwestern United States; cattle industry grew during 1850s (47°15'N/111°45'W) 517, *519*

Montgomery capital of Alabama located in the central part of the state; site of 1955 bus boycott to protest segregation (32°30'N/86°15'W) *433,* 955

Montreal city on the St. Lawrence River in southern Quebec, Canada (45°30'N/73°30'W) 49, *99*

Moscow capital of former Soviet Union (55°45'N/37°30'E) 869, *1094*

N

Nashville capital of Tennessee located in the north central part of the state (36°15'N/86°45'W) *291,* 327

Natchez city in western Mississippi along the Mississippi River (31°30'N/91°15'W) 142, *291*

National Road road from Baltimore, Maryland, to Vandalia, Illinois (40°N/81°30'W) 290, *291*

Nebraska state in the central United States (41°45'N/101°30'W) 433, *519*

Netherlands country in northwestern Europe (53°N/4°E) 20, *736*

Nevada state in the western United States (39°30'N/117°W) 518, *519*

New Amsterdam town founded on Manhattan Island by Dutch settlers in 1625; renamed New York by British settlers (40°45'N/74°W) 51, *57*

New Hampshire state in the northeastern United States; one of the original 13 states (44°N/71°45'W) 67, *274*

New Jersey state in the northeastern United States; one of the original 13 states (40°30'N/74°45'W) 70, *274*

New Mexico state in the southwestern United States; ceded to the United States by Mexico in 1848 (34°30'N/107°15'W) 15, *519*

New Orleans city in southern Louisiana in the Mississippi Delta (30°N/90°W) 154, *264*

New York state in the northeastern United States; one of the original 13 states (42°45'N/78°W) 51, *274*

New York City city in southeastern New York State at the mouth of the Hudson River; largest city in the United States (40°45'N/74°W) 133, *137*

Nicaragua country in Central America (12°45'N/86°15'W) 659, *1092*

Normandy region along French coast and site of D-Day invasion, June 6, 1944 (48°N/2°W) 872

North America continent in the northern part of the western hemisphere between the Atlantic and Pacific oceans (45°N/100°W) 10, *1092*

North Carolina state in the southeastern United States; one of the original 13 states (35°45'N/81°30'W) 49, *73*

North Dakota state in the north central United States; Congress created Dakota Territory in 1861 (47°15'N/102°W) *519,* 594

Northwest Territory territorial division north of the

Ohio River and east of the Mississippi River (47°30'N/87°30'W) 158, *158*

O

Oberlin college and town in northern Ohio (41 15'N/82°15'W) 596

Ohio state in the north central United States; first state in the Northwest Territory (40°30'N/83°15'W) 152, *274*

Ohio River river flowing from Allegheny and Monongahela rivers in western Pennsylvania into the Mississippi River (39°N/85°W) 98, *264*

Ohio Valley valley of the Ohio River, which flows from Pennsylvania to the Mississippi River at Cairo, Illinois (37°30'N/88°W) 15, *1091*

Oklahoma state in the south central United States; Five Civilized Tribes moved to territory 1830-1842 (36°N/ 98°15'W) 514, *1090*

Omaha city in eastern Nebraska on the Missouri River (41°15'N/96°W) *536,* 571

Ontario, Lake one of the five Great Lakes between Canada and the United States (43°30'N/79°W) *57,* 136

Oregon state in the northwestern United States; adopted women suffrage in 1912 (43°45'N/123°45'W) 263, *438*

Oregon Trail pioneer trail from Independence, Missouri, to the Oregon Territory (42°30'N/110°W) 403, *404*

P

Pacific Ocean world's largest ocean located between Asia and the Americas (0°/175°'W) 14, *1088*

Palestine region in the Middle East now occupied by Israel (31°30'N/35°'E) 18, *1041*

Panama country in the southern part of Central America, occupying the Isthmus of Panama (8°N/81°W), *1092*

Panama Canal canal built across the Isthmus of Panama through Panama to connect the Caribbean Sea and the Pacific Ocean (9°15'N/79°45'W) 659, *660*

Pearl Harbor naval base at Honolulu, Hawaii; site of 1941 Japanese attack, leading to United States entry into World War II (21°21'N/157°57'W) 643, *874*

Pennsylvania state in the northeastern United States (41°N/78°15'W) 71, *274*

Persian Gulf gulf in southwestern Asia between Iran and the Arabian Peninsula (27°45'N/50°30'E) *1041*

Philadelphia city in eastern Pennsylvania on the Delaware River; Declaration of Independence and the Constitution both adopted in city's Independence Hall (40°N/75°W) *57, 71*

Philippines island country in southeast Asia (14°30'N/125°E) 647, *647*

Pittsburgh city in western Pennsylvania; one of the great steelmaking centers of the world (40°30'N/80°W) *291,* 292

Plymouth town in eastern Massachusetts; first successful English colony in New England (42°N/70°45'W) *57,* 63

GAZETTEER

Portugal country in southwestern Europe (38°15'N/8°15'W) 22, *736*

Potomac River river flowing from West Virginia into Chesapeake Bay (38°N/77°W) 161, *291*

Promontory Point site in Utah where the first transcontinental railroad was completed (41°45'N/112°15'W) 512, *536*

Providence capital of Rhode Island; site of first English settlement in Rhode Island (41°45'N/71°30'W) *57,* 317

Puerto Rico U.S. possession in the West Indies (18°15'N/66°45'W) 42, *50*

Pullman company town south of Chicago; site of 1894 railroad strike (41°45'N/87°30'W) 556

Q

Quebec city in Canada, capital of Quebec Province, on the St. Lawrence River; first settlement in New France (46°45'N/71°15'W) 49, *50*

R

Raleigh capital of North Carolina located in the north central part of the state (35°45'N/78°45'W) *291*

Rhode Island state in the northeastern United States; one of the original 13 states (41°30'N/71°45'W) 66, *274*

Richmond capital of Virginia located in the central part of the state; capital of the Confederacy during the Civil War (37°30'N/77°30'W) *291, 450*

Rio Grande river between the United States and Mexico in North America (26°N/97°30'W) 15, *50*

Roanoke island off the coast of present-day North Carolina that was site of early British colonizing efforts (35°N/75°39'W) 56, *57*

Rocky Mountains mountain range in western United States and Canada in North America (50°N/114°W) 263, *264*

Russia name of republic; former empire of eastern Europe and northern Asia coinciding with Soviet Union (60°30'N/64°E) 567, *1095*

S

Sacramento capital of California located in the north central part of the state (38°30'N/121°30'W) *404,* 415

St. Augustine city in northeastern Florida on the Atlantic coast; oldest permanent existing European settlement in North America, founded in 1565 (30°N/81°15'W) 44, *50*

St. Lawrence River river flowing from Lake Ontario, between Canada and the United States, through Canada to the Atlantic Ocean (48°N/65°15'W) *50,* 98

St. Louis city in eastern Missouri on the Mississippi River (38°45'N/90°15'W) 263, *264*

St. Mihiel World War I battle site in France (49 N/5 30'E) *743,* 744

Salt Lake City capital of Utah located in the northern part of the state; founded by Mormons in 1847

(40°45'N/111°45'W) 404, *404*

San Antonio city in south central Texas (29°30'N/98°30'W) 405, *714*

San Francisco city in northern California on the Pacific coast (37°45'N/122°30'W) 44, *404*

Santa Fe capital of New Mexico located in the north central part of the state (35°45'N/106°W) *264,* 410

Saratoga Revolutionary War battle site in the Hudson Valley of eastern New York State (43°N/73°51'W) 136, *137*

Savannah city in eastern Georgia (32°N/81°W) 103, *143*

Sea Islands group of islands off the coast of Georgia and South Carolina (31°15'N/81°W) 480

Seneca Falls town in New York State; site of women's rights convention in 1848 (43° N/77° W) 371

Sierra Nevada mountain range in eastern California (39°N/120°W) *404,* 512

South Africa country in southern Africa (28°S/24°45'E) 643, *1098*

South America continent in the southern part of the western hemisphere lying between the Atlantic and Pacific oceans (15°S/60°W) 10, *1093*

South Carolina state in the southeastern United States; one of the original 13 states (34°15'N/81°15'W) 62, *73*

South Dakota state in the north central United States; acquired through the Louisiana Purchase (44°15'N/102°W) 514, *519*

Soviet Union former country in northern Europe and Asia (60°30'N/64°E) 567

Spain country in southwestern Europe (40°15'N/4°30'W) 22, *736*

Stalingrad city in the former Soviet Union on the Volga River; present name Volgograd (48° 45'N/42°15'E) 870

Suez Canal canal built between the Mediterranean Sea and the Red Sea through northeastern Egypt (31°N/32°15'E) 933, *935*

Superior, Lake one of the five Great Lakes between Canada and the United States in North America (47°45'N/89°15'W) *99,* 532

T

Tampa city in west central Florida (28°N/82°30'W) *536,* 648

Teapot Dome oil field in Wyoming; played significant role during Harding administration scandals in 1920s, 769

Tennessee state in the south central United States; first state readmitted to the Union after the Civil War (35°45'N/88°W) 104, *835*

Tennessee Valley valley of the Tennessee River, which flows from the Appalachian Mountains to the Ohio River (35°30'N/88°15'W) *835,* 836

Tenochtitlán Aztec capital on the site of present-day Mexico City (19°30'N/99°15'W) 13, *14*

Texas state in the south central United States; Mexican colony that became an independent nation before joining the United States (31°N/101°W) 404, *433*

Tokyo capital of Japan located on the eastern coast of Honshu Island (35°45'N/139°45'E) 417, *1095*

Toronto city in Canada on Lake Ontario; capital of the province of Ontario (43°45'N/79°30'W) 272, *1092*

Trenton capital of New Jersey located on the Delaware River in the central part of the state; site of Revolutionary War battle in December 1776 (40°15'N/74°45'W) 133, *137*

U

Union of Soviet Socialist Republics. *See* Soviet Union.

United Kingdom country in northwestern Europe made up of England, Scotland, Wales, and Northern Ireland (56°30'N/1°45'W) *736*

United States country in central North America; fourth largest country in the world in both area and population (38°N/110°W) 144, *1090*

Utah state in the western United States; settled by Mormons in 1840s (39°30'N/112°45'W) 15, *1090*

V

Valley Forge Revolutionary War winter camp northwest of Philadelphia (40°N/75°30'W) *137*, 138

Veracruz city in eastern Mexico on the Gulf of Mexico coast (19 15'N/96 W) 411, *1092*

Vermont state in the northeastern United States; 14th state to enter the Union (43°45'N/72°45'W) 112, *274*

Vicksburg city and Civil War battle site in western Mississippi on the Mississippi River (32°21'N/90°52'W) 456, *456*

Vietnam country in southeastern Asia (16°N/108°E) 930, *1099*

Virginia state in the eastern United States; colony in which first permanent English settlement in the Americas was established (37°N/78°W) 56, *274*

W

Wall Street street in New York City at the center of the financial district (40°45'N/74°W) 572

Washington state in the northwestern United States; territory reached by Lewis and Clark in 1805 (47°30'N/121°15'W) 512, *519*

Washington, D.C. capital of the United States located on the Potomac River at its confluence with the Anacostia River; between Maryland and Virginia; coinciding with the District of Columbia (38°53'N/77°02'W) 242, *274*

West Virginia state in the east central United States (39°N/80°45'W) *438*, 455

Willamette River Valley valley of the Willamette River in western Oregon (45°N/123°W), 403

Wisconsin state in the north central United States; passed first state unemployment compensation act, 1932 (44°30'N/91°W) 152, *438*

Wounded Knee site of battle between settlers and Indians in southern South Dakota in 1890 and of native American movement protest in 1973 (43°26'N/102°30'W) 514, *519*

Wyoming state in the western United States; territory provided women the right to vote, 1869 (42°45'N/108°30'W) *519*, 594

Y

Yorktown town in southeastern Virginia and site of final battle of Revolutionary War (37°15'N/76°30'W) 143, *143*

Z

Zaire country in central Africa (1°S/22°15'E) 969, *1098*

Glossary

PRONUNCIATION KEY

Throughout this textbook, proper names, foreign words, and other vocabulary terms that may be unfamiliar are respelled in parentheses after the word. A respelling is more easily pronounced because it is a straghtforward phonetic approach to pronunciation. Each respelling consists of sounds, shown below in the first column. Sample words for each sound follow.

a	**a**pple, t**a**p	g	**g**oat, bi**g**	ow	h**ou**se, c**ow**	w	**w**et, a**w**ay
ah	f**a**ther, h**o**t	h	**h**er, **h**appy	oy	b**oy**, **oi**l	y	**y**es, **y**ou
ai	h**ai**r, c**a**re	ih	**i**s, **i**t, m**y**stery	p	**p**an, ma**p**	y	**i**ce, t**ie**, b**uy**
aw	**a**ll, c**o**rd	j	**j**ump, **g**entle	r	**r**an, **r**ace	yoo	f**u**se, m**u**sic
ay	**a**te, s**ay**	k	**k**ick, **c**an	s	**s**un, cut**s**, mi**ce**	z	**z**oo, u**s**es
b	**b**at, ca**b**	kw	**qu**ak, **qu**it	sh	**sh**e, ru**sh**, no**ti**on	zh	plea**s**ure, bei**ge**
ch	**ch**ain, su**ch**	l	**l**augh, pai**l**	t	**t**oy, ma**t**	uh	a (**a**round)
d	**d**oor, sa**d**	m	**m**ouse, ha**m**	th	bo**th**, smoo**th**		e (wak**e**n)
ee	**e**ven, pit**y**	n	**n**ice, ra**n**	u	b**oo**k, b**u**ll		i (stenc**i**l)
eh	g**e**t, **e**gg	ng	ri**ng**, so**ng**	ur	w**or**k, h**ear**d		o (weap**o**n)
eye	**i**ce, t**ie**, b**uy**	oh	**o**ld, s**o**	v	**v**ine, li**v**e		u (**u**pon)
f	**f**an, o**ff**	oo	m**oo**, r**u**le				

Primary accented syllable is shown in capitals; secondary accented syllable, in small capitals: for example, conquistador (kohn KEES tuh DOHR); lyceum (ly SEE uhm)

A

abolitionist 1800s reformer who worked to end slavery (p. 372)

agribusiness large farming operation that includes the cultivation, processing, storage, and distribution of farm products (p. 922)

amendment alteration to the Constitution (p. 167)

amnesty act of a government by which pardon is granted to an individual or groups of persons (p. 481)

antebellum customs, manners, and institutions that existed before the Civil War (p. 596)

appeasement policy of compromising or giving in to demands in an attempt to avoid trouble and maintain peace (p. 861)

arbitration hearing and resolution of a disagreement between two parties through an impartial third party (p. 562)

armistice temporary suspension of hostilities between opponents (p. 745)

armory place or building where arms and military equipment are stored (p. 790)

artillery weapons for discharging missiles (p. 124)

astrolabe instrument used to observe positions of celestial bodies (p. 29)

automation technique of operating a machine, manufacturing process, or system that will do a job formerly performed by humans (p. 924)

B

balance of payments difference between the value of a nation's imports and its exports; also known as balance of trade (p. 1008)

bicameral political system based on two legislative chambers (p. 150)

bipartisan involving members of two political parties (p. 891)

blacklist record kept by companies of employees or former employees who are disapproved of or are to be punished or boycotted (p. 558)

bond certificate that earns interest and is redeemed for cash on a specific date (p. 233)

bounty money paid to recruit soldiers for military service; payment to encourage an action (p. 463)

boycott refusal to buy goods or have dealings with a country or other entity, usually to express disapproval or force acceptance of certain conditions (p. 103)

buffer area designed to separate and serve as a protective barrier; neutral area separating conflicting forces (p. 891)

business cycle sequence of economic activity, usually consisting of recession, recovery, growth, and decline (p. 557)

busing transportation of children to a school outside their residential area to establish racial integration in that school (p. 1008)

C

capital money invested in a business (p. 28)

caravel small ship with a broad bow (p. 29)

capital gains profits made on investments (p. 1075)

carrack large merchant ship (p. 29)

charter formal document granting the right of self-rule (p. 19)

classical relating to ancient Greece or Rome (p. 20)

closed shop system where all workers in a particular industry are required to be union members or employer agrees to hire only union members (p. 319)

coalition alliance, **combination**, or union of parties, people, or states formed for a specific action or purpose (p. 844)

collective bargaining negotiation between organized workers and management to reach an agreement on wages, hours, and working conditions (p. 559)

commodity economic good; product of agriculture; article of commerce (p. 524)

commonwealth self-governing political unit of independent states associated in a common allegiance (p. 64)

commune group of people living together with collective ownership and use of property, often having shared goals, philosophies, and ways of life; large cooperative farms (p. 992)

communism system of government in which the Communist party controls the political, economic, cultural, and social life of the people; economic system in which society as a whole, represented by the Communist party, owns all means of production, distribution, and exchange of goods (p. 890)

compact covenant, agreement, or contract between two or more parties (p. 350)

company town village built and run by a company where workers are required to live (p. 556)

compass device for determining direction by means of a magnetic needle (p. 29)

confederation nonbinding political alliance of independent countries or states (p. 15)

congregation body of church members; people meeting for worship and religious instruction (p. 64)

conquistador (kohn KEES tuh DOHR) Spanish adventurer in the sixteenth century (p. 42)

conscientious objector person who refuses to perform military service or to bear arms on the grounds of moral or religious principles or beliefs (p. 991)

conscription compulsory enrollment of people for military service (p. 462)

consensus general agreement; judgment arrived at by most of those concerned; group solidarity in sentiment and belief (p. 978)

constitution plan of government in America; basic principles and laws of a nation, state, or social group that determine the powers and duties of the government and guarantee certain rights to its people (p. 67)

consul official appointed by a government to reside in a foreign country to represent the interests of the citizens of the appointing country (p. 408)

containment policy of preventing the expansion of a hostile power; 1947 foreign policy stating the United States would hold Soviet influence within its existing limits (p. 892)

contraband goods or merchandise whose importation, exportation, or possession is forbidden (p. 738)

cooperative enterprise or organization owned by and operated for the benefit of those using its services (p. 608)

corollary proposition added to another as a natural consequence or effect (p. 661)

corporation business form consisting of a group of people authorized by law to act as a single person and having an identity that survives its incorporators (p. 540)

counterculture one with values and mores that run contrary to those of established society (p. 992)

covenant formal and binding agreement between two or more parties (p. 752)

covert secret or undercover; not openly shown or engaged in (p. 930)

craft union labor union in which all members practice the same occupation or skill (p. 845)

creditor nation a nation that lends money (p. 1068)

creole (KREE OHL) resident of the Spanish colonies born of Spanish parents (p. 44)

currency paper money that is in circulation as a means of exchange (p. 159)

D

dark horse political candidate unexpectedly nominated, usually as a compromise between groups (p. 406)

debtor nation a country that owes money (p. 1068)

deficit spending government practice of borrowing money in order to spend more money than is received from taxes (p. 833)

deflation economic condition in which the volume of available money or credit decreases, resulting in the decline of the price of goods and services (p. 611)

deport removal from a country of an alien whose presence is unlawful (p. 756)

depression economic condition marked by an extended and severe decline in production and sales, and a severe increase in unemployment (p. 159)

détente (day tahnt) relaxation of cold-war tensions between the United States and the Soviet Union that began in the early 1970s (p. 1012)

direct primary election in which nominations of candidates for office are made by voters (p. 679)

direct tax one paid directly to the government rather than being included in the price of goods; a tax collected directly from the person on whom the tax burden is expected to fall (p. 102)

disenfranchised having had the legal right to vote taken away (p. 486)

disestablished deprived of the status and privileges of an established position (p. 151)

dissenter protester; one who differs in opinion from the majority (p. 63)

dole money or goods given as charity; grant of government funds to the unemployed (p. 834)

double-digit inflation annual rate of inflation amounting to ten percent or more (p. 1038)

duty tax on imported goods (p. 94)

dynasty series of rulers from the same family; powerful family that holds its influence for a long time (p. 21)

E

economies of scale ability of large businesses to operate more cheaply and efficiently than smaller ones, resulting in lower per-unit costs for the products of large companies (p. 536)

effigy crude image or representation of a hated person (p. 107)

emancipation freeing of slaves; act or process of freeing from restraint, control, or the power of another; freedom from bondage (p. 150)

emigration departure from one's place of residence or country to live in another (p. 316)

encomienda (ehn KOHM ee EHN duh) system of rewarding *conquistadores* with tracts of land, including the right to tax and demand labor from native Americans who lived on the land (p. 44)

entrepreneur person who organizes, manages, and assumes the risks of a business or enterprise (p. 533)

enumerated commodities colonial products that Parliament said could be shipped only to Britain (p. 94)

enumerated powers those mentioned specifically one after another in the Constitution (p. 236)

envoy person delegated to represent one government in its dealings with another; a messenger, representative (p. 136)

escalation increase in extent, volume, number, amount, intensity, or scope (p. 985)

excise tax one paid by a manufacturer and passed on to those who buy the product; a tax on the manufacture, sale, or consumption of a product within a country (p. 234)

executive privilege principle that the executive branch of government is exempt from disclosing information when such disclosure would adversely affect the functions and decision-making processes of the presidency or national security (p. 1023)

expatriate person who leaves his or her native country to live elsewhere (p. 598)

extraterritoriality exemption from the application or jurisdiction of local law (p. 416)

F

fascism system of government that is strongly nationalistic and allows private ownership of property while controlling general economic policies; government characterized by racism and militarism; a repressive one-party dictatorship (p. 860)

favorite son presidential candidate supported by the delegates of the candidate's native state at a national political convention (p. 331)

featherbedding requiring of an employer under a union rule or safety statute to hire more employees than are needed (p. 906)

federal deficit difference between the amount of money the government receives and what it spends (p. 1047)

federalism system of government in which power is distributed between national and state governments (p. 167)

feudal system political and social system of Europe during the Middle Ages, characterized by self-sufficient manors owned by nobles and obligations of service and loyalty in exchange for protection for those who lived on their lands (p. 21)

foreclosure legal procedure for reclaiming a piece of property when the owner is unable to keep up the mortgage payments (p. 836)

franchise right to vote; a constitutional or statutory right or privilege granted to an individual or group (p. 150)

free-trader one that practices or advocates trade without taxes or tariffs (p. 592)

frigate medium-sized warship smaller than a destroyer; used for escort and patrol duties (p. 273)

G

glasnost policy in the Soviet Union of speaking openly about problems, introduced by Mikhail Gorbachev in the 1980s (p. 1051)

gold standard monetary system in which a nation's currency is based on the value of gold (p. 612)

graft acquisition of money or power in dishonest or questionable ways while in public office (p. 582)

greenbacks paper money that was not backed by gold or silver; legal-tender notes issued by the U.S. government (p. 466)

grievance formal expression of a complaint (p. 125)

guerrilla soldier who barrages the enemy with surprise attacks, harassment, sabotage, and other nontraditional warfare (p. 892)

H

habeas corpus legal principle which requires that people who are arrested be brought to court to show why they should be held; writ inquiring into the lawfulness of retaining a person who is imprisoned or detained in custody (p. 460)

holding company one that gains control of other companies by buying their stock (p. 543)

holocaust systematic mass murder of more than six million European civilians, especially Jews, by Nazis before and during World War II (p. 873)

horizontal integration joining of businesses together that are engaged in similar business activities or processes (p. 543)

humanism interest in classical Greek and Roman arts, literature, knowledge, and culture (p. 20)

I

impeach to bring charges of a crime against a federal or state public official with the intent of removing the official from office (p. 487)

impeachment case in which a government official is accused of wrongdoing in office or the formal charge against such official (p. 180)

imperialism act of creating an empire by dominating

other nations (p. 640)

implied powers those suggested but not directly stated in the Constitution (p. 236)

impound to refuse to spend congressionally allocated funds; to seize and hold in the custody of the law (p. 1026)

impressment form of military and naval conscription, usually by force, practiced by Britain and other European countries (p. 268)

income tax one on the net income of an individual or business (p. 705)

incumbent current officeholder (p. 1076)

indemnity security or protection against hurt, loss, or damage; exemption from incurred penalties or liabilities (p. 662)

indentured servant person who agreed to work for an employer in colonial America for a specified time in exchange for passage to America (p. 59)

industrial union one that represents every worker in a single industry regardless of his or her job (p. 564)

inflation decline in money's value when more money is printed, resulting in increased prices of goods and services (p. 611)

initiative procedure enabling citizens to propose a bill by petitioning with a specific number of signatures from registered voters (p. 679)

injunction court order requiring an individual or company to do something or to prohibit a given action; used frequently to stop strikes (p. 565)

installment buying system of paying for goods at regular intervals, usually with interest added to the balance (p. 794)

interlocking directorate system under which the same people serve on the boards of directors of several firms within the same industry (p. 716)

internal improvements roads, canals, and other transportation needs inside a nation's boundaries (p. 285)

isolationism policy or belief that a nation should limit its alliances and involvement in international political and economic affairs (p. 640)

isthmus narrow piece of land connecting two larger land areas (p. 40)

J

joint-stock company form of business organization; pooled funds of many investors or stockholders who can independently sell their shares of the company (p. 28)

judicial review Supreme Court's power to review all congressional acts and executive actions and reject those it considers unconstitutional (p. 188)

jurisdictional strike one resulting from a dispute between unions over which union should represent the workers in a company or industry (p. 906)

K

kickback payback of a sum received from increased fees because of a confidential agreement or act of coercion (p. 583)

L

laissez-faire (LEH SAY FAHR) government doctrine of noninterference in business practices and in the economic affairs of individuals; literally, "let do" (p. 257)

land speculator person who purchases land to resell for profit; one who buys or sells land in expectation of profiting from future price changes (p. 101)

line item veto power to veto a single part of a bill (p. 1075)

line of demarcation north-south line of longitude through the Atlantic Ocean dividing lands in the Americas claimed by Spain and Portugal (p. 38)

lobbyist person who promotes or secures the passage of legislation by influencing public officials (p. 584)

lockout closed factory or place of employment caused by a strike; withholding of employment by an employer (p. 558)

locks chambers with gates at each end used to raise or lower boats as they pass from a level of higher elevation to a level of lower elevation or the reverse on a river or canal (p. 293)

long drive cattle run in which a large herd is moved across great distances to a railhead, where they are shipped to market (p. 516)

loose constructionist person who interprets the Constitution in a way that the federal government gains more powers than those listed (p. 178)

Loyalist American colonist who supported the British government; one who is or remains loyal to a political cause, party, or government (p. 124)

lyceum (ly SEE uhm) voluntary organization providing public lectures, concerts, and entertainments to promote the improvement of its members and their useful knowledge (p. 367)

M

mandate clear expression of the wishes of voters, as shown in election results (p. 484)

manor large estate owned by a noble on which peasants lived and were protected in exchange for their services (p. 18)

martial law form of military rule that suspends Bill of Rights guarantees; law administered by the military in an emergency situation when civilian law enforcement agencies are not able to maintain order (p. 449)

maverick unbranded range animal or cattle; a motherless calf (p. 516)

mechanics' lien charge against a bankrupt employer, insuring that wages owed to workers be the first payments made (p. 320)

mercenary paid soldier hired for service in the army of a foreign country; one that serves merely for wages (p. 122)

merchandising buying and selling of goods in a business for a profit (p. 576)

meridian line of longitude; a great circle on the surface of the earth passing through the poles (p. 522)

mestizo (meh STEE zoh) person in the Spanish colonies born of Spanish and native American parents (p. 44)

militia group of civilians declared by law to be called to military service and trained as soldiers to fight in emergencies (p. 98)

monopoly exclusive control of a product or service in a particular market by a single company (p. 109)

moratorium official authorization to suspend payments, as with a debt; officially authorized period of waiting (p. 836)

mulatto person born of Caucasian and African-American parents (p. 44)

multinational corporation company that has divisions in more than two countries (p. 1068)

N

nationalism feeling of loyalty and devotion to one's country, honoring that nation above all others and promoting its culture and interests rather than those of other nations (p. 284)

naval stores products of pine forests used in wooden shipbuilding and maintenance (p. 62)

new federalism Richard Nixon's policy of economic partnership between the federal and state governments whereby states and municipalities received less federal funding (p. 1006)

nomadic frequent roaming about from place to place without a fixed pattern of movement, usually following a food source (p. 510)

nonimportation agreement one between colonial merchants and planters not to import certain goods (p. 103)

nonpartisan free from party affiliation, bias, or designation (p. 246)

northwest passage water route to Asia through North America sought by European explorers (p. 47)

nuclear freeze agreement that the United States and the Soviet Union would stop the testing, production, and deployment of nuclear weapons (p. 1050)

nullification state declaration of a federal law to be invalid (p. 249)

O

obiter dictum incidental opinion that is issued by a judge or court but is not binding (p. 435)

on margin method of buying stock with a small cash down payment and the rest borrowed from a stockbroker. Stockbroker holds shares of stock as collateral for the loan; borrower repays broker from stock resale profits (p. 793)

open shop employment practice in which eligibility is not determined by union membership (p. 766)

P

Parliament supreme legislative body in Britain made up of nobility, clergy, and commons (p. 19)

partitioned division into two or more territorial units having separate political status (p. 655)

Patriot American colonist who favored separation before and during the Revolutionary War (p. 124)

patronage practice of elected officials to make appointments to unelected government positions for political advantage or repayment of favors (p. 589)

patroon landowner in the Dutch colonies who received rent, taxes, and labor from tenant farmers (p. 70)

peninsulares (puh NIHNT suh LUHR ehs) government and church officials in Spanish colonial America who had been born in Spain (p. 44)

perestroika political and economic restructuring in the Soviet Union introduced by Mikhail Gorbachev in the 1980s (p. 1051)

philanthropy actions to promote human welfare and benefit society (p. 550)

piracy robbery on the high seas (p. 267)

platform declaration of the principles and policies adopted by a political party or candidate (p. 358)

pocket veto indirect rejection of a legislative bill by the President by retaining the bill unsigned until after Congress adjourns (p. 347)

political machine party organization in big cities that holds power by controlling votes, courts, and police (p. 583)

pooling illegal agreements among individual railroads to divide the total volume of freight among their lines and to keep rates high (p. 607)

popular sovereignty principle that the settlers within a federal territory have the power to decide the legality of slavery within that territory (p. 422)

pork-barrel legislation laws, projects, or government spending that would benefit only a small part of the country's population (p. 1038)

pragmatism belief that government actions should meet the needs of society; practical approach to problems and affairs (p. 676)

preamble introductory part of a constitution or statute that states the reasons for and intent of the law; introduction to a document (p. 125)

presidio (prih SEED ee OH) Spanish fort in the Americas built to protect mission settlements (p. 45)

price-cutting reduction of prices to a level designed to cripple competition (p. 716)

privateer armed private ship commissioned by the government to attack ships of an enemy (p. 242)

proletariat working class (p. 622)

proprietor individual who received legal and exclusive right to American colonial land from the king of England and who was expected to administer the land according to English laws (p. 61)

protectionist one who advocates government protection for domestic producers and manufacturers through restrictions on imports (p. 592)

protective tariff high tax on imports intended to protect domestic products from foreign competition rather than to yield revenue (p. 233)

protectorate country that is technically independent, but whose government and economy are controlled by a stronger power; the nation or region controlled by a stronger nation (p. 653)

public land that belonging to the national government and therefore to the people (p. 151)

pueblos apartment-like buildings of adobe and cut stone built by native Americans (p. 15)

pump priming government money invested in the economy to stimulate a self-sustaining economic recovery (p. 833)

purges large-scale forced removal of officials who show signs of disloyalty to their superiors (p. 891)

Q

quadrant instrument used to measure altitudes (p. 29)

quorum number of officers or members of a body that when present is legal to transact business (p. 230)

R

ratify to officially approve a proposal (p. 151)

real wages income adjusted to compensate for reduced earning power due to inflation (p. 556)

realism European-influenced literary movement that strove for accurate representation of nature or real life without idealization (p. 597)

rebate discount in the form of a refund or part of a payment for a product or service (p. 545)

recall removal of an elected official by voters in a special election (p. 679)

recession downturn in the nation's economy marked by reduced economic activity (p. 847)

reciprocity (REHS uh PRAHS uht ee) mutual lowering by nations of tariff barriers; recognition by one of two countries of the validity of privileges granted by the other (p. 641)

redcoats derogatory term for British soldiers in the colonies, referring to their red uniforms (p. 104)

rediscount small fee charged to a member bank by the Federal Reserve Bank upon acceptance of a business's promissory note (p. 715)

referendum process by which people can vote directly on a proposed law (p. 679)

Renaissance (REHN uh SAHNTS) revival of interest in the arts, literature, culture, and learning of ancient Greece and Rome (p. 19)

reparations payments made by nations defeated in war as a penalty for damages caused to other countries (p. 763)

revenue tariff low tax on imports intended to provide income for the government rather than protection of domestic products from foreign competition (p. 233)

rider unrelated amendment attached to a bill under legislative consideration (p. 589)

right of deposit right to temporarily put goods ashore for transfer to other ships without paying import duties (p. 155)

right of self-determination right of people to choose their own government and be free from rule by a foreign country (p. 126)

S

saga prose narrative or heroic poem about legendary figures and events from the heroic age of Norway and Iceland (p. 36)

salutary neglect policy of non-interference by a governing nation in order to produce a beneficial effect (p. 95)

samurai member of the military class of feudal Japan (p. 26)

satellite nations East European nations politically and economically under Soviet domination; country dominated or controlled by another more powerful country (p. 891)

scabs nonunion replacement workers during a strike or union members who refuse to strike and continue working (p. 558)

scurvy sickness caused by lack of ascorbic acid (p. 31)

secede to withdraw from a large political body (p. 157)

secession formal withdrawal from an organization (p. 438)

securities stocks, bonds, and other financial instruments traded on a stock exchange (p. 792)

segregation enforced separation of racial groups in schooling, housing, and other public areas (p. 492)

separation of powers system in which legislative, executive, and judicial powers are divided among separate branches of government (p. 181)

serf peasant of the Middle Ages who was bound to the land (p. 18)

sharecropper agricultural worker who cultivates part of another person's land, receives supplies and equipment from the landowner, and in return gives the landowner part of the harvest (p. 477)

shogun one of a line of military governors ruling Japan until the revolution of 1867-68; Japanese commander in chief (p. 26)

social contract agreement among individuals forming an organized society that defines and limits the rights and duties of each (p. 126)

social Darwinism sociological theory that states only the fittest survive social competition and experience social advancement (p. 549)

social gospel application by religious organizations of Christian principles to social problems (p. 675)

socialism economic system in which government partly owns and controls production and distribution of goods produced (p. 378)

Spanish Armada large fleet of seemingly invincible ships dispatched by King Philip II of Spain to England in retaliation against English piracy (p. 48)

specie money in the form of gold and silver coin (p. 102)

speculation risky business venture involving buying or selling in the hope of making a large, quick profit (p. 792)

sphere of influence area in China during the late 1800s where trade was controlled by a foreign power (p. 655)

spoils system practice of dismissing government job holders affiliated with a defeated party and replacing them with supporters of the winning party (p. 346)

stock partial ownership interest in a company sold in the form of shares to raise operating capital (p. 28)

strait narrow passageway connecting two larger bodies of water (p. 40)

strict constructionist person who interprets the Constitution literally, believing the federal government has only those powers specifically listed in the Constitution (p. 178)

subsistence farming level of farming at which farmers produce only enough to feed and maintain their families (p. 61)

subversives people working secretly, attempting to overthrow or undermine a government or political system (p. 908)

suffrage right to vote (p. 239)

summit diplomatic meeting of the superpowers; conference of highest level government officials (p. 1013)

supply-side economics theory that holds that the economy can be stimulated by increasing the supply of goods and lowering taxes, which increases savings and purchase power (p. 1046)

T

tariff tax on imported goods (p. 233)

technological unemployment jobs lost as the result of machines doing the jobs formerly accomplished by humans (p. 765)

tenant farmer agricultural worker who rents and farms land from another person and pays the rent either in cash or with a portion of the crop (p. 477)

tenement city apartment building, often a crowded, run-down apartment building in the slums (p. 572)

textile fabric, especially woven or knitted; cloth (p. 316)

third party minor political party operating in addition to two other major parties in a nation or state normally characterized by a two-party system (p. 612)

toll fee charged for a privilege such as the use of a means of transportation (p. 290)

totalitarian government controlled by a single person or party; suppressing freedom and controlling every aspect of life (p. 860)

township local unit of government within a county (p. 585)

trade deficit economic condition in which the value of a nation's imports is more than the value of its exports (p. 1068)

treason attempt to overthrow the government of the state to which the offender owes allegiance (p. 122)

tribute payment by one nation or ruler to another to acknowledge submission, or as the price of protection (p. 156)

trust combination of companies to gain control of an industry and reduce competition (p. 543)

turnpike road barricaded by spiked poles where travelers stop to pay a fee to use the road (p. 290)

U

underemployed having less than full-time work (p. 1075)

unicameral legislature consisting of a single chamber (p. 152)

V

vaudeville (VAHD vuhl) stage entertainment consisting of various acts (p. 519)

vertical integration joining of businesses together that are involved in different but related activities or processes (p. 543)

veto action by which an executive rejects a bill submitted by a legislature; to refuse to approve (p. 150)

viceroy person who rules a country or province as the representative of the monarch (p. 45)

vigilance committee organization of citizens who take the law into their own hands for their protection (p. 519)

W

ward division of a city for representative, electoral, or administrative purposes (p. 583)

welfare capitalism system of benefit programs offered to workers by employers intended to reduce the appeal of unions (p. 766)

"Westerns" novel, story or Hollywood motion picture depicting life in the western United States during the latter half of the nineteenth century (p. 519)

wildcat strike work stoppage initiated by a group of workers without formal union approval or in violation of a contract (p. 880)

writ of assistance written order that allowed officials to conduct unrestricted searches for smuggled or illegal goods (p. 102)

writ of mandamus court order requiring specific action on the part of person or organization served (p. 260)

Y

yellow journalism type of newspaper reporting in the late 1890s that featured sensational headlines and stories (p. 599)

Index

Italicized page numbers refer to illustrations. Preceding the page number, abbreviations refer to a map (m), chart (c), photograph or other picture (p), graph (g), cartoon (crt), or painting (ptg). Quoted material is referenced with the abbreviation (qu) before the appropriate page number. Each boldface term in the text is also referenced in the Glossary by the page on which it first appears.

INDEX

INDEX

X

Y

Z

INDEX

Acknowledgments

6 "Constitution of the Five Nations," from William N. Fenton, ed., *Parker on the Iroquois*. Copyright © 1868 by Syracuse University Press; used by permission. **6** "Navaho Song of the Rain Chant," from Nataline Curtis, ed., *The Indians' Book*, Harper and Brothers, 1907; used by permission. **85** From William Bradford, *Of Plymouth Plantation*, ed. Samuel Eliot Morison. New York: Alfred A. Knopf, Inc., 1952. **90** From Thomas Paine, *American Crisis. Number 1*, reprinted in *The Annals of America*, vol. 2. Chicago: Encyclopaedia Britannica, 1968. **222** From James Fenimore Cooper, *The Prairie*. Albany: State University of New York Press, 1962. **258** Southgate letter from James A. Henretta, *et. al., America's History*. Chicago: Dorsey Press, 1987. **312** From Henry David Thoreau, *Walden and Other Writings*. New York: Doubleday, 1970. **392** From *Mary Chesnut's Civil War*, ed. C. Vann Woodward, Yale University Press; copyright © 1981 by C. Vann Woodward, Sally Bland Metts, Barbara G. Carpenter, Sally Bland Johnson, and Katherine W. Herbert; used by permission of the publisher. **413** Coffey "Reminiscences" from *Eyewitness: The Negro in American History* by William L. Katz, rev. ed. New York: Pitman Publishing Corp., 1971. **504** From Mark Twain, *Roughing It*. Berkeley: Univ. of California Press, 1972. **506** "Under the Lion's Paw" excerpt from Hamlin Garland, *Main Travelled Roads*. New York: New American Library, 1962. **634** From Theodore Dreiser, *Sister Carrie*. New York: W. W. Norton, Critical Ed., 1970. **658** From *Official Proceedings of the Democratic National Convention...1890*, reprinted in *The Annals of America*, vol. 12. Chicago: Encyclopaedia Britannica, 1968. **728-729** "Recuerdo" and "Midnight Oil" by Edna St. Vincent Millay. From *Collected Poems*, Harper & Row. Copyright © 1922, 1950 by Edna St. Vincent Millay. Reprinted by permission of Elizabeth Barnett, Literary Executor. **729** "Dream Boogie," reprinted by permission of Harold Ober Associates, Inc. Copyright © 1932, 1951 by Langston Hughes. Copyright renewed 1979 by George Houston Bass. "Harlem," and **730** "Dream Variations," and "I Too, Sing America" from *Selected Poems* by Langston Hughes. Copyright © 1926 by Alfred A. Knopf, Inc., copyright renewed 1954 by Langston Hughes. Used by permission of the publisher. **730** "Jazz Fantasia" by Carl Sandburg, from *Smoke and Steel*, copyright © 1920 by Harcourt Brace Jovanovich, Inc.; copyright 1948 by Carl Sandburg; reprinted by permission of the publisher. **730** Excerpt from "They Have Yarns" in *The People—Yes* by Carl Sandburg, copyright © 1936 by Harcourt Brace Jovanovich, Inc. and renewed 1964 by Carl Sandburg, reprinted by permission of the publisher. **820** From John Steinbeck, *The Grapes of Wrath*. Copyright © 1939, renewed © 1967 by John Steinbeck. Used by permission of Viking Penguin, a division of Penguin Books USA, Inc. **885** Ota excerpt from *"The Good War": An Oral History of World War Two* by Studs Terkel. Copyright © 1984. Reprint by permission of Pantheon Books, a division of Random House. **948** From *Hunger of Memory* by Richard Rodriguez. Copyright 1981 by Richard Rodriguez. Reprinted by permission of David R. Godine, Publisher. **956** Beals excerpt from Henry Hampton and Steve Fayer, *Voices of Freedom*. New York: Bantam Books, 1990. **989** "Dear America" by Robert Peterson; from *Vietnam Blues*, published by the Author, 1965. **1081** From J. Richard Munro, "Goodbye to Hollywood," *Vital Speeches of the Day*, June 15, 1990. **1122** "I Have a Dream" copyright © 1963 by Martin Luther King, Jr. Used by permission, Joan Daves Agency. **1125** Deady excerpt from Lillian Schlissel, *Women's Diaries of the Westward Journey*. New York: Schocken Books, 1982. **1127** From *Crucial American Elections*, American Philosophical Society, 1973. **1128** From Robert A. Pastor and Jorge G. Casta:eda, *Limits to Friendship*. New York: Alfred A. Knopf, Inc., 1988. **1129** From Wilson Jeremiah Moses, *The Golden Age of Black Nationalism*. Boston: Archon Books, 1978.

Illustration Credits

Unless otherwise acknowledged, all photographs are the property of Glencoe Division of Macmillan/McGraw-Hill Publishing Company. Page positions are as follows (t) top, (b) bottom, (l) left, (r) right, (c) center.

i,iii Mike Hendrickson/Andris. Hendrickson Photography **vi** Giraudon/Art Resource **vii** The Granger Collection, New York **ix** Museum of Fine Arts, Boston, M. and M. Karolik Collection **xi** The Granger Collection, New York **xii** The Bettmann Archive **xiii** Los Angeles County Museum of Art, Los Angeles County Funds, **xiv** National Archives, U.S. Signal Corps photo 52393 **xvi** Wide World Photos **xvii** © Wally McNamee, Woodfin Camp **xix** The Bettmann Archive **xxiv** Tom McHugh/George Galicz/Photo Researchers, Inc. **xxv(t)** Boatmen's Bancshares, Inc. St. Louis, MO **xxv(b)** Missouri Historical Society **xxvi(t)** Estate of Mrs. Edsel B. Ford **xxvi(b)** Free Public Library, New Bedford, MA **xxvii(t)** The Metropolitan Museum of Art, Gift of Edgar William and Bernice Chrysler Garbisch, 1963 **xxvii(b)** John Carter Brown Library **xxviii(t)** H. Armstrong Roberts **xxviii(b)** Bettmann Archive **xxix(t)** Museum of the City of New York **xxix(b)** J. L. Atlan/Sygma **xxx** General Electric Company **xxxi(t)** Ty and Julie Hotchkiss/Photo Researchers, Inc. **xxxi(c)** Ken Biggs/Photo Researchers, Inc. **xxxii(l)** Alex S. Maclean/Landslides, Boston **xxxii(1)** Larry D. Hodge **xxxii(b)** State Historical Society of Wisconsin **xxxiii(t)** Gerard Fritz/Uniphoto **xxxiii(r)** James Foote/Photo Researchers, Inc. **xxxiii(c)** Warner Collection of Gulf State Paper Corporation, Tuscaloosa, AL **xxxiv(t)** Dany Krist/Uniphoto **xxxiv(c)** John Zoiner/Uniphoto **xxxiv(b)** Thomas Gilcrease Museum of American History and Art, Tulsa, OK **xxxv(t)** David Frazier Photo Library © David A. Bast/Photo Researchers, Inc.(b) Superstock. **2** St. Louis Science Center. Photo by Dirk Bakker, Detroit Institute of Arts **4(1t)(1b)(rb)** Lee Boltin **4(rt)** Art Resource **5(1)** Lee Boltin **5(ct)** Comstock **5(cb)** John Carter Brown Library **5(r)** Pilgrim Hall Museum, Plymouth, MA **6** Cranbrook **7** National Museum of the American Indian **9** The John Carter Brown Library, Brown University **11(t)** Stewart M. Green/Tom Stack & Associates **11(b)** Lee Boltin **12** © Bradley Smith/Carousel **13** The Bettmann Archive **17** Peabody Museum, Harvard University **19, 20** Giraudon/Art Resource **21, 24** Art Resource **25** Bridgeman/Art Resource **26(t), 26(b), 27** Lee Boltin **30(t)** Giraudon/Art Resource **30(b)** National Maritime Museum, London **35** Courtesy United States Naval Academy Museum **37** The Bettmann Archive **38** New York State Historical Association, Cooperstown **41** NASA **43, 44** The Granger Collection, New York **46** Kohler Codex of Nuremberg, 1534, British Library **48** The Henry E. Huntington Library, San Marino, California **49** Public Archives of Canada **55** © Wadsworth Atheneum, Hartford **58(t)** Historical Pictures Service, Chicago **58(b)** The Granger Collection, New York **60** The Library Company of Philadelphia **65** Courtesy of the Pilgrim Society, Plymouth, MA **68** The Granger Collection, New York **70** Print Collection, Miriam and Ira D. Wallach Division of Art, Prints and Photographs, The New York Public Library, Astor, Lenox and Tilden Foundations **77** Bequest of Maxim Karolik. Courtesy, Museum of Fine Arts, Boston **78** Historical Pictures Service, Chicago **84** Drew University **86** The Metropolitan Museum of Art, Bequest of Grace Wilkes, 1922. [22.45.9] **88(1)** National Maritime Museum **88(c)** Lee Boltin **88(r)** The Science Museum, London **89(1)** Laurie Platt Winfrey, Inc. **89(rt)** Joslyn Art Museum, Omaha, Nebraska **89(rc)** American Antiquarian Society **89(rb)** Independence National Historic Park Collection **90** (detail) National Portrait Gallery, Smithsonian Institution **91** The Metropolitan Museum of Art, Gift of John Stewart Kennedy, 1897. (97.34) **93** Patrick Henry Before the Virginia House of Burgesses (1851), by Peter F. Rothermel. Red Hill—The Patrick Henry National Memorial, Brookneal, Virginia **95** The Granger Collection, New York **96** The Library Company of Philadelphia **98, 99** The Granger Collection, New York **103** The John Carter Brown Library **106** The Metropolitan Museum of Art, Bequest of Charles Allen Munn, 1924. (24.90.1566a) **108** Courtesy, Museum of Fine Arts, Boston **109** Library of Congress **110** The Granger Collection, New York **111** © Yale University Art Gallery **116(1)** American Antiquarian Society **116(c)** The Insurance Company of North America **116(r)** General Dynamics Corporation **117(1)** American Antiquarian Society **117(c)** Rare Book Department, The Free Library of Philadelphia **117(rt)** American Antiquarian Society **117(rb)** Independence National Historical Park Collection **118(1)** Boston Athenaeum **118(c), 118(r), 119(1t)** American Antiquarian Society **119(1b)** The Museum of Fine Arts, Boston, Gift of Joseph W., William B., and Edward H.R. Revere **119(r)** Courtesy National Park Service, Photo by Mark Sexton **121** Fraunces Tavern Museum, Gift of Herbert P. Whitlock, 1913 **123** Historical Pictures Service, Chicago **124, 125** The Granger Collection, New York **129** Architect of the Capitol **132** The Granger Collection, New York **134** Courtesy, American Jewish Historical Society, Waltham, Massachusetts **138** Courtesy of The Valley Forge Historical Society **139** (detail) The Newark Museum **140(t)** Courtesy of the Rhode Island Historical Society **140(b)** The Bettmann Archive **144, 149** Architect of the Capitol **151** The Metropolitan Museum of Art, Gift of Mrs. A. Wordsworth Thompson, 1899. (99.28) **156** Washington University Gallery of Art, St. Louis, Gift of Nathaniel Phillips, Boston, 1890 **157** The Williamsburg Art of Cookery **159(t)** The National Portrait Gallery, Smithsonian Institution **159(b)** The Granger Collection, New York **162** Independence National Historic Park Collection **163(t)** Library of Congress **163(b)** H. Armstrong Roberts **164** Princeton University Library, Photo by Donald D. Breza **167** New-York Historical Society **169** Smithsonian Institution, Washington, DC **174** Concord Antiquarian Society/ © Rob Huntley, Chromographics. **178** Superstock **180** Photo by Paul Conklin **183** © Michael J. Pettypool/Uniphoto Picture Agency **184** © J.L. Atlan/Sygma **185** © Larry Downing/Woodfin Camp **186** © Wally McNamee/Woodfin Camp **187** Gary Cameron/Reuters **188** Boston Athenaeum **190(t)** Latent Image **190(b)** Wide World Photos **195** © Ruth Dixon **201** Light Source **202** Supreme Court Historical Society **206** Ted Rice **208** Lloyd Timmerman **209** George H. Matchneer **210, 216** © Doug Martin. **218** Worcester Art Museum, Worcester, MA, Gift of Mary Chandler Stone **220(1)** Bridgeman/Art Resource **220** (c) Giraudon/Art Resource **220(rt)** From the Aaron Douglas Collection, the American Missionary Association of the United Church Board for Homeland Ministries **220(rb)** Art Resource **221(1)** Archives Division Texas State Library **221(ct)** Peabody Museum, Harvard University, Photo by Hillel Burger **221(r)** Kim Nielson, Smithsonian University **222** Yale University Art Gallery **223** John Carter Brown Library **224** New York State Historical Association, Cooperstown **227** Independence National Historic Park **229** The Granger Collection, New York

232 Print Collection, Miriam and Ira D. Wallach Division of Art, Prints and Photographs, The New York Public Library, Astor, Lenox and Tilden Foundations **234, 235, 236** The Granger Collection, New York **237** Shelburne Museum, Shelburne, Vermont **240** Rare Book Department, Free Library of Philadelphia **242** Library of Congress **243** The Library Company of Philadelphia **244** Brown Brothers **247** The Granger Collection, New York **248** American Antiquarian Society **253** Chicago Historical Society **256** University Archives, Special Collections Department, University of Virginia Library **258** Courtesy, The Henry Francis duPont Winterthur Museum **259** *(detail)* National Portrait Gallery, Smithsonian Institution, The Thomas Jefferson Memorial Foundation, and the Enid and Crosby Kemper Foundation. Owned jointly with Monticello **260** The Time Museum, Rockford, Illinois **265** Missouri Historical Society **266** Field Museum of Natural History, Chicago, Neg. no. 93851.1C **268** New-York Historical Society **269** The Granger Collection, New York **272** Independence National Historic Park Collection **273(t)** Courtesy United States Naval Academy Museum **273(b)** New Orleans Museum of Art, Gift of Edgar William and Bernice Chrysler Garbisch **278(l)** Asher B. Durand. Kindred Spirits, 1849. Collection of The New York Public Library, Astor, Lenox and Tilden Foundations **278(r)** Rare Book Department, The New York Public Library, Astor, Lenox and Tilden Foundations **279(l)** The National Portrait Gallery, Smithsonian Institution **279(r)** © Van Bucher/Photo Researchers, Inc. **279(b)** L.N. Phelps Stokes Collection, Miriam and Ira D. Wallach Division of Art, Prints and Photographs, The New York Public Library Astor, Lenox and Tilden Foundations **280(l)** Gibbes Museum of Art, Carolina Art Association Collection **280(tc)** The National Museum of Racing and Hall of Fame **280(bc)** New York State Historical Association, Cooperstown **280(r)** Museum of the City of New York **281(l)** Patent Reproduction Company **281(r)** Peabody Museum, Salem **283** Courtesy, Historical Society of Pennsylvania, Philadelphia **285** *(detail)* The National Portrait Gallery, Smithsonian Institution, Transfer from the National Gallery of Art; gift of Andrew Mellon, 1942 **286** The Granger Collection, New York **290** Shelburne Museum, Shelburne, Vermont **292** National Museum of American Art, Smithsonian Institution/Art Resource **293** The Bettmann Archive **294(t)** American Antiquarian Society **294(b)** The Granger Collection, New York **295** Ohio Historical Society **298** Library of Congress **299** The Bettmann Archive **306** New-York Historical Society **308** Collection of Mr. and Mrs. Wilson Pile **310(c)** Giraudon/Art Resource **310(1)** Peabody Museum of Salem. Photo by Mark Sexton **310(r)** The Bettmann Archive **311(t)** The Fine Arts Museum of San Francisco, Gift of Eleanor Martin **311(c)** Historic New Orleans Collection **311(b)** The Philbrook Art Center **312** Concord Free Public Library **313** Collection of Pembroke Herbert **315** Superstock **317** Rhode Island Historical Society **318(t)** American Heritage Collection, Colby College Museum of Art **318(b)** Philadelphia Museum of Art, The Edgar William and Bernice Chrysler Garbisch Collection **319** Yale University Art Gallery, Bequest of Stephen Carlton Clark, BA 1903 **320** *(detail)* The National Portrait Gallery, Smithsonian Institution, **323(t)** The Bettmann Archive **323(b)** The Granger Collection, New York **324** William Gladstone Collection **325(t)** Maryland Historical Society, Baltimore **325(b)** State Historical Society of Wisconsin **326(t)** Thomas Gilcrease Institute of American History and Art, Tulsa, OK **326(b)** Cincinnati Public Library **328** Lee Boltin **331** National Portrait Gallery, Smithsonian Institution, Transfer from the National Gallery of Art; gift of Andrew W. Mellon, 1942 **332** Library of Congress **334** The Metropolitan Museum of Art, Gift of I. N. Phelps Stokes, Edward S. Hawes, Alice Mary Hawes, Marion Augusta Hawes, 1937. (37.14.34) **335** © Richard Pasley/Stock, Boston **339** From the Art Collection of The Boatmen's National Bank of St. Louis **341** The Nelson-Atkins Museum of Art, Kansas City, Missouri (Nelson Fund) 54-9 **342** Chicago Historical Society **344** The Granger Collection, New York **347** *(detail)* The National Portrait Gallery, Smithsonian Institution **350** City of Boston Art Commission, Photo by Richard Cheek **351** The Bettmann Archive **355** Eric Newman, Numismatic Education Society **358** The Granger Collection, New York **363** The Brooklyn Museum, 67.205.2, A. Augustus Healy Fund B **365** Massachusetts Historical Society **368** The Metropolitan Museum of Art, Gift of I. N. Phelps Stokes, Edward S. Hawes, Alice Mary Hawes, Marion Augusta Hawes, 1937. [37.14.22] **370(l)** Private collection **370(r)** The Granger Collection, New York **371** Brown Brothers **372** Sophia Smith Collection, Smith College **373** Cincinnati Art Museum, Subscription Fund Purchase **376** New-York Historical Society **377** Museum of Fine Arts, Boston, M. and M. Karolik Collection **379** The Granger Collection, New York **380** The Concord Free Public Library **386** American Antiquarian Society **388** Massachusetts Art Commission, Photo by Mark Sexton **390(1t)** National Portrait Gallery, Smithsonian Institution, Washington, DC **390(1b)** The Bettmann Archive **390(c)** Kunstbibliothek SMPK Berlin **390(rt)** Laurie Platt Winfrey, Inc. **390(rb)** Public Archives of Canada **391(1)** Photograph Courtesy of The Oakland Museum **391(ct)** Friends of the Governor's Mansion, Austin, TX **391(cb)** State Historical Society of Wisconsin **391(1t)** Courtesy of the New-York Historical Society, N.Y.C. **391(1b)** Collection of Larry Williford. **392** National Portrait Gallery, Smithsonian Institution, Washington, DC. On loan from Serena Williams Miles Van Rensselaer **393** Hampton University Museum **394** Library of Congress **397** Courtesy of Mrs. J. Maxwell Moran **401** National Museum of American Art, Smithsonian Institution, Washington, DC, **402(t)** The Granger Collection, New York **402(b)** National Cowboy Hall of Fame and Western Heritage Center **403** The Kansas State Historical Society **404** The Church of Jesus Christ of Latter-day Saints **405** Nebraska State Historical Society **409(t)** State Department of Archives and History, Raleigh, NC **409(b)** Chicago Historical Society **413** US Department of the Interior Geological Survey **415** Library of Congress **416(t)** The Chrysler Museum, Norfolk, Virginia, Photograph by Scott Wolff **416(b)** The Historical Society of Pennsylvania **421** Courtesy Robert M. Hicklin, Jr., Spartanberg, South Carolina **423(t)** Library of Congress **423(b)** Thomas Gilcrease Institute of American History and Art, Tulsa, OK **427** American Antiquarian Society **432(t), 432(b)** Culver Pictures **437** The Granger Collection, New York **442(l)** American Antiquarian Society **442(tc)** Courtesy of the Trustees of Amherst College **442(bc)** The John Carter Brown Library **442(r)** Essex Institute **443(l)** American Antiquarian Society **443(tr)** F&F Laboratories, Inc. **443(br)** Massachusetts General Hospital **444(tl)** The John Carter Brown Library **444(bl)** Library of Congress **444(r)** The Metropolitan Museum of Art, Morris K. Jesup Fund, 1933. 33.61 **445(tl)** Free Library of Philadelphia **445(bl)** The Bostonian Society **445(r)** Saratoga Springs Historical Society **447** West Point Museum, Alexander Craighead Collection. Photo by Joshua Nefsky **449, 451, 454** The Granger Collection, New York **456** Culver Pictures **457** Library of Congress **462** *Detail* from *Camp Near Corinth* by Chapman, Valentine Museum **463** The Bettmann Archive **464** US Army Military History Institute, Carlisle Barracks **465** The Granger Collection, New York **468** Culver Pictures **469(t)** The Granger Collection, New York **469(b)** The Bettmann Archive **470** H. Armstrong Roberts **475** National Museum of American Art, Smithsonian Institution, Gift of William T. Evans **477** Culver Pictures **478** *(detail)* National Portrait Gallery, Smithsonian Institution **479** Lightfoot Collection **480** The Granger Collection, New York **482** The Bettmann Archive **483** Museum of the Confederacy, Richmond **484** Culver Pictures **486, 487, 488** The Granger Collection, New York **489** *Harper's Weekly* **491** *Harper's Weekly,* March 26, 1887 **498** Library of Congress **500** Museum of American Textile History **502(1)** Library of Congress **502(ct)** Culver Pictures **502(cb)** Culver Pictures **502(r)** Embassy of Brazil **503(1)** Library of Congress **503(c)** Chicago Historical Society **503(r)** National Park Service Collection/Gift of Angelo Forgione. Photo © 1991 Karen Yamauchi, MetaForm Inc. **504(1)** The Granger Collection, New York **504(r)** The State Historical Society of Wisconsin **505** Culver Pictures **506** The Metropolitan Museum of Art, Bequest of Miss Adelaide Milton de Groot (1876-1967), 1967. [67.187.131] **509** Buffalo Bill Historical Center, Cody, WY. Whitney Purchase Fund **511** Courtesy Department of Library Services, American Museum of Natural History **512** Thomas Gilcrease Institute of American History and Art, Tulsa, OK **513** Oregon Historical Society **514** Southwest Museum **515** *(detail)* Taft Museum **516** The Granger Collection, New York **517** Amon Carter Museum **518** California State Library **520** Culver Pictures **522** Solomon D. Butcher Collection, Nebraska State Historical Society **523** Kansas State Historical Society **525** Colorado Historical Society **531** Putnam County Historical Society **533** Museum of the City of New York **534, 535(t)** The Bettmann Archive **535(b)** Courtesy of the American Petroleum Institute **537, 538** Chicago Historical Society **541** Culver Pictures **542(t)** Courtesy Levi Strauss & Company, San Francisco, California **542(b)** Culver Pictures **545** The Bettmann Archive **547(t)** UPI/ Bettmann Newsphotos **547(b)** The Bettmann Archive **548** The Metropolitan Museum of Art, Gift of Frederic H. Hatch, 1926. (26.97) **549** The Bettmann Archive **555** The Brooklyn Museum, 40.339. Dick S. Ramsay Fund **557** Kansas Collection, University of Kansas Libraries **558** The Granger Collection, New York **559** Culver Pictures **561** Massillon Museum, Ohio **563, 564** The Bettmann Archive **568(t)** Library of Congress **568(b)** Arnoldo Mondadori Editore, Milan **569** Library of Congress **570** The Granger Collection, New York **572** *(detail)* The National Portrait Gallery, Smithsonian Institution, Gallery Purchase and Gift of Mrs. Nancy Pierce York and Mrs. Grace Pierce Forbes **573** Museum of the City of New York **574** The Bettmann Archive **575** Museum of the City of New York **576** The Granger Collection, New York **581** Philadelphia Museum of Art. Given by William Alexander Dick **584** The Granger Collection, New York **585** Keystone-Mast Collection, California Museum of Photography, University of California, Riverside **586** Library of Congress **588, 589** The Granger Collection, New York **590** The Bettmann Archive **592(l)** The Granger Collection, New York **592(r)** Culver Pictures **593** The Granger Collection, New York **596** The Bettmann Archive **597** The Butler Institute of American Art **598(l)** Mary Cassatt (1844-1926), *The Bath,* oil on canvas, 1891/92, 39 1/2 X 26 in., Robert A. Waller Fund, 1910.2, photograph © 1990, The Art Institute of Chicago. All Rights Reserved **598(r)** Jefferson Medical College of Thomas Jefferson University **599** The Harry T. Peters Collection, Museum of the City of New York **600** Library of Congress **601** Culver Pictures **605** Private collection **608(l)** The Granger Collection, New York **608(r)** Brown Brothers **609, 610** The Granger Collection, New York **612** Culver Pictures **614** State Historical Society of Wisconsin **615, 616, 617** The Granger Collection, New York **618** Library of Congress **619** The Granger Collection, New York **620** Museum of American Textile History **621(t)** The Bettmann Archive **621(b)** Wide World Photos **628** Thomas Gilcrease Institute of American History and Art, Tulsa, OK **630** Los Angeles County Museum of Art, Los Angeles County Funds **632(1)** © SEF /Art Resource **632(C)** Giraudon/Art Resource **632(r)** The Bettmann Archive **633(1t)** © James P. Rowan/TSW—Click/Chicago Ltd. **633(rt)** David Austen/Stock Boston **633(rb)** Library of Congress **633(cb)** From the Collections of Henry Ford Museum and Greenfield Village **633(ct), 634** Brown Brothers **635** Library of Congress **636** Chicago Historical Society **639** Courtesy United States Naval Academy Museum **641** Picture Collection, The Branch Libraries, The New York Public Library **642** Franklin D. Roosevelt Library **643, 646(t)** Culver Pictures **646(b)** Brown Brothers **648(t)** Theodore Roosevelt Collection, Harvard College Library **648(b)** Courtesy Frederic Remington Art Museum, Ogdensburg, NY **651(l)** The Granger Collection, New York **651(r)** Culver Pictures **653** Courtesy of Dole Package Food

ILLUSTRATION CREDITS 1165

651(l) The Granger Collection, New York 651(r) Culver Pictures 653 Courtesy of Dole Package Food Company 658 Library of Congress 660 The Granger Collection, New York 661 The Bettmann Archive 666(1) Boston Athenaeum 666(c) Brown Brothers 666(rt) Culver Pictures 666(rb) The John Carter Brown Library Photo by Brooke Hammerle 667(l) Collection, The Museum of Modern Art, New York. Gift of Alfred Stieglitz 667(c) Museum of the City of New York 667(r) The Bettmann Archive 668(1t) U.S. Department of the Interior, National Park Service, Edison National Historic Site Photo by Edward Steichen 668(1b) John Hay Library, Brown University 668(rt) Courtesy RCA 668(rb) Courtesy, Boston Symphony Orchestra 669(1) Courtesy, Ford Motor Company 669(c) Missouri Historical Society 669(r) BIRDS EYE and BIRDS EYE symbol are registered trademarks of Kraft General Foods, Inc. Reproduced with permission 671 (detail) National Gallery of Art, Washington, DC, Collection of Mr. and Mrs. Paul Mellon 674(t) Brown Brothers 674(b) Historical Pictures Service, Chicago 675 Culver Pictures 676(l) Brown Brothers 676(r) Culver Pictures 680(l) Imagefinders, Inc. 680(r) Nebraska State Historical Society 681, 682 Library of Congress 683 Collection of Oliver Jensen 687(t) Library of Congress 687(b) Chicago Historical Society 688 American Jewish Historical Society 689 The Byron Collection, Museum of the City of New York 691 Lewis Hine/Library of Congress 695 National Museum of American Art, Smithsonian Institution 697 Theodore Roosevelt Collection, Harvard College Library 698 Brown Brothers 699, 700, 703 Theodore Roosevelt Collection, Harvard College Library 704(t) The Granger Collection, New York 704(b) Library of Congress 706 Theodore Roosevelt Collection, Harvard College Library 707(t) The Granger Collection, New York 707(b), 708, 712 Brown Brothers 715 The Bettmann Archive 716 (detail) The National Portrait Gallery, Smithsonian Institution, Gift of Walter Waring in memory of his wife, Laura Wheeler Waring, through the Harmon Foundation 722 Jacob Riis, Museum of the City of New York 724 Collection of Ivan E. Prall 726(1) United Nations 726(rt) U.S. Air Force 726(rb) © SEF/ Art Resource 727(1) Culver Pictures 727(c) Museum of the City of New York 727(r) Courtesy Franklin D. Roosevelt Library, Hyde Park, NY 728(t) Brown Brothers 728(c) The Bettmann Archive 728(r) Brown Brothers 729 Boston Athenaeum 733 West Point Museum/Photo by Joshua Nefsky 735(t) Brown Brothers 735(b) Bradley Smith/Carousel 737 UPI/ Bettmann Newsphotos 738 The Bettmann Archive 742(t) Collection of Pembroke Herbert 742(b) National Archives 744(t) National Archives, U.S. Signal Corps photo no. 52393 744(b) The Bettmann Archive 745 Bayerisches Hauptstaatsarchiv, Munich 747 Courtesy Bethlehem Steel Corporation 748(t) Collection of Pembroke Herbert 748(b), 749 Brown Brothers 750 The Museum of Modern Art, Film Stills Archive 751 Minnesota Historical Society 753 The National Portrait Gallery, Smithsonian Institution, Transfer from the National Museum of American Art, Gift of an anonymous donor through Mrs. Elizabeth Rogerson, 1926 754 UPI/Bettmann Newsphotos 755 Wide World Photos 761 National Museum of American Art, Smithsonian Institution, Washington, DC 763 The Bettmann Archive 767 Library of Congress 768(t), 768(b) Culver Pictures 772 The Bettmann Archive 773 The Granger Collection, New York 774 Brown Brothers 778(t) The Bettmann Archive 778(b) Historical Pictures Service, Chicago 779(t) The Granger Collection, New York 779(b) Wide World Photos 780(l) Culver Pictures 780(r) The Bettmann Archive 781 Historical Pictures Service, Chicago 782 Caufield and Shook Collection, Photographic Archives, University of Louisville 783 The Granger Collection, New York 785 Gallery of Art at Howard University 789 Collection of Whitney Museum of American Art. Purchase 37.44 791(l), 791(r) Museum of American Political History, photo by Sally Anderson-Bruce 792 The New York Times Company, October 29, 1929 793 Brown Brothers

794 The Granger Collection, New York 795 Boston Athenaeum 798 The Detroit News 800 UPI/Bettmann 801 Paul Dorsey, Life Magazine, © Time Warner, Inc. 803 Library of Congress 805 Margaret Bourke-White, Life Magazine © 1937 Time Warner, Inc. 806 Library of Congress 807 © 1982, The Oakland Museum, The City of Oakland 808(l), 808(r) UPI/ Bettmann Newsphotos 809 Franklin D. Roosevelt Library 810 Whitney Museum of American Art 811 Franklin D. Roosevelt Library 816 Museo Nacional de Arte Moderna 818 Collection of the Southland Corporation, Dallas, Texas 820(1) The Bettmann Archive, 820(c) Photo by Joshua Nefsky. Collection of Haya Gordin 820(r) Hugo Jaeger/Life Magazine © Time Warner Inc. 821(1) Combat Art Center, Department of the Navy 821(rt) Franklin D. Roosevelt Library, Hyde Park, NY 821(rc) United Nations 821(rb) NASA 822 UPI/Bettmann News Photos 823 Library of Congress 824 National Museum of American Art/Art Resource. 827 John Butler Talcott Fund, New Britain Museum of American Art 829 UPI/Bettmann Newsphotos 830(t) Brown Brothers 830(b) Franklin D. Roosevelt Library, Yousuf Karsh 831 Franklin D. Roosevelt Library 834 Minnesota Historical Society 835 UPI/Bettmann Newsphotos 836 Library of Congress 837(t) UPI/Bettmann Newsphotos 837(b) Dorothea Lange/ Library of Congress 838 Library of Congress 839 The Butler Institute of American Art 843(l), 843(r) UPI/Bettmann Newsphotos 843(b) Conde Nast Publications, Inc. 844 Department of the Interior 846, 847 Library of Congress 850 UPI/Bettmann Newsphotos 851(l) Collection of Ernest Trova, Photo by Neil Sayer 851(r) CEM Property 852 Franklin D. Roosevelt Library 857 Courtesy D. Wigmore Fine Art, Inc., New York, NY 859(t), 859(b), 860 Wide World Photos 861 Hugo Jaeger, Life Magazine, © Time Warner, Inc. 862 UPI/Bettmann Newsphotos 864 Wide World Photos 865 UPI/Bettmann Newsphotos 866 Wide World Photos 867 Franklin D. Roosevelt Library 868 UPI/Bettmann Newsphotos 870 UPI/Bettmann Newsphotos 872 The Bettmann Archive 873(t) UPI/Bettmann Newsphotos 873(b) UPI/Bettmann Newsphotos 875 UPI/Bettmann Newsphotos 877 Wide World Photos 880 Culver Pictures 882(l) Douglas Aircraft Co./FDR Library 882(r) Library of Congress 883(t) Wide World Photos 883(b) UPI/Bettmann Newsphotos 884 Wide World Photos 885 Library of Congress. 889 Collection of Whitney Museum of American Art. Purchase with funds from the Juliana Force Purchase Award. 50.23 891 UPI/Bettmann Newsphotos 896 Wide World Photos 898 UPI/Bettmann Newsphotos 899 Wide World Photos 900 The Bettmann Archive 904 Detail from Homecoming, Norman Rockwell. Printed by permission of the Norman Rockwell Family Trust, © 1945 the Norman Rockwell Family Trust 905 Library of Congress 907 UPI/Bettmann Newsphotos 908 UPI/Bettmann Newsphotos. 913 Columbus Museum of Art, Museum Purchase, Howald Fund 915(t) The Bettmann Archive 915(b) The Bettmann Archive 918 The Margo Feiden Galleries, New York 920(l) The Archives of Labor and Urban Affairs, Wayne State University 920(r) © Michael Ginsburg/Magnum Photos 921(t) © Herblock/Washington Post 921(b) Grant Heilman Photographer 924 Erich Hartmann/Magnum Photos 925 Wide World Photos 926 The Bettmann Archive 927 Photo by Rob Huntley/Chromographics 928 The Bettmann Archive 930 UPI/Bettmann Newsphotos 931(t) After the Prom, Norman Rockwell. Printed by permission of the Norman Rockwell Family Trust, © 1957 the Norman Rockwell Family Trust 931(b) The Bettmann Archive 932 Wide World Photos 936 Bob Henriques/Magnum Photos 942 Wide World Photos. 944 From the Permanent Collection of The Museum of American Folk Art, New York. Gift of Museum of American Folk Art Scotchguard collection of contemporary quilts. 1986.14.1 946(1t) United Nations 946(1b) © 1991 Peter Turnley/Black Star 946(rt) The Bettmann Archive 946(rb) © 1991 Peter

Turnley/Black Star 947(1t) Steve McCutcheon 947(1b) Courtesy of Texas Heart Institute, Houston, Texas 947(r) Bettmann Newsphotos. 948 Courtesy David Godine Publishers 949 Copyright © 1923 Curtis Publishing Company 950 J. Lawrence, 1960. National Museum of American Art. 953 Collection, Museum of Modern Art, New York, NY. Gift of Mr. & Mrs. Robert C. Scull 955(t) Reuters/The Bettmann Archive 955(b) The Bettmann Archive 956 Ed Clark, Life Magazine, © Time Warner, Inc. 957 Burt Glinn/Magnum Photos 960 UPI/Bettmann Newsphotos 961 UPI/Bettmann Newsphotos 962 NASA 963 NASA 964 Wide World Photos 967 UPI/ Bettmann Newsphotos 968 The Peace Corps in Ethiopia, Norman Rockwell. Printed by permission of the Norman Rockwell Family Trust, © 1966 the Norman Rockwell Family Trust Courtesy American Illustrators Gallery/Judy Goffman Fine Art, New York City 969 Wide World Photos 970 Sygma Photo News 971 © Herblock/Washington Post 972 UPI/Bettmann Newsphotos 973 Courtesy Sonnabend Collection, New York. 977 US Army Photographic Agency, Washington, DC 979(t) Don Uhrbrock, Life Magazine © Time Warner, Inc. 979(b) UPI/Bettman Newsphotos 980 Paul Fusco/Magnum Photos 981 H. Armstrong Roberts 986 Wide World Photos 987 © Philip Jones Griffiths/Magnum Photos 988 Fred W. McDarrah 990 Detroit Free Press/Black Star 991(t) Wide World Photos 991(b) Lisa Law/The Image Works 992 © Elliott Landy/Magnum Photos 995 Wide World Photos 996 Wide World Photos 997 Wide World Photos 998 UPI/Bettmann Newsphotos 1000 Wide World Photos 1005 The Kiplinger Collection, Washington, DC 1007 UPI Bettmann Newsphotos 1008 © Charles W. Ashley 1009 © Jim Pickerell 1011 UPI/Bettmann Newsphotos 1014 Christopher Morris/Black Star 1013(t) Gamma-Liaison Network 1013(b) Hugh Haymie, © The Courier-Journal, Louisville Times Co. Reprinted with permission 1016 UPI/Bettmann Newsphotos 1017 Don Wright. Reprinted by permission. Tribune Media Services 1019 Gamma-Liaison Network 1020 Wide World Photos 1023 Tony Auth, Courtesy, Philadelphia Inquirer 1024 © Roland Freeman/Magnum Photos 1025 © Alex Webb/Magnum Photos 1026 © George Hall/Operation Sail, NYC. 1030(1) National Museum of American Art/Art Resource 1030(c) © 1990 The Estate and Foundation of Andy Warhol/Art Resource 1030(r) UPI/Bettmann Newsphotos 1031(1t) Jerry Ohlingers Movie Posters 1031(1b) UPI/Bettmann Newsphotos 1031(rt) UPI/Bettmann Newsphotos 1031(rb) Rob Huntly/ Chromographics 1032(1t) © 1989 McDonald's Corp., Courtesy McDonald's Archives 1032(rb) Doug Martin 1033(1) St. Bartholomew's Hospital/Science Photo Library/ Photo Researchers, Inc. 1033(r) NASA 1033(c) NASA 1035 Jay Johnson America's Folk Heritage Gallery, New York City 1038 Wide World Photos 1040 The Bettmann Archive 1041 © Magnum Photos 1042 © Ledru/Sygma 1043 Stock Boston/© Diane M. Lowe 1045(t) Mike Keza/ Gamma-Liaison Network 1045(b) Owen Frank/Stock Boston 1048 Rochereau/Gamma-Liaison Network 1049 Dennis Brack/Black Star 1051(t) NASA/Black Star 1051(b) Herblock/Herbert Block, Through the Looking Glass. (W. W. Norton + Co. New York, 1984) 1053 © Dan Bosler/Tony Stone Worldwide, Chicago, Ltd. 1054 Rick Friedman/Black Star 1059 © Ira Wyman/Sygma 1061 © Patrick Piel/Gamma Liaison Network 1062, Reuter/Bettmann Newsphotos 1065, Steve Liss for Time Magazine 1066, Wide World Photos 1069 © Gale Zucker 1070, Reuters/Bettman Newsphotos 1071 © Tony Stone Worldwide, Chicago, Ltd. 1074 © Terry Ashe/Gamma Liaison Network 1075, UPI/Bettmann Newsphotos 1076, (both) Reuters/Bettmann Newsphotos 1077 © John Ficara/Sygma 1078, courtesy Congressman Jay Kim 1084 © 1985 David Em 1088-1099 R.R. Donnelley & Sons Company 1100/other interior maps, Maryland Carto Graphics, Incorporated 1104-1111 White House Historical Association. 1111, courtesy the Governor's Mansion, Little Rock AK.

ILLUSTRATION CREDITS